The Wiley-Blackwell Handbook of Group Psychotherapy

The Wiley-Blackwell Handbook of Group Psychotherapy

Edited by Jeffrey L. Kleinberg

A John Wiley & Sons, Ltd., Publication

This edition first published 2012
© John Wiley & Sons, Ltd.

Wiley-Blackwell is an imprint of John Wiley & Sons, formed by the merger of Wiley's global Scientific, Technical and Medical business with Blackwell Publishing.

Registered Office
John Wiley & Sons Ltd, The Atrium, Southern Gate, Chichester, West Sussex, PO19 8SQ, UK

Editorial Offices
350 Main Street, Malden, MA 02148-5020, USA
9600 Garsington Road, Oxford, OX4 2DQ, UK
The Atrium, Southern Gate, Chichester, West Sussex, PO19 8SQ, UK

For details of our global editorial offices, for customer services, and for information about how to apply for permission to reuse the copyright material in this book please see our website at www.wiley.com/wiley-blackwell.

The right of Jeffrey L. Kleinberg to be identified as the author of the editorial material in this work has been asserted in accordance with the UK Copyright, Designs and Patents Act 1988.

All rights reserved. No part of this publication may be reproduced, stored in a retrieval system, or transmitted, in any form or by any means, electronic, mechanical, photocopying, recording or otherwise, except as permitted by the UK Copyright, Designs and Patents Act 1988, without the prior permission of the publisher.

Wiley also publishes its books in a variety of electronic formats. Some content that appears in print may not be available in electronic books.

Designations used by companies to distinguish their products are often claimed as trademarks. All brand names and product names used in this book are trade names, service marks, trademarks or registered trademarks of their respective owners. The publisher is not associated with any product or vendor mentioned in this book. This publication is designed to provide accurate and authoritative information in regard to the subject matter covered. It is sold on the understanding that the publisher is not engaged in rendering professional services. If professional advice or other expert assistance is required, the services of a competent professional should be sought.

Library of Congress Cataloging-in-Publication Data

The Wiley-Blackwell handbook of group psychotherapy / edited by Jeffrey L. Kleinberg.
    p. ; cm.
  Handbook of group psychotherapy
  Includes bibliographical references and index.
  ISBN 978-0-470-66631-9 (hardback)
  1. Group psychotherapy. I. Kleinberg, Jeffrey L. II. Title: Handbook of group psychotherapy.
    [DNLM: 1. Psychotherapy, Group–methods. 2. Mental Disorders–therapy. WM 430]
  RC488.W48 2012
  616.89′152–dc23
                                                                            2011015216

A catalogue record for this book is available from the British Library.

This book is published in the following electronic formats: ePDFs 9781119950899; Wiley Online Library 9781119950882; ePub 9781119979975; eMobi 9781119979982

Set in 10/12.5 pt Galliard by Toppan Best-set Premedia Limited
Printed and bound in Malaysia by Vivar Printing Sdn Bhd

1   2012

Contents

Contributors ... ix

1. Introduction to Group Psychotherapy ... 1
   Jeffrey L. Kleinberg

Section One: Building the Frame: Theoretical Models ... 9

   Introduction ... 9

2. Psychoanalytic Group Psychotherapy: An Overview ... 13
   Priscilla F. Kauff

3. The Interpersonal Model of Group Psychotherapy ... 33
   Molyn Leszcz and Jan Malat

4. Towards an Integrative Intersubjective and Relational Group Psychotherapy ... 59
   Victor L. Schermer and Cecil A. Rice

5. Integrative Cognitive-Behavioral Group Therapy ... 89
   Greg Crosby, with Donald Altman

6. Functional Subgrouping and the Systems-Centered Approach to Group Therapy ... 113
   Susan P. Gantt

7. The Functional Group Model ... 139
   Sharan L. Schwartzberg and Mary Alicia Barnes

8. It's All About Me: Introduction to Relational Group Psychotherapy ... 169
   Richard M. Billow

9. Resonance among Members and its Therapeutic Value in Group Psychotherapy ... 187
   Avi Berman

10. The Dynamics of Mirror Reactions and their Impact on the Analytic Group — 197
    Miriam Berger

11. Meeting Maturational Needs in *Modern Group Analysis*: A Schema for Personality Integration and Interpersonal Effectiveness — 217
    Elliot Zeisel

12. Developing the Role of the Group Facilitator: Learning from Experience — 231
    Orit Nuttman-Shwartz and Sarit Shay

13. From Empathically Immersed Inquiry to Discrete Intervention: Are There Limits to Theoretical Purity? — 249
    Steven L. Van Wagoner

Section Two: Groups for Adults — 271

   Introduction — 271

14. Support and Process-Oriented Therapy Groups — 275
    Lise Motherwell

15. Working with the Difficult Group Patient — 299
    Phyllis F. Cohen

16. Working with Primitive Defenses in Group — 321
    Martha Gilmore

17. Structured Techniques to Facilitate Relating at Various Levels in Group — 335
    Albert J. Brok

18. Effective Management of Substance Abuse Issues in Psychodynamic Group Psychotherapy — 345
    Marsha Vannicelli

19. Single-Gender or Mixed-Gender Groups: Choosing a Perspective — 381
    Darryl L. Pure

20. Sexual Diversity in Group Psychotherapy — 397
    Morris Nitsun

21. Group Therapy For Females Molested In Girlhood — 409
    Shoshana Ben-Noam

22. Couples Group Psychotherapy: A Quarter of a Century Retrospective — 431
    Judith Coché

23. The Large Group: Dynamics, Social Implications and Therapeutic Value — 457
    Haim Weinberg and Daniel J. N. Weishut

24.	Dreams and Dreamtelling: A Group Approach *Robi Friedman*	479
25.	Group Interventions Following Trauma and Disaster *Suzanne B. Phillips and Robert H. Klein*	499
26.	After the Conflict: Training of Group Supervision in Guatemala *Elisabeth Rohr*	517
27.	Group Psychotherapy for Patients with Psychosis: A Psychodynamic (Group-Analytic) Approach *Ivan Urlić*	547
28.	Care for the Caregivers *Richard Beck*	571

Section Three: Groups for Children — 587

Introduction — 587

29.	Group Therapy with Children *Seth Aronson*	589
30.	Adolescent Group Psychotherapy: The Real Work *Andrew P. Pojman*	609
31.	The Earth as a Classroom: Children's Groups in the Aftermath of Mass Trauma *Emily Zeng*	623
32.	A Multidisciplinary Treatment Team Model for Youth Offenders in Correctional Treatment Centers: Applying Psychodynamic Group Concepts *D. Thomas Stone Jr. and Anne Carson Thomas*	645

Section Four: Diversity — 665

Introduction — 665

33.	Diversity in Groups: Culture, Ethnicity and Race *Siddharth Ashvin Shah and Razia Kosi*	667
34.	A Spiritually Informed Approach to Group Psychotherapy *Alexis D. Abernethy*	681

Section Five: Through a Personal Lens — 707

Introduction — 707

35.	Group Psychotherapy as my Career Path *Walter N. Stone*	709

36. My Development as a Group Therapist 731
    Marvin L. Aronson

37. Group Psychotherapy with High-Functioning Adults Or,
    People Like Me! 745
    Bonnie J. Buchele

Author Index 771
Subject Index 785

Contributors

Editor

Jeffrey L. Kleinberg, PhD, CGP, FAGPA, is a Fellow and the current President of the American Group Psychotherapy Association. He has served as Training Analyst, Supervisor and Senior Faculty Member at the Postgraduate Center for Mental Health in New York City. He was the President of the Eastern Group Psychotherapy Society on 9/11/01. He helped co-ordinate a large relief effort for the financial community and as part of Project Liberty and has trained more than 1000 mental health professionals in trauma counseling and group treatment. Recently, he conducted a 4-day workshop on group in Chengdu, China. He is Professor Emeritus at LaGuardia Community College, City University of New York, where he taught psychology, served as director of counseling, and later as dean of students. He is the former editor of the journal *Group*. He is a Licensed Psychologist and maintains a private psychotherapy and organizational consultation practice in Manhattan.

Authors

Alexis D. Abernethy, MA, PhD is a Clinical Psychologist and Professor of Psychology in the Graduate School of Psychology at Fuller Theological Seminary. She received her BS in Psychology from Howard University and her graduate degrees in Clinical Psychology from the University of California, Berkeley. She was the editor of a special edition of the journal, *Group* (2004), *Special Edition on Spirituality in Group Therapy*.

Donald Altman, MA, LPC is a practicing psychotherapist, former Buddhist monk, a Board Member of The Center for Mindful Eating, and Adjunct Professor at Portland State University and at Lewis and Clark Graduate School of Education and Counseling. He conducts mindfulness workshops around the country and is author of *The Mindfulness Code, One-Minute Mindfulness, Meal by Meal, Living Kindness*, and *Art of the Inner Meal*.

Marvin L. Aronson, [†] PhD, ABPP, served as the Director of the Specialty Training Program in Analytic Group Therapy at the Postgraduate Center for Mental Health in New York City from 1970-2000. He co-edited *Group Therapy: An Overview*, from1974–79, as well as *Group and Family Therapy: An Overview*. Dr. Aronson passed away in 2011.

Seth Aronson, PsyD, FAGPA, is Fellow, Training and Supervising Analyst at the William Alanson White Institute in New York. He is co-chair of the American Group Psychotherapy Association's Special Interest Group on Child and Adolescent Group Work. Together with Saul Scheidlinger, he is co-author of *Group Treatment of Adolescents in Context: Outpatient, Inpatient and School* (IUP, 2002).

Mary Alicia Barnes, OTR/L, is Fieldwork Co-ordinator in the Department of Occupational Therapy at Tufts University. With over 25 years of experience, she has co-lead therapeutic, process, and mentoring groups in educational and clinical settings and has co-authored publications related to group theory and professional development.

Richard Beck, LCSW, BCD, CGP, FAGPA, is a Psychotherapist in private practice in New York City who specializes in the treatment of Psychological Trauma. He is Past-President of the Eastern Group Psychotherapy Society, an Adjunct Professor at Fordham University Graduate School of Social Service and has conducted well over 1000 hours of trauma treatment post 9/11/01.

Shoshana Ben-Noam, PsyD, CGP, FAGPA, is a trauma specialist; Adjunct Professor, Pace University Doctoral Program in School/Clinical/Child Psychology; Faculty, Eastern Group Psychotherapy Society Training Program; and a Board Member of the American Group Psychotherapy Association. She has Guest Edited two issues on Trauma and Group Therapy, *Group* journal; trained more than 600 mental health professionals in trauma work and group therapy; and is in private practice in New York City.

Miriam Berger, MA, is a Senior Clinical Psychologist, Group Analyst, and a Founding Member and Past Chairperson of the Israeli Institute of Group Analysis. She also serves on the Faculty of the psychotherapy program at Bar Ilan University, Israel. She is a member of the editorial board of *Maarag*, The Israeli Annual of Psychoanalysis.

Avi Berman, PhD, is a Clinical Psychologist, Psychoanalyst, and a Group Analyst. He is a member of the Tel-Aviv Institute of Contemporary Psychoanalysis and the Israeli Institute of Group Analysis. He is the initiator and co-founder of the Israeli Institute of Group Analysis and its former chairperson. He teaches at Tel-Aviv University.

Richard M. Billow, PhD, is a Diplomat in Group Psychotherapy, a Clinical Psychologist and Psychoanalyst, an active contributor to psychoanalytic and group journals, and the author of *Relational Group Psychotherapy: From Basic Assumptions to Passion* (2003), and the just-published *Resistance, Rebellion, and Refusal in Groups: The 3 Rs* (2010). He is Clinical Professor and Director of the Group Program at the Derner Postgraduate Institute, Adelphi University, and maintains a private practice in Great Neck, New York.

Albert J. Brok, PhD, CGP, is Director of Group and Couples Therapy Training, at the Training Institute of Mental Health, New York City. He is on the Faculty of both the The Derner Institute at Adelphi University and the Postgraduate Center for Mental Health and is Guest Lecturer at the Argentine Psychoanalytic Association. He is on the Board of the Division of Psychoanalysis, American Psychological Association, and maintains a private practice in New York.

Bonnie Buchele, PhD, ABBP, DFAGPA, is a Training and Supervising Psychoanalyst and Group Psychotherapist practicing in Kansas City, Missouri. She is a past president and Distinguished Fellow of the American Group Psychotherapy Association and Board Member of the International Association for Group Psychotherapy and Group Processes.

Judith Coché, PhD, is the founder and director of The Coché Center, LLC. She is Clinical Supervisor with the American Association of Marriage and Family Therapy and a Fellow of the American Group Psychotherapy Association. Currently she is Clinical Professor at of the Medical School at the University of Pennsylvania. She has been awarded the Diplomate status in Clinical Psychology from the American Board of Professional Psychology. Dr Coché has been in practice since 1975. She has authored *Couples Group Psychotherapy, Second Edition* (2010), and has co-authored two books: *Couples Group Psychotherapy* (1990) and *Powerful Wisdom* (1993). *The Husbands and Wives Club: A Year in a Couples Psychotherapy Group* (2010) was written by prize winning journalist Laurie Abraham, about Dr Coché's clinical work.

Phyllis F. Cohen, PhD, is on the Boards of the Group Therapy Foundation, the American Group Psychotherapy Association and the National Council for Creative Aging. A Faculty Member and past Chairman of the Board of the Center for Group Studies, she has recently left the position of Chair of the Committee on Accreditation for the American Board for Accreditation in Psychoanalysis.

Greg Crosby, MA, LPC, CGP, FAGPA, is a Mental Health Group Co-ordinator at Kaiser Permanente in Oregon and Washington, Adjunct Faculty at Maryhurst University, Portland State University and Lewis and Clark Graduate School of Education and Counseling. He is a Group Therapy Consultant and Trainer to Health Maintenance Organizations, Community Mental Health Centers and Residential Centers.

Robi Friedman, PhD, a Clinical Psychologist and Supervisor, and Group Analyst, is President of the Israeli Institute for Group Analysis, a Board Member of the Group Analytic Society (London), lecturer at the Haifa University, Israel, and Past President of the Israel Association for Group Psychotherapy.

Susan P. Gantt, PhD, ABPP, CGP, FAGPA, FAPA, is a Psychologist and Assistant Professor in Psychiatry at Emory University School of Medicine where she co-ordinates group psychotherapy training. She is the Director of the Systems-Centered Training and Research Institute and co-author of the books *Autobiography of a Theory, SCT in clinical practice* and *SCT in Action* with Yvonne Agazarian.

Martha Gilmore, PhD, CGP, FAGPA, is a Licensed Psychologist, Certified Group Psychotherapist, and Fellow of the American Group Psychotherapy Association. She has a private practice in Davis and Sacramento, California and is Associate Clinical Professor of Psychiatry at University of California, Davis Medical School.

Priscilla F. Kauff, PhD, DFAGPA a Distinguished Fellow of the American Group Psychotherapy Association, is a Clinical Psychologist and Psychoanalyst in private practice with a specialty in analytic group psychotherapy. She is a Clinical Associate Professor of Psychology in Psychiatry at Weill Medical College, Cornell University and a Faculty Member of the Adelphi University Postdoctoral Program in Group

Therapy. She is also a Faculty Member and Supervisor in the China American Psychoanalytic Association, training Chinese mental health professionals in psychoanalytic treatment. She is the author of several articles and book chapters, the majority of which focus on aspects of psychoanalytic group treatment.

Robert H. Klein, PhD, ABPP, FAPA, DLFAGPA, CGP, a Faculty Member at the Yale School of Medicine for more than 25 years and is Past President and Distinguished Life Fellow of the American Group Psychotherapy and in private practice. He is the author, co-author or co-editor of numerous publications, including: *Group Psychotherapy for Psychological Trauma, Handbook of Contemporary Group Psychotherapy, Public Mental Health Service Delivery Protocols: Group Interventions for Disaster Preparedness and Response, Leadership in a Changing World and On Becoming a Psychotherapist: The Personal and Professional Journey*.

Razia Kosi, LCSW, has experience in working in school settings with adolescents, behavioral issues and healthy youth development. She has also worked extensively with women and issues related to cultural identity. Her training is in family systems and cross-cultural communication. She also works with groups and created the model for the CHAI Women's Wellness Group.

Molyn Leszcz, MD, FRCPC, CGP, FAGPA, Professor and Vice-Chair of Clinical Services, University of Toronto Department of Psychiatry, Psychiatrist-in-Chief Mount Sinai Hospital, Joseph and Wolf Lebovic Health Complex, Toronto, Canada. His academic and clinical work has focused on broadening the application of psychotherapy within psychiatry. Dr Leszcz's recent research has explored group psychotherapy with the medically ill and those predisposed genetically to cancer. Dr Leszcz co-chaired the American Group Psychotherapy Association's Science to Service Task Force, the working group that published AGPA's Clinical Practice Guidelines for Group Psychotherapy in 2007. He has co-authored with Dr Irvin Yalom the 5th edition of *The Theory and Practice of Group Psychotherapy*.

Jan Malat, MD, FRCPC, ASAM, Assistant Professor of Psychiatry, University of Toronto, is the Clinic Head of the Integrative Group Therapy Clinic, in the Addictions Program at the Centre for Addiction and Mental Health, Toronto, Canada.

Lise Motherwell, PhD, PsyD, CGP, FAGPA, is a Licensed Psychologist in private practice in Boston, Massachusetts, an Instructor at Harvard Medical School, Clinical Assistant in Psychology at Massachusetts General Hospital, and a Supervisor at the Boston Institute for Psychotherapy. She specializes in divorce therapy groups and developed *Pack Your Parachute*, a small-group seminar to help women negotiate the psychological, financial and legal aspects of divorce. She is co-editor with Joseph Shay, PhD, of *Complex Dilemmas in Group Therapy: Pathways to Resolution* which was published in 2005, and has written numerous articles on group therapy.

Morris Nitsun, PhD is a Consultant Psychologist in the National Health Service in London UK, a Senior Trainer at the Institute of Group Analysis and a Private Practitioner at the Fitzrovia Group Analytic Practice. His work spans individual and group psychotherapy and he runs weekly and twice-weekly groups. He is actively involved in the development of group psychotherapy training, both as a Training Analyst at IGA and a Senior Trainer and Supervisor in the NHS. With considerable experience as a clinician and manager, he also undertakes organizational consultation to individuals and groups, drawing on his concept of "The Organizational Mirror." He is a widely published author and his books, *The Anti-group – destructive forces in the group and their creative potential* (1996) and *The Group as an Object of Desire – exploring sexuality in group psychotherapy* (2006), have been described as "classics in the field."

Orit Nuttman-Shwartz, PhD, MSW, CGP, and Group Analyst, is a Senior Lecturer, Founder and Head of the Department of Social Work at Sapir College in Israel. Her research focuses on personal and social trauma, group work and therapy, and life transitions and occupational crises. Working near the Israeli border, she also studies the effects of on-going exposure to threats on individuals, communities, and organizations and the impact of a shared-trauma environment on students, supervisors, and social workers. She has recently been appointed as Chairperson of the Israel National Social Work Council.

Suzanne B. Phillips, is a Psychologist, Psychoanalyst, Diplomat in Group Psychotherapy and Fellow of the American Group Psychotherapy Association. She has been an Adjunct Full Professor of Clinical Psychology in the Doctoral Program of Long Island University, New York. She is the Co-editor of *Public Mental Health Service Delivery Protocols: Group Interventions for Disaster Preparedness and Response* and *Healing Together: A Couple's Guide to Coping with Trauma and Posttraumatic Stress*.

Andrew P. Pojman, EdD, CGP is a Licensed Psychologist in private practice specializing in adolescent and group treatment along with forensic assessment. He is an Adjunct Professor of psychology at the Wright Institute in Berkeley California. He is the author of *Adolescent Group Psychotherapy: Method, Madness, and the Basics*.

Darryl L. Pure, PhD, ABPP, CGP, FAGPA, is a Clinical Psychologist, a Diplomat of the American Board of Professional Psychology, a Certified Group Psychotherapist, and a Fellow and Treasurer of the American Group Psychotherapy Association.

Cecil A. Rice, PhD, is a Distinguished Fellow of the American Group Psychotherapy Association, President and Co-founder of the Boston Institute for Psychotherapy, Associate Editor of the *International Journal of Group Psychotherapy*, serves on the Faculty at Harvard Medical School, has written widely in the field of group therapy and has a private practice in Needham, Massachusetts in group, individual and couples therapy.

Elisabeth Rohr, PhD, is a Social Psychologist, a Professor of Intercultural Education at the Philipps-University of Marburg, Germany, and is a Group Analyst. She is engaged as a Consultant in national and international organizations and works in her own practice as a Supervisor. She holds membership in the Group Analytic Society, London, the International Association of Group Psychotherapy, the Deutsche Gesellschaft für Supervision, the Institut für Gruppenanalyse in Heidelberg, and the Deutsche Gesellschaft für Erziehungswissenschaften.

Victor L. Schermer, MA, LPC, CGP, FAGPA, is a Psychologist and Psychoanalytic Psychotherapist in private practice and clinical settings in Philadelphia, Pennsylvania. He is a Fellow of the American Group Psychotherapy Association, author/editor of seven books and numerous articles and book chapters on group psychotherapy, and is a frequent lecturer and workshop leader internationally.

Sharan L. Schwartzberg, EdD, OTR/L, FAOTA, is a Professor of Occupational Therapy and Adjunct Professor in Psychiatry at Tufts University. She has published, conducted research and presented in a wide array of professional arenas on the subject of group theory and practice. Recognized for her leadership in education and occupational therapy, her work is known internationally.

Siddharth Ashvin Shah, MD, MPH, specializes in behavioral medicine, is Clinical Instructor in Preventive Medicine at Mount Sinai School of Medicine, and is Medical Director of Greenleaf Integrative Strategies, a firm dedicated to psychosocial problem-solving and wellness in settings of trauma. He has provided group interventions and trauma consultation to community leaders, CBOs, NGOs, mental health professionals and emergency managers who serve vulnerable ethnic groups and the general population.

Sarit Shay, MSW, is a Group and Individual Psychotherapist, and Lecturer at the Bob Shapell School of Social Work, Tel Aviv University, Israel. She focuses on methods of intervention, group work and therapy, as well as clinical supervision.

D. Thomas Stone, Jr., PhD, CGP, FAGPA, is a Consulting Psychologist in private practice in San Antonio, Texas and has consulted with the Bexar County Juvenile Probation Department for thirteen years in their Institutions Division. He is an Assistant Clinical Professor at the University of Texas Health Science Center in San Antonio.

Walter N. Stone, MD, is Professor Emeritus of the University of Cincinnati. He has served on the Board of Directors of the American Group Psychotherapy Association and is a past president of the San Antonio Group Psychotherapy Society. He is author of more than 40 articles and four books on group psychotherapy. He is Past President of the American Group Psychotherapy Association, and has served as treasurer and as a member of the Board of Directors, the International Association of Group Psychotherapy.

Anne Carson Thomas, PhD, is a Clinical Psychologist and Clinical Director of Institutions for the Bexar County Juvenile Probation Department. She is an Assistant Clinical Professor at the University of Texas Health Science Center in San Antonio.

Ivan Urlić, MD, PhD, is a Neuropsychiatrist, Psychoanalytic Psychotherapist, Group Analyst, Professor of Psychiatry and Psychological Medicine at the Medical School, University of Split, Croatia. He serves as Secretary of the International Association of Group Psychotherapy. His professional interest is in the field of group psychotherapy with patients suffering from psychosis and from severe psychic traumas. He is the author of many papers, chapters, and a book, and lectures internationally.

Steven Van Wagoner, PhD, CGP, FAGPA, has been practicing group psychotherapy for 30 years in inpatient and outpatient settings, and more recently in private practice in Washington, D.C. He is on the Faculty of the National Group Psychotherapy

Institute and Group Psychotherapy Training Program at the Washington School of Psychiatry, and has served as an Adjunct on the clinical Faculty at Georgetown University, the George Washington University, and the University of Maryland. He is a Fellow of the American Group Psychotherapy Association, and has presented on group psychotherapy locally and nationally.

Marsha Vannicelli, PhD, FAGPA, is a Clinical Associate Professor of Psychology in the Harvard Medical School, and teaches group psychotherapy courses at the Massachusetts School of Professional Psychology. She is the author of two Guilford Press books: *Removing the Roadblocks: Group Psychotherapy with Substance Abusers and Family Members* and *Group Psychotherapy with Adult Children of Alcoholics: Treatment Techniques and Countertransference Considerations.* Previously Director (and founder) of the Appleton Substance Abuse Clinic at McLean Hospital, she is now in private practice in Cambridge, Massachusetts.

Haim Weinberg, PhD, CPG, FAGPA, is a Clinical psychologist (Israel, USA), Group Analyst, Certified Group Psychotherapist. Member: American Association of Group Psychotherapy, International Association of Group Psychotherapy, and Group Analytic Society. He is President of the Northern California Group Psychotherapy Society and Past President of the Israeli Association of Group Therapy.

Daniel J. N. Weishut, MA, MBA, is a Clinical Psychologist and Organizational Consultant, with special interest in issues of diversity and human rights. He has a private practice in Jerusalem, Israel. He is a Board Member of the Israeli Association for Group Psychotherapy.

Elliot Zeisel, MSW, PhD, FAGPA, CGP, a graduate of the Philadelphia School of Psychoanalysis, Dr Zeisel is a Fellow of the American Group Psychotherapy Association and serves as the Vice-Chair of the AGPA Foundation Board. He is a founder of the Center for Group Studies. Dr Zeisel is also a Training Analyst at the Center for Modern Psychoanalytic Studies and is the Director of the Group Department. He is an honorary member of the Israeli Institute of Group Analysis.

Emily Zeng, PsyD, is a Licensed Psychologist in New York City serving children and families with special needs. A native Chinese, she volunteered extensively during the 2008 Chinese earthquake. She currently is the Co-Chair of the Diversity Special Interest Group of the American Group Psychotherapy Association.

1

Introduction to Group Psychotherapy

Jeffrey L. Kleinberg

Group psychotherapy is widely practised with *different* populations, in *different* settings, using *different* approaches based on *different* theories of the mind, with *different* degrees of success. The accent here is on *differences*. How is a clinician new to this modality to make sense of this diversity and formulate a personal approach to leading a group? One's group leadership supervision, course work, and conferences, are indispensible for professional development. But what has been lacking is a current, ready-reference that briefs the leader on forming, beginning, and sustaining the treatment in ways that address the therapeutic needs and developmental status of the patients. By ready-reference I mean one that is accessible to the reader who does not want to get bogged down in jargon and a "one-size-fits-all" approach. I believe that our authors – representing the best in the field – have composed a reader-friendly text that "speaks" directly to the needs of current group therapists who want to refresh their leadership approach, to those of individual therapists who wish to expand their practices to include group treatment, and to the concerns of graduate students in mental health and allied fields wishing to learn this modality. Accordingly, an experienced or would-be group leader can turn to just about any chapter and pick up words of wisdom that will come in handy as a group is being put together or is trying to stay on track.

The chapters herein can guide the new practitioner of a group through the phases of selecting members, treatment planning, beginning the group, and developing carefully crafted strategies, reaching treatment goals.

This Handbook presents a variety of theoretical models, conducted in a variety of settings, within diverse cultures – with patients presenting many types of problems and personalities – and using technical approaches relevant to all these factors. My hope is that exposure to many models of thinking and working will help each new group leader find a voice and develop personalized, but informed operating assumptions.

The Wiley-Blackwell Handbook of Group Psychotherapy, First Edition. Edited by Jeffrey L. Kleinberg.
© 2012 John Wiley & Sons, Ltd. Published 2012 by John Wiley & Sons, Ltd.

The publication of this Handbook comes at the right time. The context within which groups are conducted has changed from what it was 20 years ago, when the last edition appeared. Today, a greater percentage of groups are taking place in agency, hospitals, schools and other community settings than before when so many groups were held in private offices and were primarily an adjunct to individual treatment. Significantly, groups today are not only geared to those suffering from mental illness, but are also geared towards others finding themselves in stressful circumstances. Group has spread to other nations, and is no longer a Western cultural phenomenon. Groups are used to respond to trauma, ranging from terror attacks to natural disasters. Group strategies are now based on a variety of theories, some of which have come to fruition in the last 20 years, and have arisen in response to emergent cohorts who did not respond to more traditional approaches. New challenges call for newer responses.

There is also a shift in the political and economic climate. There is less money for training. Managed care and the need for evidenced-based treatment modalities put additional strain on the clinician. Now, more than ever, the group therapist needs to be able to state what she does, and why she does it, and at the same time be competitive in the market place for the shrinking available dollars. Group does offer help here in that what we do is cost-effective and can be described in terms that objective observers can understand. Improving interpersonal communication skills, stress reduction, overcoming the effects of trauma, providing peer support, strengthening couple ties, and addressing mood instability can be clearly depicted. Group treatment still complements individual counseling and can enhance its impact, yet even alone, can treat the psychologically impaired or stressed.

What is the Role of Group in a Treatment Plan?

- Group is a platform through which the therapist and the individual can assess deficits in emotional functioning.
- Group experiences can promote insight into what establishes and continues dysfunctional behavior in interpersonal situations, such as family life, intimate relations, work and friendships.
- Group is an arena for patients to experiment with new behavior that could lead to improved relationships.
- Group is a place to get feedback from peers as to how one's behavior is experienced by others.
- Group is a setting in which distorted perceptions of others can be identified and revised.
- Group enables the patient and therapist to agree on what the barriers are to more satisfying relationships.
- Group interaction provides behavioral samples for measuring the extent to which treatment is progressing, and for making mid-course corrections in the clinical strategy.

Of course these are the potential benefits of group. Unfortunately, too many group patients drop-out before realizing them. My experience as a teacher, supervisor, group leader (and as a group patient!) tells me that we need to be more thoughtful in selecting patients, constructing the group, preparing each potential participant, overcoming barriers, and consolidating gains. While the Handbook is organized by topic, I have created an outline that correlates therapist required knowledge, attitudes and skills with specific sections. Thus, the text can be read in a linear fashion, or by identified need.

The group leader needs to have the relevant clinical skills, knowledge of theory, knowledge of group dynamics, a self-reflective capacity to track and incorporate ongoing emotional responses, and a commitment to continuous professional development.

I am reminded of what Ornstein (1987) said about the four phases of learning to work as an individual therapist. Adapting his formulation to group training, one learns how to feel as a group therapist; how to behave and talk as a group therapist; how to think as a group therapist; and, how to listen as a group therapist.

Leading a group *feels* different from working as an individual therapist. The novice experiences himself as more exposed, more strongly influenced by the collective needs of his patients, more confused by what is going on and as a cumulative result of these variables, less certain as to how to proceed. These stressors often place roadblocks in the way of training.

Behaving and talking as a group therapist one is directed to the goals of establishing and maintaining an effective working alliance with each patient and the group-as-a-whole. These alliances make the work of therapy possible. Without sufficient safety and tension regulation members can become closed to reflection, and change, and the group could breakdown.

Thinking as a group therapist is based on a set of assumptions as to what would lead to positive change. Specifically, the leader needs to be concerned with what contributes to the development of each patient within the group and what could strengthen the therapeutic climate of the group-as-a-whole. Thinking about groups requires a theoretical base from which clinical strategies can be launched. Theories must explain both individual and group dynamics, and the effects of their interaction. Insights about human behavior, what makes people mentally ill and what makes them better can be drawn from a number of theories. The leader, herself, has the task of integrating these viewpoints until she develops her own therapeutic stance.

If you are like most group therapists, you started out as someone who worked with individuals. In contrast to many professionals, I think leading a group requires skills that are different from one-to-one work. The challenge of a group therapist is to simultaneously track and respond to the individual's responses, the dyadic relationships as well as the group-as-a-whole dynamics. Since all three domains affect one another, the therapist does indeed act like a conductor – bringing to the fore one or two elements, and focusing the group on a particular part of the process. Which one to spotlight depends very much on where the affect is, where the conflict is or where the action is as a major a common theme is played out. To make the right choice of focus at the right time requires a quick decision within the therapeutic moment – where the biggest gains in understanding and therapeutic change may be found.

The multidimensional arena of group can best be understood through the application of theory drawn from the literature of the various components of the group process – individual, dyadic, group, organizational and cultural dynamics. Adding to the challenge is the likelihood that the therapist will have different, albeit sometimes complementary, reactions to her experience with the different constituencies. The task of the leader, then, is to be able to select what is the figure and what is the ground, and to understand and respond, according to the therapeutic needs at a particular time. Factoring in the role of one's own emotional reactions in the perception of what is taking place is essential for empathizing with the members and to be objective in the choice of interventions.

From my experience as a clinician, first, and then as a supervisor and trainer, I think it is helpful to break down the job of the group therapist in ways that help her assess what she needs to strengthen her performance. The leader should be able to apply clinical skills, to assess prospective group members, to select who is appropriate for a given group. They must have the ability to develop a treatment plan for each member, compose the group so that the patients can form a therapeutic climate, begin the group, and implement strategies for achieving the goals established for each participant. This array of skills is informed by knowledge of three kinds of theories: personality, developmental (curative), and group dynamics. Integrating and applying these theories to a specific group of patients, with specific needs, in a particular setting is necessary in the design of a treatment strategy. Self-awareness enables the group leader to use her feelings to gain insight into what the members experience and to identify when one's own issues get in the way of the clinical work. Knowing how one learns, and can learn, to be an effective leader forms a roadmap to leadership development.

This role and task analysis in Table 1.1, serves as the basis for a functional index as an alternative access point to the sections herein. Specifically, this reference list can bring the reader into contact with authors who speak specifically to the skills and knowledge expected of a group leader. In other words, using this functional index enables the learner to create a personalized menu of sections to meet her training needs. (In presenting this table I do not imply that other sections may not be relevant to a particular task or role. Rather, I am pointing to primary resources, but encourage the reader to explore other sections as well in their personal search.)

What my group of authors has sought to accomplish in this Handbook is to address these competencies and underlying rationales – each from their own experience and insights. Their rich backgrounds have enabled them to apply what they know to a variety of settings, including those based in other countries and with many different populations (children, adolescents, couples and adults) and desired outcomes (including relief from trauma and or psychiatric symptoms). In addition, several authors comment on the development of the group psychotherapist and the field of psychotherapy as the reader develops her own professional persona as a group psychotherapist.

The more traditional way of organizing a book such as this is through broad topical sections: Building a Frame: Theoretical Models, Groups for Adults, Groups for Children, Diversity and personal perspectives on one's development as a group leader. Our Contents table does that. This linear format builds a knowledge and skill base for the leader planning to launch or maintain a group. It is also a way to structure a course on group treatment that differentiates among patient populations and expected treatment outcomes. Moreover, the sections offer a diversity of opinions on how one should operate the group, allowing the leader to pick and choose what would likely

Table 1.1 Knowledge and skills required of group therapists and sectional references in handbook.

I. Clinical Skills (CS)
   a. Evaluating prospective group members: Sections 2 and 3.
   b. Developing a treatment plan: Sections 2 and 3.
   c. Designing treatment strategies: Sections 1, 2 and 3.
   d. Deciding optimal group composition: Sections 1, 2, 3, and 4.
   e. Preparing patients for group: Building working alliances: Sections 1, 2 and 3.
   f. Preparing group for new members: Strengthening cohesion and empathic attunement: Sections 1, 2, and 3.
   g. Monitoring tension levels of individual patients and of group-as-a-whole: Sections 1, 2, and 3.
   h. Managing tension to maintain optimal levels so work can proceed:
      1. Responding to empathic failures: Sections 1 and 2.
      2. Building listening and expressive capacities: Sections 1, 2, and 3.
   i. Identifying and responding to resistance (individual and group-as-a-whole): Sections 1, 2, 3, and 4.
   j. Identifying, clarifying and working through transference distortions: Sections 1 and 2.
   k. Helping patients with the working-through process that translates what has been gained in group to outside settings: Sections 2 and 3.
   l. Planning and managing termination: Sections 2 and 3.

II. Knowledge of Multiple Theories (KT)
   a. Personality development and derailments: Sections 1, 2, and 3.
   b. Group, family, organizational, and cultural dynamics: Sections 3 and 4.
   c. Psychological disorders: Sections 2, 3, 4, and 5.
   d. Restoration of mental health: all Sections.

III. Self-Reflective Capacity (SR)
   a. Knowledge of one's own emotional responses to ongoing group events: Sections 2 and 5.
   b. Tracking one's empathic capacity and its accuracy from moment to moment: Sections 1, 2, and 5.
   c. Monitoring one's own anxiety levels and potentially counterproductive activities: Sections 1 and 2.
   d. Awareness of what one does not know about the treatment group: Section 5.
   e. Ability to be both in the group and be able to look from above at process at the same time: Sections 1 and 5.

IV. Consultation Skills (CS)
   a. Ability to consult with referring individual therapist prior to start of conjoint treatment: Sections 2 and 3.
   b. Ability to give feedback to referring individual therapist and correlate treatment in individual and group modalities: Sections 2 and 3.

V. Capacity to Develop as a Group Leader (SDL)
   a. Ability to present accurately the process of treatment group: Section 5.
   b. Ability to articulate needed focus of supervision: Section 3 and 5.
   c. Openness in supervision to ideas of supervisor and peers: Sections 3 and 5.
   d. Ability to try recommended approaches to group treatment: Sections 3 and 5.
   e. Ability to examine possible links between dynamics of supervisory group and dynamics of treatment group: Section 5.
   f. Ability to track what one has learned in supervision and update goals for learning: Sections 3 and 5.
   g. Knowledge of when to seek personal treatment when blocks to learning are identified: Sections 4 and 5.

work for her. A marketplace of ideas can advance the development of the leader as she crafts her own therapeutic style.

As group leaders develop they need to be aware of how the world will look in the next decade or longer. After all, what happens in the greater global society will influence what therapists do, the nature and availability of group treatment, and training and supervisory resources made available to those leading groups.

Group therapy today is practised in agencies, schools, hospitals, and in private practices. Its leaders are drawn from the mental health professions, who differ widely in training and experience. While the American Group Psychotherapy Association Registry certifies group therapists based on an evaluation of courses taken, supervision received, and professional continuing education completed, there is no specialized license required to be a group therapist.

While much of the early development of the group modality arose in medical settings, major contributions were made in the human relations area as psychologists studied group dynamics in laboratories. These two streams of group data came together as military veterans returned to civilian life suffering from battle fatigue and the psychological effects of their wounds.

Many of the breakthroughs in technique and theory were made by psychoanalysts trying to apply psychodynamic theory to treatment in a group setting. It soon became clear to many, that group was not just a more cost-efficient way to handle large numbers of patients, but that the group setting, itself, added to the therapeutic factors seen in individual treatment. In recent years, with the rise of client-centered, cognitive and behavioral modalities, group treatment is conducted with different understandings of mental illness and curative influences.

Today, group techniques are applied to a variety of populations presenting with different needs: patients suffering from mental illness continue to be a primary target of this form of treatment, but today, we see group applied to survivors of natural disasters and man-made trauma as well. In the aftermath of 9/11 and the Gulf Coast hurricanes, group was a major way to reach out to people who experienced acute levels of stress. Modifications of existing group strategies had to be made to serve the needs of this emerging population.

The outlook for group is in many ways going to be influenced by political forces: how much will government and private insurance companies pay for group treatment versus individual work and or medicine. The field needs to assemble research evidence that will make the case for group as a proven contributor to recovery. Limited funds to support that research and the complexity of designing studies that will be considered valid and reliable remain as huge challenges.

It is also likely that the availability of electronic means of communication will bring about distance group experiences, ranging from training and supervision, to treatment. The popularity of social media makes a wider appearance of internet-based groups a probability.

Another trend line points to the preparation of more and more allied professionals on group techniques, and their deployment to fill the gaps within the licensed and highly-trained mental health labor force. This expectation will likely come true in countries outside of the United States, in which there are so few psychologists, psychiatrists and social workers, and in other cultures where the majority of existing healers are drawn from the religious sects and not from the professional community.

How to select and develop allied professional and paraprofessional group leaders remains an unanswered question. Cultural diversity, then, will also require greater attention as group therapy reaches new populations with different belief systems.

Finally, the field of group psychotherapy will probably place more emphasis on integrating theories and techniques and tearing down the silo-like organization, in which disciples of one approach disdain or discount the contributions of their counterparts from other schools of thought. Bridges between institutes, disciplines, and disciples will need to be built for this integration to happen. The role of conferences, journals, long-distance Skype-type communications, and textbooks will also need to adapt to this global context.

Just like the group process, the dynamics of change within the field are influenced by outside forces. The group leader must be alert to them to stay current and relevant.

A personal note: in creating this Handbook, I turned to many of my colleagues I met through the American Group Psychotherapy Association (AGPA). Their appreciation of the group modality and their dedication to the development of group therapists are reflected in each chapter. They have enriched this experience for me: working on a common goal, in sync with one another, but yet free to be themselves, open to feedback and valuing dialogues have illustrated what good could come from an effective working group!

Reference

Ornstein, P. H. (1987). Selected problems in learning how to analyze. *International Journal of Psychoanalysis, 48*, 448–461.

Section One
Building the Frame: Theoretical Models

Introduction

What is the role of theory in conducting groups? How we see patients and decide what they need therapeutically is based on a set of operational assumptions: about what derailed the patient's emotional development and what is the nature of that deficit, what therapeutic factors, both intrapsychic and interpersonal, in the group process, can help the member work through these blocks.

This section can help the group leader explore what the different frames of reference offer by way of understanding what occurs in the group, and what is needed to promote patient growth. It may be that certain theories apply to some patients and groups, and not to others. Having a full repertoire of potential treatment rationales allows the leader to formulate her own therapeutic stance specific to the circumstances at hand.

There of course is an added dimension to this review of theories, namely the role of the *group* dynamic in the work. So that in addition to personality and developmental theories presented in this section, the reader will also see how such foundations as the group-as-whole viewpoint or the subgrouping defenses provide a richer understanding of what is taking place and what needs to happen next.

The chapters that follow do not attempt to define the various theories; rather the authors illustrate how a theory informs their clinical observations and decision-making. I am hoping that this style of presentation will give the reader insights about the theory-in-action, and not just an "academic" theory with little practical application.

Kauff's approach to "Psychoanalytic Group Psychotherapy" focuses on how a psychodynamically-oriented leader helps members learn more about themselves, including aspects of their personality that have been repressed, but may influence their day-to-day lives. Using the classical notions of transference and resistance and creating a safe climate, we gain insight into a process well-established as a long-term therapeutic process.

Leszcz and Malat in their chapter, "The Interpersonal Model of Group psychotherapy," do not emphasize unconscious processes. Rather the group tracks observable interactions among members in the here-and-now that often reveal cognitive distortions and disturbances in ways of relating. New and more satisfying ways of securing attachment are then sought.

Schermer and Rice, in an attempt to bring a number of contemporary analytic perspectives together to inform treatment, aim "Towards an Intersubjective and Relational Group Psychotherapy." Among the operating assumptions of this theoretical umbrella is that the leader and the group need to attend to empathic failures, and their impact, and ways in which the group members co-create a world that points to individual and collective deficits that require repair.

In contrast to the psychodynamic and interpersonal approaches is Crosby's discussion of "Integrative Cognitive-Behavioral Group Psychotherapy." Emphasizing interpersonal and social skills building, the therapist creates a climate in the group in which learning can occur. Specific techniques are included that can assist the leader in conducting such groups.

Susan Gantt presents a different frame-of-reference through which she helps the group identify and utilize "Functional Subgrouping and the Systems-Centered Approach to Group Therapy." She sees the formation of groups within the group as motivated by differences and conflict among the members. Exploration of these subgroups frees the individual to identify the feelings that might have been hidden by being in a subgroup that collectively avoids conflict.

Examining four forms of action within a group, purposeful, self-initiated, spontaneous, and group-centered, Schwartzberg and Barnes present their "Functional Group Model." They hold that structured techniques give participants the opportunity to learn more about themselves and their styles of social participation.

Billow in his chapter, "It's All About Me (Introduction to Relational Group Psychotherapy)," stresses the importance of the leader knowing how he or she impacts the group and how the group impacts him or her. Ways to collectively explore this relational issue are clearly depicted.

A rationale for focusing on the subtle but palpable vibrations among group members is presented by Berman, in "Resonance Among Members and Its Therapeutic Value in Group Psychotherapy." Dramatic case examples highlight this important aspect of communication that reveals much about the people involved.

Berger, Berman's colleague in Israel, focuses on mirroring and its role in producing interpersonal conflict and intrapsychic deficits. Mirrors can help us find ourselves – an outcome sought by many who enroll in group.

Zeisel's approach to group leadership is aimed at "Meeting Maturational Needs in Group Analysis...." Through specific tactics, the leader helps members to expand their self-knowledge and their ability to manage their emotions (and lives).

Shwartz and Shay integrate multiple theories of communication and relationships in the supervisory process and describe their approach in, "Developing the Role of the Group Facilitator...." They conduct training groups that not only build skills and deliver support but also can be mined for information about the groups they conduct.

Finally, one should read Van Wagoner's "From Empathically Immersed Inquiry to Discrete Intervention: Are There Limits to Theoretical Purity" as a proposal to learn about the many theories of group process and look for commonalities and select among the differences identified. His hope is that each leader will construct what works for her and responds to the needs of the members.

This rich section serves as a fascinating introduction to the controversies among schools of thought, while it suggests that the "truth" may be found somewhere in the space among them.

2
Psychoanalytic Group Psychotherapy: An Overview
Priscilla F. Kauff

Introduction

Psychoanalytic group therapy is analytic treatment conducted in a group setting. While the differences between the group venue and the dyad (one-on-one) have implications for therapeutic technique and in some respects for the process of the therapy itself, both the task and goal of the treatment remain the same. The task of analytic treatment is to help patients explore what is going on inside themselves with special emphasis on that which is out of consciousness or otherwise out of control. As it would be in a dyad, the role of the group therapist is to help each member in the process of self-exploration by establishing the appropriate conditions for treatment. The goal, ultimately, is to enable the patient to use the acquired self-knowledge to maximize personal control or "agency" in order to achieve the greatest possible satisfaction in living. As Ogden and Gabbard (2010) asserted, the analytic approach is not to eradicate symptoms (although that may occur during the process) but rather to "..provide meaning and understanding that will help the patient become the principal agent in his own history and in his thinking."

A Psychoanalytic View of Treatment

Self-exploration

What goes on inside each one of us determines to a great degree how we perceive, experience and interact in the world, both cognitively and emotionally; it is this same internal world or psychological terrain that will distort perception to a greater or lesser degree, often trumping reality. Furthermore, when the outside world is not as we want, need or expect it to be, our perception will be transformed so that it conforms to our internal demands. Consequently, the world we occupy is an amalgam

---

The Wiley-Blackwell Handbook of Group Psychotherapy, First Edition. Edited by Jeffrey L. Kleinberg.
© 2012 John Wiley & Sons, Ltd. Published 2012 by John Wiley & Sons, Ltd.

of reality and the unique alterations we impose upon it. As often as not, even in "normal" functioning " . . . we see what isn't there, believe what isn't true and remember what didn't happen" (Gilbert, 2010).

In this context, pathology may be broadly defined as the kind and degree of disconnect between what is going on psychologically inside and what is actually going on in reality. This disconnect is what can, in fact, be altered in treatment and requires that the patient become as familiar as possible with his or her own internal terrain, as well as the manifestations of that terrain in feelings and behavior. As Aristotle (448 B.C.) wisely said, "This only is denied to God, the ability to change the past." Likewise, while treatment cannot change the past, it can be the forum for thoroughly exploring present functioning, that is, how one perceives, reacts and interacts. This process ultimately permits patients to identify what they contribute to their own pathology or to that which interferes with their optimal functioning. Analytic treatment in groups is one method for achieving this goal.

The group process

The spontaneous, free-flowing interaction between group members, here called the "group process," is the vehicle which makes the group a uniquely powerful instrument of, and venue for, conducting psychoanalytically oriented therapy as defined above. The group process consists of each member's responses to one another, to the therapist and to the group as a whole. These responses may or may not be conscious, and they may be verbal or non-verbal in form. Individual members will resonate differently and with different intensity to any particular communication (Foulkes and Anthony, 1957), but each communication and response will stimulate another, and move the process forward. *The group process is equivalent in analytic group therapy to free association in the dyad.* A crucial job of the analytic group therapist is to establish and maintain the condition for this process to exist and to manage the obstructions (resistance) that interfere with it (Kauff, 1979).

The Psychoanalytic Group

Group composition

While it is certainly possible that participation in group therapy will be of help to anyone who chooses or is invited to join, some people are better suited than others to an analytic group. At the end of the day, one cannot predict how any individual will respond to such a group; it is really an empirical issue. Nonetheless, there are several characteristics that have proven to contribute to successful membership:

1. A prospective member ought to be able to pay attention to others, to listen with at least some continuity, and to speak the language of the group. Individuals vary enormously in their ability to attend, understand and articulate but some minimal ability to do so is necessary, especially in an analytic group. It should be kept in mind that disturbances in attention and ability to articulate may be psychological in origin and can improve over time as anxiety is reduced and comfort is increased.

2. The prospective member should have some amount of "psychological mindedness," or the capacity to think about the meaning of his or her thoughts, feelings and actions. At the same time it should be noted that this capacity may improve during treatment and therefore it may be best to give a promising prospect room to develop.

3. It is important to determine that the patient can financially afford the group and is able to attend with regularity. Introducing individuals to a group that they cannot afford or which conflicts significantly with their work or lifestyle may well create more problems than it will solve.

4. Anyone being considered for group membership should be willing and able to abide by the formal aspects of the contract described below, and the therapist must appraise whether the patient can uphold his or her end of the bargain. Of course, it is always expected that deviations from the contract will occur and that these will be analyzed in the group.

Diversity

In order to create a psychoanalytic group, an important consideration is diversity in the membership. When a group is uni-dimensional on any demographic or diagnostic axis, there is an increased likelihood that members will share many unconscious defenses as well as conscious beliefs, prejudices, and expectations. This will, in turn, heighten or reinforce the resistances that occur naturally in any treatment, group or otherwise. It is virtually axiomatic that enough psychological heterogeneity should exist to assure that individual distress or disturbance will not be disguised by the mask of similarity. While it is certainly possible, for example, to conduct a group with a psychoanalytic orientation composed of only one gender, it is generally a richer experience to have groups that include males and females, heterosexual and homosexual.

The same is true for diagnostic categories, shared symptoms or shared experiences. While the initial coming together of the group may be easier if everyone in the group has suffered abuse in childhood, loss of a parent, panic attacks or depression, for example, such commonalities are more likely to hinder the development of the group process going forward than to facilitate it. The group process depends upon a wide variety of responses, which will cast light on the presence of pathology. This is especially true with respect to character pathology, which is evident in repeated, anxiety-free behavior usually experienced as "just me." Without some discomfort or anxiety, it may be impossible to get any traction at all in dealing with such symptoms. Identifying them is the first and often the hardest step.

A therapy group in which every member was female and significantly obese illustrates the problem of homogeneity or the lack of sufficient diversity. While the members all joined the group with the conscious intention of bettering their lives, their shared symptom (obesity) and the prevalence of depression fueled a resistance that virtually paralyzed the group. The therapist found himself struggling to stay awake through countless sessions in which the members were unshakeable in their focus on foods they knew and loved, diets they tried and failed, clothing they could no longer wear, and so on. The affect in the group, which varied from despair to hopeless resignation, reflected the intensity of the depression, which afflicted each member. No amount of effort on the therapist's part to shift the focus to other aspects of the members' lives much less their internal state was successful as the shared resistance became more intense and entrenched over time. The group eventually was disbanded and the members reassigned to groups with varied symptomatology.

Among the great values of group treatment is that at least one member will almost inevitably react to another member's pathology regardless of how heavily disguised it may be, perhaps by questioning some behavior or responding in an unexpected way. This in turn will call attention to the pathological aspects of behavior (which are usually completely out of awareness) in a far less threatening way than if the therapist attempts to do the same thing. It is unique to the group venue that a new stage is provided upon which old behaviors, responses, and perceptions are played out in full view of other people (members) who often do not respond in a way that the individual has come to expect (Kauff, 1993). This will ultimately encourage the person to take a second look.

Ms D, an intelligent and well-spoken patient who was insightful and helpful to other group members, regularly became vague and elusive when talking about herself. Her use of language, although seemingly sophisticated, was often too obscure to follow and she was hard put to give concrete examples, which would clarify what she was trying to say. When attempting to describe a feeling of being distant, for example, she said, "A piece of me is somewhere else and I think it is more virtual than real." If she reported a dream, usually rich in imagery, it would go on for so long that no one could remember the beginning by the time she got to the end. For some time the group listened patiently but finally, as their frustration increased, they began to interrupt and tell her that they could not pay attention, they were getting lost, and could she give an example or get to the point? At first Ms D was quite surprised by the group's response, as she was accustomed to being considered an entertaining raconteur. She was also unaware of the defensive aspects of her delivery. As the group continued to challenge her, Ms D became aware that this was a pattern that allowed her to increase distance both from others and from her own feelings and anxieties. This awareness became sharper over time and helped her to focus upon her own contribution to the problems she encountered in dealing with people in her life, especially in intimate relationships.

As important as diversity is in a group, however, it is equally important that no one member stand out as dramatically different from the rest. Although this situation may in fact occur in a therapy group, it tends to be a set-up for resistance both for the deviant member ("These people are not like me . . . I do not belong here .. they cannot understand me") and for the group ("We cannot help him and he will not be able to help us"). While such resistance can profitably be explored and potentially resolved, modulating the diversity is to the ultimate benefit of all concerned. Ideally an analytic group will consist of 6–8 members of mixed gender, with an age range of not more than 30–35 years. Diagnostically, all prospective members but those with serious organic issues or those who are very severely borderline or overtly psychotic should be considered for membership.

Ultimately, as indicated previously, the composition of the group is one that needs to be tested in real life. It is not possible to predict either the behavior of any one patient or the compatibility of the group as a whole without actually trying it out.

Of course, it is very important to try to keep an ongoing group together and functioning. Ejecting a member or disbanding a group is a dramatic and sometimes traumatic event. Obstructions or problems should be subject to analytic exploration before it is determined either that an individual member is inappropriate or that the group composition as a whole is unworkable.

Preparation

How the therapist prepares a patient to join a group can and will vary depending upon the setting – private practice versus a clinic/hospital or other institution. However, the process should include introducing the idea of a group, explaining as simply as possible why being with other people can expand the breadth and depth of self-exploration, and some review of the formal aspects of the contract (which should be reiterated in the first as well as subsequent sessions of the group when necessary).

The preparation of a new patient – one who is not already being seen individually by the therapist – for an analytic group allows the therapist to begin forging a bond or working alliance, to create some familiarity, comfort and trust that can grow over time. This is important in keeping the treatment moving successfully. The preparation should not be used, however, to eliminate anxiety, which is always present and should be explored but *not* eradicated. Some anxiety is critical to the process of exploration and consequently to the possibility for change.

The contract

When psychoanalytic treatment is begun in whatever venue, a "therapeutic contract" that parallels Freud's (1913) original analytic contract is agreed to by the patient. The intent is to clarify the roles of the therapist and patient(s) as well as the nature of the process to be engaged in and its desired outcome. In the dyad, the contract specifies that the patient will, as much as possible, report everything that comes to mind without editing. This part of the psychoanalytic contract defines "free association." In the group, the corresponding agreement is that members will verbally share whatever they are thinking and feeling as freely as possible, again without editing, including their responses to one another, to the therapist and to the group as a whole. This outlines the substance of the "group process" and is, as previously indicated, the equivalent of free association in the dyad.

The contract agreed to by all the group members and the therapist is one of the prime building blocks of the psychoanalytic group. The contract makes it possible for the group process to function with maximum potency as a vehicle for the exploration of the self within the group. In this context, it is important to note that analytic therapy groups are not democratic. With very few exceptions, any prospective member has the freedom to choose whether or not to participate. But once joining a group, the participant must agree to abide by the contract as specified by the therapist. This is not a *legal* contract; it is neither written out nor does it require a patient's signature. Rather, it is an oral agreement among all the parties that makes it possible to initiate treatment and manage it going forward in such a way as to maximize the impact of the group. It forms the basis for the working alliance among the members and with the therapist.

Indeed, because there are multiple people in the frame and therefore multiple opportunities for boundary violations, certain contractual matters require more attention in the therapy group than in the dyad. This is especially true of *confidentiality*, which is absolutely necessary to the development of trust. Confidentiality must be addressed very specifically, both at the initial group meeting and whenever it arises as an issue during the life of the group. It is imperative that each member understand and agree that what goes on in the group is to be kept in the group, that only first names are to be used with one another or when talking about people who are not members of the group. It is also imperative that members agree never to speak about another member in a way that might reveal his or her identity if they refer to the group outside of its confines.

Ideally, the contract is initially presented in an individual meeting before the prospective patient enters the group. It is then reviewed in the group with all members present. In order for the group process to proceed successfully, the members must feel safe and trusting of one another and the therapist, which, of course, cannot be mandated! The role of the therapist is to explain the details of the contract and then to help the members of the group explore their responses to it. This will include feelings about being in the group, about the prospect of sharing with one another their own thoughts and feelings, and about being exposed to one another's reactions and comments. In exploring these concerns and anxieties, the emotional basis for the contract and the working alliance will be established. It can be seen that one of the first instances of initiating the process of self-exploration actually occurs in the course of discussing and agreeing to the group therapy contract. In examining feelings related to trust, safety and comfort as well as their more troubling opposites, namely suspicion, danger and vulnerability, patients enter directly into an exploration of what is going on inside of them at the moment. In turn, this exploration will lead the way to uncovering less conscious or unconscious material related to these important feelings.

Feelings of safety, comfort, and trust are not constant. They will develop differently among individuals and vary in degree over time. Trust requires the attention of the therapist and group members throughout the life of the group. For example, unless the group always has the same membership (a rare situation in a long term group), the arrival of a new member will necessitate some review of the contract regarding acceptable and appropriate behavior, especially that which relates to the confidentiality agreement. In training settings, the leaders usually change on a yearly basis, and the contract must be reviewed every time this occurs. There are also certain events, such as a pending divorce or other legal action that may raise questions about confidentiality requiring special attention.

Occasionally, even in large cities where anonymity is usually assumed, a new patient will come into a group and recognize someone who is already a member. As the group leader does not reveal the identity of any incoming member in advance, an awkward situation can arise which must be addressed by the entire group as well as the individuals directly involved. In dealing with such an event, the therapist must protect both the on-going life of the group and the well-being of all members whether old or new. It sometimes happens that individuals who already are acquainted or who have mandatory contact outside the group, e.g., in professional or training settings, knowingly join the same group. While this is an exceptional situation and not ideal, such members should be able to participate in the same group provided that confidentiality is very carefully preserved. Only in the rare instance where negative interaction between the members becomes so intense that it cannot be resolved should the therapist consider referring the newest arrival to another group.

A related boundary issue is the occurrence of outside or extra-group contact among the members (which, incidentally, can even occur in the waiting room before group begins). While opinions to the contrary can be found in the literature even among analytic therapists (DeShill, 1973), it is this author's opinion that the power of the group is undermined when outside contact is sanctioned. Any material that relates to the feelings and thoughts that members have toward one another and especially towards the therapist belong within the group and should be heard by all. This aspect of intra-group communication is critical to the transference process (see below), and loss of any such material diminishes that which is available and necessary for self-exploration. In fact, the content of the material usually lost in extra-group contact tends to be both the most difficult to express and the most important to deal with, namely the negative thoughts, fantasies and feelings directed to other group members and most importantly to the therapist. An agreement should be made among the members from the start that contact outside of the group will be as limited as possible and that accidental contact will be kept superficial and reported back to the group. This will help to ensure that important interactions and information will remain within the boundaries of the group and will afford an opportunity for all responses to be explored.

Formal aspects of the contract

Creating the conditions in which treatment can occur involves some formal arrangements along with the therapeutic agreement outlined above. In both instances, the point is to guarantee the best possible venue for the development of the group process upon which the therapy depends. This in turn requires that patients feel secure. Keeping the "frame" of the treatment (specified in the formal aspects of the contract) as consistent as possible is one important element of that security. The formal aspects of the contract are equally important in clarifying the boundaries of the group and the expected behavior within it.

Psychoanalytic groups in the US typically meet once a week for 1¼–1½ hours each time unless the therapist specifically cancels a session. The time and place are determined by the therapist and should be maintained as consistently as possible. Make-up sessions are understandably rare as it is difficult to change the schedules of several people at once. Patients agree to pay for sessions whether they attend or not, as their place is guaranteed to them as long as they are members. It is advisable to stipulate that patients will notify the therapist and the group in advance of an anticipated absence and will contact the therapist in the event of an unexpected failure to appear. This kind of agreement will help to clarify when absences are an indication of resistance and should be further examined.

There are occasions in which the group membership becomes dramatically reduced, sometimes resulting in a session with three or even fewer members present. Although it is tempting to cancel such a session, the value of a constant frame for treatment should not be violated in that way. It is highly recommended that the therapist proceed with the group session regardless of how many people show up. The feelings of those included and those absent (when they return) can be a rich source of material, which should not be sacrificed. A session with only one member is still a "group" session as the absent members are present mentally in any event.

Fees for sessions should be uniform for all members. If a member has a special need, it should be worked out with the therapist and communicated to the group. It is advisable to avoid fee variations, but any alteration in the basic contract will give rise to feelings among the members that should be articulated and explored.

Ultimately it is the contract that creates the basis for identifying and analyzing "resistance," the counterforce to change, which is ubiquitous in every treatment (see below). It is understood in the analytic framework that the conscious agreement to engage in therapy will *always* be subject to the force of resistance. However, as Szasz (1961) pointed out, a patient's behavior may not be considered resistance unless there is an agreement as to expectations. Unexplained absences, excessive silence, missed payments, indeed any kind of acting out in violation of the agreement can only be subject to analysis if inappropriate behavior has been specified in advance. Violations of any part of the contract should be addressed immediately in the group.

The initial session

The initial session of an analytic group is the one in which the creation of the conditions for analytic work begins. It is also the one in which the contract is negotiated for the first but certainly not the last time.

After the members have arrived at the appointed hour, it is advisable to wait briefly to see if anyone will begin speaking. If there is only silence, the therapist may invite members to share their feelings and thoughts about starting the group. The first session should be conducted in a manner that will model how the group will operate going forward. In this and subsequent meetings, the leader does not "direct" or determine the content of the session. In an analytic framework, the *goal* is defined (exploration of the self) but the material presented by members is *not* defined. The agenda for the therapist is to encourage the development of the group process. In subsequent sessions, she or he will wait for someone to start. If no one speaks, the therapist will, as in a dyad, enquire as to what is going on or what is happening in the group and with the individual members. This will allow the therapist and the group to explore the observable resistance and will also help to create the condition that will maximize the accessibility of transference.

Parenthetically, "going around" or asking each member to speak or comment is *not* an analytic technique for at least two reasons: First, it disguises resistance because it offers the member something to talk about that may or may not relate to the cause of his or her silence. Second, it interrupts spontaneity because it dictates content. When the content is determined by the therapist's request for responses to a specific question, the actual or hidden material belonging to the patient is preempted and, at least for that time, lost. This does not mean that the therapist should never invite an individual member to speak. However, it is preferable that the intervention be a response to a communication (often non-verbal) from the member. The therapist might say, for example, "I see that you are staring at the ceiling!" or " You seem to be frowning." Similarly, the therapist might say, "Did you notice that you just changed the subject?" In such a case, the purpose is to invite a verbal restatement of a non-verbal communication and thereby open a channel of exploration rather than to introduce or dictate content that is part of the therapist's own agenda.

More typically, someone will begin to speak, just as in the dyad. The material presented will cover a very wide range: outside life events, dreams, fantasies, as well as interpersonal reactions from within the group, immediate feelings and/or thoughts about the therapist, the other members, or alternatively the group. One important difference, however, between the group and the dyad is the increased availability of non-verbal communication. Traditionally it is through verbal communication of thoughts, feelings, fantasies, memories, dreams and the recounting of events that material enters into analytic treatment. In the dyad this comes primarily from one source, the patient, although certain kinds of information are also accessed in the interaction between the therapist and patient. Material presented by individuals is, of course, important in the group as well, but the group format greatly amplifies and enriches access to non-verbal behavior (*including both the nature of verbalization itself and the way it is conveyed*) and the cues to unconscious factors that such behavior provides. In addition, members' responses (or lack thereof!) to one another provide non-verbal material, which can be identified and explored as it happens in the immediate moment.

It is worth repeating that group members are encouraged to observe each other's behavior, and to comment on each other's style and mode of communicating as freely as possible. Members can respond more spontaneously than can the analytic therapist who is always constrained by the requirements of neutrality and objectivity. Group members are also able to point out repetitive behavior – including that which is non-verbal – that is almost always out of awareness and serves important defensive and often pathological functions intrinsic to character defenses and entrenched character pathology.

An illustration of this process involved Mr L, whose childhood memories were dominated by the deterioration of a parent with a neurologically degenerative disease. He was the designated caretaker from an early age. Mr L appeared to have a minor learning disability that made it difficult for him to follow the flow of another person's thoughts without saying them out loud repeatedly until he "understood." This practice was eventually quite annoying to the group and the therapist, whose efforts to intervene were summarily rejected. He was "only trying to understand so he could help." But it became clear that this characterological response was allowing him to fend off the observations and reactions of the group and finally to provoke their hostility. Eventually a new member, Ms R, entered the group and reacted immediately and strongly to Mr L, whose behavior made her extremely anxious. She got angry with the therapist for putting her into a group with this man who "was exactly what she was worried about from the beginning, that the group was only a place for crazies and was the last thing on earth she needed."

As sometimes happens, a meeting occurred during very bad weather in which Mr L and Ms R were the only members present. Ms R was angry with the therapist for not cancelling the group. She was sure that the therapist "must have known in advance that only the two of them would appear. . . . wasn't it clear that it would be a fiasco?" Mr L felt similarly beleaguered and both members were ready to quit the group. Fortunately, at the next meeting, other members were able to react to both Mr L and Ms R and to help them explore their mutually powerful and hostile responses to one another. Ms R recognized that her response coincided perfectly with her feeling that she was never protected by her father from a mother she viewed as crazy, like the "crazies" in the group. The therapist had failed her in the same way. As the group repeatedly (and eventually successfully) stressed, Mr L was far from "crazy" though he could be bothersome and sometimes exasperating. This in turn helped Mr L to reconsider his "innocent attempts to understand" the other members in terms of the frustration it produced in them, making it at once difficult for them to help him and leaving him feeling abandoned to their anger as he had felt to his father's illness. In this case, the group and the group process played a special role in dealing with the resistance of both members against recognizing the non-verbal, provocative aspects of their communication style and in helping them explore their transference both to each other and to the therapist.

Dreams

While an extensive examination of the use of dreams is beyond the scope of this chapter, it should be noted that dreams may be very productively treated as shared psychic material in the group (Edwards, 1977). For example, it can be very useful, in the context of the group process, for the therapist to invite the members to associate to a dream recounted by one of them as if it were their own. In that way, the communication in the dream is treated like all other material in the group, as part of the spontaneous, conscious or unconscious interaction between members – the group process – and will hopefully provide new paths into each individual's self-exploration. In addition, the variety of associations to any dream coming from many members helps to reinforce the fact that perception is individually tailored and determined. When patients understand this, their perceptions become amenable to alteration in order to better fit reality.

Transference, Resistance and Regression

Transference

Psychoanalysis is distinguished from other forms of treatment by its focus on what goes on inside, in the inner psychological terrain of the person, where the "psychological lens" or the "templates" through which that person views and participates in the world may be found. This terrain includes the entire universe of conscious and unconscious expectations, needs, desires, and beliefs whether in the cognitive or emotional spheres, laid down both by hard wiring and experience, invented and reinvented throughout life. It may be understood as equivalent to what Freud (1912) called "a stereotype plate (or several such), which is constantly repeated and constantly reprinted afresh in the course of the person's life . . ." As such it dictates, to a significant degree, important components of human experience and behavior. As a focus of exploration in treatment, the internal psychological terrain offers "...a cumulative statement of the psychological life of the patient that is dominant at any given moment in time and would reflect the internal psychological processes active at that moment (Kauff, 2009)."

In this context, as mentioned previously, pathology is measured by the difference between one's internal psychological terrain and what is actually going on outside ("reality"). In other words, pathology reflects the amount of distortion that occurs when internal factors take over perception and behavior. And it is this very distortion or transformation that we label "transference" in psychoanalytic terminology.

As a treatment method, psychoanalytic therapy utilizes the analysis of transference as a primary vehicle of self-exploration. Access to psychic material comes into the treatment in its most reliable and purest form in the transference process that continually exists between patient, therapist and group. Transference is unconscious and its presence as an active force in the treatment appears concretely in the attribution of meaning, motives, or behavior, which are *either not relevant or not actually occurring*. In other words, when external reality is altered by the imposition onto the therapist, onto group members or onto the whole group of some aspect(s) of the patient's *internal* reality, the transference process is in action.

The analytic treatment situation, whether dyadic or in group, is deliberately structured to maximize the development and accessibility of the transference process and to make it analyzable. In a dyad, the couch may be used to make projection and displacement, the primary mechanisms of transference, easier to identify. In the group, when all people present are upright and visible to one another, the verbal and non-verbal interaction of the members (the group process) will expose the transference. Both the neutrality and objectivity of the leader as well as the reliable boundaries of the group make this spontaneous interaction a possibility, allowing the free exchange of thoughts, feelings, and especially distortions in perception to emerge.

Ms M entered the group from an individual treatment with a somewhat idealized view of her therapist whom she experienced as "warm and nice." Encouraging her to acknowledge any negative feelings, much less to express them openly, had been unsuccessful. When she began work in a group led by the same therapist, however, her experience was quite different; she complained that the therapist was "cold and bitchy" and no longer interested in her as a person. This kind of transferential response is one that entry into the group may easily stimulate. Because it was clear that the therapist was the same person that Ms M had seen in individual therapy, it became possible to introduce the idea that Ms M's experience was being redefined in her own perception and was different from reality. Although the therapist had not changed, the sanctity of the dyad had been significantly altered. It became necessary for Ms M to confront the fact that the therapist had other patients which, in turn, opened the dynamics of envy and rivalry to exploration. Both the group members and the therapist participated in the discussion; the members by challenging Ms M's perception of the therapist (they did not agree with the "cold and bitchy" description), and the therapist by encouraging the group members to express their differing views.

Transference in the group can be directed toward another member, the therapist or the whole group (this is known as "multiple transference"). The actual role of the therapist, to establish and foster the best functioning of the group, necessarily involves authority, unique expertise and some degree of control. These aspects of the therapist's role can provoke the most primitive and powerful transference responses, such as rage, dread, and sometimes fierce power struggles against the perceived "enemy." Articulating such responses directly toward the therapist can be extremely threatening to the patient who unconsciously vests the therapist with excessive, even life-threatening power. In the group context, it is possible for a member to experience such feelings and responses toward one or more members and safely away from the therapist, at least at first. Thus the opportunity for multiple transference increases the likelihood that important feelings and dynamics will ultimately be revealed and made available for exploration.

Group members will inevitably challenge distortions of one another, whether directed toward themselves or the therapist or the group. Indeed, they are uniquely able to do so as they are freed of the demand for neutrality by their contract, which explicitly invites the open expression of negative as well as positive reactions. These challenges (as illustrated in the example above) will afford patients an opportunity to further explore their own distortions, the first step to being able to do something about them. The process becomes even more dramatic when a patient experiences either the therapist or another group member as hostile or attacking. When it is the therapist who is viewed as attacking, the distortion is usually readily identifiable. One or more members of the group are very likely to point out that the therapist (in their view) was not being hostile but was instead trying to help. Any such response, even from only one other member of a group, can help the patient reconsider his or her perception and response.

Mr J entered the group after a long individual treatment, which had ended badly. The previous therapist, Mr J felt, constantly "intruded" when offering any suggestion as to the meaning of what he was saying. Mr J's theory about this was that his parents never took seriously what he said and rarely believed him when they bothered to listen. His rage toward them was as active in the present as if he were still a little child. Predictably, he began to experience the group therapist and very soon the group itself as similarly intrusive and potentially harmful. Even simple questions were felt to be hostile, threatening intrusions. The therapist was somewhat protected by the group, which acknowledged Mr J's painful experience while raising questions (gently) as to whether the intention was really hostile on the therapist's part. The therapist had no choice but to remain silent toward Mr J while encouraging the group to be open with him about their reactions. This was a very tricky situation and remained static for some time, during which Mr J would repeatedly threaten to quit the group and then change his mind. It was clear that he had at least a rudimentary bond to the group that overrode his anxiety.

Another member, Ms H, was also prone to reject the therapist's comments but was not as profoundly threatened by them as was Mr J. She was able to voice her annoyance or disagreement with the therapist and was able, at least on some occasions, to explore the possibility that she was distorting the therapist's intent. Mr J found this somewhat reassuring although he was critical of Ms H's exoneration of the therapist. Finally, in one group session, Ms H observed that Mr J seemed unusually sad. When she mentioned the look on his face (reacting to his non-verbal communication) he quickly came in touch with this feeling, of which he had previously been totally unaware. More compelling, however, was his surprise and gratitude toward Ms H for having been so empathetic, for having "heard" him in a way that he could not hear himself. It marked the first time that he was able to seriously consider the possibility that someone else's thoughts or perceptions, even if different from his, might *not* violate his boundaries and cause him pain but might, instead, make a contribution to his self-understanding.

It is true, of course, that members can and do actually become hostile to one another or to the therapist from time to time. In such instances, the role of the group is to explore what was going on that led to the hostility as well as the response to it. The exploration will inevitably highlight some aspect of the internal process for each person involved that precipitated or provoked the hostile interchange. Quite often it will become obvious that the hostile member chose the target because that person was unconsciously perceived, rightly or wrongly, as particularly threatening. Another possibility is that the chosen target was perceived as more vulnerable or significantly less likely to respond in kind and was therefore seen as "safer." In either event, uncovering the internal factors at play in a hostile interchange is exactly the kind of rich, therapeutic experience that the group provides. Responses to hostility in a group can be especially revealing because group members are not essential parts of one another's outside life (and the contract in the group is intended to keep that boundary firm). When the conflict takes on undue importance, it becomes even clearer that what is coming from the member is mediating his or her own behavior or response. This is the desired outcome of analyzing what are best understood as transferential events between members.

When the hostility is directed toward the therapist, the exploration is slightly different because the therapist guides the exploration but typically does not personally participate in it. If the therapist has actually felt hostile it is his or her responsibility to examine that countertransferential response *outside* of the therapy setting and still be prepared to lead the exploration in the group. Although there is much disagreement on this matter coming from other treatment approaches, it is not advisable in the context of psychoanalytic treatment that the therapist share his or her actual feelings with the members. The responses of the patient are the *prime* focus in analytic treatment and the intrusion of the therapist's experience adds a dimension that should not be the patient's responsibility. Of course if there is an occasion when the therapist does in fact reveal negative or hostile feelings and they are observed by one or several members, the therapist can and should acknowledge the reality but shift the focus back to the patient(s) reaction as quickly as possible. Technically it is of utmost importance to solicit responses to such events, starting in the group by noting whether the other members comment spontaneously. If they do not voluntarily share their reactions, it is understood that a group resistance is in progress and this should be observed by saying, for example, "It is interesting that no one seems to have reacted to what just happened in the group!" All members of the group do have reactions and exploring the meaning of such events is both critical to the group process and potentially very informative for everyone involved.

The exploration of transference as it, manifests in the way each group member views the therapist, the group or other individual members is a powerful demonstration of how unconscious beliefs, expectations, wishes and internal templates can dictate perception and override reality. Drilling down into this experience leads to an understanding that it is one's own psychic input that accounts for the distortion, which in turn means it is something that one can actually alter. This is where the treatment ultimately grabs hold and change can occur. It is also the ideal opportunity to help patients learn more concretely about how the process works in themselves. In group, the transference is subjected to the responses of all the other members in addition to that of the therapist and is often more reliably (even dramatically) made known to the member involved than would be the case in the dyad. All aspects of the members' functioning become available to many observers, each with their own unique and particular view to bring to bear. Further, as members respond to other members, they both contribute to the other members' self-understanding and can also learn a great deal about themselves by examining their own reactions.

Resistance

Transference is an unconscious process that is neither recognized nor acknowledged under ordinary circumstances. It is also zealously guarded by "resistance," the psychological force that operates against revealing anything unconscious and that opposes change regardless of a person's conscious intent. Resistance is built into the transference process. Making it analyzable is crucial to the role of the analytic therapist in whatever venue in order for the therapy to proceed. As in individual treatment, resistance must be dealt with in order for transference to become accessible; it must therefore take precedence over anything else going on in the group. It can arise in an individual member, between pairs of members or, on rare occasions, it can involve the whole group.

One of the most important contributions that the group makes to analytic work is that it can be a powerful antidote to resistance, and can, therefore, help individual members to become aware of their own transference process. In the group, the therapist is neither the sole object nor the sole interpreter of transference (Racker, 1968). Instead, the opinions and observations of group members provide alternative views of "reality" that are easier to accept than the same opinions or observations voiced by the therapist. In a therapy group as in life, no two people experience the same event in precisely the same way. So, in sharing perceptions, group members can help one another work through their resistance in order to identify and resolve transferential distortions.

For example, group members can say, in response to any co-member's perception, "I don't see it that way" and be far more persuasive than the therapist who tries to address the same distortion. They will often comment to one another, for example, "There you go again. . . you always have that kind of reaction even if it is not called for." As long as even one member has a different view, the possibility exists that an individual patient will be able to understand that his view may be distorted by his own inner needs, feelings and fantasies. The corollary is that these same distortions, generated as they are from inside the individual, will appear elsewhere in the patient's life and experience and not just in the therapy room.

Consider a person coming into a group for the first time. There are aspects to this experience, some conscious and some not, which inevitably arise and include anxiety related to all that is "unknown" in the new situation (Durkin, 1964). Since (with rare exceptions) neither the group nor its members are familiar to one another, new members tend to be self-protective and sometimes quite guarded. The expectation of danger will vary in degree for each individual and have very specific components, reflecting the particular nature of that individual's internal world. One new patient may experience the group as a potentially friendly ally while another may see it as a potential enemy, for example, a rejecting or damaging father, a disinterested or competitive mother or a volatile, irrational family. Whatever the specific content of the transformation might be, each new member will view the group, at least in part, through an internal lens which will reflect that member's general approach to the world, including the pathology she or he brings to it.

Sooner or later, if the group or the therapist do not behave in a way that the new patient expects, the patient will likely attempt to provoke them to do so. Consider, for example, the patient who regularly includes too many details or leaves too many out when describing an event. It will not take long for a well-functioning analytic group to start noticing this behavior, calling it to the member's attention. If the behavior persists, the group's response is likely to intensify, perhaps even becoming provoked into frustration or anger. The patient in such a situation will either begin to work on changing this defense of obfuscation or feel progressively more criticized and attacked. This may or may not be accompanied by memories of feeling similarly misunderstood, unheard, or attacked in the past. In any event, the group will work to help the patient understand that her or his behavior actually provoked their response. The patient will be helped to explore over time, as deeply as possible, what actually happens that leads to this behavior. Other members will identify with the patient and sometimes take the lead in describing their own similarly confusing ways of communicating. Ultimately, it will pave the way for both the patient and other members to become increasingly aware of their defensive efforts to hide behind a barrage of words or an absence of important facts. This in turn will lead to further exploration and an opportunity to alter responses and behavior accordingly, both in and ultimately outside of the group.

While it may seem counter-intuitive, offering support or concrete advice in an analytic setting is generally understood to be countertransference if coming from the therapist or resistance when it occurs between members. Offering support or giving advice takes the focus away from what is actually going on inside the person that may be leading to the conflict he or she has reported, and it is precisely that which should be the focus of the analytic process. "Support" in the traditional sense is not encouraged both because it distracts from self-exploration which is the primary task and because it can reinforce dependency. Real support in analytic group therapy comes from members helping one another to understand their own reactions and experiences in the most profound way possible.

To this end, the most therapeutically appropriate and valuable responses from members are the associations, reactions or feelings that each one has to the communication of the other members, to the group as a whole and to the therapist (Foulkes and Anthony, 1957). So, for example, if a patient reports an argument with his spouse, the role of the other members is *not* to suggest ways in which he might handle the conflict but rather to report their own associations or reactions to similar problems. Resolution of actual conflict or other situations in the real world is the job of the individual, not the group or the therapist.

All group therapists are familiar with the patient who, often after years of individual treatment, arrives with a mental notebook full of personal genetic hypotheses ("My mother was that way so I am this way." "My father did this so I cannot do that."

"My life was so bad that I did not have a chance."). While there may be some reality in such statements, the conclusions to which these hypotheses lead are often self-defeating, explaining little, assuming a lot, and above all, transferring the responsibility for present behavior onto an absent and often unwitting player from the past. Such patients are comfortably, albeit immovably, fixed in the role of a victim of forces beyond their control. They have, in other words, forfeited their agency or the power to be in command of their own lives. Groups learn to question the tendency of fellow members to blame others or external situations or events for their current condition. There are enough people in the group reacting in their own unique ways to challenge fixed, self-defeating ideas. Eventually it becomes clear, as Oscar Wilde is reputed to have said: "The truth is rarely pure and never simple!" As this becomes absorbed and understood, the transformation begins from passive to active, slowly increasing self-empowerment.

This function of the group process may be thought of as a "Rashomon" effect. That at least one member will see things differently from everyone else almost always guarantees that the group will ultimately challenge resistance and facilitate exploration and analysis. In the transference experience, when the patient views the therapist in a certain way and has to deal with the disagreement of fellow members, there is at least the possibility of the patient's being open to reconsidering these views. That very process is what must ultimately occur for patients outside of the therapy, as they view their behavior and their lives. The group invites its members to reconsider their automatic categorizing, to explore how they actively (if unconsciously) transform their own world. The group will challenge the theories each member creates, especially when those theories result in abandoning responsibility and blaming others for self-perpetuated difficulties.

Regression

Whether viewed as a return to earlier developmental levels in thought, feelings and behavior or a retreat into more primitive defensive functioning, regression is a very important element in psychoanalytic treatment. While the group modality is clearly not constructed as a venue to facilitate the deep, continuous regression that is deliberately cultivated in traditional dyadic analytic treatment (using the couch and multiple sessions per week), shorter and intense regressive experiences for members and for the group as a whole are typical of group functioning (Bion, 1959). Durkin and Glatzer (1973) agreed that regression in group therapy was neither as linear nor as continuous as it typically appears in the dyad. They stated that: "..the periods of regression are profound both in the sense of intensity and in the depth of the genetic levels which are partially re-lived..Regressions are rarely prolonged or pervasive. There is reason to believe that this 'dosage' of small, intense regression, frequently repeated, is at least as effective as are the extensive regressions."

Equally important is that regression may be most critical as a trigger or release mechanism for effect which is central to how the group is able to facilitate the treatment of entrenched character pathology (Kauff, 1997). Thus, it is not uncommon that the emergence of intense emotion in the group will occur, often to the surprise of the person involved, leading to a deeper exploration of the meaning and origin of the regressive experience. Such experiences tend to occur spontaneously, as a result of the group process or intra-group stimulation.

Mr W was a controlled, somewhat over-intellectualized man who considered overt displays of anger beneath his dignity. He was shocked at his outburst toward the therapist within a few sessions after entering the group, during which he shouted "How can you not understand what it feels like when you don't pay attention to me? How could you put me into a group? Don't you see how much this takes away from me?" Merely coming into the group had set off a reaction, which was affectively intense and well beyond his defensive limit. The therapist joined the group in inviting Mr W to further explore his reaction, which was unusual enough to engage his interest. Over time, he was able to identify profound feelings of abandonment and ultimately of betrayal which he felt in the group each time the attention was turned from him. Thus, both the intensity of affect and the return to very primitive anxieties were elicited and explored in the group setting.

Analytic groups are structured and conducted in such a way as to encourage the spontaneous interaction of the members rather than being directed by the therapist to fulfill some other agenda such as the deliberate inducement of regression. Unfortunately, other types of group therapy encourage such practices with the intent of creating a cathartic experience. While induced regression has indeed been shown to generate the explosive release of powerful negative emotion, it has also been shown to be a short-lived and sometimes damaging solution to long-term problems.

Working through

It is well known that insight, even insight with feelings, does not suffice to eradicate symptoms or dislodge entrenched character pathology. Identifying pathology in any form as well as the cognition and affect attached to it is not sufficient to eliminate it. Most pathology, as Freud (1914) describes, is deeply embedded in the fabric of the individual's functioning and not resolvable by discovery or suggestion. While this is especially true of character pathology, even acute symptomatology can inveigle itself into the personality in a most debilitating and persistent way. Working through actually means going back, over and over, to the same issues, the same pathological perceptions and responses and distortions until they no longer can stand on their own.

Every individual analyst knows that the "working through period" in treatment is one of the most treacherous in terms of keeping the patient involved and committed. Resistance often deepens as the process demands more sustained energy than the patient can muster or maintain. Glatzer (1969) discussed the problem of working through in group therapy, detailing how group members can be enormously helpful to one another in this long and arduous undertaking. By identifying repetitive patterns of behavior in one another, which are often out of consciousness, they help to reduce the potency of such patterns in determining behavior. The embarrassment that people feel when they find themselves repeating old behaviors is lessened as it is shared among the members. Group members also respond positively and encouragingly to one another when it is clear that old characterological patterns are being dislodged or altered. This kind of approval, which again is not generally part of the acceptable repetoire of the analytic therapist, serves as a positive reinforcement function which will strengthen the changing of old patterns as they begin to occur.

Over time, members get to know one another as psychological beings. They can associate for one another, remember for one another, identify with one another and offer one another models for change as yet untested and growth yet to be achieved. It can be extremely difficult for the therapist to help patients reflect upon their patterned inappropriate behavior, to help them say, "Oh there I go again." But when members of a group say to one another "Oh, there you go again!", the growth of understanding accelerates significantly.

Combined therapy

Group therapy is often the only treatment that is available or offered to a patient, especially in hospital settings and clinics. Unfortunately group therapy once a week is rarely sufficient, at least in the initial period of treatment. There is not enough opportunity for the patient to bond with the therapist to progress deeply into his or her interior life. In England and other locales analytic group therapy is sometimes conducted on a bi-weekly or tri-weekly basis. This format seems to successfully avoid some of the problems that arise when group is the only treatment, but it still is desirable for the patient to meet with the group therapist individually (at least occasionally) to maintain the appropriate and necessary working alliance. It should also be noted that group alone may be adequate in some cases and even desirable in the final stage of treatment as a route to termination.

This author has written extensively on the subject of combined therapy (Kauff, 2009), that is when the patient is simultaneously in group and individual treatment with the same therapist. It is also possible to have congruent therapy, which is group and individual treatment with two different therapists. The combination of individual and group treatment can maximize the power of both modalities. This is particularly true in dealing with resistance to treatment that can arise in one or the other venue over time. It is possible, for example, to work out resistance to entering a group during individual treatment. It is also possible that the group experience may help the patient continue individual treatment when it becomes particularly difficult for whatever reason. Less frequently a patient will be more comfortable starting treatment in a group and including or moving to the dyad at a later date. The important point is that dealing with resistance can be easier for some patients in the group than in the dyad and vice versa. Combined therapy can be a very helpful tool in this endeavor.

Termination

With individual treatment, much attention is directed to the termination process between therapist and patient. The dynamics and feelings are very rich and inevitably include abandonment, separation, fear of annihilation, despair, loss, and rage (Kauff, 1977). All of these are central to analytic work and need to be addressed throughout treatment, whatever the venue. Typically in the dyad, they come to the forefront when either the patient or therapist misses a session, as vacations or other breaks approach, in the case of illness or death of the therapist, and in the course of the actual termination of the treatment. In group therapy, situations involving separation arise far more frequently than in the dyad. Any member's absence or departure is a termination experience for the whole group. Understandably, a death in a group, either of a member or the therapist, is an event with far-reaching impact requiring a great deal of attention and analysis.

Again one of the advantages of group therapy is that the importance or urgency of any of the above feelings or dynamics will vary among the members. As each member articulates and attempts to deal with his or her own reactions, other members will be exposed to feelings and thoughts that they may not have had or of which they may not have been aware. This exposure will enrich the treatment of each member, by multiplying the opportunities for exploration and analysis (Fieldsteel, 1996).

A Final Note

It is important to remember that psychoanalysis is a way of thinking, of understanding human functioning and pathology, as well as a method for engaging in a treatment process. Throughout its history, psychoanalysis has provided a conceptual framework to explore and elucidate many aspects of human behavior and to enrich the study of history, economics, all forms of art, biography, and anthropology, among other subjects. While this chapter has concerned itself with the rationale, theory, and technique of conducting analytic groups with a relatively high functioning population, the principles described should not be considered *limited* to such groups. On the contrary, part of the magic of psychoanalytic thinking and technique is that they have proven applicable to a wide range of populations and in many different settings, often far beyond the analyst's office. This author, for example, created and ran groups as a part of a crisis intervention effort after 9/11 in a major corporation (Kauff, 2002; Kauff and Kleinberg, 2008). The use of analytic theory and technique was significant and enormously helpful. Hopefully the reader of this chapter will find that an analytic approach can enrich and deepen his or her group work in whatever venue or form it may occur.

References and Bibliography

Aristotle. (448–400 B.C.). Nicomachean Ethics, VI.
Bion, W. R. (1959). *Experiences in groups*. London: Tavistock Press.
DeSchill, S. (1973).The challenge to group psychotherapy. *American Mental Health Foundation*.
Durkin, H. E. (1964). *The group in depth*. New York: International Universities Press, Inc.
Durkin, H. E., & Glatzer, H. T. (1973). Transference neurosis in group psychotherapy: The concept and the reality. In L. R. Wolberg & E. K. Schwartz (Eds), *Group therapy: An overview* (pp. 129–144). New York: Intercontinental Book Corporation.
Edwards, N. (1977). Dreams, ego psychology and group interaction in Analytic group psychotherapy. *Group, l*, 32–46.

Fieldsteel, N. D. (1996). The process of termination in long-term psychoanalytic group therapy. *International Journal of Group Psychotherapy, 46*, 25–39.

Foulkes, S. H., & Anthony, E. J. (1957). *Group psychotherapy: The psychoanalytic approach.* Maryland: Penguin Books.

Freud, S. (1912). The dynamics of transference. *Standard Edition, 12*, 99–100.

Freud, S. (1913). On beginning the treatment: Further recommendations on the technique of psychoanalysis. *Standard Edition, 12*, 134–135.

Freud, S. (1914). Remembering, repeating and working – through. *Standard Edition, 12*, 155–156.

Gilbert, D. (2010, July 25). Review of Kathryn Schulz's *Adventures in the Margin of Error,* Ecco/Harper Collins, 2010. *New York Times Book Review*, p. 16.

Glatzer, H. T. (1969). Working through in analytic group psychotherapy. *International Journal of Group Psychotherapy, 19*, 292–306.

Kauff, P. F. (1977). The termination process: Its relationship to the separation-individuation period of development. *International Journal of Group Psychotherapy, 27*, 3–18.

Kauff, P. F. (1979). Diversity in analytic group psychotherapy: The relationship between theoretical concepts and technique. *International Journal of Group Psychotherapy, 29*, 51–65.

Kauff, P. F. (1993). The contribution of analytic group therapy to the psychoanalytic process. In A. Alonso & H. Swiller (Eds), *Group therapy in clinical practice* (pp. 3–28). Washington, DC: American Psychiatric Press.

Kauff, P. F. (1997). Transference and regression in and beyond analytic group psychotherapy: Revisiting some timeless thoughts. *International Journal of Group Psychotherapy, 47*, 201–210.

Kauff, P. F. (2002). Analytic group psychotherapy: A uniquely effective crisis intervention. *Group, 26*, 137–147.

Kauff, P. F., & Kleinberg, J. (2008). Crisis intervention at the organizational level. In R. H. Klein & S. B. Phillips, (Eds)., *Public mental health service delivery protocols: Group interventions for disaster preparedness and response* (pp. 159–170). New York, American Group Psychotherapy Association.

Kauff, P. F. (2009). Transference in combined individual and group psychotherapy. *International Journal of Group Psychotherapy, 59*, 29–46.

Ogden, T. H., & Gabbard, G. O. (2010). The lure of the symptom in psychoanalytic treatment. *Journal of the American Psychoanalytic Association, 58*, 533–544.

Racker, H. (1968). *Transference and countertransference.* New York: International Universities Press.

Szasz, T. S. (1961). *The myth of mental illness: Foundations of a theory of personal conduct.* New York: Hoeber-Harper.

3

The Interpersonal Model of Group Psychotherapy

Molyn Leszcz and Jan Malat

As this handbook demonstrates very well, multiple approaches to group therapy are practiced to good effect. None is a pure culture and there is substantial overlap between models. Each approach is predicated upon the link between theory of development or pathology and technical interventions that in turn follow for the group therapist.

The task in this chapter will be to address the theoretical underpinnings and practical applications of the interpersonal model of group psychotherapy best characterized in the writings of Yalom (1995) and Yalom and Leszcz (2005). Elements of this chapter are also reported elsewhere in a recent chapter, *Interpersonale Gruppenpsychotherapie* by Leszcz and Malat (2010). This model of group psychotherapy centers upon the role of interpersonal interaction, interpersonal feedback and interpersonal learning as the heart of the mutative forces in group psychotherapy (Leszcz, 1992; Leszcz and Malat, 2010). The contemporary practice of psychotherapy places ever increasing emphasis on the centrality of interpersonal processes in therapy and the core task of processing the therapeutic relationship (Hill and Knox, 2009; Shedler, 2010). The group is intended to function as a social microcosm for the members of the group utilizing the here and now of the group experience as a vehicle to illuminate how the individual authors his relational world for better or for worse, and how feedback, insight and a healing therapeutic experience can be used to gain or restore a sense of interpersonal efficacy. The group provides multiple relationships that are examined and processed with regard to their meaning, impact and the beliefs, fears and wishes that underlie the relationship experience. The interpersonal approach to group therapy is widely utilized in ambulatory, inpatient and day hospital settings and across a range of diagnostic foci from addictions to geriatric depression (Leszcz, 1997; Malat et al, 2008; Yalom, 1983; Yalom and Leszcz, 2005).

The role of specificity of models in psychotherapy is the subject of much debate (Wampold, 2001). Although it appears that factors common across treatments account for a substantial amount of patient improvement in psychotherapy (Lambert and Ogles, 2004; Wampold 2001), clarity about the application of a model serves to provide the therapist and her patients with a coherent approach to therapy that generates consistency, hope, confidence and congruence in expectancies and central elements that are important in achieving and sustaining a strong therapeutic alliance (Martin et al., 2002).

Theoretical Constructs

The model of interpersonal group psychotherapy is rooted in the original work of Harry Stack Sullivan (1953) and his emphasis on the central imperative of achieving interpersonal attachment and reducing anxiety interpersonally as the guiding developmental thrust in human existence. The pursuit of secure interpersonal attachment and the experience of self as accepted, affirmed and coherent within the context of relationships are critical forces.

Sullivan's pioneering work has ebbed and flowed in its importance in contemporary psychotherapy but has received more scientific attention of late, emerging from the domains of infant observation (Stern, 1985), clinical applications of attachment theory (Fonagy et al., 2004), the refocusing on psychotherapy from a one-person to a two-person psychology (Stolorow et al., 1987; Mitchell 1994) and the move towards integration within contemporary psychotherapy linking cognitive and interpersonal processes (Kiesler, 1996; McCullough, 2000; McCullough, 2006; Safran and Segal, 1990).

A core principle is that psychological disturbance reflects interpersonal disturbance (Horowitz and Vitkus, 1986). The interplay of the individual's temperament and biological predispositions, and early interpersonal environment shape the individual's sense of self and view of self in relation to the world. Stern's infant-observation predicated on concepts of affect attunement (Stern, 1985) has added credibility in many ways to Sullivan's principle, that an individual's sense of himself emerges from the reflected appraisals of significant others. Attunement of caregivers to the unfolding sense of self of the infant and child contributes to the individual having a fundamental belief in what is acceptable and desirable about him, and from him in his relationships to others, generating shaping beliefs about relatedness. According to Sullivan, when the infant/child experiences aspects of himself, such as ideas/emotions/action tendencies to which the caregivers have previously responded with negative emotion or neglect as opposed to attunement, intense and disorganizing anxiety may be generated in the individual. This can be experienced as a dangerous, foreign, "not-me" experience (Sullivan, 1953). The implication for the child is that the emergence of such aspects of self may lead to catastrophic relational outcomes such as abandonment and rejection. The growing child tries to engage her environment in a fashion that avoids the experience of "not-me" elements of its selfhood.

Giesler and Swann (1999) argue that much of this adherence to the negative, and the avoidance or denial of positive but foreign feedback, coupled with the selective processing and evaluation of information about the self that confirms and preserves the self-view can be explained by the self-verification theory. Regardless of the valence of self-view, they argue that individuals are motivated to confirm their firmly held self-views out of the desire to bolster perceptions of predictability and control. We seek what is known and familiar – not necessarily what is best for us.

Emde (1992) has commented further from the domain of infant observation about the importance of attention paid not only to the avoidance of negative and adverse interpersonal experiences, but to the shaping influence of attunement that endorses positive emotional experience. This helps to consolidate the infant's sense of mastery and achievement as important developmental imperatives in their own right. McCullough similarly emphasizes the importance of addressing and restoring the patient's sense of agency and interpersonal effectiveness (McCullough, 2000; 2006).

Within this framework, the child's development unfolds with the child developing internalized maps for relatedness, based upon core cognitions and beliefs that generate subsequent interpersonal patterns of behavior, emerging and following logically from these core beliefs. Safran and Segal (1990) refer to this as the cognitive-interpersonal schema, a roadmap for relatedness that each individual carries within himself. The interpersonal model of group psychotherapy focuses on both arms of this schema, identifying both interpersonal patterns of behavior and over time elaborating the core beliefs and cognitions that underlie this pattern of interpersonal interaction. Strupp and Binder (1984), in their elaboration of psychotherapy, refer to this as the misconstrual-misconstruction sequence, the link of pathogenic beliefs that alter one's construal of the world and consequent maladaptive, rigidly applied interpersonal constructions that flow from and perpetuate the sequence.

Within the framework of the interpersonal model central principles include the proposition that interpersonal disturbance manifests itself in characteristic, recurrent, disturbed interpersonal communication including not only verbal patterns of communication but non-verbal and paraverbal communication patterns, encompassing body language and styles of communication and interaction. Much of this is woven into the individual's character pattern, resulting in significant blind spots to the individual who may be aware only of the failures of interpersonal engagement, but is often unaware of his direct contribution to the interpersonal difficulties. In part, this reflects the egosyntonicity of the character pathology in that it has emerged for the individual in a logical and understandable sequence based upon early life experience. The individual relates to the contemporary world cast in the cognitive-interpersonal template from the past with an attendant lack of empathy and appreciation for new relationships and the opportunities for a present that is different than the one shaped by transference.

If psychopathology is a reflection of interpersonal rigidity and the rigid application of a pathological cognitive interpersonal schema, then a central element of effective treatment is the broadening of the patient's interpersonal repertoire. This entails both dynamic and genetic insight arising in the context of new relational experiences. This is in turn coupled with interpersonal learning and the acceptance of responsibility for the authorship of one's interpersonal life with the subsequent commitment to modify maladaptive interpersonal behaviors.

The control mastery model developed by the San Francisco Psychotherapy Research Group addresses related principles from a psychodynamic perspective (Weiss, 1993). Psychotherapy centers upon the therapist's identification of the unique plan that each patient brings into treatment. The plan, as described by Weiss (1993), focuses on the individual's conscious and unconscious pursuit of growth and restoration of a full developmental line that has been obstructed by pathogenic beliefs that reflect early life disappointments, traumas and failures in attunement. These pathogenic beliefs can be categorized as falling into six main concerns: self-doubt; doubt of others; fear of anger/assertiveness; fear of closeness; guilt of success; guilt and responsibility for others (Sammet et al., 2007).

The patient enters into treatment seeking disconfirmation of these pathogenic beliefs. Adherence to these beliefs obstructs growth and development as the patient, hoping against hope, relates in ways that recruit responses that, if unchecked, may confirm these pathogenic beliefs. Disconfirmation is achieved through the therapist's capacity to engage with the patient's testing within the transference, and provide pathogenic belief – disconfirming feedback and relational experience along, importantly, with insight as to the nature of the transference test and the pathogenic beliefs. In this model each patient's plan is unique and the therapist's tasks center around responding in ways that promote disconfirmation, alert to the hazard of inadvertent and unwitting confirmation of pathogenic beliefs by virtue of the failure to identify the transference test, or the failure to react in new and different ways, from those that historically are recruited by the patient. The transference test may be expressed in a direct displacement of past onto present – for example, submissiveness and fearing assertion in the therapy relationship or alternately through a form of mastery by inversion in which the transference test is expressed in the patient's projecting onto the therapist or co-members the experience that is dreaded – for example, treating others in a contemptuous fashion whilst fearing that engagement will generate humiliation and dismissiveness. The key question is: Will the experience of humiliation rule the relationship, or will the transference test be passed by identification and working through rather than re-enactment (Foreman, 1996).

These principles are an important link to the interpersonal work in group psychotherapy and to the interpersonal model of treatment. It is the failure to provide disconfirmation, or worse yet, the confirmation of pathogenic beliefs that Kiesler (1996) has labeled the maladaptive transaction cycle. This refers to the unbroken causal loop in which the patient continues to recruit interpersonal behavior that confirms her pathogenic beliefs while failing to integrate readily schema-disconfirming feedback and information (Carson, 1982). Sullivan described this original failure of the patient to make use of feedback that would challenge the interpersonal beliefs and behaviors in his description of the patient's selective inattention (1953). In this framework Sullivan identified the ways in which the individual continues to see the present in the spirit of the past through parataxic distortions and appears unable to incorporate new information that could liberate the individual from adherence to the original relational template.

A factor that relates to the maintenance of cognitive distortions and their resistance to modification also emerges from current developments in cognitive psychology. Misconstrual is maintained by cognitive processes that quickly link negative cognitions to streams of other negative cognitions and interfere with the individual's capacity to delineate accurately external and internal personal stimuli. This can be understood as a form of priming, in which well-worn paths of construal, referred to as associative networks in cognitive neuroscience, are much more easily set alit than are underdeveloped lines of cognitive associations (Westen, 1999).

Hence, in a moment to moment fashion, treatment provides the potential for self-fulfilling or self-defeating sequences in the form of a transference enactment (Viederman, 1993).

One of the core tasks in the interpersonal model of psychotherapy is to interrupt this maladaptive transaction cycle as it manifests itself in the treatment situation, interrupting the sequence of interpersonal recapitulations in which the patient recruits familiar patterns of response perpetuating the status quo, providing verification for the cognitive-interpersonal schema.

Clinical Illustration

A 35 year-old woman was referred for an evaluation for group psychotherapy by her family physician. Working as a mental health professional, the woman, Dawn, was referred for treatment related to chronic depression and vocational difficulties regarding feelings of isolation and interpersonal conflicts. At the initial consultation, a moment into the interview, Dawn asked the interviewer what the inscription read on his wedding band. Taken somewhat aback by this intrusive, overly familiar question a moment into the interview the therapist thought it best to provide some semblance of an answer without a premature confrontation with the patient about the inappropriateness of her request. He responded that it was a Hebrew wedding inscription – implicitly offering information that he was married and positively connected to his culture and heritage, a point of potential relevance to the patient whose name clearly signified her ethnic background. Dawn's response was, "I know that," dripping with hostility and antagonism. Dawn's response had a clear impact on the therapist putting him back on his heels, feeling chided and irritable – and quietly noting this sequence for later attention.

Dawn went on to describe that she found it impossible to relate to people. Try as she might, she described always getting into hostile exchanges with people at work and with friends. The results were repeated ruptures in relationships and job dislocation and consequent depression. She was able to speak openly about her sadness and her puzzlement, claiming that she tried as hard as she knew how to, to make better relationships. The therapist, privately reflecting upon their initial exchange about the ring, attributing the prematurely familiar and intrusive question as an attempt to offset the power imbalance she likely experienced in the interview and now feeling less irritated after the initial intrusive, hostile and dismissive response by Dawn, asked if it might be possible to look at their initial encounter as a way of gaining some awareness of these patterns of difficulty.

Attempting to speak dispassionately, the therapist inquired about Dawn's initial experience of walking into the consultation and the response to her first question. Dawn was willing to explore the here-and-now elements within the consultation and recounted coming in feeling angry and on the spot, anticipating that the consultant would be angry with her for having canceled the previous appointment and needing to reschedule this. Further inquiry about

> the motivation behind the question and her response to the therapist, allowed the therapist to articulate that he felt her retort to him carried with it elements of anger, dismissiveness and rebuke and wondered how this could have manifested itself so early in a relationship that had not yet really begun. Trying to metabolize and remove any elements of judgment or antagonism in response to Dawn, the therapist suggested how it would be easy to see in another situation how that might have led to a hostile response back to her. Indeed, such thoughts had passed through the therapist's mind before a better metabolized response could be articulated. Dawn's response to this feedback was a sudden rush of emotion and a recounting that began with her statement of, "Do you know what it's like to grow up as the only girl in a family of seven brothers in a newly emigrated family?" She went on to describe how she chronically felt humiliated, diminished and under attack by her father and brothers, viewed as someone whose responsibilities lay only in maintaining the home and facilitating the growth and development of the brothers. There was no expectation for her to have an advanced education or career and she felt chronically belittled. The emotional outpouring was quite intense and extraordinary, in particular, for such an early point in the therapeutic process. After ascertaining her consent to further processing of this, the therapist suggested that if these are the fundamental ways in which she experiences the world relating to her, then the interpersonal behavior that follows from her may well carry those same elements, in that he felt diminished and dismissed by her, recruiting potentially a self-perpetuating maladaptive cycle. Issues of antagonism, power and humiliation and potential rejection were introduced into this encounter within moments. As this was further processed, Dawn added that it was scary to see how this manifested itself so quickly – but she was also encouraged that the pattern could be so readily accessed for therapy.

Even in the initial consultation the core principles of effective treatment can be accessed: working in the here-and-now; the focus of treatment being the interactional world of the patient, setting the stage for later therapeutic work between peers within the group; provision of a corrective emotional experience; and the importance of meta-communication and feedback. Furthermore, the initial consultation provides an important opportunity for early identification of pathogenic cognitive-interpersonal schemas which can enhance the precision and effectiveness of subsequent therapeutic work.

Ultimately, the social microcosm of the group becomes the clinical laboratory for the study of interpersonal interactions and the illumination of each individual's cognitive-interpersonal schemas. Therapist interventions that are congruent with the patient's cognitive-interpersonal schema and that are plan concordant (Fretter, et al., 1994) have a significant correlation with effective outcome in psychotherapy. Hence, the greater the precision that is achievable in the identification of the cognitive interpersonal schema; in the plan of the patient; or, in the misconstrual-misconstruction sequence, the greater the likelihood is that a durable, collaborative relationship and treatment will develop that will ultimately be successful and effective. If feedback about the individual's authorship of his interpersonal world can be provided in a way that does not feel fault-finding or attacking, but rather reflects the emergence of information that the patient can utilize constructively and adaptively, then the stage is set for effective treatment (Stone, 1996). Indeed, a sense of empowerment may emerge as the patient understands his contribution to interpersonal relationships and benefits from the experience of disconfirmation of the narrow, constricted, pathogenic belief-shaped schema for relatedness. Understanding and interrupting the maladaptive interpersonal circularity provides not only a more meaningful and supportive relationship experience in the moment, it also sets the stage for the transfer of knowledge and skills into the real world of the patient (Malat and Leszcz, 2005).

Recent scholarship has further elaborated the contemporary model of interpersonal theory. Writing mainly about individual therapy, Donald Kiesler (1996) posits that the interpersonal model is the ideal integrative model for contemporary psychotherapy. In his text, Kiesler reviews the way in which interpersonal behavior can be described and understood as reflecting issues around control – the pursuit of domination or the acceptance of submission along one axis of relatedness, and issues around affiliation – friendliness and hostility along the second axis. Interpersonal circumplex construction can plot, making use of interpersonal checklists and inventories, the prototypical pattern of interpersonal relatedness for any individual, positioning that individual at a nexus that reflects the conjunction of control along the vertical axis and affiliation along the horizontal axis. This lends itself to a greater precision in understanding the cognitive interpersonal schema for each patient and enhances the therapist's ability to reflect upon not only the patient's interpersonal behavior, but the behavior and response that may be recruited by the patient in his maladaptive bid for predictability and self-verification (Giesler and Swann, 1999). The interpersonal circumplex can further illuminate the patient's interpersonal patterns and the predictable interpersonal pulls which the patient will exert on others (MacKenzie and Grabovac, 2002).

Kiesler (1996) utilizes the concept of the "impact message" to capture the patient's interpersonal behavior by studying the internal reactions and perceptions it pulls in others, in relationships, through processes of interpersonal complementarity. It includes not only manifest behavior but also the patient's covert powerful communication, expressed often through paraverbal and non-verbal means. Kiesler describes complementarity as an interpersonal behavior and its most probable interpersonal reaction. A central construct of interpersonal theory designates that interpersonal actions are designed to pull, elicit or evoke specific, often restricted classes of reactions from the other person involved in the interaction. Complementarity is reflected in the pursuit of reciprocity along the axis of control and domination and correspondence along the axis of affiliation. Non-complementary, less familiar responses may generate much anxiety in the patient as these non-complementary responses tend to elicit foreign and hence, less acceptable interpersonal experiences of the self. This may in turn lead potentially to a redoubling of the patient's effort to recruit the complementary response.

As Kiesler has noted, it is impossible for one close to the patient not to become hooked responsively, but the challenge for the therapist and in the group for other group members is to be able to recognize the experience of being hooked into a complementary response so that a non-complementary response can be offered that promotes reflection rather than reenactment. Hence the challenge is not to avoid getting hooked: the key therapeutic challenge is getting unhooked in order to process therapeutically with the patient the maladaptive interpersonal sequence.

Also, the person reacting to the individual is not a blank screen, but rather comes into the interaction with his or her own cognitive-interpersonal schema. Hence, the recruitment of complementary responses is more easily achieved with some than with others, and similarly, the unhooking process or disconfirmation of pathogenic beliefs may be more readily achieved by some rather than by others.

The impact message, in interpersonal terms, refers to the range of responses of the interactant/therapist, covering the whole gamut of direct feelings, images, cognitions and actional tendencies evoked within the interactant by the individual's interpersonal communication. From the therapist's perspective this can be understood as countertransference. It is essential that the therapist be able to recognize her characteristic interpersonal responses and subjective reactions and responses, in order to be able to discern what particular impact message is evoked by the patient's behavior. The group therapist, within herself and through exploration and inquiry with other members of the group, must look at the elements of the impact message including direct feelings induced; tendencies towards interpersonal actions that are induced; recognition of the perceived evoking message of the patient as well as access to more covert, less conscious material such as fantasies. Bringing this material into the realm of exploration within the psychotherapeutic process is essential in order to provide feedback to the patient, to foster reflection and deeper awareness of her pathogenic beliefs and to foster new and more adaptive behaviors.

Clinical Illustration

Karen, a 35-year-old college professor had been referred for group therapy to work on improving her interpersonal interactions with her students. She was a highly effective teacher with outstanding teacher evaluations but she found herself resenting her students. She experienced them as intrusive, cloying, and she could scarcely wait to get back to her office after class and put the "do not disturb" sign on her door. Her personal life very much resembled this. She had once been married for five years but had not consummated the marriage, and experienced relationships as intrusive and controlling. Giving anyone access to her meant a complete loss of autonomy and control. She had made it clear when she sought group therapy that she was not interested in getting closer to people: she wanted to learn how to tolerate their intrusion. She noted an important background, growing up with a controlling and devaluing mother whom she identified as "the Ice Queen." It was impossible to feel close to this woman and impossible to resist her unrelenting demands and control.

Karen had been in the group for several months when two new members joined the group. One of the new members, Joe, a middle-aged man, was interested in gaining familiarity with people in the group, determined to reduce his chronic feelings of isolation and alienation. Shortly after beginning the group he asked Karen what her personal life was like. Was she married? Was she in a relationship? Karen snapped at him, saying in essence – "Do not ever ask me personal questions about myself. I do not want to talk about that, least of all with someone I do not know." Joe was very much taken aback. He looked at the group therapist imploringly and then went on to say "I thought we were here to get to know one another and to develop more openness. I'm confused by Karen's response. Is this how the group operates?"

Another member of the group who had known Karen from the time of her entry into the group was critical of her shutting Joe down and in essence said – "If you are so committed to not sharing or talking with us, how do you expect to make use of the group?" The group leader also felt mounting frustration and concern that Karen's defensiveness and rigidity would confuse the new members and undermine the establishment of group norms of openness, self-disclosure and feedback. Cohesion would suffer. He was further taken aback when Karen's response to this feedback from a co-member resulted in her saying – "I am not going to be one of the group leader's trained monkeys, responding to every overture with complete submission to his request."

The "trained monkey" comment felt like a further attack on the group function and group norms and the group leader found himself hooked into an antagonistic position and in essence quietly mouthed the words to himself – "yes, why are you here if you refuse to engage?" It was at the moment of recognition of his hostile rejection of Karen, thankfully not articulated, that he recognized Karen had engaged the group and him in a maladaptive transaction cycle. She was exercising control over the group, and group leader, emerging from her fear of being controlled and colonized. Recognizing that dynamic allowed the group leader to say to Karen and the group that although in principle it was important for members of the group to be as open as possible and self-disclosing in order to create opportunities for interaction and feedback, he believed something important was happening for Karen at this moment. She needed to know that in fact no one wanted her to be like a trained monkey. Contrary wise, it was important for her to know that she could be in the group on her terms, and proceed at her pace, challenging her negative beliefs that she would be forced to submit or be extruded. Being hooked in this instance was an important part of the data that led to a more effective process of reflection and generated a therapeutic response. In this instance, the group leader, and group, passed the transference test created by Karen, lessening the polarizing tension and enabling her to choose to engage.

The concept of the impact message connects directly to reflection and investigation of the maladaptive transaction cycle (MTC). Four key elements serve as a guide for reflection on the MTC: the identification of the overt behavior of the initiator; the overt interpersonal response of the respondent/therapist; exploration of the covert or less conscious experience of the respondent/therapist; and finally the examination and exploration of the deeper, covert experience and covert self-representation of the patient. This methodology deconstructs the cognitive-interpersonal schema and misconstrual-misconstruction sequence into its key elements facilitating further exploration in treatment.

In the same fashion that Sullivan noted, the focus in psychotherapy should be on the interaction between the patient and therapist as the locus of clinical study; the same principles are articulated here, making maximum use of interpersonal communication *in-vivo* within the here-and-now of the group, rather than only relying on the patient's report. This further reduces limitations that emerge from the patient's genuine, good faith blind spots into his pattern of communications and relationships. Hence, the fact that the patient inevitably recreates the core interpersonal difficulties within the frame of treatment must be welcomed as an opportunity. This systematic focus on current interpersonal transactions distinguishes the treatment from other "interpersonal" treatments which focus on interpersonal problems and situations occurring outside of the treatment milieu (Wilfley et al., 2000).

Capitalizing within the group on the social microcosm of relationships and the principle that: what occurs *outside* of the group is likely to have expression *inside* the group sets the stage for illumination of interpersonal patterns articulated within the here-and-now of the life of the groups. In effective therapy this leads then to congruent interventions that are schema disconfirming, interrupting MTCs. Hence treatment provides new and less restricted opportunities for interpersonal relatedness, opportunities for understanding of the core beliefs and their roots, along with the opportunities to begin to experiment with new, more adaptive, accurately construed behaviors. Having reviewed the theoretical underpinnings of the interpersonal model, the remainder of the chapter will focus on treatment constructs and the way in which these powerful avenues for change can be accessed within the group setting.

Treatment Constructs

Group cohesion

Interpersonal feedback and learning are at the heart of the interpersonal model of group psychotherapy. It is essential to underscore, however, that this therapeutic focus can only unfold in the context of a group that is experienced by its members as cohesive and relatively safe. Although a range of therapeutic factors have been described in group psychotherapy (Bernard, et al., 2008; Yalom and Leszcz, 2005), for the purposes of this chapter the emphasis will be on interpersonal processes and cohesion. If the patient is to be able to enter into the life of the group and to bring himself as he genuinely is, into the treatment process, cohesion is essential in that a sense of collaboration and trust between members of the group and the therapist is a prerequisite for other psychotherapeutic opportunities to emerge.

It may be useful to conceptualize cohesion as both a therapeutic factor in its own right, and as a meta-therapeutic factor upon which other therapeutic mechanisms grow. Group cohesion has been described in terms of the overall sense of group cohesiveness or *esprit de corps* within the group that draws people to belong and to participate, and an allied concept of acceptance, as it relates to the individual experience of the member in terms of his feeling of being personally valued. Similarly there are both task and bond elements within cohesion, reflecting that group cohesiveness emerges in the context of both relational attachments and a sense of task-effectiveness (Yalom and Leszcz, 2005).

MacKenzie and Tschuschke (1993) have further differentiated cohesion into elements of engagement that reflect the working climate of the group as a whole, and, the experience of relatedness of individual members, demonstrating that it is the personal experience of belonging that is a more reliable predictor of positive outcome, than is the experience of a positive working climate as demonstrated through group-wide engagement. Elements of cohesion may reflect relationships between patients, between patients and the group as a whole, and between patients and therapist. Group cohesion has been likened to the working alliance in individual psychotherapy with its clear, significant contribution to successful outcome across psychotherapies (Martin, et al., 2000). Congruence of expectancies between the patient and the therapist, and between the patient and the group, regarding therapy's tasks, goals and the emotional bond is critical; misalliances or ruptures in the sense of cohesion must be quickly identified and addressed. The early positive experience of alliance and relatedness predict a more positive outcome in group psychotherapy (Piper, et al., 2005) – even more so in time-limited group therapies, where a slow process of engagement may leave little subsequent time for meaningful interpersonal exploration (Burlingame et al., 2002).

The therapist has an essential role in establishing and maintaining group cohesiveness. This entails attention to use of group structure, modes of verbal interaction and establishing and maintaining a therapeutic emotional climate (Bernard, et al., 2008). Aspects of group structure include selection of members and preparation of new members, instructing them about how to make the best use of the group; clarifying group norms and expectations and then modeling them in the group. Elements related to verbal interaction encompass feedback and interaction tied to individual need and the group's stage of development and fostering a sense of safety. Finally, the therapist is encouraged to maintain a posture that balances affiliation and control, demonstrating warmth and caring, and reinforcing the value of openness and risk taking, ensuring always the attribution of meaning to experience.

Clinical Illustration

Following a group session in which she received some critical feedback regarding the impact on the group of her excessive sensitivity, Sally, a 30-year-old member of the group, missed the next meeting, offering an excuse in a phone message to do with work commitments. Sally had recently entered the group after a series of failed courses of individual therapy – indeed her interpersonal sensitivity had led her to withdraw in the face of feeling uncared for or criticized by her individual therapist(s). She had experienced in her life significant early loss and neglect, leaving her feeling mistrustful and in anticipation of rejection. Her withdrawal from the group was foreboding, not the least part of which was the group members' reaction in her absence that Sally's withdrawal made a bad situation worse for her, and for them. They felt guilty on the one hand if Sally were to drop out of the group, and angrily fearful on the other hand,

> that Sally would return and restrict their openness or worse, blackmail them into avoidance and collusion. The therapist contacted Sally after the first missed meeting to express his concern for her and the importance of a quick return to the group, to which she agreed.
>
> In the next meeting the therapist welcomed Sally back and suggested that it was essential to process the last several group meetings and that an important therapeutic opportunity existed. Sally described with some encouragement how hurt she felt by the group's feedback; it evoked in her the dread of further rejection and failure and as a result she did what she always did – withdraw and cut her inevitable losses. The group members responded that in so doing she deprived herself of any chance to learn and change. They hoped that she would persist in the group; they thought they could be helpful to her. This feedback surprised Sally as she expected the group members to want her to leave. The therapist encouraged Sally to examine her reactions to the feedback and to consider that the group members cared about her and were operating in good faith – the work would be challenging but he hoped that she could trust that no one intended to hurt her. Her historical response of withdrawal may have served a protective purpose in the past and was understandable but what was required now was her commitment to keeping the group experience as stable as possible – missing meetings would not be protective but in fact would ensure that the group experience ended badly, an outcome no one wanted to see materialize.

Moving forward in the description of the clinical and therapeutic features of the interpersonal model there are four main concepts that need to be examined. They include the group as a social microcosm; working in the here-and-now; the corrective emotional experience; and, the processes of interpersonal learning.

Social microcosm

It is an axiom of most psychotherapies that the part represents the whole. In other words, there is a fundamental assumption made that an individual's characteristic patterns of relating to significant others in his outside world will, given enough time for initial social unease to dissipate, emerge within the treatment environment. Indeed, in interpersonally oriented group psychotherapy it is essential that the group function as a social microcosm in which each member is encouraged to bring himself as he or she genuinely is to the group, beyond compliance and politeness.

Part of the strength of the social microcosm is the way in which it creates an interpersonal laboratory in which maladaptive patterns of relatedness can be exhibited and can be addressed through the mechanism of feedback and meta-communication, resulting ideally in newly emerging and more adaptive behaviors. A key principle is that rather than relying on the report of individuals about experiences and relationships outside of the group every opportunity is seized upon and generated to look at the *in-vivo* experience of relatedness. At times the identification of the cognitive-interpersonal schema in the preparatory phase prior to entry into the group helps illuminate these patterns; at other times the cognitive-interpersonal schema is fleshed out by the experience of relatedness experienced and described within the group. Bellak (1980) has commented on the limits of dyadic treatment in terms of its inability at times to access information that is outside the patient's conscious awareness or capacity to report, in particular, as it relates to ego syntonic character pathology. The result at times is a two-dimensional rather than three-dimensional treatment, without full comprehension of the patient's own contribution to the difficulties experienced, since the patient's self-report mostly highlights the end results and not the process by which it was created. Additionally, there is the strength of the inherent face validity of the experience-near exploration that occurs when members of the group are able to comment to one another about patterns of relatedness that they have witnessed in the group. By operating at this lower level of inference, it becomes at times easier to confront maladaptive interpersonal behavior, and harder for the individual to refute it. Indeed, groups are powerful illuminators of interpersonal pathology, but in order to make maximal use of this, the group needs to be able to work effectively in the here-and-now and to provide both corrective and schema disconfirming experience and awareness.

The emphasis on the *in-vivo* behavior further reduces blind spots that might emerge from the synchronicity between the patient and therapist, or limitations because the individual treatment may not catalyze a particular pattern of relatedness; for example: gender or culture issues, or any of the other multiplicity of interpersonal interactions, that can emerge within the multiplicity of interpersonal interactions in the group. Furthermore, by not relying only on the patient's report, there is more access provided to non-verbal and paraverbal methods of communication.

Clinical Illustration

Peter, a 62-year-old university professor was referred to group therapy by his individual therapist. He sought treatment initially due to a lingering depression that emerged after the death of his wife of 38 years, the previous year. She was not only his beloved spouse, she was his social agent – the one responsible for maintaining social connections with family and friends. Without her he felt bereft and increasingly isolated. He quickly developed a good therapeutic relationship with his individual therapist – he felt supported and well cared for, but continued to be isolated everywhere else. Both he and his individual therapist thought a group might help reduce the isolation.

In the pre-group session, Peter described his painful situation in compelling fashion – a main lament being that since his wife's death, not one colleague at work had invited him to dinner. He labeled them all as "jerks." Furthermore, contact with his two adult sons reduced since his wife's death and felt to him as perfunctory without much evident care.

In the first meeting of a newly formed group that Peter entered, he told his story in a similarly compelling fashion, eliciting to his great pleasure, much

> support and care. After several sessions however, what emerged in his interactions with other group members was an opinionated, judging and haughty attitude. Peter believed that he always had the right answer to any problem and he berated other group members for their foolishness and poor judgment. Peter quickly became marginalized in the group that he initially idealized, which led to productive feedback that perhaps he had become isolated in his life as he was becoming in the group, not because his colleagues were jerks and his sons were callous, but because he was constantly devaluing others and putting them down. He caused others to submit or to withdraw. He was stunned to learn about his impact in the group, and to his credit, welcomed the feedback. He had no awareness of contribution to the problem. He had always seen his intent as being helpful to others, hoping to earn others' respect and appreciation. The feedback helped make sense of his difficulties and he invited the group to point this behavior out directly; he wanted so much to change and saw the group's feedback as invaluable.

Attention to the idea of the group as a social microcosm also focuses attention on the life of the group as a whole. Although the emphasis in the interpersonal model is on the individual and his interpersonal interactions, it is essential to recognize that this does not occur in a vacuum, and that the life of the group as a whole must be addressed. However, the focus of intervention is not, as it is the case in group-centered or systems approaches, focused on the group entity. Nonetheless, important group-wide phenomena that emerge in regard to group developmental stages; group pressure; or events that impact on the group as a whole such as transitions, terminations or threats to the group's integrity are explored. The group process must be addressed effectively at those times in order to reduce obstructions to genuine interpersonal engagement.

Working in the here-and-now

The concept of working in the here-and-now is both the most essential element of effective interpersonal group therapy, and the most difficult to foster. Working in the here-and-now demands a form of attention to interaction that is the antithesis of normal social intercourse, in that working in the here-and-now focuses on those elements of interpersonal communication that convey deep impact stemming from the *process* of interpersonal communication and less so from the *content*. For example, in the simple illustration of one person asking another person for directions, the content is very clear. There is a simple question and a response. Within the framework of the here-and-now, however, what would be examined is the entire subtext and process of that communication – what does it feel like to ask for directions? How does it feel to offer directions? Is the question asked in a way that is engaging? Entitled? Irritating? Shame-ridden? Is the response trustworthy? Dismissive? Devaluing? Hence, working in the here-and-now is a much more intimate and exposed, and also much more anxiety provoking, manner of communicating. Within the group it is likely to be resisted by members of the group because of the bilateral exposure that it creates, both for the sender and the receiver of feedback.

It is, however, the engine that makes group psychotherapy unique and moves it beyond offering only support, advice and commiseration. It demands that all of the members of the group be alive to the moment and to the immediacy of the experience of engagement. It emphasizes experience-near rather than experience-far process. Working in the here-and-now is bimodal. The first element involves plunging the members of the group into the experience of emotion and affect, looking at thoughts, feelings, fears, wishes and associations, followed by a second element of moving back into a self-reflective loop focused on the attribution of meaning and cognitive integration of their experience (Yalom and Leszcz, 2005). The importance of this bimodal capacity is also supported by recent neuroscience research which shows that psychotherapy helps patients access reflective capacity while their attachment system is simultaneously being activated (Fonagy and Bateman, 2006). Effective therapy generates a capacity for reflection and mentalization about the internal experience of self and others. This capacity to contextualize contributes to interpersonal skill development by increasing empathic awareness of interpersonal difficulties.

Activating interventions are those that stimulate engagement between members of the group, bridging from one member to another (Ormont, 1990), fostering the group members' capacity to examine themselves and to find words to describe their experience. In addition, bridging experiences stimulate the group's interactional flow. Working in the here-and-now also requires scrutiny of the potential analogues of extra-group situations and relationships, and their potential manifestation within the group. These activating techniques often generate an interpersonal marker (Safran and Segal, 1990). This represents a subtle shift in affect, relatedness or engagement that serves as an iceberg tip of a deeper, personally relevant experience. The interpersonal marker is an access point to addressing what might be triggering a loss of self-esteem; increase in anxiety; or, an increase in insecurity and the resultant compensatory strategies.

Working in the here-and-now also requires scrutiny of the potential analogues of extra-group situations and relationships, and their potential manifestation within the group. The clinical example below illustrates how effective activating techniques within the group can deepen understanding of an extra-group relationship problem.

Clinical Illustration

Murray, a 42-year-old business man was referred to group psychotherapy by a family physician upon the urging of Murray's wife who claimed to be at the end of her capacity to live with him. Murray seemed relatively undisturbed by his wife's agitation which centered upon his lack of responsiveness to her and his emotional distance.

In the group Murray's behavior was marked by a passive, observing stance. He would occasionally comment on how amazed he was at the level of emotional engagement experienced by people in the group, but he himself felt that it was going to take him much more time to be able to engage. Although he seemed superficially valuing of the group, he made little self-disclosure and over a period of several months he remained aloof from the group, notwithstanding many overtures on the part of the group members and therapist. On an afternoon prior to the regular meeting of the group, the group therapist received a phone call from Murray's wife who left a message saying that she was exasperated with Murray and was seeking some reason to remain hopeful that Murray was working in the group. The group therapist did not respond to the call but presented in the group that evening that he had received this highly unusual call. When the announcement was made in the group at the beginning of the session, Murray merely shrugged his shoulders, and in essence, responding – that it was a free world and if his wife wanted to make that call it was certainly her right to do so. Others in the group recognized how out of the ordinary this kind of phone call was and commented on the kind of exasperation that his wife must be feeling to have made such a call. Upon questioning, Murray described again in sparse detail the nature of his marital relationship. After some fruitless discussion the focus shifted to an elaboration of what it would be like for the women in the group to be married to someone like Murray, based upon their experience of Murray in the group.

This led to a much more affectively charged and meaningful engagement with Murray about how little he gives in relationships and despite seeming to be a decent man, there is absolutely no emotional connection extended from him to others. If they were involved with him in an ongoing way they too would feel the kind of exasperation that his wife reported. One woman stated – she felt that she would wither on the vine if she were married to him. Upon further examination Murray commented that this was not what he wishes to communicate, but he feels unable to find the words for emotional expressiveness and fears that he will say the wrong thing that will alienate and antagonize. The group members provided feedback that the offense of omission was more disturbing to his relationships than the potential hazards of commission and that he would need to take risks in order to engage or face the likelihood of the very situation that he dreads which is the end of a relationship that he values. The defense was not the solution – it was the problem. When encouraged to examine in more detail how he has come to this belief that he would say things that would alienate and destroy relationships he began to recount life in his own family, growing up in a family in which he learned at a young age "to keep my head down and my mouth shut," and avoid showing any emotions because of the certain expectation that any emotional expression would infuriate his overburdened parents and result in their critical attack of him. Concealing affect was essential in maintaining some degree of interpersonal predictability and safety growing up; now however it was experienced by others as being angry, provocative and exasperating.

Another important principle related to this clinical illustration is the challenge patients face in creating new ways of relating, despite learning that the past had an important and understandable shaping influence in the establishment of pathogenic beliefs and their cognitive-interpersonal schema. They cannot alter the past, but they can assume responsibility for the present. Indeed, at times the adherence to the past as an explanatory model is utilized to avoid making change in the present (Slife and Canyon, 1991).

Working within the here-and-now demands attention not only to vertical disclosure – the sequence of events and historicity – but also and most importantly, horizontal disclosure – what is the experience of the moment? How does it feel to put into words the affect of the moment; how does it feel to receive feedback; how does it feel to challenge or to confront? When the group works in this fashion it maintains very much a centripetal focus in which every member of the group is deeply engaged and close to the center of each meeting. This protects the group from devolving into a turn-taking model in which each person quietly waits his turn for his allocation of the fraction of time in the group that he feels is his entitlement.

As noted, groups will likely resist this at first because of the anxiety generated by the face-to-face, person-to-person communication. Hence, it is important to model and demonstrate this early on as a group norm, emphasizing that feedback need not be hostile confrontation, but may provide opportunities for meaningful expressions of support and engagement. Certainly, many patients seeking treatment have no less difficulty with expressions of intimacy and tenderness than they do with expressions of assertion.

Group members are not likely to be able to provide feedback effectively without some guidance and modeling by the group leader. Effective feedback addresses interactions occurring within the contemporary life of the group; are here-and-now related; involve some kind of emotional risk on the part of the sender of feedback directed towards the receiver; are specific rather than generalizations; focus on a specific, observable behavior in the group; and invite, but do not demand change. Ideally, feedback balances both positive and negative elements and is provided in a collaborative spirit of exploration, attempting to illuminate patterns of circular causality, rather than condemning maladaptive interpersonal behavior (Morran et al., 1998; Rothke, 1986).

The group therapist often has a choice point analysis to undertake, determining how feedback will best be provided at any moment in time. Hence, in response to an interaction or interpersonal sequence in the group, the group leader may invite the patient to process his own experience: he may invite others in the group to comment and provide feedback, or, he may provide feedback himself. Each has utility, but may be differentially more effective, and appropriately metabolized.

The corrective emotional experience

It is one thing to be able to create a social microcosm within the group and to illuminate interpersonal pathology. It is, however, another matter to make use of these elements such that maladaptive transaction cycles are interrupted and opportunities for self-awareness and newly emerging behavior that is more adaptive is fostered and supported. Yalom and Leszcz (2005) have built upon the original conceptualization of the corrective emotional experience of Alexander and French (1946) and as further articulated by Weiss (1993). Treatment provides an opportunity to disconfirm the pathogenic beliefs shaping the interpersonal misconstruction through an accumulation of experience, awareness and insight, all molded together. This disconfirmation is extended to the individual by the group members and the leader. Having stated this, it is essential that this be experienced as genuine and authentic and not as a fabricated response. Rather, it is through the understanding of both the overt behavior and the covert forces driving that behavior that it becomes possible to confront empathically maladaptive behavior. This involves a process of beginning to examine the patient's interpersonal impact, its origins, and, endorsing and valuing new and more adaptive emergent behaviors. The more the group leader is able to keep in mind the cognitive-interpersonal schema for each member of the group, the more he will be able to seize upon the significance of seemingly benign behavior within the group that may be reflective of attempts at broadening one's interpersonal repertoire. Newly emerging behavior that is not reinforced is vulnerable to being extinguished – an empathic, thoughtful question or statement of support articulated by a self-absorbed, narcissistic group member will be less dramatic than a disclosure of trauma, but may be no less important to acknowledge. Reinforcing the request for time and support made by a group member who is undervaluing of self and sees herself as only a care provider to others may have very different meaning. Hence, it is often useful to revisit the original formulation to ensure alignment on these issues, and to keep that front of mind to maximize reinforcement of new behaviors and reduce risk of colluding with old behaviors.

At times, the interpersonal behavior can be provocative and hook both the therapist and members of the group into a complementary response, meeting hostility with hostility or submissiveness with domination. Recall that the complementary interpersonal response generally elicits concordance on the axis of affiliation and reciprocity on the axis control. It is important to be able to step back from the interaction and reflect on the nature of the experience in order to provide an opportunity for feedback and meta-communication. At times, this will necessitate the therapist helping group members disengage from a critically provocative antagonist, helping them to not bite at the bait, and buy time for reflection in order to interrupt enactments that would be mutually destructive. It is often challenging to retain empathic attunement with the members in the group whose behavior is destructive to themselves and potentially destructive to others in the group. While it is essential to protect the group from toxic influence, it is also important to recognize that patients are likely operating at the highest level of adaptive capacity that they experience and the adaptive effort even beneath the maladaptive result must be understood and acknowledged. Murray's behavior made sense growing up in the environment in which he did. There are times when it makes sense in his contemporary environment. What clearly does not, however, make sense adaptively for Murray is to behave in this fashion all of the time or in all instances.

Clinical Illustration

George entered an ongoing group motivated by his impending fatherhood. He knew that he intimidated people and was viewed as aggressive and bullying at work. He recalled his own upbringing – humiliated and bullied by his father and was determined to break that mode as a father. One of the pivotal memories he recounted in the group was how his father would routinely engage him in what began as friendly father-son wrestling together, only to end each encounter typically atop George, mocking him for his weakness. He was derided and told that if he does not toughen up people will always push him around confirming his disgusting, pathetic state of weakness. George viewed the world through this cognitive, interpersonal lens. His pathogenic beliefs were that closeness was an invitation to humiliation, and illumination of his weakness, and the interpersonal behavior that flowed from that belief was to attack first as a way of ensuring safety. He manifestly resisted emotional engagement in the group, challenging the honesty of people's care for one another – yet he came on time to each meeting and rarely missed sessions.

In a central session, a co-member, Diane, recounted a depressing weekend in which she slept with three different men and asked the group for help in understanding why emotional intimacy was so hard for her but sex came so easily. She often felt that her body was the only appealing and worthwhile aspect of herself.

George offered that he knew what her problem was: "You are a slut." The impact of that statement was predictable and dramatic – Diane burst into tears and the group attacked George for his destructiveness. At first he held his ground – saying that "he calls them as he sees them." The group leader persisted, balancing support for Diane with questioning of George about his feedback to Diane – what was his intent with that feedback? What did he think his impact was? How did he think Diane felt? What did this generate in others toward him? The group leader added that this comment was so provocative it had to be understood and not only reacted to. George went on to add that he did not want to hurt Diane – in fact he liked and was attracted to her – but felt more vulnerable with her as a result and worried about her rebuff of his care. The growing closeness in the group also felt unsettling and he responded as he did to feel less vulnerable and more in control. Further exploration underscored how his defense was not a solution – it was the problem. Attacking others to reduce his vulnerability ensured only more of the same – witness the group's anger and counter attack. He had the power to turn a safe and welcoming environment into a hostile one. He obtained further feedback that in fact he had a substantial amount of control to wield – he could engage and make people allies and supports or he could turn them into rejecting attackers.

Diane then commented – she could understand George's issues but added pointedly "how much longer do I need to sacrifice myself for George's therapy?" leading both to his heartfelt apology to her and the opportunity to explore and strengthen her strong statement of deserving good and respectful care. He asked for her forgiveness and Diane responded that she needed to see him work consistently and durably to build her trust – it would not happen overnight but she was open to it. This was a key aspect of her work and the group members and therapist noted it was heartening to see her stake her claim in particular in the face of George's painful opening comment.

It is a demanding but essential task for the therapist to be able to align himself with the subjective experience of multiple members of the group at the same time (Gans and Alonso, 1998).

Occasionally, patients will protest by arguing that only in the group do people respond in this kind of empathic and sensitive fashion and that the group is an artificial environment. This is an important resistance to challenge. Indeed, the group is an unnatural place, but it is an unnatural place for natural forms of relationships rather than being a natural place for unnatural forms of relatedness. Working in this context contributes to the development of the capacity for mentalization – the reflective ability to think about the workings of another person's mind – feelings, motivations, desires and fears (Choi-Kain and Gunderson 2008; Fonagy and Bateman, 2006). This is linked to empathy and emotional intelligence but is overarching and encompasses both implicit and explicit awareness, along with attention to cognitions and affects. One can only develop the capacity for mentalization having first experienced being the object of mentalization – the therapy group may be the first opportunity for our patients to be the object of mentalization and in turn transduce that experience into a relational resource in other relationships.

The interpersonal learning sequence

Uniting the elements of the group to the social microcosm, working in the here-and-now, and the corrective emotional experience generate the interpersonal learning sequence, as described by Yalom and Leszcz (2005) (see Figure 3.1). It is this kind of interpersonal intervention that is most highly valued by patients and correlates with improved psychotherapy outcome (Flowers and Booraem, 1990). When the group is operating in this capacity there is a sense of excitement and energy in the room, revolving around the focus on interpersonal interactions.

Clinical Illustration

Following a group meeting in which there had been much focus on people's capacity to change in the present and emancipate themselves from the past, Susan arrived to the group visibly distressed noting that she had been tremendously upset after the last meeting. She had slept poorly and in fact she had missed work for the first time because of emotional distress. What upset her, she went on to add, was the upbeat focus in the group in the meeting before about people being able to emancipate themselves from the past and live in the present. She understood the importance in the group of working in the here-and-now but she struggled every day with being consumed by the past. For her, she noted, the past was not distant but very present, evident in traumatic nightmares and re-experiencing of sexual and physical abuse that had been perpetrated throughout her childhood. Although the group leaders knew of this background, Susan had yet to speak about it in the group and made a determination that she would either have to leave the group or speak to this.

> She went on to describe a range of traumatic symptoms reflecting this abuse and how she had never been able to speak about this or protest, let alone express anger. In her childhood any protest or expression of anger would lead only to greater abuse and mistreatment. In this meeting she determined that she would speak her truth and bear the consequences of what she feared would be going against the group's excitement and upbeat tone of the last several meetings. She anticipated that her protest would be met with disapproval, criticism and attack and was surprised to see that the group leaders and group members were tremendously supportive and encouraging of her protesting their apparent lack of sensitivity and empathy.
>
> The group members endorsed her courage in coming forward rather than shutting down and avoiding, which she has done throughout her life, and endorsed her action in claiming her emotional space within the meeting. The feedback had a profound impact on disconfirming Susan's pathogenic beliefs but required time for processing her lingering concern that group members or the group leaders were annoyed with her drawing attention to her hurt, or wanted to silence her, so that they could continue to do what they wished disregarding her state. She was ultimately able to settle a bit and engage more fully with the group, recognizing that in fact the group provided opportunities for her to do in the present what she had never been able to do in the past – which is to ensure that people did not inadvertently "deny or glaze over my emotional abuse." She felt heartened that if she could in fact do this in the group she would seek further opportunities to do this in new relationships she hoped to develop outside of the group.

Therapeutic meta-communication

As noted, the therapist working in this model of group psychotherapy exercises significant responsibility for activation of the group through his own level of participation. A persistent posture of disciplined personal therapeutic involvement is essential (McCullough, 2000; 2006). Clearly, the therapist will need to be transparent with his own reactions and feedback, maximizing opportunities for interpersonal learning through the process of communicating about communication – meta-communication (Kiesler, 1996). Particularly, the therapist needs to find a safe, empathic way to disclose the interpersonal impact of the patient, linking it to specific behaviors from the patient where possible. Once the patient becomes aware of authoring his interpersonal impact through his interpersonal behavior, he can assume responsibility for authoring and changing his interpersonal patterns. This is a key to enhancing the patient's interpersonal effectiveness and restoring a sense of agency in one's life.

Guidelines for therapist transparency address the importance of boundary maintenance, recognizing that transparency should always be in the interests of the treatment and the patient, and the therapist must be circumspect to ensure that he is not motivated by unrecognized, unmetabolized reactions or by his own self-aggrandizement. In a related vein, Kiesler encourages feedback when the therapist's

The individual manifests his characteristic style, reflected in verbal, non-verbal and paraverbal communication.
⬜
This stimulates reactions through the interpersonal impact evoked by the patient on others in the group.
⬜
This generates exploration of interpersonal impact, and more accessible aspects of the cognitive interpersonal schema,
⬜
What follows from this elaboration is feedback and meta-communication around the interpersonal communication, illuminating blind spots and challenging distortions, and highlighting the individual's specific contributions to the reactions of others
⬜
This feedback is ideally presented in a mutual, collaborative, non-attacking and schema-disconfirming fashion, cognizant that despite the risks of recapitulation and reenactment, what the patients seeks is disconfirmation of the pathogenic beliefs.
⬜
Processing the feedback about interpersonal impact leads to exploration of the covert cognitions and their genesis, linking dynamic and genetic insight.
⬜
A more objective, reality-based cognitive-interpersonal schema begins to take shape with modified cognitions and modified interpersonal constructions that reflect the individual's exercising of responsibility over his presentation of self to others.
⬜
Recognition exists of the capacity to make choices at the interpersonal level, generating a feeling of empowerment and embodiment.
⬜
New, more adaptive interpersonal behaviors emerge.
⬜
Risk taking stimulates affirmation of newer, more adaptive interpersonal relatedness.
⬜
A broadened interpersonal repertoire emerges within the group.
⬜
Illumination of the patient's interpersonal distortions and disconfirmation of pathogenic beliefs generate a greater feeling of boldness, self-referential activity, engagement with self and others.
⬜
An adaptive spiral is stimulated in which changes evidenced in the group begin to gain expression in the patient's life at large.

Figure 3.1 The Adaptive Interpersonal Spiral (Yalom and Leszcz, 2005).

iron has cooled in contrast to exploring interpersonal markers when the patient's iron is hot (Kiesler, 1996). The therapist must metabolize his affective responses before reacting, as a way of reducing the risks of negative reenactments. The therapist must be able to distinguish between subjective and objective countertransference, recognizing the difference between what resides within him routinely, and what gets triggered or elicited by the patient (Gabbard, 1995). Transparency is a tool, not an end in itself and it is part of the skill of the therapist to find palatable ways of saying unpalatable things. Therapist transparency should not replace self-exploration on the part of the therapist and should emphasize an empathic linkage to the patient's subjective experience, confronting maladaptive sequences, and endorsing actively and enthusiastically new, adaptive patient behaviors emerging from a broadened interpersonal repertoire.

Therapeutic meta-communication is best applied within the context of a stable therapeutic alliance and group cohesiveness, to reduce the risk of feedback being experienced by the patient as hostile or attacking, confirming rather than disconfirming pathogenic beliefs. It models furthermore authentic engagement and the responsibility of both parties in interaction for reflection and for open communication, ultimately facilitating a less restrictive, non-complementary interpersonal sequence. Therapeutic meta-communication reflects the encouragement of overt rather than covert communication, leaving as little unsaid as possible about the actual here-and-now relationship.

Throughout the process of meta-communication, manifestation of positive regard for the patient must be evident, blending tact with authenticity. The aim is not to rebuke, but rather to illuminate interpersonal patterns and exploration of the covert and less accessible aspects of more overt behavior. Other principles in the process of meta-communication include a certain degree of tentativeness and humility in the offering of feedback such that it does not come across as an edict from on high. Balancing positive with negative feedback can sometimes serve to lower the stakes for the individual. Finally, we seek to encourage the collaborative exploration of the identified pattern, seeking to either refine understanding or corroborate understanding with a view to creating further opportunities for growth and development. Sometimes an unchecked, hostile or complementary response may emerge. This too may be grist for the therapeutic mill (Yalom and Leszcz, 2005).

Conclusion

The chapter has reviewed the theoretical and therapeutic constructs of interpersonal group therapy. This is an effective model of group therapy that capitalizes on the use of the group as a social microcosm that illuminates interpersonal patterns with a view to identifying challenges and opportunities within the here-and-now experience of relatedness. Opportunities are created to address both core pathogenic beliefs and the interpersonal misconstructions that flow from these beliefs leading to the patient's capacity to author a new way of experiencing self and others relationally.

References and Bibliography

Alexander, F., & French, T. (1946). *Psychoanalytic therapy: Principles and applications.* New York: Ronald Press.

Bellak, L. (1980). On some limitations of dyadic psychotherapy and the role of the group modalities. *International Journal of Group Psychotherapy, 30,* 7–21.

Bernard, H., Burlingame, G., Flores, P., Greene, L., Joyce, A., Kobos, J., Leszcz, M., MacNair Semands, R. R., Piper, W., Slocum McEneaney, A. M., & Feirman, D. (2008). Clinical practice guidelines for group psychotherapy. *International Journal of Group Psychotherapy, 58*(4), 455–542.

Burlingame, G. M., Fuhriman, A., & Johnson, J. E. (2002). Cohsesion in group psychotherapy. In J. C. Norcros (Ed.), *A guide to psychotherapy relationships and work.* England: Oxfrd University Press.

Burlingame, G. M., Mackenzie, K. R., & Strauss, B. (2004). Small-group treatment: evidence for effectiveness and mechanisms of change. In M. J. Lambert (Ed.), *Bergin & Garfield's Handbook of psychotherapy and behavior change* (3rd ed., pp. 647–696). New York: John Wiley & Sons.

Carson, R. C. (1982). Self-fulfilling prophecy, maladaptive behaviour and psychotherapy. In J. C. Anchin & D. J. Kiesler (Eds.), *Handbook of interpersonal psychotherapy* (pp. 64–77). Elmsford, New York: Pergamon.

Choi-Kain, L. W., & Gunderson, J. G. (2008). Mentalization: Ontogeny, assessment, and application in the treatment of borderline personality disorder. *American Journal of Psychiatry, 165*, 1127–1135.

Emde, R. N. (1992). Positive emotions for psychoanalytic theory: Surprises from infant research and new directions. In T. Shapiro & R. N. Emde (Eds.), *Affect: Psychoanalytic perspectives* (pp. 5–44). Stanford, Connecticut: International University Press.

Flowers, J. V., & Booraem, C. D. (1990). The frequency and effect on outcome of different types of interpretation in psychodynamic and cognitive-behavioral group psychotherapy. *International Journal of Group Psychotherapy, 40*, 203–214.

Fonagy, P., & Bateman, A.W. (2006). Mechanisms of change in mentalization-based treatment of BPD. *Journal of Clinical Psychology, 62*(4), 411–430.

Fonagy, P., Georgely, G., Jurist, E. L., & Target, M. (2004). *Affect regulation, mentalization and the development of the self*. UK: Karnac Books.

Foreman, S. A. (1996). The significance of turning passive into active in control mastery theory. *Journal of Psychotherapy Practice and Research, 5*, 106–121.

Fretter, P., Bucci, W., Broitman, J., Silberschatz, G., & Curtis, J. T. (1994). How the patient's plan relates to the concept of transference. *Psychotherapy Research, 4*, 58–72.

Gabbard G. O. (1995). Countertransference: the emerging common ground. *International Journal of Psychoanalysis, 76*, 475–485.

Gans, J. S., & Alonso, A. (1998). Difficult patients: their construction in group therapy. *International Journal of Group Psychotherapy, 48*(3), 311–326.

Giesler, R. B., & Swann, W. B. (1999). Striving for confirmation: the role of self-verification in depression. In T. Joiner & J. C. Coyne (Eds.), *The interactional nature of depression* (pp. 189–217). Washington: American Psychological Association.

Hill, C. E., & Knox, S. (2009). Processing the therapeutic relationship. *Psychotherapy Research, 19*(1), 13–29.

Horowitz, L. M., & Vitkis, J. (1986). The interpersonal basis of psychiatric symptomatology. *Clinical Psychology Review, 6*, 443–469.

Kiesler D. J. (1996). *Contemporary interpersonal theory and research*. New York: J. Wiley & Sons Ltd.

Lambert, M. J., & Ogles, B. M. (2004). The efficacy and effectiveness of psychotherapy. In M. J. Lambert (Ed.), *Bergin and Garfield's handbook of psychotherapy and behavior change* (5th ed., pp. 139–193). New York: John Wiley & Sons.

Leszcz, M. (1992). The interpersonal approach to group psychotherapy. *International Journal of Group Psychotherapy, 42*, 37–62.

Leszcz, M. (1997). Integrated group therapy for the treatment of depression in the elderly. *Group, 21*(2), 89–113.

Leszcz, M., & Malat, J.(2010). Interpersonale gruppenpsychotherapie. In V. Tschuschke (Ed.), *Gruppenpsychotherapie* (pp. 296–305). Frankfurt: Georg Thieme Verlag Stutgartt Publishing.

MacKenzie, K. R., & Grabovac, A. C. (2001). Interpersonal psychotherapy group (IPT-G) for depression. *Journal of Psychotherapy Practice and Research, 10*, 46–51.

MacKenzie, K. R., & Tschuschke, V. (1993). Relatedness, group work and outcome in long-term inpatient psychotherapy groups. *Journal of Psychotherapy Practice and Research*, 2(2), 147–156.

Malat, J., & Leszcz, M. (2005). Interpersonal group therapy for concurrent alcohol dependence and interpersonal problems. In W. J. W. Skinner (Ed.), *Treating concurrent disorders – a guide for counsellors* (pp. 287–309). Toronto: Centre for Addiction and Mental Health.

Malat, J., Leszcz, M., Negrete, J. C., Turner, N., Collins, J., Liu, E., & Toneatto, T. (2008). Interpersonal group psychotherapy for comorbid alcohol dependence and non-psychotic psychiatric disorders. *The American Journal on Addictions*, 17, 402–407.

Martin, D. J., Garske, J. P., & Davis, K. M. (2000). Relation of the therapeutic alliance with outcome and other variables: a meta-analytic review. *Journal of Consulting and Clinical Psychology*, 68(3), 438–450.

McCullough, J. P. (2000). *Treatment for chronic depression: Cognitive behavioral analysis system of psychotherapy (CBASP)*. New York: Guilford Press.

McCullough, J. P. (2006). *Using disciplined personal involvement to treat chronic depression: CBASP*. New York, New York: Springer Press.

Mitchell, S. A. (1994). *Hope and dread in psychoanalysis*. New York: Basic Books

Moran, D. K., Stockton, R., Cline, J., & Teed C. (1998). Facilitating feedback exchange in groups: Leader interventions. *Journal for Specialists in Group Work*, 23, 257–260.

Ormont, L. (1990). The craft of bridging. *International Journal of Group Psychotherapy*, 40, 3–17.

Piper, W. E., Ogrodniczuk, J. S., Lamarche, C., Hilscher, T., & Joyce, A. S. (2005). Level of alliance, pattern of alliance and outcome in short-term group therapy. *International Journal of Group Psychotherapy*, 55(4), 27–550.

Rothke S. (1986). The role of interpersonal feedback in group psychotherapy. *International Journal of Group Psychotherapy*, 36, 225–240.

Safran, J. O., & Segal, Z. V. (1990). *Interpersonal process in cognitive therapy*. New York: Basic Books.

Sammet, I., Leichsenring, F., Schauenburg, H., & Andreas, S. (2007). Self-ratings of pathogenic beliefs: A study based on the psychodynamic control-mastery theory. *Psychotherapy Research*, 17(4), 494–503.

Shedler, J. (2010). The efficacy of psychodynamic psychotherapy. *American Psychologist*, 65(2), 98–109.

Slife, B. D., & Canyon, J. (1991). Accounting for the power of the here-and-now: issues in group psychotherapy. *International Journal of Group Psychotherapy*, 41, 145–168.

Stern, D. N. (1985). *The interpersonal world of the infant*. New York: Basic Books.

Stolorow, R., Brandschaft, B., & Atwood, G. (1987). *Psychodynamic treatment: an intersubjective approach*. Hillsdale, New Jersey: Analytic Press.

Stone, W. N. (1996). Self Psychology and the higher mental functioning hypothesis. *Group Analysis*, 29(2), 169–181.

Strupp, H. H., & Binder, J. H. (1984). *Psychotherapy in a new key: A guide to time-limited dynamic psychotherapy*. New York: Basic Books.

Sullivan, H. S. (1953). *The interpersonal theory of psychiatry*. New York: Norton.

Viederman, M. (1999). Presence and enactment as a vehicle of psychotherapeutic change. *Journal of Psychotherapy Practice and Research*, 8, 274–283.

Wampold, B. E. (2001). *The great psychotherapy debate: Models, methods and findings*. Nahwah, New Jersey: Erlbaum.

Weiss, J. (1993). *How psychotherapy works: Process and technique*. New York: Guilford Press.

Westen, D. (1999). *Psychology: Mind, brain and culture* (2nd ed.). John Wiley & Sons, Somerest, New Jersey.

Willfley, D. E., Mackenzie, K. R., & Welch, R. R. (2000). *Interpersonal Psychotherapy for Group*. New York: Basic Books.

Yalom, I. D. (1983) *Inpatient group therapy*. New York: Basic Books.

Yalom, I. D., & Leszcz, M. (2005). *The theory and practice of group psychotherapy* (5th ed.). New York: Basic Books.

4

Towards an Integrative Intersubjective and Relational Group Psychotherapy

Victor L. Schermer and Cecil A. Rice

Intersubjectivity and relational psychology are contemporary psychoanalytic perspectives with broad implications for the theory and practice of group psychotherapy. They are now merging within an eclectic multi-person systems viewpoint that includes crossovers with self psychology, object relations theory, cognitive-behavioral therapy, "mindfulness" therapy, attachment theory, trauma studies, and other points of view and schools of thought that embody their own sets of principles and practice (Wachtel, 2008). Therefore, the "intersubjective-relational perspective" has become so widespread in its impact that it can best be thought of not so much as a school of thought as it is a "sensibility" (Orange, Atwood, and Stolorow, 1997: p. 9) that leads to useful understandings and strategies in multiple clinical and theoretical contexts. Because the interpersonal, contextual, and systems emphases are also a part of group work, this perspective has a particular relevance to group psychotherapy.

Historical Perspective

The importance of the intersubjective and relational outlooks becomes apparent when we realize that for decades, psychiatry and psychoanalysis were based on a "one-person" model in which the mind and behavior were contained within the individual. Indeed psychiatric diagnoses and treatment protocols are still formulated in that way, as evidenced by the standard manual, the DSM-IV (American Psychiatric Association, 1994) used for that purpose.[1] While interpersonal and social interpretations of

---

[1] To the best of the authors' knowledge, the only formal diagnosis of a multi-person system in the psychiatric literature (other than the so-called V-Codes of situational difficulties which are not on the DSM Axis I of disorders) is the *"folie a deux."* This diagnosis appeared in the latter part of the nineteenth century depicting a couple (parent-child; lovers, etc.) who became embroiled in mutually reinforcing delusions (cf. Speck, 1964.)

psychoanalysis emerged in the 1930s–1950s (Lionells, Fiscalini, Mann, and Stern, 1995), mainstream psychoanalysts, under the watchful eyes of Freud, Anna Freud, Melanie Klein, and their followers, believed such viewpoints obscured the deeper unconscious infantile layers of the personality. According to these analysts, depth psychology could only be properly understood from the individualistic "intrapsychic" vantage point.

Atwood and Stolorow (1984, 1993) were the first to articulate a well-formulated intersubjective multi-person perspective within mainstream psychoanalysis. They sought to demonstrate that the notion of a detached, opaque clinician objectively observing the patient's mental complexes was a myth. In reality, they argued, the theories and interpretations used by the therapist invariably reflected his life history and personality as well as the mutual influence between himself and the patient in the consulting room. Psychoanalysis, they argued, is an intersubjective discipline of empathic inquiry rather than a detached "surgical" procedure. Stolorow (2010), in particular, found in Kohut's (1959, 1971, 1977) emphasis on empathy and mirroring in lieu of "experience-distant" interpretations a simpatico viewpoint, creating a confluence of the new intersubjectivity with Kohut's self-psychology and its underpinnings in mother-infant development (Mahler, Pine, and Bergman, 1975; Stern, 1985). A rich interpersonal, developmental, and contextual understanding of intersubjectivity and emotional self-regulation in infant and child development then emerged.

Intersubjectivity has also more recently focused upon non-conscious and latent aspects of the self, such as one can see in patients who enact their emotions rather than experience them and those whose empathic capacities never developed into an intuitive understanding of significant others. Moreover, confluences with motivational systems theory (Lichtenberg, 2001), attachment theory (Fonagy, 2001), affect regulation, and the study of "mentalization" (the ability to grasp another's subjectivity) (Fonagy, Gergely, Jurist, and Target, 2005) have all contributed to the ongoing study of the mutual influence of one subjectivity or another. The central idea of intersubjectivity is that the experiential, phenomenological worlds of individuals are co-created in mutual exchanges among them and with the sociocultural context.

Relational psychoanalysis emerged around the same time, but independently of the intersubjective perspective. In particular, Mitchell's (1988) interest in British object relations theories led him to the conclusion that they were inherently interpersonal, echoing Sullivanian theory (1953). Mitchell elaborated the notion stated by Fairbairn (1952) that the infant is inherently "object-seeking," i.e. seeks a relationship with the caregiver, and that relationships constitute the primary phenomena while "minds" are not *sui generis*, but by-products of human interactions. Even the deepest unconscious processes and memories, Mitchell argued, are not sequestered like the repressed archaeological sites that Freud represented them to be, but rather are alive in the immediacy of current relationships. Mutuality and dialogue are the common coinage of all humans and, in particular, psychoanalytic events (Aron, 1996). Subjectivity, and the ability to know another's internal states, are themselves acquired in the context of primary caregiving relationships. We are always encountering, absorbing, inferring, and interpreting each other's inner experience, a matter which is supported by neuroscience findings regarding mirror neurons (Schermer, 2010.) For these and other reasons, transference and countertransference inevitably co-occur in relation to one another (Hoffman, 1983). It is easy to see how the common emphasis on interaction and mutuality betokens a strong bridge between relational and intersubjective points of view, hence the confluence of the two in the New Millennium.

The intersubjective and relational literature is rich and complex. However, the more limited scope of this chapter is to focus on specific applications to group psychotherapy. In what follows, we will try to formulate a set of intersubjective and relational principles we have found to be useful and, in a positive way, challenging, in group therapy as such. We will also consider clinical examples and suggest how the intersubjective-relational sensibility can lead to productive outcomes for our groups and the patients who comprise them.

Since intersubjective and relational perspectives developed in the context of particular treatment modalities and populations, they have greater importance in some clinical situations than in others. Therefore, a brief consideration should be given to a) therapist qualifications, b) presenting problems/diagnoses, and c) types of groups and treatment contexts which might best utilize the perspectives we are advocating.

Appropriate Therapist Qualifications, Diagnostic Criteria and Treatment Settings

Training and supervision

The ideal preparation of the therapist to conduct groups centered in intersubjective and relational principles would consist of two components:

1. Training in psychoanalytic psychotherapy at an institute with an emphasis on both intersubjective and relational principles;
2. A professionally-approved certificate program in group psychotherapy.

This training combination can provide didactic education and supervision to allow for a rich, sophisticated utilization of this perspective in a variety of treatment situations.

When such extensive as well as costly and time-consuming training is not possible or readily available, it is nevertheless possible for the "generalist" therapist to pursue independent readings and continuing education that prepare him to include relational and intersubjective perspectives in the work. An important caveat, however, is that the therapist should adhere to a treatment model for which he is trained and qualified. For example, a cognitive group therapist can and should incorporate relational insights into his work while staying well within the parameters of cognitive therapy. He should consistently address cognitive distortions while placing greater emphasis on treating those distortions which impact relationships in and outside the group. For example, Young (1999) has developed a protocol for cognitive therapy of personality disorders which includes an emphasis on relational factors. If the therapist, however, attempts to go beyond cognitive therapy interventions, for example by a dynamic analysis of transference-countertransference enactments, it could contaminate the therapeutic alliance and lead the group astray from its primary therapeutic tasks. The same applies to any other school of psychotherapy and its systematic principles. Intersubjective and relational based interventions can have a powerful impact on the therapy process and must be used judiciously in conformity to a set of sound working principles for conducting groups. As yet, there are no specific intersubjective and/or relational group treatment protocols. It is hoped that this chapter will serve as a beginning step in that direction.

Clinical supervision

This is a key aspect of running groups. It begins during the therapist's training, but, for many, continues to be valuable throughout their career. The intersubjective-relational approach regards supervision as reflecting a "parallel process" to the therapy itself. The supervisor not only provides "advice and consent," he also engages with the supervisee at a mutual feeling level within an interpersonal relationship.

The feelings and dilemmas that emerge can then be explored in a productive manner, in fact providing additional information about the therapy group itself. However, consistent with traditional supervisory guidelines, supervision should not "therapize" the supervisee, but rather direct him to proper help for personal problems when the supervisor thinks they may be consistently interfering with either the treatment or supervisory process. Relationally speaking, supervision, especially when it takes on a therapeutic tone, as distinct from growth as a clinician, can unfortunately become interpersonally "incestuous," and such pseudo-mutuality and merger of selves can seriously interfere with relational group work.

Diagnoses and treatment populations

Relational and intersubjective formulations include generalities about human nature and development, but their clinical application requires sufficient patient engagement to make them treatment-relevant. For example, patients with antisocial personality or sociopathic features could sabotage such therapy, since intersubjective and relational interventions require levels beyond their capability of honesty, personal integrity, and vulnerability. While it is conceivable that well-attuned interventions might ultimately mitigate sociopathy in some patients, this is a risky process that requires great skill and experience.

With the exception of such subpopulations, intersubjective and relational interventions are highly relevant for other personality disorders, and in particular narcissistic and borderline personalities, because, in part, these interventions developed in treating those populations within the then "widening scope of psychoanalysis" (Stone, 1954), the expanding effort to treat severe personality disturbances. In addition, a wide range of interpersonal conflicts, dysfunctional family dynamics, and attachment disorders include relational components that respond well to multi-person understanding.

Psychological trauma and PTSD also have relational factors that respond to such an approach. Attention deficit and autistic spectrum disorders, on account of the interpersonal and neuropsychological deficits involved, present interesting possibilities, but involve complexities that require specialized knowledge and skill. The psychoses always require special care, although there have been promising breakthroughs using intersubjective inquiry in such cases (Stolorow, Brandchaft and Atwood, 1987).

Generally, an intersubjective-relational perspective works well with both homogeneous and heterogeneous group compositions. Homogeneous groups have the advantage that there is a built-in commonality of concerns that promote empathy and fuel goal-directed dialogue. They are also experienced as supportive by the group members, who quickly identify with one anothers' similarities and common issues. However, such groups often too easily de-generate into repetitious clichés rather than genuine dialogue. In addition, members often reach a point of development where homogeneous or topical groups hamper their further growth in the wider communities in which they participate on a daily basis. A multiphasic model where members "graduate" from a homogeneous to a heterogeneous therapy group is often helpful in this respect (Herman, 1997).

As a rule, therapists using the relational approach are more inclined to conduct heterogeneous groupings. For one thing, such groups provide more varied stimulation, and intersubjective-relational therapists appreciate excitement and lively interchange in their work. From the members' standpoint, the varied mix of patients activates multiple aspects of their self systems, with opportunities for enhanced personal growth and development. However, it appears that some individuals, for example, those with recent or severe psychological trauma, have trouble coping with the empathic lapses and informational overload of a rich mix of group members. That is one reason why homogeneous structured support groups are so important to their healing processes.

Screening, setting and context

With respect to the treatment setting, intersubjective and relational insights are most fruitful with long-term, open-ended, unstructured interpersonal and/or dynamically based group psychotherapy, which permits the greatest opportunity for the thorough working through of relational dilemmas. However, such insights can be useful in time limited groups of any "brand" provided the group modality permits a degree of unstructured member interaction, as opposed to groups such as prolonged exposure therapy for trauma (Foa, Hembree, and Rothbaum, 2007), which follow a strict protocol. On the other hand, dialectical behavior therapy (Linehan, 1995), which may utilize group interactions to effect change, incorporates relational principles.

For relational therapists, a group process truly begins when a therapist first considers a patient for admission to a group. Their initial encounters set the stage for a patient's initial experiences with the group. Screening, selection, and preparation take place simultaneously. Therefore, the authors recommend several preparatory individual sessions for members prior to joining the group. In these sessions, the therapist listens to the individual's concerns, assessing the prospective member's emotional insight and awareness, and his capacity for participating in an intersubjective-relational group. Such capability may come not only from the preparation process, but also from prior therapy, innate personality traits, and history with family and peer groups. Screening and preparation should also include a preliminary assessment of whether the therapist, prospective member, and group are a suitable match that will facilitate a working alliance among them. A multi-session intake allows the therapist to obtain some sense of the prospective member's needs, attachments, and personal goals as they may evolve over a more extended time in the group.

Both inpatient and outpatient groups, as well as private practice, mental health centers, and clinics can afford appropriate settings for relational work, although it is probably the case that outpatient private practice is most consistent with the intersubjective-relational perspective because it allows for maximum therapist and patient autonomy.

Co-therapy is often, but not always, desirable for intersubjective-relational therapists. Not only are the mutual support and multiple observational perspectives of co-therapists helpful in maintaining a strong therapeutic alliance with the group, in addition, the co-creative process that occurs between them stimulates the intergroup dialogue and provides a model of mutual engagement. Moreover, co-therapists can help each other become aware of each other's countertransference. However, it is essential that therapists be assured in advance that they make for a satisfactory working relationship. Such a match-up of co-therapists has indeed been compared relationally to a marriage in terms of the degree of compatibility and mutual support that is involved. Intersubjective and relational thinking can elucidate the elements of co-therapist compatibility that are important in their collaborations. For instance, their inner worlds and shared meanings and values should overlap sufficiently that they not only approach therapy from compatible standpoints, but also can relate empathically to one another's experience in the groups they co-lead.

Intersubjective and Relational Principles for Group Psychotherapy

The following are a set of working principles which the authors believe are central to the application of intersubjective and relational understanding to therapy groups. These guidelines derive, of course, from our inevitably selective (and intersubjectively interpreted!) knowledge base and our experience as group therapists. Both authors were schooled in classical psychoanalysis and dynamic group therapy and also have an abiding interest in the interpersonal and sociocultural aspects of human development. Our colleagues, even like-minded ones, may have a different take on what should be emphasized in the treatment process. For instance, Billow (2003; also see current volume), a relational group psychotherapist, emphasizes Bion's group-as-a-whole and psychoanalytic concepts. While the present authors consider Bion's thinking of utmost importance, they do not consider it to exemplify the intersubjective-relational "sensibility."

In addition, there is considerable variation in the literature about reliance upon empathic introspection versus research-based models in formulating interpretations and interventions. For example; Atwood and Stolorow (1984) and, with respect to group psychotherapy with a self psychology orientation, Stone (2009) emphasize the "phenomenological field" (perception and experience in the here-and-now) as the source of understanding, while attachment theorists such as Fonagy (2001) directly apply complex developmental research in his work with patients.

Importantly, the therapist must "translate" such theories into "user friendly" terms that the members can grasp emotionally. Wholesale application of pre-existing theory may interfere with in-depth relational understanding, while the use of member-shared metaphors may be both clarifying and evocative. For example, a patient remembered from her childhood concealing a book she secretly was reading by covering it with another book when her parents were around. This recollection became an evocative metaphor for the group's tendency to conceal erotic and seductive aspects of their relationships from the therapist.

Intersubjective and relational formulations suggest that the group is a spontaneous co-creation of all the participants, both therapists and members, and results from the coming together of their "inner worlds" shared and experienced intersubjectively. In this respect, the group is a transitional object (Winnicott, 1971) which is both a subjective "group illusion" (Anzieu, 1984) and an organized outer reality that serves as a "not-me possession" of the participants and can be used to promote separation-individuation (Mahler, Pine, and Bergman, 1975). Like the proverbial transitional object, namely the teddy bear, the group serves its "holding" function and is then discarded (time after time!) as the members internalize that function in their daily lives. This view of the group as a spontaneous and alive dialogical process differs considerably from the approach in which the therapist is an opaque, detached consultant and the group members are passive recipients of his interpretations and interventions. Rather, as part of the co-created group interaction, the therapist is an engaged participant whose role is to promote empathy and authenticity (Fosshage, 2003) in the group and facilitate those mutual meanings and understandings which lead to symptom abatement, interpersonal connectedness, and emotional growth. His humanness, subjective perceptions, and developmental history are not incidental, but rather part and parcel of his functions as a therapist as the group co-creates its own destiny.

Intersubjective-relational psychotherapy is in accord with self-psychology in giving high priority to rectifying the therapist's and group's empathic failures as a way of sustaining patients' self-cohesion and self-esteem. Such failures occur when the therapist (or group) is not fully attuned to a patient and responds in ways that cause narcissistic injury. Empathic failures are unavoidable in therapy (Wolf, 1988), since full attention and attunement are ideals that can only be approximated. However, therapists too often gloss over them, creating unresolved hurt in the members. When therapists or patients become aware of empathic failures, they should be discussed openly. To restore the necessary attunement, and undo the patient's implicit feelings of shame and abandonment, it is necessary to acknowledge them and explore their impact. It also helps if the therapist accesses the co-transference elements which caused his lapse in empathy.

The present approach differs, however, from self-psychology in that we do not regard empathy as the only viable therapeutic stance. Confrontive and authentically distressed/concerned responses to patients' negative attitudes and behaviors are important and sometimes essential. Empathy is restored when the patient "hears" the confrontation or distress as ultimately constructive and useful. From a relational standpoint, self-cohesion and esteem are acquired not only from empathy but also from tolerating interpersonal dissonance, conflict, and even hate as part of constructive dialogue and lively interchange.

Based upon such premises, what follows is a suggested set of intersubjective and relational working principles for group interventions. These principles, in the authors' opinions, reflect the theories and guidelines that bear the intersubjective-relational stamp. Such tenets, while they represent a paradigm shift from a one-person to a multi-person psychology, retain in many respects the psychodynamic framework from which they emerged. For example, the developmental model and the notions of transference and defense remain important for intersubjective-relational work, although they are re-interpreted contextually rather than individualistically. The defining characteristic of the intersubjective-relational perspective is the combination of depth psychology, with its attention to early developmental phenomena and unconscious dynamics, with sensitive attunement to the here-and-now and the mutual, reciprocal, self-organizing, and generative nature of human interaction.

Here are eight principles the authors consider foundational for intersubjective-relational group psychotherapy:

Principle I
The primary function of the therapist is to facilitate co-created meaningful interactions in the group, including himself as co-participant.

In the traditional dynamic model, meaning emerges in the transference and is resolved through interpretation. By remaining "neutral" and "opaque," the therapist evokes projections and displacements from the past, which are then "made conscious" and gradually resolved by a process of "working through." Group-as-a-whole transference consists of "basic assumptions" (Bion, 1959) which interfere with the "work group" until they are resolved. From an intersubjective and relational standpoint, insight into the early relationships and internalized fantasies and defenses such as those of the Oedipal Complex may be useful, but only in the context of meaningful experiences and interactions co-created by the group, the latter of which merit the primary attention and engagement of the therapist.

Gayle (2009), taking a cue from the philosopher Strasser (1985), has noted a process of meaning-making called "the hermeneutic spiral" in which the group evolves a set of meanings (symbols, group culture, etc.) in a process of regression and progression which moves from *experience*, through *expression*, to *understanding*. A simple illustration of such a process might occur when the group *experiences* a log-jam in which one member monopolizes the group. In the process of communicating various *expressions* of anxiety and concern, whether in metaphors, dreams, or statements of fact, the group may move to a co-created *understanding* of the member's monopolization of the group, which helps the group and individual members move forward to a more functional, egalitarian, and co-creative pattern of group relations. Such a spiral of experience, expression, and understanding itself spirals upward in a "double helix" of repeated cycles, evolving higher levels of group development. Gayle's hermeneutical conceptualization parallels the traditional psychodynamic notions of transference, interpretation, and working through (Greenson, 1967), but is seen as a natural process of group development which allows for a wider berth of human experience and creativity and gives the group more room to promote its own "therapeutic factors" (Yalom and Leszcz, 2005).

The therapist facilitates experience, expression, and understanding not so much by sooth-saying interpretations as by empathic attunement to the group, and by forming a "thinking couple" (Bion, 1962) between himself and the group, not unlike the way the mother facilitates the child's understanding via their verbal and non-verbal interactions. The listening process itself becomes the therapeutic "strategy," and not only leads to understanding as such, but also facilitates the trust, containment, and security that result from attunement. It also frees the child or group to have spontaneous experiences that invoke deeper levels of the personality and involve risk-taking of new ideas and behaviors. Harwood (2006), for example, used empathic attunement in her innovative groups of traumatized mother-child pairs, where standard interpretations would very likely have further traumatized and derailed the caregivers' relationships with their children. Instead, Harwood introspected empathically as a participant-observer, using shared language and culture, non-verbal interactions, play, and metaphors that the mothers and children could grasp, and engage to negotiate new, non-traumatizing attachment patterns.

Principle II
As part of the co-creative spiral, the therapist elucidates implicit (non-conscious, un-conscious, and un-articulated) meanings.

The importance of psychological insight in the change process has always been a subject of debate (Rangell, 1981; Valenstein, 1981). While classical analysis and object relations theorists have stressed insight as the basis of change, both self-psychology and the intersubjective-relational perspectives have emphasized qualities such as mirroring as curative factors, especially as they contrast with and rectify the originally traumatizing or deficient interactions with primary caregivers. However, this does not mean that clarifications and interpretations by the therapist are unimportant. Rather, they serve the function of consolidating the gains made through the already meaningful exchanges, while also defusing potential obstacles to growth and change. For example, in a group of substance abusers, the therapist's interpretation of one member's angry verbal assaults on the others, as a reflection of his early abandonment and abuse and internalization of his father's harsh ideas about masculinity, led to a mutual understanding among the group members that not only helped the individual member overcome his anger and shame about being regarded as a "sissy," but also led to a partial lifting of the group's implicit taboo against intimacy. From the current standpoint, such insights are effective only to the extent that they both a) echo and supplement the members' shared experience, expression, and understanding in the here-and-now and b) facilitate a change in the relationships and "intersubjective field" of the group interaction. In other words, co-create an upward spiral leading to new and meaningful group experiences. Meaningful experience, which also implies interpersonal connectedness, provides the crucial bridge between insight and change.

Principle III
The therapist facilitates group norms such as empathy and authenticity.

Since the dysfunctional sociocultural and familial contexts in which group members live are often not conducive to self-awareness and mutual understanding, the therapist plays an important role in promoting group norms which lead to a therapeutic milieu rather than recapitulating societal and peer group pressures towards avoidance, deception, and emotional suppression. To facilitate this process, it helps if the therapist has a strong personal motivation towards empathy and authenticity in his relations with others.

Scapegoating, for example, is fueled by a loss of empathy, authenticity, and mutuality, where the "victim" is treated as a less-than-human object by the group (Cohen and Schermer, 2002). In an open-ended outpatient group, one member himself evoked scapegoating by distancing himself from the group, frequently pointing out how he was different from the others. The members mirrored him by withdrawing from emotional contact with him and attacking him for his uncooperative attitude. The patient became angry back, and threatened to leave the group. The therapist authentically disclosed his own concern that the member was avoiding emotional contact and preventing the members from helping him. He then empathically reflected on how the patient's lifetime of vulnerabilities may have led him to become distant and withdrawn, and similarly spoke about the group's hostility as a paradoxical reflection of their healthy desire to have a more cohesive group experience. Finally, he encouraged the group members to share their life experiences of scapegoating and its impact on them. This led to a "clearing of the air" and a restoration of dialogue among the members, including the scapegoated individual.

Principle IV
Transference (defined as a displacement of past experience, fantasy, and defense into the present implicit in the current group relations and extra-group life experience of the members) is always to be understood and clarified as mutual, intersubjective "co-transference."

In the history of psychoanalysis, the analyst's countertransference, early regarded as unconscious conflict that interfered with treatment, came to be seen as a not uncommon occurrence that includes useful information about the patient (Langs, 1976). The intersubjective-relational perspective goes a step further, holding that transference and countertransference always occur together, and that the therapist must candidly acknowledge the "co-transference," understood as the unconscious, non-conscious, fantasy-laden, and historical aspects of the intersubjective field. For example, a chronically angry and resentful patient accused the therapist of trying deliberately to make him angry. The therapist initially believed that this was simply the patient's transference. He did not feel that he was the cause of the patient's anger, but introspecting, he thought that he might indeed be frustrated with the patient's passivity and thus behaving in ways that might over-stimulate the anger already present in the patient's transference. Acknowledging his countertransference to the patient cleared the intersubjective field, so that the patient could then acknowledge his own anger while not having to maintain the deception that the therapist was "neutral." The mutuality of such a "systems" analysis of co-transference, done sensitively and circumspectly, not as part of an "argument" or "apology," can have salutary effects on treatment impasses, group resistances, and other difficulties.

In groups, of course, such co-transference not only involves the therapist's interaction with a particular patient but also in the group-as-a-whole. From the current point of view, all transference manifestations are mutual, co-created experiences, and embed themselves in current interpersonal and group reality.

Principle V
Groups re-capitulate, re-enact, and express early attachment patterns, attunements versus derailments, and traumatic caregiver-child interactions. The therapist facilitates experience, expression, understanding, and resolution of such patterns.

Most intersubjectivists and relationalists regard current interactions as developmental derivatives of early relationships with caregivers. They often look to studies of attachment, primitive object relations, mother-infant interactions, mentalization, and affect regulation (Fonagy, Gergely, Jurist, and Target, 2005) to provide models for understanding ongoing adolescent and adult relationships as a function of early life experiences with significant others. The purpose of incorporating such understanding is to assess and treat the relational "damage" that led to the patients' current dilemmas and blockages.

For example, a borderline patient experienced recurrent states of distress and helplessness which she verbalized as, "I feel as if I don't exist," and which led episodically to suicidal thoughts and gestures which dramatized this feeling. Exploring her developmental vicissitudes brought out the fact that her early relationship to her mother consisted of an "anxious-avoidant" attachment pattern (Prior and Glaser, 2006) in which her mother withdrew from contact precisely at times when her daughter sought her attention. This led to a problem of affect regulation because the child could not use her mother to contain and moderate extreme feelings of love and hate. As an adolescent and adult, the patient re-enacted her mother's withdrawal by becoming involved in love relationships that invariably led to rejection. By at first playing out, and then co-creating new, reparative mutual experiences with the therapist and the group members, the patient was gradually able to attain a sense of being held, contained, and "existing," which in turn enabled her to understand and moderate her extreme emotional states. At the same time, she learned that others had feelings similar to her own. She became able to "mentalize" her relations with other group members, that is, to experience herself and others intersubjectively as sentient agents and beings rather than like her mother, whose motives and thoughts felt impenetrable to her.

One of the ways that such early relational derailments and dilemmas initially express themselves in group is in trauma-based "enactments" (Grossmark, 2007). Such enactments frequently take the form of "mindless" (un-mentalized) impulse-driven actions that repeat the original trauma in the group, and which often catch the other members and the therapist off guard (themselves "mindless"), in a collusive replay of the complementary roles.

For example, a patient shocked her group by coming to a session in an unusual-for-her state of intoxication, which became apparent in her disorganized appearance and talk. The group members felt trapped by her dramatic transformation, with one member becoming a harsh critic, another attempting to rescue and placate her, and still another threatening to leave the group. The therapist became a helpless "bystander," unable to respond in a helpful manner. It was not until the next session that therapist, patient, and group could begin to sort out what had happened. A key clarification came when the patient herself noted that her bizarre behavior might have been an enactment of pent-up hostility towards the group deriving from intense feelings of loneliness and abandonment during her adolescence when she felt that her parents, in process of divorce, became harsh and unavailable. Intersubjective and relational perspectives are especially helpful in resolving such enactments because they enable the therapist to awaken the intersubjectivity, attunement, and connectedness that is missing in the mindless actions that disrupt the group.

Principle VI

Intersubjective "I" statements are more readily assimilated by group members than confrontive "cybernetic" feedback and should generally be encouraged.

Many therapists are acquainted with the notion of "I" statements as a principle of assertiveness training (Smith, 1985). As such, it is simply about good communication that allows the individual to assert and express preferences and differences in a way that the other person will not hear as attacking or judgmental. Similarly, with regard to groups, Cohen (2000) made a distinction between what he called "intersubjective" and "cybernetic" feedback, which has some bearing on the perspective we are advocating here. Intersubjective feedback consists of one member (or the therapist in some cases) relating what another says to her own experience, for example, "When you said that you felt abandoned by the group, *I* realized that I was reacting in the same way," (an "I" statement). By contrast, cybernetic feedback consists of a member stating something he observes or thinks about another member: "You felt abandoned by us because *you* think poorly of yourself and think that none of us like you." (Cohen used the term "cybernetic" from information theory to refer to input which attempts to regulate an external system, such as the way a thermostat changes room temperature.) Intersubjective "I" feedback is "user friendly," minimizing narcissistic injury. It incorporates assumptions of the intersubjective-relational approach because it directly acknowledges the mutual engagement of the participants rather than singling out group members as isolated individuals with a "problem." Cohen found that intersubjective feedback promotes personal growth and group development. From our perspective, intersubjective feedback is consistent with the notion of the hermeneutic spiral of co-created meanings, allowing members to build on each other's experience through a mirroring process.

Principle VII

Judicious self-disclosure by the therapist is essential to generate meaningful interactions.

When a therapist himself makes an "I" statement, it adds an aspect of self-disclosure to an intervention or interpretation. The therapist becomes an engaged participant in the group. Nevertheless, the therapist, even with an active relational orientation, must maintain a certain distance and silence, giving him an "asymmetry" with respect to the group. Therefore, although essential to sustaining mutuality, self-disclosure on the part of the therapist must be judicious and well considered so that he may retain the role of facilitator or "conductor" (Foulkes, 1964).[2] Yet without such disclosure, the therapist is not fully engaged in the group process, and moreover cannot fully explore and elucidate his role in the co-transference elements so essential to the relational approach. For relationalists, the question becomes not "whether" but "when and how" to self-disclose.

From an intersubjective-relational perspective, therapist self-disclosure is essential to full accountability, transparency, and mutuality between the therapist and the

---

[2] Trigant Burrow, a pioneering psychiatrist and group analyst, recalled that he had a patient who insisted that he, Burrow, be a co-participant in the treatment, and Burrow consented. However, he soon wisely started therapy groups, partly so that the members could provide the mutual disclosures rather than the therapist becoming the identified patient (!) (Galt, 2010).

group. The important criterion for such disclosures is whether it will promote the development of the group and/or significantly help a member of the group. In a sense, the therapist is always implicitly disclosing herself to the group by his interventions, tone of voice, body language, and spontaneous reactions. Explicit self-disclosure is indicated when a relational dilemma in the group cannot be fully resolved without it.

For instance, a group member chastised the therapist for what he felt were the latter's inadequacies in running the group. Although the patient was verbalizing a transference reaction that had to do personally with his father's unavailability, he was also expressing frustrations that the group-as-a-whole was feeling about the therapist. The group members then wondered how the therapist was coping internally with the attack. The therapist decided to share his own feeling of hurt, anger, and competition with regard to what the patient said about him. Importantly, the therapist did this in the context of helping the group sort out the various ramifications and dynamics, so that each member could authentically experience, express, and understand his own feelings and thoughts. The intersubjective-relational sensibility suggests that, while the therapist might have interpreted the group experience without self-disclosure, avoiding the latter would have left a co-transferential knowledge gap that would in effect continue to influence the group outside of awareness.

Intuitive judgment plays an important role in determining when and how to self-disclose. From an intersubjective-relational perspective, the important question is whether the therapist's self-disclosure will promote or interfere with the reparative relational matrix of the group.

The manner of therapist self-disclosure is important. It should be done introspectively, with care and purpose. However, one could argue that relational therapy allows for spontaneity on the therapist's part, and even his "mistakes," so long as they are acknowledged and worked out, are part of what makes for therapist-group mutuality.

Principle VIII
   Context, including group rules, contracts, and goals as well as norms and expectations of the group, organizations, families, society, and culture are to be taken into account in elucidating relationships evolving within the group.

Both intersubjectivists and relationalists are interested in the context of interpersonal experience. For a long time, psychoanalysis focused on the personal life of the patient and paid less attention to the sociocultural milieu and "collective unconscious" in which "a life" evolves. The intersubjective-relational approach, not unlike group-as-a-whole and family systems therapy, regards the cultural "situation" as a crucial determinant of human interaction. Obvious examples include cultural diversity and minority marginalization (Schermer, 2002), the changes in sex roles brought about by feminism (Schermer, 2008), and the impact of catastrophic events like the 9/11 attack on the World Trade Center in New York City (Galea, 2002). More subtle factors might include the institutional context of the group, the therapist's professional privileging, and even the food in the hospital cafeteria! Fidler (personal communication, 1989) conducted an inpatient group where the bland quality of the institutional meals became a symbol of deprivation and oppression.

As Hopper (2003) has suggested, therapy groups are strongly conditioned by the "social unconscious," that is, familial, social, cultural, political, and economic factors that are often tacitly impactful. Analysis of groups needs to address these elements. Without the awareness of contextual totality, patients may inadvertently and mistakenly attribute to themselves that which is externally conditioned. For example, a group member from a Latino culture had trouble bonding with her White Anglo-Saxon Protestant cohorts and felt very alone in the group and in her life. It turned out that the manner of social bonding in her home country was quite different from that in her new residence. People in her place of origin use strong language and gestures to bond, while those in her therapy group and her social network are much more reserved. The patient incorrectly believed herself to be a "social reject" until the cultural factor was clarified and she was able to appreciate the value of her own spontaneous manner for herself and the group.

Illustrative Clinical Vignette of the Eight Principles

There are no specific therapeutic tactics and techniques associated with an intersubjective-relational approach. Indeed this perspective emphasizes the spontaneous co-created aspects as opposed to a set of pre-ordained rules and strategies. Structure, strategy, and technique are of course necessary, and within the relational sensibility, these are employed with special attention to their impact on the quality of the evolving relational matrix of the group. To illustrate intersubjective and relational insights in conducting groups, the following depicts four sessions of a group conducted by a senior psychotherapist, interspersed by his own running commentary in italics, with the chapter authors inserting and underlining the relevance of the above eight "principles." We hope in this way to suggest how one might "think about" a group from the current vantage point without making final judgments about what is "right" and "wrong" technique.

The vignettes are taken from a heterogeneous long-term free-flow dynamically-oriented therapy group that has met weekly with periodic vacation breaks for approximately thirty years with changes in membership over time. The current seven members are within the age ranges of 45–75, hence are dealing with mid-life and later life issues. Names and identifying features have been changed for confidentiality purposes. The sessions, selected by the therapist from his case notes, are spaced approximately four weeks apart.

Session 1

PRESENT	Carl, Maureen, Ted, Bob, Nancy, Marcia.
ABSENT	Frank (out of town).
TED	I had a really successful two-day retreat for our company. I've really made some gains. The employees were very pleased at our success. I organized them and led them in confronting the administration, and improving the treatment of employees. *(Becomes visibly very upset.)* Then after all the congratulations this friend/colleague – jerk really – thanked me

Towards an Integrative Intersubjective and Relational Group Psychotherapy

	from the podium for my hard work – then called me compulsive, suggesting that was what made me able to succeed – Could have killed the bastard.
CARL	All right – fill us in.
TED	(*by this time furious*): Don't you get it? – This is what it was like for me as a kid, when other kids beat me up, and made me eat gravel – humiliating, humiliating, humiliating!
MAUREEN	Yeah, I'd find that very hard to take also if it was me, especially knowing how much you did for the employees.
MARCIA	I agree it was very unpleasant. He's not worth the sweat. Let him go f– himself. How did he get to you, anyway?
TED	Besides the other kids, my parents used diagnostic and other labels for me rather than relate to me as a real person. *(They were two mental health workers. Ted then looked to the leader for confirmation.)*

Therapist commentary: Indeed, I did confirm Ted's experience for him and the latter slowly regained his composure. Over the years, I had learned from Ted that making interpretations for him were devastatingly painful and not at all helpful. Such interpretations he experienced as a return to his earlier humiliations of parental interpretations. It worked best to join him and stand by him. (*Principle I: Co-creating meaningful interactions in response to an empathic failure.*) He needed understanding. Initially observing his reactions to interpretations, (statements such as "You are doing or experiencing this with me, or the group because of that in the past") in individual therapy and later in group therapy led me to acknowledge openly to him that those kinds of comments seemed to hurt him and make matters worse for him. He agreed readily and angrily, and added, "Just listen to me, hear me out." In these situations, I had also been aware that I wanted protection from Ted's anger and pain. (*Principle IV: Co-transference.*) Ted's anger could be as searing as his own humiliations. Thus interpretations protected me! Once I acknowledged this to myself, the client and I began to create an effective way to do business.

Later in the same session:

MARCIA	I have something to talk about. I'm having a very difficult struggle. My marriage is over; I closed my last business, I returned the dog to my ex-husband, and I'm now living in a large empty house that was once my home. I can't do anything and it scares me. I just sit around, can't get motivated even to look for a job. I sit and eat, and drink coffee. The place is going to hell and so am I.
CARL	Yeah, I know what its like to live alone, though after all these years I've adapted to it. (*Principle VI: Use of intersubjective "I" feedback.*) On the other hand, I never was married. In the group I went through a downward spiral – could not get a job and my mood was black. That frightened the group members – they gave me all kinds of advice that was not especially helpful.

TED	Yeah, we learned from that. The advice was good but, he (*referring to me*) made clear we gave advice because your despair was unbearable for us. It was.
CARL	Yeah, I know, but let's get back to Marcia. Marcia?
MARCIA	That's about it. It feels awful being unable to act especially after many years as a successful business woman.

Therapist commentary: The group then enabled her to look at a number of contributory factors including the grief she was experiencing, that in many ways was a repeat of an earlier loss, and also a repeat of her more recent losses. The early loss happened when as a child her favorite aunt, who took care of her on an almost daily basis, disappeared suddenly – that is, she was more like a mother to her than her own mother and thus the key figure in her life. (*Principle V: Resolving early attachment patterns and enactments.*) It turned out that her mother had told the aunt to leave. To this day, she has no idea why she did it, but she never forgot it. However, one of the greatest sources of sadness was that her mother missed the emotional content of most communications. That was true of the loss of her aunt. In later life, Marcia coped by attaching herself to different women for short periods, to salve her loss, and to forestall the women from leaving her, that is, she left first. In addition, recently she nursed her father through the last few months of his life.

TED	(*in a strong voice*) Marcia, I know what it's like – I've lost so many friends – Bill's wife died of cancer at a young age, my consultant and mentor Joe died of a long miserable cancer. I could go on and on – it takes its toll.
MAUREEN	Oh God, yes. I've lost my marriage, though in many ways it was also a relief, but I also lost contact with my family for many years.
BOB	(*with a touch of melancholy*) As you know both my parents were dead by the time I was twenty, and all through my adolescence I was waiting for them to die, they were so sick. (*Principle VI: Use of intersubjective "I" feedback.*)

Therapist commentary: These exchanges normalized Marcia's experience for her, while allowing her to acknowledge her unsuccessful attempts to cope with loss through brief encounters with women. Her relations lasted three months give or take, at which point she lost interest, found fault with them and felt compelled to leave. Marcia also entered the group excited, and continued to be excited for a number of weeks. When talking about her women, each of which began with the same excitement, I wondered aloud if the same thing might happen in the group. After a good beginning, as in her love relationships, I wondered if Marcia might become disappointed in the group and want to leave. In these events, the group along with myself and Marcia had co-created a reflective space of shared observations for her, that gave some meaning to her experience, and in joining her, gave her a chance to tolerate her despair.

Still later in the same session:

BOB	*(with a mixture of force and guilt)* I need to take time to talk about my weight. I know Carl you have been on my case, as you should, suggesting that my behavior may be suicidal, but now I need to take responsibility for it. My sugar count is high again – my blood pressure is up.
SEVERAL GROUP MEMBERS	*(forcefully, emphasizing Bob's high risk)* Yes, Bob, the grandkids need to have you around!
CARL	*(with some anger)* We're also concerned about you, Nancy; you're so fatalistic about your weight.
NANCY	*(with authority)* I know where Bob's coming from. I make a lot of money, the kids are all set for college, there's a lot of money for them in the future. All the bases are covered. What else is there to do?
MAUREEN	Carl's right. That does sound like you're throwing in the towel. You're just going to eat yourself to death. *(Nancy is obese: 5'3" and over two hundred pounds.)*
MARCIA, CARL, and TED	*(pressed her to return to a special program for food addicts. with which she had had some success next Tuesday even if it meant missing the group. It might save her life.)*
NANCY	I'll see what I can do.

Therapist commentary: I was sure that Nancy would not follow their advice. I chose not to comment on it at this time, as the session was about to end. The life-threatening behavior of Bob and Nancy regenerated earlier anxiety for the members and me because several years earlier a member of the group, Mary, had died as the result of a congenital illness. She remained in the group until a few days before she died. On occasion, I had noted to the group the ongoing effect of Mary's death. I was also acutely aware of its effect on myself. Her death and her preceding illness, garnered respect from myself and the group and led Mary to make significant progress in her own development. Seeing Bob and Nancy behave in ways that jeopardized their health invited a need in me to "shake" them, psychologically, if not physically, to avoid another loss.

Session 2

PRESENT	All group members: Carl, Maureen, Bob, Nancy, Marcia, Frank, Ted.

(I noticed that everyone was present when I entered the room, except for Bob, which was a little unusual. He arrived later, but was quiet throughout most of the session.)

MARCIA	I was very sad after last session – how is it that a bunch of regular folks like us seem to have missed out on basic emotional support as kids? *(Principle V: Resolving early attachment patterns and enactments.)*
MAUREEN	*(speaking vividly and dramatically. It was typical of her to bring up experiences that generated strong feelings in the group.)* I know, that reminds

	me. This week I was in my doctor's waiting room. We were all sitting around. In comes this elderly couple. She's obviously very sick. Her husband helped her in. He found a larger seat – not a seat for two – just a larger one. He sat her down and squeezed in beside her. It choked me up. It was so lovely and so painful – no one ever did that for me. He said to his wife, "If you are not well enough to go on the cruise this summer, we'll find somewhere else to go." It was so lovely, hell, I could not bear it. *(Principle I: Co-creating meaningful interactions; Principle VIII: Importance of context. The "doctor in the waiting room" became a symbol for "the therapist and the group," an emotionally laden metaphor that the group could use to understand its relationship with the therapist and it's "medical" context.)*
MARCIA	*(enthusiastically)* Oh god – that's what I mean. There was no one there for you when you needed it. *(Principle IV: Co-transference; an indirect allusion to feeling abandoned by the therapist.)*
TED	What a moment! That would have choked me up, too. *(crying a little)* I've never experienced anything like that. It would have made me so pissed, too!
NANCY	*(triggered by the story – looking at Carl sitting beside Maureen)* I've been wondering about you two. Are you having an affair? Like that old couple, you seem pretty cozy.
CARL	*(without hesitation)* I like Maureen a lot, but we're not having an affair. I've never had a loving relationship with a woman in my life. My mother was so brutal that I was scared off women for life. But since coming to this group – since the beginning of time, it seems – I've been able to talk with a few women. Maureen has been one of those women. I feel supported by her and safe around her. *(Principle V: Resolving early attachment patterns and enactments via a reparative group experience.)*
MAUREEN	Me too. Carl has been very helpful to me. He even called me once during last summer vacation when I was in despair just to ask how I was doing. Not the usual group protocol I know, but it helped me.
NANCY	That's nice. I just needed to know. I've had trouble with men, too.

Therapist commentary: Nancy is often quite mischievous in the group – when she is not despairing herself. But she is also very good in those mischievous moments at drawing attention to events in the group itself. In this instance, the story Maureen told was indeed very moving. Nancy brought it into the room and to an important relationship in the room. The couple in the doctor's office appeared in the group. Though she was also being seductive as was her wont, she was also highlighting a set of relationships with roots dating back to before she joined the group about which she was unfamiliar and to which we will return later.

The phone call reaches back to earlier in group history. It reflected a new protocol developed by the group in the face of Mary's dying. Mary, a very isolated woman and an effective professional person, revealed herself very slowly to the group over seven and a half years. One evening she told the group that she had learned that she had a life-threatening illness. The prognosis was very poor. Months later she was unable to drive her car but wanted to continue in the group. After much conversation the members decided that one member would pick Mary up and bring her to the group and another member would drive her home. They followed this plan until Mary entered a hospice where most members including the leader visited her until she died.

As I watched the group struggle with this I felt some discomfort. In working this out, the members changed our group agreement of keeping all contacts within the group. It also tested my wish to maintain control. *(Principle IV: Co-transference.)* However, I sat with those discomforts, which I later shared *(Principle VII: Therapist self-disclosure)* and joined the group in modifying its agreements to allow Mary a very rich death among friends – she had few others – and gave her a chance to continue growing to the end. At the funeral service Ted spoke movingly about Mary and the members and I cried together.

This modification of the agreement continued on and off for sometime afterward and is seen in Maureen's appreciation of Carl's phone call. Then it happened less and less. *(Maureen and Carl's pairing, Nancy's "mischief," and the change of rules in the group constituted a set of relatively benign enactments – Principle V: Resolving early attachment patterns and enactments. – of unresolved grief related to the loss of Mary.)*

TED	Bob, how are you doing? You came in late and you seemed a little out of it.
BOB	I'm OK, thanks for asking. I'm a little tired. I'll be visiting the doctor this week for a check up.
CARL	*(angrily)* Yeah, I know, but this is not like you.
TED	Carl's right, it's not like you.
BOB	*(speaking very softly.)* Yeah, I'm OK. I'm undergoing a lot of tests. So far they are all OK but I'm a bit anxious.
CARL	It's good you're getting checked out. You know how you often fail to take care of yourself. It bugs me.

Therapist commentary: I noted to myself that Bob did not seem as sharp as he usually does. It was unclear whether he was getting depressed again as he had in the past, or whether there was a medical problem beginning to emerge. I was very aware of Bob's family medical history, which was poor and much later in life he seemed to be following their trajectory. I did not add anything at this moment, but decided to keep a careful eye on things. Remembering Mary's death earlier in the group's history generated some anxiety for me, and I felt conflicted between acting too soon, or not acting at all and remaining in role. In a later session, this would find expression among the group members whose anxiety around Bob came to a head. Bob's characteristic response to his health was to neglect it, a pattern set earlier by his parents. It evoked anxiety among the members and in me as well. As became clear in a later session, this seemed to be Bob's way of letting the members and me know how anxious he felt as a child living with sick parents.

Additionally, I noticed that when I felt anxious about Bob's health, the members did not, but when the members felt anxious and expressed it, I felt less anxious *(Principle IV: Co-transference)*. When Bob, often with pressure from the members, began to take care of himself everyone felt less anxious. He also felt more aware of this fear and for the moment was more able to tolerate it. Together the members, Bob, and I gradually created a context in which Bob could speak his fears however tentatively, bear the distress without projecting it into and onto others. *(Principle I: Co-creating meaningful interactions. Throughout the above sessions, the group is co-creating a vocabulary, images, and context for addressing loss, grief, and broken attachments.)*

> MARCIA (*changing the mood*) Hi Gang, I've been dating Rita for four months, the longest I've dated in a long time. I'm still in love with her and I've not been finding excuses to avoid her. I'm very pleased.
> THERAPIST And you're still with us.
> MARCIA Yes I am. I remembered what you said. I've not gotten disappointed in here yet, but you never know.

Therapist commentary: The problems one brings to therapy often reappear in the group itself giving an opportunity for a close-up look at the problem. When Marcia told her story to the group of her difficulty dating – and with intimacy more generally – I noted the possibility that she may have the same experience in the group which would give her and the members a closer look at what she was struggling with. The session ended, leaving, as is usually the case, unfinished business. That unfinished business around Bob's health would become a very key issue in the next few weeks.

Session 3

PRESENT (All) Carl, Maureen, Nancy, Frank, Ted, Marcia, Bob

(Bob did not show the previous week. His no-show generated considerable anxiety around him with a lot of pressure on me to do something. This time Bob came on time.)

> TED (*very forcefully and angrily*) OK so what's going on Bob? You didn't show up last week and scared the shit out of me.
> CARL (*also angrily*) I'm pissed at you. No matter what I say, you still do this crazy behavior. If you want to kill yourself so be it, but don't do it on my watch.
> MAUREEN I'm with Ted and Carl. It is very troubling when you behave this way. Not getting checked out – not showing up. I worry about you.

BOB	I know, I'm not very good at this stuff and do need to get prodded by you folks.
THERAPIST	Maybe Bob when we get anxious about you not taking care of yourself you're letting us know what it was like for you living with sick parents who might die at any moment – as they ultimately they did, when you were relatively young.

Therapist commentary: Frequently, I included myself in group comments or interpretations. The members and I shared the anxiety: Hence the use of "we" and "us." *(Principle IV: Co-transference.)*

TED	You got that right! We get it. We get it, now take care of yourself.
NANCY	Bob, I know where you're coming from. I cannot stop eating even though it's killing me. I'm getting heavier and heavier.
FRANK	Maybe you should return to the overeaters group that was so helpful to you before.
NANCY	Maybe – but besides the eating, I hate what's going on with me. I make a lot of money – hundreds of thousands a year working in a man's world, but I'm tired of the work that gets me that money. I also know that the second in command at the company would like to get rid of me – he's jealous of me. But, Paul, the owner of the company likes me and wants me to stay – but I've had enough. I need to stop, but I don't know where to go or what to do. I also don't want to disappoint Paul. I'm plain stuck.
MARCIA	I've been stuck also as you know. You said once that you rarely take a vacation – you work all the time – I've been there – goes with being a businesswoman. Maybe it's time to ask for a three month sabbatical before you make any final decisions. Would Paul go for that?
NANCY	I don't know maybe I could. I hate to ask him. I think life is pretty much over for me.

Therapist commentary: Marcia and other group members give advice to Nancy. Much of it very good, but it also seemed to help the members contain their anxiety about Nancy's despair and life-threatening behavior. Frank, a recovering addict himself, usually supported Nancy with brief directive comments while also acknowledging that she will do what she has to do when she is ready. He is the member of the group who usually says the least. When members ask what he's getting from the group he has a hard time saying what it is. Yet, he rarely misses and is always the earliest to arrive as much as 40 minutes early. He likes to sit in the office and relax. I was aware of Frank's limited feeling responses. A crucial event in his life was the day his father had a heart attack and died in his arms while his mother was upstairs sleeping off a drinking binge. He was sixteen. It moved me and the members, which we all shared with him. For Frank it was something that happened and not something that troubled him. I also noted Frank's attempt to engage me apart from the group.

I decided it would be helpful to join Frank. I said, "Frank, you and I have something in common. When I was your age in the house alone, my grandfather had a stroke, behaved bizarrely, and later died. It's not something I forget." *(Principle VII: Therapist self-disclosure; Principle III: Therapist promotes empathy and authenticity.)* Frank then began to open up and talk about how overwhelmed he felt at the time.

> CARL   *(pissed)* Come on guys, you've given me advice like this when I was despairing about my work. Doesn't help.
> NANCY   It's OK Carl this does help.

Therapist commentary: I noted this exchange by Carl and the group. I thought it was an indirect exchange between Carl and Marcia. Marcia is the cheerleader of the group and a generous giver of advice, Alan is reflective and thoughtful. I sensed that Carl was angry with Marcia for her cheerleader role. It is also important that while I liked Marcia, I did find her cheerleading a little hard to take. So who really was angry? *(Principle IV: Co-transference.)*

> MAUREEN   Nancy, Marcia has a point. I went through a crisis like this when I left the business world and started my own business designing and laying out large properties. Best move I ever made, but it took a while. Not knowing where you are going next is part of it.
> THERAPIST   Nancy, this crisis seems to have begun following your uncle's death.
> NANCY   Yeah, he was very special to me – the only member of my f–ing family that seemed to give a damn about me. I loved that man. Now he's dead – it takes getting used to. But since then my cousin died. I did not know her well, but she was very young – under 30. Man that struck me terribly – I just cried and cried – even though I did not know her well. Now I might lose Paul.

Therapist commentary: Nancy relaxed after this. Sat back in her chair and said she was OK. This material also replicated Nancy's earlier reflections on some of the roots of her problems. Parallel to Nancy's uncle was the fact that her aunt died when she was a few years older than she is now. This anxiety about history repeating itself feeds his despair.

> MAUREEN   All this reminds me of a recent recollection of my family that I had long forgotten – not sure I even remembered before. I was moving some furniture in my home when I recalled hearing furniture banging and being thrown around upstairs in my home when my father was fighting with one of the boys. It terrified me. Then I realized how little I know about my parents.

Therapist commentary: Is Maureen also wondering who I am – keep an open eye? *(Principle IV: Co-transference; Principle V: Resolving early attachment patterns and enactments. The group is working through depressive affect and traumatic life history, and the therapist is an engaged participant in this process, aware of his personal involvement.)*

BOB	Not surprised – there were six of you – by default you were one of the parents. Father was angry much of the time and mother overwhelmed. When you became pregnant as a late teenager, you took yourself from Mississippi to New York City by bus to get an abortion and then got yourself back home – shit, nobody supported you or took care of you in that.
MAUREEN	There's a lot that remains hazy.

Therapist commentary: Maureen first recalled the abortion trip when she was in the group. She recalled going through the motions, but forgot most of the details. Earlier, Maureen had learned that her love relationships including her ex-husband were all with men who were distant and revealed very little feeling or attachment. She had learned that this reflected how she used taking care of others while remaining distant from herself to cope with what she initially described as an uncaring and distant family. This will add another dimension to those roots. For Maureen, the group has become like a family where she has been learning a new set of experiences and becoming alive and strongly attached. She sits beside me. *(The parallels between the small "stranger group" and the nuclear family provides an optimal setting for Principle I: Co-creating meaningful interactions. It brings in many dimensions of the earliest caregiver and "group" attachments. And it stimulates connections and identifications among the members that are "ready for use.")*

Session 4

PRESENT	Carl, Maureen, Marcia, Ted, Frank, Bob.
ABSENT	Nancy (at retreat in Maine for food addicts).
FRANK	So how was the bike trip in France?
MARCIA	Man – was that ever great. We covered miles and miles up many steep hills. God was I proud of myself. I kept going strong to the end, though I felt pretty tired afterwards. I'd do it again. *(Marcia spoke with high excitement for close to 15 minutes)* So how was it here?
TED	You don't want to know. It was hot as hell, storms, flooding, trees falling.
FRANK	Down where I live trees came down, the power went out and boats were endangered. A couple of trees fell right through the roofs of houses.
MARCIA	That reminds me of my old home. Once, I was sitting downstairs reading while the rain was pouring outside. My then lover was out for the evening. The house rattled and outside I heard a loud crash. I had no wish to go outside so I just sat there. My lover returned and said what the hell are

	you doing? A tree has just fallen through the roof of our house! I went upstairs to check and there was this huge branch sticking through our bedroom ceiling and stopping a few inches from our bed. Glad I wasn't lying on it.
CARL	Where I live everything comes down at the best of times, this time it was just worse. Fortunately, we missed the hurricane, but I checked out safe spots in my apartment. I went to the nearest part of my apartment to the middle of the building.

For another forty minutes the members regaled a host of horror stories locally, in the news and in their pasts. *(Principle I: Co-creating meaningful interactions; Principle V: Resolving early attachment patterns and enactments. The stormy weather becomes a co-created meaningful metaphor for catastrophic anxieties rooted in the earliest abandonments and derailments of caregiving.)*

THERAPIST	This sounds like the apocalypse, the beginning of the end.
MARCIA	What the hell's he talking about?
TED	He's right. I forgot – next week is our last meeting before the August break. *(Principle VIII: Importance of context. The summer break and the loss of group support during that time is the adaptive context that has stimulated catastrophic fears of fragmentation.)*
BOB	I agree – makes me nervous – it's a long break.
CARL	It's not that big a deal.
TED	You forget, you don't usually take the vacation break this easily.
CARL	What's he getting at?
THERAPIST	Probably that you get very lonely over other summer vacation breaks and have had difficulty doing your regular tasks.
CARL	That's true but I think I'll do better this year. I've got more friends and am much better established in the world. But it's true I'll miss it anyway.
BOB	*(angrily.)* It scares me – do you have to go off for so long? Good news is my psychiatrist will be around.
FRANK	I wonder how Nancy is doing and does she know about this? *(This reflects real concern about Nancy, which Frank experiences but is scant in expressing – see earlier.)*
BOB	She was told like the rest of us some months ago – doesn't mean she remembers.
MAUREEN	This will be better for me than in the past. My depression has lifted – I'm thinking more clearly and faster. Does that happen when depression lifts?
THERAPIST	True, check with Bob.
BOB	It certainly does. When I get depressed everything slows down and fortunately speeds up when it clears.
MAUREEN	That's good to know. It'll make the break easier.
BOB	Remember last year at this time – Shoshana left – wrapped up her treatment then went to into individual psychoanalysis.
MARCIA	Who was Shoshana?
BOB	She was a very loveable member of our group.
FRANK	She was in search of something, visiting different retreats in the dessert.
CARL	She was very important to me – first woman I really trusted.
THERAPIST	You loved her.
CARL	Yes I did, being in the group with her turned my life around. Maureen's a bit like that for me now.

Therapist commentary: The first hour or more of this session was a mystery to me. I knew something was going on. Initially I was intrigued by the various war stories that had been happening locally and in the past. They were also well based in reality. My interest waned and I realized that the members did not seem to be doing any "work" as they usually would, though it was very pleasant and sometimes very funny – a sure enticement for me not to work either! I waited for a long time before intervening. This was not easy to do, but I determined it was important to wait and bear the discomfort of it until this fog began to clear. I was thinking, it does not usually take this long.

It was a group struggle not just a struggle of some individuals or couples in the group – so I asked himself, what is the group trying to cope with at this moment? Nothing came for a while. Clearly, I was denying something. Then I remembered that my summer break was coming up. Not the kind of thing one would forget. Now I had a focus, but not an easy response to the group. Any thought I had if given voice would probably drop and rattle like a clanging cymbal – not that that is necessarily bad, but there seemed to be a better way, something closer to the affect. Someone in the group mentioned the word revelation. I associated to the book of Revelations and the coming of the apocalypse for the Roman empire of the time. On a less grand scale it seemed to me that this indeed was a sign of end times for the group, hence my response of "This sounds like the apocalypse, the beginning of the end." *(The therapist here is struggling with four basic principles – I: Co-creating meaningful interactions, II: Therapist elucidates unconscious meaning; III: Therapist promotes empathy and authenticity; and IV: Co-transference. This is because his vacation acts like a powerful lens for the issues of grief, loss, and abandonment the group has been struggling with for many weeks. He becomes a "container" for the strong affects projectively identified into him by all the members. The intersubjective field is saturated with meaning and significance. Such moments represent important milestones in the group's development and have great potential for healing of relational dilemmas.)*

I was not sure it would work until I got the response from the members. If it had fallen flat I would have had to reconsider. That reconsideration would have involved some complex reflection, which among other things might have simply included wondering with the members what they thought was going on.

Discussion

The preceding several sessions and some of the therapist's self-analysis of the experience illustrates how both internally (intersubjectively) and externally (relationally) one particular therapist led a group. Other therapists, even with a similar orientation, might perceive and approach the same group sessions quite differently. In general, this therapist appeared to proceed from a traditional psychodynamic and group dynamic orientation, but with a "sensibility" that reflected intersubjective-relational principles. However, there were several opportunities where a more specific strategic application of such principles might have advanced the group development and depth of awareness still further.

For example, this therapist made minimal use of self-disclosure, mostly expressing himself through a quiet, reflective, empathic "presence" conveyed by his silence and perhaps body language. There were ample opportunities, for example, in Maureen's recollection of the doctor's office, to further engage the co-transference in which the group felt some abandonment by the therapist, thereby enriching and deepening their interactions with her.

The group made ample use of intersubjective "I" feedback, suggesting a healthy therapeutic alliance and group norms in this group. They worked through many aspects of derailed attachments, abuse, abandonment, and losses. However, more "mileage" could have been obtained by helping the group to "mentalize," i.e. put words, thoughts, and images around their relatively benign enactments involving seductive pairing and rule-breaking. The therapist's hesitancy to do this may have coincided with co-transference issues. His countertransference may have had an aspect common to many therapists, namely anxiety about aggression, and an effort to maintain empathy, albeit perhaps at the expense of authenticity. The group members often shared angrily, yet little was said by the therapist regarding this prevalent emotion, much less about his own anger. Anger, as we know, is one of the stages of grief, which was constantly alluded to by the group. Anger is an emotion which is especially difficult to address intersubjectively because by its very nature it challenges relatedness.

The therapist could also have further elucidated contextual elements that impacted the members. The "doctor's office" experience and metaphor perhaps referred to the use of the traditional medical model in therapy and its norms of "surgical" detachment. (The group appeared to feel deprived of intimacy with the therapist.) Maureen, Nancy, and Marcia all seemed to struggle with issues common to women in our culture. Bob, Carl, Ted and Frank maintained a "macho male" type of assertiveness, often at moments when they felt quite vulnerable. Further, the group sessions occurred in the decade of the 9/11 attacks and the course of the wars in Iraq and Afghanistan, whose echoes of fear and traumatic loss echoed in the society. Such contextual "background effects" are too often neglected in therapy groups. They surround all our relations as intersubjective contexts.

By and large, however, the therapeutic interaction in this group was productive and healing for the members. The therapist's traditional stance of minimal intervention combined with empathic attunedness and awareness of countertransference gave the members a feeling of security which allowed for considerable exploration of issues, and they readily co-created ample opportunities for experience, expression, and understanding in the safe sanctuary that this group offered.

Conclusions

Intersubjective and relational psychoanalysis are overlapping and complex perspectives on dynamic psychology and psychotherapy. Here, they have been applied as a set of guiding principles that can provide a useful "sensibility" for working with patients in groups. The extended case vignette suggests how they can be used flexibly and adaptively in accordance with the therapist's own orientation and style. When successfully employed, they can deepen and enrich the intimacy and depth of the therapy experience for all concerned. As Michels (2011) has noted, "Psychotherapy is praxis, not a gnosis," an art rather than a science, although it may apply scientific findings and theories, as, in the present examples, theories of communication and attachment, and research on early development. The perspectives we have depicted are continually evolving, and the scientific basis will change over time. But the emphasis in "praxis," namely the relational and intersubjective aspects of psychotherapy and of the development of self, offers a context for treatment that has been long in coming but here to stay. Its sensibility is in the modern *zeitgeist*, and its value in promoting and deepening the change process is available to therapists of diverse orientations. Perhaps its most important requirements are the therapist's access to his own self experience and his willingness to engage in the group.

Acknowledgments

The authors would like to dedicate this chapter to the memory of their late beloved friends and colleagues, Drs Anne Alonso, Bert Cohen, and Ramon Ganzarain, each of whom taught us by example the true meaning of "intersubjective" and "relational."

References and Bibliography

American Psychiatric Association. (1994). (Text revision 2000). *Diagnostic and statistical manual of mental disorders*, (4th ed.). Text Revision (DSM-IV-TR). Washington, DC: American Psychiatric Association.

Anzieu, D. (1984). *The group and the unconscious*. London: Routledge & Kegan Paul.

Aron, L. (1996). *A meeting of minds: Mutuality in psychoanalysis*. Hillsdale, New Jersey: Analytic Press.

Atwood, G., & Stolorow, R. (1984). *Structures of subjectivity: Explorations in psychoanalytic phenomenology*, Hillsdale, New Jersey: Analytic Press.

Atwood, G., & Stolorow, R. (1993). *Faces in a cloud: Intersubjectivity in personality theory* (2nd ed.). Northvale, New Jersey: Jason Aronson.

Billow, R. M. (2003). *Relational group psychotherapy: From basic assumptions to passion*. London: Jessica Kingsley.

Bion, W. R. (1959). *Experiences in groups*. London: Tavistock.

Bion, W. R. (1962). The psycho-analytic study of thinking. *International Journal of Psycho-Analysis*, 43, 306–310.

Cohen, B. D. (2000). Intersubjectivity and narcissism in group psychotherapy: how feedback works. *International Journal of Group Psychotherapy*, 50(2), 163–179.

Cohen, B. D., & Schermer, V. L., (2002). On scapegoating in therapy groups: A social constructivist and intersubjective outlook. *International Journal of Group Psychotherapy*, 52(1), 89–109.

Fairbairn, R. W. D. (1952). *Psychoanalytic studies of the personality*. London: Routledge & Kegan Paul.

Fidler, J. (personal communication, 1989)

Foa, E., Hembree, E. A., & Rothbaum, B. O. (2007). *Prolonged exposure therapy for PTSD: Emotional processing of traumatic experiences*. New York: Oxford.

Fonagy, P. (2001). *Attachment Theory and Psychoanalysis*. New York: Other Press.

Fonagy, P., Gergely, G., Jurist, E., & Target, M. (2005). *Affect regulation, mentalization, and the development of self*. New York: Other Press.

Fosshage, J. (2003). Contextualizing self psychology and relational psychoanalysis: Bi-directional influence and proposed syntheses. *Contemporary Psychoanalysis*, *39*, 411–448

Foulkes, S. H. (1964). *Therapeutic group analysis*. New York: International Universities Press.

Galea, S. (2002). Psychosocial sequelae of the September 11 terrorist attacks in New York City. *New England Journal of Medicine*, *346*, 982–987.

Galt, A. S. (2010). Trigant Burrow and the laboratory of the "I". Webpage accessed September, 17, 2010 at http://www.lifwynnfoundation.org/trigant.htm.

Gayle, R. G. (2009). Co-creating meaningful structures within long-term psychotherapy group culture. *International Journal of Group Psychotherapy*. *59*(3), 311–333.

Greenson, R. R. (1967). *The technique and practice of psychoanalysis*. (Vol. 1). New York: International Universities Press.

Grossmark, M. (2007). The edge of chaos: Enactment, disruption, and emergence in group psychotherapy. *Psychoanalytic Dialogues*, http://www.informaworld.com/smpp/title%7Edb=all%7Econtent=t783567626%7Etab=issueslist%7Ebranches=17 - v17 *17*(4), 479–499.

Harwood, I. (2006). Head start is too late: Integrating infant research, neurobiology, attachment, and trauma theories to groups with pregnant and new mothers – PIDA Project. *International Journal of Group Psychotherapy*. *56*(1), 5–28.

Herman, J. (1997). (Original work published 1992). *Trauma and recovery*. New York: Basic Books.

Hoffman, I. Z. (1983). The patient as interpreter of the analyst's experience. *Contemporary psychoanalysis*, *19*, 389–422.

Hopper, E. (2003). *The social unconscious: Selected papers*. London: Jessica Kingsley.

Kohut, H. (1959). Introspection, empathy, and psychoanalysis. *Journal of the American Psychoanalytic Association*, *7*, 459–483.

Kohut, H. (1971). *The analysis of the self*. New York: International Universities Press.

Kohut, H. (1977). *The restoration of the self*. New York: International Universities Press.

Langs, R. (1976). *The bipersonal field*. New York: Jason Aronson.

Lichtenberg, J. (2001). *Psychoanalysis and motivation*. (Psychoanalytic Inquiry Book Series). London: Routledge.

Lionells, M., Fiscalini, J., Mann, H. & Stern, D. B. (Eds). (1995). *A handbook of interpersonal psychoanalysis*. London: Routledge.

Linehan, M. M. (1995). *Understanding borderline personality disorder: The dialectic approach program manual*. New York: Guilford Press

Mahler, M. S., Pine, F., & Bergman, A. (1975). *The psychological birth of the human infant*. New York: Basic Books.

Michels, R. (2011). Foreword to Bernard, H., Klein, R., & Schermer, V. (Eds.) *On becoming a psychotherapist: The personal and professional journey*. London: Oxford University Press.

Mitchell, S. A. (1988). *Relational concepts in psychoanalysis*. Cambridge, Massachusetts: Harvard University Press.

Orange, D., Atwood, G., & Stolorow, R. (1997). *Working intersubjectively: Contextualism in psychoanalytic practice*. Hillsdale, New Jersey: Analytic Press.

Prior V. & Glaser D. (2006). *Understanding attachment and attachment disorders: Theory, evidence and practice*. Child and Adolescent Mental Health, RCPRTU. London and Philadelphia: Jessica Kingsley.

Rangell, L. (1981). From insight to change. *Journal of the American Psychoanalytic Association*, *29*, 119–142.

Schermer, V. L. (2002). Introduction. The implications of multicultural diversity and ethnopolitical conflict for working with groups. *Special Edition of Group: the Journal of the Eastern Group Psychotherapy Society, 26*(3), 175–188.

Schermer, V. L. (2008). Commentary: The complexity of gender. In Special Edition on Gender Issues in Group Psychotherapy. *Group: the Journal of the Eastern Group Psychotherapy Society. 32*(1), 57–70.

Schermer, V. L. (2010). Mirror neurons: Their relevance for group psychotherapy. *International Journal of Group Psychotherapy, 60*(4), 485–511.

Smith, M. J. (1985). *When I say no, I feel guilty.* New York: Bantam.

Speck, R. V. (1964). Foreword. English translation and bibliography of "La folie à deux: ou folie communiques", C. Laseque & J. Falret, Annales Medico-Psychologiques, 1877. (Monograph published as supplement to *The American Journal of Psychiatry.*) Washington, DC: American Psychiatric Association.

Stern, D. (1985). *The Interpersonal world of the infant.* New York: Basic Books.

Stolorow, R. D. (2010). My long-distance friendship with Heinz Kohut. *International Journal of Psychoanalytic Self Psychology, 5*(2), 177–183.

Stolorow, R., Brandchaft, B., & Atwood, G. (1987). Treatment of psychotic states. In *Psychoanalytic Treatment: An Intersubjective Approach* (pp. 132–172). Hillsdale, New Jersey: Analytic Press,

Stone, L. (1954). The widening scope of indications for psychoanalysis. *Journal of the American Psychoanalytic Association, 2,* 567–594

Stone, W. (2009). *Contributions of self psychology to group psychotherapy: Selected papers.* New International Library of Psychoanalysis Series. London: Karnac.

Strasser, S. (1985). *Understanding and Explanation.* Pittsburgh: Duquesne University Press.

Sullivan, H. S. (1953). *The interpersonal theory of psychiatry.* New York: Norton.

Valenstein, A. F. (1981). Insight as an embedded concept in early historical phase of psychoanalysis. *Psychoanalytic Study of the Child, 36,* 307–318.

Wachtel, P. L. (2008). *Relational theory and the practice of psychoanalysis.* New York: Guilford.

Winnicott, D. W. (1971). Transitional objects and transitional phenomena. In Winnicott, D.W. *Playing and Reality* (pp. 1–25). New York: Basic Books.

Wolf, E. S. (1988). *Treating the self: Elements of clinical self psychology* New York: Guilford.

Yalom, I., & Leszcz, M. (2005). *The theory and practice of group psychotherapy* (5th ed.). New York: Basic Books.

Young, J. E. (1999). *Cognitive therapy for personality disorders: A schema-focused approach* (3rd ed.). Sarasota, Florida: Professional Resource Exchange.

5
Integrative Cognitive-Behavioral Group Therapy

Greg Crosby, with Donald Altman

Author's Historical Perspective

There has been a true evolution in the history of groups in just the past 35 years, and I believe it is important to understand the history of treatment in psychotherapy in order to fully appreciate how far we have come and where we may be going. This is what is sometimes missing from graduate school curricula. For example, back in 1972 when I got started organizing and running a group program in Spokane, Washington, it was to serve 300 clients who were discharged from Eastern Washington State Psychiatric Hospital to Goodwill Industries. That time period was notable for a major de-institutionalization of mental hospitals across the country. What we had in mental health hospitals in the 1950s is what you have in prisons today. We locked people away. Because the institutionalization model was dominant, we even had people who had been born in the hospital and grew up there. In addition, at that time, women were often institutionalized for not behaving in a stereotypical way. I was fortunate to start my group programs at the time of the deinstitutionalization of mental health hospitals.

At the time (1972–1976), our program at Goodwill was considered to be *avant-garde* because we tried to develop group programs that would help clients be able to work at Goodwill, while at the same time, develop family relationships and enhance their ability to function out in the world. Further, these were mixed groups – including patients diagnosed as bi-polar, depression and schizophrenic – because the common purpose was to maintain and increase one's ability to function in the world. Every client had a supervisor at Goodwill, so we had to help him learn to communicate to his supervisor, family, as well as other persons. We helped clients identify their feelings and needs and practised a skill-based approach.

In retrospect, there were two important things we did. First, patients told their story of what it was like to be in the hospital; what it was like to work in Goodwill, and what it was like to be out in the community. The narrative story is vital in making groups work because it creates bonding and relationships, as well as helps participants learn from their story.

Second, patients learned practical skills: communication skills, problem-solving skills, stress management skills, planning and organization skills, constructive relationship skills, and self-care skills. The value of group work is that it helps people adjust to a new life and builds support within and outside the group. Clients gained confidence in working outside in the world by being in the group.

All the groups we ran consisted of co-therapy with two therapists, which was more typical than is the case today. Co-therapy is a wonderful way to learn how to facilitate a group, and I recommend that if you're out of school and can possibly do it, run a group with someone who is more experienced. Hopefully, groups would be mentored for you during internship, but co-therapy is not done as much as it could be – often because organizations struggle getting enough people in the groups. At Kaiser Permanente, where I have organized and developed group programs for the past 20 years, any mental health employee or intern gets mentored if she wants to run groups. So this is doable and important if we are to continue to provide high-quality group treatment.

The Goodwill Industries job was something I accidentally fell into. My second job was at a residential and day treatment program conducted at Waverly Children's Home (now called Trillium Services) in Portland, Oregon. When I started working at Waverly in 1977, we started the in-home prevention program for abuse. We ran groups whenever there was abuse. That resulted in national recognition for a group designed especially for fathers who had abused their children physically – and it was recognized by the National Institute for Mental Heath in 1979. We learned that fathers could change when in a group, and that they were motivated to work on a relationship with their children as a result of being able to connect with other group members and change skills. They were able to transcend their aggression and life struggles. Again, it was working with a combination of narrative stories and skills that got people inspired to work through their suffering when in groups.

Why the Cognitive-Behavioral Model?

I have been running groups for 37 years, and if someone were to ask me; "Why are you attracted to the Integrative Cognitive-Behavioral Model?" I'd have to answer this way: People who are in this type of group get inspired to work through their suffering – and they do this through a combination of relationship-building and skills. These groups show that relationships matter. While people need to tell the stories of how they got in the problem, the focus is not just talking about the problem, but working on *how* to solve the problem. That's critical because this type of group also provides tools for how to deal with your suffering. I like that skills can be learned in a group setting and that people realize they are not alone. This gives them hope.

But the Integrative Cognitive-Behavioral Model that I am going to be describing in these pages also has an historic context and evolution of its own. In 1986, I was recruited to Kaiser Permanente because of my experience as a group coordinator. I was hired in Spring 1987, and Kaiser Permanente at that time had just a few groups that were mixed, disordered, process groups – but no skills groups or health education groups were being offered. To prepare for my new job, I decided that the best preparation would be to study the *Harvard Health Plan*, which was a highly regarded mental health plan in the 1980s.

At that time, groups were divided – and still often are – as process groups or skills and tools groups. I was thinking that what you need to do is combine those two. I decided it was important to have group programs based on diagnostic themes, and that the art of running a group was being able to tell your story, but also learning and practising skills.

Part of my own development in the field of group work came when I met Roy MacKenzie, MD, who was a former Clinical Professor of Psychiatry at the University of British Columbia, as well as a former president of the AGPA. He helped increase the level of understanding in the group field with regards to blending what are often perceived as polarized paradigms – the process and the tools. In MacKenzie's book, *Time-Managed Group Psychotherapy: Effective Clinical Applications*, he defines the five key levels of process focus in group therapy (MacKenzie, 1977: p. 120). These are listed below and can be viewed as being on a continuum from the most structured (pscyhoeducational) to the most flexible (interpersonal/psychodynamic):

1. Psychoeducational
2. Social Skills
3. Cognitive-behavioral
4. Interpersonal-semi structured (basically this is skills and process together)
5. Interpersonal/psychodynamic – process-oriented.

I consider the groups that I do as being a flexibly-structured model of cognitive behavioral therapy (CBT) – half on group support and half on skill. You integrate the ability of people to blend stories with the ability to blend skills and the result is a blended model. It is true that teaching can be empowering and people need skills. It is also true that people need to share with other people in the room. There doesn't have to be a war between group models. At the same time, this can be understood as a bio-psycho-social-cultural model because it addresses all these aspects of a patient's needs. I purposely developed this as a model to reach the general patient.

People with depression don't want to just learn cognitive skills, they also want to tell their stories and interact with other people – but it needs to be done within the context of their learning styles and by including an understanding of brain science. These two additional elements (as discussed in the Core Skills section) are crucial in effectively motivating patients and helping them to get a clearer understanding of their behavior and how to engage in change. This is, I believe, what makes my groups a truly integrative model. If you are focusing only on skills or only on process, you might miss the opportunity of identifying how someone can effectively share their story.

One real-life example of this was the time I was working with a woman, Cathy, who did not do well in individual or group therapy because she had a difficult time describing her feelings and her story. She was flustered in front of the group, and at one point said "I just can't put it in words."

Then I asked her, "If you can't put it in words, what can you put it in?"

She answered, "I can put it in pictures."

Finally, I asked, "What it would be like for you to draw two pictures – one of what it is like to be depressed, another depicting how you could pull out of depression." To confirm her visual and spatial learning styles, I also asked if she normally drew pictures of things to help her make sense of out her life. Cathy confirmed this. Later, she brought pictures to the group and while looking at these visual images she was able to express herself clearly and calmly while telling her story. This also reinforced what Cathy had learned in the group about the importance of engaging the frontal cortex as a way to calm down the brain's emotionally reactive center, or limbic system.

An entirely different question needing to be answered, in the development of my groups at Kaiser Permanente, was how to deliver groups to a large health maintenance organization (HMO) population. *The Harvard Health Plan* had successfully implemented thematic groups, and I felt they provided the basis for how a population-oriented practice model of group therapy could be adapted to Kaiser Permanente. Further, *The Harvard Health Plan* based their groups on the *population needs* of the members. This meant that if 70% of the members were diagnosed with anxiety and depression, then 70% of the groups would be themed to meet those needs. Previously, therapists would run groups based on **their** preference. To me, this change represented a shift from the individual to the community that your organization serves.

After all these years, I am still excited about how the Integrative Cognitive-Behavioral Model can benefit both organizations and the individuals who share their stories, learn skills, and find energy and hope to move forward and transcend their difficulties.

Theoretical Base and Research Evidence

There are three fundamental theories – cognitive, behavioral, and interpersonal – that support Integrative Cognitive-Behavioral Groups. These three therapies and their related practices are often used separately, but I decided to put them together because they are complementary and provide a full range of skills. You can learn all the best cognitive and behavioral skills, but it won't stick if you don't have: good trust, positive regard, active listening, and the group cohesion that comes from the interpersonal therapy. When you experience these things you don't feel depressed. A treatment group needs all three aspects to fully thrive.

Let's briefly look at the theory and evidence behind each of these three therapies. Psychiatrist Aaron Beck initially wrote about cognitive-behavioral therapy in his 1948 dissertation. It wasn't until 1976, however, that Beck published *Cognitive Therapy and the Emotional Disorders*. Beck's formulation of depression and anxiety was a cornerstone for creating tools, skills, and pathways that are learnable for patients. Basically, his theory is based upon the idea that if you change your thoughts, then your mood will change as well. In the development of his "automatic thought record," Aaron Beck produced a collaborative model for therapists and clients to work together to get a balanced view. The automatic thought record describes the situation and has clients rate their emotions on a 1–100 scale. Later, this model included the annotation of the history for that situation by asking, *How far back in time does this situation go?*

The cognitive model works as a visual guide that can be written on a board or on a sheet of paper. Columns clearly show the situation, the automatic thoughts, and then a balanced view with a constructive action. This framework shows that therapy does not have to be verbal, but that it can be visual and collaborative, and therefore highly interpersonal. This represents a shift in how other senses are brought into therapy, and it makes it easier for people to imagine a visual lesson plan for how to get out of the problems of their life. Other major contributors to this theoretical view are Christine Padesky (Padesky and Greenberger, 1995) and Jeff Young (Young, Klosko, and Weishaar, 2003).

Evidence strongly supports the efficacy of cognitive therapy in treating depression. According to *The Practitioner's Guide to Evidence-Based Psychotherapy*, "Evidence supports the efficacy of CBT in treating depression (Gloaguen, Cottraux, Cucherat, and Blackburn, 1998), and outcome studies suggest that CBT is at least as effective as pharmacotherapy and may be more effective than pharmacotherapy alone in preventing relapse of the disorder (Butler and Beck, 2001)." In addition, new research with Mindfulness-based cognitive therapy (MBCT) shows it to be effective in preventing relapse. Mindfulness plays a role in Integrative Cognitive-Behavioral groups because it aids in noting pleasantness and the ability to observe mental states in a more neutral and less judgmental way.

Integrative Cognitive-Behavioral Groups strongly integrate behavioral theories. Peter Lewinson, the psychologist who wrote *Control Your Depression* in 1967, drew upon robust research around noting pleasantness. He found that if depressed persons started pleasant activities that their mood improved. That was a cornerstone event in treating depression – which can be resistant to thinking about pleasant activities. Lewinson's research also focused on the idea of daily planning and scheduling because those abilities are deficit for those who are depressed. The behavioral practices of pleasant activities, planning and scheduling helped people see how they could make an immediate impact on their lives.

In his 1980 book *Feeling Good*, psychiatrist David Burns took academic research and wrote the first popular book to delineate dozens of behavioral methods that helped transform depression. The ideas in Burns' book made behavioral methods accessible to a broader base of clients. In 1989, Burns wrote *The Feeling Good Handbook*, which extended the behavioral approach beyond depression to include anxiety. Burns paid particular attention to procrastination and provided a step-by-step method for overcoming distractions and achieving goals.

There is a long history of evidence-based practices supporting behavioral therapy. While researcher Peter Lewinson focused on scheduling, planning, and pleasant activities, it was cardiologist Herbert Benson who, in the late 1960s and 1970s, conducted a series of experiments on managing stress through the practice of diaphragmatic breathing. Benson showed that diaphragmatic breathing, or belly breathing, reduced the body's stress response in several ways for reducing anxiety. The ability to self-regulate and calm oneself is vital for those with anxiety and depression.

The third leg of Integrative Cognitive-Behavioral groups is Interpersonal Therapy. This theory posits that improving relationship skills results in better moods. Interacting with others – such as friendships, daily interactions, and doing service for others – increases one's energy and reduces depression. According to this viewpoint, depression is caused by poor relationships and interpersonal difficulties. The group model is ideal for addressing unresolved and incomplete grief, role disputes, and interpersonal deficits. Interpersonal therapy has been shown to be very effective for rapid onset of major depression, as well as for preventing relapse.

Supervision and Training

Initially, because there were no comprehensive trainings on this integrative model, I read about and went to trainings on each of the three models – cognitive, behavioral, and interpersonal. I have created trainings for Integrative Cognitive-Behavioral groups since 1987. Whenever possible, I recommend that therapists who are new to this model sit in on an integrative CBT group prior to starting their own group.

Because it is difficult to find this model in the literature, it's important to obtain training prior to running a group. Training is best done in a workshop format. Training is a visual, interpersonal means of demonstrating skills – such as diaphragmatic breathing – that gives a person direction on how to implement these ideas. Trainees learn how to adapt the material in the program, as well as have follow-up training, readings, and supervision. Part of the training includes setting dates and times for the prospective groups.

Another option prior to running groups is mentoring – sitting in with someone who is experienced in running this model. Mentoring provides first-hand experiential learning, and it helps with the nuances of adapting the model into the group. The expectation is that after going through the experience it's easier to implement this group model.

Supervision is necessary to provide support in learning how to adapt the skills and teach them within the stages of group development. Running groups at an agency requires ongoing training, ongoing individual supervision and ongoing supervision with other therapists – which can even be done via telephone conferencing. For those in private practice, I recommend getting a group supervisor or getting a group of people together to do consultations.

Another aspect of training in Integrative CBT groups is making sure that the infrastructure supports these groups. Sometimes this means meeting and communicating with others in the health system. If the agencies are not trained to refer to group training, it will not automatically be supported. As many as fifty percent of my consultations in agencies are interventions regarding infrastructure issues relating to groups – including group room space, referrals, and group times.

Group Setting

Integrative Cognitive-Behavioral groups can be implemented in a variety of settings, including within private practices, agencies, schools, and community programs. These groups can address population needs regardless of the particular setting. To be available on an as-needed basis, groups can be designed to run for 8 or 10 weeks, and then be repeated. One reason groups are open-ended is that it helps to accommodate a large client population. I like to tell patients in my groups that it's like subscribing to a magazine – you can always re-order. Because open groups can produce turnover and concerns with group members, client screening and preparation are vital to integrating new group members and maintaining a well functioning group.

Client Preparation and Screening

Screening is an important tool for several reasons. First, it is a tool for ensuring the success of the group. Screening has been shown to drastically reduce group dropouts. Further, it answers numerous questions in the assessment of potential group members for their readiness and willingness to be part of a group. Here are the primary areas that need to be considered during the screening process.

- Bonding – Explore any concerns someone has about being in a group.
- Orientation – Describe the group orientation, including the purpose, goals and homework. It helps to ask potential members how they think the group would benefit them.
- Client's Concerns – To help answer any possible concerns, identify the time and date of the groups. During the screening process, try to problem-solve any barriers that the client may need to address, such as transportation issues, or childcare needs.
- Goals and Commitment – Examine the "goodness to fit" of the client to the group. What are the client's goals? Are they committed to attend the group? After reaffirming their commitment, always review the date and time that the client will start coming to group.

While Integrative Cognitive-Behavioral Groups are time-managed at 90-minutes per session, they are not time-limited. I make a point of contracting with the person as to how many sessions they need – which is done at the initial screening. The reason for this is that it gets group members motivated to think about what it will take to make the progress they want. They need to assess how much time is needed because you do not want the rose bush to bloom in December. Every situation is different.

- Inclusion/Exclusion – Screening gives the therapist an opportunity to rule out or exclude someone who would be inappropriate for the group. For example, this might be someone who is actively experiencing suicidal ideation with a plan and intent to carry it out.

It is helpful to create an ongoing document that provides clearly written group criteria and description of all groups within a particular track. A Mood Disorder Track, for example, could include a variety of groups and educational classes. Here are just a few ideas for how to expand this to a mood disorder track for depression and anxiety: *Orientation to Understanding Mood Disorders, Medication Education Class, Medication Management Group, Panic Group, Bi-Polar Group, OCD Group, PTSD Group, Family Life Support Group, Managing Depression and Pain Group*, and *Integrative Cognitive-Behavioral Depression–Anxiety Group.*

Table 5.1 Weekly mental health group report.

Group Names	Openings	Start Date	Time	Weeks	Day & Location	Referral to
Depression/Anxiety	Full	Enroll Anytime	4:00–5:30pm	Open-ended	W/TMH	William Mays
Depression/Anxiety	Full	Enroll Anytime	5:00–6:30pm	Open-ended	W/EIN	Herman Ruthe
Depression/Anxiety	4	Enroll Anytime	6:00–7:30pm	Open-ended	W/EIN	Vernonica Law
Depression/Anxiety	4	Enroll Anytime	6:00–7:30pm	Open-ended	TH/SLM	Ernesta Banks
Depression/Anxiety	5	Enroll Anytime	7:00–8:30pm	Open-ended	T/LK	Mary Schmidt

It can also be useful to create a table, or chart that lists all groups, including the time, date, location, the number of openings, and the therapist who is running the group. It is a very worthwhile exercise to create a brochure for clients; this can help them identify those groups that best meet their needs. Table 5.1 illustrates how a group program can be depicted in table form.

The Process of Change

How people change has been the object of considerable study. Historically in psychotherapy, it was thought that solely identifying the causes of a person's disorder would produce change through catharsis. Today, however, research is finding that we need to tell our history so we can clearly recognize the factors that got us to the place we are in now. In this context, history prepares us for change by and moving us past old triggers. As researchers de Shazer, Berg, Lipchick, Nunnally, Molnar, Gingerich and Weiner-Davis concluded, "The aim is to start the solution process rather than to stop the complaint" (Miller et al., 1997: p. 127).

Prochaska, Norcross, and DiClemente (1994) identified six stages within the change process. Their model focuses on pre-contemplation, contemplation, preparation, action, maintenance, and relapse. Open-ended groups often have all six stages present. This accelerates change because those who are further along in the change process influence new group members. For example, there was an individual who was depressed and pre-contemplative when it came to engaging in pleasant activities. Another group member, who was in the maintenance stage, shared how participating in pleasant activities was a key tool for managing his depression. After hearing this, the pre-contemplative group member was able to shift his opinion and start practising pleasant activities.

Another model of change that fits well with Integrative Cognitive-Behavioral Group Therapy is the Acceptance and Commitment framework for change – a therapeutic model grounded in techniques borrowed from Steven Hayes, chairman of the University of Nevada at Reno's psychology department, and his work in addictions treatment. This is a mindfulness-oriented approach that focuses on accepting the problem and committing to the steps necessary to bring the situation under control. This model is a non-shame, non-blame approach that creates a positive expectation for change and represents a very solution-focused therapeutic stance. This stance relies on two concepts: therapeutic teaching and the teachable moment. It gives the therapist permission to problem-solve with the client. For the client, this means accepting that there is a tendency to relapse when stress increases; likewise, there is a commitment to the tools and skills in order to regain balance.

Therapeutic Factors

The more you work with groups, the more you may find yourself like the juggler who is trying to keep many different balls in the air simultaneously. This can be an exciting and creative endeavor! Consider that each group session is designed to provide time for interpersonal experience, vicarious learning, cognitive work, and obtaining skills. How can you be sensitive to blending these elements – especially since clients have their own unique problems and agendas? This is where therapeutic factors – those supportive elements at work in any group – come into play by enhancing flexible-structured Integrative CBT groups.

As far back as 1946, psychiatric pioneer Franz Alexander pinpointed the importance of therapeutic factors. He believed it was crucial during group interaction for the client to achieve what he called "the corrective emotional experience" or the therapeutic turnaround that creates healing. According to Alexander, the client needed exposure to emotional situations that he was unable to deal with in the past. He believed that the client would experience a reparative emotional experience through reality testing (Irwin Yalom, 1970).

A good illustration of a corrective emotional experience is Joseph, a man who struggled with long-term anxiety and depression – especially during the holidays. One day, after growing more comfortable with the group, Joseph disclosed that it was on Christmas when he was falsely accused of child abuse. Even though he was acquitted by a grand jury in only 14 minutes, that was the beginning of Joseph's difficulties because he continued to ruminate on his losses year after year. When he revealed this in the group, another participant said, "Joseph if you can talk about this, I feel I've been given permission to talk about the root of what's bothering me." This second person then shared the story of how shameful deaths in his family had affected him. This powerful exchange let Joseph see that through connection with others he could heal his own pain, as well as contribute to the healing of others.

Unlike what happens in an educational class where the goal is simply to learn, the above mentioned story illuminates how an interpersonal CBT Group offers the potential for therapeutic factors to exert a positive effect. Let's look at more of these curative factors – in particular, four that were identified by K. Roy MacKenzie (1990) – and which operate in every group in a mutually reinforcing way:

1. **Supportive factors** – Group members feel included, accepted, and that they are part of a caring and altruistic alliance.
2. **Self-revelation factors** – Group members feel safe enough to open up to others through self-disclosure and the expression of cathartic emotions. This produces a sense of bonding and interpersonal connection between group members.

3. **Learning from others factors** – Group members learn to locate a broader perspective on their condition, as well as discover new ways of being and behaving through modeling, vicarious learning, guidance and education.
4. **Psychological work factors** – Group members gain self-insight that is permanently integrated into the individual's perception of self and the world.

In addition to Mackenzie's factors, there are also the four fundamental and curative elements present in therapy that Miller, Duncan and Hubble (1997) found when reviewing the major literature on the effectiveness of all kinds of therapeutic techniques. By order of importance, these four beneficial elements in therapy are:

1. **Extra-therapeutic factors** – Comprises an individual's environment (relationships, work, money, health, unemployment, religious and group affiliations) can act as either stressors or strengths that affect motivation and change.
2. **Therapy relationship factors** – This is defined by an individual's level of trust, empathy, feeling understood, and having a secure attachment with the therapist.
3. **Model and technique factors** – These refer to specific therapies, like CBT, Family therapy, interpersonal or psychodynamic group, and mindfulness.
4. **Expectancy, hope, and placebo factors** – The expectancy factor is based on the belief that whatever the client and therapist do in therapy will bring about change. Evidenced-based practices, for example, increase the belief that therapy can work for both client and therapist. This factor requires preparation in understanding why a technique or a therapy works and then practising it and getting results. The hope factor emphasizes having simple realistic and achievable goals that give you greater efficacy in directing your future. Hope is increased when someone is able to move toward a goal using problem-solving skills, as well as the energy and will. The placebo factor centers on the positive response of an individual to an intervention – such as taking an inert medicine or following a therapist's instructions to use expressive therapy for social phobia – when there is no evidence to support that treatment.

Authors Miller, Duncan and Hubble (1997) examined the research and found that as much as thirty percent of the variance in psychotherapy outcome is due to so-called "relationship factors." The core conditions of relationships as encouraged by Carl Rogers – empathy, respect, unconditional positive regard, and genuineness – are modeled by the therapist and later assumed by the group. Therapeutic technique, on the other hand, only accounted for fifteen percent of change in clients.

Therapeutic factors alone are only part of what helps make group therapy work. It is important for the therapist to take a leading role in helping the client to establish and maintain therapeutic goals. One of the subtle ways in which this is done is for the therapist, in conjunction with the client, to focus on the achievable tasks of self-care early in the therapeutic process. As you will find in the **Overall Treatment Strategy** section of this chapter, the focus starts with action-oriented, behavioral skills and then transitions to cognitive work. This makes sense because behavioral skills are learned more quickly and easily and result in faster change. Then, through participation and sharing of stories, therapists can learn about the context or origin of a disorder. This lets group members support each other in taking small actions to improve their lives, and eventually take over for the group leader in creating motivation for change.

Mixed Anxiety-Depression Groups

There are clinics specializing in anxiety and clinics that focus on mood disorders. I believe, however, that there are many good reasons to bring people with these distinct diagnoses together in Integrative Cognitive-Behavioral Groups. Over the years, I started to see the commonalities of depression and anxiety, and I started putting together groups that included both diagnoses. One of the most compelling reasons is that depressed group members slow down the anxious members, and the anxious members speed up the depressed members. Let me share with you a very vivid example of this dynamic that occurred in a group I was running.

> At his check-in, anxious group member Jim said to a depressed and lethargic group member, Michelle, "Look honey, do you realize that the floor could collapse here at any given moment? There are always problems in construction. The ceiling could cave in due to earthquakes and that could happen at any given time. That's not even talking about the Mt. St. Helens blowing up again!"
> Michelle's eyes opened wide as she exclaimed, "I'm awake!"

And that's what makes mixed depression-anxiety groups work – the hyperactive energy and the imaginative quality of anxiety counterbalancing the depressive lack of energy.

Overall Treatment Strategy

Outcome measures

It is important to use an outcome measure at the start of each group and integrate results during the check-in. Why are outcome measures useful? For one thing, they help monitor progress and teach self-monitoring skills. Clients may communicate more information in a questionnaire than they might verbally, especially early in the therapy process. Also, the act of taking the measure helps members feel included in the group by being noticed. In addition, if someone's score has changed we want to know the reason, such as losing a job or experiencing a loss, etc. Lastly, these weekly measures complement and extend clinical impressions that the therapist may have from other formal measures.

I use outcome measures such as David Burns' "Brief Mood Survey" that measures depression, suicidal urges, anxiety, anger, and relationship satisfaction. This is a significant point to keep in mind because people are more comfortable about reporting suicidal ideation on a form instead of in person. An outcome measure is used at the screening and at each session to get a sense of how people are feeling at the beginning of the session. It also offers the advantage of having group members rate their week, as well as share a story that fills in the context.

Here is a resource list of useful outcome measures and clinical practices.

- David Burns' *Therapist's Tool Kit*.
- Beck Depression Inventory (BDI-II) and Beck Anxiety Inventory (BAI).
- *Measures For Clinical Practice and Research*: A Sourcebook Vol. I & II, Fourth Edition, (This contains over 500 instruments). (Fisher and Corcoran, 2007).
- *CORE Battery-Revised*: An Assessment Tool Kit for Promoting Optimal Group Selection, Process and Outcome. American Group Psychotherapy Association.
- Group Cohesion Scale.

Group check-in

Every group, starting with the initial one, will use half of the time for process work and half for skills. It is best to sit in a circle, if possible. Or if using tables, have tables form a square shape. It is helpful for the group leader to set the agenda for skills and to remind the group of the goals for the week. Keep in mind that any goals need to be simple, realistic, and achievable.

The check-in process, as described in detail below, is designed to incorporate both interpersonal exchange and narrative storytelling. This is important because it promotes participation and reduces the dropout rate. In addition, a strict cognitive approach that focuses primarily on the symptoms can miss the overall context in which the symptom appears. Symptoms do not appear out of thin air, and even Fritz Perls (1973) – the founder of Gestalt therapy who introduced the here-and-now process into group therapy – knew that the past was an important factor in treatment that could not be ignored. For this reason, integrative CBT groups need to make space at check-in for patients to share how their weekly experiences have affected their symptoms.

Check-in also sets the stage for modeling and leadership. As a group leader, you will want to become familiar with the CBT group leadership qualities that are described by White (White and Freeman, 2000). White's recommendations are for group leaders to model active participation, model tolerance and openness to individual differences, use collaborative and Socratic dialogue, to communicate the universality of experiences using "we" language, and, to use consistent nonverbal behaviors – such as stand when teaching and sit when intervening in group process. Cultivate these qualities and you will be an effective and helpful leader from check-in through to the end of each group session.

Below is an ordered list of items that help make for a seamless check-in.

- Complete the outcome measures prior to the start of group.
- Review outcome measure and homework and any new developments in their lives.
- Have current group members check-in first. Current members introduce themselves to any new member(s) and offer the following:

- Why they attend the group.
- How many weeks they are committed to doing and which week they are on. (They also have the option to renew.)
- Tips for the new member on how to get the most out of the group.
* Group members talk to entire group not only the leader.
* At any point group leader can ask if it is okay for other members to comment on what was said or discussed.
* The group leader emphasizes skills that are utilized or not utilized during each check-in.

Group cohesion is essential for a well-working group, and this process can be supported even at check-in. This means, for example, that group members are encouraged to talk about the skills that they used during the week. The therapist further encourages cohesion by making connections between two or more members' experiences. Cohesion is also built by avoiding two person private conversations. Through modeling, the therapist provides a safe environment for self-disclosure. In particular, the act of reviewing what has been learned during the group at the end of the session – as well as having individuals state what they are taking away from the group – helps to create a strong sense of togetherness.

Core behavioral skills

As mentioned earlier, Integrative Cognitive-Behavioral Group Therapy blends stories, skills, and cognitive work. Because behavioral change happens faster through skills learning, let's explore these first. Behavioral core skills – which are basic self-care skills for managing mental disorders – include such things as breathing, relaxation, stress management, diet, exercise, adequate sleep, and planned daily activities. Self-care activities are often talked about by therapists but may never be integrated into a therapeutic model. In fact, many clients and therapists are unaware of how basic daily behaviors can affect mood.

When core skills are coupled with cognitive skills in later sessions – as well as interpersonal feedback from group members once trust and safety have been established – they often lead to therapeutic breakthroughs and corrective emotional experiences. People begin to reflect on their own lives, imaginatively trying on new behaviors and insights while learning from others. The structured activities of our integrated group format requires the engagement of group members who support each other's learning through eye contact, listening, and the rituals of hello and goodbye that signal the beginning and end of the group.

How are skills integrated into the group design and structure? Without getting lost in details, the overall group structure is weighted at the beginning with behavioral skills to enhance mood management. The middle sessions incorporate a Cognitive-Behavioral component and integrate it with depression issues, such as loss, relationship, inadequacy, and lack of assertiveness. The last sessions are focused on developing a maintenance or relapse response plan to better manage relapse into depression. The group is designed so that it can be repeated if necessary, and the goals adapted to individual client needs.

Each weekly session, for instance, can focus on a core self-care behavioral skill. Brain Basics would be introduced in Week 1, followed by Breathing and Stress management, pleasant activities, Diet and Nutrition, and so on. This particular order that follows is effective because it directly addresses issues relating to increasing positive affect. Because these are open groups that allow clients to enter at any time, new participants will naturally learn about other skills from other group members.

Core Skill: Brain Basics

Using a framework of interpersonal neurobiology, group members learn why the brain is profoundly emotional and interpersonal. This teaching gives them an insight into how their brain works and how environment affects the brain. A visual map of the brain helps group members learn how to describe their brain – both when they're depressed and when they're balanced. Within each core skill, brain basics are reviewed for how they apply to that particular skill. Two useful resources on the brain and interpersonal neurobiology are *Healing the Mind through the Power of the Story* by Lewis Mehl-Madrona (2010) and *Mindsight* by Daniel Siegel (2010). Brain basics are friendly for group therapy because the emphasis is on how relationships shape the brain and that relationships are crucial for balanced brain integration and development.

The key brain basic topics include:

- How environment affects the physiology, structure, and function of the brain.
- How the brain is profoundly interpersonal.
- How emotions organize the brain.
- How awareness of learning styles increases the effectiveness of therapy.
- How narrative is fundamental to brain function and attachment.

Core Skill: Breathing and Stress Management

In Donald Altman's book *The Mindfulness Code: Keys to Overcoming Stress, Anxiety, Fear, and Unhappiness*, he writes:

> For centuries, our wisdom traditions have told of a sacred connection between the breath and the divine... the ancient word *prana* refers to the essence of the life force itself. In Buddhism, the breath is a microcosm through which one can gain insight into all phenomena; it is a way to directly grasp the nature of impermanence, grasping, and letting go. The Hebrew word *ruach* is often translated as the divine spirit in the Old Testament and literally means breath... Can the simple act of breathing help us recover this link to our deepest self? (D. Altman, 2010: p.79)

It was in the early 1970s when cardiologist Herbert Benson studied what he called the Relaxation Response – the calming of the body and brain through the practice of diaphragmatic breathing. Many people breathe higher up in the lungs, which makes them vulnerable to panic and the stress response.

I remember working with Helen, who on the first day of a new group identified her problem as anger – especially while driving. Helen said, "I get really angry if someone cuts me off. I can't control myself and before I know it, I'm giving someone the unkind gesture." Helen not only felt guilty after such events, she was fearful that she might put herself at risk. Helen learned belly breathing that first day. When she returned the next week, she shared during check-in that someone had cut her off. But what happened next surprised her. "When I got cut off," she explained, "I did the belly breathing. It was weird, because I could notice my anger, but it didn't seem to bother me as much. I kept my hands on the steering wheel and didn't even give the unkind gesture!"

Diaphragmatic breath, or belly breathing, increases air intake by as much as ten times. Breathing into the lowest part of the lungs causes the diaphragmatic wall to press on the abdominal cavity, making the abdomen move outward. It is this movement that presses on the vagus nerve – a cranial nerve that runs down the inside of the spine, connecting with the heart and the gut. When the gut presses on the vagus nerve, the body's relaxation system is activated. It then produces the following effects:

- Lowers the pulse rate, respiration rate, and blood pressure.
- Cleanses out the lactate from the blood (lactate increases feelings of anxiety).
- Increases alpha brain waves (produces a sense of calm and clarity).
- Increases the level of serotonin (a neurotransmitter that improves mood and reduces rumination). In fact, ninety percent of the body's stored serotonin is stored in the lining of the stomach and released into the blood stream when breathing diaphragmatically.

In the past, efforts at teaching patients belly breathing failed because the instructions were too complicated. Belly breathing is made easy simply by clasping your hands behind your back. Patients can do this by scooting forward in their chair or placing their arms behind their chair. This movement stretches a group of muscles running through the ribs (the intercostals) and naturally opens the rib cage.

It only takes 30 seconds for the body's relaxation response to take effect. It helps to have patients practise this for 1–3 minutes in the group and then ask for feedback. While breathing, patients should be directed to notice their breath and to place attention on the abdomen as it rises and falls.

There is an added benefit to relaxing individual clients in a group session. This technique enables members to feel included and accepted within the group body as well. A discussion of when to use breathing as a means of managing stress and preventing emotional upset (such as when driving, waiting in lines, etc.) can be helpful and illuminating for the entire group.

Core Skill: Pleasant Activities

If you ask ten different people in a group to identify a pleasant activity, you will likely get ten different answers. Pleasant activities turn one's attention toward that which is pleasing – thus shifting attention away from negative triggers, thoughts, or emotions. Because the brain is relational and experiential, the act of focusing on pleasant experiences literally shapes the brain's neural circuitry from the inside out.

However, it's not uncommon for some people to have problems locating activities they find pleasant. Take the example of Betty, a widow who had seven suicide attempts on the anniversary dates of her husband's death. She told the group that there was no pleasantness left in her life and that was why she wanted to kill herself. I asked her if she could observe 1–2 seconds of mild pleasantness, even with negativity, during the week. She agreed that this was an achievable goal, but she doubted she would find it. On the third day of trying to find pleasantness, she looked up at the moon and discovered it was glowing and iridescent, and she was amazed at the wonder of nature. In subsequent weeks, Betty started reading about the moon, writing poetry about the moon, and continued to look at the moon nightly. Once she located pleasantness, she began to appreciate her activities and her mood began to improve. Betty's example shows that if you break down a person's goals into something that is small, realistic, and achievable that big breakthroughs are possible.

A good way to work with pleasantness is to have group members identify simple, realistic and achievable pleasant activities to implement. If someone can't imagine a pleasant activity, it may be helpful to explore those activities that have been pleasant in the past. Rather than recreate the wheel, individuals can draw upon past histories to reveal hobbies, interests, and learning styles. I like to match my group therapy interventions to the learning styles of the members, and the benefit is that it makes change easier because I'm talking to them in a way that they learn. Often, for example, a pleasant activity can be identified from this information. One resource for understanding learning styles is Thomas Armstrong's book *Seven Kinds of Smart: Identifying and Developing Your Multiple Intelligences* (1999), which is a useful tool for helping people locate their learning styles, strengths, and interests – as well as pleasant activities.

After identifying a pleasant activity, it is important for these to be planned and scheduled, and for patients to know how much time they will spend doing pleasant activities. Patients can select a time and date for each activity. In addition, activities need to be achievable. For example, it is better to begin and complete a 15-minute walk than to avoid walking because a 2-hour trek was unrealistic. For patients, even reaching the smallest of goals can lead to an improved mood and a sense of hope.

Core Skill: Healthy Eating Habits

Healthy eating is a universally recognized factor in feeling better about one's body and mind. Food is a true bonding topic in the group experience (even if healthy eating habits are not always part of that experience!). For years, the psychology field has recognized the link between substance use and depression and anxiety. The behavioral health issues related to unbalanced consumption of foods – such as caffeine and sugar – can also contribute to mental health issues but are rarely probed for when treating depression and anxiety.

Caffeine, for example, accelerates the nervous system and increases the heart rate. Research studies have shown that caffeine can provoke panic attacks in people with panic and generalized anxiety disorder, as well as increase anxiety and cause insomnia. Caffeine consumption was an issue for a patient named Joe, who arrived in treatment with a chief complaint of extreme work stress. Joe's health problems included a lengthy list, from diabetes to mitral valve prolapse and mild epilepsy seizures. When it was discovered that he was drinking 75 cups of coffee per day, the addiction and primary care departments became involved and his depression was eventually managed.

Meal skipping can produce some of the same symptoms as those occurring in panic attacks, such as lack of energy, fatigue, lightheadedness, and rapid heartbeat. Barry was one such patient who regularly missed meals, especially breakfast – and who regularly struggled with lack of concentration, depression, and anger. Since protein is associated with concentration and impulse control by activating the frontal lobe of the brain, Barry developed a plan for eating that included a peanut butter sandwich in the morning before going to work. He got in the habit of carrying either a hard-boiled egg or an extra sandwich with him for a mid-morning or afternoon snack. After this simple nutritional adjustment, he noticed an immediate improvement in his ability to concentrate, as well as a reduction in irritability.

Another area of concern is the connection between high sugar consumption and mood. Joe, a chef at an upscale restaurant suffered from Attention Deficit/Hyperactivity Disorder. At the restaurant, he would prepare healthy food all day long. However, when he returned home at night he would retire to the couch in front of the TV where he would inhale a box of Cocoa Puffs. The Ritalin-like effect of the chocolate would calm him. Unfortunately, when the effect wore off he became depressed. For many like Joe, right diet plays an important role, as does exercise.

In the group session, patients can identify their eating patterns, such as under-eating or over-eating, as well as learn how eating affects their ability to sleep and manage moods. They can develop simple, realistic and achievable goals and strategies for inviting healthy behaviors into their lives, as well as a plan for tapering down from overuse of caffeine, sugar, and other unbeneficial substances.

Core Skill: Exercise

Research has shown that stress can produce a chemical soup of hormones in the brain and body that inhibit us from coping, as well as put the brakes on the immune system. With stress the eyes dilate, and there is either too much or too little oxygen to the brain, causing dizziness. The jaw, neck and shoulder muscles grow tense. The heart rate and blood pressure increase as adrenaline is released. Tension accumulates in every organ of the body. Digestion shuts down.

Fortunately, regular exercise is a primary stress reducer. In his book psychiatrist John Ratey (2008) chronicles the science behind the mind-body connection and adds to the evidence that exercise stimulates the production of neurotransmitters necessary to reduce depressive symptoms and reduce anxiety, as well as improve learning. In fact, many studies to show that simply moving the arms and legs for even a few minutes each day can make a difference.

Therapists can encourage clients to take on medically appropriate exercise – walking, dancing, swimming, hiking, biking, rollerblading, running, skiing, weight training, stretching, yoga, rowing and water aerobics – whatever works for the individual. With some clients it may be necessary to discourage exercise plans that fall into the all-or-nothing category. For example, one patient in a depression group announced he was going to begin by running 28 miles. When I asked him when was the last time he ran this distance he replied, "Oh, twenty years ago!"

Invite clients to simply augment what they are used to. As they get enough exercise they will frequently begin to notice mood improvement and an enhanced ability to sleep.

Core Skill: Managing Procrastination

Procrastination is a core skill because the inability to complete tasks makes individuals feel stuck, helpless, and hopeless. Any of the core skills can be used as practice for overcoming procrastination. In his book, David Burns (1999) writes that many people believe motivation comes before action; however, he suggests that action occurs before motivation. This understanding is particularly helpful to a client who is depressed. It is also useful to introduce the idea of "partial success" or "incomplete success" to patients who may harshly judge themselves for not sorting stacks of mail or cleaning up clutter that has been bothering them for months. In this new context, even a few minutes of time spent organizing can still be viewed as success.

I remember a patient who was in her early 40s who was facing serious heart problems. The doctor's recommendation to prevent further issues was for her to walk for thirty minutes a day. In the group she said, "I've procrastinated doing my exercise for a year, and I don't know how to get started because I don't have any motivation." In group, I asked what she was capable of doing and she said: "I could probably do 30-seconds just to get started."

The group helped her problem-solve in order to find a realistic start time for the activity. Not only did the patient complete her goal, but also once she got walking she continued. Returning to group she reported that she had actually walked for 30-minutes, not 30-seconds! Twelve years later, she has stayed with the 30-second goal, but continues to walk for 30-minutes each day.

One exercise that is helpful when dealing with procrastination is to have group members rank order 3 to 5 items that they typically procrastinate on – and then choose the easiest of these to implement. A client might include exercise, balanced diet and/or planned pleasant activity as items that have been put off. Activities can be broken down into small parts if necessary, along with setting a date and time to implement that activity.

Core Skill: Sleep Hygiene

Most people who pass through a time of crisis in their lives experience a disruption in their sleep pattern. Most adults need about eight hours of sleep. Although the lack of sleep can seem like an obvious factor, the quality of sleep, particularly that of deep sleep (REM sleep) is very important. Preston (2006) notes that after only two nights of sleep deprivation of stages 3 and 4 sleep, volunteer subjects experience significant daytime fatigue, difficulties with thinking such as poor concentration and impaired memory, and changes in emotional functioning, including irritability, lowered frustration tolerance and decreased ability to control emotional responses. Dawson and Reid

(1997) found that a lack of sleep could lead to functional impairment equivalent to or greater than driving under the influence of intoxicants.

Even just three consecutive days without enough sleep can put the body into a chronic stress state and make it difficult to regulate mood. Preston states that three actions help to regulate our natural circadian rhythms and promote normal sleep. These are: 1. establishing regular bedtimes; 2. exposure to early morning bright light; and 3. regular exercise. The key on the first two actions is to establish a regular pattern between exposure to light and darkness. In wintertime, when darkness out balances light, it is sometimes helpful to add the artificial assistance of a light box.

Here are ten useful techniques for clients who need to improve their sleep patterns:

1. Stretch before bedtime.
2. Get into an evening routine for winding-down at the end of the day.
3. Watch what you're reading before bedtime. (Some reading material, for example, can produce nightmares.)
4. Participate in activities that are soothing and have low stimulation. (Avoid electroluminescent light from computers, TV, and cell phones that can stimulate the retina and delay melatonin production.)
5. Write down thoughts and worries that occur to you, and remind yourself that they are on paper.
6. If you wake up, do not look at the clock.
7. Drink a non-stimulating herbal tea before bed.
8. If you awake, do not turn on the light as this affects the body's melatonin level.
9. Practice self-hypnosis to induce sleep, a modern version of counting sheep.
10. Upon awakening, say to yourself, "I know I got enough sleep."

Individuals with sleep issues needs to review the amount of medication they are taking, the mix of medication, and their caffeine intake. Putting structure to and creating bedtime rituals is also useful, allowing clients to review and ruminate on the day as they perform a calming activity such as watching a wilderness program on TV.

If clients are oversleeping, try to determine when and how much. I once had a client, Rachel, who had lost her husband in an auto accident. She had a deeply ingrained habit of oversleeping. It was discovered that she associated over stimulation with a time before the auto accident when her husband was still alive, and it grieved her to participate in such liveliness. Gradually, as she worked to decrease her naps, her energy returned and she started working full time again.

Core Skill: Social Networks

Social networks may be one of the most important recovery factors in the treatment of depression. It has been demonstrated, for example, that heart attack patients increase their survivability by participating in a support group once a week. The same holds true for cancer patients. The concept of social networks was formulated in the early 1950s following on the research of Bott, an anthropologist who studied the fishing villages of Nova Scotia and discovered that families were more interactive when fishermen were at sea.

Anthropologist Carolyn Attneave (Speck and Attneave, 1973) incorporated social network theory into her work and this began to be taught in social work schools by the late 1960s. She learned that when clients plotted their social networks before and after key events in their lives, losses often resulted. Attneave found that after divorce, women lose up to fifty percent of their social network and men lose up to forty percent.

Others who report low social support include single parents, children of divorce, and victims of a serious illness. Clients should be encouraged to augment their social networks. Setting achievable objectives such as a phone call, a planned group outing, or scheduling a date for a face-to-face with another person can do this. One red flag for therapists and group members is if a network consists of fewer than five people. After identifying their existing network, members can be encouraged as a group to look at their own histories and to notice how they have used and located resources in the past. This is a good example of how, through modeling and vicarious learning, group members locate their own strengths.

Core Skill: Daily Problem Solving

Many clients lack problem-solving skills. Others may complain that they lack the motivation to accomplish what they want to do, or that they procrastinate. Research shows that people become more motivated to perform a task *not before* they start the task, but *shortly after* they actually initiate the task. In fact, the real motivation to repeat an action comes about 30 to 90 seconds after we have already started. Knowing this, the trick is to set simple goals, select a time to do each, and to start on some, not on all at once.

A tool called the weekly organizer also helps. This is a basic calendar filled with days and times where clients can write such things as when to eat, when to see the doctor, when to exercise, etc. This brings focus to necessary tasks. Clients with ADHD, for example, find such planners useful. It is also useful for documenting rituals, behaviors, appointments, and activities. Planning focuses on the change process, too, because group members can share their weekly organizers. In this way, clients identify treatment issues and become accountable to the group.

The planner can also indicate an action or change a client may not be ready for. By making the action small enough to occur the therapist can actually precipitate change. Problem-solving has the benefit of helping clients achieve mastery over core skills through the two-pronged process: 1. setting goals; and 2. identifying small, realistic and achievable steps to achieve those goals. Best of all, they can apply this approach to tackle any life problems that they may be facing.

Cognitive-Behavioral Skills

Playwright William Shakespeare understood that both drama and humor were caused by distorted thinking. His writings were filled with mistaken identity, thinking errors, assumptions, and beliefs. A character misinterprets an event or story and shares it with another, who mangles the facts even more! Because of a single, past-perceived injury, two families or groups end up feuding for generations.

The truth is that no one is immune to the erroneous conclusions the mind can draw. These cognitive traps run the gamut from irrational thoughts such as exaggerating risk, control-at-all-costs, forecasting bad news, perfectionism/all-or-nothing thinking, emotions-as-evidence, giving up, and asking the unanswerable why question. However, the antidote to distortion can be found in fact-finding, challenging fears, and seeking a broader and more informed perspective.

At times, thinking styles can be passed down from generation to generation. When a client recognizes the origin of a particular thinking style within the group process, the results can be dramatic. Such was the case with Jim, who found himself in CBT group therapy for depression. In his thirties, he had an accomplished career, but found himself unable to be at peace with his endeavors and saw himself as lazy, stupid and cowardly. As his co-therapists began to work with his automatic thoughts of "I am lazy, etc.," Jim recalled a time in high school when his father was coaching the football team of which Jim was a member. His father had asked him to go out into a field where the boy was reluctant to go. When he refused, the father told him he was lazy, stupid and not brave. Jim walked off the field and quit football forever. As the group gave him feedback, Jim came to realize that the old, distorted labels had nothing to do with his real-life contributions.

Jasper, a young machinist, was being treated for panic disorder. Convinced that his pounding heart and difficulty breathing were symptoms of a heart attack, he made several trips to the emergency room before his symptoms were identified as panic. When he made a connection in group therapy between the deaths of his father, uncle and cousins from heart failure due to heroin overdoses and his own fear of harm, he resumed his active life with a new understanding that he was not like the other men in his family.

As Jasper shared his new understanding about his life with the group, it was soon obvious that his insights were significant for other group members as well. Through vicarious learning, group members recognized the link between past events and current dilemmas. They also witnessed that what are often considered to be uniquely personal problems are often similar or identical to the experiences of others. This universality of the nature of suffering helps make one's own challenges seem less daunting. Finally, group members gain hope for their own progress by seeing another member make a major breakthrough.

One technique that helps a group to organize around thinking styles is the Cognitive Worksheet. Used during group time, the worksheet assists the therapist and group members to track the designated client's narrative and document the integrating process. There are many ways to adapt the worksheet for various demographics, but the goal is always to help clients make the link between current behavioral problems and their link to the past. Usually one of four basic themes emerges: "I am unlovable," "I am incompetent," "I am unworthy" or "I am inadequate." Countering these self-defeating thoughts is essential to overcoming conditions such as depression and anxiety. The cognitive worksheet, together with establishing and maintaining core skills, forms the foundation for relapse prevention.

Response Plan for Relapse Prevention

It is no secret that conditions such as depression and anxiety have a high relapse rate. With depression alone the rate can be as high as fifty percent. The acceptance/commitment change model mentioned earlier is much more effective in working with clients because it allows for the inevitable relapse. From this vantage point it is useful to prepare clients for possible times of difficulty.

G. Alan Marlatt of Seattle's Behavior Research Center at the University of Washington was one of the first researchers in the field of drug and alcohol addiction to introduce what has been called the relapse prevention plan. Relapse planning has now extended itself into the healthcare field. Personally, I prefer to label such activity as response planning, and the very act of writing a response plan acts as a powerful symbol for change. All group members complete a response planning exercise when exiting the group. Below is an outline of that plan:

Response Plan

1. **Identify Triggers** – These might involve *internal triggers*, such as negative self-talk like "I'm no good," "The world's no good," and "The future is hopeless," or *external triggers* such as *events and anniversaries*. Elizabeth Carter, Betty Carter and Monica McGoldrick (1998) and Evan Imber-Black (1989) pioneered work in the use of anniversaries as they re-stimulate landmark events of loss in clients. Any unmourned loss can result in a corresponding internalized depression. Key triggers to be addressed in a response plan include the following:
   a. Anniversary dates (Historical losses).
   b. Stressful events.
   c. Relationship issues.
   d. Physical challenges (hormonal shifts, illness, chronic medical conditions).
2. **Identify Core Skills** – Core skills need to be clearly identified and implemented in order to counteract triggers. Most importantly, there needs to be a commitment to use core skills on a daily basis. Intentional breathing, medically appropriate aerobic and non-aerobic exercise, right diet and nutrition, regular sleep, daily activities planning, and social networking are important sources of self-healing for clients. Each of these areas can be adapted to suit a client's personal plan.
3. **Future Plans, Services and Support** – Most clients begin to understand that response planning is a part of lifelong learning. So it is useful for individual group members to explore ways in which they might enhance their expertise regarding their condition with the resources mentioned here:
   a. Additional therapy (group and individual).
   b. Support groups.
   c. Identify and maintain social networks.

Relapse is not a dirty word. Today we find that adopting an acceptance of relapse as a part of one's life journey actually averts magical thinking and encourages people to get back on track when they falter. Response planning can be viewed as a predictive science. In the end, the key elements of a response plan include predicting a trigger (being very specific about what sets the client off) and delivering a plan that is proactive and has a regimen for what to do after the fact. It should take into account the short-term, the long-term and include a mission statement or vision, as well as a safety plan. In addition, it helps to add a prediction about the client's ability to respond to various situations. Response planning is key to recovery and a successful Integrative Cognitive-Behavioral Group.

References and Bibliography

Altman, D. (2010). *The mindfulness code: keys to overcoming stress, anxiety, fear and unhappiness.* Novato, California: New World Library.

Armstrong, T. (1999). *Seven kinds of smart: identifying and developing your multiple intelligences.* New York: Plume.

Bieling, P., & McCabe, R. (2006). *Cognitive-behavioral therapy in groups.* New York: Guilford.

Bloomquist, H. (2006). *Skills training for children with behavior problems* (Revised Edition). New York: Guilford.

Burns, D. *Therapists Toolkit.* www.feelinggood.com/therapist's_toolkit.htm

Burns, D. (1999). *Feeling good: The new mood therapy.* New York: Harper.

Butler, A. C., & Beck, J. S. (2001). Cognitive therapy outcomes: A review of meta-analyses. *Tidsskrift for Norsk Psykologforening, 38,* 698–706.

Carter, E., Carter, B., & McGoldrick, M. (Eds.) (1998). *The expanded family life cycle: individual, family, and social perspectives.* New York: Prentice Hall.

Dawson, D., & Reid, K. (1997). Fatigue, alcohol and performance impairment. *Nature 388,* 235.

Fisher, J., & Corcoran, K. (Eds.). (2006). *Measures for clinical practice and research: A Sourcebook* (Vol. I & II, 4th ed.). Oxford, Usa Trade Publishing.

Fisher, J., & O'Donohue, W. (Eds.). (2006). *Practitioner's guide to evidence-based psychotherapy.* New York: Springer Science and Business Media.

Gloaguen, V., Cottraux, J., Cucherat, M., & Blackburn, I. (1996). A meta-analysis of the effects of cognitive therapy in depressed patients. *Journal of Affective Disorders, 49,* 59–72.

Heimberg, R. G., & Becker, R. E. (2002). *Cognitive-behavioral group therapy for social phobia.* New York: Guilford.

Imber-Black, E. (Ed.) (1989). *Rituals in families and family therapy.* New York: W. W. Norton & Co.

Kendall, P. (2000). *Child and adolescent therapy.* New York: Guilford.

Lewinsohn, P. M., Muñoz, R., Youngren, M. A., & Zeiss, A. (1986). *Control your depression.* Englewood Cliffs, New Jersey: Prentice-Hall, Inc.

MacKenzie, K. R. (1990). *Introduction to time-limited group psychotherapy.* American Psychiatric Press.

MacKenzie, K. R. (1997). *Time managed group psychotherapy: Effective clinical applications.* Washington DC: American Psychiatric Press.

Marra, T. (2004). *Depressed and anxious: The dialectical behavioral therapy workbook for overcoming depression and anxiety.* Oakland: New Harbinger Press.

Mehl-Madrona, L. (2010). *Healing the mind through the power of the story.* Rochester, Vermont: Bear & Co.

Miller, S., Duncan, B., & Hubble, S. (1997). *Escape from Babel.* New York: W. W. Norton & Co.

Najavits, L. M. (2001). *Seeking Safety: A treatment manual for PTSD and substance abuse.* New York: Guilford.

Padesky, C. A., & Greenberger, D. (1995). *Clinician's guide to mind over mood.* New York: Guilford.

Paleg, K., Jongsma, A. (2000). *Group psychotherapy treatment planner.* New York: Guilford.

Perls, F. (1973). *The gestalt approach and eyewitness to therapy.* New York: Bantam Books.

Preston, J. (2006). *Integrative brief therapy.* Atascadero, California: Impact Publishers.

Prochaska, J. O., Norcross, J. C., & DiClemente, C. C. (1994). *Changing for good.* New York: Avon Books.

Ratey, J. (2008). *Spark: The revolutionary new science of exercise and the brain.* New York: Little, Brown & Company.

Segal, Z. V., Williams, J., Mark, G., & Teasdale, J. D. (2002). *Mindfulness-based cognitive therapy for depression: A new approach to preventing relapse.* New York: Guilford Press.

Siegel, Daniel. (2010). *Mindsight: The new science of personal transformation.* New York: Bantam.

Speck, R., & Attneave, C. (1973). *Family networks.* New York: Pantheon Books.

Weisman, M. M., Markowitz; & Klerman, G. L. (2000). *Comprehensive guide to interpersonal psychotherapy.* New York: Basic Books.

White, J., & Freeman, A. (2000). *Cognitive-behavioral group therapy for specific problems and populations.* Washington, DC: American Psychological Association.

Yalom, I. (1970). *The theory and practice of group psychotherapy.* (2005, 5th ed.). New York: Basic Books.

Young, J., Klosko, J., & Weishaar, M. (2003). *Schema therapy.* New York: Guilford Press.

6
Functional Subgrouping and the Systems-Centered Approach to Group Therapy
Susan P. Gantt

An on-going systems-centered group started a session with a group member, Jennifer, who was sad over having lost a special ring given to her by a dear girlfriend. She was very upset, reported being unable to quit obsessing about where it could be and then judging herself for being upset about it. One member, Theresa, started to respond to her from her memory of losing an earring years ago and then having found out how to have a new one made to replace it. Theresa was interrupted by the leader and asked if she was joining or care-taking. Theresa recognized care-taking and elected to wait rather than try again to join. Other group members began joining, expressing sadness both over Jennifer's loss and others of their own. In joining this subgroup, Tom remembered a lapel pin his daughter had made him, and that at the time, he had told a funny story that made others laugh about losing it. As Tom related this to the group, he was sobbing deeply as for the first time he experienced his strong grief about his lost pin.

This excerpt illustrates two important aspects of the systems-centered therapy (SCT) approach to group: foremost, all SCT groups use functional subgrouping, where members learn to join on similarities and emotional resonance. In the above example, Tom joins Jennifer and in joining, he discovers feelings he did not know he had. Other members then joined on resonant similarities and then built on by adding their small differences that amplify and develop the subgroup exploration. Equally important, the norm for functional subgrouping with its requirement for joining meant that Theresa's enacting care-taking at the expense of joining, or even the groups' joining, was discouraged. In fact, the group was emerging into two subgroups at that moment; one voiced by Theresa of wanting to care-take and solve Jennifer's problem and the other subgroup of members who felt resonant with the sadness and grief and blocking their experience of it. Once the "grieving" subgroup weakened their blocks to grieving (obsessing, judging the grief, or turning it into a humorous story) and could freely explore their grief, those who felt the impulse to care-take started a second subgroup to explore their care-taking impulse. In this, they discovered how hard it had felt to hear Jennifer's deep feelings. And, in the "grieving" subgroup, Jennifer began to feel relieved as she opened to her grief and sadness with others in the grieving subgroup.

As the work developed, the two subgroups began to recognize what they had in common, the deep feelings of grief and the challenge of opening to their feelings, instead of judging them, telling stories about them or care-taking others, all at the expense of their feelings, exactly the conflict that Jennifer had held at the beginning of the session when her self-judgment had blocked her deep grief.

Functional Subgrouping

Functional subgrouping is the heart of every systems-centered therapy group (Agazarian, 1997). Group members learn to form subgroups that relate to the group goal by joining around similarities, and in the comfortable environment of similarity discover "just tolerable" differences within their similarities. Bigger differences are contained and explored in separate subgroups. Thus, SCT group leaders train group members to join others with whom they feel similar and explore these similarities together, by joining and building on each other. Members learn to start a new subgroup whenever there is a difference that is too different from the first. Exploration continues in each subgroup until members begin discovering similarities between the initially different subgroups, and there begins to be an integration or resolution of the conflict in the group-as-a-whole.

Functional subgrouping stands in sharp contrast to Yalom's (Yalom and Leszcz, 2005) emphasis on subgrouping as a negative phenomenon. Yalom has stressed subgrouping outside the group boundary or social or stereotyped subgrouping within a group. They found that both of these kinds of subgrouping led to premature termination. They also suggested that goal-oriented subgrouping could be useful but did little to elaborate or expound on this. In fact, systems-centered has introduced a method for goal-oriented subgrouping, that is, the method of functional subgrouping that deliberately develops a subgrouping pattern in the service of the group goal.

Theoretical basis for functional subgrouping

Agazarian (1994, 1997) developed the method of functional subgrouping by applying her theory of living human systems to group therapy. She developed this theory after working in the American Group Psychotherapy Association (AGPA) General Systems Theory committee with Helen Durkin, Jim Durkin, Don Brown, and Jay Fidler who were interested in applying systems theory to group psychotherapy. After this group dissolved, Agazarian went on to develop her theory of living human systems and its systems-centered therapy. She developed each of the constructs of the theory and operationally defined each. These operational definitions then served as hypotheses that could be tested by the clinical methods that implemented the operational definitions. Each intervention then tests a hypothesis of the theory.

For example, functional subgrouping was developed to implement and test the hypothesis that change and maturation is a process of discriminating and integrating

Functional Subgrouping and the Systems-Centered Approach to Group Therapy

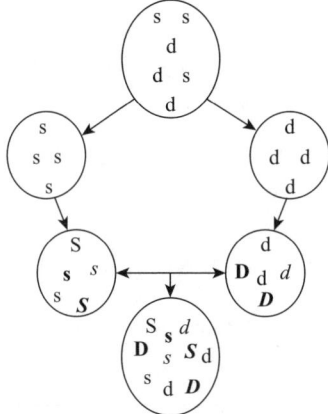

From Agazarian, Y.M. & Gantt, S.P. (2000). *Autobiography of a theory*. London: Jessica Kingsley.

Figure 6.1 Developing from simpler to more complex by discriminating and then integrating differences. © Agazarian and Gantt, 2000. Reproduced by permission of Jessica Kingsley Publishers.

differences (Agazarian, 1997). Further, groups survive, develop and transform from simpler to more complex through the process of discriminating and integrating differences, both differences in the apparently similar, and similarities in the apparently different. This hypothesis is a central theoretical construct in systems-centered therapy and is illustrated above in Figure 6.1.

In putting this theoretical hypothesis into practice, Agazarian developed the method of functional subgrouping which implements and in effect tests the hypothesis that if a group discriminates and integrates its differences, it will survive, develop and transform from simpler to more complex and move through predictable phases in its development. Functional subgrouping is fundamentally a conflict resolution method used in a systems-centered group any time there is conflict or difference within the group or within an individual.

The picture below, Figure 6.2, illustrates the process of functional subgrouping. At time 1, the group meeting begins. At time 2, a difference emerges in the group and in using functional subgrouping, the differences, represented by squares and circles, are contained in two subgroups. At time 3, each subgroup explores in turn and discovers differences within their initial similarity. At time 4, group members discover the similarities across initial differences, leading to an integration in the group-as-a-whole at time 5.

Importantly, functional subgrouping is a necessary and sufficient condition for establishing a systems-centered group. The systems-centered perspective provides an alternative to leader-centered, person-centered, group-centered or even member-centered groups in providing an overarching systems theory that links from person to member to the transient subgroup systems to the system-as-a-whole. Functional subgrouping is also the easiest to implement of the SCT methods in that it requires less training for mastery. For example, two members with minimal training applied functional subgrouping in three different work groups and reported success in using functional subgrouping (Kunneman and Ritz, 2010).

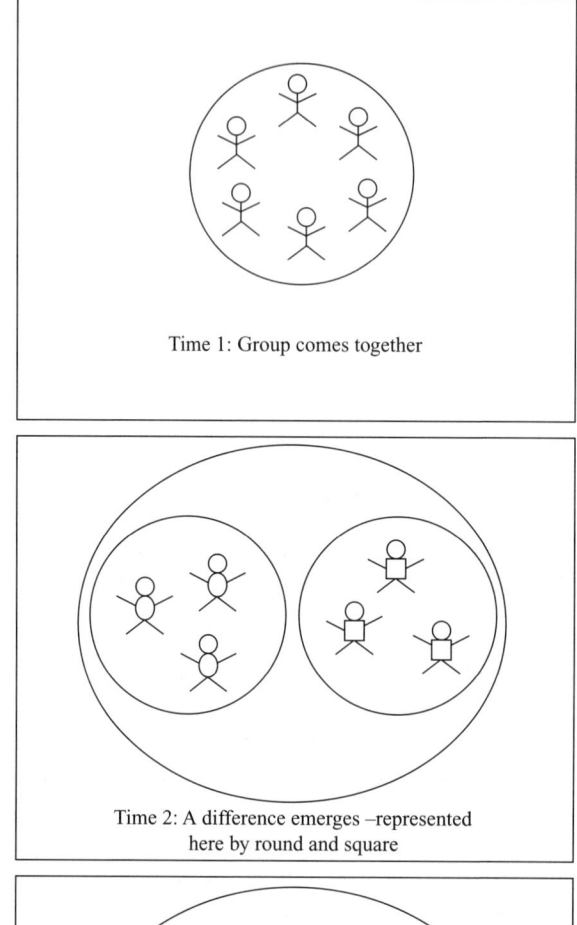

© 2010 Susan Gantt. Adapted and with permission from Agazarian, 1997.

Figure 6.2 Illustration of functional subgrouping.

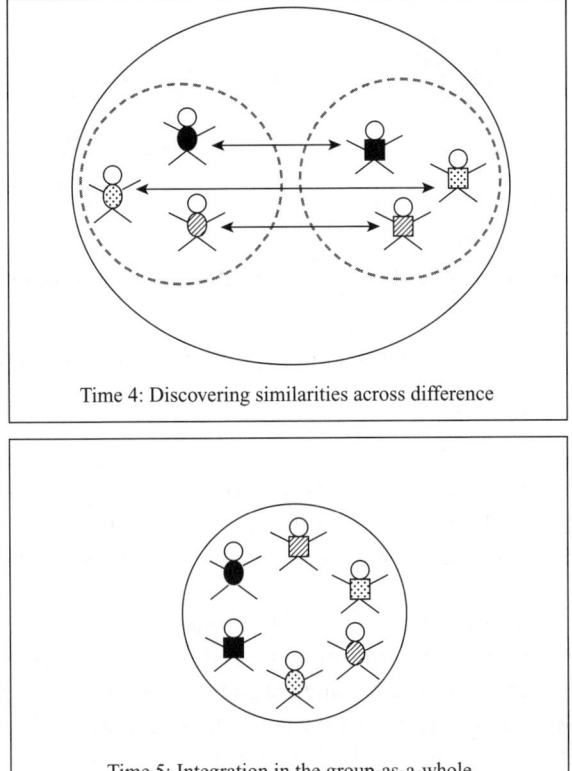

Time 4: Discovering similarities across difference

Time 5: Integration in the group-as-a-whole and greater complexity

© 2010 Susan Gantt. Adapted and with permission from Agazarian, 1997.

Figure 6.2 (*Continued*)

How functional subgrouping changes the communication pattern

Festinger (1953) linked the process of communication in a group with how a group is able to function. SCT deliberately develops a communication pattern that facilitates the group functioning to discriminate and integrate its differences instead of scapegoating them. To this point, functional subgrouping deliberately creates a communication process where members talk to those who are similar: joining and building on each other's similarities (Figure 6.3) toward the goal of potentiating the group functioning in a way that differences can be integrated.

This stands in contrast to the communication pattern to a scapegoat where the group focus is on talking to the difference: persuading or attacking or extruding a deviant member (Figure 6.3b). From an SCT view, the member with the difference (represented by the solid circle in Figure 6.3b) represents a difference that is too different for the group to integrate at that time. Groups are prone to scapegoat differences that are too different to integrate, especially in the fight phase of development (Agazarian, 1997).

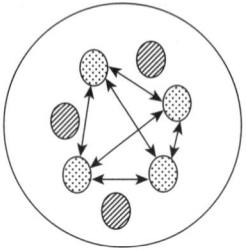 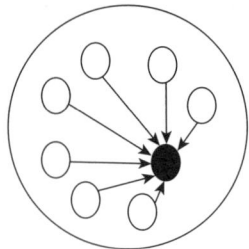

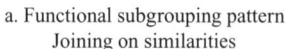

a. Functional subgrouping pattern: Joining on similarities

b. Communication to a difference

Figure 6.3 (a and b) Functional subgrouping pattern versus communication pattern to a deviant.

Scapegoating in therapy groups has long raised concerns (Gemmill, 1989; Horwitz, 1983; Rutan, Stone and Shay, 2007). With its focus on *how* a group communicates, SCT has added an emphasis on how scapegoating is enacted in the communication pattern itself.

As Agazarian (Agazarian and Gantt, 2000) described it: in the early phase of scapegoating, deviant members are often ignored, while in the later phases, they are often attacked or urged to leave. A scapegoating communication pattern is a particular form of the "communication to a deviant" pattern which can be diagnosed by a "who-talks-to-whom" coding where a frequency count is collected for the number of times each person in a group talks to every other person. For example, in one excerpt of an interpersonal group, a "who-talks-to-whom" analysis showed that out of 18 communications, 45% were directed to Alice and 38% were Alice's response to the group with the remaining 17% talking about Alice. In this example from the communication pattern, Alice is clearly in the role of a deviant in the group and holding a difference for the group (Agazarian and Gantt, 2000).

This contrasts with a "who-talks-to-whom" in an SCT group when functional subgrouping was being used in one group sample of 28 communications; "who-talks-to-whom" showed 29% of the communications to Curt, 37% to Barb and 28% to Betty. In this comparison, functional subgrouping facilitates a more balanced communication pattern making it less likely that the group will split off and deny information by "institutionalizing it in a stereotypical-role relationship" (Agazarian and Gantt, 2000: p. 96). From the SCT perspective, enacting a group role through the communication pattern not only stabilizes a group at the expense of the member but also does so at the cost of the information needed for the group's development since the role encapsulates information that is then unavailable to the group. Functional subgrouping provides an alternate pattern for containing differences that supports discrimination and integration of differences rather than attacking or extruding them through scapegoating. Moreno (2007) described an example of a group starting to scapegoat a member who was angry. Using functional subgrouping enabled the group to explore their different relationships to anger, with one subgroup joining the angry member to explore being angry and another subgroup exploring the pull to withdraw and avoid the anger.

The technique of functional subgrouping

The basics of the technique for implementing functional subgrouping are simple. Each person makes their contribution to the group, then ends by looking around to the group and saying "anyone else?" This both lets the group know when one is finished, and also lets the group know when one wants to be joined. The next person contributing starts by speaking to this member, looking at them, and reflecting what the speaker has said and joining with their similarity and resonance. When he or she is done, they look around the group and say "anyone else?" This next person then joins the last speaker, reflecting what the speaker has said and then looks around the group while adding their own version, and says "anyone else?" This continues as the subgroup works together in roving eye contact to explore their experience together. This pattern both develops the group system by establishing a "building" communication pattern as members learn both to contribute and to attune to their subgroup (this is part of developing the member system) and develops security for the group members. Though functional subgrouping is essential to an SCT group, functional subgrouping is actually only one of four methods that SCT introduces to group psychotherapy practice.

A Theory of Living Human Systems

Since SCT is the outcome of operationally defining its theory and developing methods and techniques for implementing it, it is useful to first review the whole of a theory of living human systems before describing systems-centered therapy further. In developing a theory of living human systems (TLHS), Agazarian drew from systems thinking (von Bertalanffy, 1976), communication theory (Shannon and Weaver, 1964), the force field and life space from Lewin (1951), the theory of stress from Howard and Scott (1965), and the theory of group development from Bennis and Shepard (1956), students of Bion's. Specifically, a theory of living human systems defines a hierarchy of isomorphic systems that are "energy-organizing, goal-directed and system-correcting" (Agazarian, 1997, 2010). Agazarian then defined each of these constructs and developed operational definitions for each which provided the building blocks for putting the theory into practice.

Hierarchy

Hierarchy defines a living human system as a set of three systems, where each exists in the context of the system above it and simultaneously is the context for the system below it in the hierarchy. Visualize three concentric circles. Thus, living human systems always exist in context, never in isolation. This hierarchy of interdependent systems organizes the system toward its goals of survival, development, and transformation.

Operationally defining hierarchy and applying this to a psychotherapy group leads to seeing the psychotherapy group as a set of three systems which can be drawn as three concentric circles. The innermost circle is the person system, the source of energy for the hierarchy. In the middle circle, member systems, which emerge from the person system, organize to form transient subgroup systems. In turn, the group-as-a-whole, the outermost circle, integrates its subgroups. Each system impacts the other systems in the hierarchy, and each system both influences the development of the system above and below it, and is simultaneously influenced by them. This theoretical view has led to SCT techniques for learning to shift from the perspective of the person system where there is often anguish when we take something just personally, to the member system where that anguish is always less when it is no longer just about us, to the subgroup system where the focus is no longer just one's self and much more to do with the context, and to the perspective of the system-as-a-whole and its system dynamics. It is not uncommon in SCT groups for members to be exploring what it is like when they take something just personally and what it is like when they change to first a member perspective, then a subgroup view, and then a system-as-a-whole perspective and discover that their experience of the event changes for the better when it is not experienced just personally. It was exactly this experience that first drew me to SCT, when I participated as a member in an SCT two-day training as part of an institute at the American Group Psychotherapy Association's annual meeting in 1991. I recognized right away the freedom of not taking myself or even others so personally. Included below is an example from a therapy group illustrating this:

> In this therapy group, Jim had been exploring his feelings. Lee turned to Jim with strong feeling and enthusiasm. Jim did not feel joined and Lee withdrew and blamed herself for missing the join and for not attuning to Jim. Later, the group began to recognize that attunement was a system process and attuning depended on both people for the communication to happen. In fact, Jim recognized that when he did not let Lee know he did not feel joined, he perpetuated his misunderstood feeling and did not enable the attunement process to get the feedback that the system needed to correct itself. [Tronick's (2007) research with infants demonstrated the importance of the corrective feedback for restoring an attuned relationship.] Once Lee understood this, she relaxed again and was no longer suffering from taking the challenge of attuning just personally.

Isomorphy

In TLHS, the systems in a defined hierarchy (remember the three concentric circles) are *isomorphic*. Isomorphy is defined as similar in *structure* and *function*. Structure is defined as boundaries that open or close to the flow of energy/information. (Open boundaries are illustrated in Figure 6.2, time 4). Living human systems *function* to discriminate and integrate information (finding differences in the apparently similar and similarities in the apparently different) in the service of survival, development, and transformation. Thus, whatever one understands about the flow of energy/information in one system in the defined hierarchy of three will be useful in

	Driving Forces →	← Restraining Forces
AUTHORITY PHASE Flight subphase		
	Functional subgrouping and dialoguing →	← Stereotyped subgrouping and monopolizing
	Descriptive language and exploring →	← Opinion language and explaining
	Reality-testing and collecting data →	← Worrying, negative predictions, speculations
	Being specific →	← Being vague and ambiguous, generalizing
	Bottom line or nuts and bolts communications →	← Redundancy and repetition
	Clarifying real differences →	← "Yes, but" rebuttals
Fight subphase Exploring differences in functional subgrouping →		← "Yes, but" communications
	Exploring one's reaction to differences →	← Scapegoating differences or boomeranging back against one's self
Roles and role locks with peers		
	Exploring pull to one-up/one-down roles →	← Enacting roles and role locks that manage fight impulses
	Shifting from habitual roles to member role →	← Stubbornly holding onto habitual roles
Barometric Event		
	Working cooperatively with the leader →	← Sabotaging the leader in compliance or defiance
	Taking one's own authority to participate and influence the context →	← Blaming the leader and disowning one's own authority
INTIMACY PHASE		
	Exploring pull to alienation and going it alone →	← Going one's own way when difference is encountered
	Exploring pull to fusion and affiliation →	← Affiliation at the expense of the context
PHASE OF WORK, LOVE AND PLAY		
	Knowing what one knows →	← Denying and avoiding what one knows
Using what one knows in role, goal and context →		← Self-focused or personalizing at the expense of the context

© Susan Gantt 2010   Adapted from Yvonne Agazarian.

Figure 6.4 Force field of the driving and restraining forces in the phases of system development.

understanding all other systems. For example, with a psychotherapy group, understanding something about how the subgroups in a group are discriminating and integrating information informs us about both the individual members and the group-as-a-whole.

Note that function is implemented through the method of functional subgrouping as discussed earlier. As *structure* relates to boundaries, SCT methods have been developed for modifying the permeability of boundaries so that the boundary can open or close to support the goal. A simple example is that starting and stopping a therapy group on time gives a clear boundary that is impermeable enough to contain the group and support its functioning. Modifying boundary permeability also relates to communication. Communication is defined as the transfer of information. Agazarian (Simon and Agazarian, 2000) applied Shannon and Weaver's (1964) theory of communication to boundary permeability. Shannon and Weaver demonstrated an inverse relationship between the transfer of information and the amount of noise (defined as ambiguity and redundancy) in the communication channel. Agazarian then noted that system boundaries open to information and closed to noise and she identified a third source of noise in communication: contradictions (Simon and Agazarian, 2000). This has led SCT to develop techniques for reducing noise in communication. For example, when communications are high in ambiguity, members learn to shift from vague to specific. When the group is focused on explaining what is already known (redundancy), the group learns to shift to exploring the unknown. Whenever a contradiction comes into the group, most typically in the form of a "yes, but" communication, group members are asked to see who will explore the "yes" side in one subgroup together and who will explore the "but" or the difference in the other subgroup.

Energy-organizing, goal-directed and system-correcting

As noted above, TLHS defines all living humans as energy-organizing, goal-directed and system-correcting. Structure and function relate to energy-organizing and system-correcting. The third characteristic of living human systems is goal-directed. This construct is defined as a force field of vectors that move toward or away from the system goal. Energy, defined as information in living human systems, is always vectored toward or away from the system goal. Every system has the primary goal of survival, development and transformation and a secondary goal related to its specific context. Psychotherapy groups have the secondary goal of enabling their members to live their lives with fewer restraints and a primary goal of surviving, developing and transforming from simpler to more complex. SCT then tracks whether the energy is oriented toward or away from its primary developmental goals. SCT has adapted Lewin's (1951) force field to depict the vectors of driving and restraining forces in a group (Agazarian and Gantt, 2000) in relationship to its primary goal. In developing his force field map, Lewin (1951) demonstrated that change was less stressful when achieved by weakening restraining forces than by trying to increase driving forces. Agazarian also built on this finding in developing the SCT sequence of defense modification, where restraining forces are systematically weakened, related to the context of the group's phase of development (phases are discussed in more detail below). When SCT leaders get caught in trying to push the group, that is, trying to increase the driving forces, they label it the "Sisyphus problem" in that once the leader is no longer pushing the group to change, the "stone" will roll back down the hill.

Phases of System Development and Hierarchy of Defense Modification

SCT works explicitly with the phase of system development as the context for the work that can and cannot be done in a therapy group. Building on the work of Bennis and Shepard (1956) and Bion (1959), SCT defines three major phases of system development: the authority intimacy and work phases. Each phase of development is dominated by the relevant developmental challenges of the phase and can be operationally defined by a force field of driving and restraining forces related to the developmental goal of the phase (Figure 6.4).

The developmental goal in the authority phase is to weaken the tendency to externalize and blame all one's difficulties on external authority and thus enable taking one's own authority. Within the authority phase, the group moves from the subphase of flight to fight, role locks with peers, and then the role lock with the authority or the barometric event with the leader where the group explores its hatred of authority *vis á vis* the relationship with the leader. SCT operationally defines each subphase and phase by its predictable force field of driving and restraining forces.

Flight, fight and role locks in the authority phase

In each subphase, SCT works to weaken the restraining forces that characterize the phase of development, thus freeing the group's own driving forces to move it forward in its development. For example, in the flight phase, SCT groups learn to functionally subgroup which weakens the fixation of stereotyped subgrouping and social defenses. Also, SCT groups learn to shift from vagueness to specificity, modifying a defense in communication. And importantly, SCT teaches a skill for undoing anxiety that enables members to learn the difference between: anxiety that is generated or reiterated by thoughts, from the anxiety stimulated by sensations, and still different from the anxiety at the edge of the unknown. SCT also introduces the "fork-in-the-road" of choice in the flight subphase, first with discriminating the fork-in-the-road between explaining and exploring. The group members choose which side of the fork to *explore*, the impulse to explain or the experience itself. Linking to the theory, the fork-in-the-road identifies a discrimination and members choose which exploratory pathway to take to their goal. Exploring is a process of discriminating and integrating.

Excerpts from the first 30 minutes of a new group in the flight subphase are below: (names are pseudonyms)

MANDY	I feel very anxious.
LEADER	Then say "anyone else?"
MANDY	Anyone else?
PENELOPE	Yes. I am anxious too, anyone else?
BARNEY	I'm also anxious.
NAOMIE	I was going to say "alarmed." Is that the same? [Group laughter]
LEADER	Ah. Does it feel close?
NAOMIE	It feels close.
LEADER	Okay. I think you get on board the subgroup then. Yeah? Because that's the job in subgrouping. You keep coming on in, whenever it's similar, whenever it's close. And the subgroup you are joining will let you know if it is too different. And remember to say "anyone else?"
NAOMIE	Anyone else?
DORIS	I'm very anxious. Anyone else?
CRAIG	Yes. I suppose . . . I'm . . . tense. It's, uh . . .
LEADER	Okay. Is . . . is . . . uh . . . tense or anxious, Craig? Those are . . . those are two different spots.
CRAIG	That's true.
LEADER	Anxiety is the butterflies in the belly . . . little short on breathing . . . uh, maybe a little light-headed. And tension is the muscular constriction. Which one you got?
CRAIG	Uh . . . anxiety, more like. Yeah.
LEADER	Anxiety. Okay. So you've got a big subgroup. So is everybody in the anxious subgroup . . . take a look around, so you know who's with you. And if you'd sort of raise your hand for a moment so you know who's . . . who's with you in the anxious subgroup. Okay. Yeah. Now . . . first step in the anxious subgroup is to find out the source of the anxiety. Anxiety always has a source. So will the six of you talk together and find out if you're getting anxious by anything that you're thinking. See if any of the anxiety is coming from your thoughts.
PENELOPE	I know for me, it's . . . I'm very new at this, at group work, and . . . nervous . . . anxious . . . Not knowing what to expect. Oh, anyone else?
LEADER	Okay. So you're nervous, anxious, not knowing quite what to expect. So anxiety always has a source, uh, are you thinking about what's going to happen, or is it more not knowing, edge of the unknown?
PENELOPE	I'm . . . no. I'm not . . . foretelling anything or thinking anything about what will happen.
LEADER	Uh-huh?
PENELOPE	Just that I know I'm inexperienced and feel a little uncomfortable and anxious about that . . . so.
LEADER	Okay. So you feel un . . . un . . . uncomfortable about being new to what's happening.

(*Penelope nods.*)

LEADER	Okay. Which is how we all get. You know that? Everybody gets a little, uh, anxious around uncertainty and not knowing? Yeah. Okay. 'Cause if you two will hold onto that one for just a minute, Penelope, and Craig, we'll . . . and we'll get back to that once we have undone the anxiety

	from thinking. Anybody else noticing whether or not you're thinking of something that's making you anxious?
MANDY	Anxious about what might happen.
LEADER	Okay. And do you have a specific thought about what might happen that is making you uncomfortable?
MANDY	Well, one of the things I thought about was what if I start crying, and everybody sees me crying? What would that be like?
LEADER	Okay. All right. So you've got the thought, "what if I start crying?"
MANDY	Mm-hmm.
LEADER	Yeah. And anybody else with Mandy, noticing that you have a thought that's making you anxious? [Pause] Anybody else . . . Barney?
BARNEY	I have a . . . I have a thought that, uh, I would like to be engaged as well as, uh, my therapist would like me to be. Um, I guess I wanted to do that and show her I can.
LEADER	Mm-hmm? And you're thinking, "What if I don't live up to her expectations?"
BARNEY	Right.
LEADER	Okay. Because if you notice, what you . . . the two of you have in common is you both have a thought about the future . . . about what's going to happen in the future.
MANDY	Yeah. Mm-hmm.
LEADER	Yeah. Anybody else in the subgroup got a thought about what's going to happen in the future that's making you anxious?
CRAIG	I don't know if it's similar, but it's, uh . . . I have this feeling of before diving into something . . .
LEADER	Uh-huh.
CRAIG	You know, on a trampoline or . . . whatever it's called . . . and, uh . . . if I dare to dive or not. More like . . . [looks to Naomie]
NAOMIE	Mm-hmm. Not knowing what to expect.
CRAIG	Exactly. Yeah.
LEADER	Okay. So we've got three people with edge of not knowing what to expect and the kind of anxiety that comes there, and we've got two people with the anxiety that comes from going into the future. Right? Okay? Now let's work with the future one first. Uh-huh? Now for you, Mandy, and for you, Barney . . . do you believe you can tell the future? Do you believe . . .
MANDY	Within limits.
LEADER	Okay. And do you believe you know whether or not you're going to cry in this group?
MANDY	No, I don't know that.
LEADER	Okay. So that's an unknown.
MANDY	Right.
LEADER	Okay. And what happens inside as you recognize that's an unknown?
MANDY	My anxiety goes down.
LEADER	So you're discovering when you move, uh, back from the future, to find out that you actually don't know . . . that your anxiety goes down.
MANDY	Yes.
LEADER	Yes. Okay. And how about for you, Barney? Do you believe you can tell, right now, whether or not you'll live up to your therapist's expectation?

BARNEY   No, I . . . No I don't. [Group laughter]
LEADER   Okay. [Group laughter]
BARNEY   I can't say that now.
LEADER   Uh-huh. And what happens inside as you know that?
BARNEY   I feel much less anxious.
LEADER   Okay.
BARNEY   I, uh, feel kind of, uh . . . well, now I feel kind of silly. [Group laughter]
LEADER   Okay. All right. Well let's do that one, too, okay? 'Cause "silly" is . . . "silly" is . . . you just made a judgment of yourself.
BARNEY   Yeah. I'm kind of embarrassed.
LEADER   Yeah. And did you remember that you're working with Mandy?
BARNEY   Uh . . . no I didn't.
LEADER   Okay. Yeah. Because what . . .
BARNEY   I lost her.
LEADER   Yeah. If you, uh . . . make eye contact. Because what you and Mandy just did was you worked with a piece we all do. Okay? Because as human beings we time-travel into the future all the time. Okay? And we go into our heads and we start to think something about this may happen, or that may happen, and we get anxious.
          Yeah? So what the two of you are doing, is you're undoing that piece of anxiety for yourself and for the group.
BARNEY   Mm-hmm.
LEADER   Yeah. And when you remember that, which is coming back into member . . .
BARNEY   Yes it is. Yes.
LEADER   Yeah. And back with Mandy. How's that inside? Better, worse, or the same?
BARNEY   Oh, it's, I, uh . . . I like looking at Mandy.
LEADER   Yeah.
BARNEY   I feel . . . less anxious.
LEADER   Mm-hmm? Okay? And then we've got, uh . . . Naomie and Doris . . .
DORIS   Focusing on what people are saying.
LEADER   Okay. So your anxiety's going down?
DORIS   Yes.
LEADER   Okay. And how about yours, Naomie? What's the source of yours? Is it coming from a . . . we work with the notion that anxiety always comes from either a thought, or a feeling, or being at the edge of the unknown. And so far we've got two pieces of anxiety from a thought, three pieces from being at the edge of the unknown, and let's find out where yours is coming from.
NAOMIE   Mine feels like anticipation.
LEADER   Uh-huh? And is it anticipation right at the edge of not knowing?
NAOMIE   Yeah.
LEADER   Yeah. So you're with Craig? Yeah. And with Penelope and Jill? Yeah. Now for the four of you, would you do an experiment? Because what we find, and I'd like you to test it out and see if it's true for you, is that when we get that "edge of the unknown," that uncertainty, as human beings we by and large don't like it. Okay? And there's always some apprehension, there's always a little apprehension right at the edge? Uh . . . and the thing that we've discovered makes a difference is to get curious. That when we get that kind of apprehension, if we, uh, remember to get

	curious, it makes a difference. So would you, the four of you experiment . . . uh, access your curiosity, and talk together and see if that makes a difference. So what happens when the four of you get curious?
PENELOPE	I suppose we should be asking one another questions. [Laughs] One does not come to mind right away for me.
LEADER	Well . . . asking questions would be doing something. Which would be different than just seeing what happens if you start to open up to feeling curious, eh? And then telling your subgroup what it's like when you start to get curious.

[5 second pause]

CRAIG	[To Naomie] Well, I . . . am interested to know . . . know more about . . . you. So I can discover you as a person somehow.
LEADER	Uh-huh? And as you get curious, does the anxiety feel better at the edge of the unknown . . .
CRAIG	Yes.
PENELOPE	Uh-huh.
LEADER	. . . worse . . . or does it stay the same?
PENELOPE	Better for me. Uh-huh.
LEADER	Better for you. Mm-hmm. And how about for you, Naomie?
NAOMIE	I'm getting worse. [Group laughter]
LEADER	Now, uh, so that's great. So we get a chance to practice again, which is what we're doing as a group. The first question with anxiety is, did you get a thought that made you anxious?
NAOMIE	I got worse when he wanted to know more about me.
LEADER	Okay. And did you think something about Craig's wanting to know about you that made you anxious . . . ?
NAOMIE	Yes, that I needed to respond now, in a certain way.
LEADER	Okay! So you started talking to yourself, uh . . . telling yourself that you needed to do something in a certain way. Is that right?
NAOMIE	Right. I started to think, what does he want?
LEADER	Okay. Now . . . now when you did that, when you started thinking "I need to do something in a certain way" . . . uh, how did you feel inside?
NAOMIE	Anxious!
LEADER	Okay. Now do you see that that anxiety is coming from how you're thinking?
NAOMIE	Yes.
LEADER	Yes. Okay. Now, what happens if you let that thought go?
NAOMIE	Then I go back to where I was before.
LEADER	Okay. Would you rather be hanging onto the thought and staying anxious, or would you rather let it go?
NAOMIE	I'd like to let it . . . I did. I've let it go.
LEADER	Okay. So let it go. Back to the edge of the unknown.
NAOMIE	Yeah. I like it here.
LEADER	Uh-huh. Got some curiosity?
NAOMIE	Yeah.
LEADER	Yeah. Okay. [Pause] Anybody else resonating with the curiosity? Or . . .

Each SCT group develops in its own way through its predictable phases of development. The above example illustrated a group early in the flight subphase. When the norms for functional subgrouping have been established and enough of the restraining forces in flight have been weakened (e.g., negative predictions about the future) and the group has begun to establish a reality-testing culture, the group transitions to fight. In this transition, the group then no longer actively avoids the real differences between group members as it does in the flight subphase and instead the group begins to notice their reactions to each other's differences: this marks the shift into fight. This is an important transition for the group and often not a smooth one in that one subgroup will begin to get frustrated and another quickly gets anxious in response and usually making negative predictions that frustration will lead to members losing control. Importantly, at the group-as-a-whole level, one subgroup is in flight and one in fight. The alternating subgroups in effect titrate the pace of the work for the group-as-a-whole so that the group can move forward in its work at a pace that the group can integrate, undoing negative predictions and slowly testing to see if the experience of frustration leads to loss of control. SCT leaders legitimize the role of each subgroup both for itself and its own work and also its role in the group-as-a-whole. As the anxiety subgroup works to undo its anxiety, the whole group gets less anxious and the frustrated subgroup becomes more free to explore its frustration. Exploring frustration and the inevitable irritation that arises in response to differences surfaces the developmental task of learning to weaken the restraining forces of tension or withdrawal that move away from experiencing the knowledge grounded in the body and one's sensory and emotional experience. The skill of centering into one's body and one's experience is also taught in those early subphases as the group is learning to weaken the restraining forces from the emotional knowledge of the body. This lays the groundwork for the next step of undoing the restraining forces that result in depression or outrage at the expense of the experience of one's retaliatory impulse. This is an important exploration in the fight phase as many of us have little capacity to open to our irritation and anger, and the retaliatory impulses that go with these feelings, leaving us vulnerable to act – in against ourselves in depression or out against others in acting out outrage or fury. Again, in all of this exploration, functional subgrouping is used so that those who notice they have lost their energy and turned an irritation or retaliatory impulse back on themselves explore with others who have recognized that pattern as well. As the group begins to explore the impulses in fight, it also identifies and weakens the pull into one-up, one-down or dominant/submissive roles and role pairings that often defend and manage the impulses to fight. When enough of these roles with other group members have been weakened that the group has established a new level of cohesion and confidence in working together, the group is ready to explore the authority role locks with the leader.

Barometric event in the authority phase

In effect, the work in each phase and subphase prepares the group for its next phase of work, and all of the work in the flight, fight and role lock phases has prepared the group with the resources to explore the challenges and hatred of authority *vis á vis* the relationship with the leader and the compliant/defiant roles with authority. This may emerge subtly, as when the group jokes about not wanting to hear what the leader is saying, or suggests that the group is having more trouble because their leader has introduced a new method that is causing the group to be more hesitant, or it may be more vociferous as when the group elects a member to start arguing with the leader, or even explosive when someone erupts in fury with the leader and the real belief that the leader is blocking them from succeeding in the group. All of this is an opportunity for the group to subgroup and to explore either the roles members go into with the leader that manage the relationship or the feelings toward the leader that the roles often prevent. [More detailed descriptions of these phases in an SCT group can be found in Agazarian (1994, 1999) and Agazarian and Gantt (2003).]

Again each group finds its own pace and path in this exploring, some jokingly put down the leader the first time through the authority issue work and return later to explore the deeper layers of virulence and hatred for the leader. Other groups move more quickly. Ultimately, the group explores the sense that if only one of us can live, the group will choose itself and sacrifice the leader, an important moment of recognition in the group and the beginning of the group freeing itself from the tyranny of the roles they have been locked into with the leader. This is often a very poignant moment in a group that leads the group to great relief, sometimes somberness and a sense of greater freedom to take its own authority and also much gratitude toward the leader for containing the hatred until the group is free to experience it and know it.

Intimacy

The group then shifts into the intimacy phase where there is much less preoccupation with the leader and much more interest in relating to each other. The developmental goal in intimacy relates to exploring the challenges in separation/individuation and issues of closeness and distance with one's self and with others. There are often two subgroups exploring the two sides of the intimacy conflicts, those who are enchanted and see the group as enabling a very special kind of closeness, and the disenchanted who feel different and alienated and expect no different. As each subgroup explores in turn, the enchanted subgroup starts to discover differences in its initially blissful experience and the disenchanted members begin building bonds and comfort with others in their subgroup. The habitual roles explored in this phase relate to this basic split between merger and alienation and have roots in early attachment patterns. The tendencies to join subgroups quickly or slowly early in a group often foreshadow the attachment issues that can be explored in the intimacy phase. For example, those of us with a skew toward an avoidant-attachment style will tend to see every subgroup as "too different" to join, while those with more of an ambivalent-attachment may lose our own experience by moving from subgroup to subgroup and joining every one that comes by. It is also in the intimacy phase, after the basic split of right and wrong has been undone in the work of the barometric event, that group members can then visit their pasts for information instead of for ammunition against oneself or one's parents. It may be that the micro-attunements (Schore, 2003a, 2003b) that occur in the secure environment of the subgrouping process directly affect early implicit attachment patterns in the direction of greater security. Group is a very useful context for surfacing our automatic, out-of-conscious-awareness relational patterns and offers the possibility of changing these relational patterns and implicit maps through the experiences of connecting and being understood; this potential is heightened in the intimacy phase.

Work

The third phase of development is the work phase, where the major goal is to be able to work with any of the on-going challenges of taking one's role to support the goal of one's context. Particularly important in on-going work is to explore the restraining forces against knowing what we know and using our common sense and emotional intelligence in context. In the work phase, groups often revisit earlier phases and can easily contain subgroups working different phase dynamics.

SCT Methods

SCT leaders work to build the systems-centered system that makes a context for the group and its members to develop. Each of the methods described previously was derived from applying the theory and refining the techniques for applying it in the trial and error process of working with training groups who were learning SCT (Agazarian and Gantt, 2000). These methods were then further refined and honed in working with them in clinical practice. The four major methods SCT introduces are: functional subgrouping, vectoring and the fork-in-the-road of choice, contextualizing and shifting from person to member, and boundarying techniques. Just as functional subgrouping implements the construct of function, techniques and models have then been developed to implement each of the other theoretical constructs.

Contextualizing

SCT methods for contextualizing include an on-going emphasis of learning to contribute one's voice as information for the group and learning not to take one's self or one's experience just personally. As discussed earlier, this includes learning to shift from a self-centered perspective to a member perspective, then to a subgroup perspective and to a systems-centered perspective. Ultimately, this translates into patients learning to proactively take their membership role in whatever context they are in, to support the goal of the context. SCT frames this as "role, goal and context" so that orienting to one's role, for example in one's marriage, means seeing if the marriage context is parenting or sexual intimacy or business, and then taking one's role to support the goal of the context (Agazarian, 2002, 2006).

Goal orientation and vectoring

SCT introduces the fork-in-the-road of choice, where members choose each time whether to explore their experience or the restraining force blocking their experience. In this process, group members learn how to deliberately direct their attention and focus and energy with the on-going choice of exploring any restraining forces to the goal or deliberately using the driving forces to move toward the goal.

Boundarying and the hierarchy of defense modification

Of central importance are those methods developed for boundarying (some of which were discussed earlier in terms of titrating the noise in communication) and the sequence of defense modification that links to the phase of system development. SCT introduces a set of skills that group members learn to use to modify the defenses or restraining forces that relate to the common symptoms that bring most clients to therapy. For example, group members first learn the skills for modifying the social defenses of communication – ambiguity, contradiction and redundancy – and then learn how to undo the negative predictions and mind reads, or other cognitive distortions, that generate anxiety from top-down thinking. As the group gains some mastery in undoing anxiety and weakening the defenses related to thinking, the skills for undoing tension and withdrawal are introduced. Once the group has restored the relationship to the emotional knowledge of the body by undoing the body-related defenses of tension and withdrawal, the group learns to undo depression caused by turning the retaliatory impulse back on the self or the parallel defense of outrage generated by righteous thinking. Lastly, SCT introduces skills for weakening the pull into repetitive maladaptive roles, like one-up or one-down, that manage the impulses to fight. Modifying these defenses in sequence weakens the predictable restraining forces as they relate to the phase of development.

SCT is a highly integrative approach so that in the flight phase, some of the SCT skills for undoing the cognitive distortions of negative predictions and mind reads resemble cognitive behavioral techniques, while some of the skills in centering and undoing tension are reminiscent of Gestalt therapy's sensory awareness exercises and mindfulness practices, and the skill for undoing low energy and withdrawal pulls from bodynamics (Brantbjerg, 2009). For example, SCT weakens the negative predictions and mind reads common in the flight phase that generate experience, often anxious experiences, from top-down maps and at the expense of sensory knowledge and experience grounded in the body. Once enough of the cognitive restraining forces have been weakened, the work shifts to modifying the restraining forces that relate to the body and our sensory and emotional knowledge.

What is unique to SCT is that it offers an overarching map where each of these methods and skills are tied to the phase of development of the group which is always the context for the group leader's interventions so that members learn the skills relevant to the phase. At the same time, using the skills develops the group which then further develops the members by providing a context of increasing complexity from building and developing the group system.

The Uses of SCT in Psychotherapy Groups

SCT has been applied extensively with patients with a variety of diagnoses in both inpatient and outpatient settings. For example, in one pilot study in the UK, SCT has been introduced in a psychoeducational format where patients learn and practice a different skill each week and then participate in an SCT therapy group session. These patients, 80 in total, split into 18 groups, had diagnoses ranging from severe depression, anxiety disorder and personality disorders, and many of whom had long-standing difficulties. Many patients showed enough improvement so that many of them elected to continue in a longer term group where their gains were even greater (Haddock and Viskari, 2006).

Other SCT practitioners have reported success using SCT group methods with inpatients, in outpatient clinics, in private practices, with alcoholic patients, with veterans in trauma groups, with couples, with adolescents in school settings, and with a wide spectrum of diagnoses.

Research

Action research is built into the SCT model in that each intervention is designed to test the validity of the theory and its hypotheses and the reliability of the SCT practice. In addition, some of the SCT techniques include research questions. For example, the distraction exercise is done typically at the beginning of each group whenever a member reports being distracted and not able to be present in the group. Members first identify the facts of their distraction, then how they feel about the facts, and then cross the boundary into the group by looking around and bringing their feeling into the relationship as they make eye contact with group members. At the end of this, the member is asked the research question, "Do you feel more here, less here or the same?"

We have also developed a number of research hypotheses and in 2003, as a first informal step in testing them, surveyed members of the non-profit organization, Systems-Centered Training and Research Institute. Eighty members participated and generally reported favorable findings from their own clinical applications of SCT. These results are summarized in Figure 6.5.

Formal research has not developed as rapidly and has lagged behind the reports of success from clinical practitioners. Still, several formal research studies are promising. In one study using single case methodology, SCT was used with three individual patients with generalized anxiety disorder in a ten-session treatment (Ladden, Gantt, Rude and Agazarian, 2007). All three subjects improved to the extent of no longer meeting diagnostic criteria at the end of treatment and these gains were maintained at a one-year follow-up. Though this study was of SCT applied in individual therapy, the same SCT hierarchy of defense modification was used as with groups, making the results promising for the group application as well.

In another study, O'Neill and Constantino (2009) compared the process and outcome of SCT training groups to other training groups in a quasi-experimental design. The SCT groups compared positively overall to other groups led by experts in their area. Interestingly and as was hypothesized, SCT groups reported less conflict and avoidance, as well as more self-confidence, more activity, and better relationship quality than the other training groups. Surprisingly, SCT groups showed less engagement than the other training groups though SCT groups reported more engagement over time in a way that was consistent with successful groups. There was also a suggestion in the findings that what SCT groups learned appears to be different than what the other groups learned, and consistent with the SCT theory and model. Also, SCT groups reported high satisfaction with their overall learning.

Functional Subgrouping Hypotheses	% YES	% NO
Functional subgrouping increases the ability of a group to integrate differences	100	0
Functional subgrouping is introduced when scapegoating is aroused	97	3
Functional subgrouping reduces targeting behavior and scapegoating in the group	100	0
SCT groups have a norm that no member works alone	92	8
Using functional subgrouping reduces the identified patient energy in the group	97	3
Using functional subgrouping to explore the impulse to create an identified patient establishes the drive to care-give and care-seek as normal human impulses	85	15
Vectoring Hypotheses		
Using the Fork-in-the-Road technique decreases compliance/defiance	88	12
Introducing Time Travel concepts increases ability to deliberately vector attention to the present and away from the past and future	100	0
Learning Containing and Centering increases access to emotional information in groups	98	2
Vectoring to the present increases goal-oriented behavior in the group	95	5
Using the Fork-in-the-Road technique facilitates weakening restraining forces	97	3
Reducing the restraining forces in the phases of group development increases the group task-oriented energy	94	6
Weakening restraining forces increases the ability of a group to do its work	100	0
Boundarying Hypotheses (Titrating boundaries to information)		
Reducing ambiguity, contradiction & redundancy increases information transfer in a communication	99	1
Reducing ambiguity, contradiction & redundancy increases the group energy for work	100	0
Boundarying Hypotheses: Defense Modifications in the Phases of Group Development		
Exploring identified patient dynamics reduces the volunteering for the roles of taking care of or being taken care of	94	6
Weakening tension increases the access to frustration and emotional information in groups	100	0
Undoing the boomerang defense of turning the retaliatory impulse back on the self decreases depression in groups	97	3
Reducing depression increases access to anger and the retaliatory impulse in your groups	100	0
Undoing outrage increases the access to the experience of aggression and the life force in your groups	100	0
Bringing anger into relationship with the leader increases the energy and spontaneity in your groups	99	1
Weakening role locks increases the group's ability to explore issues around dominance and power and control	99	1

Figure 6.5 SCT research hypotheses and frequency that SCTRI members endorsed the hypothesis from their own clinical practice.

Experiencing the crisis of hatred decreases externalizing in your groups	93	7
Exploring enchantment and idealization increases the recognition of differences in the apparently similar in your groups	94	6
Recognizing differences in the apparently similar increases separation in your groups	87	13
Exploring alienation increases the recognition of similarities in the apparently different in your groups	100	0
Finding similarities in the apparently different increases the individuation in your groups	95	5
Contextualizing Hypotheses		
Decreasing the defenses against the intuitive and rational knowledge in your groups increases the ability of your groups to reality-test and solve problems	100	0
Increasing contextualizing and decreasing personalizing increases common sense, sense of humor and emotional intelligence	100	0
Percentage of members increasing in ability to see group events from more than one perspective		
A. Within 3 months	48%	
B. Within 6 months	59%	
C. With 12 months or more	75%	
Percentage of group members who decrease their tendency to take things just personally with one weekend of training (approximately 12 hours)	73%	

Data collected by Yvonne Agazarian and Susan Gantt, 2003.

Figure 6.5 (*Continued*)

Preliminary research based on a rudimentary self-report scale of functional subgrouping has also been promising. Specifically, participants reported a positive experience related to functional subgrouping where in one small sample, 40.8% of the words used to describe their experience of functional subgrouping were emotionally positive words, such as "connected, supported, energy, excitement, fun, warm" while only 5.1% of the words were emotionally negative, for example, "sad, painful, frustrating." This same study also reported on a small sample where self-reported depression and anxiety at the end of a training group experience was negatively correlated with functional subgrouping (O'Neill, Smyth and Mackenzie, 2010).

In another unpublished study, group members who report more functional subgrouping also report more learning in relationship to becoming an effective leader than those reporting less involvement in functional subgrouping (O'Neill and Constantino, 2010).

More research is underway. Data collection has just been finished for the development of a scale, *How This Group Works* (O'Neill, 2010), that discriminates based on participants' observations between groups that use functional subgrouping and those that do not. This will then enable more comparison with groups that use functional subgrouping and those that do not to see if the use of functional subgrouping correlates in any way with outcome, and if so, how and for what outcomes.

In addition, the informal pilot done with SCT psychoeducational groups is now becoming a formal pilot research project to ascertain more specifically which patients benefit from the SCT psychoeducational group model and to serve as a formal pilot for a randomized comparison study between short-term SCT and CBT groups.

Learning SCT

Functional subgrouping itself is relatively easy to learn and, from informal reports, leaders experience large differences in their groups after introducing this method. Learning functional subgrouping starts with learning to join on similarities and gaining some experience of SCT's functional subgrouping in a classroom practice or an experiential training group like those offered at group conferences such as the American Group Psychotherapy Association (agpa.org), the International Association for Group Psychotherapy and Group Processes (iagp.com), or the Systems-Centered Training and Research Institute (sctri.org).

Much more extensive training is needed to gain mastery of the SCT theory and the skills that both test the theory, and also put the theory into practice. Learning to apply the skills starts with learning how to build the systems-centered system, anchored by functional subgrouping so that the skills can be applied in context and attunement with the group process, and with an awareness and understanding of the group dynamics and the group system's phase of development.

Trainees in SCT training are discouraged from using methods and techniques with others that they have not used with themselves and integrated. Thus, systems-centered training starts with participating in an on-going SCT training group where participants gain experience of functional subgrouping and learn to take membership in an SCT group, learning to bring their person into their membership role in the group. In this setting, participants learn both to see the group system and to apply the methods and techniques with themselves in the process of developing the group in which they are a member. This experiential work is augmented with a theory group and at the intermediate level with intensive skills training. Advanced training is for those committed to gaining licensing as an SCT practitioner and includes participation in a three-year closed group that meets twice each year in a five-day block, followed by working as a member of a peer licensing group which sets criteria for assessing and assesses its members based on work samples submitted for qualification for licensing.

Summary

This chapter has described the method of functional subgrouping and the systems-centered approach to group therapy. Functional subgrouping itself introduces a radical difference for group leaders in that the leader deliberately shapes the norms of the group communication in a way that supports the discrimination and integration of differences (which SCT posits as a central change principle). This is especially useful for lowering the acting out of scapegoating which is endemic to groups. SCT also provides a comprehensive systems theory and practice for group therapists and group leaders that enables a practice where every intervention is tied to a theoretical hypothesis which is tested in the ongoing practice.

References and Bibliography

Agazarian, Y. M. (1994). The phases of development and the systems-centered group. In M. Pines & V. Schermer (Eds.), *Ring of fire: Primitive object relations and affect in group psychotherapy* (pp. 36–85). London: Routledge, Chapman & Hall.

Agazarian, Y. M. (1997). (Re-printed in paperback, 2004). *Systems-centered therapy for groups.* New York: Guilford Press. London: Karnac Books.

Agazarian, Y. M. (1999). Phases of development in the systems-centered group. *Small Group Research, 30*(1), 82–107.

Agazarian, Y. M. (2002). A systems-centered approach to individual and group psychotherapy. In L. Vandecreek & T. Jackson (Eds.), *Innovations in clinical practice: A source book*, (Vol. 20, pp. 223–240). Sarasota, Florida: Professional Resource Press.

Agazarian, Y. M. (2006). *Systems-centered practice: Selected papers on group psychotherapy.* London: Karnac Books.

Agazarian, Y. M. (2010). *Systems-centered group psychotherapy: A theory of living human systems and its systems-centered practice.* Manuscript submitted for publication.

Agazarian, Y. M., & Gantt, S. P. (2000). *Autobiography of a theory.* London: Jessica Kingsley.

Agazarian, Y. M., & Gantt, S. P. (2003). Phases of group development: Systems-centered hypotheses and their implications for research and practice. *Group dynamics: Theory, Research and Practice, 7*(3), 238–252.

Bennis, W. G., & Shepard, H. A. (1956). A theory of group development. *Human Relations, 9*(4), 415-437.

Bion, W. R. (1959). *Experiences in groups.* London: Tavistock.

Brantbjerg, M. (2009). *Hyporesponse – the hidden challenge in coping with stress.* Unpublished manuscript.

Festinger, L. (1953). Informal social communication. In D. Cartwright & A. Zander (Eds.), *Group dynamics, research and theory.* New York: Row, Peterson & Co.

Gemmill, G. (1989). The dynamics of scapegoating in small groups. *Small Group Behavior, 20*(4), 406–418.

Haddock, R., & Viskari, S. E. (2006, March). SCT and psychiatric treatment: Short-term groups in the UK and Sweden. Presented at the SCT Annual Conference, Boston.

Horwitz, L. (1983). Projective identification in dyads and groups. *International Journal of Group Psychotherapy, 33*(3), 259–279.

Howard, A., & Scott, R. A. (1965). A proposed framework for the analysis of stress in the human organism. *Journal of Applied Behavioral Science, 10,* 141–160.

Iacoboni, M. (2008). *Mirroring people: The new science of how we connect with others.* New York: Farrar, Straus & Giroux.

Kunneman, P., & Ritz, H. (2010). Can "subgrouping only" survive, develop and transform? *Systems-Centered News, 18*(1), 7–9.

Ladden, L., Gantt, S.P., Rude, S., et al., (2007). Systems-centered therapy: A protocol for treating generalized anxiety disorder. *Journal of Contemporary Psychotherapy, 37*(2), 61–70.

Lewin, K. (1951). *Field theory in social science.* New York: Harper & Row.

Moreno, J. K. (2007). Scapegoating in group psychotherapy. *International Journal of Group Psychotherapy, 57*(1), 93–104.

O'Neill, R. M. (personal communication, August, 2010).

O'Neill, R. M., & Constantino, M. J. (2008). Systems-centered training groups' process and outcome: A comparison with AGPA institute groups. *International Journal of Group Psychotherapy*, 58(1), 77–102.

O'Neill, R.M., & Constantino, M. J. (2010). Multi-level systems-centered training in large group: Functional subgrouping, goal-setting, mood, and outcome. Unpublished manuscript.

O'Neill, R. M., Smyth, J. M., & Mackenzie, M. J. (2010). Systems-centered functional subgrouping: Trainees love it but what is it, can it be learned, and is it useful? Unpublished manuscript.

Rutan, J. S., Stone, W. N. & Shay, J. J. (2007). *Psychodynamic group psychotherapy* (4th ed.). New York: Guilford Press.

Schore, A. N. (2003a). *Affect dysregulation and disorders of the self.* New York: W.W. Norton & Co.

Schore, A. N. (2003b). *Affect regulation and the repair of the self.* New York: W.W. Norton & Co.

Shannon, C. E., & Weaver, W. (1964). *The mathematical theory of communication.* Urbana, Illinois: University of Illinois Press.

Simon, A., & Agazarian, Y. M. (2000). The system for analyzing verbal interaction. In A. Beck & C. Lewis (Eds.), *The process of group psychotherapy: Systems for analyzing change* (pp. 357–380). Washington, DC: American Psychological Association.

Tronick, E. (2007). *The neurobehavioral and social-emotional development of infants and children.* New York: W.W. Norton & Co.

von Bertalanffy, L. (1976). (Original published in 1968). *General system theory: Foundations, development, applications.* Revised edition. New York: George Braziller.

Yalom, I. D., & Leszcz, M. (2005). *The theory and practice of group psychotherapy.* New York: Basic Books.

7
The Functional Group Model
Sharan L. Schwartzberg and Mary Alicia Barnes

Introduction

The Functional Group Model (FGM) is an approach that seeks to enhance adaptive behavior by mobilizing the dynamic elements of group processes in accordance with four forms of action; purposeful-action, self-initiated action, spontaneous-action, and group-centered action (Schwartzberg, Howe, and Barnes, 2008). In doing so, a group context and climate is developed that has "the potential to positively shape people's understanding of themselves [and] or their abilities" (Kielhofner, 2009: p. 112). The model is inter-subjective and relationship-based in that it encourages access to unconscious material and feelings that impact social participation. The FGM also allows therapists' to incorporate frames of reference according to member needs. The Functional Group Model (Schwartzberg, Howe, and Barnes, 2008) was first introduced in 1986 (Howe and Schwartzberg, 1986) and is based on theory and research in five areas: group dynamics (Bales, 1950; Benne and Sheats, 1978; Bennis and Shepard, 1956; Cartwright and Zander, 1968; Garland, Jones, and Kolodny, 1965; Lifton, 1961; Tuckman, 1965), effectance motivation (Barris, Kielhofner, and Hawkins, 1983; White, 1959; 1971), needs hierarchy (Maslow, 1970), purposeful activity (Fidler and Fidler, 1978; Reed, 1984), and adaptation (Burke, 1983; King, 1978; Reed, 1984).

The FGM approach allows leaders to titrate the amount of group structure using a variety of leader techniques to create a group-centered process. One of the key components of the FGM is adherence to monitoring the four forms of action (purposeful-action, self-initiated action, spontaneous-action, and group-centered action) to facilitate group process. These four forms of action are represented by the use of time, energy, and activities to promote adaptation to improve functional performance and quality of life.

Purposeful-action is the "doing" that provides the context or lens through which members perceive the group as meaningful and congruent with their needs and goals. Purposeful-action helps group members become acquainted with each other and develop an understanding of what may be accomplished. In many regards, purposeful-action drives meaning and a sense of "fit" between the individual and the group. Self-initiated action is how members attempt to be a part of the group, in whatever way they are capable. Self-initiated member participation, be it verbal or non-verbal, becomes representative of members' willingness or ability to engage in the opportunities the group may provide to improve their skills, understanding of themselves, or quality of life.

Spontaneous (here-and-now)-action allows experiential learning in a safe and supportive environment. As the group develops, members' active engagement in the group tasks and processes can facilitate self-discovery about areas of strength or skill deficit. Members' actions and responses, when examined in the here-and-now, can be a source of feedback or insight about what behaviors or beliefs may interfere with, or enable, their participation in interpersonal interactions or other meaningful activities. Spontaneous-action can support exploring perceptions of self and other as they directly impact intra-and interpersonal relationships. When carefully facilitated, it can offer members a venue in which to experience risk-taking, decision-making, choice, and self-control or self-regulation.

Group-centered action reflects a sense of emerging group identity as the group as a whole begins working to address the diverse physical, cognitive, emotional and social needs of all members. Group-centered action can be fostered through changing or adapting group structure, environment, and goals as members come to understand and realize the interdependent nature of group process and outcomes. Maximal involvement of members in the group's process is a form of group-centered action. As a synthesis of the four forms of action, group-centered action helps members develop a cohesive group. Working towards a shared understanding becomes a collective experience through which the group builds consensus to identify and achieve a common purpose or goal.

The FGM can be applied with different populations in a variety of contexts and settings. For the purposes of this chapter, *Group Narratives* will illustrate how the Functional Group Model (FGM) (Schwartzberg, Howe, and Barnes, 2008) is used in an educational environment (*see* Box 7.1). The narratives are composites based on the authors' combined years of experience leading training groups (T-groups) and feature common themes that emerge in groups. Features of the FGM approach, such as a *Group Assessment, a Functional Group Protocol,* and *Session Evaluations,* are shown via Displays 7.1–7.4 in an abbreviated manner to provide background material to the *Group Narratives* and demonstrate application of the model. The *Session Evaluations* in Displays 7.2–7.4 will highlight leader reflections identifying FGM action components as they are represented in the group process. Additionally, leader reasoning related to addressing forms of action through each stage of a Functional Group: Formation, Development, and Closure (Schwartzberg, Howe, and Barnes, 2008), will be shared, along with relevant literature that informs the reasoning process in subsequent ***Discussions***. The ***Discussion*** sections will further demonstrate how the Functional Group Model easily incorporates leaders' preferred frame(s) of reference and group theory concepts.

Display 7.1

Group assessment and Functional Group Model protocol

Assessment of context: general group program description

Training group (T-group) for students in post-baccalaureate educational program offering degrees in competitive healthcare field.

Group purpose

Explore the dynamics, communication, and action patterns of small groups to build understanding of personal as well as organizational culture, in relation to group development. Experience and reflect on group process, leadership, and membership.

Frames of reference

Psychodynamic (Azima and Azima, 1959), systems-centered (Agazarian, 1997), developmental (Mosey, 1970), and task-oriented (Fidler and Fidler, 1978).

Facilities and materials

Group will meet in classroom/conference room with chairs set up in circle and tables removed to periphery of room. Leader and members will have access to closet of materials within the room (various art supplies, such as paper, drawing tools, collage materials, therapeutic games, 'icebreaker,' and psycho-educational activity manuals).

Physical and emotional climate

The physical and emotional environment of the group may be a challenge for members due to setting (e.g., group a course requirement and associated with academic expectations, members socialize with each other outside of group, leaders and members see one another outside of group in other social, educational and training situations). There may be competition in the group around educational and career achievement. Transitional stressors may exacerbate possible anxiety related to understanding and meeting expectations in a rigorous healthcare training program. Members may have heard 'via the grapevine' about T-group experiences from previous students, with descriptions ranging from T-groups being highly meaningful and intensely rewarding to their being arduous learning experiences laden with awkward silences. Members may present with anticipation and desire to do well, mixed with fear and uncertainty about being "judged" or "evaluated."

Established norms

Prior normative educational experiences of learner as passive recipient of knowledge and "teacher" as leader or expert may impact members' comfort and self-initiation.

General description of members

Mixed gender and sexual orientation, ages 24–50 with diverse educational, economic, and socio-cultural backgrounds.

Occupational roles of members

Student, self-care, family member, significant other, worker, friend, and community member (encompasses civic, religious, athletic, philanthropic, artistic, etc.).

Assessment of group members

Group members are highly intelligent, with a variety of health and social concerns such as chronic pain, anxiety or learning disorders, histories of loss/trauma such as divorce, sudden or untimely death of family member, natural disasters (earthquake, hurricane, tsunami, and severe storms), job loss secondary to economic downturn, and immigrant status. Members hold expectations for themselves related to successful performance in chosen area of study and future career.

Prior group experience

Some members have previous group experience as leaders, managers, or employees in health related fields. Some have previous group experience as recipients of healthcare services, participants in support groups or self-help groups (e.g., Alcoholics Anonymous, Grief group), or spirituality groups (organized religious or faith-based). Others have no identifiable group experience outside of primary group (family) or educational and recreational settings (seminar classes, sports teams, clubs, etc.). Members are undergoing life transitions of returning to student role, as well as marriage or ending of relationships, childbirth (expecting or recent birth of child) or assuming care for family members (siblings, parent or in-laws, grandparents, etc.).

Functional group protocol

Group format

Closed group of 12 members.

Dosage

14 Weeks; 1 hour per week.

Rationale

Group size, closed group format, and dosage are needed to provide adequate leader: member ratio, allow ample time for individual member participation, support establishment of trust and sense of safety in the group. Small group format allows for leader to adequately observe and interact with members as needed.

General group goals
1. Observe and describe communication and action patterns of self and others, as group leader and member.
2. Observe and evaluate one's repertoire of group leadership and membership roles, accurately describing one's effect on others, reflecting on one's own culture and development, and identifying directions for growth as a group leader.
3. Engage in the identification and problem solving process to address (organizational, behavioral, intra-group) problems that interfere with group's objectives.

Group contract
1. Absences reported to leader in advance.
2. No cell phone use (extenuating circumstances such as child care/emergencies will be managed on a case-by-case basis).
3. Outside group communication is brought back to group.
4. Confidentiality is respected (peers and client) and required.

Rationale

Members are expected to be able to abide by group contract that outlines expectations for attendance, participation, confidentiality, and ethics. Members' ability to accurately interpret small group dynamics will be assessed through their ability to articulate an understanding of group theory as applied to T-group experience.

Anticipated outcomes

Members will be able to articulate understanding of group theory and practice through verbal processing of personal perspectives of being a group leader and a group member. Members will be able to assume group leader and member roles through actively engaging in group process and reflective dialog.

Leader role and functions

Monitor member performance, reiterate group contract and purpose, provide input integrating meaning attribution and executive functions (Yalom and Leszcz, 2005; *see* Box 7.2), including limit setting or redirection as needed. Assess degree of emotional activation and caring (Yalom and Leszcz, 2005) needed to support exploration while attending to member safety (versus vulnerability) and needs of group as a whole. Ensure forms of action (i.e., purposeful, self-initiated, spontaneous, group-centered) support process, motivate members to participate, and enhance members' sense of control and wellbeing. Encourage and role model limiting self-disclosure to moderate amounts to ethically maintain safe personal boundaries within context of professional training program. Follow principles of group members needs relative to action in keeping with the phases of group development (see Tables 7.1, 7.2, and 7.3), as appropriate.

> *Methods*
> Adjust activity or environmental demands to balance amount of novel versus familiar activity. Encourage verbalization and self-reflection. Empower members' decision-making and engagement through titrating forms of action using leadership techniques such as transparency (Yalom and Leszcz, 2005) process commentary (Brown, 2003; *see* Box 7.3), bridging (Ormont, 1990), redirection, concrete language, feedback, clarification, and reality testing as indicated.

Group Narrative: Process Training Group

Formation stage

It is the second session of a 14-week long process group. There is a lengthy silence as the group opens. Susan asks, "Is there something we should be doing?" The leader explains, "The group's purpose is for members to learn about group dynamics through participation in the group, so our degree of structure will vary based on members' needs. As per our agreement last session, today we are starting off with a set of members co-leading the group. I had understood we agreed this would continue until everyone has had an opportunity to co-lead the group. I would like to remind today's co-leaders to leave time for the group to share process reflections." Susan states, "I am just not used to this type of learning." Bob, an older student, comments, "I rather like the opportunity to have things somewhat open-ended."

The two students who had volunteered to co-lead the session begin running an icebreaker. One of them explains to the group, "During a workshop at my previous job we did this icebreaker as a means to get to know one another better." The group is divided into two subgroups and members are then asked to stand and change sides of the circle according to their responses to a series of questions related to travel experiences, birth order, relationship status, and health and life experiences such as pet ownership or high-risk adventure activities. After a short period the icebreaker ends and members look over at the leader.

The leader suggests to the volunteer co-leaders and group members, "Perhaps it might help the group to learn about the group's process by sharing your feedback and reflections about the experience with each other." Many members respond to this prompt with superficial answers such as "I liked the chance to move around" or "I am surprised how many of us have certain experiences in common." The leader shares her observations, "It seemed to me at times as if there were moments of chaos and what I felt to be nervous laughter as you all were moving around." The leader also shares her observations of members' verbal and nonverbal expressions during the activity: "Did anyone else notice someone stating, 'Am I the only person who is confused here . . .?' and other members frowning or seeming hesitant to move during the exercise?" One member responds, "Yeah, it did get a little out of control at one point when so many of us were up and moving about – I actually got a little confused, wanting to stay in the middle of the room because my situation didn't quite fit the question."

Susan then remarks, "I'm confused about what we are supposed to be doing right now. Is this what we should be doing or not?" Another member, Li, looks at the leader and states, "Aren't you supposed to be teaching us about group leadership and group process?" Susan adds, "I feel like we are wasting time." The leader then asks, "Are there others who can identify with what either Susan or Li is feeling?" The leader shares, "I am wondering if there were times in the past when anyone might have felt what they're feeling in the here-and-now." She indicates, "My reasoning for asking about this is that reflections about past experiences might help guide you in exploring what is going on in the present moment in the group."

Bob responds, "Truthfully, my problem is that I can't recall who identified with what during the icebreaker exercise. In a way, I wish we could revisit the questions while staying put, that way each person could tell the group whether it applied to them or not and maybe give more details." Susan states, "I don't see how that will help" and looks down. Bob looks to the leader, who, sensing Susan's affect is starting to impact her ability to participate, nods reassuringly towards Bob and asks, "What do others think about Bob's suggestion? Are there other ideas for how we might proceed to use our time today?" A group silence ensues.

Another member, Rita, who is the oldest member of the group, states, "I like Bob's idea, but I'm wondering how exactly we would go about it. Maybe since we don't know each other that well, we could just agree to one or two of the more conversational questions for this week?" She looks over at Susan and asks, "Would that be okay with you, Susan?" Susan looks up startled and says, "It's not up to me! I'll do whatever . . . ."

The leader reflects, "You seem surprised Susan." She asks the group, "Does anyone else feel surprised?" Bob tentatively ventures, "Well, I felt like you sort of snapped at me Susan, so I guess I was surprised by your reaction to my idea. I can understand why Rita might want to make sure you feel comfortable with whatever gets decided." Susan apologetically states to Bob, "I have a hard time with lack of structure, especially when I'm not sure what the expectations are of me." Other members chime in stating, "I didn't realize the decision for what to do with the time would be up to us" and "I was unsure about what was allowed, but I like Rita's suggestion." Another member states, "Let's start with the fun stuff-like travel and birth order." Li states, "Sure, anything besides another awkward silence!" A ripple of laughter again runs through the room. Rita states, "Well, I guess I'll start by telling you I was the only child in my family, so I guess that makes me both oldest and youngest!" Laughter resumes and members begin to settle into taking turns sharing information about birth order and number of siblings.

As the session comes to a close, the leader encourages members to reflect again about the activity and the group process, "Does anyone have thoughts, feelings, or feedback about how things went this time round? I am curious if there are any observations regarding how the degree of structure afforded in the icebreaker activity did or did not facilitate the stated goal of learning more about one another?" After a brief moment of quiet, Susan states, "It seems ironic, but I felt more meaningful interaction and information exchange occurred when we adapted the exercise." Once we allowed the questions to be more open-ended, it seemed like we took more control over the process. Does this make sense?" The leader smiles at Susan and shares, "It seemed to me that your group decision-making process, which resulted in slowing down the icebreaker activity process by remaining seated, limiting the number of questions asked, and allowing each other choice about what you would disclose and discuss, seemed to bring the group closer." Bob states, "I agree, it really was a combination of everything that happened today – sort of the whole being greater than the sum of its parts. In the past I might've just written this group off, you know, lowered my expectations for learning anything and figuring I'd just have to 'suck it up' as an hour a week spent going nowhere. Once we got into it, time seemed to fly by. I must admit, now I am really curious to see what happens next week!"

Display 7.2

FGM Session evaluation of formation stage narrative

Outcomes addressed enhancement in areas of occupation:

- ■ Activities of Daily Living (ADL)
- ■ Instrumental Activities of Daily Living (IADL)
- ☒ Education
- ■ Work
- ■ Play/Leisure
- ☒ Social Participation
- ■ Rest/Sleep

Outcomes addressed enhanced performance skills in:

- ■ Motor and Praxis
- ■ Sensory-Perceptual
- ☒ Emotional Regulation
- ☒ Cognitive
- ☒ Communication/Social

Outcomes addressed client factors related to:

- ☒ Values/Beliefs/Spirituality: _____
_____
_____
- ■ Body Structures: _____
_____
_____
- ☒ Body Functions: <u>Specific/Global Mental Functions pertaining to affect, cognition and perception (i.e., higher level cognitive/metacognitive, concept formation, insight, coping, self-concept, motivation)</u>

Group structure allowed for:

- ☒ Purposeful Action
- ☒ Self-initiated Action
- ☒ Spontaneous Action
- ☒ Group-Centered Action
- ☒ Flow state
- ☒ New learning
- ☒ Evaluation and Feedback re: Group process
- ■ Evaluation and Feedback re: Member progress

Leader reflections (preparedness, behavior/roles, effectiveness, emotional response):

Susan, Bob, Li, and Rita's self-initiated actions helped the group spontaneously examine group member's perceptions regarding the leader as authority or person in charge. Leader actively utilized the self-initiated action of Susan's self-expression to try bridging other member's viewpoints, observations or reactions into the discussion (Ormont, 1990). Leader monitored spontaneous-action to address group task, maintenance, and individual roles (Benne and Sheats, 1978; *see* Box 7.4). Members seemed to adopt task roles such as initiator-contributor, energizer, elaborator, information seeker, opinion giver and seeker, and evaluator critic. Some members appeared to assume maintenance roles such as encourager, gatekeeper, harmonizer, observer-commentator, and follower (Benne and Sheats, 1978). As these roles emerged naturally in the process, support and redirection helped to facilitate group-centered action. At times, conflicting levels of comfort expressed about the degree of structure in the group appear to be a source of tension for the group and to drive possible emergence of individual roles such as blocker, help-seeker, and dominator (Benne and Sheats, 1978).

Leader utilized spontaneous-action to see if possible subgroups of members exist who may share similar feelings of confusion or uncertainty. Leader facilitated members' joining with others as a form of safely bringing diverse perspectives into the discussion by identifying possible subgroup formations (Agazarian, 1997). In doing so, group members were able to explore and address underlying anxieties that may be driving tension and work on conflicts they are ready to address (Agazarian and Gant, 2003). Leader, familiar with and accepting of feelings of anxiety that emerge as natural part of Formation Stage of groups, adopted task and maintenance roles as needed to balance out these functions in the group process. Leader also used concrete language to help clarify members' understanding of their own affect and expectations. These interventions combined with self-disclosure and process commentary facilitated more effective group decision-making.

Group members were able to air their feelings of confusion, surprise and frustration with encouragement and slight prompting from leader. Self initiated and spontaneous action facilitated members dealing more adaptively with their tension by sharing perspectives of the impact of Susan's negative remark. As more members' input was sought, then spontaneously shared, a group-centered agreement was reached to proceed with Rita's suggested modification of Bob's idea. Purposeful-action of revisiting questions from icebreaker members felt safe to self disclose answers to, began the process of achieving the goal of members getting to know each other. Increased member comfort and cohesion seemed evident in further release of tension through more relaxed laughter with more spontaneous member-to-member interaction and personal sharing. The process that ensued allowed for member perception of a "flow state" (Csikszentmihalyi, 1975, 1990) whereby their abilities fit with the possibilities for action in the group.

Discussion

Novice or student therapists may be reluctant to engage in therapy training groups for a variety of reasons. Markus and Abernethy (2001) explain unwillingness can stem from cognitive, behavioral and affective concerns such as:

1. Misunderstandings of the value and attitudes toward various group psychotherapy treatments.
2. Resistance because of their own early group experiences such as family of origin or peer groups.
3. Multiple threats to self-esteem and sense of competence.
4. Fear of self-disclosure of own feelings and strong emotions due to fear of rejection or personal socio-cultural experience.

Further, there is evidence of perceived differences between novice and experienced therapists regarding the importance of therapeutic factors in group psychotherapy (Vostanis and O'Sullivan, 1992).

In short-term training groups, members' perceptions of the leader, themselves, and the group as emotionally engaged and willing or able to confront conflict, can be seen as more predictive of learning than depth of relationships to other members (Tschuschke and Greene, 2002). As a group moves through the "Formation Stage" (Schwartzberg, Howe, and Barnes, 2008), feelings of dependency and fears of abandonment are triggered (Harpaz, 1994). To effectively support member needs and counter dependency, the leader's role is to:

1. Hold anxieties of group.
2. Quickly establish a therapeutic environment.
3. Shift the group toward issues that can be addressed in time available.
4. Protect loss to self-esteem and damages of over self-disclosure.
5. Assist the group to conclude well (Aveline, 1993).

The FGM approach allows members opportunity to identify, experience, and explore aspects of group formation and development such as anxiety, themes of narcissism (Battegay, 1990; Weber and Gans, 2003), and power and rivalry (Battegay, 1990) as they emerge. In the Formation Stage, purposeful-action is used to structure the process to be respectful of opinions and feelings of all members while clarifying expectations for participation. Members' self-initiated action, often in the form of expressing positive or negative feelings, is woven into the process via process commentary (Brown, 2003). In doing so, the leader is able to model listening and responding to support member interactions and comfort with risk taking. Self-initiated action can drive spontaneous-action in the group through members sharing perceptions and reactions. Using activities in addition to verbal exchange, leader(s) and members can work in the here-and-now on themes of diversity and acceptance. Group-centered action evolves as awareness of the group process develops. Nascent themes related to patterns of behavior or concerns over acceptance and belonging become a basis to support the group-centered action, which shifts the group process from a leader-dependent to a member-driven process.

The interaction between the leader and the members in the Formation Stage focuses on helping the group define its purpose and goals. As members begin to address what the group will do, issues of choice and control as well as group member roles more fully emerge (Benne and Sheats, 1978). Group norms may evolve that reflect the different roles (e.g., task, building and maintenance, individual) members assume. The roles members take in the group influence the group process and resultant leader actions. The leader looks to balance the group process by assuming task and maintenance roles as a means of facilitating the group process. Addressing emergent individual member roles is necessary to build trust and safety. Members need a safe context in which to explore their levels of comfort with conflict, as well as, with intimacy (Schwartzberg, Howe, and Barnes, 2008). The leader encouraging dialog and discussion that supports members learning to tolerate anxiety and ambiguity, while exploring options for decision-making, furthers group-centered action. (*See* Table 7.1).

Group Narrative: Process Training Group

Development stage

It is week five in the 14-week long process group. The more verbally active members sit on one side of the circle and, for the most part, the more silent members across the room. A self-identified "talker" states he feels resentful of the "silent" members, gesturing to the other side of the circle, and feels burdened with the responsibility to "carry the group." The silent members withdraw physically (folding arms, crossing legs, looking down or at each other). The leader asks, "I am wondering if anyone feels hurt by what is being suggested?"

"I am not usually a quiet person outside of this group," a withdrawn member declares. Another explains, "I was taught to be respectful and abide by the rule, 'If you can't say something nice, don't say anything at all'." A few members, who have not been very verbal in their participation, join in the discussion in agreement. "As a Quaker, I am comfortable with silence," one "silent" member declares. "I use the silence to reflect about what others have said and what I feel or think about it." Another states, "I prefer talking while doing something, it's so artificial to just sit around and stare at each other. If we were doing something or talking about something specific, besides who's talking and who is not, I *would* participate." Another "silent" member states, "Usually someone has already said more or less what I was thinking and I don't feel it is necessary to say the same thing over again." Yet another declares, "By the time I've figured out what it is I want to say, we've moved on to another topic." The leader sits quietly for a moment, then states, "You've given us a lot to think about in terms of what your silence means for each of you. I find myself resisting my own urge to say more, which leads me to wonder if we might view silence as a form of resistance? Any thoughts?"

Table 7.1 Group Issues and Membership Needs Related to Action: Formation Stage

Formation Stage issues: Concern over belonging and acceptance, formation of individual and group goals, dependence on leader, testing leader style.

Group Members Needs: related to action:

Purposeful action provides:	Self-initiated action allows for:	Spontaneous action occurs via:	Group-centered action yields:
Structured activity that includes all members and can provide successful outcomes	Safety of polite social behavior	Encouragement of expression of ideas, feelings, and thoughts related to "here-and-now"	Building knowledge of group resources
Guidance regarding expectations of members	Avenues for expression of negative and positive feelings	Opportunity to interact with leader and test extent of freedom and control	Gradual sharing by members taking initiative
Clear options and alternatives in goal selection	Opportunity for safe behavior risk-taking	Member sharing of perceptions and reactions as to what is going on in the group	Examination of group goals and exploration of norms appropriate to achieving group goals
An accepting climate	Group support and encouragement for individual roles and goals	Overt support and acceptance of diversity or difference	Group-centered decision-making
Expression of respect for opinions and feelings of members			Developing consensus and awareness of group's own process
			Establishing patterns of behavior/norms

Leader actions and Skills Employed

Discussing confidentiality
Clarification of individual or group goals; use of group contract; establishing group rules
Strong leader involvement in task analysis, selection and adaptation
Encouragement of member roles exploration
Structuring action and interactions for member comfort and growth
Modeling
Genuineness and empathy
Listening and responding
Tolerance of ambiguity and tentativeness in planning
Giving and receiving feedback
Sharing rationale for leader action
Using concrete language
Classifying themes
Climate setting for supportive interpersonal relationships
Leader input and support as needed

From Schwartzberg, S. L., Howe, M. C., & Barnes, M. A: *Groups: Applying the functional group model.* F. A. Davis, Philadelphia, 2008, (p. 137), with permission.

A member who has often reflected he is concerned about dominating the group, states, "Each week I say I'm not going to say anything, then I can't stand the silence so I start talking. Last week I spent the whole session focusing on not talking and it really made me dread coming today." The leader states, "Let's see what it might feel like to 'move to action' for a moment. Would anyone like to try taking a seat on the opposite side of the circle? I do have one caveat though, action will need to be put into words, meaning, once you switch seats, explain, to whoever's sitting in the seat you asked to take, why you did so, **and** in turn, invite the person who switches seats with you to do the same." After a prolonged moment of silence, a "silent" member initiates taking the seat of the self-identified "dominant" member. She shares what she sees and how it feels, literally and figuratively stating, "It seems as though I'm on stage and have an audience in those across from me who are expecting me to say something brilliant. I almost feel compelled to speak, and yet am unsure what to say." She turns toward the leader and reports, "Now I'm feeling frustrated that I have been put in this situation." She looks anxiously at the dominant member, who articulates, "Do you want your seat back? I feel as though I'm being held hostage and am unsure what to do!" He turns to the leader and states, "You must have known something like this would happen! Now what do we do?"

The leader asks the dominant member, "Can you identify what feelings might underlie your wish for me to take charge of the situation?" The member replies, "In my past job, if people weren't performing up to my expectations, I would take over to be sure the project was done right and ready for the client on time. It got to be so difficult and draining. There was so much tension around the office." A "silent" member states to the dominant member, "Well, I am sorry, but I am not going to compete with you. It is not worth it to argue with you about what we should talk about in the group. It's not like you are very open to other's ideas truthfully. Well, that's just my opinion. As the youngest child in my family, I have learned to just 'go with the flow.' Besides, I would rather we just 'do' something."

The leader asks this member, "Can you be a little more specific about what you would like the group to 'do'?" The member replies, "I don't know . . . it's not my place to tell others what to do. I'm not the leader. Can't you be more directive and just tell us what we should be doing? Isn't that really *your* job as our leader? I feel like you know what is supposed to be happening and aren't telling us. Isn't it your role to tell us what the best thing to do in a situation like this is?" The leader states, "This is very helpful for me to hear what you are thinking and feeling. I feel torn between a desire to grant your request and perhaps rescue us from this discomfort, and a sense that what we are doing right now is important. Perhaps our coming to understand our roles in the group may be what it is we need to 'do'? Are there others in the group who might be feeling frustration or disappointment with my leadership approach?"

The "talker" who had disclosed feeling burdened at the opening of the session states, "I'm not sure if it's you I am disappointed with, or myself for not just 'taking the bull by the horns', so to speak, or all of us for retreating in the face of a challenge. In some way, I'm glad no one person 'took over', because I realize now, wherever we go from here, we need to feel we're genuinely headed there together. Otherwise I see us riding this merry-go-round again. For sure." He looks over at the "silent" subgroup grinning and asks, "So what *do* you think we should **do** next week that would help us understand what roles we play in groups?"

Display 7.3

FGM Session evaluation of development stage narrative

Outcomes addressed enhancement in areas of occupation:

- ■ Activities of Daily Living (ADL)
- ■ Instrumental Activities of Daily Living (IADL)
- ☒ Education
- ■ Work
- ■ Play/Leisure
- ☒ Social Participation
- ■ Rest/Sleep

Outcomes addressed enhanced performance skills in:

- ■ Motor and Praxis
- ■ Sensory-Perceptual
- ☒ Emotional Regulation
- ☒ Cognitive
- ☒ Communication/Social

Outcomes addressed client factors related to:

- ☒ Values/Beliefs/Spirituality: _____

- ■ Body Structures: _____

- ☒ Body Functions: <u>*Specific/Global Mental Functions (i.e., higher level cognitive/metacognitive, judgment, awareness, insight, coping, self concept, motivation)*</u>

Group structure allowed for:

- ☒ Purposeful Action
- ☒ Self-initiated Action
- ☒ Spontaneous Action
- ☒ Group-Centered Action
- ■ Flow state
- ☒ New learning
- ☒ Evaluation and Feedback re: Group process
- ■ Evaluation and Feedback re: Member progress

Leader reflections (preparedness, behavior/roles, effectiveness, emotional response):

Leader took the risk to make a process commentary, observing that the members who have been identified as "silent" seem to have reacted physically to what is being said, adjusting their bodies to what might be interpreted as a protective or closed-off manner. Leader worked with the subgroups, the more silent and the more verbal, to have all voices heard so that other points of view would be seen and accepted. "Silent" members became more verbal, expressing roles in primary, spiritual, or peer groups that may be impacting their participation in the T-group. Leader used purposeful-action to drive more group-centered action, encouraging the members to do an activity of changing seats as a symbolic form of changing perspective. This purposeful-action created a safe forum in which spontaneous and self-initiated actions of "silent" and "dominant" members help them to explore issues, uncovering commonalities meaningful to the group as well as individual members. The leader though uncertain as to group's readiness at times, made the decision to address possible anger in the group. Leader invited the group members to further explore what is being said as well as "not said" by inquiring about related feelings and possible transferences (*see* Box 7.5) that might be occurring in the here-and-now of the group. Members' self-initiated actions in the form of their verbal and nonverbal responses became a source for spontaneous-action; examining possible transferences towards leader, as well as leader counter transference. Leader, though feeling somewhat defensive, took this internal cue as possible state of anxiety or fear in members and calmly assured the group that she values and can tolerate their input and feelings. By sharing her own feelings and thoughts, the leader became a vehicle for more in-depth intra-and interpersonal exploration and communication. Members were able to tentatively approach possible underlying feelings of anger, expressing frustration and disappointment that leader was "not doing her job." Once these feelings were aired and contained, leader felt more confident and relaxed, which allowed her to probe further. This spontaneous-action allowed some members' opportunity to examine their own possible feelings and motivations for their choices around group participation.

Discussion

Issues of power and control emerged in the form of subgroups and resistance. Member roles were becoming imbalanced, potentially creating group norms that could have led to the group being "stuck." This imbalance of task versus group building and maintenance in the process became represented in the members' articulated struggle around "doing something" besides "talking" or verbal processing. An unconscious wish for the leader to take care of the group appeared in the form of multiple members' verbal or nonverbal expressions, and projections of affective material onto the leader or each other. Comments related to who was "in charge" or "responsible" for what goes on in the group session and active attempts by members to "silence" themselves spoke to concerns about control. One member stating she was "not the leader" spoke of an apparent desire to return the process to one of leader-centered as opposed to group-centered action.

Members struggled with resistance as it emerged in themselves and in the group, but were able to address material related to possible underlying fears of exposure and rejection. In actuality, members found many commonalities (anxieties about uncertainty, disappointment in lack of group participation and decision-making), even though they actively began the discussion about differences in level of participation. As members were more open about what they were thinking and feeling, they were able to come to explore their feelings about the leader and what leadership meant to them as individuals. In a T-group, members are often faced with a juxtaposition of feelings about the leader, who happens to be a source of formative feedback in their chosen area of study. Ambivalence may become evident in their feeling uncertain about trusting or allowing others who may also be future colleagues, to see different, often more vulnerable, sides of their true selves. Group members who are grappling with the notion that the group has to be "fun" in order for them to consider it "safe" may be experiencing a possible "flight" (Bion, 1959; *see* Box 7.6) reaction as well. Subgrouping can be a response to feeling anxious about the work, a need for leader approval, and perceived absence of leadership.

It is typical to see continuous recycling of concerns around need for leader structure and approval in short-term groups, perhaps even more so in those that are a training requirement. Members are expected to attend the sessions and to actively participate. The academic or professional setting provides an additional complexity to the group context, challenging the notion of freedom in the group. Members' sense of choice and control paradoxically requires risk taking, and thus calls upon the "courage" (Gans, 2005) of both members and leader to explore personal issues as they emerge, without any certainty that the outcome of the exploration will be successful. In this population, members often arrive with idealized images of about how a therapist should feel and act. Leaders are vulnerable to "shame," given the deep challenges of their work and ego ideals (Weber and Gans, 2003). Moderate leader "self-disclosure" and "transparency" (Yalom, 1995) facilitate the development of trust and group cohesion. The leader's expression of feelings is fine-tuned in accordance with the needs of the individual, subgroups, and the group as a whole. In the FGM, leader's judgment and decision-making about how to proceed incorporates what might be needed at each level (individual, subgroup, group as a whole) to discern group and member needs related to action (purposeful, self-initiated, spontaneous, group-centered). Discussion becomes a means to identify what might be objective or "real" concerns as well as possible "subjective" projections and projective identifications on the part of the members (Van Wagoner, 2000). Action is used as a means to clarify and validate member concerns while continuing to empower members' safe participation in the group process. (*See* Table 7.2).

Group Narrative: Process Training Group

Closure stage

It is the second to last session and a member is absent from the group. The leader keeps a chair in the circle as a means to recognize the member's place in the group. A few members express dislike of the "empty chair." Jane, who is seated next to the chair, touches it and says, "This reminds me of when my brother went off to war, no one would dare take his seat at the table. Even though he died in combat, no-one ever sits where he used to sit at the table." Another member, Deborah, responds, "It's like an empty chair at Seder dinner to remember all who were lost." Silence ensues. "Now I feel like we are waiting for Elijah the Prophet!," she exclaims. "I can't believe we are back to the awkward silences!"

The leader remarks, "These are very powerful associations. Just to clarify, my intent was to recognize our missing member and acknowledge that, while not present today, he is a part of our group. I am wondering if some of you might have feelings about someone being absent, or perhaps, about the fact that we are close to our final

Development Stage issues: Concern over acceptance or rejection as result of change; testing the safety of the group; struggle between safety and involvement; control and power struggles (conflict) with leader and other members (Corey & Corey, 1977, 1982).

Group Members Needs (related to action):

Purposeful action provides:	Self-initiated action allows for:	Spontaneous (here-and-now) Action occurs via:	Group-centered Action yields:
Structured activity that includes all members and can provide successful outcomes	Support of exploratory behavior	Encouragement of expression of ideas feelings, and thoughts related to, here-and-now	Leadership emerging from group membership
Guidance regarding expectations of members	Encouragement of task involvement and expression	Opportunity to interact with leader and test degree of freedom and control	Sense of ownership as "our" group
Clear options and alternatives in goal selection	Opportunity to express positive and negative reactions and feelings	Member sharing of perceptions and reactions as to what is going on in the group	Increased member-to-member interaction
An accepting climate	Accepting environment	Overt support and acceptance of diversity or difference	Members looking less to leader for approval or needs to be met
Expression of respect for opinions and feelings of members			Increased cohesiveness and support
			Increased tolerance for limitations of group (time, materials, attention)

Leader actions and Skills Employed

Reviewing confidentiality
Continued clarification of individual and group goals; use of group contract; redefining group rules
Continued leader involvement in task analysis, selection, and adaptation; activity demands must match member abilities for task and social interaction
Leader encouragement for members to assume group task and maintenance roles
Gradual increase in expectations for action to level of member tolerance and growth
Modeling
Genuineness and empathy
Active Listening
Giving and receiving feedback
Assurance that conflict can be worked through if not acted out or avoided
Sharing process commentary as indicated
Using concrete language; reframing potential hostility and anger as possibly related to disappointment with leader, frustration with limitations of group context, unmet needs, etc.,
Connecting themes
Creating a climate or holding environment that allows for supportive interpersonal relationships
Leader input, support, and limit-setting as needed

From Schwartzberg, S. L., Howe, M. C., & Barnes, M. A: *Groups: Applying the functional group model*. F. A. Davis, Philadelphia, 2008, (pp. 179–180), with permission.

session." A member, Li, states, "I feel it is impolite to talk about someone who is absent." Another member, Susan, states, "I wouldn't mind it being acknowledged if I was absent, but not to the extent I would feel as though I should've come to group even if I wasn't feeling well. It feels like being accountable to the group would take precedence over my own wellbeing." One member expresses, "I hope that I would not be overlooked when absent, yet I wouldn't want too much focus on the absence upon my return – just enough to fill me in as to what I missed."

Another member states, "I think we can acknowledge a missing member without having to hold their place with a chair!" Jane rejoins, "I don't mind the chair, but I guess maybe I'm at a different place in my life with facing loss. Truthfully, I am sorry Bob isn't here today to help plan our last session. I realize I've really begun to value his energy and ideas for the group. I look forward to having this time once a week where I don't feel pressured, sort of a time for me. I will miss it." The leader replies to Jane, "I will miss you Jane. I have enjoyed the opportunity to get to know you better. I have been impressed by your openness and willingness to share your perspective with the group." Rita responds, "I want to second that sentiment. Jane, you've really taught me that it's alright to have your own opinion about things. I am so much more assertive now with others outside of the group, really able to say what I am feeling and thinking more. Oh, and I'd like to state for the record that I miss Bob's energy today too; it really does feel hard to plan for our last session without him."

Susan replies, "It's not like we aren't ever going to see each other again. We'll still run into each other as we finish up our training." Li remarks, "True, but it won't be the same. Too bad we can't reconvene as a group meeting next semester - having this time really did help me to reflect on what I have been learning and my own professional growth." Deborah remarks, "It would be a good idea to have someplace to take our concerns as we continue in our training program. I'm not sure I'm really 'ready for prime time' yet. The thought of being responsible for someone else's wellbeing scares me to death, if you want to know the truth. I guess I should have made more of this opportunity to really focus on my professional development goals. I feel in some ways like I 'missed the boat' and am just now realizing how much I still need to learn." Jane replies, "Oh Deborah, I think you are more ready than you give yourself credit for – you know how the saying goes; 'the more you know, the more you know you don't know.' Don't be so hard on yourself!" Li looks to the leader and asks, "Have you ever thought about doing a voluntary continuation?" The leader replies, "Li, your wish is very tempting. I love running groups and have enjoyed watching each of you grow and develop this semester. But I think my job today is to help support you all through this process of coming to a close as a group, facing the reality of change that is part of our lives and participation in a training program."

Susan interjects, "Maybe we should plan for our final meeting to be like a celebration – we could all bring refreshments and just talk about what our future plans are or whatever people feel like." The leader remarks, "Susan, I appreciate your bringing our attention to the future, but am wondering if we could stay for a minute with some of what's being talked about right now? Often, when we face endings, it may bring about reminders of other losses, or even a revisiting of where we began. For our group, there have been some different metaphors raised, one being that of a journey for some. We have also had some very poignant concerns raised that I'd like us to take a moment to acknowledge before we move on."

Deborah replies, "That's just it I guess. I can't believe that when we've finally gotten to the point where we are alright with all the scary and uncomfortable aspects of being in a group, we have to end. Sort of just when we've gotten to the good part . . ." Li replies, "I'd rather focus on what was gained than opportunities lost. I feel in life there is always a master plan, I have learned I have to trust that things are happening for a reason." Rita responds, smiling, "I agree with you Li, and now I feel I can add 'trust the process' to my core philosophy. When I think back, and admittedly, look back over all that reading we were assigned, I can't believe how 'classically' our process unfolded." Another member quips, "I guess I'd better finish all the readings, then so I can 'know' how the story is going to end." As the group laughs, another member comments to the leader, "It is amazing how you masterminded all of this." Jane replies, "We did the work, and deserve the credit. At least, that's what I believe." Jane looks toward the leader, smiles and states, "Not that you weren't masterful as our guide and true north, oh fearless leader!"

"Ok, enough of this mushy stuff!," Susan interjects. "Can we get back to party planning for next week already? Maybe Rita and Jane can come up with an activity that will help us all reminisce and reflect on our goals? It would be neat if we had something tangible to take away with us to remember our time together by – any ideas anyone?" Looking at the empty chair, she remarks, "Perhaps the question is, 'What would Bob say we should do?'" Rita, smiling, replies, "Let's figure this out together Susan, that way next week there are no big surprises. Though I must say, you really have grown in your ability to 'go with the flow'." "Thanks Rita!" Susan replies. "I guess my motto has become, 'always expect the unexpected' when it comes to group! But seriously, I do appreciate that you noticed that I have tried to learn to 'sit' with what goes on in here, or should I say, 'comes up'? Obviously though, it's still pretty hard for me."

Another member, Sally, replies, "You are not alone Susan. I still like when I know what the 'plan' is for the group." Turning to Jane, she remarks, "I think you are so *brave* Jane to talk about your brother. I could never do that." She looks away, tears forming in her eyes, "I'm sorry, I'm so embarrassed. It's just been a hard week for me personally, as my significant other and I have decided to call it quits. I didn't mean to make such a fuss just now. As some of you know, it's been a long time coming, excuse my language, but her timing really sucks. I'm so conflicted about it. Relieved that it's over, but angry that it is taking my energy and attention away from everything else right now, as we sort through who gets what, including our dog." Li replies, "Wow, that's awful! Are you sure you are alright?" "Yes" she replies, "I didn't mean to get so carried away and unburden on you all."

The leader remarks, "It is hard for many of us to sit with our feelings. It can especially be difficult to sort through mixed feelings. Perhaps there are some mixed feelings in others about our group ending too? I sense an urge in myself, and others perhaps, to want to take care of you in your distress. It tugs at the caretaker in me . . . and conveniently might serve to distract me from my own feelings of losing the opportunity to work with you all more? Or possibly, keeping a focus on you provides a means to channel my feelings into what looks like a purposeful action? And so, I wonder, what would be most helpful right now, for you, and the group, in the time we have left today? Would it be useful to reminisce and highlight what people have accomplished? Or, maybe to identify other resources or future opportunities that might exist in terms of personal and/or professional development?"

"Just to let you all know, I'm alright" Sally replies, "I have lots of support with this, honest. But thanks for your understanding. What would help *me* most right now is if we just got back to our planning for our next, or I guess I should say more accurately, last, session."

Display 7.4

FGM Session evaluation of closure stage narrative

Outcomes addressed enhancement in areas of occupation:

- ■ Activities of Daily Living (ADL)
- ■ Instrumental Activities of Daily Living (IADL)
- ☒ Education
- ☒ Work
- ■ Play/Leisure
- ☒ Social Participation
- ■ Rest/Sleep

Outcomes addressed enhanced performance skills in:

- ■ Motor and Praxis
- ■ Sensory-Perceptual
- ☒ Emotional Regulation
- ☒ Cognitive
- ☒ Communication/Social

Outcomes addressed client factors related to:

- ☒ Values/Beliefs/Spirituality
- ■ Body Structures: _____
- ☒ Body Functions: <u>Specific/Global Mental Functions pertaining to affect, cognition and perception (i.e., higher level cognitive/metacognitive, memory, awareness, insight, coping, self esteem, motivation)</u>

Group structure allowed for:

- ☒ Purposeful Action
- ☒ Self-initiated Action
- ☒ Spontaneous Action
- ☒ Group-Centered Action
- ■ Flow state
- ☒ New learning
- ☒ Evaluation and Feedback re: Group process
- ☒ Evaluation and Feedback re: Member progress

Leader Reflections (include: preparedness, behavior/roles, effectiveness, emotional response):

Leader used self-initiated action of members' disclosures regarding loss and sadness to acknowledge the importance of the issues raised and to validate members' concerns and feelings. Purposeful-action was used to clarify intent behind symbolic 'empty chair' while remaining clear with members about the group coming to a close. Transparency was used to role model self-disclosure

> of ambivalence as well as providing summative feedback to another member. Self-initiated and spontaneous-action became a means to re-direct individuals back to the 'here-and-now' affect that was emerging. Feedback, transparency, and process commentary was used to bring members' attention to ways in which talking about meeting in future venues and focusing on peers' distress might serve as a potential means to avoid affect and engaging in the process of saying goodbye. Leader, though slightly surprised by strength of attunement with wish to continue and counter transference regarding caretaking, was able to effectively use all forms of action, as well as balance task and maintenance roles through transparency and self disclosure to guide group towards addressing needs for closure.

Discussion

Klein 1972 aptly points out that group closure can bring up affect related to loss, sadness, grief or abandonment: "It leaves one with the dread of loneliness and of having to 'go it alone.' It reactivates the fear of risk and the anticipation of inadequacy and hence failure" (p. 283). Klein further relates, if the group has been successful, intermingled with such feelings of loss and fear, are feelings of hopefulness, accomplishment, and anticipation. The termination process is shaped by several factors: the extent to which earlier issues were resolved, the socio-cultural background of members, and the group structure and culture (Wardi, 1989), as cited in Schwartzberg, Howe, and Barnes, 2008, pp. 210–211

Group members may have difficulty facing the reality of a group coming to a close (Cohen and Smith, 1976; Klein, 1972). Members may engage in behaviors related to premature termination, denial or avoidance, raising new issues for discussion, anxiety and fear, anger, depression or sadness.

Raising new issues may represent members' wish for the group to continue. Identifying other resources for addressing their concerns may be necessary. Others may not talk about feelings at all, or, put off dealing with feelings until the last few moments when it is too late to discuss them thoroughly. Group members may also engage in denial by making plans for the group to meet again in another context. In such a case, the end of the group sessions is acknowledged, but the end of the group relationship is denied (Schwartzberg, Howe, and Barnes, 2008). Anxiety may emerge in the form of regressed behavior, moving apart from the group to gain closure, or a return to behavior more typical of Formation and Development Stages (Schwartzberg, Howe, and Barnes, 2008). Some members may withdraw from the group before closure is discussed. Withdrawal may become evident in lack of participation (Cohen and Smith, 1976; Corey and Corey, 1982), lateness, or absenteeism. It is essential for leaders to maintain realistic expectations regarding termination or closure. Rice 1996, postulates, "There can be no complete resolutions or perfect terminations . . . The leader aims to support "'good-enough' terminations . . . one that fulfills the treatment contract, including its refinements during therapy", (p. 8). (*See* Table 7.3).

Table 7.3 Group Issues and Membership Needs Related to Action: Closure Stage

Closure Stage issues: Denial and avoidance, premature termination, anxiety and fear, depression and anger, sadness, raising new issues for discussion.

Group Members Needs or Behaviors related to action:

Purposeful Action:	Self Initiated Action:	Spontaneous Action (here-and-now):	Group-centered Action:
More focus on maintenance roles, but less on task	Power struggles emerge or re-emerge	Becoming more concerned about individual needs	Review of group's history and process over course of sessions
Trust versus mistrust re-emerges as theme	Withdrawal from group	Wish or appeal for group to continue may be expressed	Reminiscing about member participation
Participation declines	Regressive behavior(s) may be revisited or re-expressed as means to demonstrate uncertainty about future or ability to function without group (i.e., question if "ready" for group to end)	May devalue importance of group and learning or growth that occurred (Viewing work done as worthless)	Recognizing and/or celebrating individual & group accomplishments
More structure is needed		Anger toward leader and/or other members (possibly to avoid sadness about loss or anxiety about separation)	Group conflicts may predominate
		Feedback to other members provided with less intensity	Silences and inactivity may prevail
			Unresolved issues may be raised

Leader actions and Skills Employed

Review terms of group contract regarding number of sessions and confidentiality
Re-enforce group rules
Structure process to facilitate members addressing feelings about termination issues
Genuineness and empathy
Listening and responding
Modeling acceptance and tolerance of ambiguity
Giving and receiving feedback
Classifying themes
Use of metaphor or narrative in reviewing group stories and reminiscing about member participation
Structuring activity to allow for "transitional object"
Confrontation
Reality testing
Self-disclosure

Conclusion

The Functional Group Model demonstrates an approach to group work that is unique in its action-oriented approach. Adherence to the model and protocols determine leader competency relative to "treatment distinctiveness" – behaviors that are unique to the model and essential to it (Waltz, Addis, Koerner, and Jacobson, 1993). Intervention strategies such as setting goals, use of empathy, self-disclosure and feedback are essential but not unique to the model. The use of process exploration is encouraged, if feasible given members' capabilities, but not necessary to the model. Exploration for the sole purpose of insight and examination of transference alone is advocated when it is in support of the action orientation. Adherence to the combined use of the four forms of action (purposeful, self-initiated, spontaneous, and group-centered) is required and assessed in evaluation of leader competence. Trained therapists are expected to follow the guidelines offered, to ensure the model is carried out in a competent manner.

Box 7.1

Common questions about the Functional Group Model

What is the difference between this approach and a therapeutic approach?

The FGM is a unique model of systematic group intervention that can be flexible in its application across settings and populations. As such it provides general principles, protocols, and guidelines that can be used therapeutically in settings such as hospitals, outpatient clinics, and private practice with individuals who have a diagnosis. It is also of value in educational settings, community settings, and other natural settings such as the workplace. Wherever individuals and groups need to enhance function, the functional group model provides a structure to guide leadership and intervention with a population or setting. Using the FGM approach might be considered analogous to teachers applying behavioral theory as part of their reasoning for using behavioral techniques to manage and motivate students in a classroom. In the educational context, the work is not called therapy, but may have therapeutic-like qualities and personal growth outcomes.

What are the confidentiality agreements that are in place?

Ideally, before members start a group, pre-group interviews are conducted as much as possible. In these interviews or the first session of the group an agreement is reviewed orally and at times in writing. The expectations for confidentiality are set forth: whatever is discussed in group should remain in group and not reported in a way that would make individuals recognizable. The contract, as set forth in the course syllabus and reviewed in the first session, indicates members are to bring outside discussions with other members about group back to the group.

What kinds of emergencies can come up in these groups?

In educational settings, our members are prescreened by virtue of the graduate admissions process. The students are oriented to services on campus and specific academic policies as well as expectations related to occupational role development when they arrive. As in a therapeutic setting, when a member appears to be in significant distress for emotional or physical reasons, leaders may refer them to means of individual support (health service provider, academic advisor or resource center, Rehabilitation Act 504 officer) with a plan for individual follow-up. Group members are expected to let the leaders know of absences in advance of sessions when possible. The leaders are easily available by phone and email.

How does your approach differ from other group training approaches?

The Functional Group Model capitalizes the use of action components of a group to enhance self-awareness and understanding of group process and dynamics. The group expectations include requiring members to co-lead a group session. Principles of the model and structured formats for activity selection are provided in verbal and written form to guide the co-leaders addressing individual and group needs. Forms of action become the medium by which resistances, fears and feelings about leadership competencies are explored. Members learn through firsthand experience how to facilitate a group that is purposeful, self-initiated, group-centered, and operates within the here-and-now (spontaneous). Through the process of doing, the action components become the metaphorical mirror for self-reflection regarding group as a therapeutic intervention as issues inherent to forming, developing and concluding a group are replicated.

Box 7.2

Leader functions (Yalom and Leszcz, 2005)

Research into client perceptions of group leaders showed four key leadership functions; higher amounts of caring and meaning attribution showed significant relationship to positive outcomes.

1. *Emotional activation* (challenging, confronting, modeling by personal risk-taking and high self-disclosure).
2. *Caring* (offering support, affection, praise, protection, warmth, acceptance, genuineness, concern).
3. *Meaning attribution* (explaining, clarifying, interpreting, providing a cognitive framework for change: translating feelings and experiences into ideas).
4. *Executive function* (setting limits, rules, norms, goals; managing time; pacing, stopping, interceding, suggesting procedures). (Yalom and Leszcz, 2005: p. 536)

Box 7.3

Process commentary (Brown, 2003)

Brown (2003) explains; "Process commentary makes visible what and how the group and its members are acting in the here-and-now . . . members often lack awareness of what is happening and this can lead to feelings of being stuck and accomplishing little, a very uncomfortable and distressing atmosphere. The leader speaks of what is hidden or not understood and the effect of these on the group and its members" (p. 238).

A leader needs to gauge whether there is sufficient trust before making "process commentary" (Brown, 2003). In the early stages of a group, making tentative statements rather than posing questions might be warranted to avoid being seen as critical or blaming. Process commentary can be useful to move a group forward when it seems stuck, loses energy, or discussions are circular. Members may resist responding to leader(s)'s process commentary, but it is likely the group will revisit the content when ready. Withdrawal, dependency on leader, and sub-grouping serve members' sense of safety. Until trust and cohesiveness are felt, aggressive feelings, such as jealousy and competition, or loving feelings, such as admiration or interpersonal intimacy may remain unconscious or be experienced as too threatening if they emerge openly in the group.

(Adapted from Schwartzberg, Howe, and Barnes, 2008: p. 181.)

Box 7.4

Member roles: group task, building and maintenance, and individual

Benne and Sheats (1978) identified roles group members might adopt, clustering them within three categories:

1. "Group task roles" which assist the group in coordinating its efforts to define and solve common problems. These roles assist the group in completing specified tasks or goals.
   a. **initiator–contributor** suggests or proposes new ideas or new ways of viewing the group problems or goals.
   b. **information seeker** asks for clarification of suggestions made and for authoritative information and facts pertinent to the problem being discussed.
   c. **opinion seeker** is less concerned with the facts but looks for clarification of the values pertinent to what the group is doing.
   d. **information giver** offers facts or generalizations that are authoritative or relates his or her experiences to the group problem.
   e. **opinion giver** states a belief or opinion related to a suggestion made or to an alternative suggestion.

    f. **elaborator** makes suggestions in terms of examples and offers a rationale for suggestions made previously.
    g. **coordinator** clarifies the relationships among various ideas and suggestions, tries to pull ideas together, or tries to coordinate the activities of members or subgroups.
    h. **orientater** defines the position of the group with respect to its goals.
    i. **evaluator–critic** subjects the accomplishments of the group to standards of group functioning within the context of the group task.
    j. **energizer** prods the group into action or decision-making and attempts to stimulate the group to a "greater" or "better" activity.
    k. **procedural technician** facilitates group movement by doing things for the group.
    l. **recorder** makes a record of group suggestions and decisions by writing down or recalling for the group the products of discussion.
2. **"Group building and maintenance roles,"** which help enable everyone to work together as a group and strengthen or alter the group's processes in terms of social and emotional elements. These roles focus on maintaining group-centered behavior by building group processes and supportive attitudes:
    a. **encourager** praises, agrees with, and accepts the contributions of others. Through these attitudes, he or she indicates warmth and solidarity toward the other group members.
    b. **harmonizer** mediates differences between members, attempts to reconcile disagreements, and relieves tension in conflict situations.
    c. **compromiser** operates from within a conflict in which his or her ideas or positions are involved. The compromiser may compromise by giving up power, admitting error, or in agreeing with the group by altering his or her opinion.
    d. **gatekeeper** or **expediter** attempts to keep communication channels open by encouraging and facilitating the participation of other group members or by regulating the flow of communication in the group.
    e. **standard setter** or **ego ideal** expresses standards for the group to achieve in its functioning or applies norms in evaluating the quality of the group process.
    f. **group observer** or **commentator** keeps records of group process and helps the group to evaluate its own procedures by presenting feedback.
    g. **follower** goes along with the sense of the group, serving as an audience for group discussion.
3. **"Individual roles"** which are assumed by individual members of a group, consciously or unconsciously, solely to satisfy personal needs. When group members are exhibiting a high incidence of any of these roles, the group is experiencing "individual-centered" as opposed to "group-centered" participation, which suggests the group is not functioning well:
    a. **aggressor** lowers the status of others; disapproves of the values, acts, and feelings of others; and attacks the whole group or an issue on which the group is working.

b. **blocker** tends to be negative, stubborn, disagreeing, and oppositional beyond reason.
c. **recognition seeker** works in various ways to draw attention to him or her.
d. **self-confessor** uses the audience that the group provides to express personal, non–group-oriented communications.
e. **playboy** displays a lack of involvement in the group's processes.
f. **dominator** tries to assert personal authority or superiority by manipulating the group as a whole, or selected members of the group. Domination may be in the form of flattery, asserting a superior status, or interrupting the contributions of others.
g. **help seeker** tries to elicit expressions of sympathy from the group through unreasonable expressions of insecurity or self-deprecation.
h. **special interest pleader** speaks for special interest groups, usually as a mask for his or her prejudices and biases.

(Adapted from Schwartzberg, Howe, and Barnes, 2008.)

Box 7.5

Transference and the Functional Group Model

The leader strives to help members examine and explore both subjective and objective aspects of transference concerning the action components of the group. Through such exploration, blocking and facilitating behaviors are revealed with the aim of promoting a more group-centered versus leader-centered group. A group-centered process is maximally self-initiating as well as purposeful to individual members and the group as a whole. Insight and integration of thought and action is sought through "doing" and "verbalizing." The "examined action" in the group is means to goal achievement, rather than viewed as "acting out" of interpersonal and intrapersonal conflict.

Box 7.6

Group tensions (Bion, 1959)

A psychoanalytic point of view regarding tensions experienced by group members and possible ways members can be viewed as coping with and working through their tensions postulates members go through three stages:

1. fighting or fleeing,
2. dependence and counter-dependence on the leader, and
3. a process of pairing.

> Pairing in the third stage can be seen in the form of subgrouping and may become a means for members to form closer bonds and thus overcome underlying fears. This stage of coping with tension may suggest the group is progressing in their development and readiness to work together.
>
> (Adapted from Schwartzberg, Howe, and Barnes, 2008: p. 20.)

References and Bibliography

Agazarian, Y. M. (1997). *Systems-centered therapy for groups.* New York: Guilford Press.

Agazarian, Y. M., & Gant, S. (2003). Phases of group development: Systems-centered hypotheses and their implication for research and practice. *Group Dynamics: Theory, Research and Practice, 7*(3), 238–252.

Aveline, M. O. (1993). Principles of leadership in brief training groups for mental health care professionals. *International Journal of Group Psychotherapy, 43*(1), 107–129.

Azima, H., & Azima, F. (1959). Outline of a dynamic theory of occupational therapy. *American Journal of Occupational Therapy, 13*(5), 215–221.

Bales, R. (1950). *Interaction process analysis.* Reading, Massachusetts: Addison Wesley.

Barris, R., Kielhofner, G., & Hawkins, J. H. (1983). *Psychosocial Occupational Therapy Practice in a Pluralistic Arena.* Laurel, Maryland: Ramsco.

Battegay, R. (1990). Complementary individual and group analytic training for future psychotherapists. *Psychotherapy and psychosomatics, 53*(1–4), 130–134.

Benne, K. D., & Sheats, P. (1978). Functional roles of group members. In L.P. Bradford (Ed.), *Group development*, (2nd ed., pp. 52–61). La Jolla, California: University Associates.

Bennis, W. B., & Shepard, H. A. (1956). A theory of group development. *Human Relations, 9*(4), 415–457.

Bion, W. R. (1959). *Experiences in groups.* New York: Basic Books.

Brown, N. W. (2003). Conceptualizing process. *International Journal of Group Psychotherapy, 53*(2), 225–244.

Burke, J. P. (1983). Defining occupation: Importing and organizing interdisciplinary knowledge. In G. Kielhofner (ed.), *Health through occupation: Theory and practice in occupational therapy,* (pp. 125–138). Philadelphia: F. A. Davis.

Cartwright, D., & Zander, A. (Eds.) (1968). *Group dynamics research and theory* (3rd ed.). New York: Harper & Row.

Cohen, A. M., & Smith, R. D. (1976). *The critical incident in growth groups: Theory and technique.* La Jolla, California: University Associates.

Corey, G., & Corey, M. S. (1977). *Groups: Process and practice,* Monterey, California: Brooks/Cole.

Corey, G., & Corey, M. S. (1982). *Groups: Process and practice,* (2nd ed.). Monterey, California: Brooks/Cole.

Csikszentmihalyi, M. (1975). *Beyond boredom and anxiety: The experience of play in work and games.* San Francisco: Jossey-Bass.

Csikszentmihalyi, M. (1990). *Flow: The psychology of optimal experience.* New York: Harper Collins.

Fidler, G. S., & Fidler, J. W. (1978). Doing and becoming: Purposeful action and self-actualization. *American Journal of Occupational Therapy, 32*(5), 305–310.

Gans, J. S. (2005). A plea for greater recognition and appreciation of our group members' courage. *International Journal of Group Psychotherapy, 55*(4), 575–593.

Garland, J. A., Jones, H. E., & Kolodny, R. (1965). A model for stages of development in social work groups. In S. Bernstein (Ed.), *Explorations in group work*. Boston: Boston University School of Social Work.

Harpaz, N. (1994). Failures in group psychotherapy: The therapist variable. *International Journal of Group Psychotherapy, 44*, 3–19.

Howe, M., & Schwartzberg, S. L. (1986). *A functional approach to group work in occupational therapy*. Philadelphia: J B Lippincott.

Kielhofner, G. (2009). *Conceptual foundations of occupational therapy practice*, (4th ed.). Philadelphia: F A Davis.

King, L. J. (1978). 1978 Eleanor Clarke Slagle Lecture: Toward a science of adaptive responses. *American Journal of Occupational Therapy, 32*(7), 429–437.

Klein, A. F. (1972). *Effective group work: An introduction to principle and method*. New York: Association Press.

Lifton, W. M. (1961). *Working with groups: Group process and individual growth*. New York: John Wiley & Sons.

Markus, H. E., & Abernethy, A. D. (2001). Joining with resistance: Addressing reluctance to engage in group therapy training. *International Journal of Group Psychotherapy, 51*(2), 191–204.

Maslow, A. H. (1970). *Motivation and personality* (2nd Ed.). New York: Harper & Row.

Mosey, A. C. (1970). The concept and use of developmental groups. *American Journal of Occupational Therapy, 24*(4), 272–275.

Ormont, L. (1990). The craft of bridging. *International Journal of Group Psychotherapy, 40*(1), 3–17.

Reed, K. L. (1984). *Models of practice in occupational therapy*. Baltimore: Williams & Wilkins.

Rice, C. A. (1996). Premature termination of group therapy: A clinical perspective. *International Journal of Group Psychotherapy, 46*(1), 5–23.

Schwartzberg, S. L., Howe, M. C., & Barnes, M. A. (2008). *Groups: Applying the functional group model*. Philadelphia: F A Davis.

Tschuschke, V., & Greene, L. R. (2002). Group therapists' training: What predicts learning? *International Journal of Group Psychotherapy, 52*(4), 463–482.

Tuckman, B. W. (1965). Developmental sequence in small groups. *Psychological Bulletin, 63*, 384–399.

Van Wagoner, S. L. (2000). Anger in group therapy Countertransference and the novice group therapist. *Journal of Psychotherapy in Independent Practice, 1*(2), 63–75.

Vostanis, P., & O'Sullivan, D. (1992). Evaluation of therapeutic factors in group psychotherapy by therapists in training. *Group Analysis, 25*, 325–332.

Waltz, J., Addis, M. E., Koerner, K., & Jacobson, N. S. (1993). Testing the integrity of a psychotherapy protocol: Assessment of adherence and competence. *Journal of Consulting and Clinical Psychology, 61*(4), 620–630.

Wardi, D. (1989). The termination phase in the group process. *Group Analysis, 22*, 87–98.

Weber, R. L., & Gans, J. S. (2003). The group therapist's shame: A much undiscussed topic. *International Journal of Group Psychotherapy, 53*(40), 395–416.

White, R. W. (1959). Motivation reconsidered: The concept of competence. *The Psychological Review, 66*, 297–333.

White, R. W. (1971). The urge towards competence. *American Journal of Occupational Therapy, 25*(6), 271–274.

Yalom, I. D., & Leszcz, M. (2005). *The theory and practice of group psychotherapy* (5th ed.). New York: Basic Books.

Yalom, I. (1995). *The theory and practice of group psychotherapy*, (4th ed.). New York: Basic Books.

8
It's All About Me: Introduction to Relational Group Psychotherapy

Richard M. Billow

With what fear and avoidance does the analyst write about his own method of coming to conclusions, about his own thoughts and impressions! The devil himself could not frighten many analysts more than the use of the word 'I' does in reporting cases. . . . In our science only the psychical reality has validity. It is remarkable that the unconscious station which does almost all of the work is left out of analytic discussions. . . .
Analyst, analyze yourself. (Theodore Reik, 1983/1948: pp. 147–148)

As psychoanalytically oriented therapists and group leaders, we have come a long way from Reik's lament, written over sixty years ago. In his revolutionary text, *Transference and Countertransference*, Racker (1968) described the analyst as a conflicted individual – no freer of unconscious influence than anyone else, despite training and personal psychotherapy. As a beginning group therapist, then, you might be relieved to discover that the "I" of even the seasoned professional is an admixture of healthy and neurotic tendencies. The therapist's "internal and external dependencies, anxieties, and pathological defenses . . . [respond] to every event of the analytic situation" (Racker, 1968: p. 132). The chair of a panel at the august American Psychoanalytic Association declared, "In today's world countertransference is God" (Friedman, 1997), and hailed Racker as his prophet.

The therapist's countertransference – his or her "irreducible irrational involvement" (Renik, 1993) – is inevitable and cannot be eliminated; and this is not even a desirable goal. For it is out of our full participation that we bring our own unconscious into the relationship, potentiating key interactions related to the participants' difficulties in living (Harry Stack Sullivan's phrase) that would not otherwise be discovered.

Transferences and countertransferences do not resolve but evolve, continuing to provide a rich source of potential meaning. And, while the therapist's unconscious conflicts, character structure, and misunderstandings lead to inevitable resistances in the group and its members, they also provide vehicles for learning and transmitting information.

The nineteenth century Danish philosopher, Soren Kierkegaard, offered a profound truth: "Life can only be understood backwards, but it must be lived forwards." To some extent, we characterize the therapeutic process similarly. The basic premise of the relational approach is that psychoanalytic data are mutually generated by therapist and patients, co-determined by their conscious and unconscious organizing activities, in reciprocally interacting subjective worlds (Stolorow, 1997). Relational theorists (e.g., Chused 1992; Renik 1993; Spezzano 1996) presume that patients and therapists do much if not most of their thinking unconsciously, and intersubjectively, each affecting the other.

Therefore, the participants may learn only retrospectively about what has been going on mentally, when the derivatives emerge into preconsciousness or consciousness. By that time, words and actions have produced "enactments" (Boesky, 2000; McLaughlin, 1991). These are co-created symbolic and behavioral scenarios that are learned about with the benefit of insight, hindsight, and often, with mutual feedback (*see* clinical illustration).

Relating to our topic of "me," I argue that the therapist's increasing self-awareness and understanding of one's own (inter)subjectivity is a driving force in the group and its members' development and growth. Since self-other awareness is the linchpin of any psychodynamic approach, it behooves the beginning group therapist to have had some prior experience, preferably in both individual and group treatment, as well as on-going supervision.

In my work (Billow, 2003; 2010a), I have attempted to bring relational thinking to the theories and practice of group psychotherapy. I have reconsidered W. R. Bion's seminal contributions, *Experiences in Groups* (1961), and his later writings (1962, 1963, 1965, and 1970), which have supplied the metapsychological underpinnings of my work.[1]

A Basic Human Conflict: to Think or Not to Think

Like Freud and Klein, Bion postulated basic underlying conflicts within the individual that contribute to intrapsychic and interpersonal difficulties, but also stimulate symbol and cultural development – the constructive social participation involved in talking, thinking, and learning. Freud mythologized an antagonism between the pleasure and reality principles, and between the life and death instinct. Klein narrated dynamic interplays between love and hate, and envy and reparative gratitude. Bion described how the human need to think conflicted with a desire to avoid the mental pain that accompanies thinking.

---

[1] However, my interactive style of intervention differs from Bion's, which could be "oracular" and epigrammatical. In my opinion, Bion's apparent abdication of leadership magnified his importance and increased his groups' anxiety and reliance on primitive defenses (which he referred to as the group's "*basic assumptions*" [see footnote 2]).

Aristotle declared "all men by nature desire to know" (in *Metaphysics*). Bion emphasized the relational dimension. He reasoned that we share a particularly human need to learn about our psychology and the psychologies of others.[2]

> There is a need for awareness of an emotional experience, similar to the need for an awareness of concrete objects that is achieved through the sense impressions, because lack of such awareness implies a deprivation of truth and truth seems to be essential for psychic health. The effect on the personality of such deprivation is analogous to the effect of physical starvation on the physique. (Bion, 1962: p. 56)

As group therapists, we attempt to create and sustain an evolving truth-seeking culture, inviting our members to reach for and communicate psychological awareness. But this type of thinking often hurts, since it may be confusing, anxiety arousing, and disturbing. Its truths may feel "not nice," primitive, socially inappropriate and personally embarrassing.

If experience is food for thought, one becomes what one eats, and no longer is what one was. Emotional thinking leads to the possibility of growth and change in the personality, disorienting and reorienting the thinker to past, present, and future. Again, mental pain. The person who bears to think and to learn risks ever-greater separation from established, conventional relations with others, as well as with one's previous ideas. Freud and Klein emphasized that self-knowledge brings forth the primacy of self-integration over repression and splitting; hence self-knowledge brings inner peace and social harmony. Bion emphasized that integration entails the capacity and the courage for even greater levels of emotional turbulence, existential risk, and personal and social disharmony.

A basic conflict exists within the self, and within the group and its members: tensions between motives to tolerate, develop, and integrate thought and feeling, and motives to evade the truth-seeking process. The leader displays a "questioning attitude," stimulating a group to think, to function as a "*Work Group*" (Bion, 1961). Such a group encourages both individuality and collaboration.

However, to avoid the hard work and loneliness of maintaining a "mind of one's own" (Caper, 1997), and the anticipation of painful consequences, the members of all groups have the tendency to band together with patterns of thought-evading group defenses, which Bion termed, "*basic assumptions.*"[3]

---

[2] Recent theorists have referred to this type of thinking involving emotional awareness of self and others, as "mentalizing" (Fonagy and Target, 1998).

[3] "*Basic assumptions*" refer to modes of avoiding thinking. They describe three types or constellations of primitive object relations, fantasies, and affects, which individuals come to project and act out together in social settings. The basic assumptions are *Dependency* (*baD*), *Fight/Flight* (*baF/F*), and *Pairing* (*baP*).

In *Dependency*, the members are preoccupied with seeking ministrations from, or ministrating to, the leader. In *Fight/Flight*, the members mass against an enemy, within or outside of the group; or, members may maneuver to ignore or avoid underlying hostilities. In *Pairing*, the group fastens on two members, one of whom may be the therapist, and they become the focus of group activity.

But I suggest that the therapist also participates in basic assumptions. No one is exempt from the conflict between thinking and avoiding pain and all of us may detour, delay, and obstruct learning from experience. In my opinion, all of the defining characteristics of group life – its progressive and regressive influences – are co-created, maintained, and processed intersubjectively.

The therapist is not a blank screen, oracle, or sole arbiter of psychological truth or the methods of reaching truth. He or she is a powerful presence whose subjectivity the group monitors and perceives with varying accuracy. Group members form valid and significant insights regarding the therapist's personality and the complexities of their therapist's psychology, and respond accordingly (Gill, 1994). The dynamic factor involving the group leader's psychology – the "me" – is always prominent and influential, and often apparent to group members, although not always articulated consciously or publicly.

Thinking and its evasion describe psychological dimensions of all group members' consciousness and unconsciousness, and of group's structure, culture, and process. As I illustrate in the case example, groups generate their structure, process, and meaning from the interaction between the ambivalent, conscious, and unconscious "desires to know" of the group members and the group leader.

"All About Me:" Two Broad Principles

Now, to clarify. When I declare "it's all about me" I am asserting two broad principles.

1. Every intervention the therapist makes (including silence) is filtered through his or her subjectivity, of which the therapist has imperfect knowledge. Given the leader's importance to what occurs and does not occur in group, the therapist needs to keep a "third ear" acutely attuned to "me."

    And then, there is the old joke: "Well, enough of 'me.' Let's hear about you. What do *you* think of me?" We have limited access to our own unconscious, our character, and reactivity, so we need to hear about "me" from other group members. The members respond directly and indirectly, through what they say and do not say, via symbolic derivatives (metaphors, dreams, jokes, scapegoating, *basic assumptions*), and by participating in individual, subgroup, and group resistances, rebellions, and refusals (Billow, 2010a).

2. The members' variable perceptions of who the therapist is impacts everything that takes place in group. We have just met as reader and writer. Although existing in different time and space, we are linked in a relationship, defined in part by our mutual "desire to know," and reconfigured as you confront "me."

I keep in mind the words of Emily Dickinson, the nineteenth century American poet: "Tell all the truth, but tell it slant. . . . The truth must dazzle gradually, or every man be blind." I think about "me" in planning to "go public," that is, to introduce and present my psychic truths whether in print or in a group. I try to anticipate your emotional as well as intellectual response to "me" in what you read. Thus, as we move along in this chapter, we "co-create" your experience.

I now show you how this process of being involved with "me" can work, by providing a clinical example of it not working the way I believed and wanted, until the group's interventions. Something about "me" emerged unexpectedly; it occurred in the course of a day's conference I offered during an annual meeting of the American Group Psychotherapy Association.

Clinical Illustration

Talkers and non-talkers

We began as I asked the attendees – about 30 – how they would like to spend the day, and what they wanted to accomplish. This process allows me to present myself and to make eye-to-eye contact with individuals, and for the whole group to bear witness to the ideas presented and the persons behind them. Not everyone took the opportunity to talk, of course, but there was general agreement that I would present some didactic material that would address some of the members' questions and interests, do a "fishbowl" demonstration group in the morning, and spend the afternoon conducting a full-group process experience, and end with a return to concepts and a debriefing.

From these initial interactions and onward, my impression was confirmed that this was a lively, interactive group, with some large personalities dispersed through the wide range in age and clinical training. But as we resumed after lunch, I realized that some of the attendees had spoken only minimally or not at all. I had tried to involve them, such as inviting participation with a welcoming smile, picking up on body language, and "bridging" (Ormont, 1992), as by having one member "translate" another's feelings about a third member's feelings.

Now I addressed their lack of verbal participation specifically: "You will get more from this afternoon's meeting if you say something. Even one comment gives you a new sense of the group." The room remained quiet. Then I said: "It's okay even if you grunt or groan." My humorous intervention met with some success.

"I've been wanting to talk, but I've been afraid. Thanks for noticing." The member then filled in some biographical data, as did several others who followed. Some of the active members made appreciative and encouraging gestures, but the process ran out of emotional steam, and the group turned to other interactions.

Still, I felt unsatisfied, and curious, and near midpoint in the afternoon, I said: "There seems to be two groups here – the talkers and the nontalkers." That drew the group's eyes to the verbally nonparticipating, and then I felt anxious about scapegoating them by applying peer pressure.

Someone came forth: "In my family, I was always very quiet. At home, I let my mother speak for me until I left for college."

"Who reminds you of your mother?" I asked. My goal was to encourage more individual participation and member-to-member involvement, and also, to introduce transference analysis and intrapsychic exploration in the group setting.

"I don't know . . . maybe anybody who dared to speak."

I had found a useful angle to extend participation: who reminded someone of whom, and why, and how did it feel. I was feeling relaxed and successful, until an attendee broached what seemed like a change of direction:

"If I were running this group, I'd want to know what I did to cause the 'two groups'."

I felt embarrassed, as if accused of not practising what I preach about considering the impact of "me," but the comment was delivered respectfully, and I answered in the same way.

"What do you think I did to cause subgrouping?"

"You like people who talk."

Several members came to my rescue: "Well, he was faced with a new group, of course he wanted people to talk." "He tried to bring people in, he's doing it now [and to the person who posed the challenge], you tried too."

But I thought the comment deserved a fuller consideration and, in thinking about it, I felt inspiration in the question I had posed a few moments earlier: the topic of family relations and intragroup transferences. I shared an insight that felt sudden and intense: "Well, I was the first born in my family, and I maintained my position by doing a lot of talking."

In conducting groups, I do not make a habit of intentionally self-revealing, but here saw no reason to be evasive. Now other people pressed to talk, and we discovered that for the participants of the non-talker subgroup, silence had different meanings and motivations. I kept further introspections to myself.

"This is my first workshop as a member. I did not know what to expect. I never heard of you but I liked the topic [the "3 Rs," see Billow, 2010a]. Since I'm going to start working with drug addicts next month, I thought I better learn about refusing. I'm learning a lot anyway. Am I resisting, rebelling, or refusing? I don't know yet."

"I'm here because my professor is here, and [humorously] she threatened to flunk us if we didn't come. She didn't say we had to talk."

"Yes, me too, we read your papers in her class. They were real good, although I can't say I understood them or this group [laughter]."

I reflected that it takes courage for the students and teachers to mix it up in this group setting, with expanded boundaries and rules of exchange.

A woman spoke up: "I must come out of the closet. I'm the 'mean' teacher. I've been so impressed by your writings, Dr Billow, that I guess I feel intimidated."

I lightened the atmosphere by saying that other people must be a lot less impressed because they seem comfortable calling me "Richard" and challenging me to think about what I've been doing.

More people took chances with themselves in reflecting on the "two groups":

"I was the 'golden boy' in my family. Talking, but not talking too much. I want to be the golden boy in your group. Just me. [Humorously] Am I being it now?"

"I was the second fiddle. I feel like that here, and that's why I haven't revealed myself. I have to think about my responsibility. You welcomed me, several times."

"I was my parents' 'joy', their 'ray of sunshine.' [and with irony] See how I always smile and am seen and not heard."

A young man volunteered: "Maybe I've been Cinderella here, waiting to be invited to the ball. I need to man up, I got my own balls."

We turned to the professor self-described as "mean," who seemed to be crying: "In my family, I was the oldest, and my job was to take care of my siblings, as they arrived, one by one. But I liked it. My parents weren't close, I was afraid of my father and my mother wasn't very warm either. I wanted to have my students here. [Turning to them] I felt you would make me feel safe and secure. Thanks for coming. . . . You all get an A," she said, smiling between visible tears.

One of the members who had tried to shield me from criticism joined in: "I had to protect my mother. She has 'issues' and gets depressed. When you blamed Richard for creating the 'two groups,' I worried that he would fall apart. I'm always worried that my patients are going to fall apart, and then my psychotherapy group that I run. I see that not happening here."

With some sadness, we drew the group process to a close. During the debriefing and evaluation, one of the members complimented me for the day, but wondered: "Could you have achieved the same results if you had stayed out . . . and not worked so hard?"

Discussion

1. "Me": A fratricidal leader

Cain said to his brother Abel, "Let's go out to the field." And while they were in the field, Cain attacked his brother Abel and killed him. (Genesis 4:8)

It snowed last year too: I made a snowman and my brother knocked it down and I knocked my brother down and then we had tea. (Dylan Thomas, 1954: p. 12)

To illustrate the effect of intersubjective factors on group formation and process, I share some personal thoughts.

Freud (1921, pp. 120–121) traced the development of our inclination to group (gregariousness) to the reaction against the initial envy and aggression an older child experiences to the arrival of a younger sibling – who now is a rival for the leader's (i.e., the father's) attention. Whereas this hypothesis seems not applicable universally,[4] it may partially explain my own interest in groups and my style of leadership.

I could easily justify my technical approach to the silent members: after all, people unfold at different times, and not always verbally. And besides, some of them had asked questions at the workshop's beginning – and I kept in mind and addressed the questions throughout the morning. However, I came to realize that projection, envy, rivalry, guilt, and reparation were among the emotional elements I utilized – for better and worse – in conducting the workshop. As we know, silent members and subgroups exert power, and may even hold a group hostage, demanding special attention by their very quietness. In terms of my psychology, of which I was not conscious at the time, such individuals represented my younger brother.

I felt envious of the attention he received, and interested in him too. His emotional unavailability was irritating and intriguing, and both stimulated and frustrated my curiosity. I provoked him to respond, teasing, wrestling, socking him when necessary, which was often. In my reflective, adult consciousness, I know (and probably knew as a child) that he wished to isolate himself from any unpleasant intensity of our family. Selective withdrawal seemed to be beyond my emotional capabilities. In my on-going unconsciousness, he was (and is) a rivalrous model of a "better" type of individual, one self-contained and without need.

In the group, the quiet members entered my unconsciousness as rivals too, competing with the talkative ones, which included me, for my attention (as father-leader) and for the group's attention (my "parents"). I could easily express curiosity, fight and embrace the talkative ones. Whether they were friendly or hostile, I knew who they were, and I "liked" them. In terms of infantile narcissism, they were reflections of "me." I resented the quiet ones, the "better than us," who deigned not to participate in the intensity of our group. Caught between deciding to kill or love – ignore or attend to – the quiet ones, I tried both.

2. The group reveals "me" before I find myself

Self-disclosure is inevitable and continuous in any human interaction. Even classically oriented psychoanalysts, such as Ralph Greenson, have acknowledged that as therapists, "everything we do or say, or don't do or say, from the décor of our office, the magazines in the waiting room, the way we open the door, greet the patient, make interpretations, keep silent, and end the hour, reveals something about our real self and not only our professional self" (1967: p. 91).

Some writers have argued that because the therapist cannot help being self-disclosing, why not consider the opportunity to make explicit that which reveals

---

[4] Freud contradicted Trotter's view, stating that man is not a herd animal but a horde animal that seeks and follows a leader to assure mutual protection against siblings and the leader himself. Ethnologists confirm Trotter's hypothesis over Freud's. In studying diverse animal groups, schools of fish, flocks of bids, herds or packs of animal, Lorenz (1952) found little evidence of autocratic authority. At seemingly all levels of the animal hierarchy, instinctive gregariousness manifests as complex inter-relational social behavior (Conacher, 1998: p. 225). Trotter characterized three types of herds: defensive herds, which band together for survival against predators; predatory packs, which coordinate their behavior to secure prey; socialized groups, in which the individual devotes itself to the group, as the bee, ant, or sheep (Conacher, 1998).

oneself to be emotionally involved? Relational therapists reserve the option to gradually and purposefully reveal aspects of themselves, in an attempt to model openness, to propel patients to deal more realistically with the nature and basis of their beliefs, to encourage mutual exploration of interactional dynamics, and to take responsibility for their actions and effects on the other (Blechner, 1996; Ehrenberg 1995; Davies, 1994; Gerson, 1994; Jacobs 1991; Little, 1951; Searles 1979; Winnicott 1949).

The lines between intentional and unintentional self-disclosure are ambiguous and fluctuating. The therapist's behaviors may range from spontaneous exclamation to measured revelation, from those that are seemingly consciously determined to those unconsciously enacted. Levels of meaning, revealed by subtleties in timing, tone, and cadence, may contradict what is verbally spoken (Chused, 1991; McLaughlin, 1991).

When the group therapist utilizes him or herself in an open, spontaneous manner, the therapist may be producing more obvious disclosures, or different types of disclosures, than those that also occur in traditional individual or group technique.

One issue to consider in taking or avoiding the opportunity for self-disclosure is whether it serves to open or close things up, a question that may be answered only retrospectively, and even then without certainty that another way may not have been better (Aron, 1996; Greenberg, 1995). Group members see a therapist-in-action, responding to intense group, subgroup, and dyadic situations. The perspectives are multiple, and members may not be in agreement with each other, and much less with the therapist. Still, the therapist learns about "me" by attending to these various perspectives: listening to the members' expressions in feelings, fantasies, symbols (e.g., metaphors, jokes, dreams), thoughts, behavioral reactions, and reflecting on how he or she impacts the group culture (e.g., as in co-creating the "two groups").

We may directly invite members to share their opinions. I question my work, often asking members what they think I am doing, and why, and could they or I have done it differently, and better. I respect that I do not have full command of how I feel and respond; I cannot and do not want to be a "blank screen." Signs that I "like people who talk" were many and obvious to certain members and not all of them are evident to me now. I am now more acutely aware of the possible differences in enthusiasm in which I invite, meet, and sustain the gaze of various group members, and also, more aware of their visual and bodily reactions to me. My "liking" was co-regulated, encouraged by some (the talkers), and held in abeyance by others (the nontalkers).

In the development of human attachment, a prolonged period of mutual, "eye love" (Beebe and Stern, 1977) between mother and infant occurs, involving not only the visual sense, but also touch, sound, and movement (exteroception-interoception). In this "dance," each partner enjoyably takes into account and makes moment-by-moment adjustments in response to the other's shifts in behaviors (Beebe and Lachmann, 2002; Beebe and Stern, 1977; Stern, 1971; Tronick, 1989).

So, who did what to cause the "two groups"? It was not me alone who decided whom I "danced" with, and when. The therapist cannot expect to be aware and in control of all, or even, many of the group members' varied and variable transferences to the leader, other members, and to the group situation itself. Like the mother, the therapist needs to maintain relaxed but intense interest, empowering the members to seek and avoid engagement, without anxiously "chasing" after them. I believe that even with my inevitable clinical and personal shortcomings, my behaviors of "liking" were sufficiently well distributed to propel bonding, mutual recognition, and the development of the group's identity. In being (selectively) self-revealing, I took responsibility for "me" – acknowledging and expanding on the group member's insight regarding my contribution in "sucking" (Horowitz, 1983) members into their respective roles. This seemed to encourage members to take responsibility for their "me's" too: discovering in their respective psychologies and personal histories the emotional equipment for the part they played and their influence on others. In our group, the technical decision seemed to have facilitated greater openness among members and furthered the development of group autonomy and cohesiveness.

3. Emotional co-participation: loving, hating, and being curious in the group

In my view, psychoanalytic treatment is not about cure, but about transforming pain into the richer capacity to "suffer" meaning. To drive change and stimulate creative growth, the therapist needs to provide an on-going sense of security, but also must encourage a breaking down of pre-established and safe emotional attitudes. Leadership entails aiding the group and its members to tolerate, communicate, and eventually integrate a wide range of emerging, contradictory, and intense feelings.

However, often our group members come to treatment to be relieved of pain, and they initially may display little tolerance for increasing the range of felt feelings, or for understanding and integrating them in their communications to others. It is often left to the therapist to suffer mental pain, to think about the feelings of the group, including one's own, and those operative and those denied. Hypothetically, our emotions derive from basic affects, drives, or "instincts," involved in loving (attachment or bonding), expressing frustration-aggression (hating), and exercising curiosity.[5] While these affects are basic, they do not operate in pure form. Like everyone else, it is difficult for the therapist to "know" what he or she feels, or "really feels." Feelings hide behind their opposites, and defense mechanisms of denial, dissociation, reaction formation, and projection are to be expected, particularly in situations of anxiety and conflict.

I function as leader with a sense of anxiety, co-existing with confidence, that something unknown about myself will emerge, and that I will learn and grow from each group session. I attempt to monitor my affects, and to be open to the feedback from others. How loving and empathic do I feel? How frustrated, impatient, angry, or hateful do I feel? How interested am I in myself and in the group? How am I utilizing these affects to link up with the members and with the group as a whole? Thinking about my affects brings some self-awareness to the therapeutic reality of the group, as I experience it.

In the group under discussion, one simple sentence jarred me out of any complacent fantasy being in full command of how I felt and what I was doing. "You like people who talk." My "not nice" feelings were exposed, and I felt guilty, personally and professionally deficient. For the group member was implying that I did not like

---

[5] Bion (1962) provided a shorthand, *L*, *H*, and *K*, respectively, the drive to love, to hate, and to know about.

people who did not talk (H), and did not embrace them with full curiosity (K). The communication had a ring of truth, and "suffering" the meaning-making process provided access to my love and compassion (L) towards these same members, my brother, and myself as well.

I had believed I was working with professional ease and competence, eliciting involvement from a significant segment of the attendees. I do not think too many observers would disagree with this perspective. But other perspectives jarred me out of any tendency to rest secure in my relative comfort zone: "You like people who talk;" "If I were running this group, I'd want to know what I did to cause the 'two groups';" "Could you have achieved the same results if you had stayed out?"

I cannot say I found these remarks to be pleasant – but they were on point and deserved to be respected as legitimate responses to "me" and my impact, and not prematurely interpreted as "transference," "resistance," an expression of a "*basic assumption*," and so forth. In terms of my functioning as a clinician, I had to re-evaluate my feelings, technical actions, and even, my very way of "being."

Freud counseled the analyst: "It must not be forgotten that the things one hears are for the most part things whose meaning is only recognized later on" (Freud, 1912: p. 112). I could only understand my feelings about what I was experiencing some of the time, and my understanding was partial. Most difficult to sort out and bring to meaning were probably the very reactions that had the most "causal" influence on the group!

Becoming aware of avoided feelings allows the therapist some control over expressing them, and to function with fuller emotional co-participation. I did not wish to banish my negative feelings towards the non-talkers, but I wanted to know where they came from, and how they affected my group relationships. Then I would be able to use a fuller array of feelings, and with greater clinical acumen.

Racker (1968) suggested that a neglected aspect of the Oedipus complex was the analyst's wish to be master or king, not only of other people, but also of one's own unconscious. The best the therapist can do is to eradicate, as much as he or she can, not anxieties, resistances, wishes, and fears, but their repression. In being receptive to the infantile, primitive, and neurotic aspects of one's own personality, the therapist may more fully experience one's own experience, and this is, I believe, the precondition that allows the therapist to help the group members do the same.

We are humbled by the awareness that our words and actions are partially derivatives of an unfolding (and evolving) conscious/nonconsciousness, and that we cannot fully understand ourselves before or even after we communicate. Authentic communications represent the therapist's most profound insights and powerful intentions. Yet, they remain only "best guesses" of emotional truth – what we feel, think, and decide is appropriate to express – to be reevaluated and revised as we continue to participate in here-and-now clinical experience.

4. Activity level of the relational group therapist

Of all the comments, questions, criticisms directed to me during our six-hour group, one rankles my retrospections: "Could you have gotten the same results if you had stayed out and not worked so hard?" I heard my mother's voice behind the question: "Why can't you behave like your brother!" Who was this questioner, I wondered, a junior colleague or critical competitor, friend or foe? Given my emotional involvement with my family of origin, I could not be sure of the accuracy of my judgment, then, or now. As much as I hated the comment and the commentator, I took it and him as sincerely curious, and I respectfully replied that my way of working was something he and other people could think about. The nineteenth century poet, William Blake, penned these cautionary lines:

> The questioner, who sits so sly,
> Shall never know how to reply.
> He who replies to words of doubt
> Doth put the light of knowledge out.
>
> William Blake, *Auguries of Innocence*

I did not wish to intellectually reduce the experience and provide premature closure. Besides, a didactic rationale would have felt defensive. But here I will offer my point of view, which puts the "me," the group leader or therapist's experience, as a center of action. The major group theorists have described groups as organic entities, evolving through stages, rebounding from one defensive position to another in accordance with developmental conflicts consequent to group membership. According to their theories, successful groups depend on the therapist's effective performance in pre-therapy tasks such as patient selection, composition and preparation, and in negotiating the novice group through its formative stages of boundary formation, structuring, resistance, and goal direction. It follows that the mature group more often treats itself, coming to appreciate the therapist as a consultant rather than as the continuing mesmerizer of transference (Agazarian, 1997; Ettin, 1992; Foulkes and Anthony, 1957; Rutan and Stone, 2001).

The founder of the Group Analytic movement, Foulkes, wrote that the group therapist "does not step down but lets the group, in steps and stages, bring him down to earth. . . . [the group] replaces the leader's authority" (Foulkes, 1964: p. 61). Along this line of thinking, Yalom presented the maxim: "Unlike the individual therapist, the group therapist does not have to be the axle of therapy. In part, you are midwife to the group: you must set a therapeutic process in motion and take care not to interfere with that process by insisting on your centrality" (Yalom, 1995: p. 216).

In my opinion, while the classic contributions in theory and in descriptive phenomenology are fundamentals of every group therapist's thinking and practice, the emphasis on member-inspired dynamics seriously underplays the enduring role of the therapist, most particularly, the authority of the therapist's evolving psychology on what occurs and does not occur in group. The therapist remains the figure of inspiration, and the most important member of any group, no matter its focus or duration. Therapist-influenced dynamics supersede the clinician's theoretical or technical orientation, and we sometimes achieve more, or less, in our practise than what we preach. Our amiable, sincere, and patient efforts to reach the group count for a lot, and we fumble and are forgiven for our fumbling more than we know. No school of thought owns exclusive or automatic rights to empathy, or to understanding of the self and others. In our striving for depth, clinicians of all theoretical persuasions may miss what is timely and most relevant.

Whereas the focus of this chapter is on the leader or therapist's affects, thought, and clinical behavior, and their influence on the group, subgroup, and individual members, I appreciate that change flows not only from the efforts of that individual. A restrictive focus on the leader, or for that matter, any predetermined theoretical-technical orientation, neglects other important group, subgroup, and intrapersonal factors, other ways in which experience may be generated and understood.

Indeed, although I conceptualize leader or therapist-inspired dynamics as a prevailing influence behind group interactions, I appreciate that the force of these dynamics are modulated by the nature of the group situation. Transferences (and countertransferences) and other intersubjective interactions are multiple in group, and may be directed to individuals other than the leader of course, to dyads, subgroups and the whole group (as in the case example). Leader or therapist-specific transferences are also deflected onto the group and its members, where their diverse manifestations may be understood and eventually interpreted.

Members and leaders derive benefit from multiple factors of group participation; each group is unique and its constituents provide a wide range of interpersonal options and therapeutic effects. Important, too, are cultural, ethnic, and political factors that contribute to the group's organization, functioning, and goals (Hopper, 2003).

We may think about the question: "Could you have achieved the same results if . . .?" without concluding that there is one way, or a best way. Each group leader or therapist plays his or her own music, as well as captures a particular version of the music of others. While some notes resound forcefully, others remain faint, distant, or unheard, and they wait for their development on other occasions, with other players from within and without the group.

I believe it is important to interact spontaneously and maintain a down-to-earth manner. After all, we want this type of verbal behavior from our group members. The inexpressive leader appears self-absorbed, an artifact that calls attention to itself. The infrequency of this type of leader's interventions augments their strength and tendency to sound oracular. It is quite possible that the technique of minimalist intervention derives from the classical model of psychoanalysis, in which, theoretically, interpretations are reserved to associative blocks connected to transference (Halton, 1999).

I share my thinking often, even when it may not be entirely welcomed. While I do not rush to make judgments and form conclusions, I value the interpretative mode in group as well as in individual analysis, which may be addressed to the group-as-a-whole, subgroups, or individuals. An intervention does not become a "group interpretation" because it is given in the form "we," "all of us," or "the group seems to believe that." Neither does it become an individual interpretation because it is directed to and concerned with any particular individual (Foulkes 1964: p. 163). An interpretation directed to the group may not be experienced as applying to all the members, and certainly, no therapist can be certain that the interpretation does apply to all, or reaches each member equally or in the same spirit. And on the other hand, interventions directed to an individual or subgroup are witnessed by the group at large, and are reflected upon and integrated by the entire membership to varying degrees.

I believe that there are no clear demarcations between interpretation and other forms of interventions. As do most contemporary therapists, I keep in mind the members and the group's developmental and on-going needs, and accept the legitimacy of noninterpretative activity involved in symbolic play and certain other forms of enactments.

Being "active" and "leader-focused" may eventuate in being attentively quiet. Bion wrote about nonverbal containment: how the therapist's capacity for "reverie" (dream-like, internal free-association), patience, and inner security communicate something crucially important, even curative, furthering the group members' capacity to tolerate powerful affects and develop emotional thoughts. Such introspective activity relating to self-other containment is particularly important when the therapist or leader feels a rising tide of anger and disappointment – whether emanating from the self or membership.

A group therapist's respectful silence or brief appreciative acknowledgment in the face of an apprehensive member's challenge or overt hostility may be a powerful, even decisive intervention. Conversely, verbal formulations that reach into the realm of unconscious phenomena, involving constellations of fantasy, desire, anxiety, character, and defense, rightly may be valued for their effort and concern as much as for their acuity and depth.

This brings us to the question of "truth," the accuracy of the therapist's interpretative thoughts and interventions. Group leadership involves holding the tension of truth as best as one understands it, and deciding how, when, and how much to convey, and to whom. Values and practical considerations exist in tension. We rarely live up to the "should books" provided by theorists and writers such as myself. To lead well, we must live with inconsistency and paradox, attempt to find balance without definitive solutions, and accept the nonexistence of the perfect option, flawlessly applied. Growth remains possible and likely, if the leader remains thoughtful, invitational to feedback, and self-critical as to what is achieved.

I have offered my opinion: groups – small and large – intuit their therapist or leader's orientation, both technical and personal, and to some extent respond accordingly. As in this example drawn from an experiential workshop but applicable to psychotherapy groups, members adapt to the leader's personality characteristics – and vice-versa. When groups function constructively, participants learn from each other how to tolerate difference, and also, to come together to function as a working unit. They negotiate, compromise, and "match up" to assure efficacy.

I attempt to be personable, maintain a light touch, and not function as a mysterious figure, invulnerable to feeling or feedback, or a "know-it-all." When I am confused or unsure, which is often, I may seek clarity from other group members, although I do not necessarily agree with or follow their guidelines. In the group under discussion, I asked for help, and achieved insight, which inspired me to develop the thoughts in this chapter. And also, I received several jolts of pain; their effects linger.

Concluding Remarks

The leader or therapist's subjectivity – the complex of basic affects, feelings, thoughts, fantasies, many of which remain out of awareness – affect how we comport ourselves, how we relate to our groups, and how they relate to us. Using myself as an example,

I have illustrated how unresolved Oedipal and sibling dynamics were involved in my perceptions, theory, and technique – perhaps in every micro-action and interaction that comprised the group experience.

The variety and flexibility of the group leader or therapist's activity, internal and interpersonal, exposes the qualities of care and establishes authenticity (Billow, 2010b, 2010c). Through his or her behavior, the group leader or therapist defines the working group culture: how group relationships and experiences are to be regarded, and the emotional depth to which exchanges may be considered.

The technical focus may be *intrapersonal,* concentrating on the individual, *transactional* or *interpersonal,* concentrating on the subgroups and dyads, *group-as-a-whole,* concentrating on group dynamics (Parloff, 1968), or more likely, an eclectic mix of the three approaches. The clinician's basic patternings of subjective experience influences, often determines, not only the focus, but also the group's depth of functioning, even the particular process and contents of the session.

All psychoanalytic psychotherapy is grounded on Freud's belief that the understanding of others is based on self-understanding. However, self-understanding is an evolving, affective process, stimulating strong and often painful emotions that influence and are influenced by others. Self-awareness remains tentative and uncertain, and is revised according to the shifting currents of present-day reality. Inspection, introspection, retrospection, the longevity and stability of a group, these factors do not vouchsafe objectivity or inoculate therapists from the tendency to rationalize who we are, how we feel, and what we are doing.

We cannot be sure of all the factors that drove the process of the group under discussion, the accuracy of my evaluations of the interactional dynamics, or even the emotional realities that I have described. The leader or therapist cannot neatly separate self from others and from the group at large. Emotional reality is not a concrete, unchanging something, from which truth can be derived with certainty or finality, but an ever-incomplete process of becoming. The group leader and member's communications are intersubjectively constructed; their intent and effect remains highly personal, and no final, or even fully objective, assessment is possible.

Whatever the leader or therapist is attending to, he or she is also reflecting upon and revealing oneself, influencing other members – and you, the reader – in this process. Contemplating one's evolving mental relationship to the group, and its influence on the group, brings layers of meaning to the here-and-now clinical situation, however conceptualized. All benefit from a group leader or therapist unequivocally involved in "me," in personal discovery and growth.

References and Bibliography

Agazarian, Y. M. (1997). *Systems-centered therapy for groups.* New York: Guilford.

Aron, L. (1996). *A meeting of minds: mutuality in psychoanalysis.* Hillsdale, New Jersey: The Analytic Press.

Beebe, B., & Lachmann, F. (2002). *Infant research and adult treatment: co-constructing interactions.* Hillsdale, New Jersey: The Analytic Press.

Beebe, B., & Stern, D. N. (1977). Engagement-disengagement and early object experiences. In N. Freedman & S. Grand, (Eds.), *Communicative structures and psychic structures* (pp. 35–55). New York: Plenum Press.

Billow, R. M. (2003). *Relational group psychotherapy: From basic assumptions to passion.* London & Philadelphia: Jessica Kingsley Publishers.

Billow, R. M. (2010a). *Resistance, rebellion and refusal in groups: The 3 Rs.* London: Karnac.

Billow, R. M. (2010b). Modes of therapeutic engagement: Part I: Diplomacy and integrity. *International Journal of Group Psychotherapy, 60,* 1–28.

Billow, R. M. (2010c). Modes of therapeutic engagement: Part II: Sincerity and authenticity. *International Journal of Group Psychotherapy, 60,* 29–58.

Bion, W. R. (1961). *Experiences in groups.* London: Tavistock.

Bion, W. R. (1962). *Learning from experience.* London: Heinemann. Reprinted in 1977: *Seven servants: Four works by Wilfred R. Bion.* New York: Aronson.

Bion, W. R. (1963). *Elements of psycho-analysis.* London: Heinemann. Reprinted in 1977: *Seven servants: Four works by Wilfred R. Bion.* New York: Aronson.

Bion, W. R. (1965). *Transformations.* London: Heinemann. Reprinted in 1977: *Seven servants: Four works by Wilfred R. Bion.* New York: Aronson.

Bion, W. R. (1970). *Attention and Interpretation.* London: Tavistock. Reprinted in 1977: *Seven servants: Four works by Wilfred R. Bion.* New York: Aronson.

Blechner, M. (1996). Psychoanalysis in and out of the closet. In B. Gerson (Ed.), *The therapist as a person.* Hillsdale, New Jersey: Analytic Press.

Boesky, D. (2000). Affect, language, and communication. *International Journal of Psychoanalysis, 81,* 257–262.

Caper, R. (1997). A mind of one's own. *International Journal of Psychoanalysis, 78,* 265–278.

Chused, J. (1991). The evocative power of enactments. *Journal of the American Psychoanalytic Association, 39,* 615–640.

Chused, J. (1992). The patient's perception of the analyst. *Psychoanalytic Quarterly, 63,* 161–184.

Conacher, G. N. (1998). Disorders of mythopoiesis. *Journal of the Royal Society of Medicine, 91,* 225–228.

Davies, J. (1994). Love in the afternoon: A relational reconsideration of desire and dread in the countertransference. *Psychoanalytic Dialogues, 44,* 155–170.

Dickinson, E. (1960). Tell all the truth but tell it slant. In: Thomas H. Johnson (Ed.), *The complete poems of Emily Dickinson.* Boston: Little, Brown.

Ehrenberg, D. B. (1995). Self-disclosure: Therapeutic tool or indulgence? *Contemporary Psychoanalysis, 31,* 213–228.

Ettin, M. (1992). *Foundations and applications of group psychotherapy.* Boston: Allyn & Bacon.

Fonagy, P., & Target, M. (1998) Mentalization and the changing aims of child psychoanalysis. *Psychoanalytic Dialogues, 8,* 87–114.

Foulkes, S. H. & Anthony, E. J. (1957). *Group psychotherapy.* New York: Penguin.

Freud, S. (1912) The dynamics of transference. *Standard edition, 12.*

Freud, S. (1921) *Group psychology and the analysis of the ego. Standard edition, 18,* 67–144.

Friedman, L. (1997). Classics revisited: Heinrich Racker's *Transference and countertransference.* Panel held at the Spring Meeting of the American Psychoanalytic Association. L. Friedman (Chair), Los Angeles, May 3, 1996. Also, *Journal of the American Psychoanalytic Association, 45,* 1253–1259.

Gerson, B. (1994). An analyst's pregnancy loss and its effects on treatment: Disruption and growth. *Psychoanalytic Dialogues, 4,* 1–17.

Gill, M. M. (1994). *Psychoanalysis in transition.* Hillsdale, New Jersey: Analytic Press.

Greenberg, J. (1995). Self-disclosure: Is it psychoanalytic? *Contemporary Psychoanalysis, 31,* 193–205.

Greenson, R. (1967). *The Technique and Practice of Psychoanalysis.* New York: International Univesities Press.

Halton, M. (1999). Bion, Foulkes and the Oedipal situation. In C. Oakley (Ed.), *What is a group? A new look at theory in practice*. London: Rebus.

Hoffman, I. Z. (1996). The intimate and ironic authority of the psychoanalyst's presence. *Psychoanalytic Quarterly*, 65, 102–136.

Hopper, E. (2003). *The social unconscious. Selected papers*. London: Jessica Kingsley.

Horowitz, L. (1983). Projective identification in dyads and groups. *International Journal of Group Psychotherapy*, 33, 259–279.

Jacobs, T. (1991). *The Use of the Self: Countertransference and Communication in the Analytic Situation*. Madison, Connecticut: International Universities Press.

Little, M. (1951). Counter-transference and the patient's response to it. *International Journal of Psychoanalysis*, 32, 32–40.

Lorenz, K. (1952). *King Solomon's Ring*. New York: Thomas Y. Crowell.

McLaughlin, J. (1991). Clinical and theoretical aspects of enactment. *Journal of the American Psychoanalytic Association*, 29, 595–614.

Ormont, L. R. (1992). *The group therapy experience*. New York: St. Martins.

Parloff, M. (1968). Analytic group therapy. In J. Marmor (Ed.), *Modern Psychoanalysis*. New York: Basic Books.

Racker, H. (1968). *Transference and countertransference*. Madison: Connecticut: International Universities Press.

Reik, T. (1983). (Original work published 1948). *Listening with the Third Ear*. New York: Farrar, Straus & Giroux Paperbacks.

Renik, O. (1993). Analytic interaction: Conceptualizing technique in light of the analyst's irreducible subjectivity. *Psychoanalytic Quarterly*, 62, 553–571.

Rutan, J. S., & Stone, W. (2001). *Psychodynamic group therapy* (3rd ed). New York: Guilford Press.

Searles, H. (1979). *Countertransference and related subjects*. New York: International Universities Press.

Spezzano, C. (1996). The three faces of two-person psychology: Development, ontology, and epistemology. *Psychoanalytic Dialogues*, 6, 599–621.

Stern, D. N. (1971). A microanalysis of mother-infant interaction. *Journal of the American Academy of Child Psychiatry*, 10, 501–517.

Thomas, D. (1954). *A child's christmas in Wales*. New York: New Directions.

Tronick, E. (1989). Emotions and emotional communication in infants. *American Psychologist*, 44, 112–119.

Trotter, W. (1953) *Instincts of the herd in peace and war, 1916–1919*. London: Oxford University Press.

Winnicott, D. W. (1949). Hate in the countertransference. *International Journal of Psychoanalysis*, 30, 69-75.

Yalom, I. (1995). *The theory and practice of group psychotherapy* (4th ed.). New York: Basic Books.

9
Resonance among Members and its Therapeutic Value in Group Psychotherapy
Avi Berman

"Resonance" is one of the basic concepts in group analysis which represents a psychodynamic perspective of group therapy. Based mainly on psychoanalytic theory and practice, group analysis explores the matrix of communication between people, which may be transformed into therapeutic contribution. Resonance is a primal unconscious and spontaneous communication between people in which all-human themes inspire each other, forming an interpersonal group mind and common emotional experience.

In psychotherapy, "Resonance" is an acoustic metaphor for human interaction, which draws on the phenomenon in which "a sound is reinforced by reflection or specifically by synchronous vibration" (Oxford English Dictionary). The sound (vibration) of one string may evoke a different sound from another nearby string of the same pitch (frequency).

In group analysis the term "Resonance" was suggested by Foulkes (1977) as he noticed some spontaneous unconscious, verbal or non-verbal interaction between members in the group that resembled for him strings that vibrate and reinforce each other. "The individual resonates in the key to which he is attuned, in which his specific personality structure is set. . . . the term resonance underlines that this happens quite instinctively and inevitably. Each individual member picks out from the common pool what is relevant to him" (Foulkes, 1977: pp. 298–299).

According to Foulkes (1977), resonance always takes into account the unconscious meaning and the "wavelength of the stimulating event," faithfully and correctly. In the analytic group individuals not only resonate on a large scale to each other, simultaneously and reciprocally, but also to the group as a whole and particularly to the group conductor, who in turn is influenced by his own resonance. Under the conditions which we create in these groups, that which is deeply individual material is also shared in the group itself. Thus what is unknown and unknowable to each individual member is nevertheless activated by this common process and is in this way also fed back into the common matrix.

The term resonance is introduced today into psychoanalysis especially through the relational perspective which underlines reciprocal unconscious influence of both the patient and the analyst. Resonance is considered as a basic aspect of human communication. For example, Mitchell (2000) uses the term as being a part of human affective permeability. He writes in surprisingly similar terms to those used by Foulkes decades earlier. "Affect is contagious, and, on the deepest level, affective states are often transpersonal. Intense affects like anxiety, sexual excitement, rage, depression, and euphoria tend to generate corresponding affects in others. Early in life, on the deepest unconscious levels throughout life, affects are evoked interpersonally through dense resonance between people, without regards for who, is feeling what" (Mitchell, 2000: p. 61).

It seems that the psycho-neurological discovery of the mirror neuron system (Iacoboni, 2008) had created a basis for better understanding resonance (and mirroring) as the innate and earliest form of human communication. Mirror neuron systems demonstrate how expressions of feelings, behavior and verbal communication in one person stirs the same reaction in another person's brain and duplicates the experience in someone else's mind. "The registration of other people's experience is 'wired' into brain structure, much like vision, hearing, or movement itself" (Seligman, 2009). Minds that are mutually connected through mirror neuron systems form together what we may term a "we-self." Reis (2009) suggests that resonance is one form of mirror neuron communication. It is immediate and prereflective.

When resonance is elaborated through self-reflection and verbal conceptualization it may create more developed forms of communication. Our conscious experience of empathy and identifications are probably based on spontaneous and immediate resonance reactions elaborated by reflection and thinking. Projective identification may demonstrate what is probably a phase in the reflective and verbalization of resonance into more developed communications forms. In this phase, mutual emotional experience is still preconscious and the sense differentiation between subjects is blurred.

I would like to demonstrate the spontaneous enactment of resonance between two members in a therapy group through the following example.

Clinical Illustration

Sara is a new member in the group. She is 28 years old, an intelligent and elegant looking woman. She never imagined herself turning to therapy, let alone going to a group therapy. It had been always difficult for her to self-disclose herself to other people. Although she yearned for love and intimacy, her relations with men were short and superficial. She had been referred to my group by a psychiatrist who met Sara after talking with one of her superiors in the bank where she worked. Her superior told her that she was a good candidate for promotion, but they noticed how difficult it was for her to talk with other people, work colleagues and clients alike. She looked tense and avoidant. They needed her to be more open and friendly. They suggested that she speak to a psychiatrist. She did, and started taking some medication that really calmed her down but unfortunately made her more shameful and even more socially avoidant.

The group members welcomed her warmly. At that stage they had already gained significant trust in each other and in me as their conductor. They could identify with her anxiety of feeling like a stranger among strangers. Sara came to each session hesitantly, smiling, not talking, sipping silently from a small bottle of water and trying to hide herself throughout the meeting. The other members turned to her from time to time, inviting her in but mainly they just let her be.

As a conductor I preferred to avoid putting any pressure on this young woman. I made sure to address her at least once during every session and wait patiently for further developments. In group therapy, as I see it, the members, partly through resonance, take part in building the psychotherapeutic value. In this case, something new happened spontaneously through the participation of another member, Daniel.

Daniel was a young man in his twenties. He had been a member in the group since its beginning. He worked in a software company as a programmer and was an amateur actor. He was shy and hesitant and had some difficulties addressing women and forming relations with them. He was greatly encouraged in the group, firstly by understanding his experiences of exclusion, having come from a lower social class into an arrogant high school class. As he gained more self confidence in the group, through the support and empathy of the other members, he began to dare more and took more risks in his life. He began to sing and play his guitar in front of young audiences. When he shared this with the group he was loved and admired by all the members.

This proved to be an inspiring event for others and for several weeks some other members came back to the group with some new beginnings in their lives.

Yet, the atmosphere in one of the next sessions was very different. Daniel asked to speak first. He looked tense and sad. The group became very attentive immediately. Daniel took us back five years to his great journey to India. This was, as we could understand, some sort of an initiation quest for him. It had begun joyfully: a small group of three friends went together to India on their own, into the unknown, far away from their parents. They had had some great times together, enjoying parties on the beach, dancing to Indian music and trying some local Indian drugs.

Daniel went into great detail. Gradually the group members and myself grasped that some important punch-line was waiting for us further on at some point. There in India Daniel met a girl, they fell in love and they became a couple. They traveled together for three months. At first they enjoyed closeness and harmony but later Daniel became tense and reserved and she became angry and dissatisfied. The drugs didn't work too well any more. On the contrary: he then felt more anxious and suspicious. Conflicts caused distance between them and eventually they broke up. Daniel went to Thailand and then traveled back home.

At this point in the group, Daniel became silent for a couple of minutes. Then came the punch-line: as he came back home he was so anxious and frightened that he needed to see a psychiatrist. He had to take psychiatric medication and. . . . Yes he is still on them.

Daniel's self-disclosure was elaborated in the group for several sessions, among other themes. It became clear that he could not enjoy the members' affection and appreciation without telling them the painful (shameful) truth about himself. Most of the group members could understand him. Most of them reacted with empathy and support. Yet two members expressed their reservations. One woman, Hanna, who was older than most of them said that drugs probably ruined both Daniel's relationship with his girlfriend and his mental stability. She was angry at all the members who did not object to using drugs as she did. Three months later she told us that her son used to take drugs. He quit his job and his relationship with his girlfriend fell apart. She blamed herself for not knowing enough about his life.

I often focus on Daniel's group sessions when I am talking about the emergence of the "true-self" (Winnicott, 1965) in the group and the basic need of a person to be loved and appreciated for what he really is, and not only for the grandiose self-impression he wishes to make. Yet, now I would like to focus on the impact on Daniel's story in the group in terms of resonance.

Let's go back to Sara. As a conductor, I observed every other member's reaction to Daniel's story. Sara had a clear and acute response from the moment Daniel mentioned his anxiety in India. She was moving nervously in her chair, looking at me as if she needed my attention and help, smiling all the time as if she felt constantly observed by others or maybe even psychically transparent to others. (They did not seem to notice her reaction, being so concentrated on Daniel.) She was clinging to her bottle of water sipping from it intensively. When Daniel disclosed his weak spot, taking psychiatric medications, it seemed that Sara couldn't take it any longer. She had sworn to herself that she would keep her private life behind her walls of privacy even at the expense of being socially distant and banal. Yet now she just had to speak. Moreover, although she did not say anything yet, she felt so exposed that she felt she had nothing to lose. She spoke after David, who was the first to address Daniel in consolation, and expressed appreciation for his sincerity. Sara said: "I understand you Daniel (the first time she ever mentioned anyone's name in the group), I am like you. I take those drugs too. I always had difficulties talking to other people. My boss at my work told me that people don't know how to deal with me. They think that I am cold." She said. "I know I am not, and I know that I really need people and do not express it. So I went to a psychiatrist, like you did, Daniel, and he told me that I am Agoraphobic. He gave me some tranquilizers and recommended group therapy."

As you can imagine, following her very personal sharing in and her soft and warm relating to Daniel she was welcomed in the group. Daniel thanked her for joining him in his lonely planet of psychiatric cases.

Until that point in the group process, I intervened almost not at all. My main intervention in that session dealt with identifying common themes in the group and giving words to difficult, disavowed feelings. I referred to Daniel's

> and Sara's experiences as representing other members' unconscious experiences too. I suggested that shame could be one of the barriers that might cause members to refrain from sharing similar experiences, and that maybe Daniel and Sara consciously overcame their shame and fear of rejection, despite being reluctant to reveal secrets.
>
> In later sessions, other members joined Daniel and Sara, each revealing his own version of shameful secrets. As Daniel gradually believed them more, he could benefit from their mirroring. He became more assertive and self-confident and his life continued to change.

The Therapeutic Value of Resonance

Foulkes referred to resonance as a universal aspect of human communication. Yet in his analysis of the clinical implications of resonance, he focused on pathology and mechanisms of defense. According to his perspective, understanding the phenomenon of resonance makes it easier for the conductor to respond to destructive development and narcissistic character formation. "All well known 'defense mechanisms' such as repression, denial, somatic or conversional representation, acting out, isolation, projections, introjections and projective identification come into operation" (Foulkes, 1977: p. 298).

While many of the resonance responses express exact attunement to the emotion that is brought up in the group and identification with its content, it is clear that others express defenses against the vulnerability they may cause in members who feel suddenly confronted with their denied psychic aspect. Therefore, as Foulkes suggested, members in the group may react with spontaneous (sometimes hostile) rejection of the possible personal significance of issues brought up in the group. A member who stirs emotional response in others might be answered by projection of the relevant denied content in another member. This process facilitates better self-recognition of split-off self-states that are projected on others (Bromberg, 1998). Let us consider, for example, Hanna's response to Daniel in the above clinical description. She blames him for damaging his own psychic condition by using drugs. Three months later, she tells the group about her own remorse over not detecting her son's similar behavior in time. This later sharing of hers gives additional meaning to the projection of her angry reaction to Daniel. Therapeutic benefit in the group takes time. This is the time Hanna needed to reflect on the meaning of Daniel's story for her. Following Foulkes, I suggest that what begins as a resonance expression of rejection, projection or other mechanism of defense, may be elaborated into beneficial self-reflection. It is true that many times the raw resonance reaction may present not only simple identification with the theme that is brought up, or with the person who brought it, but rather a form of denial, or even some hostile reaction formation of this very subject. We all might jump to deny something that is most relevant to our hidden painful issues in life. Nevertheless, raw reactions give way to further elaboration much more than supportive, positive responses, let alone safe avoidance.

Yet, in our contemporary thinking resonance reactions in the group do not always have to carry pathological meanings. They often present our universal psychic lives. Every theme that is brought up through resonance is a part of our common inner reality. Therefore, resonance clarifications in the group may enhance each member's sense of belonging and enable a benign transformation from loneliness and detachment into meaningful relationship.

Sara's response to Daniel's story is an example of a spontaneous inevitable resonance response. In the above example, Daniel's decision to self-disclose his psychiatric situation was a risk that made it possible for resonance responses to occur in the group. Sara just couldn't help expressing herself in a form of identification with his anxieties. On one hand her agoraphobic symptoms presented some aspects of the pathological condition which brought her to group therapy, as Foulkes argued. On the other hand it enabled her to step in and belong to the group for the first time. Moreover, she helped Daniel feel less lonely in the group by joining him as a twin patient. Her equivalent self-disclosure, made with such an effort, meant more to him than the support of his veteran friends in the group. I believe it meant even more than what I, as conductor, had to say at that moment. Daniel and Sara could understand each other a little bit better than all those who had never experienced this kind of shame and fear.

Moreover, the universal themes that Daniel and Sara brought up in the group were broader and deeper: Everyone might feel shame and fear of rejection by others for his secret truths. Sometimes people find it hard to resist the temptation of being accepted and loved and therefore keep up their false self presentation. We all oscillate between feeling hidden and safe and the risk of exposing our true-self among others. The wish for intimacy entails self-disclosure which may be experienced as crossing an interpersonal barrier for anyone who pursues it. The inevitability of resonance responses makes those leaps of self-disclosure surprisingly more possible, especially for avoidant or self-critical people. On many occasions, I noticed that their ability to engage in intimate relations benefitted from initial resonance in the group.

In this group process, it is no wonder that other members followed Daniel and Sara through their own resonance responses. The whole group process was inspired by the possibility of sharing hidden self-states and overcoming shame and fear of rejection. The growing acceptance in the group that was demonstrated in this case encouraged other members to be more daring. Following Sara and Daniel's example, group members shared feelings of inferiority over self-doubts about body image, lack of formal high education, and unsatisfactory marriages. Their anxieties turned into new unexpected experiences of confidence. This experience had significant therapeutic value for them and for other members as well.

In group therapy resonance reinforces self-expression. Growing self-expression in the group enhances mutual recognition (Benjamin, 1988). Personal private contents may be transformed into group-as-a-whole themes and at the same time mirroring of other members amplifies everyone's sense of subjectivity and uniqueness.

The experience of resonance and the group mind enhance the sense of belonging. Experience of belonging in itself is considered (Foulkes, 1977; Fromm, 1947) as a therapeutic factor in human life. Resonance promotes both psychic and interpersonal transformation from loneliness to belonging. The here-and-now realization that "my sharing of personal content in the group inspires others" may create a personal feeling of togetherness. At the same time being deeply touched by somebody else's personal and unique aspect may result in feelings of closeness, empathy and concern.

Resonance: The Subjective Experience

Resonance is a professional term given by an observer to some group process. The personal experience of the participant is not that objective. I suggest that there are two main aspects of a participant's subjective experience whenever he is unconsciously involved in that interpersonal process. The first is an experience of emotional over-involvement. In the process of resonance one may feel that he is getting extremely emotionally involved in some theme in the group. This theme is usually represented in the group by some other member who becomes charged by one's emotional reaction. Strong identifications or antagonisms are typical in these emotional reactions. For example, a woman in the group complains at length about being constantly rejected by men despite her devoted efforts. Two other members respond immediately by intense emotional involvement: One man goes out of his way to promise her his help in every future session. Another woman gets very angry at her and mocks her dependency. (In future sessions it would become clear that these resonant reactions are relevant to each of these participant's personal therapeutic work in the group.) The man had been emotionally abused by his mother who wanted him to be almost unable to separate from her. He reacted to the suffering woman with some regressive overdoing of trying to save her. The woman had had to overcome her wishes for benign dependency as a child after the death of her parents resulted in depression. She expressed her life-long counter-dependency by projecting her antagonism on her group-mate whom she considered childishly dependent.

The second form of subjective experience of a member involved in the process of resonance is the feeling of being transparent to others. In other words, the member may feel that when some very relevant theme is brought up in the group, his emotional reaction is so obvious that he loses the social manners that usually help him defend his privacy. He may feel that his inner world has become exposed to others without his control. That might be a very difficult moment for any participant.

Most of the patients usually choose to self-disclose themselves more, provided they feel that the group has become a safe place to do so. Others may feel extremely unsafe and even paranoid. In one case, a new member joined the group in a session during which another member had just told the group about his fear of failure in his final medical exams. Examination anxiety had always been the new member's ultimate nightmare. She felt she wasn't ready to speak about it yet. At the end of the session she approached me and said she decided to quit: "Do you remember the film Roger Rabbit?" she asked. "Roger Rabbit is hunted by the evil Tune figure when this bad guy plays a song that rabbits sing. Roger Rabbit cannot help singing the song and that's how he is caught. This man with his fear is singing my song. I don't want to speak about it yet because it might ruin my inner balance. So I have to leave." She left and turned to individual therapy.

The conductor should bear in mind how strong resonant reactions might be. I will return to this issue at a later point.

The Role of the Conductor

Therapeutic elaboration of resonance in a group requires safety. Unlike in individual therapy, the patient in the group rarely feels completely safe among people who have their own needs and unexpected behaviors and who are not professionally committed to him as a therapist is. Yet most of the patients who join group therapy are ready to take some risks, provided they experience the conductor as a professional figure who bears in mind their need for safety and promotes it.

Holding the group in accordance with fixed rules of time, place and roles contributes to the members' experience of safety. Reminding the group members of the basic rules of confidentiality is of elementary importance. Yet, in my view, the conductor should also detect any premature self-exposure in the group and bear in mind that the intensity of the resonance process might cause members to lose their social defenses and over-expose themselves too soon. This might result, in some cases, in paranoid anxieties or even masochistic submission to other people's voyeuristic needs. I suggest that the role of the conductor in these cases is to remind members of their conscious choice to regain self-control of their sharing in the group and to decide when, and which aspects of their life and their inner realities, they want to share with the group. By these interventions, not only does the conductor enhance the members' ability to use their ego-functions but he is also better regarded as their protector against interpersonal pressures in the group.

In time, group participants gradually come to agree upon their basic mutual needs for safety. They form mutual concern and sensitivity for each member's personal pace of self-disclosure. They learn how to help each other to express more and at the same time how to respect needs for privacy even in the presence of other people. Under these conditions, resonance may be most therapeutically fruitful.

It seems that once good enough safety in the group is established the basic role of the conductor is to contribute to the elaboration of resonance into mutual self-reflection and verbal communication.

I suggest that working with resonance requires that the conductor have countertransference belief, or should I say "faith" in the sense of Eigen (1981), that everything that happens in the group, verbal as well as non-verbal, may be the result of resonance and the reason for further resonance. Empathic response as well as antagonism, excitement as well as over-expressions of boredom, gestures of closeness as well as going to the restroom at a certain moment – all may be forms of resonance. For instance: one woman gathers the courage to say in the group that she had been cheating on her ex-husband. Another woman intervenes quickly and asks her: "How long have you been married?" It turns out later that the second woman was dealing with exactly the same issue in her marriage, with similar experience. Her attempt to quickly change the subject proved to be her resonance response to something that bothered her. The basic criteria for detecting resonance should be the "now moment" (Stern, 1998) of the events and the time proximity of behaviors. The conductor should ask himself, "Why now?" Then he may explore those reactions with the members.

The conductor's other function is, of course, identifying similar themes within the discourse of different members. Usually resonance is most powerful when it reveals themes that are so emotionally loaded that they are usually consciously hidden, denied or split off. Deep shame and diminished self-esteem (as I demonstrated in the above clinical example) may be brought up sometimes only through inevitable resonance. Resonance may touch upon disturbing or repressed memories of archaic psychic pain. The conductor should bear in mind that however lonely and exceptional a group member might feel, no man is an island. There are always other group members who share similar pain. Practically it may be useful for the conductor to listen to each member while systematically exploring the others' reactions.

The conductor may contribute a lot to the group when he suggests what might be the hidden or unconscious theme that needs resonance to be amplified in the group. He may say: "What Ann just said about marriage, unfaithfulness and secrets may occupy the mind of others in the group." This kind of group intervention may help other people join in and talk about their own most difficult issues and at the same time help Ann to feel more at home with her fears of being considered a bad wife and a bad person.

Resonance reactions need space. This kind of space may be provided in the group when the conductor refrains from intervening too soon and lets members respond first. I refer here to the therapist's emotional ability to wait, contain and pay attention to his reverie (Bion, 1962; Ogden, 1997a, 1997b).

An over-controlling conductor might arrest the process of resonance in the group. Some interpersonal reactions among members might be difficult to contain and rouse the conductor's annihilation anxieties in his counter-transference. Consider, for instance, the reaction of the woman in the group who became angered by another woman who complained of being constantly rejected by men. The conductor might worry that some member in his group might get hurt and even quit, or that aggressive motivations would get out of control, or indeed, that members would accuse him of not protecting them.

Last but not least: The conductor should be aware of his own resonance reaction which may cause him to feel exposed with his own over-emotional reaction. In this case he may withdraw his possible intervention. It is often much better for the conductor to use his inner reaction as a reverie (Ogden, 1997a, 1997b) for better understanding the unspoken agenda in the group and to come forward with his ideas of what may be the theme that is difficult to talk about.

References and Bibliograpy

Benjamin, J. (1988). *The bonds of love: psychoanalysis, feminism, and the problem of domination.* New York: Pantheon.
Bion, W. R. (1961). *A theory of thinking. Melinie Klein today.* London, The New Library of Psychoanalysis. London: Routledge.
Bromberg, P. (1998). *Standing in spaces.* Hilsdale, New Jersey: The Analitic Press.
Eigen, M. (1981). The Area of Faith in Winnicott, Lacan and Bion. *International Journal of Psycho-Analysis, 62*, 413–433.
Foulkes, S. H. (1977). *Notes on the concept of resonance.* Selected papers. psychoanalysis and group analysis. London: Karnac Books.
Fromm, E. (1947). *Man for himself.* Greenwich, Connecticut: Fawcett.

Iacoboni, M. (2008). *Mirroring people: The new science of how we connect with others*. New York: Farrar, Straus & Giroux.

Mitchell, S. A. (2000). *Relationality: From attachment to intersubjectivity*. Hillsdale, New Jersey: The Analytic Press.

Ogden, T. (1997b). Reverie and metaphor: some thoughts on how I work as a psychoanalyst. *International Journal of Psycho-Analysis, 78*, 719–732.

Ogden, T. H. (1997a). Reverie and interpretation. *Psychoanalytic Quarterly, 66*, 567–595.

Reis, B. (2009). We: Commentary on papers by Trevarthen, Ammaniti & Trentini, and Gallese. *Psychoanalytic Dialogues, 19*, 565–579.

Seligman, S. (2009). Anchoring Intersubjective Models in Recent Advances in Developmental Psychology, Cognitive Neuroscience and Parenting Studies: Introduction to Papers by Trevarthen, Gallese & Ammaniti, and Trentini. *Psychoanalytic Dialogues, 19*, 503–506.

Stern, D. N., Sander, L., Nahum, J. P., et al., (1998). Noninterpretive mechanisms in psychoanalytic therapy. *International Journal of Psycho-Analysis, 79*, 903–921.

Winnicott, D. W. (1965). Ego distortion in terms of true and false self. *The maturational processes and the facilitating environment: Studies in the theory of emotional development*. London: Hogarth Press and The Institute of Psychoanalysis.

10

The Dynamics of Mirror Reactions and their Impact on the Analytic Group

Miriam Berger

The purpose of this paper is to present the concept of mirroring and to explore its various developmental and relational aspects as formative and transformative factors in group dynamics. The term itself defines a process by which the mutual reflections of emotions between persons enhance their ability to communicate effectively with each other and to move from withdrawal to fruitful participation in personal and social relationships. Mirroring is harnessed by group participants and conductor alike to activate a move towards growth and, where necessary, to assist in a process of healing distorted development. I will discuss how various psychoanalytic thinkers have handled the concept and draw on experiences from my own analytic group as examples of how its use may succeed or fail.

Introduction

Since ancient times, mirrors have played a part in mythology, literature, and folklore across various cultures around the world. The mirror serves as a metaphor for a person's perception of himself, his relationships with others and with reality in general. It represents the central place we allocate to the human face, to the significance we attach to the eye as an expression of one's inner world and a window to his soul. The mirror signifies an emotional crossroad between subjective and objective realities; it stands for the complexity of self/other interconnectedness. The idea of mirroring as a developmental process that is also inherently relational provides us with a bridge that connects the private with the social dimensions in human affairs, the affective factors with the cognitive ones. In group therapy, members reflect each other's realities both consciously and unconsciously. In such a setting, this process of mutual reflection can be harnessed to promote more effective communication.

Mirrors and Mirroring: The Wonder of the Looking Glass

Psychoanalysts offer various definitions of mirroring that illuminate different developmental aspects and clinical implications of the process in both individual and group settings. The writings of J.D. Lichtenberg can serve as a general frame for thinking about mirroring as a meaningful factor in human relationships.

Lichtenberg (1982, 1985, 1989) suggests that the Latin root of "mirror" combines "miracle" and "mirage" into one notion and points to the mirror's magical and illusory aspects as an intertwined entity that has always aroused man's wonder. He further suggests that our fascination with mirrors is rooted in the human longing to know the unknown. It represents two unknowns that are emotionally charged for us:

1. Man cannot see his own face.
2. He cannot see the unconscious of the other upon whom he depends for his welfare and safety.

For Lichtenberg, mirroring represents the longing of man to penetrate the secret recesses of mind and soul (his own as well as others') and to create a bridge over the elusiveness inherent in the attempt to really "know" oneself and the other. Lichtenberg believes that the discernment of facial expressions is an essential guide that informs a person about his situation subjectively and objectively. It provides him with a map for an emotional orientation in any given situation. The ability to read faces is crucial both for self-knowledge and for relational orientation. Since a person cannot read his own face, he must learn to find his way into his own life and into relationships with others through becoming "literate" about the meanings other faces convey. In other words, people provide each other with a compass that guides them in reading the emotional map needed for orientation.

Thus, the ancient dictum "Know Thyself" acquires an additional dimension of "Know the Other": One must know the other's emotional make-up, his feelings and intentions, in order to navigate one's way in one's own personal world more effectively.

Lichtenberg represents a growing number of contemporary psychoanalysts and group analysts who believe that people develop through a continuous process of mutual responsiveness and an active involvement with each other. The notion that our lives are interwoven with those of others and that there is no human existence outside the context of social relationships is a basis for exploring the working of mirroring as a major therapeutic factor in groups.

I would like to start the discussion of mirroring processes in groups with two tales that might at first seem rather removed from our subject matter. The first is an old Jewish folk tale taken from a collection of stories called "The Wise Men of Helm," which can serve as an illustration of man's fascination with the elusive nature of mirroring. The second, though a story about pelicans, shows how the magic of a mirror can influence the neuropsychological dimension of human social life.

"The Wise Men of Helm": How to Trap the Moon in a Barrel

As the story goes, the Helm sages knew about the magical powers of mirrors and decided to harness them for the benefit of the village. The idea was to capture the moon, that is, its reflection, to lighten their darkened nights. Many possibilities were considered in the effort to find the best strategy to achieve their goal; finally they decided to place a barrel full of rainwater in the courtyard of their synagogue on a night with a full moon, and thus to trap its image in the barrel.

This strategy proved successful: indeed, they managed to catch the full moon. But alas, on the following day, its image had begun to shrink; and so it proceeded to shrink gradually every consecutive night. Finally, after several days, the moon slipped away and disappeared from their barrel, to their utter chagrin. The wise men of Helm did their best to harness the powers of nature to better their communal living. They strove to reach out and grasp what was "really real" beyond appearances. But the illusive nature of the mirror reflection defeated them.

However, sometimes the magic powers of mirrors do work. The following tale about a group of pelicans in Tel Aviv University provides us with an example of such a successful outcome.[1]

Contagious Social Moods

The pelicans: a group tale

Once upon a time, in the zoological gardens of Abu–Kabir (the region where Tel Aviv University began its life), several pelicans were gathered into a fenced area in the yard behind the university building. The zoologists who put the pelicans in this area meant to study their behavioral patterns and explore the dynamic processes that governed their communal lives. The flock consisted of a number of males and females that were expected to court, mate, lay eggs, hatch them and finally raise a new generation of pelicans that would bring pride to Tel Aviv University. Several hatching seasons passed, but none of these events occurred.

The puzzled department professors gathered to examine the situation and consider possible solutions. They thought about the difficulties of the pelicans: What could be inhibiting them? What was keeping them from going ahead with the natural sequences of procreation? What could be done? Finally, someone suggested the following (bizarre) idea: to order a huge mirror and put it in their cage. Thus, a large mirror was brought to the yard and placed next to the fence, facing the pelicans. Strange as it seemed, this idea turned out to be very productive: The pelicans looked in the mirror, understood that their number had doubled, and strengthened by the thought that they had now become part of a massive group, got down to the business of courtship. They found mates, laid eggs, and in that very same spring sat upon them together, letting the natural life cycle take its course. Since then, the pelicans continue to produce new generations of babies and live the life of a happy flock unto this very day.

---

[1] As told by Dr Ilan Golani, an ethologist from Tel Aviv University.

German ethologists such as Konrad Lorenz have offered an explanation for this phenomenon. Apparently the natural course of procreation in pelicans is activated only if the flock consists of a certain number of birds. Only when such a "critical mass" has accumulated certain hormonal mechanisms are activated, which in turn generate courting and mating behaviors. This is part of an inborn mechanism referred to as contagious social moods.[2] It seems that upon viewing their reflection in the mirror, the pelicans believed they were encountering other birds like themselves; this doubling of their numbers released their natural potential for procreation and enabled them to undergo the developmental process that was engraved in their genes.

Returning to the phenomena of mirroring in group therapy, we may speculate that human affairs are subjects in some ways to similar mechanisms. Namely, a similar yet different other (or group of others) has to be positioned in reality outside an individual in order to provide him with the adequate responsive reflection that is needed to sustain certain developmental processes which make humans into the social beings they potentially are.

Apparently, pelicans and humans alike live within an essentially psychobiological matrix; they create networks of continuous mutual resonance and mirroring with each other that may be defined as a communicational matrix. Apparently human society, along with its individual members, is more closely connected with the larger biological makeup than we have realized.

The Group as a "Hall of Mirrors"

The group analytic approach contends that the group framework promotes the development of the ability to read a complex emotional roadmap and to use it to find one's way both personally and socially.

S. H. Foulkes, the founder of Group Analysis, (1948, 1957, 1964, and 1990), believed that the group is the backdrop against which the individual delineates his personal boundaries, develops his creativity, and finds his unique idiom. He perceived the therapy group as "A Hall of Mirrors" and defined a factor he called "Mirror Reactions" as a process that has a central group-specific therapeutic value. The mirror reaction factor encompasses a range of dynamic processes such as identifications, projections, projective identification, internalizations, externalizations, and so on. It consists of echoes or reflections evoked in group members by each other while struggling to become relevant, reach out, connect and communicate with each other. Foulkes states that:

---

[2] Generally speaking birds are tribal animals; they live in flocks and their behaviors (including inner hormonal processes) are somehow synchronized with each other. Observations show that a flock of birds tends to imitate any of its individual members that initiates a certain behavior – any move that one of them starts is immediately followed by the whole group; thus, if one bird begins to preen its feathers to peck and eat or takes off to change a position – all the other birds around join in to do the same. It seems they have an inborn mechanism *for contagious social moods*. This phenomenon has been coined as Socialshteimung (social mood in German). Ethologists hypothesized that this phenomenon of synchronization within the flock may have some survival value for the birds. For instance "communal raising of offspring" that consists of nestlings hatching at the same time by all pelicans in a given flock seems to have an advantage against predators. Pelicans may band together for common protection of offspring if the hatching occurs simultaneously.

A person sees himself, or part of himself – often a repressed part of himself – reflected in the interactions of other group members. He sees them reacting in the way he does himself, or in contrast to his own behavior. . . He also gets to know himself and this is a fundamental process in ego development- by the effect he has upon others and the picture they form of him (Foulkes, 1964: p.110).

The "eyes" of others in the group, participants and conductor alike, are the emotional "training map" upon which the individual constructs his world. (Foulkes' definition of the analytic group as *"ego training in action"* captures this idea.) Mirroring is a crucial factor that allows this developmental process to take place from infancy onward. Thus, we can think of the analytic group as a developmental playground on which participants construct and define their unique subjectivities through a continuous exchange with each other.

Members of the group, as well as conductor, sit face-to-face in a circle, exposed to each others' look, with nothing to hide behind. They are all equally *"vulnerable to the eye"* (Foulkes and Anthony, 1990: p. 63). They are seen and revealed for what they are, for better and for worse. This quality of being "vulnerable to the eye" encompasses a large spectrum of beliefs about mirroring that range between the crucial need for an accepting, affirming look of a significant other and fear of the "evil eye" another person's look may evoke.

Sitting face-to-face in the analytic group invites equality, mutuality, and the openness to diverse viewpoints that are all allotted a valid chair. This positioning further delineates the boundaries for a space that enables reciprocal democratic exchange between members. Seeing and being seen is identified with acceptance, affirmation, recognition, and validation ("I see" means "I understand"); it is closely related to being perceived as a valued member in one's community; it means to have a say, to make a difference, to be included and to belong. Many of us are too familiar with the painful experience of becoming "transparent" to others; namely, ignored, overlooked, excluded and discredited.

Group therapists may find it useful to keep in mind that both poles (the need to be seen and the fear of being seen) are relevant in shaping the interactions between group members. Awareness of both possibilities as well as the continuous shifting of viewpoints in any given situation enhances the conductor's ability to be effective in containing the emotions of the members.

The following vignette from a therapeutic group illuminates the dynamics of being caught between the need to be seen and the equally devastating fear of being overlooked.

Clinical Illustration

Tanya missed two consecutive group sessions in a row. At her first session back, she sits silently for a long time (as is her habit) and follows the conversation with a tense and worried look on her face. About half an hour before the end of the session, she gathers her courage and asks in a barely audible voice: "What had you been talking about in the group when I was away? Could you fill me in?" Hesitatingly, members begin to respond to her request and to recall details from previous meetings; however, it quickly becomes apparent that she had something else in mind. Her question was really intended to call the group's attention to her absence and to express the fact that she felt hurt. It turns out that she felt ignored: nobody noticed her absence. Nobody phoned to ask what had happened. Had they even noticed that she wasn't there? Was she missed? Did anyone "see" that her chair was empty?

In any event, Tanya states that she doesn't expect anything from anyone; she insists (with a tinge of cynicism in her voice) that the fact that they don't notice her is "natural", since "I never have anything interesting to say."

Knowing some of Tanya's vulnerabilities, I understand she longs for a warm responsive look from others, while she fears being discredited and shamed; she ends up shutting herself off by cynical remarks. Her difficulty in being in touch with her need to be taken into account results in withdrawal and social isolation. She is, indeed, generally silent and it is rather easy to pass her over and to become involved in subjects that others bring up. Thus, her fear of being ignored becomes a self-fulfilling prophecy. Tanya has settled into waiting passively for someone to "see" her, to invite her to join in. Too often, she sits there with a silent grudge on her face; her stance irritates others and evokes in them a wish to shake her out of her helplessness.

I suggest the group members would like to invite her into the circle, to relate to her more empathically, but may be afraid she will ignore them; they don't seem to believe they have a real chance to reach her.

Gradually they respond by talking about their own experiences of self-abnegation that are at times unbearable. Tanya seems to bring out those feelings without leaving too much room for a redeeming quality to evolve. The readiness of group members to share their own vulnerabilities softens some of Tanya's bitter closing off. The tension in the group atmosphere lessens a little and the flow of communication is resumed with more warmth.

Comment

As a conductor, I struggle continuously with the tendency of mirroring processes to lean in negative directions; I strive to protect the group from becoming trapped in prolonged malicious cycles of negative mirror reactions that may prove destructive for all members.

When mirroring processes evolve favorably, the group space creates a juncture for the diverse viewpoints of its participants to be played out and enrich each of its members. The reality of actually seeing each other, of being continuously exposed to mutual reflections, opens participants' eyes to new aspects of themselves; it enables them to reorganize their sense of who they are, to have a more coherent view of themselves and their impact on each other. Since what we see defines what we know, and vice versa, the analytic group circle with its open vistas for all can become a transformative space that facilitates development, promotes new self knowledge and generates the creation of new self definitions.

(*"The symptom mumbles to itself with the hope of being overheard"* is a known Foulksian aphorism; it expresses the belief that symptoms are relational messages; they speak an autistic language of isolated individuals who seek to connect to others and to restore the broken ties with their community. Thus Tanya's prolonged silences and the group's irritated responses to her complaints can be perceived as coded messages that struggle to become a communicative process that enhances growth.)

Isolation

The Malady of Narcissus and Echo

The transformative move from withdrawal to participation in the group is achieved through mirror reactions between group members that confirm each others realness even while they disagree or fight. According to group analytic ideas, "no man is an island"; isolation from adequate social interactions blocks and distorts one's development. The group provides a space for a vital exchange with others. The process of healing neurotic distortions is marked by a continuous struggle of each member to negotiate between objective and subjective viewpoints simultaneously. The many self-images offered by others provide an opportunity to escape from an infinite web of self-projections that can entrap the isolated individual who is enclosed in a world without sufficient exchange with others. We can imagine the group as a provider of vital oxygen supplies that rescues one from emotional suffocation.[3]

The myths of Narcissus and Echo (discussed by M. Pines in 1998 in his extensive exposition of mirroring processes in groups) depict symbolically the dangers posed by withdrawal into one's inner self. Narcissus and Echo are both trapped in vacant relationships: He drowns in his own reflection and she is responded to only by her own voice. Their worlds are empty of objects. They have no relationships with others who can see or hear them and confirm their existence as separate unique subjects. Their only resource is their self-projections; hence, they are deprived of the vital connectedness with the "really real" others and turn into mythological warning posts for the dangers of isolation.

As mentioned, "the hall of mirrors" has been used to describe the nature of the group space that enables the mutual reflections of its members to be played out. In addition, it is possible to envision the interactions of each member with others in his group, as an X-ray portrayal of the relationship between his own conscious and unconscious aspects; each member's personal world is populated by numerous different parts that are sometimes as alien to each other as the real group members can be. In other words, one's inner world (comprised of an "inner group") and one's relationships with others, the intra-personal and the inter-personal facets recapitulate and reflect each other. This idea can be instrumental in understanding complex group

---

[3] Winnicott's concept of the capacity for "object use" versus object relating can add a relevant facet to this idea.

processes and assist the conductor in formulating hypotheses about the prevailing dynamics in a given situation.[4]

The way we see ourselves is closely related to the way others see us. The perception of others become an integral part of our inner self-experience and affects the manner in which we shape reality in a myriad of ways.

Toward the end of a group session Mila (a member) says:

"The work we're doing here is like cleaning the mirror. When we talk, I can begin to see myself and understand what happened to me when I was growing up. It is as if there was a thick layer of dust on the mirror and we are wiping it off together; simply cleaning years and years of neglect. Through your looks, I can see the lost girl I used to be, despite the comfortable life I had at home."

Her words express the transformation she underwent when she was able to start making connections between the images she has of herself and the new facets that others in the group have been discovering in her over time.

Patterns of Mirroring in Group Therapy

Pines (1981, 1998, 2000), Zinkin (1983, 1992), and others who explore the dynamics of mirroring define some specific patterns of mirror reactions which are activated in group therapy and have a decisive impact on its overall functioning. Pines (1998) describes three forms of mirror reactions which are prevalent in groups: antagonistic mirroring, dialogic mirroring, and absence of mirroring. Zinkin offers the term "malignant mirroring" to emphasize his belief that mirroring processes may have destructive facets that should not be overlooked by group therapists.

The Antagonistic Mirror Reaction

The antagonistic mirror reaction develops when two participants who evoke in each other feelings of impatience, fury, or despair confront each other incessantly. Their mutual allergy to one another and their continuous fights threaten to drive the whole group into a stance of defensive withdrawal. Pines attributes this process to early primitive destructive relationships that are reactivated on the stage of the group. The conductor faced with this process may be helped by an understanding that "it takes one to know one"; that the protagonists in such fights are entrapped by the coercive power of their own projections onto each other and that they need firm mediation in order to prevent a prolonged stalemate that may destroy the group.

Here is a short clinical vignette that illustrates such a process.

---

[4] Hopper (2003) and Dalal (1998) have each contributed meaningful conceptualizations to promote and enrich this view. It can also serve to bridge the gaps between psychoanalysis and group analysis and open new vistas for both individual and group therapy.

Clinical Illustration

Keren often turns to Naomi in the following manner: "I cannot say anything without you shutting me down. You remind me of my mother. When I would come home hurting because the boy I liked left me for another girl, or I'd received an undeserved reprimand from a teacher, or I was excluded by classmates from a game, she would shrug me off saying in Yiddish, "Ein kleinikeit" [Loosely translated as "this is all just petty nonsense"]. She was a holocaust survivor; my problems seemed petty and insignificant to her. She never had room for my 'little' sorrows. You're doing the same thing here."

Naomi is a bereaved mother whose eldest son David was killed in a military action in Lebanon and whose husband died a few years later of a "broken heart". At times, her losses are almost too much for the group to bear.

Naomi would usually become irritated and discredit whatever Keren would complain about. She would respond with a hurt and despairing tone: "You're like my sister-in-law; after David was killed, she set Yali against me (Yali is now Naomi's only remaining daughter with whom she has a stormy and painful relationship). She (the sister-in-law) even blamed me for my husband's death. I was accused of being too demanding and harsh. She was unsupportive, venomous to me just like all my husbands' relatives were, when I most needed them. Last year, she died of cancer. I must tell you that I did not feel sorry at all; I went to her funeral, stood there alone at some distance from that whole bunch of my relatives and kept saying to myself: 'It was coming to them. They finally know what real suffering feels like'."

The ferocity of these interactions between Keren and Naomi threaten to draw the group into unending cycles of injury and retribution; members often retreat into periods of prolonged heavy silences. The vengeful threat implicit in the exchanges is mostly resistant to transformations, despite the numerous prolonged attempts of therapist and members to respond empathically and connect to the intense feelings that these two women evoke in each other.

These interactions present a painful impasse to therapist and members alike. It appears that they recreate a hard core of despair, isolation, and utter loneliness that recapitulates the violent reality of trauma that is part of the lives of most of these group participants. It may also be that this hard core impasse reflects parts of our social reality in Israel and is woven into our collective matrix in a more general way.

The Dialogic Mirror Reaction

The dialogic mirror reaction occurs when group members are able to respond to each other's experiences and subjective viewpoints without becoming overly defensive; they can see themselves through the eyes of the others and accept their perspective as valid. Such interactions create a communicative space and constitute an introspective culture within which each member can be sufficiently in touch with himself and with others. Dialogic mirror reactions enhance a sense of shared reality, enable learning, and strengthen the emotional resilience of the individual and the group-as-a-whole.

Following is a short vignette taken from a group session; it illustrates the compassionate responsiveness that emerges within the group space when painful experiences of one member resonate with and mirror those of others.

Clinical Illustration

Alia starts the session by telling us she has felt burdened by the state of her eighty-three-year-old mother, who recently suffered a minor stroke that was followed by deterioration in her overall condition. She had been a strong, industrious woman who raised six children on her own and ran her houseware store for years; now, after being released from the hospital, she insists on continuing her business as she always did, despite the fact that her functioning has declined markedly – she confuses the store's accounts, misplaces administrative forms, transfers money irrationally from one project to the next, orders unnecessary merchandise, and so on.

Alia's mother did ask for help from her busy children, but she demands non-negotiable obedience and disregards their own constrains. She discredits their offers to give what they can and leaves them feeling helpless, guilty and frustrated. Alia finds herself traveling from afar to her mother's home with pots full of cooked food, only to return home with most of them untouched, because her mother "would not eat food that was not cooked in front of her eyes in her own kitchen."

Alia's account is met with diverse mirror reactions that resonate with her experience. Other members share similar life situations they have encountered and struggled with. They talk about the sense of helplessness, shame or rage they felt when their wish to help a needy relative was turned into a painful fight that made them look insensitive, indifferent, or even cruel to the ones closest to them.

Gradually, as the flow of associations in the group proceeds, the members find the ability to feel compassion for all parties in this rather tragic entanglement. Despite the heaviness and sadness of Alia's situation, the atmosphere in the group becomes one of acceptance and empathy; members are able to understand the point of view of both the stubborn old mother who is struggling to hold on to her independence and human dignity in such a castrating and domineering manner, and of Alia, who returns home with her pots, angry, helpless and deeply sad.

The Absence of Mirroring

Vampires tales, that hold such horror and fascination for us provide us with a colorful idea about the damaging effects that the lack of a responsive and affirming look may have on man. These gruesome mythological creatures, neither dead nor alive which have occupied our imaginations for generations are marked by two signals: The first is a thirst that can be quenched only by drinking the blood of a human being; the second, more relevant to our discussion, is the absence of a mirror reflection. When a vampire looks into the mirror, the mirror remains empty.

If we examine the vampire myth through a psychoanalytic lens, we could say that a being without a mirror image, one that is not adequately seen by others, is doomed to feel empty. It would seem that the creators of Dracula, or Frankenstein's monster, joined psychoanalysts in their belief that a consistent benevolent mirror reaction is essential for feeling alive and real. Apparently, vampires are deprived of this vital provision; hence they have no "inside" that can be reflected in the mirror and are doomed to live off the inner lives (or blood) of others. It would make psychological sense to offer them a therapy group, a specialized form of a hall of mirrors to heal their lonely isolation.

The absence of mirroring occurs most often in groups consisting of members who suffer from serious personality disorders. It is attributed to a dearth of internal representations of others and to a deficiency in the ability to be cognizant of the impact one has on others. As a result, the process of communication is distorted and the ability to have a sense of shared reality is damaged. The connection of such group members' inner world to the common social fabric they belong to demands a conscious effort of the conductor and a specific understanding of the works of dissociation mechanisms.

Here is a short vignette which presents some group interactions that can illustrate an absence of mirroring that reactivates some aspects of the traumatic histories of group participants.

Clinical Illustration

Mona was born in Poland right after the occupation ended in 1945. She was an only child of rather older parents who lost most of their family members in the war. She was raised as the single prodigy child in a group of elderly holocaust survivors. They adored her youth and talents and placed in her their hopes for retrieving some of their colossal losses.

Mona is a very bright, rather arrogant, domineering woman of sixty-two. She often declares disdainfully that she "needs nothing from nobody." Since childhood, she has had difficulties in forming close relationships with peers. She entered the group because she felt depressed and demoralized after numerous unsuccessful attempts at individual therapy. Growing up with a serious deficiency of mirror reactions from peers, she finds it very frustrating to share a common space with others in the group and has continuous claims on my exclusive attention as her own therapist.

> Mona is amazed to discover that things she says have an impact on others; over time, she learns that she can be perceived as conceited and arrogant with her seemingly objective remarks. Her initial disregard for others is matched only by her disregard for her own feelings, to which she has been mostly quite oblivious. It's a tedious and arduous effort (by conductor and group participants alike) to help Mona realize that she does need the affection and acceptance of others in the group, that she does care about what they think of her and that she does affect them with her opinionated remarks. As a child, she was the only Jewish girl in school, ostracized, ridiculed and blamed for using her outstanding achievements to become her teachers' favorite. She protected herself by insulating herself from peers and also from the threats posed by living in an anti-Semitic neighborhood. The extreme traumatic history she was born into and grew up in turned into an inner reality of isolation and loneliness that was reactivated in the relationships with group members.
>
> Group members struggle with Mona's cynical attacks on neediness; somehow she taps into their longing to become meaningful and valuable to each other. They do not give up, nor does she. Although progress is very slow, Mona has made quite a change in the way she participates in the group: She is now able to actually acknowledge that she feels attached to the group and becomes anxious if a member considers termination. Her fellow group members have become valuable mirrors for her, and for the first time in her life, she believes that she is being seen as she really is. She has started to realize that her depression is connected with the isolation she grew up with. The interactions in the group are marked by a continuous struggle to reconnect with Mona, to heal her broken ties with others.

Malignant Mirroring

As mentioned, this additional form of mirroring in the therapy group was posited by Zinkin (1983, 1992), who maintains that while mirror reactions are helpful in promoting one's self-awareness, they can also be experienced as intensely persecuting. They may cause distancing and alienation and become quite catastrophic for a person who suddenly is faced with a truth with which he is not prepared to deal. Zinkin believes that these types of mirror reactions are not sufficiently explored by Foulkes or Pines and claims that their assumptions about the therapeutic value of mirroring are therefore too simplistic. Zinkin uses his concept of malignant mirroring to define the pathological attraction which can arise between two participants who get into a deadlock with each other and evoke destructiveness in the whole group. Zinkin (1992) thinks that participants with borderline personality organization are prone to create such pairings; each one attributes to the other unbearable emotional parts of himself, while denying their existence in their own inner world. Thus, they both become trapped in a vicious cycle of mutual projections and drag the group down into an irreversible abyss. At times, some of the antagonistic mirror reactions between Keren and Naomi threaten to become "malignant" in Zinkin's terms. The endless conflicts that arise between two such protagonists can overwhelm the group and usurp its creative energies; group culture becomes dominated by pointless arguments, and an atmosphere of tension, fear, and hopelessness prevails for prolonged periods of time. These interactions may increase the personal vulnerabilities of individual members, damage their self-images even further, and threaten to become traumatic for the group-as-a-whole.

The awareness of the conductor when such a malignant cycle is put in motion can help him or her set more realistic goals for the group, be more cautious about group composition, and intervene more actively in order to prevent deterioration and protect the safety of the group.

Mirroring in Psychoanalysis

Following is a brief account of some psychoanalytical ideas about mirroring that are relevant to group therapy.

The psychoanalytic significance attributed to "seeing" runs the full gamut from the joyful "gleam in the mother's eye" of Kohut[5] to the persecutory and paranoid look of the other posited by Klein. The more traditional approaches of Freud, Klein, and Bion, among many others, tend to emphasize the working of inborn, internal aggressive drives that shape man's relationships with self and other. According to this theory, the gaze of the other symbolizes the threat inherent in the existence of others with whom one must share the limited resources available in reality. Furthermore, in order to maintain the necessary social bonds with one's community one must appease powerful others and relinquish aspirations for total satisfaction.

The "softer" approaches like those of Winnicott, Fairbairn, Kohut and a whole range of Relational writers emphasize that acknowledgment and recognition are essential human needs that are encompassed in a responsive benevolent look. According to this theory, mirror reactions enable and validate the formation of a unique subjective self. The fear of an envious, overpowering evil eye is not generated by a repressed innate destructiveness but, rather, it is an outcome of empathic failures and traumatic real-life experiences.

A scene from Atura Skola's movie "The Family" captures the essence of the delicate balance that is continuously negotiated between one's need for privacy (or even fear of impingement) and one's need to be seen. It illustrates poignantly Winnicott's saying:

> It's a joy to hide. It's a disaster not to be found (Winnicott 1965: p. 185).

---

[5] Kohut's "gleam in the mother's eye" represents the continuous provision of vital narcissistic supplies needed throughout life, whether one is a child or an adult. If these narcissistic supplies are meager, one is doomed to feel pessimistic about his prospects; a sense of narcissistic vulnerability governs his life and weakens his belief in his chances to realize his hopes.

> **Scene from the Movie:** *The Family*
>
> The family has gathered in the drawing room to celebrate a festive event; little Tony enters the hall hiding playfully behind his father's broad pants. The scene begins in a joyful atmosphere; everyone participates in the hide-and-seek game that has evolved; Tony's grandfather cries out repeatedly and loudly: "Where is Tony? Where is Tony?" The "invisible" Tony is excited and happy to hear his father declare "anxiously" that Tony has disappeared. The game is played out: Everyone continues to search for the "lost" Tony. However, after several more minutes have passed with grandfather's declarations that he does not see the child clinging to his father's pants, Tony becomes panicky. He tries desperately to put an end to the game and to let his father see him and confirm his existence. He starts crying and screams repeatedly and frantically: "Here I am! Look at me! See me. You do see me!"

We feel with Tony and identify with his urgent, frightened need to retrieve the sense of safety that was so necessary in order for him to tolerate, and even enjoy being "invisible" for a few moments.[6]

The participants of an analytic group hide, seek, and find each other continuously. Thus, Foulkes's "Hall of Mirrors" can be envisioned as a playground where this "hide-and-seek" game can be played out creatively provided it is protected, controlled, and safe for members and conductor alike.

"Psychobiological Mirrors": Contributions of Child Developmental Studies and Psychobiological Research

The belief of the softer psychoanalytical approaches in the crucial role of mothers as Psychobiological Mirrors is validated by the findings of child developmental studies which explore the relationships between infants and their caretakers in a microscopically detailed way. The formulations of Schore (1994) and Stern (1990) echo the ideas of many others in this field who believe that adequate face-to-face (mirroring) interactions are absolutely essential for healthy development. They stress particularly the value of positive feelings, such as joy and enthusiasm as factors that substantially increase the physical and mental resilience of infants. Receiving these feelings guards their health, provides them with a protective shield, and enables them to have a hopeful outlook on life. Moreover, reciprocal cycles of affirmation and acknowledgment gradually enable the infant to experience a greater range of feelings and promote emotional flexibility. Hence, his affect tolerance, his ability to process emotions and

---

[6] It's a keen reminder that we can bear fantasy (be creative and "play" in Winnicott's sense) only to the extent it is grounded in "real reality" that is safeguarded by others who do "see" us and recognize us as equal subjects.

manage them effectively is substantially increased. In short, such positive mirroring processes may be perceived as a kind of emotional immunization system.[7]

According to these ideas, the group space can be perceived as a reservoir of collective positive affective provisions, while the paucity of appropriate mirror reactions in the therapeutic group can result in deprivation that blocks growth. Keeping this duality in mind can help the conductor cast a benevolent look on his or her group members without becoming overly suspicious about the unconscious, destructive tendencies they defend themselves against. The conductor should also be aware that too many group-level interpretations might be experienced as abandonment or as a de-legitimization of normal personal longings for acknowledgment and affirmation.

A fascinating addition to this subject is the recent discovery of a neurological phenomenon termed "Mirror Neurons" (Damasio, 2003 pp. 115–116). It has generated a whole range of new research and thoughts about mirroring processes in individual psychotherapy, group therapy and human relationships in general.[8]

Without going into detail about this phenomenon and the potential vistas for exploration it opens up, we can now hypothesize that monkeys, birds and men alike are connected in a common neurobiological matrix and shaped by its processes in many ways about which we are mostly unaware. The concept of mirror neurons provides an additional rationale for placing people in therapy groups with the expectation that they will become curative caretakers for each other.

To state it simply, emotions are contagious. We are continuously "infected" by the moods of others, and vice versa: A smile breeds a smile and a sorrowful face generates sorrow. According to these new findings, feeling states and even intentions may be transmitted by mirror neurons and related neural networks. It appears that biologically we are natural mimes, just like the tribal birds that were presented at the beginning of this paper.[9]

Mitchell, one of the central figures in the relational tradition in psychoanalysis, summarizes these thoughts and findings in a concise way:

> Human beings, starting as small babies, seek other human minds to interact with, not for satisfaction of some discrete needs, but because we are wired to respond visually to the human face, olfactorally to human smell, auditorially to human voice, and semiotically to human signs. (Mitchell, 2000: p. 106).

---

[7] Kohut relates to this issue with a poignant question: "Why can't we convince our colleagues that the normal state, however rare in pure form, is a joyfully experienced developmental forward move in childhood, including the step into the oedipal stage, to which the parental generation responds with pride, with self-expanding empathy, with joyful mirroring, to the next generation, thus affirming the younger generation's right to unfold and be different?" (Kohut, 1982: p. 402).

[8] The "*International Journal of Group Psychotherapy*" (2010, Vol., 60/4) and "*Psychoanalytic Dialogues*" (2009, Vol. 6) have recently come out with special issues devoted to discussions that explore the potential implications of the new neurobiological findings for psychoanalysis, group analysis, human development and relationships in general.

[9] Dalal (1998) claims that although imitation has a bad name in the world of psychoanalysis, all learning has an element of imitation, copying from others and from external reality. Hence, all learning and development are generated by society. As an example that shows how "deep, personal" taste is actually the product of imitation he presents the bell-bottom trousers that appeared strange and ugly to him twenty-five years ago and now seem completely acceptable. In a paragraph that is subtitled "In Praise of Imitation," he says: *"This is an uncomfortable realization that to some extent we are behavioral and cultural sheep."* (Dalal, 1998: p. 216).

To conclude this discussion I will present two clinical vignettes that illustrate some of the mirroring processes which have been discussed throughout this chapter. The first is an example of positive mirroring cycles at work, while the second describes a process of thwarted mirroring.

Clinical Illustration

Coming out of the closet

Nir opens a group session: "I want to tell you something I've really avoided touching upon for a long time; now I feel closer to you and I decided to risk it: I was in therapy for nine years and did a lot of work on myself, but something always remained empty inside; finally, I stopped it. I felt I could no longer go on with this routine and I consulted a psychiatrist. Since last year I have been on antidepressants and my life has changed. I feel completely different, as if I've suddenly put on a pair of glasses and begun to see. I'm afraid you'll look down on me. We are all therapists here [the group consists of mental health workers]; we believe in dynamic processes that bring about inner changes; so I felt ashamed to admit that I need medication. It is as if I gave up on myself, admitted to being weak, inadequate. I never talk about this; it may mark me as different and unworthy; I'm afraid it will hurt me at work, damage my reputation. I did expect to handle my life on my own; it is a disappointment for me, too, that I really couldn't. But I feel good for the first time in years. I hadn't meant to talk about this in the group, but everyone is revealing something about himself here, and I want to be part of you. If I don't speak about it now, I am out of the circle. It's important for me to be myself here and to belong to this group. I am afraid but I do want you to see me as I really am."

Nir's confession evokes a lot of feelings and draws everyone in.

Lisa reveals that she can't sleep at night and is struggling not to use the help of medication. She sees her difficulties as a sign of pathology; something is probably very wrong with her; she is ashamed to admit that her nights are tortuous and that she cannot find rest. "Sleep comes so naturally to everyone else." She feels that she is marked as different; less than they; deficient in some shameful way.

Guy tells the group about a crisis he went through in adolescence, when he spent almost a year at home, not being able to go to school despite the many consultations with mental health professionals his family arranged. He had never mentioned this before, even though it had an indelible effect on his life.

Tally tells us that she went through a period when she was plagued with incapacitating anxiety attacks; she could not take her final exams and lost the chance to graduate with her classmates. Finally she asked for help; a family doctor prescribed her tranquilizers, a fact she shared with no one out of shame and fear. This secrecy was damaging in its own right because she isolated herself from friends and family when she most needed them.

As conductor, I barely intervene throughout these exchanges. I note the flow of communications, the resonance and mirroring group members offer to each other. I say briefly something about their wish to be open and accepted for what they really are; about the courage it takes to risk humiliation yet not avoid reaching out for contact.

Nir's decision to be real, to come out of his hiding place and present himself in full view to the eyes of others, initiated a developmental move for other group members. They followed his example much like the tribal birds in the flock. As this vignette illustrates, such gestures of courage are contagious; they enhance the developmental potential for each member and enrich the value of the group-as-a-whole for all of them.

Clinical Illustration

The covered mirror

The mirror reaction has to be mutual and reciprocal, as it was in the previous illustration. If the group doesn't become a truly benign hall of mirrors, if members avoid self-disclosure or don't respond openly to their fellows, an atmosphere of caution, constriction and aloofness prevails and may even intensify. When such a state of mind controls the group, it becomes too risky to reveal personal failings; members tend to keep to themselves, to avoid sharing. Mirrors are cautiously covered up.

Tamar turns to Gadi (her protagonist during many tense exchanges): "You don't say anything about yourself. You claim that you are very much 'with me' without talking, but it doesn't help me a bit, your sitting there silently. I do not need your understanding if you do not reveal something about yourself too. I got myself down in the mud here, while you always stay clean. It makes me very angry. You can come down into this mud, just like me. Don't you ever feel as rejected as I do? Didn't you ever have a door shut in your face? I feel you look down on me."

I suggest that there are probably others in the group who feel vulnerable, anxious about getting down "into the mud," afraid they will be met with ridicule or indifference. The need to share feelings, to open up, to be understood seems too risky a venture at the moment.

My comment does encourage members to volunteer hesitantly some remarks about their experiences. But overall, they are cautious about their moves, careful not to expose their "dirt"; the risk of being shamed by the "clean" ones, to feel embarrassed or stupid stops them. The reserved atmosphere in the group prevails.

Tanya (whose long silences were mentioned in a previous clinical example) says that she always gives up and avoids talking. She will be laughed at . . . she doesn't have anything clever to contribute . . . others have more urgent issues to deal with . . . she doesn't want to bother them . . . she cannot find the right words . . . and in any case, she can't remember what she wanted to say.

> Gabrielle plucks her courage and says that she still feels hurt over an interaction that occurred in the group several weeks ago when she shared some intimate details about her relationship with her husband. She received plenty of "clever advice" from others who told her what she should do in order to fix her marriage. "You all kept your clothes on and only I took them off." She went home feeling humiliated and guilty. "Why did I have to tell you those things? What good did it do me?"

Gabrielle's pained question is a poignant reminder of Zinkin's caution against an over-idealized view of mirror reactions; the look of others is not always benevolent; it can be intrusive, envious, threatening; it can be critical or denigrating. Seeking an acknowledging and accepting look becomes a risky venture when the longed for "good eye" turns into an evil one.

Final Comments

Two things come to mind as I conclude this chapter. The first is a question that an elderly widowed patient poses when speaking about his daily routine: *"Do you have any idea what it means to go through the whole day with no one who looks at you?"* It's a poignant statement about the essential human need to be seen and about the pain of being overlooked.

The second is a comment I found in Caroline Garland's (1980) paper:

> Group Analysis taught me to make use of mirrors, to find one's self in and through others; Not just to retrieve the lost or buried parts of the self but to discover some, I did not even know where there" (Garland, 1980: p. 43).

This personal note is a keen reminder that people create each other's realities while they reveal them to each other. It's a paradoxical process that evolves continuously in group therapy, as well as in relationships in general.

It makes a difference to realize that one has an impact on others; this does not mean it's always a positive experience. Rather, it denotes a struggle to feel real, connected, and responded to adequately and personally. It enables group members to experience the ways they affect each other and to use this newly acquired knowledge beneficially. The active participation in the group circle brings out a person's uniqueness and crystallizes his subjective individuality.

It opens up new vistas for renegotiating relationships and enables a richer emotional spectrum to come into play. Group therapy provides a frame in which the mirroring phenomenon, which is inherent in human social connectedness, is harnessed to assist in a process of healing and personal growth.

References and Bibliography

Brown, D., & Zinkin, L. (Eds.) (2000). *The psyche and the social world. developments in group analytic theory.* London & Philadelphia: Jessica Kingsley Publishers.

Dalal, F. (1998). *Taking the group seriously. Towards a post-foulkesian group analytic theory.* International Library of Group Analysis 5. London & Philadelphia: Jessica Kingsley Publishers.

Dalal, F. (2001). The social unconscious: A post – Fouksian perspective. *Group Analysis, 34*(4), 539–555.

Damasio, A. (2003). *Looking for spinoza, joy, sorrow, and the feeling brain.* New York & London: Harcourt.

Foulkes, S. H., & Anthony, E. J. (1957). *Group psychotherapy. The psychoanalytic approach.* Harmondsworth, Middlesex: Penguin Books.

Foulkes, S. H., & Anthony, E. J. (1990). (2nd ed.) *Group psychotherapy. The psychoanalytic approach.* London: Karnac Books.

Foulkes, S. H. (1948). *Introduction to group analytic psychotherapy. Studies in the social interaction of individuals and groups.* William Heineman Medical Books Ltd. London.

Foulkes, H. S. (1964). *Therapeutic group analysis.* London: Allen & Unwin.

Foulkes, H. S. (1990). *Selected papers. Psychoanalysis and group analysis.* London: Karnac Books.

Garland, C. (1980). Face-to-face. *Group Analysis, 13*(1), 42–43.

Hopper, E. (2003). *The social unconscious. Selected papers.* London & Philadelphia: Jessica Kingsley Publishers.

Kohut, H. (1989). *The analysis of the self. A systematic approach to the psychoanalytic treatment of narcissistic personality disorders.* International Universities Press Inc. Madison Connecticut.

Kohut, H., & Wolf, E. S. (1997). The disorders of the self and their treatment: An outline. *International Journal of Psycho-Analysis, 59*, 413–425.

Kohut, H. (1982). Introspection, empathy, and the semi-circle of mental health. *International Journal of Psycho-Analysis, 63*: 395–407.

Lichtenberg, J. D. (1985). Mirrors and mirroring: developmental experiences. *Psychoanalytic Inquiry, 5*: 199–210.

Lichtenberg, J. D. (1989). *Psychoanalysis and motivation.* Hillsdale, New Jersey: The Analytic Press.

Lichtenberg, J. D. (1982). Reflections on the first year of life. *Psychoanalytic Inquiry, 1*: 695–729.

Mitchell, A. S. (2000). *Relationality. From attachment to intersubjectivity.* Hillsdale, New Jersey: The Analytic Press.

Nitsun, M. (1998). The organizational mirror: A group analytic approach to organizational consultancy, Part I – Theory. *Group Analysis, 31*, 245–267.

Pines, M. (1998). *Circular reflections. Selected papers on group analysis and psychoanalysis.* London & Philadelphia: Jessica Kingsley Publishers.

Pines, M. (1981). The frame of reference of group psychotherapy. *International Journal of Group Psychotherapy, 31*(3).

Pines, M. (2000). The group as a whole. In D. Brown & L. Zinkin (Eds.), *The psyche and the social world. Developments in group analytic theory,* (pp. 47–59). London & Philadelphia:Jessica Kingsley Publishers.

Schore, A. N. (1994). *Affect regulation and the origin of the self – the neurobiology of emotional development.* Hillside, New Jersey: Lowrence Erlbaum Associates Publishers.

Stern, D. N. (1990). Joy and satisfaction in infancy. In R. A. Glick & S. Bone (Eds.), *Pleasure beyond the pleasure principle*, (pp. 13–25). New Haven: Yale University Press.
Stern, D. N. (1985). *The interpersonal world of the infant.* New York: Basic books.
Winnicot, D. W. (1971). *Playing and reality.* London & New York: Tavistock Publications.
Winnicott D. W. (1965). *The maturational processes and the facilitating environment: studies in the theory of emotional development.* The International Psycho-Analytical Library.
Zinkin, L. (1992). Borderline distortions of mirroring in the group. Group analysis. *The Journal of Group Analytic Psychotherapy*, 25(1).
Zinkin, L. (1983) Malignant mirroring. *Group Analysis*, *16*(2), 113–129.

11

Meeting Maturational Needs in Modern *Group Analysis*: A Schema for Personality Integration and Interpersonal Effectiveness

Elliot Zeisel

Modern Group Analysis is an outgrowth of the pioneering work of Dr Hyman Spotnitz. He began developing modern psychoanalysis and psychoanalytic group therapy in the mid-1940s and 1950s. Spotnitz's work centered on developing a new psychotherapeutic method for the treatment of narcissistic disorders, starting with schizophrenia and borderline conditions. Modern Psychoanalysis is a theory of technique that places an emphasis on joining and reflective techniques in the engagement of patients who are walled off from interpersonal experience. People previously thought to be untreatable have been helped to live more comfortably with themselves and others.

Spotnitz was also one of the first psychoanalysts to advocate the use of groups and to promote combined (one therapist treats the patient in individual and group) and conjoint treatment (two therapists treat the patient in individual and group). His approach to group treatment, also originally developed with schizophrenic clients, emphasized the therapist's use of his or her feelings induced by the group and is an early proponent of using countertransference feelings in formulating interventions. One of Spotnitz's students, Louis R. Ormont, PhD., expanded on the theory and practice of group treatment and placed the emphasis on the group's curative effect, the healing power of relationships that develop member to member and member to leader, and the leader's emotional availability and engagement in meeting maturational needs and resolving resistance. This chapter will highlight how the group's culture is organized and developed so that a member's maturational needs can be met in a way that leads to personality integration and maturation.

Generally, patients who enter group treatment have a desire to acquire a greater degree of emotional freedom and interpersonal availability. In Modern Group Psychoanalysis we have the unique opportunity to help our patients and ourselves become better acquainted with the full spectrum of emotions and in the process learn how to best utilize feelings in relationships. As Ormont (1999) said, "Those who are effective in group are effective in life."

The process begins with the screening interview where we meet our prospective patient for the first time. Our experience from that moment on becomes a series of rich opportunities for modeling immediacy and interpersonal availability. I define immediacy and interpersonal availability to mean: *the individual's ability to know what he is feeling in the moment, to know why he is feeling that way, and to be able to use his feelings effectively in the service of living.* To arrive at this ability requires maturity.

> ### Clinical Illustration
>
> A patient arrived in my office for a screening interview in preparation for joining a group. As he walked from the waiting room, he was munching on an apple. As soon as he took a seat on the couch he reached into the paper bag he was carrying and proffered an apple. I took the apple without saying a word and bit into it, with my mother's voice in my head warning, "Never take candy from a stranger." I felt frightened, nevertheless I began to eat the apple, not knowing exactly why but, sensing that I was being invited by this prospective patient into a relationship and that my actions constituted entry into his world. I felt a guarded affection for him as he told his life story and convinced me that he was in need of much more attention than he could get in a group. We agreed to begin individual therapy in preparation for entering a group. Many months later, when we revisited our first encounter, the patient explained that the apple, a symbol from the bible story of Adam and Eve and the tree of knowledge, represented his hope that he would find self-understanding in his work with me. By joining this man, without questioning the offer of the apple, he said, I opened a door that allowed him to step into treatment.

In group treatment there is great opportunity to develop into a mature person by having your maturational needs met and by developing a greater capacity to *know, regulate and utilize your feeling life* (Maroda, 1991). As Spotnitz (1976) delineated, each of us has maturational needs that require attention and satisfaction in order for us to move through the developmental stages and have our character grow and become better integrated. One definition of a mature person is someone who knows what she wants and knows how to get it (Laquercia, 1983). Needless to say, no one gets all of her maturational needs met in a timely and helpful way; we all arrive in young adulthood with maturational deficiencies. Some of our needs were met too vigorously or weakly while others went unattended, resulting in a personality in need of development. Add to this mix, the functional and dysfunctional method and style of relating that we absorb in our formative years and the result is that for most young adults there will be some aspects of intimate life that are difficult to tolerate. For example, patients often describe an unwillingness to deal with conflict and the feelings associated with it such as frustration and anger. One patient summed it up when he said, "If the other person causes me too much grief, I just get rid of 'em!" This response to interpersonal tension worked for this patient until he grew lonely enough to want a more flexible approach in resolving interpersonal conflicts.

Expanding the Emotional Range

Patients who are new to treatment often say that they are unwilling to tolerate "bad or negative feelings." This means they have a system for living that places a priority on staying in close contact with their "good or positive feelings" at the expense of any feeling state that might cause discomfort. Countless people suffer because of an inability to metabolize and tolerate what they refer to as their negative feelings: frustration, anxiety, sadness, rage, fear, shame, and hate resulting in a broad population who are addicted to the pursuit of feelings associated with pleasure. This comes at an enormously high price on an intra-psychic, interpersonal and societal level.

As modern analysts we embrace an all-inclusive attitude toward feelings and suggest that all feelings are positive, all feelings are a welcomed event in psychic life and treated as primitive messages from your psyche to you, raw data that the mind makes available for negotiating life as it unfolds. We work with a paradigm that shifts the emphasis from good or bad feelings to helpful or unhelpful. For example, it might not feel good to be anxious on the way to an interview for a new job, but if you can respect the anxiety, it might be helpful in guiding you through the process, alerting you to events more acutely as they unfold. Within the experience of the anxiety, there is likely some useful information that can contribute to a desired outcome (Lichtenberg, 1989).

In group, we study the members resistance to engaging each other in progressive emotional communication, that kind of communication that helps the group know them as individuals and helps them know the other members' more intimately. To do this requires a working knowledge of one's feeling life and as the leader works to develop the group's culture he delineates the difference between self-feelings and object-feelings.

> Self-feelings include: **Frustrated, Sad, Anxious, Happy, Frightened, Ashamed, Guilty, Jealous, Hurt, Envious, Angry, Enraged**.
> Object feeling or feelings directed toward another person: **Love, Hate, Affection, Anger, Sexual Excitement**.
> And finally we distinguish between Feelings and States of Mind: all of the above and: **Disgusted, Exhausted, Identified, Cautious, Confused, Suspicious, Confident, Mischievous, Depressed, Smug, Overwhelmed, Hopeful, Surprised, Grateful, Admiring, Shocked, Shy, Bored, Protective, Distraught, Disappointed, Lost**.

For example, if someone said, "I feel disappointed in you," he is not actually talking about his feelings, he is reporting a state of mind usually with the intention of inducing guilt and controlling the other person. If the person said, "I'm hurt and frightened by what you said and angry with you for not considering me!" the communication is clear and the other person is in a better position to respond emotionally. When someone says, "I'm frustrated," she is actually reporting on her condition, and a more complete communication would be, "I'm frustrated and angry with you." We also highlight the difference between thinking and feeling, so that when someone says, "I feel you're doing that just to get back at your mother," she is actually reporting a thought. A statement with a feeling and a thought would be, "I'm sad and angry with you for doing that to your mother, it looks like you're trying to get back at her." As the members struggle with the finer points of progressive emotional communication, resistance to many feelings and thoughts emerge. The group then sets itself to the task of exploring these objections, to thinking anything and saying what might draw them into closer emotional contact. This puts group members at greater risk, but makes them more accessible to learning about unconscious process and opportunities for meeting life as it presents.

A similar approach is taken by the Modern group leader when resistance is encountered. Rather than labeling resistance as bad and something to overcome, we adopt a positive view of resistance as: the best adjustment the patient was able to make to life given the nature of their experience. Resistance to cooperation with the group contract is the royal road to understanding the unmet needs that the patient has brought to treatment. The five elements of the contract include:

1. Arrive on time.
2. Take up one portion of the total talking time.
3. Avoid socializing with group members outside the treatment room.
4. Pay on time.
5. Maintain confidentiality.

Ormont called these the "parameters of progress," since over time members will resist cooperating and provide a chance to study their particular way of relating. How they resist cooperation is key to understanding their personality difficulties. For example, a patient repeatedly brought a check for his monthly fee that underpaid by one session. As the leader and group members explored his resistance, "to pay at the last session of the month and to pay the correct amount," they discovered that the patient was quietly busy, grading each session for its utility, and deciding whether or not he'd pay the full fee. He was the product of demanding, judgmental parenting and frequently would have his allowance reduced for minor infractions at home and school. He was applying the same strict measures for performance to the group's leader, grading his performance and withholding money as a form of protest over what he deemed insufficient. With the help of the group, the patient was encouraged to verbalize his displeasure in the session as he was aware of it and as close to the event as possible. For him, the verbal pathway of expression was less developed than the acting out pathway (Zeisel, 2009) and this episode set him on a course that was designed to strengthen his verbal expressive ability.

As the process in group progresses, the leader and members develop a road map of each individual's maturational requirements so that anyone at any given moment in the treatment process can provide what was missing from the patient's original experience and thereby contribute to personality integration. Setting aside any genetic contribution, people made them who they are and people can help them learn to feel differently about themselves. As Cody Marsh said, "By the crowd were they broken, by the crowd they shall be healed."

The Role of Feelings in Everyday Life

In any close relationship conflict is inevitable. It is as regular as the tides. The laws that govern nature apply to human nature as well. No organism can expand endlessly. At a cellular level a nerve fires but then requires a period of rest before firing again. As in nature, where the sun comes up and the sun goes down, flowers bloom in daylight and contract and close at nightfall, relationships are subject to an endless cycle of expansions and contractions. No matter how loving a relationship may be, it is likely that every seventy-two hours some tension will arise and lead to conflict. Love alone will not make for a lasting, dynamic relationship. Most young adults are poorly equipped to negotiate the rigors of an emotionally intimate life. The high divorce rate in Western civilization is testimony to the fact that we do a poor job preparing people for the rigors of connected life. We are highly organized when it comes to educating students cognitively but we do little to provide an emotional education. Group treatment is an excellent vehicle for educating people about their emotions and many people can benefit from the experience. This is primarily because group therapy is an excellent venue for the experience of love and hate to emerge (Levine, R. 2001), so the members can learn to negotiate a full spectrum of emotions that accompany being intimate with other people.

The process in group lends itself to an exploration of how relationships are formed and maintained over time, so that the members get to learn cognitively and experientially what is helpful or unhelpful in getting along with others. For example, group is an environment in which conflict develops (Yalom, 1970: p. 168) given the fact that time is limited (usually one meeting a week for an hour and a half) and the experience is shared by a number of others who also want to be heard. Moreover, there is an agreement to limit contact to the group session. The process is further complicated by the inevitable experience of transference, where group members find in other members the character traits of people who are most important to them in their life outside the treatment room. Thus, conditions are ripe for conflict to erupt. As this happens, members get to see, hear and experience behaviors, some adaptive, others maladaptive, making for an emotionally rich environment. A patient said it best when he said, "I didn't know that there was an alternative to developing a stomach ache when someone got me angry!"

Clinical Illustration

Susan, an attractive 38-year-old woman, arrived in group with the following request: "I want you all to help me know why I'm so fucked up, why I haven't been able to do what my two younger sisters have been able to do, marry and have kids!" With that statement, the group members were invited into a therapeutic function, namely to help Susan understand the parts of herself that discourage relationships and ward off intimate emotional contact. In the weeks following, Susan told the group some of her history that highlighted her combative relationship with her father, a brainy engineer, and her emotionally withdrawn mother, who worked as a librarian. During these sessions I took note of the fact that Susan never made eye contact with me and avoided including me as she addressed the group. She also began to quietly study how emotional business was conducted in the group, occasionally asking for clarification from group members about why they said what they did to each other.

In the eighth session, after I intervened in a conflict between two other group members, Susan said in a challenging tone, "What makes you the final arbiter of what just happened between Jack and Gretchen?" My "understanding" and "delivery" of what transpired had aroused a strong reaction in Susan. I felt my pulse quicken in response to the combative tone Susan assumed and I thought to myself, "This is a measure of what we're dealing with." Sensing conflict that I thought would be unhelpful to the new, tentative relationship we had, I decided to bridge to a veteran group member, Rachel, and ask, "When Susan addressed me, what did she want me to feel?" Rachel had worked very hard over the course of several years to better understand her own aggressive response to men; she was well acquainted with the scene that was unfolding. She turned to Susan and said, "Sounds like you want Elliot to feel scared and doubtful about his ability to lead this group." "That's just not true!," Susan exclaimed, "Why would I give a shit about his ability to lead this group, he looks like he's doing just fine?" Susan's stridency caught the attention of several members and so began a process that linked Susan's internal agitation to her behavior. As simple as it seemed, this was new information for this bright, high-achieving woman who had very little understanding of her impact on people. She had adopted, in spite of her best efforts, her father's interpersonal density and combative stance.

Subsequently, Susan garnered a lot of recognition when she spoke directly and candidly to other members of the group, particularly when there was tension in the room. On one occasion, a man was monopolizing the time in a way that the group had grown tolerant of even though it was clearly irritating. Suddenly, Susan spoke up and voiced her irritation and displeasure and said that we seemed not to be helping him once again in a tone that was simultaneously interested, sympathetic and irritated. A few people acknowledged Susan for saying what they felt they couldn't say and for saying it with compassion. This kind of emotional nourishment agreed with Susan, who had never felt recognized in a family in which all interpersonal resources were consumed by her father.

Therapist Commentary: This process repeated itself many times and as it did Susan's maturational need for recognition as a person who had something of value to contribute began to be satisfied. At work, Susan began to assert herself in meetings in a way that garnered more respect and responsibility. Although she worked hard to avoid me, her transference to me found a way to assert itself in group. As we explored the process between us it became apparent that I had assumed the role of her "all-knowing father." Every time we entered this realm of exploration it exposed her conflict with men. This was a process that got repeated many times over the next two years. Each exchange helped us understand how determined Susan was to, "never submit to a man," in spite of her yearning for an intimate relationship with a man. Gradually, the group helped Susan develop a keen awareness of her sensitivity to frustration and the anger that ensued. She saw how others managed their angry feelings, how they found language to discharge tension in a way that engaged rather than enraged, and slowly her ability to talk in the thick of conflict increased. In a parallel process in individual treatment with me, she got to examine her failed relationships from the past and slowly relinquish her grip on these missed opportunities. This, along with encouragement from group, set Susan on a new course of engagement with men and women where her new found skills are beginning to meet with success.

The Group's Culture

In a Modern Analytic group the leader works to establish a culture that values the contributions of the members. We avoid making the group a leader-centric experience, so that knowledge flows from anyone to anyone in the process. Informally, the leader identifies unique skills in the participants, in a subtle process of empowerment. Ultimately this contributes to the healing in group, as members learn about their value to each other as emotionally resonant people.

For example, someone might be expert in identifying the meaning of non-verbal gestures or body language, another might be sensitive to aggression while someone else might be superb at labeling sarcasm when she hears it. This orientation puts the members at the center of the experience and, while the leader plays a crucial role in facilitating the process and lending himself to resolving transference issues with members, in the end it is largely the members who heal each other. We work to create a culture in group treatment in which all feelings are welcome and available to the crucible of learning and relearning. As members hear new ideas and experience new feelings for each other, the negative introjects, those voices from the past that inhabit the mind, are slowly moved to the side making way for introject substitution whereby we incorporate the ideas and feelings that group members have for each other leading to a better integrated personality (Leibenberg, 2009).

The emphasis is on emotional experience not interpretation, exploration not explanation. It is through the process of repeated exposure to *emotional interactions* that members of the group learn to feel and think in new ways about themselves, expand their capacity to tolerate a wide range of emotions and learn more adaptive and appropriate ways of discharging tension (Zeisel, 2009).

The emphasis on the members as healers has three other functions. First, it conveys to them that their participation, week in week out, is crucial to the process of treatment and that it is their relationship to one another that will heal them. Second, it has an ego reinforcing effect and strengthens the member's idea about himself and his ability to observe, identify and talk about his feelings in a way that is valued. Third, it allows the leader to ally himself with the unconscious ego of the patient and contributes to the building of a therapeutic alliance; the leader is less of an irritant and more of an ally.

Attraction and Sexual Feelings in Group

Over time, the members learn that while conflicts from their life outside can be enlightening, the more compelling experience resides in the ever unfolding group room as relationships get formed and maintained (Ormont, 2003). As difficult as it is for some members in group to tolerate their aggressive feelings, it is often the case that members have difficulty accepting recognition, affection and sexual interest as it is expressed towards them. A member who arrived with a distorted sense of self can be helped to develop new ideas and feelings about himself provided that there is sufficient emotional nutrition available in the group process (Zeisel, 2009).

For this emotional activity to flourish, we rely on the contract with each incoming patient that includes two provisions that work to ensure that all of the emotional activity will be conducted in the presence of the entire group and that it will be limited to talking. All of our patients agree not to socialize outside the treatment with fellow group members and while in session, nothing is acted out, only words are used, no one leaves their seat. With these agreements in place the stage is set for interpersonal exploration of an intimate nature that is not invited in polite society. In group you will hear and experience exchanges that might take place between intimates, more often than not these days recalling exchanges on the internet, but with the added advantage of resistance analysis in real time. So that when an interaction grows close and sexual and arouses resistance, it can be explored and yield new information about the character of the participants. In group we have the advantage of moving reported experience into *in vivo* experience making for a rich exploratory process.

Clinical Illustration

The group, ongoing for several years, has been engaged in this session since its opening phase, in a series of information exchanges whereby members report on some issue from life outside the room. One member lets the group know how helpful their recommendation was in resolving a conflict with a supervisor at work, while another told of some minimal progress in a mediated divorce process that had been stalled for months. The emotional attention shifted suddenly, when Jeff turned to Lois and told her he is feeling a lot of affection for her. Lois seemed pleased with his approach and sat up in her chair as if to better receive what was coming. Jeff then said that the exchange they had the week before, in which Lois declared how attractive she found Jeff, how masculine he was and how effective he had been in resolving a problem with another member of the group, left him with an enhanced sense of himself. In fact, Jeff went on, "I think you helped me land a new job this week, I had a terrific interview on Wednesday!" Lois looked at Jeff and said, "Well I'm glad I had a good effect on you." Jeff then launched into a description of his interview and the manner in which he conducted himself, highlighting how he remained present focused with his potential employer, bantered and responded to hypothetical problems that had been posed. However, the irony was that he was not present with Lois and left his initial connection with her at the "speed of psychological light." I felt sad and just as I was noting this in my mind, a groan could be heard from the left side of the room. Judy said, "Ooogh, Jeff I'm really glad you had a good interview but, I hate it when you speak to a woman like you just did to Lois. What does anything have to do with her! It's all about what she said that made you feel good and do well in your interview." Jeff looked stung and blanched as he took Judy's words in. He responded with anger and defensiveness and accused Judy of raining on his parade and behaving just like his sister who was always competing with him. A couple of other members chimed in, in an effort to reach Jeff in his agitated state. The effect was soothing and gave Jeff some psychological breathing room from which he could better assess what was being said to him. Slowly, Jeff could see that while he was feeling affection for Lois he wasn't free to tell her what it was specifically about her character that had such a nutritive effect on him. What he could do was tell her the effect she had on him and how useful it had been. Once again Jeff's self-absorption trumped his interest in another person, an issue we've been working on for several months. Jeff, a determined man, said, "Well, ok, I can see that now, let me try again." He turned toward Lois and with a faint smile and affection in his voice he said, "You are a very generous and beautiful woman. I love your energy, your sense of humor and being around you, what's difficult in life seems more manageable and your presence in my life made my interview this week more manageable." Lois smiled and said, "Well, I think you're a terrific man, I'm loving your flexibility at the moment, the way you shifted and could make room for seeing new possibilities between us." The sexual tension in the room was available for all to feel. Jeff looked pleased by her words and said, "I find you very attractive, I've always loved how you welcome attention from people in group." Lois smiled and said, "I think you're sexy and I'd go to bed with you in an instant!" Jeff looked delighted for a second and then grew uncomfortable and squirmed in his seat. He said, "Well what about we have a date first?" With those words the tension that connected them dissipated as if someone had pricked an inflated balloon. Lois responded with some disappointment in her voice and became slightly self-attacking when she said in an agitated voice to the group at large, "Did I go too far, too fast?" A resounding chorus of "NO" helped Lois to see that Jeff put the brakes on their engagement; they

> urged her back into contact with him. "Ok then," she said, "I can go slower if that's what's needed, where would you like to go on our date?" This lead to an exchange that Jeff was able to participate in and as they elaborated on the details, Jeff's resistance to being vulnerable became more apparent. Lois said, "Well, I'd want to feed you some dessert on my spoon." Jeff's voice tensed as he said, "That sounds nice." His words lacked energy and sounded hollow.
>
> I intervened and asked, "What happened Jeff, where did you go?" He looked down at the rug and in a muffled voice said, "I just can't take it, beyond a certain point I get scared." "What scared you?" I asked with interest, "What's so scary about Lois at the moment?" "It's not Lois, it's all women, I just get frightened that I'm going to be either criticized or left in some way that I can't bear," he said in a plaintive way. "What's your objection to being criticized or left? What feeling don't you want to experience?" I asked with genuine interest. "What do you mean!," he exclaimed, "Who wants to be ridiculed or left?!" "Nobody," I said, "But we know from experience that when people get to talking, they can end up feeling hurt or sad and then angry, you have an objection to any of those feelings?" I can see Jeff soften slightly as he said, "So you mean all I have to do is be open to pain and then I'll be able to go further with women?" "Exactly, all you have to do is be open to whatever unfolds as you're interacting with Lois or anyone else for that matter. You stay receptive and watch where it takes you. You can't go wrong. With Lois, if you tell her you're having trouble staying present, you're going to get interest." Lois chimed in, "He's right about that, I'm very loyal and determined." "Ok, I get it," Jeff said smiling and the group shifted its attention to another member who had asked for time to speak.

In this example, it is apparent that the group culture allowed for an emotionally laden exchange to take place in the safety of the circle. The group is contending with its resistance to the reproduction constellation – forces that make themselves felt in desires for sexual congress and procreativity (Spotnitz, 1976). Jeff is the "carrier" of the group's resistance; his narcissism and need for meaningful human connection are apparent. His bungled effort to recognize and stay in emotional contact with his group compatriot, Lois, led to an exploration of need and desire that everyone in the group could identify with. There was an empathic break in their relationship and with the help of the group, Jeff and Lois were able to re-engage after their connection faltered. Lois' availability to people and her determination to have more, bumped up against an old part of her that is afraid of being seen as "too aggressive." As soon as Jeff withdrew she quickly moved in the direction of self-attack and worried that she was responsible for the break in the contact. However, this time her mind was free to consider her contributions to the stalemate and with a gentle nudge from the group which had learned their way around her character, Lois was free to forsake the tortured experience of seeing herself as wrong or bad, in favor of being self-accepting. The energy that would have been devoted to self-attack became available for Lois to redirect toward Jeff. This is a theme in the lives of a number of members in the group and each of them was bolstered and encouraged by her new found freedom.

The evolution of the exchange, gave the group a deeper look at Jeff's primary objection to progress namely, he doesn't want to feel hurt or sad and angry with anyone; he's had more than enough of that for one lifetime. This resistance is shared by several other members of the group. Nevertheless, he is determined to expand his experience with people and to his credit he allowed me to work with his resistance in an exchange that named the obstacles to progress and enlisted an observing part of his mind in the ongoing study of the problem. The goal is not for Jeff to change his behavior, but to get intimately acquainted with the internal operation of his resistant pattern. We want Jeff to have greater access to his observing ego, that part of the ego that is separate from the interaction and available for observation and learning. For Jeff, this constitutes a break from the past and his commitment to see himself as flawed beyond repair (negative introjects); his allegiance to depression was momentarily suspended while new ideas and sensations became available to him (introject substitution). *It is the combination of experiential learning and cognitive learning that made this episode into the healing experience that it was for Jeff and for all of the members who identified with him. He got to have a new emotional experience and that, combined with a new understanding of his internal dynamics, will set the stage for consolidation of this learning into his character.* This kind of experience accrues over time and contributes to an expanded sense of self and a willingness to face life as it unfolds, no matter how difficult.

The Preparation of the Therapist

For the group to be willing to face what is challenging in human interaction, the therapist must first become a master of his own process. He must be a flexible communicator who can model emotional availability and expressiveness. As Martin Grotjahn said, "The therapist must be a man who has experienced life to the fullest or at least is willing to do so. He may be young or old but he must have the courage to experience life on many levels; he must know how it feels to be alive. He must have known fear and anxiety, mastery and dependency, and he must not be afraid to love, nor be a stranger to hate. An analyst should look back on his lifestyle as a proud expression of a lifelong creative effort. He may as well consider himself his own favorite patient – one who has to learn as long as he lives" (Grotjahn, 1977: p. 213). A difficult task to master. However, when viewed as the work of a lifetime, the analyst's job is enviable. Others (Hoffman, 1983, Rosenthal, 1987: p.105; Wolf, 1975) have suggested that the analyst is in a position to learn from his patients. It is therefore likely that through a lifetime of exposure to group process, the group leader will have some of his own maturational needs met as well. The analyst occupies a key position in the group process, and while he strives to lead he must also help the members feel that he is one of them, too. If the leader listens attentively to what his patients say about him, he is likely to expand his understanding of his craft and himself (Ormont, 1992: p. 51, 190; Wolf, 1975: p. 12).

Another critical function that the leader assumes is to operate within the process as an emotionally responsive person who is himself free to live in the moment, demonstrating what living with freedom feels, sounds and looks like. Recent research into the phenomenon of mirror neurons suggests that in establishing the tone for how relationships can be lived, the analyst sets in motion a process of contagion and before long members are attempting to contact one another with new freedom (Schore, 1994). And, when resistance to new experience appears, they are encouraged to explore the obstacles that have been erected. If the analyst hides his affect life, the group members will do so as well. We all learn from watching and participating in the development of relationships in the group as well as from observing the resolution of conflicts that inevitably arise member to member and member to leader. *If he is going to succeed, the leader's capacity for tolerating charged feeling states must expand over the course of his career.* This will aid him in facing the challenge of the group process, where the intense expression of emotion is commonplace. *How to be present emotionally without being activated by his countertransference resistances (resistances that derive from something in the leader's life) is a key component of skilled leadership.* The interpersonal and intra-psychic pressure that the group leader must tolerate is sizable. The conscious and unconscious forces that we contend with are considerable and their impact is sometimes unknown.

The benefits of leading multiple groups each week should be seen as a supplement to the leader's own treatment and supervision and not a substitute. Any process that contributes to flushing our psychic systems clean is bound to contribute to more psychic availability over time. Through the study of patients, we have come to know that the safest way to discharge tension is by exercising our verbal pathway of expression; talking helps. The alternative is to encourage the visceral pathway to dominate and lead to somatization, or the acting out pathway, which may be momentarily gratifying but have devastating consequences. Freud's patient Anna O called it "chimney sweeping." Or as someone else said, "If you put a cat in the kitchen to catch a mouse, you can't expect it to ignore the rat in the cellar." Through the work with patients there is the potential for a build-up of toxic psychic waste that can be readily attended to by participating in a group treatment or supervision. I am an advocate of lifelong treatment, supervision and training for anyone working with unconscious material and intersubjective experience in a therapeutic matrix. Choosing to do so will preserve and maintain your psychic apparatus and contribute to a more robust career and help you avoid compassion fatigue. Along with regular physical exercise, a healthy diet and some spiritual practice that could take a variety of forms like painting, meditation or church, group is the key to a long and satisfying practice.

Our own group process is also one of the ways we learn best how to deal with the variety of people we encounter in our work. Through parallel process and the group's unconscious experience light is shed on dark corners of complex interactions that make group treatment challenging and exciting. To master the craft of group leadership requires a prolonged immersion in cognitive and experiential learning. Group treatment and supervision is the best place to accomplish this. How many times have you been in a situation that you find dense and impossible to contend with that someone in the group has clarity about. And, in addition to the considerable body of written work in our field there is a great oral tradition to our learning and teaching. I cannot count the times in group that I have been helped to develop an understanding of a patient or sub-group and an intervention that addressed a thorny resistance or complicated interaction. Gradually, we incorporate these experiences, and if successful, we end up with three ready sources that can be turned to at moments of heightened tension in group process for consultation. The first is your analyst's voice, the second is the voice of your group analyst (sometimes the same person) and the third is the sum of all of the people you have ever been in group with, either as co-members or patients you have worked with. Something you experienced in the past will remind you of the challenge you are facing at the moment and where there were no words, suddenly you will find a phrase or an understanding that addresses the issue at hand. As my colleague Dr Leslie Rosenthal said, "My groups dragged me into mental health!"

References and Bibliography

Grotjhan, M. (1975). Growth experiences in the leader. In Z. Liff (Ed.), *The leader in the group*, (p. 148). New York: Jason Aronson.
Grotjahn, M. (1977). *Art and technique of analytic group therapy*. New York: Jason Aronson.
Laquercia, T. (personal communication, 1983).
Leibenberg, B. (2008). *Address to the Fellows of the American Group Psychotherapy Association*, Washington, D.C.
Levine, R. (2007). Treating idealized hope and hopelessness. *International Journal of Group Psychotherapy*, 57(3), 297–315.
Lichtenberg, J. D. (1989). *Psychoanalysis and motivation*. Hillsdale, New Jersey: The Analytic Press.
Maroda K. (1991). Motivations for treatment: The pursuit of transformation. In K. Maroda (Ed.), *The power of countertransference*. John Wiley & Sons.
Ormont, L. R. (personal communication, 1988).
Ormont, L. R. (1992). *The group therapy experience*. New York: St. Martin's Press.
Ormont, L. R. (1996). Bringing life into the group experience: The power of immediacy. In L. Blanco Furgeri (Ed.), *The technique of group treatment* (p. 355). Madison, Connecticut: Psychosocial Press.
Ormont, L. R. (personal communication, 1999).
Ormont, L. R. (personal communication, 2003).
Rosenthal, L (1987). *Resolving resistance in group psychotherapy*. Northvale, New Jersey: Jason Aronson.
Schore, A. N. (1994). *Affect regulation and the origin of the self – the neurobiology of emotional development*. Hillside, New Jersey: Lawrence Erlbaum Associates Publishers.
Spotnitz, H. (1976). *The psychotherapy of pre-oedipal disorders*. New York: Jason Aronson
Wolf, A. (1975). The role of the leader in the advanced and terminal phases of group psychotherapy. In Z. Liff (Ed.), *The Leader in the group* (p. 12). New York: Jason Aronson.
Yalom, I. (1970). *The theory and practice of group psychotherapy*. New York: Basic Books Inc.
Zeisel, E. M. (2009). Affect education and the development of the interpersonal ego in modern group analysis, *International Journal of Group Psychotherapy*, 59(3).

12

Developing the Role of the Group Facilitator: Learning from Experience

Orit Nuttman-Shwartz and Sarit Shay

Group facilitation is a skill that requires integration of theoretical knowledge and practical skills. The group facilitator needs to be attentive to the main issues raised in the group sessions, and to choose an appropriate intervention strategy. In that context, the facilitator needs to be aware of several dimensions of group dynamics: the individual, the individual in the group, the group as a whole, and the group as a socio-cultural microcosm (Foulkes, 1964; Karles and Wandrei, 1994).

Bollas (1987) and Ogden (1994) highlight the importance of the unique encounter between two or more individuals, who constitute a unique "third space." As such, the group is a complex, multidimensional space, which is in a perpetual state of transition. When instability is encountered – even if it happens momentarily – the dynamic nature of the group and the choice of behavior patterns are affected. In those complex situations, professionals need to integrate three levels of knowledge in their activities:

Theoretical knowledge: which relates to how the situation faced by the facilitator at a given moment can be understood.

Practical knowledge: which includes strategies and techniques that are relevant to the field, and are selected on the basis of a specific event that has taken place.

Knowledge based on beliefs and values: that affect the facilitator's style of group leadership and interventions.

In this chapter, we will discuss two types of knowledge: *espoused theory*, which includes theoretical knowledge, professional perspectives, and skills that relate to the process of socialization; and *theory in use*, which reflects beliefs and values that affect the choice of group facilitation strategies.

In reality, group facilitators – particularly those with less experience – do not always feel that what they have learned corresponds with what is happening in the "here-and-now." Schon (1987) relates to those feelings as critical experiences in group facilitation, and argues that even if an activity has been conducted, the facilitator is often left with questions, feelings of helplessness, and confusion. In these situations, facilitators feel that the familiar conceptual model is not effective enough, because it does not fit the reality that they have encountered. As a result, the facilitator's equilibrium is often upset, and the professional self-image of the facilitator as a group leader and therapist is adversely affected. This further highlights the importance of examining questions such as:

1. What was the critical event?
2. What caused the facilitator to feel a sense of imbalance?
3. Is there a gap between espoused theory and theory in use?

These issues are addressed through professional supervision, which should be conducted in a group format in the case of group facilitators. Participation in group supervision enables the supervisor and supervisee to deal with situations of ambiguity, experiences of imbalance, and activities ranging from the level of work to the level of basic assumptions. It also enables the participants in the group to gain self-confidence.

Moreover, according to Pedder (1986), supervision is a process of professional development and growth, which is more than education but less than psychotherapy. It involves learning self-awareness, and is based on complex and supportive relationships (Towel, 1972). As such, supervision is a common professional tool that practitioners use throughout their professional lives. Hence, the supervision space needs to be updated with current learning and therapeutic approaches. Toward that end, this chapter will relate to group supervision as a recommended tool for group therapists in general and groups of trainees in particular. Supervision groups can be regarded as a special tool for group psychotherapists in training, which is based on dyadic interaction, and which can help them gain practical experience as facilitators through their own participation in a supervision group (Bransford, 2009; Tylin, 1999).

Between Theory and Practice

Theories of supervision have related to three main functions of the supervision process: the didactic-educational function, the supportive function (sometimes referred to as "meta-therapy"), and the function of oversight, which relates to administrative management, ethical components, and the supervisor's responsibility for the supervisee's clients. These three elements must exist simultaneously, but can be present to varying degrees, depending on the process, the developmental stage of the group, the context of the group process, and the type of clients. Essentially, group supervision is a didactic, containing and supportive–space that is conducive to professional development. Thus, beyond performing the actual task of supervision, it is important for the supervisor to make the group a *potential space* which strengthens openness, comfort, cognitive and emotional learning, and learning from experience (Nuttman-Shwartz and Shay, 1998). The supervisor needs to be skilled in the supervision components as well as in group facilitation. In that capacity, the supervisor functions as a learning facilitator who balances the group in a number of key areas, such as: the role of group members as spectators versus co-supervisors; structure versus lack of structure; group facilitation versus supervision; challenge versus support; and group needs versus individual needs (Nuttman-Shwartz and Shay, 1998).

With regard to the supervisees, many practitioners have indicated that the availability of clinical support and consultation is crucial to their professional competence. This kind of support also serves as a useful tool for the development of a professional sense of self, and as a way of preventing compassion fatigue or burnout (Reed, 1982; Worden, 2000). Other researchers (e.g., Anderson et al., 1972) have found that participation in a supervision group encourages the group members to take responsibility for learning, enhances their sense of belonging, and creates a sense of meaning (Berman and Berger, 2010; Bogo, Globerman, and Sussman, 2004; Bransford, 2009). Such professional development occurs because the key contributor to the group is not the facilitator but the group itself, and each group member has a different perspective on the therapeutic situation. Members of the supervision group, who are somewhat removed from their groups in the field, can see existing or unconscious elements relating to countertransference among supervisees who make presentations in the group. To use Schon's (1991) term, the participants in the supervision group can explore unique elements of theory in use that affect the facilitator's behavior. On the one hand, they are similar to each other and have universal characteristics (Yalom, 2005). On the other hand, they need to solve problems and cope with the unique characteristics and the specific experiences of each group member (Foulkes, 1964). At a certain point, the individuals in the group can identify with the other participants and see themselves as others see them (i.e., similarities and differences gleaned through mirroring). The basic assumption is that most people operate intuitively, on the basis of the knowledge they gain from common experience. Reflective examination depends on the supervisee's confidence and ability to function in a situation that relates not only to theory and techniques learned in the classroom, but is also an outcome of theory in use. It can even involve the ability to create new theories relating to a specific case and test their implementation (e.g., Argyris and Schon, 1974; Fook, 2002). To reach a point that allows for reflection, supervisees need to be in a situation that Bion (1967) has referred to as "no wishes, no desires." That is, they have to be able to contain the situation of "not knowing" to a point where knowledge is used as an organizing factor, and where words and meaning are attributed to events.

Scanlon (2000) and Schon (1987) used terms that relate to practice – "knowing how," "knowing that," and "knowing in action" – which are the essence of practice wisdom. According to those researchers, the knowledge that is accumulated by the therapist-facilitator can be divided into two dimensions, as indicated: espoused theory, and theory in use. These elements guide therapists in conscious or unconscious choices, as well as in implementation of strategies of action. Schon (1987) argued that knowledge acquired at universities cannot provide answers to the complex questions and situations that emerge in the field. Hence, there is a gap between knowledge that is learned, and the knowledge that is needed in practice. Reflective examination makes it possible to develop professional knowledge by raising dilemmas that have been encountered in the field, analyzing how those dilemmas have been resolved, and considering the outcomes of these activities. To establish a dialogue between theory in use and espoused theory in the supervision group, there has to be a safe space that allows for "role playing" and "conceptualization." All of this must take place in a situation of security, open communication, contact, and cohesion. As mentioned, the way to bridge between the two types of knowledge is through reflection.

Schon (1987) identified two types of reflection: reflection *on* action, that is, retrospective thinking; and reflection *in* action, that is, "thinking on your feet". Regarding the first type of reflection, the facilitator attempts to gain insights into the situation after it has occurred; and with regard to the second type of reflection, the professional engages in a process of examination while the event is taking place.

Reid referred to reflection as an active process rather than as passive thinking: "Reflection is a process of reviewing an experience of practice in order to describe, analyze, evaluate, and so inform learning about practice" (Reid, 1993: p. 305). It is also a personal process that usually changes the individuals' perspectives of a situation, and that creates new learning. In addition, reflection is a decision-making process in which clinical developments are discussed, and in which the understanding of what happened can serve as the basis for personal and professional development. To sum up, the supervision group aims to enable translation of the different narratives in the supervisory matrix into a more articulate understanding of how the supervisees experience their respective training groups.

Taking all of this into consideration, we sought to develop a conceptual framework that can be applied to group supervision in an attempt to maximize its productivity, minimize its disadvantages, and allow for the development of a potential learning space for all of the participants in the supervision group. This training model is an integrative one, which combines developmental and psychodynamic orientations based on the theories of Bion (1961), Foulkes (1964), and Winnicott (1971) as well as an on educational theories that seek to update professional learning concepts (e.g., Argyris and Schon, 1974; Fook, 2002). Theories of supervision are also integrated into our model (Kadushin, 1992). Personal growth and the adoption of new clinical skills enable trainees to try out new behaviors, and to begin adapting to the demands of their upcoming role in a more or less protected environment – the supervision group. In the "potential space" of the supervision group, trainees are expected to internalize the demands of the group therapist's role, and to function autonomously as group therapists. In the following section, we will integrate literature on group psychotherapy with literature on professional education.

The Reflective Action Model for Group Supervision

Our model is based on the understanding that the group supervision process enables participants to gain new knowledge and perspectives on a particular situation, which can be applied toward conducting their groups. This is done through a process of reflective examination, where participants in the group present a narrative or critical event, and raise difficult dilemmas that they have encountered as facilitators. The process of reflection also focuses on the encounter between espoused theory and theory in use, as well as on exploring different patterns of group leadership and how selected strategies of action affect the outcomes of intervention. One of the advantages of group supervision lies in its format, which is parallel to that of clinical groups and is characterized by many of the same dynamics.

Bernard and Goodyear (2004) and Coleman et al., (2009), argued that the supervisee or trainee experiences *in vivo* the nuance and power of the group dynamics while receiving extensive feedback from peers. In order to provide feedback, group members need to engage in open communication, in keeping with the assumption that "everything can be thought about and articulated" (Foulkes, 1964). Therefore, in our model, the first step is to provide the participants with a safe space for learning and interaction, and enable them to develop a sense of belonging – a meaningful feeling that promotes homeostasis and facilitates professional growth (Bernard, 1999; Coleman et al., 2009; Fook, 2002; Kleinberg, 1999; Yerushalmi, 1999). To use Yalom's (2005) term, there is a sense of "universality" among the group members, which develops when the presenters see that other facilitators deal with the same problems and experiences, and which enables the presenters to contain their sense of inadequacy and lack of homeostasis. Being a supervisee in a group of equal members puts feelings of anxiety into perspective, and allows each to be more tolerant toward their own difficulties and failures as well as toward the difficulties and failures of others in the group. Although the proposed model is chronological, it is not always clear where one stage ends and the next one begins.

The ability of the group members to observe events in the "here-and-now" while also exploring the events that the presenter shares with the group is an important part of the learning process. The theoretical literature on group supervision has emphasized that each member of the group plays a double role, as a participant and as a group leader. In addition, each participant is both an integral part of the group as-a-whole and an independent entity. These complementary processes play a role in holding the group. They enable each participant to "enter" the minds of the other group members, and integrate those individuals into the matrix of the group. In that way, participants can experience regressive and fragmented aspects as well as explore internal and unconscious parts of themselves (Berman and Berger, 2010). Foulkes and Anthony (1957) stated that the mirror reaction of the group and the process of transference enhance the members' understanding of their own conflicts, cultural assumptions, individual norms, and behavior patterns. As such, the matrix of the supervision group becomes a source of assistance for the other group members, and the group's task is to turn the personal narrative of each participant into a group narrative shared by all of the members. That is, the group aims to translate and contain the narratives, and uses free associations and feedback from the group members as a means of gaining new insights into the participants' experiences at various levels: the personal level, the level of interpersonal relations in the supervision group, and level of the group in the field.

Operative Principles of the Supervision Model

The group supervision process consists of two dimensions: the technical dimension, which is reflected in the narratives presented by each participant in the group sessions; and the dynamic dimension, which includes the relationships among the members of the group. Another noteworthy dimension relates to the parallel processes of group supervision. The supervisor needs to be aware of the complexity of this work, which includes professional and personal exposure relating to the establishment of a safe space. At the same time, the supervisor is obligated to focus on the task at hand, that is, supervising facilitation of groups in the field, while revealing the dynamics within the supervision group itself.

Stages of Work

Our model is a circular one, which consists of stages recurring in each supervision session and in the process of the group's development over time. Each session and the process as a whole begin with a phase referred to as "tuning in," which aims to lay the foundation for work. The second phase is "reflective work," where each member of the group is invited to engage in reflection and examination; and the third phase is "conceptualization and summarization." The process continues at the beginning of the next session, when the supervisor invites the presenter from the previous session to share thoughts and feelings that arose since that session, and the other group members offer feedback.

Principles of Work ("What and How")

The supervisor. The supervisor possesses theoretical knowledge relating to the context of group supervision and facilitation. This knowledge is accessible to the members of the supervision group, and is transmitted through sharing and conceptualization. Thus, the supervisor is not the one who transmits the knowledge. Rather, the group members are invited to participate in the process of reflection and apply practical and theoretical knowledge that they have accumulated from their experience as facilitators of groups in the field. The supervisor needs to weigh the developmental stage of the group and adapt the style of supervision to the dynamics of the group at a given moment. Various models of group supervision have argued that the supervisors go through developmental stages themselves. Each stage has unique characteristics, which range from relative dependency to professional autonomy (Coleman, Kivligham, and Roehlke, 2009). That is, the supervisor needs to move from content to process, and integrate psycho-educational elements with the dynamics of the group in order to hold the group-as-a whole and the participants as individuals. In that process, the supervisor applies methods relating to reflection in and on action.

To enhance their own understanding and the participants' perspective of what takes place in the different spheres, supervisors need to use parallel processes known as the "here-and-there" – for example: the supervisor *vis-à-vis* the group; the facilitator alone; and the group. Although supervisors are primarily responsible for the supervision group, they are also responsible for the groups in the field. Toward that end, the supervisor needs to implement a model for leading the supervision group and training the supervisees to facilitate the groups in the field. Hence, the participants need to be equipped with tools for coping with that task, and they need to be able to promote the group process in the field.

The Stage of Building the Group

The process of group supervision aims to provide an opportunity for participants to listen to each other and reflect on case materials, while at the same time, minimizing the potential for defensiveness. This process depends on the ability of the supervisor and the participants to engage in reverie at the level of open dialogue (Bion, 1962). The term reverie refers to the supervisor's ability to reach a stage characterized as "without memory and desire" (Bion, 1970), in which the supervisor believes that something meaningful will evolve. The supervisor's ability to be in that kind of position will determine the extent to which the participants can engage in free association, learning, and change.

At this stage, the aim is to create conditions for optimal learning in the supervision group, in order to enable participants to attain the goals that they sought to achieve in the group sessions. Toward that end, the tasks of supervision focus on the following: creating the supervision setting; working on the dimension of relationships among group members, and creating a safe space; establishing the principles of work, while addressing the supervisor's expectations of the group and the group members' expectations of each other; creating a group language by using concepts related to group theories and supervision and conceptualization of the process experienced by the group; and demonstrating events in the "here-and-now."

The tasks at this stage are a precondition for engaging in dialogue and for reflective thinking. Therefore, the supervisor does not focus on the groups led by facilitators (or that the facilitators are supposed to lead). Rather, emphasis is placed on creating a space that is conducive to containment. The style of supervision is structured, and sometimes it is directive. Time is allotted for the members of the supervision group to get to know each other. These interactions can also relate to the aims and character of the group, how well the participants know each other, and their familiarity with group facilitation. In the context of creating the setting for the initial sessions, the facilitator engages in the function of "holding," and focuses on the following questions: What are the aims of supervision? What domains of work will they focus on, and how? The supervisor also seeks to establish norms and patterns of work, and attempts to provide a concrete theoretical and practical rationale for the method and style of work. The supervisor shares thoughts and feelings with the participants that are relevant to the "here-and-now" process, and also involves them in decisions about facilitation, on the assumption that modeling based on openness, explanation, conceptualization, and speaking at eye level will considerably reduce anxiety and increase understanding. For example, at the beginning of the first session the group members get to know each other. Afterwards, the supervisor explains the nature of the work in the group, and clarifies why a certain type of introduction was chosen and why certain words were used. Toward the end of that session, the supervisor can stop and ask the participants how they felt at the beginning of the session and how they feel at the end. In that way, they will be able to identify experiences of anticipation and ambivalence in the process of positioning themselves in the group.

In the initial stages of the learning process, it is important to devote time to examining the participants' educational needs. This can be done, for example, through questions about their previous experience with facilitating groups, their perceptions of incentives and obstacles in facilitation, and their desires and expectations. At this stage, the supervisor relates to characteristics that the participants share in common, as well as to differences between them. Common characteristics strengthen the feeling of togetherness and the experience of partnership, whereas the differences represent the distinctive characteristics of each participant. For example, participants with a high level of anxiety often hold basic assumptions that unconsciously elicit nonverbal emotional behaviors, and that prevent exploration, understanding, and conceptualization. Hence, the supervisor needs to be able to identify this process (the relationship between basic assumptions and the working group), and to understand why the group has not succeeded in learning and engaging in behaviors characterized as "attacks on linking."

Afterwards, the supervisor needs to help the participants identify these processes and enable them to move from the level of basic assumptions to the level of a working group. Specifically, the supervisor helps the participants learn from experience, and invites them to share their experiences in the here-and-now, to examine all of the feelings that arise, and to conceptualize those feelings through theories that deal with group processes. At the same time, the events in "here-and-now" can be applied to the groups that the participants facilitate in the field. At that point, the group can move to the stage of work and reach a process of reflection or free association, which is essential for creating the personal and group narrative.

The Stage of Group Work

In every group supervision session, participants are selected to make a presentation to the group and raise a dilemma or question about events that take place in the groups they facilitate in the field, or about the way that those groups are being conducted. The presenters know when they are scheduled to make a presentation, and can prepare in advance.

The Narrative Stage

At the beginning of each session, the presenters briefly describe the characteristics of the group they are facilitating: how many people are in the group, the type of population, the aim of the group, the duration of sessions, the main topics that arose in group sessions, etc. Based on the approach of Schon (1987) and Fook (2002), the presenter will choose a critical event as the focus of the supervision session.

In some cases, the participants in the group will feel frustration or general worry, but they will not verbalize it. According to our model, the supervisees are invited to address any issue they choose in their presentations to the group. In the supervisor's work with the supervisees, an attempt is made to identify any gaps between espoused theory and theory in use, conflicts that arose at the end of the activity, and sources of frustration, in addition to determining what interventions were not effective and why that happened. It is important to bear in mind that in keeping with the reflective approach, supervisees refrain from talking about "right and wrong" or "good and bad." Rather, they emphasize "what *went* wrong," and why. After the supervisees have made a general presentation about their group, they are asked to present their personal narrative. In some cases, the presenters talk about a specific event that took place in their group, and that raised questions in their minds. In other cases, they raise a general question or share vague and confused feelings. In those cases, the supervisor's task is to ask the presenter to give examples, and direct the presenter toward an event or several events that are associated with the espoused dilemma. Sometimes, when supervisees are unable to present a specific event, they are asked to describe the last session of their group. It is important to notice when the presentation of the event becomes lifeless or repetitive, or when it becomes unclear. When the participants in the supervision group comment on the presenter's narrative, the supervisor needs to emphasize that they should not try to evaluate or interpret it; rather, they should only ask questions for clarification. In that way, the participants in the group "reflect on action," so that the presenter's personal narrative can become a narrative that involves all of the members of the group.

It is assumed that the comments and questions of other group members will provide a basis for expanding the presenter's narrative, and will allow latent aspects or aspects that were put aside to come to the surface. In light of those comments, the supervisor will reflect on questions such as:

- Did the presenter focus more on the group-as-a-whole than on the individuals in it (or the opposite)?
- Did the presenter focus more on the process than content?
- How was the presentation made?
- What language was used?
- What did the presenter avoid?
- What was placed in the background, and what was in the foreground?
- What were the presenter's emotional reactions?
- To what extent did the presenter respond to the questions, and what were the responses?

In that process, it is important to make sure that the responses to the intervention in itself are not judgmental, and that they focus on examining questions in an attempt to enhance understanding and expand on the content (Miehls and Moffat, 2000). The method of work, as mentioned, focuses on the presentation of a topic at the beginning of each group session and on the discussion that ensues. The presenter learns through modeling the supervisor and through verbal articulation. The supervisor tests the boundaries of the presenter, and chooses what topics to focus on and when. In that process, the participants in the supervision group learn how to conduct themselves in the group context.

As mentioned, the work takes place only on the cognitive level. The supervisor observes the group, and considers the extent to which the participants support the presenter, the extent to which they relate to the topic presented, and whether the narrative becomes a group narrative or whether there is avoidance among the participants. The supervisor relates to the role of the group in the process, and attempts to understand the relevance of those responses to the process, how much they represent a certain difficulty, and whether the group is engaging in actual work. The process ends when the supervisor feels that the first stage has been completed. At that point, the presenter is asked to describe personal thoughts and insights relating to that stage of the work.

The Stage of Reflection

Participants in the supervision group are invited to share their reactions to the presenter's narrative. In so doing, they can allow themselves unlimited space for free association and creative thinking. For example, they can discuss situations of unconscious enactment by the presenter or other participants in the group. As they learned in previous stages of the group supervision, the participants relate to their case material, and not to countertransference. This minimizes vulnerability and enables openness and sharing, although the supervisor continues to be aware that the countertransference discussion might seep in and hurt the presenter. Notably, the supervisor is in a position to protect the presenter, and if the supervisor identifies countertransference, the group should be made aware of it.

Through free association, the group creates a unique matrix. The narrative analysis is an outcome of active listening, and represents the main topics that unconsciously concern the presenter, that is, topics that the presenter cannot contain, or other conflicts and dilemmas that are projected onto the group members. The analysis can also relate to blind spots that serve as incentives or obstacles, or to the personal narratives of other participants in the group. Furthermore, it can relate to the dynamic narrative of the group-as-a-whole in the here-and-now. First, the presenter is asked just to listen, and to refrain from responding. That is, the presenter is supposed to be in a "dream state," which is a state of relaxation that enables the individual to learn from experience without having to react to what is taking place. It is assumed that when the presenters are in a dream state, they refrain from using defense mechanisms and justifying previous behaviors and emotions. Therefore, they are more open to absorbing new content. In the subsequent stage, cognitive learning takes place.

As the discourse progresses, the personal narrative becomes known to the group; it contains the ideas and interpretations of the group, and becomes a group narrative. In addition, the narrative contains free associations and reactions of the group members based on the experiences of all of the members. It also contains the changes that took place in the group, and the narrator's responses to the group discussion.

The relative distance created between the personal and group narratives is conducive to raising unconscious personal and group content. The goal of this process is for the participants in the group to be more open to their inner experiences as a way of deepening their contact with and understanding of the presenter. As mentioned, the participant is in a receptive position, and can connect with emotional responses. In the process of reflective sharing, participants experience a process of translating feelings and unconscious thoughts into emotional and cognitive experiences that are articulated in words so that their meaning becomes clear. At that point, they move from the notion of unknown thought (Bollas, 1987) to a state of professional and personal awareness.

At this stage, the supervisor attempts to examine the main conflicts that arise, and to assess gaps between theory in use and espoused theory at the levels of the presenter and the other members of the group. The supervisor needs to decide what type of reflection to use in facilitating the group, when to stop the free associations and intervene, on what level to intervene, and whether to emphasize the level of content or process. It is also important to determine whether the group process takes place at the level of work and the primary task, or whether it takes place at the level of basic assumptions. While the discussion is taking place, the supervisor can make use of the concept of "parallel processes," and connect the topics raised at the group level with the personal topics raised by the presenter. These topics can be related to the theme of the supervision group or to professional development (emotional attitudes and countertransference).

The Summary Stage

This stage of the supervision process includes identifying and exploring the principles that guided the group and the supervisor in the supervisory sessions. Dynamic elements relating to the events in the "here-and-now," and in the "there-and-now" are emphasized. This enhances the participants' self awareness, and enables them to consider what the discussion aroused in them, what personal insights they gained, and what insights they can apply to the groups they facilitate. Toward the end of the session, the focus returns to the presenter and to practical questions, such as, what the presenter has gained from the group, how the experience will affect the presenter's behavior in the future, and how those outcomes can be conceptualized. The supervisor focuses on establishing organization and order, and provides definitions and conceptualizations of the process from a theoretical and practical perspective: group, supervision, and developmental theories relating to the problems of clients and to the organizational and political context in which the group operates.

An Example of a supervisory Group

This illustration is based on one supervision group, which was conducted as part of an internship in group facilitation in the Masters of Social Work program at one of the universities in Israel. Sessions were held once every two weeks for the entire academic year. The group of supervisees consisted of 12 graduates in psychology and social work, which were between the ages of 27 and 50. Two of the participants were men.

Clinical Illustration

A woman named Michal asked to present a dilemma relating to silence. At the beginning of her presentation, the supervisor asked the presenter in the previous meeting to briefly describe any developments since the last session, and to indicate whether she had gained any new insights. As mentioned, the supervision model highlights the importance of following up and giving the presenter in the previous meeting a chance for closure, by briefly sharing new insights and experiences since the presentation.

Afterwards, Michal proceeded with her presentation:

MICHAL   My group has eight participants – two men, and six women. Three of them are Arab women who live in the area. Two of the Arab women dress traditionally, and one is secular. The two religious Arab women have been silent since the beginning of the group sessions. The group has been meeting for three months, and I've tried to get them [those two women] to speak, but nothing seems to work. It really irritates me, and I don't know what to do about it. On the one hand, I'm concerned about them and want to protect them. I don't want the others in the group to hurt them or treat them as a minority or as an enemy. On the other hand, I'm angry about their silence and lack of cooperation. Even when I know that they're just expressing resistance, and even if their behavior reflects the reality we live in, I don't feel any calmer. Even now, as I talk about the problem, I still feel angry.

(The participants in the supervision group were invited to comment on Michal's story and ask her for clarifications.)

NAOMI   I really identify with you – but do the other members of your group participate all the time?
MICHAL   Well, not all the time – but these two women have stayed silent from the very beginning.
GILA   Do they communicate nonverbally?
MICHAL   At first I thought they did [say things nonverbally]. I thought I could feel their message . . . But the more time goes by, the angrier and more frustrated I feel. I'm afraid the group is going to lose them.
DAPHNA   What do you do in the group? Can you tell us a bit more?
MICHAL   In the last meeting, after they had been silent for so long, I specifically asked each of the participants to react to the fact that not everyone talks. When their turn came up, these two women still refused to say anything. Then I addressed Nur [one of the women]. I said to her: "You've been here for three months already. I really want to get to know you. So does the whole group. Can you tell us anything? I waited for a long time. It seemed like forever to me . . . She just kept silent. I asked the group if anyone wants to respond – and the people in the group said that if someone doesn't want to talk they don't need to . . . Most of the others in the group said that it doesn't bother them at all.

At that point, the supervisor felt it was important to clarify how frustrating it is to choose a strategy that doesn't yield the desired outcome.

SUPERVISOR Michal, I get the impression that you are very upset about this – that you show it both in your group and in this group.
MICHAL   I feel that my personal self is confused with my professional self. I understand from the reactions of my group that I didn't do the right thing – but I just don't know what to do.
SUPERVISOR What did you think would happen when you asked the group to go around and respond to your question?
MICHAL   I don't know what made me choose that strategy. I was sure it would work – but it didn't, and that's what's frustrating.
SUPERVISOR But what did you expect? Even if you weren't aware of your expectations, try to explore . . . go back and reconstruct the session.

(Michal is silent. It's hard for her to respond.)

SHAUL   If you were having the same problem with a Jewish participant, would you still have chosen to go around in the group and talk about it?

MICHAL	In the last session, silence was the main characteristic of the group as a whole, and not just a problem that characterized a certain sub-group. That is, it wasn't just those Arab women. Maybe the question should have been "What is the significance of talking in the group?"
SUPERVISOR	Right now, is there anything that has become clearer to you?
MICHAL	What's going on right now is that I don't feel like I'm a good enough facilitator [she smiles] – or, in my family's terms, I'm not outstanding.

At that point, the supervisor saw that she had touched on an important theme. As part of the transition to the "in-action reflection" stage, she asked the participants to share any associations that came to their minds at that moment.

GILA	Michal said that the silence makes her angry . . . she doesn't know what to do about it. Like "didn't these people come here to get help? So why are they shutting up?" (She says this in an angry tone).
DAPHNA	It's always the same story. The "here" and "there" always get mixed up. I don't understand why we always have to reconstruct the conflict.
ELI	In my group the people who keep silent are different. I have a homosexual participant, who stopped talking in the group ever since he came out of the closet. And there's another girl in my group who is small and thin . . . I don't know anything about her.
BATYA	I'm totally discouraged. If things go well, then fine. But if they don't . . . It reminds me of my parents' home. After we had arguments, there was interminable silence.
MICHAL	I come from a home where silence is considered a disaster. My parents are divorced, and ever since they split up I've been living in thunderous silence. And it's not at all like me to talk about problems with others. It only reminds me of difficult family incidents.
SHAUL	Just don't go back to the Holocaust [he laughs cynically].

Regarding this comment, the supervisor noted that the reference to the Holocaust reflects a sense of anger, which was expressed as behavioral enactment in a cynical voice. There was a feeling of dissatisfaction, difficulty, and anxiety that cannot be articulated in words. That the explanation for this group situation relates to key topics such as majority-minority relations and similarities versus differences, which are present in the room but generate tension because they do are not verbally articulated. The transition to group discourse made it possible to moderate Michal's level of anxiety and examine the process of mirroring in the group.

At that point, the supervisor assumed that the anger expressed in the supervision group reflected a general experience of helplessness which was directed against people who are silent. The supervisor's assumption might explain the anger and frustration that Michal felt toward the participants in her group who refused to talk. Through free associations, the supervisor noticed that the group had moved from talking about external conflicts to internal, personal conflicts that were aroused by the reference to violence in the home or the experience of divorce. The supervisor proposed that both of these familiar aspects might be a mechanism for coping with the difficulty of staying in a new, conflictual place that represents uncertainty about one's role, insecurity about facilitation skills, and confusion about the professional languages. Regarding unconscious responses, the participants in the group decided not to talk about topics they were unfamiliar with or unsure about. The discourse that ensued about when people are silent or whether silence is a form of resistance was interpreted by the supervisor as the use of a distancing strategy that represents insecurity.

The supervisor returned to Michal, and asked her what strategies she uses when she feels insecure. Michal replied that she moves between two directions: on the one hand, she has an urge to be silent and unconsciously believes that silence is a bad thing; on the other hand, she aspires toward excellence. Michal said that she had difficulty reconciling the gap between what is desirable and what exists. Therefore, she could not reconcile herself to the need for creative thinking and active responses based on theory in use. Essentially, she had difficulty adapting to reality, and did not translate espoused theory into theory in use. This was the source of her own frustration and the frustration expressed by the other group members, which resulted in a rigid and formal approach that conflicts with the underlying perspective of our model.

In this case, the supervisor chose to conceptualize the situation as one in which the participants in the group were trapped in a familiar process, and where silence reflected their stagnation and lack of courage to raise alternatives. Based on that approach, the supervisor could show that Michal's strategy was also reconstructed in the event, and that by trying to force the participants in her group to talk, she was relating to them in the language that was familiar to her as a facilitator. However, that language represented the values of Western society, as reflected in the assumption that silence does not bring progress. Michal attempted to ignore sociocultural differences among members of her group and did not make room for members of the "other" group to express their perspective. This was also evidenced in the fact that she referred to the two Arab participants as if they were one person, and no one in the group mentioned anything about that. This kind of activity does not maximize the relative advantage of the group as a forum for expanding the group matrix.

In this context, it also important to bear in mind that the two "silent" students were Arab. According to Fook (2002), the social situation is reconstructed in the process of reflection. In the above-mentioned supervision group as well, the sociopolitical structure of Israel was reflected in Michal's case description, which raised the issue of power relations, silence and silencing, and ambivalence about the extent to which people are interested in voicing their perspectives, listening, and engaging in dialogue. Notably, the participants in the supervision group were all Jewish students. Therefore, the issue of silence and silencing went beyond the sociopolitical level and moved to the personal level, which reflected life in the shadow of family violence and even references to the Holocaust. In the process of summing up, the supervisor made references to reconstructing social, political, and cultural elements as a dimension that needs to be considered in the process of supervision. Those elements can manifest themselves on various levels – intrapersonal, interpersonal, and social. Nonetheless, the question arises: how much should this issue be addressed, and to what extent should the supervisor stick to the primary task of supervision? On the one hand, the Israeli-Palestinian conflict was addressed in this case. On the other hand, the conflict was not addressed sufficiently or directly. This might reinforce the dimension of supervision in the above-mentioned group (Nuttman-Shwartz and Shay, 2006), and it supports the contention that in psycho-educational groups it is important to work on the cognitive function (Ettin, 1999). In our case, the conflict in the group enabled the members to fashion a relatively safe space and accept cultural and individual differences. In that connection, Ettin (1999) proposed that the therapist should raise emotional events pertaining to the group while ensuring that those issues do not deflect the group from engaging in its espoused task. In that way, it might be possible to enhance the participants' understanding of each other and prevent the use of destructive defense mechanisms such as splitting and projection. That approach might serve as a model for acceptance of cultural, ethnic and racial diversity which enables the participants to become familiar with the Arab students and support them.

At that point, the supervisor asked Michal what she had learned from the session, and invited her to reconsider what strategy is relevant to her and her group in the field. That led to the Summary stage.

Conclusion

The chapter presented a model for training students in group facilitation and group therapy. Based on a phenomenological perspective, we combined the Person In Environment approach with reflective approaches to teaching. According to those approaches, in real life the individual possesses knowledge and experience that broaden theoretical understanding and promote dynamic therapy.

The present chapter demonstrates the unique contribution of an approach that combines theoretical knowledge with group supervision while students are being trained or while students or group therapists are engaging in group facilitation. Multidimensional work, which breaks down the various components of professionalism into espoused theory and theory in use can enhance the students' awareness and enable them to distinguish between what the facilitator or therapist knows ("classic" learning), and what is learned through practical experience (practice wisdom). In addition, the model stresses learning from peers in the process of examining and conceptualizing group work as a participant on the one hand and as a facilitator on the other. When the "what-and-how" come together, the processes of change are internalized, and the participant's identity as a therapist or facilitator is strengthened. These processes are intensified by enhancing the supervisees' awareness of the knowledge they have acquired through their experience as group facilitators in the field.

This integrated model highlights the complexity of the supervisor's role. Even though it is accepted that experienced therapists move from individual to group supervision, this chapter highlights the importance of group supervision as a distinct field. Contemporary approaches to professional supervision are based on knowledge in the field of adult education, in addition to knowledge relating to individual and professional development. Specialization and experience are not sufficient for teaching and supervision. An examination of the case description presented in this chapter emphasizes that the supervisor needs to move between different roles and make an effort to encourage active learning in the "here-and-now" and the "now-and-there". This is also important in light of the supervisor's professional responsibility for the clients facilitated by the participants in the supervision group. Because the supervisees in those groups are usually experienced professionals, the supervisor needs to be able to maneuver in the different spheres that relate to the supervision process. Hence, we recommend that supervisors specialize in the field of supervision, and not just in therapy and group facilitation. A difficulty commonly mentioned in the literature relates to the distinction between supervision and therapy. Quite a few supervisors fail to make that distinction, and essentially turn the group sessions into therapy sessions. As a result, the boundary between supervision and therapy often becomes blurred (Nuttman-Shwartz and Shay, 2006). Another source of confusion relates to the tendency to turn these groups into forums that work only on the individual narratives of the participants. In those cases, the primary task changes, and the sessions no longer focus on supervision. These difficulties highlight the need for awareness, as well as the need for substantive learning of the working model.

Supervision is a learned skill, and supervisors who facilitate supervision groups also need room for reflection. They need to strengthen their capacity to maneuver and enhance their specific knowledge in order to distinguish between the therapeutic and didactic components of the group process. It is important for them to recognize that group supervision is neither therapy nor teaching, and to take responsibility for how they use the "time and place" of the supervision sessions. As such, supervisors who facilitate supervision groups need to achieve a proper balance between theory in use and espoused theory. They also need to facilitate the supervision sessions "without memory or desire" (Bion, 1967), and they need to create an atmosphere that is conducive to exploration and reflection from a position of "knowing and not knowing" rather than from a position of omniscience. Even though the educational models of Fook (2002) and Schon (1987) are well-known, to the best of our knowledge they have not been applied to practice in contexts of group therapy and facilitation. One explanation for this might be that the kind of work described in this chapter is highly complex and has not yet been implemented comprehensively in group therapy and facilitation. Nor has it been examined beyond its application in casework supervision.

In summary, group supervision is an accepted and desirable tool for supervision of facilitators. However, there is a lack of literature on that kind of supervision and, as mentioned, there is often confusion and ambiguity about that context. A good facilitator can become a supervisor, but the difference between the roles of therapist-supervisors and facilitator-supervisors is not always taken into account. In addition, there is often a lack of integration in the field. Hence, the new model proposes an integrative approach that links different roles and disciplines, in addition to linking the spheres of supervision, facilitation, and therapy.

The supervisors of these groups engage in the complex task of observing multidimensional events. Therefore, they need to acquire knowledge in various fields, including adult education, group therapy and facilitation, and the supervisors need to make effective decisions about which of those dimensions to focus on at a given moment. Toward that end, they need to consider the best interests of the supervision group, the presenter, and the group in the field. All of those dimensions together require specific, comprehensive training. Essentially, group supervision is an ongoing process, which combines supervision and learning, and in which peers in the group play an active role in enhancing awareness, acquiring appropriate knowledge, and expanding skills. This combination of reflective work based on the two types of theories (espoused theory and theory in use) was integrated into the proposed model for group supervision and facilitation of psychodynamic groups.

References and Bibliography

Anderson, C. M., Harrow, M., Schwartz, A.H., et al. (1972). Impact of therapist on patient satisfaction in group psychotherapy. *Comprehensive Psychiatry, 13*, 33–40.

Argyris, C., & Schon, D. A. (1974). *Theory in practice: Increasing professional effectiveness.* San Francisco, California: Jossey-Bass.

Berman, A., & Berger, M. (2010). Matrix and reverie in supervision. *Group Analysis, 40*, 243–249.

Bernard, H. S. (1999). Introduction to the special issue on group supervision of group psychotherapy. *International Journal of Group Psychotherapy 49*, 153–157.

Bernard, J., & Goodyear, R. (2004). *Fundamentals of clinical supervision.* (3rd ed.). Boston, Massachusetts Allyn & Bacon.

Bion, W. (1961). *Experiences in groups and other papers.* London: Tavistock.

Bion, W. (1962). *Learning from experience.* New York: Basic Books.

Bion, W. R. (1967). *Second thoughts: Selected papers on psychoanalysis.* London: William Heinemann Medical Books.

Bion, W. R. (1970). *Attention and interpretation.* London: Tavistock.

Bollas, C. (1987). *The shadow of the object: Psychoanalysis of the unthought known.* New York: Columbia University Press.

Bogo, M., Globerman, J., & Sussman, T. (2004). Field instructor competence in group supervision: Students' views. *Journal of Teaching in Social Work, 24*, 199–216.

Bransford, C. R. (2009). Process-centered group supervision. *Clinical Social Work, 37*, 119–127.

Coleman, M. N., Kivligham, M. D., & Roehlke, H. J. (2009). A taxonomy of feedback given in the group supervision of group counselor trainers. *Group Dynamic Theory: Research and Practice, 13*, 300–315.

Ettin, M. F. (1999). Group development: Building protocol for psychoeducational groups. In M. F. Ettin (Ed.), *Foundations and applications of group psychotherapy: A sphere of influence* (pp. 223–259). London: Jessica Kingsley Publishers.

Fook, J. (2002). *Social work: Critical theory and practice.* London: Sage.

Foulkes, S. H. (1964). *Therapeutic group analysis.* London: Allen & Unwin.

Foulkes, S. H., & Anthony, E. J. (1957). *Group psychotherapy: The psychoanalytic approach.* London: Marshfield Library.

Kadushin, A. (1992). *Supervision in social work.* New York: Colombia University Press.

Karles, J. M., & Wandrei, K. E. (1994). *Person-in-environment system: The PIE classification system for social functioning problems.* Washington, DC: National Association of Social Workers.

Kleinberg, J. L. (1999). The supervisory Alliance and the Training of Psychodynamic Group Psychotherapy. *International Journal of Group Psychotherapy 49*, 159–179.

Miehls, D., & Moffatt, K. (2000). Constructing social work identity based on the reflexive self. *British Journal of Social Work, 30*, 339–348.

Nuttman-Shwartz, O., & Shay, S. (2006). Supervision groups and political-social conflict. *The Journal for Specialists in Group Work, 31*, 291–309.

Nuttman-Shwartz, O., & Shay, S. (1998). Transition to leadership: An innovative program to prepare helping professional to lead parents groups. *Social Work with Groups, 21*, 117–128.

Ogden, T. H. (1994). The analytical third: Working with intersubjective clinical facts. *International Journal of Psychoanalysis 75*, 3–20.

Pedder, J. (1986). Reflections on the theory and practice of supervision. *Psychoanalytic Psychotherapy, 2*, 1–12.

Reed, H. (1982). Burnout and self-resilience. *Public Welfare, 40*, 29–35.

Reid, B. (1993). But we're doing it already! Exploring a response to the concept of reflective practice in order to improve its facilitation. *Nurse Education Today, 13*, 305–309.

Scanlon, C. (2000). The place of clinical supervision in the training of group-analytic psychotherapists: Toward a group dynamic model for professional education. *Group Analysis, 33*, 193-207.

Schon, D.A. (1987). *Educating the reflective practitioner.* San Francisco, San Francisco: Jossey Bass.

Schon, D. A. (1991). *Educating the reflective practitioner.* San Francisco, California: Jossey Bass.

Towel, C. (1952). *The learner in education for the professions.* Chicago: University of Chicago Press.

Tylin, I. (1999). Group supervision and the psychoanalytic process, *International Journal of Group Psychotherapy, 49*, 181–195.

Winnicott, D. W. (1971). Transitional object and transitional phenomena. In D. W. Winnicott, (Ed.), *Playing and reality.* London: Penguin Books.

Worden, B. (2000). Using fieldwork experiences as a tool for teaching: A multi-layered approach. *Groupwork, 12*, 56–76.

Yalom, I. (2005) *Theory and practice in group psychotherapy.* New York: Basic book

Yerushalmi, H. (1999). The roles of group supervision of supervision. *Psychoanalytic Psychology, 16*, 426–447.

13
From Empathically Immersed Inquiry to Discrete Intervention: Are There Limits to Theoretical Purity?

Steven L. Van Wagoner

Training programs in Group Psychotherapy abound for clinicians who have completed their graduate studies in their respective fields, and yet seek to expand their knowledge and skills at post-graduate level. Through the American Group Psychotherapy Association (AGPA) and its local affiliate societies alone, there is a wealth of group therapy training venues available across the United States, and this list does not include many of the fine training programs outside of AGPA through other private and public organizations.

Some training programs adhere to a specific theoretical framework (e.g. The Center for the Advancement of Group Studies offers training in Modern Analytic Group Principles and Techniques), while others train their students through multiple theoretical lenses (e.g. The National Group Psychotherapy Institute of the Washington School of Psychiatry). Each approach has its merits. In the former, a student can be immersed in a specific theoretical approach, learning in great detail how that theory views the central elements of group therapy: interpersonal and intrapsychic development, group development, understanding group dynamics, the leader's role, and how group can be an agent of change in the lives of its members. The latter provides the student with exposure to multiple approaches, tailoring learning toward integrating knowledge from several theoretical perspectives, comparing and contrasting each theory along the central elements listed above. In addition, both models typically provide experiential and didactic learning of basic and/or theory specific group principles, which are both experienced in the here-and-now as well as through readings, lectures, and/or discussion.

The purpose of this chapter is to explore whether deviation from a specific theory has certain benefits, and moreover, whether integration of theories has its place in our work. While I believe that thorough study of a particular theoretical approach is laudable, even desirable, I think that there are also benefits to being not only knowledgeable of, but also appreciative of, other group therapy approaches. As a result,

---

The Wiley-Blackwell Handbook of Group Psychotherapy, First Edition. Edited by Jeffrey L. Kleinberg.
© 2012 John Wiley & Sons, Ltd. Published 2012 by John Wiley & Sons, Ltd.

the group therapy student can avoid the trap of becoming an overzealous disciple of one approach, and instead a thoughtful integrator of the myriad approaches at his disposal when the situation calls for it, even when he tends to work predominantly from a specific school of thought. I will restrict my focus to approaches that have a foundation in psychoanalytic and psychodynamic theories, in which there are many differences, but also similarities, even though I recognize that the psychodynamically oriented group therapist might, on occasion, employ techniques from non-analytic approaches (e.g. cognitive-behavioral, gestalt). It is my hope that what will emerge are some central concepts of group psychotherapy that can be a kind of connective tissue between the various theories to which we adhere.

Models of Group Psychotherapy

I invite you to think about the model of group therapy from which you operate most of the time. Does a specific theory come to mind (e.g. modern analytic, Self psychology, relational) or do you tend to practise from an integration of one or more theories? If the latter, do you find you have an organized way of thinking about group dynamics, development, and interventions? If you consider yourself what I will call a theoretical purist, do you ever do something that seems outside the framework from which you typically work? Can you explain these *instances* without resorting to characterizing it as countertransference or a lapse in theoretical adherence? Might there be deviations from theory that are thoughtful, or even when seemingly spontaneous or impulsive, might emerge out of an appreciation for other ways of working when the situation calls for it? Perhaps in our enthusiasm to fully explicate and promote our theories, we gloss over similarities between theories, or unique ways of assessing group dynamics that another theory might lend to our cherished models.

I believe that there are pan-theoretical concepts that could as easily explain our divergence from our chosen theories as countertransference, counterresistance or some other form of acting out or acting in. In many ways, these pan-theoretical concepts might be what many integrationists adhere to when working effectively in their groups. I think that many group therapists combine methods and theories to inform their leadership style, ways of assessing and viewing group dynamics, and their interventions. Before presenting these pan-theoretical elements of psychoanalytically oriented group therapy, I would like to review some of the more prevalent theories.

Psychoanalytic approaches

While all of the approaches I plan to review fall under this broad category, I would like to make finer distinctions between various analytic methods. Brook (2001) pointed out that Alexander Wolf had initially proposed that any focus on group dynamics was the therapist's resistance to employing the basic analytic tools of free association and dream interpretation to understanding the individual patient, and that Wolf emphasized that the goal of group treatment was for the individual patient to gain insight. In essence, he was envisioning a group of individuals getting psychoanalysis in the presence of others. Brook (2001) also reports that Slavson, who founded the American Group Psychotherapy Association and the *International*

Journal of Group Psychotherapy, concluded that individual analytic techniques and concepts could be applied to group psychotherapy.

Slavson (1950) also explicated that within groups there exist powerful dynamics of sibling rivalry in relation to the jealousy and competition that emerges between members of the group. So while Slavson might have leaned toward using individually oriented analytic techniques in group (i.e., free association, dream interpretation), he also introduced an appreciation for the unique opportunity to use emerging group dynamics to understand individual group members. Multiple transference interpretations are central to the work, as is of course free association and dream interpretation.

Nevertheless, Slavson, as well as Wolf, could be viewed as struggling between an appreciation of the existence of group dynamics, and actually employing group oriented methods in their interventions. Indeed, Rosenthal (2005) points out that Slavson still adhered to the notion that group therapy is merely an application of individual analytic techniques to the group situation. This is similar to Wolf, whose book, Psychoanalysis in Groups, presented a model of conducting analysis in the presence of other group members (Wolf and Schwartz, 1962). Many of us have seen the well-known cartoon of a group analyst, armed with pad and pen, surrounded by a circle of couches with group patients lying on their backs, heads toward the analyst.

Group dynamic approaches

Group dynamic approaches grew out of Lewin's Field Theory, which moved away from an emphasis on the individual in isolation in the group toward understanding an individual's emotions and behavior as a function of forces operating in the group-as-a-whole. While differing in emphasis, terminology, earlier theoretical foundations, and interventions, the theories of Ezriel, Bion, and Foulkes exemplify the group dynamic/group-as-a-whole approaches (Rutan and Stone, 1993; Shaffer and Galinsky, 1974).

Bion, who was heavily influenced by Melanie Klein, thought that individuals attempting to manage the complexities of emotional life in the group would resort to regressive mechanisms reminiscent of the earliest phases of life (Bion, 1959). He relied on interpretations of the group attitude toward the leader, toward the individual, and the individual's attitude toward the group, that interfere with the group working toward its task. These unconscious "basic assumptions" obstruct and divert the group from its task, and each assumption is common to the whole group. Individual resistances are often viewed as and interpreted as whole group resistances. Bion recognized that in the regressed states of the basic assumptions, each member has a uniquely personal experience of them, and yet he focused on the shared elements of these states. He had been known to reflect about the individual transference meanings of a member's participation, only to struggle to find the meaning for the entire group (Sutherland, 1985).

Ezriel (1973) operated from an object relations perspective, but suggested that the group analyst focus his attention on the transference with the group analyst, rather than on reconstructions of earlier relationships with the parents. Interpretations were made around three types of object relations:

1. The type the patient attempts to have with the analyst.
2. The avoided relationship, that which the patient most fears; and
3. The calamitous relationship, which would emerge if the avoided relationship could not sidestepped.

While Ezriel appears most similar to the psychoanalytic approach, it is his view on the importance of the group tension, group forces and the imperative of interpreting group resistances that sets him apart. He acknowledged the existence of the lateral transference between members, but viewed them as displacements from the leader (Brook, 2001).

Foulkes, whose approach was formally labeled "group analysis," takes into account individual and group dynamics, thus wedding group-as-a-whole with individual analytic approaches. Foulkes described what he called "group association," which he had hoped would be a group-wide free association, but what he observed was more of a "discussion circle" (Foulkes, 1964: p. 23). While Foulkes believed that transference existed in group, he thought it to be diluted by the "horizontal dimension" of the group interactions (Shaffer and Galinsky, 1974). His interventions were a blend of group-as-a-whole interpretations as well as individual interpretations, but make no mistake, Foulkes always viewed the group as reacting as a whole, and not the sum of the individual members. He saw the group analyst more as a conductor and educator, than a blank screen for projections. He educates when accepting verbalization of thoughts and feelings, and facilitating deeper communication.

The interpersonal approach

The interpersonal tradition, most completely elucidated by Irvin Yalom, is a radical departure from the methods thus described. Yalom too focuses on the here-and-now in the group, but deemphasizes group as whole phenomena in favor of careful examination of the interpersonal interactions in the group as they reflect a person's manner of interacting with others in life outside of group.

Process illumination is the core method b y which the interpersonal group therapist promotes learning. The therapist is concerned with what the interactions between members as well as with the leader, tell us about the individuals, their relationships in the group, the problems in relating that vex them in their relationships outside of group, and the group-as-a-whole (Yalom and Leszcz, 2005). In the early stages of the group, the leader is the primary process commentator, but Yalom believes that it is incumbent upon the members to also comment on the process. In process illumination, members learn about how others see them and how their behavior affects others' feelings. Through this feedback loop, members also develop self-evaluations and can decide based upon the information provided, whether they want to change, and how they should change.

The therapist serves as the primary authority as he or she promotes cohesiveness and shapes the group culture, but the members can also be authority figures, as well as the more traditional sibling representation. The group therapist promotes exploration over explanation, yet Yalom saw a place for judicious use of interpretation. While Yalom thought the primary focus should be in the here-and-now, he also recognized that the past is always present, and at times deserves some attention, especially as it relates to some current dilemma or interpersonal impasse. In this sense, the "past is the servant, not the master" (Yalom and Leszcz, 1985: p. 191).

Relational approaches

Group therapists working from the relational perspective place great emphasis on enactments that take place in the group. The relational group therapist examines the interactions in the here-and-now, but more with an eye toward the subjective experience of the therapist and the other members as a co-participants and perhaps co-contributors to what takes place in the interactions. Wright (2004) posits that relationists view transference "as an effort by patients to induce or compel a complementary response from others to meet their needs," and therefore, "is not a distortion of the present by the past but rather a creation of a past reality in the present and it may serve either adaptive or destructive purposes depending on how it fits with the present social environment" (Wright 2004: pp. 210–211). It follows that the therapist's corresponding response to this pull might be called countertransference. Aron (1996), however, argues the terms transference and countertransference too easily imply a one-way influence, obscuring the more reciprocal influences of which relational therapists speak. The term enactment captures these mutual influences present in the transference-countertransference matrix.

Enactments at times can feel disruptive and chaotic, and can involve dissociated self states (Grossmark, 2007a). The therapist balances these dynamics, allowing the enactment to unfold by containing the inchoate feelings that emerge, and attempting to make meaning. To do the latter too soon is to rob the group of potential data, but to allow the group to remain too long in the chaos risks damaging the trust in the group. The challenge, therefore, is to provide a safe container in which the enactments can unfold so that the group can then examine what is taking place in order for the members to learn about the effect that they have on others and vice versa. Billow (2010) calls this endeavor to make meaning discovering the truth "with a small t" recognizing that "truth is neither certain nor unchanging" (Billow, 2010: p. 3). The task is for the therapist and members, once engaged in these enactments, to "strive to work their way out of these entanglements, hopefully finding new, healthier ways of relating to each other" (Wright, 2000: p. 185).

Relational therapists believe that the group members are often a resource to the therapist. They rely on the multiple perspectives at their disposal to lend to the task of examining and understanding what is going on between members and the therapist. All perspectives are subject to examination, including that of the therapist (Wright, 2004). The group therapist is no longer simply a mirror for the members, but may also be required to subject himself to the group's scrutiny (Richarz, 2008; Wright, 2004). In addition, these extra sets of eyes can help the group therapist regain footing when her observing capacities are impaired by her subjective experience and reactions. This is not dissimilar to Ormont's (1991) technique of using the group to resolve the subjective countertransference, which will be described later in this chapter. Relational group therapists believe that this openness and authenticity meet our patient's needs to have an impact on us and with our assistance make meaning of that impact.

Self psychological approaches

Sustained empathic immersion into the subjective world of the patient is a central tenet of the self psychologically oriented group therapist. This method involves a periodic, but temporary stepping into the shoes of the patient, feeling what he feels, and sensing what he senses, perceiving the inner life of the patient while maintaining his or her stance as an observer. The therapist becomes immersed while maintaining her boundaries, such that this mode of inquiry is used only for understanding the subjective experience of the patient, illuminating the emergence of specific developmental needs, and informing interpretations (Harwood, 1998). During this process, the therapist and other members will occasionally fail each other through various and inevitable misunderstandings. Hopefully these moments of misattunement are nontraumatic, and similar to the relational approach, can be explored and understood more fully.

Central to individual development from this perspective is the notion that significant people in the lives of our patients provide certain functions that contribute to the individual's sense of self, growth, and psychological equilibrium. This is what Kohut (1971) referred to as a selfobject function. The selfobject is not an actual object in the person's life, but rather a subjective experience of another as (s)he provides an important function in the face of its absence in the individual, or temporary disablement (Stolorow and Brandchaft, 1987). In this sense, we might refer to the interaction between the subject (i.e. infant, patient, group member) and others (i.e. caregiver, therapist, group therapist/group member) as a selfobject experience, such that it leads to the creation or restoration of self cohesion and vitality (Lichtenberg et al., 1992). Through the process of transmuting internalization (Kohut, 1971), psychic structure is established as the developing child takes over critical selfobject functions heretofore provided by a caretaker (e.g. mirroring). This takes place when the child (or later in life, the patient), experiences an optimal failure or frustration, which is then explored and empathically understood in a manner that either promotes, consolidates, or restores a stable sense of self (Stolorow et al., 1987).

Some group members may reveal their selfobject needs readily, while others may defend against these needs lest they be retraumatized (Stone, 2009a). Through the process of occasional failures to meet selfobject needs thereby resulting in narcissistic injury, by therapist and group members alike, the member must rely upon the therapist's "recognition of the meaning of patients' responses to such injuries . . . ," and his ability to link these experiences to those of other group members (Stone, 2009b: p. 110).

One can readily identify some similarities between self psychology approaches and the relational approach. A key distinction, however, is with respect to the use of the therapist's subjectivity. While relational group therapists will not only invite their members to explore the subjective experience of the therapist in the group, they will authentically bring their subjective experience (Billow, 2003; Wright, 2000; 2004). Wright (2004), however, suggests that the self psychologically oriented group therapist will use his subjectivity to formulate understanding, and may explore the impact of his subjectivity on the group or group members, but he will unlikely expose his subjective experience directly to the group.

Modern analytic group

Modern group analysis, probably the most technique oriented theory of group psychotherapy approaches, was developed by Louis Ormont (2001), a modern psychoanalyst who took the innovations in technique developed by Hyman Spotnitz, and adapted and expanded them for group therapy (Brook, 2001). Ormont's writings on technique were based upon the observation that what analysts were witnessing in the group sessions between members was typically a reenactment of what occurred between members and significant people in their lives, both past and present (Ormont, 1995). Ormont used these observations to critique the prevailing group techniques of delving into member's personal histories, when their histories were coming alive before the therapist's eyes.

The goals of modern group analysis are to encourage emotional communication and interchanges between members, relying heavily upon the technique of bridging. Bridging is any technique designed to get members to expose their characteristic ways of relating to others through the group interactions, and it tends to illuminate similarities between members as well as differences (Ormont, 1990). Brook (2001) points out that bridging is far more than helping members make emotional contact, but rather is a technique based upon complex rationales, including but not limited to bringing object representations into lateral transferences in the group (i.e. objectification of the ego), facilitating partial identifications, and promoting full participation by all of the members (Brook, 2001: p. 17). Modern group analysts might bridge two people with similar resistances, or opposing viewpoints (Ormont, 1997). Bridging can also be used to protect members from undue or premature exposure, when their ego states are severely threatened, or to turn up the heat on members who seem impervious to their effect on the other members, or the member's attempts to have an effect on them. Ormont (1994; 1997) called this use of bridging "modifying" insulation barriers, helping those with impenetrable insulation barriers to soften them, and those with too little insulation to strengthen the barrier.

In modern group analysis, as in the relational approach, the therapist's reactions are also a source of study. When the group therapist's feelings seem to spark something from his own past that is interfering with his objectivity in the group, Ormont (1991) calls this the subjective countertransference and proposes using the group to help him resolve them through exploration of their reactions to his behavior. Ormont discovered that group members are often eager to share their frustrations with the leader when that frustration reaches an optimal pitch. These therapist feelings and thoughts are distinguished from the objective countertransference, which becomes one of the most valuable tools in the therapist's repertoire. Group therapists often have feelings that are induced by the reality of the group in which they sit, feelings that might be shared by other group therapists sitting in the same seat. Rather than explain these feelings away, they are a critical source of data about what takes place in the group (Ormont, 1970). It is through analysis of this data that the group therapist is eventually able to understand the resistances to immediacy and emotional communication, both in him, and in the group. Resistances can be toward intimacy (Ormont, 1988), progressive emotional communication (Ormont, 1999a), or meeting each other's maturational needs (Ormont, 2002). Resistances are studied in the group, first by the therapist, and then by the group, and explored to the point of understanding and resolving the fears underlying them (Ormont, 1988), thus allowing them to gradually establish more mature ties in the group.

The Connective Tissue Between Group Approaches

As I was researching and writing the review of the theoretical approaches emerging out of psychoanalytic, I was struck by how much I value what each has to offer, even though I work largely from a relational framework. This was not the first time I felt this, but somehow it seemed more salient given my interest in writing about the limits of theoretical purity. I began to appreciate the oft-cited quote attributed to Bernard of Chartres by the English philosopher John Salisbury (McGarry, 1955):

> We are like dwarfs sitting on the shoulders of giants. We see more, and things that are more distant than they did, not because our sight is superior or because we are taller than they, but because they raise us up, and by great stature add to ours. (John of Salisbury, Metalogicon [1159]).

I could have written exhaustively on the contributions of Freud (psychoanalytic), Kohut (Self Psychology), Hoffman or Mitchell (relational), and others, not group therapists in their own right, but some of the giants on whose shoulders major proponents of these and other schools of thought stand, but it would have been beyond the scope of this chapter. Nevertheless, these theories do not stand separately when viewed with an unbiased eye, but are interwoven into the larger fabric of all psychoanalytically oriented group approaches. It is these inherently intuitive connections, I believe, that explain some theoretical deviations. As we see in the previous review, what once might have been viewed as a deviation from theoretical orthodoxy evolved into new theorizing and its concomitant revolution in technique. As a result, in the next section I have attempted to extract dimensions of our work as group therapists that span our theories, and with which there might be more similarity than difference.

Setting the frame

Ormont (1962) lamented the lack of discussion in the literature about how to prepare our patients for group therapy. Indeed, many early approaches allowed group dynamics to evolve with little direction or instruction. Ormont believed that this resulted in wasted time as group members floundered about trying to understand what was expected of them, and therefore proposed the group contract as a method for not only communicating expectations, but also studying resistances manifested in deviations from the contract.

Yalom (1985) sets up expectations in individual pre-group preparation meetings emphasizing "ground rules" such as honest communication of feelings in the moment, maintaining confidentiality and avoiding contact between members outside of the group. To avoid the impression of setting forth "hard and fast laws," Rutan and Stone (1993) essentially describe a set of agreed upon group behaviors and objectives (i.e. "group agreements") that reflect ego cooperation, recognizing all too well that unconscious motives might influence circumvention of the agreements. They see the agreements as a way of directing the group toward the most therapeutic activity, as well as establishing a frame within which the group members can feel safe enough to do the work. Fehr (2003) believes that a stable contract with "rules and regulations" is essential, and that it matters not whether it's called the "Magna Carta of group," so long as "these rules are understood and accepted by all group members" (Fehr, 2003: p. 80).

It is astonishing how many books and articles on group therapy prior to Ormont's 1962 article did not mention the group contract or some similar tool or approach for setting the frame or culture in the group, so it is difficult to ascertain how widely used contracts are, or what diverse methods might be used to establish a frame. There is widespread agreement among those addressing this topic, however, that some form of group rules, whether in preparation meetings or in writing, help to establish a group structure (Goodman and Weiss, 2000). Indeed, review of the empirical evidence suggests that pre-group preparation not only increases attendance and reduces premature termination, but also increases therapeutic alliance (Bernard et al., 2008).

Even more important than setting expectations for the group members, however, a contract can provide the lens through which to study resistances to immediacy and emotional communication toward each other. For Ormont (1987), the contract is critical to the conduct of resistance analysis. By studying deviations from the contract we are studying resistances to Oedipal level functioning and communication (Brook, 2001), not to attack them directly, but to inquire and explore these resistances and their function until which time as the group member fully understands them and thereby relinquishes them.

Whether the purpose of a contract or set of rules is to set the therapeutic frame, communicate expectations, construct boundaries, or a tool for analyzing resistances in the group, not setting a stable frame might create the following situation.

Clinical Illustration

In a group in a college counseling center, a male group member Rob let slip that he and several members of the group had met for coffee after the previous group sessions. The co-therapists of the group were startled about this revelation. They knew that this could spell trouble, but were unsure what to do about it. Attempts to explore it were met with chiding resistance by those who had met, and silence by those who were excluded. There was much feeling in the room, but no one was expressing it to anyone else, other than irritation expressed toward the leaders who were clearly upset that a subgroup was acting out. In the time between this meeting, and the subsequent meeting, the therapists decided to establish a rule that contact outside of group should be avoided, and if it occurs should be reported back to the group, which as one can imagine, fomented more resistance and hostility.

Fehr (2003) cautions that to change a contract can cause enormous problems for the group, especially if it seems to emerge out of some special treatment given to an individual.

The therapists had not created a group contract and yet they knew that the members were not engaging in therapeutic interaction and they needed to address the resistance. While they knew about pre-group preparation, they had never prepared a formal contract for the group. They also never thoroughly learned how to explore group resistance or enactments, even though their training had a strong component of process commentary and illumination indicative of an interpersonal approach to group therapy. Eventually they figured out how to explore the meaning of the out-of-group meetings by maintaining a focus on the enactment, rather than challenging the resistance directly, and the needs being expressed in the enactment. Asking excluded members why they thought the subgroup needed to meet outside of the group, was the beginning of unlocking the resistance.

In the above example, these therapists, who did not know the relational literature and its emphasis on identifying enactments and making meaning from them, or modern analytic resistance analysis, intuited it early enough to resolve the group resistance. A modern analyst would use the group contract emphasizing putting thoughts and feelings into words, not action, to focus the exploration and analysis of the resistance, as would some psychodynamic group therapists (Fehr, 2003; Rutan and Stone, 1993). In this example, the therapists spoke of their countertransference, which led to "setting a specific rule" to deal with the crisis at hand. In addition, they were in such conflict about their own behavior that they were tempted to refer to it as countertransference acting out. On the other hand, might it be equally plausible to think of their behavior as intuitively directed toward exploring a group resistance, even though they had a bumpy start? Establishing a group contract would have made this exploration more readily available when the resistance first emerged, but their solution was rational, even though it would have been more effective had it been implemented at the outset of the group. While the therapists in the above example were clearly aware of their induced feelings, not having a framework for analyzing the feelings created challenges that did not need to be so intensely felt. If any error were to be identified in this vignette, it would be around the failure to prepare members adequately for therapeutic group activity, not for their course correction *per se*. Even if they had a contract or a set of rules, it is naïve to believe that members would adhere to the rules. In fact, we can expect group members to deviate from the contract as they reveal those aspects of themselves that obstruct mature interpersonal relating (Ormont, 1992).

Fostering cohesiveness

Related to setting the group frame, but deserving special mention, is the therapeutic factor of cohesion. Cohesiveness is defined by Yalom and Leszcz (2005) as a sense of belonging and trust that is felt between group members. Research has established cohesiveness as linked to preventing premature dropouts (MacKenzie, 1987), fostering increased feedback (Tschuschke and Dies, 1994), and symptom improvement (MacKenzie and Tschuschke, 1993). Although Cohesion has been correlated to positive group outcomes, this relationship is more complex, and is probably better understood in its relationship to group structure, verbal interaction, and maintaining an emotional climate (Bernard et al., 2008). To carefully set the group frame is likely to increase cohesiveness, but it also appears that other factors are also related to cohesiveness in groups.

While cohesiveness is clearly an important factor in fostering a productive group, we need to exercise caution in thinking of group cohesion merely as a function of, or a strategy for promoting trust, support, and togetherness. There are inevitably times when groups can feel untrustworthy and painful (Billow, 2003), and during these potentially destructive processes, the group therapist helps the members contain and tolerate these intensely affective moments while still maintaining a commitment to understanding what is taking place. When members experience pent up aggression, it is our role to help them express their aggression, all the while making sure that we also protect the more fragile members from attack (Ormont, 1984). It is not a matter of unleashing aggression all at once, but helping the group to regulate both its aggression and its resistance to its expression (Ormont, 1984, 1988). A group that withstands and works through such difficult periods will certainly contribute to its cohesiveness.

> Years ago, a therapy group of mine that had been running approximately two years and had developed into a well-functioning, cohesive group, gradually began to lose life. Members were still interacting, but in a more self-manner and devoid of real feeling. I was feeling increasingly frustrated and all attempts to make meaning of what I knew to be an enactment, but of what I did not know, failed. It was clear that the group was becoming increasingly frustrated, and the feelings induced in me were anger and helplessness. Some members were showing up late or missing sessions during this period. Finally when one member announced that she was thinking about leaving, and when a couple of others acknowledged similar thoughts when I inquired, I found an opening. I said that I didn't blame them for wanting to leave. When they asked me to explain myself, I pointed out that through deviations from the contract they were telling me something about their experience in the group through their symbolic communications (i.e. lateness, absences, and emotional withdrawal). I suggested that they were also angry with me for not being more of a stickler with the contract and that without my help they felt powerless to stop the withdrawal. The members shared their anger and frustration without restraint, and suddenly the feeling was real, and directed, in this case toward me. As they expressed their feelings, many members were able to share how this experience reminded them of parental failures in their own lives. Subsequent groups continued to be more vital, with members expressing feelings in the moment and toward each other and the leader, while at the same time exploring the meaning of enactments that had taken place that threatened the life of the group.

There are two things I would like to note in the above vignette. One is that the resolution of the group resistance involved supporting a substantial subgroup's expressed desire to leave. On the surface this could engender anxiety about the group falling apart if it were not already evident that this is exactly what was in danger of taking place (Van Wagoner, 2008). As members got in touch with their frustration, there was a renewed sense of cohesiveness as feelings that had been suppressed for months, were finally coming out. In this case, the road back to a cohesive group was through some threatening territory. It is imperative that the therapist can contain the feelings well enough for members to tolerate expressions of aggression so that they can be worked through. Perhaps, as research suggests, cohesiveness is less a central factor in treatment outcome, but rather a necessary condition for things like confrontation and interpersonal learning to take place (Joyce et al., 2007).

Secondly, here is an example of theoretical integration. Would the relational group therapist find fault with me for employing techniques of the modern analytic group therapist to resolve the treatment destructive resistance that had developed in the group, or view the intervention as necessary to move the group toward its ongoing activity of making meaning of what was being enacted? Sometimes a group cannot tolerate the chaos that emerges in some enactments without a more sure hand from the group leader. In addition, I employed an interpretation that neither approach would readily advocate, albeit I kept my interpretation centered on what was taking place in the here-and-now between me and the group members.

Empathic immersion

We must persistently attend to the myriad verbalizations, actions, symbolic expressions, and feelings that are constantly presented and shifting in our groups. We are also like conductors, as Foulkes would say, directing the music, paying careful attention to the resonances and dissonances between the members as they struggle to relate or avoid relating. Some might also see us as technicians, constructing and employing interventions that we believe will keep the group moving in an enlivening and progressive direction resulting in interpersonal learning and maturation.

But a central aspect of our work is being able to help our group members understand what they need to promote greater interpersonal maturation, and to understand what obstacles appear in the way of achieving this goal. Sustained empathic inquiry, what Stolorow (1994) defines as the investigative stance the analyst assumes in attempting to understand the world of the patient from within, includes attending to the analyst's own subjective affective responses, or absence of them. Stolorow is suggesting that our attention is not just outward toward the other, but inward as the other impacts us.

Even the most well analyzed and reasonably mature group therapist cannot help but be profoundly emotionally affected by her groups. This is an unavoidable, but more importantly, necessary aspect of our role. Part of being empathically immersed is to affectively resonate with the feelings of the group member (or group-as-a-whole), and thereby study what is induced in us. This type of inquiry can be seen in many of the approaches described earlier, but might come to be known by different terms that have slightly different emphases, whether as sustained empathic inquiry (Self psychology/intersubjective), emotional analysis of and by the group therapist (modern analytic), or examination of mutual impact (relational). Greenson (1960) observed that we make a trial identification with the patient to be empathically immersed in his world, but that when this identification goes awry (for example, overidentification), countertransference behaviors can emerge. This is similar to what Ormont wrote nearly 40 years later – we must make transient identifications with our patients that involve temporarily "letting go of who we are to experience the feelings of another, followed by a return to ourselves" (Holmes, 2009: p. 257). It requires the ability to partake of the emotional experience, but also to step out of the affective resonance and view what took place from a more objective stance (Greenson, 1960; Reich, 1960). Just as we ourselves use our empathic experience to understand others, we also teach our group members these very same skills so that they can move from a stance of narcissism to object relatedness (Ormont, 1999b).

Enactments

Although much has already been stated about this concept elsewhere in this chapter, enactment deserves brief mention as a distinct category. Relational group therapists speak directly about enactments and their place in group therapy, while others describe what are essentially enactments using different terminology. Whether we are speaking of lateral transferences as representations of object impressions as they are externalized in the interactions between group members (Brook, 2001), recapitulation of the primary family (Yalom and Leszcz, 2005), or recognizing behavioral patterns in the social microcosm (Yalom, 1985), many psychoanalytically grounded group approaches emphasize the central value of these enactments in a) identifying character pathology as it relates to members' interpersonal difficulties, and b) through their careful and systematic exploration, resolving obstacles to mature interpersonal relatedness (i.e. resistance analysis). Sometimes our language and terminology are critical to explaining nuances in our work and making fine distinctions in our theories and techniques, but sometimes they obfuscate the myriad ways our theories overlap. The term enactment as put forth by relational theorists, however, also emphasizes that these interactions are the result of co-constructed influences between therapist and members in the intersubjective field, and not just the result of a transference pull for the therapist to objectively understand from a neutral and expert position.

Therapist authenticity

Interpersonal group therapists call it transparency. Relational therapists refer to it as authenticity. Ormont (1970, 1984) has repeatedly written about the necessity of the therapist's study of his own induced feelings, and feeding it back to the members in digestible form.

Central to our work in groups is the use of ourselves to forward understanding and maturation. None of these approaches proposes unbridled or impulsive sharing of the therapist's own emotional and subjective responses, but rather through careful study, make thoughtful determinations about how to communicate our group members' impact on us such that it will produce a progressive effect on the group. There are no hard and fast rules about how much the therapist should disclose about his reactions in the group, although it is generally agreed that such disclosures, when volitional, should be made with the group's benefit in mind (Billow, 2003). It is crucial to understand, however, "that if the leader hides from his affect life, the group will do the same" (Zeisel, 2009: p. 429).

Exploration versus explanation: A dialectic

Modern group analysts are far more interested in the group members' feelings than in any interpretations or insights about their feelings (Ormont, 1997). They strongly believe that many interpretations fall flat because our members' difficulties in group stem from character formation that took place before words were available. The preferred activity is to explore the feelings, how they are being communicated, the resistances to their communication, and the way group members feel toward others. If there are interpretations to be made, they will be most effective coming from other members through the technique of bridging (Ormont, 1990).

There is wide variation in the literature and among differing approaches as to how central interpretations are to the group therapy endeavor. For example, within the relational approach, there are many who favor non-interpretive interventions (Aron, 1996; Grossmark, 2007a; Wright, 2004), but also those who value the use of interpretation (Billow, 2003). Self-psychological approaches offer interpretations tentatively, not so much as explanations, but hypotheses to be further explored (Stone, 2009c). Regardless of the degree to which interpretations are used by any particular approach, there has clearly been movement away from interpretations being the centerpiece of group psychotherapy since the heyday of the psychoanalytic and group dynamic approaches.

What is widely agreed upon, however, is that interpretations serve no purpose if the patient cannot hear it (Yalom and Leszcz, 2005). This understanding obviously has informed the major contemporary approaches reviewed here. Interpretations can be directed toward understanding vertical transferences, lateral transferences, and group-as-a-whole phenomenon. Nevertheless, most group therapy approaches would favor interpretations that maintain a here-and-now focus, targeting what is unfolding between the members of the group and the group therapist.

Group-as-a whole

As with the use of interpretations, there is variation in the degree to which the group-as-a-whole, and interpretation of group-as-a-whole dynamics, occupy a central place in the theory. Modern analytic theory tends to de-emphasize the group as whole, especially as a target of interpretation except in instances when there is a group resistance. This should be distinguished from the approach's emphasis on keeping the whole group involved and seeing the whole group as an agent of change. Even so, Ormont (1970, 1984) will attempt to find a spokesman for the group resistance, and through exploring the resistance with that individual, elicit expressions and analysis of the resistances in the other members.

Relational theories give more attention to the group-as-a-whole, especially as it is involved in enactments with the individual members and the therapist (Grossmark, 2007a). This does not mean interpreting group-as-a-whole dynamics, but rather containing them while the group itself attempts to make meaning of what is transpiring (Grossmark, 2007b). Other relational theorists will use group as whole interpretations sparingly when it forwards group progress (Billow, 2003). Interpersonal therapists will also judiciously use group-as-a-whole interpretations or commentary when the whole group, or a significant part of it, is engaged in anti-therapeutic behavior (Yalom and Leszcz, 2005). This process involves describing for the group its process and the negative impact it has on the group's progress. Stone (2009c), operating from a self-psychological perspective, suggests that group-as-a-whole interpretations can go further when the purpose is to understand the group, rather than explain something to the group. Rutan and Stone (1993) divide group-as-a-whole interpretations into those focusing on the transference to the leader (for example, anger at the leader for taking vacation, thus awakening abandonment fears), and those involving transferences to the group (for example, the group as dangerous, engulfing, or protective).

Awakening emotional vitality

The group therapist's role in keeping the group engaged in emotional communication should be evident in each of the components described before, but I wanted to bring it into stark relief here. This is a central task of group therapists in each of the contemporary psychodynamic approaches described here. We engage in a kind of affect education, helping group members to learn about what they are feeling and toward whom, and then expressing those feelings to the other group members (Zeisel, 2009). We want our patients to put their feelings into words, not action (Ormont, 1992; Zeisel, 2009), in the here-and-now (Yalom and Leszcz, 2005), and toward other members (Brook, 2001; Ormont, 1999a). We accomplish this through modeling our own authentic expression of emotion (Wright, 2000, 2004), bridging and fostering progressive emotional communication (Ormont, 1990, 1997, 1999a), and communicating empathic recognition of affective states (Stone and Gustafson, 2009).

Even when feelings are being expressed, and toward other members, there can at times be a quality of repetition in the sense that we have covered this ground before, and nothing new seems to be emerging. What may seem on the surface to be emotional engagement by anyone seeing a particular session out of context, can be felt by the therapist as already traveled territory. Ormont (1999a) stresses that when this sense of repetition emerges in the experience of the group therapist, we must devise strategies to make the exchanges progressive, meaning that new features of each member's personality are revealed as relationships develop, feelings deepen and become further nuanced, new risks are taken, and the relationships continue to develop in new ways.

Sometimes obstacles to emotional expression can be weakened through the use of humor and play, in addition to other methods for resolving resistances to emotional communication identified elsewhere in this chapter. Wright (2000) describes how humor, playfulness, and teasing can ease tensions and anxiety allowing for greater freedom of emotional expression and cohesion in the group. Billow (2003) cites the containing function of the therapist's ability to creatively and constructively play in the group, and encourage play from the group members. He sees constructive play as a sign of mature thought. Indeed, play can unlock the member's creative capacities, reduce fear of the therapist as an austere authority, and in fact create greater space for emotional vitality in the group. Use of humor and play are other strategies we use to bring life into the group room.

Implications for Theoretical Choice

Many of the contemporary theoretical schools briefly described above, share similar central concepts that seem to play a shared role across theoretical disciplines. One might conclude that I am leading the reader toward a rationale for integrated theory. While this suspicion is understandable, it is not my intention; rather I want the reader to appreciate that many of our psychoanalytically based theories were further developments of previous theories, and while often using different terminologies, share much in common when considering some of the central concepts elucidated above. Where they differ, which can be the subject matter for another chapter, is typically with respect to emphasis, technique, and each theory's historical underpinnings and development.

The group therapist's development

One might argue that the beginning group therapist would benefit from an introduction to multiple theoretical approaches. This is typically how graduate programs with a group therapy curriculum proceed, exposing students to myriad approaches. But what about the post-graduate student? Might she benefit from a similar method? Or is it better for the post-graduate student to begin study of a particular approach?

I believe one can make arguments for either method; however, I think it desirable to think about the special needs of the group therapist who has now completed his degree, internship, and perhaps a post-doctoral/graduate fellowship and is exploring setting up a group therapy practice, or leading groups in some other clinical setting. I think that there are merits for someone at this level of training, to learn a particular approach thoroughly, with both related supervision and personal group therapy experience. In fact, regardless of whether one learns a particular theory, or integrates theory, it is well-established opinion that supervision and personal group therapy be a part of any clinician's group therapy training (Billow, 2003; Fehr, 2003; Spotnitz, 1976; Yalom and Leszcz, 2005). Because the clinician at this level of professional and clinical development is still learning (a process that hopefully never stops), it can be argued that learning a singular approach can reduce ambiguity and bolster confidence as the emerging group therapist gains mastery of a single approach. As the approach is mastered and internalized, the student therapist's identity as a group therapist might also be internalized into a stable, cohesive sense of one's competency.

The above rationale notwithstanding, I also believe that the post-graduate student of group therapy could benefit enormously from exposure to core concepts and language that while indicative of a particular approach, has relevance to another theory or theories, perhaps using different terminology. For example, modern group analysts attempt to externalize object representations by promoting and observing the lateral transferences that develop between members. This is similar to what relational group therapists refer to as observing and making meaning of the enactments that develop in the group (i.e. when the past is recreated in the present interactions), sharing those observations and cultivating adoption of this approach in the members. Group therapists from both approaches at times will differ on how they work with these enactments, but at times they simply exercise patience, wait and watch what unfolds, verbalizing their observations and encouraging the same from others so that understanding emerges from the most complete data available.

The experienced group therapist, after developing mastery of a particular theory, also amasses years of group experience that enables her to readily recognize patterns in group dynamics and functioning, and intuitively responding to various group scenarios. Her experience enables her to more readily understand and integrate multiple theories, recognizing convergence and divergence, and appreciating more fully what other theories might offer. Her experience also allows her to easily critique each theory for its shortcomings in light of particular group situations and dilemmas. In addition, her experience will likely contribute to greater flexibility of approach, without fear of "doing it wrong." She is more likely to recognize how a particular theoretical perspective can often offer a new perspective to a thorny group dilemma, enhancing or complementing her own theoretical approach. Finally, by having a firm understanding of foundational concepts that span multiple psychoanalytically informed group theories, she is not merely mixing and matching theories, but blending them in fluid and meaningful ways.

The group member's development

Many contemporary theories of group psychotherapy address the special needs of some patients, particularly those who present a borderline or narcissistic character structure. Some theories offer prescriptions for dealing with this special population. In modern group analysis, Ormont (1974) describes the use of joining with preoedipal resistances when the group is no longer functioning cooperatively, but only after the group has developed some maturity in functioning, has an attachment to the group leader, and no longer responds to other interventions like confrontation or interpretation. Ormont (1989) added to this technique, a repertoire of additional interventions such as engaging the other group members, observing egos or insulating the preoedipal member from overstimulation, to name but a few. Psychodynamic theorists point out that interpretations might have to be replaced by other techniques with this population such as confrontation, pointing out similarities among members, empathizing with hurt or defensiveness, and interpreting certain behaviors of other members that are relevant or similar to the borderline member without putting him on the spot (Rutan and Stone, 1993).

Narcissistic members deserve special mention, because while borderline patients might be exquisitely sensitive to emotional injury, narcissistic members are well defended and seemingly impervious to it (Rutan, 2005). This is not to say that these patients are not vulnerable to emotional injury as they most certainly are; they are just more defended or insulated. In the case of these patients, we might employ techniques that carefully reduce their insulation barrier (Ormont, 1994), while maintaining an empathic stance toward what these defenses are protecting (Rutan and Stone, 1993). We are titrating their exposure to emotional stimulation according to their capacity to feel it. Self psychological group therapists emphasize the centrality of establishing a therapeutic alliance with these difficult patients, but will also offer interpretations such that they highlight unmet maturational needs or underlying fears in an empathic, non-judgmental manner. Modern group analysts (Ormont, 1989) and interpersonal group therapists (Yalom and Leszcz, 2005) also suggest conjoint therapy with open communication between therapists (concurrent individual and group treatment) as a way of containing these patients in group.

What is clear from this discussion is that each theory has a conceptualization about the defensive structure of these special populations and the interventions designed to be effective. As a result, it does not appear that any particular theory promises more to members at a particular stage of maturational development. Moreover, many theories attend to the role of individual development as it relates to certain challenges and dilemmas for individuals in group therapy.

It appears that choice of theory depends not upon a mix and match approach of particular theories to specific stages of group member development, but rather the completeness and thoroughness of any theory at addressing the complexities of personality development, the structure of defenses, and how these give rise to interpersonal difficulties. In addition, the extent to which theory informs the use of technical strategies or interventions and the conceptualization of group dynamics and group functioning should also be critical to one's theoretical choice.

The therapy group's development

Might the maturity level of the group dictate theoretical choice? Again, I would argue that it is not a critical factor, but rather theoretical choice should be predicated on how well and how completely that theory describes individual and group development and the accompanying strategies informed by this understanding. Many theories of group psychotherapy even discuss special considerations to attend to in the beginning phases of group development that often diminish as the group matures. What seems more relevant to theoretical choice is how well each theory can chart group development and distinguish a floundering group from a mature, well-functioning group. Again, the contemporary group theories (e.g. relational, modern analytic, self psychological, interpersonal, psychodynamic) all describe in their own language what a mature group looks like.

Summary

I hope it is clear that deviation from theory as I have treated it here, is not so much a theoretical leap, as a nuanced shift in the lens through which we might view our groups, its members, and specific challenges, dilemmas, and scenarios. I have attempted to weave together core concepts of contemporary psychodynamically and psychoanalytically informed theories that form a connective tissue between these approaches described here. In a sense I hope that I have provided a persuasive argument that what we might sometimes think of as deviations, are really more subtle shifts in perspective and resulting technique. While it is always useful to be open to any change in our approach as reflecting a countertransference pull, it is equally useful not to assume that it is always so. While theory organizes the way we conceptualize our groups and inform our technical strategies, the run the risk of offering "the security of the familiar," while potentially limiting our capacity to appreciate "the complexity of exploring new possibilties for understanding [our] patients" and our groups (Stone and Gustafson, 2009: p. 155). For this reason, we should strive to use our theories as roadmaps toward understanding and improving the lives of our group members, appreciating that sometimes we will necessarily and thoughtfully change course along the way as the situation merits.

I want the reader to know that I appreciate that there are specific theoretical approaches that have been found effective with specific problems or populations treated in homogeneous groups (e.g. anxiety management groups, anger management groups, borderline personality groups) where non-psychodynamic, cognitive-behavioral therapy and dialectical behavior therapy groups are the approach of choice. Even though these theoretical approaches are quite different from the psychoanalytically informed theories reviewed here, they too share some of the central concepts (e.g. setting the frame, fostering cohesiveness), although with differing emphases. Moreover, I am aware that some psychodynamically oriented group therapists have integrated some of these approaches into their groups. The extent to which this is useful and desirable, as well as the special problems or challenges that this practice might pose, is beyond the scope of this chapter but also bears careful consideration.

References and Bibliography

Aron, L. (1996). *A meeting of the minds: Mutuality in psychoanalysis.* Hillsdale, New Jersey: The Analytic Press.
Bernard, H., Burlingame, G., Flores, P., et al. (2008). Clinical practice guidelines for group psychotherapy. *International Journal of Group Psychotherapy,* 58(4), 455–542.
Billow, R. M. (2003). *Relational group psychotherapy: From basic assumptions to passion.* London: Jessica Kingsley Publishers.
Billow, R. M. (2010). Models of therapeutic engagement part 1: Diplomacy and integrity. *International Journal of Group Psychotherapy,* 60(1), 1–28.
Bion, W. R. (1959). *Experiences in groups.* New York: Basic books.
Brook, M. (2001). The evolution of modern group process: An overview. In L. B. Furgeri (Ed.), *The technique of group treatment: The collected papers of L. R. Ormont* (pp. 11–20). Madison, Connecticut: Psychosocial Press.
Ezriel, H. (1973). Psychoanalytic group therapy. In L. R. Wolberg & E. K. Schwartz (Eds.), *Group therapy* (pp. 183–210). New York: Stratton Intercontinental Medical Book.
Fehr, S. S. (2003). *Introduction to group therapy: A practical guide* (2nd ed.). New York: The Haworth Press.
Foulkes, S. H. (1964). *Therapeutic group analysis.* New York: International Universities Press.
Goodman, M., & Weiss, D. (2000). Initiating, screening, and maintaining psychotherapy groups for traumatized patients. In R. H. Klein & V. L. Schermer (Eds.), *Group psychotherapy for psychological trauma* (pp. 47–63). New York: The Guilford Press.
Greenson, R. R. (1960). Empathy and its vicissitudes. *International Journal of Psychoanalysis,* 41, 418–424.

Grossmark, R. (2007a). The edge of chaos: Enactment, disruption, and emergence in group psychotherapy. *Psychoanalytic Dialogues, 17*, 479–499.

Grossmark, R. (2007b). From chaos to coherence: Unformulated experience and enactment in group psychotherapy. In M. Suchet, A. Harris & L. Aron (Eds.), *Relational psychoanalysis: New voices* (Vol. 3., pp. 193–208). London: Routledge.

Harwood, I. (1998). Advances in group psychotherapy and self psychology: An intersubjective approach. In I. Harwood & M. Pines (Eds.) *Self experiences in group: Intersubjective and self psychological pathways to human understanding* (pp. 30–46). London: Jessica Kingsley.

Homes, L. (2009). The technique of partial identification: Waking up the world. *International Journal of Group Psychotherapy, 59*(2), 253–265.

Joyce, A. S., Piper, W. E., & Ogrodniczuk, J. S. (2007). Therapeutic alliance and cohesion variables as predictors of outcome in short-term group psychotherapy. *International Journal of Group Psychotherapy, 57*(3), 269–296.

Kohut, H. (1971). *The analysis of the self.* New York: International Universities Press.

Lichtenberg, J. D., Lachman, F. M., & Fosshage, J. L. (1992). *Self and motivational systems: Toward a theory of psychoanalytic technique.* Hillsdale, New Jersey: The Analytic Press.

MacKenzie, K. R. (1987). Therapeutic factors in group psychotherapy: A contemporary view. *Group, 11*, 26–34.

MacKenzie, K. R. & Tschuschke, V. (1993). Relatedness, group work, and outcome in long-term inpatient psychotherapy groups. *Journal of Psychotherapy: Practice and Research, 2*, 147–156.

McGarry, D. D. (*Trans*) (1955). *The metalogicon of John of Salisbury: A twelfth century defense of the verbal and logical arts of the trivium.* Berkeley: University of California Press.

Ormont, L. R. (1962). Establishing the analytic contract in a newly formed therapeutic group. *British Journal of Medical Psychology, 35*, 333–337.

Ormont, L. R. (1970). The use of the objective countertransference to resolve group resistance. *Group Process, Winter*, 96–111.

Ormont, L. R. (1974). The treatment of preoedipal resistances in the group setting. *Psychoanalytic Review, 16*, 420–432.

Ormont, L. R. (1984). The leader's role in dealing with aggression in groups. *International Journal of Group Psychotherapy, 34*(4), 553–572.

Ormont, L. R. (1987). The importance of the contract in resolving resistances to progress: A critique of a therapy group. In L. B. Furgeri (Ed.), *The technique of group treatment: The collected papers of L. R. Ormont* (pp. 77–84). Madison, Connecticut: Psychosocial Press.

Ormont, L. R. (1988). The leader's role in resolving resistances to intimacy in the group setting. *International Journal of Group Psychotherapy, 38*(1), 29–45.

Ormont, L. R. (1989). The role of the leader in managing the preoedipal patient in the group setting. *The International Journal of Group Psychotherapy, 39*, 147–171.

Ormont, L. R. (1990). The craft of bridging. *International Journal of Group Psychotherapy, 40*(1), 3-17.

Ormont, L. R. (1991). The use of the group in resolving the subjective countertransference. *International Journal of Group Psychotherapy, 41*(4), 433–444.

Ormont, L. R. (1992). *The group therapy experience.* New York: St. Martins Press.

Ormont, L. R. (1994). Developing emotional insulation in group. *International Journal of Group Psychotherapy, 44*(3), 361–376.

Ormont, L. R. (1995). A view of the rise of modern group analysis. *Modern Psychoanalysis, 20*(1), 31–43.

Ormont, L. R. (1997). Bridging in group analysis. *Modern Psychoanalysis, 22*(1), 59–77.

Ormont, L.R. (1999a). Progressive emotional communication: Criteria for a well-functioning group. *Group Analysis, 32*(1), 139–150.

Ormont, L. R. (1999b). Establishing transient identification in the group setting. *Modern Psychoanalysis*, 24, 143–156.
Ormont, L. R., (2002). Meeting maturational needs in the group setting. *International Journal of Group Psychotherapy*, 51(3), 343–359.
Reich, A. (1960). Further remarks on countertransference. *International Journal of Psychoanalysis*, 41, 389–395.
Richarz, B. (2008). Group processes and the therapist's subjectivity: Interactive transference in analytical group psychotherapy. *International Journal of Group Psychotherapy*, 58(2), 141–161.
Rosenthal, L. (2005). S. R. Slavson – an Appreciation. *Modern Psychoanalysis*, 30B, 88–94.
Rutan, J. S. (2005). Treating difficult patients in groups. In L. Motherwell & J. J. Shay (Eds.), *Complex dilemmas in group therapy: Pathways to resolution* (pp. 41–49). New York: Brunner-Routledge.
Rutan, J. S. & Stone, W. N. (1993). *Psychodynamic group psychotherapy* (2nd ed.). New York: Guilford Press.
Shaffer, J. & Galinsky, M. D. (1974). *Models of group therapy and sensitivity training*. Englewood Cliffs, New Jersey: Prentice Hall.
Slavson, S. R. (1950). Transference phenomena in group psychotherapy. *Psychoanalytic Review*, 37: 39–55.
Spotnitz, H. (1976). *Psychotherapy of preoedipal disorders*. New York: Jason Aronson
Stolorow, R. D. & Brandchaft, B. (1987). Developmental failure and psychic conflict. *Psychoanalytic Psychotherapy*, 4, 241–253.
Stolorow, R. D., Brandchaft, B. & Atwood, G. E. (1987). *The psychoanalytic treatment: An intersubjective approach*. Hillsdale, New Jersey: Analytic Press.
Stolorow, R. D. (1994). The nature and therapeutic action of psychoanalytic interpretation. In R. Stolorow, G., Atwood & B. Brandchaft (Eds.), *The intersubjective experience*. Northvale, New Jersey: Jason Aaronson.
Stone, W. N. (2009a). A self psychological perspective of envy in group psychotherapy. In W. N. Stone (Ed.), *Contributions of self psychology to group psychotherapy: Selected papers* (pp. 91–106). London: Karnac.
Stone, W. N. (2009b). Frustration, anger, and the significance of alter-ego transferences in group psychotherapy. In W. N. Stone (Ed.), *Contributions of self psychology to group psychotherapy: Selected papers* (pp. 107–122). London: Karnac.
Stone, W. N. (2009c). Group-as-a-whole: A self psychological perspective. In W. N. Stone (Ed.), *Contributions of self psychology to group psychotherapy: Selected papers* (pp. 35–54). London: Karnac.
Stone, W. N., & Gustafson, J. P. (2009). Technique in group psychotherapy of narcissistic and borderline patients. In W. N. Stone (Ed.), *Contributions of self psychology to group psychotherapy: Selected papers* (pp. 155–172). London: Karnac.
Sutherland, J. D. (1985). Bion revisited: group dynamics and group psychotherapy. In M. Pines (Ed.), *Bion and group psychotherapy* (pp. 47–86). London: Jessica Kingsley Publishers.
Tschuschke, V. & Dies, R. R. (1994). Intensive analysis of therapeutic factors and outcome in long-term inpatient group. *International Journal of Group Psychotherapy*, 44, 449–464.
Van Wagoner, S. L. (2008). What to do when the group is falling apart? In S. S. Fehr (Ed.), *101 interventions in group therapy* (pp. 409–413). New York: The Haworth Press.
Wolf, A. & Schwartz, E. K. (1962). *Psychoanalysis in groups*. New York: Grune & Stratton.
Wright, F. (2000). The use of the self in group leadership: A relational perspective. *International Journal of Group Psychotherapy*, 50(2), 181–198.
Wright, F. (2004). Being seen, moved, disrupted, and reconfigured: Group leadership from a relational perspective. *International Journal of Group Psychotherapy*, 54(2), 235–250.

Yalom, I. D. (1985). *The theory and practice of group psychotherapy* (3rd ed.). New York: Basic Books.

Yalom, I. D. & Leszcz, M. (2005). *The theory and practice of group psychotherapy* (5th ed.). New York: Basic Books.

Zeisel, E. M. (2009). Affect education and the development of the interpersonal ego in modern group analysis. *International Journal of Group Psychotherapy, 59*(3), 421–432.

Section Two
Groups for Adults

Introduction

Adult groups are offered in hospitals, correctional facilities, outpatient clinics, private offices, and college campuses. Often they are general psychotherapy groups the aim of which is to alleviate emotional distress, including psychiatric symptoms. Sometimes, they are thematic groups, through which adults have chosen to develop personal skills that they feel they lack, such as assertiveness, or coping strategies to deal with life threatening situations, such as physical illnesses. More recently, group approaches have been established to help survivors of natural and man-made disasters go through the recovery process.

Leadership of groups for adults requires the assessment of patient or member problems, their emotional resources and limitations, identifying treatment goals, considering whether group should be part of the treatment plan, designing therapeutic strategies within the group process, putting together a group that allows the goals to be met, preparing the members for the group experience, and monitoring outcomes. Underlying every phase of the group development should be a personality and curative theory that informs treatment decisions as well as an understanding of how group dynamics can drive the group towards its intended results.

This is an area of clinical work that has a multiplicity of clinical approaches which may all be aimed at similar treatment outcomes. Their commonalities and differences will be explored in this section.

Lise Motherwell begins this section comparing "Support and Process-Oriented Therapy Groups." Both have a therapeutic goal, but the former focuses on coping strategies and managing emotions, while the latter emphasizes personal growth and interpersonal learning.

How to treat the fragile patient is creatively discussed by Phyllis Cohen in "Working with the Difficult Group Patient." She differentiates the patient who alienates others

---

The Wiley-Blackwell Handbook of Group Psychotherapy, First Edition. Edited by Jeffrey L. Kleinberg.
© 2012 John Wiley & Sons, Ltd. Published 2012 by John Wiley & Sons, Ltd.

and is hard to reach. What the therapist should do to meet the needs of this member is explored.

Martha Gilmore, in "Working with Primitive Defenses in Group," continues to offer insight and assistance to the leader trying to respond to the patient who becomes overwhelmed by anxiety in group. She explores issues of emotional attachment and how greater stability can be achieved through developing a more secure connection with such patients.

Al Brok is also concerned with managing the tension levels within a group that can be serious barriers to therapy unless managed carefully. In "Structured Techniques to Facilitate Relating at Various Levels In Group," he offers specific activities that begin to explore important emotional issues but permit a gentle easing into difficult material.

Continuing the focus on members with special needs, Marsha Vannicelli's "Effective Management of Substance Abuse Issues in Psychodynamic Group Psychotherapy," provides an excellent state-of-the art description of ways to offer an insight-oriented experience that can address the needs of the patient who wants to work on addiction. Her guidelines about utilizing community resources and supervision prepare the group leader for offering group-based help to this important group of patients.

Leaders seeking guidance on composing a group can turn to Darryl Pure's "Single-Gender or Mixed-Gender Groups. . . . " Based on the needs of his patients and their respective developmental histories, the therapist can weigh the advantages and disadvantages of having a same-sex group or a group with men and women, together.

The focus on sexuality continues in Morris Nitsun's "Sexual Diversity . . . " The group leader is advised to be sensitive to sexual orientation in the group process. Concerns about prejudice and pathologizing different orientations are addressed. This is a much-neglected topic in training and Nitsun opens an important door for our field.

Shoshana Ben-Noam's chapter offers assistance to the therapist working with sexually abused clients. Her paper, "Group Therapy for Females Molested in Girlhood," considers the importance of this group approach and through detailed clinical examples and treatment strategies prepares the leader to establish such a group that might otherwise be considered daunting.

The section, then turns to specialized approaches and "cutting-edge" programmatic models to address emerging mental health needs.

Judith Coche's "Couples Group Psychotherapy . . . ," provides a creative introduction to establishing an effective means for working on intimate relationships. Her wisdom flows from more than 25 years of experience in helping hundreds of couples in distress.

Haim Weinberg and Daniel Weishut turn our focus to another contemporary development in our field, "The Large Group. . . . " This format, consisting of at least thirty participants plus the leaders, is usually offered in group conferences and promotes learning about large group dynamics and how each individual responds to the forces at play. Insights can be applied to the understanding the larger community, including organizations and society. The authors make sense of what can be experienced as chaotic.

Robi Friedman in "Dreams and Dreamtelling . . . ," shares with us his well-honed approach to learning about individual and group relationships. Here, the reader will see how one can work with dreams in a way that is not threatening, but is likely to yield many insights.

The next two chapters in this section consider the application of group to survivors of trauma. Suzanne Phillips and Robert Klein, in their "Group Interventions Following Trauma and Disaster," draw from their experience in training, supervision and direct service, and consider the differences between a trauma group and a general group therapy model. They present extensive guidelines for running a trauma group that takes the survivors through the recovery process. Concerns for the leader and her responses to this difficult work are also addressed.

Elisabeth Rohr, who has been supported by the German government for her work in conflict-torn Guatemala, describes a group-based supervision and training effort related to victims of torture. Teaching coupled with emotional support characterize her contribution to the Guatemalan effort. Detailed curricula are provided.

From Croatia, Ivan Urlich in "Group Psychotherapy for Patients with Psychosis," continues the effort to apply group models to challenging populations. This chapter is of great importance to clinicians working with the patients suffering from severe disorders within hospital settings. Urlich discusses structuring a group approach that is not merely a holding, or socializing activity, or an opportunity to check the impact of medication, but rather a laboratory offering insight and emotional learning.

Finally, Richard Beck in "Caring for the Caregiver," allows us to take a deep breath after immersing ourselves in challenging and anxiety-producing situations, and discusses how the group leader can avoid vicarious traumatization, a form of professional and personal burn-out. The challenge of leading a group demands that we monitor and respond to changes in mood, motivation, interpersonal patterns, and health that may be the result of immersion in our work.

14

Support and Process-Oriented Therapy Groups

Lise Motherwell

Introduction

Our world is a relational world, where mental health is promoted through deep, meaningful, and lasting connections with others. Most of our patients' problems come from feelings of isolation, low self-esteem, and difficulties with relationships. When a dramatic event occurs or patients suffer from psychological issues, they often feel more isolated and alone. Support and therapy groups offer patients a safety net and an opportunity to develop close connections with others in a confidential environment. With proper boundary maintenance, good leadership skills, appropriate patient selection and preparation, and an awareness of group development and group dynamics, groups can be therapeutic.

A support group focuses on coping strategies and emotional re-enforcement. An on-going, process-oriented therapy group emphasizes personal growth and interpersonal learning. Clinicians should know the difference between the two groups and how basic concepts in group dynamics are applied to each. In this chapter, I discuss similarities and differences in the two types of groups and how the leader intervenes in each.

Selected Review of the Literature

Social support has been proven to be an important component of coping when people face stressful situations (Cohen and Wills, 1985; Leavy, 1983). A meta-analysis of twenty randomized clinical trials studying the effectiveness of nursing and cancer support groups found significant improvements in levels of depression and anxiety, illness adaptation, quality of life, and marital relationships (Zabalegui et al., 2004). Further, in a meta-analysis of randomized psychosocial interventions with adult cancer patients, Meyer and Mark (1995) found improved emotional adjustment, functional adjustment, and medical symptoms. In the first study of support group effectiveness with minority breast cancer patients, Taylor et al., (2003) found that African-American women who participated in an 8-week psychoeducational support group for non-metastatic breast cancer resulted in improved mood and increased breast cancer knowledge. Sikkema et al., (1995) demonstrated the effectiveness of a cognitive behavioral support group for those who have experienced an AIDS-related loss. They found significantly reduced depression, intrusive experiences, grief reactions, demoralization, and overall psychological distress immediately following the group and at a 3-month follow-up. In a qualitative research study, Oygard et al., (2000) found four therapeutic factors that support the effectiveness of divorce support groups: universality, interpersonal learning, group cohesiveness, and catharsis. Participants also found meeting others with similar thoughts and feelings and increased insight into themselves and others helpful. Norberry (1986) asserts that leader-led divorce support groups helps women over the age of 50 mourn their losses and help them to move forward. Sharing within a small group of like individuals validates their experiences and helps them overcome adversity.

Similar results have been found in group therapy studies. Group therapy has been found effective for schizophrenics (Kanas, 1986), manic-depressive illness (Wulsin et al., 1988), mood and anxiety disorders (Oei and Browne, 2006), somatization disorder (Kashner, 1995), and chronic trauma related stress disorders (Kanas, 2005). Davenport et al., (1977) found that lithium treatment with couples therapy decreased hospitalization, marital failure, suicides, and improved social functioning and family interaction. Volkmar et al., (1981) found dramatic decreases in hospitalizations and increased full-time employment for bipolar patients who took lithium and participated in a psychotherapy group and Kripke and Robinson (1985) found that group therapy coupled with lithium treatment decreased hospitalizations and improved socioeconomic functioning in bipolar patients.

The efficacy of process group therapy has been more difficult to assess because group interactions are complex and sensitive to many different conditions (Piper, in press). Jensen et al., (2010) found short-term psychodynamic group therapy effective for symptom relief in a public out-patient setting, but suggested longer term treatment might be even more effective. In a meta-analysis of outcome research on process group therapy, Callahan et al., (2004) found interpersonal-psychodynamic group therapy to be an effective treatment approach for survivors of childhood sexual abuse. While process group therapy needs to be further researched, there is a growing body of evidence that group therapy and support groups provide significant help with psychiatric symptoms, social support, catharsis, and an opportunity to share and validate one's experiences with others who have experienced similar circumstances.

The Support Group

Clinical Illustration

Joan has been married for 15 years and has just learned her husband is having his second extra-marital affair. Two weeks ago, he moved out of the house and asked her for a divorce. She has three children under the age of 12, many friends, and family nearby. She has not worked in 15 years and worries about how she will support herself, her children, and the house she and her husband bought ten years ago. Devastated, and afraid she might be wearing out her friends, Joan wants to meet with other women who have gone through a similar situation.

High-functioning patients who experience an acute, unexpected event would benefit from a support group. By and large these patients function well in the world: they have strong relationships with others, have meaningful work, and are able to manage normal amounts of stress, but under acute distress due to changing circumstances have trouble coping or feel isolated. They are able to be empathic and supportive of others, but need additional information and coping strategies to deal with their current situation. They often want to be in a group with others who are experiencing similar circumstances (e.g., a divorce or newly diagnosed medical problem). They may have minor characterological issues, but are not interested in the deep exploration of their personalities. Normally high functioning, but now feeling overwhelmed due to the break-up of her family, Joan would benefit from a support group as she navigates the divorce process.

The purpose of the themed or diagnosis-centered support group is to provide symptom relief and emotional support as patients develop coping skills, build an extended social network, and strengthen their resilience so they can return to their normal level of functioning. Self-help support groups include 12-step groups such as Alcoholics Anonymous, Overeaters Anonymous, and Gamblers Anonymous that provide peer support and sponsors and psychoeducational groups such as Parents Anonymous, which are leaderless or peer-led and emphasize skill-acquisition. Support groups that are theme-focused life event groups (e.g., bereavement, AIDS, or divorce) and medical illness support groups are led by qualified professionals. In this chapter we will focus on support groups that are led by trained mental health professionals.

All support groups bring together people with the same problem or concern. Homogeneous groups are more advantageous for shorter-term and support groups because they ". . . gel more rapidly than heterogeneous groups, have a better attendance rate, are more cohesive, offer more immediate support, have less conflict, and provide more rapid relief of symptoms" (Salvendy, 1993: p. 76). Some support groups are unstructured groups that provide a supportive environment for patients to share their experiences and provide empathic connections to one another. Other more structured support groups offer information about the condition, teach coping strategies such as cognitive reframing, mindfulness, meditation, stress management techniques, and visualization exercises, and encourage the development of a support network. Therapeutic factors in support groups include supportive help-giving comments, personal disclosure, information sharing, positive interactions, and empathy (Abramowitz and Coursey, 1989; Kurtz, 1997; Toseland, Rossiter, Peak, and Smith, 1990). While support groups may be therapeutic, unlike therapy groups, their goal is not to promote change of enduring personality characteristics.

Organizations that specialize in a particular concern or illness or non-profits like churches often offer support groups. A cancer hospital, such as Dana Farber in Boston, may offer support groups to patients with cancer, family members of patients with cancer, parents of children who have cancer, or bereavement groups for families who have lost a loved one to cancer. Many of these groups are open to anyone who wants support and are often "drop-in" groups where members have the option to go when they want rather than committing to weekly attendance, although a core group may attend regularly. The support group is often free of cost, and each meeting usually has a duration of between 60 and 90 minutes. Often the leader provides refreshments before or after the group so additional social interaction can occur.

Other support groups are found in private practices where the leader has some specialty training in the topic or issue. In these closed-membership groups, the leader selects and prepares members and charges a fee. Leaders in either setting may structure the group session (see Figure 14.1).

The Therapy Group

> ### Clinical Illustration
>
> Paul, a 60-year-old gay male with few friends, has suffered from depression and low self-esteem for 45 years. Well-educated but underemployed because of his inability to tolerate stress, he recently took a medical leave from work to participate in a 3-week partial hospitalization program after his partner of 10 years unexpectedly died of a heart attack. He felt despondent and suicidal after his loss. He has had a good experience in groups at the hospital and would like to continue in a group after he finishes his partial program to better understand himself and to develop better connections with others.

Therapy groups, whether time-limited or on-going, are for patients who have long-standing characterological issues that interfere with healthy functioning at work or in relationships. These patients often get stuck in maladaptive ways of functioning which leads them to feel depressed, unfulfilled, anxious, and lonely. They want to improve or build new relationships that are deep and meaningful. Paul would benefit from a psychotherapy group because of his chronic depression, low self-esteem, long-standing character issues, and low stress-tolerance. His positive experience in hospital groups and interest in learning about himself and others make him a strong group therapy candidate.

The purpose of a process-oriented psychotherapy group is to provide a therapeutic environment for interpersonal learning and personality change (Brabender, 2002; Motherwell and Shay, 2005; Rutan, Stone, and Shay, 2007; Yalom, 1995). Patients are encouraged to share their feelings and reactions to others and to be self-reflective. There are many types of psychotherapy groups. Dialectical Behavior Groups, often used with borderline patients, provide skills training to teach affect regulation and coping skills. Psychodynamic groups offer a safe environment in which group members explore interpersonal and intrapsychic conflicts. Structured short-term groups in hospitals, clinics, and partial-hospitalization programs teach cognitive-behavioral skills. Interpersonal groups focus on social learning in a group setting. In this chapter we will emphasize process-oriented psychotherapy groups which focus on group development and the interpersonal, here-and-now interactions among group members.

Process-oriented therapy groups may be theme focused (e.g., depression, social phobia, gay men, women's group, parents of children with learning disabilities, etc.) where members are referred based on diagnosis or affinity group, or they may have a general membership of patients with diverse issues who are brought together to work on intrapsychic or relational concerns. Whitaker and Lieberman (1964) recommend maximum heterogeneity in the patients' intrapsychic conflicts and homogeneity in their psychological functioning in long-term, insight-oriented, and interpersonal groups. Members in these groups explore peer and authority relationships, learn conflict resolution, develop empathy toward others and the self, learn effective communication and assertiveness skills, and learn to express feelings appropriately. They may have a corrective emotional experience, recognize behavior patterns in a social milieu, develop insight, and work with multiple transferences (Yalom, 1995). They may reenact characterological dilemmas, expose shameful secrets, reintegrate split-off aspects of the self, and express difficult affects (Alonso and Swiller, 1993). In addition, seven therapeutic factors are associated with successful group therapy: instillation of hope, universality, altruism, imparting information, the corrective recapitulation of primary family group, development of socializing techniques, and imitative behavior (Yalom, 1995). These factors, along with meaningful connections with others, provide a healing experience.

Process-oriented therapy groups may be time-limited or open-ended, but are often longer term than support groups. They are held in private practice, hospitals, and clinics and are run by trained mental health professionals. These groups most often have closed membership; that is, there is a specified limit to the number of patients in the group, and once filled, no new members enter unless someone terminates and a seat becomes vacant. In time-limited groups, the leader usually closes the group to new members by the second or third meeting. In an on-going group, the group is open to new members as long as seats are available. However, the leader interviews, selects, and prepares each new member to make sure the patient and group are a good match, that the patient understands the way the group will be run and that he/she develops goals before joining the group. Members generally pay for sessions and do not meet outside the group.

Basic Concepts of Groups

While support and therapy groups differ widely in function and process, underlying concepts of how a group functions are present in both. Knowledge of these concepts – stages of group development, leadership functions, patient selection and preparation, the importance of hellos and good-byes, resistance in groups, countertransference, and working with difficult patients – is crucial to running an effective group. All groups go through stages of development. Effective leaders provide the frame and maintain the boundaries. Leaders of therapy groups, and if possible, support groups, should select and prepare their members for group. At some point, all groups face resistance. All groups have beginnings and endings. And most leaders have faced difficult patients or groups. An understanding of these basic concepts and how they are used in support and therapy groups will help the leader provide more effective care.

Stages of Group Development

The leader should pay attention to what stage the group is in and be prepared to make interventions that support the healthy development of that stage. In therapy groups, the leader uses that knowledge to respond to and understand the group and individual dynamics. In support groups, the leader uses the information to provide empathy and to create further support.

There is some disagreement about what the stages of group development are (Rutan, Stone and Shay, 2007), but the concept is useful to understand what tasks the group may be working on at any one time. Tuckman (1965, 1977) described a five stage model that includes forming, storming, norming, performing, and adjourning. Typically, the first stage is a formative phase where the group works on issues of joining, building trust, and belonging to the group (Rutan, Stone, and Shay, 2007). Patients look for ways in which they are similar and can connect with one another. In the second phase, storming, group members respond to how they feel about being part of a group. They may act out the group agreements, have conflicts with one another or the group leader, or feel ambivalent about their commitment to the group. In the third phase, the group develops a set of implicit agreements or norms by which the group operates. In the fourth stage, the group becomes a well-functioning, working group. The group members share leadership responsibility, are open with feelings and to feedback, tolerate and manage conflict, and pursue their goals for personal growth. In the final termination stage, the group members let each other know how much they mean to each other, celebrate what they have accomplished, acknowledge unfinished business, and say good-bye.

Effective groups will move through all the stages (not necessarily in order), and often go back and forth between stages as group membership changes and the group develops. In an on-going therapy group, the forming and adjourning stage will occur over and over as new members join and older members terminate. In contrast, in a time-limited support group, patients may not have time to move through all the stages well or for long due to the shorter length they will be together. Nor will all patients or groups go through all stages at the same time. For example, some patients never learn to say good-bye and either bolt from the group without notice, or stay forever, avoiding the inevitable termination. Other patients may avoid conflict or the working phase of group.

Clinical Illustration

Paul and Jim have been in a therapy group for two years. Several weeks ago, Paul confronted Jim about taking too much time in the session. Jim became furious and then sat silently for several weeks. Since then, Jim has arrived to group twenty minutes late each week. He looks down when he enters the room and mumbles an apology. Several members ignore him and continue the conversation; others smile at him.

Response in a support group:
  LEADER Welcome, Jim. Come join us. Joan was just telling us about her
     experience at the hospital this week.

A few minutes later, the leader might say: Up until recently it was unusual for you to come late. Has something changed that is making it difficult to get here on time?

JIM	I've had to stay at work late, which means I pick up my children late. I have to take them across town to their mother's, which then takes me a half an hour longer to get here.
LEADER	What has been others' experience with logistics getting here?
CHARLENE	I had the same problem a year ago. I finally asked my next door neighbor if we could exchange babysitting nights one night a week. Now she picks up my kids on Tuesdays. I feel relieved and a lot less stressed. I actually can give myself a night to do something for me.

Response in a therapy group: This group knows each other well and has been able to manage conflict. On this day, the leader waits several minutes to see if anyone comments on how they feel about the lateness or its possible personal or interpersonal meaning. If not, he says:

LEADER	Jim, I notice you have been late these last few groups. You look distressed. I wonder what your lateness is telling us about how you are feeling about what goes on here?
JIM	It's not about the group. I have been asked to stay late at work so now I hit traffic.
LEADER	Sometimes practical issues can get in the way of getting to group on time. Other times, there may be something deeper. I wonder if anyone has any thoughts about what else Jim's lateness might mean?
CHARLENE	I'm not sure, but I feel irritated by the disruption. And then we have to repeat what has gone on.
PAUL	Me, too. But I also appreciate Jim's remarks when he's here.
LEADER	It sounds as though people are irritated by your lateness, but they value you and miss your input when you are not here.

This relational comment models positive connections and reminds group members that sometimes behaviors are misguided efforts to communicate difficult feelings.

The intention of each of these interventions is different. In the first case, the intent is to help the member feel included and supported, and to develop better ways of coping. In the second case, the leader is trying to help both the late member and the group articulate how they feel about the lateness and what it might mean to each individual and the group as a whole to promote insight and connection.

The Role of the Leader

The primary role of the leader in both therapy and support groups is to create a safe environment in which group members can do the work they have come to do. The boundaries and group agreements help group members to feel safe and provide a frame within which the group functions. They let the group members know what the tasks of the group are and how they will be expected to do them.

The boundaries in a support group include where and when the group will meet, the cost if there is one, who will lead, confidentiality or anonymity, a safe container, and the group agreements. Since the leader may not know who will be in the group from week to week, he may strengthen a support group's boundaries by providing structure – for example, the leader may conduct round robin introductions, have members share the time equally each session, or provide a structured exercise. The structure provides continuity and reduces the possibility of interpersonal conflict.

Typical support group agreements are to share the time, provide mutual support, and to share experiences and information. Members are expected to tolerate differences, avoid personal confrontations, and keep all names and personal information confidential. The leader must keep stress within the group environment to a minimum, reinforce positive and productive activities in the group, and focus on progress (Kurtz, 1997). The eight support group process goals proposed by Wasserman and Danforth (1988) are:

1. Information exchange.
2. An atmosphere of mutual respect.
3. Group cohesion.
4. Increased coping and self-efficacy.
5. Reduction of social isolation.
6. Stress reduction.
7. An atmosphere of safety.
8. Reinforcement of positive behaviors in and outside of group (cited in Kurtz, 1997: p. 100) can be reinforced through the group agreements.

Clinical Illustration

A support group member, Danielle, spews negative remarks about her husband each time the divorce group meets. She revisits his infidelities, talks about what a terrible father he is, and refuses to acknowledge any positive attributes he might have.

LEADER Danielle, your situation is very painful and I can see that you are really angry. I wonder how you might channel that anger into a positive force. Does anyone have any suggestions about how they have handled those difficult feelings?

If Danielle cannot be redirected over several sessions, the group leader will need to meet with her individually to coach her on more positive behaviors. If she cannot abide by the agreement to maintain a positive attitude, she may need to be referred to a therapy group or individual treatment. This is not to say that a support group member cannot express negative affect; however, chronic negativity in a support group will lead to high drop-out and depression rather than hope and progress. The leader must address any violations of the contract right away. If the behavior displayed or discussed is self-destructive (e.g., getting drunk the night before after an argument with a spouse), the support group leader would use it as an opportunity to teach skills and talk about more adaptive coping skills.

In process-oriented groups, the leader's primary role is to provide a therapeutic frame and to maintain the boundaries while paying attention to process. Boundaries are important to maintain in this type of therapy because of the emotional and regressive nature of the work (Cohn, 2005). Members are asked to share painful memories and to risk interacting with others on a deep level. There are both emotional and physical boundaries in therapy groups. Emotional boundaries include here-and-now versus there-and-then experiences, how it feels to be in or out of the group, and the distinction between self and group (i.e., other). External boundaries include where and when the group will meet, session length, and membership. Internal group boundaries include billing, confidentiality, and the group agreements (Cohn, 2005). It is the leader's responsibility to start and end the group on time, manage difficult group members, emphasize confidentiality, and to determine who is in or out of the group.

In process-oriented groups where interpersonal learning is primary, the group agreements promote safety and provide guidelines for how the group will work. In typical agreements members agree to:

1. Be present each week, to be on time, and to remain throughout the meeting.
2. Allow the members of the group to have an impact on me and talk about the feelings, thoughts, observations, and fantasies that might arise from that impact.
3. Use the relationships in the group therapeutically, not socially.
4. Put my feelings into words, not actions.
5. Pay for all group visits at the beginning of each session. I understand that I must pay for my membership whether or not I attend the group.
6. Protect the names and identities of the other group members.
7. If I should decide to discontinue the group, I will give advance notice of my intention to leave and give the members a chance to discuss with me my decision to leave the group.
8. Once I have decided to leave the group, to give the group time to say good-bye (Rutan, Stone, and Shay, 2007).

One significant difference between the two sets of agreements is that support groups encourage members to meet outside the group whereas outside contact is prohibited in therapy groups. This difference highlights the difference between group as support and groups that emphasize interpersonal learning and intrapsychic change. Support groups encourage outside contact to promote the development of additional support systems. In therapy groups, members are discouraged from outside contact with each other so that interpersonal work can occur among members in the safety of the therapeutic setting and to minimize sub-grouping outside the office. Imagine being part of a therapy group where all the members decide to go to dinner together without inviting a "difficult" member or the impact on the group dynamic if two members decide to have a secret tryst? While these events can and do happen in therapy groups, the group agreements and leader encourage members to bring in any outside contact for processing by the group. Thus, in therapy groups the explicit and implicit message is, "We will learn about ourselves and each other through understanding the meaning of our behaviors and communications."

Support group example

A patient comes into a cancer support group and sits on the floor.
Support Group Intervention:

LEADER   Julia has made herself comfortable. Why don't we all find a way to get comfortable?

Or if she wants to tighten the frame:

LEADER   Susan, it looks like you've made yourself comfortable there on the floor. In this group I encourage everyone to sit on a chair so that each member can see other members equally. Why don't you sit in that empty chair there and we can get started?

This intervention acknowledges the deviant behavior, offers an alternative, and welcomes the member into the group.

Therapy group example

On the first week of a therapy group, a new member, Julia, took off her shoes as she sat down on the couch. The second session, Julia sat on the floor and commented that the group seemed "a little stiff." The third week, Julia was the last to enter the group room and as she did asked the group leader, "Can I have a hug?"

LEADER   If I give you a hug we will lose the opportunity to understand more about what you are asking for. Let's sit down with the group and talk about what you want.
JULIA   I'm not sure this group is right for me. It seems so formal. In my last group, we always hugged each other after the group. I feel lonely and unwanted.
CELIA   If we hugged after group, I would feel scared rather than closer to others.
LEADER   In this group, we agree to tell each other how we feel just as you two just did rather than act on impulses. Julia, can you tell us more about how you are feeling?
JULIA   I want to feel closer to both you (the leader) and the other group members. I don't feel a part of the group.

> CELIA I would feel closer to you if I got to know you better first. You've only been here three weeks and I don't really know anything about you. I think you may feel more a part of the group after we get to know each other better.
>
> The new member learned that while she wants closeness, she often engaged in behaviors that drove others away.

Therapy group agreements are intended to be guidelines rather than sacrosanct rules; broken group agreements are communications or enactments to be processed where therapeutic work can get done. A group member who is consistently late, for example, may be expressing discontent with the leadership, an unresolved conflict with another group member, ambivalence about his or her membership in the group, or a conflict for the whole group. The group leader should take a curious, non-punitive, and empathic stance about the behavior and help the individual member and group to understand its meaning.

Patient Selection and Preparation

Aside from boundary maintenance, patient selection and preparation are crucial to well-functioning therapy groups. The most important factor in patient selection is to have all members functioning at the same developmental level. If a high-functioning group has a member who cannot share the time or modulate his affect, is acutely suicidal, is psychotic or manic, or is sociopathic, the group will never reach the working stage, and it is likely that the group will have a high drop-out rate. That said *mature* groups can often incorporate a member that functions at a lower or higher level. To determine appropriateness for a group, leaders should meet with potential group members at least twice and if possible, three times in order to develop a therapeutic alliance and to assess and prepare them for group. These meetings should include three components: a general history, group preparation, and the group agreements and patient goals, and should answer three important questions:

1. Is this patient suitable for group therapy?
2. Is this patient suitable for the specific group I have in mind?
3. If so, is he or she ready to join the group now? (Gans and Counselman, 2010: p. 204).

The leader of an open-ended support group may not have the opportunity to meet with new group members before they join the group. I encourage all support group leaders of closed-member support groups to meet with their potential group members at least once even if they cannot exclude a group member from the group (which may happen in hospital and clinic settings). The leader tells the potential group member that he wants to meet with her to discuss the nuts and bolts of the group and to make sure that the group is the right support group for her. The leader builds an alliance by hearing the potential member's story, and tells her about the structure of the group, how she might participate, and why it might be useful. The leader can encourage or discourage the potential group member from joining (and refer her to a more appropriate group) and know how an addition might change the group dynamic.

In preparation for a therapy group, the leader tells the potential patient that they will meet several times to get to know each other and to decide if the patient and group will work well together. In order to avoid narcissistic injury, I emphasize the importance of the group being a good match for the patient. The leader needs to do a standard intake that includes a chief complaint, developmental history, family history, psychiatric history, medical history including hospitalizations, medications, history of suicidal ideation, gestures, and attempts, and a social history including current social supports; however, this intake should emphasize the patient's relational and group history. The leader should ask about past group experiences (sports teams, church groups, Scouts, friendship groups, sibling groups, work groups, etc.), including that all-important first group, the family. In the second interview, the leader should conduct a group therapy interview that begins to prepare the patient for group. Possible questions include:

- What has been your best group experience? Worst?
- What made it good/bad?
- What kind of person do you imagine you would connect with in the group?
- Who would you *not* want in the group?
- How do you manage interpersonal conflict?
- How did your family manage anger/sadness/joy?
- Who do you consider a great support in your life?
- Tell me about a relationship disappointment in your life? What happened? How do you understand what happened?

The purpose is to obtain information on the person's relational capacity, history, ability to be self-reflective, readiness for group, and vulnerabilities so that the leader can help the patient with potential difficulties and prepare the patient for the group experience.

The next task is to go over the group agreements. I ask potential members which group agreement they will have the most trouble following (Vannicelli, 2006); the answer gives me information about which agreement may be broken and reminds them that they are likely to feel some conflict about the group agreements, which we can talk about. We then discuss the group member's goals, which give members a measure of their progress and help them determine when they are ready to leave the group. After I meet with the potential group member, we talk about any questions or concerns and whether the group is right for them. If we agree it is a good match, I give my current group members two weeks notice before having a new member join. This gives the current group members time to express their concerns about a new member (no one likes a new sibling) and gives them the opportunity to say good-bye to the group as they have known it. Each new member necessarily brings with them a new group, so the old group needs to mourn its loss. If the patient is not a good match for the group, the leader should be honest about why and refer the person to another group. An appropriate group member for one group may not be good for another group.

> ### Clinical Illustration
>
> A 35-year-old, childless woman who had been abandoned by her father at an early age and now was going through a divorce after being married for two years wanted to join a divorce support group. She felt rejected and worried that she would remain childless if she did not find a new husband right away.
>
> *Support group intervention*
>
> LEADER I know how much you want to be in my group, but I think you would be better served in a group where there are others who are in your situation. My group has older women in it, all of whom have children. Much of the discussion is about custody issues and parenting. I think you would get more out of a group where you have more time to talk about the divorce and relationships. I have a colleague who runs a co-ed group for people at your age that would work well for you.
>
> *Therapy group intervention*
>
> LEADER My group has a mix of men and women, some of whom are divorced, some of whom are not. While I can understand the need to meet someone right away, I think you would benefit from understanding yourself and your relationships better so you can make a good choice in your next partner.

Beginnings and Endings

Beginnings and endings are critical times. To agree to join a group marks a major commitment to start a difficult and exciting personal journey. In support groups, the leader begins the group by introducing himself and actively encouraging members to introduce themselves to each other. Sometimes the leader creates a structure for these introductions; for example, he might ask each member of a divorce support group to introduce themselves and let the group know where they are in the process. A structured "hello" reduces anxiety because the members know what is expected of them. In support groups, the leader may give a "pass" to anyone who does not want to share that first night or he may just ask the person to introduce himself with his first name.

In a process-oriented therapy group, the leader gives the group time to decide how they are going to say hello. This can lead to minutes of anxiety-ridden silence for both the leader and the group members as the group and each individual member contemplate how to begin. This is an important moment because how a group member says hello is often a clue to how they relate in the world. Who speaks first? Who doesn't speak at all? Does someone spill information? Who dominates or disappears in the group? By the end of the first therapy group, the leader should make sure that all members speak so that each member has "joined" the group.

> ## Clinical Illustration
>
> In a first group therapy session, Joan sat quietly throughout the group. Each of the other new members introduced themselves and told the group why they were there.
>
> *Therapy group intervention*
>
> LEADER   We have 15 minutes left and not everyone has spoken.
>
> LAURA   (to Joan) I've been thinking about you for most of the group. You've not said anything and I wondered why.
>
> JOAN   In my house everyone talks so fast and loudly, it is impossible to get a word in edgewise. I was afraid it would seem rude if I interrupted the others.
>
> LEADER   So you took a real risk to speak up. How might it feel to take some more time now to tell us about you?
>
> JOAN   Like I had taken the last brownie on the plate. With six children in the family there wasn't enough to go around at home, so to take anything felt like I would deprive someone else.
>
> LEADER   In this group, you have an opportunity to learn how to ask for what you need, even if others have needs too.

Endings are as important in support groups as they are in therapy groups, but they may be handled differently. Loss is something that everyone experiences in life, so learning to say a healthy good-bye is a crucial part of the therapeutic process. In many support groups, members join the group because good-byes are current, unexpected, and often painful. For example, in cancer support, bereavement, or divorce groups loss or potential loss is the foremost issue. Cancer patients may have to say good-bye to their families and friends long before they had hoped or planned. People going through a divorce often say good-bye not only to their marriage, but to their in-laws, friends, homes, lifestyle, financial security, and full-time parenting. The primary focus in bereavement groups is on mourning and loss. Each of these groups requires patients to mourn so that they can move on.

In closed membership, time-limited support groups and therapy groups, saying good-bye is a major part of the group's work. Because the group has a known ending, the leader highlights it by announcing each week what week the group is on ("We are in our fifth week. We have seven more weeks to go."). In addition, much of the content is about loss and mourning. In a support group, the leader may talk about the stages of loss, symptoms of complicated bereavement, the differences between sadness and depression, and how people say good-bye in different cultures. The emphasis on endings places a high level of importance on the meaning of good-byes, and allows the group to deal with their feelings about them. The leader actively encourages group members to talk about their feelings about the end of the group and past good-byes. As the group comes to a close, the group members often talk about their feelings about each other and express gratitude for the support. Often, support groups develop a ritual for the last group (the sharing of food, cards, gifts, etc.).

In therapy groups, the group agreements encourage group members to give adequate notice to the group when they are planning to leave the group. This allows the group members time to say good-bye, to process feelings about the member and their decision to leave, and to grapple with their own issues about endings. When a member announces a plan to leave, the therapist encourages over weeks or months the verbal expression of here-and-now feelings about the group, the ending, and hopes and disappointments by all group members. Since the group membership will now necessarily be different, the group also mourns the "old" group. The leader discourages members to express any wishes to say good-bye through action (e.g., gifts, food, or hugs) and encourages a verbal expression of feelings related to good-byes.

In both types of groups, members may have social contact after they leave group. In therapy groups, however, group members who have left group and begun to socialize with members still in the group would be excluded from rejoining the group. This and other considerations (e.g., an unwillingness to truly terminate) should be discussed as members leave group and contemplate whether they will remain in contact with each other. In support groups, the leader encourages continued social contact after the group ends or a member leaves.

Resistance

All individuals and groups face resistance at some point in treatment (Freud believed that uncovering and understanding resistance was *the* focus of treatment). Resistance is a set of primitive defenses against knowing, feeling, or experiencing parts of the self that are difficult to acknowledge or integrate. When a patient or the group is faced with unbearable affects or painful truths, they will unconsciously avoid the work of the group through defensive maneuvers.

In support groups, resistance may manifest as unwillingness to bond with others or express feelings, a refusal to mourn, excessive joking or other avoidant behavior, or advice giving. In short-term groups, resistance is less likely to occur than in longer-term support groups or therapy groups because of the time pressure to get work done. Large (2005) found additional resistances in on-going cancer support groups: monopolization in the group, avoiding intense affect, scapegoating, complaints about doctors, inflexible attitudes or personality, subgroups, victimization, and resistance to termination from the group. When the group process is curtailed by unconscious wishes, drives, and feelings, it is the leader's job to point out the resistance and to help the group members move forward. Yet, as Large (2005) has pointed out, it is difficult if not impossible to address resistances in support groups without group agreements that reinforce interventions that address resistance, or an agreement to do personal or interpersonal work.

Typical group therapy resistances include group silence, social conversation, labeling, sub-grouping, acting out, and transference (Weiner, 1993). Leaders can use a four step approach to working with resistance in therapy or on-going support groups:

1. Identify the resistance.
2. Help the group acknowledge the fears that underlie the resistance.

3. Elicit discussion about the fear from the group members.
4. Appreciate and reinforce intimate connections when they occur between members (Large, 2005).

I find that the leader can perform steps two, three, and four in any order.

> ### Clinical Illustration
>
> After three weeks of closeness and shared intense feelings in a bereavement support group, the group members reverted to complaining about how inadequate the medical profession is and surmising if it were more competent their loved ones may still be alive.
>
> LEADER   I noticed that for several weeks you shared a great deal about yourselves and had developed an intimate connection. Now you are talking more about your dissatisfaction with the medical profession than about your loved ones. What do you think might be going on?
> MARIE   (bursts into tears) I just miss my father so much I can barely stand it.
> LEADER   I think others may feel the way you do. It feels unjust that your family members were the ones to die. You wish the medical profession could have done more and are angry that it couldn't. Perhaps it feels easier at this point to be angry with the medical profession than it does to feel the deep sadness of your losses. Yet I have seen the poignant connections that you have made with each other over the past few weeks. I wonder if you are afraid to remain connected for fear you may lose again someone that has become important to you.
>
> In this comment, the group leader highlights the current behavior, asks what it might mean, reflects upon the fear it might mask, intervenes, and connects the members, once again, to each other.

Countertransference

Countertransference in the broadest sense includes all of the therapist's conscious and unconscious reactions to the client which may manifest as thoughts, feelings, or behaviors. In group therapy, dealing with countertransference reactions is often complex because the therapist may have reactions to individuals in the group, dyads, subgroups, or to the group-as-a-whole (Counselman, 2005). An effective group leader pays attention to and uses her own reactions to better understand individual and group dynamics.

Common difficult countertransference feelings in group that may be evoked in the therapist are shame, hate, anger, envy, insecurity, love, sexual attraction, and the wish to be a member rather than the leader of the group. These feelings may be evoked in support or therapy groups, but are handled differently. A support group leader informed about group dynamics would use the feelings to understand where the individual and group are, but probably would not address the feelings unless the group seems stuck as we discussed in the section on resistance.

> **Example**
>
> A client in a divorce support group brought in copies of her financial statements and bills after photocopying them at work. She did not want her abusive husband to know she had copied them and was about to give him a ride home in her car, so she asked the therapist if she would keep them for her. The therapist wanted to help, but also felt worried about keeping confidential files for a client. She fantasized the client's husband might find out and retaliate. Besides, to keep confidential files for a client was a boundary she did not feel comfortable crossing.
>
> A support group leader might agree to keep the files until the group met again because there was a real possibility of physical or verbal abuse by the husband if he found the files. The leader should also have an agreement with the client that she would take the files back and have another safe place to keep them.
>
> A process-oriented group therapist might do the same (for safety reasons), but would later ask the client what else she might be wanting or asking for, how it felt to her for the therapist to refuse or accept, and what it meant that she had asked the therapist to keep her records safe for her (a gift or a burden)?

The therapist would consider what the client's gesture meant for the group – was she speaking for the whole group about safety issues, wishes to be special to the therapist, expressing aggression, or some other group dynamic? Leaders may also feel frustration or boredom in support groups due to group or individual resistances. Support groups can feel superficial at times because there is no agreement to "go deeper."

Often a client will say or do something at the end of a group that stirs strong countertransference reactions in the therapist. A client might reveal suicidal thoughts or say that this is the last session she is coming to two minutes before group ends. Often the group therapist feels on the spot and that there is some urgency to respond. Experienced therapists learn to sit with the discomfort and modulate the feelings before responding.

Difficult Patients and Groups

Both experienced and inexperienced therapists are often faced with difficult patients or the difficult group. Rutan (2005) asks ". . . whether difficult patients are difficult to *treat*, difficult to *sit with*, difficult to *help*, difficult to *like* (Rutan, 2005: p. 41)" . . . or do they evoke difficult feelings in the therapist? Many difficult patients have deficits in affect regulation, conflict resolution skills, anger management, or social skills. They can disrupt the group process with angry outbursts, suicidal threats, overreaction to narcissistic injuries, refusal to consider feedback of others, or by monopolizing the time. Too many difficult patients can result in a difficult group, but so can a lack of proper screening, a sudden unexpected statement or behavior, contagion, or the leader's failure to intervene quickly enough (Shay, 2009). When working with difficult patients or groups, the group leader may feel incompetent, deskilled or paralyzed to intervene. Inexperienced leaders often believe that their group will run better if they eject the difficult patient. Experienced leaders know that groups often co-construct group roles and if a member is ejected another member will happily step up to fill that difficult patient's role. How does one manage the difficult patient in support or therapy groups?

In support groups, the leader should model appropriate group behavior and be active. If a group member talks too long, for example, the leader might say, "Helen, in order to give everyone a chance to speak, we will need to move along. Please take a minute to finish your thought, but then let's give someone else a chance to speak." If a group member needs more time than he or she can get in a group, the leader should refer them to concurrent individual treatment.

To handle difficult patients in therapy groups, Shay (2009) proposes the following interventions:

1. The leader should stop the action right away and assess for danger. If physical danger is present (e.g., suicidal threat or gesture or physical threat or action from one member toward another), stop the action and name the danger.
2. Decide who is most in danger and help that person. You may need to leave the group with a distressed group member to keep the group or member safe. If you return without the member, let the group know the person is safe and immediately process the event with the group (you may need to do this over several sessions). If no one is in immediate physical danger, the leader should ask the group members how they feel and to reflect on what they think is happening.
3. The leader can ask for help from group members to find out what they think the difficult member might be communicating. Leaders can use the members' responses to guide their intervention/interpretation.
4. If possible, make sense of and verbalize what you think is going on (Shay, 2009).

Clinical Illustration

A group member, Charlotte, monopolized a therapy group for several sessions. Each week she droned on about every detail of her chemotherapy visit to the hospital. The other group members wait patiently for an opening, but one rarely arises. Several members have cancelled before group, and those who come seem to tune out for much of the session.

LEADER   Charlotte, I notice you have been doing a lot of work for the group lately. I wonder whether you might like some help from the others? Or,
LEADER   Paul, I've noticed Charlotte has been working hard for about 20 minutes now, and I wonder what you think she might be communicating. Or,
LEADER   Charlotte, you are talking about something that seems really important to you, but I've noticed some people have checked out. Let's check in with the others and see what's going on.

The group leader should not encourage or participate in scapegoating the member. If scapegoating starts to occur, the leader should pull the attention and affect to himself with (for example), "I note that people are expressing anger at Charlotte, but I wonder if the group is really angry with me about something." When the leader pulls negative affect towards himself, he lets the group know that he can handle the situation and that he is not going to allow the group to destroy a group member.

If a group member continues to be difficult, the leader should set up an individual appointment with them to reinforce the group agreements, discuss their behavior, and to coach them on positive group participation. If the group member cannot participate appropriately in group, then the leader needs to decide whether to permanently remove the patient. This should only happen in the most extreme of circumstances (e.g., threatening behavior toward other members or the leader, acute suicidality, inability to empathize or share the time) as removing a patient is often painful for the patient.

Other Considerations

It is possible for clients to participate first in a support group and then move to a process-oriented therapy group. The support group experience can educate the client about the value of sharing one's experience in a group setting and how to use the group effectively. The therapist can learn more about how the client functions in a social setting and can give valuable feedback to the client about why he thinks group therapy would be useful and how it would be different. The therapist should meet with the client and explain that process-oriented therapy groups focus on intrapsychic and interpersonal learning. He or she should assess whether the client is capable of doing that work and whether the group and client are a good match. Similarly, clients who have been in 12-step programs who want to join therapy groups need to know that cross-talk is encouraged and expected in therapy groups.

It is tempting to move a designated support group into a process-oriented support group as the support group matures or is ready to end; however, changing the boundary from support to therapy mid-stream is dangerous. Without proper preparation, an agreement to focus on personal or interpersonal work, and group agreements that provide safety for that kind of work, group members are likely to feel confused, dropout, and become resistant. If one wants to make a shift, the first group should be terminated as planned and the group members, if they would like to continue, should be prepared and selected for this new endeavor.

Sometimes people come to a support group, but want or need to do therapeutic work as well. They may have decided to get a divorce, but can't seem to leave their spouse, or they may suffer from a complicated bereavement that has led to depression. They may not have an adequate support network because they have difficulty with relationships. Or they may have a history of post-traumatic stress and the new event has triggered old feelings and responses. These patients would benefit from what I call a process-oriented support group, a therapeutic group whereby members are brought together for support over a particular acute concern (e.g., divorce, depression, bereavement, becoming HIV positive), but also come to do interpersonal and intrapsychic work that leads to improved relationships and personalchange. Process-oriented support groups have two goals: to provide support and promote change. The leader selects and prepares patients as they would for a therapy group, because group members will develop skills and find support, but will also need to be reflective and willing to process the interpersonal interactions in the group. I use group therapy agreements rather than the support group agreements to provide clearer boundaries and a safe, therapeutic environment in which interpersonal work can be done.

Because members come together over a similar issue and have an immediate way of identifying they belong to the group, they tend to bond and show support to each other quickly. The group leader initially emphasizes providing support because the group members join group in an immediate crisis. As the group develops and matures, the leader shifts the emphasis toward interpersonal learning and intrapsychic change. Often this is a time of resistance in the group; members feel better and question whether they need or want to change. As the group moves into the working phase of development, the group process goes deeper and the patients become more intimate with one another. In this mature phase, these support groups ". . . can be indistinguishable from well-functioning psychodynamic or interpersonal psychotherapy groups. (Large, 2005: p. 566)" When group members terminate from group, they often stay in contact with each other to continue the support they provided one another in the group.

Training and Supervision

There is an unfortunate lack of group therapy training opportunities available in graduate psychology programs. Group therapy training may be an elective or not available. Students and early career clinicians often lead groups with no experience or are supervised by clinicians who have no group therapy training. My bias is that those who run support or therapy groups should be trained in group dynamics and group therapy. Even if one does not address the group dynamics (for example, in a support group), one should know what dynamics are occurring. In the real world, however, support groups are often led by non-clinicians due to a lack of available resources. To run a group without training and supervision is to invite chaos and high anxiety in both clients and the group leader. This is likely to lead to high dropout rates. Group dynamics are complex and, as we have seen, even the most senior clinicians can feel confused, stuck, or unsure, even in a well-functioning group.

Certification is available in group therapy through the International Board for Certification of National Registry of Certified Group Psychotherapists. This certification allows clients, referring therapists, and insurance companies to know that one has significant training and expertise in group therapy. Regional and national group therapy professional organizations such as the American Group Psychotherapy Association offer the 12-hour group therapy coursework for the Certified Group Therapist Certificate. Supervision is also required, and all group therapists should seek individual or group supervision even after completing the CGP training. Difficult scenarios, complicated countertransference feelings, and complex group dynamics are regular occurrences in group therapy. Good supervision from an experienced group therapist is crucial to better understand the group process and one's own countertransference reactions so that one can run emotionally safe and effective groups.

Week 1: What is Depression?
- Introductions and sharing individual stories about depression
- Symptoms and treatment of depression
- Exercise: "What was bad about this week? Name two things that were good about this week."
- Open conversation
- 2 minute meditation

Week 2: My Depression
- Structured exercise on You and Depression: "Choose an image that represents your relationship to depression."
- Discuss with the group
- "Choose a second image that represents your improved relationship with depression."
- 2 minute meditation
- New ways of thinking (Exercise on irrational thought patterns)
- Relaxation exercise
- Open discussion

Week 4: My Family Myself
- Structured exercise: How does my family see me?
- Who are your supports?
- Building a support network
- Open discussion
- Relaxation exercise

Week 5: Coping
- Structured exercise on how do you cope?
- Improving coping
    - A network of friends and family
    - Funny movies
    - Walks on the beach or in the woods
    - Warm baths and hot showers
    - Massage or Yoga
- Open discussion
- Visualization exercise

Week 6: Lifestyle
- Exercise on taking care of oneself
    - Exercise
    - Healthy diet
    - Regular sleep
- Name three things you are grateful for (encourage members to write down three things each night before bedtime).
- Open discussion
- Visualization exercise

Week 7: Building and Following a Dream
- Structured exercise: Describe a time you felt really good about something you were doing – it doesn't have to be work-related. What were you doing? What made it good? How did you feel?
- Create a dream of where you would like to be in life. What is the first step to get there?
- Open discussion
- Meditation or relaxation exercise

Week 8: Where from Here and Good-byes
- Next steps
- Good-byes

Figure 14.1 Example of an 8-Week, closed-member, depression support group.

Conclusion

Support and therapy groups provide opportunities for significant therapeutic work to be done. In support groups, the goal is to return patients to their normal level of functioning after they have experienced an unexpected, challenging life event that may place excessive stress upon them. Process-oriented therapy groups are for patients who want to work on deep, personal growth and change. The group leader who understands the differences and similarities between the two will know when and how to intervene in order for either to be effective.

References and Bibliography

Abramowitz, I. A., & Coursey, R. D. (1989). Impact of an educational support group on family participants who take care of their schizophrenic relatives. *Journal of Consulting and Clinical Psychology*, 57(2), 232–236.

Alonso, A., & Swiller, H. (1993). *Group therapy in clinical practice.* Washington, DC: American Psychiatric Press.

Brabender, V. (2002). *Introduction to group therapy.* New York: John Wiley & Sons.

Callahan, K. L., Price, J. L., & Hilsenroth, M. J. (2004). A review of interpersonal-psychodynamic group psychotherapy for adult survivors of childhood sexual abuse. *International Journal of Group Psychotherapy*, 54(4), 491–519.

Cohen, S., & Wills, T. A. (1985). Stress, social support, and the buffering hypothesis. *Psychological Bulletin*, 98, 310–357.

Cohn, B. (2005). Creating the group envelope. In L. Motherwell & J. Shay, (Eds). *Complex Dilemmas in Group Therapy: Pathways to Resolution* (pp. 3–12). New York: Brunner-Routledge.

Counselman, E. (2005). Containing and using powerful therapist reactions. In L. Motherwell & J. Shay, (Eds), *Complex dilemmas in group therapy: pathways to resolution* (pp. 155–165). New York: Brunner-Routledge.

Davenport, Y. B., Ebert, M. H., Adland, M. L., et al. (1977). Couples group therapy as an adjunct to lithium maintenance of the manic patient. *American Journal of Orthopsychiatry*, 47, 495–502.

Foulkes, S. (1964). *Therapeutic group analysis.* London: George Allen & Unwin.

Gans, J., & Counselman, E. (2010). Patient selection for psychodynamic group psychotherapy: Practical and dynamic considerations. *International Journal of Group Psychotherapy*, 60(2), 197–220.

Jensen, H. H., Mortensen, E. L., & Lotz, M. (2010). Effectiveness of short-term psychodynamic group therapy in a public outpatient psychotherapy unit. *Nordic Journal of Psychiatry*, 64(2), 106–114.

Kanas, N. (2005). Group therapy for patients with chronic trauma-related stress disorders. *International Journal of Group Psychotherapy*, 55(1), 161–165.

Kanas, N. (1986). Group psychotherapy with schizophrenics: A review of controlled studies. *International Journal of Group Psychotherapy*, 36(3), 339–351.

Kashner, T. M. (1995). Enhancing the health of psychosomatization disorder patients: Effectiveness of short-term group Therapy. *Psychosomatics: Journal of Consultation Liaison Psychiatry*, 36(5), 462–470.

Kasner, T. M. (1996). Enhancing the health of somatization disorder patients: Effectiveness of short-term group therapy. *Psychosomatics: Journal of Consultation Liaison Psychiatry*, 36(5), 462–470.
Kripke, D. F., & Robinson, D. (1985). Ten years with a lithium group. *McLean Hospital Journal*, 10, 1–11.
Kurtz, L. F. (1997). *Self-help and support groups*. Thousand Oaks, California: Sage Publications.
Large, T. R. (2005). Resistance in long-term cancer support groups. *International Journal of Group Psychotherapy*, 55(4), 551–573.
Leavy, R. L. (1983). Social support and psychological disorder: A review. *Journal of Community Psychology*, 11, 3–21.
Meyer, T. J., & Mark, M. M. (1995). Effects of psychosocial interventions with adult cancer patients: A meta-analysis of randomized experiments. *Health Psychology*, 14, 101–108.
Motherwell, L., & Shay, J. (2005). *Complex Dilemmas in Group Therapy: Pathways to Resolution*. New York: Brunner-Routledge.
Norberry, L. P. (1986). Divorce over 50: A program of support. *Journal for Specialists in Group Work*, 11(3), 157–162.
Oei, T., & Browne, A. (2006). Components of group processes: Have they contributed to the outcome of mood and anxiety disordered patients in a group cognitive-behavioral therapy program? *American Journal of Psychotherapy*, 60,(1), 53–70.
Oygard, L., Theun, F., & Solvang P. (2000). An evaluation of divorce support groups: A qualitive approach. *Journal of Divorce and Remarriage*, 32(3–4), 149–164.
Piper, W. E., Ogrodniczuk, J. S., Joyce, A. S., et al. (in press). *Effects of process variables on therapeutic outcome*. Washington, DC: American Psychological Association Press.
Rutan, J. S., Stone, W., & Shay, J. (2007). *Psychodynamic group psychotherapy* (4th ed). New York: The Guilford Press.
Rutan, J. S. (2005). Treating difficult patients in group. In L. Motherwell & J. Shay (Eds.), *Complex dilemmas in group therapy: Pathways to resolution* (pp. 41–50). New York: Brunner-Routledge.
Salvendy, J. (1993). Selection and preparation of patients and organization of the group. In H. I. Sadock & B. J. Sadock (Eds.), *Comprehensive group* (3rd ed., pp. 72–84). Baltimore: Williams & Wilkins.
Shay, J. (2009). *Fear and loathing in group therapy*. Workshop presentation (with Jerry Gans & Lise Motherwell) at the American Group Psychotherapy Association Annual Meeting, San Diego, California.
Sikkema, K. J., Kalichman, S. C., Kelly, J. A., et al. (1995). Group intervention to improve coping with AIDS-related bereavement: model development and an illustrative clinical example. *AIDS Care*, 7(4), 1–17.
Taylor, K., Lamdan, R. Siegel, J. E., et al. (2003). Psychological adjustment among African American breast cancer patients: One-year follow-up results of a randomized psychoeducational group intervention. *Health Psychology*, 22(3), 316–323.
Toseland, R. W., Rossiter, C. M., Peak, T., & Smith, G. C. et al. (1990). Comparative effectiveness of individual and group interventions to support family caregivers. *Social Work*, 35(3), 209–216.
Tuckman, B. (1964). Developmental sequence in small groups. *Psychological Bulletin*, 63, 384–399.
Tuckman, B., & Jensen, M. A. (1977). Stages of small-group development revisited. *Group and Organization Studies*, 2(4), 419–427.
Vannicelli, M. (2006). (Personal Communication.)

Volkmar, F. R., Bacon, S., & Pfeffferbaum, A. (1979). Group therapy in the managment of manic-depressive illness. *American Journal of Psychotherapy*, 35, 226–234.

Volkmar, F. R., Bacon, S., Shakir, S. A. et al. (1981). Group therapy in the managment of manic-depressive illness. *American Journal of Psychiatry*, 35, 226–234.

Wasserman H., & Danforth, H. E. (1988). *The human bond: Support groups and mutual aid.* New York: Springer.

Weiner, M. (1993). Role of the leader in group psychotherapy. In H. I. Sadock & B. J. Sadock (Eds.), *Comprehensive Group Psychotherapy* (3rd ed). Baltimore: Williams & Wilkins.

Whitaker, D., & Lieberman, M. (1964). *Psychotherapy through the group process.* New York: Atherton.

Wulsin, L., Bachop, M., & Hoffman, D. (1988). Group therapy in manic-depressive illness. *American Journal of Psychotherapy*, XLII(2), 263–271.

Yalom, I. (1995). *The Theory and Practice of Group Psychotherapy* (4th ed). New York: Basic Books.

Zabalegui, A., Sanchez, S., Sanchez, P., et al. (2005). Nursing and cancer support groups. *Journal of Advanced Nursing*, 51(4), 369–381.

15
Working with the Difficult Group Patient
Phyllis F. Cohen

Psychoanalytic literature describes the "difficult" patient in a number of ways. In the vernacular, they are likely to be spoken of as very sick, requiring extra effort therapeutically, unpleasant, resistant, uncommonly hard to understand, obnoxious, impervious, demanding, manipulative, suicidal, depressed, possibly violent, and rigid and inflexible both in stance and in thinking. Truly demonstrating Freud's "stone wall of narcissism," the inaccessibility of such patients and their frequent bizarre behavior create alienation and prevent the taking in of any "good milk" that might be proffered by the therapist.

According to Hopper (2001) such "difficult patients are those with pronounced borderline and narcissistic elements in their personalities and characters." (p. 140) Often they are irascible and intimidating. Eigen in a classic description, calls such people the "unwanted".

> These patients tend to drive therapists away, as they do people. They generally present severe narcissistic character deformations which are more than usually exasperating or repulsive. They may oscillate between an over-cloying and obnoxiously negativistic manner in apparently endless repetition of extreme forms of hostile dependence. They can appear needy and demanding but seem to present intractable resistances if one tries to help them. In some instances they may appear snake-like and cynically chilling. If they are vegetative, they are also willful and proud, even when in seemingly masochistic and silent ways. They are very sensitive to slights . . . carry a hope tinged with resentment made heavy with an accusing sense of deprivation and self-pity. They seek relief from pain but have a high tolerance for feeling that things will never change and nothing good can happen to them . . . all this despair (in) an atmosphere of muted want and rage. Their identity is formed by a chronic sense of injury together with a primitive union with the phallic mother-male or female – who injured them. Thus one moment they may enact the role of helpless victim and then become a terrifying active mass, impulsive, tyrannical or biting. (Eigen, 1977: p. 119)

The Wiley-Blackwell Handbook of Group Psychotherapy, First Edition. Edited by Jeffrey L. Kleinberg.
© 2012 John Wiley & Sons, Ltd. Published 2012 by John Wiley & Sons, Ltd.

These are the patients who so often appear in our groups. Without the knowledge and the trained ability to work with preoedipal disorders it becomes impossible. So what is it that a group therapist needs? First, it is a theoretical model, complete with a body of clear, clinical techniques that have been tested successfully and second, the advantage of a sense of humor.

History

"Modern group analysis is a theory of techniques designed to reach patients who were until recently, considered difficult or unable to benefit from a psychodynamic approach . . . (It) is more a method of exploration than a method of explanation by way of interpretation" (Brook, 2006: p.177). This discipline first emerged during the early 1950's through the work of Hyman Spotnitz, a neurologist and psychoanalyst whose seminal work with schizophrenia laid the base for therapy with preoedipal, (that is, narcissistic) patients. Group techniques that protected the fragile ego, thereby aiding the patient in staying in treatment, were conceived here. According to Ernsberger, (1991) what the Modern school offers "is a unified body of knowledge, a clinically confirmable theory of the etiology of narcissistic illnesses and a unified technique based on this theory for the management of all sorts of cases" (Ernsberger, 1991: p. 23).

The work of Spotnitz was followed by that of Lou Ormont, a brilliant therapist who only conducted groups, believing the group-as-a-whole to be the best agent of change. Through his research and the many comprehensive articles he published, Ormont added the importance of what has come to be known as the three "I's."

The *Insulation barrier*, a defensive structure "that enables a person to withstand toxic stimuli and that also permits nutrient experiences to flow through."
Immediacy, meaning that one works in the here-and-now and is seen as a key to the development of understanding relationships which permit members to form a cohesive group.
Intimacy, is a mature expression of closeness, developed through the resolution of those resistances which served as a defense against the fears and anxieties triggered by early traumas. All of these then translate into the possible formation of beneficial relationships outside the therapy room. (Ormont, 1988, 1993, 1994, 1996) This is one of the ultimate aims of what is termed, "emotional education."

Fortunately for me, my first graduate courses were taken at a university where the faculty included four professors who had been trained in Modern Psychoanalysis and the practice of group psychotherapy that rested on its premises. The value of the embodied techniques was made clear to me while serving an internship in Family Court. There, three of us, students who would "practice" under the eyes of a supervisor, treated groups of family members mandated to us by a judge. Understandably, resistance on the part of those patients rapidly emerged.

The other students had not taken the same classes as I had and the differences in the ways in which we spoke to those sent to our office soon became obvious. Their interventions, either interpretations or ego-based questions, could be seen as intensifying patient discomfort and frequently resulted either in silence or disappearance. I took the risks of using the unusual but simple techniques Modern Group therapy is based on, and the fact that they worked became demonstrable. Therapy with families was indeed doing group work. Patients settled comfortably enough to speak in the sessions so that progressive communication became possible. At the same time I grew more comfortable in a role that had us interacting in a safe and cooperative therapeutic alliance, a partner, rather than the expert know-it-all. Such sessions became easier to conduct, both with practice and with the expert guidance of training supervisors at the university.

The Theory

What differentiates Modern Analytic psychotherapy from more classical is basically that to the importance of transference and resistance has been added the careful attention paid to countertransference and the narcissistic defense. These emphasize the value of recognizing nonverbal, acting-out and symbolic communications; all of which are utilized by more primitive patients. The benefits are derived from the therapeutic ability to respond to the covert rather than the overt message from the patient.

Let me define those terms. As we understand it, transference is a repetition of older attitudes towards people from the patient's early life, who had special importance in that past. These feelings are now being re-enacted and directed in both actions and words, toward the therapist in the present. Resistance is any force within the individual which opposes that which will lead to positive change. Countertransference is a feeling experienced by the therapist that has been induced by the patient's own transference or resistance. It can be either subjective or objective. The former is based on the therapist's personal life history while the latter is solely a product of the patient's life story as it is reactivated in the therapy room. The narcissistic defense appears when the patient attacks the self to protect the object (i.e. the therapist) from hostile feelings. The best explanation of such self-destructive behavior lies again in early life. The child, totally dependent on the parent for all forms of support, cannot take the risk of expressing anger at that source of life. Yet, to the regressed patient, the only place where such negative feelings can go is inward. Under these circumstances, in its extreme form, attacking the mind would result in schizophrenia and attacking the body would activate psychosomatic symptomology.

The "more primitive patient," understood as a preoedipal patient, demonstrates specific behaviors in group that reflect behaviors in their outside life . . . Such a person is:

> . . . occupied exclusively with his own needs. To him the wants and reactions of others are irrelevant. His obsessive aim is to suck from others, to draw them into solving his "unique" problems for him. The love he receives is never enough. Indeed, his insatiable demand for it prevents him from operating in a way that would lead to fulfillment. It distorts his behavior. Such a patient regards the group room as the emergency ward of some psychological hospital designed to minister to his every need, and the hospital staff is failing. (Ormont, 2001: p. 145)

Assessing such patients in an initial interview, before working with them can be very difficult. This is why if the person being considered for group is not already in one's private practice, a therapist will frequently say "Let's try working together for a few sessions and see how it goes. That way I have a better sense of what group might be a good fit." When the therapist feels that such a person will respond positively to what a group can offer, it has been found to be more effective placing them in an on-going group with a mixture of seasoned members. If the sense is that they are still too fragile, more individual work would usually be suggested. It is recommended that groups consist of people with differing symptomology. This permits interactive support from areas where there is ego strength. As stated by Yalom and Leszcz:

> There appears to be a general clinical sentiment that heterogeneous groups have advantages over homogeneous groups for *long-term interactional group therapy* . . . This principle – *that change is preceded by a state of dissonance or incongruity* – is backed by considerable clinical and social-psychological research." (Yalom and Leszcz, 2005: pp. 272–273)

The Techniques

What takes place in group practice in my private office is based on those specific Modern Group techniques which emanated from this theory. They have demonstrated that successful therapy with difficult patients can be successful in part through their ego-strengthening effect. There is a clear avoidance of any intervention that might damage the already fragile sense of self. These methods are designed to work with early stages of the narcissistic group patient and are classified as "psychological reflection." They include joining the resistance:

> . . . where the analyst responds as if he sees and perceives the world from the same perspective, thereby protecting the defensive structure; and mirroring the resistance, where the patient's defenses are accepted as though one's own and indication is given of having or (having had) similar feelings, thoughts and experiences. (Spotnitz, 1969: p. 32).

In the mirroring of the unconscious, the analyst attributes to himself the unconscious impulse that is being defended against; a method whereby the patient can look at himself in the analyst until he feels strong enough to face himself. Discussing the analyst's "problems" rather than his own, enables the safe exploration of the projection on an outside ego and thereby permits the patient to avoid the unnecessary pain his ego is not yet prepared to master. This is recognized as the "twinning stage" of the narcissistic transference, clearly still a time where it is necessary to safeguard the damaged ego until it can heal.

In these difficult patients, boundaries are either absent or overly fluid. This frequently results in great fears of being taken over, engulfed, abandoned or erased. In too many cases, there is a ready capacity to feel hurt or humiliated, along with an acutely vulnerable sensitivity to criticism or rejection. Self-examination is painful. The awareness of differences between self and others poses a threat. Poor impulse control with abounding rage is accompanied by a hunger for admiration.

In our private practices there are patients shaped by myriad cultures, religions and social strata. The work that we do must therefore be capable of successfully crossing any number of hidden boundaries. To accomplish this we must draw on those same basic techniques of joining and mirroring. I well remember the woman of Island heritage, high up in a corporate structure; so self-destructive in her dealings with authority that it was suggested she come into therapy. Rosa walked into my office; took one look at me and said, "This will never work. There is no way that you could understand me." I asked "Why?" and was told that I was the wrong race, the wrong culture and the wrong social milieu. I agreed that these were possible stumbling blocks but asked if she would be willing to gamble a few weeks of her life to satisfy the authorities that had sent her. "At the same time," I commented, "it would make me look better to your superiors." In these interventions, one joining with her wish of being able to be rid of me and the other, mirroring her wish to be seen and recognized as successful at work, permitted her to accept our beginning contract.

To treat such an intelligent woman it was necessary to capture her curiosity. Then we could explore together the minefields she seemed to step into time and time again. Weeks became months as we carefully interacted, and one day Rose came back in with a big smile. "You know," she said, "I've been thinking about it and we're really very much alike. Both of our origins are Mediterranean and not from cold-climate ancestors." Here is the first indication of identification, marking the start of the narcissistic transference. Such cases are always reminders of the remark apocryphally attributed to Freud: "We must treat our patients the way that porcupines make love. Very carefully!"

How then do we try to communicate and work with difficult patients? The primary contact method evolved for use with delicate egos is the "object-oriented question." This is a question formulated "to direct the patient's attention away from his own ego and towards objects or events external to himself" (Margolis, 1983: p. 70). For such a person, self and object are not distinctly different; the unstable ego would experience an ego-oriented question, directed towards the "you," as an attack or threat. Rather than saying to a patient coming late for the therapy hour, "You are twenty minutes late. What kept you?" we might say, "Was the traffic bad today?" This circumvents the sense of accusation which might well echo early parental criticisms and therefore further concretize resistance. However, by offering the out of dealing with an external circumstance, rather than an internal flaw, the patient's comfort level can be maintained, which aids in preserving the treatment in early days.

Numerous requests had come from students, to give more examples of how to begin such interventions. In answer I composed a two-page list entitled "The Secret Weapon for Dealing with Narcissism: The Object-Oriented Question." It included such phrases as "What if I were to tell you that. . . . ? How would it be if . . . ? Is there anything familiar about that? and, Where did that come from?" While the therapist is using such phraseology, new ways are being modeled for group members to experiment with, as questions are posed when they speak with each other.

In the beginning, when we start working with a patient we establish a contract based on the premise that the patient will put into words all thoughts and feelings as best she are able. All else is the responsibility of the therapist. What are the subjects spoken about in therapy? The past, the present, the future, dreams, sex, money and thoughts about the analyst. If patients are seen both individually and in group, these areas are indeed a focus of exploration in their private sessions, particularly as a source of uncovering past trauma. In the group, by contrast, there is movement to bring those elements into the present. How does each group member display personal forms of resistance within and among the other group members? Basically, this unconsciously occurs by their replicating within the group, outside difficulties and impediments that block healthy relationships outside. When this takes place the therapist then sits back and silently observes how each person reenacts early blocks; resorting to silence, acting out, compliance, defiance or digression.

Ormont (1988: p. 32) characterizes resistances as either verbal or attitudinal. The fact-seeker, the fault finder, the fighter, the setter of conditions for closeness, the diverter and the humorist are using verbal resistances. Attitudinal resistances are expressed non-verbally by the self-absorber, the detacher, the unsatisfied one, the distruster and the complier. I have added my own additions: "The ice-queen, haughty, superior, condescending and isolated; the intimidator, given to pounding on the couch or chair, raising his voice, threatening; the bored one, yawning and falling asleep, symbolically trying to 'bore the therapist to death'; the disappearing one who slides further and further down until one is reminded of the Cheshire cat, leaving behind only his sneering smile; the baby who whines and verbally pees all over; and the schlemiel who, no matter what, can succeed in making himself look bad" (Cohen, 1996: p. 27).

Once these resistances are full-blown and easily recognized, interventions are offered to help resolve them with the aim of translating the symbolic message into words. The therapist notices, studies, investigates with object-oriented questions, reconstructing while simultaneously using joining, mirroring and role modeling new ways of making contacts. These reflective techniques are conceptualized as interventions that communicate to the preoedipal patient at the same maturational level on which he is functioning. They also preserve, strengthen and reinforce early ego defenses that had served essential self-preserving functions in the difficult patient. It has been hypothesized that by so doing, such a procedure reverses the original process of negative ego formation which occurred when the infantile mental apparatus was unable to release hostile feelings towards its earliest object. Such techniques have proved to be effective in those cases where interpretation could have little effect on the destructive patterns that patients often feel compelled to repeat.

These interventions are offered in a manner described as "contact functioning." This refers to any attempt, verbal or symbolic, on the part of a patient to contact either the therapist or another group member for the purpose of attempting connectedness. In permitting this initiative, rather than calling on someone, the patient is encouraged to control his own level of frustration and stimulation. This is somewhat like relying on self-demand feeding for an infant. How the contact is made is assumed to clarify what the patient needs. That way the patient can control what he can mentally and emotionally digest and in so doing maturational growth takes place. By contrast, there are those who might retreat and not speak, sometimes for lengthy periods. Rather than permitting this lack of contact to solidify, the patient's introspective tendencies might be countered with a carefully worded object-oriented question once in each session. In these early periods with the difficult patient, the first purpose would be to extricate the group member from a self-absorbed state.

For example, in the midst of a group discussion about bullies, a silent member might be contacted with a question such as "Nancy, are there any people like that in your life?" If we were then to get a possible response, perhaps Nancy monosyllabically responding that she had been mistreated by an employer; rather than commiserating, we might ask, "When did this happen?" or "What kind of person would do that?" These are two innocuous questions that literally refer to "outside" the therapy room. Such a query serves to interrupt the self-involvement. It models a new and different behavior, now fashioned on an interpersonal exchange in a safe environment. Our hope is that the possibility of a beginning dialogue has taken place. Our purpose is to offer training that will first enable the frightened patient to abandon a state of self-absorption; and second, to model for the other group members ways in which isolated states can be breached without endangering the contacted person. Through all interventions, we must be careful to protect the insulation barrier which serves as the defensive structure. Such a structure is conceived as "a meshwork that enables a person to withstand toxic stimuli and that also permits nutrient experiences to flow through" (Ormont, 1994: p. 362).

Once such ways of forming connections become a function of group awareness, a technique called "bridging" can be introduced to evoke identification and to intensify intimacy. As Ormont described:

> The term *bridging* refers to any technique designed to strengthen emotional connections between members, or to develop connections where they did not exist before. Loosely speaking, bridging is the group therapist's way of uniting what sociologists term a *scattered community*, namely a collection of people with similar problems, but who are not as yet communicating in a meaningful fashion. (Ormont, 2001: p. 164).

This is particularly useful in the early stages of a group, where each member is likely to want contact only with the leader and wishes to feel like "the special child." To avoid a too early reawakening of sibling rivalry within the group, we use our knowledge of individual lives to foster a link across the room. How might this look?

> Harry, who is still mourning the loss of his father many years before, is speaking of the wish for some male figure to care enough about him to help him. Primarily, he focuses on his repeated difficulty in "satisfying" his professors in law school, partners in the law firm where he served his internship and his uncle who was in *loco parentis*. Slouching down in his chair he appears apathetic and hopeless. Facing him in the circle is Paul, an older man who is constantly complaining bitterly about his "thoughtless" son. A question is directed to Paul. "What would it be like, do you think, to have someone like Harry for a son?"
> Both men sit up a little straighter and look at each other. In the here-and-now, there is a beginning connection. This takes place not only between the two men, but also provides an opening for others to enter in and conjecture.

> In this manner, Harry gets the attention he craves from an older, caring man that will also eventually help him to understand his role in sabotaging past relationships. Paul, through external exploration with Harry, will be led to feel less threatened in his parental role by their developing interactions. Hopefully, this will lead to a better understanding of how and why his son misbehaves, what his role in the misunderstandings has been and how he might help to change it in the present.

Two Often "Unsung" Additional Ways of Creating Connections

There are two other tools that we use, yet don't think of as part of our professional therapeutic repertoire. One is the use of metaphors, a valuable shortcut to the unconscious. People present themselves to others by telling stories. It has been said that scientists believe in statistics but ordinary people are more often moved by stories. At the heart of a story is usually a metaphor. Gardner has written, "I am a firm believer in the value of the storytelling mode of communication – especially when allegory and dramatization . . . are utilized. Messages so communicated are more palatable and more likely to be appreciated and retained" (Gardner, 1977: p. 2). For this reason the use of a metaphor can indeed be powerful.

> In one of my groups there was a woman who had no affect, none at all. There were no apparent facial expressions, no smiles, no tears, no rage, no humor, only an icy control. One evening while sitting in a group session, a light bulb unexpectedly blew, darkening the room. She commented suddenly, "That's how I feel all the time. Darkened!" In the weeks that followed, being "in the dark" was the metaphor that group members used in speaking with her. Questions would be asked "Are we still in the Dark Ages?" "Is your light bulb working yet?" "How is the Dark Lady today?" Small changes began to unfold as she began to respond to her new role in the group.
>
> She would come into the room and often, as her "share of the talking time," report on the state of her dullness. As weeks went on, though, the faintest beginning of brightness began to appear. It was readily acceptable now for her to speak since it was all centered around the metaphor of "electric" as a synonym for being alive. It could be spoken of as it was essentially external to her feelings. Each successive week brought more frequent interactions with others in the group and were accompanied by new bits of expressiveness: a smile, a look of astonishment, a frown. Finally the day came when she announced with laughter that she felt "illuminated" or as several other group members commented, "enlightened" and "all lit up." Working together, the group had incorporated the metaphor into its ability to affect change.

The second therapeutic way of being, not often recognized as a technique because of its spontaneity, is the use of humor, often recognized as a redeeming salve of painful experience in therapy. Laughter can remove super-ego pressure from the ego and assist in creating warmer feelings. The laugh of recognition shows that the humorous contact has had some intrapsychic importance for the patient, and is recognized as such within the group ethos. When used appropriately, not to make fun of but to touch humorously in a manner that still permits dignity, and with a sense of correct timing, it can have a powerful, lasting effect. "Humor used by the therapist can help to alleviate excessive tension, overcome resistances, provide alternate methods of coping, furnish a correcting emotional experience and form a healthier identification with the therapist." (Reynes and Allen, 1987: p. 269). The result of these kinds of contacts can be a positive emotional experience that therapist, group and patient have together; a moment of shared, empathic amusement.

In one group, a very obese woman would speak constantly of two themes: how difficult it was to get her husband to do what she wanted and how difficult it was for her to lose weight. When she had heard this long enough, another member had what is called an "ah-hah moment." "I finally get it," she said to the first, "If you get thinner then what he wants will carry more weight!" Someone gasped, the room went silent, and then there was a burst of spontaneous laughter. Now there was a place to explore the covert block that had impeded healthy behavior.

In another group there was a man who had been given the sobriquet of "the great procrastinator." A talented, promising architect, now in his late thirties, he was sabotaging his career by continually putting off the advanced exams required by his firm to attain the needed certification. His family history included a competitive, denigrating older brother and a father who favored the eldest child. One day he brought a dream into the group. He said, "It was really queer. I was running down the street but my head was on backwards and there were watches strapped all the way up my legs. I just don't understand it." Fortunately his group siblings did. "It's time you stopped looking backwards at all the people who said you would never make it," was the first comment. Then came the second interpretation, from another. "And you are really running out of time!" As dreams frequently make use of puns and witticisms as metaphors, they afford excellent material to enable group members to tap into covert messages from the unconscious.

The Association for Applied and Therapeutic Humor officially defines therapeutic humor as "any intervention that promotes health and wellness by stimulating a playful discovery, expression or appreciation of the absurdity or incongruity of life's situation. This intervention may enhance health or be used as a complementary treatment of illness to facilitate healing or coping, whether physical, emotional, cognitive, social or spiritual" (Sultanoff, 2000: p. 1). The value of such interventions lies in the way in which they open a path towards further examination of here-to-fore buried feelings.

And Yet Two More Vital Components of Therapeutic Practice

It would be a disservice to omit brief discussion of two additional factors that play an important role in our work. The first is research and the second is supervision.

There is at present a dearth of empirical evidence as demonstrated by Modern Analytic group research. The primary work done in the field has been about the single case studies. As Shepherd has written, "Modern analysts have spent over three decades refining a methodology for single-case study research that is appropriate for psychoanalysts and acceptable to the canons of scientific inquiry" (Shepherd, 2004: p. 163). Specific guidelines have been set out by Meadow that include methodology, design, measurement, reliability and validity (Meadow, 1996, pp. 308–333). Clearly, the need is now to encourage formal group research based on professional standards as evinced in these earlier citations.

Supervision, as it says in the introduction to the AGPA training book, "is a delicate undertaking in the best of circumstances. A good supervisory experience can make an important contribution to the development of a professional, resulting in an abiding commitment to offering group psychotherapy for the duration of his/her career" (Bernard and Spitz, 2006: p. 4). Like love, it comes in many different forms, the most common being individual, that is one-on-one with a supervisor, and in group, with an experienced practitioner capable of providing both expert guidance and professional consultation within a protected environment.

The advantages are numerous. "As the presenter tells about his or her therapy group, the members of the supervisory group experience reactions that mirror, parallel, or identify with dynamic processes that originated in the first place. In response to the creative interaction between presenter, presented, and receivers, the consultation group can arrive at formulations that provide the consultee with new understandings and action plans" (Ettin, 1995: p. 3). It is a true working relationship that often appears as a parallel process to the case that is being supervised, and it is here that the therapist can serve as an alter ego when support is needed. The value and importance of group supervision is underscored by the reality that even seasoned practitioners often either continue in such groups, or return to them from time to time, such as when attending an American Group Psychotherapy conference.

The Practice

At the end of sessions with difficult patients, I am occasionally left with two strong opposing feelings, not dissimilar from those that the borderline patient experiences. They are that either the treatment (and I) have been a success or that we have been a failure. In this examination of the phenomena of what occurs between such patients and therapists, where the process is of equal importance to the outcome, a number of past cases come to mind. I offer here two instances of success and two of failure.

Four Case Studies

Paula

A 35-year-old woman had been sent to me for group and individual therapy by a colleague (whom I later learned had dissolved his own group of which she had been a member, as the only way of getting rid of her). A practicing doctor, Paula came from a prominent New York banking family. Her mother had been emotionally absent and physically distant, both from her husband and her child. Her father was intrusive, seductive and controlling, and as I later understood, Paula identified strongly with him. She had had one short failed marriage where her money had been used as a control issue and was unable to form any healthy relationship, either with men or other women. What she wanted from therapy was a miracle that would gift her with a "perfect" life.

Little (1958) has said that borderline patients are known for wide fluctuations in their clinical presentation. One can see normal, neurotic and psychotic transference in the same patient in the course of one therapeutic hour. Paula demonstrated this, coming in to a group session with a smile and saying "I'm so glad to be here," to be followed minutes later with the dismissive comment to me, "You don't do very much, do you?" Later in the session, should I join with her on a comment she had made, her response could be a vitriolic attack. "Stop trying to use analytic techniques on me. You're so stupid and I'm much smarter than you. You're ugly and an idiot and I don't know why I come here!" Realizing that she was giving me a true picture of the way she had been raised, it was clear that my only chance of succeeding in treating her was to mirror both her moods, tone of voice and aggression. Understandably, I had no trouble expressing the last. Members of her group cooperated in occasionally siding with her; occasionally defending me; utilizing the expressions of aggression either to examine hidden negative feelings or to maintain an ongoing dialogue. One of the men in the group commented that he appreciated her being there as it enabled him to work out some of his furious feelings about his wife. By the fourth month it seemed that we were proceeding well. Her words to me then were "You really are just like me." I assumed this to be an excellent example of a positive narcissistic transference statement.

However, the sabotage continued to escalate. Paula seemed to embody all the descriptive words of Eigen as an "unwanted person," and added to it her own ingredient of seductive behavior. She came to group in increasingly short skirts and low cut blouses. The final blow-up occurred on the evening when she appeared in a leopard-print blouse cut half way down to her navel and a skirt that nearly met it. When questions arose as to the non-verbal message she was giving, she stood up and viciously attacked the men in the group for being perverts, of sexually assaulting her with their eyes, of wanting to "screw" her and not being men enough to say so. As for me, I was running a group where a woman could be sexually abused and she had no intentions of staying. With that she stormed out of the room, never to return, and shouting over her shoulder, the ultimate "fuck-you." "Besides, I've been in another group for three weeks, and they're the good one, appreciating me, not like you wimps!" and that was the last she was heard from. Paula did not answer a phone call nor a closing letter and did not pay her last bill; definitely, a failure with a difficult patient.

In retrospect, what had gone wrong became increasingly clear. The therapy or perhaps the therapist, in this instance, could not penetrate Freud's "stone wall of narcissism." In studying my own countertransfernce, it became apparent that my feelings towards her were a very mixed bag. I came to realize that my distaste, often in her presence, had to be the way her mother felt and why she had distanced herself from the child. This was also replicated in her last therapy. It was exactly what her last therapist had done, acting out on his own induced negative feelings, to get rid of her. The aggression and pseudo-sexuality the group and I experienced in the room with her was a reflection of her own identification with the rageful and seductive father at too early an age and with too symbiotic a relationship. Most of all I was acutely aware of the nursery rhyme often running through my head while with her: "Humpty Dumpty sat on a wall. Humpty Dumpty had a great fall. And all the King's horses and all the King's men, Couldn't put Humpty together again." Such unrecognized countertransference feelings had led her previous therapist to go into action and had led me to be overly cautious in my interventions. This unconscious awareness of her underlying fragility and the fear that if she "cracked" she might not be put back together again, obviously played a part in the failure of the therapy

According to Lathrop, "The abrasive patient . . . seizes upon the mistake as a wonderful opportunity to berate the therapist. This is one of those exquisitely delicate points in an intimate relationship. If the patient succeeds in "killing off" the therapist, the healing value of the relationship is destroyed. If the therapist fails to accept full responsibility for the mistake or permits the patient to beat him/her up, maladaptive patterns will be perpetuated . . ." (Lathrop, 1984: p. 63). In this instance, both dreaded possible outcomes occurred.

Tim

One of my favorite stories tells us of the power of a group whose members have assimilated these new ways of contacting each other. Tim, an author suffering from writer's block, which he blamed on chronic insomnia, came in for a consultation. Sleep clinics, nutritionists, neurologists and frauds who prescribed (among other things) keeping pasta under the bed to eat when he awakened at night, had done nothing to help. Therapy was a last resort. There was only one problem: he didn't believe in it! However, he did dream a lot. He asked, "Would it be possible to just talk about my upsetting dreams?" When I agreed that we might do that, he came into group ostensibly only to get their help in examining his nightmares. When this was presented to the group before his appearance they agreed to try it out and see if someone could be cooperative as a group member under such limiting circumstances.

Tim's dreams were always of some form of transportation that could not, either due to some failure on his part or some malevolent force, move him fast enough to save him from pursuers ultimately seeking to jail him for some horrendous crime. The themes were always the same. He came too late for the takeoff of a plane, a train was carrying him in the wrong direction, a bus never arrived, a street that was foreign and he was repeatedly "missing the boat," thus feeling permanently endangered. The group tried to adhere to the original agreement; to ask questions only about the dream work. Very cleverly, in spite of it, curiosity eventually won out.

Tim stayed in the group only presenting his dreams but as he involved himself more in other peoples' presentations, his nightmares intensified. They began to change in ways that raised the sensations of acute danger. Men were chasing Tim and he was to be arrested for some crime he hadn't committed. Extreme punishment of some sort was going to be executed. With this motif now in the middle of the room, true therapeutic work could begin. Piece by piece we began to be allowed to connect the feelings and symbols in his dreams to what had existed in his real life. "What crime had he as a child been held accountable for?" someone asked. Another wanted to know, "What might you have been unjustly accused of doing?" A third woman in the group, also an author, utilized her sense of metaphor to explore whether "'missing the boat' related to the missing years when he was unable to work on his book?" In my mind I wondered if it could be related to a disappearance, "the missing" of his mother at the birth of his younger brother, when at the age of three he was sent to the "evil" grandmother's house to get him out of the way? This, coupled with his old feelings of guilt at hating the new baby, who literally took his place in the house, seemed to have compounded whatever was the original crime. Tim, now willing to widen the areas which could be spoken of, the group, and I began to understand and put together all the pieces of the puzzle.

Dreams, as we know, are multi-determined. What came to light through interested and sustained group questioning was the story of his brother's near drowning when they were aged 10 and 12. The two boys were playing near a pond at their grandfather's home. Suddenly, the younger boy was in the water. Tim grabbed a tree branch and threw it in the pond, thinking his brother could hold on to it and float. Then, not knowing how to swim, he ran to the house for help. When rescue came, his brother accused him of being the villain who had pushed him into the water and then tried to drown him by hitting him on the head with the tree branch. Some family member muttered the words, "Just like Cain, trying to kill his brother." Another looked at him with loathing and said "You little murderer." These devastating words caught in Tim's memory and the unconscious, emotional damage was done.

A woman in the group asked sympathetically, "Could your brother have been afraid of being punished for playing so near the pond and needed to put the blame on you to save himself?" Another commented, "Isn't it possible that his version never really happened? You **were** trying to rescue him with that tree branch, not kill him." And still another, "Didn't you realize that you really were the one who saved him by going for help?" Finally, one of the women who had a strong sense of moral outrage, said forcefully, "What was wrong with those relatives that they attacked you instead of pinning on a medal?" These ego-protective questions asked by peers demonstrating care, made possible the exploration of an early trauma from an entirely new prospective.

> Here we come to the difference between thinking of oneself as a Cain, a murderer, or as a superman, a rescuer. By offering a change in the script we helped recreate an image of a life that could be allowed to be successful in the present. Tim can now say, "They shouldn't have treated me that way. I really did save him!" and walk out of subsequent sessions feeling capable of going on living without the punitive, self-destructive impulses. He would now be allowed to experience the joy of being creatively productive, with a sense of strength. What the group has done was to uncover and validate this new life story. "Really saving his brother" was now accepted as a fact. "Tim" no longer stood for "Cain," a symbolic role undeservedly based on an external authority figure's definition. Newly defined as the hero of the story, the writing block was successfully resolved and his book could be completed. As another group member put it, "Now Tim can catch the right train."

In this kind of adventure the group and the therapist become true partners. It is the therapeutic alliance at its finest. What we must do together is very clear. Together we externalize the internal dialogue for fundamental revision. How people construct "truths" about themselves and how we can help reconstruct them, requires our imagination and free floating attention. As we see daily, the legends of lives repeatedly playing on internal tapes are immensely powerful. The difficulty is that they are determinants that can be self-defeating or affirming; ranging from "I'm not good enough," to "That's easy. I can do that." Collectively we must look to rewrite the plot and recreate the character, hoping for the response that says, "I never thought of it that way before."

With Tim's case, we had unearthed the "crime" and in so doing, we could resolve the "punishment" that had blocked his progress in his chosen career. Several years later his novel was completed as was his therapy. Our early work together was based on the theory of "joining the resistance;" thus honoring his wish to only examine his dreams. My mantra during that period was a passing comment that Spotnitz had once made. "You can't tell a baby when or how to cry." Tim had been a truly difficult patient. When he became safe enough to speak of his personal demons, progress could be made. To a great extent it was creative and empathic group interventions that made it possible. With increased understanding and willingness to participate in the therapeutic alliance, it finally moved towards success.

Difficult patients do induce difficult reactions in their therapists. Their primitive defenses, particularly splitting and projective identification, contribute to a pattern of intense, chaotic and potentially problematic countertransference reactions. Projective identification is understood to mean fantasies and a body of feelings having to do with a desire to rid oneself of unwanted, painful aspects of the self. These unwanted parts of the self are then deposited on another person; in therapy it would be the therapist or other group members. When identified they can be neutralized and returned to the patient in a modified, more acceptable form. Perhaps for those very reasons, when countertransference feelings have caught us unawares, these become the cases that are best remembered and understanding them is particularly helpful in the training of a therapist and in our own life-long learning curve.

Stanley

Many years ago I made a colossal error with a patient; colossal was not too strong a word. A huge man came to see me in consultation. Well over six feet tall and weighing more than three hundred pounds, Stanley came in (unlike March) not like a lion but like a lamb. He had recently lost his good position with a glamorous company and was experiencing deep trouble with his wife. According to his report, he was trapped in feelings of worthlessness. Totally depressed, he expressed not knowing what he wanted to do with the rest of his life. My first error was to miss a strange point. There was a total omission of anger and resentment at all that had gone wrong for him.

Stanley had a background of years of alternate schools of therapy, much of it with well-known and highly regarded therapists. After four individual sessions, during which he seemed to be thoughtfully able to use the material we spoke of in a progressive manner, I put him in a group, since that had been his presenting request. This was my second error. It came as a result of subjective countertransference feelings based on the idea that all those "important" psychoanalytic figures must have helped him work through early narcissistic trauma. I accepted his veneer of therapeutic sophistication and agreeing to his request for group therapy seemed to make perfect sense. It was only after he entered a well-functioning group that his violent, out-of-control rage at women became obvious; an emotion that had been carefully hidden in our earlier preparatory, individual sessions.

In one of those private sessions I had learned that his mother had been psychotic and reportedly murderous to the small child. In our talk he had excused her with a tiny smile and expressed only sadness. What emerged however in the group sessions (and there were only two as that was all that participant could tolerate), was that toward the men in the room he had first, contempt, that tranferentially had come from feelings for the weak father who could not protect him from his mother's hatred; and second, a deep yearning to be loved by the men in the group which came again, transferentially, from what he had not received from the father who had absented himself rather than risk having to do battle to protect his son.

For the women in the group he voiced disgust and venom, easily triggered and fiercely spewed out. Weirdly, in the midst of a raging outburst, he would turn to me and smile with great sweetness. For me there was "best behavior" and idealization as I appeared to represent the good mother he had wished for but never found. With his primitive "magical thinking," this goddess/doctor up on the pedestal would make everything right. The frustration I experienced heightened as I realized that no technique I had ever utilized in the group setting could either contain him or properly protect the group. Any intervention on my part resulted in a displaced attack on a group member. After his second session it was clear that he had to go, for his sake and for theirs. It was necessary to go back to individual sessions with the knowledge that there was no short cut. This was for the long haul and once again, the value of using only joining techniques and object-oriented questions "for as long as it takes" became apparent. It served as a clear reminder to question my own assumptions about where a patient had developmentally reached, particularly if there was any danger of being influenced by subjective countertransference feelings.

Rauel

This case was, modestly, one of great success. It is the story of a life conditioned by abandonment, fear and foster homes, and of the hero's journey that took Rauel from abject object to fulfilling maturity.

He came to me at the age of 35. A tall, handsome man of mixed African and Island heritage, he presented yearnings and obstacles that offered a confused picture of what he wished to accomplish in therapy. According to him, he found it impossible to speak before an audience, even a small one made up of good friends, without shaking. As an adult he had failed at every relationship, always selecting someone either unavailable or unsuitable and turning himself inside out to try and make it work. There had been too many drug-related experiences and too many painful feelings. His life as he described it was filled with amazing contradictions.

Rauel had been born to a jailed "crack" mother and never knew who his father was. His infancy had been spent in the Foundling Hospital, to be followed by foster homes for the next seventeen years. The two saving graces had been that the last home was a fairly nurturing one, with foster-siblings who became a substitute family. At the same time, he had become an accomplished athlete and a swimmer of Olympic quality, whose record in a particular length still stands.

His athletic accomplishments were encouraged by a woman coach who took a special interest in him. She saw that he graduated from high school with athletic honors and high enough marks to earn a college scholarship and then ensured that he graduated college. She taught him how to dress and behave socially, and stayed in *loco parentis* through these growing years. Unfortunately, the destructive part of the relationship was the seductiveness that culminated in a lengthy sexual relationship that defied the disparity in their ages.

At this stage of his life, Rauel was filled with despair. He had gone from graduate school to become an attorney, but as he said: "What's the use of knowing why everything feels so terrible when you can't change the past and it all seems so hopeless?" The next question was "Can you help me and how long will it take?" The answer given was "How could I not help you and how long did it take you to get to this place?"

It was decided to utilize both individual and group therapy; the latter to work out his fear of speaking in front of people. For an attorney, this was a truly crippling limitation; one that would restrict him to research work in the back room of the law firm and prevent him from ever achieving partnership status.

For the first year Rauel sat outside the group circle in the farthest corner of the room from me, wrapped up in the small blanket kept on the couch for winter chills. The atmosphere in the room was filled with fear; his fear that somehow the ghosts of past horrors would enter the room through a door that words from group members or me would cause to open. My fear was that I might not be able to keep him safe enough to stay in group. Admirably, he found the courage to do so. During that early period in individual sessions, we carefully looked back on childhood experiences and how they "might" touch on the present. Again I kept in mind Freud's dictum as to how porcupines make love. The group slowly began to learn of his early self-destructive wishes; to die, to jump out of a window, to disappear. The ability to soften these toxic feelings was aided by group members who shared the misery of having had similar ones. When it appeared that we might be getting too close, Rauel cleverly found a way to circumvent the possible danger by communicating his negative feelings through e-mail! Fortunately, there is a written record of the course of both the narcissistic defense and the negative narcissistic transference. "I think about death every day. Sometimes I still think about suicide but I don't have the guts to do it. I've watched three foster mothers die." This was a clear transference communication that expressed both his fear and his wish about me.

At this point in his therapy I suggested that, with his permission, I could help him bring these feelings to group sessions. There, empathic others could interact with him and create a safe enough climate that risks could be taken in the immediacy of their interchanges. One of the most meaningful connections made to him came from a woman who had been adopted at birth, sexually abused by older siblings and as a result, had never felt either safe or that she belonged. She was exactly the right person to build a bridge to him. "Look Rauel," she said. "Don't you think I know those feelings? Do you have any idea how scary and lonely it is, even at this age? I'm a single woman, petrified to be with anyone, man or woman, but at the same time, wanting it dreadfully. And I shake too. What disaster is coming next? What monster is going to come after me?" Visibly moved, Rauel thanked her and said that he wished he could protect her. Finally, his attention began to be focused externally on someone other than himself.

At a later date, when it seemed apparent that Rauel too had been sexually abused, I asked what I thought was a carefully worded question about the possibility. "What is so hidden and can't be let out?" This was greeted in the group with silence. I waited a minute and then asked "What would be the danger in putting it into words?" Still silence. In a protective maneuver, group members collaborated in quickly introducing another topic; entering into a discussion about holidays with great verve. It was clear that I had to join the resistance. The e-mail that followed from Rauel, however, was far from silent. Fiercely he wrote, "I am so mad at you. When you asked me that question in group on Tuesday my heart started racing. I didn't remember anything so I couldn't understand what was happening to me. I already told you all things I had never told anyone . . . things that were painful and difficult for me to tell. Why did you have to put me on the spot? I thought you understood! Oh no. You started this and then left me to deal with it after the session by myself!"

During this period my task was to contain the rage, accept and explore my "bad, abandoning" behavior and essentially, to sit tight and wait and let the group hold him. As a result of doing so, one day a communication arrived that marked the end of this developmental stage. "I sent you a message saying that I hated everybody in the group and most of all, you. I couldn't sleep after I sent it so I had to get up and take it back. I realized that it wasn't any of you that I hated. It was me . . ." With the narcissistic defense now fully conscious and verbalized, we were able to move on to the next phase of work. The strength of the therapeutic alliance and the empathic willingness of group members to refuse to be shut out had been strong enough to withstand the emergence of his early horrors.

The therapy continued, with greater ease to bring bits of history into the sessions. More and more difficult material surfaced. One memorable story was of his hunting down his birth mother when he was 21. He had found her in a filthy tenement, ill, alone and drug-ridden. Rauel stayed for three days and nursed her. He then began weekly visits, cleaning the apartment and bringing food. Once after winning an important swim meet, he brought her the huge championship trophy, wishing for admiration and signs of love. At his next visit he found that she had sold it for the money to buy "coke." That was the end of the idealized myth that all could be changed if he were only good enough, and of his realization that no matter what he did, she could never become the mother for whom he had wished. Happily, this maturational gap was being filled in the here-and-now by group members. There is an old adage that groups serve as "Second-chance families." In other words, those surrounding him in the therapy office became the good surrogate mothers, fathers and siblings that had been longed for and never existed. In these new relationships, Rauel could himself experiment with novel ways of being; and as time went on he was able to speak more freely and easily.

At this point in his therapy he came into group one day and said "Something you've all been saying made me think I should make a list of what I need to work on. This is what I came up with:

1. Get over my mother
2. Accept not knowing who my father is
3. Sex
4. Stage fright
5. Get into a healthy relationship
6. The unspeakable, whatever that might be.

I guess we're all going to be together for a few more years, huh?" He laughed. "That will give me lots of time to be there for all of you for a change." Now working primarily with some sense of object relations, much could be accomplished more rapidly. It was to be expected that there would be periods of old regressive behaviors, between and among the group members and when this happened I retreated to early techniques of joining until it worked through.

> Intermittently, I experienced countertransference feelings of hopelessness and failure; of rage and ambivalence; of grandiosity, pride and delight. For Rauel and fellow group members, there were also times of rage that now could be expressed aggressively while the climate of the room maintained its sense of being a safe place. At last came the times when immense joy followed successes in Rauel's life that could be shared. He could now speak up in the legal office where he practiced. He could appear in court on behalf of a client. When a large group of friends gave him a surprise party for his 40th birthday, he was able to take the microphone, thank them and give a witty extemporaneous speech – without shaking! He had begun to date women who were not only right for him but were caring, smart and most of all, available.

During those three years, recognition of my own countertransference continued to serve as a reliable gauge of what was needed. Did I feel hate, did I feel distant, did I feel like running away, did I feel love? Why? Any of these feelings were open to investigation. We all explored together where in the group they might have emanated from; then we would use the conjectures to further progressive communication. For Rauel this was a period where the anaclitic (psychological dependency) countertransference was being worked through. "Upon analysis and the confirmation from the patient, these feelings turn out to be the very feelings of which the patient was deprived during his dependent years, yet which were needed for his maturation" (Liegner, 1991: p. 154).

When we mutually decided that it was time for therapy to terminate, Rauel was engaged to a lovely woman who was both a corporate executive and an artist. Several years later, I received a photograph of the couple at the one-year anniversary of their marriage with the accompanying message, "Life is wonderful. I never would have believed it possible." This was definitely a hard-earned success for Rauel, the group and for me.

In one of my groups long ago, when someone was leaving with the mutual understanding that the important work had been successfully completed, a farewell ritual was begun. Through the years, the ritual was passed as if by osmosis, to my other groups as well. First, the special person would go around the room and tell something to each person. It might be a remembered shared story, an interchange that had been deeply touching; an intervention that spoke so strongly that it stimulated change or an expression of intense feelings such as admiration, aggression, love. It was understood that this piece of their work together would always stay with the leaver. After that it becomes the turn of the group members to give a parting gift in the form of a wish for the departing colleague. I remember two in particular that were given to Rauel in his "sending off." One was the wish that he have a magic carpet with a built–in security system that could take him anywhere in the world so that no place would ever be out of his reach. The other wish was for a crystal chalice to hold his heart safely until the right woman appeared with the right key. In a more realistic manner, these ephemeral tokens of care were a legacy to make difficult future times easier to work through.

As can be seen from these cases, once the therapeutic work has succeeded in aiding the patient in reaching a place of object constancy, object transferences are achieved. Now both therapist and other group members are seen for whom they really are, real people, no longer transference figures from the patient's past. At this point the more advanced techniques of interpretation and direct "you" questions can come into play because the ego is now strong enough to tolerate them. In classical language, the patient has now reached the Oedipal stage. Here, interpretations, explanations, and a true dialogue between therapist and patient and among group members can be effectively taken in, rather than being experienced as a narcissistic blow. This usually marks working through the last part of therapeutic needs and often signifies the coming of the termination period.

Conclusion

These descriptions and the selected cases presented, provide samples of the wide variety of induced feelings that arise in therapists working with difficult patients. They include guilt, rescue fantasies, transgressions of professional boundaries, rage, hatred, helplessness, despair, worthlessness, anxiety, aggression and even terror (Gabbard and Wilkinson, 2000). Clearly, such emotions are reflections of the pain-filled feelings of those we treat. With all of these feelings and more that are experienced in our offices daily is it any wonder that on some days we sense that we are going into mortal combat? However, there are the other feelings as well; those of pride, elation, happiness, pleasure and sometimes, even sexual stirrings that make it worthwhile. The reality remains that the aim of our therapeutic work is ultimately to aid patients in resolving those resistances to intimacy and meaningful socialization that inhibit their lives.

Ormont (1988) talked of the ability to achieve mature intimacy as one of the goals of group therapy. I believe this is one of the results we seek for patients in our group practice. Patients' abilities to affect object constancy and to demonstrate maturational growth can serve as a measurement for successful treatment. We know that these states can be achieved, even with the most difficult of patients. But first the therapist has to provide a "safe-enough" space for the group to serve as the agent for change. Second, techniques that are sophisticated, though they sound so simple, promote maturational growth while at the same time protecting the fragile ego structure. Progressive movement follows, which encourages intimacy in the here-and-now and strengthens the insulation barrier. Third, a conscious awareness of one's own subjective countertransference must be maintained while optimally using one's objective countertransference for the benefit of the patients. (Here supervision can play a vital part.) Ultimately, deeply imbedded resistances can then be resolved.

Modern Analytic psychotherapy interventions have been designed to comply with the requirements of acceptable therapeutic practices. They benefit patient and therapist alike. The ability to use them is based on a foundation of careful training in an approved institute; on supervision, preferably over time with more than one supervisor and to make note of the old joke about how one gets to Carnegie Hall: practice,

practice, practice. In truth, the practice of Modern Analytic group therapy is both a craft and an art.

References and Bibliography

Bernard, H. S., & Spitz, H. I., (2006). *Training in group psychotherapy supervision* (p. 4). New York: American Group Psychotherapy Association.
Brook, M. (2006). Introduction to the special issue. *Group, 30*(3), 177.
Cohen, P. F. (1996). Symbolic communication in modern group therapy. *Modern Group, 1*(1), 19–31.
Eigen, M. (1977). On working with "unwanted" patients. *International Journal of Psychoanalysis, 58*(1), 119.
Ernsberger, C. (1991). Modern psychoanalytic training: the first four decades. *Modern Psychoanalysis, 16*(1), 15–24.
Ettin, M. F. (1995). From one to another: group consultation for group psychotherapy. *Group, 19*(1), 33.
Franzini, L. R. (2001). Humor in therapy: the case for training therapists in its uses and risks. *Journal of General Psychology, 128*(2), 170–194.
Gabbard, G., & Wilkinson, S. (2000). *Management of countertransference with borderline patients.* Lanham, Maryland: Jason Aronson.
Gardner, R. A. (1977). *Modern fairy stories* (p. 2). Cresskill, New Jersey: Creative Therapeutics.
Hopper, E. (2001). Difficult patients: phenomenology and the case of Pandoro. *Group, 25*(3), 140–143.
Lathrop, D. D. (1984). *Abrasion: wearing down and transformation* (pp. 61–67). New York: The Haworth Press.
Liegner, E. J. (1991). The anaclitic countertransference in resistance resolution. *Modern Psychoanalyst, 20*, 153–164.
Little, M. (1958). On delusional transference (transference psychosis). *International Journal of Psychoanalysis, 39*, 134–138.
Mackay, N., & Poser, S. (2004). The case study in psychoanalytic education. *Modern Psychoanalysis, 29*(2), 171–192.
Margolis, B. (1983). The contact function of the ego: its role in the therapy of the narcissistic patient. *Psychoanalytic Review, 70*, 69–81.
Meadow, P. W. (1996). Issues in psychoanalytic research. *Modern Psychoanalysis, 21*(2), 308–333.
Nagelberg, L., & Spotnitz, H. (1952). Initial steps in the analytic therapy of schizophrenia in children. *The Quarterly Journal of Child Behavior, 4*, 57–65.
Ormont, L. (1988). The leader's role in resolving resistances to intimacy in the group setting. *International Journal of Group Psychotherapy, 38*, 32.
Ormont, L. (1993). Resolving resistances to immediacy in the group setting. *International Journal of Group Psychotherapy, 43*, 399–418.
Ormont, L. (1994). Developing emotional insulation. *International Journal of Group Psychotherapy, 44*(3), 361–375.
Ormont, L. (1995). Cultivating the observing ego in the group setting. *International Journal of Group Psychotherapy. 45*, 489–506.
Ormont, L. (1996). The group as agent of change. *Modern Group: Journal of the Center for the Advancement of Group Studies, 1*, 9–18.
Ormont, L (2001). The craft of bridging. In L. B. Furgeri (Ed.), *The technique of group treatment* (p. 264). Madison, Connecticut: Psychosocial Press.

Ormont, L. (2001). The role of the leader in managing the preoedipal patient in the group setting. In L.B. Furgeri (Ed.), *The technique of group treatment* (p. 145). Madison, Connecticut: Psychosocial Press.

Reynes, R. L., & Allen, A. (1987). Humor in psychotherapy: a view. *American Journal of Psychotherapy*, 41(2), 260–270.

Shepherd, M. (2004). Single-case-study methodology and the contact function. *Modern Psychoanalysis*, 29, 163–170.

Spotnitz, H. (1969). *Modern psychoanalysis of the schizophrenic patient* (p. 32). New York: Grune & Stratton.

Sultanoff, S. M. (2000). Web site: http//www.humormatters.comm.definiti.htm. Definitions, p.1.

Yalom, I. D. (with Leszcz, M.) (2005). *The theory and practice of group psychotherapy* (pp. 272–273). New York: Basic Books.

16
Working with Primitive Defenses in Group
Martha Gilmore

Introduction

Clinicians have often struggled when an apparently innocuous event in treatment abruptly results in a patient decompensating into chaos, paranoia, misunderstanding and injury. Suddenly, the clinician is off-balance, struggling to understand why the patient is reacting so strangely and trying to manage the difficulty, often unwittingly sliding into increased wounding and further chaos. This feels like a clinician's nightmare, but it often presents the opportunity for carefully protected wounds to be finally understood and worked through. This paper hopes to help clinicians anticipate such sudden descents into primitive anxieties and develop methods of understanding and working with the issues underlying such events.

Theoretical base

I was initially trained in both humanistic and psychodynamic orientations along with some interpersonal and Gestalt methods in group therapy. As time went on, I developed more interest in the modern developments in psychodynamic thought, in particular, the intersubjective and relational models. On a somewhat separate track, I developed some expertise in the treatment of trauma and dissociative disorders, especially from a relational perspective. These interests have come together synergistically, supported on a base of attachment theory and allowing me to work effectively with a wide variety of patient issues. I find this basis helps me to understand both the etiology of many of the difficulties my patients face, and how to intervene in ways that support patients' development of new attachment security and improved functioning in the world.

Attachment theory basics A brief review of attachment theory will provide the theoretical base for our discussion. Bowlby (1982) first understood that the attachment of the baby to the caregiver was a biological imperative – a bond necessary for the physical and emotional survival of the infant. He theorized that since the infant has to attach to the caregiver to survive, the infant will adapt in order to ensure that bond. Thus, behaviors (and the underlying thoughts and feelings) that support the attachment bond will be integrated into the self of the infant while those that threaten the attachment will be excluded. Infant attachment serves to ensure infant survival by regulating the proximity to the caregiver, serving as a source of comfort and security and providing a secure base from which an infant can explore. Bowlby (1973) postulated that out of attachment experiences we develop mental representations of self and others in the context of close relationships which he labeled internal working models (IWM). As later updated by Main (Main et al., 1985) IWMs provide rules for processing information that influence how we are able to think, feel, remember, and act throughout our lives, long beyond infancy.

Ainsworth took Bowlby's theory and applied it in a series of studies of the attachment behavior between children and their caregivers, culminating in the Ainsworth Strange Situation studies (Ainsworth, Blehar, Waters, and Wall, 1978) and the identification of the first three attachment patterns – secure, insecure-avoidant, and insecure-ambivalent. Main extended Ainsworth's studies and identified a fourth subset of infants she labeled as insecure-disorganized (Main and Solomon, 1990). Later, George, Kaplan, and Main (1984, 1985, and 1996) developed the Adult Attachment Inventory to assess the adult versions of attachment relationships. Main (1991) later found that individuals who were not secure, exhibited multiple contradictory models that were state-dependent which could be activated by both external and internal circumstances. Further research has demonstrated that attachment patterns are lifelong and difficult to change (Mikulincer and Shaver, 2007).

Since the specific types of attachment are quite relevant to our discussion I will discuss them in some detail including both the infant-caregiver origins (as seen in the Ainsworth Strange Situation) and the adult versions.

Secure attachment results when the caregiver responds predictably and helpfully to the infant's distress. Securely attached infants seek proximity to their caregiver when reunited after a separation, communicate distress openly, and then easily return to exploration. Secure infants use their attachment figures appropriately for emotional regulation and adults are able to use self-regulation and self-reflexivity as coping strategies. Recent studies (Fonagy et al., 2002) have shown that secure attachment also helps the brain develop the ability to mentalize which will be discussed below.

Insecure-avoidant attachment results when the caregiver predictably responds with neglect or punishment to the infant expressing distress. The caregiver may respond positively as long as the infant does not express negative affect. The infant tends not to show distress upon reunion and to ignore the caregiver. The coping strategies of the infant serve to avoid punishment by denial and suppressing distress and/or by care-giving and are understood as a reaction-formation. The adult attachment style is labeled dismissive. This is considered a deactivating strategy in that it defends against the activation of attachment needs by avoiding noticing threats or attachment figures which are seen as unhelpful in emotional regulation (Mikulincer and Shaver, 2007).

Insecure-ambivalent/resistant attachment results when the caregiver responds unpredictably to the infant's distress. Infant behaviors include strong attempts to seek proximity and maintain contact while also pushing away and remaining unsoothable.

These infants are unable to return to play or exploration after reunion with their caregiver. This coping strategy is seen as an attempt to increase caregiver predictability. The corresponding adult attachment style is labeled "preoccupied" and is seen as an activating strategy where the person becomes more needy and emotional in an attempt to elicit a response.

The final type of attachment is labeled **insecure-disorganized/disoriented** in infants and unresolved in adults. It results when the caregiver is both dangerous (either frightening or frightened) and unpredictable. The infant shows contradictory or undirected behavior and copes using both defended strategies to avoid punishment and coercive strategies to increase predictability.

In further exploration of the effects of attachment relationships on psychological functioning, Main (1991) and Fonagy (Fonagy et al., 2002) pointed out that secure attachments are associated with the ability to have a reflective stance towards experience. In examining the contradictory internal working models of her insecure subjects, Main (1991) identified that only secure subjects had a unitary model and could use metacognition. Metacognition is the ability to think about thinking; to realize that our thoughts are merely representations of reality and not reality itself. Fonagy (Fonagy et al., 2002) expanded Main's work to include a focus on the thoughts of others as well as one's own and developed the concept of mentalizing. Mentalizing is the ability to consider experience in the light of the mental states that underlie it. "It enables us to respond to our experience on the basis not only of observed behavior, but also of the underlying mental states – desires, feelings, beliefs – that make behavior understandable and give it meaning" (Wallin, 2007: p. 44). We can therefore see that internal reality is separate from, but related to, external reality. This reflective function is a key benefit of the secure attachment experience. All types of insecure attachment result in deficits in the ability to mentalize. Instead, insecurely attached people tend to be trapped in a mode of psychic equivalence where the internal and external worlds are equated or in a pretend mode where the internal and external worlds are disconnected and whatever is imagined to be real holds sway.

Wallin (2007) posits that co-created relationships are the key context for development and that new attachments can spur new development throughout life. However, it is clear that most of our early attachment relationships occur on the preverbal level and are not accessible through words. Those parts of experience which have been excluded from awareness will also remain inaccessible verbally. Therefore, they remain what Bollas (1987) called the unthought known, and must be uncovered by how they are evoked with others, enacted with others, or embodied (Wallin, 2007).

Revealing the unthought known The clinician has several methods to reveal what goes on underneath the verbal representations of difficulty that the patient presents. One particularly powerful tool is understanding projective identification as a communication about the patient and the relationship. The therapist must remain highly attuned and use her own subjectivity to understand the internal life of the patient and the likely relational and attachment experiences that contributed to the patient's particular development. For example, if the therapist regularly feels deadened in the session, wonders how she is being useful to the patient, and is surprised that the patient continues to schedule appointments, a dismissive attachment style should certainly be considered.

> Jim[1] grew up with parents who pushed him to excel academically and to never bother them with any needs, emotional or otherwise. The sole exception was any physical complaint which was immediately responded to with a visit to the doctor. He came to therapy with me after a suicide attempt, several years of therapy (which he experienced as just telling him what to do), and long-standing somatic complaints – each diligently investigated by his HMO without any physical problems diagnosed. In our work together, I must constantly guard against slipping into advice-giving and open myself to the wordless pain and shame that is before me. Not surprisingly, I easily can feel useless, avoid the pain by getting drowsy, or go back to the old advice-giving strategy and participate in an as-if therapy. The pull to respond to Jim in the same emotionally neglectful way his parents did is incredibly strong.

Another important tool is to be aware of and utilize enactments within the therapy. I think of enactments as projective identification put into action; going beyond feelings and awareness into words and actions. An enactment demonstrating a preoccupied attachment pattern might involve a therapist regularly forgetting to inform her patient of upcoming vacations out of an unconscious attempt to avoid the panicked clinging that results.

Yet another way that the unthought known presents itself is how things are embodied within the patient. Wallin (2007) points out that the unresolved patient lives in a mindless body that feels without any understanding what the bodily experience is. I have seen this in patients that hit their chair while talking unemotionally about something that would make most of us angry or in others that flinch and scowl without any apparent awareness. One dissociative patient of mine presented as a cheerful, sweet man as he entered and left the room. His entire demeanor changed once he sat down. While remaining almost wordless, he changed into a menacing presence; grimacing and clenching his fists while shooting killer looks with his eyes. This man had little awareness of this transformation and could give only the barest outline of his traumatic childhood.

The dismissive patient lives in a disembodied mind on the other hand (Wallin, 2007), and is likely to have a poker face and minimal physical cues. Jim (in the example above) lives in his mind and can only guess about his feelings. He has many somatic complaints but is unable to connect physical sensations or distress with any thoughts or feelings. In addition, while he complains of extreme hopelessness, depression, and anxiety, he is unable to communicate these in a way that is believable to the listener. One psychiatrist even accused him of faking his depression and his suicidal ideation.

Mutiple self-states Let me bring your attention to an oversimplification that I have inadvertently been leading you toward in the above examples. Remember that attachment styles are state-dependent so that most of us have multiple self-states that exhibit different attachment styles based on the current circumstances. This makes things much more complicated but also leads to important possibilities for change.

---

[1] All names and identifying information have been changed to protect client confidentiality.

When one is caught or embedded in a particular self-state, the ability to mentalize about what is going on is quite compromised. However, when the group and/or the therapist can bring in new experience, a different self-state may become accessible and change the entire picture. Repetitive experiences within this new self-state are then needed to rewire the maladaptive attachment pattern into one of earned secure attachment which can create long-standing change (Wallin, 2007; Flores, 2010).

The fact that each of us has multiple self-states is part of what creates the phenomenon that I am addressing in this paper. One key benefit of secure attachment is a solid integration of these multiple self-states so that the self has good access to all of its own experience (Wallin, 2007). My experience is that many patients reach a point in treatment (or start treatment) where they are functioning very well in many areas of life but have some significant vulnerabilities that occasionally intrude on their lives in dramatic, powerful, and intense ways. I am generally looking at these vulnerabilities through the lens of attachment theory so I think about how patients cannot manage the thoughts, feelings, and behaviors that were not allowed within their attachment relationships. These experiences are then dissociated and undeveloped until a different self-state emerges and puts them in focus. One can also see these vulnerabilities as fears of abandonment, annihilation, and disintegration. Patients are thus very motivated to do their best to defend themselves from entering the self-states that contain their wounding and so prevent themselves from entering into such dark territory. Hopper (2003) points out how such patients need to seal off annihilation anxieties in order to survive. However, such pockets of wounding are difficult to shield without major compromise. Patients may defend against such anxieties with autistic encapsulations, splitting, distortions, projections, etc. Adams (2006) powerfully describes a psychotherapy group full of high-functioning patients who struggle with such self-states that erupt in certain circumstances in the group (and in their lives). These issues are seen most powerfully and dramatically with patients with an unresolved attachment style since the unintegrated, unresolved experiences of loss and trauma cannot be easily recalled and are walled off behind a dissociative defense. Group therapy can be particularly effective in eliciting these problematic self-states and providing a framework within which healing can occur.

Group psychotherapy

Group psychotherapy provides multiple attachment objects and transferences and thus can evoke multiple self-states depending on the current context. Different members provide different perspectives, a range of intensity, and a range in the dialectic between embeddedness (being trapped in one's own perspective and reality without being able to consider others – the mode of psychic equivalence) and mentalizing at any point in time. Members model thoughts, feelings, memories, and behavior that have been excluded from the repertoire of others. They spend time thinking about thinking (metacognition) as seen in such questions as, "What made you think I was angry with you?" They explicitly model mentalizing when they voice their assumptions and make interpretations about others' motivations and internal experiences and implicitly model it when they empathize with each other.

Members' multiple perspectives help them relate internal and external reality rather than equate or dissociate them.

> Joe had difficulty leaving his job on time and so chronically came late to the group to face much anger and frustration from the group. He felt targeted and controlled by the group's pressure to be on time. The group felt mistreated and angry that Joe could not make the commitment that they had. Further exploration revealed Joe's investment in doing a good job at his work and difficulty in asserting himself with co-workers out of a deep sense of responsibility and fear of displeasing them. Understanding this, the group was able to support Joe's values and his developing self-assertion while also communicating their own feelings of unimportance when he came late and fears that he did not value them or the group. This process of making meaning allowed the group and Joe to move beyond their mutual anger, support Joe's development, and in the end resulted in Joe coming on time consistently.

The role of the group therapist

I see my task as a group therapist as creating a safe and contained space and helping members to develop therapeutic norms so that the group can become the agent of change. The metaphor I use in explaining this to patients is that of a hike leader. I put the group together, decide the place and time and other boundaries of the group. Each group member carries her own backpack and hikes under their own power. The group generally sets the pace, though if someone gets too far ahead or too far behind, I will point this out so the group can remember to stay together. The group will hike along, doing its thing at its will. If someone is getting too close to the cliff and no one notices, I will point it out. If no one notices the beautiful flowers, I will bring attention to them. When the hike is going well, I am just another person hiking along, carrying my own stuff. When something is not going well, I am there to help the group notice and focus her efforts to deal with the problem.

Another role I carry as group leader is to keep the group focused on what is happening in the here-and-now. This starts in my initial meetings with a potential group member when we discuss the issues the client wants to address in terms of how they are likely to arise within the group. I take some time to educate the patient about the importance (and the inevitability) of their having their problems in the group, rather than just talking about their problems. This helps them understand the group focus on what is actually happening in the group and on the relationships between people in the group, and see that the difficulties that arise can be contained, examined, and worked through for great therapeutic benefit. From the very beginning, I am making it clear that we will be working in the here-and-now, that the work will be challenging, and that ideally, the kinds of difficulties patients have in their lives will reoccur in the group. This is what provides the opportunity for something new to happen and change to occur.

As part of my initial assessment of a potential group member, I ask about their relationship history and attempt to determine what kind of attachment relationships they had in childhood and how these have developed throughout their life. Getting a sense of the kinds of experiences that could or could not be accommodated within these attachment relationships helps me determine what kinds of issues are likely to come up in group and what kinds of corrective experiences they are likely to need. I often even do some (somewhat paradoxical) predicting of the themes that are likely to develop. A recent addition to my group described a series of relationship betrayals, starting in childhood and most recently with her last therapist. In addition, her description was confused, dramatic, and overly detailed in a way that indicates preoccupied attachment, in this case overlapping with some unresolved pieces. I pointed out the theme of betrayal throughout her life and predicted that she would likely feel betrayed in the group, probably by me, and that the opportunity for change would exist if she could stay in the group and struggle to work through and understand what was going on that she ended up feeling betrayed. I pointed out the courage it would take to put herself in the position of trusting me, a stranger, and a whole group of strangers, knowing that she would be entering into the experience of being betrayed again. I find that this kind of prediction primes both of us to keep a foothold on our mentalizing functions when we are sliding into a repetition of that very attachment wounding that needs to be worked through.

I mentioned that one of my tasks is to help the group develop norms so that the group can be the agent of change. As you can see from the above, this starts in the initial contacts as I educate the potential member about what is important in the group and model talking about the relationship in the here-and-now. This continues in the group and, when it works well, the members become a powerful force in noticing what is going on, expressing a range of thoughts and feelings, and using their mentalizing and metacognitive functions. This is what makes group such an incredible asset. At any point in time when people become entrapped in some sort of enactment or other version of an early attachment wound, there are likely some people who are not in the same place and retain the ability to understand what is going on. As Grossmark (2007) so eloquently puts it:

> The process of group therapy unfolds through enactments that involve the whole group and the group therapist entering into the grip of repetitive and unmentalized self-states. These enactments are resolved when the group members, with the therapist's help and containment, can access alternative self-states that allow for new and unformulated experience to emerge (Grossmark, 2007: p. 479).

Combined treatment There are times when combined treatment (group plus individual therapy) is particularly helpful, if not essential, for the patient. I find that when patients are prone to descending into primitive anxieties the use of combined treatment may be necessary to work through the issues involved. The individual therapy can provide a forum for solidifying access to the new attachment experiences that have been primed in the group. Whether the individual therapist is also the group therapist or someone else closely coordinating, they can help the patient retain access to the self-states that are able to mentalize and escape the embeddedness of the old attachment scripts. One long-term client I had in group only managed to stay because of the solid relationship she had with her individual therapist. Whenever Mary took a risk in group she collapsed into a kind of paranoia where she was certain that both the group and I hated her and that I was preparing to expel her from the group. She thought she had better quit before I had the chance to fire her. Initially, she would call her individual therapist in crisis about this and after receiving reassurance from her and having the therapist check with me, she could contain her anxiety and return the next week. Eventually, she could wait until her regular individual session to check, and later, she could talk with me directly to see if her paranoia was just that "thing that she did" and without any basis in reality.

Let me point out that the benefits of combined therapy can also be seen in the reverse. That is, sometimes the group can provide the supportive and flexible environment needed for a patient to work through a stuck place in individual therapy. For example, Laurie was referred to group by her individual therapist who felt quite stuck in breaking through her helpless victim persona. The group tried and tried to reach Laurie, repeatedly ending up in an advice-giving mode in response to her helplessness. Laurie could not, would not, be helped. By moving to a group-as-a-whole focus, I was able to help the group recognize the way that Laurie was helping the group experience her feelings of helplessness and inadequacy. The group could then move to an empathetic stance with her which helped her to drop more vulnerably into her emotional experience. She took this deepened affective connection back to her individual therapy and the therapy started to make progress.

Clinical tactics

Wallin (2007) suggests that good psychotherapy can learn much from what good parenting does to provide an experience of secure attachment with the infant (Lyons-Ruth, 1999) and must take into account the patient's mentalizing capacity at the moment. The therapist should mostly empathize with and note, name, and explore the moment-to-moment shifts in the patient's emotional experience. Wallin says:

> We should be aiming for:
> 1. An affective as well as linguistic dialogue that accommodates as much of the patient's subjective experience – feelings, thoughts, desires – as possible;
> 2. A sensitivity to disruptions in the relationship and readiness to initiate repair;
> 3. A stance of acceptance combined with an expectation of a little more from the patient than she currently believes herself capable of;
> 4. A willingness to confront, set limits, and struggle with the patient – as is often appropriate during periods heralding change in the patient's identity and in the therapeutic relationship" (Wallin, 2007: p. 194).

Interpretations should be limited to occasions when the patient's metacognition is high.

Clinical examples

Working with what is evoked In order to use the unthought known that is evoked in the group, we must stay attuned to our own subjective experience, understand it, and find ways to work with it within the group. Our feelings, thoughts, and body sensations all become valuable therapeutic resources. We must consider our experiences as co-created with the group and not clearly the property of just the group or just ourselves. We must take the risk of having experiences that we would rather not have and find ways to bring them into the group as seen in the following example.

Mary, mentioned above, had a long history of self-destructive behavior including bulimia and cutting herself with a razor on her thighs. Her childhood was full of neglect, highlighted by never-revealed sexual abuse by her brother. She had a great deal of difficulty trusting anyone, including the group, and after several years in group had never revealed the abuse or her self-destructive behavior. Her unresolved attachment style was seen in her desire for closeness and security in relationships, and her terror and anger at the impossibility (in her perception) of achieving that. One hot summer day, she came into group wearing shorts and crossed her legs in a manner that revealed long lines of scabs and older scars on her thighs. None of the members seemed to notice and no one commented on this. I spent long minutes acutely aware of Mary's legs and questioning whether and how to say something. At one moment, I felt that all eyes were on Mary's legs and on me, watching for my reaction and at the next that I was inventing the problem and no one could see anything. I was certain that if I said anything, Mary would be angry and humiliated. Finally, I convinced myself that Mary was disclosing something in the only way she could and that my silence would only serve to reenact the family dynamics around her abuse and neglect. I pointed out the scabs and scars on her legs with the expected reaction from Mary. What surprised me was the group's response. Members were angry at me and shamed me for exposing Mary in this way. I was caught up short, embarrassed, full of self-doubt. Clearly, it was I who was being abusive and the group was not-so-kindly letting me know. Sitting quietly trying to withstand the criticism, I suddenly understood that the experience that was being evoked in me was the experience of an abused child telling the secret of the abuse. I gathered my wits about me and shared my thoughts saying, "I can understand how uncomfortable it is to see me pointing out something so significant that Mary usually tries to hide. What interests me though is that the group seems focused on my motivations for pointing out Mary's scars and does not seem interested in exploring the meaning of Mary's injuries and of her revealing them today." As the conversation settled down, I worked internally with how to introduce the feeling that telling of the abuse was worse than the abuse itself since this seemed like a crucial piece for Mary in undoing her profound shame. Finally, I disclosed that my feelings while hearing their criticism reminded me of what I imagined a child reporting incest might feel in revealing the abuse to the family. My hope was that, in verbalizing the feelings evoked in me, Mary would be able to put some context to the feelings she had not been able to integrate as part of her history. Mary went silent, but another member who had previously discussed her own sexual abuse was able to explore such feelings. Mary never did take that step in group, but was an avid listener and through seeing the group's acceptance of the other group member, and working in individual therapy she made some progress of her own.

In working with what is evoked in us by our patients and groups, we need to remember that the process of influence is bi-directional and take the risk to be emotionally available to both ourselves and our patients. Whether we chose to use what is evoked explicitly, as I did in the above example, or implicitly depends not only on what we think is good for the group but also on our own acceptance of our internal experience. Making sense of the experience is what will help patients integrate disowned, unthought or unfelt parts of themselves.

Working with enactments One of my groups has a structure that involves a significant portion of the group membership changing each fall. Shortly after the group had reconstituted with about half of the members being new, one of the continuing members, Sue, started to talk about an interaction she had had with her mother. She described feeling that her mother wanted to minimize the negative affects Sue was reporting and change the topic to something more positive and neutral. Sue started to become angry and tearful and to reveal some of the history of her wounding in relation to this dynamic with her mother.

Feeling quite aware that this was a new group in many ways, I became concerned about Sue's disclosures being premature for the group and potentially resulting in her feeling overexposed, the group beginning to identify her as "the patient," and the norm of self-disclosure being set in a way that would be threatening to new members. I intervened by interrupting Sue rather clumsily and inviting the other group members to relate to her story. The group was horrified. Sue cried even more heartily. I was astonished. The group soundly criticized me for doing to Sue exactly what she was describing her mother doing. In effect, I ignored and minimized Sue's feelings and changed the subject. We went through a few rounds of my trying to explain my positive intent and repeatedly pouring more salt on the wound and the group unrelentingly telling me that I was continuing the same pattern while Sue continued crying, mostly wordlessly. Eventually, I was able to get through my own defensiveness and see how I was playing my part in a powerful enactment. No matter how well-intentioned I was, and how protective I felt I was being of Sue and the group, there was no way for her not to see me as another version of her mother. Once I could truly see the pain I was causing, empathize with Sue and put her emotional needs of that moment in focus, then she could feel that something new was happening. As she could see my pain in causing her pain and feel met in that, then she could begin to really feel my concern and care for her rather than my wanting to shut her up. Put another way, taking in my changing perspective, Sue then could step out of the wounded self-state she was in and begin to think about what was happening in a new way. She moved from an embedded stance where her truth was the only truth, to one in which she could think about how things were seen by me. She regained her ability to mentalize even in this context.

In this example, we can see that Sue was describing a recent interaction with her mother that distressed her and revealed that a typical dynamic between them was that if Sue took the risk to reveal distress to her mother, she was neglected or punished for it; prime territory to develop a dismissive attachment style. If I had been able in that moment to think about what I knew of Sue and her relationship with me, I might have found some elegant way to speak to her longing for my attention to her distress and for my soothing. But perhaps that would not have been nearly as effective. It was not until I enacted the dynamic with Sue that she really fell into the pain of the childlike self-state and that created the opportunity. Sue dropping into her pain represented a more activating strategy that she was able to reach with me and the group, unlike with her mother. This may have indicated some development of more secure attachment with me and the group had already occurred. Her evident distress was much easier to recognize than a dismissive withdrawal would have been, but I was caught in my own dismissive, logical stance and just as stuck as Sue was without the group's help. The group was able to be outside the enactment and watching it with horror, they persisted in confronting me with my role until I was able to step outside of my perspective and begin to understand what was happening.

Intersubjective/relational theorists put a premium on enactments as *the* work of psychotherapy and suggest that we are continually involved in enactments that are by definition, initially unconscious (Wright, 2004). At some point, enactments become conscious, either because they become so uncomfortable that we cannot continue to ignore them, or ideally, when our self-awareness brings them into focus before they have become that extreme. A mindful stance of self-awareness of what we are actually doing with a patient, without judgment, is particularly helpful here. Noting some behavior with a patient that is either repetitive or is uncharacteristic of us can cue us about the nature of the enactment as can one's personal therapy or consultation. In group, the consultation often comes from members of the group as seen above. Once we are aware of our participation in an enactment, we become free to move, think, feel, and act in ways that we were not able to earlier. Then we have the chance to move from a repetitive enactment into a reparative one that helps the patient integrate new experience.

Working with what is embodied

> Mary (mentioned above) and Kelsey competed for the position of most needy patient in group and regularly fought with each other, mutually targeting each other with the hate they had experienced from their families of origin. One day, over some slight I cannot remember, Kelsey decided she could take it no more, made a suicidal threat and ran out of the group. Mary, who had felt quite in control a moment earlier, panicked. Without any reason to think of it, Mary decided that Kelsey had gone to the parking lot to vandalize her car. Mary's panic was visceral. She became breathless and shaky and the group resonated with her. She got up and peered through the blinds, trying to see into the parking lot but too afraid to go out into it. No amount of reassurance could calm her.
>
> Mary's reaction of panic did not fit the context of the moment as is often true of these kinds of somatic reactions. In noting the intensity of her physical reactions and her thoughts (that Kelsey would scratch Mary's car with her keys), and the group's mirroring we were eventually able to make some meaning of these events. Over the next several weeks, when the group's fear had subsided somewhat and I reported that Kelsey did not kill herself but felt unable to return

> to the group, we began to work with the self-hate and annihilation anxiety that was so clearly embodied in both members and communicated non-verbally. Mary revealed how hated she had felt in her family, how suicidal she could feel about that and how much rage she felt toward those who had a sense of belonging in their own families. She even made sense of her particular fantasy about the car being "keyed," revealing that she had expressed her own rage towards co-workers with that very act.

Talking about the body and bodily cues presents a number of difficulties. Asking a patient to focus on their physical sensations may increase their arousal beyond a level they can tolerate and thus short-circuit any hope of developing understanding of the body cues. Therapists need to carefully titrate their interventions and use grounding techniques to turn the arousal level down when it threatens to become disruptive. Such grounding techniques can include asking patients to focus on just the present moment, to focus on something in the room, or to focus on breathing more slowly and deeply. I often ask group members who are getting a little too aroused or seem to be avoiding their feelings by rushing through their words just to slow down and take a breath.

Another difficulty is the self-consciousness and exposure people often feel when their non-verbal behavior and body cues are commented on. We are really breaking the social rules when we make such comments and need to be very respectful and tentative. Just think of how difficult it is to point out someone's sweating, digestive noises, smell, or even change in weight. When such comments can be made as a non-judgmental observation with an invitation to explore the meaning together, we are most likely to help in making connections between bodily states, feelings, and thoughts. Then we can begin to make further meaning by linking the current context with the historical antecedents that have been kept disconnected and unintegrated into the self.

Cautionary notes

One concern in working with the issues I have been addressing, is how to handle the occasions when a patient is pushed too far by the therapist or the group and becomes overwhelmed. In some ways, I posit that this is inevitable and when it happens, the focus needs to be on repair and on understanding or making meaning of the event. In other ways, it is possible and important to try to decrease the intensity of these kinds of events so that they have an affective charge but are not overwhelming. I find that close attention to the non-verbal and somatic signs of arousal can help in this regard. Helping a patient turn down the intensity, either with the grounding techniques I discussed before, or by backing up to a more empathic approach, can be quite helpful. Sometimes it is only the strength of our convictions, our containing capacities, our clear boundary-setting and our therapeutic contracts that can provide the time and space for some shift to occur that will help us get through such impasses. Close colleagues and consultants can help clarify the issues and determine appropriate courses of action. Sometimes, no matter what we try and how well intentioned we are, we will fail. Such failures can remind us of our own limits and of the need to be gentle with ourselves and our colleagues when we make mistakes.

Intersubjective/relational theorists have helped shift the focus in psychotherapy from one which only examined the patient's contribution to what happens in the consulting room to one in which the therapist's contribution is equally important. Attachment theorists are beginning to explore the particular contributions of the therapist's attachment styles on the therapy as well (e.g. Muller, 2009; Rubino et al., 2000). It is essential that, as therapists, we have a well-developed understanding of our own psychology and attachment patterns and be willing to remain open and exploratory of our thoughts, behaviors (verbal and non-verbal) and feelings. Our own psychotherapy and on-going consultation are necessities in this pursuit. Wallin (2007) suggests that an ongoing practice of mindfulness can cultivate a non-judgmental awareness of ourselves which can help us be more aware of our contributions to stuck places in enactments and move us towards initiating understanding and repair. In addition, he points out that while a securely attached therapist has some innate advantages in doing psychotherapy, the asymmetry of the therapeutic relationship "creates a context in which we may well feel both more secure than the patient and more secure than we ordinarily do" (Wallin, 2007: p. 261).

Group supervision/consultation can provide a uniquely valuable context for group therapists since the parallel processes can be explored as another source of information and understanding.

In conclusion, the multiple perspectives and transferences in group psychotherapy are particularly useful in eliciting well-defended but problematic self-states in our patients. Close attention to how attachment wounds are evoked, enacted, or embodied in the therapy group can provide unique opportunities to make meaning of what has remained out of awareness and to provide new experiences of secure attachment where all parts of the self can be integrated. This newly earned secure attachment then promotes significant growth in intrapsychic and interpersonal functioning.

References and Bibliography

Adams, K. A. (2006). Falling forever: The price of chronic shock. *International Journal of Group Psychotherapy*, 56, 127–172.

Ainsworth, M. D. S., Blehar, M. C., Waters, E., et al. (1978). *Patterns of attachment: A psychological study of the strange situation*. Hillsdale, New Jersey: Analytic Press.

Bollas, C. (1987). *The shadow of the object: Psychoanalysis of the unthought known*. New York: Columbia University Press.

Bowlby, J. (1982). (Original work published 1969). *Attachment and loss: Vol. 1 Attachment*. London: Hogarth Press and the Institute of Psycho-Analysis.

Bowlby, J. (1973). *Attachment and loss: Vol. 2. Separation: Anxiety and anger*. New York: Basic Books.

Flores, P. J. (2010). Group psychotherapy and neuro-plasticity: An attachment theory perspective. *International Journal of Group Psychotherapy*, 60, 547–570.

Fonagy, P., Gergely, G., Jurit, E. L., et al. (2002). *Affect regulation, mentalization, and the developent of the self.* New York: Other Press.

George, C., Kaplan, N., & Main, M. (1984). *Adult attachment interview protocol* (1st ed.). Unpublished manuscript, University of California at Berkeley.

George, C., Kaplan, N., & Main, M. (1985). *Adult attachment interview protocol* (2nd ed.). Unpublished manuscript, University of California at Berkeley.

George, C., Kaplan, N., & Main, M. (1996). *Adult attachment interview protocol* (3rd ed.). Unpublished manuscript, University of California at Berkeley.

Grossmark, R. (2007). The edge of chaos: Enactment, disruption, and emergence in group psychotherapy. *Psychoanalytic Dialogues, 17*(4), 479–499.

Hopper, E. (2003). *Traumatic experience in the unconscious life of groups: The fourth basic assumption: Incohesion: Aggregation/massification or (ba) I:A/M.* New York: Jessica Kingsley Publishers.

Lyons-Ruth, K. (1999). The two-person unconscious: Intersubjective dialogue, enactive relational representation, and the emergence of new forms of relational organization. *Psychoanalytic Inquiry, 19,* 576–617.

Main, M. (1991). Metacognitive knowledge, metacognitive monitoring, and singular (coherent) vs. multiple (incoherent) model of attachment: Findings and directions for future research. In C. M. Parkes, J. Stevenson-Hinde & P. Marris (Eds.), *Attachment across the life cycle* (pp. 127–159). London: Tavistock/Routledge.

Main, M., Kaplan N., & Cassidy, J. (1985). Security in infancy, childhood, and adulthood: A move to the level of representation. *Monographs of the Society for Research in Child Development, 50*(1–2), 66–104

Main, M., & Solomon, J. (1990). Procedures for identifying infants as disorganized/disoriented during the Ainsworth Strange Situation. In M. Greenberg, D. Cicchetti & E. M. Cummings (Eds.), *Attachment during the preschool years: Theory, research and intervention* (pp. 121–160). Chicago: University of Chicago Press.

Mikulincer, M., & Shaver, P. R. (2007). Attachment, group-related processes, and psychotherapy. *International Journal of Group Psychotherapy, 57,* 233–245.

Muller, R. (2009). Trauma and dismissing (avoidant) attachment: Intervention strategies in individual psychotherapy. In *Psychotherapy: Theory, Research, Practice, Training, 46,* 68–81.

Rubino, G., Barker, C., Roth, T., et al. (2000). Therapist empathy and depth of interpretation in response to potential alliance ruptures: the role of therapist and patient attachment styles. *Psychotherapy Research, 10,* 407–420.

Wallin, D. J. (2007). *Attachment in psychotherapy.* New York: The Guilford Press.

Wright F. (2004). Being seen, moved, disrupted, and reconfigured: Group leadership from a relational perspective. *International Journal of Group Psychotherapy, 54,* 235–251.

17
Structured Techniques to Facilitate Relating at Various Levels in Group
Albert J. Brok

Introduction

You are a new clinician in a mental health clinic, a senior center or day hospital and have been asked to run your first group. Or perhaps you are in your own practice building up the courage to start your first group. You are interested, excited and a little worried. How will it go? What do you say as the leader? How do you get things started? Do you wait for the patients to start or do you give some kind of orientation or warm up? And what do you do, or say, once things have started? You wonder about all these conundrums more and more as you sit at home surrounded by a pile of ubiquitous group books ranging from the umpteenth edition of Yalom's "Theory and Practice of Group Therapy," theoretical texts by Bion, and various "here-and-now" Group Counseling treatises. What to do, what to read, and how to prepare? You ponder, realizing that you can never read all of your books by tomorrow. So, when you start your first group, you decide to just wing it, go by your experience in the group and use common sense. Anyway, you have a supervisor to discuss things with, although the supervision session may seem short as there is so much to cover.

The above paragraph is illustrative of a situation that many new clinicians face. Many have limited theoretical knowledge, and are compelled by their agency to deal with many different kinds of patients. Selecting members for a group is not always the mental health professional's prerogative in a clinic, or in any institutional setting. In private practice this is of course the group therapist's responsibility. Though sometimes well-trained, a new group therapist in private practice, can also experience anxiety and uncertainty.

In this chapter, I will address the issue of levels of group interaction based on the experience and proficiency of the group therapist. I will offer some suggestions based on the value of a structured technique which gives the new group leader options to stay at low anxiety levels or to move the group to deeper more profound levels of interaction.

People are complex, and so are groups. Just as each individual has many dimensions, so are groups similarly complex. There are many theoretical and clinical models to draw from when trying to understand people, and so it is when understanding a group.

Groups and the people comprising them operate at many different levels of experience. Indeed it is a judicious challenge for a group therapist to discern which level is most relevant at any given moment. Implied is the issue of when and how to make an intervention. To help with this, I will present a flexibly-structured modular approach I have developed, which is intended to facilitate group interaction at the level most appropriate to the group's needs and the therapist's experience (Brok, 1976, 1977). For all therapists, whether novice, or seasoned, how we deal with any clinical situation, depends on our level of knowledge and experience. It is very important to have comfort with the paradox of conflicting truths. In any given situation there are many truths, the issue for me as a therapist, is which truth is the most relevant at the moment and how competent am I to deal with it.

Structure and anxiety

In general it can be said that the more structure there is in a group, the less manifest anxiety there will be, and where there is less structure the more manifest will anxiety be (Caligor, Fieldsteel and Brok, 1993). Thus, for the beginning therapist, doing a beginning group, it might be best to initiate the group with a structured exercise. Such an approach diminishes the level of manifest anxiety for the less-experienced leader as well as for group members.

Beginning a group in a structured manner, may be highly beneficial for individuals who are depressed or manifest weak or fragile senses of self. Less structured groups which focus on interpersonal relations and the ongoing flow of inter-subjective experiential states tend to generate a modicum of anxiety in members. Such groups are of great value in working with individuals who have been well prepared by individual therapy and have a stronger sense of self and good reflective capacity (Caligor, Fieldsteel and Brok, 1993; Brok, 1996). In any beginning group it is the leader's task to create an optimally safe and nurturing environment. Thus all groups ought to begin with a degree of structure, whether it be provided by active verbal leadership, or structured exercises – the focus of this chapter.

The more structured a group is, the less anxiety for the novice leader as he is not faced with the degree of paradoxical judgments one needs to make in a more interpersonal group. The more free flowing the group, the more a leader has to choose between many different levels of possible intervention. This calls for considerable experience.

The more structured group

One structured method I have developed involves a short term module , The "Life Enrichment Counseling Approach" (Brok, 1976; Weiner, Brok and Snadowsky, 1987). This approach aims to help individuals recognize problems and develop approaches to make meaningful use of time. People who are depressed or conflicted find difficulty making choices about how to use their time in a satisfying manner.

The module can be used with all age groups, and is a good conversation starter while giving the less-experienced group leader options about where and how to intervene. The guiding philosophy of the module is proactive rather than rehabilitative in that it aims at enhancing developmental potential. It is of course not solely concerned with use of time, but also serves as a relatively low anxiety conversation starter which can yield important and relevant personal material for group work. Essentially, the module encourages group interaction in a low anxiety context.

The module comprises of a set of group exercises that can be used to provide a focus for discussion and promote interaction in a leader-guided way. The exercises can be used in sequence or in whatever order the leader feels is appropriate for the group in question.

What follows is a typical sequence I have found useful. All approaches minimally depend on the initial introduction followed by the first exercise.

Exercises

Introduction to the exercise   In the initial phase, the rationale for using the module is presented by the leader. This can vary depending upon the setting and purpose involved. For example, in a Senior Center, the module can be introduced as a potentially diverting activity involving discussion and exchange of ideas about how to use leisure time. With the group leader acting as moderator, such a discussion can serve the purpose of an "ice breaker" or way for people to get to know something about each other. This module can also be introduced as a theme oriented discussion on the philosophical issue of use of time from a religious or other point of view. In more clinical settings, it might be used as a structured projective method for elucidation and discussion of in depth feelings about the self. Use of the module ultimately depends on the purpose of the group and the skill of the leader. It is important that all leaders be aware that they are dealing with what can rapidly become a sensitive topic area. The leader has options to deal with things either on a superficial activity level, or at a greater depth.

Exercise A: Self-generated list of leisure activities   As part of the introduction to this exercise group members are presented with the *Self Generation of Leisure Activities Form,* (see Activity Form A) This is a structured form in which each group member is asked to make a list of things he or she does during leisure time.

Of great importance, is that this is a list made by participants – there are no constraining pre-set categories such as checklists. Participants are encouraged to make their lists as long as they wish, although it is sometimes useful to have a time limit such as five minutes. Each person ought to have sufficient time to feel comfortable writing the list. Since initial thought associations to a word or concept tend to be normative or stereotyped, with enough time, more unusual and creative responses may emerge. This is especially true for individuals with higher anxiety levels.

Some people when doing the exercise may ask: "What is work and what is leisure?" It is useful to defer this question for later discussion so that participants can decide the issue for themselves. The leader's most useful response is to suggest that group members list whatever meets their own criteria for leisure. For example, some people put down such things as "housework" which many consider a non-leisure activity. Nevertheless, housework may subjectively be experienced as leisure by certain people.

> ### Activity Form A
>
> **Self generation of leisure activities**
>
> *Instructions:* List below the kinds of things that you do in your leisure time.
> Put down anything that comes to your mind.
> The order in which you write these activities is not important.
> After you have listed everything that you can think of, rate each activity according to the degree of enjoyment you experience using the scale below.
> The scale goes from 1 which represents the low end to 5 which represents the high end.
> Circle the number that best expresses your degree of enjoyment.
>
> | Leisure Activities | Degree of Enjoyment
Little   Much | Gains |
> |---|---|---|
> | A | 1 2 3 4 5 | |
> | B | 1 2 3 4 5 | |
> | C | 1 2 3 4 5 | |
> | D | 1 2 3 4 5 | |
> | E | 1 2 3 4 5 | |
> | F | 1 2 3 4 5 | |
> | and so on. | | |

This approach is in keeping with the existential-humanistic concept that people need to construct their lives and to subjectively determine the meaning of their own activities. It also allows for the possibility of explaining, understanding and perhaps changing the idiosyncratic belief systems of participants. There are those, for example, who find doing housework a terrible chore, which might have more to do with the attitude brought to the activity, rather than anything intrinsic to the task, and vice-versa.

Exercise B: Self-evaluation of enjoyment Upon making their lists, group members may be asked to evaluate the degree of enjoyment they experience when involved in each activity. Each member does this by circling the number that best expresses his or her degree of enjoyment for each activity recorded in the self-generated list. As seen in the form (see Activity Form B), the numbers to be circled are printed in the *Degree of Enjoyment* portion of the *Self Generation of Leisure Activities Form*. It is convenient to have a range from 1–5 where 1 stands for "little enjoyment," and 5 stands for "much enjoyment." This structured exercise can provide a general picture of how people feel about the kinds of activities that they subjectively list as part of their leisure time. It can provide an opportunity for discussion about specific activities that are enjoyed. This discussion also allows for each participant to discover similar interests and enjoyable experiences in others, thereby providing the opportunity for validating feelings of self-esteem and self-worth. It also allows for people to discuss the differences between each other in terms of their different enjoyment of the same activities.

Activity Form B

Activity gains

Instructions: Take some time and read the list of paragraphs below.

Then choose the one or ones which might best apply to each activity you have listed in Activity Form A.

If no paragraph seems to apply for an activity you have listed, that's all right, just leave the column to which it corresponds blank.

For paragraphs which DO apply, please place their number in the "Gains" column which is on Activity Form A.

1. This activity gives me the feeling that other people support me in my interests, my confidence in other is affirmed.
2. This activity gives me freedom to be separate and a sense of standing on my own two feet. This activity reinforces my belief of being able to take care of myself.
3. This activity gives me a chance to explore and be creative. I enjoy this activity because there are no set rules. I decide what the activity consists of, and how I will do it.
4. This activity gives me a sense of accomplishment and helps me to gain a sense of achievement.
5. This activity helps me to learn more about myself and to find out who I am. It gives me a chance to try different ways in which to do things and by which to discover new things about myself.
6. This activity allows another person to find out more about me and encourages me to find out more about another person in depth. It involves sharing meaningful feelings with another. Through this activity I get close to another person and expose my personal side.
7. This activity allows me to feel that I am contributing something worthwhile to others or to society. This activity helps me to feel that I am giving something, helping others, or making my mark on another person's life, or an organization or in a community.
8. Through this activity, I can appreciate the difference between people and can accept myself and others. This activity helps me to feel satisfied with the manner in which I have led my life.

Exercise C: Personal assessment of developmental experience through leisure Upon completion of their lists and their enjoyment ratings, participants may be presented with a list of developmental task descriptors (see Activity Form B). These descriptors consist of eight phrases that describe developmental stages, based on the original concepts of Erikson in 1959, and modified by Brok in 1976 and again 1997 and Weiner, Brok and Snadowsky (1987) to reflect the positive pole of each Eriksonian stage-related psycho-social crises. In this structured exercise, each group member is asked to indicate which phrase best expresses what might be developmentally relevant or experienced from each activity listed during the self-generation phase. Theoretically, this exercise provides a developmental meaning in Eriksonian terms of each group member's activity repertoire. These are listed by number on the right hand side of the *Self-Generation of Leisure Activities Form*. Provision can be made for members to indicate more than one descriptor for each activity listed. For example, participants may be asked to list the numbers of as many descriptors as they feel apply to each leisure activity. Members ought not to be required to provide descriptors for activities that do not seem to meet any of their developmental needs – as phrased by the descriptors. The descriptors used here are meant as illustrative phrases, based on my own experience and research. Other descriptors may be substituted, depending on the situation and client population. *The descriptor approach is useful for purposes of subsequent discussion by the group, rather than for assessment.*

There are many further exercises in the complete module but here I will only touch on one more which is

Exercise D: Qualitative descriptions In this exercise, each group member is requested to describe in his or her own words what they experience during or as a function of the activities they described. These qualitative descriptions are written or listed in the "Activity Gains" column of the first form. This exercise leads to a final activity: the *Theme Oriented Group Discussion*.

Before turning to the "theme oriented group discussion" it is relevant to note that these exercises are presented as guidelines. It has been my experience that the exercises do not have to be followed in a sequential manner. In many cases, only some of the exercises may be relevant. Indeed, each exercise may be carried out as a separate unit over a period of days or weeks. Their appropriateness depends on the kind of group and on time allowances.

Guidelines for theme oriented group discussion

I will now present some approaches to using the exercises in a *"leader friendly way."* By this I mean, a situation where depending upon training and experience, a leader has the choice of staying at a basic interaction level or moving the group to deeper and more profound levels. All the while, the intrinsic interest in and the structure provided by the exercises help group members slowly move into guided group discussion with minimal anxiety in comparison to an open ended unstructured group experience led by a relatively silent non-directive leader.

So, for example, once exercise "A" and any of the optional exercises B, C, or D are completed, a situation is organized in which group members are encouraged to focus on themes or issues of common concern and interest. The theme-oriented group is especially useful for the beginning group therapist, because the focus remains on a *tangible* topic. As I have suggested in this chapter, one such topic might be various uses of leisure time. A discussion of the underlying belief systems, thoughts, approaches, and alternatives to "free time" may preclude the necessity of spending time focusing on the emotional relations within such a group. As a result, the beginning group leader is freer to focus on creating an atmosphere of mutual participation through which a sense of group cohesiveness may develop. The more experienced psychodynamically oriented leader will find ample material for opening up emotionally laden areas, should this seem appropriate or if the participants expect such a discussion. Thus, this cognitively based theme approach to group provides *flexibility*, for various therapeutic-educational needs.

The cognitively-based, theme-oriented group is less stressful for participants because its structure provides the opportunity to share feelings and ideas about specific topics of mutual interest. For example, by virtue of each member's involvement in the series of exercises and discussions about the uses of leisure time, a sense of "connectedness" among participants is established. In general, sharing common interests provides a "launching pad" for deeper discussion. In this light, what follows are some suggestions for leaders guiding discussions in terms of the exercises previously described.

Uses for the self-generated leisure activities form

The simplest discussion technique requires that the leader ask each participant to read out loud the items that he or she has written. This exercise encourages members to reveal something personal and subjectively meaningful about themselves that can be shared with others. It encourages group members to find similarities between themselves and others, and it enhances "connectedness" and group cohesion. As a result, an open theme-oriented discussion may ensue about the variety of activities in which people engage. Such a discussion can serve as an "ice-breaker" for a newly formed group whether privately, in an out-patient setting, or in community or senior center. Although this exercise promotes the disclosure of material that is personal, it also allows people the choice of not becoming involved in any underlying emotional content if they do not wish. Further it is important to note that the group leader should emphasize that participants do not have to read every item on their lists if they so choose. Analysis or consideration of resistance to the process is not a suggested part of this technique. Such approaches can come later on if the group proceeds beyond a short-term process and as the need for structured material lessens.

Material which emerges from the Self-Generated lists can also be used to develop a more philosophical or topical discussion about the use of time. In this approach the leader can suggest that participants discuss "what is defined as leisure, and what is not." The attempt to clarify differences between work and leisure is not always simple and can often lead group members into a stimulating discussion about the meanings given and underlying beliefs concerning various life activities. The discussion can also help group members comprehend the subjective element in one's personal value system This, in turn, can encourage the appreciation of difference between oneself and others.

One specific way of implementing these aims is to ask members to read their lists out loud (this should be on a voluntary basis), and then discuss whether or not they agree on what is work and what is leisure. For example, the leader might ask: "Do some of you consider what anyone else describes as leisure to be work? Why? Did anyone not include what Mr Brown put down because you thought of it as work? How many people put down cleaning house as a leisure activity? Would we all go by the same set of definitions?"

In my clinical use of this process, I have noted that some group members characteristically omit or prefer not to immediately discuss certain items. For example, some do not list sex as a leisure activity. With some humor, leaders have occasionally suggested that this might mean that it is considered work! In a more serious vein, focusing on the issue of sex can lead to fruitful therapeutic discussions about an area of human functioning that is very emotionally sensitive. For some it may be an embarrassing topic and considered inappropriate, while for others, revealing they have sexual needs may be poignant and/or conflicted. Many people however find it easier to discuss sensitive topics such as sex, upon discovering that others in the group find it to be an appropriate topic that can be talked about. Thus we can see how the exchange and sharing of the self-generated leisure items and the discussion of what is or is not a leisure activity can yield a number of important social learning experiences at many different levels.

Uses for the self-evaluation of enjoyment form

Perhaps the simplest use for the material generated by this exercise requires that each group member share out loud (on a voluntary basis) the activities that he or she has rated highly enjoyable, that is those rated 4 or 5. Sharing these highly enjoyed activities with others encourages members to experience a sense of mutuality and cohesiveness. This approach also provides the opportunity for a lively discussion about the different ratings given by members who engage in similar activities. This exercise can serve as a stepping stone towards an in-depth discussion about the uniqueness of one's experiences. It has also been of use in "singles" groups where potential couples have a sense of compatibility of interests.

Leisure ought to be joyful, but unfortunately for many it is not. This opens up another choice for the leader. If warranted, the group leader can suggest that members compare their lists for areas that show the least enjoyment. This is done by discussion of activities given a 1 or 2 rating. This part of the exercise can launch a discussion of such problem areas as boredom, underlying negative beliefs about the self, depressive affect, ennui and alienation. It also can lead to cognitive re-framing about possible solutions or needed acceptance of one's current abilities. Here the sensitive group leader can use this material to enter an in-depth discussion about areas of psychological apprehension and can encourage problem-solving behaviors. For example, the group might discuss how individuals can do more of what they enjoy or how they can discover new enjoyments. Sometimes, low ratings imply areas of considerable guilt.

Group members can also be asked to sum up the number of activities that they rated "4" or "5" and compare them with those they rated "1" or "2" (little enjoyment).

The use of the enjoyment ratings can lead to the creation of a *human resources group* (Blocher, 1974, 1996) during which emphasis is placed on helping members to extend their levels of functioning to the upper limits of their potential. The group leader focuses on the positive potential that each member has, rather than on any pathology. The group leader can use the enjoyment rating scale for such a purpose by focusing discussion on those items that each member most enjoys.

Related to the above notion is the issue of *Ideals vs. Reality* and their relation to beliefs about the self. This can be approached by suggesting that each group member review their highly rated enjoyment items and ask that they indicate how often they *actually experience* each particular activity. It has been the experience of group leaders that members not only list activities that they have not done for some time (or only do infrequently), but that they also list things they would like to do, but have never done.

The goal here is to enable group members to better live up to their ideal self-concept as well as to understand and cope with their real selves. One such technique is the *action program method* (Blocher, 1974, 1996; Wiener, Brok and Snadowsky, 1997; Brok, 1997). Essentially this involves having the group encourage a particular member to develop a plan (in addition to talking about what he or she would "like" to do) that would increase or facilitate the development of the person's strengths. Homework assignments are then given to carry out the plan.

A specific example of this approach is one leader's experience with a Senior Citizen's Group in which a member had listed "playing the piano" as something she enjoyed greatly. It the ensuing discussion, it became apparent that the last time this person had actually played the piano was some 15 years ago. There was clearly an incongruence between her actual self and her ideal self. When asked why she no longer played the piano, a number of important factors emerged. First it had nothing to do with physical disability. Second, and more important, her playing was an activity to which she had given only cursory thought and that she had been timid about revealing this interest. This exercise permitted her dormant potential to emerge. Once it emerged, group discussion provided the opportunity for others to express interest in her activity. In addition the participants inquired as to why she had not been playing the piano recently and began to motivate her to develop an *action plan*. The other group members thus became *potential resources*. One member noted that a piano was available in the lounge of the Center where this discussion took place. This led to the group considering how and when the piano could be used by her not only to play at Senior Citizen events, but also to teach others. The group was thus able to activate an interest that had been dormant for some years. The interest would probably not have emerged without the structured technique.

Uses for the assessment of developmental experiences exercise

A discussion about what is gained through involvement in the various activities can lead to profound reflection about member's life experiences in developmental terms. Use of the Activity Gains form provides a relatively low anxiety way to approach such developmental material. The group leader can use each person's self-assessment to encourage a deeper discussion of life goals.

Uses for the qualitative description of leisure experiences

Perhaps the simplest use of the qualitative description of experiences is for the leader to initiate a group session by suggesting that each participant discuss and share the kinds of things that she or he does with free time. Simply having a topic to discuss, lowers anxiety as it serves an "environmental prop" through which to relate (Brok, 1973, 1997; Weiner, Brok and Snadowsky, 1987). It is not necessary to require that each member refer to his or her list of self-generated activities. Here, the format can be more free-wheeling in order to encourage general discussion. However, the more structured approach lowers anxiety, even more than a mere topic, and seems to yield more interesting and profound material. Thus, the qualitative description approach can be incorporated as part of the discussion of the self-generated activities list. This is done by asking members to discuss and compare what they gain from each of their listed activities. For some populations this may be the least threatening way to introduce group discussion.

Group approaches to treatment involve a wide variety of techniques. The present chapter emphasizes the value of a structured approach without stifling opportunity for the leader to move into more interpersonal and psychodynamic themes if warranted. The structure of the approach generates the content, which can be handled in various ways by the group dependent upon its interests, requirements and goals.

This is just one approach especially for new group therapists. It gives the group leader the flexibility of staying at a comfort level they can best function with, but also allows for going deeper if one chooses. It does not obviate the more profound usefulness of a psychodynamic ongoing approach to therapeutic treatment as I have delineated elsewhere (Brok, 1996).

References and Bibliography

Blocher, D. H. (1974) (1996). *Developmental counseling*. Ronald Press.

Brok, A. J. (1976). *Existential, instrumental and developmental issues in leisure relevant to counseling and applied human development.* Society and Leisure, 3, 60–71.

Brok, A. J. (1996). *Preparing group leaders for an analytic perspective, Psychologist-Psychoanalyst. Official publication of Division 39.* American Psychological Association, 16, 1, 34–35.

Brok, A. J. (1997) A modified cognitive-behavioural approach to group therapy with the elderly. *Group, 21*, 2, 115–134.

Caligor, J., Fieldsteel, D., & Brok, A. J. (1993). *Combining individual group therapy*. Northvale, New Jersey: Aronson.

Erikson, E. (1959). Identity and the life cycle. New York, International Universities Press.

Weiner, M., Brok, A. J., and Sandowsky, A. (1987). *Working with the aged: practical approaches in the institution and the community*. Norwalk, Connecticut: Appleton Century Crofts and Fleschner Publishing.

18
Effective Management of Substance Abuse Issues in Psychodynamic Group Psychotherapy

Marsha Vannicelli

Historical Context

There is likely no population more commonly linked to group treatment in the United States than individuals who suffer from substance abuse. The public has probably seen, heard, and read more accounts of alcoholics in groups than all other clinical populations combined. Despite the fact that these groups (mostly AA) are not what most clinicians would call "therapy groups," they have influenced the climate of group treatment for this population for more than half a century.

Beginning with the Uniform Treatment and Rehabilitation Act (Hart, 1977; Kurtz and Reiger, 1975) in the early 1970s when alcoholism was decriminalized and, instead, treated as a disease requiring treatment, thousands of treatment programs were set up around the country. Supply matched demand for 30-day inpatient programs, partial hospital programs, and outpatient programs – all heavily group-oriented, mostly with a solid emphasis on the teachings of AA (through psycho-education groups involving the 12 steps and active participation in AA meetings). Group therapy that was more psychodynamically oriented was much less common with this population – and in fact strongly eschewed in many quarters.

When I entered the field in the early 1970s, right after my clinical internship – inexperienced, uniformed, and flying pretty much by the seat of my pants – I was given the task of helping to set up the first alcohol inpatient treatment unit at McLean Hospital, and five years later was asked to develop and direct the hospital's first outpatient program for this population (the Appleton Outpatient Clinic). I had fallen in love with psychodynamically oriented/interpersonal group therapy as a psychology intern, co-leading a long-term outpatient group (which is still thriving nearly 40 years later). Impressed with the effectiveness of this model in a generic population, I assumed it would be equally effective for alcoholics. Thus, this model of group work (along with AA) became an integral part of the Appleton Treatment Program (both inpatient and outpatient). Several years later, I began reading "informed literature" of the past (Alexander, 1949; Gordis, 1987; Wolberg, 1948) and learned, fortunately too late, that dynamically oriented group work supposedly could not be done with this population.

While the Appleton Inpatient and Outpatient programs, both highly group-oriented, were initially focused solely on clients with alcohol problems, in the early 1980s these two programs, like so many others across the country, began expanding to include clients with other substance abuse problems. Initially added were those who abused cannabis and prescription drugs, and much later those who were addicted to "street drugs," such as heroin and crack. With this came a broadening in population diversity of groups for substance abusers.

Another change that positively impacted the effectiveness of group work with this population was the increasing reliance on psychopharmacological adjuncts. Medications were commonly prescribed to deal with alcohol cravings (campral, naltrexone) and to help reinforce the drinker's resolve not to drink (antabuse), to assist with urges for opiate abusers (cyboxin), and to help manage the uncomfortable mood states and other concomitant disorders often associated with substance abuse (antidepressants, anxiolitics, and mood stabilizers).

But perhaps the most significant change in the treatment zeitgeist began in the late 1980s and early 1990s with the advent of managed care which dramatically affected substance abuse treatment and group treatment, as well. Whereas through the early 1990s insurance companies provided inpatient treatment for virtually any substance abusing client who felt he would benefit from a 30-day "get away," under managed care, intensive 30-day rehabs gradually became available predominantly to those with considerable means who could afford to self-pay. This change meant that inpatient group experiences of 30-days or more which had been common earlier became relatively rare, and as a result, the number of group-oriented aftercare programs decreased. In keeping with the general tightening of resources, the number of outpatient programs for substance abusers also dramatically decreased and long-term groups, common in outpatient programs through the mid-1990s, became increasingly difficult to find outside of private practice. Today, substance abusing patients enter such private practice groups following detox, a day or evening program, or for the few who are fortunate, a 30-day rehabilitation, but often without any prior inpatient or outpatient treatment for their substance abuse.

The terrain also shifted considerably in my own private practice. Initially all of the groups that I ran or supervised that involved substance abusers were homogeneous (early on all members had problems with alcohol; later all members had problems with alcohol and/or another chemical substance). Gradually, however, I began integrating substance abusers, once they had achieved stability with regard to their substance use, into my long-term psychodynamically oriented therapy groups. (This modification will be discussed further in the section on heterogeneous groups.) The treatment contract (detailed later in the chapter), pivotal to the homogenous groups (Griefen, Vannicelli, and Canning, 1985; Vannicelli 1982, 1988, 1992, 2001a; Vannicelli, Canning, and Griefen, 1984; Vannicelli, Dillavou, and Caplan, 1989) remained central for substance abusers entering heterogeneous groups. It provided explicit guidelines for bringing into the group any changes in a member's relationship to alcohol or drugs (including urges as well as possible lapses).

But perhaps the greatest shift in my group treatment of substance abusers occurred in the mid-1990s as I increasingly worked with problem drinkers who were reluctant to embrace abstinence but were willing, instead, to embark on a course of systematic Moderation Training (Vannicelli, 2001b, 2002). Whereas in my earlier writings (Griefen, Vannicelli, and Canning, 1985; Vannicelli, 1982, 1988, 1992, 2001a; Vannicelli, Canning, and Griefen, 1984; Vannicelli, Dillavou, and Caplan, 1989), I had consistently emphasized the importance of *abstinence* to the patient's eventual emotional stability, I was now introducing the possibility of a different approach for managing alcohol abuse. I began incorporating into my long-term groups those drinkers who wished to moderate (once they were stabilized with regard to specific moderation goals), along with those with abstinence goals. (This will be discussed further in the section on heterogeneous groups with mixed goals for alcohol abusers.)

Having described some of the changes that have occurred in the national landscape with regard to group treatment of substance abusers over the past 40 years, as well as some of the changes in my own clinical practice, I will now discuss the utility of the psychodynamically oriented interactional model for this population, highlighting special issues that are important to attend to when working with substance abusers in groups. Though I will be discussing these issues within the context of an outpatient psychodynamic-interactional group therapy model, the reader will find many of the issues equally relevant in other group contexts (e.g., inpatient, day and evening programs) and also with groups based on other theoretical models.

The Psychodynamic Group Psychotherapy Model

The prevalence of group treatment with this population is not only a result of the historical connection between substance abuse treatment and 12 step programs, but also the recognition among professionals that group work offers substance abusers unique opportunities to:

a. Share and identify with others who are going through similar problems;
b. Understand the effect of alcohol and drugs in their lives and the defenses that keep them adversely entangled with chemical substances;
c. Learn more about their own and others' feelings and reactions;
d. Learn to communicate needs and feelings more directly (Vannicelli, 1992).

Although these goals can be achieved in a variety of group formats with different theoretical orientations, the model that I will be discussing is the psychodynamic-interactional therapy model which has been described in detail by Yalom and Leszcz (2005), and shares many features, as well, with the work of Rutan, Stone and Shay (2007).

The format involves weekly 90-minute meetings of 8–10 members who come together to learn about themselves in the context of a group. Under the leadership of a trained therapist, the group provides a unique "learning laboratory" in which members interact openly and honestly with others, while at the same time assuming a self-reflective stance. The behaviors that members bring to the group mirror in important ways their reactions to people and situations in their lives outside the group. By paying attention to what is alive in the group and giving and receiving feedback, members learn more about themselves and one another, and how to trust and connect in more satisfying ways.

The group provides a safe, supportive place to share problems and concerns, and to learn from and with others. Like many individuals, substance abusers often carry the disquieting feeling that they are very different from other people and that if others really knew them they would not be accepted. The group presents an opportunity to be truly known, understood, and accepted. In addition, work in the group provides a forum for understanding family of origin issues as they are replayed in the present. As past conflicts are recreated in the present, the group provides an opportunity for old non-adaptive behavior patterns to be challenged and new behaviors to be tested out.

Adaptations to the Model to Deal with Substance Abuse Issues

The psychodynamic-interactional group therapy techniques that I will be describing with substance abusers are similar in many ways to the techniques that I use with non-substance abusers. They differ, however, in that stability with regard to use of alcohol and drugs is seen as essential to the patient's eventual emotional growth. While this is stressed in pre-group interviews and throughout members' tenure in the group, membership is not contingent on absolute, unswerving adherence to a member's specific parameters (either moderation or abstinence) but on his willingness to struggle honestly with conflict about drinking or drug use and his clear commitment to returning to his agreed upon goal. Toward this end, group leaders firmly and explicitly encourage simultaneous use of other supports that will be helpful in maintaining abstinence or moderation (including the use of self-help programs and medications).

In addition, effective treatment of substance abusers in group therapy requires attention to several other important issues that can pose challenges for the group (and for leaders). Twelve of these are detailed in the sections that follow. The first seven issues have been discussed in many of my writings since 1982 (Griefen, Vannicelli, and Canning, 1985; Vannicelli, 1982, 1988, 1992, 2001a; Vannicelli, Canning, and Griefen, 1984; Vannicelli, Dillavou, and Caplan, 1989). Four of these issues are **generic** – that is, important regardless of whether a substance abuser is treated in a homogeneous group where all members have substance abuse histories or in a heterogeneous (integrated) group where other members may or may not have such histories. Three of the seven issues are **specific to homogeneous groups**. The four final issues that are discussed are **specific to heterogeneous (integrated) groups**.

Table 18.1 distinguishes among a variety of psychodynamically oriented interpersonal psychotherapy groups in which these issues are relevant. Though not within the purview of this chapter, the reader will readily recognize that many of the issues discussed are also relevant in non-psychodynamically oriented groups such as Skills Training, CBT, and Relapse Prevention groups.

Table 18.1 Overview of substance abuse groups consistent with a psychodynamically oriented interactional model.

Homogeneous Groups Abstinence Goals	All members are substance abusers who are committed to abstinence. They join at various stages of recovery when ready to work on interpersonal issues in a group and prefer to do so with others who have had substance abuse histories.
Homogeneous Groups Mixed Goals	Same as above except for goals specified for drinkers (either *abstinence commitment or explicit moderate drinking parameters*). This model allows for more liberal criteria for defining a successful outcome for drinkers, in keeping with the general philosophy of harm reduction approaches.
Early Recovery Groups Abstinence Goals	Substance abusers who are committed to abstinence but join the group when abstinence is still relatively untested. Generally designed exclusively for those with abstinence goals, members stay until stable abstinence has been reached (generally 6–12 months, sometimes longer).
Readiness Group Ultimate Goals Undecided	Substance abusers who are exploring their substance abuse issues, but not yet committed to a course of action. Attention is paid to cost/benefit analysis of what drinking and drug use does *for* them as well as *to* them, the meaning of drug and alcohol use in the context of their own and familial histories, and feelings that emerge as they consider behavioral changes with regard to chemical substances.
Heterogeneous/Integrated Groups Abstinence *or* Mixed Goals	Substance abusers who are treated along with other members who do not have substance abuse issues. Likely the most common model since most therapists, either by design or by unanticipated circumstances, will, at some point, have individuals in their groups with substance abuse issues. Substance abusers may all have abstinence goals, or may be mixed in terms of goals (either *abstinence commitment* or *explicit moderate drinking parameters*).

Overview of Key Issues to be Addressed

Generic issues potentially relevant for any group with one or more substance abusers

1. Specification of an explicit contract regarding drug and alcohol use and how urges and/or actual "use" will be handled clinically.
2. Clarification of group expectations for members who have had histories in other kinds of groups (e.g., A.A, psycho-education).

3. Active outreach by the group leader to provide early intervention when patients miss a group session and may be having a hard time with regard to alcohol and drugs.
4. Clarity regarding the handling of information that comes in from outside the group.

Issues specific to homogenous groups where all members have substance abuse histories

In addition to the four generic issues above, three other issues are important:

5. Group defensive maneuvers that involve the drinking and drugging theme (i.e., talking about alcohol and drug use as a defense against group work).
6. Recovery-related defenses, including tensions among members who are advocates of 12 step programs and those who prefer other supports (and/or may even dislike AA).
7. Challenges to the group leader to disclose information about his own drinking and drug use.

Issues specific to heterogeneous groups where substance abusers are integrated with non-substance abusers

In addition to the first four generic issues, four other issues are important:

8. Group resistance to seeing use as problematic.
9. Group seeing the problem as "too big" or "too different" for the group to handle.
10. Substance abuse problem emerging in an individual with no prior history (thus no pre-group contracting about how problematic use will be handled).
11. Leader resistance to contracting.
12. Challenge of mixed goals (abstinence or moderation) for alcohol abusers.

In the sections that follow I will address each of these 12 issues, and then discuss a treatment adjunct – Moderation Training – that is especially useful in heterogeneous groups, ending the chapter with a discussion of countertransference issues.

Generic Issues Relevant for Any Group with One or More Substance Abusers

The contract regarding alcohol and drug use

An explicit contract is needed regarding drug and alcohol use that specifies the parameters to which each group member has agreed with regard to his use of substances. The contract also makes explicit the expectation that any difficulties encountered in sticking to his parameters (in the form of either urges or actual use) will be discussed with the group and may require the addition of supplemental supports.

Attending to alcohol and drugs problems can be facilitated when group therapists include in their basic ground rules for all group members (regardless of whether there is a known substance abuse problem or not) an agreement that *any changes* that occur with regard to use of either medications or any substances such as alcohol and drugs will be discussed in the group.

It is also important for the group leader to keep in mind that in groups with substance abusers, some "slips" will inevitably occur. It is thus helpful for a therapist to view the recovery process favorably if clients substantially increase the duration of time periods in which they are in compliance with the goals they have set for themselves, and decrease the number and length of lapses from their goals. A slip should not suggest to either the patient or the therapist that all that had been gained has now been lost. In fact, a lapse that is handled properly by the patient (i.e., he solicits help or stops drinking or drug use soon after the onset of the episode and discusses it openly with the group) can be a useful learning experience for the patient as well as for other group members, underscoring the need for continued vigilance and adequate supports for staying on track.

The well-prepared group leader will treat slips seriously but not rigidly. Clarity, fast action, and good clinical judgment are called for. While it is extremely important that the patient come into the group and talk about slips, it is also important that a philosophy be adopted by the group and reinforced by the leader's behavior, that if a slip does occur – in particular, if the slip becomes a slide – that the member must embrace other supports in order to remain in the group. The importance of *sequential contracting* is introduced during the pre-group interviews – underscoring that slips frequently point to gaps in the support system that require shoring up. Thus, to sustain the patient's commitment regarding alcohol and drug use, supports are added progressively as needed, including self-help programs (e.g., AA, NA), psychopharmacological interventions, and/or individual therapy. If these prove insufficient, the added support of a detox, a day or evening program, or a residential rehabilitation program may be needed.

A carefully negotiated contract will offer gradations of increasing support that the patient is actively involved in selecting and can readily endorse (Griefin, Vannicelli, and Canning, 1985; Vannicelli, 1992). The therapist's job is to help the patient work with the group to decide what would be an effective and workable plan, challenging "ready-made" solutions proposed by the patient, such as "90 meetings in 90 days."

As this vignette illustrates, patients should be encouraged to embrace plans that they can realistically manage, rather than more ambitious plans that they may verbally endorse but are unlikely to carry out.

> ### Clinical Illustration
>
> Mary, after 4 months of solid abstinence came into group, tearful about an *in situ* breast malignancy that she had learned about during the week – news that she dealt with by drinking heavily on two nights. The group responded with caring to her understandable fears about both her diagnosis and pending treatment, and also how important it would be for her to be able to "muster" for all that lay ahead. She accepted the group's support and reaffirmed her commitment to abstinence – assuring the group (and herself) that she knew what to do and would go to some AA meetings to help her "shore up." When she came in the next week, filled with remorse at having drunk even more extensively, she stated, "Starting next week, I'll do 90 in 90." To this the leader asked, "Is that realistic for you? Given the many other things that you have on your plate right now, will you be able to do that? Perhaps it would be better to start with a more modest plan that you can count on doing." With the group's help Mary decided that she would go to at least three meetings every week and also get back on antabuse – which she had successfully used during her first month of abstinence.

Good judgment on the group leader's part is also needed in terms of a decision about whether a patient can participate in the group the same day in which substance use has occurred. Clearly the group is not effective either for the member himself or for the group as a whole if a member attends who is visibly under the influence of alcohol or drugs. However, the precise definition of "under the influence" is not an easy one, and there is a lot of territory between an obviously high or intoxicated patient whose behavior is not appropriate for the group (discussed in the next section) and a member who, a few hours earlier, had a relatively contained slip (perhaps one beer). Rather than having a rigid rule that members cannot participate if they abuse any chemical substances within 24 hours of the group (a rule that is common in homogeneous groups, and often leads to withholding information about slips), it is preferable to have a rule that clearly states that patients must be in appropriate condition to participate in order to be in the group. This allows the therapist to make a clinical judgment on a case-by-case basis as to whether or not a patient who has slipped may benefit from being in the group that night.

> ### Clinical Illustration
>
> Andy called the group leader, Dr Jones, a few hours before the group saying that he "got really scared" earlier in the day after he took a single Percodan from an old bottle that had just resurfaced, moments later throwing the rest down the toilet. He added that although he was a little high, he felt he needed the group that night and had asked his wife to drive him if the Dr Jones agreed

> that he could attend. Dr Jones decided that Andy sounded capable of appropriate participation and could really benefit from being in the group that night to discuss, in a timely way, the situation and emotional triggers that got him so close to being in trouble again, and the tools he used to stop himself before things got more out of hand. Andy came to the group, recommitted to abstinence, and relieved to have group support to stop his slip from becoming a slide.

So far we have been discussing appropriately handled slips. However, there is a lot of ground between an appropriately handled slip and other kinds of substance abuse that occur within the context of group psychotherapy. Four of the most common drinking and drugging landmarks (Vannicelli, 1982, 1992), from least to most common, are:

a. The patient who comes to group visibly under the influence of alcohol or drugs;
b. The patient who is drinking or using drugs between sessions but refusing to acknowledge it;
c. The patient who is using drugs or drinking outside his specified parameters and is willing to talk about it, but has no intention of stopping;
d. The patient who continues to use drugs or to drink outside his agreed upon parameters – simultaneously giving verbal endorsement of his commitment, while his behavior contradicts it.

Coming to the group under the influence: The patient who comes to the group high or intoxicated makes it difficult for the group to proceed. If it is immediately obvious upon arrival to the group that a member is too impaired to participate, the leader should ask the member to leave and return to the group in a condition appropriate for participation the following week. Provision must also be made for assuring the patient's safety if he is not in a condition to get himself safely home. Checking with the patient prior to the next group session is also generally indicated – at least by telephone and preferably in a face-to-face meeting with the leaders.

The patient whose impairment is not immediately apparent but becomes so during the group presents greater challenges. He should be told that his specific alcohol- or drug-related behaviors (e.g., talking while others are talking, inability to keep up with what is going on in the group) indicate that he is not able to participate reasonably that evening. Ideally, in such an instance the patient would simply leave and let the group continue, but patients who are under the influence are rarely so accommodating. Thus, it is often helpful for the leader to couple her observation that the patient is having difficulty participating with the suggestion that he go out and get some fresh air and return only when he feels that he can participate appropriately. Because this is somewhat less rejecting than simply asking a patient to leave, it is less likely to evoke a struggle and compliance is more likely – an especially important consideration once the session has already begun.

Whether or not the patient returns that evening, the other members should be encouraged to share their feelings about what has transpired – including possible anger from some members who may see the leader's invitation to the patient to leave as punitive or rejecting. When the patient does return, group members should also be encouraged to share their concerns with him and also to engage with him around embracing more supports.

Using alcohol or drugs but refusing to acknowledge it: At times, it may become known that a group member is having trouble with alcohol and drugs but is not talking about it in the group. For example, the group leader may obtain information from a patient's individual therapist or spouse. Ideally, the group leader would be able to use this information to help the patient disclose the substance abuse "on her own" – facilitated by a general comment to the patient, such as, "I understand, Sandy, that you have been having a rather tough time for the past few weeks." If the patient acknowledges this, she should be encouraged to talk more about it. However, if she does not mention or denies any problems with alcohol or drugs, the therapist should share the information he has received. (Saying, for example, "Your husband called in today, concerned about the shape you were in when you left the house this morning." Or, "Your therapist let me know that you came to your last session noticeably high.") If denial continues, the patient should be asked how she understands the discrepancy between the outside information and her own report.

It may be that the patient does not trust the group enough to talk about her substance use. This can be addressed by saying, "It must be hard for you to find yourself in a group in which you don't feel safe enough to talk about what's really going on." (This may also provide an opportunity for the group as a whole to explore feelings of safety in the group and each member's sense of what she feels she can and cannot share.)

In any case, the patient must be reminded of her contract with regard to substance use that includes talking about slips if they occur, as well as adding supports to get back on track. If the substance abuse continues and still is not discussed, the group leader will need to let the patient know (preferably in the group) that there is an untenable impasse that has to be resolved in order for her to remain in the group.

A related situation arises when a patient comes in showing very slight signs of intoxication (a faint odor, mildly tangential, or slightly pressured speech) who denies that he has been using substances. To this individual, it might be appropriate to say something like, "Bill, you don't seem quite yourself tonight, and there is a faint smell of alcohol in the room. I am concerned that you may be drinking." If Bill denies drinking, the leader might add, "I have a hunch that it's been hard for you to acknowledge your use of alcohol because you care a lot about what people in here think of you and don't want to disappoint them." This empathic response communicates to the patient that his not leveling with the group is not because he is a bad person trying to put one over on the group but, rather, that he is worried about what people will think of him. Patients are sometimes willing to assent to this kind of empathic comment even when direct questions about drinking or drug use continue to be refuted. Group discussion would then focus on what needs to happen next in order to get Bill back on track – additional supports that need to be added, a timeframe for the resumption of abstinence, and possibly some way of establishing a safer forum so that Bill will be able to talk about the drinking if it does happen again.

At times such as this, the possibility of alcohol screens may also be helpful as in the following case (Vannicelli, 1992).

> **Clinical Illustration**
>
> Over a three month period, Mr Stone intermittently appeared at group with bloodshot eyes and emotionally somewhat labile. One co-leader or the other frequently believed that he was under the influence of Valium, but they rarely agreed about this on any given night. It was difficult for them to confront him given their lack of clarity. Occasionally one or the other would ask him if the problems he was having had anything to do with use of drugs but this question was always met with denial. Finally, they brought this to their supervisor and the three of them collectively decided that the uncertainty about his status (as well as their intermittent concerns that he might not be leveling with the group) was jeopardizing the effectiveness of his treatment and needed to be more directly addressed in the group.
>
> The following week they said, "Mr Stone, for several months now we have wondered off and on whether you might be back on Valium and last week we both had that concern again. We think it's bad for our relationship with you to be worried about this – and must also be troublesome for you to have your therapists wondering and doubting. We would like to find a way to resolve this so that doubt and worry will not stand in the way of work that needs to be done in here. One possible solution if you come into group again in a condition that raises concern is that you agree to have a urine screen." He agreed, though no screens were ever needed. The impact of this clear intervention was that the next week he checked himself into a 30-day program. When he returned to the group, he acknowledged that the group leaders had been right all along and he thanked them for confronting the issue.

Regardless of whether or not screens are suggested, it is essential that the group leader tackles the problem by:

a. Empathic joining with the patient that expresses understanding of what might make it hard for him to acknowledge his substance use;
b. Making the impasse explicit – namely, that it is important to both the patient and leader(s) to feel that they are in a credible relationship and that this is difficult when doubts continue;
c. Problem-solving to get past the impasse.

Using and talking about it with no apparent desire to change course: The patient who returns to group week after week talking about his continued drinking/drugging incidents, while showing no apparent investment in modifying his behavior, provocatively flaunting the group contract regarding the importance of actively addressing substance abuse issues. He and other group members should be asked to discuss their feelings about his participation in the group when his behavior so clearly contradicts the central premise that dealing with one's substance abuse is part and parcel of what it means to be effectively working in the group. It may be useful to help the patient see that some part of him wants help making changes in his life (the likely motive for his continued attendance), and that the struggle that is now being played out between him and the group (his behavior being in conflict with group expectations) may well be an externalization of his own conflict.

However, it is also important that the patient (and other group members) understand that keeping this struggle alive indefinitely is not productive for either the patient or the rest of the group, and that his ability to remain in the group is contingent on his re-establishing a contract that is consistent with the initial parameters to which he agreed when he joined. A lively example of this occurred in one of the first groups that I supervised (Vannicelli, Canning, and Griefen, 1984).

> Mr Binds drank frequently, while rebuffing the group's effort to intervene by presenting a sophisticated explanation of his difficulties with authority and control. His aversion to control, expressed as a threat to leave the group if coerced into a contract, was a powerful deterrent to a "nice" group, highly concerned about driving others away. However, as group members began talking about their own fears regarding confrontation, they ultimately made progress. They lucidly presented to Mr Binds the dilemma that he was posing: he desired their support while actively opposing any of their suggestions about plans for containment (meetings, a sponsor, antabuse, etc). Members expressed understanding of his difficulty acceding to imposed limits and suggested, instead, that he develop his own contract that would be shared in group. The group thus successfully sidestepped an immobilizing struggle with Mr Binds. While affirming the necessity of limits, members allowed him to negotiate a viable, self-designed agreement with the group. The work done around this issue was not only effective in bringing Mr Binds' drinking under control but equally important, helped to elucidate the self-destructive control struggles that he frequently found himself in with others, and the frustrations he experienced, especially when he had to thwart his own purposes to avoid feeling controlled.

Continued use while verbally endorsing the importance of tackling the problem: The patient who continues to use or who frequently slips while at the same time endorsing "the importance of dealing with my problem" can pose even more difficulty for other group members than the patient who is outwardly struggling with the group. The verbal endorser frustrates the group in a more subtle way by continuing to fail. However, since she is at least verbally on board, it is easier for the group to set up contingency contracts with her.

The therapist may say, "It's clear, Mary, that you feel it is important to address your substance abuse issue. Since what you have been doing so far has not been working adequately, it is important that we find more effective ways to help you make headway." Mary and the group should then be asked to set up specific requirements that she will have to follow (e.g., taking naltrexone, going to four NA meetings per week), in order to maintain her group membership.

In concluding this discussion of various deviations from the contract, it is important to underscore the following. First, it is essential that the lapsing member is utimately engaged with the group and the leaders in making tangible headway. This means that the group leader must assume responsibility for setting limits (or, ideally, getting the group to do so). Second, when using direct confrontation, it is important to remain mindful of the intended purpose. The goal is to help the patient, and the group looks squarely at what is going on with the aim of providing clarity and understanding, as well as support for behavioral changes that may be needed.

However, the leader should not lose sight of the fact that the group will grow from an opportunity to explore each member's feelings about the deviating member's behavior, the leader's and group's reactions to it, and the member's departure if he cannot ultimately commit to getting back on track. In addition to feelings of concern and/or anger at the member who has slipped, members may also feel concerned about themselves and the security of their own sobriety. Doubts may also emerge about the skills of the leader and the value of the group.

Clarification of group expectations for members with histories in other kinds of groups

In pre-group interviews, as patients are prepared for their membership in the group, it is important that all of the ground rules are clearly spelled out (preferably in a written handout, as well as discussion) to include not only each member's specific contract regarding alcohol and drug use, but also the basic ground rules that provide the "frame" for any psychodynamically oriented group. Patients are told that a unique feature of this kind of therapy group is that it provides a mirror of other important groups to which people belong. Thus, as basic patterns of behaviors with both individuals and groups are replicated, these patterns can be understood and new ways of relating can be tried out. The importance of inter-member participation is emphasized, as well as the therapist's role in facilitating this.

Ground rules, in addition to members advising the group of any changes in their use of alcohol and drugs and/or medications, include expectations (Vannicelli, 1992) of regular and timely attendance (notifying the group if unable to attend or likely to be late), payment for all sessions whether in attendance or not, and several weeks' advance notice prior to terminating. The importance of confidentiality is emphasized and operationalized by the expectation that members will not discuss what happens in group in any way that might disclose the identity of another member. Group members are also told that they will be expected to talk about issues that interfere with making intimate connections or living life fully, as well as processing what is going on in the group itself as a way of better understanding their own interpersonal dynamics. Finally, in order to maximize the energy available for the work of the group, patients are encouraged to keep outside-of-group contact to a minimum and to discuss with the group any contact that does occur.

Self-help group versus group therapy: Because past experiences in self-help groups and more didactic psycho-education groups are likely to strongly influence new member's expectations about group psychotherapy, it is important to clarify the ways in which the expectations of members in a therapy group are different. Thus, after ascertaining that a patient is familiar with one of the self-help programs, I might say, "Good. Many folks in recovery find that AA can be a very helpful support, along with group therapy. But there are also some differences between what happens at an AA meeting and in a therapy group that will be highlighted as we review together the written group ground rules. In a therapy group, you are expected to attend every week and on time; continuity of the therapeutic work is very much affected by members being able to count on one another to be regularly present. In addition, unlike AA, in the therapy group it would matter a great deal to other members if somebody left prior to the end of the session. As you can see, the boundaries are much tighter in a therapy group than in AA and there is a lot more accountability."

Other differences between a therapy group and a self-help group should also be clarified. These include the expectations that outside-of-group contact is to be brought back into the group and that what goes on in the group **itself** will be talked about (i.e., exploration of the group process itself). The latter is especially important to attend to given that most of the exchanges in large, open AA meetings occur between the "leader" (i.e., the speaker) and individual members (i.e., serial dyadic interaction). "Cross talk", the "meat and potatoes" in a therapy group, is explicitly discouraged.

Finally, the importance in a therapy group of attending to feelings and learning to communicate them more clearly should be underscored, as well as attending to both the past and the present, with the goal of better integrating and understanding one's feelings and experiences. Though patients may at times feel that there is conflict between AA and group therapy since the expectations are so different, the therapist should be clear in his own mind that the two provide support in distinct but complementary ways that are not in any way mutually exclusive.

Education and structured task groups versus group therapy: Many substance abusers may also have had prior experience in more structured groups, for example, groups with role plays and substance abuse education groups, which also have ground rules that differ from those of a therapy group. It is thus helpful in the pre-group interview to prepare new members by saying, "Although you will learn a great deal in this group, the purpose of a therapy group is not so much to provide specific information, but rather, to explore feelings and situations that you find difficult and to help you better understand where you fit in with the difficulties that you experience."

It may also be useful, if the new member's past group experiences have included role plays, to let him know that that kind of structuring will be less prominent in the group he is now joining. However, like any agreements and clarifications that are made in the pre-group interview, at times of stress in the group such agreements will be challenged. This is illustrated in the following example from an early group that I supervised (Vannicelli, 1992).

> Several months into a new psychodynamically oriented group, a member suggested (with the support of several others) that the leader provide "more structure" by doing role plays. This request for structure came following several sessions in which members had become more intensely involved with one another and was a way (unconsciously) of controlling the intensity of the emotional life of the group and providing a sense of greater safety. The leader responded by asking, "How would it help to have role plays in here? What more would you hope we could accomplish?" To each response the group made, she further explored, "What do you suppose gets in the way of our doing this in the format we now have?" Ultimately, she asked, "Do you suppose there could be a connection between what has been going on in the group the last few weeks, particularly the fact that members have been more direct with one another and sharing more personal material, and the group's request for a change that would structure things more?" As the group processed these questions, members came to understand that their request for more structure was a way of slowing things down and that even the discussion about it served as a temporary detour.

Need for active outreach

The patient who misses a meeting without advance notice to the group, or who leaves a message that he will not be able to make it, accompanied by an explanation that seems flimsy or ambiguous, needs prompt attention from the group leader. These may be warnings that the patient is in trouble, and may sometimes even be a cry for help. Given these possibilities, it is generally useful for the therapist to make contact as soon as possible – before the group session if the patient leaves a message that suggests that with a bit of prompting he might make it in, or immediately after the group session if the patient gives no advance warning.

Though this outreach has definite advantages in terms of early intervention with patients who may have relapsed, it also has certain disadvantages. In particular, repetitive reaching out and following-up, especially if the therapist communicates disappointment or irritation, runs the risk of infantilizing the patient and/or setting the leader up to be perceived by the patient as a punitive "parental" figure. To avoid this, it is helpful for outreach calls to focus specifically on what is getting in the way of his attendance and what he may be communicating by his absence.

Communications to leaders from outside the group

Ground rules about information exchange and what is and is not confidential need to be made explicit as part of the initial treatment contract, given that such exchanges can be complicated in groups with substance abusers. For example, in multifaceted treatment programs a patient may have several treatment providers and he needs to be told explicitly what kind of information will be exchanged between them. It may be simply, "We feel that it is important that the entire treatment team knows what is going on that may be relevant to your problems with substance use. Thus, any information that is clinically relevant will be made available, as we feel appropriate, to other therapists in this program."

Equally as important as communications among treatment providers (and often considerably stickier) are communications that come from other sources outside the group (for example, a concerned call from a spouse about her husband's drinking). Two policies are useful for the handling such information. First, that any information received will be handled in a manner in which the therapist feels is clinically appropriate. She should thus make no promises to family members that what they tell will not be shared. The second policy is to view outside information as further input – possibly useful, but not necessarily more valid or reliable than information supplied by the patient. (Significant others can also be wrong.) Thus, when the therapist presents such information to a patient, it should be presented as data to explore. For example, the therapist might say, "Your wife called me worried that you might be using again. Do you know anything more about her concerns?" Any discrepancies between what the patient shares and the information that the group leader has received should be pointed out, and the patient should be asked what he makes of the discrepancy. The involvement of other group members in the discussion and their attempts to understand what has gone on can also be very helpful in cutting through the patient's denial.

Issues Specific to Homogenous Groups where All Members have Substance Abuse Histories

Talking about substance use as a defense against group work

In the early stages of group therapy with substance abusers, discussions about alcohol and drugs commonly predominate, including reminiscences about the "good old days" when using was still fun and "war stories" about how bad things finally got, as well as concerns about current wishes to use. A sense of cohesiveness is established by focusing on substance abuse – the one thing known to be held in common. In addition, although group members have picked a relatively safe way of beginning, the discussion *is* relevant to one of the stated group goals.

At times, however, a group may persist in a narrow substance abuse focus long beyond the first few weeks, or may later relapse to this limited form of group interaction. The group leader, faced with this, is likely to feel baffled – the group seems to feel stuck and a bit dull, yet on the surface it appears to be on track. (After all, what could be more legitimate than sharing alcohol and drug-related experiences in a treatment group for substance abusers?) It is the apparent legitimacy of this kind of discussion that makes it such a beguiling group defense against exploring deeper issues and achieving greater intimacy.

The leader's job is to help the group understand what is happening. For example, following the second session in which a patient further details her "drunkalogue" (with encouragement from others in the group), the leader might comment, "I am puzzled at the amount of time the group has spent attending to details regarding

Pauline's past drinking. I wonder if talking about it at such length may serve a function for the group."

Another common example of defensive talk about using that temporarily stalls the group is illustrated by the following:

> In a therapy group for substance abusers, members were caught up in an intense here-and-now focus in which two members were struggling to express their anger and competitive feelings towards one another. A third member interrupted to say, "I really don't see how Bob and Amy's feelings about one another have anything to do with the work that we are supposed to be doing here. I thought we came to group to understand the role of alcohol and drugs in our lives." This comment was heralded by a chorus of support by other group members – a protest mounted as a defense against the painful feelings that were alive in the group and reflecting a wish to return to safer territory.

It should also be noted that while talking about drinking and drugging may be a way for the group to protect itself, such discussions may serve a very different purpose for the group member who feels particularly unworthy. For this individual, talking about drugs or alcohol may seem to be the only "legitimate" way to get a share of the group's time. When this seems to be the case, it is important for the leader to encourage and support this member's fuller participation.

Recovery-related defenses

The program proselytizer: A member who has had success with "the program" (AA, NA) may be disquieted about the presence of others in the group who "don't get it." A considerable amount of his time and energy may be spent proselytizing about "the necessity of regular attendance at 12 step meetings and the impossibility of recovering without it" – even registering concerns about his own participation in a group where other members are not sufficiently attached to the program. For such individuals, their own sense of precariousness about maintaining abstinence can create tremendous anxiety about the possibility of anyone else deviating from a program that they have successfully embraced. When a patient raises such concerns, it may be useful for the leader to underscore what a critical support AA has clearly been for him while at the same time stating, "There may be more than one way to skin a cat, and other members may find different supports beneficial."

The group leader should also be aware that a continued struggle around this issue may serve a function for the individual involved, as well as for the group as a whole. As the group becomes polarized, group process becomes stalemated and intimacy is lowered. In one group, a particularly graphic example of this occurred (Vannicelli, 1992).

> All group members had been totally abstinent for many months. Two had recently graduated who were staunch AA members, leaving behind Bill, the only other staunch supporter, with four others – two members of whom attended AA occasionally but were not particularly avid program supporters, and two who did not use AA at all. The week after the second graduate departed, Bill called me in a rage. He insisted that I find him a new group where AA would be supported, since, as far as he was concerned, "failing to attend AA regularly was tantamount to having a slip." While initially he created a polarized situation in the group – members trying to convince him that his position was absurd (while he fought valiantly for the other side) – group members ultimately pointed out to him, "You're afraid of being in here and getting close to us." With the help of the leaders, it became clear that Bill was frightened of remaining in a group in which a higher level of intimacy might be achieved. After several weeks of processing the struggle, as well as the entire group's involvement in keeping the defensive stalemate going, the group was able to effectively move on, with Bill's continued participation.

The program sloganizer: For other members, resistance to full engagement may take the form of overly concrete and literal acceptance of AA's dictums. For example, slogan resistance may first be apparent when a leader asks, during the second week of a new group, what thoughts members may have had about the previous session, and a member responds, "I just think about what is happening for today. I don't think about the past, and I don't project into the future." This individual, in a sense, is a good student who has learned her lessons well – even if she has taken them too literally. A useful response from the leader might be, "It's clear that you have learned a lot in AA that's been really helpful for you and also about the ground rules for successful participation in the program. Though some of the ground rules in here are a little bit different, I think you will find that they operate in a complementary fashion." It is important that the leader underscores not only in the pre-group interview, but also whenever indicated throughout the life of the group, that in group therapy it can be extremely useful to revisit the past in order to understand how old patterns get repeated in the present – often an important step in being able to modify current behavior.

"Program talk" can also be used in other ways as a defense against exploring issues in greater depth. Thus, at times of stress in the group, members may limit exploration with comments such as, "That's typical alcoholic thinking," or, "That's what addicts do." Such assumptions about "sameness" can create a "you know how it is" mentality in the group, aborting exploration of "the obvious," thus preventing the group from moving from one stage of group life to the next. It is important that leaders challenge these kinds of statements, helping the group to understand that assumptions of sameness represent attempts to temporarily close the door on painful issues, providing a simple surface explanation without really addressing what is going on. To statements like, "That's typical alcoholic behavior," the leader should explore further, inquiring what specifically was going on for the individual involved and also pulling for additional kinds of feelings or reactions that others in the group might have. This furthers differentiation, rather than supporting the defense of "sameness."

Pressures on leaders to disclose their own histories with alcohol and drugs

Often group leaders – even those who generally disclose relatively little about themselves – feel pressured by members' queries about the leader's use of alcohol and drugs. Pressures for this kind of self-disclosure are particularly common with substance abusers (and may feel "legitimate" to both the client and the therapist) because of the prevalence of the 12 step culture in the United States which promotes the idea that help for one's problems comes from others who have the same problem (the sponsor as well as others in the 12 step program). While it may seem "natural" that a patient may be curious about this, the well-prepared group leader will understand that requests for this information, like any other request for personal information about him, is rarely just a matter of curiosity. The request has meaning that can be usefully explored. Like many such requests – "Do you have kids?" "Are they in trouble?" "Are you married?" – the client is asking for reassurance that you will understand her issues and will be able to help. Thus, despite the aura of legitimacy about these questions, the group therapist's policy about handling them should be no different than his policy about other questions regarding his personal life. A useful response to this kind of question might be, "I have a hunch that at this point you have lots of questions about me, but above all, are wondering whether you'll be able to get the kind of help here that you need." Some group leaders may feel that, in addition to exploring the meaning of the request for information or framing a possible interpretation (as in the "hunch" above), a direct answer should also be given. This decision should be guided by, and consistent with, their views and general behavior regarding self-disclosure.

Issues Specific to Heterogeneous (Integrated) Groups

While there are advantages to homogeneous groups, particularly in terms of the cohesion created by belonging to a group where all members have struggled with substance abuse, heterogeneous groups also offer some unique advantages for the substance abuser, the non-substance abuser, and the therapist. For the substance abuser, treatment within the context of an integrated group provides an opportunity to understand and address his problems within a more general framework of over-learned (often maladaptive) strategies for coping – and in so doing to realize that in many ways his problems are not so different from the problems of those who do not abuse substances. The non-substance abusing group member, on the other hand, gains from the opportunity to actively contract with members who have alcohol and drug problems, modeling the kinds of commitments that group members can make to one another when non-substance-related problems arise that call for new behavioral strategies. In addition, integrated groups are advantageous to the leader in terms of allowing for more flexibility in filling a group with members who will work well together. Moreover, the reality of life in groups is such that substance abuse issues can surface at any time, even if one had not intended to be working with substance abusers – creating, by default, an integrated group.

However, despite the advantages of heterogeneous/integrated groups, management of substance abuse issues in these groups is more complicated than in homogeneous groups. Though the issues themselves will be dealt with similarly, the group leader has to work harder to mobilize the group for appropriate engagement around drinking and drugging behavior, and also has to deal with several kinds of resistance – his own, as well as the group's.

Group resistance to seeing substance use as problematic

In integrated groups there will often be some non-substance abusers who do not understand addiction, proclaiming, "I don't see why occasionally drinking too much is such a big deal." Or, "I use a little pot myself from time to time and don't understand why John's use is getting so much attention." When such protests arise, the therapist needs to actively engage the group in exploring the issue, asking, for example, "Do you think it might be different for John to be 'dabbling,' than it is for you to do so, given the serious problems he has had in the past with cocaine and weed, and his own sense that using undermines his ability to grow in the ways he is hoping for?" Members may also have difficulty understanding, initially, some of the subtle differences between the leader's usual stance in the group and his stance when addressing substance abuse issues. Negative reactions are especially likely in response to his directness in labeling a problem or putting data on the line when a patient's substance use needs to be actively addressed (as exemplified in the two clinical examples that follow, describing group member reactions to leader interventions with Jill and Sheila).

Seeing the problem as "too big" or "too different" for this group to handle

While minimization of alcohol and drug issues in a heterogeneous group is common, so is its opposite – the concern that the issue is "too much for a group like this to handle." Protests from fellow group members may include statements such as, "I've never had to deal with anything like this." In addition, whereas in the homogeneous group there may be a pull towards maximizing the sense of "sameness" among members (e.g., by talking about "our disease" and "the way alcoholics and druggies are"), in heterogeneous groups the opposite may be occur. Namely, those who do not abuse substances find ways to distance and differentiate themselves from those who do – seeing it as a problem unlike any they have known.

The sense of being out of control and overwhelmed that is experienced by the lapsing substance abuser, as well as his sense of hopelessness and despair, can also be experienced by other members of the group, adding further to their wish to take distance. When this occurs, it is the leader's job to help group members understand that the uncomfortable feelings alive in the room are all too familiar to the lapsing member, and that he is in the right place. With the help of the group, he has an opportunity to get "back on track" and regain control.

The challenge of a substance abuse problem emerging after entry into the group

At times, a member's drinking or drug problem comes to light only after her entry into the group. This poses special challenges for the leader, regardless of whether he intended to be running an integrated group (i.e., having some members with known substance abuse issues) or had intended to have a group in which he would not be dealing with substance abuse issues at all. If a member develops an alcohol or drug problem after joining the group, the leader must deal with it without the advantage of the extensive pre-group preparation and upfront contracting that would have occurred had the leader known at the outset of a substance abuse problem. On the other hand, a preliminary contract specifying for all clients that "any changes with regard to substances (prescribed or non-prescribed) need to be brought into the group," provides some leverage – conveying that one's use of substances is relevant to an individual's overall well-being and emotional growth, and is thus relevant for the group to address.

The challenge of "contracting"

For many psychodynamically oriented therapists, particularly those leading heterogeneous groups, the idea of contracting with individuals in the group around management of substances (or any issue) may be quite foreign – seemingly inconsistent with the model in which they generally work. However, contracting can be smoothly incorporated as part of the group process when the contract is negotiated with sensitivity to the lapsing member's alliance with both the group and the leader.[1]

When it becomes apparent that an individual is having a substance abuse problem, there are several important steps to attend to:

a. Naming it – that is, calling it a "drinking problem" or a "drug problem";
b. Discussing whether it would be useful to make a contract with the group about how to manage the drinking or drug use;
c. Adding external supports that may help the wavering member move forward – for example, attendance at self-help meetings (AA, NA, Smart Recovery, Moderation Management), a psychopharmacology consult to evaluate for medications to help with cravings and/or to deal with anxiety or depression that may be related to the alcohol and drug use, or, in groups with mixed goals in which moderation may be an option, enlisting the support of an individual therapist to do Moderation Training.

The following clinical example illustrates aspects of this process, as well as the richness of the group dynamics.

---

[1] It should be noted that when I bring substance abusers into a mixed group, they enter with the same contract that I use in homogeneous substance abuse groups – namely, a stated commitment to continuing to work toward each individual's stated goals with regard to alcohol and drugs. The contract includes talking about urges, temptations, and near slips; and if actual slips occur, a commitment to contracting with the group for resumption of added supports (Vannicelli, 1982: pp. 88–89). Patients understand that although the focus of the group is not substance abuse *per se*, any issues around their use or feared use are relevant to their work in the group.

In a seven member group, four members have substance abuse problems: Gina, an ardent devotee of AA, has been stably abstinent for three and a half years; Karla, with the help of a sponsor and sporadic attendance at AA, has been in the group and solidly abstinent for more than two years; Brian, the newest member, eight months into his group tenure is struggling to maintain abstinence; and Jill, who has just begun to recognize that her drinking is causing serious problems.

Jill entered the group three years earlier for depression and suicidal ideation following the end of a relationship. With the aid of Prozac, her depression has considerably attenuated. However, she has gained considerable weight and is feeling increasingly out of control with both her eating and her use of alcohol – in recent months drinking to excess once every few weeks (5–7 drinks while socializing with friends or on weekend visits with her family). On such occasions she wakes up the next morning feeling sick, having difficulty remembering what transpired the night before, with regrets about "having over done it."

The "invisible" middle daughter, she suffers from a long-standing sense of being "less important" to her parents and siblings than they are to her and of "not quite fitting in." Her frequent visits home generally add more fuel to the fire – increasing further her need/desire to be with them, and her disappointment about "not being seen." After a particularly demoralizing weekend, she comes to the group with a clearly articulated wish that her parents would be more interested in her and would want to know her better. The group leader asks, "Do your folks know about your depression?" She responds, "I don't know, they never ask me anything about it." The leader follows by asking, "What do your folks know about your problem with alcohol?" At this point, another member asks, "Has it ever been called that before – I mean, labeled as a 'problem with alcohol'?" She is joined by others, especially the three without histories of substance abuse, who challenge the leader about the usefulness of her characterization. Jill, herself, is taken aback by the pronouncement of "an alcohol problem."

The next week Jill shares how shocked she was by the leader's words and also the enormous impact they had on her – adding, "Dr V is right. I do have an alcohol problem and I want to do something about it." When asked if it would be helpful to make a contract with the group, she indicates that she is still not sure what she wants to do, but is determined to think more about how to make her intentions more concrete. While the group members are generally supportive, Gina makes a lengthy and zealous pitch for AA.

The following week begins with a comment from Karla about Gina's "over the top" proselytizing for AA the week before, and Karla's continued difficulty with aspects of AA ideology, which she insists "is definitely not everyone's cup of tea." Jill agrees that AA doesn't feel like it would be useful to her at this point, but indicates that she has decided, for now at least, to stop drinking altogether. She has also decided, at her psychopharmacologist's suggestion, to take naltrexone to help with possible urges that may arise. As she put it, "I don't want to ever again throw up, and wake up not having remembered something."

When Brian walks in a few minutes later reeking of alcohol, the leader decides that a prompt intervention would be useful. She briefly summarizes the discussion about alcohol problems and how various members have chosen to deal with them, and then adds, "You have come in a very different condition tonight than usual. How long has it been since your last drink?" He responds, "Two weeks ago." Dr V says, "No, how long ago *today*?" To this he says, "I haven't drunk today. Why do you ask?" She replies, "There is a distinct odor of alcohol in the room. I wonder if you feel it would be possible for you to let the group know if you were drinking." He says, "Yes, I would. But I have been working in the lab all day and what you are smelling is the lab preparations that I used."

Other group members look dismayed, express concern for him, and concern about the strong statement that Dr V has made. She says, "It must be hard for you, Brian, to have me doubting." And he responds, "Well, the truth is half in what I said and half in what Dr V said. I do smell of lab fumes, and I also had a couple of drinks today." Within minutes he is tearful and apologetic to the group about having lied to them.

This is a major turning point in Brian's work – the first time he has acknowledged his drinking in close proximity to a drinking event. (Routinely, his wife points out when she picks him up from work that she knows that he has been drinking, which he consistently denies). Although he is embarrassed at having lied, group members are quick to point out that covering up is something they have all done, including the non-drinkers. They have all misrepresented things, fooled themselves, and tried to fool others when they were in pain or when they felt shame. Members go on to share experiences where their own behavior mirrored his – providing enormous support and acceptance for him.

The next week Brian returns to the group feeling relieved and appreciative, but still drinking almost daily at work. With the help of the leaders and the group, he agrees to go into a detox at a local hospital, followed by step-down day and evening treatment, while residing on the hospital grounds in a three-quarter way house. He continues to attend the group (on "pass") during the next six weeks of step-down care, also using antabuse and AA with some regularity. He is abstinent, but feeling deprived and very much aware of having given up something that was important to him.

Jill, during this period, has done well with abstinence, recounting nearly a month and a half of continuous success in situations in which she had drunk to excess in the past. She is pleased with how this has made her feel about herself – not only an increased sense of being in control of her life, but also an increased sense of self respect. As she formulates her progress in this way, Brian realizes that instead of giving something up, which is how he has been experiencing his own period of abstinence, he can now think of it as "doing something positive for himself and getting something back by working on self respect."

The next example (Vannicelli, 2001a) illustrates, in addition to the importance of directly addressing the problem and contracting for increased supports, the importance in an integrated group of underscoring the substance abuse contract, both in the pre-group interview and throughout the life of the group. It also illustrates the discomfort that group members may experience when they see the leader intervening with uncharacteristic vigor around a substance abuse issue that she feels requires immediate intervention.

> Sheila was an engaging 50-year-old woman who had made strong attachments to several members of the group. One night as she entered the group and walked by me I had a vague sense that I smelled alcohol. I decided to wait to intervene until I had a little more data – hoping that I might be able to muster support from the noses of other group members. She talked at the outset about conflict with her husband and about feeling extremely low. Fifteen minutes later, when her eyes began to droop, I addressed her, saying, "I wonder, Sheila, how some of the difficulties you've been describing might relate to drinking." She said, "I haven't been drinking." I responded, "I have a hunch that it is difficult right now for you to let the group know the full extent of the difficulties you have been having around alcohol use, given how much you care about people in here and how badly you'd feel about disappointing them." To this, Sheila nodded in assent, and I added, "It's important that we put some supports in place to help you get back on track; perhaps the group could help you to work out some kind of a contract." (My empathic confrontation to Sheila put the situation clearly on the table so that the group and she could begin to actively grapple with it.)
>
> Another group member, at that point commented, "Dr V seems to think Sheila has been drinking, even though Sheila says she hasn't." In response, another member added, "I wasn't going say anything but I thought I smelled alcohol when Sheila walked in, and sitting next to her I've had a sense of it off and on for the past 15 minutes. It's also unlike her to 'nod off' in here."
>
> The next week, when Sheila called in sick, members worried that my confrontation of her had been too direct. One member contrasted my behavior with Sheila to my general way of behaving in the group. As he put it, "It seems to me that in here, we are usually allowed to work on our issues at our own pace. If we don't want to do something about a problematic behavior – at least not right away – that's our choice. I think it would have been better if Sheila had been given the same option." Another member of the group, a pot abuser several years into recovery, indicated that she felt that it was different with substance abuse – stating, "Early intervention can prevent a slip from becoming a major slide. I can't imagine being as passive when we know that somebody had slipped as we might be with other issues in the group."
>
> I asked the group, at that point, whether members remembered that Sheila had come into the group with a specific contract about her drinking, in which there was a clear expectation that this issue was not to go underground and

was to be dealt with immediately whenever there were difficulties – feared or actual. Though few had remembered, all agreed that that shed useful light on my behavior with her.

The next week Sheila returned to the group and talked about the AA meetings that she had returned to, her reconnection with her sponsor, and her great relief that the group had "helped her to get back on track."

The challenge of mixed goals for alcohol abusers

In the two previous examples, all members of the integrated group with prior histories of substance abuse joined the group with commitments to abstinence. When one adds the possibility of mixed goals for managing the alcohol abuse[2] – either abstinence or moderation – there are additional factors for the leader to consider. In particular, tension may arise among members who are dealing in different ways with their problems – with those who are committed to abstinence potentially experiencing longings to be able to moderate and/or envy of others who are doing so. These complicated feelings can give rise to condescending interpretations about "how the moderator is fooling himself and will learn soon enough that moderating is just another way to avoid dealing with the problem." These can be challenging discussions, but when handled well they provide grist for the mill, as the abstainer's longings are uncovered, as well as resentments against those who do not have to give up alcohol altogether. This is illustrated in the following case example.

The unexpected death of Larry's slightly older brother to complications related to alcohol raised concerns about "the long-term wear and tear" of his own 15 years of near nightly drinking (5–7 beers). Years before, he had briefly tried a therapy group where members were dealing with alcohol problems but, though he found the interpersonal aspect of the group useful, he had been "turned off" by the "hard-line" abstinence orientation of the leader. Determined that he would like to continue drinking but at a safer level, he wanted to join a group that would provide support for moderation. He understood that such a group might be possible, but only once he had successfully completed a course of Moderation Training and was able to stably commit to a specified set of drinking parameters. He embarked on 30 days of abstinence while building a repertoire of alternative activities for the evening drinking hours, and deciding on drinking limits for the future (not more than three drinks per occasion, not more than two times per week). Feeling pleased with the ease of the first 30 days, he continued abstaining for an additional four months. In the fifth month, he began drinking moderately, guided by the drinking parameters he had set

---

[2] Though mixed goals (abstinence or moderation) for drinkers are more likely in heterogeneous groups, and hence presented in this part of the chapter, the mixed model is also tenable in homogenous groups.

> for himself. A month later he joined a long-term integrated therapy group with the understanding that the group would continue to address the self-esteem and interpersonal issues that he had begun to work on in his individual sessions with the group therapist, while also providing continuing support for his controlled use of alcohol.
>
> The eight-member group that Larry joined had two members with prior histories of alcohol abuse, both now stably abstinent – one with extensive involvement in AA, the other with the help of antabuse and naltrexone. They were uneasy about Larry's decision to moderate (having repeatedly flirted with their own "bargains at control" before becoming stably abstinent), and expressed "guarded optimism" that while this might work for him, they knew it was not an option for them. While Larry's way of dealing with his alcohol problem, initially and intermittently, stirred anxiety in these two members, the concerns they expressed (as well as their openly expressed envy that perhaps **he** could do it even if they could not), ultimately served to reinforce for each of them their own hard-won resolve that "a totally closed door" for them, at least, seemed like "the only viable choice."

The example above of an integrated group with mixed goals (abstinence or moderation) for those with drinking problems demonstrated the group's need to grapple with the possibility of "different roads to success" – a very different matter from no direction at all. Moderation Training, discussed in the next section, is one relatively new way of providing useful direction.

Moderation Training: As an Adjunct for Effective Management of Drinking Problems

As mentioned earlier, it is not uncommon for an alcohol problem to surface in an integrated group for a member who had not been known to have a problem with alcohol prior to entering the group, or in a group in which the leader had not intended to be dealing with substance abuse issues at all. It is the leader's responsibility to help the group attend to the drinking problem – contracting with the wavering member to modify his use of alcohol and to embrace supports to help with this. Moderation Training (Vannicelli, 2001b, 2002) is one such support – carried out as a treatment adjunct in individual sessions, with the understanding that the group will be kept informed of the member's progress with the journey.

Research documentation

There is an extensive body of research, including controlled comparisons with traditional abstinence-based approaches, that supports the effectiveness of moderation approaches for appropriate populations (Alden, 1988; Baer et al., 1992; Brown, 1980; Graber and Miller, 1988; Heather, et al., 1987; Hester and Delaney, 1997;

Kivlahan, et al., 1990; Marlatt, et al., 1993; Miller, et al., 1992; Pomerleau, et al., 1978; Sanchez-Craig, et al., 1984; Skutle and Berg, 1987; Sobel and Sobel, 1976, 1984). Moderation approaches are also supported by the Institute of Medicine's recommendations (1990) that the level and intensity of alcohol treatment match the severity of the problem.

During the first 20 years of my professional life, in addition to my clinical work, I was actively involved in the alcohol research community as a clinical investigator and member of peer review panels reviewing the research of others. I was thus aware of the growing body of research that demonstrated positive results with moderation approaches. Though I was intrigued, there seemed no feasible way to integrate these approaches with the traditional abstinence-oriented outpatient program that I was directing at that time. When I left my hospital position for full-time private practice in 1993, I began developing the program of Moderation Training that has become an important part of my clinical practice.

The model and its applicability

Moderation Training (MT) draws from the work of Sobel and Sobel (1993) at the Addictions Research Foundation which they refer to as Guided Self Change and from the self-help program, Moderation Management, outlined by Kishline (1994). Like other moderation approaches, MT fits within the general model of harm reduction (Marlatt, 1998; Marlatt et al., 1993) in which treatment strategies are designed to reduce the harm associated with addictive behaviors. Examples include:

a. Nicotine-replacement methods for smokers.
b. Weight management programs for the obese.
c. Safe sex programs (e.g., condom distribution in high schools).
d. Methadone maintenance programs for opiate users.
e. Needle exchange programs to reduce the spread of HIV and hepatitis among addicts who might otherwise share needles.

Moderation as a goal is an ideal approach for those at the lower end of the alcohol abuse continuum, often characterized as problem drinkers (classified in DSM IV as alcohol abusers). However, it also can serve as an effective motivator for others whose drinking problems are considerably more serious (classified in DSM IV as alcoholics or alcohol dependent) but who would never commit to abstinence without first convincing themselves that they cannot moderate. Thus, for many, it can be a stepping stone for ultimately achieving abstinence.

Though many in the alcohol treatment community in the United States have viewed it as almost heresy to even consider moderation approaches, for more than three decades these approaches have been seen as mainstream treatment in other parts of the world (Heather and Robertson, 1983, 1997; Skutle and Berg, 1987). In Canada, Great Britain, and much of Europe, alcohologists have long recognized that most of the serious costs to society of heavy drinking derive not from alcoholics, but from problem drinkers – the majority of those with serious drinking problems.

In fact three out of four individuals who have problems with alcohol are *not* alcoholics (Institute of Medicine, 1990). Moreover, for many of these problem drinkers who do not see abstinence as appropriate, moderation is an appealing alternative.

Philosophy and treatment course

Moderation Training is a collaborative, non-labeling approach which "lowers the gate," making it easier for clients to enter treatment. It is not necessary to have "hit bottom" or to see oneself as "diseased" in order to get help. In the spirit of motivational interviewing (Miller and Rolnick, 2001), the MT therapist helps the patient gather and look at data – treating him as an adult capable of making his own decisions. Rather than being told what to do, the client is encouraged to try things out and see what he can learn from it. The approach is very different from simply encouraging the patient to "use control" – or supporting his bargains at control.

Patients begin their work with 30 days of abstinence, during which they develop alternative strategies for dealing with situations where in the past they might have drunk to excess, find new ways of rewarding themselves, and develop a detailed set of parameters to guide future drinking should they decide to begin moderation at the end of the 30 days. These parameters include specific limits on the number of drinking days per week, and the number of drinks per drinking occasion, as well as a detailed list of situations that are high risk in which drinking should be either more tightly restricted or avoided entirely. Through the course of their work, some realize that, for them, abstinence is preferable to moderation as a long-term goal.

A case example follows of Moderation Training in combination with an invitation to join an integrated group with mixed goals (either moderation or abstinence) that was pivotal to a successful outcome.

> Marge, a 38-year-old scientist, was referred by her individual therapist of 12 years, after a number of years of feeling that her client's drinking was complicating attempts to appropriately medicate her depression. A "light weight" as far as problem drinkers go, Marge recognized that her nightly consumption of two or three drinks was nonetheless causing problems. She reported shame about "fading out" nightly before her kid's bedtime, and feeling "under the weather" and confused at the lab every morning.
>
> Alongside her weekly appointments with her individual therapist, I saw Marge weekly for Moderation Training. After a very gradual diminution of drinking, the 30 days of abstinence went well. Then began her attempts to drink moderately – within her specified parameters (no more than one and a half drinks per day, no more than three times per week, and never alone). Marge would follow through for a few weeks, soon to report glumly that she had "messed up." We would use "misses" as data to learn from, attempt to understand what was getting in the way of her success, and reaffirm useful parameters.
>
> After several months of this, I learned that in her family of origin, attention was given only when an individual was seen as "legitimately needy" by virtue

of being weak or sick. Such reward was never accorded accomplishment or success. Some of Marge's fondest memories (and among the few in which she recalls being tenderly treated by her alcoholic mother) were those occasions in which she would be sick enough to stay home from school. This rang a bell. I recalled suggesting at several points in our initial months together that Marge might cut back to every other week with me and use a portion of her sessions with her individual therapist to discuss her progress with moderation. She consistently resisted, saying that she valued the weekly time with both of us. It finally occurred to me that her failing to achieve success with moderation might have less to do with her ability to do so than a wish to keep me as an additional therapist – a second therapy appointment each week seeming unacceptable unless she was "weak."

I raised this hypothesis with Marge, and suggested a possible option in which success (rather than weakness) could be rewarded – namely, by joining a weekly therapy group for high-functioning professional women that I was beginning in two months. She was excited about this prospect. I also pointed out that no members would be accepted who were not stabilized in terms of their alcohol use – either abstinence or moderation; if she were set on this course, she could enter as soon as she had shown herself to be consistently on track. By the next session, she had decided to stop drinking altogether so she would be "ready to join the group right at the start." She did; and now five and a half years later she is still in the group and has not had another drink.

Countertransference Issues

The special challenges presented by group work with substance abusers and the active role that the leader plays in effectively dealing with these challenges provide a fertile playing field for countertransference reactions (detailed in Vannicelli, 1992, 2001a). Even the well-trained group leader is likely to experience feelings of frustration, inadequacy, and helplessness at times given that this population of patients who have felt the pain of being out of control or devalued may engender similar feelings in those who work with them. The countertransference issues posed by this patient population can be even more challenging for the many caregivers in the substance abuse field who are either in recovery themselves or are from families troubled by substance abuse; both of which can further heighten the potential for intense feelings to be aroused.

Countertransference reactions, when properly understood, can guide and inform the therapeutic work, shedding light on what is transpiring in the group. In contrast, countertransference reactions that are not understood can seriously impede the work. In the sections that follow, several key countertransference issues will be addressed:

a. countertransference related to therapist's personal or familial history with substance abuse;
b. feelings of rage when patients slip and are not forthright about it;
c. feelings of uncertainty that are aroused when members relapse.

Countertransference related to the therapist's personal or familial history

Many therapists have personal or family histories with substance abuse – experiences that may motivate them to work with this population and make them especially sensitive to the needs of substance abusing patients. However, these experiences may also impede their work if the inevitable countertransference issues are not given adequate attention. It is, thus, particularly important for therapists personally impacted by substance abuse to be reflective about the feelings that get stirred up for them in the course of their work.

Therapists who have successfully used self-help programs for their own recovery may at times find themselves torn between the role of group therapist and the more collegial, mutually self-disclosing relationships that they are familiar with in AA or NA. Because the pull towards the self-help model may create pressures to share personal experiences, it is important for the group therapist to be thoughtful about what he shares, considering carefully how it will be helpful to the patient. As Langs (1975) warns, such decisions often are not made primarily because of the patient's needs but, rather, "are rationalizations of the extensive countertransference gratifications they offer the psychotherapist"(Langs, 1975: p. 117). It is thus important for the group leader to have a clear sense of his general stance with regard to self-disclosure, and to pay attention to any deviations that occur (or that he may be considering).

Countertransference feelings when patients are not forthcoming about slips

When the group leader learns that a member has been using for some time and keeping this information from the group, she may be silenced by feelings she fears she will leak – anger about having been betrayed and feelings of utter helplessness. To manage these feelings, it is important to recognize that the patient who "covers up" does so not because "all addicts lie" or because "this is part of the psychopathology of addiction," but rather, to protect two things that are of great concern to him while he is using. First, he wants to continue using alcohol or drugs (and talking about it risks having sanctions imposed if he continues to do so). Second, he wants to protect his relationship with the leader and the group.

It may be difficult to comprehend how someone who is not being forthright might be trying to "protect" the relationship. What is required is an understanding of the differing perspectives of the patient and therapist about the treatment alliance and what it means. Whereas for the therapist, the alliance means that the patient will talk honestly about what is going on in his life – including discussion of urges as well as slips – for the patient, the alliance often means having a connection with an idealized caregiver. Thus, after a slip occurs, the patient has the difficult task of managing his profound feelings of shame about letting down a person he cares a great deal about while also dealing with his fear that he may lose this important person if he talks about his use (particularly if he is not ready to stop). In addition, he may also have concerns about group members that he cares about and how they will feel about him if they discover that he is using.

It is also important to consider that the patient who is using and hiding his use may also be ambivalent – his wish to hide in opposition to a wish to finally have his secret known so that he can be back in connection (honest again) with people that matter to him. The following case (from Vannicelli, 2001a) is illustrative.

> When Ronald returned to the group, following an inpatient detox, he reported that on several occasions he had "shot up" in the parking lot just outside the group therapy office. Upon learning of this, the group leader asked, "Should we have known? Were there signs that we missed along the way?" Ronald responded, "I wasn't leveling with you or with the group. You did all point out to me, several times that I didn't seem myself, but I gave lots of excuses about problems with my liver, my weight loss, my teeth. I felt so scared and ashamed. I did everything I could to get you all off my case. But another part of me was dying to be rescued and wished that you and the group had pushed even harder."

The therapist who is feeling betrayed and angry may fail to understand that group members may be experiencing very similar feelings, and along with this, may be acutely disappointed that things can get so out of hand despite participation in the group. All members (including the one who has lapsed) may have feelings about the ways in which the leader has failed. These feelings may be matched by the therapist's own feelings of failure. Often, in retrospect, she may recognize that there had been signs that the patient might be using (e.g., sleepiness, labile affect, runny nose) but that she had "optimistically" overlooked them (hoping that she was wrong). It is important that all of these feelings – the therapist's, the lapsing patient's, and the group's – are addressed.

Feelings about the therapist may be raised by inquiring, "What's it like to have a therapist who did not pay enough attention?" Group members' reactions may range widely from trying to protect the leader by defending her humanness, to devaluing her for disappointing their idealized image of omnipotence and infallibility. Both sets of feelings (and others, as well) are likely to be alive in the group leader herself. It is thus important that she guard against behavior that might covertly encourage the group to deal with her feelings by getting group members to either chastise or absolve her. Instead, she needs to help them stay in touch with the full range of feelings that are alive (requiring her to sit with her own powerful mix of feelings, as well).

Feelings of uncertainty about how to address alcohol and drug relapses

The therapist faced with a silently lapsing patient may worry that the therapy has been a sham – the patient, the therapist, or both fooling themselves into believing that they have been doing useful work together. These feelings may be accompanied by tremendous feelings of inadequacy and uncertainty, not only about the quality of his past work, but also about how to proceed in the future. No group leader who treats substance abusers is immune to such feelings, since none are immune to the possibility of a group member lapsing and not talking about it.

It is not uncommon for therapists to respond to these complex emotions by becoming punitive, rationalizing that they have been "too lax" and must now "tighten up." This may even lead to precipitous discharge of patients from the group. What is needed, instead, is careful and courageous attention to early signs – asking direct questions to get the substance abuse issues more clearly on the table, as illustrated in the following situations.

Alcohol odor in the room with source unknown: Feelings of uncertainty in the therapist may be especially pronounced when there is a distinct odor of alcohol in the room indicating that someone has been drinking, but it is not clear who. The leader may be reluctant to process the data, given his uncertainty about the source. However, it is essential that he actively attend to it, by inquiring, for example, "I wonder how what is going on in here right now might relate to the faint odor of alcohol in the room?" (thus presenting the presence of the odor as a fact). Alternatively, he might state, "There is a faint smell in here that seems like it could be alcohol," followed up by exploring members' thoughts and feelings about this. Even if it is not immediately apparent who the drinker may be, the issue has not been ignored, and with time, clarity is likely to emerge.

After the fact confessions: Yet another set of conflictual feelings may arise in group leaders when a member, some time after he has resumed abstinence, confesses to the group that months earlier he had a prolonged period of drinking that he never discussed. When presented with this information, the leader may feel conflicted about whether to deal with the deception of the past or to help the group appreciate the group member's present forthrightness and the courage it has taken for him acknowledge his past cover-up. However, the most useful approach is to help the group actively deal with both – inquiring, "How does it feel for the group to have Jeff's honest disclosure about his slip at this point and also to know that for a long time he was not able to be open with the group about it?" Or the leader might ask, "Along with the positive feelings group members may have about the fact that Jeff is now able to share this with us, what other feelings might there be about the period when he was not?"

At those moments when countertransference feelings are the most painful, it can be helpful for the group leader to keep in mind that substance abuse problems are as bedeviling for the patient as they are for the therapist, and that no one would ever choose to have an alcohol or drug problem or the life situations that go with it. Often I tell patients, "I have an enormous respect for this illness – one, clearly, that no one would ever choose."

Conclusion

Though there is much to consider if substance abusers are to be treated effectively in group psychotherapy, the group leader who takes on this undertaking need not be an "expert" in substance abuse. He does, however, need to be a well-trained, competent group therapist willing to face the challenges of extending his skills to treat this population. He also needs a certain amount of courage, backed by knowledge of available resources and the wherewithal to call on the expertise of others.

More specifically, he needs to be aware of resources in his community for supporting both abstinence and moderation, including knowledge of the range of self-help programs that may be available (including Moderation Management and Smart Recovery, as well as AA and NA), and psychopharmacologists who are comfortable treating substance abusers and willing to prescribe naltrexone, campril, antabuse, and cyboxin. He also needs to be able to maintain a clear focus on the substance abuse issues, while remaining mindful of countertransference. Errors of omission (failure to take action, for example, in dealing with patient slips) and errors of commission (doing something inappropriate, such as becoming excessively punitive, or over-involved) need to be guarded against – sometimes helped by having a co-leader with whom to check out clinical impressions, to examine reactions to patients, and to work through some of the painful feelings that can be generated. Finally, he needs to know where he can get appropriate supervision, either on an ongoing basis or for brief consultation, to help set up adequate support systems for lapsing clients, as well as to attend to the many complicated issues raised for the group as whole (and for the leader).

Acknowlegements

The author wishes to thank Roberta Caplan, PhD and Lawrence Kron, PhD for their thoughtful suggestions for this manuscript as well as Sanden Averett, MTS, for her ongoing support and detailed editorial assistance.

The chapter in part draws on material previously published by the author.

References and Bibliography

Alden, L. E. (1988). Behavioral self-management controlled-drinking strategies in a context of secondary prevention. *Journal of Consulting and Clinical Psychology*, 56, 280–286.

Alexander, F. (1949). *Fundamentals of psychoanalysis*. New York: W. W. Norton.

Baer, J. S., Marlatt, G. A., Kivlahan, D. R., et al. (1992). An experimental test of three methods of alcohol risk reduction with young adults. *Journal of Consulting and Clinical Psychology*, 64, 974–979.

Brown, R. A. (1980). Conventional education and controlled drinking education courses with convicted drunken drivers. *Behavior Therapy*, 11, 632–642.

Cooper, D. E. (1987). The role of group psychotherapy in the treatment of substance abusers. *American Journal of Psychotherapy*, 41(1), 55–67.

Gordis, E. (Ed.). (1987). *Alcohol and health: Sixth special report to the Congress (US Department of Health and Human Services, publication No. ADM 87-1519)*. Washington, DC: US Government of Printing Office.

Graber, R. A., & Miller, W. R. (1988). Abstinence and controlled drinking goals in behavioral self-control training of problem drinkers: A randomized clinical trial. *Psychology of Addictive Behaviors*, 2(1), 20–33.

Griefen, M., Vannicelli, M., & Canning, D. (1985). Treatment contracts in long-term groups with alcoholic clients. *Group*, 9, 43–48.

Hart, L. (1977). A review of treatment and rehabilitation legislation regarding alcohol abusers and alcoholics in the United States: 1920–1971. *The International of the Addictions*, 12(5), 667–678.

Heather, N., Robertson, I., MacPherson, B., et al. (1987). Effectiveness of a controlled drinking self-help manual: One year follow-up results. *British Journal of Clinical Psychology*, 26, 279–287.

Heather, N., & Robertson, I. (1983). *Controlled drinking*. London: Methuen.

Heather, N., & Robertson I. (1997). *Problem drinking*. Oxford: Oxford University Press.

Hester, R. K., & Delaney, H. D. (1997). Behavioral self-control program for windows: Results of a controlled clinical trial. *Journal of Consulting and Clinical Psychology, 65*(4), 686–693.

Institute of Medicine. (1990). *Broadening the base of treatment for alcohol problems.* Washington, DC: National Academy Press.

Kishline, A. (1994). *Moderate drinking: The moderation management guide for people who want to reduce their drinking.* New York: Crown Trade Paperbacks.

Kivlahan, D. R., Marlatt, G. A., Fromme, K., et al. (1990). Secondary prevention with college drinkers: Evaluation of an alcohol skills training program. *Journal of Consulting and Clinical Psychology, 58*(6), 805–810.

Kurtz, N., & Reiger, M. (1975). The Uniform Alcoholism And Intoxication Treatment Act: The compromising process of a social policy formulation. *Journal of Studies on Alcohol, 36,* 1421–1440.

Langs, R. J. (1975). The therapeutic relationship and deviations in technique. *International Journal of Psychoanalytic Psychotherapy, 4,* 106–141.

Marlatt, G. A. (Ed.). (1998). *Harm reduction: Pragmatic strategies for managing high-risk behaviors.* New York: The Guilford Press.

Marlatt, G. A., Larimer, M. E., Baer, J. S., et al. (1993). Harm reduction for alcohol problems: Moving beyond the controlled drinking controversy. *Behavior Therapy, 24,* 461–504.

Miller, W. R., Leckman, A. L., Delaney, H. D., et al. (1992). Long term follow-up of behavioral self-control training. *Journal of Studies on Alcohol, 53,* 249–261.

Miller, W. R., & Rollnick, S. (1991). *Motivational interviewing: Preparing people to change addictive behavior.* New York: The Guilford Press.

Pomerleau, O., Pertshuk, M., Adkins, D., et al. (1978). A comparison of behavioral and traditional treatment methods for middle income problem drinkers. *Journal of Behavioral Medicine, 1,* 187–200.

Rutan, J. S., Stone, W. N., & Shay, J. J. (2007). *Psychodynamic group psychotherapy* (4th ed.). New York: The Guilford Press.

Sanchez-Craig, M., Annis, H. M., Bornet, A. R., et al. (1984). Random assignment to abstinence and controlled drinking: Evaluation of a cognitive-behavioral program for problem drinkers. *Journal of Consulting and Clinical Psychology, 52*(3), 390–403.

Skutle, A., & Berg, G. (1987). Training in controlled drinking for early-stage problem drinkers. *British Journal of the Addictions, 82,* 493–501.

Sobel, M. B., & Sobel, L. C. (1976). Second year treatment outcome of alcoholics treated by individualized behavior therapy: Results. *Behavior Research and Therapy, 14,* 195–215.

Sobel, M. B., & Sobel, L. C. (1984). The aftermath of heresy: A response to Pendery et al.,'s (1982) critique of "Individual behavior therapy for alcoholics." *Behavior Research and Therapy, 22*(4), 413–440.

Sobel, M. B., & Sobel, L. C. (1993). *Problem drinkers: Guided self-change treatment.* New York: The Guilford Press.

Vannicelli, M. (1982). Group psychotherapy with alcoholics: Special techniques. *Journal of Studies on Alcohol, 43*(1), 17–37.

Vannicelli, M. (1988). Group therapy aftercare for alcoholic patients. *International Journal of Group Psychotherapy, 38*(3), 337–353.

Vannicelli, M. (1992). *Removing the roadblocks: Group psychotherapy with substance abusers and family members.* New York: The Guilford Press.

Vannicelli, M. (1995). Who's unmotivated? Treating the ambivalence in substance abusers. Presented at Annual Meeting of the American Group Psychotherapy Association. Washington, DC.

Vannicelli, M. (2001a). Leader dilemmas and countertransference issues in group psychotherapy with substance abusers. *International Journal of Group Psychotherapy*, *51*, 43–62.

Vannicelli, M. (2001b). Moderation training for problem drinkers: Treatment techniques and clinical considerations. *Cognitive and Behavioral Practice*, *8*(1), 53–61.

Vannicelli, M. (2002). A dualistic model for group treatment of alcohol problems: Abstinence-based treatment for alcoholics, moderation training for problem drinkers. *International Journal of Group Psychotherapy*, *52*, 189–214.

Vannicelli, M., Canning, D., & Griefen, M. (1984). Group therapy with alcoholics: A group case study. *International Journal of Group Psychotherapy*, *34*(1), 127–147.

Vannicelli, M., Dillavou, D., & Caplan, R. (1989). Dynamically oriented group therapy with alcoholics: Making it work despite the prevailing bias. *Group*, *13*(2), 95–101.

Wolberg, L. R. (1948). *Medical hypnosis* (Vol. *1*). New York: Grune & Stratton.

Yalom, I. D. (1974). Group therapy and alcoholism. *Annals of the New York Academy of Sciences*, *233*, 85–103.

Yalom, I., & Leszcz, M. (2005). *Theory and practice of group psychotherapy*. New York: Basic Books.

19
Single-Gender or Mixed-Gender Groups: Choosing a Perspective
Darryl L. Pure

Introduction

In composing a group a common question which a group therapist must confront is whether the group is to be heterogeneous or homogeneous (Rutan, Stone, and Shay, 2007). While groups generally thrive on heterogeneity, there are times when therapists prefer to constrain the group to be homogeneous on one or more dimensions that relate to the purposes of the group or the time constraints with which it must contend. Thus, time-limited groups are often limited to a single problem or diagnosis as a way of focusing the group within the time allotted. Examples of this are groups for grief, eating disorders, depression, anxiety, etc. Other groups have a diagnostic focus so that members may benefit from others who are similar to them with regard to their presenting problem. Examples include groups for breast cancer, peripheral vascular medicine, or single parenting.

One frequently considered dimension in forming homogeneous groups is gender. At first blush, this seems to make sense; after all men and women are different (Dore, 1994; Walker, 1981). On further consideration, however, therapists owe their clients a more thorough explanation, as even within gender there are many differences such as age, socio-economic status, education, marital status, etc. Whenever therapists distinguish between groups on one dimension and thus achieve homogeneity, they leave other dimensions free to vary between individuals. Furthermore, while some patients seek group therapy to work on issues related to gender, many more seek treatment to work on their cross-gender relationships. Consequently, there needs to be a clear reason to assign a prospective patient to a single-gender group instead of suggesting that they work on their vocational and intimate relationships in a mixed-gender group. This chapter will focus on the reasons that therapists typically assign patients to single-gender groups, the efficacy of such groups, and finally suggest a novel developmental framework for deciding between single-gender and mixed-gender group psychotherapy. In general, though there is not yet empirical support, the framework is assumed to hold for both hetero-sexual and homosexual clients.

Single-Gender versus. Mixed Gender Groups

There are four general reasons that group therapists assign people to single-gender groups instead of mixed-gender groups:

1. They request a single-gender setting and there is no contra-indication nor does the request seem to be defensive in nature.
2. The presenting problem occurs more often in one gender than in the other or is of a nature that would be frightening to the other gender (e.g., men who batter or are sexually abusive, or women with a history of molestation or who struggle with eating disorders).
3. The focus of the group is unique to one gender or the other (e.g., menopause or pregnancy groups, fathering groups, coming-out groups, and women's consciousness raising groups).
4. As I will argue in this chapter, there are developmental issues that remain unresolved with same-gender mates, rendering premature the desire for cross-gender intimacy.

These reasons divide into cases with different possible outcomes. There are situations where the clinician must cede to the patient's request for a single-gender group (e.g., when the patient comes seeking a single-gender group and there are no contra-indications). There are situations where the therapist can only offer single-gender treatment regardless of the patient's request (e.g., the clinician only has space in a single-gender group and does not know of other co-ed resources for the patient). Sometimes the clinician can reasonably offer a unisex group but could also suggest, provided the patient has sufficient ego-strength, a co-ed group that would work on the same issues. There are other times, as I will propose in this chapter, that in spite of the patient's request for a co-ed group, a therapist applying a developmental approach would do well to suggest a single-gender group.

The remainder of this chapter will focus on each of these reasons. I will also briefly review the literature concerning the development of intimate and romantic relationships. Finally, I will use this review to propose a developmental approach to intimate and romantic relationships that will help the clinician discern the conditions under which a single-gender group would be valuable despite the patient's request for a mixed-gender setting.

The general thrust of single-gender groups has been to meet what many see as the unique needs of one gender or the other. They argue that seeing men and women in the same group, results in stereotypical gender roles that prevent the participants from exploring deeper aspects of their psyches or achieving the desired behavioral goals (Walker, 1981). According to this line of reasoning, everyone should be placed in single-gender contexts in addition to having experiences in mixed-gender groups, as it is only in the single-gender context that certain outcomes are likely to ensue. As we shall see, things are not always so obvious.

Requests for placement in single-gender groups

It is common for people to request being seen in a single-gender setting, which is in part an outgrowth of the Women's Movement and the corresponding Men's Movement. Influenced by the culture, where such individuals seek a particular sort of experience that they believe can only occur in the single-gender context, they should not be swayed unless there is a contra-indication, or the request seems to be avoidant of some anxiety that requires more direct challenge. It is not clear that patients presenting for a men's or women's group could not have their needs met by a mixed-gender group; it is simply that by removing a stressful variable (sexual tensions and gender role expectations) participants can more quickly lower their defenses and explore themselves.

Women in groups

Single-gender groups emerged in the 1970s in part as a function of the Women's Movement, its focus on consciousness raising (Brodsky, 1973; Lieberman, et al., 1979), and the benefits of all female therapy groups (Glaser, 1976; Klein, 1976). The Women's Movement is widely thought of having started its "second wave" with the release of oral contraception in 1961 and the publishing of Betty Friedan's *The Feminine Mystique* (1963). In her book, Friedan identified a myth of womanhood that was defined by a patriarchal society and that stifled women and their ability to express themselves as independent human beings. Many other works followed this, including Germaine Greer's *The Female Eunuch* (1972), which challenged women to increase their awareness of their bodies, sexuality, sexual roles, and their domination by men. A movement was born that resulted in a need for women to raise their awareness of themselves and their need for independence and emotional freedom.

A natural outgrowth of this era was women's groups. Walker (1981), for example, notes that while women's groups, similar to mixed-gender groups, focus on improved interpersonal relationships, resolution of self-concept concerns, emotional support, and honest, open, direct, meaningful communication; that they differ from mixed-gender groups in significant ways. According to Walker, women's groups focus more than do mixed-gender groups on a socio-cultural perspective of women's personal problems and in the case of consciousness raising groups, on social action.

Carlock and Martin (1977) suggest that women's groups focus on intrapersonal issues and the development of female relationships and intimacy. They note that there is an emphasis on establishing independence, potency, eliminating self-hatred, and the expression of one's abilities, which are areas that founder in the mixed-gender setting. Women focus on their unique identity as a person independent of their primary relationships. Women's groups also lend themselves to open discussions of body image and sexuality; both topics that tend to be avoided in mixed-gender groups.

In mixed-gender groups, women tend to be more passive, talk more softly, and tend to withdraw (Carlock and Martin, 1977; Elrick, 1977). Women in mixed groups also are apt to speak less than men, are more easily interrupted, and do not defend their ideas vigorously compared to men. In general, it seems that mixed-gender groups have more sexual and power dynamics between the genders than women's groups, resulting in increased competition within each of the genders and in women having difficulty freely exploring their issues.

In a similar vein, Holmes (2002) concluded that women's groups are especially good for women who are traditionally "feminine" (i.e., have impoverished senses of self in terms of internalized objects). Holmes also concluded that women's groups are especially useful for women who are traversing milestones of female development such as adolescence, pregnancy, and menopause.

> ### Clinical Illustration
>
> Mary, a successful attorney in her late 30's presented requesting a women's group to help her deal with her poor self-image, lack of meaningful friendships, and difficulty picking men with whom she could establish an intimate long-term relationship. When asked why she was seeking a women-only setting, she explained that she had a distant relationship with her mother and never felt truly solid as a woman. In fact, she saw her professional success as a way that she could show the world a brave face while feeling empty and hollow.
>
> Upon entering the group, Mary was initially worried that the other women would not like her but quickly felt "at home" in the group as she listened to the other women talk about deep and private issues. She began to realize that she had always experienced other women as competing with her for the attention of men. Not having to perform for the men, she did not feel a need to struggle with the other women and could join with them. She quickly relaxed and began to participate in frank conversations about how she experienced herself as a woman, how she felt about her body, and her fear of being found inadequate by other women and especially her mother. Discovering how the women reacted to her and particularly how they genuinely seemed to like her, she began to report feeling better about herself. Soon she was talking about friendships that she was developing with women in the outside world and how easy it was now that she could "hear" in her head the other group members and their praise for her. After a year in the group she began talking about the men she was beginning to date which culminated in the first serious relationship in which she felt on equal footing.

Men in groups

The Men's Movement was an outgrowth of the Women's Movement and its identification of the patriarchal structure of our culture and the difficulties that pertain to it. At first blush this seems odd as the struggle of women to break free of patriarchy would hardly seem to empower men; on the contrary, it would suggest that men should be encouraged to cede power and authority to women. In fact, to many women, the Men's Movement appeared to threaten a return to the indentured servitude of patriarchy. Nothing could be further from the truth.

Observing the fledgling liberation of women, men too began to identify ways that patriarchy had shackled them; they began to yearn for freedom from sex-stereotyped roles that relegated them to sacrifice their joy for service to the family at work, often in tasks that risked their physical safety or placed them in harm's way. Similarly, men began to be aware that while they were required to relinquish the security of their attachment to mother, in our culture there were no longer paths that connected them to father, other men, or "tribe."

Men found themselves rejecting the role of warrior and the violence it espoused. Books such as *Fire in the Belly* (Keen, 1992) encouraged men to begin a journey of self-discovery by leaving the world of women behind and finding oneself within the world of men. Osherson (1986) wrote about the need of men to leave behind the trappings of patriarchy and find a new way of being partners for their women while also finding new roles as fathers. He noted the intense father-hunger that modern men experienced and needed to address.

Finally, Bly (1990; Moyers and Bly 1990) encouraged men to attach themselves to the hero's journey of yore and to search for modern rituals of initiation whereby boys could leave home and mother and emerge as men. In his book *Iron John*, Bly, (1990) outlines the journey and uses a mytho-poetic approach to it. Similarly, in a documentary television show with Bill Moyers (1990), Bly demonstrates how the tale of Iron John speaks to the hunger of men to return to a strong and nurturing masculine identity. The work of Bly (1990), Keen (1986) and others led to the growth in self-help men's groups and formal men's groups began to be created within the mental health community.

These societal trends led to men seeking men's psychotherapy groups to deal with the wounds they uniquely carried. Wright (1987), for example, notes that men respond to the demands of culture by becoming "shame phobic," a role in which the worst that a man can experience is failure and shame while the highest good is pride and success. Such a culture values competition, achievement, dominance, and power. Not to achieve these ideals is to be a disillusioned failure, and leads to despair, depression, shame, and humiliation. Often men hide their shame or failures and substitute a false pride, commonly expressed as grandiosity. Wright argues that it is only in an all-male group that men can feel sufficiently safe to lower their defenses and heal. Specifically he argues that the group mechanisms of vicarious learning, universality and altruism are of great value in allowing men to show their inner wounds in ways that are open and increasingly vulnerable.

Clinical Illustration

Tom, a mid-50's salesman, was referred to a men's group by his psychiatrist who had been treating him for depression. When asked why he was considering a single-gender group as opposed to a mixed-gender group, the referring psychiatrist explained that Tom had an idealized relationship with his long-deceased father but did not have close friendships with men nor did he seem to have a strong masculine identity. His psychiatrist felt that Tom would benefit by being

> able to be in a strong male environment for the first time in his life. Additionally, Tom explained that he could easily charm women but never felt truly close to them. He said that though he yearned to be successful like his father, he never felt like he had the drive or ambition that other men had.
>
> Upon entering the group, Tom was initially apprehensive about the all-male environment, but quickly relaxed when he heard other men opening up to each other and confronting one another in strong yet supportive ways. His "salesman personality" diminished and he started to relate to the men in the group in a much more open and less defensive way, receiving honest support from the other members. As he began to assert himself in the group, he started to talk about standing-up for himself in his marriage, and ultimately this seemed to enable him to be more assertive in pursuing his dreams for starting his own business. In a very moving session, he told the members what they meant to him and expressed how important his relationships to men outside of the group had become. He noted that as he learned to express himself and accept support from other men, he also found himself getting closer to his son and learned to help his son establish himself in the working world.

Single-gender groups for specific problems

As noted above, many single-gender groups form to serve men or women who seek a single-gender setting. Another, important reason for single-gender groups is to offer therapeutic help to populations that are suffering from gender-specific difficulties that will be best aided in a homogeneous setting or if they were present, would be offensive to the opposite gender.

There are many reports of groups that address domestic violence (Palmer, Brown and Barrera, 1992), anger (Feindler, et al., 1986), breast cancer (Goodwin, et al., 2001; Kissane, et al., 2003), rape (Hensley, 2002), sexual compulsivity (Orzack, et al., 2006), and eating disorders (Wilfley, et al., 1993) in single-gender modalities, and show good efficacy. Often these groups are designed for single genders due to the preference of the leader or members instead of being based on clear comparison studies that demonstrate that single-gender groups are more efficacious than the co-ed setting (Richards, Burlingame, and Fuhriman, 1990). Perhaps it would be useful to differentiate between those groups where it *seems* preferable to have a single-gender format from those situations where the nature of the difficulty clearly falls along lines that are gender divided.

Clear gender divisions

While there are several areas where single-gender groups seem necessary, there are probably fewer that address truly gender-unique issues. Examples include groups for menopause, pregnancy support, ovarian cancer, testicular cancer, prostate cancer, erectile dysfunction, motherhood, or fatherhood.

> **Clinical Illustration**
>
> James, a 32-year-old first time father responded to an announcement of a 12-week group for new and expectant fathers. Initially very anxious, he was eager to meet other men who were embarking on fatherhood. After introductions were made the men began discussing their hopes for the group and James was able to tell the members that he was looking forward to being a father, but as the due-date approached he found himself worried and feeling trapped. He was ashamed of these feelings, but felt reassured hearing that others experienced similar dread as the birth of their child approached. Over the ensuing weeks, the group explored many topics. The group members were able to discuss their concerns about sex during and after the pregnancy, changes in their wife's body, sleepless nights, the health of the baby, their role as provider and caregiver, the loss of freedom they experienced, and how they now felt hesitant to take risks that they formerly enjoyed. Interestingly, several of the members talked about how the discussions in the group allowed them to feel free to discuss the same issues with their partner; many for the first time.

Assumed but less clearly defined gender divisions

Many other foci may seem to call for single-gender settings, but on closer examination may or may not benefit from such group composition; unfortunately there is not much empirical research to guide us. Examples include groups for domestic violence, rape, breast cancer, and sexual issues including sexual compulsivity. On the face of it, it seems to make sense to segregate men and women around the issue of domestic violence. Nevertheless, is this really the case? It seems equally plausible that both male and female perpetrators could benefit from being in the same group. While they may or may not have similar issues resulting in their behavior, they likely have much to learn from each other.

The little empirical evidence that exists investigating mixed versus single gender groups found that mixed-gender groups were more effective for gay support groups (Lenihan, 1985; Westefeld and Winkelpleck, 1983 cited in Richards, Burlingame, and Fuhrman, 1990), group treatment overall, (Burlingame, Fuhrman, and Mosier, 2003), and for psychodrama groups (Kipper and Ritchie, 2003). Similarly, while perpetrators and victims often divide by gender, they too may benefit from treatment in the same group. There are many other issues in the group literature where seemingly antagonistic groups of individuals benefited from being in a group together including the black-white groups of the civil rights era, skin-heads and Jews, Palestinians and Israelis, and even violent felons and their victims. While certainly fraught with tension, these groups are actually similar to the common co-ed group in that they seek to help participants to expand their view of themselves and others who they initially view as hopelessly different from themselves. To be effective, the mixed group must be carefully composed and the members well prepared.

Additionally, in order to help the patients in question, the leader would need to be well versed in gender-specific aspects of the problems and alert to intervening in the group. While it is likely that the group dynamics would be more complex than would be found in a single-gender group, given sufficient time to work-through the dynamics and allow the patients to resolve the heightened frustration and anxiety, it is possible that the mixed-gender group would achieve the same outcomes, or perhaps more robust ones as the single-gender group.

In the addictions field, there have also been suggestions that single-gender groups are preferable to co-ed groups; some of these suggestions are supported by empirical evidence while others merely make the assertion. Dore (1994), for example, presented a group model that relies on this assumption without empirical support. He developed a group model to address male-specific difficulties and applied it to men recovering from addiction or coming from families with addiction problems. In this model, the issues of masculine identity addressed were "fatherlessness," the strain of men's psychological roles, and the "pervasive organization of male aggression and violence (overwhelmingly against other men) across almost all of the world's cultures." He suggested that addressing these issues in a directive group format would treat what he described as the four primary emotions which men have been socialized to and been harmed by: grief, fear, anger, and shame. He recommended a short-term, male-specific, and directive model of group treatment that is well thought-out but lacks empirical support. It is possible that this model will show more efficacy than mixed-gender treatments, but it is also possible that while preferred by many men, it is no more effective than the common mixed-gender treatment groups.

Some studies have reported better results when treating women in gender-specific groups than in mixed groups. For example, Greenfield, et al., (2007) found that developing a manualized 12-week treatment program for women substance abusers, resulted in equally good responses to treatment as did mixed-gender group counseling, but much better outcomes at a 6-month follow-up. Similarly, Greenfield, et al., (2008) found that women substance abusers with psychiatric symptoms improved more when treated in a woman-specific treatment than those treated in a mixed-gender framework. In both of these studies, Greenfield, et al., (2007, 2008) attributed the improved results to utilizing a treatment manual that focused on:

> The effects of drugs and alcohol on women's health; women's relationships and recovery; violence and substance abuse; mood, anxiety, and eating problems and substance use disorders; recovery skills; stigma, shame, and disclosure; being a caretaker and being in recovery; self-help groups; and achieving a balance. (Greenfield, et al., 2007: p. 40).

Kauffman, et al., (1995) also reported that men's and women's needs are different within mixed-gender substance abuse groups. They contrasted the experience of women in mixed-gender substance abuse groups with that of women in women-only treatment groups and found that the single-gender framework better addressed their treatment needs.

Clearly, we need research to clarify the conditions in which co-ed groups or single-gender groups are preferable. Clinically, while some conditions may seem to be best treated in a single-gender setting, there are other times when the same condition my respond equally well to a mixed group.

Clinical Illustration

His individual therapist referred Bob, a 35-year-old, four times married, professor of physical therapy for group treatment. The University fired Bob from his teaching position after having an affair with multiple female students in his charge. As his treatment progressed, it became clear that he had issues with sexual compulsivity and admitted to having had sex with hundreds of women who he described in the most demeaning fashion. He freely admitted that to him, women were "things" he used for his sexual pleasure and he was unable to understand the damage his behavior did to them. When confronted in the screening interviews, he shrugged-off any responsibility for the effects of his behavior by saying, "They were all over 18 and should have known better. When I came-on to them, I never promised anything more than a good time."

In selecting a group for Bob, I quickly ruled-out any of my co-ed groups as I thought that his disdain for women and his dismissive treatment of them would be so provocative to the women in the group as to make it unworkable. I offered him a men's group, which would have provided him a supportive yet confrontational environment where he would be accepted but also held accountable. I also thought that the single-gender setting would preclude sexual tensions that would complicate the treatment and diminish the possibility of his using his seductiveness and sexual acting-out to avoid painful emotions. He quickly declined this group because it met at an "inconvenient" time. We discussed my reservations about placing him in a co-ed group that met at a more convenient time. I considered the group's composition and the ego-strength of the women in the group, sought consultation, and warned Bob that this could result in a situation where he might be exposed to the hurt of being rejected by the group. I decided to proceed.

As expected, the group was cautious but accepting of Bob, who to his credit spoke openly about his unfaithfulness to his wife and inappropriate behavior with his students. He admitted to ongoing affairs in his marriage which he tried to justify, but was confronted by both men and women in the group. About six months into his treatment he began to talk about changes he was making; he spoke about remorse for the pain he had caused himself and others, including his wife. He told the group that he loved her and was grateful that she stuck with him as he struggled to get better. As the new year approached, he resolved to be faithful to his wife. At the beginning of April, ten months into his treatment, he turned to the group with obvious satisfaction and thanked them as he had achieved four months of faithfulness; the longest period he had ever sustained. At this point, a very quiet woman in the group spoke and said, "I don't believe you. I think you are a total liar." Bob was stunned. On his way home from group, he called and left me a furious message saying that he was done with group; he simply could not stay in a setting where he was so misunderstood and mistreated. I wondered whether or not he would be at the next session, but decided I would not contact him unless he failed to show-up the following week.

> Bob did attend the next session and uncharacteristically started the group by telling Sherry how furious he was with her. He told the group of his phone call to me, and that he expressed his intention never to return to the group. When asked why he did return, he turned to Sherry and said, "Because you were right. I have been lying and that you could see this actually makes me feel better." Bob stayed with the group for another couple of years and appeared to make progress, which was confirmed by his individual therapist and by his wife's report in couples counseling.

A Developmental Approach to Using Single-Gender *versus* Mixed Gender Group Psychotherapy

Thus far, we have seen that same-gender groups are useful for individuals who are seeking that sort of group, or who see their problems in living as being most amenable to a single-gender group. Does this preclude single-gender groups for those who seek a group for difficulties with romantic relationships and intimacy? Are they ever candidates for a same-gender group experience?

Frequently clinicians refer clients for group treatment due to difficulties in their interpersonal and romantic lives. If the client meets the usual criteria for group psychotherapy, a co-ed group is usually suggested. This seems to make sense both to clinicians and patients alike; after all, given that they are having problems with the opposite sex, what better place to learn about oneself than in relation to members of the opposite gender.

For many years this was the approach I used in assigning people to groups; I had groups of all women when working with eating disordered patients, men's groups for those working on issues directly related to their masculinity (e.g. masculine self-esteem, fatherlessness, men who were searching for a men's group), and co-ed groups for those working on intimacy and relationships. For many patients this worked very well, though I began to see that some men and some women in the co-ed groups struggled and took a longer time than others did in being ready to lower their defenses and to expose their longing for intimacy and connection. As I thought about this group of patients, a commonality began to emerge; almost to a person, they not only lacked good cross-gender relationships, but also had histories of non-existent or highly disturbed same-gender relationships from childhood onward. This resulted in my searching the literature to understand better the development of romantic relationships and intimacy. Clarifying the developmental path to intimacy led me to develop a developmental model that is useful in assigning candidates to single or mixed-gender groups.

The Developmental Path of Romantic Relationships

Dunphy (1963) proposed that a study of adolescents' peer groups might shed light on the development of romantic relationships. Specifically, he suggested two peer-structures, which he thought were important in the development of romantic relationships during adolescence. The first of these he termed "cliques" and referred to small, same-gender groups. The other, he termed "crowds," which referred to larger, mixed-gender groups of a non-romantic nature. He also suggested that as adolescents matured, their cliques eventually merged into larger mixed-gender cliques that in turn eventually merged to form crowds. It was from the relationships thus formed, that romantic relationships emerged.

This fits the observations of adolescent heterosexual romantic relationships. Connolly, et al., (1999), for example, found that while young adolescents report interest in romantic relationships, their actual participation in such is quite rare. As they age, however, this changes such that by the age of 15 or 16, approximately fifty percent report romantic involvements (Feiring, 1996), and by late adolescence, most report having had or being in a romantic relationship (Dickinson, 1975).

Furthermore, Connolly, et al., (2000) demonstrated that small groups of close friends were predictive of other-gender peer-networks, which were in turn predictive of romantic relationships. This suggests that individuals who struggle with same-gender small-group friendships will also have trouble in the establishment of good cross-gender friendships and intimate romantic relationships. They also cite evidence that those with supportive relationships with close friends during adolescence report having supportive romantic relationships (Connolly and Johnson, 1996).

Leaper and Anderson (1997) note that gender segregated peer relationships begin at about age three and continue into adolescence when cross-gender relationships gradually replace them. Similarly, as already noted, romantic relationships also become more evident. This is important as play and relationships in gender-segregated groups differ considerably between girls and boys. Girls' traditional play provides them with more opportunities than boys for practising the social-relational skills that seem helpful to intimate relationships. Boys' play focuses more on skills that are more suited to the world of work. By adolescence, girls are more prepared to approach relationships with nurturance and support while boys are more prepared to approach relationships with independence, competition, and dominance.

It is obvious that the difference between the socialization of girls and boys plants the seeds of relationship difficulties. This fits the feminist models already described in the need for women in all-female groups to increase the ability to safely assert themselves and to be able to express anger and dissatisfaction. Similarly, in keeping with Wright's (1987) notion, boys' socialization around competition, dominance and independence results in men requiring all-male groups to find ways to combat shame and find their gentler, more nurturing selves.

Good adult romantic relationships, according to Leaper and Anderson (1997), require not an equality of roles, which are often complementary, but instead equality based on shared decision-making and mutual expressiveness and support. Thus, couples who share communication styles are generally most satisfied with their romantic relationships. Furthermore, this same dynamic seems true of cross-gender and same-gender friendships. The communication skills most associated with satisfying relationships are mutual self-disclosure and the ability to express and manage conflict and disagreement. I propose that it is within same-gender adolescent groups that both men and women learn how to mitigate their gender-based stereotypical roles and to communicate with others most effectively. Not traversing this step, I suggest, causes men and women to develop cross-gender relationship preferences that are shallow, defensive, and stereotyped.

As previously noted, self-disclosure is difficult for boys and men as it leads to a sense of not being masculine, a condition which evokes shame. Conflict and disagreement may also be problematic as men often deal with them by withdrawing from the situation (flight) or by some form of violence or aggression (fight). Leaper and Anderson (1997) have found that those who have more feminine or androgynous self-concepts have higher relationship satisfaction. While many men struggle with shame, those who can accept a relational self-concept are also more available to intimate relationships with both peers and romantic partners. In contrast, women find that self-disclosure comes naturally while conflict and disagreement are problematic. Women tend to shun conflict out of fear of violence or that disagreement will lead to the dissolution of relationships. In addition, women may view conflict as overly masculine and therefore less desirable.

Given that adolescent relationship development proceeds from same-gender friendships to cross-gender groups and eventually to romantic relationships, one might assume that cross-gender relationships are the perfect "training ground" for romantic relationships. While the research suggests that this is the general path, there are also suggestions that this is not as straightforward as one might think. While in same-sex relationships, friends rarely report romantic or sexual interests, the same is not true of cross-sex relationships. When asked, it is common for one or both partners in a cross-sex relationship to acknowledge some degree of sexual attraction or romantic interest (Afifi and Faulkner, 2000). It seems likely that the presence of sexual attraction increases the anxiety levels of the participants making it more difficult to be fully open and emotionally intimate.

Using Developmental History to Choose Between Single and Mixed Gender Groups

Though not yet empirically supported, I have been using patients' developmental histories to assign them to single or mixed gender groups with some success. Though often referred for assignment to a co-ed group, I find that some have had good same-gender relationships throughout adolescence and beyond; these I assign to the appropriate mixed-gender group. For those that have trouble with intimate relationships with the opposite gender but have not ever established successful same-gender relationships, I generally suggest starting in a single-gender group, sometimes followed by a mixed-gender group experience. This is typically met by some initial resistance as to most patients it seems counter-intuitive. When I explain my rationale, many are willing to follow my suggestion, generally to good result. For those who have not had satisfactory same-gender relationships, being in a group with the opposite gender creates complex dynamics. They are usually more comfortable with the opposite sex; they have developed sophisticated protective mechanisms that allow them to interact with the opposite gender but without true intimacy. Thus, men will often tell me, "I prefer talking to women and have very little in common with men." As we explore this statement, it becomes clear that they are anxious around other men but have a seductive repertoire that works with women, though progress stalls once a relationship develops and greater intimacy is required. The same is true of women who may eschew relationships with other women who they describe as "catty," while preferring to use their sexuality to keep men at some optimal distance.

Once in a single gender group, these patients find that they are initially anxious but quickly find a sense of safety. Additionally, not having their usual seductive repertoire at their disposal, forces them to find new behaviors that result in true closeness, intimacy, and emotional vulnerability. Most are surprised to find that as they become closer to their same-gender peers, they also begin to develop deeper, healthier, and more fulfilling relationships with the opposite sex.

Clinical Illustration

Mark, an elderly man married for more than 40 years came seeking a group due to marital difficulties and what his wife determined was a "sexual addiction." He was preoccupied with pornography to the extent that it almost interfered with his job, in addition to his marriage. Additionally, he agreed that he had been "selfish throughout my marriage to the point where I wouldn't have put up with my crap either, if I were her." As his wife threatened divorce, Mark wanted to be seen in a men's group where he could work on his sexual compulsivity.

Upon entering the group, Mark was at first shy, admitting that he had never had friendships with other men and felt more comfortable with women. When asked about this he described growing up in a family that was dominated by his mother. His father was conflict avoidant and would withdraw to his study when confronted or berated by his wife. Mark slowly began to open up in the group and found that the other men were supportive but also confrontational. The firm but caring nature of their confrontations and the way they held him accountable for his behavior in the group allowed him to trust their positive regard for him. Prior to the group, if he was complimented, he would deny the praise by noting, "They're just blowing smoke up my butt." After several months he told the group that he was beginning to trust and that he must be "An okay guy 'cuz you guys seem to like me and you're sure quick to tell me when I've screwed up."

As his self-esteem began to improve, Mark began telling the group that he was more able to hear his wife's complaints without getting defensive and that when they squabbled, the disagreements were more quickly and fully resolved than they had ever been. Mark's wife became a strong proponent of the group noting that it made him "More real and less defensive."

Conclusions

Clinicians often use single-gender groups for a variety of reasons, though empirical support for doing so is scant and mixed. In the simplest case, some patients seek single-gender groups to work on issues related to the Men's or Women's Movements, or to help with deep-seeded feelings linked to their sense of femininity or masculinity.

Therapists recommend treatment to other patients in a same-sex context because their presenting problem is uniquely gender specific. Many others present with issues which seem to lend themselves to single-gender treatment, but it is often the bias of the therapist and/or patient which leans in the unisex direction when in fact a co-ed group may not only suffice but actually provide better options. It is in this instance that the empirical evidence is both scant and mixed. Clearly, we require more research.

Finally, there is a large group of patients who present for co-ed groups who, for developmental reasons according to the model I propose, can benefit from being seen in a men's or women's group. These patients are those who have never had age-appropriate same-gender relationships and thus lack skills in developing intimacy that would aid them in their quest for fulfilling romantic relationships. This model, like much of the gender-related group literature, lacks empirical support and warrants further research.

References and Bibliography

Afifi, W. A., & Faulkner, S. L. (2000). On being "just friends": The frequency and impact of sexual activity in crosssex friendships. *Journal of Social and Personal Relationships, 17*(2), 205–222.

Bly, J. (1990). *Iron John: A book about men.* Perseus Books.

Brodsky, A. (1973). The consciousness-raising group as a model for therapy with women. *Psychotherapy: Theory, Research and Practice, 10*(1), 24–29.

Burlingame, G.M., Fuhriman, A., & Mosier, J. (2003). The differential effectiveness of Group Psychotherapy: A meta-analytic perspective. *Group Dynamics: Theory, Research, and Practice, 7*(1), 3–12.

Carlock, C., & Martin, P. (1977). Sex composition and the intensive group experience. *Social Work, 22*(1), 27–32.

Connolly, J., Craig, W., Goldberg, A., et al. (1999). Conceptions of cross-sex friendships and romantic relationships in early adolescence. *Journal of Youth and Adolescence, 28*(4), 481–494.

Connolly, J., Furman, W., & Konarski, R. (2000). The role of peers in the emergence of heterosexual romantic relationships in adolescence. *Child Development, 71*(5), 1395–1408.

Connolly, J. A., & Johnson, A. M. (1996). Adolescents' romantic relationships and the structure and quality of their close interpersonal ties. *Personal Relationships, 3*(2), 185–195. doi:10.1111/j.1475-6811.1996.tb00111.x

Dickinson, G. E. (1975). Dating behavior of black and white adolescents before and after desegregation. *Journal of Marriage and Family, 37*(3), 602–608.

Dore, J. (1994). A model of time-limited group therapy for men: Its use with recovering addicts. *Group, 18*(4), 243–258.

Dunphy, D. C. (1963). The social structure of urban adolescent peer groups. *Sociometry, 26*(2), 230–246.

Elrick, M. (1977). The leader, she: Dynamics of a female-led self-analytic group. *Human Relations, 30*(10), 869–878.

Feindler, E. L., Ecton, R. B., Kingsley, D., et al. (1986). Group anger-control training for institutionalized psychiatric male adolescents. *Behavior Therapy, 17*(2), 109–123. doi:doi: DOI: 10.1016/S0005-7894(86)80079-X

Feiring, C. (1996). Lovers as friends: Developing conscious views of romance in adolescence. *Journal of Research on Adolescence*, 7, 214–224.

Feiring, C. (1999). Other-sex friendship networks and the development of romantic relationships in adolescence. *Journal of Youth and Adolescence*, 28(4), 495–512.

Friedan, B. (1963). *The feminine mystique*. New York, New York: W.W. Norton & Co.

Glaser, K. (1976). Women's self-help groups as an alternative to therapy. *Psychotherapy: Theory, Research, and Practice*. 13, 77–81.

Goodwin, P. J., Leszcz, M., Ennis, M., et al. (2001). The effect of group psychosocial support on survival in metastatic breast cancer. *New England Journal of Medicine*, 345(24), 1719–1726.

Greenfield, S. F., Potter, J. S., Lincoln, M. F., et al. (2008). High psychiatric symptom severity is a moderator of substance abuse treatment outcomes among women in single vs. mixed gender group treatment. *The American Journal of Drug and Alcohol Abuse*, 34(5), 594–602.

Greenfield, S. F., Trucco, E. M., McHugh, R. K., et al. (2007). The women's recovery group study: A stage I trial of women-focused group therapy for substance use disorders versus mixed-gender group drug counseling. *Drug and Alcohol Dependence*, 90(1), 39–47. doi: DOI: 10.1016/j.drugalcdep.2007.02.009

Greer, G. (1972). *The female eunuch* (4th ed.). New York, New York: Bantam.

Hensley, L. G. (2002). Treatment for survivors of rape: Issues and interventions. *Journal of Mental Health Counseling*, 24(4), 331.

Holmes, L. (2002). Women in group and women's groups. *International Journal of Group Psychotherapy*, 52(2), 171–188.

Kauffman, E., Dore, M. M., & Nelson-Zlupko, L. (1995). The role of women's therapy groups in the treatment of chemical dependence. *American Journal of Orthopsychiatry*, 65(3), 355–363. doi:10.1037/h0079657

Keen, S. (1992). *Fire in the belly* (4th ed.). New York, New York: Bantam.

Kipper, D. A., & Ritchie, T. D. (2003). The effectiveness of psychodramatic techniques: A meta-analysis. *Group Dynamics*, 7(1), 13–25.

Kissane, D. W., Bloch, S., Smith, G. C., et al. (2003). Cognitive-existential group psychotherapy for women with primary breast cancer: A randomized controlled trial. *Psycho-Oncology*, 12(6), 532–546.

Klein, M. (1976). Feminist concepts of therapy outcome. *Psychotherapy: Theory, Research and Practice*, 13(1), 89–95.

Leaper, C., & Anderson, K. J. (1997). Gender development and heterosexual romantic relationships during adolescence. *New Directions for Child and Adolescent Development*, 1997(78), 85–103.

Lenihan, G.O. (1985). The therapeutic gay support group: A call for professional involvement. *Psychotherapy: Theory, Research, and Practice*, 22(4), 729–739.

Lieberman, M. A., Solow, N., Bond, G. R., et al. (1979). The psychotherapeutic impact of women's consciousness-raisingnn groups. *Archives of General Psychiatry,*, 36(2), 161–168.

Moyers, B., & Bly, R. (Producers). (1990). *A gathering of men*. [VHS] Available on Amazon.

Orzack, M. H., Voluse, A. C., Wolf, D., et al. (2006). An ongoing study of group treatment for men involved in problematic internet-enabled sexual behavior. *CyberPsychology and Behavior*, 9(3), 348–360.

Osherson, S. (1986). *Finding our fathers: The unfinished business of manhood*. Free Press.

Palmer, S. E., Brown, R. A., & Barrera, M. E. (1992). Group treatment program for abusive husbands: long-term evaluation. *American Journal of Orthopsychiatry*, 62(2), 276–283. doi:10.1037/h0079336

Richards, R. L., Burlingame, G. M., & Fuhriman, A. (1990). Theme-oriented group therapy. *The Counseling Psychologist, 18*(1), 80–92.

Rutan,, S., Stone, W., & Shay, J. (2007). *Psychodynamic group therapy* (4th ed.). New York: Guilford Press.

Slusher, M. P., Mayer, C. J., & Dunkle, R. E. (1996). Gays and Lesbians Older and Wiser (GLOW): A support group for older gay people. *The Gerontologist, 36*(1), 118–123.

Walker, L. S. (1981). Are women's groups different? *Psychotherapy: Theory, Research and Practice, 18*(2), 240–245.

Westefeld, J., & Winklepleck, J. (1983). University counseling service groups for gay students. *Small Group Behavior, 14*(1), 121–128.

Wilfley, D., Agras, W., Telch, C., et al. (1993). Group cognitive-behavioral therapy and group interpersonal psychotherapy for the nonpurging bulimic individual: A controlled comparison. *Journal of Consulting and Clinical Psychology, 61*(2), 296–305.

Wright, F. (1987). Men, shame and antisocial behavior: A psychodynamic perspective. *Group, 11*(4), 238–246.

20
Sexual Diversity in Group Psychotherapy
Morris Nitsun

This paper argues that sexuality is marginalized in the group psychotherapeutic literature and that sexual diversity, in particular, is seldom addressed directly and in depth. This is out of touch with the contemporary recognition and acceptance of a broad range of sexual orientations and lifestyles. The lack of an adequate sexual discourse in group psychotherapy potentially creates theoretical and technical problems in dealing with sexual diversity, failing to challenge prejudice and unnecessary pathologization.

Sex and sexuality may be difficult to address openly in groups because of the highly personal nature of individual sexuality and its propensity for shame. Since sex is so much of the body and bodily fantasy, it may be difficult to communicate openly in a group. However, the author proposes a group psychotherapy perspective of sexuality, based on his book, "The Group as an Object of Desire" (Nitsun 2006), which respects the group process while acknowledging changes in the understanding and representation of sexual diversity. The elements of this model are:

1. An embodied view of the psychotherapy group, in which the body is given greater emphasis.
2. The recognition of an erotic imagination.
3. An awareness of the group as witness in relation to problems of intimacy and sexual relatedness, and
4. An acknowledgement of group morality as influencing the expression of sexual difference.

While some might argue that such "freedom" would encourage sexual acting-out, the author contends that an open sexual discourse in the group is likely to decrease rather than increase the potential for sexual transgression.

The role of the group therapist is crucial in facilitating an open and constructive dialogue concerning sexuality. The author is a British group analyst who writes from his clinical experience in the UK and draws on contemporary group analytic and psychoanalytic perspectives, while holding a critical position in relation to the normative and conformist tendency of some analytic traditions.

Introduction

Diversity is a key issue in group psychotherapy. Of all the psychotherapies, group therapy is the closest in spirit to a diverse society since the group approach is usually based on plural membership and the appreciation of difference (Thyssen,1992). Yet, the problem of prejudice, potentially intensified by increased diversity, remains as much an issue in therapy groups as it does in the wider society. Various publications have highlighted this and attempted to address the emergent difficulties (Burman, 2002; Weegmann, 2007; Debiak, 2007) but it is not clear how the different models of group psychotherapy deal with diversity. This is reflected in the fairly sparse literature on sexuality and sexual diversity in group psychotherapy relative to the explosion of interest in sexuality in the media and on the internet. We appear to live in a considerably more free and sexually tolerant world than existed just a few decades ago. But in some respects this has complicated individuals' sexual choice and behavior, as well as society's views, and it is important that our psychotherapeutic approaches take full account of these changes.

I have argued (Nitsun, 2006) that sexuality and intimacy are important subjects in group therapy not only because they play such a significant part in people's lives but because the group itself is strengthened by openness about these subjects. One reason why people fear and resist groups is the anxiety about intimacy, in terms of relationships both *outside* and *inside* the group. I have suggested that a group with marked anti-group tendencies (Nitsun, 1996) is likely to be one in which intimacy and sexuality cannot be openly explored and that, conversely, dissociation and repression of sexuality in the group contribute to the formation of an anti-group. Hence, the "group as an object of desire" is a group in which there is sufficient trust and safety to engage freely in the sexual discourse, including the various forms of sexual diversity.

The Background

I begin the consideration of sexuality in group psychotherapy by contrasting the individual psychotherapeutic/psychoanalytic and group analytic/group psychotherapeutic traditions: how has sexuality been dealt with in these two traditions and how have they approached the theme of sexual diversity?

The relative neglect of sexual diversity in group psychotherapy reflects a wider problem – the under-emphasis, as I see it, on sexuality more generally in our field. It is a subject that seldom appears in any depth in the literature on groups. For example, Yalom, in his otherwise comprehensive texts on groups, hardly touches on the subject and in the group-analytic field, which is my specialist area, the subject seldom appears in the literature. This is a curious situation when compared with individual psychoanalytic or psychotherapeutic approaches where sex has featured as a major discourse, albeit in a normative way. In order to make sense of the discrepancy, and its implications for both group theory and practice, I will briefly look at the psychoanalytic background which still influences some current psychotherapeutic thinking and then consider more fully sexuality in group psychotherapy

Sexuality in Psychoanalysis

Psychoanalysis was born in an explosion of interest and controversy about sexuality. It was the secrecy and hypocrisy about sexuality in late 19th century Vienna that struck Freud and what he saw as the basis of many of the problems presenting in the consulting room. Since then, sexuality has maintained a dominant position in the development of psychoanalysis. But there are ambiguities and inconsistencies in this development. Here, I highlight some of the distinguishing features and contradictions in the psychoanalytic discourse on sexuality, not only as critique of psychoanalysis in its own right but also as a framework within which we might consider the requirements of a meaningful and useful approach to sexuality in group therapy:

1. Although there is a great deal of emphasis theoretically on sexuality in the individual psychotherapeutic/psychoanalytic tradition, there is less clarity about how this translates into the consulting room. The bodily aspect of sexuality may be difficult to communicate and share between therapist and client. Confusion about these matters is complicated by concern in the last few decades about sexual misconduct between therapist and patient arising in the consulting room: there now exist more stringent rules and punishments. These tensions may account for what appears to be a decreasing emphasis on sexuality in psychoanalytic practice, a situation Mann (2003) has described as the "desexualiszation of psychoanalysis".
2. Psychoanalysis from early on adopted a normative approach to sexuality. Freud himself regarded bisexuality and early polymorphous sexuality as natural, describing how these tendencies had to be repressed in order to conform to social expectations. However, psychoanalysis increasingly represented a socially conformist position on sexual difference. This had a major influence on the perception and understanding of sexual diversity, with an overriding emphasis on perversion, a point to which I will return later.
3. The outcome of these developments was that psychoanalysis paradoxically has had both a liberalizing and a restraining influence – liberalizing in so far as it took the lid off sexuality, but restraining because it reflected orthodox social norms and tended to pathologize much of sexual diversity.

Sexuality in Group Analysis and Group Psychotherapy

Almost the opposite situation obtains in group psychotherapy. Whereas psychoanalysis is saturated by sexuality, group psychotherapy, including group analysis, is marked by an almost total absence of any discourse on sexuality. There is very little written about it and even less clarity about how it is dealt with in the consulting room.

Foulkes, who originated group analysis, put limited emphasis on sexuality and, in keeping with the fact that he wrote about 50 years ago, adopted the conservative views of the time. Similarly in the USA, where there is a much greater range of group psychotherapeutic approaches, sexuality has nevertheless been given relatively little emphasis.

This has led to the following situation:

1. Sexuality in general and sexual diversity in particular have been marginalized in group psychotherapy.
2. The lack of an adequate framework for considering sexuality in group creates ambiguity and uncertainty about how to deal with it in practice.
3. The lack of a discourse can lead to an uncritical absorption of values and norms concerning sexual diversity, with little debate about its significance and meaning in group psychotherapy.

Given this unsatisfactory situation, where do we go from here?

The Changing Landscape of Sexual Diversity

There have been significant changes in sexual norms in the last few decades with far greater openness about sexual diversity. It is not clear that psychotherapeutic approaches have kept up with these changes. In this section, I consider three alternative perspectives of sexual diversity and how they have gradually yielded to a more open and flexible contemporary perspective but with vestiges of prejudice still present in psychotherapeutic practice.

Diversity as perversion

I return here to the psychoanalytic emphasis on perversion. I agree with the views of Muriel Dimen (1995) who argues that psychoanalysis was influenced from early on by what she calls "The Discourse of Nature." Freud, writing at the time of Darwin, was influenced by the exigencies of biology and reproductive survival, within which "normal" sexuality is defined in terms of genital heterosexual intercourse. Sexual preferences outside of this biological view were generally interpreted as perversions. Although Freud himself had the imaginative ability to comprehend sexuality in its very different forms, his followers concretized notions of perversions and for many decades sexual diversity was routinely pathologized. This was reinforced by strongly conservative attitudes in psychiatry, identified with Kraft-Ebbing, and reflected in the identification and categorization of perversions based mainly on heterosexual assumptions.

Linked to this was the strong tendency in psychoanalysis to pursue a sharp division in the roles of the sexes so that masculinity and femininity were defined in opposition to each other and gender differences conceived as a polarity. This tendency was reinforced by the prevalence of the Oedipus complex as an explanation of sexual development, since the resolution of the complex in conventional terms is seen as identification with the same-sex parent and desire for the opposite sex parent. The combination of these influences led not only to psychoanalysis as a body of theory reflecting and reinforcing social orthodoxy but to treatment approaches that emphasized heterosexual adjustment. There are many accounts in 20th Century literature of homosexuals of both sexes feeling misunderstood and pathologized in psychotherapy (O'Connor and Ryan 1993).

Diversity as natural

The tide started turning when both the women's movement and the gay liberation movement of the 1960s onwards began to challenge many of these assumptions. The naturalness of women's sexuality and of people's sexual attraction to members of the same sex became key positions in these movements, undermining stereotypes and prejudices that had held sway for many years. The decentering of the sexual subject from its conventional frame was further assisted by the post-modern thinking of the later 20th century, writers like Foucault and Derrida arguing against notions of unitary identity and for the existence of diversity, *between* individuals and *within* individuals. Society, rather than biology, was increasingly seen as the constructor and mediator of sexual norms and, as such, could be challenged. A later development of the 20th century – and continuing in the 21st – are the advances in reproductive technology, resulting in new ways of having children, independent of the necessity for heterosexual intercourse (Raphael-Leff 2010). This further lessens biological necessity as the absolute criterion of sexual maturity and adds substance and openness to a wider range of sexual preferences. The outcome in the last decade or two has been dramatic. Take, for example, the civil recognition of gay partnerships in marriage – something that just 5 or 10 years ago would have been thought of as impossible and that now is common in several countries in the world.

Diversity as experimental

If the trend in the 20th century was moving toward a greater appreciation of sexual diversity, through the intellectual and social movements I have described, real expansion of diversity came through the phenomenon that has changed our culture in many ways – the internet. By extending our knowledge of sexuality and opening networks of communication between people of different persuasions, the internet has both revealed and created a vast landscape of sexual diversity. The internet caters to people of every conceivable sexual preference. This has created problems of its own, including the greater opportunity for acting out of dangerous or destructive forms of sexuality. But, on the whole, the internet has helped to universalize and normalize large areas of sexual difference that have previously remained underground.

Another way in which the internet has encouraged the acknowledgement of sexual diversity is through the creation of virtual relationships. Again, this may be of dubious value, given the retreat from actual to virtual relationships, but it allows for greater elements of play within individuals' sexual repertoire and facilitates different sexual possibilities. This is epitomized in the creation of alternative identities, sexual and otherwise – also known as avatars – which is integral to internet movements such as

Second Life, a virtual universe which is subscribed to by many millions of people and which offers opportunities for fictitious but compelling sexual lives.

The upshot of all this change in the construction and representation of sexual diversity is that psychotherapists now face a very different sexual landscape from that of just 10 or 20 years ago. For group psychotherapy, this presents a particular challenge. The group culture is naturally inclined towards diversity; most psychotherapy groups consisting of heterogeneous populations, and valuing of diversity as a condition for growth and change. Yet, given the absence of a sexual discourse in group psychotherapy, how are we to address the current situation?

Parameters of Sexual Diversity in the Group

What do we mean by sexual diversity? If we adopt a wide definition of the term, we may consider the following: homosexuality in its various manifestations – or what may be called the "homosexualities," since there is no one form of homosexuality (Stoller, 1979, 1985); the differing degrees of bisexuality, some enacted and others not; variations in sexual behavior from celibate to promiscuous; sexual preferences within both heterosexuals and homosexuals that include sadomasochistic fantasies and activities; fetishisms; and transgender identities.

The most common form of sexual diversity encountered in clinical practice is homosexuality. I am therefore focusing on this as an illustration of my views. Given the greater acceptance of homosexuality in society, it is not surprising that many more openly homosexual men and women are presenting for psychotherapy. In both my own National Health Service practice in the UK, and my private practice, I have seen a steady increase of gay individuals over the years. This filters through to all forms of therapy and certainly group therapy. In most groups I know of, either as conductor or supervisor, gay members now constitute a significant proportion of the membership.

This increase in gay referrals and self-referrals fundamentally reflects changing demographics rather than suggesting that gay individuals are inherently more disturbed than any others. At the same time, it is important to recognize that, while it is easier for people to acknowledge their gayness more openly, there are still anxieties and problems about homosexual identity. In spite of major attitudinal changes in society there remain pockets of fierce conservatism and prejudice. As recently as late 2008, Pope Benedict XVl, in his Christmas address, publically proclaimed homosexuality as evil and undermining the work of the church. While the Catholic church is not known for its liberal attitudes, this is nevertheless a sharp reminder that large tracts of society still hold conservative and reactionary viewpoints concerning sexual diversity. And this is reflected in the continuing doubts and difficulties of gay people themselves – continuing feelings of isolation and exclusion and continuing struggles with acceptance of their own sexuality – a condition widely regarded as internalized homophobia. Gay people frequently find themselves in a bind – aware of a more open society in some respects, enjoying some new freedoms but still carrying the burden of prejudice. A study in 2006 by Hegarty and Buechel has suggested that while there is greater tolerance of sexual identity differences, including homosexuality, there remains intolerance concerning sexual *practice*.

An important point is that all sexuality, not just homosexuality, may be difficult. However exciting and fulfilling sex can be, sexuality for many adults is problematic. Stoller (1979), one of the great contemporary writers on sexuality, has described much of adult sexuality as awkward, variably satisfying and often anxiety-provoking. Christopher Bollas (2000) suggests "sex is inherently traumatic." I make this point so as to widen our focus. It is not just those with minority sexual interests who have problems. We all have problems in this sensitive and important area. Part of the difficulty may be the complex nature of much sexuality, including what might be called "internal sexual diversity" – the diversity that exists within each one of us. This can include bisexual fantasies and impulses; confusion about sexual orientation; variations in the object of our sexual desire; conflicting sexual desires, say for active and passive sexual experience; the pulls of auto-erotic versus relational sex; sexual fantasies of a "transgressive" nature; and the changing nature of sexual functioning as we go through life, from youth to old age.

Perhaps the point here is not to isolate sexual diversity as something that belongs to just some individuals but to include it in the wider spectrum of sexuality, the overall pool of fantasy and desire to which we all belong. But this gets back to the problem of sexuality being such a marginal discourse in group psychotherapy. If we are hardly addressing it in our literature, where do we begin? In the next section I want to propose some ideas about how we can fill this gap.

Developing a Group Psychotherapy Perspective of Sexuality

Drawing on the ideas in my book, "The Group as an Object of Desire" (Nitsun 2006), I consider the therapy group from three main perspectives – as an embodied group, as a container of the erotic imagination and as a group representing a moral position. I also want to consider the notion of the group as witness.

The embodied group

Contrary to the impression that sexuality may be off the agenda in groups, given its marginalization in the literature, most group therapists would probably agree that sexuality is usually very present in groups, whether openly discussed or not. Among the few writers who have directly addressed this issue, Moeller (2002) described the group as "a highly charged libidinal network" and Tylim (2003) described it as a "theatre of desire." In my own writing, I have drawn attention to the bodily, non-verbal aspects of the group, where members sit in close proximity to each other, close enough to see, touch and smell. Sexual attraction, desire and fantasy enter into the here-and-now of the group, in addition to members' awareness of their sexuality and relationships outside of the consulting room. Group therapy, therefore, is not just an interaction between minds, which is how it is often described (Behr and Hearst 2005), but between bodies, and these bodies in their different ways are sexual bodies. This may seem obvious but is an observation that has so far not been developed in our field. Almost all of the emphasis has been on verbal communication and the meeting of minds. Perhaps it is time to look at bodies meeting and communicating.

The erotic imagination

I use the term "the erotic imagination" to describe not just a single individual's erotic fantasies and thoughts but a wider erotic imagination, a container of the diverse range of desires and fantasies. I suggest that a therapy group generates an erotic imagination, comprising the members' individual desire within a matrix that is greater than the sum of its parts. This includes conscious and unconscious fantasy. The more free the erotic imagination, the greater the scope it gives for exploration in the group and the more likely it will be that members will share the hidden aspects of their sexuality. Conversely, restraints on the erotic imagination will be reflected in inhibition and concealment in the group. Although this might not matter for some members, it might be crucial for others, particularly those who are anxious about "transgressive" thoughts and impulses, those who are concealing painful aspects of their sexuality and those who are especially prone to shame.

Group morality

Groups also hold a moral position, whether overt or covert. As sexuality is so constrained by social norms, the way the therapy group represents the conventional morality will strongly influence the freedom with which sexuality is addressed in the group. I want to make a plea for a generous morality. Elias (1978), a sociologist who influenced Foulkes' thinking about groups, has written extensively about the power of social restraints. He makes a distinction between "necessary restraints" and "unnecessary restraints." The former refers to restraints that are a necessary part of an ordered, sane society, the latter to restraints that reflect the operation of vested interests and arbitrary controls. Whereas the former are needed in the interest of a well-functioning society, the latter are open to challenge and revision. I suggest that this is true of the restraints surrounding sexual diversity. While restraints are entirely appropriate in situations where harm may come to an individual/s – and there are forms of sexual diversity that have a destructive potential and that are genuinely perverse – this does not hold true for the majority. Notions of perversion are too easily conflated with difference. The therapy group, rather than simply mirroring conventional restraints, is in principle, free to question them. In this sense, it has the potential to become a benign authority, a fairer, kinder morality than the morality of the super-ego, the harsh, critical function of the self and culture that is the internalization of repressive social controls (Elias 1978).

The revised morality of the group may go some way toward mitigating the shame that is so often an aspect of sexuality. Revealing sexuality in a group is usually difficult. It is one of the most private and personal aspects of ourselves, rarely discussed with others in any detail or depth. The bodily aspect of sexuality adds to this sensitivity. The body, in its nakedness, may be enshrouded in shame. This is probably true of all sexuality but more so with sexual diversity, since the shame about difference may be even greater. This is where a group that reflects a benign morality may be of real value. The emergence of such a morality in the group and how it is shaped, possibly through the therapist's attitudes and interventions, possibly through members openness and curiosity, is therefore of crucial importance in facilitating the wider reaches of the sexual subject.

The group as witness

Unlike individual therapy, where there are just two players in the room, each enacting a very different role, groups have the advantage of several members in addition to the therapist. The opportunity for a range of observations and opinions is an integral part of the group therapeutic process, adding the strength of diversity to whichever discourse is uppermost. I suggest this is another advantage for the exploration of sexuality. While revealing sexuality in a group may be difficult for the reasons outlined above, the subject nevertheless benefits from the different views that are usually forthcoming in a group. One of the difficulties of dealing with intimacy in ordinary life is the relative isolation in which this may occur. Intimacy, sexual or otherwise, usually takes place between two people. Whereas this is an appropriate condition for the expression of intimacy, it can also be the occasion for anxiety, invasion and abuse. Bringing matters of intimacy into a group opens the experience to new forms of facilitation and understanding. I have described this in my writing as "re-contextualizing intimacy" (Nitsun 2006).

These comments suggest that the therapy group can be a valuable context for the exploration of sexuality in general and sexual diversity in particular. The group, rather than constraining the acceptance of sexual diversity, may help to bridge the differences that are so much a part of sexuality.

It remains for me to consider the therapist's role in this process and to look at the ethical implications of group therapist conduct.

The Group Therapist

I suggest that the therapist has a crucial role in influencing the sexual discourse in group psychotherapy. The therapist's morality must affect the discourse. When it comes to difficult issues where prejudice may occur, group members are likely to be sensitive to the therapist's views, whether stated or not. In turn, this depends very much on who the therapist is, his or her own sexual experience and what attitudes he or she brings to the subject of sexual diversity. I say this recognizing that few of us are free of preferences of our own, as well as inhibitions and prejudices. As Mitchell (1996) points out, the requirement is not so much that we free ourselves totally of prejudice, since this is impossible, but that we are able to reflect on our prejudices and recognize how these influence our work and our moment to moment judgments.

I suggest that there are ethical aspects to the sexual subject in group therapy. In general, as Debiak (2007) has pointed out, there is an overlap of ethical and diversity issues in group psychotherapy practice. But this has particular relevance to sexual diversity. We are familiar with ethics as related to questions of sexual acting-out in psychotherapy and accept that there are fundamental boundary requirements that protect members from sexual transgression and exploitation. These are ethical considerations. But ethics also apply to the therapist's management of sexual diversity. How one makes decisions about what sexual differences to include in the group, how one approaches this difference and how one intervenes in the exploration of sexual diversity are all ethical concerns. In the past, the subject of sexual diversity has raised questions about the acceptability of difference in a largely conformist society. I suggest that has largely changed: the ethical concern now is how responsibly we deal with sexual diversity. The point is no longer whether diversity exists and whether it is acceptable: it is how humanly and imaginatively we deal with diversity as a given in society.

Clinical Illustration

Marian, a successful professional woman in her late twenties, was referred for private once-weekly group psychotherapy. She had, some years earlier, undergone individual psychotherapy in an attempt to deal with doubts and difficulties surrounding her homosexuality. She had found the individual therapy frustrating and limiting. The therapist, a psychoanalytically trained woman, regarded Marian's homosexuality as a defensive reaction to anxieties about her femininity and competition with other women for a male partner. Marian was uncomfortable with this line of interpretation as she felt intrinsically homosexual and the interpretation invalidated her own understanding of herself. She felt she had come for help with adjusting to her sexuality rather than deconstructing or changing it. However, her discomfort with the therapist's interpretation was interpreted as psychotherapeutic resistance. She was also unable to share affectionate and loving feelings she intermittently felt towards the therapist, for fear of censure or further interpretation. Increasingly frustrated, she left individual therapy after three years.

By the time she was referred for group therapy approximately eight years later, Marian had made a more active adjustment as a lesbian. She had formed lesbian friendships and met a woman with whom she established a close emotional relationship and with whom she was now living. Their relationship was proceeding well until her partner expressed a strong wish to have a child that would be reared by them as a couple. The prospect of becoming a parent to a child she had not conceived, as well as dealing with the presence of a baby, precipitated a crisis in Marian.

Returning to psychotherapy, Marian joined a twice-weekly analytic group that in addition to several straight members included a gay man, a woman with a homosexual son and a man in a heterosexual marriage struggling to deal with his homosexual wishes. The group was run by a female therapist who had been through an actively bisexual phase some years earlier but had settled into a heterosexual partnership. Although anxious about joining an ongoing group, Marian quite soon felt that she had made the right choice of psychotherapy. She felt far more able in the group to talk openly about her sexuality than she had in the individual therapy – and without a fear of censure or "corrective" interpretation. Her problems resonated with several other members and their problems in turn touched her. She also found the female therapist highly attuned to her. There was a high level of feedback in the group, with moments of pronounced intimacy, the therapist facilitating a here-and-now

> approach. This enabled members to talk about feelings of attraction and desire in the group that crossed the conventional lines of gender and sexual orientation.
>
> Belonging to this group of people struggling with issues of sexual diversity became a very meaningful experience for Marian. She was able to address some of her continuing pain about being a lesbian, her difficulties with her family's ambivalence, and her grief about the possibility of her never conceiving a child of her own. Through this, she was able to understand her distress about her partner having a child and the elements of envy, jealousy and feared exclusion that had been stirred up in her. She was gradually able to adjust to the plan and when her partner eventually gave birth, she coped relatively well. At first overwhelmed and ambivalent about the arrival of a noisy infant with all its demands, she settled into her own role as a parent and became increasingly attached to the child.

It is worth pointing out the eight years' time gap between Marian's individual therapy and her group therapy. During these eight years there had no doubt been a cultural shift in attitudes towards homosexuality: a widening of the sexual agenda and greater tolerance of diversity. The therapy group reflected these changes and at the same time exemplified several of the features of a contemporary group approach to sexuality that I have outlined in this paper. These features could be summed up as follows:

1. Sexual diversity is no longer a hidden subject but has become available for open discussion and exploration.
2. The presence of a range of sexual preferences requires a tolerant environment in which to deal with the difficulties of sexual adjustment.
3. The group approaches this not as an intellectual exercise but as an embodied entity in which it is possible to share feelings of attraction and intimacy. The group is capable of an erotic imagination.
4. The group adopts a benign morality in which fears of judgment and censure may be allayed.
5. The group re-contextualizes intimacy by providing a witnessing and containing function to the exploration of sexuality.
6. The feedback and interpretive system involves all members of the group, including the therapist, rather than the therapist solely representing social attitudes. This guards against therapist bias or prejudice.
7. However, the process benefits from a therapist who, through experience and personal morality, is open to sexual diversity.
8. The group provides a place to belong which counteracts feelings of separateness and alienation that may arise in dealing with sexual difference.
9. These group characteristics contribute to the group as an object of desire in contrast to an anti-group in which there is an alienation of desire.

Conclusion

The psychotherapeutic group, sometimes regarded as a medium in which it is difficult to deal openly with sexuality and sexual difference, emerges as a very relevant frame for dealing with diversity in contemporary society. Through its potential for embodiment, its openness to the erotic imagination, its adoption of a benign morality in keeping with progressive social attitudes and its function as a witness to expressions and problems of intimacy, it offers a potentially valuable experience for those dealing with diversity. This must be balanced with regard for confidentiality and boundary management which prevent inappropriate acting-out. This will be influenced by the group therapist's own morality, fairness and openness, all of which are reflections of the ethical imperative that guides our work.

References and Bibliography

Behr, H., & Hearst, L. (2005). *Group-analytic psychotherapy: A meeting of the minds*. London: Wiley Blackwell.
Bollas, C. (2000). *Hysteria*. London: Routledge.
Burman, E. (2002). Gender, sexuality and power in groups. *Group Analysis*, 35, 540–559.
Debiak, D. (2007). Attending to diversity in group psychotherapy: an ethical imperative. *International Journal of Group Psychotherapy*, 57, 1–12.
Dimen, M. (1995). On "our nature": Prologemon to a relational theory of sexuality. In T. Domenici, & R. C. Lesser (Eds.), *Disorientating sexuality*. New York: Routledge.
Elias, N. (1978). *The history of manners: the civilizing process, vol. 1*. Oxford: Blackwell.
Hegarty, P. & Buechel, C. (2006). Androcentric reporting of gender differences in APA articles, 1965–2004. *Review of General Psychology*, 10, 377–389.
Mann, D. (ed.) (2003). *Erotic transference and counter-transference*. Hove: Brunner-Routledge.
Mitchell, S. (1996). Gender and sexual orientation in the age of postmodernism: the plight of the perplexed clinician. *Gender and Psychoanalysis*, 1, 45–74.
Moeller, M. L. (2002). Love in the group. *Group Analysis*, 35, 484–498.
Nitsun M. (1996). *The anti-group: Destructive forces in the group and their creative potential*. London: Routledge.
Nitsun M. (2006). *The group as an object of desire: Exploring sexuality in group psychotherapy*. London: Routledge.
O'Connor, N., & Ryan, J. (1993). *Wild desires and mistaken identities*. London: Virago.
Raphael-Leff, J. (2010). "Generative identity" and diversity of desire. *Group Analysis*, 43, 539–558.
Stoller, R. J. (1979). *Sexual excitement: Dynamics of erotic life*. London: Maresfield Library.
Thyssen, B. (1992). Diversity as a group-specific therapeutic factor in group-analytic psychotherapy. *Group Analysis*, 25, 75–86.
Tylim, I. (2003). Eroticism in group psychotherapy: psychoanalytic reflections on desire, agony, and ecstacy. *International Journal of Group Psychotherapy*, 53, 443–457.
Weegmann, M. (2007). Group analysis and homosexuality – indifference or hostility? *Group Analysis*, 40, 59–76.

21

Group Therapy For Females Molested In Girlhood

Shoshana Ben-Noam

Introduction

> ### Clinical Illustration
>
> Moira[1] was sexually abused by her father since the age of 9. For the first several weeks, he playfully tickled her and she giggled. Then, the tickling changed to gentle fondling between her legs. She didn't understand the sensations in her body and was afraid to move. Gradually, the caressing became rough and she felt sore. Her father told her she was his special little girl and she better keep their special time secret to avoid trouble. She was confused and scared. The abuse stopped at the age of 11 when her parents were divorced.

Moira didn't understand her sexual arousal and the father's actions. She was confused by her father shifting from playful, seductive behavior to rough fondling. She was also constantly petrified he would return to inflict more pain. Even worse, she was afraid he would abandon her if she didn't keep the secret. "The horror . . . [was] not in the sexual act, but in the exploitation . . . and the corruption of parental love" (Herman, 2000: p.4).

Characteristics of Child Sexual Abuse

Child sexual abuse is the misuse of a child by an adult for the sexual needs and gratification of the perpetrator. To be legally determined abuse, the sexual act has to be

---

[1] No real names are used in the chapter.

between a child under the age of 18 (Doll, et al., 2004; Finkelhor, 2008) and an adult who has power over them (Gartner, 1999; Herman, 2000). This power leads to the child's compliance out of fear of rejection, punishment and abandonment, particularly in incestuous relationships.

The sexual abuser may be a member of the child's nuclear or extended family, or a non-family member as a teacher, coach or clergy. It is often that the abuser is known to the victim (Finkelhor, 1994) and the child trusts him/her. This trust, in conjunction with seductive behavior, initially leads the child to cooperate with the sexually abusive acts. These involve fondling of genitals through clothing or directly, oral-genital contact, attempted intercourse or intercourse. It also includes exhibitionism and pornography. These sexual acts destroy the child's trust in the perpetrator and very likely in other individuals. The mistrust engendered by the abuse, along with the child's real or feared threats by the abuser, often prevents the child from disclosing the molestation.

Cultural Impact on Disclosure

Disclosure of sexual abuse has undergone a cultural revolution in the last few decades. It has received unprecedented social exposure as a result of the Women's Movement in the 1960s and 1970s, and the active promotion of the disclosure of abuse by the Children's Protection Movement. In addition, the media gave center stage to celebrities such as Oprah Winfrey, Roseanne Arnold and McKenzie Phillips who came forward with their own stories of sexual abuse in their families (e.g. Gorman and Dolan, 1991). Furthermore, during this same time period more books were published on personal accounts of sexually victimized girls (e.g., Freeman, 2005; Braddock Bromley, 2007). The impact of this publicity may have encouraged an increased number of sexually abused women in girlhood to come forward with their stories or seek treatment. However, as yet, no statistics are readily available to document it.

In contrast to the extensive publicity of girls' molestation, the sexual abuse of boys has been minimized (Courtois, 2010). This changed when the sexual victimization of young boys by Catholic priests was highlighted in the press (e.g., Cooperman, 2005; Slack, 2005; Donadio, 2010) and when other instances were revealed by former scouts of the Boy Scouts of America (Boyle, 1994). However, the fact that incest of boys often goes unreported may be in part attributed to the cultural notion that boys are not traditionally the victims in their families.

The aftereffects of child sexual abuse vary considerably between men and women (Gold et al., 1999). This chapter will address the ramifications and treatment of women only.

Factors Affecting Female Survivors of Childhood Sexual Abuse

To better understand the consequences of women's childhood sexual victimization, we need to consider the circumstances in which the abuse occurred. These include the following factors:

Age of onset and developmental stage

Some studies documented the age of onset as 8–12 years old, while others suggested a younger age (Courtois, 2010). The younger the age of onset of repeated parent-daughter incest, the more likely it will be dissociated to enable the girl to establish an attachment with the abusive parent. Whereas the older latency girl maybe more aware of the abuse and therefore more distressed while it happens.

In both infancy and latency developmental stages, sexual abuse disrupts the girl's psychological and cognitive development in areas such as learning, emotional regulation and social isolation. She is consciously or unconsciously preoccupied with the abuse and has difficulties dealing with its affective impact.

Duration and frequency of abuse

Prolonged, repeated abuse is more harmful than a brief period or single occurrence of abuse since it further exacerbates the loss of trust and betrayal.

Types of sexual acts

Sexual abuse involving penetration and/or violence are more harmful than other types of acts as they cause intense pain, horror and serious traumatizing effects. However, on the continuum of noncontact to manual or genital contact, it is not clear which acts are the most damaging to the victim since the context of the abuse must be considered.

Girl's relationship to the abuser

The closer the relationship between the perpetrator and the child, the greater the psychological damage. Parent-child incest is associated with the most serious aftereffects because of the betrayal and loss of trust. Also, sexual abuse within the family is more likely to affect emotional and cognitive disturbances than abuse outside the family.

Nondisclosure/disclosure by sexually abused girls

Children's nondisclosure at the time of the abuse is often due to the fear of the abuser's threats; fear of being blamed or not believed; or, at a very young age, not understanding they were abused. Nondisclosure, then, usually prevents intervention, prolongs the abuse and often has negative consequences (to be discussed later in the chapter).

Disclosure is most likely to occur when the perpetrator is a nonfamily member, and the least likely to occur when the abuser is within the nuclear family, since incest threatens the parent-daughter, or siblings' bond. Once the victim discloses the sexual abuse to her mother, another family member, or a trusted adult, a protective and supportive response may stop the abuse and reduce damage. When the response entails blaming or shaming of the child, more traumatic manifestations might emerge at a later age.

Secure/insecure attachments

A secure mother-child (or caregiver) attachment may mitigate negative consequences of sexual abuse. The victimized girl has the mother's "safe base" to return to and be protected by, thereby decreasing the possibility of trauma.

In contrast, insecure attachments with the parent/caregiver often induce the girl to "become fearfully . . . attached . . . or anxiously obedient" (van der Kolk, 1987a: p. 32). Thus, she is more susceptible to sexual abuse inside and outside the family.

In summary, prolonged, repeated sexual abuse with an early age of onset, coupled with insecure attachments, are linked to negative consequences such as cognitive and emotional disturbances as well as interpersonal difficulties with peers during childhood. These are likely to set the stage for further symptomatology during adolescence and adulthood, especially "when the trauma has been neither acknowledged nor treated" (Krugman, 1987: p. 128) and the world awaiting the innocent victim has been tainted with violation.

Functional Definitions of Trauma, PTSD and Complex PTSD for Sexually Victimized Women in Childhood

Trauma

Psychological trauma renders the abused girl helpless by overwhelming force (Herman, 1992a: p. 33). She is horrified, experiences loss of control and intense fear of annihilation. She also feels trapped in an inescapable situation, especially in father-daughter incest. It is the fear of punishment or abandonment that keeps her compliant.

The traumatized girl often manifests symptoms of Post-Traumatic Stress Disorder such as startle reactions, flashbacks and avoidance behavior.

Post-traumatic stress disorder (PTSD)

"In PTSD the past (of childhood sexual abuse) is relived with an immediate sensory and emotional intensity that makes victims feel as if the event were occurring all over again" (van der Kolk, et al., 1996: p. 8). The onset may occur immediately after the abuse, months or even years later. The three main clusters of PTSD symptoms are "hyperarousal" (Herman, 1992a: p. 35; Van der Kolk, 1987a: p. 3) "intrusive reexperiencing" (van der Kolk, 1987a: p. 3). and "avoidance" (Figley, 1985: p. 263).

The hyperarousal cluster Includes sleeping difficulties, irritability, and easy startle. This cluster, often applicable to women sexually abused in girlhood, may be understood as a constant arousal of the autonomic nervous system in anticipation of returned danger. This ongoing elevated state of arousal may cause difficulties for traumatized women in modulating anger and anxiety, particularly in situations associated with the traumatic event. For example, a woman molested by her father may be easily startled when incidentally touched by a man or easily irritated when having a minor disagreement with a male co-worker.

The reexperiencing cluster Includes flashbacks, nightmares, and intrusive recollections of the traumatic event along with the emotional intensity of the event itself. Flashbacks or nightmares may occur when a woman, sexually molested in childhood, enters significant, emotionally charged phases or events in her life, such as a wedding or entering college. The traumatic experience is then consciously or unconsciously relived. In addition, insignificant reminders such as the smell of a pipe or the décor of a specific room may trigger a woman's memories of the abuse.

The avoidance cluster Includes numbing, a feeling of being detached from the world, emotionally constricted interpersonal relationships, and dissociation. The latter defends the sexually abused woman against the horrifying childhood trauma by keeping it "walled off." However, the dissociated material filters into consciousness through intrusive thoughts or disturbances in areas such as intimate relationships and/or compromised interests in occupational, cultural and community activities.

These three PTSD clusters, according to Herman (1992a), apply to the aftereffects of single traumatizing occurrences. She proposed the concept of Complex Post-Traumatic Stress Disorder to depict the symptomatology of victims with prolonged, repeated trauma.

Complex post-traumatic stress disorder (complex PTSD)

Expansion on the PTSD categorization to include adaptations to early prolonged interpersonal trauma where the victim feels imprisoned and controlled by the perpetrator (Herman, 1992b), as exemplified in parent-daughter incest or ongoing, nonfamilial-child sexual abuse.

The complex PTSD profile includes early prolonged disturbances in the areas of affect and sexual behavior regulation, states of awareness, somatic manifestations, perception, interpersonal relationships, and belief systems (Herman, 1992a, 1992b; van der Kolk, 1996; Wallenberg Pachaly, 2000; Briere and Spinazzola, 2009).

Difficulties in affect and sexual behavior regulation Are manifested primarily in the inability to modulate anxiety, aggression and sexual behavior. Women molested in girlhood often experience ongoing anxiety such as panic and phobias; chronic depression or alternations between repression and extreme eruption of rage; and, either manifest loss of interest in sexuality or inappropriate/risky sexual behavior. These are conscious and unconscious adaptations to the emotional impact of the original trauma.

States of awareness Characteristic of coping with childhood abuse are amnesia and dissociation. These defend the sexually abused girl against the horrifying and disorganizing trauma.

Physical and somatic symptoms Are directed toward the sexually violated body, thereby avoiding the feelings connected with the trauma. Feelings, such as self-hatred and self-blame, are manifested in physical illnesses and neglect of medical care/procedures.

Changes in perception Are noted in ongoing guilt, shame and self-accusing, as well as idealizing of the abuser. These misperceptions protect the victim from experiencing the rage, pain and betrayal induced by the trauma.

Chronic relationship difficulties Are common following prolonged sexual abuse in childhood. The woman has difficulties trusting or being intimate with others. She is also prone to being revictimized or victimizing others, thus repeating the trauma.

Belief systems Are altered as a result of the betrayal of the perpetrator. Hope is altered to hopelessness, and the belief in the goodness of others is changed to the loss of faith in others.

The complex PTSD symptoms and/or adaptations are often the presenting concerns for which women, sexually victimized in childhood, seek therapy.

Presenting problems for treatment

Women rarely enter therapy stating they are seeking help for traumatic antecedents associated with childhood sexual abuse. There might be several reasons for this: being unaware of the dissociated or suppressed memory of the victimization, disguising the abuse because of previous painful responses to the disclosure, mistrusting others, or being afraid of losing control or being rejected. Additionally, they may not connect the molestation to the problems for which they are seeking help.

However, when women molested in girlhood seek treatment, it is usually for PTSD and/or complex PTSD symptoms. The presenting problems often include clinical depression, intense anxiety, impulsive behavior, somatization, distrust, chronic interpersonal difficulties, and negative self-perceptions such as low self-esteem, guilt and shame. The following example illustrates some of these problems.

> ### Clinical Illustration
>
> Lisa entered my office for the first time, apologizing for being five minutes late. She also apologized for not knowing how to explain why she came to see me, adding: "I always apologize." She was 26 years old, and married to an emotionally abusive man. She complained of frequent anxiety, even when performing simple tasks; having difficulties concentrating on her job; and becoming petrified when arguing with a co-worker or with her husband, stating: "my body trembles, my heart pounds and my palms get sweaty. I don't know why I get so anxious."

Lisa's guilt, intense anxiety and troubled relationships may be associated with early attachment disturbances and/or maltreatment at a young age or adolescence. These hypotheses had to be explored in subsequent sessions.

Additional presenting problems that may be associated with women's girlhood sexual abuse meet the diagnostic criteria for substance abuse and eating disorders (such as bulimia or anorexia) (Levenkron and Levenkron, 2007), Borderline Personality Disorder, that is, fear of abandonment, severe interpersonal difficulties, self-destructive behavior such as self-mutilation (Rodriguez-Srednicki and Twaite, 2006), and Dissociative Identity Disorder, that is, presence of more than one dissociated personality state (Herman, 1992a). The association between these diagnostic disorders and childhood sexual abuse has been supported by extensive empirical research. Yet, the association has to be established in treatment since other underlying disturbances/occurrences may also be present.

Furthermore, female survivors of childhood molestation may present for crisis intervention or therapy following intense aftereffects of life events that symbolize the childhood trauma. The outburst of PTSD symptoms and/or trauma memories may be triggered by transitional events such as getting married, divorce, death of a family member, or loss of a job (Courtois, 2010).

Individual therapy is usually a beneficial first step in stabilizing the flood of intense memories and symptoms affected by a crisis situation. It can address the symptomatic manifestations and/or unfold the association between women's presenting problems and sexual abuse in girlhood.

Individual Therapy for Females Molested in Girlhood

In individual therapy in private practice, mental health clinics, or inpatient units, initially the therapist needs to focus on the woman's concerns in the present, including, regulating feelings such as rage and anxiety (adding medication if patient is highly symptomatic), working on sobriety and detoxification (if necessary, adding an alcohol or drug program), and relinquishing or reducing/minimizing an eating disorder or self-mutilating behavior. This process may take a long time since sexually abused women in childhood may have difficulties letting go of the complex PTSD symptoms and self-destructive behaviors they have adapted to in order not to experience feelings such as pain, shame and guilt.

To begin the process of relinquishing symptomatic/self-destructive behavior, the therapist needs to create a therapeutic relationship in which the woman feels safe. This begins with focusing on patient's concerns, validating the individual's strengths, and addressing the therapist-patient contract in reference to fees and time boundaries. In addition, clarifying that the patient can choose the material to be discussed is quite empowering. This may begin to counteract the feelings of disempowerment and clearly establish that the purpose of the relationship is neither exploitive nor sexual (Rodriguez-Srednicki and Twaite, 2006).

Additionally, by listening empathically to the patient and offering undivided attention, the therapist may further strengthen the woman's trust in the therapeutic relationship. As the trust develops, the woman may begin to let go of symptomatic/self-harmful behavior, and volunteer the childhood sexual abuse story, or access some memories of the abuse. This is usually a very long and painful process during which the therapist needs to be attuned to the woman's pace and ability to tolerate the induced feelings. Gradually, the molested female may learn about the association between the presenting problems and the trauma history. She may come to realize the harmful impact of the girlhood abuse and start to understand the intrapsychic and interpersonal difficulties in the present.

Clinical Illustration

Several months after entering treatment, Lisa (addressed in the previous section) disclosed that her mother's live-in boyfriend molested her between the ages of 7 and 9. The abuse stopped when the mother "kicked the boyfriend out of the house." Lisa was petrified to disclose the abuse since he threatened to kill her mother if she did.

As Lisa began to talk about the molestation, her symptoms worsened. She became more anxious and insomniac. Medication was added to the individual treatment. However, with time, as our therapeutic alliance strengthened, her anxiety began to regulate and the sleep pattern improved. She also gained some insight into the connection between her childhood abuse and current difficulties. Her medication was gradually reduced.

To offer Lisa the opportunity to further explore her interpersonal difficulties and symptomatic manifestations, group therapy was added to her therapeutic regimen.

Why Group Therapy for Sexually Victimized Survivors?

For several decades, group therapy has been a beneficial adjunct to individual therapy for women sexually victimized in girlhood. It offers an atmosphere of safety, respect and relational consistency that is conducive to counteracting the isolation, shame and secrecy characteristic of abused individuals. In a supportive, non-exploitive and non-judgmental group, members gradually share their painful, horrific stories of sexual abuse and learn to attend to each others' stories in an empathic, accepting manner. In this process, dissociated memories slowly emerge, starting to replace the traumatizing experience with a narrative to be brought to the group discussion.

Additionally, the victimized women learn to better understand their symptoms, and the connection between their symptoms/maladaptive behaviors and the childhood sexual abuse. Consequently, they are able to better manage and modulate affective and somatic reactions in the present.

As the therapeutic alliance with the group leader and members evolves, trust slowly develops and repeatedly tested. Once the group becomes more cohesive, interpersonal dilemmas are addressed and explored in the "here-and-now," utilizing the group therapist and members' feedback. Furthermore, the victimized women learn from each other how to communicate assertively rather than aggressively and impulsively, and, how to listen to each other rather than being self-absorbed and demanding. They begin to develop an individuated voice, a sense of personal empowerment and self-worth.

In the process of hearing and being heard in the group, women molested in girlhood begin to regain their power, enhance their sense of self, and bond with the group therapist and other members. As interpersonal connections strengthen, group members may mourn together the loss of life experiences resulting from constricting aftereffects of the interpersonal trauma. This grieving process can be liberating, and open the possibility for new life experiences. Hope may be instilled (Yalom with Leszcz, 2005; Kleinberg, 2007), beginning to replace the grim and constricted outlook on life. A safe sense of belonging emerges within the group.

Research on Group Therapy with Women Molested in Childhood

Group therapy has been used to treat women sexually victimized in girlhood (Lundquist, et al., 2006) in inpatient and outpatient settings. However, it "has not been extensively evaluated in rigorous randomized clinical trial...research, and the scientific evidence of its efficacy is limited but growing" (Committee on Treatment of Posttraumatic Stress Disorder, 2007 as reported in Ford, Fallot and Harris, 2009).

The outcomes of different approaches to group treatment with females sexually abused in childhood (Wolfsdorf and Zlotnick, 2001; Lundquist, et al., 2006) have been reported. These include psychodynamic, supportive, and trauma memory disclosure modalities. Results have also demonstrated enhanced functioning two years after the treatment was completed (Ford, et al., 2009). A randomized clinical trial, comparing present focused and trauma focused (Lubin and Johnson, 2008) groups of childhood molested females with a wait-list of women with similar histories, resulted in self-reported reduced symptomatology in both group modalities (Classen, et al., 2001).

Most group interventions for female survivors of childhood sexual abuse offer supportive or process oriented approaches, addressing patients' affect, perceptions of self/others and new behavior possibilities. The group therapist's choice of a modality is often impacted by her/his conceptual framework of group treatment.

My Theoretical Framework of Group Therapy

My theoretical framework for working with this population in a group setting includes the interpersonal approach, some conceptual formulations from the intrapsychic perspective, attachment theory, and, interpersonal neurobiology.

Interpersonal theory

My initial training in group therapy focused primarily on the interpersonal perspective. The basic premise of this approach is that growth occurs through the group interactions in the here-and-now (Yalom with Leszcz, 2005).

I find this approach effective in working with sexually abused women in girlhood. These women often manifest affective and behavioral disturbances, such as dysregulated anger or impulsive behavior. They may not be aware of the extent of these disturbances and the negative impact on others. Group members and the group leader can offer authentic, nonjudgmental feedback about how a member is perceived, "bear witness" to the painful childhood molestation story, and help the member explore and gain insight about the connection between her maladaptive behavior and the girlhood sexual abuse. When this therapeutic work is done repeatedly in a supportive, empathic atmosphere, it can improve the patient's relationships with the other group members and lessen/diminish her symptoms with time.

The role of the therapist in this context is to create a safe atmosphere in which the interactions between the members can be explored in an open and honest manner. In addition, the therapist role models how to offer feedback, encourages members to help each other grow, and demystifies the anticipation of traumatic consequences within the group. This facilitates authentic sharing of the molestation stories and genuine interchanges between members.

Intrapsychic perspective: transferential issues

The intrapsychic approach to group therapy utilizes the conceptual formulations of the psychodynamic and psychoanalytic theories. In my group work with females molested in childhood, I consider the intrapsychic transference phenomenon especially useful since the group offers opportunities to examine and work through parental, sibling and group-as-a-whole transferences.

Spiegel (1986) addressed the mistrustful transferences of abused individuals as traumatic transferences, for example, the molested patient projects the unconscious expectation of being exploited by the group therapist or group member for their own needs. These negative transferences are enactments of the original danger that induced, for example, betrayal, nonprotection or abandonment.

The nature of the projected transferences is usually affected by the severity and duration of the childhood molestation and the protection or lack of it the girl experienced at the time. The more severe the abuse and the more isolated the little girl felt, the more difficult is the working through process of the transferences. Furthermore, the projected transferences depend on the group's composition. For example, in an all-women group with a female group therapist, a woman who has been abused by a male and has not been protected by her mother may project rage toward a helpless, passive member or a perceived nonresponsive group therapist. Another transferential phenomenon maybe the patient's notion that the group-as-a-whole is a group of damaged women. I find that working through these negative transferences can be a long and difficult process which may enhance the victimized women's self-esteem and lead to more trusting and authentic relationships in the group and beyond.

Attachment theory

Attachment styles developed at an early age tend to continue into adulthood. According to Bolen (2002), childhood sexual abuse seems to be associated with insecure patterns of attachment such as anxious/ambivalent or avoidant attachments. The anxious/ambivalent attachment may stem from inconsistent responses to the child (at times starting before the abuse), such as exploitive incestuous demands from a father on one hand, and the same parent's overly nurturing manifestations on the other. In an attempt to establish an attachment with the abusive father, the girl dissociates the sexual abuse and responds to the father in a clinging/dependent manner which usually carries into adulthood. Another insecure attachment is the avoidant one, wherein the young girl responds in an avoidant manner to being unprotected and rejected by the mother following the disclosure of father-daughter incest. As an adult, this woman may be mistrustful and experience a fear of intimacy.

Working in the context of insecure attachments, I believe that issues of fear of closeness, mistrust and dependency enacted in the therapy group, can be worked through in the supportive safety of the group, and gradually facilitate more secure attachments inside and outside the group.

According to Pearlman and Courtois (2005), it is the secure attachments both with the therapist and group members which provide the therapeutic atmosphere for working through trauma-related memories/feelings and complex interpersonal difficulties, thereby enhancing relational bonding.

Interpersonal neurobiology

The concept of interpersonal neurobiology, developed by Siegel (1999) and Schore (2003), is important for understanding how the interpersonal difficulties experienced by women molested in girlhood can be worked through. This concept addresses the interpersonal healing at a neuronal level. According to Courtois (2010), the brain's neuroplasticity makes it possible for the traumatized mind to alter when interacting repeatedly with attuned, empathic group members and therapist. Thus, women sexually abused in childhood who undergo group therapy in an empathic and supportive atmosphere may, over time, change their attachment patterns from insecure to secure ones and develop close relationships.

Thus, to enhance interpersonal relationships, modify perceptions of self and others, and reduce/minimize the symptomatology of females molested in childhood, concurrent individual and group therapy is suggested.

Treatment Strategy

My work with women molested in childhood begins with individual therapy (as discussed in an earlier section) and continues with concurrent individual and group treatment. The latter consists of a trauma-focused, homogeneous time-limited group followed by a heterogeneous long-term group.

Concurrent individual and group treatment

Group therapy is an important complementary therapeutic mode to individual therapy for women sexually victimized in childhood. It counteracts isolation, offers a supportive setting for disclosing the abusive stories and working through the aftereffects of the abuse. However, the information disclosed in the group may at times evoke memories and emotions too difficult for the traumatized women to "bear witness" to or process in the group. In these situations, the concurrent individual therapy, with a trusted therapist, can be a safe place to explore the triggered stressful experiences.

In addition, simultaneous individual and group therapy is suggested for the traumatized woman as the individual therapist can offer special one-on-one attention and close monitoring of possible reactions such as re-traumatization or dissociation in response to material elicited in the group.

Group therapy for females molested in girlhood

Herman (1992a), whose group model I have been utilizing, suggested a three-stage group model of recovery for repeated traumatized individuals, such as women sexually abused in childhood over a prolonged period. The stages progress as follows: a cognitive-didactic group; a homogeneous trauma-focused group; and, an interpersonal heterogeneous group.

Cognitive-educational group

Cognitive-didactic group work is primarily geared to inpatient settings, and lasts for several sessions. It is psychoeducational rather than exploratory with the goal of establishing safety. The focus of the group is to impart information regarding the symptomatology of the trauma, and learn methods of self-care and self-protection to counter overwhelming memories and feelings. Group members typically do not share much about themselves or confront each other. No strong group cohesion evolves, and the group leader takes an active didactic role.

Homogeneous time-limited groups for females molested in girlhood

Many clinicians concur that homogeneous groups are the group mode of choice for individuals with complex PTSD disorders (e.g., Parson, 1985; Herman, 1992a). Women molested in girlhood usually benefit from being in an all-women group in which other members have had comparable experiences. The all-women group focuses on the trauma, promotes the disclosure of the abusive stories, and offers feedback/suggestions for managing/reducing the symptoms.

The homogeneous group, however, also has liabilities. These include a resistance to moving beyond a primary identity as victim (van der Kolk, 1987b; Buchele, 2000); and compromised individuation as the result of the experience of "we-ness" in the group.

All-women groups of females molested in girlhood are usually time-limited, and primarily offer psychoeducation, support and cognitive-behavioral therapy in a structured format. The supportive groups are "present-focused" (e.g., Classen, et al., 2001) whereas the memory processing modalities are "trauma-focused" (e.g., Lubin and Johnson, 2008). Psychodynamic approaches are also utilized (e.g. Lundquist, et al., 2006). The time-limited groups range from 4–20 sessions (Shea, et al., 2009), and optimally include 5–7 members.

Time-limited groups for this population have several advantages. They reduce the anxiety of joining a therapy group and pave the way for a future long-term group; focus primarily on childhood sexual abuse issues rather than the more anxiety provoking complex interpersonal difficulties in the "here-and-now"; encourage the disclosing (for some members, it is the first time outside the individual therapy) of the histories and aftereffects; and, address ways to manage the painful memories, feelings and symptoms.

Trauma-focused, homogeneous time-limited groups

Trauma-focused groups, applicable to private practice and outpatient clinics, have the goals of remembering and mourning the traumatic sexual abuse, and managing/reducing the aftereffects symptoms. According to Herman (1992a), these groups are usually structured and time-limited with minimal work on interpersonal issues amongst the members.

Group cohesion develops quickly as members feel recognized and understood by others who have undergone similar experiences. As a member reconstructs her own story, the other victimized women often recall new parts of their stories. At times, the new recollections emerge too fast for the individual or the group to tolerate. The group leader then needs to slow down the process into a pace the membership can bear.

Since trauma-focused groups are time-limited, the termination process has an integrative goal, often accomplished by formalized rituals. For example, each group member writes her personal gains in the group as well as her goals for future work. Also, each member writes a similar assessment for all the other group members. These rituals serve as a take away of one's own experience and of the group-as-a-whole.

I concur with the benefit of trauma-focused, homogeneous, time-limited groups for females molested in girlhood who are in the early stages of dealing with the victimization. However, I modify Herman's model when working with groups whose members have undergone prolonged intensive individual therapy and dealt with the sexual abuse and its consequences. In these cases, I add to the remembering and mourning goal some working through of interpersonal difficulties in the "here-and-now." I also facilitate the integrative task of the termination process verbally rather than in a written format. This enhances spontaneity, encourages interpersonal interactions, and prepares for the next group experience in an interpersonal two-gendered group.

Heterogeneous, open-ended interpersonal therapy groups

Heterogeneous groups, geared for private practice and outpatient clinics, have the goal of integrating the victimized women into the community. These groups focus on complex interpersonal dilemmas in the "here-and-now". They are composed of men and women with trauma histories at advanced stages of recovery, and also of others who have not been traumatized. In these unstructured groups, conflict is allowed to develop in a safe environment. The working through and resolution of interpersonal conflicts are facilitated in a supportive, empathic group environment, thereby contributing to the members' growth.

Heterogeneous groups also present opportunities to work through transferential issues related to the trauma, both with men and women. For example, a female molested in childhood who was unprotected by her mother may feel unprotected/

unsupported by another female member or unsafe/in danger with the men in the group. The challenge and the hope in this group is that the sexually molested woman will abandon the perception of herself as victim and establish a new sense of herself and others inside and outside the group.

Both the interpersonal therapy group and the trauma-focused group are aimed to help the victimized women work through the traumatizing aftereffects, including complex interpersonal difficulties.

Selected Clinical Tactics for Trauma-Focused Groups

Patients for a trauma-focused group need to be screened for suitability and prepared prior to being admitted to the group. This is usually accomplished in two to three individual interviews.

Patient selection

In selecting group members for a trauma-focused group, the group therapist does not need to match patients according to the severity and duration of the abuse. The compatibility of the group members is based on their ability to tolerate psychic stress, that is, being able to share their stories and listen to the painful material of other individuals.

Screening the suitability for a trauma-focused group for women molested in girlhood should include the following:

1. Taking a basic personal history, including the individual's current life situation, to determine the extent of prior loss or illness as well as the degree of available support in the present.
2. The nature of the childhood abuse and its duration. Whether it has been previously disclosed (outside of the individual therapy), and if so, what were the reactions to it. The latter information is likely to impact the extent/difficulty of disclosing the trauma within the group.
3. A diagnostic assessment must be taken, including assessment of impulse control, and the ability to modulate affect and tolerate psychic stress.

Inclusion criteria

The readiness/motivation to join a group as well as positive experiences in other group situations may be good predictors that the woman will benefit from the group. She needs to be willing/able to disclose the abuse history, accept support/feedback from others, and listen to other members' stories with empathy. In addition, a member needs to be concurrently in individual therapy. For alcohol/substance abusers, at least six months of sobriety are necessary.

Exclusion criteria

Individuals who are reluctant to join a group or cannot keep regular group meetings will not make good candidates. Also, women with the following diagnoses need to be excluded: acutely psychotic/intensely paranoid, actively suicidal, manifesting a severe eating disorder or self-mutilation, narcissistic personality disorder, multiple personality disorder, poor impulse control and mentally challenged. In addition, a woman in crisis is not suitable since the group may not be able to provide the special attention she needs.

Patient preparation

Patients usually benefit from some preparation prior to joining the group. Informing them about what to expect often reduces the anxiety. Typically, the information about a trauma-focused group includes the group's goals, that is, disclosure of the molestation histories; themes that may emerge (such as managing/reducing symptoms); the logistics including day, time and place of the meetings, and fee structure; and, an explanation of how the group works (for example, members offer feedback to one another). In addition, the patient's concerns/questions need to be addressed (for example, how many women will be in the group?). Finally, group agreements need to be presented and accepted.

Group agreements

Group agreements offer structure and contribute to the group's safety. They need to be presented and agreed upon in the pre-group interviews, and repeated in the first group session. Patients need to agree to attend group meetings regularly, notify the therapist of a planned/unplanned absence, and pay the fee on time; use no violence to self/others/office and express rage in a constructive way. Not use physical contact and instead put feelings into words. This is of special importance for women whose bodies have been violated in girlhood. Protect the names and identities of other group members. This is significant for victimized women who have issues with trust, secrecy and shame. Use relationships in the group therapeutically, not socially. This enhances group cohesion since all group members share the same experiences, and no one is hurt by being excluded from a social activity. However, some clinicians encourage socialization outside the group to counteract members' isolation (e.g., Lubin and Johnson, 2008).

Group leadership

Leading a group for females molested in girlhood requires training in group therapy; knowledge of PTSD disorders and the traumatic aftereffects; and, supervision in leading trauma-focused groups.

These groups are often co-led in outpatient settings and led by a single therapist, often for practical reasons, in private practice. The advantages of co-leadership include mutual therapist support in dealing with the intense feelings triggered in a trauma-focused group; the opportunity to share the observation and processing of the elicited material; and, the lessening of intense parental transferences as they are projected on two therapists. An additional asset to co-leadership may be the role-modeling of respectful resolution of conflict/disagreement between the leaders. This can serve as an important learning experience for women who grew up in dysfunctional families.

As for the single therapist leading a trauma-focused group, a supervision group or a peer group of colleagues is essential for dealing with the intense feelings and materials elicited in this type of group.

Furthermore, this is to note that most trauma-focused groups for women molested in girlhood are led/co-led by females. The victimized women often refuse to join a group led or co-led by men since the majority of perpetrators of females are men.

Group boundaries

The boundaries of women molested in girlhood were seriously violated, usually making them either rigid or lax regarding boundaries. The inflexibility distances them from others and keeps them isolated, whereas the carelessness makes them prone to revictimization. To counteract this maladaptive behavior, the trauma-focused group leader needs to present clear boundaries.

The external boundaries include the time and place of group meetings, duration of each session, fees and charges for missed sessions, and confidentiality. These boundaries create the frame for the group and are non-negotiable. As the group begins its work, relational boundaries are addressed to delineate communications between members, for example, being nonjudgmental. Also, the therapist will present internal boundaries, namely, boundaries within the member herself. She may realize the boundary between her experience and the experience of another group member. This may be an important learning since many molested women in girlhood grew up in enmeshed families.

Boundaries will inevitably be violated in the group. Members will occasionally be late to a session or not pay the bill on time. It is the group leader's role to monitor the violations and address them in a constructive/noncritical way to maintain the group's safety. Gradually, group members will also learn to explore their own boundary violations both in the group and during childhood.

Vignettes from a Trauma-Focused Group for Females Molested in Girlhood

The following is the 12th session of a 20-session trauma-group composed of five members:

LIZ   I am so glad to see you. I haven't slept well the last few nights. I wake up remembering my father's face sweating, and I start shaking. As I told you before, I remember he sexually abused me from age 8–11, but I have always felt numb about it. My heart is pounding fast now, and my palms are sweating. Why am I so nervous now, what's going on?

MOIRA   (introduced earlier in the chapter) It looks like you began to remember how scared you felt during the abuse. I was also very nervous when I started to remember how I felt when my father abused me.

LIZ   Do you feel nervous about it now?

MOIRA	It gets easier with time. The more I talk about it here the less anxious I feel.
LIZ	I remember his sweaty face, smiling, and his body close to mine, why is the bastard smiling? I am shaking now.
THERAPIST	You are safe here in the group. You can take some time out to re-ground. You do not have to remember everything at once.
LISA	(addressed earlier) You have a lot of guts to remember it.
SUSAN	Take your time. Take care of yourself.
LIZ	(moving back in her chair) I do feel better, I do feel safe here, but I am confused. Did it really happen to me or is it just a dream?
SUSAN	Every time I think about the abuse, I don't believe it happened to me. I think it is because it hurts so much.
LIZ	I am OK now. I don't want to talk about it anymore right now. I feel calmer now.

Liz, the first member to speak in this session, wanted to be heard and was actually heard by the group. She asserted herself, experienced in the group some of the terror she felt in response to her father's sexual abuse, and began to modulate her intense anxiety in the present. The latter was facilitated by the group's support and my re-grounding her.

I usually begin the sessions in this group in a structured manner by checking how the members are doing. This reduces the members' anxiety and offers everyone the opportunity to share. However, since Liz's assertion was productive and self-empowering, and the members joined the discussion, I decided not to interrupt the process and skipped the usual checking in go around.

SUSAN	My husband says I am a frigid woman. I have sex with him when he wants but I don't enjoy it.
MOIRA	My ex-husband used to complain I didn't enjoy having sex. That's why he found a girlfriend. The boyfriend I have now wants to have much more sex than me. He wants to get married but I don't want to. It's hard for me to trust any man after my own father betrayed me. It hurts so much that I don't want to think about it.
KATHY	I trusted my stepfather and he raped me. I don't feel any pain. I am just angry all the time. I want to hurt him. I want him to die. I want him to pay for what he did to me. I told my mother and she didn't believe me. She said he was a good man. Now, after they got divorced, she believes me.
THERAPIST	It's hard to trust both men and women after you were betrayed by your father and not believed and protected by your mother.
MOIRA	(to Kathy) Don't you trust me? I care about you.
KATHY	I do. I trust everyone in the group, but you can't change my past. I feel like I am damaged goods.
LIZ	We can't change the past, but we care about each other now. Doesn't it count for something?

KATHY	(stating in a soft voice): I guess my stepfather was damaged goods, not me.
THERAPIST	It's very important you realize you are not damaged goods.
MOIRA	Every time my father came after me and hurt me, I thought I did something wrong and I deserved it. Yes, I think we are damaged goods.
SUSAN	When I was a little girl I always thought my uncle hurt me in my pussy because I was a bad girl.

During girlhood, these women blamed themselves for being sexually abused since they were scared to get enraged with the perpetrator or lose the relationship with him, thereby setting the stage for a lasting poor self-esteem. Kathy began to change her negative self-image by noting that her stepfather was "damaged goods," and not her. The latter will have to be further reinforced in future sessions. Other members' negative self-perceptions will need to be further explored, worked through and gradually replaced by positive self-images.

MOIRA	My boyfriend wants to have a lot of sex. Many times I have sex with him when I don't want to. I am afraid he will leave me if I don't. I am already 48 years old and I don't know if I can find another boyfriend. He is good to me, takes care of me. I don't want to lose him.
LIZ	It's like you were scared to say no to your father.
MOIRA	I never saw the connection between my boyfriend and my father. I am afraid to speak up. Do you think I should?
KATHY	Did you tell your boyfriend you were sexually abused by your father?
MOIRA	No. He will think I am damaged goods and leave me.
KATHY	I think if he really cares about you he won't leave.
LIZ	I agree.
THERAPIST	It's hard for you to trust your boyfriend. You are afraid he will abandon you if you are honest with him.
MOIRA	Ya, I am afraid he will abandon me. I don't know what to do (crying).
SUSAN	I think you will have to take a chance and be honest with your boyfriend, have an open discussion about your feelings regarding having sex. I am older than you. I am 53. I took a chance and divorced my ex-husband. He was emotionally abusive to me. He didn't love me. He used to make fun of me, tell me I am fat and ugly. Now I have a boyfriend who is good to me. I care about you. I want you to be happy.
MOIRA	I will think about talking to him.

Moira expressed her difficulty to assert herself and say "no" to her boyfriend's requests to have sex more frequently than she wanted to. She felt helpless, not knowing whether to address it with him since she was afraid he would abandon her. She learned for the first time in the group that there is a connection between her reluctance to speak up in the present and her inability and fear to refuse her father's sexual abuse during her childhood. This important revelation will need to be further reinforced.

The group served as a "safe base" for beginning to integrate Liz's memories of the sexual abuse and the intense anxiety she experienced in the present as a repetition of the childhood terror. It was the support of the members and the group leader that facilitated her ability to calm down during the session. In addition, Moira's insecure/clinging attachment to her boyfriend was challenged by the group. She was receptive to the group's feedback and stated she will consider talking to her boyfriend openly. If she does, this may be a first step to developing more secure attachments in the future.

Lastly, the group addressed a group-as-a-whole transferential issue of being "damaged goods." Kathy made some strides to counteract this negative self-image. However, Kathy and the rest of the group need to further work through this negative self-concept and replace it with a positive one.

Vicarious Traumatization

Vicarious traumatization, a concept originated by McCann and Pearlman (1990), addresses the impact of traumatic material on the treating therapist. It is not a countertransference reaction to a specific patient, but a psychological reaction that develops over time by being engaged in therapeutic relationships with several traumatized patients. The therapist's specific reactions are influenced by the type and severity of the trauma, any personal traumatic history she may have, and present life stressors.

In treating women molested in girlhood, a therapist is prone to experience vicarious traumatization since she is exposed to and empathizes with the horrific stories of these women. Through empathy, the therapist identifies with the women's terror, rage and helplessness. Such ongoing therapeutic work may overwhelm the therapist and intrude upon her psyche via nightmares or intrusive memories of the molestation stories. It may also impact her relationships with others, particularly in the areas of intimacy and sexuality.

Therapist's vicarious traumatization may also affect the therapeutic alliance with patients. For example, in order to defend against the unbearable terror elicited by "bearing witness" to the sexual abuse stories, a therapist may shift the topic of discussion or assume the role of rescuer to avoid the feelings of helplessness.

To manage the unavoidable experience of vicarious traumatization, both for the sake of the patient and the therapist, the therapist's reactions to working with females molested in girlhood have to be explored and worked through in supervision or consultation with appropriately trained colleagues. Professional support in doing this work is imperative. Personal support and self-care outside the work setting further contributes to the mental health of the therapist and her effective work with patients.

Conclusion

This chapter has attempted to illustrate the impact of group therapy on traumatized females molested in childhood. A brief synopsis of the prevailing theories providing the framework for group treatment with this population has been presented. It is contended that not any one theory in itself or one type of group can adequately address the multitude of issues involved. Therefore, a group program, following Herman's (1992a) model, was suggested. This model, geared to private practice or outpatient clinics, encompasses a trauma-focused, homogeneous, time-limited all-women group, followed by a heterogeneous interpersonal, long-term, two-gendered group.

The purpose of the trauma-focused group is to provide a safe environment in which remembering the histories and triggered feelings, and managing symptoms are encouraged and accepted. Interpersonal dilemmas are minimally addressed in this group, but should be followed up in a heterogeneous group which resembles the community at large. The objectives of the interpersonal group include the resolution of complex interpersonal issues and the facilitation of the letting go of the victim image, replacing it with an integrated image of a multi-faced individual. Thus, the victim becomes a survivor who courageously defeated the odds. In addition, vignettes from a trauma-focused group illustrated and discussed the challenges in remembering and mourning the sexual abuse in a supportive/safe environment of others with similar experiences.

In the process of facilitating the trauma-focused group, the group therapist often becomes vicariously traumatized in hearing and containing the horrifying and devastating stories. The support of a co-therapist, supervision group or on-going consultations with colleagues are essential in working with this type of group. Also, self-care should be given priority while doing this demanding work.

Despite the obstacles and the potential emotional distress, it is a rewarding experience to witness the healing process when the victim becomes a victor in leading a more fulfilled life.

References and Bibliography

Bolen, R. (2002). Child sexual abuse and attachment theory: Are we rushing headlong into another controversy? *Journal of Child Sexual Abuse, 1*, 95–124.

Boyle, P. (1994). *Scout's honor: Sexual abuse in America's most trusted institution*. Rocklin, California: Prima.

Braddock Bromley, N. (2007). *Hush: Moving from silence to healing after childhood sexual abuse*. Chicago: Moody Publishers.

Briere, J., & Spinazzola J. (2009). Assessment of the sequelae of complex trauma: Evidence-based measures. In C. A. Courtois & J. D. Ford (Eds.), *Treating complex traumatic stress disorder: An evidence-based guide*. New York: Guilford Press.

Buchele, B. J. (2000). Group psychotherapy for survivors of sexual and physical abuse. In R. H. Klein & V. L. Schermer, (Eds.), *Group psychotherapy for psychological trauma*. New York: The Guilford Press.

Classen, C., Koopman, C., Nevill-Manning, K., et al. (2001). A preliminary report comparing trauma-focused and present-focused group therapy against wait-listed condition among childhood sexual abuse survivors with PTSD. *Journal of Aggression, Maltreatment and Trauma, 4*, 265–288.

Cooperman, A. (2005, February 19). *In 2004, 1000 alleged abuse by priests*. The Washington Post: Washington, D.C.

Courtois, C. A. (2010). *Healing the incest wound: Adult survivors in therapy.* (2nd ed.). New York: Norton.

Doll, L. S., Koenig, L. J., & Purcell, D. W. (2004). Child sexual abuse and adult sexual risk: Where are we now? In L. J. Koenig., L. S. Doll., A. O'Leary & W. Pequegnat (Eds.), *From child sexual abuse to adult sexual risk: Trauma, revictimization, and intervention.* Washington, D.C.: American Psychological Association.

Donadio, R. (2010, April 15). Comments by Cardinal on sexuality create a stir. New York Times: New York, New York.

Figley, C. R. (Ed). (1985). *Trauma and its wake: The study and treatment of post-traumatic stress disorder.* New York: Brunner/Mazel.

Finkelhor, D. (2008). *Childhood victimization: Violence, crime, and abuse in the lives of young people.* New York: Oxford University Press.

Ford, J. D., Fallot, R. D., & Harris, M. (2009). Group therapy. In C. A. Courtois & J. D. Ford (Eds.), *Treating complex traumatic stress disorders: An evidence-based guide.* New York: The Guilford Press.

Freeman, J. M. (2005). *A wallflower no more: Building a new life after emotional and sexual abuse.* Phoenix, Arizona: Acacia Publishing.

Gartner, R. B. (1999). *Betrayed as boys: Psychodynamic treatment of sexually abused men.* New York: The Guilford Press.

Gold, S. N., Lucessko, B. A., Elhai, J. D., et al. (1999). A comparison of psychological/psychiatric symptomatology of women and men sexually abused as children. *Child abuse and Neglect, 23*(7), 683–692.

Gorman, C. & Dolan, B. (1991, October 7). Incest comes out of the dark. *Time, 138*(14).

Herman, J. L. (1992a). *Trauma and recovery.* New York, New York: Basic Books.

Herman, J. L. (1992b). Complex PTSD: A syndrome in survivors of prolonged and repeated trauma. *Journal of Traumatic Stress, 53,* 377–391.

Herman, J. L. (2000). *Father-daughter incest.* Cambridge, Massachusetts: Harvard University Press.

Kleinberg, J. (2007). Restoring hope through posttrauma groups. *Group Journal, 31,* 4, 293–308.

Krugman, S. (1987). Trauma in the family: Perspectives on the intergenerational transmission of violence. In B. A. van der Kolk (Ed.), *Psychological Trauma.* Washington, D.C.: American Psychiatric Press.

Levenkron, S., & Levenkron, A. (2007). *Stolen tomorrows: Understanding and treating women's childhood sexual abuse.* New York: Norton.

Lubin, H., with Johnson, D. R. (2008). *Trauma-centered group psychotherapy for women: A Clinician's Manual.* New York: Haworth Press.

Lundquist, G., Svedin, C., Hanson, K., et al. (2006). Group therapy for women sexually abused as Children. *Journal of Interpersonal Violence, 21,* 1655–1677.

McCann, I. L., & Pearlman, L. A. (1990). Vicarious traumatization: A framework for understanding the psychological effects of working with victims. *Journal of Traumatic Stress, 3,* 131–150.

Parson, E. R. (1985). Post-traumatic accelerated cohesion: Its recognition and management in group treatment of Vietnam veterans. *Group, 9,* 10–23.

Pearlman, L. A., & Courtois, C. A. (2005). Clinical applications of the attachment framework: Relational treatment of complex trauma. *Journal of Traumatic Stress, 18,* 449–460.

Rodriguez-Srednicki, O. & Twaite, J. A. (2006). *Understanding, assessing and treating adult victims of Childhood abuse.* New York: Jason Aronson.

Schore, A. N. (2003). *Affect regulation and the repair of the self.* New York: Norton.

Shea, M. T., McDevitt-Murphy, M., Ready, D. J. et al. (2009). Group therapy. In E. B. Foe, T. M. Keane, M. J. Friedman & J.A. Cohen (Eds.), *Effective treatments for PTSD: Practice* guidelines from the International Society for Traumatic Stress Studies. New York: Guilford Press.

Siegel, D. J. (1999). *The developing mind: Toward a neurobiology of interpersonal experience.* New York: Guilford Press.

Slack, D. (2005, February 21). *67 clergy abuse complaints reported in 2004.* Boston Globe: Boston Massachusetts.

Spiegel, D. (1986). Dissociation, double binds, and posttraumatic stress in multiple personality disorder. In B. G. Braun (Ed.). *Treatment of multiple personality disorder.* Washington, D.C.: American Psychiatric Press.

Van der Kolk, B. A. (1987a). *Psychological trauma.* Washington, D.C.: American Psychiatric Press.

Van der Kolk, B. A. (1987b). The role of the group in the origin and resolution of the trauma response. In B. A. Van der Kolk (Ed.), *Psychological trauma.* Washington, D.C.: American Psychiatric Press.

Van der Kolk, B. A., McFarlane, A.C., & Weisaeth, L. (Eds.). (1996). *Traumatic stress: The effects of overwhelming experience on mind, body and society.* New York: The Guilford Press.

Van der Kolk, B. A., & McFarlane, A. C. (1996). The black hole of trauma. In B. A. van der Kolk, A. C. McFarlane, & L. Weisaeth (Eds.), *Traumatic stress: The effects of overwhelming experience on mind, body and society.* New York: The Guilford Press.

Von Wallenberg Pachaly, A. (2000). Group psychotherapy for victims of political torture and other forms of severe ethnic persecution. In R. H. Klein & V. L. Schermer (Eds.), *Group psychotherapy for psychological trauma.* New York: Guilford Press.

Wolfsdorf, B., & Zlotnick, C. (2001). Affect management in group therapy for women with posttraumatic stress disorder and histories of childhood sexual abuse. *Journal of Clinical Psychology, 57,* 169–181.

Yalom, I. D. with Leszcz, M. (2005). *The theory and practice of group psychotherapy* (5th ed.). New York: Basic books.

22

Couples Group Psychotherapy: A Quarter of a Century Retrospective

Judith Coché

A Couple is the Most Powerful Unit on our Planet

How fortunate is the mental health professional who is fascinated daily by the interpersonal puzzles put before her in clinical practice. She will be amply rewarded for the deep investment in the clinical skills it takes a lifetime to learn. Just as no two individuals are alike, no two couples are alike. Therein lies the unending fascination with the dynamics of interpersonal space, which engages both the intellect and the senses of every clinician who undertakes couples group psychotherapy. Tragic marriages are compelling in the human drama they create for the clinician. As complex as it is to learn the specialty areas of couples psychotherapy, family psychotherapy, and group psychotherapy, the rewards of doing so make the task worthwhile.

In the last quarter of a century since the first publication of *Couples Group Psychotherapy* in 1990, the field has begun to come into its own. Although relatively few clinicians undertake the difficulties of learning the model, couples now request couples group psychotherapy and clinicians regularly ask to be trained in it. This chapter helps the graduate student and practising clinician learn to use couples group psychotherapy.

This chapter briefly addresses topics found at greater length in *Couples Group Psychotherapy, Second Edition* (Coché, 2010). It introduces the clinician to the theoretical foundations, the structure of couples group psychotherapy, the treatment strategies, selected professional and ethical issues, a capsule of evidence-based practice, and brief future directions of couples group psychotherapy.

What is Couples Group Psychotherapy?

Couples group psychotherapy is a treatment modality founded on integration of principles from the field of group dynamics and family therapy. A small-group structure is used to promote healing and growth for married or unmarried heterosexual or homosexual couples. Conceptual origins in systems theory are drawn from the worlds of biology (von Bertalanffy, 1968) and social psychology (Lewin, 1951); clinical application in mental health services are drawn from two usually separated but not incompatible sectors: family and couples therapy and group psychotherapy, and form a unique treatment modality which treats each individual and the couple as a unit through a psychotherapy group format. Additional expertise comes from individual psychotherapy and is modified to apply to work with couples.

The Theoretical Foundations for Couples Group Psychotherapy

A brief overview of treatment skills with intimate partners precedes a discussion of theoretical foundations for couples group psychotherapy.

Treatment Skills with Intimate Partners

Key concepts from philosophy and couples therapy include an existential foundation for the process of change and an intergenerational frame for couples work.

Couples therapy is a relatively new treatment modality. Peterson (1968) stated that couples therapy was established as late as 1942. Defining terms became an early focus, crystallizing disagreements: conjoint marital therapy, family therapy, multi-family therapy, marriage counseling, marriage therapy, couples therapy, group counseling, group therapy, and network therapy meant different things to different professionals and, to some extent, still do, making communication in the field difficult. Lacking standardization of terms, the field has splintered into cognitive therapy, marriage encounter, psychodynamic therapy, psychoeducational approaches, counseling with couples...the terms are too numerous and inexact to mention. Enthusiasm and dedication is more frequent than cognitive clarity and solid research.

Early references to couples group therapy began to appear in 1960 when van Emde Boas (1962) worked with a group for couples. Leichter (1962) also recommended couples groups for couples with problems of separation and individuation. Bowen's (1971) early work with multiple-family groups was influential in Framo's (1982) model in 1973 for couples groups. Although articles on the marital treatment of couples in groups have been appearing for three decades, the field is still in its infancy in terms of research and more frequently is referred to as "couples counseling," a term that is rarely operationally defined.

Existential base

An existential foundation provides a philosophical stance for the process of behavioral and interpersonal change in the Coché model. Through clinical interventions that strengthen the use of self, Coché teaches couples basic attitudes toward being in the world. Three existential principles underlie the work:

1. *Clients seek to be more of a person in an intimate context than they have been able to achieve.* Whitaker and Keith (1981) stated that the goals of psychotherapy should be to establish a sense of belonging, to provide the freedom for persons to individuate, and to increase personal and systemic creativity. The obstacles that patients construct against desired intimacy create a dysfunctional level of stability within the personality structure, blocking growth in the desired direction. Learning to be more of a person means freeing up new levels of energy and creativity by overcoming some of the obstacles constructed by oneself and by one's family. Personal and interpersonal meaning increases, and the members of a couple need no longer return to the early frustrating Modus Operandi.

2. *Adult intimacy involves taking responsibility for one's actions.* Intimacy is at its best for adults when the partners are able to take responsibility for their own thoughts, feelings, and behavior in relation to the other person. Therefore, adult intimacy is best achieved when partners are skilful and careful in their communication with one another. One must respect personal boundaries in order to be close to someone else. Additionally, this model of successful intimacy is skill based: it necessitates learning how to experience emotions, communicate feelings, listen to the thoughts and the feelings of another person, and negotiate conflict in a respectful manner.

3. *Living life fully and responsibly entails making life choices.* No matter what happens in life, each person is faced with continual choices. Barring natural disasters, adults get to choose whether to have and raise children and how to feed and care for their bodies and intellects. Living life fully requires that people own their choices: they are entitled to fully enjoy life's pleasures and to learn from their mistakes. In the Coché model, blame is superfluous: the emphasis is on positive and constructive cognitive and dynamic handling of human concerns. Coché assumes that people make unconscious choices based on hidden conflicts that echo the legacy of an early family pain. For Coché, the therapist often magnifies the existential theme for a couple struggling with what seems to be an everyday problem. Drawing attention to the larger existential issue often opens new ways to unstick the everyday dilemma.

Clinical Illustration

Jean and Donald married despite concerns about their competitive families. Donald is American, of Italian heritage, and Jean is Australian. Both families wanted the couple in their home country and competed for the affection of grandchildren. After Jean's completion of graduate training, the couple settled in the United States where Jean was quite unhappy. Life did not mean very much to her in a society which she saw as highly materialistic: she deeply preferred the more laid back culture of her native outback Australia. Her longing produced a haunting internal battle for emotional survival, and Jean finally sought treatment for depression.

As treatment for both Jean and the couple progressed, they began to explore the reasons for marrying the other. Jean, raised in a highly self-contained British

> family culture, thought that Donald's high-spirited Italian family often acted in bad taste and she had no interest in learning to fit into their customs. Because Donald was more flexible and quite excited about the freedom that Australia offered, the couple thought through their lives and moved with their two sons to Australia where they remain. They love living near the ocean, love the freedom of the country, and find great meaning together raising their family in this society. As soon as they were able to agree on what would mean the most, they successfully overcame the daunting task of creating a meaningful culture for themselves and their children.

An intergenerational frame for couples work

Regardless of the theoretical map of the clinician, be it psychodynamic or cognitive-behavioral, clinicians need to help couples relearn dysfunctional interpersonal patterns. Couples therapy relies on cognitive interventions which stress the ability to master improved levels of interpersonal functioning, and on therapy that stresses the primacy of attachment in human bonding. Coché (2010) varies the old adage, "those who understand family history are not doomed to repeat it," emphasizing retraining interpersonal dynamics as the foundation of working though dysfunctional patterns from family of origin. For example, Whitton et al., (2008) found that adolescents who experienced more hostilities in their families of origin were more likely 17 years later to show hostility during marital conflict resolution.

> Tom found it near to impossible to be tolerant of Karen's passion for bringing home "cute" objects. As far as he was concerned there was a place for everything and everything ought to be in its place…except his papers. As an academician, Tom believed his papers deserved to be wherever he wanted them, especially on the granite kitchen counter between the sink and the designer gas oven. Years of discussion proved fruitless until Tom reflected on his own family history: as a boy his only close moments were with his father when he followed his father around as "dad repaired one thing or another in the house." Tom reflected that dad's tools were everywhere and that when his mother tried to clean up his tools his father would bellow that "the place for a man's tools is anywhere he wants to put them!" Once Tom got in touch with the meaning this behavior had in his family he and Karen were able to reach a more reasonable agreement about the place of objects in their lives.

Theoretical Constructs in Couples Group Psychotherapy

Due to "turf" issues produced by competition for the same research and client dollars, there are few acknowledged similarities among the many theoretical bases of clinicians who practice couples group psychotherapy. Some groups are primarily support groups. Others are therapy groups which do not rely on group dynamics. The Coché groups rely on a foundation of group dynamics for therapeutic power. But all couples group therapy depends on the assumption that both couples and groups form a system and that treatment interventions need to be based on understanding and shifting interactive patterns.

The Coché model integrates group psychotherapy techniques and marital therapy. Theoretical and conceptual foundations from the fields of individual personality development, existential psychotherapy, family systems theory, and group psychotherapy theory form the basis of the model. Clinicians need prior knowledge and training in both group psychotherapy and psychotherapy with couples and families. Group leaders must conceptualize client change through the psychotherapy process in contextual terms. Human change occurs within an interpersonal context and can, therefore happen most efficiently when the psychotherapy process is conducted with awareness of the power of the interpersonal arena. As Sullivan (1953) stated, "It takes people to make people sick and people to make people well." Further, a group sometimes operates like a family, and a family has the properties of a small group. Both are greater than the sum of their parts, and the subsystems of each can be fully understood only through a knowledge of the working of the whole (Spitz, 1979).

Isomorphism

A key concept in the Coché model is the principle of isomorphism, a concept well-known to systems theorists. The principle states that similar structures and processes occur on several levels in related systems. Accordingly, a troublesome issue can manifest itself, with some variations, on an individual level (that is, within a member of a couple), on a couples level (between members of a couple), on a subgroup level (for all men or for all victims of abuse), and on a group level (for each group member). Applying that principle to a couples group enables the therapist to think on several levels simultaneously, to respond with flexibility to the challenges of the group, and to unravel otherwise bewildering shifts in levels. For example, the activity of a group can take place on any one of four levels at any time and on a combination of more than one level simultaneously. A brief description of each level follows.

Personal level. At the personal level the group concentrates intensively on one member. At times, couples group therapy looks like individual therapy in the presence of others. This therapy model is often the intervention of choice because it has a very powerful effect on a person.

Couples level. At the couples level a group spends time on the dynamics of one particular couple.

Interpersonal level. At the interpersonal level, the activity of the group is directed to interpersonal relationships between members or couples in the group, a subgroup level of attention. The members learn that others are struggling with similar issues and discover that they can be helpful to each other by sharing similar struggles, and their attempted solutions with others. Many of Irvin Yalom's (1985) curative factors, such as universality and altruism, come to full therapeutic power at the interpersonal therapeutic level. At times, the mere discovery of similarities is healing; at other times, only an extensive working with group member experiences can bring about therapeutic change.

Group-as-a-whole level. At the group-as-a-whole level interventions are aimed at each member of the group simultaneously. The leader makes a statement that applies to everyone, such as "the group is annoyed." Directional shifts, group decisions, norm enforcement, and explorations of participants' roles in the group – all are topics of discussion that fall into the group-as-a-whole category (Agazarian and Peters, 1981). To be a successful working group, the group has to work out problems in its own dynamics. Lewin (1951) provided seminal thinking on the centrality of context in promoting human change. Group-as-a-whole work enables the group to progress developmentally from dependence on the leader through cohesiveness to interdependence between members. Members can gain therapeutic benefits in a group that has gained some mastery over its dynamics.

> Rebecca annoyed her husband Michael because she stashed sweets and snuck drinks when she thought he was not looking. New to a couples group, Rebecca tried to avoid discussing her cravings in public. However, Rebecca craved more than chocolate and vodka. She craved intimacy, she craved being needed, and she craved sexual satisfaction. Working in the couples group, Drs Judith Coché and Juliette Galbraith used the metaphor of craving blue cotton candy at a carnival when what was really needed was a substantial dinner. The leaders encouraged the group to discuss how "you can never get enough of what you really don't want" as a way of inviting Rebecca to discuss her severe deprivation in the marriage. Group members related through their own experiences with smoking, drinking, and binge eating. By beginning to talk about the metaphor of craving sweets to fulfil human longing, the leaders were able to impact the group-as-a-whole as well as each individual member.

Structuring Couples Group Psychotherapy

Creating a setting for couples group therapy

Professional office space reflects the taste and values of the clinicians who work within the space. Although couples group psychotherapy can be led in institutional settings just as successfully as in independent practice settings, certain characteristics need to be considered for the space to be appropriate for professional treatment. Three qualities that enhance couples group psychotherapy settings are an atmosphere of personal reflection, a comfortable setting within which to work, and a crisply professional handling of clients.

An atmosphere of personal reflection

An atmosphere of personal reflection is often evident in a psychotherapy environment. Comfortable furniture, non-intrusive background music or white noise machines, reflective reading material, fresh bottles of water, form the ingredients with which one builds an atmosphere for personal and interpersonal reflection for clients. This attitude must be communicated through appropriate attire and demeanor for professional staff in order for it to trickle down to the clients who choose to invest in increased well-being. At the Coché Center for example, staff wear casual but neat attire and speak with modulated voices. Background music is soft and non-intrusive. Paintings on the walls create a place for thinking and planning. The space beckons towards the activity done within it.

A comfortable setting

Whether chairs are in a circle or couches are in a square, couples tend to sit together in couples. In group psychotherapy especially, it is valuable to set up the room so that couples are able to sit independent of but near each other. Since the group meets for an extended period of time, comfort and special health needs, such as back problems and inability to sit still, also need to be considered. A couples group begins to think about the treatment room as "theirs" as if it belongs to their group alone. The group will negotiate how warm or cold they want the room and often will have opinions about furnishings and wall hangings. As the group becomes more cohesive, members claim their spaces and make it part of their treatment. They literally and figuratively take the space home with them.

Professional handling of clients

The structure of psychotherapy creates a foundation for interpersonal change. When therapists handle clients in a respectful manner it models respectful behavior and enables clients to handle each other in a respectful manner. Professional handling of clients requires respect for individual difference between clients, patience with the whims and individualities that clients bring to the treatment situation, and an eye for detail that fosters follow-through on every level of practice.

> Ken and Kandy had great trouble making ends meet. Despite two professional incomes their collections of animals, farm equipment, and motorcycles made it impossible for them to stay on top of their financial obligations for couples group psychotherapy. Lagging far behind the other couples in terms of payment, it was necessary to issue constant reminders in order to keep the payment nearly up-to-date. The professional staff was very careful to maintain fairness and dignity in dealing with Ken and Kandy. In so doing, the staff helped them reconsider their budget as a way of handling their financial needs more responsibly. Had impatience crept into their voices, Ken and Kandy's defensiveness could have both slowed down treatment and decreased their sense of well-being.

Structuring an effective treatment package

In order to structure an effective treatment package it is necessary to decide if one is going to do a closed or open group; one must plan the length of the sessions, one must set goals and do progress reports, and one must consider whether to require out-of-group psychotherapy. Finally, a decision about single or co-leadership needs to be reached. Each concern will be addressed briefly.

Closed or Open Group Therapy? The Coché Center has chosen groups which begin and end at the same time. Couples who sign up with the group agree to stay with it for the full duration which is usually 11 months. Closed-ended groups have a better chance to experience stages of group development together and form a tightly-knit working group. Just as a marriage is a closed contract, presumably for the lifetime of the members, a closed model of group psychotherapy provides a very powerful instrument of change. However, many clinicians prefer to run open groups in which members enter and leave as seems best for them and the group. Either approach can be viable.

Group Size. A number of authors write that the optimal group size is three to five couples in a group. Smaller groups do not maximize the power of group dynamics factors, such as roles and norms (Coché and Coché, 1990).

Length and Frequency of Sessions. Clinicians vary in their preferred length and frequency for group meetings. At the Coché Center sessions began in 1985 with a duration of two and a half hours twice monthly. After a decade of this approach, it became evident that it was more convenient and more powerful to meet less frequently for longer periods of time and the current model of six hour monthly meetings became operative. Groups of four couples meet with one or two leaders for six hours monthly, usually on a weekend. This format allows members to fully invest in their treatment. It also functions to give all members sufficient working time so that crucial issues cannot be avoided in the group. Members who travel from a distance would be unable to attend a group that met more frequently that once a month so this model has proven to be very powerful and efficient for relatively high-functioning couples.

Although actual time varies, it is crucial to adapt the frequency and length of the sessions to the needs of the members. In an institutional setting, for example, where clients would find it hard to concentrate for a longer period of time, greater frequency and shorter duration of sessions would be necessary. Clinical success requires a match between the needs served and the clinical structures built.

Screening

A number of factors are important in member selection and group composition. Most authors agree that motivation for change is of paramount importance, especially in relation to the couple's commitment to their own relationship. The couple's willingness to stick it out and work to resolve their difficulties is considered a necessary but not sufficient factor. Judith Coché and Erich Coché (1990) required an intimate relationship of at least three years duration; the desire to improve the marriage; ongoing and previous individual, couples, or family psychotherapy; an interest in learning from and participating with other adults.

Couples group psychotherapy is not for everyone. It is, for example, inappropriate for couples seriously contemplating divorce. With the use of stringent and careful screening and selection, most complications and limitations can be minimized.

Heterogeneity and homogeneity

Couples groups are heterogeneous in relation to the members' ages, diagnoses, and severity of marital problem. Couples groups can include people as old as 75 and as young as 25. A large age range prompts therapeutically useful transferences (Coché, 2010). For example, younger couples get into various aging-parent issues with the elderly members. Coché prefers groups that vary in their severity of the marital problems or individual diagnoses. Although one borderline patient in a group is difficult, two borderline patients work fairly well. The groups do not work well for members of average or below-average intelligence, nor do they work well for members who are psychotic or who have multiple personality disorders. The groups do work well for adults with learning disabilities.

Many couples are relatively high-functioning but need couples group therapy to refresh and revitalize a marriage that has gone stale. Some couples believe that their marriages are fundamentally solid but that the spark has gone out of the relationship: they choose group therapy to enhance and revitalize the marital foundation. Other members are going through a series of chronic crises and look at the group as their last hope. Many have been to marriage therapy before but found the experience disappointing. Having both types of couples in the group is encouraging. Those with the serious problems find much to learn from the others; those with stale marriages are relieved to learn that they are not as badly off as their peers in the group or as they had thought.

Such diversity offers group members concrete proof of the scope of marital function and dysfunction. The wide range of both positive and negative experiences of each couple creates a vast wealth of information at the disposal of each group member for use in making decisions or trying out new strategies for relationship improvement. Most rapid progress comes when group members are similar in intellectual and cognitive levels of functioning but who use different cognitive styles. Cognitively, the members are average or above average in intellectual functioning and have a variety of ways of organizing their experiences to form their own definitions of interpersonal reality. Some members are gifted in warm nurturing ways of thinking about others: others may be cool and distant yet insightful and incisive; some members are concrete and matter-of-fact; others are facile in thinking psychodynamically, systemically, or metaphorically. Some are remarkably articulate; others have great difficulty in knowing or expressing how they feel. Most members appreciate humor and enjoy the laughter that is central to the fluidity of group functioning.

Papp (1976) advocated separate groups for husbands and wives because of the element of surprise, intrigue, and curiosity that occurs when each partner has a same-gender group. She believed that such groups can expedite change and mollify the hopelessness that can accompany marital difficulties and can improve the work done when the groups eventually meet as a whole. Coché (Coché and Coché, 1990) finds that an individual group for one or each of the couples may

Co-therapy

Many therapists advocate the use of co-therapists in the conjoint or group treatment of couples. Besides the advantages to both therapists of convenience and sharing the workload, clinical lore claims that male-female co-therapy teams increase the likelihood and the quality of transference, ease identification, reduce therapist bias and dropout rates, and improve motivation, sensitivity, and efficacy. Unfortunately, few studies address the veracity of such co-therapy advantages. Nonetheless, the model is unparalleled for therapist support and training.

Gill H., & Temperly, J. (1974) have found the use of co-therapists to be effective in working with couples presenting with a variety of problems. Experienced co-therapists further argue that the usefulness and the ultimate success of co-therapy depend on the working relationship between the two therapists involved and should not be tried unless a sound relationship exists. The co-therapists may have different therapeutic styles, but they must agree on their basic therapeutic theoretical frame. Considerable differences in the theory of what is helpful to people in a group could severely undermine the efficacy of the therapy (Hellwig and Memmott, 1974). On a therapeutic level, the leaders provide a valuable complement to each other, if one of them either overlooks or exaggerates the importance of a particular issue at hand, the other can provide balance, bring in an additional point of view, and prevent potential iatrogenic problems. Rutan and Stone (1984) listed a variety of advantages of co-leadership but also pointed out its drawbacks, citing a number of authors who noted that the complexities of the relationship between the co-leaders may detract from the power of the group.

If the leaders are of different genders, it is a further advantage to the group (Kluge, 1974). Members of heterosexual couples have the opportunity to project their own feelings toward the opposite sex onto one of the leaders and work out those feelings in the transference (Cooper, 1976).

Group organization and functioning

Pretraining. Most pretraining programs consist of brief informative sessions which function to define the therapist's role; teach group skills; and describe the session format, confidentiality, goals, the group purpose, contracting, and other general group policies. In Piper's (1979) initial review of orientation techniques, he concluded that controlled studies show only "weak positive data in favor of pretraining for process and outcome data." In a later study, Piper (1981) found that cognitive-experiential approaches to pretraining have strong positive effects on attendance and dropout rates and mildly positive outcome effects; the weak outcome effects found are probably a result of:

1. The large time span between the pretraining period and the outcome measures.
2. The less structured training methods used in early studies.

Phases of group development. For the purposes of simplicity, this chapter suggests that five stages are involved in the development of a group. Each will be reviewed briefly:

Joining In the first stage of a group, the characteristics include fear of acceptance by group members, anxiety over the wisdom of joining a group, and social politeness. A group often depends on its leaders, and the members fear too much self-disclosure.

> A newly formed couples group was asked to read the group policies before meeting for the first time. Although a couple of members read ahead, most members did not read what was assigned to them. Instead, the group nervously asked a lot of questions and found details which occupied a lot of their clinical time. When the leader asked them to talk about how they felt about being in the group, they admitted they were too nervous to read the material ahead of time and were more comfortable once they were there. They went on to say they wanted the leader to explain the policies about the group so that they could be sure and understand. The leader acknowledged that the group was feeling dependent and this was understandable given their anxiety about beginning a therapy experience with people they had never met.

Beginning working phase In the beginning working phase, the members begin to work on marital problems. One of the hallmarks of the stage is what may be called moving from couple identify to personal identity. The members, who at first were merely seen by the others in the group as partners in a couple, begin to emerge as individuals with their own styles and their own problems.

Crisis At the end of the second stage, the group often goes into a crisis. What often begins in stage two as dissatisfaction with leaders, format, money or other group variables can turn into a real battle. The onset is usually sudden. One couple may come into a session and threaten the group with dropping out if the evasiveness does not stop. Or a member suddenly loses his or her temper and noisily attacks the leaders or another member.

Intensive working phase Once the crisis has been overcome, the group members tacitly agree on a comfortable level of self-disclosure, which creates an atmosphere in which therapeutic work can be done. The group enters its second working phase. At that stage the group is cohesive: the members express genuine liking and affection for each other.

> A group of three couples began their work as soon as the clock indicated start time. They immediately divided the time between them ensuring that each couple got at least one hour to do work. With no help from the leader they decided the couple who has having the most pressing problems ought to go first. This couple described the devastation that occurred when the husband had been let go from his job and the group wrestled with their problem with very little leader intervention. The group occasionally turned to the leader to ask for additional descriptive material based on her knowledge of the situation but did not rely on her leadership in order to work in the group. Although it might look to a naïve observer as though the leader was not necessary, the group appreciated her skill in letting the group do its own work, intervening only when necessary.

Termination About two months before the last meeting, one of the leaders reminds the group that it will end in eight weeks. During the termination phase, reconstructing becomes a major issue. Couples decide if they want to end their membership or join again for another year. They ask for feedback from the rest of the group and report to the group on their progress during the group year. Much of that progress is clearly visible to the group. An atmosphere of sadness about ending the remarkable experience of their group is mixed with the pride and the team spirit that result from hard work.

> As the contract came to a close for a group that had worked together for 22 months, members began to evaluate the importance that the group held for them. A summary of these comments, drawn from Coché (2010), indicates the power of the experience:
> - "I am more secure as an individual and as part of a team together."
> - "My partner is helping me grow by communicating more of his feelings and sticking to his positions."
> - "We are more responsible and more considerate of each other."
> - "There is a happier home life for all."

Assessment forms the foundation for treatment planning

Assessment consists of deciding how to handle an initial contact, providing a structure for the initial consultation, deciding whether to do in-depth psychological testing or psychiatric consults. Each will be dealt with briefly.

Responding to initial contacts When clients initially contact a professional for assistance they are understandably uneasy and worried. Since every contact with a client is potentially therapeutically helpful or harmful, therapists need to be both friendly and professional at all times. A quick return call to say "hello" and answer inevitable questions of cost, treatment philosophy, and other concerns sets the tone for a respectful interchange between client and professional. These initial phone calls turn out to be crucially important in allowing clients to relate to a professional with ease.

Structuring an initial couples consultation   A 90-minute independent consultation is the beginning for all client contact at the Coché Center (Coché, 2010). The purpose of this initial consult is to determine whether or not there is a match between what the client is requesting and what the clinician can provide. If this match is not present at this initial consultation, there is follow-through with client referral to an appropriate source for help. Most frequently, however, the consultation becomes the first appointment. The goal of the initial consultation is to assess the strengths and weaknesses as the couple sees them. This is done by encouraging each partner to think about why they chose their partner and what they enjoy about them. Framing the initial consultation within a positive psychological viewpoint often gives the couple hope that progress can be made with their more difficult concerns. The latter part of the consultation looks at the troubles the couple is having and the goals they have for themselves in the treatment process. In summary, an initial consult looks at what works in this relationship and what needs to be improved. Finally, it encourages the partners to think about if and how they want to move forward with treatment.

In-depth psychological testing and psychiatric assessment   It is up to the clinician to determine whether or not in-depth testing and psychiatric assessment seem important. If a clinician spends over an hour and a half with a couple but is still left with more questions than answers, further assessment is wise. In an initial consultation a clinician can begin to gather critical background information to develop a sound treatment plan and take a developmental history for each member of the couple. For in-depth assessment, advanced personality testing can be of particular value when there are diagnostic concerns. Finally, if there is a history of psychiatric consultation or a question about whether medication is necessary, it is incumbent upon the clinician to require medical consultation with a psychiatrist in order to move treatment planning forward.

Treatment Strategies for Couples Group Psychotherapy: A Guide for Clinicians

Couples group psychotherapy has benefited from recent developments related to evidence-based practice. This brief overview considers key concepts in member self-disclosure; helping client's set therapy goals, and additional psychotherapy outside of the group. A brief consideration of the handling of predictable problems and clinical emergencies in groups follows. Finally, it considers current paradigms from relational psychoanalysis, positive psychology, nonverbal dimensions, and attachment theory.

Member self-disclosure

Research during the past two decades has indicated numerous positive therapeutic effects for members of psychotherapy groups. One of the benefits in psychotherapy within a group involves the willingness of members to self-disclose (Coché, 1983). There are two kinds of self-disclosure in groups: in one, members tell the group about their life situations, backgrounds, and marriages. In the second, members reveal their dynamics by their behavior in the group in the here-and-now. Both are invaluable in promoting therapeutic power. It is wise for the leader to teach members effective self-disclosure methods, which are known to increase group cohesiveness.

Therapy goals and progress reports

Therapy goals vary from group to group, couple to couple, and member to member. Clinical treatment goals focus on a number of common areas:

1. Clear and respectful communication skills based on highy trained emotional intelligence
2. An understanding of the power of the system of couples communication and willingness to apply self discipline to harness the power of skillful verbal and non verbal interchange
3. Heightened awareness of an openness to the needs and wishes of the other
4. Increased good will and flexibility in intimacy, sexuality and daily problem solving
5. Clarification of role ambiguities and conflicts to enable stress free living
6. Improvement of the couple's maladaptive defensive styles
7. Increasing awareness and master of intergenerational issues
8. Happier and more satisfying days, weeks, months, years and decades together

> Angie was certain that her husband Sam was verbally abusive to her and her children but Sam disagreed vehemently. Sam said that it was his birthright to say what was on his mind and he was proud to grow up in a family that knew how to talk about "stuff." Because Angie was not able to have a therapy goal that included changing her partner, she was forced to look inward in order to set a goal for her own work. After a lot of thought, Angie decided that her goal for her work in the upcoming year was to "understand what I do to provoke treatment of me that I find hard to manage." Additionally, Angie decided that she wanted to learn to manage her own anger better. In this way, Angie's goal did not revolve around changing her husband; instead it concentrated on work that she was able to achieve. In the course of the year Angie met her goals and reported this in her progress reports.

In order to assess progress, a key part of the group's work is to take time near the end of the group to do written progress reports. In these progress reports each member outlines the changes they have seen for themselves and whether or not they think it is wise to return. Couples share these progress reports with one another, after which, feedback is given from the members of the group to each couple about changes seen and the wisdom of returning for another contract period. These frank discussions rely on the power of group dynamics. The group is truly a hall of mirrors when it comes to giving members feedback about what other members have seen in terms of clinical progress. This phase of the group devoted to evaluating progress for each member, is crucial in helping members see their own change realistically, and for convincing couples to return for deep work in the next contract period.

Out-of-group psychotherapy work

Working with a therapist in individual, couples, or family sessions at least once every three weeks is a necessary part of the treatment package for the Coché model (Coché, 2010). Concurrent psychotherapy is necessary, because the group moves quickly. It is impossible to contain all the issues for each member and for each couple through group interaction alone.

Concurrent treatment modalities are often used to maximize therapeutic effectiveness or to deal with special problems that arise within a couple. Popular formats are individual psychotherapy with one or both members of a dyad, couples therapy, family therapy consultations with the families of origin or the couple's children, and workshops. Greenbaum (1983) advocated a combination of individual, couples, and group therapy because he believed that the combination intensifies the therapeutic process, decreases resistance, and minimizes interpersonal distortions. Conversely, Kaslow (1981) argued against the concurrent use of treatment modalities. She asserted that group therapy alone is critical in maintaining a sense of group belonging and integrity, confidentiality and for making sure that, the values of group therapy for each couple are maximized. More recent approaches are mentioned in the next section of this chapter.

How does one facilitate psychotherapeutic change within a couples group setting?

Two facets of facilitating change within a couples group setting are worthy of brief clinical attention. First, group leaders need comfort with handling predictable problems and clinical emergencies in ongoing groups. The second involves choices of treatment paradigms for maximal therapeutic progress. In addition to recent developments in relational psychoanalytic thinking and cognitive-behavioral approaches to psychotherapy, particular mention is devoted to the impact of positive psychology on psychotherapeutic change, the nodal work on attachment theory in couples group psychotherapy, and the foundation work in the technology of neuropsychological and non-verbal aspects to couples group psychotherapy. Each will be briefly considered.

Group leadership variables in couples group psychotherapy

Assuming that leaders are aware of group dynamic principles in basic leadership styles, leaders need to be able to handle predictable problems and clinical emergencies as they crop up in groups.

Handling predictable problems in ongoing group Predictable problems in couples groups include absences, lateness, and finances. All three areas are handled with clinical follow through, eye for detail, and perseverance. A leader needs to be able to set the norm that absences are serious undertakings. For example, at the Coché Center groups are paid for whether the member attends or not. This makes the statement that the place for the member is held in the group whether or not the member is present. Member absences are discussed in detail and members are expected to attend.

In similar fashion, leaders state clearly that "the group starts on time and ends on time." Because members travel great distances to reach their destination, lateness is not tolerated in a psychotherapy group. Routine lateness is handled in a clinical manner and is taken as an indication of interpersonal patterns. Most frequently, the way in which a couple handles lateness and absence is indicative of the way they handle each other and their children. Likewise, the expectation is that members will pay promptly for group therapy at the beginning of the month for the group to come (Coché and Coché, 1990; Coché, 2010). It often happens that those members who have trouble meeting their financial obligations to the group, also have trouble meeting their financial obligations in the community. A discussion of absence, lateness, and finances, as it impacts the group members, often reveals a deeper conflict around honesty, accountability, and personality responsibility, as it exists inside the

> Angie and Sam often entered the group bickering about why it took Angie so long to get into the car before she left the house. The couple often commented that they had argued on their 45-minute drive to group therapy: why Angie was late, and why Sam had so much trouble paying the family bills on time, including the fee for monthly group therapy? Arriving late and disheveled, the couple monopolized group time through their own disorganization. Sensing the group's frustrations, Dr Coché invited the members to discuss their reactions to the pattern of lateness. By listening to the reactions their behaviors stimulated in valued group members, Angie was able to alter her own behaviors so she started earlier and avoided being late. In like fashion, Sam began to pay his monthly therapy fee on time when he realized other group members were going out of their way to do so. In this way, routine administrative concerns can be handled in a way that is beneficial to the clients and to the psychotherapy practice.

members. A group discussion around these seemingly superficial parts of group therapy is often the beginning of an important change mechanism.

Handling clinical emergencies All groups have clinical emergencies although these vary from group to group. Breaking group policies constitutes an emergency in most group settings. In this case, leaders deal with the dynamics by inviting the group to process the way they handled group policies. This level of here-and-now work in which members speak about their emotional reactions, as well as their intellectual analyses of the concern at hand, allows members to reach conclusions together which can dissolve a stalemate in the group.

Clinical paradigms in treating couples in groups Psychoanalytic practice has begun to embrace relational perspectives and cognitive psychotherapy continues to be clinically viable and powerful in treating couples. Additionally, however, three contemporary paradigms deserve mention: new energies from the educational imperative provided by positive psychology, integrating non-verbal dimensions into couples group psychotherapy, and enabling progress in primary human attachments.

Relational psychoanalytic concepts in practice Long considered the epitome of attention to individual psychodynamics, recent psychoanalytic trends have begun to concentrate on the dynamics of interpersonal engagements. Enactments (Frank 2002; Ginot, 2007), are interpersonal manifestations of disassociated relational styles. Unconsciously triggered between two people, these internalized relational patterns can be changed by experiences both inside and outside the therapeutic setting. By making automatic and unconscious patterns conscious, therapists attempt to repair and enhance chronically dysfunctional life patterns. This attention to the interpersonal dimension is a welcome addition to the traditional focus on the impact of earlier learning.

The educational imperative from positive psychology Over the past decade positive psychology has provided legitimacy for the desire to enjoy one's life fully and strive towards optimal functioning. Positive psychology does not pretend to ignore psychopathology. Instead it uses cognitive restructuring as a way to open their minds and their hearts to greater happiness. Seligman (2002) emphasizes that the goal for psychological treatment is not merely to remove the dysfunctions and roadblocks that create unhappiness and suffering, but to enable fulfilled and satisfying lives and relationships. Positive psychology stresses the importance of positive emotions and positive interaction styles to support coupled relationships. Gable, Reis, Downey (2003) have demonstrated that responding actively and constructively to a partner enhances satisfaction within coupling. Success begets success. As Gottman (1994) found, couples minimally need a 5:1 ratio of positive to negative behaviors such as compassion, forgiveness, and gratitude. For a couple to achieve happiness they need to go beyond repairing dysfunctionality and learn the assumptions and behaviors involved in choosing happiness as a lifestyle. Recent research is beginning to provide solid guidelines for this relation set (Gable, Reis, Impett, and Asher, 2004).

Integrating nonverbal dimensions into couples group psychotherapy As Coché and Gillihan found in their recent review of nonverbal communication in coupling (Coché, 2010), the bulk of couples' communication has always been nonverbal. Siegel (2006) stresses the necessity to promote neural integration into therapy suggesting that the clinician focus on attunement as the heart of therapeutic change. In similar fashion, Johnson and Greenberg (1994) concluded that emotion is central in all forms of interaction. For example, Walter et al., (2008) points out that the sexual response involves four distinct components (cognitive, motivational, autonomic, and emotional). The nature of human attachment requires nonverbal dimensions of sensuality and sexuality in order to sustain human loving.

Enabling therapeutic progress in primary human attachments As Konner (2004) states, attachment is "one of the most important determinants of human well-being." Current research suggests that psychodynamic processes underlying romantic attachment are similar to those underlying parent-infant attachment. Recent research points to the key role of the reward system in the development of human attachment. Specific focus on the centrality of sensory awareness by Damasio (1999) and others, points the way to deepening levels of intimacy by increasing positive human bonding through movement, massage, and nonverbal communication.

> Arthur and Jane were locked into a marriage of over 30 years because both refused to divorce. The marriage felt like a terminal sentence of boredom and frustration. They described themselves as "totally unconnected" but the leader was able to help them understand that they were deeply bonded to one another through withdrawal and silent anger. The couple came to understand that the work of the therapy would be to transform the nature of their bonding so that it felt comfortable and safe for each member. Although that sounded like an unbelievable goal to them, they were only too happy to dream about the day that life would be better. Through the work of the group they were able to understand that they had learned a method of human bonding, which had existed in both families of origin. Using insight, cognitive psychotherapy, and the experience of the group itself, Arthur and Jane successfully improved their relationship to a level of deep satisfaction.

Professional and Ethical Dimensions of Couples Group Psychotherapy

Three professional and ethical dimensions stand out in reviewing clinical work with couples and groups.

1. *Confidentiality* Confidentiality is the most important policy in psychotherapy. A group cannot function unless a group trusts one another (Davis and Meara, 1982). Confidentiality is complex when couples spend six hours a month together. The centrality of confidentiality in the psychotherapeutic process is magnified by couples who come from the same residential community and do psychotherapy together. In small towns, it is highly likely that one will be invited to be in a group with one's neighbor, for example. However, even in a large city the boundaries of confidentiality are complex when members of the same academic community choose the same psychotherapist. Likewise, the restriction against social contact outside of the group is complex. Written policies help by delineating clear guidelines. For example, Coché (2010) provides a written contract around confidentiality, which states "that all information discussed at all group psychotherapy meetings is to remain in the room." This policy is enforced through continued discussion whenever there is danger of breaking the confidentiality.

When a therapist works in an individual setting as well as a group setting with the same client, the therapist needs to be careful about information carried from an individual meeting into a group. Professionalism and good judgment provide standards of excellence. The consent of the group member is always obtained before revealing confidential information.

2. *Handing the financial commitment* Coché (2010) finds that the most desirable approach to handling fees is direct and firm. She suggests that clinicians might offer clients in financial need a financial need-based scholarship which supports the work. She further suggests that payment be collected at the first of each month for the group meeting to come. Finally, she suggests that payment concerns be part of the clinical life of the group when it becomes obvious that couples find it impossible to handle their own finances appropriately. Often a couple that is having trouble paying their group fee is having financial trouble in their lives. Her recommendation is to deal with finances as any business person might. Her experience is that this approach is highly successful and models appropriate financial accountability for the members of the group.

3. *Is marriage and family therapy ethical and effective?* Many psychotherapists trained in individual psychotherapy believe it is unprofessional and even bordering on unethical to work with two members of a couple. Resolving this concern in the context of couples group psychotherapy provides an ethical and professional challenge. Inspection of the website for the American Association for Marriage and Family Therapy (www.aamft.org) provides substantial documentation for an approach which includes the treatment of the individual in the context of family. Marriage and family therapy has had the benefit of 60 years of theory and research as the underpinning for clinical treatment. An extensive set of ethical guidelines are available on the website.

In addition to the theoretical and research foundation for marriage and family therapy as a treatment of choice, marriage and family therapists have pressed for mandatory licensure in all 50 states. As a result of their dedication to high standards and credentialing, the federal government considers marriage and family therapy a legitimate treatment for those individuals who are part of the military. In summary, marriage and family therapy as a treatment modality, has been validated through theory, research, high standards in clinical practice, ethical guidelines and recognition by policy makers.

The special challenge of couples group psychotherapy

As with any treatment modality responsible leadership requires an honest assessment of potential roadblocks and ethical concerns. Three thorny dilemmas come to mind in relation to couples group psychotherapy. A brief discussion follows:

1. *"Whose side are you on?"* Although couples group psychotherapists are trained to promote the welfare of the unit of the couple and family there is often misunderstanding on the part of the clients who find it hard to understand that anyone could be trained to be dedicated to the welfare of all members of the family simultaneously. For example, an attorney trained primarily in the representation of one client, often challenges the assumption that a leader will keep the welfare of both people in mind. Often the feedback from other group members helps skeptics begin to see that it is

not only possible, but useful to engage in psychotherapy which concerns itself with the welfare of everyone.

2. *"But what if we need to break up during a group?"* Often the very couples who need couples group psychotherapy the most are those near divorce. Because it is necessary to construct a group with the welfare of all members in mind, it is not responsible to invite couples into a group if it is likely that they will divorce during the period of the group contract. This frequently feels disloyal to those couples who believe that they should be able to join the group and leave it if they have to divorce. It is the job of the leader of the group to explain to them that just as a family needs to look out for the welfare of all members at all times, a couples group needs to be a viable treatment modality for all members during the duration of the contract. Explained in this way, couples frequently accept the limitations placed by the leader on their membership.

3. *"This is really hard to lead."* Frequently colleagues are excited by the power of the treatment they see as they come to know couples group psychotherapy trained in either couples or group therapy but not both. These clinicians want to start doing couples group therapy without adequate training in both modalities. Because they see the model as demanding of their time and energy, they find it difficult to create the time necessary to learn the model before practising it. Often these leaders find the model very hard to use and give up. Instead, when potential couples group therapy leaders invest in learning the various facets of leading couples in groups, they enjoy a growing fascination with the model and with their own career.

Supervision and training in couples group psychotherapy

As Coché and Coché stated in their training tape for colleagues (Coché and Coché, 1990) couples group psychotherapy is a unique combination of two separate but related fields. For best practice couples group psychotherapy, the clinician requires advanced training in both couples psychotherapy and group psychotherapy. Although the years of training may seem burdensome, the result of investing in the development of expertise in individual therapy, couples therapy, and group therapy creates a fertile and challenging career path in which boredom is never of concern.

For training in couples therapy, clinicians have major resources from the American Association of Marriage and Family Therapy, and the American Family Therapy Association. Additionally, each professional organization has its own training process.

For training in group psychotherapy, the American Group Psychotherapy Association provides excellence in academic, clinical, and research dimensions for training in all kinds of therapy groups including couples groups. Couples groups have been in existence for over 25 years. Ample opportunity for training exists in person and online.

It is assumed that any clinician undertaking couples group psychotherapy will have substantial training in individual psychotherapy because couples and groups are comprised of individuals. Best practice clinical work rests on a dual foundation of depth psychotherapy and cognitive/behavioral interventions. Practitioners need expertise in both dimensions if they are to work with individuals on long-lasting behavioral changes at the same time as they tackle issues of personality organization.

In summary, training and supervision in couples group psychotherapy is actually an amalgam that begins with training in individual psychotherapy, then moves to training in both couples and group psychotherapy. Finally, clinicians interested in couples group psychotherapy integrate all dimensions into the very powerful and dynamic model of couples group psychotherapy (Coché, 2010).

Evidence-Based Practice in Couples Group Psychotherapy

A couples group creates a microcosm of a marital community in which couples show their interactive style. The intensity of relating to the same group members for over 50 hours in a calendar year creates a hall of mirrors in which one cannot help but see one's own behavior.

A sizable body of research indicates that both couples and group psychotherapy are effective treatment modalities (Coché, 2010). Couples psychotherapy has been used to treat anxiety disorders (Monson, Schnurr, Stevens, and Guthrie, 2004), mood disorders (Barbato and D'Avanzo, 2008), substance abuse (Powers, Vadal, and Emmelkamp, 2008), and relationship satisfaction (Shadish and Baldwin, 2003). Research tells us that couples psychotherapy is better than no therapy for about 80% of individuals receiving it (Snyder et al., 2006).

Likewise, group psychotherapy has been shown to be quite effective in treating a vast array of presenting problems (DeRubeis and Crits-Christoph, 1998). Therefore, it is no surprise that, despite little research on couples group psychotherapy, couples group psychotherapy has been used to deliver treatment for partner illnesses including alcoholism, drug use, HIV, breast cancer, borderline personality disorder, partner abuse, and sexual deviance. These studies consistently show the effectiveness of couples group psychotherapy (Coché, 2010).

Couples have reported that a cohesive group is helpful to them. Perceived as less helpful were structured exercises. This finding is especially surprising because these same couples requested more structured interventions (McCarthy and Coché, 2008). The authors suspect that different patients with varied cognitive styles experience the interventions uniquely and that seemingly contradictory data may, in fact, be due to different subgroups responding consistently within their own experiences. For example, some couples need and respond well to structure; other couples grow more quickly through a group that deals primarily in the here-and-now.

The interpersonal aspects of the group are the most important factors – honesty, trust, helping, and being in a group. The structure imposed by the therapists, important though it may be to the overall functioning of the group, is not paramount in the minds of the participants.

Evidence-based practice at the Coché Center Assessments made at the beginning of a group often form the basis for later evaluations of a couple's progress (Coché, 1983). Adopting the attitude that modest research goals can be used to address key questions, Coché, Hunt, and McCarthy, designed a small study (unpublished) to address the effectiveness of the groups in assessing desired change. Coché and colleagues used the Group Climate Questionnaire, the Millon Index of Personality Styles, the Marital Assessment Inventory and the Dyadic Adjustment Scale to address how couples had changed. Couples reported that each partner had changed as well as the couple as a whole. For example, in 2009, couples stated: "We are more responsible and considerate of each other" and "We have a new model for living life" (Coché, 2010). The team concluded that many aspects of the relationship improved as response to treatment. For example, one woman said: "I feel as though my husband, for the first time in 16 years, actually desires my company, and that is awesome" (Coché, 2010). McCarthy (McCarthy and Coché, 2008) suggested that clinicians need to move forward with evidence-based practice as a way of improving our understanding of clinical work. He further suggested that evidence-based practice need not be expensive, cumbersome, or esoteric and reported that practice research could be accomplished with a simple spreadsheet.

Couples Group Psychotherapy: The Next Quarter of a Century

Couples group psychotherapy provides both cognitive and experiential learning for couples. This multilevel learning guarantees that individuals will learn to experience themselves differently by being a member of a group for couples. In the next quarter of a century, one might predict that economic necessity will combine with increased interest in optimal mental health, to create an ideal environment for the expansion of couples groups as a clinical modality. Because of the complex training in the field (*see* section on training and supervision) many clinicians who might enjoy working with couples and groups have been shy about undergoing the necessary training. In 2009, the American Group Psychotherapy Association began to offer telecourses in couples work and couples group work which allowed a clinical community to form, in which training in couples work and couples group work was available through teleconferencing. These technical advances, combined with the pressure for clinicians to treat mental health disorders quickly and efficiently, suggest that couples group psychotherapy may expand in a few key directions over the next 25 years. Three directions are briefly mentioned.

1. *Monthly couples groups.* Despite the earlier popularity of a weekly couples group, Coché and others have found that meeting monthly for up to 6 hours at a time provides a powerful clinical setting guaranteed to promote personal and interpersonal change. The ability to vary the frequency and duration of the group is a distinct advantage (Coché et al., 2006).

2. *Theoretical advances in couples group psychotherapy.* Recent work in relational psychoanalytic psychotherapy provides tremendous encouragement for psychodynamically trained clinicians. For example, the notion of enactments – interpersonal manifestations of dissociated interpersonal styles – finds support in both attachment studies and neuroscientific research (Frank, 2002; Ginot, 2007). While psychoanalytic thinking was moving forward, positive psychology quietly began to legitimize happiness as a goal for human existence for the first time in the history of clinical practice. In 2002, Martin Seligman had the courage to state that happiness is not only a legitimate goal in psychotherapy, but necessary for the welfare of individuals and couples. As this article goes to press, the field of positive psychology is beginning to do solid research on the variables that contribute to individual well-being and human thriving. It cannot be long before happiness in couples becomes a legitimate area for

theory and research. Further, psychotherapists are able to internalize theory and research in order to select therapeutic interventions from the fields of psychodynamic psychotherapy, cognitive-behavioral psychotherapy, and positive psychology. This creates a promising future for theory and practice in couples group psychotherapy.

3. *Neurobiology is a reality to be dealt with in psychotherapy.* The start of the 21st Century saw an explosion in theory and research demonstrating the centrality of neurobiology in the functioning of couples. As early as 1997, Dan Goleman reported the importance of emotional intelligence. Building on earlier work, Dan Siegel (2006) created the concept of the mindful brain. Siegel integrated meditation with brain research and challenged clinicians to recognize that talk is only a small part of human change. In Gillihan's review of the neurobiological research on coupling (Coché, 2010) he drew the conclusion that the integration of sensuality, sexuality, attachment, and nonverbal communication form a foundation of relearning sensory awareness as a part of couples group psychotherapy. Coché and Slowinski began to treat sexual dysfunction in a couples group in 2002 (Coché et al., 2006) and Coché began to integrate nonverbal communication, dance, and other forms of nontraditional movement into couples work, so that couples could learn to move together more smoothly. In the final analysis, it is the relearning of dysfunctional neuropsychological pathways that contributes to the most powerful change for couples.

Summary

Couples Group Psychotherapy has traveled light years since Coché began to develop her model in the late 1980s. Originally considered a "quirky" little modality that few understood and fewer practised, couples group psychotherapy has become a treatment of choice for many couples who seek therapists able to practise it. Both efficient and effective, the modality is founded on principles of ethical and professional practice, integrative theory and clinical work, and solid evidence-based practice. Despite the requirement of complex training, at the writing of this chapter, the popularity of the modality is mushrooming as clinicians recognize that couples psychotherapy and group psychotherapy can lead to efficient and effective change. One might predict that as this field continues to mature, more and more couples will benefit from it.

Acknowledgement

This book chapter was prepared with the assistance of Stephen Schueller, MA, who assisted in the formatting and conceptualization of the relationship between positive psychology and coupling.

References and Bibliography

Agazarian, Y., & Peters, R. (1981). *The visible and invisible group: Two perspectives on group psychotherapy and group process.* London: Routledge & Kegan Paul.

Barbato, A., & D'Avanzo, B. (2008). Efficacy of couple therapy as a treatment for depression: A meta-analysis. *Psychiatric Quarterly, 79,* 121–132.

Buber, M. (1958). *I and thou* (2nd ed.). New York, New York: Scribner's.
Bugental, J. F. T. (1981). *The search for authenticity: An existential analytic approach to psychotherapy.* New York, New York: Irvington.
Bowen, M. (1971). The use of family theory in clinical practice. In Haley, J. (Ed.), *Changing families: A family therapy reader* (pp. 159–192). New York: Grune and Stratton.
Coché, E. (1983). Change measures and clinical practice in group psychotherapy. In R. R. Dies & K. R. MacKenzie (Eds.), *Advances in group psychotherapy* (pp. 79–99). New York, New York: International Universities Press.
Coché, J. (1995). Group therapy with couples. In N. S. Jacobson & A. S. Gurman (Eds.). *Clinical Handbook of marital therapy* (pp. 197–211). New York, New York: Guilford.
Coché, J. (2010). *Couples group psychotherapy: A clinical treatment model* (2nd ed.). New York: Taylor & Francis.
Coché, J. M., & Coché, E. (1990). *Couples group psychotherapy: A clinical practice model.* New York, New York: Brunner/Muzzel.
Coché, J. M., Slowinski, J., McCarthy, K. S., & Galbraith, J. (2006). Couples group psychotherapy for sexuality and intimacy: Intensive treatment for lifelong change. *Group, 30,* 25–39.
Cooper, L. (1976). Co-therapy relationships in groups. *Small Group Behavior, 7,* 473–498.
Damasio, A. (1999). *The feeling of what happens: Body and emotion in the making of consciousness.* San Diego, California: Harcourt.
Davis, K. L., & Meara, N. M. (1982). So you think it is a secret. *Journal for Specialists in Group Work, 7,* 149–153.
DeRubeis, R. J., & Crits-Cristoph, P. (1998). Empirically supported individual and group psychological treatments for adult mental disorders. *Journal of Consulting and Clinical Psychology, 66,* 37–52.
Framo, I. L. (1982). *Explorations in marital and family therapy.* New York, New York: Springer.
Frank, K. A. (2002). The "ins and outs" of enactment: A relational bridge for psychotherapy integration. *Journal of Psychotherapy Integration, 12,* 267–286.
Gable, S., Reis, H., & Downey, G. (2003). He said, she said: A quasi-signal detection analysis of daily interactions between close relationship partners. *Psychological Science, 14,* 100–115.
Gable, S. L., Reis, H. T., Impett, E., et al. (2004). What do you do when things go right? The intrapersonal and interpersonal benefits of sharing positive events. *Journal of Personality and Social Psychology, 82*(2), 228–245.
Gill H., & Temperly, J. (1974). Time limited marital treatment in a foursome. *British Journal of Medicine Psychology, 47,* 153–161.
Ginot, E. (2007). Intersubjectivity and neuroscience: Understanding enactments and their therapeutic significance within emerging paradigms. *Psychoanalytic Psychology, 24,* 317–332.
Goleman, D. (1997). *Emotional intelligence: Why it can matter more than IQ.* New York, New York: Bantam.
Gottman, J. M. (1994). *What predicts divorce: The relationship between marital processes and marital outcomes.* Hillsdale, New Jersey: Lawrence Erlbaum Associates.
Greenbaum, H. (1983). On the nature of marriage and marriage therapy. *Journal of the American Academy of Psychoanalysis, 11,* 283–297.
Hellwig, K., & Memmott, R. J. (1974). Co-therapy: The balancing act. *Small Group Behavior, 5,* 175–181.
Johnson, S. M. (2005). *Attachment processes in couple and family therapy.* New York, New York: The Guilford Press.

Johnson, S. M., & Greenberg, L. S. (1994). *The heart of the matter: Perspective on emotion in marital therapy.* New York, New York: Brunner Mazel.

Kaslow, F. (1981). Group therapy with couples in conflict: Is more better? *Psychotherapy: Theory, Research, and Practice, 18,* 516–524.

Kluge, P. (1974). Group Psychotherapy for married couples. *Psychotherapy and Medizinische Psychologies, 24,* 132–137.

Konner, M. (2004). The ties that bind: Attachment: The nature of the bonds between humans are becoming accessible to scientific investigation. *Nature, 429,* 705.

Leichter, E. (1962). Group psychotherapy of married couples group: Some characteristic treatment dynamics. *International Journal of Group Psychotherapy, 12,* 154–163.

Lewin, K. (1951). *Field theory in social science: Selected theatrical papers.* Chicago, Illinois: University of Chicago Press.

Lloyd, R., & Paulson, I. (1972). Projective identification in the marital relationship as a resistance in psychotherapy. *Archives of General Psychiatry, 27,* 410–413.

McCarthy, K. S., & Coché, J. M. (2008). *Making an evidence base from practice: Good intentions, complications, and recommendations for group psychotherapists.* Paper presented at the annual meeting for the American Group Psychotherapy Association, Washington, DC.

Monson, C. M., Schnurr, P. P., Stevens, S. P., et al. (2004). Cognitive-behavioral couple's treatment for posttraumatic stress disorder: Initial findings. *Journal of Traumatic Stress, 17,* 341–344.

Papp, P. (1976). Brief Therapy with Couples Groups. In: Guerin, P. J. (Hrsg.) *Family Therapy – Theory and Practice.* New York: Gardner Press.

Peterson, J. A. (1968). *Marriage and family counseling: Perspective and prospect.* New York: Association Press.

Piper, W. (1981). Selecting suitable patients: Pretraining for group therapy as a method of patient selection. *Small Group Behavior, 12,* 459–475.

Piper, W., Debbane, E. G., Garant, J., et al. (1979). Pretraining for group psychotherapy: A cognitive-experiential approach. *Archives of General Psychiatry, 36,* 1250–1256.

Powers, M. B., Vedel, E., & Emmelkamp, P. M. G. (2008). Behavioral couples therapy for alcohol drug use disorders: A meta-analysis. *Clinical Psychology Review, 28,* 952–962.

Rutan, J. S., & Stone, W. N. (1984). *Psychodynamic group psychotherapy.* New York, New York: Macmillan.

Seligman, M. E. P. (2002). *Authentic Happiness.* New York, New York: Free Press.

Shadish, W. R., & Baldwin, S. A. (2003). Meta-analysis of MFT interventions. *Journal of Marital and Family Therapy, 29,* 547–570.

Siegel, D. J. (2006, March 8) *Toward an interpersonal neurobiology of psychotherapy.* Paper presented at the American Group Psychotherapy Association Annual Meeting, Austin, Texas.

Snyder, D. K., Castellani, A. M., & Whisman, M. A. (2006). Current status and future directions in couple therapy. *Annual Review of Psychology, 57,* 317–344.

Spitz, H. I. (1979). Group approaches in treating marital problems. *Psychiatric Annuals, 9,* 318–337.

Sullivan, H. S. (1953). *The interpersonal theory of psychiatry.* New York, New York: Routledge.

van Emde Boas, C. (1962). Intensive group psychotherapy with married couples. *International Journal of Group Psychotherapy, 12,* 142–153.

von Bertalanffy, L. (1968). *General systems theory: Foundations, development, and applications.* New York, New York: Braziller.

Walter, M., Bermpohl, F., Mouras, H., et al., (2008). Distinguishing specific sexual and general emotional effects in fMRI: Subcortical and cortical arousal during erotic picture viewing. *Neuroimage, 40,* 1482–1494.

Whitaker, C. A., & Keith, D. V. (1981). Symbolic-experiential family therapy. In A. Gurman & D. Kniskern (Eds.), *Handbook of family therapy* (pp. 187–225). New York, New York: Brunner/Mazel.

Whitton, S. W., Waldinger, R. J., Schulz, M. S., et al. (2008). Prospective associations from family-of-origin interactions to adult marital interactions and relationship adjustment. *Journal of Family Psychology, 22,* 274–286.

Wolf, T. J. (1987). Group psychotherapy for bisexual men and their wives. *Journal of Homosexuality, 14,* 191–199.

Yalom, I. D. (1985). *The theory and practice of group psychotherapy,* (3rd ed.). New York, New York: Basic Books.

23

The Large Group: Dynamics, Social Implications and Therapeutic Value

Haim Weinberg and Daniel J. N. Weishut

The Large Group: Typical Dynamics

For many group therapists who are used to the traditional small group, the large group format is unknown and confusing. When coming to a conference that includes a large group, some participants ignore it as if it never existed in the conference schedule or deliberately avoid it and skip its meetings. Others come once, feel overwhelmed, frustrated and perplexed, and vow that they will never come again. Still others come from time to time, wondering about the nature of this "strange beast," waiting for the features of the small group to appear. Yet some group practitioners become hooked to the large group, attending year after year, feeling that something important is happening there, and even finding that the large group becomes the highlight of the conference for them. We would like to make the large group more "user-friendly" by explaining its dynamics and pointing out its typical processes, and hope that this will assist potential participants in their learning process.

In recent years the large group has regained attention as an experiential or learning group in order to understand societal processes. When referring to "the large group" (LG) in this paper, we relate to an experiential group with membership anything above 30–35, led in an unstructured way, usually from a psychodynamic perspective. This kind of LG can be found in psychological and especially group psychotherapy conferences.[1] We "utilize the large group experience as a laboratory in which to study large group processes, both conscious and unconscious, as a way of understanding their impact and influence upon social, organizational and systemic thinking, feelings and actions" (Weinberg and Schneider, 2003: p. 17). The LG is considered to be a reflection of the society, culture or organization we are part of. In the literature emphasis has been on the social aspects of the LG, while therapeutic aspects have

---

[1] There are a range of publications on therapeutic large group intervention after disasters (e.g. Terr, 1992). Since they have a different purpose from the kind of the LG we discuss, we left these out.

been mostly de-emphasized. Still, several theorists relate to the psychodynamic processes of the LG, to how the participant learns about his or her social role, and how the LG enhances the development of connections and feelings of belonging to society.

LGs can be "crazy" and chaotic. It is difficult to follow a thread, and voices may be unheard or ignored. The individual experience can be intimidating and paralyzing. Even finding one's voice in the crowd can be difficult, and for some people just expressing their thoughts in the LG is an achievement. Members may wonder, "Do I dare disturb the universe, overcome my fears and say what I have in mind in public?" The fears are only partly imaginary, because the individual voice might be lost in the crowd, drawing no response at all, which can become a narcissistic blow for the person who dared to speak. Still it is important for the participants to be able to express themselves, as participation in the LG brings to the fore a sense of citizenship and belonging to a community.

LGs can be overwhelming and confusing. It is difficult to think clearly in this setting, and not easy to make sense of the experience. The loose boundaries and weakened container, due to unstable participation in the group sessions, enhance regression and evoke fragmentation anxieties. It takes time to understand what happened and to absorb the events. That is why usually we need small groups following a LG experience to process the individual's feelings and restore a sense of identity that is sometimes threatened by the LG. Yet it can be strengthening for the ego to go through this experience and to be able to crystallize one's boundaries and keep one's identity under the pressure to merge with the mass.

LGs can also be aggressive and conflictual. The anxieties evoked in the LG create a tendency to cling to familiar subgroups. Sometimes you just attach to the friend that came with you. Other times people identify with social subgroups such as those around gender, ethnic origin, religion, political attitude, or any other minority or majority groups. Because there are strong defense mechanisms of splitting and projective identification in the LG, the tendency to group into such social subgroups can create intense conflicts. In addition, anything said aloud in the group will be perceived in its social context. Thus a personal remark could suddenly be turned around into a stance representing a certain subgroup. In this way the LG provides a unique opportunity for people to become intensively aware of multicultural issues and social conflicts from a passionate and involved rather than intellectual and detached point of view.

The Large Group and the Social Unconscious

In psychodynamic group psychotherapy we usually focus on the personal and on the interaction between individuals in the here-and-now. We tend to avoid dealing with the social context in which the group takes place and in which its participants live. But this false dichotomy is based on the premise that the individual and society are separate entities. Western cultures (especially in the USA) praise individuality, encourage the notion of the individual as unique and independent, and focus on the process of differentiation from the family as part of becoming a mature adult. This notion is so embedded in Western cultures that it is taken for granted and creates the illusion of a truism. Other cultures may put more value on collectivism than on the individual (Hofstede, 2001). It is enough to look at Eastern, African, Latin or Arab cultures, where individuals and society are intertwined, to understand that this emphasis on individuality is only one possibility of deconstructing reality. Actually, we cannot disconnect the individual from her social context.

The Group Analytic approach believes that the individual is social through and through. Pines (1981) characterizes the evolution of group analysis as follows:

> The emergence of analytic group psychotherapy as a theory and as a technique was facilitated by a new scientific paradigm, that of the move from the study of the single entity, the item, the individual, to the study of the relationship between an entity and the field of forces in which other entities are encountered . . . . . The classical psychoanalytic model of mental apparatus will not do, as it is based on one-body psychology. In group psychotherapy we need other models; perhaps a systems model will do. (Pines, 1981: p. 276)

These ideas sound similar to those of the intersubjective approaches to psychotherapy, arguing that the mind is inherently dyadic, social, interactional, and interpersonal (Aron, 1996). But when we move from one person to two people and then apply these intersubjective ideas even beyond two-persons-psychology into multiple-people-psychology, we can no longer hold on to the idea of the individual as a separate entity from its social context in which he is embedded. The evolution of society profoundly affects individual psychodynamics. As individuals civilize their behavior and restrain their impulses, the power of the social forces inside the individual (and impacting his behavior) increases, and the structure of the psyche changes.

Experiencing the LG is experiencing oneself as part of a social matrix, as belonging to some connecting web that exists all around us but is usually invisible in ordinary day life. In the small group, we sense existence and impact of the-group-as-a-whole and experience "the group mind," which is a dynamic product of the interaction of the group members. When we move from individuals to groups and as we see groups as an entity, we also have to shift our perspective from the individual Freudian unconscious and focus on a new kind of unconscious that emerges: the group unconscious. LGs reveal what is called "the social unconscious" or the organizational unconscious. The social unconscious (Hopper, 2003; Weinberg, 2007) refers to the existence and constraints of social, cultural and communication arrangements of which people are to varying degrees "unaware." It includes anxieties, fantasies, defenses and object relations, as well as various aspects of socio-cultural-economic-political factors and forces, many of which are also co-constructed unconsciously by the members of particular groupings.

LGs, conducted in an unstructured way and developing an atmosphere of exploration, can reveal this social unconscious by focusing on shared defenses, fantasies and anxieties existing in that setting. The leaders can bring to attention the subtle ways in which members of the LG co-construct common fantasies, that are beyond the contents of the specific group, belonging to the larger context of the organization or society from which this group comes from. When members bring dreams, use metaphors, share personal stories and associate to them, the leaders might point at a deep unconscious issue connecting these dreams and stories. Utilizing the idea of parallel processes or equivalence (Hopper, 2003) they can speculate that this issue reflects a preoccupation residing in the social unconscious of that group.

The social unconscious is easier to be noticed and its manifestations in the LG are especially prevalent in traumatized societies. The specific psychological processes of ethnic, national or religious groups are influenced by shared representations of historical events and the transgenerational transmissions of ancestors' trauma. We would like to introduce here the notion that these kinds of groups tend to choose and identify with certain glories and/or traumas. *Chosen glories* are shared mental representations of a large group's ancestors' past triumphs and the heroes and martyrs associated with them (Volkan, 1988). They induce a heightened sense of "we-ness." *Chosen trauma* is the shared mental representation of a massive trauma that the group's ancestors suffered. When a LG regresses, its chosen trauma is reactivated in order to support the group's threatened identity. It is the collective memory of a disaster, which becomes a paradigm that keeps the existential threat in the national memory in order to ward off potential complacency. "Memories," perceptions, expectations, wishes, fears, and other emotions related to shared images of the historical catastrophe and the defenses against them, may become an important identity marker of the affected LG and actually construct its Social Unconscious.

Here is an example from a LG occurring in a conference in Ein Gedi, Israel, 2008, shortly after Operation Cast Lead (the war on Gaza) which had highly controversial results both in Israel and abroad.

> A Jewish Israeli woman, who identified with the suffering of the Palestinians (left wing political position in Israel) told the group that in the middle of the war, when she heard about the life-threatening danger to children in Gaza, she and her daughter started a project trying to evacuate 500 children from the Gaza strip. At first they asked Israeli Jewish families from the southern parts of Israel to host these children and were answered positively. When they understood that the Palestinians will never agree to come to Israel, they approached Palestinian families in the West Bank. The project almost started when they got a response from the families in Gaza that they were not ready to send their children away. The argument was that this was an Israeli manipulation not to feel guilty, and that after evacuating their children there would be no reason for the Israelis not to bomb them. The Palestinians said that this was a trick to take their land: First move the children, then move the adults and make them refugees again.
>
> The LG room was full with emotions: The Israelis felt hurt that their good intentions were labeled "manipulative." The Palestinians felt misunderstood as well, and the people from outside Israel felt excluded. The atmosphere changed when one Palestinian asked: so do you mean that Palestinian mothers care less about their children than Jewish mothers? In addition, a British woman associated about the evacuation of children from London in WWII, and the research that showed that the children who were evacuated suffered more post traumatic stress disorder symptoms than those who stayed with their families in London. It helped the group become less reactive and more communicative.

This stormy event in a LG shows how difficult it is to really give up one's point of view and recognize the other's subjective experience, due to chosen trauma residing in the Social Unconscious. The amount of distrust between the parties (Israelis and Palestinians, in this case) is enormous. Although the arguments of the Palestinians were clearly stated, Israelis could not listen to them, drop their righteous attitude and see the issue from the eyes of the Palestinians. What blocked their regular ability to listen was the memory of the Holocaust and the associations involved in the specific case (a well-known case of a "children transport" from Nazi Germany was mentioned in the LG). The Palestinians were not able to listen either to the well-intended Israeli wish to do something positive during the war, since they have their own trauma of the Nakba, which is the loss of their villages and houses following the Israeli Independence war, resulting in them becoming refugees and feeling misled by Arab leaders. These historical events seem to unconsciously creep into the discussion and influence its participants. Without acknowledging these traumas that are part of the Jewish-Israeli and Palestinian social unconscious, and without understanding its impact on members of both nations, dialogue will probably fail. It is also interesting that, in this LG, a historical memory of another nation, brought by a British woman, could penetrate the parties' walls and help reestablish communication.

Therapeutic Value of the Large Group

The LG is not a small group. This simple truism sounds clear on paper but seems hard to remember. A common mistake is to come to the LG expecting the familiar processes of self-exploration, cohesion and intimacy. Sometimes a member brings in a personal problem believing that she will get feedback or a personal response to her distress. She may be very disappointed when the LG fails to act like a small group and just moves on to another topic. The LG is mostly aimed at exploring societal and organizational dynamics. The focus of the leaders is not on the individual but on the group-as-a-whole, reflecting conscious and unconscious processes of the organization or the conference in which the LG is taking place, or of society-at-large. While the LG may be therapeutic – any resemblance to therapy is more like sociotherapy than psychotherapy. It lacks the setting, the boundaries and the rules (e.g. confidentiality, *see* Weinberg and Schneider, 2007) that usually characterize therapy, and does not provide a safe environment.

Having said that, we still want to argue that LGs can be therapeutic. The notion of the LG being therapeutic has encountered much resistance (Wilke, 2003), despite the fact that in psychiatric settings the large group (or community), including both patients and staff, is recognized for a long time as being therapeutic (Kreeger, 1975; Main, 1946; Springmann, 1975). De Maré (1972) stated that:

> The technique of large group psychotherapy, which would appear to be a self-evident conclusion, continues to meet with the suspicion that was once accorded to psychoanalysis and later to small group psychotherapy . . . the intensive and rigorous application of a large group technique *per se* has not yet been seriously mooted. The explanation

for this might lie in the powerful, chaotic and unpredictable nature of large group phenomena and in their tendency to ideology formation which would prove politically and economically dicey in many countries to-day. (De Maré, 1972: p. 106)

De Maré referred to the crucial role of culture as an active ingredient in psychotherapy. He claimed that "psychoanalysis in deliberately isolating the patient from a social to a psychotherapeutic frame is a psychology of the individual. Small groups, on the other hand, involve the psychology of the family. It is only in the larger group that cultural dimensions can be comprehensively explored" (De Maré, 1975: p. 79).

De Maré was not alone. Jordan (2001) called for the use of relational-cultural theory not only to help individuals move into healthier, more mutual relationships in which they can grow and contribute to the growth of others, but also to develop strategies to shift hurtful disconnections between groups of people toward an attitude of respect and mutuality. Agazarian and Carter (1993) discussed the large group as a context for therapeutic change, and put forward that "changing the structure and function of communication within subgroups simultaneously changes both the large group and the individual subgroup members" (Agazarian and Carter, 1993: p. 210). Weinberg and Schneider (2003) suggested that "the large group helps in role differentiation and integration in the developing of both an individual as well as group identity" (Weinberg and Schneider, 2003: p. 18). All these indicate that LGs have therapeutic value:

> The large group provides members with opportunities to explore and learn about the difficulties we all have, as subjects, in recognizing other subjects as "equivalent centers of experience" and enabling a move towards enhancing capacities for mutual recognition in the group. (Jarrar, 2003: p. 31).

If we take the group analytic premise seriously, and agree that the individual and society are intertwined, theoretically we cannot make a sharp distinction between sociotherapy, and psychotherapy. Any change in society deeply influences the individual. So let us focus on the therapeutic value of the LG. Specifically, we would like to explore the extent to which therapeutic factors present in the small group are relevant also in the LG. Afterwards we will suggest two more specific therapeutic factors available in the LG. The term "therapeutic factors" could be defined in various ways. We will use the term indicating factors that enhance psychological well-being and/or encourage personal growth.

Therapeutic Factors in the Large Group

Group therapy traditionally has referred to small groups – with usually between five and twelve participants – and was described extensively in many textbooks (e.g. Yalom and Lescz, 2005; Rutan et al., 2007). The therapeutic value of small groups seems indisputable. Yalom and Lescz (2005) discussed the essence of successful group therapy and proposed a list of 11 elementary factors of therapeutic change.

These therapeutic factors are:

1. Instillation of hope
2. Universality
3. Imparting information
4. Altruism
5. The corrective recapitulation of the primary family group
6. Development of socializing techniques
7. Imitative behavior
8. Interpersonal learning
9. Group cohesiveness
10. Catharsis
11. Existential factors.

Yalom and Lescz (2005) noted that there is substantial variance among groups and group leaders in the emphasis they put on each of these factors. Not all factors are always present or equally important. Thus, some groups may put more emphasis on interpersonal learning (e.g., Yalom-type groups) while other groups (for example, psycho-educational groups) would emphasize imparting information. Furthermore, group participants may differ in how much they are able to profit from each factor. For example, one participant could experience the instillation of hope as being most important, while for another, the strongest therapeutic factor could be imitative behavior. Yalom and Lescz emphasized that the distinction between these factors is arbitrary and that the factors are interdependent and do not occur separately.

Yalom mentioned that larger groups also have therapeutic value (Yalom, 1980), and that several of these same therapeutic factors are relevant in larger groups (Yalom and Lescz, 2005). However, he did not expand on this issue and thus left a gap. In an attempt to fill this gap, we will now shortly describe each of these therapeutic factors, and the extent in which they seem available in the LG. We will divide these factors in those that are fully, partly, or hardly available in the LG.

Factors hardly available

Some therapeutic factors, readily available in the small group, are hardly available in the kind of LG described previously in this chapter.

Group cohesiveness Yalom related to the term "group cohesiveness" as the experience of feelings of trust, belonging and togetherness developed in groups. The sense of belonging to a large group was proposed as one of its main benefits (Weinberg and Schneider, 2003). This seems true for the "natural" group, like a society, political party or professional community. Natural large groups create their own culture and norms; they do not dissolve easily and this provides the individual with strength. However, it is questionable whether we can see this factor as contributing to the therapeutic effect of the LG as discussed here. The boundaries of the LG are too loose, and allow for partial participation (people may attend just one session during a conference), and for joining or leaving its meeting without disrupting its natural continuity. The LG usually does not exist long enough to create cohesiveness; often not more than a few hours or maximum several days. Actually, many a LG may be experienced as "incohesive" (Hopper, 2003).

Instillation of hope One of the more difficult issues to cope with in the LG is the issue of hope. Yalom referred to the recognition that other members' success can be helpful and develop optimism for one's own improvement. Yalom and Lescz (2005) suggested that faith by itself can be therapeutic. "Group therapists can capitalize on this factor by doing whatever we can to increase clients' belief and confidence in the efficacy of the group mode" (Yalom and Lescz, 2005: p. 5). They suggested that for example self-help groups put much emphasis on hope. However, LGs often catalyze tension and chaos (Wilke, 2003). It is not unusual for conflict to remain until the closure of the group, without finding a solution. Eventually, participants may feel bewildered and lost (Hopper, 2003). Although LG facilitators may be in the position to increase hope, it seems that in the LG hope can be easily lost. It is true that, when LGs do reach conflict resolution, it does create hope for resolution of social conflicts, but this is quite rare and most of the time the value of the LG for the individual is learning how to deal with seemingly hopeless situations and still not lose hope.

Imparting information Yalom and Lescz referred to the possibility of receiving education or advice by the facilitator(s) or group members. They related to didactic instruction about mental health, illness, and general psychodynamics given by the therapists as well as advice, suggestions, or direct guidance from either the therapist or group members. They mentioned the importance of imparting information as a way to reduce anxiety. Though mental health and general psychodynamics may not be the main concern of most LGs, we may postulate that information on the group process and its reflection of society could be helpful for participants to feel more at ease within the LG. Anxiety is an unseparated part of the LG process. Still, in most of the psychodynamic LGs, leaders provide no or very limited information to the participants; not even about what is expected from them. Participants in the LG may provide information to each other. However, imparting information is considered to be of little importance in the LG, unless it is a group with psycho-educational intent (see Rausch et al., 2006). In some conferences, the large group leaders provide a short theoretical presentation and discussion with the participants after the sessions, as part of the need for credit educational units and its requirements, but actually this is not part of the setting of the LG.

The corrective recapitulation of the primary family group Yalom and Lescz related to the unsatisfactory experience most clients have had in their primary family, and to the corrective role the small group has in this respect, through reenacting critical family dynamics with group members in a corrective manner. The LG goes far beyond the primary family group in its size and lacks the feeling of family intimacy. It reflects society, not a family. In conferences where the structure includes both large and small group meetings ("Tavistock" style, group relations, also called Leicester conferences in Britain or A. K. Rice conferences in the US), the small group is associated with the family, while the LG is associated with "the street". The number and variety of stimuli in the LG exceed the capacity of the self to organize in a family-like grouping (Shields, 2001). Therefore, the LG cannot provide a corrective recapitulation of the primary family group. When the LG does remind a participant its family of origin, it lacks the capacity for corrective experience. In one of the LG meetings in a day intended to explore LG processes, a participant said: "This group reminds me of my alienated family, where no one really spoke directly to another. I feel so lonely here." There was no response from any other participant, as if to validate this alienated/isolated experience in his family.

Factors partly available

Some therapeutic factors available in the small group are also available in the LG. However, their availability is rather limited because of the large size of the group.

Interpersonal learning   Yalom linked to the term "interpersonal learning" to the possibility of gaining personal insight about interpersonal impact through feedback provided by others. It was suggested that the "group analytic model applied within a large group offers a rich opportunity to pursue the therapeutic objective to promote growth in the capacity to build and maintain caring and respectful interpersonal relationships" (Shields, 2001: p. 218). This may be more true to the therapeutic community on a psychiatric ward than to the LG in conferences. Because the LG is not focused on individual patterns of communication and connection, and feedback from one person to another is not encouraged by the leaders, it is up to the participant to do the work inside himself and draw conclusions about his interpersonal style. Some members may be able to do so (perhaps those who are more psychologically-oriented and more used to self-reflection), some not.

Development of socializing techniques   The small group may be especially helpful in the development of basic social skills, such as learning how to approach people, providing feedback, working out difficulties with particular group members (Yalom and Lescz, 2005). This may also be possible to some extent in the LG. However, both the atmosphere in the LG, which may be intense and aggressive, and its limited focus on the individual may not be conducive for individuals trying to develop basic socializing skills. This is different for the development of more advanced social skills and the ability to deal with power and conflict. If we include this arena in social skills, we can say that the LG can encourage its members to develop and strengthen these skills. We will discuss later in this chapter the ways in which the LG confronts its members with a representation of society and provides opportunities to use power.

Altruism   Altruism, seen as the experience of offering something valuable to the other without the expectation of something in return, is suggested to be a deeply satisfying experience (Rutan et al., 2007). Yalom related to the boost to one's self image through extending help to others. To do something for someone else makes people feel meaningful, which is therapeutic in itself. In addition, many times in a small group, people are touched by such generous contributions and respond to the altruist person with compliments that strengthen self-image. The LG, like the small group, provides the opportunity to support others in a variety of ways, such as expressing understanding, providing direction, sharing similar concerns, and more. What makes this more complicated is the size of the group in comparison with the time-frame, which provides space for relatively few people to participate in an altruistic act. In addition, rarely do people in the LG reciprocate with self-strengthening responses, due to the non-interactional nature of the LG, at least in its initial stages. It takes a more advanced LG, the kind that develops only in long enough conferences with enough LG sessions (from our experience there should be at least four sessions of the LG), to develop that capacity.

Factors fully available

Some therapeutic factors present in the small group are even more readily available in the LG.

Catharsis Yalom referred with the term "catharsis" to the release of strong feelings about past or present experiences. The LG is an excellent place for expressing strong emotions. The regressive forces in the LG exert their pressure on the individual and we can witness strong outbursts of anger (even rage) or uncontrolled sobbing. The presence of many people amplifies the emotions and intensifies the cathartic experience. If expression of strong emotions by itself is perceived as therapeutic and relief-bringing, then the LG would be a great place, at least for the people having this opportunity. For others, seeing someone expressing strong emotions could be a vicarious form of catharsis. One could ask though if in order for catharsis to be therapeutic there needs to be an empathetic response. In large support groups or encounter groups we may expect empathy, but in many other LGs, because of their nature we cannot expect much empathy from the group.

Universality Yalom and Lescz referred to the notion that other members share similar feelings, thoughts and problems, and add that the disconfirmation of someone's feelings of loneliness is a powerful source of relief. "After hearing other members disclose concerns similar to their own, clients report feeling more in touch with the world and describe the process as a 'welcome to the human race' experience" (Yalom and Lescz, 2005: p. 6). Some of the concerns raised in the LG may not be universal to all. However, the abundance and diversity of people in the LG ensure that often individuals will encounter other individuals or even sub-groups that have similar concerns. Therefore, this therapeutic factor could act even stronger in the LG than in the small group.

Imitative behavior Yalom and Lescz suggested that imitating others is a way to experiment with new behavior, and that "imitative behavior" can have a strong therapeutic effect. They related to the possibility of expanding personal knowledge and skills through observation of self-exploration, working through and personal development of others. The LG offers the participant an opportunity to meet with an abundance of different behaviors. Therefore, LGs – like small groups – provide ample opportunity for participants to learn from the behavior of other group participants and/or facilitators. One may think: "If she can do it, I may be able to do it as well." Imitation or making these forms of behavior one's own, can take place still within the LG or at a later occasion.

Existential factors   Yalom then added another cluster of therapeutic factors, which he named "existential factors."

> All these factors relate to existence – to our confrontation with the human condition – a confrontation that informs us of the harsh existential facts of life: our mortality, our freedom and responsibility for constructing our own life design, our isolation from being thrown alone into existence, and our search for life meaning (Yalom and Lescz, 2005: p. 98).

These factors also seem to be highly relevant in the LG. However, "existential factors" seem to be a broad spectrum of factors provided by the group, partly overlapping with other therapeutic factors in Yalom's list. For example, "hope" was mentioned by several researchers as an existential factor of therapeutic value, especially when coping with health issues (Blinderman and Cherny, 2005; Havens and Ghaemi, 2005). "Isolation" seems to be inversely related to "universality" and "altruism" (Yalom, 1980). Themes that are common in the LG are issues about life and death, personal and social responsibility, human rights and questions of (inner and outside) freedom and oppression. All these are clearly related to existential factors and are discussed many times in the LG with more depth and perspectives than in a small group.

Factors Available Uniquely in the Large Group

In addition to the factors mentioned above and cited by Yalom, we identify some unique factors that are not mentioned by Yalom, perhaps because they are usually rare in small groups, and are more typical for the LG. Two factors that are available and prominent in the LG, but almost absent from the small group are the representation of society and the struggle for power. Both factors can be connected to a higher maturity level of personality development. Helgeson's model (found in Saragovi et al., 1997) on a division of personality factors, is somewhat comparable to the proposed division here. Both factors "communion" and "agency" in this model were found to be related to "interpersonal maturity" and well-being. Let us now take a closer look at both factors.

Representation of society as therapeutic factor

We are in essence social beings. "No man is an island," said John Donne in *Meditation XVII*, 1624 (Booty, 1990). Human development is a cultural process (Rogoff, 2003) and personality is shaped among others by cultural influences (Triandis and Suh, 2002). It was suggested that the primary source of our suffering is from isolation, and that healing is the process of connection and integration with different others (Jordan, 2001). However, it takes a kind of awareness beyond inner processes to understand that we are part of a larger system, and sometimes it takes another step to actively become involved in social affairs beyond one's selfish interest.

The "representation of society" as a therapeutic factor in the LG may be considered as parallel to the "corrective recapitulation of the primary family" as a therapeutic factor in the small group. It relates to complex social abilities, and thus could also be seen as a higher level of "development of socializing techniques", another of the therapeutic factors readily available in the small group. However, being involved in social issues and developing social responsibility, which might become the result of participation in a LG, is a more complex virtue than simple social skills needed to smoothly interact with others.

The LG can more or less represent the society in which the group takes place. In any LG we can find a huge diversity of people from different ethnic groups, religious background, age and of course, gender. Thus, in the USA, LGs can include both blacks and whites, Christians, Moslems and Jews, Hispanics, Caucasians and Asians, heterosexuals and homosexuals, etc. In LGs taking place in international conferences we can find people from different nationalities as well, adding to the flavor of the encounter and creating a rainbow of diversity. Usually soon after – or sometimes even before – the start of a LG some form of subgrouping will occur. This situation confronts the participant with two essential questions, "What is my social environment?" and "To whom do I belong?" Based on these two questions, we will make a distinction between "diversity" and "pluralism."

Diversity With the term "diversity" we mean the opportunity to discover the variety of possible experiences, ideas and views present in the LG. Shields (2001) claimed that the "rich opportunity for the self in the LG is to develop 'the capacity to be alone' in Winnicott's sense, in the midst of stimulation by the overwhelming diversity that must always be present in the large group context" (Shields, 2001: p. 214).

Others related to the socializing aspects of the LG. James (1994) referred to the LG as enhancing good citizenship, while providing opportunities to learn the viewpoints of others. Weinberg and Schneider (2003) related to the LG as a tool in the understanding of social interactive processes, interrelationships within society and the so called "social unconscious." They saw the LG as a laboratory for understanding conflict and a way to create acceptance of diversity and multiculturalism. We believe that the LG is exceptional in the possibilities it provides to learn about the enormous diversity within society and one's own individual position.

There are numerous ways in which people are diverse. One LG, held at an international conference near Jerusalem (Israel, 2010), in which both authors participated, stressed, among others, differences in the particpants' language, women and men, Jews and Palestinians, the organizers of the conference and the participants.

Pluralism "Diversity" comprises the notion that we are all different, but relates neither to subgrouping, nor to the power-differential between these groups. "Pluralism" takes this idea one step further to the interpersonal level. With the term "pluralism" we refer to the possibility to gain awareness of one's own position *vis-à-vis* ethnic, religious and cultural subgroups and to the engagement between, and with, these subgroups on an equal level. It is not enough to accept diversity, and respect other points of view that are different from one's self, there also is a need to grant equal opportunities for each cultural, ethnic and social subgroup. Feeling honored and respected in one's culture was suggested to enhance well-being. Therefore, it is important to recognize the inequity of power between groups, and acknowledge everyone's right to self-determination (Waldegrave, 2009).

Belonging to a group enhances a feeling of group identity. The LG facilitates the development of both an individual as well as this group identity (Weinberg and Schneider, 2003). Jarrar (2003) related to the notion that the individual has multiple group identities. These group identities are not necessarily in harmony, and are challenged when participating in the LG. The encounter with different group identities or subgroups in the LG is anxiety provoking and threatening (Jarrar, 2003; Shaked, 2003). However, this encounter assists in getting to know one's own and others' unique subjectivities. The challenge then is to create a dialogue both internally and interpersonally in which the other is not perceived as inferior (Jarrar, 2003). Thus, it seems that the LG provides, more than any other therapeutic group, the possibility of mapping one's group identity among that of many others.

In the previously mentioned group (near Jerusalem, 2010) almost all participants were Hebrew speakers. Since the group was facilitated in Hebrew this put them in a superior position over those foreigners who did not speak Hebrew. Attempts were made to translate for the non-Hebrew speakers, but this did not always work, and some foreigners became upset. This was a good opportunity to learn among others about the limits of goodwill and the extent to which a majority can, or is willing to, adapt to the needs of a minority.

The struggle for power as therapeutic factor

In any society there are overt or covert power struggles. It was suggested that much of the distress people encounter, may be less the result of internal conflict than of disturbing events in the outside world, including the inequality or abuse of power, leaving us with feelings of powerlessness or helplessness (Mack, 1994).

Small groups do not create the difficulty of speaking we face in LGs. The small group leader focuses on creating a safe environment and the atmosphere in the small group very quickly becomes intimate, inviting shy people to speak and encouraging quiet individuals to talk. In contrast, in many – if not most – LGs we will find struggles for power taking place simultaneously in different realms: the physical (e.g., seating places, room temperature), communication (e.g., language, possibility to hear each other), content (topics of discussion), and leadership (being influential). These power struggles make it highly difficult for the participant, whether actively engaged or merely watching, to stay aloof. For some participants even the ability to overcome inner fears and open their mouths facing this monstrous LG, feels like a huge achievement.

The LG provides a social environment that – if all goes well – is relatively well-contained, and therefore a good playground to experience individual freedom and exercise one's power. The essential questions being: "What do I think about all this?" and "What shall I do with my power?" Based on these two questions we can make a distinction between "agency" and "authority."

Agency With the term "agency" we indicate the power of the individual to act independently and make one's own free choices. Personal agency is related to will,

> In an international group therapy conference held in Rome (IAGP, Italy, 2009) the leaders of the LG verbalized clearly that the language in the LG will be English without official translation.[2] There were about three hundred participants, half of them from Italy. Language became one of the difficult barriers to overcome in this LG, not only as a means of communication, but also as representing power struggles between cultures. Particularly as many Italians did not speak English well, and were frustrated because there was no translation. As an act of protest and rebellion some of them started speaking Italian in the LG and refused to be translated. Many long speeches came from Italian speaking members without translation. After long discussions and arguing it became clear that the Social Unconscious was at work. This rebellion had to do with the humiliation of the descendants of the Roman Empire who felt overtaken by "strangers." This issue connected with the fact that immigrants flood Italy nowadays. The struggle was actually around hegemony, namely the opposing of American/English as manifestations of imperialist rulers of the world, current US and the Ancient Roman. This way, the Italians could feel that they restored some of their power and pride as descendants of the old Roman Empire.

freedom, choice and responsibility. Restoring a sense of agency was seen as the main goal of therapy (Mack, 1994). Agency was linked to well-being, through a sequence of mechanisms.

1. In response to widening opportunities of life, people place stronger emphasis on emancipative values,
2. In response to a stronger emphasis on emancipative values, feelings of agency gain greater weight in shaping people's life satisfaction,
3. In response to a greater impact of agency feelings on life satisfaction, the level of life satisfaction itself rises. (Welzel and Inglehart, 2010: p. 43)

Similarly, Weinberg and Schneider (2003) used the term "inner authority" and proposed the exploration of the meaning of inner authority as one of the benefits of the LG.

Alternatively, we could use the term "empowerment" (instead of "agency"), which is the possibility the group provides in learning to think, decide and behave in autonomous ways. Empowerment was found to be related to psychological well-being and/ or mental health in many populations, like family caregivers (Tebb, 1995), refugee and immigrant women (Khamphakdy-Brown et al, 2006), people with psychotic disorders (Castelein et al., 2008), adolescents (Berg et al., 2009), and children (Romanelli et al., 2009). In our view the LG provides ample possibilities to find one's own individual way within the masses.

Agency involves taking risks. In the Ein Gedi LG (2008) the first author was one of two facilitators, while the second author was a participant. The first author was

---

[2] This is in contrast with the international conference, mentioned earlier held in Jerusalem, in which the language was Hebrew and foreign participants received simultaneous interpretation on request.

sitting in the inner circle, while the second author initially did not want to be in the spotlight and chose to sit in a circle close to the center. Then, at the start of the group session, there were annoying lights on a large screen at one side of the room. This was an issue of setting, but the facilitators did not intervene. After some deliberation, the second author gathered enough courage to get up in front of everyone, take the lead and turn off the computer causing the disturbance. For him it was an act that required strength and courage. However, the result was unexpected. The screen then said "no signal," which immediately was interpreted by another member of the LG, referring to the lack of communication in the group.

Authority "Agency" means that we are free to decide and act, but this does not necessarily include the use of power over others or the idea of leadership. "Authority" takes this one step further, to the interpersonal level. With the term "authority" we refer to the opportunity to exercise the legitimate and socially approved use of power over others in the LG. Shields (2001) suggested that the "group relations approach is an excellent means to study the impact of diversity within the social system and how covert problems in working with authority may become projected onto potential valuable subgroups in the large group context" (Shields, 2001: p. 220).

Aggression in this context is often used to maintain pressure on people or subgroups to conform to the norms of the majority (Hopper, 2003). We do not see aggression in itself as therapeutic or leading to any positive growth. We need to add that the use of authority does not necessarily include aggression or violating the rights of others. In the LG, power may take the form of verbal or nonverbal aggression.

Shields (2001) claimed that the group relations approach "offers a unique opportunity for members to learn by taking up differentiated leadership roles on behalf of the work of the group" (Shields, 2001: p. 220). Like Weinberg and Schneider (2003), our understanding is that the "large group is an ideal venue for investigating issues of leadership and authority" (Weinberg and Schneider, 2003: p. 18). When stormy conflicts burst out in the LG, every member faces the question: "Should I do something? Would it not be better for me to stay an observer and not intervene?" A decision to express one's voice when two people or two subgroups enter a fight is not only exercising good citizenship, but is also a unique opportunity to feel that one has an impact on the way things happen in one's environment. What people learn is that their actions matter. Their lesson can be "do not talk about change – be the change".

> The Ein Gedi LG, in 2008 was about to end in a rather frustrating way, in which many a participant felt that it remained too difficult to bridge the differences. Then, one of the participants staged a dramatized embrace between a Palestinian and a Jewish woman. This was an unusual and powerful step, in which a psychodramatist confronted the majority of psychodynamic oriented therapists with a, for them, different (nonverbal) way of dealing with conflict and pain. Reactions to her way of taking the lead were ambivalent. Though for some members in this LG the event created hope, others felt uncomfortable with the use of psychodrama, while still others felt that she tried to force a positive ending. In any case, she made a lasting impression.

The Intrapersonal and the Interpersonal Experience in the Large Group

We can see both factors "representation of society" and "struggle for power" as existing on two levels, an intrapersonal and interpersonal level. Initially, both of these factors may cause the individual to take a more personal or reflective stance, temporarily withdrawing from involvement with others. At a later stage both factors may cause the individual to increase interpersonal engagement with her or his environment. Thus, the recognition of "diversity" within the represented society leads to becoming actively engaged in a pluralist society. Likewise, in the process of becoming empowered, attaining an inner level of self-assurance, it takes time to develop a strong sense of agency before one can assert one's authority in the group (see Table 23.1).

Table 23.1 "Representation of society" and "Struggle for power" as therapeutic factors.

	Personal	Interpersonal
Representation of society:	Diversity	Pluralism
Struggle for power:	Agency	Authority

In summary, dealing with social issues and fully accepting diversity inside and pluralism outside, in addition to developing a sense of agency and being able to experience one's authority are strengthening for the self, and lead to a higher level of maturity. Foulkes (1975) saw the analytic group as "ego training in action," meaning that while working on intrapersonal and interpersonal issues, we train our ego to sustain more pressure, to contain inner anxieties, and not withdraw in conflictual situations. The LG is THE place to train the ego (or the self in more updated terms) in dealing with difficult situations in a more mature way.

The Role of the Leaders in the Large Group

Although this chapter is addressed to LG participants, we would like to say a few words about leading the LG and point out some important differences between leading small groups and large groups. LGs are usually conducted by two or three highly experienced group leaders. We would not like to give the erroneous impression that conducting a LG could be done by novices. It is difficult enough for novices in group work to participate in a LG, let alone conduct one. Unfortunately, there is no training program aimed at teaching how to lead a LG.[3] Some organizations that frequently organize "Tavistock" style conferences (mentioned earlier) provide a kind of "on-the-job training" for more experienced LG participants. After participating in several such LG conferences in which LG and small group sessions alternate, participants are "upgraded" and put in a small group of more experienced or senior group

---

[3] Attempts were made by the first author to set up a training track for large group leaders, when he was leading a group leaders' training program in Israel.

therapists. Later, they join the staff of such a conference, start co-leading a small group, and eventually co-lead a LG.

When conducting a LG, perhaps the main deviation from most of the group therapy approaches practised for small groups in the USA, is the focus on group-as-a-whole interventions. The reasons for doing so are both theoretical and practical. As explained before, the aim of the LG is to learn about organizations, societies, social dynamics or the social unconscious. The leaders are looking for common themes and trying to understand and interpret the process more than relating to the contents. They listen to the tone and music of the interactions in a free-floating attention, identifying it as the free-association discourse of the crowd. They will give their interpretations as if they were "wondering aloud" on what happens in the group-as-a-whole.

Focusing on the individual will not serve the purpose of the LG. The leaders do not and cannot deeply know the individuals in the group (unless from other encounters). The words of the individual are considered as expressing something beyond the specific person, and even when they are unique, the LG leaders try to understand these expressions in the background of the entire process going on. It will be a mistake to address intrapsychic dynamics based on a comment a participant utters. Sometimes, participants who feel at loss try to "invite" the leader(s) to a dyadic interaction, or "seduce" the leader(s) to help them with their problems. The leader will focus on the meaning of these behaviors in the context of the group, and not interpret them as individual dynamics or personal disorders. As said above, although participation in the LG can be therapeutic, this is definitely not the place for personal therapy. As an example, take a LG with the physical structure of concentric circles of chairs, in which most of the inner circle is empty, except for two chairs occupied by two senior therapists. It will be a grave mistake to interpret this interesting seating arrangement as a narcissistic tendency of these participants sitting in the center (whether it is true or not). It might be better for the leaders to wonder aloud about the possible anxiety of the members in taking a central role in the LG or even in the organization. Or perhaps they might explore the possibility that newcomers (to the LG or the organization) feel intimidated by senior members.

LG leaders in conference setting are often known as colleagues, teachers, supervisors or therapists to at least part of the LG participants. Leaders and participants thus may have some common history, as well as a common future. This fact creates certain challenges and ethical dilemmas. For example, we cannot apply or request confidentiality in LGs. It is also clear that it is not feasible, nor even recommended for participants to avoid talking about the LG events outside the group. This is in contrast to what is recommended in some therapy groups regarding social interaction between group members outside the group session. Weinberg and Schneider (2007) summarized some ethical considerations for the LG and recommended that the leaders avoid discussing the events in the group with participants outside the time and setting allocated for the meeting.

The LG leaders are in no way a neutral force in the group. They should be very aware of their biases and countertransference, as in any LG situation they have a choice between the various processes they could emphasize. For example, in the previously mentioned conference near Jerusalem, they opted for reflecting on the power struggle concerning the use of language. At the same time they could have introduced the idea of pluralism, the notion that there needs to be place for all. Alternatively, they could have put the focus on the many sexually tainted remarks raised in the group. In that case they could have emphasized the implicit power aspects of these remarks or refer to them in the realm of socializing, as attempts to become closer to each other. They thus could use their power to try to direct the group in certain directions. However, the forces within the group are huge, and the power of the leaders is limited – much more than in the small or median group. Furthermore, the limited timeframe and the abundance of information create a state in which many processes remain untouched. In some cases, this may aggravate participants. Individual participants or subgroups may then raise their voices and try to take control. The LG is a crowd and leaders are sometimes overruled by it; this is part of the process. As in society, leaders come and go.

How to Benefit from the Large Group Experience

Before concluding this chapter, we would like to briefly look at the requested therapeutic effects and risks related to participation in the LG. We then will provide some recommendations to make the most out of the LG experience.

The LG experience is a strong emotional experience. If all goes well, the individual may come out of the LG with a better understanding of social processes, clearer awareness of self versus the group, a strengthened feeling of identity, and a feeling of personal competence. However, because of the higher pressures of the LG compared to the small group and its powerful regressive pulls, to benefit from participation in the psychodynamic LG, one needs a relatively stable or balanced self, the capacity for self-containment, and the ability to stand high levels of uncertainty and frustration. As Weinberg and Schneider (2003) state:

> Those who are strongly identified with their own self, are able to accept the roller coaster effect that the large group has on their individual identity. However, there are those who feel lost when exposed to a large group experience (Weinberg and Schneider, 2003: p. 20).

Participating in a psychodynamic LG involves some risks. For many individuals the LG creates strong feelings of being overwhelmed or "at loss." The tough conflicts that often occur in LGs and which at times may appear insoluble could result in loss of hope. Also, those with fragile identity may experience some kind of identity diffusion. Another risk is the narcissistic blow of making an effort to say something and getting either no response, as if one's voice met a void, or an unexpected negative response, like in several of the previously mentioned examples. This can be quite a hurtful experience.

Therefore, the novice in the LG might want to consider some recommendations to enhance the experience of the group as a therapeutic tool.

1. **Expectations:** Prepare for a unique and intense experience. Remember that the LG environment is usually unsupportive and may be difficult to endure. People

may get hurt when expecting empathy or impacting others. The experience may be overwhelming to such an extent that you may find it hard to think clearly. In any case, do not come to the LG with expectations from the small group. Remember that the possibility of being mirrored, acknowledged and validated by either the leader(s) or other participants is highly limited in the LG.

2. **Focusing:** Pay attention to your emotions, thoughts, and sensations before, during and after the group. Check these *vis-a-vis* other group members, subgroups and facilitators, and see how they change over time. Try to recognize societal conflicts and power struggles both within the group and as representations of conflicts and struggles in society at large.

3. **Experimenting:** Try out different (physical) positions in the group. Check out how your position affects your experience. Consider expressing your ideas even if this is difficult for you, and be open to unexpected or no reactions from the group. If you do say something, try to interact with others. If you feel up to it, consider the possibility of trying to influence and take a leading role in the LG discourse.

Conclusion

The LG experience is a strong emotional experience. It involves regressive forces, archaic processes and primitive defense mechanisms of splitting, massive projection and projective-identification. If all goes well, the individual may gain a greater understanding of social processes and conflicts, develop a sense of agency and social responsibility, strengthen an individual and group identity, and feel empowered and influential. However, participating in a LG involves some risks. For many participants, the LG creates strong feelings of being overwhelmed or "at a loss." Those with less cohesive crystallized identity may experience some kind of identity diffusion.

In conclusion, therapeutic factors of LGs tend to be ignored, which is unfortunate, since it is quite possible to enhance personal growth through LGs. Having discussed the various therapeutic factors in the small group, it seems that at least several of these are active in the LG as well. Two more therapeutic factors were identified as available in the LG on both the personal and the interpersonal level. The representation of society encourages the development of one's group identity through issues of diversity and pluralism. The struggle for power enhances the individual's empowerment from agency to authority.

Although we tried to describe the specific dynamics and processes that develop in the LG, we did not mean to instruct the reader how to conduct a LG. Understanding the LG dynamics can enhance the benefits of the LG for the participant, reducing some of its potential hazards. It can also be helpful to those interested in learning how to lead a LG, but this is not enough. Unfortunately, there are not many programs in which one can learn how to lead a LG, but certainly if someone is interested in becoming a LG leader, he or she should first accumulate many hours of participation in LGs.

Research studies about the LG are scarce or almost absent. We would like to encourage colleagues to methodologically check the therapeutic factors existing in the LG.

References and Bibliography

Agazarian, Y. M., & Carter, F. B. (1993). Discussions on the large group. *Group, 17*, 210–234.

Aron, L. (1996). *A meeting of minds*. Hillsdale, New Jersey: Analytic Press.

Berg, M., Coman, E., & Schensul, J. (2009). Youth action research for prevention: A multi-level intervention designed to increase efficacy and empowerment among urban youth. *American Journal of Community Psychology, 43*, 345–359.

Blinderman, C. D., & Cherny, N. I. (2005). Existential issues do not necessarily result in existential suffering: Lessons from cancer patients in Israel. *Palliative Medicine, 19*, 371–380.

Booty, J. E. (1990). *John Donne: Selections from divine poems, sermons, devotions, and prayers*. Mahwah, New Jersey: Paulist Press.

Castelein, S., van der Gaag, M., Bruggeman, R., et al. (2008). Measuring empowerment among people with psychotic disorders: A comparison of three instruments. *Psychiatric Services, 59*, 1338–1342.

De Maré, P. B. (1972). Large group psychotherapy: A suggested technique. *Group Analysis, 5*, 106–108.

De Maré, P. B. (1975). The politics of large groups. In L. Kreeger (Ed.), *The large group: Dynamics and therapy* (pp. 145–158). London: Constable.

Foulkes, S. H. (1975). *Group analytic psychotherapy, method and principles*. London: Gordon & Breach.

Havens, L. L., & Ghaemi, S. N. (2005). Existential despair and bipolar disorder: The therapeutic alliance as a mood stabilizer. *American Journal of Psychotherapy, 59*, 137–147.

Hofstede, G. (2001). *Culture's consequences: Comparing values, behaviors, institutions, and organizations across nations*. Thousand Oaks, California: Sage Publications, Inc.

Hopper, E. (2003a). *The social unconscious: Selected papers*. London: Jessica Kingsley Publishers.

Hopper, E. (2003b). Aspects of aggression in large groups characterised by (ba) I:A/M. In S. Schneider & H. Weinberg (Eds.), *The large group revisited: The herd, primal horde, crowds and masses* (pp. 58–72). London: Jessica Kingsley Publishers.

James, D. C. (1994). 'Holding' and 'containing' in the group and society. In D. Brown, & L. Zinkin (Eds.), *The psyche and the social world: Developments in group analytic theory* (pp. 60–79). London: Routledge.

Jarrar, L. K. (2003). A consultant's journey into the large group unconscious: Principles and techniques. In S. Schneider, & H. Weinberg (Eds.), *The large group revisited: The herd, primal horde, crowds and masses* (pp. 29–43). London: Jessica Kingsley Publishers.

Jordan, J. V. (2001). A relational-cultural model: Healing through mutual empathy. *Bulletin of the Menninger Clinic, 65*, 92–103.

Khamphakdy-Brown, S., Jones, L. N., Nilsson, J. E., et al. (2006). The empowerment program: An application of an outreach program for refugee and immigrant women. *Journal of Mental Health Counseling, 28*, 38–47.

Kreeger, L. (1975). *The large group: Dynamics and therapy*. London: Constable.

Mack, J. E. (1994). Psychotherapy and society: Power, powerlessness, and empowerment in psychotherapy. *Psychiatry, 57*, 178–198.

Main, T. F. (1946). The hospital as a therapeutic institution. *Bulletin of the Menninger Clinic, 10*, 66–70.

Pines, M. (1981). The frame of reference of group psychotherapy. *International Journal of Group Psychotherapy, 31*, 275–285.

Rausch, S. M., Gramling, S. E., & Auerbach, S. M. (2006). Effects of a single session of large-group meditation and progressive muscle relaxation training on stress reduction, reactivity, and recovery. *International Journal of Stress Management, 13,* 273–290.

Rogoff, B. (2003). *The cultural nature of human development.* New York: Oxford University Press.

Romanelli, L., Hoagwood, K., Kaplan, S., et al. (2009). Best practices for mental health in child welfare: Parent support and youth empowerment guidelines. *Child Welfare, 88,* 189–212.

Rutan, J. S., Stone, W. N., & Shay, J. J. (2007). *Psychodynamic group psychotherapy (4th ed.).* New York: Guilford Pub.

Saragovi, C., Aube, J., Koestner, R., et al. (2002). Traits, motives, and depressive styles as reflections of agency and communion. *Personality and Social Psychology Bulletin, 28,* 563–577.

Shaked, J. (2003). The large group and political process. In S. Schneider, & H. Weinberg (Eds.), *The large group revisited: The herd, primal horde, crowds and masses* (pp. 150–161). London: Jessica Kingsley Publishers.

Shields, W. (2001). The subjective experience of the self in the large group: Two models for study. *International Journal of Group Psychotherapy, 51,* 205–223.

Springmann, R. (1975). Psychotherapy in the large group. In L. Kreeger (Ed.), *The large group: Dynamics and therapy* (pp. 212–226). London: Constable.

Tebb, S. (1995). An aid to empowerment: A caregiver well-being scale. *Health and Social Work, 20,* 87–92.

Terr, L. C. (1992). Mini-marathon groups: psychological "first aid" following disasters. *Bulletin of the Menninger Clinic, 56,* 76–86.

Triandis, H. C., & Suh, E. M. (2002). Cultural influences on personality. *Annual Review of Psychology, 53,* 133–160.

Volkan, V. D. (1988). *The need to have enemies and allies: From clinical practice to international relationships.* Northvale, New Jersey: Jason Aronson.

Waldegrave, C. (2009). Cultural, gender, and socioeconomic contexts in therapeutic and social policy work. *Family Process, 48,* 85–101.

Weinberg, H. (2007). So What is this social unconscious anyway? *Group Analysis, 40,* 307–322.

Weinberg, H., & Schneider, S. (2003). Introduction: Background, structure and dynamics of the large group. In S. Schneider, & H. Weinberg (Eds.), *The large group revisited: The herd, primal horde, crowds and masses* (pp. 13–26). London: Jessica Kingsley Publishers.

Weinberg, H., & Schneider, S. (2007). So what is this social unconscious anyway?. *Group, 31,* 215–228.

Welzel, C., & Inglehart, R. (2010). Agency, values, and well-being: A human development model. *Social Indicators Research, 97,* 43–64.

Wilke, G. (2003). Chaos and order in the large group. In S. Schneider, & H. Weinberg (Eds.), *The large group revisited: The herd, primal horde, crowds and masses* (pp. 86–97). London: Jessica Kingsley Publishers.

Yalom, I. D. (1980). *Existential psychotherapy.* New York: Basic Books.

Yalom, I. D., & Lescz, M. (2005). *The theory and practice of group psychotherapy* (5th ed.). New York: Basic Books.

24
Dreams and Dreamtelling: A Group Approach
Robi Friedman

Introduction

Dreams are dreamt in the process of digesting excessively stimulating emotions. Moving beyond the traditional consideration of dreams as a religious or prophetic experience, Freud conceptualized Dreaming as a mental processing mechanism (Freud, 1900). Since then, Dreaming has occupied a special place in psychoanalysis. It is considered an on-going autonomic digestion of stimuli, even though, ironically, the dreamer creates a dream without being in control of what he/she is doing. The dream is an outcome of the processing of excessively threatening and exciting emotions and is considered to reflect the mind of the dreamer. Dreams were considered by Freud the "royal road to the unconscious." There are many aspects of a dream that render it so: its authenticity, depth and ability to lead us to deeper understandings of latent and manifest emotional difficulties. The plethora of the symbolic meanings found in dreams is impressive, stimulating our curiosity and calling on our ability to decipher their secrets. Working with our dreams and those of others is a highly satisfying way of answering our hidden wishes to be a Sherlock Holmes or even a Freud.

It is astonishing that from the multitude of our dreams we usually remember only a few. And of these, we rarely tell other people.

Some have offered physiological explanations for this selectivity in remembering and telling dreams. Others have devalued the significance of dreaming altogether. Psychoanalysis, starting from Freud, attributes the ability to recollect dreams to the availability of the dream's content to consciousness. I have extended this understanding by conceptualizing that this ability is also a function of the dreamer's relationships with others. While dreaming is a common nocturnal phenomenon, remembering a dream and especially Dreamtelling needs a container, usually another person with whom the dreamer is in a relationship, who is able to "hold" the content of the dreamer's dream. Such a person meets the dreamer's need for external containment of difficult feelings when his/her internal container is insufficient. Groups can be such a container, offering potential space to facilitate remembering dreams. Telling them in groups can promote a process of external, complementary elaboration.

Differentiating between Dreaming and Dreamtelling

In contrast to Dreaming, which is an autonomous, intrapersonal function – part of our "unconscious thinking" (Palombo, 1992) – Dreamtelling always involves an interpersonal exchange. Groups, being multi-personal situations, are a particularly interesting setting for the intersubjective interaction of Dreamtelling. The notion of inter-subjectivity assumes the existence of mutual mental and emotional influences in relationships. Emotional movements communicated through telling dreams cross psychological boundaries between people-in-connection. The individual is no longer considered a "closed entity" (Stolorow, Atwood and Orange, 2002). Rather, he/she is influenced in relationships and social activity by inter-subjective mechanisms. These mechanisms are conceptualized somewhat differently by respective psychological approaches. Here, I use the overall inter-subjective model to highlight the fact that affects embedded in the relationships between people, particularly in groups, will undergo reciprocal, though sometimes asymmetrical, influences. These influences will go beyond the group and affect participants' entire relational world.

> A two-day workshop at the start of a two-semester university course began with participants expressing their feelings of being stuck. In the previous year many had felt abused by their charismatic teacher, a powerful personality known for his condescending attitude towards students. He was felt by many in this class to be cruelly critical. At the workshop's outset, they seemed depleted of energy and without emotional movement. Nearly half the class was not able to participate. Others were bitterly passive/aggressive. In the first session some identified with a group member who described himself as "castrated."

Following, is a brief account of the group's significant communications concerning an outspoken and particularly injured member:

In the middle of the second session a member told me she thought I was too protective. I was allowing the group to avoid "the real issue," which in her opinion was the phenomenon of aggressive 'sub-grouping' (Agazarian, 1994). She said that the group seemed to be split into small entities that were not openly communicating with each other. Some hours later, another member repeated a story similar to that of the first one, namely, that she had left the class under the prior leadership because she felt highly criticized and attacked by him. In the last session, she shared with the group a dream she had had the night before: I will now use this dream and the reactions to it to demonstrate how I work with Dreamtelling.

> She and a male friend found a baby who was wrapped in clothes in such a way as to appear to be tied up. They freed it, cleaned it up and began to take care of it. Suddenly they realized the baby's hands were still tied behind its back. At this point in the telling, members of the group started to cry along with her.

I was extremely moved by the group's and my own emotional response to the dreamteller. Even though the dream's content was not clearly understood, many participants seemed to share the dreamteller's sorrow. Why? Was there something moving about the image of "finding a baby?" Was the fact that the baby appeared tied up in his clothes so touching? Could it be that more than being moved by the content of the dream, participants were touched by the courage and openness of members sharing their personal experiences, some of which were as vague and unconscious as the dream? I found myself thinking that the possibility of creating, remembering and telling a dream in this group may mean that their "castration" by the prior leader had been overcome: a new baby can be born... Yet, at the same time, the crippled baby with its hands tied behind his back may have suggested that the group still feels held back.

It was very interesting to note that despite the strong emotions provoked by the dream, the group at first resisted "working" with it, that is, associating to it personally or trying to find a meaning to the dream. I thought of several possible explanations for this reluctance:

1. The immediate emotional reaction had been extremely strong. Perhaps people simply needed time to mull over the dream.
2. Most participants may have preferred to stay in the experience rather than beginning to think or associate.

As with many acute and overloaded emotional events, some people will often prefer to silently contain an emotional influx rather than share their feelings about it. Another possible explanation for the group's silence was that members may have been angry because of an earlier attempt by the dreamteller to establish a "pairing" bond with me (Bion, 1962). In spite of her position of positive leadership, in which she seemed to be carrying many of the group emotions, trying to get close to me may have been perceived by members as crossing certain boundaries.

These kinds of relational considerations make it possible to connect the contents of the dream with the group's reactions to them. Seeing that someone had remembered her dream and was willing to relate to it was a welcome surprise for her. What did she consciously and unconsciously expect by telling her dream? Why was she telling it at this point? These are the kinds of questions that help me differentiate between Dreaming and Dreamtelling.

The concept of "containment" was first put forward by Bion (1962). By containment he meant an activity that transforms someone's unmanageable and excessive feelings in such a way that they are easier to manage. This patient's Dreaming seemed to be the first step in the containment of stimuli from her inner life. Her attempts to cope with issues of being-in-a-relationship with a man are reflected in her dream, together with the many implications of the appearance of a baby, such as, being like a baby, having a baby and taking care of a baby. In the next session, she continued to talk of personal issues, more specifically, her struggle with dependency, inferiority and authority. We can see in this example how Dreaming, the more visible part of our mental digestive apparatus, which Meltzer (1983) called "dream life," seems to process overwhelming emotions 24 hours a day.

Aside from reflecting the dreamer's struggles in his personal life, telling the dream to participants may reflect the way he is tolerating, organizing and coping with difficulties in the group. Specifically, Dreamtelling serves two important intersubjective functions;

1. The request for containment and/or
2. The wish to influence.

These functions will be elaborated upon later in the chapter. However, at this point, I want to suggest a main developmental paradigm in working with dreams, which may help further clarify the social aspects of Dreamtelling. In this schema, Dreaming can be seen as the first step in containing emotional difficulties. Dreamtelling is the next step, one that helps us further this process. In the example above, we can see that by telling her dream to the group, the dreamer is unconsciously sending an SOS: "I don't know if the men and babies I'll encounter here in the group are OK. Help me with the pairing efforts I wish to make."

Telling a dream, and the processes connected with it, are significant social events. In my opinion, it is incorrect to think that Dreaming is an exclusively individual activity. Dreaming may have strong interpersonal functions, a point that seems to have been quite neglected in Psychoanalytic literature.

I have already stated that a dream reflects the dreamer's individual effort to cope with certain emotional difficulties. But, more specifically the dreamer may be making efforts to bear, organize and better cope with his difficulties in his group. Finally, he may be making these efforts for the whole group as well. Our minds are more permeable than we think, which renders Dreaming, in spite of the fact that it takes place "inside" the dreamer's mind, not just an individual activity. Dreaming may function as a working-through process in the service of the dreamer's relationships and the relationships of those connected to the dreamer. In families, a mother may dream up her daughter's problem; a mature sibling may have a dream in which he/she is anxious on behalf of a younger one. In groups and society it is possible that one person will be unconsciously "delegated" to dream a dream for another (or a sub-group or the group-as-a-whole), who may himself have difficulties in containment. "All for one and one for All" was never more true than in Dreaming, a shared, unconscious activity that is of primary significance for the group therapist. Listening to a dream while at the same time keeping an eye on group processes may reveal meanings beyond the individual significance reflected in the dream's content.

> It becomes obvious in our example that the group therapist had to consider the possibility that the participant's dream may have been more than an effort to overcome her own personal difficulties. To not have done so would have been reductionist thinking that would have divorced the personal meaning from the interpersonal one. Instead, the therapist had to consider the possibility that the dreamer may have dreamt this dream to elaborate something for the group. In short, her Dreaming was an attempt to overcome not only her own "castration," that is: restriction and limitation, but the group's as well.

The phenomenon of Dreamtelling will be presented as an activity that complements the processes I have described above. Dreamtelling has an interpersonal function. It aims at transforming the dreamer's relationship with the audience. In all the examples I bring in this chapter, the significant communicative functions of Dreaming and Dreamtelling are evident. Ironically, outsiders are often more aware of these powerful functions than dreamers themselves.

Dreaming, Dreamtelling and Acting Out

Clinicians often ask themselves, will the just-narrated dream be followed by an "acting out?" Does a just-told dream in some way foretell the future, or is it only the reflection of a concrete past? "Acting out" implies a failure to contain. It occurs when an emotion is so overwhelming that reflection and elaboration become impossible. The person is "pushed" from "inside" to engage in acting/doing. Dreams actually help avert acting out, as they may facilitate elaboration of difficult emotions. Dreamtelling invites further containment. This is why group therapists should try and make the group a place for further elaboration of dreams. It reduces the probability of "acting out." The many examples of Dreamtelling in history and literature show that nothing remains the same once a dream is told. A dramatic example of this is the Biblical narrative of Joseph, in which we see the powerful impact on his brothers when he tells them his dreams. We also see later in the narrative how his work with dreams enhances his fame throughout Egypt.

> Applying these thoughts to the above-mentioned example, we can ask: about which aspects of "acting out" in the group is the dream warning? Possibly the dream is referring (and advising me, the new group conductor) to the fact that the experience of "castration" was still being felt very strongly by the dreamer (and by the group). The dream may have been communicating how group members were feeling about authority in general, and my authority in particular. It may have been "predicting" that not just the dream teller but other members

> as well might explode, rebel or resign, despite the fact that the prior problematic leader had left and a new one had taken his place. The dream suggests the existence of a large wound in the group and may be sending a warning that it is in a post-traumatic condition. The dream may have been a reflection of suspicion in general and particularly towards the group's new conductor, the setting and the organization.

Dreams often carry great energy; through projections, identifications and other intersubjective mechanisms. Dreamtelling evokes strong feelings within listeners and can result in significant emotional movement. Dreams and Dreamtelling may create space for playful change and learning (Winnicott, 1969), which can be a preparation to action or an alternative to acting out. I think of the individual and the group experiment, and learn on three *playgrounds*: dreaming, dreamtelling and sharing the dreams of others. Some patients fear the strong uncontained emotions in their dreams. It is important for the conductor to reassure them. In this way, they are helped to dream. By telling them in the group dialogue is enhanced, thereby reducing the probability of dangerous acting-out.

> Judging from the group's post-dreamtelling development, it appears that the dream's successful containment of anxieties and aggressions enabled it to then be told as a "good-enough dream".

At first glance it may seem a paradox that dreams can function as containers of excessive emotions and yet be acted upon in an interpersonal space (Steiner, 1995). The explanation for this is as complex as life itself. Dreaming as a mechanism of elaboration functions in a manner similar to that of the process of elaboration in therapy. Dreaming processes affects in emotionally saturated or overloaded relationships. Dreamtelling "pushes" the listener towards emotional reactions, either by "requesting containment" and/or by transforming relationships with the dreamer or both. Dreams, Dreaming and Dreamtelling are links in a chain of "metabolism" that is ignited both in the individual and the social minds and may lead to mature responses that need not be viewed as "acting out."

Three Uses of Dreams

An informative approach to dreamtelling

The dream's structure, which is a creation and reflection of the dreamer's mind, contains information about the dreamer's psyche (Friedman, 2002). Freud, who rediscovered the value of the dream as a diagnostic tool that can help reveal the dreamer's inner truth, believed that dream censorship and many other devices for hiding truths could be circumvented by searching for the dream's *latent*, hidden meaning. This classic approach focuses on the inner world of the individual. I am suggesting here that when the *social context* in which a dream is told is taken into consideration, it is possible to see interpersonal meanings as well. In other words, Dreams can be used to accumulate information, understanding and knowledge about the groups and society in which the dreamer is functioning.

It is impossible here to elaborate the whole psychoanalytic approach to dreams. I will restrict myself to the insights I have gained from my basic clinical toolbox, namely, Ego Psychology, Kleinian contributions and Projective Identification-in-the-Dream. I will also draw upon important Jungian and self-psychological contributions. All these approaches are basically part of the informative approach to Dreamtelling in group therapy.

> The dreamer in the example above has told a dream that seems to reflect a wish to repair the disconnection between herself and the group. Something hidden in the content caused the listening group members to weep and perhaps identify with her. In the manifest aspect of the dream we can see significant symbolic situations, for example, being handcuffed, having an encounter with a man, having parental responsibilities and being like a baby. Perhaps all these were dreamt in an effort to cope with emotional issues touching the audience of participants. This is suggested by the fact that each of these symbolic situations was related to and discussed in depth by the group.

Freud mistrusted the dream's manifest narrative. He believed that in order to understand a dream, its "latent" and unconscious elements had to be discovered. This was to be done by interpreting defense mechanisms, such as symbolization, displacement, reaction formation and condensation, which hide the dream's unconscious content (Freud, 1900, 1933). In his view, dreams are created to circumvent censorship and camouflage. They must be overcome in order to get to know the dreamer's inhibitions, motivations and "transference" reactions.

Adding to the contributions made by the various analytic schools, I espouse the view that dream structure reflects the dreamer's ego and his typical psychic and behavioral patterns (Friedman 2002). The nature and movement of human figures may reflect aspects of the dreamer's energy and/or relationships. The organization of its narrative and the quality of its script are also significant. All these can help us assess the dreamer's personality and his/her interpersonal patterns (Friedman, 2002).

> In our example, it is possible to see a hidden, romantic significance to the image of the dreamer's friend, to note anxiety evoked by the baby and the fact that it is tied up and to recognize the dreamer's terror on realizing that the first attempt to free the baby was not enough. In the subsequent group dialogue, it became particularly apparent to relate to the fact that the baby, that is, the group, was not yet freed. The narrative is frightening but nonetheless

> well-organized, with a clear beginning, middle and end. The subsequent discussion revealed feelings of closeness and even dependency on one another amongst participants. The overwhelming feeling of weakness depicted in the dream may have been a reflection of the group's feeling of recurring impotence and a general lack of emotional motion among members.

Freud was particularly interested in how the Oedipal Complex manifested itself in dreams. For him, and subsequent psychoanalytic thinkers, health and pathology are intrinsically connected with the way in which this complex is "solved." We can see references in dreams to the way in which the dreamer has found solutions. These references can be inferred from such things as the dreamer's position in his family, the mental evolution of his/her feelings and his place in mother/father/child triangles and in subsequent similar triangles.

> In the dream we are puzzled by the appearance of a man and a baby. In our initial discussions, members didn't understand much beyond the obvious symbolic and manifest meanings of different parts of the dream. Perhaps, some suggested, the triangle made by the man, woman and baby might refer to an oedipal relationship, in the spirit of Freudian thinking. It took several more sessions for members to realize that the dream may also have been referring to the dreamer's attempt to pair with the leader. The group had negative feelings about this, which may have been reflected in the dream and certainly was in the subsequent group process. In the dream, there had been an expressed wish for a loving relationship. One can wonder whether the abused baby was a punishment for the dreamer's prohibited pairing. This line of reasoning is very characteristic of (early) psychoanalytical thinking.

Among the many significant post-Freudian developments, object-relations psychology has contributed important, complementary understandings of dreaming mechanisms. This psychoanalytic approach holds that our mind reacts to intense emotional situations – those characterized by anxiety and/or by aggression – by splitting perception of these situations into "good" and "bad." In our dreams "good" is felt as "me" and is acceptable. Disowned feelings and/or relationships are unconsciously felt as "not-me". Also in dreams there is an attempt to cope with difficult situations by splitting and "disowning" the unbearable feelings, such as fears, aggressions or impotence. Specifically, unwanted feelings are put into particular subjects or objects. These are perceived in the dream as being bad and "not me." Projecting (externalizing difficult emotions) on to others may spare us painful recognition that these threatening emotions may actually be part of the "me." Dreamers haunted in their dreams by aggressors, threatened by other people's envy and persecuted by sexual invitations can only develop and grow when they "re-own" the split off parts of their Self.

> The dreamer's "not-me" in our example is the tied and re-tied baby. This abused newborn, who is not able to remove his own clothes, may also represent the group's disconnected impotence, which is displaced onto the "not me" figure, for example, the baby. Through this image the dreamer may be unconsciously touching her own dependent feelings and also the group's feelings of impotence and "castration." In short, the dream communicates the overlapping difficulties of the individual and the group and their efforts to overcome them.

The Informative approach to dream looks for connections between the personal and interpersonal aspects of dream contents, particularly in the context of relationships in the group. Dreamtelling is used to gather information about individuals and groups, their manifest and hidden patterns and, emotional movements. The roles of protagonists are examined.

In addition to representing the "not-me," the protagonists may reflect the dreamer's effort to develop particular emotional abilities. Figures are recalled and "recruited" from the dreamer's past to help the dreamer deal with qualities he/she is struggling to deal with today. In Dreaming, the figures are manipulated so as to experience and "play" from a distance with overwhelming feelings. The integration of such figures into the dream-script – their "use" by the dreamer, – is the process I call Projective Identification-in-the-Dream (Friedman, 2002). Projective Identification means that someone close is "forced" to identify with a needed projection and serves as a soothing and teaching container. Thus, the dreamer's externalizations are met in the dream protagonist's identifications. This process is maybe the most profound explanation for deep interpersonal communication and relations. It also contributes to "movement" in relationships.

> In the group process, it became important to find out what the Dreamer attributed to her "male friend," as well as what she felt the baby's qualities were. It was clarified that the friend was someone who, in the dreamer's eyes, represented security. He also had an ability to emotionally touch others. The latter quality was particularly difficult for the Dreamer.

In general, the group therapeutic approaches to dreams are remarkably individual-oriented, with the exception of the few contributions that refer to "group dreams" (Pines, 2002). The implication of these contributions is that, rather than ascribing an excessive importance to the dream's content, the whole group should be helped to "own" such a dream. In effect the whole group will have "redreamt the dream together." The experience of sharing and jointly elaborating dreams is unique to group therapy. It carries powerful, curative benefits. It is a way to gather information about the group's dynamics and the relationships between members and is an important element of any group therapeutic technique. (It is important to note that not every dream containing a manifest group image is necessarily a group dream. Whether a group can "own" the dream of a participant may well depend on the dreamer's relationship with the group.

> The dream's context may imply that the baby is the group's newborn, which, like the members, must struggle with great difficulties in growing. The horror and identification resonating in the group suggests that the dream may have been born out of social pain. Perhaps the dream reflects hope of repairing relationships in the group. The baby's dependency may also represent the group's need for a good caretaker. The newborn's twice-binding – to which I personally associated Isaac's binding by Abraham – may point to members' ambivalence about my authority. They are both hopeful and suspicious. The dream also suggests that although the conflict between the group and the dreamer is not yet over, participants strongly identify with her. This bodes well for repairing the relationships among them. While the group may still be post-traumatic, it seems to be organizing itself and seeking external help.

One unique aspect of working with dreams in groups is the appearance of multiple resonances and mirroring. If there is a culture of free, individual reactions to Dreamtelling, a significant accumulation of information, experiences and connections will take place. The echoing of a moving dream-segment and associating with one's own personal experience may enable participants to have "moments-of-meeting" (Stern et al., 1998) with each other. This will promote new awareness.

> In the subsequent session I suggested that group members echo that part of the dream that moved them "as if it were their own." This produced highly touching revelations, such as a woman who told about her abortion, a man who revealed he had been in prison and another woman who told of her great yearning to be intimate with her husband who had left her. These responses in turn elicited powerful reactions in the dreamer, who said she had been touched in "more ways than she can talk about now."

Deep interpersonal encounters sometimes seem magical in the way they can reflect deep meanings of the unconscious in the latent dream content. It is experienced as though participants who share their associations to a dream have somehow "X-rayed" the dreamer and had a "transpersonal" experience with him/her (Foulkes, 1973). Such events are powerful and authentic encounters among the unconscious worlds of the participants. They give new meanings to the dream and help reveal important and unexpected information about the dreamer. Dreamtelling is "the Royal Road through the Other" (Friedman, 2002), informing the dreamer, the listeners and the conductor and eliciting as it does personal resonance. The word "informative" suggests change, as does the word "transformation," which contains the words *trans* and *form*. The higher levels of consciousness implied in transformation enhances the possibilities of choice. Deeper awareness of one's own feelings expands one's ability to think and to control behavior. In the sessions I have been describing, we can see that the mutuality and circularity of dialogue, as opposed to monologue (Schlapobersky, 1993), is not always a linear phenomenon. It is important to keep this in mind while working with Dreamtelling in a group.

A Formative Approach to Dreamtelling

My first response to a dream is to let my own "feeling" tell me something about the emotional movement the dream sets off in listeners. Next, I try to estimate the characteristics of the dream's structure in order to make certain strategic decisions. Specifically, I evaluate the coherence of the dream narrative, asking myself whether it has a clear beginning, middle and end. I also look for human figures in the dream (or in children's dreams, animals) and note whether they are moving about. If these elements are present, I conclude that the dreamer's mind is capable of healthy emotional movement and is strong enough to not be harmed by interpretations, even those that may cause mental pain. While I would never disregard any dream, it is important to differentiate more structured, organized dreams from fragmented and chaotic ones. The former can be worked with interpretatively; work with the latter must be more supportive. Chaotic, terrifying dream contents are a sign that while important information is being provided, the dreamer should be handled with the support and care implied in the formative approach. This carefulness is necessary so as to deflect the possibility of increasing anxiety and fragmentation.

> A disturbed patient of Bion's (1993) could only dream "in the presence of his psychoanalyst." This meant that he could only "dream with precautions" (Bion, 1993: p. 40). The dependent quality of this dreamer is an indication for the kind of non-interpretative, supportive approach which I have been calling "formative."

Too often therapists offer deep interpretations to dreamers or to groups that are fragile and lacking coherency. Intense interpretations do not help the dreamer and others in the group expand awareness of the relationships among each other. Rather, they lead to a premature unveiling of threatening and over-stimulating, hidden content and may contribute to the formation of strong, hierarchical relationships and/or threaten a shaky Self.

The formative approach holds that a fragmented, chaotic and unstructured dream may reflect an immature state of mind and contain a request for a more holding "dream skin"(Anzieu, 1989). Non-interpretative, supportive responses to dreams, which remain at the level of manifest content, can and should be learned and practiced. A partner who retells, draws or rewrites a dream, for example, a supportive partner, is preferable to being one who makes "plunging interpretations" (Foulkes, 1964). A therapist should try and maintain a position in the group that allows him/her to choose an appropriate intervention, for example, one that falls between the poles of uncovering and support. Self-psychology, which is concerned with a cohesive Self-State in Dreams (Livingston, 2002), and Jungian psychology advocate approaches to dream interpretation that are relatively descriptive and experience-near and reflect a formative approach to working with Dreams.

Dreamtelling is inherent in the formative approach. The goal is not just the building of containment for a particular individual. The "mind" of the group (de Mare, 1998) must be developed. Telling the dream "in the presence" of others is a first communication and a testing out of just how secure a space will be available in the group.

> In a first session of a closed, long-term group a frightened participant reported he had dreamt that a donkey was dragged uphill and ripped to pieces. For some reason, the group, including the conductors, could not respond and remained silent. Several sessions later the dream was referred to, briefly, as a symbol of "beginner's panic." Only months later was the dream mentioned again. This time one of the co-conductors reminded the group of its paralyzed reaction upon initially having heard the dream. The participant who had dreamed the dream then shared with the group that in fact he had been deeply strengthened by the group's response of silence, since he had been fearing a direct rejection.

External, supportive containment of unbearable and dreadful emotions has been examined by therapists from various approaches (Fonagy, 2000). Fragmented dreams told in a group are viewed as a warning both about the fragile state of the dreamer's mind and the group's capacity to contain. In the example given immediately above, the therapists' lack of familiarity with the group and/or the intensity of the dream affects made it unwise to delve too deeply into the dream's painful content. The most that could be done when the dream was initially told was to verbally acknowledge the dreamer's needs and courage, his willingness to share his dream with others and the group's ability to tolerate the difficult affects it aroused.

A dream told in a group often seems to be searching for an elaborating Partnership. Sharing a dream with other participants often contributes to the formation of the group's mentality (Puget, 2002; Stone and Karterud, 2006). The "same group and the same leader must create their own style anew with each dream presented" (Stone and Karterud, 2006: p. 183). The Self-psychology approach to dreams "is particularly aware of affective shifts and vulnerability and looks for the group's emotional responses and reactions rather than for interpretations." (Stone and Karterud, 2006: p.184).

Finally, it is important to realize that a group's formative abilities grow as the group itself develops. A mature group is much better able than a beginning one to contain deficient mental structures and frightening and threatening dreams. Dreamtelling is a uniquely potential fertilizer for the associative matrix of the group, acting as a bridge between the individual dreamer and members of the group. In the example, above, the group matrix became more open and showed greater commitment to group processes after the dreamer told her dream.

> In the "handcuffed baby" dream there are indications for the possibility of good containment. The dream has clear structure, an understandable narrative with beginning, middle and end and human motion. Furthermore, it produces an affective echo in the dreamteller's audience. In the dream, there is a soothing relationship between a man and a woman. While the ending is frightening, it is not terrifying. All these suggest that the dreamer's Mind is cohesive and coherent. She appears strong-minded enough to work interpretatively once a holding space had been re-secured (the group's structure had been damaged by the difficult relationship with the prior leader and had to be repaired). Therefore, the leader began with formative work, dealing with the dream in an empathic and accepting way.

To conclude, the decision as to whether to do formative rather than interpretative work is based both on the content of the dream and the group's ability to contain the dream's unconscious emotional material.

Diversion: Formative Aspects of Disclosure and Protection

The most important task of a group conductor is to form a protected space in which disclosure is possible, and the individual can feel him/herself "used" but not "abused" (Winnicott, 1969). Before the group therapist decides on using an "informative" approach, he/she should evaluate both the dreamer's and the group's capability to embark on a therapy which includes disclosure. Some members should not work (at least at the beginning) with threatening, disclosing interpretations. Neither should they be asked to address hidden and frightening aspects of their dreams in the here-and-now interaction that follows dreamtelling.

The same is true regarding the group-as-a-whole. Not all group therapy members are ready to listen to and contain frightening dream material related by one of the members. They must feel protected (Friedman, 2002; Ullman, 1996). It is important for the entire group to go through a process of maturation and preparation for containment. The group therapist provides protection to the whole group by forming a group "space" strong enough to contain increasingly difficult emotions. At this point "plunging interpretations" (Foulkes, 1975) should be avoided.

Transforming Relationships through Dreamtelling

Dreamtelling is an interpersonal event. Whether told in public by a politician or related in a more intimate sphere, dreams told to others are consciously and unconsciously meant for the audience's ears and minds. There is an inter-subjective encounter between a dreamer, his dream and the listeners. These kinds of encounters are extremely significant in groups.

Dreams shared in the group space, that is, the matrix, have several interpersonal purposes. One such purpose in the telling of a dream is to ask the listeners for containment, such as, a mutual elaboration of the dreamer's emotional difficulties. A second purpose is to exert influence on the listeners. Dreamtelling in the group space starts as a search for a partner, one who can further the dreamer's "mental digestion" (Bion, 1993: p. 50). This is certainly so in the case of frightening nightmares or dreams of overwhelming desire. But, there are other strong emotions as well, such as fears of rejection, which can be worked through with the help of trusted partners. It is essential that not only the group therapist but the whole group must communicate some willingness to be in a partnership with the dreamer. Such conditions facilitate Dreamtelling and subsequent containment.

> When the first dream has been told, I usually say to the group: "It's very tempting to interpret this dream, but I suggest that instead, you respond to it as if it were your own dream. Let's leave interpretation for later . . . and first share the points at which the dream touches you in your own life, where it moves you and awakens memories." Usually this is enough to help participants become involved in a personal way. It is important for group therapists themselves to refrain from precocious interpretation, as the conductor's interventions will be immediately copied by group participants.

The group then "dreams the dream" by resonating and mirroring it. It processes the undigested parts by echoing its emotionally unconscious aspects and functioning as a "container-on-call." This is a parental function of immediately available concern and identification.

Another interpersonal, intersubjective function of Dreamtelling is the unconscious wish to move the audience by "making the dream public."

> "You had red lips. I came close. We kissed passionately, and you embraced me." This was a dream dreamt by a very timid man who was undergoing therapy. The dream and its subsequent processing helped him approach the woman he loved. It both unconsciously communicated his difficulty in making contact and his desire to seduce her into falling in love with him (Friedman, 2004).

This point highlights a great difference between seeing dreams as if they were merely "contents" to be examined, like the Rosetta Stone, or viewing this "content" as having a certain energy that can alter a particular interpersonal situation. The dream above, for example, is characterized by highly loaded emotions, hidden projections and communications reflecting the dreamer's identification. It should not come as a surprise to the sensitive group therapist that, together with a request for containment, the dreamteller is also pushing inadvertently for a unique change in his relationships with women.

> In our "dream of the newborn" the dreamer has put forward a number of concurrent communications. She was asking for help with her fears of relationships with men and help with anxieties stemming from the traumatic experiences she had had with the authority figure of the prior year. These anxieties may have been exacerbated by life-time, relational patterns. Finally, she may have been appealing to the group to see her not simply as a woman competing for the attention and affection of the male group therapist but also as the baby who needs to be cared for.

From what I have presented above, it is clear that Dreamtelling can produce alternative and complementary perspectives regarding the dream's content and the dreamteller's motivations and goals.

The transformative perspective of dream work raises two additional questions for the clinician. First: what is it the dreamer or the group cannot process by themselves? And second, how is the dreamer trying to affect his/her relationship with the group? Though it may not be possible to answer these questions at the outset, it is important to keep them in mind. Regarding the first question, we often see that a request for containment repeats itself, becoming a pattern. Regarding the second question, the dreamer's wish to influence the audience and affect the quality of relationships with them may not be immediately apparent. What is important is that telling a dream is the beginning of emotional movement, which is important for the group therapist to monitor.

> It is her ambivalence about pairing that the dreamer in our "newborn dream" had difficulty in containing. Her strong wishes for contact were accompanied by great fears, and she was requesting containment of both her needs and her anxieties. She seemed to be communicating, too, her inability to cope with conflict between herself and the group. Separation anxiety caused her to regress to older patterns of pairing and dependency. She is not able to sufficiently digest anxiety evoked by triangular situations. This is true particularly in situations in which she competes with other women or has wishes to possess a man. She unconsciously uses the dream to get the "soothing" she needs, resorting to a time-tested pattern: evoke in others strong identifications and closeness with her. In the case of the dream, she had presented herself as a victim, that is, the tied-up baby. In addition, this image may also represent unconscious fears of punishment for her earlier, prohibited pairing with me. She may be "using" Dreamtelling to ask the group to legitimize an intimate encounter with a man and help her to bear the anxiety at the thought of potential rejection.
>
> The image of the baby served the additional purpose of revitalizing hope. Her inner "scriptwriter" was pushing for a group atmosphere that would be willing to accept care and also willing to try again to establish a relationship with a new conductor.

Echoes, shared thoughts and other responses – including interpretations – are at the base of group discourse. This is the essence of the notion, "dreaming the dream," in which feelings, relational patterns and fantasies of members are discussed and further elaborated.

Working with Dreams in Group Therapy – Summary of Technique

1. At the telling of the first dream, the conductor suggests that no interpretations be made. Optimally, the participants, including the dreamer and the group therapist, resonate with the dream by bringing associations from their personal experience, (i.e., "as if it were your personal dream").

2. The group therapist uses his/her skills to decide whether this dream can be worked-through by deep, interpretative exploration, or whether a less intrusive, more formative approach is called for. Indications for a particular approach lie in the therapist's assessment of the dream's structure, its narrative and timing, the dreamer's level of development and the group's maturity and ability to cope with emotional difficulties.

3. Working-through starts by accepting rather than rejecting the dream. All processes relating to the dream are considered relevant to the interpersonal context. In the first example, discussion of the dreamteller's complaint that the present conductor was "too protective," the group's culture was too "leader-orientated" and the participants' feelings of rejection all reflect this attitude of acceptance. The contents of the dream, the feeling of group "stuckness," the fact that the dreamer waited many hours before telling the dream and the image of the foundling are all part of the dream matrix, waiting to be worked through. The reactions by three members – telling about an abortion, a jail term and difficulties in "couplehood" – reflect hidden reactions to contents in the dream. On the group level, the strong identification with the handcuffed newborn became a significant aspect of the dream matrix.

4. After sharing their resonance to the dream, both the group therapist and the participants join together in "analyzing" it (Foulkes, 1975). Summing up the group's responses and relating them to individual and group levels are done later. By and large, I do this mainly by myself but I try and relate to the comments of others. Addressing a dream can be done repeatedly over time. In long-term, experienced groups, these references to earlier dreams are preferably made by participants themselves. Regarding the "foundling" dream above, I acknowledged the significance of the participant's dreamtelling and the strong resonance it evoked in the group. In the following session, I asked her whether she recognized her dependency patterns and how they might have been affecting her role in the group. As always, I also tried to lend necessary support to the group and strengthen formative aspects of the group processes.

5. I address the interpersonal side of Dreamtelling by asking the dreamer what she felt about the responses. In the baby dream, the dreamer said she felt very touched. I felt she was pleased that her Request for Containment had been answered,

and I went on to explore a similar request for containment by the group that had been hinted at in their various identifications with the dream. From their responses, I understood that her dream had supplied containment for their own "castration anxieties." These had been moments of connection among the participants, the dreamer and the dream contents. I tried to reinforce these by active acknowledgement. I asked the dreamer how she felt in the group. She responded that she felt wonderfully cared for; and I understood she was pleased at her impact on the group. In fact, interpersonal influence is an important issue in groups. The examination of this issue must wait until the dreamer and other participants experience the group as a Safe Space in which to share their unconscious worlds. An indication that the group has become such a safe place can be seen in the quality of the group's emotional movement (i.e., there are signs of increasing security and freedom). Other indicators are found in members' associations, in the sharing of more dreams and fantasies and in an increasingly open resonance in the group matrix. Emotional difficulties from the past drive Dreamers to Dream. Dreamtelling creates a present. Resonance among members helps co-create future relationships. In the specific case described above, elaboration of emotional damage incurred by participants during sessions with the prior leader made it possible to examine long-standing patterns and old vulnerabilities, Something new could be born. A new period of group development had begun.

6. In therapy, I use a progressive interpretation technique. I start by evaluating the coherency of the dream as well as the group's capacity to contain unconscious and difficult affects. Bearing in mind, the possibility of using a supportive or interpretative intervention, I shift gradually from discussing the dream contents to discussing how the relationships of the listeners have been affected. In doing so, I remind myself that I can usually trust the group and take therapeutic advantage of members' reactions.

Research

Dayan (2010) studied the interpersonal ramifications of Dreamtelling in families, looking at, among other things, the effects of gender. A questionnaire, filled out by 90 women and 90 men, included questions about childhood Dreamtelling and Dreamtelling in current relationships with a spouse and children. Dreams told ranged from "a very pleasant dream" to "a nightmare" and were studied with an eye to the dreamer's ability to tell them in different relational contexts.

The research found links between adult and childhood Dreamtelling. It corroborated preliminary findings that Dreamtelling is a request for interpersonal containment that produces an emotional influence on dream-listeners. The research also found evidence that the experience of Dreamtelling in original families prepares a person for Dreamtelling in marriage and other present-day relationships, contributing to these relationships by enabling better elaboration of emotional difficulties. Connections with mother which were characterized by Dreamtelling are more meaningful than those with father, suggesting that gender differences must be taken into consideration in assessing the effect of Dreamtelling on the dreamer.

References and Bibliography

Agazarian, Y. M. (1994). The phases of group development and the systems-centered group. In V. L. Shermer, & M. Pines, *Ring of Fire*, 36–86. London: Routledge.

Anzieu, D. (1989). The film of the dream. In S. Flanders (Ed.), *The dream discourse today* (pp. 137–150). London & New York: Routledge.

Bion, W. R. (1962). *Learning from experience.* London: Heinemann.

Bion, W. R. (1963). *Elements of psycho-analysis.* London: William Heinemann. [Reprinted London: Karnac Books]. Reprinted in 1977: *Seven servants: Four works by Wilfred R. Bion.* New York: Aronson.

Dayan, D. (2010). Relationship between interfamily childhood dream telling patterns of adulthood dream telling patterns. Unpublished Master Thesis, Haifa University.

De Mare, P., Piper, R., & Thompson, S. (1991). *Koinonia, from hate through dialogue to culture in the large group.* London: Karnac.

Fairbairn, W. R. D. (1963). Synopsis of an object-relations theory of the personality. *International Journal of Psycho-Analysis, 44*, 224–225.

Fonagy, P. (2000). Dreams of borderline patients. In R. J. Perelberg, *Dreaming and thinking. Psychoanalytic Ideas.* London.

Foulkes, S. H. (1964). *Therapeutic Group Analysis.* London: Maresfield Library.

Foulkes, S. H. (1973). The group as matrix of the individual's mental life. In E. Foulkes, (Ed.), *S. H. Foulkes Selected Papers*, (pp. 223–233). London: Karnac.

Foulkes, S. H. (1975). *Group analytic psychotherapy: Method and principles.* London: Karnac.

Foulkes, S. H. (1984). *Therapeutic Group Analysis.* London: Karnac.

Foulkes, E. (Ed.). (1990). *S. H. Foulkes Selected Papers.* London: Karnac.

Freud, S. (1900). *The Interpretation of Dreams.* Standard edition 4/5.

Freud, S. (1933). *New Introductory Lectures on Psycho-Analysis, SE 22:5.* London: Hogarth Press.

Friedman, M., & Vietze, P. (1972). The competent infant. *Peabody Journal of Education, 49*(4), 314–322.

Friedman, R. (2002). Dream-telling as a Request for containment in Group therapy – The Royal Road through the Other. In M. Pines, C. Neri & R. Friedman (Eds.), *Dreams in group psychotherapy* (pp. 46–67). London, New York: Jessica Kingsley Publishers.

Friedman, R. (2004). Dreamtelling as a request for containment – Reconsidering the group-analytic approach to the work with dreams. *Group Analysis, 37*(4), 508–524.

Friedman, R. (2008). Dreamtelling as a request for containment – Three uses of dreams in group therapy. *International Journal of Group Psychotherapy, 58*(3).

Grinberg, L. (1987). Dreams and acting out, Psychoanalytic Quarterly, LVI. *Group Analysis, 30*(2), 187–202.

Grotstein, J. S. (2003). Introduction. In R. M. Billow, *Relational, group psychotherapy: From basic assumptions to passion.* London: Jessica Kingsley Publishers.

Hopper, E. (2001). The social unconscious: Theoretical considerations. *Group Analysis 34*(1), 9–27.

Hopper, E. (1981). [2003] Social mobility: A study of social control and insatiability. Oxford: Blackwell. Excerpts reprinted in Hopper.E. (2003) *The Social Unconscious: Selected Papers.* London: Jessica Kingsley Publishers.

Khan, M. (1972). The use and abuse of dream in psychic experience. *International Journal of Psychoanalytic Psychotherapy, 1.*

Livingston, M. (2002). Self-psychology, dreams and group psychotherapy – working in the playspace. In M. Pines, C. Neri & R. Friedman (Eds.), *Dreams in group psychotherapy* (pp. 46–67). London, New York: Jessica Kingsley Publishers.

Medici De Steiner, C. (1995). Analyzing children's dreams. *International Journal of Psychoanalysis*, 76(1), 45–49.

Meltzer, D. (1983). *Dream-life*. Worcester: Clunie Press.

Mitchell, S. A. (2000). Response to commentaries. *Psychoanalytic Dialogues*, 10(3), 505–507.

Ogden, T. H. (1979). On projective identification. *International Journal of Psychoanalysis*, 60, 357–373.

Ogden, T. H. (1994). The analytical third: Working with intersubjective clinical facts. *International Journal of Psychoanalysis*, 75(1), 3–20.

Palombo, S. R. (1992). The eros of dreaming. *International Journal of Psychoanalysis*, 73, 637–646.

Puget, J. (2002). Singular dreams – dreams of link scene and discourse. In M. Pines, C. Neri & R. Friedman (Eds.), *Dreams in group psychotherapy* (pp. 46–67). London, New York: Jessica Kingsley Publishers.

Schlapobersky, J. (1993). The language of the group: monologue, dialogue and discourse in group analysis. In D. Brown & L. Zinkin, *The psyche and the social world: developments in group-analytic theory* (pp. 211–231). London: Routledge.

Stern, D., Sandler, L., Nahum, J., Harrison, A., Lyons-Ruth, K., Morgan, A., Bruschweiler-Stern, N., & Tronick, E. (1998). Non-interpretative mechanisms in psychoanalytic therapy. *International Journal of Psychoanalysis*, 79, 903–921.

Stolorow, R. D., Atwood, G. E., & Orange, D. M. (2002). *Worlds of experience: Interweaving philosophical and clinical dimensions in psychoanalysis*. New York: Basic Books.

Stone, W., & Karterud, S. (2006) Dreams as portraits of self and group interaction. *International Journal of Group Psychotherapy*, 56(1), 47–61.

Ullman, M. (1996). Appreciating dreams – A group approach. London: Sage.

Winnicott, D. W. (1958). *Anxiety associated with insecurity. Through pediatrics to psychoanalysis* (pp. 97–100). London: Tavistock.

Winnicott, D. W. (1962). The theory of the parent-infant relationship. Further remarks. *International Journal of Psychoanalysis*, 43, 256–257.

Winnicott, D. W. (1969). The use of an object and relating through identifications. In D. W. Winnicott, *Playing and Reality*. London: Tavistock.

25
Group Interventions Following Trauma and Disaster
Suzanne B. Phillips and Robert H. Klein

The solidarity of a group provides the strongest protection against terror and despair, and the strongest antidote to traumatic experience. (Herman, 1997: p. 214)

The goal of this chapter will be to examine and demonstrate the suitability and efficacy of multiple different group interventions in the aftermath of trauma and disaster. Toward this end, the authors will address the nature and impact of traumatic events, common reactions, mediating variables and stages of recovery. They will develop the rationale for group interventions after trauma, delineate the specific core principles that underlie such interventions and provide a set of guidelines for conducting group interventions. The role of the leader, as well as a comparison of the salient differences between a trauma group and a psychotherapy group, will be highlighted. The proposed guidelines will be illustrated by examining evidenced-based group intervention models best suited to address the needs of diverse populations as those unfold across the time spectrum of trauma and recovery. Finally, the chapter will conclude with a consideration of the countertransference issues stirred in trauma group leaders and the necessary tenets of self-care needed to counteract secondary post-traumatic stress and vicarious traumatization.

Introduction

Traumatic events, be they natural disasters or man-made atrocities, push us to our limits. By definition, they overwhelm our usual abilities to cope and adjust, and call into question the basic assumptions that organize our experiences of self, relationships, the world and the human condition. In the case of disasters, the destruction that unfolds is thought to exceed the coping capacity of the affected community.

The Wiley-Blackwell Handbook of Group Psychotherapy, First Edition. Edited by Jeffrey L. Kleinberg.
© 2012 John Wiley & Sons, Ltd. Published 2012 by John Wiley & Sons, Ltd.

Traumatic events generally involve threats to life and bodily integrity; a close personal encounter with violence and death; witnessing an event that involves death, injury or threat to the physical integrity of another; or learning of the death, serious harm or injury of a family member. According to the *Diagnostic and Statistical Manual of Mental Disorders* (4th Ed.) 1994, the criteria for psychological trauma include the experience of intense fear, helplessness and horror. These most certainly are salient features in the definition of what is traumatic for many trauma survivors. However, intervention with uniformed personnel or combat veterans, suggests that while they may be quite traumatized in the aftermath of a critical incident or combat, their mission focus and battlefield mentality often overrides the experience of fear, helplessness or horror at the time the event occurs.

In this vein, some trauma experts (Shalev and Ursano, 2003) underscore the importance of broadening the dimensions of "trauma" to include the experiencing of other feelings including profound loss, be it concrete or symbolic; isolation like that experienced with captivity or kidnapping; dehumanization and degradation as in prisoners of war or rape victims; uncertainty as experienced by those waiting on rooftops during Hurricane Katrina; and a sense of incongruity with the assumptive world as rescue workers handling children's body parts. Shalev and Ursano suggest such incongruity to be at the core of mental traumatization.

Common Reactions to Trauma

The human response to trauma is a complex, integrated system of physical, psychological and neurophysiological reactions. These reactions manifest in symptom clusters in three categories: hyperarousal; intrusion or re-experiencing; constriction and avoidance. Hyperarousal, as described by Judith Herman (1997), is the persistent expectation of danger. It is reflected in an intense startle response, sleep difficulties, agitation, irritability, and anger common after experiencing a traumatic event. Intrusion involves the re-experiencing of the trauma in the form of intrusive and disruptive recollections, flashbacks, nightmares and traumatic memories. Traumatic memories, neurologically imprinted in the right brain as sensation during a state of hyperarousal to danger, are different from conscious narrative memory. The intrusive re-experiencing of trauma represents the continued attempt to assimilate the "imprint" of trauma. It most often persists longer than the symptoms of hyperarousal. The constriction or numbing that is frequently a response to trauma can constitute an escape from the traumatic situation by an altered state of consciousness. Manifested as the detached calm in the face of terror, rage or pain, this dissociative response is, as Herman suggests, "one of nature's small mercies, a protection against unbearable pain" (Herman, 1997: p. 43).

According to van der Kolk and McFarlane (1996), avoidance in the aftermath of trauma may take many different forms, including keeping away from reminders, ingesting drugs or alcohol in order to numb awareness of distressing emotional states, as well as the unconscious use of dissociation to keep unbearable aspects of experiences from consciousness. Avoidance differs from dissociative symptoms as it involves a more conscious withdrawal and detachment from everyday activities. It is frequently one of the most tenacious symptoms as a person feels relieved by putting constraints on daily life to avoid re-experiencing the traumatic symptoms (Herman, 1997: p. 49).

It is important to recognize that most survivors experience these symptom clusters in the immediate aftermath of trauma. They appear to be "normal" reactions to an abnormal, terrifying and overwhelming situation. Such early symptoms tend to subside over time, usually within a matter of weeks for most survivors. Responses from the majority of individuals exposed to a traumatic event fail to meet criteria for a diagnosable mental disorder and will not need formal psychological intervention (McFarlane and Girolamo, 1996).

Accordingly, it is not the initial presence of such symptom clusters that mark any individual's responses to trauma as pathologic. Rather, it is their persistence, intensity, and disruptive impact on overall level of pre-morbid functioning that is critical to evaluate. If such symptoms do not begin to dissipate or resolve and cannot be overcome through the normal range of available personal, family and community supports, but instead continue to interfere with and disrupt more adaptive functioning, then careful professional assessment and treatment may be required.

Furthermore, because of the nature of the particular symptom clusters aroused in response to trauma and the social stigma that can be associated with the trauma and/or help-seeking behavior, the survivor may not come forward requesting help. Often it is those who know him/her who first recognize that the survivor is not doing well and does indeed need professional assistance. Similarly, there may be individuals suffering from lingering sub-clinical and/or delayed or disguised reactions that may require formal intervention to resolve.

Mediating Factors

The reaction to traumatic events and the persistence of post-traumatic stress cluster symptoms are a function of a number of factors that can exacerbate or mediate their impact. These factors include the nature of the event, meaning of the event, individual crisis experience variables, personal resiliency or vulnerability, and the networks of available social support.

Nature of the event

There is evidence that a man-made trauma, like rape or a terrorist attack, escalates more extreme responses than the pain and suffering caused by an accident or natural disaster (Herman, 1997). An event that involves unanticipated traumatic loss of life tends to be complicated as one is first assaulted with trauma and then expected to deal with loss (Rando, 1993). Events of catastrophic proportion like 9/11 which involve the elements of a man-made atrocity assaulting safety, the death of thousands and the loss of social networks, community structures, financial and personal resources spare no one in their impact. Similarly, wars like those waged in Iraq and Afghanistan involving multiple deployments, a different type of warfare, the lack of safe zones, the use of improvised explosive devices (IED's), and the risk of extensive injuries, escalate combat stress and post-traumatic stress disorder (PTSD).

Meaning of the event

According to van der Kolk, McFarlane, and Weisaeth, (1996) the critical element that makes an event traumatic for a survivor is the meaning s/he attributes to it. The survivor's assessment of it in terms of threat, helplessness, and overall impact on body, mind, spirit and future is more fundamental in terms of response than the event itself. Hence, what may be traumatic for one individual, need not be for another.

Individual crisis experience variables

The meaning and impact of a traumatic event is quite often a function of individual crisis experience variables such as degree of exposure, duration, proximity to the danger and/or relationship to the victim(s). For example, the location of children on a playground versus in the school when a sniper shoots other children, the amount of time someone is trapped in a vehicle after an accident, or witnessing the explosion of your friend in the vehicle immediately ahead of you all weigh into the meaning and impact of the event.

Personal vulnerability and resiliency

Children, the elderly, those who have a prior psychiatric diagnosis as well as physically ill or infirm are at higher risk for suffering from the impact of traumatic events. Similarly, factors such as culture, job, or gender may significantly affect the impact of trauma. Personal resiliency traits such as intelligence, problem-solving, spirituality, physical mastery, independence, social skills, artistic ability, and creativity have all been shown to offset the impact of trauma and foster recovery (Boss, 2006; Norman, 2000).

Available social support networks

The presence and connection to familiar networks of care and support have also proven to be a crucial variable in mediating responses during the acute stage of trauma (Ørner and Schnyder, 2003) Similarly, the unavailability of such support networks evident in the form of negative social appraisal can have an adverse impact as can be seen when a rape victim is blamed for her assault or when Vietnam Veterans suffer social stigmatization.

The time-line of trauma

Another factor that bears on the experience and impact of traumatic events is its phase-specific nature. Trauma unfolds across a time spectrum. Interventions, therefore, must be designed to address different needs at different points in time. The stages of trauma include:

1. The Acute Stage usually extends from the time of impact to the first four weeks;
2. The Post-Acute Stage, usually identified as the time when rescue is complete and recovery begins, may span from one to several months after the traumatic

event. This stage is often extended by additional unrecognized traumatic events like the impact of injury, loss of resources, relocation etc.;
3. The Long-term Stage is often considered to begin six months or more past the event. As seen after 9/11, with the closing of Ground Zero almost 9 months later, or the multiple deployments and combat stress experienced by those serving in the military, the long-term impact from trauma may unfold for many years thereafter.

A Rationale for Using Group Interventions to Address Trauma

How, then, might group interventions (either alone or in combination with other interventions) be useful in addressing responses to disaster and trauma? The rationale for the use of groups in such circumstances is based upon multiple considerations. To begin with, group psychotherapy has been a widely accepted treatment option for more than 50 years. Substantial evidence has been compiled attesting to the empirical effectiveness and cost-efficiency of group psychotherapy for the treatment of a variety of psychological as well as physical problems (Bergin and Garfield, 1990; Burlingame, MacKenzie, and Strauss, 2003; Burlingame, Fuhriman, & Mosier, 2003; Garfield & Bergin, 1994; Lambert, 2003).

Specifically with regard to the treatment of trauma, the current literature provides consistent evidence that group psychotherapy, regardless of type, is associated with favorable outcomes across a number of symptoms. PTSD and depression are the most commonly targeted symptoms, but efficacy has been demonstrated for a range of other symptoms as well including global distress, dissociation, low self-esteem and fear (Foy, Glynn, Schnurr, Janowski, Wattenberg, Marmar, and Gusman, 2000).

A critical component of group efficacy rests upon the notion that groups can provide a safe, nurturing, non-judgmental environments where participants can feel accepted and emotionally supported (Klein and Schermer, 2000; Klein and Phillips, 2008; Buchele and Spitz; 2004). This is especially valuable because groups can offer relief from the aloneness, isolation and disconnectedness that disaster survivors frequently feel. Group participants meet together with others who have endured similar frightening, overwhelming and deeply disturbing experiences. Such experiences are difficult to put into words and difficult to talk about with others.

A holding container can be established that enables group members to find their voices, share their experiences, disclose painful feelings, and find words for the unspeakable. The dreadful nature of such experiences, along with the accompanying feelings of shame, loss, rage and anguish, often interfere with and sometimes totally preclude broaching these concerns anywhere else, with anyone else, particularly in an on-going fashion. In fact, many trauma survivors find it difficult to seek help. Participating in a group with other survivors rather than seeking individual attention, can relieve the social stigma and cultural barriers that often impede help-seeking and enable emotionally isolated survivors to recognize that they are not alone.

Furthermore, the presence of other people in the group generates opportunities to reveal, validate and to bear witness to what has happened. In the process of so doing, members begin to restore their disrupted external connections with others as well as begin to repair the often profound rifts in their internal assumptive worlds about themselves, relationships, life and the way the world usually works (Klein and Schermer, 2000; Kauffman, 2002). In the early stages, the very act of sharing information about what happened can quell misinformation and upsetting rumors. The group can provide a context for education and the proper dispersal of information, especially with regard to needed available resources and how to secure them. The courage, strength, compassion and resilience displayed by group members often serve to inspire participants and to stimulate a renewed sense of hope about the future.

By helping other group members, individual participants can both augment their own damaged sense of self-esteem and relieve the collective sense of helplessness survivors experience. In addition, groups enable members to share and learn new ways of self-care and new strategies for coping. The acquisition of such tools can promote healing and restore more effective levels of functioning. Finally, by providing opportunities for sharing, emotional support and new learning in a safe environment, groups can help disaster survivors to begin to repair their disrupted sense of trust in their leaders, the world around them, and other people (Schein, Spitz, Burlingame, Muskin, and Vargo, 2006; Klein and Schermer, 2000).

Core Principles: A Comparison of Trauma Groups and Psychotherapy Groups

Psychotherapy groups come in different sizes and shapes. So, too, do time-sensitive intervention groups following disaster and trauma. Different theoretical orientations have given rise to a host of different approaches, including psychodynamic, cognitive-behavioral and supportive models. The specific nature of the disaster situation has contributed to the development and implementation of a variety of group interventions. In the aftermath of 9/11 for example, the American Group Psychotherapy Association pioneered a series of group interventions that included both large and small groups, with different selection and composition criteria, and various leadership structures that met for varying lengths of time. These groups adopted different formats in pursuit of a variety of goals at different points in time following the disaster (Buchele and Spitz, 2004; Klein, Bernard, Thomas, Block, and Feirman, 2007; Klein and Thomas, 2003, 2005; Klein and Phillips, 2008). It is, therefore, an oversimplification to speak about a single type of group intervention for disaster.

Differences between trauma groups and psychotherapy groups

An important consideration in understanding group intervention for trauma and disaster is a clarification of the similarities and differences between trauma group interventions and psychotherapy groups in terms of therapeutic factors, group goals, the nature of the participants, leader roles and techniques.

Therapeutic factors

In terms of similarities, both types of groups clearly rely upon common therapeutic factors that underlie the efficacy of all groups (e.g., Yalom and Lesczc, 2005; Bernard et al., 2008). This is especially the case with regard to factors such as acceptance, support, belonging, universalization, and establishing a sense of cohesion and trust in a safe environment. Both types of groups encourage self-expression, the sharing of information and emotional ventilation/catharsis. Each provides opportunities for new interpersonal learning to occur.

Goals

Decisions regarding the specific nature and form of any group intervention ideally should be based upon the overall purpose of the group, that is, what is it that one wishes to accomplish. Depending on the time and stage unfolding after trauma and disaster, we believe that the goals for group intervention would include safety, support of feelings, assessment, triage, normalization of responses, acceptance, development and facilitation of coping skills, recognition of resiliency traits, connection and restoration of functioning. The unspeakable is contained and defenses are supported.

These are different from the goals of most on-going outpatient psychotherapy groups. Regardless of the model, on-going outpatient psychotherapy groups work toward relief of anxiety, depression, interpersonal problems, discontent with life by facilitating change or development of existing personality structures over time. Toward this goal, the group is utilized to uncover or confront unconscious conflict, resistance, defense, and transference. The here-and-now in the group serves as an important new experience as well as a reference point toward examining historical patterns and transference reactions.

Participants

This fundamental difference in goals follows on from the fact that participants enter post-disaster groups under different circumstances, in a different state of mind and with different expectations compared to those who enter psychotherapy groups. More specifically, something unexpected and tragic has occurred which has left survivors feeling frightened and overwhelmed. Post-disaster group participants do not identify themselves as patients intent upon resolving conflicts in their own personal histories. They do not come into the group seeking treatment or psychotherapy. Rather, they see themselves as survivors, people who have experienced and emerged from a deeply disturbing situation. They are struggling to understand what has happened, to examine their own responses to the situation and to learn how to go on being. Frequently what is most helpful is psycho-education and emotional acceptance. In addition, participants may not wish to see the group leader as a psychotherapist with expertise in treating psychopathology. Rather, they want to view the leader as someone with expertise in dealing with trauma who can guide them through their terrible ordeal.

Role of leader

The goal of a group has a direct bearing on the role of the leader in the group. Specifically, s/he must make differential use of the available therapeutic factors, emphasizing the development of certain factors, that is, cohesion, while limiting the operation of others, such as, transference analysis and insight. Working successfully with a group of disaster and trauma survivors requires that the group leader always remain aware that the group goal is to facilitate re-integration and recovery, not to uncover and work through unconscious material to promote personality change.

The traditionally more neutral and detached stance of the leader in the psychotherapy group must give way to one that can be best described as more emotionally-near and available. Skillful interpretations need to be replaced by modeling a compassionate presence. Because the sense of trust in self and other is often assaulted by trauma, the leader must be more attentive to providing clear structure, limiting disruptive anxiety, and carefully titrating emotional expression and exposure. S/he must help the group to make sense of what has happened, and what needs to occur for them to be able to cope more successfully.

With this in mind, the leader must be especially patient in post-disaster and trauma groups. S/he must allow the group to develop at its own pace, not push individual members to do more than they are capable of doing, and respect the fact that the group, as a whole, will need to go slowly. The typical stages of group development (MacKenzie, 1994, 1997; Brabender and Fallon, 2009) may at times seem delayed. However, it is important for the leader to recognize that re-establishing a sense of trust and re-connecting with others are core components at the heart of what is helpful in such groups. It is well worth spending additional group time and energy to ensure that participants feel heard and accepted, gain relief from isolation, learn about and normalize responses to disaster, and begin to re-discover their own voices.

Dealing with the here-and-now of the group is important in both psychotherapy and post-disaster groups. However, examination of the deeper, unconscious interpersonal patterns that are being replicated between members in the group does not constitute a primary focus for post-disaster groups. Emphasis is placed instead on helping participants to cope with their current life situations, normalizing their responses, and aiding them to assist and learn from one another in order to strengthen and support more adaptive functioning and thereby promote recovery. These efforts can best be served by making use of conscious and pre-conscious mental content, not probing for unconscious material.

Technique

Disaster intervention group leaders frequently make use of a variety of other techniques that they may not ordinarily use during their more traditional psychotherapy groups. These may include, for example, the use of mini-lectures, structured exercises, written materials, specific suggestions and guidance, homework assignments, etc. Many of the principles underlying the operation of short-term or time-limited groups are also relevant in this regard (MacKenzie, 1996; Klein, 1985).

In the aftermath of disaster, technique is often driven by circumstances. As described by Kauff and Kleinberg (2008), post-disaster groups are often conducted on site in the community, not in the safety and security of the mental health professional's office. The surrounding situation may still remain frightening and chaotic. It is often the case that group service has been described and presented by someone other than the group leader, thus making it more difficult to establish a realistic and coherent group contract with the group participants. Furthermore, it may not be possible for the group leader to attend to issues of group selection and composition, or to prepare members for what to expect and how best to make use of the group. In addition, many post-disaster groups are conducted in schools, community centers and organizations where group participants will continue to work with each other during and after the group. Determining what is safe to express in the group and what are the boundaries surrounding confidentiality may well take on additional meaning and importance.

General Guidelines for Group Intervention after Trauma and Disaster

The following is a list of general guidelines for group leaders who choose to utilize group interventions in the aftermath of trauma and disaster. They essentially reflect the core principles of response discussed above that should underscore group intervention regardless of the type of model being used. These guidelines are consistent with those endorsed by the American Group Psychotherapy Association (AGPA website; Bernard et al., 2008; Klein & Phillips, 2008).

- Try to restore, promote and ensure safety in the group. This is essential for any group treating trauma survivors, many of whom are stunned and dazed.
- Establish initial safety and mitigate anxiety levels by introduction of the leaders, and clarification of time, place and purpose of the group.
- Go slowly; it will take time to develop a climate of safety and trust in the group. Encourage members to join the group in their own ways and at their own pace. Let members know they can listen and participate as they wish.
- Remember that fears of stigma and cultural barriers may impede help-seeking and interfere with becoming a group member. Participants in such groups often enter burdened with deeper feelings of shame that may well be stimulated during the joining process.
- Utilize opportunities to normalize responses and provide information that legitimizes feelings, fears and physical symptoms in the aftermath of trauma. It is often useful to incorporate a psycho-educational component into the group.
- Model support, acceptance and active, non-judgmental listening.
- Try to remain experience-near, emotionally attuned and soothing to counter members, feelings of aloneness and isolation and to pave the way for subsequent interpersonal reconnection
- Highlight similarities/commonalities/universalities to relieve aloneness and to promote group cohesion.
- Pay careful attention to basics, especially with regard to establishing and examining boundaries and boundary violations (task boundaries; time boundaries; role boundaries; confidentiality boundaries).
- Recognize that the frame may be different in a trauma group. For example, outside social support and networking by members may be encouraged in the trauma group but not the typical outpatient psychotherapy group.
- Give members the opportunity to find their voices; to share/discuss accurate information about unfolding events and disclose their experiences.

- Remember that "emotional avoidance" may be an important and necessary defense for some in the early aftermath of trauma; trauma groups do not confront or challenge defenses, they support existing healthier structures.
- Contain/control the level of emotional stimulation and the anxiety level of the group; titrate stories of trauma so that group members can take in what is being said without becoming overwhelmed and re-traumatized.
- Assess in an on-going way and verbally check how speakers and listeners are doing with the material shared or feelings expressed. A critical aspect of the group as a container is its capacity to assist members to detoxify and metabolize what has happened and their roles in it.
- Attempt to re-establish trust; remember that this is a core issue and that members are likely to feel severely shaken, distrustful and suspicious.
- Encourage members to help one another, especially in terms of sharing coping strategies and self-care activities. Such activity enables individual members to experience increased self-esteem and relieves the collective sense of helplessness in the group.
- Facilitate members' use of existing family and social networks as well as fostering new networks of support. Promote the use of available resources both inside and outside the group.
- Look for opportunities to identify and support resiliency traits, such as: creativity, intelligence, spirituality, interpersonal strength, art, athletic ability, sense of humor, etc.
- Avoid making interpretations; stick with conscious material. Focus primarily on the current life situations, the here-and-now of the group, and what lies ahead.
- Make provisions prior to the group for managing referrals and emergency interventions, for those in need of immediate individual assessment, medications, or hospitalization.
- Be alert to members who manifest persistent, intense or incapacitating symptoms of anxiety, depression, and PTSD. Be aware that such responses may be triggered during group sessions; think through ahead of time interventions that could be used to deal with emotional over-arousal, re-experiencing, withdrawal or dissociation.
- Work with a co-leader, if possible. Co-leadership facilitates on-going assessment and individual member attention, if needed. It also affords support for the leaders in terms of containment of traumatic material, physical and emotional fatigue, processing of countertransference issues, and reducing vicarious traumatization.
- Establish an on-going relationship with a supervisor/consultant. It is especially important to be able to process leader responses outside of the immediate, often intense, emotional line of fire.
- If possible, participate in a support group for leaders where you can examine your own reactions.
- Monitor your countertransference responses; be alert to signs of vicarious traumatization in yourself, especially the cumulative effects of prolonged exposure.
- Be sure to take proper care of yourself; leaders who are emotionally overburdened, overworked and unsupported are more vulnerable and less effective.

Trauma Group Interventions

The following section contains examples of endorsed and evidenced-based group interventions applicable across the time spectrum of trauma and disaster. More detailed comprehensive discussions of time and population-specific group interventions can be found elsewhere (e.g., Klein and Phillips, 2008; Schein et al., 2003)

Acute stage

There is ample evidence that early psychosocial intervention is a crucial dimension to a comprehensive response to trauma and disaster (Ørner and Schnyder, 2003; Schein, Spitz, Burlingame, Muskin and Vargo, 2006). The most widely endorsed response in the acute stage of trauma is Psychological First Aid (PFA) (US Department of Health and Human Services, 2001). Psychological First Aid is defined as "a supportive and compassionate presence designed to reduce acute psychological distress and/or facilitate continued support, if necessary" (Everly and Flynn, 2005). The Core Actions of Psychological First Aid (Uhernik and Husson, 2009) include:

- Establish a human connection: non-intrusive, compassionate manner.
- Enhance immediate and on-going safety: physical and emotional comfort.
- Help survivors to articulate immediate needs and concerns.
- Connect survivors to social support networks, including family members, friends, and community helping resources.
- Support positive coping, acknowledge coping efforts and strengths.
- Offer practical assistance and information.
- Provide psycho-education.
- Refer to higher levels of care.

Given that trauma and disaster most often impact natural groupings, be they a family, community, corporation or school, it is important to note that these Core Actions can be effectively implemented in a group context. Group Psychological First Aid (GPF) was developed by Everly, Phillips, Kane, and Feldman (2006) for homogeneous cohorts who have experienced a traumatic event, such as a school team who has lost a member to a tragic accident, a bank staff who has faced a robbery, or uniformed service personnel (fire, police, emergency medical services and military) who have suffered a traumatic incident.

Group Psychological First Aid draws upon the pre-existing cohesion of the existing group as a protective factor and aims to reduce distress, assist with current needs, and promote adaptive functioning by active listening, normalizing, identifying coping skills, supporting and providing opportunities for higher levels of care. Unlike former debriefing models (Everly and Mitchell, 1999), this is a consensus model that does not elicit details of traumatic experiences and losses.

The Core Actions of Psychological First Aid can also be invaluable components of broader community, corporate or school programs that seek to restore the social networks of connection and care necessary for recovery after a traumatic event.

Post-acute stage interventions

As noted earlier, a number of group treatment interventions have proven effective in response to the diagnosis of PTSD or the prolonged presence of sub-clinical levels of symptom clusters of intrusion, hyperarousal, numbing and constriction, as well as anxiety, depression and substance abuse (Foy et al., 2000).

Two programs that have statistically demonstrated reduction of symptoms with adults include Trauma-Focus Group Therapy (TFGP) (Unger, Wattenberg, Foy, and Glynn, 2006) and Present Centered Supportive Group (PCGT) therapy for adult trauma survivors (Wattenberg, Unger, Foy, and Glynn, 2006). Both are time-limited programs that include a specific pre-determined number (often sixteen) of sessions.

TFGP draws upon the cognitive behavioral techniques of systematic prolonged exposure and cognitive restructuring to process each group member's trauma experience. More specifically, each member works at describing a personal narrative of trauma experiences in the context of non-judgmental group support. In addition, this model makes use of psycho-educational material for normalizing trauma reactions and supporting coping skills when dealing with trauma-related reminders and symptoms.

PCGT is based on the finding that inherent in the suffering of trauma survivors is the inability to observe themselves in relation to their current physical and interpersonal situation because trauma-based intrusions, affects and attitudes interfere with their daily and automatic processing of new information. The dual focus of PCGT includes Symptoms That Diminish Attention to Everyday Life and Trauma-Based Alteration in Beliefs, Attitudes, Habits and Behaviors. The main objective is to support movement from a trauma-based worldview to a broader perspective that includes the present environment.

Less structured than TFGP, this model involves an active leader working to facilitate client strengths, process encouraging interventions and keep the here-and-now focus. Interpersonal comfort is supported. The flexibility of this model has proven effective as an adjunctive intervention to other types of intervention. Both TFGP and PCGT have been used effectively with civilian and veteran populations.

Long-term intervention

Regardless of the model used, an understanding of the issues related to the longer-term impact of trauma or disaster are crucial for effective intervention (Cecil Rice, 2004). It is worth recognizing, for example, that the unconscious is not bound by literal time. Traumatic memory and intrusions can haunt survivors for years. It is often the avoidance of such triggers that causes a survivor to withdraw from life and remain locked in the past.

Traumatic intrusions whether manifested as feelings and sensations on anniversary events or in traumatic memories and on-going nightmares can be contained, understood, normalized, and addressed in group treatment. With intervention, they can become opportunities for healing and integration.

Long-term trauma centered group therapy

An excellent example of a long-term group intervention for trauma is the model described in *Trauma Centered Group Psychotherapy for Women* by Lubin and Johnson (2008). This model addresses the historical, chronic, childhood and adult trauma of women in a way that integrates cognitive behavior, exposure, supportive and psychodynamic perspectives and techniques. Accordingly, it accomplishes two tasks rarely found together in most models. It uses a manualized protocol that enhances the possibility of quality control and assessment, and it recognizes the power of group dynamics and the *group process* as a crucial component and therapeutic change agent for addressing the interpersonal ramifications of traumatic experience.

Care of the Trauma Group Leader

It almost goes without saying that the trauma group leader must be willing to enter into and contain the feelings, words and protective patterns ancillary to the insult of childhood or adult trauma, natural disaster, war and catastrophic violence. To do so, one must put himself/herself in harm's way (Stamm, 1999). As such, there will be inevitable countertransference reactions which can include feelings of helplessness, anger, empathy, fear, and over identification, etc. (Phillips, 2004; Klein and Phillips, 2008; Pearlman and Saakvitne, 1995). There are times when a trauma group leader may actually experience Secondary Posttraumatic Stress (SPTSD), that is, the same cluster of PTSD symptoms of hyperarousal (cannot relax, sleep, concentrate), intrusion (nightmares, traumatic memories, intrusive thoughts), numbing (protection by not feeling) and avoidance (personally and professionally) suffered by those with whom he/she is working.

As identified by Pearlman and Saakvitne (1995) it is not uncommon for those working with trauma to suffer vicarious traumatization in addition to SPTSD. Vicarious Traumatization includes an altered and negative view of self, the world, and one's capacity to access joy, hope and maintain connection with others. Pearlman and Saakvitne offer guidelines for ameliorating Vicarious Traumatization which include the ABC's of self care: *A*ssessment of needs and limitations, *B*alance of personal and professional life; and *C*onnection to others professionally and personally (Saakvitne and Pearlman, 1995; Pearlman, 1999; Stamm, 1999).

Group programs for leader self-care

It has been the experience of the authors and other AGPA colleagues who have offered "Care of the Caregiver" programs both nationally and internationally that the use of a group venue to address the impact of trauma on caregivers is invaluable (Andronico, Cleary, Einhorn, Miller, Shapiro, Spitz, and Ulman, 2008; Phillips, 2004). The group provides its members with opportunities to arrive at a deeper, more personal understanding of the potency and emotional impact of the psycho-educational material, specifically information on countertransference, SPTSD and vicarious traumatization.

It is the nature of caregivers whether civilian, uniformed service or military to prefer to be "trained rather than treated." A group venue that offers caregivers, in some cases, the first "safe" opportunity to hear about the impact of trauma on other caregivers and to disclose and bear witness to the unspeakable pain and suffering that they have held alone for others is therapeutic for all involved. A group program for caregivers offers an opportunity "to actually experience in the group context" the ABC's of caregiver care being recommended.

Summary and Conclusions

In this chapter we have described typical and pathologic responses to trauma and provided a rationale for the use of group interventions in the treatment of trauma. We have examined the phase-specific nature of responses to trauma, have identified a core set of principles that underlie group interventions by contrasting trauma and more traditional psychotherapy groups, and have provided a set of guidelines for the trauma group leader. Examples of evidenced-based trauma group intervention strategies and programs have been highlighted along with the role and techniques of the trauma group leader and the importance of self-care activities.

Our experience suggests that in order to work effectively with trauma survivors group leaders require special preparation and training. Such training, we would argue, must include not only increased intellectual understanding but opportunities for emotional exposure, sharing, support, inspiration and learning that can be best accomplished through the use of the group. Joining a network of trauma group leaders who meet in a group on a regular basis and are committed to self-scrutiny, new learning and mutual support can be invaluable.

We want to conclude by emphasizing that the world of trauma is dangerous territory to venture into alone. This is equally apt for both survivors and caretakers. Judith Herman, commenting upon the value of group for trauma survivors, states:

> Trauma isolates; the group re-creates a sense of belonging. Trauma shames and stigmatizes; the group bears witness and affirms. Trauma degrades the victim; the group exalts her. Trauma dehumanizes the victim; the group restores her humanity. (Herman, 1997: p. 214)

References and Bibliography

Ajdukovic, D., & Ajdukovic, M. (2003). Systematic approaches to early intervention in a community affected by organized violence. In R. Ørner & U. Schnyder (Eds.), *Reconstructing early intervention after traumatic trauma: Innovations in the care of survivors* (pp. 82–92). Oxford: Oxford University Press.

American Group Psychotherapy Association. (2010). *Practice Guidelines for Group Psychotherapy, guide to developing and leading psychotherapy groups*. Available from the American Group Psychotherapy Web site, http://www.agpa.org/guidelines/index.html

American Psychiatric Association. (1994). *Diagnostic and statistical manual of mental disorders* (4th Ed.). Washington, DC: Corporate Author.

Andronico, M., Cleary, T., Einhorn, F., et al. (2008). Support for disaster response helpers and service delivery workers. In R. Klein & S. Phillips (Eds.), *Public mental health service protocols: group interventions for disaster preparedness and response* (pp. 127–144). New York: American Group Psychotherapy Association.

Bergin, A. E. & Garfield, S. L. (1994). *Handbook of psychotherapy and behavior change*. New York: Wiley.

Bernard, H., Burlingame, G., Flores, P., et al. (2008). Clinical practice guidelines for group psychotherapy. *International Journal of Group Psychotherapy*, *58*(4), 455–542.

Boss, P. (2006). *Loss, trauma, and resilience: Therapeutic work with ambiguous loss*. New York: W. W. Norton & Co.

Brabender, V., & Fallon, A. (2009). *Group development in practice*. Washington, DC: American Psychological Association.

Buchele, B., & H. Spitz. (2004). *Group interventions for treatment of psychological trauma*. New York: American Group Psychotherapy Association.

Burlingame, G. M., Fuhriman, A., & Mosier, J. (2003). The differential effectiveness of group psychotherapy: A meta-analytic perspective. *Group Dynamics: Theory, Research and Practice*, *7*(1), 3–12.

Burlingame, G. M., MacKenzie, K. R., & Strauss, B. (2003). Small group treatment: Evidence for effectiveness and mechanisms of change. In M. Lambert, A. E. Bergin, & S. L. Garfield (Eds.), *Handbook of psychotherapy and behavior change* (5th ed., pp. 647–696). New York: John Wiley & Sons.

Everly, G. S., Jr., & Flynn, B. W. (2005). Principles and practices of acute psychological first aid after disasters. In G. S. Everly & C. L. Parker (Eds.), *Mental health aspects of disasters: Public health preparedness and response* (Rev. ed., pp. 779–789). Baltimore, MD: Johns Hopkins Center for Public Health Preparedness.

Everly, G. S., & Mitchell, J. T. (1999). *Critical incident stress management: A new era and standard of care in crisis interventions*. Ellicott City Maryland: Chevron Publishing Corporation.

Everly, G. S., Phillips, S. B., Kane, D., et al. (2006). Introduction to and overview of group psychological first aid. *Brief Treatment and Crisis Intervention*, *6*(2), 130–136.

Foy, D. W., Glynn, S. M., Schnurr, P. P., et al. (2000). Group therapy. In E. Foa, T. Keane & M. Friedman (Eds.), *Effective treatment for PTSD: Practice guidelines from the international society for traumatic stress studies* (pp. 155–175, 336–338). New York: Guilford.

Garfield, S. L., & Bergin, A. E. (Eds.). (1990). *Handbook of psychotherapy and behavior change*. New York: Wiley.

Herman, J. (1997). *Trauma and recovery*. New York: Basic Books.

Kauff, P., & Kleinberg, J. (2008). Crisis intervention at the organizational level. In R. Klein & S. Phillips (Eds.), *Public mental health service protocols: Group Interventions for disaster preparedness and response* (pp. 159–170). New York: American Group Psychotherapy Association.

Kauffman, S. (2002). *Loss of the assumptive world: A theory of traumatic loss*. New York: Brunner-Routledge.

Klein, R. H. (1985). Some principles of short-term group therapy. *International Journal of Group Psychotherapy*, *35*, 309–330.

Klein, R. H., Bernard, H. S., Thomas, N., et al. (2007). Reacting to a national mental health crisis: Developing the use of groups for disaster preparedness and response. In L. VandeCreek & J. Allen (Eds.), *Innovations in clinical practice: Focus on group, couples and family therapy*. Florida: Professional Resource Press.

Klein, R. H., & Phillips, S. B. (Eds.). (2008). *Public mental health service delivery protocols: Group interventions for disaster preparedness and response*. New York: American Group Psychotherapy Association.

Klein, R. H., & Schermer, V. L. (Eds.). (2000). *Group psychotherapy for psychological trauma*. New York: The Guilford Press.

Klein, R. H., & Thomas, N. K. (2005). Preface. In Buchele, B. & Spitz, H. (Eds.), *Group Interventions for treatment of psychological trauma* (pp. 4–7). New York: American Group Psychotherapy Association.

Klein, R. H., & Thomas, N. K. (2003, February/March). Disaster outreach task force rallies after 9/11. *The Group Circle, 1*.

Lambert, M. J. (Ed.). (2003). *Bergin & Garfield's handbook of psychotherapy and behavior change*. New York: Wiley.

Lubin, H., & Johnson, D.R. (2008). *Trauma-centered group psychotherapy for women: A clinician's manual*. New York: Haworth Press.

MacKenzie, K. R. (1994). The developing structure of the therapy group system. In H. Bernard & R. MacKenzie (Eds.), *Basics of group psychotherapy*. New York: Guilford Press.

MacKenzie, K. R. (1996). Time-limited group psychotherapy. *International Journal of Group Psychotherapy, 46*, 41–60.

MacKenzie, K. R. (1997).Clinical applications of group development ideas. *Group Dynamics: Theory, Research and Practice, 1*(4), 275–287.

McFarlane, A. C., & De Girolamo, G. (1996). The nature of traumatic stressors and epidemiology of posttraumatic reactions. In B. van der Kolk, A. McFarlane & L. Weisaeth (Eds.), *Traumatic stress: The effects of overwhelming experience on mind, body, and society* (pp. 1129–1154). New York: Guilford Press.

Norman, E. (2000). *Resiliency enhancement: Putting the strengths perspective into social work*. New York: Columbia University Press.

Ørner, R., & U. Schnyder (Eds.). (2003). *Reconstructing early intervention after trauma: Innovations in the care of survivors*. Oxford: Oxford University Press.

Pearlman, L., & Saakvitne, K. (1995). *Trauma and the therapist: Countertransference and vicarious traumatization in psychotherapy with incest survivors*. New York: W. W. Norton.

Pearlman, L. (1999). Self-care for trauma therapists: Ameliorating vicarious traumatization. In B. Stamm (Ed.), *Secondary traumatic stress: Self-care issues for clinicians, researchers, and educators* (pp. 51–64). Lutherville, MD: Sidran Press.

Philips, S. B. (2004). Countertransference: Effects on the group therapist working with trauma. In B. Buchele & H. Spitz (Eds.), *Group interventions for treatment of psychological trauma* (pp. 194–227). New York: American Group Psychotherapy Association.

Phillips, S. B. (2009). The synergy of group and individual treatment modalities in the aftermath of disaster and unfolding trauma. *International Journal of Group Psychotherapy, 59*(1), 85–107.

Rando, T. (1993).*Treatment of complicated mourning*. Chicago: Research Press.

Rice, C. A. (2004). The later stage: The role of group interventions in coping with the aftermath of traumatic events. In B. Buchele & H. Spitz (Eds.), *Group interventions for treatment of psychological trauma* (pp. 180–193). New York: American Group Psychotherapy Association.

Schein, L., Spitz, H., Burlingame, G., Muskin, P., Vargo, S. (Eds.). (2006). *Psychological effects of catastrophic disasters: Group approaches to treatment*. New York: The Haworth Press.

Shalev, A. Y., & Ursano, R. J. (2003). Mapping the multidimensional picture of acute responses to traumatic stress. In R. Ørner & U. Schnyder (Eds.), *Reconstructing early intervention after traumatic trauma: Innovations in the care of survivor* (pp. 118–129). Oxford: Oxford University Press.

Stamm, B. (Ed.). (1999). *Secondary traumatic stress: Self-care issues for clinicians, researchers, and educators*. Lutherville: Sidran Press.

Uhernik, J. A., & Husson M. A. (2009). Psychological first aid: An evidence informed approach for acute disaster behavioral health response. In G. R. Walz, J. C. Bleuer & R. K. Yep (Eds.), *Compelling counseling interventions: VISTAS* (pp. 271–280). Alexandria, Virginia: American Counseling Association. http://counselingoutfitters.com/vistas/vistas09/article 24 UhernikHusson.pdf, accessed 11/28/10.

Unger, W. S., Wattenberg, M. S., Foy, D. W., & Glynn, S. M. (2006). Trauma-focus group therapy: An evidence-based group approach to trauma with adults. In L. Schein, H. Spitz, G. Burlingame, P. Muskin & S. Vargo (Eds.), *Psychological effects of catastrophic disasters: Group approaches to treatment* (pp. 731–786). New York: The Haworth Press.

US Department of Health and Human Services, US Department of Defense, US Department of Veterans Affairs, US Department of Justice and American Red Cross. (2001). *Mental health and mass violence: Evidence-based early psychological intervention for victims/survivors of mass violence.* Airlie Conference Center, Warrenton, Virginia http://www.nimh.nih.gov/health/publications/massviolence.pdf. Accessed 11/2/10.

Van der Kolk, B. A., McFarlane, A. C., & L. Weisaeth (Eds.). (1996). *Traumatic stress: The effects of overwhelming experience on mind, body, and society.* New York: Guilford Press.

Wattenberg, M. S., Unger, W. S., Foy, D. W., & Glynn, S. M. (2006). Present-centered supportive group therapy for trauma survivors. In L. Schein, H. Spitz, G. Burlingame, P. Muskin & S. Vargo (Eds.), *Psychological effects of catastrophic disasters: Group approaches to treatment* (pp. 505–579). New York: The Haworth Press.

Yalom, I., & M. Leszcz. (2005). *The theory and practice of group psychotherapy* (5th ed.). New York: Basic Books.

26
After the Conflict: Training of Group Supervision in Guatemala
Elisabeth Rohr

The Political and Social Background

After having signed a peace treaty in 1996, marking the end of a devastating war that lasted more than 36 years, Guatemala was confronted with the challenge to reconstruct a society that had known only violence, savage persecution, random killings and massacres for almost half a century. More than 200 000 people had lost their lives during the "armed conflict," 45 000 disappeared without any trace, one million fled to Mexico to live in refugee camps and more than 400 indigenous communities were completely erased from the landscape as a result of the military strategy of scorched earth, leaving a toll of more than 600 massacres in rural and ethnic regions of the country (Comisión de Esclarecimiento Histórico, CEH, 1999).[1]

This Guatemalan tragedy had a global as well as a local dimension: In times of the cold war, the resurgent movement threatened the hegemonic power of the USA in Central America, already weakened by political transformations that had taken place in Nicaragua and in El Salvador (Molkentin, 2002; Kernjak, 2006).[2] Therefore, American interventions in Guatemala were a political strategy to maintain and to re-enforce the status quo and the hegemonic power of the USA in the region.

Beyond these global factors, the war developed a strong and home-bred racial and even genocidal dynamic. It turned out to be one of the longest, bloodiest and most

---

[1] Two Truth Commissions under the guidance of the UN and the Catholic Church stated unanimously that more than 93% of the atrocities had to be attributed to the army and 3% to the guerrilla (Recuperación de la Memória Histórica – REMHI 1998, CEH, 1999).

[2] Under Reagan US-military interventions, CIA-intelligence, weapons and counter-insurgency trainings increased to support the Guatemalan army in their efforts to fight the guerilla, whereas Carter minimized military support, when human rights violations by the army provoked international protest (Bornschein, 2009).

violent wars of South America (Kurtenbach, 2003).³ Both "Truth Commissions" left no doubt that a considerable part of the population was psychologically damaged and heavily traumatized (REMHI, 1998; CEH, 1999).

However, the devastating effects of war and of human rights violations especially affected the marginalized and impoverished indigenous population, representing 60% of the total population. Since the army perceived indigenous people, mostly of Mayan descent, as natural allies of the rebel forces, defenseless civilians were mercilessly and with extreme cruelty slaughtered, "en masse" (CEH, 1999).⁴ As a result, the rural ethnic population made up 83% of the victims of the war (Bornschein, 2009: p. 61).⁵

The main reasons behind the armed conflict were the extremely unequal distribution of wealth and of land,⁶ in combination with racial discrimination and social exclusion of the indigenous population (CEH, 1999). To be Indian always equated to being poor. This is still true today. According to the United Nations Development Program (UNDP) 56% of the 13.4 million of Guatemalans are poor, 16% extremely poor, living on less than one US-Dollar per day (UNDP 2009: p. 228). But within the indigenous rural population 74.8% are considered to be poor and 24.4% are defined as destitute: extremely poor.⁶ Today Guatemala has the fourth highest rate of chronic malnutrition in the world and 70% of indigenous children under the age of five are malnourished.⁷

The cultural, social and economic polarization within Guatemalan society has always been structured along racial lines. War has aggravated this situation, adding to poverty and violence, trauma and impunity. Even though the UN-Verification Mission in Guatemala (MINUGUA) was set up to monitor the peace accord implementations, which included strategies for greater democracy, equality and justice within Guatemalan society, the political elite of the country has managed to maintain an attitude of denial and willful ignorance, concealing a past that left deep scars and open wounds in the social fabric of society.

Therefore, a repressive strategy of censorship over those who wanted to uncover the dreadful acts of the past has prevailed in Guatemala. None of the well-known perpetrators was ever taken to court and convicted of human rights violations (Bornschein, 2009). Since the Guatemalan army was convinced of its victory in war,

---

³ This racial dimension of the war was one of the reasons why the armed conflict in Guatemala, in contrast to the wars in Chile and Argentine, did not find too much of a media echo outside of the country and hardly any international protest. The impoverished, illiterate and politically barely organized indigenous population had no international political lobby to denounce their human rights violations.
⁴ "In the majority of the massacres there is evidence of multiple acts of savagery, which preceded, accompanied or occurred after the deaths of the victims" (http://shr.aaas.org/guatemala/ceh/report/english/conc2.html)
⁵ Whereas in urban areas people did not even want to believe that there was an ongoing civil war, asking "where is the war?" or "it can't be that there were so many atrocities, we would have noticed them" (Molkentin, 2002: p. 278).
⁶ 20% of the population receives two-thirds of all income (http://en.wikipedia.org/wiki/Economy_of_Guatemala). Last reading: 11.7.2010; A small percentage of the population owns more than 80% of the country's best land (http://www.undp.org/execbrd/pdf/ADR-Guatemala.pdf). Accessed 24.05.2011.
⁷ http://en.wikipedia.org/wiki/Economy_of_Guatemala, accessed 11.7.2010.

it only signed the UN-enforced peace treaty reluctantly. As a result, the government in power felt no urgency in fulfilling the requirements of a peace-building process. President Arzù even refused in 1999 to officially receive the 12 volumes of the "Report of the Truth Commission," thus publicly rejecting any recognition of the atrocities of the past and the suffering of the victims of the war (Öttler, 2004).

This post-war political atmosphere of denial and repression had severe psychosocial consequences: There was no public space to mourn the dead or to demand justice in the wake of large scale human rights violations, committed during a dirty and irregular war. The politically repressive climate did not allow any critical reflection on the past. Those who did not adhere to this unwritten law of silence were stigmatized as enemies of the state or, in some cases, even eliminated as was the anthropologist, Myrna Mack, who dared to investigate the tragic situation of Guatemalan refugees. She was one of many who were brutally executed in order to maintain the law of silence (Mack, 2004). The message was clear: To mourn the dead, to denounce the atrocities of the past or to demand justice simply meant risking one's life!

How then would it be possible to rebuild trust in a society whose social fabric had been severely damaged and almost destroyed, where democracy, justice, peace and human rights existed only in theory, but in reality, social and political life was organized according to utterly repressive and quite authoritarian laws and motives?[8]

How then would training in group supervision, relying on trusting relationships, working with theoretical and methodological concepts based on the notion of the unconscious, function, if life and work in society obliged its members to silence the past and to deny any historic memory? How would its participants dare to develop a desire to explore and to reflect upon critical incidents in their professional life, if, at the same time, all other desire to explore experiences of the past had to be suppressed? What kinds of difficulties, inhibitions, anxieties, defenses and strategies of resistance have to be expected in a training group, under these circumstances? The central question therefore is: How can training in group supervision work, under repressive political conditions, in a post-conflict society and within a population that has been heavily traumatized and confronted with injustice in its daily working experience?

The Organizational Background

After the war, a whole armada of international organizations entered the country trying to support Guatemalan efforts to rebuild trust and peace in society. An international network of support and pressure was the only way to ensure the implementation of the peace treaty. Otherwise, the government would simply allow the peace-building process to fade away.

One of these organizations was the German Technical Cooperation (GTC), an official government agency that had been working in the country for many years and therefore was quite familiar with political and social structures in Guatemala. Drawing

---

[8] Guatemala is by no means an exception. For example Cambodia, Rwanda, Chile and South Africa have all required a combination of economic, social, cultural and psychosocial measures to meet the complex challenges of a post-conflict society, to reestablish peace, democracy and human rights, to break the silence and to mend the broken connections between people.

from experiences in other post-war societies, the GTC decided to put more emphasis on psychosocial projects in Guatemala, thus strengthening the few already existing national efforts that were reaching out to the victims of the war.[9]

An investigation had shown that a large number of social workers and psychologists were working in rather difficult areas: Some of them organized exhumations of mass graves in indigenous communities, counseling Indian families, who expected to find their dead family members in the ground. Some worked with lawyers defending criminals in prison, who had been law breakers and also victims of torture. Others worked in ethnic communities, supporting groups of widows, who had experienced sexual atrocities, helping them to cope with the effects of gang rape and the loss of their husbands and children during the armed conflict.

All of these social workers and psychologists were highly engaged and motivated young people, often carried away by their desire to help, trying to heal the wounds and soothe the pain of people, they worked with. All were part of an environment that Becker (2006) defined as a "traumatizing situation." They witnessed and experienced immense suffering by victims of the war and, at the same time, saw that the majority in society continued to deny the despair, pain and extreme poverty of the victims of the war and that there was no justice. Often enough they felt overwhelmed by the misery they experienced and felt left alone with their sorrow and grief, bearing and sharing so much suffering and pain. There seemed to be nobody, who wanted to listen to them, who wanted to share their sadness and helplessness. Within Guatemalan institutions, counseling the counselors or group supervision was unknown.[10] Therefore, any desire to speak out had to be suppressed. It would have been misunderstood as a sign of professional deficiency. Therefore, they always had to be strong, never failing, never showing any signs of exhaustion, desperation or frustration. They were simply required to function.

There could not be any doubt that an enormous, desperate need for counseling existed. If the healthcare experts would not find a way to digest their painful experiences, the risk of burn-out, exhaustion and of being traumatized themselves would increase. Without continuous and professional support they might become contaminated by the surrounding trauma, not allowing them to stay healthy and sane, while fulfilling their professional tasks. Instead, they would be drawn into what is called "secondary traumatization" (Figley, 1995), which is the injury of experts working with, observing and attempting to heal traumatized patients.

Considering this complex situation, the GTC decided to establish training in group supervision, promoting supervisory skills and support, capacity building and tools to prevent burn-out and secondary traumatization.

The Participants

Before the training started, the GTC offered various workshops to find out, if supervision would be accepted as a specific form of counseling in Guatemala. It turned out that these workshops were always well attended by about 20–25 people, so that

---

[9] The projects aimed at empowering indigenous women, at reconciliation processes in indigenous communities, at capacity building efforts, and at strengthening community mental health services.
[10] A Masters in counseling has been established meanwhile, at the Universidad del Valle, in Guatemala.

the person in charge was quite confident in finding the necessary quota of 18–20 participants to begin the training. There was no prior assessment, simply an announcement was sent out to institutions which were engaged in the peace and reconciliation process, hoping to attract those who felt a strong need for additional qualifications. Since it was training sponsored by the German Government, there were no costs involved for the participants of the training. This might have been one of several factors contributing later on to the difficulties of reliable and continuous participation.

Twenty-two young people showed up on the first day of training, amongst them four indigenous women, one man of Mayan descent, three Germans and one Austrian. They were all working in peace and reconciliation programs inside the country. The majority of those attending were social workers and psychologists, but there were also three psychiatrists, one law student and one university professor. Almost all of them identified strongly with the victims of war, emphasizing that their engagement had to be understood as a humanitarian effort to compensate for the damages that the war had inflicted upon so many, mainly indigenous people. Of course, not all of those present shared these views. At least two of the participants supported and defended the government's interpretation of past and present events.

Undoubtedly, we had the political conflict, which had been splitting the country apart for ages, right in the midst of our training group. This proved to be a major challenge for the training. From the beginning there were strong tensions, fears and signs of resistance as a result of several important and hidden issues, emerging either as a joke or a whispered question at break time – Is there a "spy" among us? How safe are we in this unknown environment with this unknown group conductor and with unknown theories and methods, all coming from Europe? Is this a new way to "colonize" our minds and to impose new "imperialistic" ways of thinking, endangering our own culture and our Latin American identity?

Tendencies to split, project and scapegoat emerged throughout all phases of the training and demonstrated deeply entrenched feelings of anxiety and insecurity, pointing to the loss of trust in society and in human relationships.

Clinical Illustration

A young man kept on asking about the cultural background of the theories that were mentioned in the curriculum, doubting their validity for the Guatemalan context. At the same time, he was eager to present case material from his working experience. One day, after having discussed one of his cases in depth, he came to the conclusion that he had gained quite important new insights and understanding. He appeared to be very grateful for his newly acquired knowledge. But then he would regularly choose to be absent from the next stages of our working phase.

He seemed unable to bear sharing strong emotions within a group context. He always had to distance himself, in order to regain his emotional balance. Feeling close to others, seemed for him to be an overly frightening experience. After all, one could always be abandoned again, as had happened so many times throughout the war.

This ambivalence of wanting to be close, share experiences and at the same time being frightened of emotional intimacy inside the group was a recurrent and upsetting issue throughout the two and a half years of the training. These issues had to be understood as an emotional echo from the war and without the knowledge of the political, social and cultural background of the conflict these group dynamics would never have been understood. The question now was would the training in group supervision be able to overcome this mistrust and restore some hopeful trust back to other members and even throughout society itself, even though it was not considered a psychotherapeutic experience?

There were reasonable doubts at the beginning. After the first week's training, two of the Mayan women, who had been quite engaged throughout the five days, left without any explanation, leaving us alone with our speculations. Within the next two and a half years five others also stopped attending. Some of them changed jobs, others left the country and there were those who could not participate anymore, since it required too much time away from their employment.

In the end, a group of 15 people participated more or less regularly throughout the two and a half year period, four men and eleven women.

The Theoretical Background of the Training

The training course of group supervision was based on the theoretical principals of Group Analysis, a theory and method that had been founded by Sigmund Heinrich Foulkes, a German-Jewish refugee, who had been forced into exile, fleeing from Nazi Germany to Great Britain in 1933. At the beginning of the Second World War, he worked in the psychiatric ward of a clinic in Northfield, England, caring for traumatized British soldiers, suffering under the effects of "shell-shock," the terror of war. Since he had so many patients suffering from the same horrifying experiences, he decided to offer therapy in a group. He thought this would be more economical, more efficient and beneficial for the healing process, since all of his patients showed similar symptoms and could share their experiences not only with their therapist, but with each other as well.

These experiences in the clinic with traumatized soldiers of the Second World War inspired Foulkes later on to develop a Group Analytic concept, mainly relying on the principals of psychoanalysis, but eventually adding ideas and elements of other theoretical concepts as well (Foulkes, 1983).

Initially Foulkes parted from Freud's idea that group dynamics work according to a concept that he had developed in his famous study about "Mass Culture and Ego-Analysis" (GW, XIII). Foulkes did agree with Freud that group dynamics always reflected the group's "transference" onto the conductor, producing an illusion of love and a lack of emotional control, associated with "regression." Through this transference process, the group empties itself of all emotions, which are redirected on to the conductor and falls back into a regressive and passive state of mind and of emotion. The conductor thus changes into an idealized, omnipotent figure, nourishing the fantasy that only he or she is able to rescue the group.

But in contrast to Freud, Foulkes (1964) saw multiple transference processes in action, some directed toward the conductor and some placed upon other members of the group. He was convinced that these transference processes were influenced by a variety of social, cultural and psychological factors that could not be understood by a merely psychoanalytic perspective. This was especially true for his understanding of group processes. Foulkes (1983) did not consider the group to be an undifferentiated conglomeration of people. He understood it as an agglomeration of individuals, insisting, at the same time, that a group was more than just a mere summation of individuals as (Slater, 1966) already had addressed.

According to Foulkes (1964), each group had a specific life on its own. This "matrix" influenced every person involved and vice versa. Consequently, he looked at the individual not as an isolated, but as a social human being by nature and, as such, always in connection to others. Foulkes now could explain why every change of an individual within the group affected every other member and the group as a whole. Theoretically, this meant that changing one element had an effect upon all other elements in the system.

This is one of the main differences between a group analytic concept of understanding and a psychoanalytic approach to the comprehension of group processes.

To conduct a session with group analytic tools is therefore an ambitious task, because the role and the task of the conductor change dramatically. In a dual psychotherapeutic situation, the professional always has a prominent position, whereas in a group analytic situation the conductor is considered to be an important person on the edge of the group, taking care of its boundaries, making sure that there is always a protected and safe space available to work in, thus being a safeguard, maintaining the rules and regulations within the group context.

Foulkes (1964) once compared the function of a group conductor with his musical counterpart in an orchestra. But this metaphor fits only at first sight, because this image is connected with a strong dominating, male position, aimed at training an orchestra to play together beautifully, erasing all mistakes and erroneous notes. This, however, is in no way the aim of group analysis, which is interested principally in the irritations that arise out of any group's communicative and interactive efforts to understand each other. This is not achieved by suppressing irritations or misunderstandings, but by allowing them to surface and then carefully uncovering the reasons for their existence. Only an error-accepting and accommodating attitude will aid in understanding unconscious anxieties and desires within a group. Therefore, group analysis is not a training technique designed to reach a perfect harmony or to overcome all dissonance. On the contrary, it is a proven and complex instrument created to explore these dissonances and their roots.

From a feminine perspective another image would be preferred. That of a midwife helping the group to explore its hidden issues, inhibitions and anxieties, examining and exploring obstacles, bearing pain and sharing hard labor that always connects to creative processes. Giving birth to new awareness, we find new ways of understanding, thus paving the way for real change, new insights and a more satisfying method of relating to oneself and others.

Group analysis wants to strengthen people's potential to resolve their conflicts in a more productive and creative way and to be more in touch with one's own and other people's desires. Group experiences always work on an individual as well as a group level. Therefore, Foulkes' notion of multiple transference processes is one of the key issues of group analysis, because it helps to explain the effectiveness of the therapeutic group process. Of course, there are numerous controversies concerning the effectiveness of group analysis and there cannot be any doubt that there are limitations of the method. Not all patients (for example psychotic patients) can be treated in a group, no matter what instruments would be used.

It is easy to understand that multiple transference processes are quite effective and that they are quite a powerful tool in dealing with the complexity of group dynamics. There are simply more options offered to understand and gain insight. However, that is not the only reason for the effectiveness of group analysis. Another reason comes from the fact that these multiple transference processes are always connected to specific experiences of group reality. When transference processes of sibling rivalry occur in a group, one can be sure that participants do not accept these transference emotions like a conductor would, interpreting these emotions, reacting in an accepting way, staying calm and at a certain distance. Group members will react in a different way, since they might feel attacked and therefore are inclined to reject these transference emotions, responding with aggression and maybe even with fearsome attacks. Therefore, there is always a two-fold process of transference and of real life-experiences happening in the group at the same time, thus increasing the effectiveness and the benefit of group analytic therapy. Group Analysis is training in action.

Clinical Illustration

The young man, who always left whenever he had strong, emotional experiences in the training group, hardly reacted to my interventions concerning his attitude of leaving. Usually he simply left without excusing or even announcing his forthcoming absence, producing a lot of annoyance in the group. One day, one of the psychiatrists told him, in a very friendly, but firm tone of voice that she wanted him to stay in the group; she felt disturbed, irritated and frustrated and she simply wanted him to be there. This had quite an impact on him, he did not leave the training as often as before and when he left, he would announce it.

This intervention was quite effective, because he could hear and feel not only her concern, but also her anger and he could, in part at least, react to her desire, to have him in the group and be less defensive.

From a group analytic perspective, she did not only speak for herself, but she dared to pronounce a desire that most surely others in the training group felt as well, but did not dare to pronounce. She spoke for herself, but also for the group and even for me as group conductor and this made her intervention so psychotherapeutically effective.

This concept of group analysis as developed by Foulkes differs from essential notions of psychoanalysis, but without overthrowing core psychoanalytic issues like the unconscious, just including more social psychological and systemic ways of understanding group processes. To illustrate these differences once again, but in a more tangible manner, it helps to look at the famous Russian matryoshka dolls.

Freud would look at the Russian doll as the perfect image of an individual, detecting in every one of the Russian dolls another one and the further he would search, the more dolls he would find, one hidden inside the other one. Freud's thinking revolved around a model of intra-psychic processes, which is still the core of psychoanalytic theory and practice. But Foulkes would take the Russian doll, pull them all out and put them in a circle, then watching what would happen between them and the conductor and between each one of the dolls. He externalized the intra-psychic processes Freud had been talking and writing about (the topographic model) and tried to investigate what was happening on an inter-personal and inter-psychic level. Foulkes (1964) was interested in the communicative and interactive dynamics, developing in the group, always understanding them as an externalization of intra-psychic processes of the individuals involved, now being mirrored and acted out in the group.

He looked at these processes from five different perspectives: They represented according to his understanding:

- dimensions of society (the social class, ethnic background, organizational realities)
- dimensions of the family (biographic material, significance of parents and siblings)
- dimensions of the psychic reality of the individual (projections, introjections, resistances, etc)
- images of the body (who is the head of the group, the heart?)
- the archaic unconscious (culture, legends, myths).

To reach this complex way of understanding, Foulkes had to revert to the findings of social psychology as outlined by Norbert Elias in his famous book about the "The Civilizing Process" (Elias, 1994) and to more philosophical and sociological thoughts as outlined by Adorno, Marcuse and Horkheimer. He also benefitted from the works of the psychoanalysts Balint (1957) and Bion (1961) and from new findings in neuroscience. Goldstein (1995) had experienced in his practice that patients, who had lost one of their eyes, would eventually learn to substitute the loss of the one eye with an amplified way of looking at the world with the other eye. The brain helped to substitute the deficiency, by expanding the functions of the other eye. Foulkes (1986) took up these thoughts, applying them to his understanding of group processes. Now he could explain why any group would always establish a dynamic matrix of the ongoing group process, the group functioned like a brain: If there was an individual's neurotic conflict that had to be resolved the whole group, and each participant, would in different ways be involved in this process and finally benefit from the group's efforts to find a resolution. There was never just one individual benefitting from the group, but the group always benefitted from each individual as well.

This theoretical concept not only works in a clinical and psychotherapeutic setting, but can be applied in a supervisory setting as well.

The Concept of the Training

It took altogether five years before the first group analytic training course of supervision could start in September of 2005 in Guatemala. I was entrusted with the task to work out a design for the training in group supervision in cooperation with Dr Vilma Duque, a dedicated Guatemalan psychologist, who turned out to be the heart of the project. Since I spoke Spanish, it was not necessary to work with a translator; however, the theoretical readings and the learning exercises had to be translated into Spanish. As it was not possible to rely on any books or articles about supervision that had been published in Central or South America, some books from Spain were copied for all participants.

The theoretical design of the training was basically group analytic. Since supervision does not share the clinical intentions of psychotherapy, even though it applies the same theoretical and methodological tools, some changes had to be introduced: To apply group analysis in the field of supervision and in a cultural foreign context, it is necessary to focus strongly on the dimension of society (ethnic, social, political, historical and institutional level), whereas the dimension of the family and the individual as well as the dimension of the body have lesser significance. But the dimension of the archaic unconscious again is important, because here cultural images, as represented in legends, mythology, fairy tales, songs, poems and literature can be used to clarify hidden issues in supervisory case work. Additionally, and due to the conflict burdened history and presence of Guatemalan society, methods of conflict resolution like mediation were introduced, as well as elements of organizational consultancy. Special attention was also paid to team supervision and to the history of the development of group theories.

The training did not include experiential elements. They would have been helpful, of course, but since the GTC would not finance two trainers, it was not possible to mix the role of a teacher and trainer and a group therapist. However, some of the participants had previous experiences of psychotherapy.

The training courses took place in six five-day sessions, spread out over a period of two and a half years. They ran from Monday to Friday, 9am–5pm, in a beautiful colonial style villa in Guatemala City, with plenty of coffee and refreshments during the breaks, and a delicious lunch at noon on the terrace under a huge avocado tree.

The morning sessions were all dedicated to theory and methodological questions, as well as to learning exercises, to present difficult theories in a more digestible form. The afternoon sessions were exclusively dedicated to case work.

A. Theoretical introduction	B. Casework: Life supervision
1. What is supervision and how does it work? 2. Historical developments of group theory therapy. 3. Essentials of Psychoanalysis and Group Analysis. 4. Common grounds and differences. 5. Team supervision. 6. Forms of intervention in group supervision. 7. Supervision and mediation.	The afternoon sessions were life-supervisions focusing on casework and issues brought in and discussion by the participants. Sometimes these were enriched with casuistic evaluations. For example: psychological mechanisms were explained with the help of material that had been discussed.
At the end of the training, the film "Babette's Feast" (1987) was presented and discussed as if it was a case that had been brought in for supervisory discussion.[11]	

[11] Babette's Feast is a famous Danish film, based on a story by Isak Dinesen (Karen Blixen) that brings to life, group processes with all its different features and helps to understand psychological defense mechanisms, like regression, resistance, suppression of desire, projection, projective identifications etc.

C. Supervisory experiences and supervision in a group	D. Self-organized theoretical control discussion
After the first block of the training, participants were expected to start with supervisory processes on their own, organizing a continuous process/supervision in a group.	Planned self-organized discussion groups in intervals between the training blocks. This never worked though, since controlled autonomous learning is not widely applied in Guatemala.
E. Feedback by e-mail	
Feedback by e-mail was also offered. This worked on rare occasions, but was not used as frequently as had been hoped for and promised.	

The Structure and Contents of the Training

Training Course – No. 1

What is Supervision and How Does it Work?

What is supervision? Supervision is a specific method of counseling, analyzing and reflecting the dynamics of working relationships. It is not a "little sister" of psychotherapy, because supervision is not concerned with biographical issues of the participants. Relationships with parents, sisters and brothers are not explored and supervision does not try to uncover infantile psychological conflicts. Instead, supervision does focus exclusively on working relationships, especially on relationships between professionals and their clients. In team-supervision relationships and/or conflicts between colleagues and between professionals and their superiors are being explored. The aim is always to try to find out what is the hidden issue that people in a group, the group-as-a-whole, or the team, is struggling with, using the group as a resonance body to mirror the conflicts, the participants are talking about. By doing this, the supervisor will always focus on the here-and-now of the group, trying to understand the conflict between a participant and his or her client, just being mirrored and acted out as a scenic play in the group.

How does it work? By establishing a secure space and a setting with well-defined boundaries, applying group analytic theory and techniques for the interpretation of group dynamics and by relying on a conductor, who is capable of containing the process and promoting confidence in the group's own resources. The primary focus of attention is the case, a critical incident that has been experienced by one of the participants in a working context and which is offered for discussion. After the case has been presented, the supervisor will invite the group to describe their observations, their thoughts and feelings, encouraging the participants to freely express what they might have observed or what caused irritations. The supervisor might point out some contradictions or hidden issues that were noticeable, until finally closing up the case, summarizing the results of the discussion. Maybe new perspectives on managing a case had developed and professional strategies to work with a client could now be reviewed and changed, but perhaps the reflection of the case just helped to relax and feel reassured that the professional strategies applied in this case were adequate and more could not be accomplished.

What are the historical roots? Historical roots date back to social casework and to clinical applications of psychotherapy. Throughout the great depression in the USA (around 1930) social workers dealing with impoverished families were increasingly confronted with misery and suffering that were hard to bear and even harder to deal with. Some of them decided to get together and share their experiences with colleagues, to be able to stay healthy themselves and be able to continue and offer support to the families they worked with. This was one of the roots of supervision, which was professionalized later on, relying on an expert, a counselor, who would act as an independent, but reliable person from the outside, coming at regular intervals to counsel the social workers, thus helping them to professionalize their case work and avoid burn-out.

Around the same time, Freud established a network of friends and colleagues to share his experiences with psychotherapeutic cases and theoretical ideas. He eventually came to the conclusion that psychotherapy needed an external control. To explore psychic structures and to deal with unconscious conflicts was quite a risky affair and therefore needed an external advisor. Until today, any psychotherapeutic training, no matter what theoretical background, always will be accompanied by years of clinical supervision, to ensure that the future psychotherapist will not damage his patients, or himself.

Supervision therefore has two roots, the case work of social workers and clinical psychotherapy.

In which fields is it applied? Supervision today is essential within all psychotherapy professions, but also within psychiatry and in all medical professions, as well as in many profit and non-profit organizations. This, of course, depends strongly on where, and in which, countries supervision takes place. Within the USA and in central and northern Europe supervision it is very well known and applied in almost all social, educational, medical and ecclesiastical fields of work. Outside these countries, supervision is usually only applied in clinical professions; for example, in Germany almost all social workers and many teachers and directors of social institutions are involved in supervisory work and supervision has turned out to be a profession all on its own.

What forms of supervision do exist? There are essentially three types:

1. Supervision of a single person, sometimes also closely related to coaching, especially if it is asked for in profit organizations.
2. Supervision of a team of colleagues (i.e. team-supervision).
3. Supervision of a group of professionals, coming from different institutions and a different professional background, also called Balint-Group.

What are the formal requirements? Supervision needs a secure and protected space, continuity, a set rhythm of reliable times, an agreement of confidentiality and a contract to keep to the rules that have been agreed upon in the beginning (for example, abstinence), including to pay the supervisor on a regular basis, to participate regularly, to announce any unavoidable absence, and not to take drugs or arrive intoxicated when coming to the sessions.

What is the role of the supervisor? The supervisor is a professional with a sound background of either psychotherapeutical or specific supervisory training experiences, responsible for the boundaries, space, time, rules and regulations, which are necessary to establish supervision. He or she stays on the edge of the group, intervenes only when it is necessary and supports and accompanies the individual's or the group's struggle to analyze, reflect and finally understand the conflicts or critical incidents presented. A supervisor helps the group or the individual with his theoretical and methodological tools to find adequate answers to the questions that have been raised. Only very rarely will he or she give direct answers.

Supervision Case

After the first training week some started with their own supervisory experiences:

One of the female participants had been asked to start a supervision group with policemen. When she arrived at the police department, a friendly group of policemen awaited her and she explained what supervision is, how it works and then asked them what they wanted to talk about. First the group talked about their job, long hours, difficult clients and bad pay. Soon they started to get into a heated discussion about a slogan that was popular between them: "A good thief is a dead thief." Some agreed and some thought this was an awful thing to think and to say, and soon some started accusing the others of being bad policemen, aggressively attacking each other. The supervisor feared that one of them would draw a pistol and start shooting, so she broke off the supervision and simply left the room and hurried home.

That was the end of any further supervision efforts with this group of clients.

In the training we came to the conclusion that this was too big a challenge for a beginner and probably not even a case for supervision. These policemen needed capacity building and specific training, but not supervision.

There were obviously tremendous anxieties in this group of policemen, perhaps even enhanced by the presence of a female supervisor. Therefore, they unconsciously reverted to a "murderous" image, presenting themselves as dangerous men, thus "killing" the supervision and saving themselves from any further attempts to reflect upon their professional actions, behavior and their relationship amongst themselves.

Training Course – No. 2

Historical developments of group theory and therapy

In this training course, we focused upon historical developments of group theories, starting with Freud, continuing with Lewin, Bion, Balint, Schindler and Foulkes, trying to point out differences as well as similarities. Looking at the cultural background of these authors and the historical and political evolution of their theories it became evident that all of them had a transcultural heritage. Participants of the training connected easily to the idea that all of the group therapists mentioned were refugees, and that early in Latin America, in Argentina, a group of psychotherapists (Grinberg, Rodriguez and Langer, 1957) had already applied group analysis in the 1950s very successfully, even with factory workers. It was important to draw attention to political and transcultural elements of group analytic theory (Dalal, 2002), thus contributing to the acceptance of a group analytic-orientated supervision training in a non-European country, and in a post-war society like Guatemala. These refugee biographies influenced to a considerable degree the elaboration of group theories, focusing strongly on social, cultural and political issues and not only on the individual.

Freud's model of mass-psychology mirrors his understanding and knowledge of the individual, of its intra-psychic forces that govern its soul, transferred upon a mass of people, reaching a surprising depth of understanding, but not really crossing psychoanalytic borders to reach a broader and not only intra-psychic understanding of group processes. Whereas Lewin (1947) like Freud, concerned with the mass hysteria under Hitler in Germany, asked himself what are the forces behind dictators like Hitler, who seem to be able to manipulate masses of people, transforming individuals to blind followers of a faith or a political ideology. He set up an experiment with groups of ten-year old boys, who had to fulfill certain tasks first under the guidance of a democratic, then an authoritarian, then a laissez-faire leader. It proved that the groups under the guidance of a democratic leadership were most productive and creative, fulfilling their tasks with pleasure and to the utmost satisfaction. In contrast, the groups under the authoritarian rule only worked whenever they were forced to and behaved aggressively within the group. The laissez-faire group was not at all able to fulfill its task and behaved as if it had been abandoned.

Lewin, who was considered a pioneer of social psychology and the founder of Gestalt-therapy, was able to separate Freud's model and show how different styles of leadership influence the behavior of a group and its members. Bion (1961) also has to be considered a pioneer of group theory and practice. He was very much concerned with the question of how group dynamics developed and how they could be explained and understood. Through his psychotherapeutical practice and his experiences with patients in a group, he came to the conclusion that group dynamics could be understood as an expression of basic assumptions:

Of dependency – of fight and flight – of pairing

- If the group process revolves around issues of dependency the group hopes to be saved by an almighty figure, the conductor (a God), the group feels very dependent, passive and overwhelmed by infantile desires.
- The group, that is concerned with fight and flight, is trying to avoid a conflict with the conductor, (the administration, an organization, a project, a superior) either by getting rid of him or her, or by taking refuge, themselves, challenging the setting.
- The group, that produces processes of pairing (two or more persons), is concerned with hope and utopian desire and illusion, feeling creative and productive, hoping that a Messiah (an idea) will be born out of the group. Pairing, a defense mechanism, helps to control anxieties and fears of a breakdown or an ending of the group.

Bion's understanding of group processes introduced the idea of the group-as-a-whole, but in contrast to Freud he did not try to apply the individual's intra-psychic structure as a model to explain group dynamics. Instead he invented the idea of basic assumptions, thus helping to understand group processes from within, but with the eye of a psychotherapist.

Balint (1957), a student of Ferenczi and a psychoanalyst from Hungary, having fled like Freud, and Bion, into exile to Great Britain, developed the idea of a group of medical doctors, coming together to talk about their patients, discussing difficulties, disturbances and irritations in their relationships with their patients in order to understand, also on the level of the unconscious, their physical suffering and pain. The idea of the Balint-Group was born, one of the most well-known forms of supervision until today. The core of Balint's concept is the idea that the unconscious issue between the professional coming into supervision and his or her client will be mirrored within the relationship of supervisor and client. The classical model of Balint-group is centered upon the idea of a case that is being presented for discussion in supervision. What is ignored is the internal dynamic of the group. Only the case counts and nothing else will be considered.

Schindler (1957–58) looked at groups more from a social dynamic point of view, insisting that there are four basic positions, that determine the behavior of human beings in a group. He called the central figure "Alpha," the representative of a group's initiative, with whom all other members of the group, the "Gamma" – individuals, will identify. Thus Alpha turns out to be a secret leader of the group. Alpha represents the identity of the group and invites all other Gammas to identify with him or her as an aggressor. This functions because this allows the Gammas to become norm setters on their own. Gammas are like a mirror of the unconscious projections of Alpha, expressing Alphas, hidden or suppressed desires. These identifications with the aggressor are usually used to rally against the weakest members in the group, the Omegas. Omegas search for a safe space, identifying with the enemy of the group. Omegas thus turn out to be the representative of the enemy of the group; they are the ones, who will break rules and norms.

Schindler looked at group processes from an individual's point of view, elaborating different roles that members of a group might take at different phases of the group, but he did not take into account the group-as-a-whole or the group's dynamics deriving from internal conflicts.

Foulkes (1964, 1983) in his exile in Great Britain was familiar with these authors and most surely knew their writings and their ideas about groups. Because Foulkes benefited in many ways from the writings of Lewin, Schindler, Balint and Bion and, in addition, to the contacts he had in Germany with Elias, Adorno, Horkheimer, Marcuse, Fromm and Goldstein, he systematically included social structures in his efforts to understand unconscious dynamics of group processes. Foulkes finally managed to combine both an individual's and group's perspective, considering the individual with its specific intra-psychic structures and the group-as-a-whole with its specific group dynamics at the same time. However, Foulkes insisted that the individual is always a social being whose individual psychic structures will be reflected in the way this individual relates to significant others. These relationships are always a mirror of the individual's disturbances, as well as its hidden anxieties and desires. To analyze the modes of interaction and communication and their unconscious expressions in a group thus helps to understand an individual's neurosis.

Foulkes' model of group analysis therefore is very beneficial for any group supervision, because it allows us to use the group as an instrument to analyze unconscious processes happening in the here-and-now of the group. These theoretical models were discussed and applied to the Guatemalan situation, trying to figure out, which theory can explain what kind of political, social and cultural experience and which elements help to understand the working experiences of the participants.

> ### Supervision Case
>
> After the second block training another experience with supervision was reported:
>
> Two female participants from the training group had been asked by a women's shelter organization for supervision. When they arrived, they saw a nice new building, very modern, brightly painted, the doors guarded by armed policemen. Three social workers were working there and they were eager to start. They did not want any explanations, they immediately started to talk about their clients, the violence these women experienced and how difficult their job was. They went on to explain how sad and depressive they felt, realizing how little they could do for these women. Then one of their mobile phones rang, a screaming woman on the other end, crying out loud, that her husband was trying to kill her and that she needed help immediately. The social workers grabbed their bags, one of them still on the phone, asking for the address of the victim and then all three of them rushed out of the door, jumping into a cab and off they went leaving the two supervisors abandoned in the building. When the supervisors noticed that they were alone in the shelter, they panicked and left as hurriedly as they could, jumping in the first cab that came along and went home.
>
> They said that they were overwhelmed with anxieties and fears and as soon as they arrived at home, they shut all the doors and windows.
>
> They felt threatened, persecuted and extremely helpless.

Discussing this case, we came to the conclusion that supervision under these circumstances is not possible, since minimum standards of a safe and protected space to work in, did not exist. We suggested that it might be a healthy move for the three social workers to leave their office and meet for supervision in a place offered by the supervisors and then clarify the working conditions, such as, mobile phones should be shut off during supervision to enable an emotional and psychological space to talk about difficult experiences.

At the end, the two supervisors said they could not imagine working with these three professionals, because the issues they talked about were too frightening and they feared they would be unable to keep their professional attitude and composure.

This case very clearly showed a fight or flight situation and that supervision needs not only a safe and protected space to work in, but also adequate working conditions, to be able to reflect, without any outside disturbances, about the existing and difficult relationships with clients. Additionally, the case illustrated transference and countertransference processes in action, producing in the supervisors all the emotions that the endangered women felt: abandonment, panic, fears, anxieties, the feeling of being threatened, persecuted and to feel alone and helpless.

Probably these same transference feelings drove the three social workers to always just act and react, without ever finding a space to reflect.

Training Course – No. 3

Essentials of psychoanalytic and group analytic theory

Since the essentials of psychoanalytic and group analytic theory have already been discussed, it is now important to concentrate on techniques and upon the question: how knowledge and understanding of basic elements of psychoanalysis, as well as group analysis, were transmitted in the training.

At first it seemed quite a challenge to convey knowledge and understanding of basic psychoanalytic and group analytic principles to participants, who had hardly any previous knowledge of psychoanalytic or group analytic theory and method, much less psychotherapeutic experiences on their own. Two examples dealing with the unconscious and with resistance might illustrate our approach:

First we referred to a theoretical scheme explaining modes of communication developed by a German scientist, Friedemann Schulz von Thun (1998), a scheme that would allow a faint glimpse of the unconscious. According to von Thun, there are at least four different levels in every communicative interaction:

- a factual message
- a relationship-oriented message
- a self-explorative message
- a message of appeal.

He called this the four–ear model:

Example

A man comes home from work, very weary, lies down on the couch in front of the TV and says to his wife: "I am so thirsty".

Anybody in command of the English language will be able to understand this sentence.

The factual message on this level of communication is clear: "I am thirsty."

On the level of the relationship between this man and his wife, he insinuates: "Darling, I have worked so hard today and I bring home the money, therefore it's your duty to serve me. I need something to drink."

On the self-explorative level the message implies: "Darling, I am so tired and I don't feel like getting up from this comfortable couch, but I would love to have a nice, cold beer, please get me one."

On the appeal level he says: "Darling, please bring me a beer."

This scheme helps to introduce a glimpse of the unconscious, clarifying that a message always has different meanings, depending on the social and emotional circumstances of the speaker. Supervision always tries to unravel these different meanings, offering different possibilities for understanding a working hypothesis, which has to be clarified further in the developing process of supervision.

In our training, the participants were now asked to work in small groups and think about examples they had experienced to clarify this scheme even more. One group chose an example from our training that they interpreted according to the above mentioned model, referring to a sentence I once had said:

> **Example**
>
> As the majority of participants would come in late in the morning, I said:
> "I thought we had agreed upon a 9 o'clock to start with our work. I am not able to work well under these conditions."
>
> The factual message is: "We had agreed upon 9 o'clock to start with our work."
>
> On a relationship oriented level this meant: "You don't keep to our agreement. Are there any doubts concerning the time to start our program? You make it difficult for me to work well."
>
> On a self-explorative level it meant: "I feel quite frustrated and in my role as a trainer not taken seriously. Under these circumstances, I am not able to do a good job."
>
> On an appeal level it meant: "Please come on time and keep to our agreement. I would like to do an excellent job for you."

These examples helped to understand that there are always different messages hidden behind any statement and that it is the aim of group analytic supervision to bring to the surface these hidden meanings.

Resistance Besides the "unconscious" we also dealt with other mechanisms, for example, resistance. It was first explained on a theoretical level. Resistance has to be considered quite an important issue in supervision, because resistance will manifest itself in any given process and has to be dealt with on a professional level. Resistance is always significant, because it points to unconscious anxieties, difficulties and inhibitions of the client that he or she might not be aware of, but that cannot be expressed in any other way. So resistance always has to be taken seriously and should not be ignored. This is one of the most important rules in dealing with groups, teams or individuals in supervision as well as in therapy.

Resistance can have different meanings:

- When changes are frightening, resistance serves to keep up the status quo.
- Resistance might be a creative, but desperate option to express something that cannot be expressed in any other way.
- Resistance should never be suppressed.
- Resistance always points to a hidden, but not yet available option for change and development.

Therefore it is important to realize that: supervision tries to work with the resistance and not against it.

> **Example**
>
> It turned out to be a very productive experience, when I managed to handle the group's resistance coming late in the morning in a less reproachful manner, by saying: "It seems very difficult for you to come on time at 9 o'clock in the morning. I wonder why?"
>
> Without hesitation they agreed that it was difficult for them to arrive on time and then started telling me, why they almost always were late: one of the participants had just been robbed of her cell-phone. Another one had to get off the bus, because heavily tattooed young men entered the vehicle, probably gang members, ready to rob and steal, whatever they could get. Another one talked about a car accident, she had been involved in.

This approach, to working with the resistance and not against it, opened up new perspectives of understanding and of trust, because now they started to share some of their heartfelt reality with me and the others in the group. This produced confidence and, at the same time, diminished their anxieties concerning this new training program.

Therefore in supervision:

- It is important to recognize and accept resistance, because it is like a locked door that cannot be opened by force, but only with a lot of caution, taking care that nobody will be hurt.
- Resistance usually has nothing to do with the supervisor and should not be taken as an attack on his or her integrity.
- For any supervision, it is important to deal in a creative and productive way with resistance. This might be a model for the team, maybe even for the organization on how to deal with difficulties and different forms of resistance.

Of course, coming late is quite a common form of resistance, but this does not mean, that there are not many other forms of resistance to consider. For example:

- Clients keep on asking for more information about the qualifications and credentials of the supervisor.

- They keep on questioning the methods used.
- They seem to agree a lot, but then keep on having doubts: "yes . . . but"
- They maintain that problems have an unalterable social, political and historical background and they cannot be changed by any means.
- They keep projecting blame by always insisting that it is the fault of others and that the existing problem has nothing to do with their own performance at work.
- They want a prefabricated solution and are not interested in the process itself.
- They have already solved all problems on their own and now there are no more difficulties to be discussed.
- They agree with everything the supervisor says.

This list is only an example of a few standard situations that illustrate various forms of resistance which may occur in any supervisory process. There are many expressions of resistance. Groups as well as individuals are usually very creative when it comes to devising sophisticated forms of dissent.

The training group was, therefore, asked to look for examples of resistance they had experienced in their working practice, discuss them in a small group and later on present their results in front of the entire group.

The task was to describe how they had managed the situation and what kind of strategy had been used. If their approach had not worked, they were asked to explain why, elaborating different options on how the situation could have been acted upon in a more creative and productive manner.

In the afternoon, case work was used to enhance the theoretical explanations offered in the morning session. The group was split, one half sitting in a circle in the center, the other half forming an outer circle around them, tasked with observing the following psychological mechanisms in action: resistance, regression, projection, mirroring, identification, introjection, pairing, sub-groups and resonance. The group sitting in the inner circle would discuss a case that a participant had presented and the observers had to notice when and in what situation they were able to recognize what kind of psychological defense mechanism was used. After closing the case, all observations were collected and a second term of case work started, then including and evaluating the findings of the observers.

This exercise helped, in almost all cases, to deepen the understanding of the hidden issues involved and to grasp on an experimental level the meaning and the feeling of psychological defense mechanisms.

Supervision Case

In between the third and the fourth training course an invitation had reached some of our participants to start supervision in a social organization.

The director had been worried, since a strong fluctuation amongst his employees weakened the organization and inhibited a high working output.

He decided that all of his 160 employees had to participate in a supervisory process. How could this be managed?

> We discussed several possibilities and came to the conclusion that out of the 160 employees 13 teams should be established, so 13 supervisors were needed. Each one would be responsible for one team unit. The supervisions were to take place once a month, for three hours on a Friday afternoon in a secure and safe space outside of the organization. Since this supervision was considered as part of their employment, it was mandatory for employees to participate.

Training Course – No. 4

Team diagnosis and organizational dynamics

Team-Supervision is considered to be one of the most difficult types of counseling, because it means bringing balance among supervision, organizational consultancy, team counseling and conflict resolution. Therefore it is important to clarify first, what is team-supervision and what is its aim and task in any given institution.

- Team-supervision is contracted when teams ask for a professional and systematic reflection of their working relationships, usually because there are conflicts that reduce their capacity to work. These conflicts might be located within the team, between the team and its clients, between the team and its superiors or the team and the organization. Since institutions are not created to satisfy human needs of their employees, but are created to fulfill specific tasks, team-supervision is asked to support or to increase the employee's capacity to work and to help them in fulfilling their professional objectives.
- Team-supervision never works within an isolated space, because it cannot be separated from the structures, culture and institutional realities of the organization. Team-supervision has to reflect this reality and take into account any changes that team-supervision might induce.
- Team-supervision always has to bear in mind the tasks it has to fulfill within the institution. This includes the study of relationship-oriented aspects or conflicts within the team or between single team-members or between the team and its superiors. These aspects cannot be treated in isolation from the reality of the surrounding organizational context.
- Team-supervision always offers an opportunity for institutional self-reflection with open results. If the organization rejects this potential, team-supervision will not function at all.

On the basis of this short introduction, the training group was asked to split up again and to work out a team diagnosis of a group in an institution, where they observed social workers, psychologists, psychiatrists, according to the following criteria:

- **Institutional realities and how does the team deal with them?**
  - What is the institutional task of the team?
  - Where and when do disturbances occur and how do they manifest themselves?
  - What are the expectations of the clients of the institution?
  - Are there contradictions between the task of the team and the expectations of the clients?

- Are the team-members identified with their institutional task?
- Are the organizational structures transparent?
- Is the distribution of tasks and roles clearly defined and is it acceptable?
- According to what criteria are resources distributed? Is the distribution transparent?
- Is the flow of information clearly regulated?
- How does the team deal with the existing relationships of power, with hierarchies, differences of status and payment?

Well-prepared with this diagnostic manual, the same small groups, which had worked out the institutional diagnosis, were now asked to evaluate a team process, which they had experienced as social workers, psychologists or psychiatrists, but now from the position of a (fictitious) team-supervisor, according to the following criteria:

- **Individuals in the team and their communication and interaction:**
  - Who spoke and who did not speak?
  - Who took over what role?
  - What relationships were observed?
  - What constellations existed in the team?
  - Were there any sub-groups? Any alliances? Outsiders?
  - Communicative culture: how were decisions made: in a democratic, in a non-transparent, in a friendly way?
  - Were there friends, pairs or enemies in the team?
- **Contents of the meeting, the "supervision":**
  - What did the participants speak about and what did they not address?
  - Which problem was first mentioned?
  - Which case was mentioned, but not put up for discussion?
  - Which case was offered for discussion?
  - What was mirrored in the case about the team?
  - What was mirrored in the team about the problem of the clients?
  - What was mirrored in the team about the organization and their conflict?
- **Interaction with the social worker, psychologist, psychiatrist (supervisors)**
  - Were there any specific circumstances accompanying the request for support? (late in the evening, on a weekend, very urgent).
  - Was it difficult to come to an agreement between the organization, the team and the social worker, psychologist, psychiatrist?
  - What was the expressed aim of the counseling?
  - Was there a secret agenda?
  - Who wanted help and support and who did not? Who took over a leading role in contacting the professional?
  - Who showed significant resistance? Who did not cooperate and why?

This manual proved to be very helpful in grasping the dynamics of the supervisory process and in concentrating on significant structures as they develop in any process of counseling.

> ## Supervision Case
>
> The supervision in the above mentioned social organization went exceptionally well.
>
> Many questions arose in the course of this process: Some of the teams kept on complaining about their superiors, bad working conditions, political threats, about being very afraid at times, because there were secret cars without license plates stalking them.
>
> It was difficult for many of the participants to accept and understand what supervision is about and what it is not about:
>
> For example, some of the supervisors were asked by several teams to write letters on their behalf to their superiors, telling them about their concerns and anxieties. The supervisors were not only ambivalent, but felt trapped inside of a serious conflict: They could comprehend the concerns of their clients and thought they were correct in demanding more protection and actions from their employers. At the same time, they felt very unsure if it was advisable to write letters on their behalf.
>
> We discussed the case at length, looked into their identifications and counter-transference reactions and finally at their impulses, wanting to help, needing to do something in order to protect their clients. They felt utterly helpless and insecure, because of not knowing what to do and if this was allowed or not by their role in supervision.
>
> Taking their wish to help seriously, we analyzed the possible effects of their desire to actually help and write these letters of reference. Would it not be better to inspire the teams to communicate on their own, thus supporting them in their desire to do something positive and to change things within their own organization?
>
> Yes, certainly, this would be an excellent suggestion! But, they felt very guilty, refusing to write these letters. We explored the matter a little more: Supervision is not action, but a method to empower clients to take destiny into their own hands. Why allow them to become dependent or passive? Politically speaking, not to write the letters, would help their clients to become more autonomous as individuals and teams in taking proper care of themselves. This argument convinced the training group not to act and the supervisors decided not to write any letters.
>
> Not to act turned out to be a difficult challenge for this group of politically motivated people, because now their doubts became obvious: is it really worthwhile to work as supervisors, not getting involved, just reflecting and analyzing complex situations? Will this really be effective and produce results?

Training Course – No. 5

Different forms of intervention

There are different forms of intervention which become relevant to any group analytic supervision. Those frequently used are listed below. They were presented, explained and discussed in the training. Afterwards, the group was divided into pairs and asked to work on at least five of these interventions looking into Guatemalan literature, films and songs, to find examples and discuss the effects these interventions had caused in this context.

- **To summarize**

Significant information will be emphasized. Less important information will be ignored.

For example, significant information is usually material that tends to suggest a potential solution of a problem, including precise questions and explanations concerning the emotional state of mind of the person involved. Less important information is trivial and has nothing to do with the case in question. Summarizing the information helps to structure the process of supervision.

- **To focus**

Within the material presented, priorities are pointed out by emphasizing or repeating and reinforcing certain aspects, thus drawing the attention to the core of the problem. This helps to steer the supervisory process.

- **To mirror**

To point out and repeat irritating formulations. This is a very effective way to draw the speaker's attention to the hidden meaning of his words that might have been mentioned unintentionally.

- **To support**

To understand and accept whatever is said. This helps to reduce anxiety and to create a friendly atmosphere.

- **To ask**

To clarify something, in order to understand more precisely a specific context.

- **To point to an issue**

To put into words a sensation or a hidden issue that can be felt, but not yet expressed verbally. This helps to promote an improved understanding of a problem.

- **To confront**

To point out blind spots. This helps to draw the attention to the unintentional effect of words and actions (it has an aggressive component).

- **To interpret**

To try to understand the unconscious message of a story or a plot, searching with utmost caution and very carefully for adequate words to express what might be the hidden issue. Interpretations are supposed to support the client in his effort to change perspectives, opening up new horizons of understanding. The aim of the interpretation is always to comprehend unconscious motivations and meanings.

- **To normalize**

To modify exaggerated demands thereby opening up new perspectives toward a more realistic approach.

- **To explain**
  To offer professional knowledge, thus helping to promote the solution of problems.
- **To moderate**
  To determine the direction of the process of supervision.
- **To examine and revise a working hypothesis**

To offer tentative interpretations of the problem that has to be examined, of the task that has to be elaborated and of the way the clients arrange their process of interaction and communication in the supervisory context. These tentative interpretations are the basis for any supervisory intervention. They should always be re-examined, varied or even discarded up, if additional material emerges that raises doubts or if the participants of the supervision reject the working hypothesis. This serves to reformulate the context of the problem.

Training Course – No. 6

Supervision and mediation – a tool of conflict resolution

Mediation is considered a very effective tool of conflict resolution. Considering the conflict burdened history and present state of Guatemalan society it was necessary to provide the participants with effective and powerful tools to deal with conflicts in their supervisions. First of all mediation was introduced and the five stages of the process were discussed:

STAGE 1: Opening statement

Purpose:

- Explain procedures and ground rules (structure, time, commitments, confidentiality)
- Discuss expectations
- Define roles and responsibilities

Techniques:

- Make contact with parties
- Balance communication
- Demonstrate competence and confidence

STAGE 2: Uninterrupted time

Purpose:

- Give each party equal opportunity to present from his/her point of view
- Mediator identifies key issues for discussion

Techniques:

- Listen for keywords, significant feelings
- Summarize
- Reformulate complaints

STAGE 3: The exchange

Purpose:

- Assist each party to understand how the other is affected by the situation
- Examine issues
- Identify underlying interests
- Move from positional statements to problem-solving

Techniques:

- Set agenda
- Paraphrase, mirror
- Translate, reframe, reformulate to open new perspectives
- Acknowledge to validate speaker
- Summarize to move process forward

STAGE 4: Building the agreement

Purpose:

- Develop options
- Explore possibilities using objective criteria

Techniques:

- Offer support to develop creative options, fantasies are allowed
- Moderate the process

STAGE 5: Writing the agreement

Purpose:

- Symbolic of shared commitment to resolution
- Memorializes specifics of agreement to reduce likelihood of future misunderstandings

Techniques:

- Support to verbalize the resolution

STAGE 6: Closing statement

Purpose:

- Acknowledge and reinforce efforts of parties
- Review results of mediation and follow-up procedures
- Formal closing on a positive note[12]

---

[12] The mediation process according to the San Diego Mediation Center.

While discussing this mediation scheme, it became clear that in many conflictual circumstances a more structured procedure is helpful, since this might help to maintain the composure of a supervisor and guide the group in trying to find a resolution to their disputes. For any supervision, Stage Two, uninterrupted time, and Stage Three, the exchange, are essential and might be deepened as well as extended to reach an understanding of the hidden issues.

For beginners, this mediation scheme is extremely helpful, because it offers more structure and orientation. Within the training group the participants were asked in small groups of three to apply this model to a conflict they had experienced either themselves or in their role as professionals and try to work it out according to this scheme. Later on results were presented to the entire training group. It turned out that this mediation approach was very helpful, especially when reviewing past conflicts they previously had tried to resolve, but at that time did not manage, since they simply did not have adequate tools at their disposal.

At the end of our training, the group was invited to watch a movie "Babette's Feast," which had been possible to acquire in a Spanish version, to enjoy images of a foreign culture: In a Danish village of fishermen in the 19th century, followers of an evangelical faith, encountered a female refugee from the revolutionary upheavals in France, who turned out to be a famous cook, spending her fortune to celebrate and share a luxurious meal with the villagers.

The film was treated like a turbulent case offering the opportunity to watch psychological processes and mechanisms in action as there were: suppressed desires and their negative social effects, seduction, anxieties, projections, regression, libidinous affects, shame, guilt and finally through a sumptuous feast and meal, the liberation of hidden and suppressed signs of love, and desire.

To enjoy a movie that was far from their own reality and be able to follow the plot and the process of interpretation with much empathy, showed how much the participants had gained through our training and how much they were capable of opening themselves to new perspectives, minimizing their anxieties, and developing at least some trust and confidence within themselves and within others.

Supervision Case

The supervision with the 160 employees of the social organisation prospered as well. All of them had resisted to writing letters on behalf of their teams. However, now, the teams seemed to have found ways to communicate their complaints to their superiors, and doing this in a way that their superiors were now able to listen to and even accept their critique. Things started to change:

- The cleaning women happily reported that there was not that much paper on the floors and that toilets were not that dirty any more.
- The group of the superiors reported that there were no more organized strikes in front of the building, but that employees would now come and talk to them.
- The employees received security trainings, enough toilet paper was supplied, as well as masks to avoid being infected, whilst working with dust and old documents.

- New hygienic standards were introduced as was a more transparent way of communication.
- Teams now said they felt like a family; supervisors learned there were parties on weekends and birthdays were celebrated within the institution.

Supervision worked, the culture within the institution had changed, there were fewer destructive conflicts, less sick-leaves and lower turnover and employees developed friendships and high standards of transparent communication with their superiors. There was more peace, trust and good working relationships developed as a result of the supervision. Therefore the director decided to extend the supervisory contract for one more year.

References and Bibliography

Balint, M. (1957). *The doctor, his patient and the illness.* London: Pitman.
Becker, D. (2006). *Die erfindung des traumas – verflochtene geschichten.* Berlin: Edition Freitag.
Bion, W. R. (1961). *Experiences in groups.* London, Tavistock Publications.
Bornschein, D. (2009). *In den tentakeln der macht. Vergangenheitspolitik im prozess der demokratisierung Guatemalas (1990–2007).* Mensch and Buch.
Bornschein, D. (2009). *In the tentacles of power: the Past in the process of democratization in Guatemala (1990–2007).* Berlin: mbv.
Comisión para el Esclarecimiento Historico – CEH. (1999). *Informe: Guatemala – Memoria del Silencio, Tomo1-12.* Ciudad de Guatemala, Guatemala.
Dalal, F. (2002). *Race, colour and the process of racialization.* East Sussex: Brunner Routledge.
Elias, N. (1994). *The civilizing process.* Oxford: Blackwell.
Figley, C. R. (1995). *Compassion fatigue: coping with secondary traumatic stress disorder in those who treat the traumatized.* New York: Brunner.
Foulkes, S. H. (1964). *Therapeutic group analysis.* London, Unwin.
Foulkes, S. H. (1971). *Dynamische prozesse in der gruppenanalytischen situation.* In Heigl-Evers, *Psychoanalyse und gruppe.* Göttingen.
Foulkes, S. H. (1983). (Original published, 1948). *Introduction to group analytic psychotherapy.* William Heinemann Medical Books. London: Karnac Books.
Foulkes, S. H. (1986). *Gruppenanalytische Psychotherapie.* Frankfurt am Main. Fischer.
Freud, S. *Mass culture and ego-analysis.* GW. XIII.
Goldstein, K. (1995). (Original published 1939). *The organism: a holistic approach to biology derived from pathological data in man.* New York: Zone Books.
Grinberg, L., Langer, M., & Rodrigué, E. (1971): *Psychoanalytische Gruppentherapie. Praxis und theoretische Grundlagen.* München, Kindler.
Jonas, S. (2000). *Of centaurs and doves – Guatemala's peace process.* Boulder.
Kernjak, F. (2006). *Tote suchen – Leben finden.* Exhumierungen in Guatemala. Historische ufarbeitung und psychosoziale Arbeit. Studien Verlag. Innsbruck, Österreich.
Kurtenbach, S. (2003). Guatemala: The blocked peace. In M. A. Ferdowsi, & V. Matthies (Eds.), *Comparative studies on the consolidation of peace processes in post-conflict societies* (pp. 302–319). Bonn.

Lewin, K. (1947). Frontiers in group dynamics, I. Concept, method and reality in social sciences; social equilibria and social change. *Human Relations*, 1(1), 5–41.
Mack, M. (2004). *Apuntes sobre los engranajes de la impunidad den casos de derechos humanos de Guatemala*. F & G Libros de Guatemala.
Molkentin, G. (2002). *Kriegsursachen und friedensbedingungen in Guatemala. Europäische Hochschulschriften. Reihe 31*. Frankfurt am Main.
Öttler, A. (2004). *Erinnerungsarbeit und Vergangenheitspolitik in Guatemala*. Vervuert. Frankfurt am Main.
Recuperación de la Memoria Histórica – REMHI. (1998). *Guatemala: Nunca más. Ciudad de Guatemala*. Oficina de Derechos Humanos del Arzobispado de Guatemala (ODHAG), Guatemala.
Schindler, R. (1957–58). Grundprinzipien der Psychodynamik in der Gruppe. *Psyche*, 11, 308–314.
Schulz von Thun, F. (1981). *Miteinander Reden. 1: Störungen und klärungen*. Reinbek bei Hamburg: Rororo.
Schulz von Thun, F. (1989). *Miteinander Reden 2: Stile, werte und persönlichkeitsentwicklung*. Reinbek bei Hamburg: Rororo.
Slater, P. E. (1966). *Microcosm*. John Wiley & Sons. New York, London, Sydney.
Torre Rivas, E. (2002). El desarrollo democrático a la luz de un lustro de paz: un balance preliminary. *In Revista Debate 51: A 5 años de la firma de la paz en Guatemala. Un balance critico*. FLACSO. Guatemala.
United Nations Development Programme, May (2009). (http://www.undp.org/execbrd/pdf/ADR-Guatemala.pdf). Accessed 24.05.2011.
Walker, T. W., & Armony, A. C. (Eds.). (2000). *Repression, resistance and democratic transition in Central America*. Wilmington, Rowman & Littlefield.

27
Group Psychotherapy for Patients with Psychosis: A Psychodynamic (Group-Analytic) Approach

Ivan Urlić

Introduction

A psychodynamic approach to patients suffering from psychosis

Psychosis occurs as a disabling process in the affective, cognitive and relational aspects of psychic life. The psychological problems are manifested in groups: psychotic disorder/processes are mirrored in the group and by the group. Diagnostic and therapeutic decisions aim to place the very disturbed patient in an appropriate group to optimize the recovery process.

A diagnosis can be verified in the group process. After the diagnosis is confirmed, a correlated group treatment plan can produce better results than individual work alone. It is, however, always important to remember that attainable treatment aims should be formulated along with specially tailored group interventions. Then the role of the conductor in such a group and what is expected from the consultant/supervisor can be clarified.

The focus of this chapter is on the nature of the psychotic process present in the group patient and specific ways of addressing the presenting problems associated with this highly disabling disorder.

The schizophrenic disorder is not a single illness. It may be said that the term "schizophrenia" covers an array of disturbances in the functioning of specific brain areas and their interconnectedness. These disturbances influence mind, behavior, cognition and social roles. While the core essence of the psychotic processes has not been clearly identified, certain common features regarding psychotic personality structure have become evident, especially in relation to reality-testing and interpersonal behavior, reflecting problems in the perception of the self and others.

Specific defense mechanisms prevailing in patients with psychotic disturbances include strong projections, primitive idealizations, fears of annihilation (mostly due to paranoid perceptions), dissociative phenomena, and splitting, denial and projective identifications. For patients functioning at the psychotic level, transferential and countertransferential issues play a very important and sometimes decisive role in establishing interpersonal contact between the patient and psychiatrist, the patient and other members of the therapeutic team and relationships with peers in group psychotherapy.

Biological and psychological research has identified the high-risk factors for the onset of psychosis. Specific studies have focused on predisposing, facilitating and precipitating factors (e.g., Rose, 1994; Howells and Guirguis, 1985; Cannon and Mednick 1993) but they still do not provide a clear etiological picture. Consequently, Boyle (1990) even wonders if schizophrenia may be just a scientific delusion. Many authors, on the contrary, stress the impact of the individual's biological and social background: a disturbance in the thinking process followed by difficulties in affectivity, interpersonal relationships, feelings of the self, will and psychomotor activity (Kanas, 1996). Additional difficulties include a number of social disturbances, inadequate self-care and overall disruption in the quality of life.

Symptom patterns, together with the degree of the intransience of the underlying biological factors, should affect the choice of therapeutic approaches to the schizophrenic patient as well as the roles that the group therapist will be able to play in his/her relationship with the patients. Prior family patterns will also influence the treatment plan. The development of a person as an individual is inseparable from the group from which he/she comes (Urlić, 1989; 1994). The individual receives a basic communication and interaction model from his/her primary family group. The first dyadic relationship, with the mother or motherly figure, represents the cornerstone of further development. During such development, relationships toward the environment are multiplied and transformed until a certain level of maturity is reached. In this way, the experience of oneself and one's own environment is gradually formed.

In reconstructing the emergence of a pathological state, we can follow two directions. The first focuses on the individual: we try to reach and experience him/her and his/her primary group, and observe the constructive and destructive situations in which he/she is involved. The other direction concerns the group, when we try to approach the individual through social communication. Both offer diagnostic and therapeutic possibilities.

The history of psychology, psychiatry and psychodynamics shows that the dyadic form was always the preferred approach to both the study of psychic phenomena and therapy. Writing about the long evolution of the psychotherapeutic approach to psychosis, Frieda Fromm-Reichmann (1953) mentioned that it took a decade to understand the patient, another decade to learn how to establish contact with the patient, and a third decade to use all of this knowledge and experience.

The therapeutic use of groups in the treatment of patients with psychosis began as early as the 1930s. However, it was only in the 1950s that clinicians recognized the advantages of a supportive group setting for schizophrenic patients. This approach was considerably facilitated by the development of psychopharmacotherapy. Skolnick (1994) points out the following:

> There are a multiplicity of meanings embedded in processes that culminate in breakdown, whether the breakdown is categorized as major depression, bipolar disorder, addiction, borderline disorder or schizophrenia. Meaning, relevant for the self of the patient, the family and the larger social system, is buried when the field of inquiry and action is reduced to the study and treatment of the patient's diseased or "chemically imbalanced brain." When individuals identified as mental patients do not respond to treatment and remain in states considered diseased or socially disruptive, they tend to become dismissed as mad and are stripped of a meaningful voice in the human community. (Skolnick, 1994: p. 241)

Accordingly, in the treatment of patients with psychosis it is important to apply a group setting starting from the hospital experience, as well as in transitional therapeutic institutions and outpatient conditions. The consideration of the value of group psychotherapy is primarily based on the view of a person as a being who is socially determined and intertwined. The therapeutic group may facilitate the surfacing of interpersonal problems but can also help us find clues as to how dysfunctional patterns began in the early family and were sustained. Kanas (1996) states the following:

> Both biomedical and psychosocial treatment approaches are necessary. Although antipsychotic medications are a major treatment intervention, not all patients with psychosis respond optimally to these drugs, and others do not take them on a regular basis due to serious side-effects. Therefore, counseling, individual, group and family therapy, and social services are important components of a complete biopsychosocial treatment plan. Given the characteristics of schizophrenia, group therapy would seem to be an especially valuable treatment modality, because its interpersonal nature offers the sheltered ambience for these patients to share ways of coping with their symptoms, to gain support and test reality in the here-and-now of the sessions, and to improve their ability to relate with other people (Kanas, 1996: p. 141).

What did not seem to be addressed were the particular effects that antipsychotic and other medications have on the various dimensions of the psychotherapy of schizophrenia, such as transference and countertransference, quality of relatedness and engagement, the therapeutic alliance, freedom of the expression of affects, ability to process interpretative interventions, and the development and depth of insight.

Medications are administered to decrease anxiety, the level of regression and cognitive disorganization, and to facilitate interpersonal contact between the patient and his/her environment. When the patient is stabilized, psychosocial treatment, including the creation of a therapeutic community, can promote recovery.

Understanding Changes in Psychotic Psychic Functioning

Reasons for introducing group methods in therapy

The medical records of patients suffering from psychosis usually indicate that during the adolescent or post-adolescent period, important changes in behavior, interests and communication occur. Hallucinations and aggressive behavior toward others or oneself (sometimes attempted or committed suicide is considered as the first manifest episode of psychosis) represent triggers for the first psychiatric hospital treatment experiences. Especially in cases of agitated and extremely fearful patients, the first contacts can prove to be decisive for later long-term therapeutic activities, resocialization, and cooperation between the therapist and patient.

While the first medical contact the acutely psychotic patient has is usually one-to-one, groups are also inevitably present: family, medical and social, including police, emergency medical service, etc. In keeping with the group mode, an acute psychiatric unit should be organized according to the principles of a therapeutic community. This means that the first phase of psychiatric intervention, the vertical one, includes the prospect of horizontalization, as is illustrated in the following case example.

Clinical Illustration

The patient was brought to the acute psychiatric unit accompanied by the emergency medical service and police because of openly aggressive behavior and threats to the lives of his parents. He was accusing them of intending to poison him and was also hearing voices telling him about their plans.

During the administration of antipsychotic medication, he was cursing the doctors and all the staff, whom he perceived as guilty for taking actions against his life. No reassuring words, explanations or acknowledgements of his extremely fearful feelings could soothe the patient's suffering. As the psychiatrist on duty, I took responsibility for the therapeutic team and was observed by everyone on the ward. I told the patient that I was responsible for his well-being and that we would talk about his fear after he calmed down. The patient was completely defiant. At that point, some other patients suffering from various types of psychoses told the newly admitted one to trust the doctor. The patient still looked defiant but now showed some surprise. Obviously, he was more influenced by what his peers were telling him than by what the treatment team was saying!

After becoming less frightened and in better contact with reality, he was very surprised when I asked him to come to my consulting room, which he did without any comment. We were able to talk about his fears that were provoked by his paranoid ideations and auditory hallucinations. He looked at a poster for an upcoming psychiatric event. The artist understood the essential element of psychiatric work as trying to help patients come out of their chaotic state of mind. What he created was black unstructured spots, reminiscent of the Rorschach test, and in the middle of the poster was the well-structured pattern of the board game Ludo. Pointing to the spots, the patient asked whether he used to be "like that." Then he asked: "And you, would like me to become like this?" He pointed to the structured patterns but relaxed his posture when I nodded.

Many patients through the years have responded in that way. The vast majority of them have become functioning members of the ward therapeutic community, then of inpatient groups and later of outpatient groups.

> **Clinical Illustration**
>
> From an inpatient group psychotherapy session for patients with psychosis:
>
> Lisa's dream: She is going to a party. Many of her friends will be there. She is curious to see whom she will encounter. In the next scene, she is meeting her friend (in actuality he suffers from schizophrenia and has attempted suicide several times) who greets her: "Hello, how are you?" In the dream, he is so normal. He is man of culture and very intelligent . . .
>
> After having related her dream, Lisa added that she is still puzzled and excited that a "crazy" person can feel so well and appear so normal. In the group discussion, many agreed that they sometimes felt normal and sick at the same time. That was a sign of hope for each of them. The therapist emphasized the importance of continuous cooperation with the therapeutic team. Many group members nodded.
>
> After a brief silence, Mary said that she would like to share her secret: she was divorced because she couldn't bear to live with a rigid man. She's had many partners since then. Her mother, a widow, says that women should not be alone. Comments in the group concerned difficulties in establishing more stable relationships within their families. Sometimes these difficulties resulted in the avoidance of close interpersonal contacts. One group member said that he felt good in this group because of his feeling of confidence in all the team members and the group.

Mutual trust building was the core element in enabling group members to disclose their difficulties in establishing secure and trustful relationships with important persons in their environment. The group members were becoming aware of the corrective emotional experience within the therapeutic group and could compare diverse kinds of experiences. This benefit is illustrated in Sebastian's dream.

> **Clinical Illustration**
>
> Sebastian relates his dream: In the dream, he wants to travel to France with a Croatian passport. The French do not let him enter the country because the document is not theirs. Then he returns to Croatia with a French passport and the Croatians do not accept it because it is not their document. He remains in a "no-man's land" and feels desperate. After a while, he adds that on the previous day he almost cried, although when he was a child his father told him that men do not cry.
>
> This dream and the previous clinical illustration reflect a diffusion of identity, a lack of more stable object relations and feeling lost in a "semi-structured" or chaotic world of one's own. Several group members could recognize some of their feelings in Sebastian's dream. Some developmental features that could

> bring about heightened vulnerability to a stress situation might be seen in Anna's and George's stories below, associations from their early childhood experiences.
>
> During the subsequent development of the group dynamics, Anna added her recollections that she was always good in school. Her mother sometimes would beat her for minor errors and Anna cried and screamed. Her mother used to say if she continued that way, she would become crazy.
>
> George said: "Does it mean if you protest, you're crazy?" He said he was angry at his father. His mother was 17 when she bore him. The father had his affairs, the mother hers. In his house, there were no rules . . . When he was 15, his father used to tell him about his relationships with women. George was in a state of confusion. He wanted his father and not his secrets (he was close to tears).
>
> Jane said that her mother became a widow after she was born and her father's brother married her. She learned that family secret when she was an adolescent. There was another secret in her family: her mother's sister had committed suicide. She asked why it was not possible to have more open and sincere talks inside the family.
>
> Julie said that her late mother was a seamstress. Her mother never asked Julie how she would like to have a dress done. Julie was always fat but her mother used to sew very tight dresses for her that she could barely pull on. Strange.
>
> At this point, the therapist asked who listened better to whom in this group? Through projections and identifications, it was possible to enhance insight into the patients' inner worlds and better understand their reactions to the "no-man's land," which represented an important element of their affective deficits. On the other side, the group members could express their basic trust in the therapeutic team and the group as having provided a new emotional experience inducing greatly increased freedom in a context of mutual confidentiality.

Group Psychotherapy Under Hospital Conditions

Despite extensive experience in the application of group psychotherapy for the treatment of psychotic disorders, the literature on the subject appears to be relatively meager. According to Hummelen (1994), this is more due to the vagueness of the concept of psychosis than to clinical practice. Such conceptual vagueness gives rise to differences in diagnostic criteria and therapeutic approaches, which in turn hinder comparison among particular groups of psychotherapeutic approaches in terms of their efficiency in the treatment of patients with psychosis. In any case, today it is impossible to imagine a psychiatric ward without various forms of group therapy in use as basic methods of treatment (Hummelen, 1994; Milders, 1994; Plante, Pinder and Howe, 1988; Sandison, 1994; Scheidlinger, 1997; Schlachet, 1989).

When group psychotherapy is applied under hospital conditions, it includes patients with a variety of psychiatric disorders. The number of indications for this kind of treatment is much greater under hospital than outpatient conditions. What seems to dominate current theoretical conceptualizations and therapeutic approaches may be regarded as a tendency toward positive eclecticism due to the increasing "emphasis on diversity and on the integration of diverse perspectives into one's own personal 'style' and perceptual gestalt" (Schermer, 1994: p. 11).

With regard to analytically oriented therapy, only "targeted or focal" therapy is predominantly applied under hospital conditions. Such therapy is aimed at eliminating the manifest picture of the disorder and establishing "meaningful and supportive interpersonal exchange and repair" (Yalom, 1985). It is more directed at current conflicts and less at the interpretations that relate the present state to the past, particularly childhood and adolescent experiences. However, the same can generally be said about the group psychotherapeutic approach to patients with psychosis under both transitional and outpatient conditions.

Agreeing with the tendency toward positive eclecticism, Kanas (1996) advocates an integrative approach that would include all the constructive elements from all types of approaches in the group psychotherapy of patients with psychosis. The strengthening of ego functions by means of group therapy, especially the possibility of feeling and testing reality, still remains the basic aim of this approach. In other words, coping with symptoms and improving interpersonal relationships should be constantly worked on as the basic aims of treatment. Along this way, psychopharmacotherapy and psychotherapy represent two parts of a whole, together with psycho-social interventions.

Since there is still no satisfactory conceptualization of psychosis and its etiology is most probably multifactorial, multidimensional thinking regarding a patient suffering from psychosis is preferred in clinical practice. Within this context, the psychoanalytic, that is, group-analytic approach, cannot represent the basic theoretical approach as with neurotic patients. It may be questioned for whom and why psychiatrists and other members of the therapeutic team learn about the psychodynamic approach to a patient with psychosis. First of all, it is to attempt to understand the patient – his psychotic transference that stimulates the therapist's countertransferential reactions – which should be contained in order to ease coping with the patient's psychotic states. From the clinician's standpoint, multidimensionality of the therapeutic approach to the patient with psychosis under both hospital and outpatient conditions should also include other types of treatment. This primarily refers to antipsychotic medication, family therapy and various social and rehabilitative interventions.

The integrative therapeutic approach to psychotic patients demands selectivity, continuity and a long, often "endless" time perspective. Selection occurs in relation to the level of the regression and intensity of the psychotic symptoms, regardless of the domination of productive or unproductive, – positive or negative, symptoms. Acute or exacerbated chronic psychotic states indicate the need for hospitalization, a "privileged regressive setting," as termed by Haynal and Pasini (1984). The structured, albeit regressive, hospital environment represents a framework for the symbiotic experience, which in the corrective and constructive sense offers the following (Urlić, 1999; Restek-Petrović, Orešković-Krezler, and Mihanović, 2007; Gans and Counselman, 2010):

a. A structured, personal and dyadic relationship toward the doctor and medical personnel (if adequately trained).
b. Medications, which in addition to their pharmacological effects are also imbued with the meaning of a transitional object which is often ambivalently invested and incorporated, and consequently experienced independently of its pharmacological properties.
c. Group experience as a place of exposure as well as the possible "practising" of a triadic situation, which determines the assessment of the patient's capacity for social readjustment or the defusion level of partial objects and the degree of establishing their integrity and constancy.

Most frequently, hospital treatment is the first phase that leads to outpatient group psychotherapy after discharge.

Group Psychotherapy for Outpatients Suffering from Psychosis

The characteristics of an outpatient group of patients with psychosis can be described as follows:

a. It includes patients suffering from psychosis who are already sensibilized and motivated (many ambivalently) to engage in group psychotherapy.
b. The transference relationship to the therapist, although regressive and ambivalent, represents the essential factor for the establishment and continuation of treatment. (In this respect, the initial contact with the doctor can play a decisive role through the perception of introjected "good" or "bad" characteristics.)
c. Such groups offer the opportunity for constancy, spatial-temporal continuity with either a limited or open perspective (with the ocean-like element of "infinity," which is important for the experience of acceptance and containing).

A small or extended therapy group is conceived as a setting for encounters and confrontations, as well as a transitional space that stimulates projections and introjections, and in which reality and phantasy exist in parallel.

Reality is mainly observed in the function of experiencing and distinguishing the quality of internal or external, past or present, pleasant or unpleasant, protective or threatening and regressive or progressive. This distinction and experience occurs as follows:

a. In the encounter with the structured setting, new people and different ways that stimulate meaningful interpersonal communications;
b. In the encounter with diseased experiences in the world of others and in one's own world, which stimulates the development of a more adequate relationship toward the disorder and facilitates insight into the necessity of treatment;
c. With the possibility of focusing certain relationships in the "here-and-now" situation, which are of particular importance for one or more patients or the whole group.

The value and importance of the "here-and-now" strategy should be pointed out. Yalom (1985) says: ". . . more accurate, alive data will result from the patient's observation of direct interpersonal behavior in the 'here-and-now' situation," and "the patients who correct unadjusted interpersonal behavior and take the risk of new behavior in the here-and-now group situation will be able later to transfer the acquired knowledge to life situations outside the group." According to the same author, two components are needed for a therapeutic process to develop in this direction: experience acquired in the group and the understanding of this experience in the reflection of oneself.

Fantasies primarily relate to the patient's own world of disordered ideas, experiences and corresponding feelings. Generally, the following three conditions must be met in group psychotherapy:

1. The group primarily relies on verbal communication.
2. The individual group member is the object of the treatment.
3. The group itself is the main therapeutic factor.

The analytic group is basically a transference group. However, all relationships in the therapeutic situation should not be called transference. It would be better to consider the total situation, with its specific features, as the therapeutic situation.

According to Foulkes (1964), three levels of communication in the group could be distinguished: transferential, autistic and realistic. Work with patients with psychosis at the transferential level is characterized by part-objects being transferred onto the therapist, other therapeutic team members and other group members. During the psychotherapeutic process, psychotic transference should be distinguished from transference psychosis, when reality testing is temporarily lost (almost) completely.

The application of the principles of group analysis seems to be appropriate for the understanding of manifest and latent processes in the group of acute hospitalized patients with psychosis mirrored in the matrix, reflecting the personal and interpersonal dynamics of the "here-and-now" situation.

However, if the therapist integrates the psychodynamic approach according to the group analytic principles into his/her professional culture and practice (Klain, 1996; Cividini-Stranić, 1996a, 1996b; Moro, 1996), he/she will bear them in mind and will be able to introduce them into the methodology of work whenever they appear to be appropriate, thereby improving group work.

As illustrated by the previous clinical examples, psychodynamic understanding of group processes requires attentiveness to several features occurring during psychotherapeutic group work, such as; the basic assumptions described by Bion; the roles of group members during group psychotherapy described by Foulkes and Anthony; specific phenomena in group psychotherapy/analysis according to Foulkes, and therapeutic factors in group psychotherapy according to Yalom.

How the above-mentioned notions can facilitate understanding the group processes within the frame of reference of the group psychotherapy of patients suffering from psychosis will be explained through the following clinical examples.

Clinical Illustration

Outpatient group psychotherapy. The group has 13 patients including two new participants, Peter and Miriam. Roberta started the group interactions by saying that today she will take her name, Roberta, again . . . otherwise she can't recollect her life . . . She is happy to be with the others, she likes them.

THERAPIST Last time somebody missed you.
ROBERTA My absence is felt everywhere. This is normal for someone like me because I am very open.
PETER I have been in many groups where I felt good . . . There was always something new to say . . . like in a factory . . . When there were strikes, there were meetings as well . . . This group could be like that and everybody could express his sentiments.

He then explained that he wasn't thinking about therapeutic groups but about workers' groups, where they discussed various problems. They would vote and the majority won.

ROBERTA (addressing Peter) Were you my sister's boyfriend?

Peter said that he was going around with his friends and was never close to her sister. The dialogue turned into a brief silence.

DON I would like to know from a group of friends what it means to work . . . I believe that to work means to live . . . There are people who think that work is sweat and getting tired, while others feel good when working.
ROBERTA Work is a spiritual initiative. When I am recovered, I always try to work and to put everything in order. There is always something that could be done, but very few or no one, does anything. If you don't work, you don't have money for holidays.
PETER I looked many times for work during the last twenty years but I always ran into controversies and couldn't express myself. For example, what does it mean to be a trainer for the handicapped and think that we are all handicapped? I think that when I give something I gain something (thinking about an earlier experience). To be with a handicapped adolescent means to meet his needs completely.
ROBERTA Work is mental gymnastics, as well.
RICKY I am very unhappy because I don't work. I am unemployed and I am desperately searching for a job. Nevertheless, I have my retirement money and my wife's salary . . . If I don't work, I don't feel equal to others. I hope to find a job and to go to the night hospital, and then into the community.
ROBERTA I am the only one who is working.
RON I had a nice job, even creative, but I didn't succeed in keeping my job.
PAULA They changed my role and I was working more and more.
ROBERTA When I used to go to work, on the bus, they were always playing the song "A Wish to Die." I was depressed and had the worst jobs to do . . . I had an accident and was in a coma for three days. However, afterward I continued to work because work is a source of life. Who doesn't work becomes mad. My life was always full of effort. I felt inferior when confronted by others.

> The talk in the group continued about reasons for becoming depressed and lacking affects.
>
> ROBERTA   had the following association: When I was in the hospital, I was feeling out of reality and had a mystic crisis . . . Depression is an illness that could happen to anyone, even to normal people. Then I started to realize that I have become mad.
>
> MONICA   I have difficulties including myself now because I am feeling anxious. Two days ago, my father came to visit me. We are physically alike but we have different characters. My father was trying to stimulate me to become more active but that is difficult for me.
>
> The therapist underscored that the group was talking about the value of work and the meaning of its loss in the context of depression, and asked the group whether there were some connections.
>
> DON   For me, depression means void of meaning, life without meaning. I thought that life was something light but it is like an engine trying to speed up or else it stops.
>
> PETER   Once I said to my chief that he was mad and I had to go to the hospital. Otherwise, I would have been fired.
>
> MIRIAM   I have many positive sides and I can't see depression as a lack of meaning.
>
> PAT   Before I attempted suicide, I was feeling bad. There are external and internal circumstances. Often, you have one face inside and one face outside of the family. When harmony is lacking, one can feel depressed. Love can help. Someone from the family, usually the father, can take out outside problems on his son, and that could result in problems and depression.
>
> MIRIAM   That is not my case or it is something that I don't understand.
>
> GEORGE   In depression, we all have something that is breaking up inside ourselves.
>
> Many group members talk and don't try to listen to the other members of the group.

The group was sending the message that talking about the capacity and meaning of being included in the working environment could foster positive feelings of personal value. In parallel, many ambivalent feelings could be distinguished when inclusion in the social tissue was in question; for example, defined structure and boundaries, together with explicit regressive phenomena and defense mechanisms such as splitting, projections, projective identifications, as well as difficulties in learning from mutual mirroring.

Clinical Illustration

> A month later, three new patients became members of the same outpatient group: Anthony, Gill and Marc.
>
> Once more, Roberta started the group discussion:
>
> ROBERTA   My name is Clara (it was more than a month since she had introduced herself using another name). I had nightmares the whole night. In my

	dream, I had to say many prayers. I encountered a demon and if I weren't praying the whole night I would have remained entrapped in my dream.
MONICA	I had nightmares, too. I was dreaming of being ill, vomiting.
ROBERTA	Monica and I were in a small town, not far away from here. My sister's boyfriend was there and I was with John.
MONICA	Roberta is imagining things.
BENT	Perhaps it was another Daniel.
ROBERTA	(bad tempered) No, we were there and we were even making love.
THERAPIST	Bent thinks that every now and then, Roberta has fantasies . . .
ROSA	(in an ironic mood) Daniel doesn't lose his equilibrium.
THERAPIST	Perhaps what we are talking about is not the truth . . .
ROBERTA	It is the truth, and if Daniel denies it, that will mean that he didn't like it.
DANIEL	It is not true, and if you continue in that way I'll leave the group.
ROBERTA	Previously when I had a nervous breakdown, I heard God's voice saying that he would like to make love to me and telling me to throw a bomb on the world.

At this point, the therapist asks the group what they think about Roberta's story.

ZOE	Perhaps it is a fantasy.
BENT	God could have so many women, could be a Latin lover, but he didn't have them. He knew how to talk with everybody, men and women.
ROBERTA	(Very excited, she tries to say something but it is unintelligible.)
MONICA	Perhaps what Roberta said was just a dream.
ROBERTA	(irritated) It is the truth.
CLARA	What Roberta said is not true. That is my opinion.
THERAPIST	Perhaps she would like to say that there are fantasies that could be exchanged for reality.
ROBERTA	I could remain in the trap of my dreams and not wake up. I really heard God's voice and a demon's voice.
MONICA	Voices are something belonging to psychology and mental functioning.
ROBERTA	No, it is telepathy. Many people are thinking but only a few can hear voices. With telekinesis, I can go where I wish.
BENT	(talking to Monica) When you were hearing voices, were you thinking as you do now?
MONICA	No, I was confused in my mind. I was thinking in a different way, I mean that they gave the impression of reality.
BENT	From this silence, I conclude that they were the only ones who had sensations of that type.
MARY	I never heard voices.
BENT	Sometimes in the past I had phases of hearing voices and not being able to see anyone.
GILL	I had phases when I was hearing voices and couldn't see anyone but I think that I was dreaming with my eyes open.
ROBERTA	I was always hearing voices and songs in my head that were accompanying me during the day.
MONICA	I believe these are a psychic-mental phenomenon and if you don't take any notice of them, you could be less aware of them.

BENT	Years ago, in the hospital, I found my body lying in bed but in my mind I felt that I was in the dining room, among others. It was as if I were in a trance.
ZOE	I never heard voices.
ANTHONY	There are things that one can hear or see, even if they don't exist. However, one experiences them as real.

Some group members were nodding.

ROSA	Such stupid talk!
GILL	Whoever experiences them has the impression that they are real.
BENT	It is possible to see or feel strange things, even strange smells . . . You, Rosa, what do you think about?
GILL	It happened to me, as well.
BENT	(turning towards Rosa) Is it something you are familiar with?
ROSA	I believe it is.
MONICA	It might be something like a sixth sense.
MARC	I believe in voices because when I was in my house sometimes, I heard someone talking but I was alone in the house. Once, in my garden, I was looking at the sky and saw Jesus and Our Lady. I lowered my eyes and when I looked up again they were still there.
THERAPIST	What did you think about?
MARC	I was thinking that this was reality.
ROBERTA	(singing) God appeared to me.
CLARA	I don't hear voices but my mind is greatly confused.
THERAPIST	(turning to Gill) You're rather silent . . . ?
GILL	(new group member) Yes, I don't feel like talking. Something personal.
ROBERTA	When I eat meat, I have dreams with warning contents but not if I eat macrobiotic food.
ANTHONY	I am always talking in a pessimistic way but now I would like to say something nice and to feel good. My hygienic standard is much higher than the one in this environment. I would like to distance myself from ugly things. During my life, I did many wrong things and I received many bad things. I sense that people are saying various things and I am very scared.
THERAPIST	Now we were talking about voices but fears were coming to your minds. Is there any connection?
ANTHONY	I would like to distance myself from bad things that make me feel fearful.

Addressing the whole group:

THERAPIST	Is it that when talking about voices, smells and visions, we are looking at the sources of our fears?
GILL	I believe that bad things provoke fears. Only when they pass can one understand that they weren't real.
CLARA	Sometimes one is afraid to confront some problems.
GILL	When feeling fear, one becomes even more ill.
DANIEL	Perhaps I lost my equilibrium more than usual but now I would not like us to talk about this any more. It is OK to look forward.

In the psychodynamically-informed conducting of a group of patients suffering from psychosis, it often happens that members reveal uncertainty about their identities. The challenge of that precarious state of thinking about oneself and the outer world was the starting point of this last clinical illustration. Lack of certitude between inner and outer realities found resonance in almost all the members of the group. Each member was expressing deep anxieties and psychotic fears that were mirrored among them, creating a special field with pre-genital elements of perceptions or, in a Kleinian manner, these would be recognized as pertaining to the paranoid-schizoid position. In order to fill the gap created by dissociative phenomena (that try to protect their personalities from deeper splitting and regression), the group members were disclosing the spectrum of the productive psychotic symptoms that accompanied these processes. The way in which they described their experiences from psychotic episodes helped them to achieve a better understanding of how dissociated parts of experience have a prevailing impact on the thinking and feeling processes, in comparison to external reality. In this way, a psychotherapeutic group conducted in the group-analytic manner provides containing capacity, which, together with a trusting relationship with the therapist/therapeutic team, facilitates the expression of some degree of regressive psychic functioning and allows a corrective emotional (symbiotic) experience to occur.

Some Basic Elements of the Relationship Between a Patient with Psychosis and the Therapist

In the application of group psychotherapy to patients with psychosis, the following are of fundamental importance:

1. The assessment of the patient's capacity to establish a relationship with the therapist and, through him/her, also with others, and
2. The personality traits and training of the therapist.

1. The capacity of a patient with psychosis to establish a relationship with another person primarily refers to the capacity for introjection. The integrity of a patient's intrapsychic experience is interwoven with his/her capacity to perceive the outer reality and to introject the therapist from this reality as a separate external object. Another dimension of the relationship to the outer reality is projection, which is interwoven with introjection. The constant exchange of introjection and projection determines the experience of the self and the definition of external objects and the environment.

For the assessment of a patient's capacity to establish a relationship with the therapist, along with the mechanisms of projection and introjection, the mechanism of splitting, which protects the personality from threatening further regression, also plays a decisive role. The depth of the personality split will also determine the possibility and level of the transference experience, that is, the therapeutic level.

The capacity to establish relationships with others is related to the possibility for patients suffering from psychosis to establish positive transference. By definition, transference is the repetition of relationships to primary objects. The transference of the psychotic patient is a projection from very early "psychotic" phases of development (i.e., "normal autism" and "normal symbiosis," according to M. Mahler, together with a differentiating subphase of the S-I process). Therefore, such transference exists considerably outside the situation in which it occurs. In the case of the favorable development of a relationship between a patient with psychosis and therapist, the therapist will become a new primary object for the patient. Through the repetition of the earliest phases of childhood relationships, this process could bring about the development of a new object with corrective constancy (nevertheless, almost always ambivalently). Transference by the patient with psychosis will also represent the repetition of the relationship to the therapist from their first encounter(s). This enables the patient to reduce the regression depth and improve his/her relationship to reality through the therapist. The therapist interferes between the patient and reality in the achievement of the therapeutic goals, which are based on the objective assessment of the patient's capacities for more adequate structuring and functioning, with the important possibility of establishing a corrective symbiotic (emotional) relationship. It is assumed that the therapist feels the need to develop this relationship toward higher levels or the more autonomous functioning of the patient.

2. On the other hand, the therapist should introduce the following therapeutic features into the therapeutic relationship (Urlić, 1999):

a. Unpossessive warmth (primary, unidirectional and nonverbal capacity that the therapist generally has);
b. Empathy (the therapist's capacity to introject the patient as an object and to structure the image of the patient with as much data as possible from all the developmental phases. The image of the patient in the therapist is shaped through the arrangement of nonverbal and verbal data perceived unconsciously and consciously);
c. Genuineness (enabling the therapist to direct and measure his/her behavior toward the patient spontaneously).

It is known that the educational experience and orientation of the therapist, as well as the integrated theoretical framework within which the phenomena observed in the group are defined, are also important. Although, on the one hand, they are necessary aids in the structuring and understanding of intrapsychic and interpersonal relationships and the manifold meanings thereof, on the other, they can also represent certain limitations, especially if strictly observed.

The Necessity and Meaning of the Leadership Role during Work with Groups of Patients with Psychosis

The role of the leader logically results from a situation that in its initial phase of working with the group, or when a new member joins the group, is observed as the prevailing dynamics in the relationship of the group toward the therapist. In such situations, the group usually establishes a regressive, dependent relationship with the therapist, expecting leadership and gratification of infantile needs from him/her.

Realizing the needs of the group, the psychotherapist has two possibilities: to acquiesce to or resist their wishes. In fact, the only thing the group has in common at the beginning is its conductor and psychic difficulties (Foulkes and Anthony, 1965). At first, the group shows the tendency to place its leader in the center and expect instructions from him/her.

The therapist and the group can represent different objects (e.g., husbands, wives, friends), while individual members can mutually react within transference in a narrower sense (as to sisters, brothers, mothers, spouses, etc). Their feelings for these persons or their inner images of them can be projected in the group. At times, the therapist may be seen almost as an idealized godlike parent, while sometimes he/she can be experienced as a bad parent whom they dread and reject, as if he/she were "God" sitting by him/herself, having everything and giving nothing. The therapist can also be perceived as a realistically powerful individual who treats the group as a bunch of weak and helpless people.

The therapist can be further seen as a potent healer in comparison to them as patients, as normal in relation to them as disturbed, as a parent in relation to them as children, as strong in relation to them as weak and helpless etc. He/she can also be experienced as immune to emotional provocations, capable of maintaining stability and cheerfulness when faced with volcanic eruptions of emotions. The therapist is generally regarded as the embodiment of progress directed toward maturity, who meaningfully and professionally improves healthy patterns of life.

On account of the immature need of the group for a leader, the therapist's activity may result in the authoritative "fixation" of the group. After creating an appropriate and dynamic situation for the therapy, the group analyst, as well as the psychoanalyst, can leave the patient to face his/her problem, treating him/her with the least possible interference. The therapist plays an important role in encouraging the group members to expose their thoughts, feelings and experiences, and to engage in stimulating interactions within the group.

Therefore, it is not sufficient to view the therapist's contribution as one among others within the general scheme of interactions. It is the interaction of the therapist's psychology with the psychologies of the other participants that gives each group its specificity. Even in a more advanced stage, the two psychologies remain present and patients often put pressure on the therapist to become a patient like themselves, while at the same time they are afraid that he/she might really do so and make them "a leaderless group," left to their own resources to save themselves under the burden of all the regressive, destructive forces present in them. The therapist's attitude basically involves the rejection of the authoritative role and the inclination to work through the group and with the group while exerting as little interference as possible. The aim of the therapist is to wean the group from its orientation to the leader, that is, to transform the leader gradually into the conductor of the group whenever possible. During this process, Slavson (1973) warns against permissive behavior by the group therapist at the very beginning of therapy, which might result in a very disturbing atmosphere.

From the psychotherapist, as the group leader, the group demands various roles according to its needs. On the other hand, the psychotherapist has his/her own ideas about his/her role in the group context, as well as his/her needs. Here, the therapist's personality with all the countertransference moments revealed by such situations, education and integrated training become expressed. Wolf and Schwartz (1962) write about authoritative therapists dominated by either the id or superego: "In the id dominated group every expression is intense. In the superego dominated group any intense affect is either disapproved or regarded as acting out. Too permissive or too repressive therapy negates the meaning of group experience" (Wolf and Schwartz, 1962).

Within this context, Yalom (2005) points out that some therapists prefer to be seen as almighty, while others can have a discouraging effect on patients. Some therapists feel so threatened when patients search for their autonomy that they unintentionally "do not allow them to grow up" and can sometimes be so provocative and sarcastic that patients in the group form a permanent alliance against them. The same author says that the most difficult thing to define, considering the differentiation between the therapist and the patient in the patient-therapist relationship, is not related to what the therapist does or really is but to what he/she evokes in the fantasies of each patient. Transference distortions evoke parental authority, dependency, power, revolt and autonomy, which are all frequently personified in the therapist's person. The clarification and working out of transference distortions in the patient-therapist relationship bring about significant changes in the therapeutic process. However, such development of the group process is not characteristic of a regressive group of patients with psychoses, while comparatively brief hospital treatment is also unconducive to the development of such group dynamics. It is, however, important that the therapist does not lose sight of this potential perspective in his own experience and the conducting of the group.

One of the central problems in a group is the conflict over authority. Cividini-Stranić (1980) mention that due to ambivalence in the life of every group, conflicts and crises of authority are unavoidable.

Solving the authority crisis contributes to the process of the separation and differentiation of the patients' selves from the therapist's self, which further offers the possibility for differentiation among the members. The essential part of the crisis is the desire for individual and group autonomy, as opposed to fear and the desire to remove the leader. The problem is how to deal with, make understandable and work out the authoritative and powerful role of the therapist, which is at times needed by the group and at times by the therapist, when during the entire group process it is both rejected and demanded by the group from the therapist. The members of the group expect the therapist to give them all his/her knowledge. They hope that they can be easily cured by him/her, while they themselves do not have to make contributions. They frequently see the therapist as an expert on a given situation and openly or indirectly request a solution from him/her. The psychotherapist is aware that many members of the group need the function of the therapist's strength and power to feel safe. The group often expects the therapist to be "the one" who gives orders, makes decisions, which means that the therapist represents authority.

Much more has been written on the roles and meaning of the group therapist than on his/her personality. The fact that the therapist is the cause of the existence of the group and its organizer, who for many reasons is assigned a special place within the group, does not mean that he/she must be special. The personal and professional qualities required of the therapist belong to the sphere of basic humanity. He/she should be a person who accepts risks in life situations as a member of the community to which he/she belongs, whose rules he/she either accepts or is able to disapprove of calmly in a way that facilitates further dialogue (Moro, 1996). This means that the therapist should, from the onset, enable each member of the group to feel safe and welcome in the group, and to trust the therapist, knowing that he/she will not harm him/her intentionally. This level of professional and personal integrity is difficult to achieve and maintain. On the one hand, "the regressive impact is unlikely not to touch the conductor, while on the other, the leadership function emanates from the deeper recesses of internalized models of authority" (Nitsun, 1996). The achievement and maintenance of this level of professional and personal integrity require continuous learning from interpersonal relations, consultation and supervision.

The above propositions can best be followed through clinical experience.

Clinical Illustration

The group of outpatients has eight members, who meet at the day center.

The session starts with Grazia talking about her disagreements with her mother. Then she switches to another subject: Marc lost his false teeth and thinks she is to blame. Then she said that "nothing goes well here . . . Marc doesn't like her . . ."

Others say that this is her perception.
Rosaria should tell a secret. Marc told her that a person who steals false teeth should die. She thinks that perhaps the cleaning women could be blamed . . .
Tony said that his dog died. He got a new one and named him Winnie.
They talk about dogs. Somebody says that he has a German shepherd.
Another participant has a new dog that she likes very much.
There is a question why she doesn't bring him here. She said that she can't because it is a valuable dog.
Thomas goes out of the room.

The conversation is about dog sitters and places where one can leave a dog. Tony said that there is a nice house for that purpose. The owner has a barn where an old woman and her daughter used to live. Hay was stored in the barn. Tony said: "My father used to take the hay and place it on a scale for sale." Who knows who will take that scale? The scale belonged to my father."

The talk continues about the scales and what will happen to them.
The conductor poses a question: "Why don't you take it?"
The patient would like to have the TV but he doesn't want to take either the scale or the grass.
Somebody said that the scale could be a TV set.
Another participant said: "All of you know everything but you are staying here."
Somebody asked where they were supposed to go.
"To the Moon, we are lunatics." Laughter in the group.

It is always important to bear in mind that patients with psychosis have a psychotic personality structure. This means that there is always the possibility for them to live in their different realities, the one that is externally exchangeable and recognized as mutually acknowledged experience, while the other is a private, split-off psychotic experience. This psychopathological configuration requires a specific conceptual and therapeutic approach, modified and need-adapted to the specific requirements of the patients suffering from psychosis.

Concluding Remarks

Various theoretical schools view the functions of the therapist in relation to the hypotheses and focus to which they are directed. Revising and summarizing earlier experiences, Scheidlinger (1997) holds that the majority of group therapists would agree that their activity in therapeutic groups consists of the following:

1. Structuring the group's composition, time, meeting place and remuneration procedures;
2. Structuring the conduct of the sessions with reference to confidentiality, agenda, physical contact and therapeutic techniques;
3. Empathically accepting and caring for each patient, coupled with a belief in the latter's potentiality for change and growth;
4. Encouraging the open expression of feelings and concerns;
5. Fostering a climate of tolerance and acceptance of variance in feelings, behaviors and peer helping;
6. Controlling drive expression, tension and anxiety levels in individual patients within acceptable limits;
7. Controlling group-level manifestations;
8. Using verbal interventions including simple observations, confrontations and interpretations aimed at reality testing and eliciting meaning and genetic connections.

With respect to the principles of group analysis (according to Foulkes and other group-analytic authors), the aforementioned would provide a broader framework, in which the creation and understanding of the group matrix concept, the conduct of the group-as-a-whole, as well as the evolutionary concept of the therapist's role from leader to conductor would represent some of the fundamental assumptions. According to them, the therapist should organize the group, understand group phenomena and make interventions in the "here-and-now" situation.

Conducting a group of patients with schizophrenia or some other psychosis, the therapist acts differently than in a group of persons able to function at a higher level. The aims of group work are related to the needs of the patients. Due to the difficulties patients with psychosis have in experiencing and interpreting both inner and outer realities, Kanas (1996) describes the functions of the therapist in such groups in the following way: the therapist is

1. Active and directive in keeping group members focused on the topic;
2. Clear, consistent and concrete with interventions;
3. Supportive and diplomatic with comments;
4. Open and willing to give opinions and advice that are appropriate to the discussion;
5. Here-and-now (rather than there-and-then) focused; and
6. Encouraging of patient-to-patient (rather that patient-to-therapist) interactions.

Within the context of the therapist's role in a group of patients with psychosis (Yalom and Lieberman, 1971), there is a dilemma between the two basic types of conductor: "energizer" or "provider." In terms of measured action, it seems that the patience of the "provider" is more acceptable, as it appears that the therapist's role as a "new primary object" is more adequately realized in this way, although it requires fuller and longer engagement from the therapist.

The question can be raised as to how to conduct the group psychotherapy of patients with psychosis using elements of the group-analytic approach under hospital conditions, where patients stay for a short time, when even a brief interruption in work creates the situation of a new beginning every time. According to the experience presented, group psychotherapy represents a therapeutic and diagnostic method that should take both the time factor and the number of patients into account. Some patients are admitted to the hospital when others are discharged. For each of them, there is the possibility to reveal his/her social communication potentials through interactions with other members of the group. Such potentials are a reflection of the very personality and its current possibilities. The group appears to be a good container for the deeply regressed parts of the personality structure, as well as a medium for the stimulation of healthy ego potentials. Since the time span is narrowed, the group remains focused around its therapist, who has the function of the leader. Most often, this structuring role cannot be modified without a high risk to the members with very weak and fragmented egos.

In addition to therapeutic and diagnostic purposes under hospital conditions, group work prepares the patients for the continuation of group treatment (along with psychopharmacological therapy) under outpatient conditions. In outpatient group psychotherapy, the expected extent of reality is higher and more constant than in hospital groups.

A question can also be raised with regard to the roles and their range or flexibility that the group therapist can assume in a group of patients with psychosis in hospital and outpatient settings.

In conclusion to these considerations on small and medium-sized groups of inpatients and outpatients suffering from psychosis, as well as the therapist's role in such groups, the following could be said (Urlić, 1999):

1. The therapist conducts the individuals in the group. From experience, this situation does not change considerably from the beginning to the end of group treatment under hospital conditions, due to the deep regression and fragmentation of the psychic functioning of the patients. In an outpatient group, a more flexible approach is possible, with the transformation of the "infinite" into a more defined course of treatment.

2. In hospital groups, due to time constraints in terms of ward treatment and heterogeneity in the regression depth, the therapeutic aims are necessarily limited.

3. An outpatient group, on the contrary, needs constancy or spatial and temporal continuity, with an open and adjustable perspective at the level of the ego functions and stability of the patient's object relations.

4. In an outpatient group of patients with psychosis, the possibility of the evolution of the therapist's role from leader to conductor is more realistic and often more adequate than under hospital conditions. This means that the distinctions between these two types of settings become more amenable to a wide range of influences and, therefore, considerably more flexible in their exchange.

5. Therapeutic work in a group setting can be aimed at corrective symbiotic experience, as well as at the "dilution" of the dyadic transference relationship in terms of development directed at a triadic, socially better-adjusted one.

6. Under both hospital and outpatient conditions, group psychotherapy of patients with psychosis, together with psychopharmacological therapy, represents an essential complementary part of the treatment of patients with psychosis (with the exceptions of manic patients or those inclined to acting-out, and with questionable benefits to patients suffering from acute paranoia). The social component of the biopsychosocial approach should always represent one of the basic working frameworks.

7. Group psychotherapy of patients suffering from psychosis represents an important part of both the diagnostic and therapeutic procedures. It can represent a technique for a professional approach as part of the usual routine or it can reach high levels of creativity and represent a challenge for further scientific investigation.

Therefore, the psychodynamic (group-analytic) approach should be considered to be the body of concepts stemming from essential psychoanalytic notions and a wealth of long-term clinical experience, subject to appropriate modifications when the psychodynamically-oriented group psychotherapy of patients with psychosis is in question.

References and Bibliography

Boyle, M. (1990). *Schizophrenia: A scientific delusion?* London & New York: Routledge.

Cannon, T. D., & Mednick, S. A. (1993). The schizophrenia high-risk project in Copenhagen: three decades of progress. *Acta Psychiatrica Scandinavica*, (Suppl 370), 33–47.

Cividini-Stranić, E. (1980). *The psychotherapist in group psychotherapy (Croatian)*. Belgrade: Zbornik radova III kongresa psihoterapeuta Jugoslavije.

Cividini-Stranić, E. (1996a). *The group matrix* (Croatian). In E. Klain (Ed.), *Grupna analiza*. Zagreb: Medicinska naklada.

Cividini-Stranić, E. (1996b). The use of group analysis (Croatian). In E. Klain (Ed.), *Grupna analiza*. Zagreb: Medicinska naklada.

Foulkes, S. H. (1964). *Therapeutic group analysis.* London: George Allen & Unwin Ltd.

Foulkes, S. H., & Anthony, E. J. (1965). *Group psychotherapy. The psychoanalytic approach.* London: Penguin Books.

Fromm-Reichmann, F. (1953). *Principles of intensive psychotherapy.* Chicago & London: The University of Chicago Press.

Gans, J. S., & Counselman, E. F. (2010). Patient selection for psychodynamic group psychotherapy: Practical and dynamic considerations. *International Journal of Group Psychotherapy*, *60*(2), 197–220.

Haynal, A., & Pasini, M. (1984). *Médecine psychosomatique (French)*. Paris: Masson.

Howells, J. G., & Guirguis, W. R. (1985). *The family and schizophrenia*. New York: International Universities Press.

Hummelen, J. W. (1994). Group analysis and the psychoses. *Group Analysis*, *27*, 389–391.

Kanas, N. (1996). *Group therapy for schizophrenic patients*. Washington, D.C. & London: American Psychiatric Press, Inc.

Klain, E. (1996). The group as a whole (Croatian). In E. Klain (Ed.), *Grupna analiza*. Zagreb: Medicinska naklada.

Milders, C. F. A. (1994). Kernberg's objects-relations theory and the group psychotherapy of psychosis. *Group Analysis*, *27*(4), 419–432.

Moro, L. (1996). The Group Conductor (Croatian). In E. Klain (Ed.) *Grupna analiza*. Zagreb: Medicinska naklada.

Nitsun, M. (1996). *The anti-group*. London & New York: Routledge.

Plante T. G., Pinder S. L., & Howe, D. (1988). Introducing the living with illness group: A specialized treatment for patients with chronic schizophrenic conditions. *Group*, *12*(4), 198–204.

Restek-Petrović, B., Orešković-Krezler, N., & Mihanović, M. (2007). Patient selection for group psychotherapy of patients with psychoses (Croatian). *Socijalna psihijatrija*, *35*(3), 133–139.

Rose N. D. B. (1994). *Essential psychiatry* (2nd ed.). Oxford: Blackwell Science Ltd.

Sandison, R. (1994). Working with schizophrenics individually and in groups: Understanding the psychotic process. *Group Analysis*, *27*(4), 393–406.

Scheidlinger, S. (1997). Group dynamics and group psychotherapy revisited: four decades later. *International Journal of Group Psychotherapy*, *47*(2), 141–159.

Schermer, V. L. (1994). Between theory and practice, light and heat. In V. L. Schermer & M. Pines (Eds.), *Ring of fire. primitive affects and object relations in group psychotherapy*. London & New York: Routledge.

Schlachet, P. J. (1989). The metabolization of primary process in groups. *Group*, *13*(3) and (4), 217–224.

Skolnick, M. R. (1994). Intensive group and social systems treatment of psychotic and borderline patients. In V. L. Schermer & M. Pines (Eds.). *Ring of fire*. London & New York: Routledge.

Slavson, S. R. (1973). *An introduction to group psychotherapy*. New York: International Universities Press.

Urlić, I. (1989). The influence of the symbiotic experience and factors of developmental stages on the onset and development of the schizophrenic process (Croatian, doctoral dissertation). *Medicinski fakultet Sveučilišta u Zagrebu*.

Urlić, I. (1994). On some characteristics of group psychodynamics in group psychotherapy with patients with psychosis: Inpatients and outpatients (Italian). In N. Benedetto (Ed.), *Pensare l'apprendere. la formazione in gruppoanalisi*. Torino: UPSEL Editore.

Urlić, I. (1999). The therapist's role in the group treatment of psychotic patients and outpatients. a foulkesian perspective. In V. L. Schermer & M. Pines (Eds.), *Group psychotherapy of the psychoses. concepts, interventions and contexts*. London & Philadelphia: Jessica Kingsley Publishers.

Wolf, A., & Schwartz, E. K. (1962). *Psychoanalysis in groups*. New York & London: Grune & Stratton.

Yalom, I. D. (1985). *The theory and practice of group psychotherapy* (3rd ed.). New York: Basic Books.

Yalom, I. D., & Lieberman, M. (1971). A study of encounter group casualties. *Archives of General Psychiatry, 25*(1), 16–30.

Yalom, I. D., & Leszcz, M. (2005). *The theory and practice of group psychotherapy* (5th ed.). New York: Basic Books.

28

Care for the Caregivers
Richard Beck

Introduction

There is at the very minimum an isolation inherent in doing clinical work that is amplified when the modality we choose to work with is group therapy.

To counteract the impact of such loneliness, I often chat with people in the building where my private practice office in New York City is located. One morning, the person who delivers packages to the building commented to me, "You have the easiest job in the world . . . all you do is sit in your chair and get paid to listen to people. How hard could that be?"

Pondering how to respond to Ivan's perspective on therapy and group therapy in particular, I answered; "There is more than meets the eye when listening to people in pain in order to help them, especially when the therapy takes place in the form of group therapy."

This interaction stayed with me during my encounters with Bruce, a novice group therapist whom I was mentoring. I continued to ponder the toll, or rather, the potential types of tolls that leading/conducting/running a therapy group takes on the group leader, therapist or conductor; how group therapists recognize the impact our work takes on us, and the strategies available to ameliorate the impact of leading therapy groups. Much has been written addressing the impact of leading what we commonly call "trauma groups" on the therapist, but are those the only groups that have the potential to negatively impact the inner and outer life of the group therapist? I think not.

Bruce, who had fought in the Gulf War, was all too familiar with the effects his wartime experience had on his life and how this impacted the lives of those he loved. Initially, Bruce did not describe his florid PTSD cluster symptoms, rather he described the loneliness and isolation upon his return home – leaving behind his unit, his group, his "band of brothers," each of whom he trusted because they "had each other's backs."

The Wiley-Blackwell Handbook of Group Psychotherapy, First Edition. Edited by Jeffrey L. Kleinberg.
© 2012 John Wiley & Sons, Ltd. Published 2012 by John Wiley & Sons, Ltd.

"Bruce," I said, "returning alone is traumatizing." I continued, "Group therapists, working alone, hearing the types of stories that you lived through, may experience similar emotional reactions, vicariously, just as you have experienced them firsthand."

We agreed that it is a privilege to be able to do therapy, either individual or group, and there are definite rewards and challenges for group members and group leaders alike. As members begin to trust one another and the group therapist, they begin to share unspeakable truths, as in the case of trauma groups. "We are all human," I told Bruce, "listening and bearing witness to the experiences and lives of other human beings is an emotional liability, if we listen deeply with an open heart and mind."

During my own training in group therapy at The Postgraduate Center for Mental Health, I formed and ran a group for male survivors of childhood incest and sexual abuse. The idea of leading such a group was quite anxiety-provoking. Would I be able to understand their experiences and what it meant to the group members? How would I react to hearing their stories of physical, psychological and sexual abuse? How would I, a student of group therapy, "do no harm" so as not to retraumatize these men who have been both abused and left unprotected by parents to mature into emotionally healthy adults?

I chose not to share this experience with Bruce, but pondered the impact leading such a group had on me, as well as on any therapist, working with this population. Would a neophyte therapist be more at risk for different emotional repercussions in doing such work than a seasoned, more clinically mature therapist?

To assuage my anxiety, before each group session, I would eat a large Japanese meal at a restaurant near the clinic where the group was run. A senior colleague informed me that when he led groups with chronic schizophrenics he too would eat a meal before each session, filling himself up with food in anticipation of the emotional void and deadness that he would contain as he held the group's psychotic projections week after week. Simply knowing that a well-respected senior colleague was soothing himself with food in the same fashion had normalized my reaction and reduced my shame about eating in anticipation of hearing details of horrific pain, abuse and neglect. Most importantly, along another dimension, this reduced my sense of isolation in my experience of leading such a group and led to a deeper understanding of how my self-care took the form of eating.

Judith Herman (1997) writes that no survivor of trauma can heal alone and no clinician can perform trauma work alone. Herman eloquently expresses a realistic and pragmatic assessment of the group therapist's need for a forum to discuss his work so as to minimize the impact this work can take. The more a group therapist listens to traumatic life experiences, the more open and present he may be with those who have survived traumas. Yet this may also allow for an increased vulnerability as we listen empathetically to the pain of others.

When we lead a therapy group we experience our countertransference to the group members, to the group itself, and to the setting. We experience both our subjective and objective countertransferences all the time. Depending on one's theoretical orientation, the reader might view objective countertrasferences differently, but I prefer the totalistic model in which the entirety of the emotional reactions of the group therapists are considered and used (Beck and Buchele, 2004).

Each time Bruce shared his concerns about becoming a group therapist, he hesitatingly described his emotional reactions to being in a war zone and how he felt upon his return. All of the criteria for diagnosing PTSD were present, as PTSD cluster symptoms were present in Bruce: hyper-arousal; re-experiencing and constriction, avoidance and numbing. I informed Bruce that his were normal reactions to the type of life experiences he had survived. I also informed Bruce that a group therapist, listening to people who experienced such symptoms, can begin to experience them for himself.

This is one of the potential hazards of doing group work: There is an affective amplification that, if we are emotionally open to the group members, we are also at risk of experiencing ourselves. Actually, those who listen to the lives of others in group expose themselves to the emotional slings and arrows others have endured and are radiating out of their pores during each group session.

Another senior colleague described his routine of taking a shower after a long day of doing group work to "wash off" the projections he absorbed during each group session. Over time, listening to people's traumatic life stories can affect the therapist, yet no one session will cause the group therapist to alter his world or the experience in leading such a group. Rather there is a gradual process that impacts the group therapist.

Perhaps in a theme-centered group, the group therapist has some idea as to the nature of how the group members will relate to each other, to the group itself and to the group therapist, and he can anticipate his countertransferences to the group members and the group-as-a-whole. There are many common countertransferential reactions that group therapists feel both in anticipation of and while leading homogeneous trauma groups. Some of these, as delineated by the American Group Psychotherapy Society's Distance Learning Course, and Trauma Training Course include feelings of depression, sadness, anger, inadequacy, shame and blame, and guilt. Fears include connection with loss and desperation of group members, witnessing details of the trauma, members' anger or conflict, and the need to know ALL details coupled with the need to rescue. These common countertransferential reactions occur regardless of the nature of the traumatic event, for example, a natural disaster such as an earthquake, flood, an act of terror, or industrial accidents such as the Gulf Oil Spill, or the nuclear disasters at Three Mile Island and Chernobyl.

Other potential sequalae to immersing oneself in the emotions expressed verbally and non-verbally in group are: secondary traumatic stress, compassion fatigue and vicarious traumatization. These experiences differ from countertransferential reactions that are unique to the emotional reaction experienced in a particular session, be it to the group itself, to a group member, or theme in a particular session.

As defined in presentations by AGPA's Trauma Course, Secondary Traumatic Stress (STS) is a syndrome of symptoms nearly identical (cluster symptoms) to PTSD, resulting from knowledge about or helping a traumatized person. Whereas Compassion Fatigue is defined as deep sorrow plus the drive to alleviate pain in another, it is more often used by the medical community to explain stress and fatigue.

Vicarious traumatization

Vicarious Traumatization: The transformation of the therapist's or helper's inner experience as a result of empathic engagement with survivor clients and their trauma material (McCann and Pearlman, 1990). Vicarious traumatization (VT) is a cumulative process and does not occur as the result of listening to one particularly emotionally charged session. Rather, it is a gradual experience that occurs within the self of the therapist, as he listens to and bears witness to unspeakable events and experiences that people have endured and survived. It should be noted that VT is not an inevitable result of doing work with trauma survivors; however, therapists are at risk the longer they listen to such accounts.

I experienced this firsthand after leading over one thousand hours of trauma groups in New York City after September 11th, 2001 and after the hurricanes that devastated the Louisiana and Mississippi regions a few years later. Week after week, year after year, I led trauma groups composed of survivors who worked in and around the Twin Towers. I treated hospital employees who themselves had treated families of survivors or families who lost loved ones. I treated police officers, firefighters, emergency response personnel, and therapists who treated survivors. In addition, I worked with colleagues from the South who lost everything after the hurricanes and broken levees.

Slowly, I began to feel I knew what it was like to be in the Towers when the planes hit and the buildings shook. I began to imagine walking down over one hundred flights of stairs in the dark with co-workers hand in hand. For years, I would look up at the New York Skyline and visualize the impact of a plane crashing into a building. Hyper-vigilance, numbness, constriction and re-experiencing were cluster symptoms that I experienced. My colleagues who were doing similar work experienced this as well.

Fortunately, much of the work I did was funded by AGPA and, as a condition of doing such work, all group therapists conducting trauma groups were assigned a consultant – someone who was both knowledgeable about trauma treatment and not directly exposed to the traumatic event. Having a consultant, supervisor or peer group is crucial when doing any form of group therapy and essential when leading trauma groups. Without such self-care, the impact on the group therapist can be enormous. Thus, the group leader needs to be aware of the potential cumulative effects of listening to patients, to recognize and take the appropriate steps to reduce these effects.

Burn out

Burn Out: A state of physical, emotional and mental exhaustion caused by long-term involvement in emotionally demanding situations (Beck and Buchele, 2004).

When I have worked too hard for too long, my batteries flash "low energy" and I need to take time off in order to recharge my inner core, my emotional batteries. Burn out is just one effect that leading groups can have on the leader, regardless of the type of group the leader is running.

Bruce and I began to discuss burn out. Bruce listened closely to my description of how leading a group and listening to the verbal and nonverbal expression of feelings can take its toll on the group therapist. He admitted he was beginning to recognize the complexity of leading a therapy group. I agreed and further informed Bruce that leading a group means being comfortable with uncertainty – being comfortable with not knowing-regardless of the many theories group therapists have to organize their thinking about leading a group.

Hypothetically, if a group is composed of therapists who treated students where a university shooting took place, then the therapist might have an idea as to what to expect from group members, but still he wouldn't know their personal histories or if any trauma was present in their developmental years. This is even truer in "garden-variety" therapy groups when people come to treatment for help with symptoms that are distressing them and affecting their current life's functioning. The group therapist, even when screening someone for a group, may find himself in the midst of a recollection of a traumatic event that might trigger similar recollections in other group members. The idea that traumatic material is only to be found in formal "trauma groups" is naïve at best.

Shame

"Bruce," I said, "you don't have to tell me, but think for a moment about your life before you served and fought in the Gulf. Perhaps there were painful moments you endured throughout your childhood, adolescence and young adulthood. These experiences, especially if they occurred very early in life, are encoded in your memory system and filed away. Sometimes memory may be stored in the body itself if the trauma occurred before a person has developed the capacity for using words." Bruce stared at me and said that this was something he never considered: how the body might store memories of trauma. As a war veteran, he had somatized experiences that were repetitive and unavoidable. Bruce whispered to me that at times he was ashamed of himself and his symptoms. I comforted him (hopefully) by letting him know that how he dealt with his wartime experience was a normal reaction to being repeatedly exposed to traumatic events.

Group therapists often feel the shame that group members describe as having experienced or are currently experiencing. Group therapists can experience both witness shame as well as witness guilt when we listen to horrific stories. At the same time, we feel powerless to change what the group member has lived through. Witness shame and survivor shame are very powerful, toxic feelings that need to be expressed and worked through.

It would be inappropriate for the group leader to work through his own witness shame in the group itself because there needs to be an appropriate forum, an appropriate place, where the shame can be expressed, understood, and forgiven in order for such healing to take place.

A group therapist can share his emotional reactions with:

- A consultant who has expertise in treating trauma
- A peer supervisory group where there is safety to share shameful reactions and feelings
- A supervisor with expertise in working with trauma
- Personal therapy if the work is very close to issues in the group therapist's life.

There is a soul weariness that comes from caring. From doing business with the handiwork of fear. Sometimes it lives at the edges of one's life, bruising against hope and barely making its presence known. At other times, it comes crashing in, overtaking one with its vivid images of another's terror with its profound demand for attention, nightmares, strange fears and generalized hopelessness. (Stamm, 1999)

How, then, can the group therapist, like a veteran returning home from war, transform his inner experience from that of fatigue to a more positive view of life, to shift to hope and resiliency (Stone and Beck, 2010)? The key element in this transformation is recognizing that just as providing group therapy is a process, so too is the toll that this process takes on the clinician and so too is the process of regaining an internal sense of mastery and normalcy over one's life, both inner and outer.

I used the analogy of working with firefighters to illustrate the impact of conducting therapy groups with any population, be they garden-variety groups or groups identified both by members and therapist alike as "Trauma Groups." Not every firefighter who enters a building will be burnt or suffer from smoke inhalation – occupational hazards of being a firefighter. However, the more fires the firefighter fights, the greater the likelihood becomes that at some point he may suffer from smoke inhalation or a burn of one degree or another. Thus, conducting trauma therapy is akin to being an emotional firefighter. We are trained to enter the lives of people who are in tremendous emotional pain and not flee the flames of the unspeakable traumas they have endured and survived. Most civilians flee from fires and most people flee from stories of trauma survivors, regardless of the nature of the trauma.

That is what puts therapists at risk to the potential consequences of listening to the unspeakable. Even when conducting garden-variety groups, we are never fully aware, nor are our patients fully aware, of the traumatic histories that might unfold throughout the course of being a group member. Much of our training is focused on the "how" of providing group therapy and not on the impact or effects leading therapy groups "might" take on the group leader. Most graduate students in psychology or social work, residents in psychiatry, nursing students, or ministry students focus their attention on the task of the work, not on the potential risks involved in providing such work. In addition, the risks involved in leading such groups are not formally or academically addressed. Therapists should periodically observe themselves in order to recognize the effects of conducting therapy groups. These include:

- Compassion fatigue
- Secondary traumatic stress(STS)
- Vicarious traumatization.

Compassion Fatigue: The result of being repeatedly exposed to a patient's stories or experiences of trauma. It is the experience of empathy and the degree of exposure that cause some to develop it and others not (Figley, 1995). Figley also describes Compassion Fatigue as "the stress and fatigue of duty-related experiences" (Figley, 1999). Adams, Boscarino and Figley, (2006) says: "It is caregivers' reduced capacity or interest in being empathic or 'bearing the suffering' of patients."

Secondary Traumatic Stress (STS): A natural behavior and emotion resulting from knowledge about and/or helping or wanting to help a traumatized or suffering person (Stone and Beck, 2009). This is in contrast to "burnout", which is viewed as something that emerges gradually over time as emotional exhaustion from any job (Stone and Beck, 2009).

Secondary Traumatic Stress is a syndrome with the same symptoms used to describe PTSD except that the trauma involves the concern and care for a traumatized person (Figley, 1999).

Vicarious Traumatization (VT), as reported by Stone and Beck, involves a pervasive impact on the therapists in terms of their: view of self and the world, belief systems, interpersonal relationships, and cognitive, emotional and spiritual functioning (Saakvitne and Pearlman, 1995).

Vicarious Traumatization is a process and does not result from conducting one group session in which traumatic material is worked on. Vicarious Traumatization is the gradual shift in the inner self of the group therapist after openly listening to horrific experiences time and time again. It is the repeated nature of listening to the traumatic material that may cause a shift in the core of the therapist. Listening to one horrific experience, being present to traumatic countertransferences, can have an impact on the group therapist, but experiencing a traumatic countertransference during a group therapy session is different from the cumulative experience of helping trauma survivors over years (Beck and Buchele, 2004). A group therapist must also understand the differences between Compassion Fatigue, Secondary Traumatic Stress, and Vicarious Traumatization. The question we need to ask ourselves is: *How often am I exposed to traumatic material?*

A colleague's doctoral thesis demonstrated that the traumatic impact on police officers working with trauma was determined not by the magnitude of the traumatic events they responded to, but the frequency of traumatic events the officers were exposed to, regardless of the size or magnitude of the traumatic event (Hammer, 2008).

> I experienced this firsthand in 2007 when I was invited to lead a workshop at a Training Institute in New York City entitled, "When Healing Hurts: The Impact of Listening to Trauma." The workshop was marketed to anyone whose work involved listening to traumatic material and included mental health professionals and non-mental health professionals: police officers, firefighters, teachers, insurance company employees, etc. Over fifty people attended this ninety-minute workshop. Despite how I planned to conduct the workshop, when I began with a go-around, asking members to introduce themselves and briefly describe the types of trauma they listened to, I observed a hunger to be heard. I let the group supervise me and, as a result, the go-around took up almost the entire amount of time allotted for the workshop.
>
> After the last person shared her experience, I simply asked the audience, "How do you take care of yourself as you listen to traumatic material day in and day out?" The experience was powerful and palpable, as people shared horrific details with one another, as in the case of an insurance claims worker who had to examine graphic photographs included in insurance claims she had to process.

There is a loneliness that occurs when we listen to traumatic material. People tend to identify us with the trauma we listen to and do not want to hear about our work (Beck and Buchele, 2005). Therefore, it is important to find a safe place among colleagues to share this traumatic material.

> A colleague and I were invited to present at a conference whose attendees were all interfaith, spiritual caregivers. The audience was composed of priests, nuns, rabbis, ministers, and Imams – these were New York City clergy who had all heard 9/11 horror stories from members of their congregations. When it came time to present, my colleague and I gave a theoretical talk about the impact listening to trauma can take on a person. After the didactic presentation, we asked those in attendance to break into small groups and discuss how they took care of themselves. Amazingly, the entire audience ignored our instructions, stayed together as one large group, and spent the rest of the conference speaking amongst themselves, sharing how they cared for themselves. We chose to respect both the audience's decision to stay as one large group and the boundary of their group by not joining them.
>
> As Judith Herman notes, they were able to bear witness to each other's experience.
>
> At the end of the workshop, they thanked us for providing them with the opportunity to speak to each other about what they had listened to and contained for many years without a formal outlet. This was a very moving experience for all of the clergy as well as for the facilitators who witnessed this phenomenal experience in the lives of these spiritual caregivers and healers.

When people are constantly exposed to trauma, some common reactions to feeling overwhelmed may be manifested by: anxiety, numbing, confusion, dread of meeting new patients, distractibility, physical discomfort, excessive planning or rumination, disengagement, over-distancing, avoidance of interpersonal engagement, intellectualism, extended use of silence, giving concrete reassurance, depression, sadness, anguish, despair, and loss of hope; sleep problems, social withdrawal, poor concentration, and appetite changes and somatic complaints (Stone and Beck, 2009).

We might over-identify with the loss and desperation the survivor presents us with and might indicate, either verbally or non-verbally, directives such as: "Feel better," "Be less frightened," "Get on with life," or offer false reassurances, such as, "It will be ok, you will be ok, and it will be over soon" (Stone and Beck, 2009).

To make ourselves more comfortable after hearing traumatic material we might: silence the patient, change topics, control the process, and become overly intellectual, either experience empathic avoidance or repression, or empathic enmeshment for a previously-traumatized therapist (Stone and Beck, 2009). We might get angry with an angry or unappreciative patient; we might get angry with patients in the group who are not "sufficiently empathic"; we might feel inadequate because we can't "undo" the traumatic event; or we might base our self-worth on our ability to "heal the patient" (Stone and Beck, 2009).

Thus, there needs to be a strategy for self-care (Ulman and Beck, 2010). This strategy needs to include:

- A balance between work and play
- Meeting one's physical needs
- Connecting with family and friends
- Connecting with professional peers
- Engaging in activities that reinforce a sense of self
- Identifying and attending to personal triggers
- Know when to "say no"
- Using stress reduction techniques when appropriate
- Taking a "no heroes welcome" approach.

As illustrated in the examples of the clergy and the workshop I gave on the impact of listening to traumatic material, groups serve as an ideal intervention for people conducting therapy, as they provide:

- Support and psycho-education
- Validation
- Normalization
- Universality.

Groups also provide:

- A sense of community
- Reduction of isolation and emotional disconnection from self and others
- Continuity
- Reality testing
- Help with affect regulation
- Encouragement of resiliency and mastery
- Encouragement of self-care
- Help with remembering, mourning and reconnecting (Ulman and Beck, 2010).

Groups are necessary for trauma group leaders, as well as other caregivers and helpers. A caregiver group model would be:

- Flexible with time-frame options
- Offered regularly while caregiver is providing services
- Offered at anniversaries of major events.

> The leader of the caregiver group needs to be well-trained and experienced in working with trauma groups.
> There needs to be group guidelines regarding confidentiality.
> The group culture needs to be supportive and non-judgmental.
> If these groups are conducted in the workplace, the leader must be aware of the hierarchy of the organization's infrastructure and its impact on the group members.
> The group may be homogeneous or heterogeneous in composition.
> The caregiver/group leader is best served when consulting with or in supervision with another trauma expert – preferably a consultant/supervisor not in the immediate proximity if the caregiver group leader was exposed to the same trauma as the members of her/his group.

During such caregiver groups, the leader can encourage resourcefulness adaptation and affective stability as well as provide containment and watch for adverse reactions such as dissociation and overwhelming affect (Ulman and Beck, 2010).

Group leaders must find a place to process their experiences and share their reactions with one another, just as the clergy did in the workshop described, as they formed one large group and shared in confidence their unique and personal experiences and reactions.

> ## ABC
>
> According to Saakvitne and Pearlman (1996) we group therapists must be aware of the ABC's of addressing Vicarious Traumatization:
>
> **Awareness**: Being attuned to one's needs, limits, emotions and resources, that is, knowing when to say "no" – focusing on the mind/body connection and using eating, breathing and sleeping to regulate stress.
>
> **Balance**: Maintain balance among activities, especially: work, play and rest. Balance between self and other:
>
> *Response – reaction*
> *Safety – Danger*
> *Life – Death*
> *Hope – Despair*
> *Joy – Suffering*
> *Vibrant – Bored*
> *Engaged – Disengaged*

Questions to ask ourselves about our inner balance:

- What happens when we get pulled too much one way or the other?
- When are we most likely to lose our balance?
- How do we get our balance back? (Stone and Beck, 2010).

As group therapists, we need to nurture all sides and monitor ourselves for:

- Over-identification with our work.
- Practising good coping skills and mechanisms; meditation, yoga, all forms of recreation, sex.
- Doing something that you always wanted to, for example, travel, learn to play the guitar, tennis, etc. (Stone and Beck, 2010).
- Learning what your sources of resiliency are! Is it your intelligence, love of art, music, social connections, sense of humor, love of nature, creativity, spirituality or athletic ability, to name but a few (Ulman and Beck, 2010).

Connection: Connection to oneself, to others, and to something larger.

The most pervasive experience in the aftermath of trauma is isolation from self, others and belief systems. Reconnection is key to recovery and resiliency for ourselves and for those we care for (Philips, Klein, Ulman, and Beck, 2010).

- Cultivate your circle of friends.
- Cultivate professional connections, (i.e., peer supervision, co-leadership).
- Cultivate spiritual connections.
- Attend conferences.
- Attend continuing educational seminars.

Cultivate a space where you can share the little and the big events in the groups you lead, as well as find a place to share the little or big experiences which are taking place in your personal life. This sounds so intuitive, but so few colleagues take the time to cultivate places and spaces to share both their personal and professional experiences.

Hope

Hope is the ability to have options. When people look into the future and see only their traumatic past – they feel hopeless. . . . the greatest source of hope is belonging. (Yael Danielli, 1994)

Cultivate **Hope**. In trauma groups as well as in garden-variety groups, the cultivation of hope is essential for the group and group members. This is critical for our suicidal patients, be they seen in individual treatment or group, in that they have lost hope and the belief that life is worth living (Yalom, 1980, Existential Therapy).

"So, hope is key for group therapy patients?" asked Bruce. I replied, "Not only for the members of therapy groups, but for the group leaders themselves. It is really easy, in the face of listening to the atrocities that people have survived, for the group therapist to lose hope." This is a signal, a big signal, to reach out. Feelings are contagious, and feelings of sadness, despair and depression are as contagious as feelings of joy and happiness. The perspective of awareness, balance, and connections helps to ameliorate the overwhelming onslaught of feelings that we group therapists are exposed to on a regular basis.

It is imperative that we not lose hope as we work with people who have lived through awful life experiences. People are quite resilient and knowing and believing in that is so very useful and important. Often our patients have endured and survived experiences that cause us to wonder how we would have survived if these events happened to us! You cannot teach people resilience, but you can remind them of how they have been resilient during difficult times in life.

Hope, like resilience, can be cultivated like a charcoal ember that needs just a whisper of breath upon it to restore its vibrant glow. That breath can come from the group members, the group leader, or both. That breath blows both ways, as the group members and the group itself restore hope in the group leader along the way.

The group therapy process, the care for the caregiver process, is on-going and reciprocal, just as the discussion back and forth between Bruce and me has been on-going during the years I mentored and supervised him.

The comment that I have the easiest job in the world because I get paid just to sit and listen to people's problems stirred up feelings in me. In addition, as Bruce and I spoke, I highlighted the challenges, the risks, and the risks that listening deeply to people's feelings exposes the group therapist to, as well as the rewards that this experience offers the patient and the therapist alike.

As Bruce and I spoke, we discussed the group therapist's need to be aware of potential hazards. We need not suffer from these hazards to recognize the manifestations of the toll of listening to people's life experiences and how to develop strategies to address this. Nothing is more important to anyone leading groups than trusting the group and having hope for the group and its members.

I informed Bruce that I have stopped smoking cigarettes now and am cultivating healthier ways to deal with the effects that conducting therapy groups can take on me. I hope that Bruce can find healthy ways to deal with his stressors and that you, the reader, having learned about caring for the caregiver, can give conscious thought as to how best to address your own needs as well.

Acknowledgments

The author wishes to acknowledge and thank Drs Thomas D Stone and Kathleen Hobbs Ulman, with whom he has presented this material at conferences; the American Group Psychotherapy Distance Learning Trauma Faculty. Drs Suzanne Phillips, Jeffrey Kleinberg, and Robert Klein, his co-instructors, and Angela Capodanno for her editorial expertise.

I would like to acknowledge my thanks to the AGPA for funding and providing me with the opportunity to conduct over one thousand hours of trauma group work.

References and Bibliography

Adams, R. E., Boscarino, J. A., & Figley, C.R. (2006). Compassion fatigue and psychological distress among social workers: A validation study. *American Journal of Orthopsychiatry*, 76(1), 103–108.
American Psychiatric Association (1954). Psychological first aid in community disasters. Prepared by the American Psychiatric Association Committee on Civil Defense. *Journal of the American Medical Association*.
American Psychiatric Association. (2000). *Diagnostic and statistical manual of mental disorders* (4th ed.). (DSM-IV-TR). Washington, D.C.: American Psychiatric Association.
Beck, R. (2004). Unique aspects of group work with trauma. In B. J. Buchele & H. I. Spitz (Eds.), *Group interventions for treatment of psychological trauma*. New York: American Group Psychotherapy Association.
Beck, R., & Buchele, B. (2005). In the belly of the beast: Traumatic countertransference. *International Journal of Group Psychotherapy*, 55(1), 31–44.
Beck, R., Bergmann, U., Broden, A., et al. (2008). Lessons learned in group strategies for survivors, witnesses and family members. In R. Klein & S. Phillips (Eds.), *Public mental health service delivery protocols: Group interventions for disaster preparedness and response*. New York: American Group Psychotherapy Association.
Benson, H., & Klipper, M. Z. (2000). *The Relaxation Response*. Harper Paperbacks, UPD edition.
Boulanger, G. (2002). Wounded by reality: The collapse of the self in adult onset trauma. *Contemporary Psychoanalysis*, 38,(1), 45–76.
Buchele, B., & Spitz, H. (2004). *Group interventions for treatment of psychological trauma*. New York: American Group Psychotherapy Association.
Danielli, Yael. (1994). Countertransference, trauma and training. In J. P. Wilson & J. Lindy (Eds.), *Countertransference in the treatment of post-traumatic stress disorder* (pp. 368–388.). New York: Guilford Press.
Figley, C. R. (1995/1999). Compassion fatigue: Toward a new understanding of the costs of caring. In B. H. Stamm (Ed.), *Secondary traumatic stress: Self-care issues for clinicians, researchers, and educators* (pp.3–28). Lutherville, Maryland: Sidran Press.
Figley, C. R. (Ed.). (1995). *Compassion fatigue: Coping with secondary traumatic stress disorder in those who treat the traumatized*. New York: Brunner/Mazel.
Graham, S. (2002). Study shows New Yorkers suffered most 9/11 stress (accessed 10 May 2011) http://www.scientificamerican.com/article.cfm?id=study-shows-new-yorkers-sandSID=mailandsc=emailfriend
Hammer, E. P. S. (2006). Cumulative trauma in police officers. *Dissertation Abstract International*, 66(12), 6922. (UMI No. 3199389).
Herman, J. (1997). *Trauma and Recovery*. Basic Books, NewYork.
Johnson, K. (2003, February 14). Chronicling history and finding a role in it; Interviewers shaping an oral account are entangled in the stories of September 11, 2001. *New York Times*.
Kauff, P. (2002). Analytic group psychotherapy: A uniquely effective crisis intervention. *Group*, 26(2), 137–147.
Kauff, P. F., & Kleinberg, J. (2008) Crisis intervention at the organizational level. In R. Klein & S. Phillips (Eds.), *Public mental health service delivery protocols: Group interventions for disaster preparedness and response*. New York: American Group Psychotherapy Association.
Kernberg, O. (1965). Notes on countertransference. *Journal of the American Psychoanalytic Association*, 13, 38–56.

Klein, R. H., & Schermer, V. L. (Eds.). (2000). *Group psychotherapy for psychological trauma.* New York: The Guilford Press.

Klein, R., & Phillips S. B. (2008). *Public mental health service delivery protocols: Group interventions for disaster preparedness and response.* New York: American Group Psychotherapy Association.

Lesczc, M. (personal communication, 2004)

Lubin, H., & Johnson, D. (2008) *Trauma-centered group psychotherapy for women: A clinician's manual.* NewYork & London: the Haworth Press.

Maltsberger, J. T., & Bure, D. H. (1974). Countertransference hate in the treatment of suicidal patients. *Archives of General Psychiatry, 30,* 625–633.

McCann, I. L. & Pearlman, L. A. (1990). Vicarious traumatization: A framework for understanding the psychological effects of working with victims. *Journal of Traumatic Stress, 3*(1), 131–149.

Miller, M., Shapiro, E., Spitz, H. et al. (2008). Support for disaster response helpers and service delivery workers. In R. Klein & S. Phillips (Eds.), *Public mental health service delivery protocols: Group interventions for disaster preparedness and response.* New York: American Group Psychotherapy Association.

National Child Traumatic Stress Network and National Center for PTSD *Psychological first aid: Field operations guide,* September, 2005.

Pearlman, L. A. (1995/1999). Self-care for trauma therapists: Ameliorating vicarious traumatization. In B. H. Stamm (Ed.), *Secondary traumatic stress: Self-care issues for clinicians, researchers, and educators* (pp. 51–64). Lutherville, Maryland: Sidran Press.

Pearlman, L. A., & Saakvitne, K. W. (1995). *Trauma and the therapist: Countertransference and vicarious traumatization in psychotherapy with incest survivors.* New York: W. W. Norton.

Pearlman, L. A., & Saakvitne, K. W. (1995). *Trauma and the therapist: Countertransference and vicarious traumatization in psychotherapy with incest survivors.* New York: W. W. Norton & Company.

Phillips, S. B. (2009). The synergy of group and individual treatment modalities in the aftermath of disaster and unfolding trauma. [Special issue] *International Journal of Group Psychotherapy,* 85–107.

Phillips, S. B. (2004). Countertransference: Effects on the group therapist working with trauma. In B. J. Buchele & H. Spitz (Eds.), *Group interventions for treatment of psychological trauma.* New York: American Group Psychotherapy Association.

Phillips, S. B. (2005). The role of the bereavement group in the face of 9/11: A self-psychology perspective. *International Journal of Group Psychotherapy, 55*(4), 507–527.

Phillips, S. B., & Kane, D. (2008). *Healing together after trauma : A couple's guide to coping with trauma and post-traumatic stress.* Oakland, California: New Harbinger Publications. www.couplesaftertrauma.com.

Phillips, S. B., & Klein, R. H., Ulman, K. H., et al. (2010). American Group Psychotherapy Society Annual Conference. Proceedings of the trauma training course. New York. http://member.agpa.org/source/Orders/index.cfm?section=orders&task=3&CATEGORY=OLARRCNTTC&PRODUCT_TYPE=SALES&SKU=AUTRAUMASESS1&DESCRIPTION=Audio-recordings%3A%20Recent%20Teleconferences&FindSpec=&CFTOKEN=78594555&continue=1&SEARCH_TYPE=find

Racker, H. (1968). *Transference and countertransference.* New York: International Universities Press.

Raphael, B. (1986). *When disaster strikes.* New York: Basic Books.

Saakvitne, K. W., & Pearlman, L. A. (1996). *Transforming the pain: A workbook on vicarious traumatization.* New York: W. W. Norton.

Stamm, B. H. (Ed.). (1995/1999). *Secondary traumatic stress: Self-care issues for clinicians, researchers, and educators.* Lutherville, Maryland: Sidran Press.

Stone, D. T., & Beck, R. (2009). American Group Psychotherapy Society Annual Conference: Care to military caregivers: From fatigue to hope and resiliency. San Diego, California. http://www.agpa.org/mtgs/2010_annmtg/2010%20Institute/institute_index.html

Ulman, K. H. (2004). Group interventions for treatment of trauma in adults. In B. J. Buchele & H. I. Spitz (Eds.). *Group interventions for treatment of psychological trauma.* New York: American Group Psychotherapy Association.

Ulman, K. H., & Beck, R. (2010). Northeastern Society for Group Psychotherapy annual conference: Group interventions in the aftermath of disaster: How we can help. Boston, Massachusetts.

Ursano, R., McCaughey, B., & Fullerton, C. (Eds.). (1994). *Individual and community responses to trauma and disaster: The structure of human chaos.* Cambridge, UK: Cambridge University Press.

Williams, M. B., & Sommer, J. F., Jr. (1995/1999). Self-care and the vulnerable therapist. In B. H. Stamm (Ed.), *Secondary traumatic stress: Self-care issues for clinicians, researchers, and educators* (pp. 230–246). Lutherville, Maryland: Sidran Press.

Wilson, J. P., & Lindy, J. D. (1994). *Countertransference in the treatment of PTSD.* New York: Guilford Press. www.nsgp.com/PDFs/Web_brochure_update2.pdf

Yalom, I. D. (1980). *Existential psychology.* New York: Basic Books.

Yalom, I. D., & Leszcz, M. (2005) *The theory and practice of group psychotherapy* (5th ed.). New York: Basic Books.

Youcha, I. (personal communication, 1994).

Section Three
Groups for Children

Introduction

There is increasing need for groups designed for children. With concern growing for children with special needs and strengthened school-based systems for identifying them, parents in greater numbers are looking at treatment options. The realization that children traumatized by natural and man-made events are also in need of care has resulted in special opportunities for children in trauma-related groups, some school-based, and others offered in the community.

Working with children requires collaboration with parents and other primary caregivers, teachers and counselors and frequently pediatricians. Typically, parental guidance sessions create the climate at home that will help the child build upon what she has gained in the treatment. Teachers and counselors will also collaborate to facilitate the further development of the child in a way that supports the group therapy. Physicians are consulted to identify any possible biochemical issues involved and where needed to prescribe the appropriate medications. It is obvious that demands of seeing children in group often exceed those involved in running adult groups.

The techniques for conducting children's group treatment will vary widely from those deemed appropriate with adults, and the age and developmental levels of the youngsters will further dictate how the leader works. One's view of personality development will also shape the therapist's style of working. Finally, the arena in which the treatment takes place will also influence the nature of the group.

When working with groups of traumatized children, the leader faces additional challenges. Dealing with shock and continuing threats needs to be part of the therapist's repertoire. Cooperating with governmental and other agencies may be a necessary task not associated with conventional treatment.

Seth Aronson in "Group Psychotherapy with Children," provides a how-to-do manual and rationale for establishing a group for children. Explaining their developmental needs, he suggests ways of organizing and leading such a group. The leader needs to determine the stance needed to achieve optimal benefit. The roles of parents and other external resources are considered.

What Aronson does for children, Andrew Pojman does for adolescents. In "Adolescent Group Therapy," Pojman describes how he works with this population. Issues regarding screening, group composition, ethics and confidentiality are clearly discussed. The leader interested in working with specialized populations, such as those needing assistance in anger management, will find a framework here through which to respond in group.

In "The Earth as a Classroom: Children's Groups in the Aftermath of Mass Trauma," Emily Zeng brings her approach to working with children to the earthquake zone in China. Using mentors and supervisors in group, she has developed a multi-modal approach to a very traumatized population. In ways that are depicted she also responds to community needs and pressures as she works outside of the consulation room. The importance of considering culture is underscored here. Her work is particularly impressive since group treatment in China is reatively new.

Tom Stone and Anne Thomas work with troubled youngsters in an institutional setting. In their, "A Multidisciplinary Treatment Team Model for Youth Offenders in Correctional Centers . . . " they consider the application of group treatment to clients with severe behavior problems and deficits in the ability to socialize. This chapter is also important in its coverage of organizational dynamics that facilitate or impede treatment.

29
Group Therapy with Children
Seth Aronson

Introduction

Donald Winnicott, the renowned British pediatrician/psychoanalyst, began one of his essays with an epigram from Tagore, "On the seashore of endless worlds, children play". (Winnicott, 1971: p. 95). Group therapy provides children with such a setting – there are any number of media available to them – talking, playing, doing – and 'endless worlds' of relational possibilities – with each of the other members individually, in pairs or a group-as-a-whole, and with the group leader. The world of children is a "network of groupings ranging from loosely organized play groups in the schoolyard or neighborhood to special purpose clubs, athletic teams and cliques" (Aronson, 1998: p. 432). Children's perceptions of self and other are rooted in their actual experiences; Sullivan (1953) discussed the widening scope of social-interpersonal awareness as a result of exposure to group life outside the home, as well as the subsequent establishment of in-groups and out-groups in childhood society, ideas later echoed by Erikson (1959). The importance of children's group life, of organized games (Bettelheim, 1987; Sutton-Smith, 1986) and of manual activities for the expression of emotion, identity formation and for learning spatial skills have all been noted in the literature. All of these factors lend credence to the findings of many studies that "the group format is equal in effectiveness and efficacy to individual treatment and superior in cost-effectiveness" (Shechtman and Mor, 2010).

Historical Background

Many of the pioneering child group therapists were originally trained as educators, and used their knowledge of classroom management to therapeutic effect. August Aichhorn, in 1920's Vienna, coordinated a series of group homes for youth, in which principles of group therapy were paramount in creating a therapeutic milieu (Aichhorn,

1936). Later, in this country, Slavson (1943, 1950) and Redl (1944, 1966) continued the application of children's responsiveness to group experience to beneficial effect. These approaches were welcome in child guidance clinics, where clinicians were learning that, in some cases, it was difficult to elicit verbal communications in elementary school-aged children in a one-to-one treatment context (Scheidlinger, 1982). Slavson called his modality "activity group therapy" (AGT), stressing the expression of fantasies and feelings through activity and play. The interactions of the children with each other and with the therapist constituted the major therapeutic ingredients.

Slavson's model was extended to work with adolescents (Gabriel, 1939), and preschoolers, (Schiffer, 1969) as well as to more severely disturbed young children (Frank, 1976; Scheidlinger, 1960). More recent applications of group work with various populations include group work with sexually abused children (Mandell et al., 1989), children who have lost a parent to AIDS (Aronson, 1995), children with learning disabilities (Mishna and Muskat, 2004), expressive arts therapies (Weber and Haen, 2005), groups for children with trauma-related symptoms (Keyser, Seehaus and Kahn, 2000; Shechtman and Mor, 2010) and ADD (Chasen, 2005), to name just a few.

Classifications of Children's Groups

Using Scheidlinger's (1985) model of adolescent groups, different types of group therapies may be distinguished, such as psychoeducational groups and support groups. In this chapter, the focus will be on *clinical group psychotherapy*. Clinical group psychotherapy always entails a trained mental health practitioner who is working with a carefully balanced group. The idea of balance, originally described by Slavson (1943), is achieved via the screening process (to be discussed below), with each group member being assessed and judged suitable for the particular group. In contrast, in psychoeducational and support groups, there may be little screening and assessment process, as these groups tend to be aimed at prevention, education and do not necessarily have the *explicit* goal of reducing symptoms. Examples of this type of group include therapeutic community meetings held on inpatient units, or daily meetings held at group residences. In these groups, there is no selection of members; the group is open to everyone on the unit or in the residence at the time. To be sure, each type of group has its own value, and the distinction between types is made in the interest of conceptual clarity, and planning and implementation of the group.

Curative Factors in Group

Yalom and Leszcz (2005) have described several curative factors in group experience: installation of hope; universality; imparting information; altruism; corrective recapitulation of the family experience; interpersonal learning; group cohesion; catharsis; existential factors; development of socializing techniques; imitative behavior.

Not all of these factors apply equally to children's groups. Shechtman and Gluk (2005) found the three most relevant therapeutic factors for children to be group cohesion, catharsis and social techniques. For other children, especially those from abusive families, the corrective experience of being in a family-like group can be extremely powerful. (This may coincide with fantasies about the leader, or leaders, as parent figures.)

> In one children's group, the two leaders disagreed about planning the next week's activity. Jennifer, a nine year old girl from a home characterized by domestic violence, became visibly agitated. She explained that she was concerned that a fight would ensue and "someone would get hurt." The leaders explained that they could agree to disagree without resorting to violence.

Some group members develop an increased capacity for empathy in group, which fosters a sense of altruism, enabling them to give to others in the group, and receive the benefits of such altruism. Other children's groups described in the literature (Aronson, 1995) highlight the power of universality in creating a sense of group cohesion.

> In one of the first sessions of a group for children whose parents had died of AIDS, the children began asking each other in which cemeteries their parents were buried. The leader was, understandably, uncomfortable with the subject matter, but realized it was the group's way of bonding and making explicit the commonalities among them.

Redl (1966) has described the importance of group as an arena for social and interpersonal learning, as well as for imparting information that children may not gain otherwise. For example, street-wise pre-adolescent boys may not have basic facts about sex; or, children who have been sexually abused may require help in basic self- and body-care. The group also provides a space in which children received direct feedback about the impact of their behavior on others.

In addition to the curative factors described, there are several elements common to all groups.

Each group develops its own *code*. The code refers to the procedures, assumptions and commonly held beliefs which are specific to each group. For example, a school-based group may decide that they are the "bad group," and that everyone in the group has been sent there by the principal. Or, there may be elaborate seating rituals ("hey, that's my seat" – as if seats were assigned!). There may be beliefs about the group leader which are tacitly or overtly expressed.

Every group has its own *infrastructure*. In one course on group process for classroom teachers taught by the author, a teacher presented a diagram with the rooming requests for fifth graders as they prepared to visit a nature retreat. The ensuing diagram was quite revealing as to who were the most popular students, who were the outliers, where cliques lay, and so on. Every group – be it a classroom of 25 students, or an activity group with six members – will have subgroups, cliques, and in and out groups.

In addition, every member plays a *role*. The role may be fluid or fixed. Some are easier to identify, others more difficult. Common roles include the leaders' assistant, the clown, the monopolizer, the silent member, the storyteller, and the scapegoat (to be discussed further).

It is important to note that each role fulfills a purpose on an individual and group level. For example, a child who clowns around is probably reflecting his/her own anxiety and regressive propensity, but is also helping to distract the group from the task at hand. A silent group member may not necessarily be withdrawn from the group, but rather, provides a sense of mystery and a potential group cohesive activity as the rest of the group tries to draw the silent member out, and figure out what he/she might be thinking. A monopolizer is clearly fulfilling some narcissistic need, but the monopolizer also allows the other members to be silent and not participate. Thus, it is extremely helpful to the group leader to ascertain each member's role and how the role serves the group as well as the individual, so he/she may interevene in a thoughtful, timely manner.

Each group also has a sense of the group as a unique entity unto itself, the "*group-as-a-whole.*" The group is not only a number of individuals, but also has its own identity as a group *qua* group. This idea, in practice, can be a powerful supportive force, much like Winnicott's "holding environment" (Winnicott, 1960); Scheidlinger (1982) has described this element as the "mother-group" (to be discussed later).

The leader, or what Redl has termed *central person* is also intrinsic to every group. This is a figure around whom the group is organized, even briefly. The central person may shift, depending on the needs of the group at any given time.

> The group began talking about parents' substance use. There was much anxiety, giggling and laughter. Jimmy, an eight year old who was generally quiet and reserved, recently witnessed his brother taken away to a wilderness retreat for his brother's severe substance use. He began to recount what he had learned at family Alanon meetings. The group listened attentively to this quiet member who held the group's attention for the remainder of the session as well as several subsequent meetings.

The *group climate* varies from group to group. This atmosphere is determined by any number of factors, including style of leadership, such as democratic, authoritarian, or laissez-faire. The personality characteristics of the members will also contribute to the group's climate as well as the task confronting the group.

Curative factors in children's groups also include models of parental care, with the group members akin to the infants and the therapists compared to the caregivers. Winnicott's (1960) idea of the "holding environment," mentioned above, is relevant. In Winnicott's thinking, the holding that the infant experiences in relation to his/her mother allows the infant to begin to develop a sense of self, separate from its caregiver. Holding "includes the whole routine of care throughout the day" and through this care, the infant "is able to have a personal existence and so begin to build up a continuity of being" (Winnicott, 1960: p. 54). The group, if run in a "good-enough" manner, allows its members to develop a stronger sense of self and a "continuity of being," which then leads to further enrichment of the self. More recently, Winnicott's ideas of holding have been applied to many other therapeutic settings (Slochower, 1996).

Scheidlinger's idea of the mother-group is also relevant here. This refers to "an aspect of identification with the group entity connoting a covert wish of group members to restore a state of unconflicted well-being characteristic of an earlier tie to the mother" (Scheidlinger, 1974: p. 23). This longing for a return to this relationship and its unequivocally positive need-gratifying elements, is brought directly to bear in and by the group. Used wisely, it can be a powerful force of identification with and connection to the group-as-a-whole.

Bion described the importance of containment (1962). The infant, in his/her effort to survive, rids itself of disturbing, uncomfortable feelings (such as being hungry, wanting attention and care) via the unconscious fantasy of projection. These feelings and psychological experiences are represented via the baby's physical and bodily activities. In fantasy, the infant believes he can evacuate these bad feelings and in turn these feelings will be received by the caregiver. The attuned caregiver accepts these feelings (again, in fantasy), makes sense of them and responds accordingly to the infant's distress. By accepting these feelings and responding, the caregiver is "containing" difficult feelings and, in essence, returning them to the infant in palatable form. In actuality, the caregiver's response to the infant will demonstrate if such containment is taking place. A caregiver who changes the baby's diaper or recognizes the need for feeding is containing the infant's feelings. In contrast, a caregiver who neglects a crying infant is demonstrating lack of containment. In groups, the leader may be called upon to handle and contain disturbing and powerful feelings as they arise (in the members as well as in themselves), helping the group members to make sense of them. The leaders' actual intervention will either demonstrate containment or lack thereof. Such interventions by the therapist can be a powerful force for therapeutic change.

> In a group for young children who were sexually abused, Alisa an eight year old girl who had been repeatedly molested, began inappropriately touching other members. The leaders met with her individually about her behavior, putting into words some of her previously unarticulated experience of being victimized. In the group, the therapists led a discussion of how a child may feel angry after being touched inappropriately, and how this rage may lead that child to want to hurt or touch others. However, the group needs to be a safe place, and rather than act on those feelings, they are better expressed in words. The leaders devised various activities designed to allow for expression of some of the feelings harbored by abused children. This led to further discussions by all the children as to their anger at their abusers and how they might more appropriately and assertively express their feelings.

Caspary (1993) has described a sequence that involves the child projecting disowned difficult self-characteristics and attributes (e.g. flagrantly cheating at a game while accusing the therapist or other members of doing just that), which the therapist accepts, empathically scrutinizes and eventually responds to, thus allowing the child to reinternalize a transformed self-representation. This requires both the holding and containing described by Winnicott and Bion, respectively. In this way, the therapist does not judge the child, but rather attempts to make sense of the child's experience. In the above example, rather than harshly condemning Alisa for her behavior, the leaders met with her in an effort to understand the origins of her actions (which were unknown to her at the time) and, subsequently in group, help her shift her self-representation from helpless, angry, "bad" victim to a more empowered, assertive, non-victimized child.

Developmental Considerations

In determining the structure of the group as well as the "goodness of fit" factors, such as each child's age, gender, developmental level and diagnosis must be considered (Schamess, 1986). For the pre-school child, play groups are a developmentally comfortable and syntonic modality. Pre-schoolers also relate with ease in co-educational groups and generally speaking, accept the authority of adults of either sex. As children enter elementary school, their verbalization skills continue to develop, as do their abilities for reflection and self-awareness. The group becomes a major source of support and self-esteem enhancement.

Games, sports, crafts and other creative and competitive efforts become the building blocks for a sense of identity (see Bettelheim, 1987; Erikson, 1959). The developmental level of the group will also help the group leader in planning activities – does the group require a good deal of structure? Less structure?

> In one group of elementary school aged boys with ADHD, the group leader planned the group's activity each week. In another group for children adjusting to a new school setting (and less impulsive), the same leaders began each session with a group discussion of how the group might decide together what that day's activity should be.

An excellent, useful comprehensive scheme relating children's developmental phases and differential diagnoses to varied group treatment models was proposed by Schamess (1986). In organizing a group for children according to developmental needs, it is necessary to consider the following:

1. A safe physical environment that facilitates peer interaction.
2. Furnishing and play material that are developmentally appropriate.
3. Clearly defined therapist/leader ratios to help the group members individually, and the group-as-a-whole, to master specific developmental tasks.

Indications and Contraindications (the Screening Interview)

A screening appointment with each child and the family can help determine the suitability of the match of group with child. This initial interview also allows the therapist to balance the prospective group (Slavson, 1950). Balancing entails careful consideration of who the group members should be, based on developmental factors and presenting difficulties as well as race, ethnicity, gender, sophistication levels, etc. Some degree of homogeneity is essential to the group. Attention to the group's make-up helps to maximize the group's therapeutic potential and effect. For example, placing an anxious, inhibited nine year old girl into a group for eleven and twelve year old boys with ADHD is a recipe for disaster! On the other hand, the screening interview can allow the therapist to devise a trial for some group members.

> A ten year old boy, bullied at school, was referred for group. The existing group members were boys, ten to twelve, who had difficulties with affect and impulse regulation. The group leaders were concerned that this boy could potentially be scapegoated. Together, with the family, all parties agreed on a four week trial to see how this boy acclimated to group (as well as how the group adjusted to him). At the end of the four week trial, the leaders would meet with the boy and his family and evaluate the "goodness of fit."

The screening interview also creates the opportunity to begin to establish a treatment alliance. During the session, treatment goals can be formulated. For example; "What do you hope to accomplish in the group? How do you envision the group helping you?" These questions can be posed to the potential group member. The goals can help in establishing a treatment plan.

The screening process is essential to establishing an alliance with the family. Particularly with children's groups, the therapist must have the family's support. Without it, the child may have no access or transportation to the group. The parent may use the group as reward or punishment ("If you don't behave, you're not going to your group!"). It is the task of the therapist to show the family that the group is not a special treat or privilege, but a treatment modality necessary for the child's wellbeing.

The frame of the group should be explained during the screening process. Cancellation policies, fees, and group rules should be explained. In addition, it is very important to explain the confidentiality of the group. Most children's group leaders will meet with the family before the child enters the group and at termination, with other meetings scheduled if necessary. It is imperative to explain to the family that the child's privacy must be respected. Obviously, if the child reports that he/she is in danger of harming him-/herself or others, confidentiality must be broken. Confidentiality with children is a tricky business, as some parents may demand to know what is discussed in session, but if the group is to function successfully, the child patient's privacy must be respected. It is also essential, in this day and age of mobile phones and internet messaging that this is made clear to the children that "what is said in the group stays in the group!"

There are some clinicians who draw up a written contract with the rules, framework, number of acceptable number of absences, cancellation policies, etc., for the potential group member and family to sign (Kahn, personal communication). The screening interview can also provide information as to how the child functions in group. Children's lives are replete with group experience – such as religious groups, sports teams, and after-school activities. Asking about the child's involvement in such activities provides a window into the child's life in groups.

As for contraindications, children who are very fragile and anxious are best seen individually prior to placement in larger group. Children who are extremely impulsive, violent or actively psychotic are also poor candidates for group therapy. Today, there are groups for many children who, in the past, would not have been considered for groups (e.g., those with Aspergers, see McAfee, 2002)). It is important to match the child with the group that best fits him/her.

It is best to select six to eight members for each group. This ensures that given inevitable absences due to illness, there will always be a critical mass of children in any given group session.

Structuring the Group

In setting up the group, one must take into account the location and furnishings of the group. A small, crowded room may precipitate frustration, especially for those children at a developmental level which necessitates space in which they can move around freely. Similarly, too large a room may be too expansive and encourage frenzied activity. A room with plush carpeting, expensive furnishings or video equipment invites trouble.

> A small group for young boys in foster care met in a room with video equipment. The boys were immediately drawn to the camera, and ignored the therapist's warning to refrain from touching the expensive equipment. By session's end, the camera was broken, creating a difficult situation in which the boys (and therapist) felt out of control and their aggression untrammeled.

The furnishings can also send a message to the participants.

> A girls group met in a room also used for Alcoholics Anonymous meetings. The furnishings were shabby and some of the chairs were broken. One girl said to the others; "See what they think of us? We're only worth a couple of broken down chairs!" Another, upon finding Alcoholics Anonymous literature on the floor said, half jokingly, "Maybe they think we're alcoholics."

Location of the group room is also critical. Running a group for very active, loud, expressive boys near the clinic administrator's office is sure to bring some degree of anger (and institutional scapegoating) directed at the group and leaders.

The materials and games should be chosen for their therapeutic efficacy and effect. For example, elementary school-aged boys will respond enthusiastically to arts and crafts materials as well as controlled sports games such as dodgeball (using Nerf balls of course!). Board games with clear direct rules are also helpful in diminishing potential fighting and conflicts. Pre-schoolers appreciate projective materials and toys, such as puppets and dollhouses, or costumes. It is important to gear the material to the developmental level of the group in order to foster progression and mastery rather than regression.

> A middle school aged boys group had to switch group rooms due to a scheduling conflict. They met in a room filled with toys for preschoolers. To the astonishment of the group leaders, the "street-wise," savvy boys began talking in "babytalk," one boy even began to suck his thumb! The leaders quickly realized how this particular setting was promoting regression.

The use of food in children's groups has been well-documented (Mishna, Muskat and Schamess, 2002). Simple foods can be used for symbolic and real feeding. In the real sense, children are hungry after school (when groups are usually held); providing snacks can also help with attendance. Symbolically, food provides nurturance and fosters a positive attachment to the group. Food can also be a means of teaching healthy, nutritional eating. Snacks may be fruit, or fruit juice rather than soda or junk food. Children can be encouraged to choose from week to week which fruit they would like for each group session. Further use of food offers a unique opportunity for social skills training. The leader can appoint a member to help distribute the snacks, encouraging sharing, and containing feelings of envy and deprivation.

> In one group, Suzanne, a severely deprived ten year old girl, grabbed nearly all the cookies for herself, hoarding them. In the next session, the leader asked her to help him distribute the snacks. She began to learn how many cookies were needed to go round to ensure each member had an equal share. Suzanne became more cognizant of how her behavior impacted on the others in group.

In this way, children can learn give and take, sharing, and table manners. Food can also help to allay anxiety. Once the children feel fed, they may talk more freely. If possible, it is best to run a children's group for at least a full hour, if not ninety minutes. This length allows for a warm-up period and for full emergence and exploration of the issues that arise in the course of a session. Once weekly is ideal for frequency.

One way to structure the session is to begin with the snacks, with the children sitting in a circle around a table. Once the snacks are distributed, discussion can be initiated, if it hasn't already begun. Some advocate a check-in (Kahn, personal communication) with each child recounting how their week was and what issues they may wish to discuss. An exchange can be initiated and intragroup connections made by encouraging each child to throw an imaginary ball to whichever group member they choose, who then picks the next member to go, and so on. This check-in gives the leader a sense of what to expect in group or what issues require follow-up. After the snack and "talk-time," the activity section can begin, with talking encouraged throughout. Following the activity, there may be a check-in at group's end, again in a circle, with the therapist asking each member how they feel, how they felt group went, etc. Groups for more disturbed children tend to be more structured, and experiential, rather than focused on discussion (Schamess, 1986; Scheidlinger, 1960; Frank, 1976). These groups have frameworks in which limits are very clear, goals are manageable and the children themselves feel contained and nurtured, making the groups more therapeutically effective.

How many rules to implement will also be determined by the group's composition.

> In the first group for children with impulse control difficulties, one girl suggested the group go around the room and say "who we were"(meaning ethnic backgrounds). The group leader asked her, if she was worried about people calling others names. She shyly nodded. The group members, including the leaders, divulged their ethnicities. The other leader then said; "You know, that's a good idea – we should talk about rules – does the group have any suggestions?" Immediately, the boys in the group began yelling out suggestions: no fighting, no spitting, no cheating, no writing on chairs. One boy said "and no pissing in the corner." It became evident to the leaders that the boys were asking for a great deal of structure!

Generally speaking, a rule about confidentiality, no one getting hurt (either physically or emotionally) and nothing being broken is a good framework with which to begin a discussion of rules. Groups requiring more structure will find ways to let the therapist know of their need for more explicit rules; groups requiring less structure will need less explicit limits.

The initial child group therapy pioneers advocated a single group leader. However, more recently, there is a growing use of a co-therapy model. This is a good idea for several reasons. Yalom and Leszcz's (1995) list of curative factors include recapitulation of the family. A co-therapy model, whether it be male-female, or two therapists of the same gender, will more readily elicit the ubiquitous fantasies regarding the leaders as parents and group as family. The children inevitably cast the leaders into paternal-maternal roles, regardless of gender.

> In one group led by a male and female therapist, the children wondered aloud all year if the leaders were married or boyfriend and girlfriend. In another group led by two men, the children commented on how one seemed strict, while the other male leader was nicer, softer and "more gentle."

There can be a teaching advantage to having a trainee conduct and simultaneously observe a group with a senior practitioner (Scheidlinger, personal communication). A two leader model is also quite practical. In the event of a group member having a difficult time and requiring individual attention, one leader can take the troubled member aside while the other continues to conduct the group. A two leader model also provides important opportunities for support, discussion, relief through humor and debriefing after each session. Of course, a disadvantage of a two leader model is that it may lead the group to pit one against the other, but this can be handled in group, collegial consultation or supervision (Soo, 1991; Schamess, Strieder, and Connors, 1997).

Depending on the needs of the group, a group may be short- or long-term, time-limited or open-ended. A short-term, time-limited group is generally a group with a focus (for example, a twelve session program for children whose parents are divorcing). In such a group, it is not prudent to bring new members into the group once it begins as the twelve sessions leave little time to foster cohesion. A longer term group, one run for the duration of the school year, for example, is more conducive to adding new members once the group has started, provided it is not too far along into the group's development. If the group is designed to allow for members rotating in and out and is part of the group's culture, the children will be accustomed to welcoming new members and saying goodbye to the more veteran members.

The Child Group Therapy Leader

Brems (1994), as quoted in Sheppard (2008), describes various positive attributes of the therapist with who works with children. They include: self-respect; self-awareness; open-mindedness; cultural and gender sensitivity; respect for the child and family; empathy; flexibility and tolerance of ambiguity (Sheppard, 2008). Other important characteristics include a willingness to play, perhaps based in part on an ability to use regression in the service of the ego (Kris, 1952). Such an ability to play, as described by Winnicott (1971), also includes the capacity to understand verbal and non-verbal material.

The leader must be able to focus on the relationships in group (and in children's groups, they are plentiful and manifold!), supporting and facilitating communication among members. By demonstrating the ability to contain difficult emotions, the therapist provides the group with the sense of "holding" (described above) as well as a sense of safety. One of Yalom and Leszcz's (2005) curative factors is instillation of hope and it is critical that the therapist believe in the group's ability to help its members with their respective difficulties, in this way holding out hope and confidence in the group's ability to heal.

Shechtman (2007) describes six types of responsiveness on the part of the therapist in group therapy: the therapist encourages, provides directives, questions, paraphrases and reframes material, gives feedback, and at times, self-discloses. Self-disclosure, or divulging information about the therapist by the therapist, should be done in a judicious fashion, if its goal is to further the therapeutic process. The therapist who simply offers personal information may flood the children with too much information, overstimulating them and increasing their anxiety. A sense of humor can also be critical in child group work as it provides perspective on what can be a difficult and challenging process.

Transference and Countertransference

Contemporary interpersonal-relational approaches to transference-countertransference (in essence, the relationship between patient and therapist) advocate an interaction between past history and engagement in the present (e.g. Mitchell, 1988; Gill, 1982; Hoffman, 1983; Levenson, 1972). Thus, the child group members approach the group experience with anticipation based on past and present relationships, and weave what they notice about the leader and other members into their expectation of understanding the world. The child's relationship to others in the group is not simply a distortion based on history, but a complex configuration that takes into account both history and the present. (Incidentally, this is also true for the group leader, suggesting that the group leader is not the arbiter of whole truth, above the action as it were, but in fact, a player and participant in the group's process. The therapist will himself have reactions to what goes on in the group, in part based on what is going on in the present, and in part based on the therapist's own unique personal history. The group therapist's reactions are natural and inescapable – ultimately, they represent important avenues of information.)

> Carlos, an appealing ten year old boy, always chose a seat beside the therapist. Admonishments to the group were immediately forthcoming: "Would you guys keep it down?" "Quit acting stupid – show the man some respect." The therapist realized how much he appreciated Carlos' help and how it was almost like having a younger brother, or trainee beside him. Over time, and with supervision, the leader began to understand how Carlos' behavior served both the boy and the leader's needs, and not incidentally, kept Carlos from fully joining his peers and the leader from doing his job in facilitating Carlos' involvement in the group (both enactments).

Thus, the transference and countertransference represent a mix of intrapsychic and interpersonal phenomena on several levels. The multiple members of the group multiply the number of opportunities for transference and countertransference. Each member may have a transference to every other member, the leaders and to the group-as-a-whole.

Group therapy with children poses several unique transference and countertransference issues. Because the therapist is an adult and the members are children, it is nearly impossible for the group not to view, in some form, the leader as a parental/authority figure. They will respond accordingly. A child who is angrily resisting limits from parents may immediately challenge the group rules.

> In the first group meeting, the therapist was going over the simple rules: confidentiality, no one gets hurt and nothing gets broken. One eleven year old boy took out a cigarette lighter he had been hiding and flicked it dangerously near one of the window curtains. "If something burns, does it count for things being broken?" he asked provocatively. It became clear that this boy was challenging authority at home and at school.

As children are more active, there is a greater chance there will be acting out behaviors that the therapist will be called upon to handle. The interaction with the child's family will raise countertransference for the child group therapist, as it is bound to trigger his own feelings towards his family of origin. Frankiel (1985) has described the wish by therapists to rescue child patients, thereby proving that the therapist is a better parent to the child. This is also related to a strong over-identification with the child, which can lead to unconscious collusion in an "us versus them" mentality. The child group members may attempt to elicit support from the leader against authority figures, such as teachers, school principals, and of course parents. "Don't you think my grounding is unfair?"; "That teacher is so mean – she hates me"; "Can't you please speak to my mom for me?" are all common conscious (or unconscious) ploys to draw on the therapist's over-identification with the child group members. Azima (1972) has described other such manifestations of countertransferential reactions, such as excessive self-disclosure in an effort to ingratiate oneself to the group, somatization and omnipotence.

In Bion's theory of containment, the difficulties of containing powerful feelings and not act on them brings heavy countertransferential pressure to bear on the group therapist. For example, listening to a horrifying account of abuse will undoubtedly elicit strong feelings in the therapist, who must take care to respond based on the child's needs and not his own feelings and reactions.

> In one group for children who were survivors of sexual abuse, Brian, aged ten, cried as he described his older cousin molesting him. "It was so weird having him touch me – I hated it." Rather than jumping in with an intervention, the group leaders let Brian continue. "But he's my cousin – I spend time with him – he teaches me how to be a better baseball player, and he even let me use his skateboard. How can I hate him?"
>
> It was clear that Brian's feelings towards his cousin were very conflicted and had the therapists rushed in with their own feelings of anger, they would have been misattuned to Brian's very real feelings of love for the same cousin who abused him.

Phelan (1974) has described the multiple roles of the group therapist who works with youth: parent, teacher and analyst. The child group leader must juggle all three – field responses as if he were the group's parent, provide education and information (Yalom and Leszcz, 2005) when called for – all the while maintaining his role as therapist. No easy task!

Stages of Group Development

Hajal, and also Riester (in Aronson and Scheidlinger, 2002) cite Tuckman's evocative naming of stages of development of group: forming, storming, norming and performing. Other writers (Corey, Corey, 2002; Garland, Jones and Kolodney, 1973; Smead, 1995) advocate different ways of conceptualizing group development.

The following scheme draws on some of these models of group development.

First stage – Pre-affiliation

This is characterized by the anxiety each child member has about fitting in – who are these strangers who are the members of this group? Where do I fit? The group leader must be very active in encouraging introduction of members, creating connections, and establishing the frame (e.g. rules, confidentiality). The limits and rules provide the group with a sense of safety and trust.

> Sean, an athletic boy of eleven and new to the group, introduced himself by informing the group where he went to school, and that he liked football and baseball. Alan, another member chimed in: "You like baseball – me too!" and then to the group – "this will be a great kid to have in group!" Jesse began to describe the fights he had with his younger brother. One of the leaders asked if other members also had difficulties with younger siblings. Several other boys began to talk about their issues with siblings. In doing so, the leader had begun to establish a commonality, leading towards increased cohesion and sense of purpose.

In this first stage, there may be much fluidity of roles and themes, making it a good time to add new members, if necessary. As the group begins to coalesce, there may be issues of power and control as members vie for status. A hierarchy based on group roles may be established, although there may be some fluidity as roles change. The therapist may be directly challenged, and the leader's ability to contain and set limits is crucial to maintaining a sense of safety within the group.

Working stage

As the group's cohesion builds, intimacy deepens. There may be noticeable personal involvement of group members with each other. A family-like feeling grows as do references to the group as a valued unit. In this working stage, children may spontaneously report on events that have occurred outside of group, and how they are trying to handle them better, based on feedback and experience in group. In this working stage, children may more readily ask for and give help to each other. There is a clarity of and trust in group purpose.

> At the end of one emotionally draining group, in which many of the members spoke movingly of their parents' battles with alcoholism, the group expressed sadness at having to end. One boy suggested: "Hey, why don't all of us who take the bus walk to the bus stop together?" The members readily agreed and talked excitedly to each other as they left the group room, clinic and, in essence, carried the group with them out into the street.

Termination stage

In the termination stage, members consolidate what learning and gains they have made. There is sadness as they mourn the loss of the group. Some members may revert to old behaviors in an effort to turn back the clock, and stall the inevitable end of the group. The group leader should encourage members to consider how they might carry the gains they have made forward, into the future. The group may excitedly recapitulate the history of the group, waxing nostalgically about their history ("remember when. . . . ?"). A party, event, or ritual with festive food items or a special activity may help to mark the group's ending.

Short-term groups undergo similar developmental stages. The time-limited nature of short-term groups forces the leaders to pay even closer attention to group selection and composition as well as the establishment of focused, achievable goals. A focus on adaptation and mastery becomes essential.

Some Common Problem Behaviors

Scapegoating, "a phenomenon as old as human history" (Scheidldinger, 1982) is an inevitable part of group process. It is a defensive phenomenon that "entails simultaneous behavioral components from the individual-intrapsychic, the interpersonal and the group-as-a-whole frames of reference" (Scheidlinger, 1982). Scapegoating is a complex process that allows the group to rid itself of unacceptable wishes, feelings, thoughts and characteristics by attributing them to the scapegoated member. It is based on a wish from the scapegoaters to conform with the initiator, a reluctance to challenge those seemingly in power, and a diffusion of responsibility (members feel less responsible for acts of omission if they can share the guilt and responsibility with others).

Scapegoating is interactive, involving both individual and group factors. Thus, the child who is prone to regressive, immature behaviors on an individual level can easily become a target. On the group level, projection occurs. By scapegoating the immature group member, the other group members can distance themselves from their own propensity for immature, regressive behavior. It can also seem to enhance cohesion among the scapegoating members (Eilenberg and Wyman, 1998). Scapegoating can be a way to repair narcissistic injury and damaged self-esteem. Sadly, this has certainly been borne out by our society, in the form of racism, bigotry and discrimination. In short, it is a way to rid oneself of unacceptable emotions.

> Denise, a ten year old girl, anticipated being scapegoated from the very first moment of group. She grabbed snacks, mercilessly denigrating herself, referring to herself a "fat pig." She often came late, persistently asking for extra help from the group leaders during craft activities. She would complain, in a voice much younger than her eleven years, "I can't do it!" The other girls began to call her names and complain about her "being such a baby – why do you bother the leaders so much? Do it yourself!" It became clear to the leaders that Denise was an easy target for the members' feelings and allowed them to distance themselves from their own wishes for dependency in the wake of pre-adolescence.

Scheidlinger (1982) has proscribed offering "psychological first-aid" to the victim. This provides a measure of support and trust that the leader will ensure that the group is safe. Once the leader firmly puts a stop to the scapegoating behavior, it is important to understand the underlying projection so that discussion can lead to the group's acknowledgement of their own behavior – the how, why and theme behind it.

Another common problematic behavior in children's groups is what Redl called "emotional contagion"(Redl, 1966).

> The group was busy decorating picture frames as gifts for Mother's Day. Suddenly, seemingly out of nowhere, one boy burst out laughing. "You're so stupid" said one girl as she began to laugh. Other members began giggling. Soon they couldn't stop. The entire group was laughing and becoming more and more silly. A frame fell to the floor, shattering the glass. The leaders felt helpless in the onslaught of the group's regression.

Redl describes the origin of such contagion. Generally, there is an acute conflict area in the group (in this case, feelings about mothers, deprivation, nurturance), a high degree of emotional liability, and an initiator with high status in the group (the boy who began laughing). The initiator must have high status if his behavior is to be accepted and spread by the others. A group that is characterized by cohesion will allow the initiator's behavior to spread quickly, especially if the initiator seems to demonstrate little guilt or hesitation about his behavior.

Stopping the emotionally contagious behavior depends on identifying the initiator and the issue/conflict area so it can be addressed. It may also involve the leaders breaking up the cohesion of the group (which, in this case, is working at cross-purposes with the best interests of group) by creating subgroups, and, at times, separating the initiator.

Ethical Concerns in Group

As noted above, a primary concern is confidentiality. This is often difficult as the family is paying for the treatment, responsible for the child and may want to know details about the group. It is essential to establish the parameters of what can and cannot be divulged at the screening interview.

Establishing rules and boundaries ensures that group members are safe and maximizes the possibility of trust in the group.

> In one children's group that met in a school, the group was assigned to a room in which, at times, teachers would inadvertently open the door, thinking the room was free (despite the prominent "Do Not Disturb" sign posted on the door!). The leader would caution the children to remain quiet until the intruding teacher shut the door. This aspect of maintaining the frame (and protecting privacy) became internalized so that after a while, the door would open, and the children would remind each other to remain silent till the door was closed again.

Shechtman (2007) has advocated instituting measures of accountability to track group outcomes, and in this way, illustrate the benefits of the group experience for its participants. Some of these measures include self-report questionnaires devised by the leaders to be completed by the children, behavior rating scales to be filled out by teachers, and pre- and post-outcome measures to be completed by the child's caregivers.

Corey and Corey (2002) and Smead (1995) suggest that the leader engage in self-evaluation following group, which can also represent a measure of accountability. Shechtman (2007), in adapting ideas from the American School Counseling Association's Code of ethics, advocates careful screening of children, as well as assessment for motivation for engagement in group, all in the service of selecting the right group for each child.

Conclusion

The economic realities of today, which include managed care, changes in national healthcare in the United States, and continued budget cuts in the public sector, increasingly suggest shifts to pragmatic and cost-effective treatment. Group therapy for children represents such a pragmatic and cost-effective approach.

Group treatment for children as originally described by its pioneers has now been extended to the public and private sectors, schools, institutions serving children and other venues. Today's children's group leaders make use of group therapy theory as well as developmental principles in helping to provide children with educational, restitutive and therapeutic experiences. The challenges remain for the child group therapist – how to withstand the outside economic pressures in addition to the pressures of the work, maintain a balance of leader and participant, demonstrate authenticity and spontaneity, while enabling the children to play in "endless worlds?" The challenges may be daunting, but the rewards are great.

References and Bibliography

Aichhorn, A. (1936). *Wayward youth*. New York: Viking.

Aronson, S. (1995). Group intervention with children of parents with AIDS. *Group, 18*(3), 133–140.

Aronson, S. (1998). Group therapy with children. In N. Alessi, J. Coyle, S. Harrison, S. Eth (Eds.), *Handbook of child and adolescent psychiatry* (Vol. 6, pp. 432–439). New York: Wiley.

Azima, F. (1972). Transference and countertransference. *International Journal of Child Psychotherapy, 1*(4), 51–70.

Bettelheim, B. (1987). The importance of play. *The Atlantic Monthly*, 39–48.

Bion, W. (1962). *Learning from experience*. Karnac: London.

Brems, C. (1994). *The child therapist: Personal traits and markers of effectiveness*. Needham Heights, Massachusetts: Allyn & Bacon.

Caspary, A. (1993). Aspects of the therapeutic action in child analytic treatment. *Psychoanalytic Psychology, 10*(2), 207–220.

Chasen, L. (2005). Spectacle and ensemble in group: Drama therapy treatment for children with ADHD and related neurological symptoms. In A. Weber & C. Haen (Eds.), *Clinical applications of drama therapy in child and adolescent treatment* (pp. 153–170). E. Sussex, UK: Brunner-Routledge.

Corey, M., & Corey, G. (2002). *Groups: Process and practice* (6th Ed.). Pacific Grove, California: Brooks/Cole Publishing.

Eilenberg, M., & Wyman, S. (1998). Scapegoating in an early adolescent girls' group. *Journal of Child and Adolescent Group Therapy, 8*(1), 3–13.

Erikson, E. (1959). *Identity and the life cycle.* New York: International Universities Press.
Frank, M. (1976). Modifications of activity group therapy: Responses of ego-impoverished children. *Clinical Social Work Journal, 4,* 102–113.
Frankiel, R. (1985). The stolen child. *International Review of Psychoanalysis, 12,* 417–430.
Gabriel, B. (1939). An experiment in group treatment. *American Journal of Orthopsychiatry, 9,* 146–169.
Garland, J., Jones, H., & Kolodny, R. (1973). A model for stages of development in social work groups. In S. Bernstein (Ed.), *Explorations in group work* (pp. 17–71). Boston: Milford House.
Gill, M. (1982). *The analysis of transference.* New York: International Universities Press.
Hajal, F. (2002).Group psychotherapy with psychiatrically hospitalized adolescents. In S. Aronson & S. Scheidlinger (Eds.), *Group treatment of adolescents in context* (pp. 123–140). Madison, Connecticut: International Universities Press.
Hoffman, I. (1983). The patient as interpreter of the analyst's experience. *Contemporary Psychoanalysis, 19,* 389–422.
Kahn. G. (2000). Personal communication.
Keyser, J., Seehaus, K., & Kahn, G. (2000). Children of trauma and loss. In R. Klein, & V. Schermer (Eds.), *Group psychotherapy for psychological trauma.* New York: Guilford.
Kris, E.(1952). *Psychoanalytic explorations in art.* New York: International Universities Press.
Levenson, E. (1972). *The fallacy of understanding.* New York: Basic Books.
Mandell, J., Damon, L., Castalso, P., et al. (1989). *Group treatment for sexually abused children.* New York: Guilford.
McAfee, J. (2002).*Navigating the social world; a-curriculum for individuals with aspergers' syndrome, high functioning autism and related disorders.* Arlington, Texas: Future Horizons Inc.
Mishna, F., Muskat, B., & Schamess, G. (2002). Food for thought; The use of food in group therapy with children and adolescents. *International Journal of Group Psychotherapy, 52*(1), 27–47.
Mishna, F. & Muskat, B. (2004). I'm not the only one: group therapy with older children and adolescents who have learning disabilities. *International Journal of Group Psychotherapy, 54*(4), 455–476.
Mitchell, S. (1988). *Relational concepts in psychoanalysis.* Cambridge, Massachusetts: Harvard University Press.
Phelan, J. (1974). Parent, teacher or analyst: the adolescent group therapist's trilemma. *International Journal of Group Psychotherapy, 24,* 238–244.
Redl, F. (1944). Diagnostic group work. *American Journal of Orthopsychiatry, 14,* 53–67.
Redl, F. (1966). *When we deal with children.* Glencoe, Illinois: Free Press.
Riester, A. (2002). The basics in establishing groups in schools. In S. Aronson & S. Scheidlinger (Eds.), *Group treatment of adolescents in context* (pp. 175–190). Madison, Connecticut: International Universities Press.
Schamess, G. (1986). Differential diagnosis and group structure in the outpatient treatment of latency aged children. In I. Kraft & A. Riester (Eds.), *Child group psychotherapy: Future tense* (pp. 29–70). Madison, Connecticut: International Universities Press.
Schamess, G., Streider, F., & Connors, K. (1997). Supervision and staff training for children's group psychotherapy: general principles and applications with cumulatively traumatized, inner city children. *International Journal of Group Psychotherapy, 47*(4), 399–425.
Shechtman, Z. (2007). *Group counseling and psychotherapy with children and adolescents; Theory, research and practice.* New York: Routledge.
Shechtman, Z., & Mor, M. (2010). Groups for children and adolescents with trauma related symptoms: outcome and processes. *International Journal of Group Psychotherapy, 60*(2), 221–244.

Shechtman, Z., & Gluk, O. (2005). The therapeutic factors in group psychotherapy with children. *Group Dynamics: Theory, Research and Practice, 9*, 127–134.

Scheidlinger, S. (1960). Experiential group treatment of severely deprived latency age children. *American Journal of Orthopsychiatry, 30*, 356–368.

Scheidlinger, S. (1974). On the concept of the "mother-group". *International Journal of Group Psychotherapy, 24*(4), 19–30.

Scheidlinger, S. (1982). *Focus on group psychotherapy-clinical essays*. Madison, Connecticut: International Universities Press.

Scheidlinger, S. (1985). Group treatment of adolescents; an overview. *Amercian Journal of Orthopsychiatry, 55*, 102–111.

Scheidlinger, S. (Personal communication).

Schiffer, M. (1969). *The therapeutic play group*. New York: Grune & Stratton.

Sheppard, T. (2008). *Group psychotherapy with children*. New York: American Group Psychotherapy Association.

Slavson, S. (1943). *An introdcution to group therapy*. New York: International Universities Press.

Slavson, S. (1950). *Child centered group guidance for parents*. New York: Internatiolla Universities Press.

Slochower, J. (1996). *Holding and psychoanalysis*. Hillsdale, New Jersey: Analytic Press.

Smead, R. (1995). *Skills and techniques for group work with children and adolescents*. Champaign, Illinois: Research Press.

Soo, E. (1991). Strategies for success for the beginning group therapist with child and adolescent groups. *Journal of Child and Adolescent Group Therapy, 1*, 95–106.

Sullivan, H. (1953). *The interpersonal theory of psychiatry*. New York: W. W. Norton.

Sutton-Smith, B. (1986). *Toys and culture*. New York: Basic Books.

Weber, A. M., & Haen, C. (2005). *Clinical applications of drama therapy in child and adolescent treatment*. E. Sussex, UK: Brunner-Routledge.

Winnicott, D. W. (1960). *The maturational processes and the facilitating environment*. New York: International Universities Press.

Winnicott, D. W. (1971). *Playing and reality*. London: Tavistock.

Yalom, I., & Leszcz, M. (2005). *The theory and practice of group psychotherapy*. (5th ed.). NewYork: Basic Books.

30
Adolescent Group Psychotherapy: The Real Work
Andrew P. Pojman

Introduction

Adolescence is defined as the transitional time between puberty and adulthood. Levy-Warren (1996) lists this time as ranging from 10–22 years of age while the American Academy of Child and Adolescent Psychiatry has the adolescence stage ranging from 13–19 years (American Academy of Child and Adolescent Psychiatry, 2001). No matter the age span, adolescence is a period of change, excitement, and passion; it is also a time of uproar, chaos, and high-risk behaviors. A variety of researchers and theorists have discussed the adolescent developmental tasks needed to make this transition into adulthood. Gemelli (1996) integrated these theorists and their models into a non-sequential biopsychosocial model of development: survive puberty; develop a sense of identity (Erickson, 1968); accomplish secondary separation-individuation (Blos, 1962); expand relationships; contemplate a realistic plan to achieve social and economic independence; achieve abstract conceptualization (Piaget, 1972); integrate a mature value system (Kohlberg, 1981). The achievement of these goals is significantly tied to friendships and the socialization process (Meeks and Bernet, 2001). Relationships and patterns of interpersonal experiences determine the development and functioning of the brain not only in adolescence but also throughout our life (Siegel, 1999). Adolescence with its emphasis on socialization and the "riotous changes" in the cerebral cortex (McAuliffe, 2007) makes group therapy an important component of any psychological treatment for this developmental stage.

Socialization is a complex phenomenon which requires neurological, psychological, and social factors – some or all of which many adolescents struggle with. These struggles may be related to psychoneurological immaturities, isolation, trauma, substance abuse, inadequate caregiving, and poverty. The group experience whether within the family, school, neighborhood, or clinic office is crucial to the successful transitioning from adolescence to adulthood. The psychotherapeutic group meets these developmental needs, offering opportunities for corrective experience, social skill development, and connection.

This chapter is written in the spirit of touching upon "The Real Work" of adolescent treatment. Because of their developmental needs, group work with the adolescent is and can be markedly different from working with adults and even children. This population innately is a high-risk group that can "pull at your heart" and "get into your head." Material from this chapter was collected from a variety of sources. It was chosen with the idea of highlighting the special aspects of working with this trying, exciting, sometimes scary, and unique patient population in a psychotherapeutic group.

The Group Culture and Pre-Group Interview

An understanding and sensitivity to the adolescent culture is imperative to successful adolescent treatment (Pojman, 2009); the adolescent culture is what drives identity formation, friendships, and social development. It is shaped by the family, school, neighborhood, media, and the Internet. A psychotherapy group has its own special culture – a culture that facilitates psychological growth, interaction, and learning. This group culture begins to form prior to the first session. Sensitivity to this process is essential since the culture of the group fosters identification and inclusion – salient factors necessary for healthy adolescent development.

Setting

The setting, by its innate structure, plays a significant role in determining the culture of the psychotherapeutic group. It defines the purpose of the group, membership, length of the session, and frequency of meeting. Groups are offered in: school, inpatient facilities, residential placements, juvenile detention facilities, or outpatient clinics. The purpose of groups in each of these settings can be different. For example, group in an inpatient facility is more focused on immediate stabilization and anxiety reduction of the psychiatrically distressed teen who will be soon be discharged while group in a school may emphasize friendships and social skill development meeting throughout the academic year.

Purpose

The purpose of the group is defined usually by the need, which refers to both individual and common adolescent concerns, desires, and problems (Malekoff, 2004). These needs can be assessed in a variety of formal and informal ways. Formal ways include interview with the adolescent, discussion with the parents, physician, or teachers. A psychiatric diagnosis may, by its very nature, help determine areas of concern and need for assistance. Informal assessment can be done in casual interpersonal interactions (hanging-out) in the classroom, on the hospital unit, or within the community setting.

The goal and purpose of the group need to be clearly identified not only to the adolescent but also to his parents, teacher, probation officer, etc. The goal needs to be developmentally appropriate, realistic, and obtainable. Failures in group therapy often come about because these goals and the purposes are not clearly articulated (Kurland and Salmon, 1998). It would not be unusual that this goal and purpose would change over time especially with a long-term group. An anger management group might shift to focusing more on loss and depression as a group member deals with the sudden loss of a loved one.

Physical site

The setting or the demands of the physical site often determine the size of the group. Rachman (1995) noted that the "emotional warmth, physical comfort, and 'psychological room to breathe and interact' are the hallmarks of such a setting" (Rachman, 1995: p. 75). In some venues, this ideal may be readily reached while in others the therapist may have to negotiate or be creative in meeting this need. For example, a group of emotionally disturbed adolescents meets in their classroom. The therapist makes sure that the group rearranges part of the classroom using a screen to separate the group space from the desks of the classroom. This physical change in the room allows for the creation of a therapeutic space for the group.

Member composition

The culture of the adolescent group is helped by having members who are more alike than different – a principle called Redl's Law of Optimum Distance (1951), that is; "the group should be homogeneous in enough ways to ensure their stability and heterogeneous enough to ensure their vitality" (Northen and Kurland, 2001: pp. 122–123). If possible, the guiding questions for group participation are:

1. Will the adolescent be able to benefit from this group? and,
2. Will the adolescent be able to participate in such a way as to not interfere with the realization of the purpose of the group? (Northen and Kurland, 2001).

The age of the group members is an important consideration since adolescents better relate to peers who are at the same developmental level facing the same kind of problems, stresses, and concerns. Large discrepancies in ages can hinder group cohesion and result in unnecessary levels of tension and worry in group members. Rachman (1995) suggests that early adolescent members should vary in age by one year; middle age adolescents can vary by up to three years; late adolescents can tolerate the widest variance.

The gender of group members is often determined by the demands of the setting and also, the developmental needs of the adolescent. A coed group can raise anxiety, competitiveness, aggression, and sexual feelings. Early adolescents with emerging sexual interest and physical development often function best with same sex group members. Middle and late adolescents may possess the maturity to manage a coed group. It is important to note that usually same sex members allows for more regressive behavior in the group. This regression can be therapeutically helpful or disruptive depending on the group.

Other considerations such as intelligence, social class, sexual orientation, and diagnosis are factors that can color the culture and ultimately the effectiveness of the group. Each group is unique and can have varying levels of tolerance for difference. It is important that the group therapist fosters the member's identification with each other – a process that facilitates the work of the group.

Logistics

The session length varies based on the needs of both the membership and the institution. Adult groups often meet for 90 minutes to 2 hours; a 2-hour group for many adolescents could easily result in physical restlessness, disruptive behavior, and verbal complaints such as "This is boring!" Groups in school often last the length of a class period. No matter the length, it is imperative that the time in group be productive and useful.

The number of sessions or whether or not the group is open to new members or closed is determined by the group needs and the demands of the setting. In some settings, such as hospitals and residential treatment, the groups are on-going with the membership shifting with the population. Anger management, dialectical behavior therapy, and social skill groups are common psychoeducational groups that have a set agenda and time-frame (e.g. eight sessions lasting one hour).

Structure

An adolescent group by its developmental nature requires operational structure. The level of this structure is determined by the purpose of the group; member's maturity; anxiety of the group (including the leader's anxiety); group cohesiveness; and therapist experience (Pojman, 2009). Leaders of adolescent groups have to be more active and involved in the group process. A group can go through periods where a high level of therapist-directed structure is required and times when little therapist involvement is needed.

Rituals and activities provide a structure for the group. They can facilitate interpersonal closeness, foster a sense of community, and help contain the emotions of the group. The rituals could include a check-in; a pizza after the member gets his or her driver's license; or a specific closing for the session ("Tell me one thing you liked about today and one thing you didn't like"). These rituals and activities also provide a way for the therapist to monitor the group process and any therapeutic changes in the group members.

Rules and Confidentiality

Concerns for the beginning adolescent group therapist are rules and confidentiality. Institutional policy and state laws dictate some of the rules and the policy on confidentiality. The issue of "rules" can be notable in the adolescent group since teenagers are often in treatment because of their inability to follow the rules at home, at school, or in society. Rules should be simple and enforceable. I have only two rules in my groups. One is that group members need to be respectful both to each other and the leader; the other rule relates to confidentiality – the legal limitations based on danger to self and others. Confidentiality in group also means that members are not to talk about what is discussed in group with others. The rule of respect is rather broad in nature and behaviorally not well defined. It does, however, cover a variety of issues, for example, talking while others are talking, profanity, physical contact, and individual private conversations within group. The group leader is in the position to define for the group what is respectful and what is not. For example, an angry adolescent discussing his or her feelings may include a profanity – it is not disrespectful; an adolescent cursing for show and out of habit is disrespectful.

The group policy about drugs and alcohol varies from setting to setting. In school or outpatient groups, I have found the best policy to be that the adolescent should not come to group under the influence of any drug or intoxicated. Violations of this rule will result in notification to the appropriate authority be it a school official, parent, caregiver, or probation officer. Any trafficking of drugs between group members either in or outside of group could result in their termination from the group.

It is important to note that total confidentiality in an adolescent group is not possible (Shechtman, 2007). It has been my experience that violations of confidentiality are based on either impulsive lapses or anxiety. An incident may happen in group that raises the anxiety of all members (including the therapist). The disclosure outside of group is a reflection of the group's inability to contain the anxiety of the event.

Pre-group Interview

An important, often overlooked element of running a successful group, is the pre-group interview. The purpose of the interview is to assess a youngster's potential for a therapeutic group experience, to prepare him or her for the group experience, and to develop and foster an alliance (Rachman, 1995). Assessing the adolescent's potential for the group experience involves taking a history of interpersonal relationships paying attention to the quality of these relationships and the level of demonstrated attachment. The interview helps determine the teen's fit for the group. This fit is based on the teen's age, diagnosis, and presenting problem. The teen is prepared for the group by discussing the group's purpose, structure, and rules. The therapist also helps identify for the adolescent clear goals that are easily understood and operationalized. An impulse-ridden, easily overstimulated youngster may have a goal of listening to others and not interrupting while others talk.

It is in this initial contact that the therapeutic alliance is developed and fostered. This alliance requires compassionate understanding of the problem and if needed a positive reframing of the issue. This reframing can help relieve any underlying anxiety and shame. It can also give the youngster a new way to look at an old problem.

While the pre-group interview is desired, in many settings this is not possible. These settings include a psychiatric hospital, a residential facility, or correctional setting. The pre-group interview can then take place in the youngster's first group session. The rules and structure of the group are reviewed. The adolescent is given a chance to recount their background and the nature of the problem that brought them into treatment. If the adolescent is not able to do this, then the therapist may need to help him or her articulate the problem. The information is then used by the therapist to develop a therapeutic goal for the youngster in group. This goal is tailored to the youngster's needs and is reachable. This process facilitates the adolescence's entrance into group.

Group Dynamics and Process

The group dynamics and process are influenced by a number of factors including the stages of group development, member roles, transference, and countertransference. An understanding of these factors is crucial to the running of a successful group.

Stages of group

Appreciation of the stages of group development help the leader track the group process, form interventions, and monitor the maturity of the group. Most of these stages have been developed using adult groups. Garfield et al.'s (1965) model was, however, developed using child and adolescent groups. These five stages include: Pre-affiliation; Power and Control; Intimacy; Differentiation; and Separation.

1. **Pre-affiliation stage**; members demonstrate approach and avoidant behavior struggling with both the wish and fear of connection. The therapist's role is to encourage involvement pointing out the similarity between members with the therapist providing structure to reduce anxiety and encourage inclusion.
2. **Power and Control**; finds the members testing the limits as they strive to assert their autonomy. The therapist clarifies issues and sets limits. More importantly, they work to encourage a balance between "full-blown catharsis and repressive conformity" (Shambaugh, 1996: p. 61).
3. **Intimacy**; the group becomes more personal and interpersonally closer. The therapist serves as the "gatekeeper" and facilitator helping to control the level of closeness – closeness that can result in anxiety if not properly modulated.

This intimacy facilitates the next stage which is:

4. **Differentiation**; The group members become aware of and see the psychological differences between the members. Members exert more leadership within the group.

The final stage according to this model is:

5. **Separation**; The member's explore resources outside of the group looking for support and activity. The therapist's role is to help the members deal with any ambivalence about leaving.

Stages of group development specifically developed by Dies (1991) follow along the same pattern as articulated by Garfield et al., (1965). These stages were developed specifically for adolescent groups. They include: Initial relatedness; Testing of Limits; Resolving Authority Issues; Working on Self; and Moving On.

Interventions sometimes fail because of the lack of congruency between the intervention and the stage of the group. Mary is 15 minutes late for group in an outpatient setting. The group is new and just forming. Given the stage of the group, the leader should simply greet her and remind her of the time parameters of the group. If the group were at the Intimacy stage, then exploration of why she (who is almost always on time) is late would be clinically warranted.

Leadership roles within the group

The members of the group often take on leadership roles as defined by Durkin (1981). These roles and the therapist's response to members in this role facilitate the group process. These leadership roles are fluid and dynamic. They are described as follows:

a. **Task Leader** – provides support to the group and individual members; helps uphold the norms of the group; facilitates members' interpersonal interactions; and accurately perceives and verbalizes incidents in the group.
b. **Emotional Leader** – is interested in and focuses on feelings; is well-liked by others; wants support from others and is highly motivated to change; models the change process.
c. **Scapegoat Leader** – is perceived by the group as markedly different from others; is generally socially unaware and out-of-step; the group uses the scapegoat to identify boundaries; needs to be protected by the leader from the anger, animosity, and projection from group members.
d. **Defiant Leader** – stimulates issues of dependency/independency; monitors the trust in the group; carries the ambivalence about the group.

Transference and Countertransference

Transference and countertransferencial reactions in an adolescent group can be particularly strong, provocative, and distressing. They offer the opportunity for psychological change and growth and also the potential for acting out by the adolescent and even the therapist. The management of transference in an adolescent group differs in a number of ways from psychotherapy with adults. These modifications include:

1. A positive parental transference is sought and fostered.
2. Negative transferences are worked through as they present in the group.
3. Transference reactions are perceived as real and genuine.
4. The therapist validates the adolescent's accurate perceptions of people, experiences, and relationships.
5. The therapist discourages the perception of himself/herself as an absolute authority.
6. The member is encouraged to develop a "real" relationship with the therapist (Rachman, 1995: p. 171).

Common countertransferencial reactions in the adolescent group include aggression, anger, over-control, sexuality, and dependency (Rachman, 1995). These reactions can be intense and overwhelming to the therapist. One of the best ways to manage these reactions within the group is through the judicious use of self-disclosure. Rachman and Ceccoli (1996) have listed a number of considerations that clinically warrant self-disclosure or transparency by the therapist.

1. Self-disclosure is done in order to enhance the group's functioning.
2. Self-disclosure can be offered voluntarily or in response to a request.
3. The therapist can and should set limits on the amount, content, and frequency to protect his or her privacy and not burden group members with unnecessary information.
4. Self-disclosure should be limited to material appropriate and germane to the group and the group process.

Self-disclosure requires maturity, thoughtfulness, and clinical savvy. It is important that any self-disclosure by the therapist becomes part of the group process, for example: "How was it for you to hear about my dating experience in high school?" While supervisors may frame self-disclosure or therapist transparency as appropriate or not appropriate, it is better to perceive it as helpful or not helpful either to the therapist, individual or the group.

Methods and Strategies for Managing Issues/Behavior in the Adolescent Group

The needs and problems of the adolescent in group often require unique interventions, strategies, and techniques. A concern, especially for the beginning therapist, is the management of any impulsive/out-of-control behavior by group members. The reality is that in some groups this level of serious acting-out is not noted. The therapist needs to keep in mind that the testing of limits is part of adolescence – an experience that helps them understand authority and better gain a sense of themselves.

Limit-setting

Limit-setting in group by the therapist is often comprised of a gentle verbal reminder or prompt such as "Shut the door," "Let Jose finish his thought," or "Don't use that word." It is important that these statements are given in a parental, compassionate fashion. Rather than individual timing-out, it is best (if the level of disruption in the group warrants such a reaction) to time-out the entire group, for example: "You need to be quiet for three minutes." Individual time-outs can also be helpful, not only for the member, but the group and the therapist. This time-out is clinically most useful when a verbal warning is first given in the face of oppositional behavior. The setting of the group determines the length and place of the time-out. It is usually not good to time-out the individual for the length of the entire group. If a member requires frequent time-out and intervention, then it may be possible that the member is not a good fit for the group and should be seen in individual treatment or referred to another group.

Paradoxical interventions

Paradoxes, or contradictory statements, by their essence, are a part of the life of the adolescent. Interventions based on paradox are innately appealing to the adolescent and can help shift them from an oppositional position. For example, a youngster who is struggling to do homework telling him/her not to do it creates a paradox especially if the skilled group therapist spells out the result, "So don't do your homework . . . getting good grades is not that important and you can always live at home, be close to your parents, and go to the local college."

Homework

While some groups such as those based on Cognitive Behavioral Therapy (CBT) require written homework. Written homework in general is to be avoided since it can readily set-up opposition, power struggles, and noncompliance. Behavioural homework can be an important therapeutic intervention since it requires the teen to "complete" some activity before the next group. This process facilitates internalization of the group. For example, Chris talked in group about his struggles with a female friend. He got feedback about how to handle the problem during the group. The therapist asked him to try one of the suggestions (homework) and report back to the group.

Modeling

Modeling is an essential part of group process. In teen groups, members may not notice the behavior of others. They may also show faulty cause-effect reasoning. The leader often needs to point out and reinforce positive behavior or identify the negative consequences of their actions.

Activities

Activities can be crucial to the success of the group stimulating interpersonal reactions, relieving stress, or tension. They can include art projects, games, crafts, watching a short video, and psychodrama. All activities need to facilitate the group process; offer opportunities for support and inclusion, and should be consistent with the stage of the group (Pojman, 2009).

Ethical and risk issues Adolescents by their very nature are at risk to act-out, engage in potentially dangerous activities, and break the rules. The group therapist needs to be aware of this potential and ways to manage these risk factors. These factors include out-of-group contact, acting-out, suicidality, adolescent sexuality, and substance abuse. The developmental struggle of the adolescent to understand and make sense of diversity, e.g. ethnicity, race, social class, and sexual orientation, can also be a risk factor.

Out-of-group contact

Out-of-group contact is not unusual between group members. It can provide an opportunity for the adolescent to increase and develop more intimate relationships.

It can also result in acting out and splitting. The group leader needs to clarify the expectations about out-of-group contact in the pre-group interview or when the adolescent first enters group. The details of out-of-group contacts that do occur may need to be discussed in group.

Acting out

The acting out of adolescents within the group can be managed in a number of ways. Careful selection of group members is imperative. It is also important that the therapist modulate the affect and its intensity within the group. Addressing conflictual or potentially over-stimulating material in the here-and-now of the group is necessary. The acting out of the adolescent can stimulate strong countertransferencial feelings (e.g., fear of acting out or vicarious enjoyment in their actions).

Suicidality

Adolescents are at high-risk for suicide. This disclosure of suicidality either ideation or a plan needs to be worked through and understood within the context of the group. The group therapist needs to assess the adolescent for suicide. This assessment can take place either in group or individually; occasionally, it should take place both within group and later in an individual session. The group therapist explores with the group what the disclosure is saying for the members. For example, is the group member carrying the hopelessness, anger, despair, or loneliness that other members feel but do not express? The group and the suicidal adolescent need to be reassured by the therapist that the teen will be kept safe. This assertion helps reduce anxiety and keeps the group safe.

Sexuality

It is important the group therapist provide accurate information about sex. In this process, it is important that the therapist reinforce values and group norms against unprotected sex that are appropriate to the age and experience of the group member (Malekoff, 2004). Narrow perceptions about sexuality need to be confronted and the relational nature of sex needs to be discussed. What it means to be a sexual person should be a topic of discussion. This discussion should also include the social influence and pressures that teenagers face in their developing sexuality.

Substance abuse

The pre-group interview and selection process help determine the adolescent's drug and alcohol history and the need for specialized drug and alcohol treatment versus participation in a general adolescent group. It is imperative that the contract around substance abuse and confidentiality be clarified early in treatment. Rachman (1995) has noted a number of ways that group can "provide an alternative to drug abuse" (Rachman, 1995: p. 258). Some of these factors include:

- (group) encourages the adolescents to bring their fantasies about substance use before the actual experience;
- open and honest confrontation by the therapist and the group;
- assessment of the personal meaning of drug or alcohol use;
- appropriate therapist role-modeling and self-disclosure around drug or alcohol use;
- maintaining a culture in the group where nondrug or alcohol use is a positive attribute.

Diversity

Differences between people can facilitate growth and also anger, anxiety, and even violence. Group offers an arena for adolescents to appreciate and grow from understanding diversity. This healthy process increases member awareness and appreciation of ethnicity, race, and Lesbian, Gay, Bisexual, and Transgender (LGBT) issues. Prejudice, stereotypic thinking, and oppression need to be directly confronted in the here-and-now of the group. It is important to promote the understanding and respect for the views and values of diverse group members.

Specialized Groups

Specialty groups are organized around a problem, a specific issue, or an experience, for example, trauma, anger, divorce, medical or psychiatric diagnosis. Specialty groups are similar in that: the membership is more homogeneous; all members have similar treatment goals; groups are often closed in format, short-lived, and highly structured. This high level of structure helps the therapist better manage the time and focus on relevant issues pertinent to the group purpose (DeLucia-Waack, 1997; Gladding, 1998).

Specialty groups also have a strong psychoeducational focus. Goals for the psychoeducational group have been articulated by DeLucia-Waack (2006) for the psychoeducational groups (DeLucia-Waack, 2006: p. 279). They include: teach and practice new skills; increase communication skills; use problem-solving skills; share emotions including positive and negative feelings; give feedback to other members when requested; request feedback about thoughts, behaviors, and situations; gain and show support for others in similar situations.

Each specialty group has its own unique purpose, content, and structure. Some of the more common groups in inpatient, residential, school, and community settings are focused on Attention Deficit Hyperactivity Disorder (ADHD), aggression/anger management, conduct disorder/defiance, depression, and trauma.

Attention Deficit Hyperactivity Disorder

The model for group treatment of ADHD teens is primarily based on behavioral and cognitive therapy. These groups are found in schools, agencies, or private practice. They are highly structured with a typical limit of 10 to 12 sessions. Goals of the group include helping the members to improve peer relationships, increasing their ability to focus and attend, improving self-esteem, and developing a better ability to regulate affect (Pojman, 2009). These goals are reached through peer and therapist feedback along with practical problem-solving. Skill training and behavior therapy are also essential components of treatment.

Aggression/anger management

These groups are crafted using a model of social-cognitive and behavioral therapy. They can be done on an inpatient and outpatient basis typically involving 12–18 sessions. In some cases, participation can be court-ordered. Recommended goals have been suggested by Fleckenstein and Horne (2004). They include: develop awareness to anger; evaluate the function of their anger and replace anger with more effective responses; learn relaxation skills to self-calm and develop self-talk that will calm the proactive response; learn problem-solving skills; and increase the effectiveness of communications skills (Fleckenstein and Horne, 2004: p. 555). Frequently used intervention methods include behavioral analysis, relaxation, modeling, and practice.

Conduct disordered/defiance

Work with this often difficult population is based on social-cognitive and interpersonal models. The form and structure of the group is frequently established by the setting with little opportunity for therapist input, such as: juvenile hall or correctional facility. Adolescents diagnosed with a conduct disorder can be successfully treated on an outpatient basis (Madonna and Caswell, 1991). Group goals include: increase empathy, develop problem-solving skills, develop social skills, and increase emotional awareness and control. Exploration of feelings, limit-setting, modeling, reality testing, and behavioral coaching are useful interventions.

Depression

The group model for the treatment of depression involves social-cognitive, interpersonal, behavioral, and psychoeducational approaches. These types of groups are found in both inpatient and outpatient setting. Group goals include: increase positive thinking, decrease depression, increase pleasurable activities, improve social skills, and improve the sense of self. To reach these goals, the therapist can use cognitive therapy, modeling, homework assignments, exploration of feelings, reframing, and activities, (e.g., art, dance, or crafts).

Trauma

Groups focused on adolescents who have been traumatized are supportive, behavioral, and psychoeducational. These groups are found in a variety of settings with the group time-limited. Aronson and Kahn (2004) have outlined important group goals. Initially, it is imperative that safety be created in the group. Safety is facilitated by the homogeneity of the group members, the use of group-as-a-whole interventions, and the high level of structure in the group. Other goals include: reduction of problematic feelings and behaviors; relieving isolation and establishing peer connections;

addressing the changes that have occurred in the assumptive world as a result of the trauma (Aronson and Kahn, 2004: pp. 98–99). Specific interventions involve education regarding the trauma and normalizing the adolescent's reaction. Coping skills are taught related to trauma-inspired behavior, and the emotional experience of the adolescent is processed with the therapist highlighting the connection between trauma and bereavement.

Concluding Comments

This chapter has been written with the goal of teaching the beginning adolescent therapist or reminding the more experienced therapist about "The Real Work" of doing groups with this challenging and rewarding population. The real work in the treatment of adolescents is learned over time as one sits in the group and interacts with the adolescents in the here-and-now of their lives.

References and Bibliography

American Academy of Child and Adolescent Psychiatry (June 2001). Normal Adolescent Development Part I. *Facts for Families*, 57. Retrieved December 3, 2010 from www.accap.org.

American Academy of Child and Adolescent Psychiatry (June 2001). Normal Adolescent Development Part I. *Facts for Families*, 58. Retrieved December 3, 2010 from www.accap.org.

Aronson, S., & Kahn, G. B. (2004). Group interventions for treatment of trauma in adolescents. In B. Buchele & H. Spitz (Eds.) *Group intervention for treatment of psychological trauma* (pp. 89–115). New York: Amercian Group Psychotherapy Association.

Blos, P. (1962). *On adolescent: A psychoanalytic interpretation*. New York: Free Press.

DeLucia-Waack, J. L. (1997). Measuring the effectiveness of group work: A review and analysis of process and outcome measures. *Journal for Specialists in Group Work*, 22, 227–293.

DeLucia-Waack, J. L. (2006). *Leading psychoeducational groups for children and Adolescents*. Thousand Oaks, California: Sage Publications, Inc.

Dies, K. R. (1991). A model for adolescent group psychotherapy. *Journal of Child and Adolescent Group Therapy*, 1, 59–70.

Durken, J. E. (1981). *Living group: Group psychotherapy and general systems theory*. New York: Brunner/Mazel.

Erickson, E. H. (1968). *Identity: Youth and crisis*. New York: W. W. Norton & Company.

Fleckenstein, L. B., & Horne, A. M. (2004). Anger management groups. In J. L. DeLucia-Waack, D. A. Gerrity, C. R. Kaladner, & M. T. Riva (Eds.). *Handbook of group counseling and psychotherapy* (pp. 547–562). Thousand Oaks, California: Sage Publications.

Gladding, S. T. (1998). *Counseling as an art: The creative arts in counseling* (2nd ed.). Alexandra, Virginia: American Counseling Association.

Garfield, J. A., Jones, H. E., & Kolodny, R. I. (1965). In S. Bernstein (Ed.), *Explorations in group work: Essays in theory and practice* (pp. 19–49). Boston: Milford House.

Gemelli, R. (1996). *Normal child and adolescent development*. Washington, DC: American Psychiatric Press.

Harris, J. R. (1998). *The nurture assumption: Why children turn out the way they do.* New York: Free Press.

Kohlberg, L. A. (1981). *The philosophy of moral development, moral stages, and the ideal of justice: Essays on moral development, Vol 1.* San Francisco, California: Harper & Row.

Kurland, R., & Salmon, R. (1998). Purpose: A misunderstanding and misuses keystone of group work experience. *Social Work with Groups, 21*(3), 5–17.

Levy-Warren, M. (1996). *The adolescent journey.* New York: Rowman & Littlefield Publishers.

Madonna, J., & Caswell, P. (1991). The utilization of flexible techniques in group therapy with delinquent adolescent boys. *Journal of Child and Adolescent Group Therapy, 1*(2), 147–157.

Malekoff, A. (2004). *Group work with adolescents: Principles and practice* (2nd ed.). New York: The Guilford Press.

McAuliffe, K. (2007). Life of a Brain. *Discovery presents the brain: An owner's manual.* Discover, 9–11.

Meeks, J. E., & Bernet, W. (2001). *The fragile alliance: An orientation to psychotherapy of the adolescent* (5th ed.). Malabar, Florida: Krieger Publishing Company.

Northen, H., & Kurland, R. (2001). *Social work with groups* (3rd ed.) New York: Columbia University Press.

Piaget, J. (1972). Intellectual evolution from adolescence to adulthood. *Human Development, 15,* 1–12.

Pojman, A. (2009). *Adolescent group psychotherapy: Method, madness, and the basics.* New York: American Group Psychotherapy Association.

Rachman, A. W. (1995). *Identity group psychotherapy with adolescents.* Northvale, New Jersey: Jason Aronson, Inc.

Rachman, A. W., & Ceccoli, V. C. (1996). Analyst self-disclosure in adolescent groups. In P. Kymissis & D. A. Halperin (Eds.), *Group therapy with children and adolescents* (pp. 155–173). Washington, DC: American Psychiatric Press.

Redl, F. (1951). The art of group composition. In S. Schulze (Ed.), *Creative group living in a children's institution* (pp. 79–96). New York: Associated Press.

Shambaugh, P. W. (1996). Developmental models of adolescent groups. In P. Kymissis & D. A. Halperin (Eds.), *Group therapy with children and adolescents* (pp. 55–75). Washington, DC: American Psychiatric Press.

Shechtman, Z. (2007). *Group counseling and psychotherapy with children and adolescents: Theory, research, and practice.* Mahwah, New Jersey: Lawrence Erlbaum Associates.

Siegel, D. J. (1999). *The developing mind: How relationships and the brain interact to shape who we are.* New York: The Guilford Press.

31

The Earth as a Classroom: Children's Groups in the Aftermath of Mass Trauma

Emily Zeng

In this chapter, we will explore some essential aspects of group intervention specific for children in the aftermath of mass trauma. We will examine closely a compelling case in the 2008 Chinese Earthquake and how children in a tent-made school near the epicenter were able to cope with traumatic experiences in the safe environment of groups even without much physical safety per se.[1] The traumatic and vulnerable nature of their circumstances was extraordinary. So were their ability and creativity in playful interaction, collective healing, and contribution to the community-at-large. The theoretical framework used in this case is deeply participatory, psychosocial, and community-based. Some universal and case-specific factors or characteristics are also presented in light of prevailing evidence-based or "best practice" principles in international disaster relief. It is hoped that this will attract, inspire, and mobilize a new generation of like-minded mental health professionals who are willing to devote themselves to working with children and families in challenging and even perilous situations around the world.

The Backdrop

The Westside Mountain tent school was perched halfway up a mountain in earthquake-ravaged Beichuan County, overlooking one of the most beautiful landscapes on earth. Two tents accommodated approximately fifty children ages from 4 to 15 gathered from several nearby schools. The tent school was conveniently divided into two classes, K–2 and Grade 3–7. When I arrived in July 2008, which was two months

---

[1] One month after the tent school ended, on September 24, 2008, four children from the school were killed in a mudslide, which also killed 20 other adults. The village was forced to move out overnight. The Westside Mountain was declared uninhabitable thereafter. A year later, in July 2009, the water of a nearby river overflowed into the refugee camp where they currently reside, causing another emergency evacuation overnight.

after the earthquake, the school was surrounded by a semi-collapsed mountain where survivors built temporary tents next to their (mostly) collapsed family houses. Like many other severely damaged areas in the quake zone, Westside Mountain had been depleted of its resources and was isolated and depressed since day one.

Of all the counties and regions struck by the deadly earthquake, Beichuan ("Beichuan Qiang Autonomous County") sustained the most unimaginable losses. An earthquake-prone region that typically experiences several tremors a year, Beichuan suffered to an unprecedented degree.[2] At Beichuan county town, where 80 per cent of its 20 000 residents had presumably been buried alive, out-of-province military and concertina wire were set up to guard this dead city for years to come. No one knows exactly how many children were killed in the earthquake. To date, while a world-class earthquake museum is under way and a 2.4-billion-dollar new Beichuan is being built 15 miles south (Larmer, 2010), countless bodies of schoolchildren are still nowhere to be found.

The Group

Due to a severe shortage of manpower, I was assigned to teach the Grade 3–7 class upon my arrival. The class consisted of thirty children – 25 boys and 5 girls ages 7–15. The average attendance stabilized at approximately twenty. Most of the children identified themselves as of Qiang descent, an ancient culture closely related to both the Han Chinese and the Tibetans (Wang, 2003). Due to the sweeping effect of the earthquake, many of the students were evacuated and transported to makeshift refugee camps hours away before they returned to the village to rejoin their families. Many of them had been exposed to horrific or grotesque scenes. More than half the class had lost one or more family members. The pupils from Beichuan Hope Primary School were evacuated more or less unscathed, but the nearby Beichuan High School, once housing 2990 students and staff, lost more than half of its population. One of our eighth graders from Beichuan High School was trapped under the debris for hours. She was one of the few students in her class to survive. A 14-year-old boy from Beichuan Middle School in downtown Beichuan lost more than 200 of his schoolmates, when a massive landslide buried much of the school grounds.

From June to September 2008, the tent school served as a sanctuary, an *ad-hoc* medical center, and a relief distribution site that provided vital sustenance such as rice, oil, matches, comforters, and infant formula. Although the acute phase of the disaster had passed, on-going aftershocks, landslides, and unstable geological conditions thwarted various attempts to rebuild. Residing close to uninhabitable zones, peace and relief were deemed transient. In the middle of class, a boy would suddenly stand up, reporting that an aftershock had been detected, and the class would stop and run a quick check verifying whether that was accurate.

I perceived the class as a free-standing, naturally occurring therapeutic group (Chazan, 2001) with on-going survival as its single-minded but elusive goal. In a

---

[2] The earthquake killed approximately 30 000 ethnic Qiang people, or one-tenth of the Qiang population in China (Lim, 2008). Thus the Qiang culture was considered in danger of being "further marginalized towards cultural extinction" (Wessendorf, 2009: p. 288).

large-scale catastrophes like this, psychological distress is often more about the difficulties of everyday living following the initial impact rather than the trauma itself (Hutton, 2001; Wessells, 2009; Fernando, Miller and Berger, 2010). Dealing with post-disaster adversities, such as poverty and unemployment, can be more draining and taxing than surviving the actual disaster itself. In fact, the term "post-disaster" can be a misnomer that is both inaccurate and misleading. "Post-disaster" implies a discrete event with a cut-off line that differentiates "before" and "after" the disaster. However, most catastrophes are often of a chronic and complex nature. A magnitude-8 earthquake, for instance, runs its course in months, or even years.

As an essential part of the tent school, I was acutely aware of my temporary, short-term, outsider status. My dilemma was how to be integrated and detached simultaneously, to be minimally intrusive but maximally productive. As in the case of all disaster relief work, the central question was: What could I do to promote recovery, resilience, and healing in this group?

Theoretical Framework

Several sources influenced my thinking behind the group, disaster psychiatry (Ursano, Fullerton, Weisaeth and Raphael, 2007), trauma literature (van der Kolk, McFarlane and Weisaeth, 1996), group therapy (Yalom, 1998; Chazan, 2001), and participatory action research (Hart, 1992, 1997, 2008). My background as a clinical child psychologist gives me a developmental and systemic view which superimposes all the above. My philosophy has its early roots in several distinguished thinkers, such as Martin Buber (1996), and Paulo Freire (1972, 1973/2002). Additionally, I also had great interest in dance therapy and had received training from two highly skillful therapists from South Korea (for an excellent introduction on dance therapy with children, see Kornblum, 2008). Being open to a variety of approaches enhanced my understanding of the impact of mass trauma and subsequent intervention. A clear cognitive framework is important as it "permits an ordering of all the inchoate events of therapy . . . a sense of inner order and mastery – a sense, if deeply felt, is automatically conveyed to patients, and generates in them a corresponding sense of clarity and mastery" (Yalom, 1998: p. 94).

One text that I used extensively as my conceptual foundation and practical guide was Roger Hart's *Children's Participation: The Theory and Practice of Involving Young Citizens in Community Development and Environmental Care* (1997). Originally written for environmental education, this book is an excellent resource on how to involve children in groups. One of Hart's often cited concepts is the "ladder of children's participation" (Hart, 1997: p. 41), an eight-rung model that describes various possibilities of involving children in groups with increasing degrees of decision-making (Figure 31.1). Hart differentiates non-participation (the lowest three rungs) from genuine participation (the upper five rungs). In this model, children are free to move anywhere within the upper five rungs, based on their age, developmental levels, and situational factors (e.g., personal interests, comfort level, etc.). To maximize the involvement of children of various backgrounds, a strong emphasis is placed on visual and interactive methods, such as drawings and collages, mapping and charting, interviews and surveys, puppetry and photography (Hart, 1997).

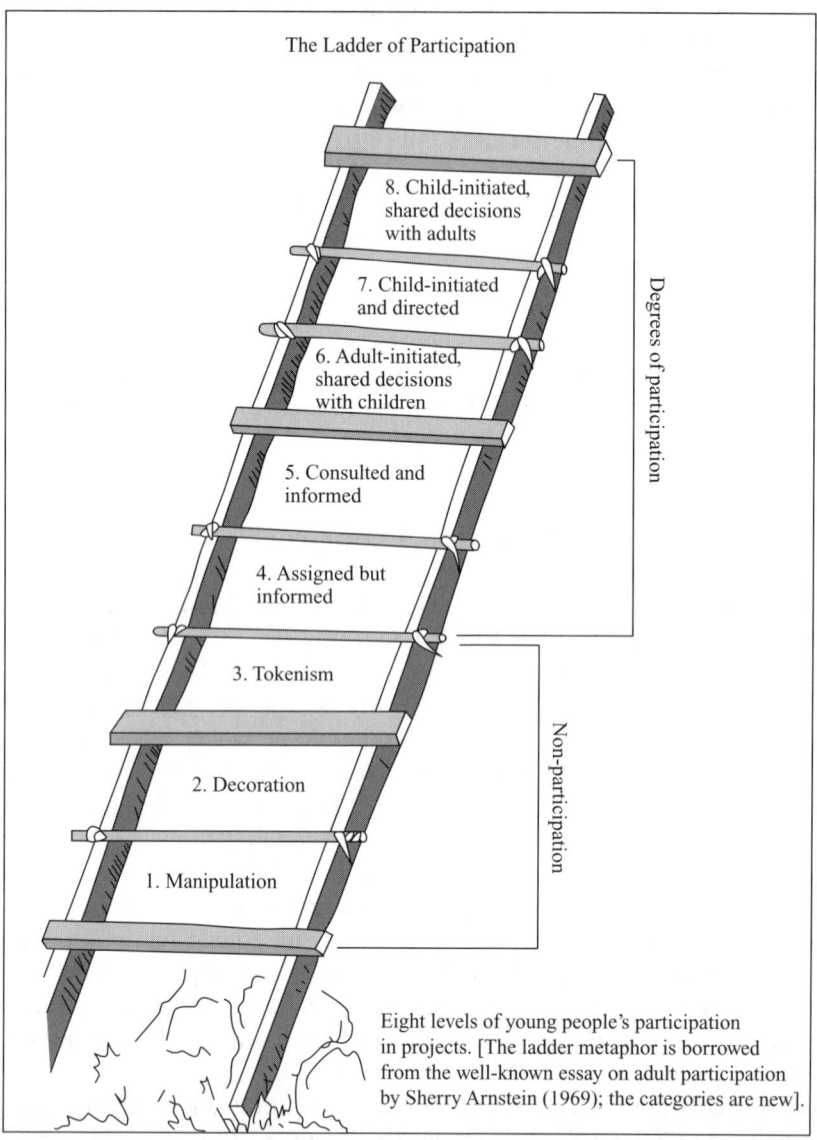

Figure 31.1 The ladder of children's participation (Hart, 1992: p. 8). *Reprinted with permission of UNICEF.*

Although he never mentions "trauma" or "treatment," Hart's model can be adapted effectively for post-disaster group intervention in conjunction with various group techniques. Because it approaches the problem from the bottom up, instead of from the top down, it lends itself to being sensitive to developmental levels, cultural values, and stages of bereavement (Zeng and Silverstein, forthcoming). Despite various criticism (e.g., Hart, 2008; Malone and Hartung, 2010), Hart's model remains one of the most influential theories on children's participation. In a playful spirit, Hart (2008) himself also envisions an expansion of his model so that children could move beyond the ladder, and "climb" into other "meaningful" and "fruitful" ways of working with others (Hart, 2008: p. 29).

The Process

I readily engaged in a process called "designing the plane while flying it" (Herr and Anderson, 2005: p. 69). For the sake of clarity, we divided the developmental progression of the group into four stages, each of which had a singular focus:

1. Restoring structure and routine.
2. Developing group cohesion.
3. Participating in research and action-oriented activities.
4. Community action (Zeng and Silverstein, forthcoming).

Nevertheless, as all stages were overlapping and intricately intertwined, it was virtually impossible to differentiate one stage from another. For instance, restoring structure and routine was an on-going task throughout the process, and action orientation was a defining feature of the school. My job was to set the stage and create a condition, so the group could do its work and, if at all possible, function on its own after I left.

To create a sense of order in the midst of chaos, everyday routines need to be restored (UNICEF, 2006). Before my arrival, there were virtually no rules. Thus, rules were spelled out on my first day of teaching. Several children quickly suggested common slogans such as "respecting teachers and peers," and "taking care of the environment." The class had a discussion about putting these terms into action. They finally agreed that "respecting teachers and peers" meant no throwing bricks or calling strikes, and "taking care of the environment" meant cleaning personal space and taking refuse to the garbage bin. Establishing rules brought an initial sense of order. To ensure a sense of continuity (Klingman and Cohen, 2004), the daily routine was structured in a way that resembled their original schools, starting, for example, with morning poetry recitation led by a student.

The tent school was quite chaotic when I arrived. Two major "school-wide" problems persisted: fist-fights among the boys and strikes among the girls. I still recall the most illuminating moment during a morning break, when I rushed to restrain an angry nine-year-old boy from throwing a brick at another child. Never in my lifetime had I been this "physical." I held him from behind for forty minutes while he was screaming and kicking. The class fell apart, and I ruefully entered an hour-long internet supervision with my mentor overseas. As I lamented my personal failure, this episode turned out to be a turning point for the school. The children seemed to realize that there were boundaries, and they were actually contained. A sense of safety and trust began to permeate among us.

Singing and dancing also promoted group cohesion. Like their ancestors, the children who were mostly of Qiang descent were natural singers and dancers. One of their popular songs, "the song of Highland Barley," involved several intricate moves that I never quite learned. Our favorite song, "I have peace like a river," starts with a brief exchange between a teacher and a few children. After morning greetings, the teacher asks the children if they all had a good night's sleep. A young child quickly reports that he did not wet his bed, another says that he had no nightmares, the third states that she even had a "sweet and wonderful" dream. Every time the song was played out on the CD player, the class chuckled. I took a quick poll on the sweet dreams and nightmares the prior night, and then started our day. By doing so, a variety of responses was accommodated. Entering August, when frequent aftershocks became the topic of the day, this little song had a welcoming effect that introduced a calm and peaceful rhythm to the school.

I have entitled this chapter "The Earth as a Classroom," based on the primary function of school as a learning environment and our primary roles as teacher and students. It is, however, equally appropriate to name it "The Earth as a Playroom" or "The Earth as a Playground." The children spent a significant amount of time in play. Due to geographical isolation, we had a limited number of toys and games. Nevertheless, as I recall, we did have a fine collection of toys, a combination of quiet games and group activities, indoor and outdoor choices, familiar games (e.g., Chinese checkers and chess) and foreign games (e.g., Tumbling Tower). Interestingly but perhaps not surprisingly, the most popular games were often self-designed or required nothing but imagination (e.g., jumping rope, the whispering game, the sentence completion game). When everything physical and visible had collapsed in front of us, we were left with each other, our psychic, innate capacity to play, and to survive together, as a group.

The importance of play can never be overstated. Athena Drewes, a psychologist who has done extensive research on children's play, exalted play to equal status as nutrition, housing, education, and "both a cause and an effect of culture" (Drewes, 2005: p. 26, citing Roopnarine, Johnson and Hooper 1994). Donald Winnicott (1971), one of the most prominent child analysts who ever lived, asserts that play is our first encounter with culture. Play is the universal, natural language of children. It promotes physical, intellectual, social and emotional development. To play actively is identified as a protective factor of resilient children (Duncan and Arntson, 2004: p. 10). David Epston, one of the originators of narrative therapy, noted that "however dire the circumstances seem . . . children usually welcome a playful spirit in which to express themselves and explore change" (Freeman, Epston and Lobovits, 1997: p. 33).

Play also serves as a natural, non-intrusive diagnostic tool. Once we were playing "sentence completion game," a popular Chinese game that involved the names of people and places. Suddenly the class erupted and the group dynamic changed. A boy had written down the name of his brother who had been killed in the earthquake. Other boys were furious, stating that he was not supposed to use a dead person's name. "Dead people don't count." I realized that the group was not ready to tolerate the traumatic reminder of a deceased peer (Samide and Stockton, 2002). The gap between life and death was too close to be imagined then.

Community mapping is the first step in getting the community to look at itself and to re-establish a "sense of place" (Prewitt Diaz, 2008; Prewitt Diaz and Dayal, 2008). As a relative stranger who was unfamiliar with the vicinity, I asked the children where they lived in the village. This led to the creation of our first group project, a child-made community map, which showed family tents, the High School and the treacherous Tangjiashan Quake Lake. For a village that was too small to be on a map, this was perhaps the first in its history. Used as an instant guide for my home visits, the map represented the potential efforts of children to contribute to the community at large.

Since we were all in a tent school, another mapping exercise involved what happened to the former schools of the children. The class divided into small groups based on their former affiliation with specific schools, detailing and labeling each area. A child mapped his future school entitled, "A school that never falls." One of the groups came up with the brilliant idea of making two drawings of their old school, Beichuan Hope Primary. The before-the-quake drawing was filled with colorful marks; the after-the-quake version was penciled with gloomy shades of gray. The children were so proud when they presented their ingenious work to the class. These activities allowed expression of their thoughts and feelings and fostered self-understanding, perspective taking, and collaboration.

Photography was an excellent tool that helped the children to carefully observe and document everyday life. It also provided additional benefits, such as promoting cognitive clarity, verbal and narrative coherence, perspective taking, and multi-layered processing. Thanks to the generous donation of a friend in New York, we had fifteen digital cameras, which the children rotated among themselves. They mastered the basic camera skills within hours and began a visual journal. Every day after school, a small group of children would gather around my laptop to review their photos and critique one another's work. As children shared their photographic work, they naturally attempted to tell a story, which I wrote down verbatim to process within the group. It was visual, verbal, and group processing all at once. The quality of photos notwithstanding, the subjects and themes were of great value to any child therapist. I was often shocked by the emotionality embedded in some of the ordinary-looking photos. A series of photos "Landslides" by a fourth grader contained haunting images with subtitles such as "[My] grandpa was buried underneath. Now it's covered with tall, green grass." One year later, when I returned to the village with a participatory video project using more technically "advanced" video cameras, a boy commented, in his exemplary honesty, that he would rather have "the camera he had before." Apparently, a smaller, simpler tool gave him more satisfaction and a better sense of control.

Interviewing was another popular activity that aided in perspective taking. The children formed small groups and took turns being an interviewer, a journalist, and a photographer. The children enjoyed interviewing one another, using classroom items such as flutes and pencil boxes for microphones. Spontaneously, they began to enquire about each other's earthquake experiences, such as the loss of family members, a forbidden topic that they had not been able to initiate until then.

A visitor who happened to come to the school during a class break would be struck by the level of noisiness and rambunctiousness, the fluidity of conversations, the "horizontal" engagement (Chazan, 2001) between students and between students and teacher. Creativity was encouraged. Individual rights and responsibilities were respected. Infinite time was given for a small child to express himself effectively. Other than practising social skills such as conflict resolution and feedback giving, the children also learned to organize themselves to manage the school; wiping the board, cleaning the desks, and sweeping the floor. Purposeful action, however minimal, produces a sense of competency and commitment (Klingman and Cohen, 2004). By the end of the summer when the tent school ended, many children were comfortable resolving conflicts using, say, simple majority rule (Hart, 1997). School-wide strikes had disappeared, and physical fights subsided. Yalom (1998) holds that cohesion is the precondition of change. In our case, cohesion was almost equivalent to change.

Opportunities came when the group became sufficiently cohesive. At the end of July, when a projector became available and electricity was steady, the children decided that a community movie night was in order. To show films on the tent-filled stadium of Beichuan High School was the first effort of community outreach and the most remarkable task the group was able to accomplish. Two children climbed up the metal fence to set up the screen. One child brought a DVD player from home. Another borrowed a power extension from his uncle. The rest of us set up tables and chairs, inviting parents and villagers to come. Almost overnight, the traumatic site of the high school was transformed into a community gathering that brought pleasurable experience to children and adults alike.

The collective life of the tent school culminated in a memorial trip to the Beichuan county seat. On August 12, a reticent 15-year-old girl who had lost her mother to the earthquake raised her hand for the first time, reminding the class of the special meaning of the anniversary[3]. Her reminder generated discussion and led to a memorial trip to commemorate the tens and thousands of people who lost their lives in the earthquake. The children decorated the tent with balloons, wrote special messages to their loved ones, and reflected on their experiences and losses. A classroom remembrance box was created. Passing the military checkpoint and troops of soldiers, we ascended the nearby mountain, and buried our remembrance box in the cave overlooking Beichuan. Of the 20 children who participated in the memorial trip, more than half of them had not seen the disaster site since the first day of the earthquake. This event had a long-lasting impression on all of us. Two months later, a non-stop rain flushed the remembrance box out of the cave. One of the boys discovered the box, and re-buried it inside the cave.

Figure 31.2 Boys playing tumbling tower during class break. © Emily Zeng.

[3] According to an ancient Qiang custom, the hundredth day after a death in the family marks the beginning of a three-day mourning period. Because so many Beichuanese were killed on the first day of the earthquake (May 12th), August 12th became a collective day of mourning for the entire region.

Figure 31.3 Beichuan three-month anniversary. Children decorate classroom in remembrance of loved ones. © Emily Zeng, August 12, 2008.

Discussion

So far, we have presented a short-term, "school-based", psychosocial intervention with a group of ethnic minority children who had narrowly escaped a cataclysmic event that killed many of their peers. Unlike dominant disaster literature which emphasizes children's needs and vulnerabilities (Garrett et al., 2007; Ursano, Fullerton, Weisaeth and Raphael, 2007), this study depicted the image of children in a seemingly contrary way. While the government was struggling to provide assistance and adults were busy making a living, children in West Mountain tent school engaged in meaningful participation. Not only did they demonstrate extraordinary strengths and capacity for post-traumatic growth, they also made significant and concrete contributions that improved the quality and scope of the rebuilding efforts. Participation is beneficial for children, families, and communities (Duncan and Arntson, 2004; UNICEF, 2007; Malone and Hartung, 2010).

In many aspects, the group was no different from many children's trauma and bereavement groups (e.g., Underwood, Spinazzola and Milani, 2004; Salloum et al., 2010). It was built upon well-established developmental principles, grief theory, and group therapy techniques. It ran its course from the beginning to the end, had its rules, vicissitudes, crises and challenges. It dealt with loss-related feelings such as denial and anger; issues with ambiguous losses, multiple losses; as well as reconnecting and closure. The desired outcomes, notably self-esteem, social skills, reduction of antisocial and aggressive behaviors (Brabender, Smolar and Fallon, 2004), are similar to many traditional children's groups. In a more general sense, many of the therapeutic factors, such as universality, self-understanding, interpersonal learning, cohesion, instillation of hope (Yalom, 1998), remain the same.

However, the group was fundamentally different from a traditional therapy group. Three defining features: participatory, psychosocial, and community-based, which are interconnected with one another. First of all, unlike most expert-driven, top down paradigms for trauma treatment, the group took a child-centered approach in which the children participated freely and voluntarily, and were allowed to set their own pace in dealing with their feelings of trauma and loss. They were in charge of what they wanted to do and determined when they wanted to do it. Consequently, the group leader maintained a minimal, supportive stance throughout the process. Indeed, as the group became more cohesive and active, the leader retreated to a more peripheral role, spending more time listening, observing, and reflecting upon children's interactions. Secondly, the group employed many therapeutic strategies and activities to promote psychosocial well-being of the individual child, which was the ultimate goal of the group. The group was community-based as it was conducted out in the field, integrated into classroom curriculum and the everyday life of the children, and embedded in pre-existing structures, resources, and cultural norms. Many of the group activities, such as singing and dancing, were derived directly from the local, indigenous culture. Moreover, it was action-oriented from the very beginning, seeking not just healing and recovery, but also opportunities for growth and learning (e.g., the village map, the movie night). In Chinese, the word "crisis" (危機, *wei ji*) consists of two parts, "danger" (*wei*) and "opportunity" (*ji*). The goal of disaster relief should not be limited to fixing or reversing damages or losses incurred (Hutton, 2001), or a return to pre-disaster functioning. Rather, it should be an opportunity for community expansion and post-traumatic growth (Calhoun and Tedeschi, 2006; Joseph and Linley, 2008).

The group was deemed successful in several ways. It started with regular classes, play and recreational activities, and concluded with community actions. Transitioning from routines to actions was a natural, fluid process that was informed by perceived safety, communality, intimacy, a sense of ownership and responsibility. The frequent breakdowns into small groups promoted greater interaction and diverse experiences. One might argue that without the publically sanctioned anniversary, the group could not have evolved so rapidly and have been bold enough to embark on the memorial trip. However, the group had acquired the ability for mature decision-making by then. Their sense of mastery and self-confidence was observed in their increasing ability to carry out effective communication and collective decisions. Therefore, it was only a matter of time before group found its way to reach a greater sense of closure. A group has its own life and course of action, which the group leader may not always be able to foresee. However, she just needs to trust that the group will take care of itself and meet the needs of its members. As I often noted, the children became very watchful and protective of themselves as well as the welfare of one another. As the memorial trip illustrated, a reluctant member was noticed, and her wish was endorsed by the entire group, even though she had rarely spoken before. One can speak of the wisdom of collective unconsciousness. However, it was no coincidence that both the culture and the group had chosen a day to address the needs for collective mourning, thereby reviving the cultural heritage.

Chazan proposes that the human need for symmetry is an important feature of the therapeutic group (Chazan, 2001: p. 71). A therapeutic group, she said, is not about conforming, but about symmetry, which means that everyone assumes equal status within the group (Chazan, 2001: p. 13). Each member has the dual status of being the agent (to give) and the recipient (to receive). To receive more than we can give begets passivity. To give more than we have received drains us. Either condition generates imbalance or disequilibrium. To be able to give and take at the same time creates a sense of balance that is important to ordinary individuals as well as the bereaved or traumatized. Not only adults but also children need to feel that they are needed, that they are beneficiaries as well as benefactors. Prior to the tent school, I had the opportunity to work at another temporary school nearby which was bigger and more easily accessible. I had witnessed truckloads of donated toys being distributed by various organizations while children abandoned classes every twenty minutes to line up to receive them. It was a well-meaning but thoughtless act that was condescending and humiliating for me to watch. However, the children (and adults alike) soon became habituated to receiving gifts and internalized their perceived "victimhood." During my tenure at the tent school, the children had to "earn" their toys by their deeds or virtue, which gave us a sense of routine, normalcy as well as self-efficacy. I never provided rewards without a very specific reason (this was perhaps the only time when I exercised power and influenced the group explicitly). By extension, I had attempted to do everything in a measured, goal-directed way. Being perceived as a thoughtful, reflective adult who viewed everything as meaningful and purposeful instilled, over time, a sense of meaning and purpose within the group.

In comparing the group and the individual dyad, Chazan describes how a group that is mature enough could be perceived as a mother figure, a secure base that is superior to any individual therapy (Chazan, 2001: p. 43). When the group is running long enough and is sufficiently cohesive, the group-as-a-whole is internalized and carried outside the group by its members; hence the notion of the inner group. The inner group serves as an auxiliary ego that gives the child a sense of safety, order, and empowerment, which infiltrates or transcends individual boundaries and defenses. It enables the child to venture out of her or his usual patterns of functioning, which results in greater spontaneity, curiosity, creativity and critical thinking, as manifested vividly in many of the children's problem-solving or brainstorming sessions. As the group becomes more self-correcting and self-governing, the group leader is no longer necessary. This was increasingly noticeable in the later stage of the group. The group decided to launch a trip, and I served as commentator and technical consultant, posing all sorts of hypothetical questions (e.g., "What if you get hungry, or thirsty?" "What if you cannot catch up with the rest of the class?"). The group still needed practical advice, but they no longer felt that they needed my permission or approval. I was happily ignored!

The children surprised me every step of the way. Growing up in the mountains, many of them had learned to help around the house from a very early age. Cooking, collecting firewood, caring for the young, feeding the animals, were common responsibilities for many of them. Like their parents, the children were hospitable towards outsiders like us. They trusted easily, and were receptive and generous. The discrepant ages among them posed an initial challenge for curriculum design, but it was also a source of strength that improved heterogeneity, empathy, and mutual awareness. It also expanded our repertoire of skills during community events. I was always mindful of the near-death experiences they all may have endured. However, had I been preoccupied by the past I would have lost sight of the vitality and aliveness of flesh and blood right in front of me. Gerard Jacobs (2007), one of our leading experts in this field, reminds us, the most important principle for a disaster mental health worker is to *be present*. Contrary to what many of us might think, it was *actually* easy.

Participation is most effective when it is grounded in children's life, in settings with which they are most familiar (Hart, 1997). As untapped resources and assets (UNICEF, 2007), children's capacity and potential have often been under-estimated or even unnoticed (Hart, 1997). As I learned later, as early as June, when out-of-province volunteers first arrived in the village, several boys had been instrumental in deciding whether or not to rebuild a school. They watched standing on the sidelines, and approached the volunteers and the village head. Their voice and concerns were considered and eventually contributed to the establishment of the tent school. One of the boys who was especially eager to have a school again, initiated the process by removing the rubble and carrying heavy stones from elsewhere to use as stools for the K–2 class (Li, personal communication, August 2, 2008). This pragmatic idea was a creative solution and, due to our limited resources, the only one.

In a chapter *Healing through Nature*, List describes how children with extensive outdoor experience do significantly better than their peers in developmental skills, such as object constancy, working memory, observation skills, spatial relationships, empathy, "deeply experienced sense of their inner life," (List, 2008: p. 77), and "theory of mind" (List, 2008: p. 85). In sharing their photographic work, the children often revealed their sentiments. "Look how pretty our village is. Look at the clouds!" And with a sense of regret, "Alas . . . the quake destroyed it all!" They often guided me to note the details of a leaf, a crescent moon that was half hiding behind a group of clouds, a scene captured from different angles or different times of the day. Their favorite subjects were the sky, the mountains, plants and flowers, animals and insects, which they often gave poetic titles such as "morning dews," "twilight," "green bamboos." Even against its disaster background, the landscape still inspired a sense of awe, mystery, and interconnectedness in a first-time visitor like myself. By meticulously documenting their environment, the children reaffirmed a deeply felt affinity and belonging to a world that was still recognizable and familiar.

Metzel (2009) defines resilience as a multifaceted and contextual process rather than an attribute or outcome, which is to say, resilience is context-specific and can be cultivated and nurtured. Masten (2001) notes that resilience "does not come from rare and special qualities, but from the everyday magic of *ordinary*, *normative* human resources in the mind, brains, and bodies of children, in their families and relationships, in their *communities*" (Masten, 2001: p. 235, my emphasis). I can think of many intrinsic and extrinsic factors. But unmediated contact and an on-going, all-embracing relationship with nature (Hart, 1997) was a unique feature that promoted resilience in many of these children.

As an integral part of the tent school, my relationship with the rest of the village, particularly the parents, also moved along a parallel line, following a continuum from stranger, to outsider, to "outsider-within" (Herr and Anderson, 2005: p. 32). Living and teaching at the tent school 24/7 allowed me to get to know the community in an intimate way that was otherwise impossible. In the Chinese culture, the role of a teacher generally carries great authority and respect. However, as I noted during home visits, since the earthquake, there was a prevailing sense of mistrust or even loss of faith towards teachers and the national education system. "What's the benefit to go to school, if you just end up dying there?" "Why couldn't the teacher save my child?" As a Chinese living overseas, I have always had a special feeling towards Chinese parents. Since the earthquake, this collective title has taken on a feel of unspeakable grief and pain that no other words can compare.

In retrospect, the group had educated and guided me in mostly unmistakable ways. Through my day-to-day contact with the children, I learned to resist my curiosity and urge to ask and to know, to tolerate ambiguity, horror, and guilt. The group also challenged me to be fully present without losing the ability to anticipate, to be spontaneous and contemplative at the same time, to maintain a non-attached stance while facilitating a sense of closeness and intimacy among them. Very early on, a 14-year-old boy approached me and disclosed his survival story. He had "misbehaved" that fateful morning, which angered his teacher so much that he was asked to change his seat from the last to the front row, which was closer to the door (an eye-opening lesson on the importance of regular fire drills). The boy survived, but his best friend, with whom he had switched seats, did not. The boy expressed his wish to revisit his old classroom, a wish that I embraced too quickly and even offered to accompany him. It was, as it turned out, a premature intervention that probably had intimidated both of us. To focus on the individual instead of the group ran a potential risk of erring on the wrong assessment of the situation. Paradoxically, as I stood on the periphery facilitating the workings of the group, I was also shielded, unwittingly, from vicarious learning and traumatization (Ryan and Cunningham, 2007).

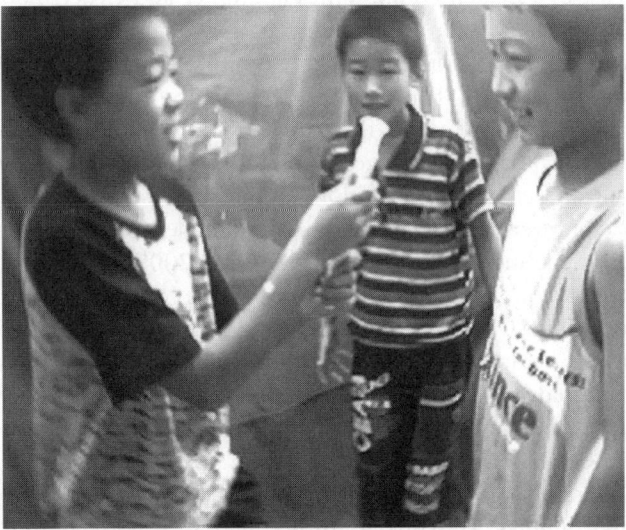

Figure 31.4 Boys interviewing each other in a small group, using flute as "microphone." Photo courtesy of Yu, then age 14 (352 × 288 resolution).

Towards a Participatory Group Therapy Approach to Mass Trauma

Among all populations affected by a disaster, children have historically been identified as particularly vulnerable and at high-risk of developing various psychiatric symptoms (Vogel and Vernberg, 1993; Peek, 2008; Silverman and La Greca, 2002; Ursano, Fullerton, Weisaeth and Raphael, 2007; Margolin, Ramos and Guran, 2010). Ethnic minority children who are already poor and socially oppressed are at a greater disadvantage in times of distress (Hutton, 2001; Marsella and Christopher, 2004; Ray, 2010). In this chapter, we present an integrated, hopefully more sophisticated, view of children, addressing both their needs for care and protection as well as their right and potential to participate (UNCRC, 1989). Assisted by dedicated and truthful adults, even those who are exposed to the most horrific events are capable of self-healing, problem-solving, and contributing to the larger community. Not only are they dignified human beings, they are also legitimate members of their community and have the rights and capacity to participate in community events *on their own terms* (Hart, 1997). While we continue our heavy-duty individual trauma work, we also need to remind ourselves that trauma constitutes a small percentage of affected populations (Hutton, 2001). To focus on trauma symptoms exclusively or excessively, as we are predisposed to do, is to lose sight of the vast majority of children who are capable of healing and recovery without formal treatment (Hutton, 2001; Jacobs, 2007). Vulnerability and resilience coexist. It is the group and the community to which they belong that should be the focus of our attention.

The tent school group was in no way an isolated existence. In recent years, participation as a viable way of working with children has been increasingly been noticed by humanitarian agencies (Steinitz, 2009; Duncan and Arntson, 2004; West, 2007; Maglajlic, 2010), by research communities (Loughry and Eyber, 2003; Cammarota and Fine, 2008; Ronan et al., 2008; Manyena, Fordham and Collins, 2008; Peek, 2008; Prilleltensky, 2010; Thomas and Percy-Smith, 2010), and by governments and municipalities (Kinoshita, 2007). Citing extraordinary examples worldwide such as the 1999 Turkey Earthquake and the 2004 Tsunami in particular, the UNICEF (2007) convinced us that, in all stages of disasters, children around the world have made significant and crucial contributions. As in the case of the tent school, many examples they cited were also self-initiated or spontaneous. Some even preceded the arrival of government and relief agencies (UNICEF, 2007: p. 10). A United Nations on-site assessment conducted in Aceh, one of the worst hit areas in the Asian Tsunami, reported that "simply having the opportunity to support rebuilding efforts is *the best therapy* we can offer . . ." (Rosati, 2006: p. 269, my emphasis). Just like we are often confused as to what is in "the best interest" for children, what constitutes "good therapy" is also more complicated than we think.

For lack of a better term I am tempted to use "participatory group therapy" as a preliminary construct to conceptualize our tent school children's group and the type of intervention it signifies. To name it "group therapy" is both comforting and unsettling. "Therapy" often implies a pathological approach, a privileged therapist-client relationship involving consent and diagnosis, which seems to be too structured and orderly to fit into the disaster scene. In addition, "participatory" and "group therapy" as two separate entities, each has a long-standing history and tradition in their respective fields, which do not seem compatible at first sight. However, the two terms juxtaposed point to a new direction that may have the potential to transform our ways of engaging children in disaster. It may even have the potential to transform our everyday practice of groups with children, to enter into their subjective world, to engage them in the process, to adapt and respond to their needs, thoughts and feelings, and to advocate for them so they can advocate for themselves in the long run. As we learn from the tent school group, participation has both therapeutic value and transformative potential. Children have distinct perceptions of what they want to do and what works for them, especially in "all matters affecting them" (UNCRC, 1989). To actually get to know them and "talk" to them is the first step to fulfill our adult obligation of protecting them from the debilitating effect of trauma. A transparent, egalitarian relationship is not only necessary, it also leads to more effective and sustaining outcomes.

Group therapy, on the other hand, is a powerful, cost-effective intervention for children (Scheidlinger, 2004; Shen, 2002). It is especially feasible in disaster context as most disasters do cause mass disruptions in various groups within the community. Even with all things being equal, children prefer the group to individual settings (Chemtob, Nakashima and Hamada, 2002). As disaster overwhelms the affected area and population, different agencies, organizations and individuals are brought together into otherwise unlikely encounters. For mental health providers, it is about being more open, flexible, and supportive (Jacobs, 2007), which are consistent with the traditional values and aspirations of group practice. In an era in which disasters are so frequent and survivors are so rapidly reduced to statistical abstractions, psychologists and other mental health professionals with the training, sensitivity, and intimate appreciation of intricacies of groups have much to contribute. Instead of limiting ourselves or maintaining the status quo, we can reach out, enter the community facilitate face-to-face dialogues and repair collapsed communications. By broadening our horizons, we can transform the communities as well as ourselves.

Participatory group therapy, therefore, is a community-based psychosocial model aiming at personal and communal empowerment and transformation. It is a therapeutic group, emphasizing individual perceptions and initiatives, and egalitarian, collaborative relationships among all involved. It focuses on the psychosocial wellbeing of its members, but it is also mindful of the needs and issues of the broader community. Through authentic participation within the group and the community, it promotes new ways of being, relating, and interacting with one another. Simply put, participatory group therapy is group therapy with an ecological and participatory orientation. It is a strength-based model, capitalizing on collective resilience and wisdom instead of problems and deficits. It builds upon existing resources and capacities instead of introducing a new structure or agenda (IASC, 2007). In doing so, it transcends cultural differences.

The participatory approach is not without its criticism (Kindon, Pain and Kesby, 2007). As a practice of power, employment of participatory work is not always easy. From my own experience, the process of "designing the plane while flying it" was both anxiety provoking and time-consuming. It requires a leap of faith, a willingness to be influenced, subverted, or even undermined. With children of diverse backgrounds, it may require us to be more playful and spontaneous than we typically are.

Thus, participation can be a genuine process of empowering and transforming the community (Hickey and Mohan, 2005). It can also be "the new tyranny" (Cooke and Kothari, 2001). A multitude of ethical, personal and institutional challenges have been noted (West, 2007; West et al., 2007; John, 2003). One of the major obstacles in working with children is the lack of competence of the adults around them (UNICEF, 2007). As a form of "childhood amnesia," we adults often act as if we had never been children before. There are times we even cause more harm than good to children. Steinitz (2009) noted that a common caveat in participatory work is "to pressure a child, make him or her feel badly or manipulated, or feel more vulnerable than he or she did before participating" (Steinitz, 2009: p. 24). As we recall the ladder metaphor, genuine participation can be easily undermined or substituted by various forms of non-participation, i.e., manipulation, decoration, and tokenism (Hart, 1992, 1997). Nevertheless, as a promising approach, participation improves the psychosocial well-being of children in disaster. It also contributes to a better, more democratic world for us all (Percy-Smith and Thomas, 2010).

A Final Note

This chapter was derived from direct, extensive engagement with the field. A cautionary note is necessary, as direct services carried out by outside providers are generally not recommended (Jacobs, 2007). Extensive training, supervision, needs assessment, and networking, are all essential parts of preparatory work. I, however, had the benefit of being a "semi-local," a fellow Chinese who grew up in the same province and spoke the dialect of the survivors. With no prior experience in any earthquakes or disasters, I had the good fortune of being supervised off-site by a "group" of extraordinary individuals who had watched over me every step of the way. Their wisdom

Figure 31.5 The clouds hovering Beichuan mountains, where the Qiang people, the "People of Clouds," reside. Photo courtesy of Wang, Y., then age 7 (352 × 288 resolution).

and concern had accompanied me as I ventured into the unknown of the catastrophe. My professor, Louise Silverstein, with whom I had "live chat" via Google Talk whenever I had access to the internet, discussed extensively every clinical, personal, and political issue I had encountered. I also stayed in close touch via lengthy emails with Suzanne Phillips and the entire outreach team of American Group Psychotherapy Association (AGPA), whom I had not yet met in person. Having an invisible group of experts, albeit at a distance, affords indispensible protection and support for anyone involved in the immense work of mass trauma.

Two years hence, I have managed to maintain an on-going relationship with the village that I once had the privilege to serve. As I prepare for the chapter reminiscing about the allure of rural life, the West Mountain tent school seems to acquire a dreamlike quality that is as memorable as the clouds the children used to photograph. In fact, the group as I experienced it speaks to the uniqueness of groups and individuals that we encounter on a daily basis. It speaks to our deep longing for genuine, face-to-face contact, our perennial needs for small and organic communities. A disaster transforms our life, prompting us to reorganize ourselves, our communities, and even our society. It triggers, as the Chinese say, both danger and opportunity. It is, indeed, an opportunity for us to learn to be a community again.

Acknowledgements

The author wishes to thank the children of Westside Mountain tent school, the volunteers, her multiple mentors Louise Silverstein, Suzanne Philips, Maureen Underwood, and her alma mater Yeshiva University for their participation, guidance, and support. This chapter was written in celebration of a participatory spirit in us all.

References and Bibliography

Brabender, V., Smolar, A. I., & Fallon, A. E. (2004). *Essentials of group therapy.* John Wiley & Sons, Inc.

Buber, M. (1996). *I and thou.* Simon & Schuster.

Calhoun, L. G., & Tedeschi, R. G. (2006). The foundations of posttraumatic growth: An expanded framework. In L. G. Calhoun & R. G. Tedeschi (Eds.), *Handbook of posttraumatic growth* (pp. 1–23). Mahwah, New Jersey: Erlbaum.

Cammarota, J., & Fine, M. (2008). *Revolutionizing education: Youth participatory action research in motion.* Routledge.

Chazan, R. (2001). *The group as therapist.* Jessica Kingsley Publishers.

Chemtob, C. M., Nakashima, J. P., & Hamada, R. S. (2002). Psychosocial intervention for postdisaster trauma symptoms in elementary school children: A controlled community field study. *Archives of Pediatrics and Adolescent Medicine, 156*(3), 211–216.

Cooke, B., & Kothari, U. (Eds.) (2001). *Participation: The new tyranny?* London: Zed Books.

Drewes, A. (2005). Play in selected cultures. In E. Gil & A. Drewes (Eds.), *Cultural issues in play therapy.* Guilford Publications.

Duncan, J. & Arntson, L. (2004). *Children in crisis: Good practice in evaluating psychosocial programming.* Save the Children Federation, Inc.

Fernando, G. A., Miller, K. E., & Berger, D. E. (2010). Growing pains: The impact of disaster-related and daily stressors on the psychological and psychosocial functioning of youth in Sri Lanka. *Child Development, 81*(4), 1192–1210. DOI: 10.1111/j.1467-8624.2010.01462.x

Freeman, J., Epston, D. & Lobovits, D. (1997). *Playful approaches to serious problems: Narrative therapy with children and their families.* New York: Norton.

Freire, P. (1972). *Pedagogy of the oppressed.* Harmondworth: Penguin.

Freire, P. (1973; 2002). *Education for critical consciousness.* Continuum Publishing Company.

Garrett, A. L. Grant, R., Madrid, P., et al. (2007). Children and megadisasters: Lessons learned in the new millennium. *Advances in Pediatrics, 54,* 189–214. DOI:10.1016/j.yapd.2007.03.011.

Hart, R. (1992). *Children's participation: From tokenism to citizenship.* Florence: UNICEF Innocenti Research Centre.

Hart, R. (1997). *Children's participation: The theory and practice of involving young citizens in community development and environmental care.* London: Earthscan.

Hart, R. (2008). Stepping back from "the ladder": Reflections on a model of participatory work with children. In A. Reid., B. Jensen., J. Nikel., & V. Simovska (Eds.), *Participation and learning: Perspectives on education and the environment, health and sustainability* (pp. 19–31). Netherlands: Springer.

Herr, K., & Anderson, G. L. (2005). *The action research dissertation: A guide for students and faculty.* Sage Publications, Inc.

Hickey, S., & Mohan, G. (2005). *Participation – from tyranny to transformation? Exploring new approaches to participation in development.* Zed Books.

Hutton, D. (2001). *Psychosocial aspects of disaster recovery: Integrating communities into disaster planning and policy making.* Institute for Catastrophic Loss Reduction.

Inter-Agency Standing Committee (IASC) (2007). *IASC guidelines on mental health and psychosocial support in emergency settings.* Geneva: IASC.

Jacobs, G. A. (2007). The development and maturation of humanitarian psychology, *American Psychologist, 51,* 932–941. DOI: 10.1037/0003-066X.62.8.932

John, M. (2003). *Children's rights and power: Charging up for a new century.* Jessica Kingsley Publishers.

Joseph, S. & Linley, P. A. (Eds.) (2008). *Trauma, recovery, and growth: Positive psychological perspectives on posttraumatic stress.* Hoboken, New Jersey: John Wiley & Sons.

Kindon, S., Pain, R., & Kesby, M. (Eds.) (2007). *Connecting people, participation and place: Participatory action research approaches and methods.* London: Routledge.

Kinoshita, I. (2007). Children's participation in Japan: An overview of municipal strategies and citizen movements. *Children, Youth and Environments 17*(1), 269–286. Retrieved from http://www.colorado.edu/journals/cye.

Klingman, A., & Cohen, E. (2004). *School-based multisystemic interventions for mass trauma.* New York: Kluwer Academic/ Plenum Publishers.

Kornblum, R. (2008). Dance/movement therapy with children. In D. McCarthy (Ed.), *Speaking about the unspeakable: Non-verbal methods and experiences in therapy with children.* Jessica Kingsley Publishers.

Larmer, B. (2010). *China's arranged remarriages.* New York Times (May 7). Retrieved from: http://www.nytimes.com/2010/05/09/magazine/09widows-t.html.

Li, H. (personal communication, August 2, 2008)

Lim, L. (2008). New lives, new ethnic identity for Chinese villagers. *NPR.* Retrieved from http://www.npr.org/templates/story/story.php?storyId=98681734andft=1andf=1001.

List, I. (2008). The secret garden: Healing through nature. *Speaking about the unspeakable: Non-verbal methods and experiences in therapy with children.* Jessica Kingsley Publishers.

Loughry, M., & Eyber, C. (2003). Psychosocial concepts in humanitarian work with children: A review of the concepts and related literature. *Roundtable on the demography of forced migration*. National Academy Press.

Maglajlic, R. A. (2010). "Big organisations" supporting "small involvement" – lessons from Bosnia and Herzegovina on enabling community-based participation of children through PAR. *American Journal of Community Psychology*. DOI: 10.1007/s10464-010-9322-0.

Malone, K, & Hartung, C. (2010). Challenges of participatory practice with children. In B. Percy-Smith & N. Thomas (Eds.), *A handbook of children and young people's participation: Perspectives from theory and practice* (pp. 24–38). Routledge.

Manyena, S. B., Fordham, M., & Collins, A. (2008). Disaster resilience and children: Managing food security in Binga district in Zimbabwe. *Children, Youth and Environments, 18*(1), 303–331. Retrieved from http://www.colorado.edu/journals/cye.

Margolin, G., Ramos, M. C., & Guran, E. L. (2010). Earthquakes and children: The role of psychologists with families and communities. *Professional Psychology: Research and Practice, 41*(1), 1–9. DOI: 10.1037/a0018103.

Marsella, A. J. & Christopher, M. A. (2004). Ethnocultural consideration in disaster: An overview of research, issues, and directions. *Psychiatric Clinics of North America, 27*(3), 521–539.

Masten, A. S. (2001). Ordinary magic: Resilience processes in development. *American Psychologist, 56*(3), 227–238.

Metzel, E. S. (2009). The role of creative thinking in resilience after Hurricane Katrina. *Psychology of Aesthetics, Creativity, and the Arts, 3*, 2, 112–123. DOI:10.1037/a0013479.

Peek, L. (2008). Children and disasters: Understanding vulnerability, developing capacities and promoting resilience: An introduction. *Children, Youth and Environments 18*, 1–29. Retrieved from http://www.colorado.edu/journals/cye/.

Percy-Smith, B. & Thomas, N. (Eds) (2010). *Handbook of children and young people's participation perspectives from theory and practice*. Routledge.

Prewitt Diaz, J. O. & Dayal, A. (2008). Sense of place: A model for community based psychosocial support programs. *The Australasian Journal of Disaster and Trauma Studies*. Retrieved from http://www.massey.ac.nz/~trauma/issues/2008-1/prewitt_diaz.htm

Prewitt Diaz, O. J. (2008). Integrating psychosocial programs in multisector responses to international disasters. *American Psychologist, 63*, 820–827. DOI: 10.1037/0003-066X.63.8.820.

Prilleltensky, I. (2010). Child wellness and social inclusion: Values for action. *American Journal of Community Psychology, 46*, 238–249. DOI: 10.1007/s10464-010-9318-9

Ray, P. (2010). The participation of children living in the poorest and most difficult situations. In B. Percy-Smith & N. Thomas (Eds.), *A handbook of children and young people's participation: Perspectives from theory and practice* (pp. 63–74). Routledge.

Ronan, K. R., Crellin, K, Johnston, D. M., et al. (2008). Promoting child and family resilience to disasters: Effects, interventions and prevention effectiveness. *Children, Youth and Environments, 18*(1), 332–353.

Roopnarine, J. L., Johnson, J. E., & Hooper, F. H. (1994). *Children's play in diverse cultures*. New York: State University of New York Press.

Rosati, M. J. (2006). Effectively addressing the mid- and long-term needs of young people affected by the tsunami in Aceh: An on-site assessment. *International Review of Psychiatry, 18*(3), 265–269. DOI: 10.1080/09540260600656183.

Ryan, K., & Cunningham, M. (2007). Helping the helpers: Guidelines to prevent vicarious traumatization of play therapists working with traumatized children. In L. C. Terr & N. B. Webb (Eds.), *Play therapy with children in crisis, third edition: Individual, group, and family treatment* (pp. 443–459). Guilford.

Salloum, A., Garside, L. W., Irwin, C. L., et al. (2009). Grief and trauma group therapy for children after hurricane Katrina. *Social Work with Groups, 32*, 64–79. DOI: 10.1080/01609510802290958.

Samide, L. L., & Stockton, R. (2002). Letting go of grief: Bereavement groups for children in the school setting. *Journal for Specialists in Group Work, 27*, 192–204. DOI: 10.1177/0193392202027002006.

Scheidlinger, S. (2004). *Group interventions for treatment of psychological trauma. module 2: Group interventions for treatment of trauma in children.* American Group Psychotherapy Association (AGPA). Retrieved from http://www.agpa.org/pubs/2-children.pdf.

Shen, Y. (2002). Short-term group play therapy with Chinese earthquake victims: Effects on anxiety, depression, and adjustment. *International Journal of Play Therapy.* DOI:10.1037/h0088856.

Silverman, W. K., & La Greca, A. M. (2002). Children experiencing disasters: Definitions, reactions, and predictors of outcomes. In A. M. La Greca, W. K. Silverman, & E. M. Vernberg (Eds.), *Helping children cope with disasters and terrorism* (pp. 11–33). Washington, DC: American Psychological Association. DOI: 10.1037/10454-001.

Steinitz, L. (2009). The way we care: A guide for managers of programs serving vulnerable children and youth. *Family Health International.* Retrieved from http://www.fhi.org/en/HIVAIDS/pub/guide/res_The_Way_We_Care.htm

Theis, J. (2007). Performance, responsibility and political decision-making: Child and youth participation in Southeast Asia, East Asia and the Pacific. *Children, Youth and Environment, 17*(1), 1–13. Retrieved from http://www.colorado.edu/journals/cye.

UNCRC. (1989). United Nations General Assembly Resolution 25 Session 44: *Convention on the rights of the child* (CRC). Retrieved from http://daccess-ddsny.un.org/doc/RESOLUTION/GEN/NR0/547/84/IMG/NR054784.pdf?OpenElement. Also: http://www2.ohchr.org/english/law/crc.htm.

Underwood, M., Spinazzola, N., & Milani, J. (2004). *Families going on after loss: Manualized curriculum and training manual.* Verona, New Jersey: Mental Health Association of New Jersey.

UNICEF. (2006). *Education in emergencies: A resource tool kit.* UNICEF East Asia and Pacific Regional Office.

UNICEF. (2007). *The participation of children and young people in emergencies: A guide for relief agencies, based largely on experiences in the asian tsunami response.* UNICEF East Asia and Pacific Regional Office. Retrieved from: http://www.unicef.org/eapro/the_participation_of_children_and_young_people_in_emergencies.pdf

UNICEF. (2010). *Core commitments for children in humanitarian action.* UNICEF. Retrieved from http://www.unicef.org/lac/CCCs_EN_070110.pdf.

Ursano, R. J., Fullerton, C. S., Weisaeth L., & Raphael, B. I. (2007). *Textbook of disaster psychiatry.* Cambridge University Press.

van der Kolk, B., McFarlane, A., & Weisaeth, A. (Eds.) (1996). *Traumatic stress: The effects of overwhelming experience on mind, body and society.* New York: Guilford Press.

Vogel, J. & Vernberg, E. M. (1993). Children's psychological response to disaster. *Journal of Clinical Child Psychology, 22*, 470–484. DOI: 10.1207/s15374424jccp2204_7.

Wang, M. G. (2003). *Between the Han and the Tibetans: The historical anthropology of the Qiang minority in Western Sichuan.* Taipei: Lianjing Publishing [in Chinese].

Wessells, M. G. (2009). Do not harm: Towards contextually appropriate psychosocial support in international emergencies. *American Psychologist, 64*, 842–854.

Wessendorf, K. (2009). *The indigenous world 2009.* International Work Group for Indigenous Affairs (IWGIA).

West, A. (2007). Power relationships and adult resistance to children's participation. *Children, Youth and Environments, 17*(1), 123–135. Retrieved from http://www.colorado.edu/journals/cye.

West, A., Chen, X. M., Zhou, Y., et al. (2007). From performance to practice: Changing the meaning of child participation in China. *Children, Youth and Environments, 17*(1), 14–32. Retrieved from http://www.colorado.edu/journals/cye.

Winnicott, D. W. (1971). *Playing and reality*. London: Tavistock Publications.

Yalom, I. (1998). *The Yalom reader*. Basic Books.

Zeng, E. & Silverstien, L. (forthcoming). China earthquake relief: Participatory action work with children. *School Psychology International*, International Response to Trauma Special Edition. SAGE.

32

A Multidisciplinary Treatment Team Model for Youth Offenders in Correctional Treatment Centers: Applying Psychodynamic Group Concepts

D. Thomas Stone Jr. and Anne Carson Thomas

The Blind Men and the Elephant

It was six men of Indostan
    To learning much inclined,
Who went to see the Elephant (Though all of them were blind),
    That each by observation
Might satisfy his mind.

The First approached the Elephant,
    And happening to fall
Against his broad and sturdy side,
    At once began to bawl:
"God bless me! but the Elephant
    Is very like a wall!"

The Second, feeling of the tusk,
    Cried, "Ho! what have we here
So very round and smooth and sharp!
    To me 'tis mighty clear
This wonder of an Elephant
    Is very like a spear!"

The Third approached the animal,
    And happening to take
The squirming trunk within his hands,
    Thus boldly up and spake:
"I see," quoth he, "the Elephant Is very like a snake!"

The Fourth reached out an eager hand,
    And felt about the knee.
"What most this wondrous beast is like
    Is mighty plain," quoth he;

"Tis clear enough the Elephant
    Is very like a tree!"

The Fifth, who chanced to touch the ear,
Said: "E'en the blindest man
Can tell what this resembles most;
    Deny the fact who can
This marvel of an Elephant
    Is very like a fan!"

The Sixth no sooner had begun
    About the beast to grope,
Than, seizing on the swinging tail
    That fell within his scope,
"I see," quoth he, "the Elephant
    Is very like a rope!"

And so these men of Indostan
    Disputed loud and long,
Each in his own opinion
    Exceeding stiff and strong,
Though each was partly in the right,
    And all were in the wrong!

Moral:
So oft in theologic wars,
    The disputants, I ween,
Rail on in utter ignorance
    Of what each other mean,
And prate about an Elephant
    Not one of them has seen!

John Godfrey Saxe

Introduction

In residential settings, group psychotherapy concepts have utility beyond the clinical group treatment room because a significant amount of work outside the treatment room is also conducted in groups or teams. These teams can be either formal or informal, and are formed in an effort to provide the best possible treatment to the residents. Moreover, regardless of the organizational structure of the residential setting, that structure is necessarily impacted by the dynamic psychological politics of the group. In residential settings involving youth offenders, the goal is to find the organizational structure that best utilizes group psychotherapy concepts to provide comprehensive care and treatment.

An adolescent who has become part of the juvenile judicial system offers a unique set of challenges. The profile of the youth offender has increasingly changed over the years. These changes are partly attributable to the reduction in services available in community-based mental health systems. Adolescents in need of comprehensive mental health services often land in the juvenile justice system because of behavior that can be attributed to their mental health disorders. These adolescents bring with them not only mental health concerns, but also medical and academic needs that require a comprehensive and well-organized approach to their care.

The nature of these aforementioned needs coupled with the behavioral conduct of the youth offender creates organizational demands that cannot be addressed purely by focusing on the individual needs of each youth. Instead, these demands require an organizational system with a comprehensive approach and a well-integrated structure. Every treatment partner and discipline needs to be in alignment with a common mission to meet the challenges of the correctional treatment of the youth offender. For this reason, we believe a Multidisciplinary Treatment Team (MTT) in which every discipline is represented can be extremely successful in the care and treatment of youth offenders in the residential setting. In order for the MTT to effectively address the challenges unique to the youth offender, however, it needs effective leadership that understands the impact of dynamics among and between the residents and the members of the team. This chapter will attempt to:

1. Identify the demographic and psychological characteristics of the youth offender.
2. Describe the structure and dynamic process of the MTT.
3. Elucidate the complex skills required of the MTT Facilitator.

Many of the ideas discussed in this chapter are the result of the 13 years we have spent organizing a treatment matrix that not only maximizes the possibility for change in the individual youth offender, but also maximizes the nature of the treatment offered by changing how the facility partners and disciplines interact with each other. Our experience then is based on our extensive involvement in leading changes over time that have challenged the institutional mind often found in youth residential facilities. The facility that we will reference from time to time is the Cyndi Taylor Krier Juvenile Correctional Treatment Center (Krier) that is located in San Antonio, Texas. It is currently a 96-bed all-male facility that has an autonomous educational program as well as a county-based ambulatory health care facility. Prior to this year there was a 24-bed unit of female residents about which reference will be made in the chapter.

What about the poem at the beginning? This poem might be thought of as a primary guiding principle in how we think about work with youth offenders. The poem illustrates how easy it is for us to close our minds and fill in the blanks with sweeping generalizations based on little bits of information. This tendency becomes strikingly apparent in working with youth offenders. Each treatment partner or discipline encounters different parts of the troubled adolescent and may blindly make "partly right" conclusions only to find out later that they were "greatly wrong." In light of this, the MTT strives to be guided by a hovering awareness of the limitations of a single perspective in its capacity to "see" the whole clinical picture.

Who is the Youth Offender?

In order to attain a full clinical understanding of the youth offender, it is important to know how they enter into the juvenile justice system and the challenges they bring to the system. In this section, we will give the reader an overview of the juvenile justice system and demographic information about the youth offender including:

1. Age and ethnicity factors.
2. Familial and cultural factors, educational factors.
3. Medical and health factors.
4. Mental health factors, including diagnostic, psychodynamic, psychotherapeutic, and countertransferential considerations.

A clear and comprehensive picture of the youth offender is essential to understanding the challenges of this work.

Entrance into the juvenile justice system

Juvenile offenders are initially brought into the justice system because they have been arrested for crimes such as possession of drugs/alcohol or assaultive behavior against other youths, family members, and occasionally teachers or police officers. Criminal mischief, such as vandalism or destruction of property including tagging, is another crime that often results in a juvenile's appearance before a judge. First offenders are usually placed under the supervision of the juvenile probation system. They are required to meet periodically with an assigned probation officer. The probation officer is charged with both protecting the community from further criminal activity and being an advocate for the youth to receive the assistance required to address the personal and external conditions that contribute to the youth's delinquent behavior. This supervision includes placement by court order in some of the wide variety of programs designed to address the specific needs of the youth. These programs often have a mental health component. If these less restricted interventions prove to be ineffective in curtailing the delinquent behavior, the juveniles will be court-ordered to a post-adjudication facility. A post-adjudication facility is usually a residential treatment facility where the youth is ordered by the court to live for a specific period of time or until they fulfill certain program requirements. Over the last 15 years, these facilities have become a mainstay of the local juvenile system aimed at combining correction and treatment.

Youths who are placed in a post-adjudication facility typically have had more extensive involvement in the juvenile justice system. They often have been referred to the juvenile justice system six or more times. Their histories are replete with numerous Child In Need of Supervision (CINS) referrals and violations of probation conditions due to truancy, breaking curfew, leaving home without permission, and positive urine drug screens. While juveniles who have committed violent or aggravated crimes would generally be expected to be placed by a court at a more stringent state-run facility as opposed to a residential treatment facility, many, if not most, of the juveniles at the Krier Center have exhibited aggressive and assaultive behaviors.

Demographics – age and ethnicity

According to national data (Sickmund, Sladky, Kang, and Puzzanchera, 2008), 83% of youth incarcerated in detention and correctional facilities in the United States are 15–17 years of age. While ethnicity within each facility varies depending upon the type of facility and the demographics of the surrounding communities, the nationwide percentage of each ethnic group in these facilities is as follows: 44% Black, 37% White, 16% Hispanic, 2% Asian/Pacific Islander, and 1% Native American. In our experience at the Krier, the vast majority of juvenile offenders are between 15 and 16 years of age and are mostly from minority ethnic groups. However, the overall age range is between 10–17 years old.

Familial-cultural factors

Social histories of youth offenders at Krier also reveal patterns much worth noting. For example, by tracking zip codes, it is clear that many of these youth come from the same neighborhoods. These neighborhoods have higher overall crime rates, higher drop-out rates, higher teenage pregnancy rates, and higher rates of chronic medical problems such as diabetes. Poverty levels are higher and age expectancy is lower. These juveniles most often come from "broken" or single-parent homes, have moved homes and schools multiple times, and were born to young mothers. These juveniles have also been exposed to disturbing levels of violence, direct or indirect, in their homes and communities. Records have confirmed that 35% of the juveniles have been physically, sexually and/or emotionally abused in their lifetimes. What is less well known is how many have been traumatized by domestic violence, including fights with siblings or between parents, and violence in the streets.

The majority of youth offenders are involved with gangs, ranging from association through friends and family members to high-ranking positions within organized criminal organizations. Tattoos reveal their loyalties, their tag names, and their stories of loss and trauma: from teardrop tattoos, to initials of fallen "home boys," to names of deceased or incarcerated family members.

Educational factors

Educational records of youth offenders show they are, on average, two years behind their expected grade in school based on their age. Typical reasons for failure in school include attendance problems, discipline problems affecting academic progress, and learning disabilities. At any given time, about 33–50% of the youth offenders at the Krier Center are special education students. Psychological evaluations indicate that most of the residents operate within the low average to average range of intellectual functioning. They frequently have language comprehension and expression as relative weaknesses. With learning problems at about 28%, the youth offenders typically have a long history of academic difficulties and are behind in academic achievement. There are current efforts to study the extent to which traumatic brain injury, resulting from reckless behavior, violence, and substance abuse, contribute to their academic failure.

Medical and health factors

Special medical needs appear to be extraordinarily high among youth offenders at about 25%. These special medical needs include hypertension, diabetes, blood disorders, Hepatitis C, cardiac conditions, obesity, sickle cell, epilepsy, encopresis, HIV, etc. All of these medical conditions are more concentrated in the female than the male population. Female youth offenders are at a higher risk for STDs and teenage pregnancy than non-offenders. As a result of often being in sexually and emotionally abusive relationships, female youth offenders have not developed a healthy sense of self or the skills necessary to effectively manage healthy boundaries in relationships.

Mental health factors

Due to the prevalence of mental health disorders among juvenile offenders and the impact of these disorders on effective treatment (Cocozza and Skowyra, 2000), this demographic factor will be examined in greater detail. Attention will be given to diagnostic, psychodynamic, psychotherapeutic, and countertransferential considerations.

Diagnostic considerations With the growing reliance on the criminal justice system to care for and treat mentally ill persons, the numbers of youth admitted to detention and correctional facilities with such problems have grown significantly over the past few decades. Wide discrepancies in estimates of the prevalence of mental health disorders in the juvenile justice population have made it difficult to conclude with any confidence how rates of mental health problems in juvenile offenders differ from those regarding the general population. A meta-analysis conducted by the Office of Juvenile Justice and Delinquency Prevention (Teplin, McClelland, Mericel, Dulcan and Washburn, 2006) illustrates this discrepancy. In the meta-analysis, over 16 different studies were examined, and the diagnosis of major affective disorder in the studies varied from 5–88%, substance abuse disorders varied from 20%–88%, and psychosis varied from 12–45%. The discrepancies are believed to be due to dissimilar population samples, the different procedures utilized to determine the presence of mental health disorders, as well as the differing definitions of mental health disorders.

One important source for the discrepancies among these types of studies is whether or not conduct disorder and possibly other behavioral disorders, such as oppositional defiant disorder and disruptive behavior disorder, are included in the definition of a mental health disorder. Although conduct disorders are included in the DSM-IV-TR (2000), many researchers do not include these diagnoses in studying juvenile offenders, based on the assumption that nearly all of the juvenile detainees will meet the criteria for one of these diagnoses due to the simple fact, they have entered the juvenile justice system. In a study conducted by Northwestern Juvenile Project (Friedman, Katz-Leavy, Manderscheid, and Sondheimer, 1996) researchers attempted to surmount these discrepancies and concluded that 60% of male and 70% of female juvenile detainees met the criteria for at least one psychiatric condition. Further, given the rates of comorbidity, many of these youths also suffered from a substance abuse disorder. For reasons stated before, these percentages exclude the diagnosis of conduct disorder based on the assumption that the conduct is what brought them into contact with the law. In our view, it is essential to distinguish studies that include conduct disorder in their definition of mental health disorders from those that do not. At the same time, the exclusion of conduct disorder does not provide a full diagnostic picture of the psychopathological dynamics of the juvenile justice population and needs to be addressed.

Psychodynamic considerations Because a diagnosis of a conduct disorder is nothing more than a behavioral description of antisocial patterns of behavior, there are great differences among youth diagnosed with this disorder. Conduct disorder includes a wide spectrum of behavioral conditions that contribute to the antisocial pattern of behavior. For example, one youth offender may engage in aggressive, explosive behavior due to fundamental problems with emotional regulation while another youth offender may engage in the calculative and strategic use of aggressive behavior in order to assume power and position within a youth group. Indeed, since the behavior problems are the most predominant problem affecting a youth offender's adjustment and ability to function within society, the inclusion of conduct disorder diagnoses is necessary since treatment planning must address these central behavior problems. Diagnostic criteria for conduct disorder provide critically important information regarding behavioral features, but tell little about the underlying psychodynamics. Conduct disordered youth, by definition, violate societal norms and impinge on the rights of others, but the etiology can be quite complex and the underlying causes for this behavior dramatically differs between youth offenders. Some incarcerated youths demonstrate personality characteristics traditionally associated with the "juvenile delinquent" such as emotional callousness and use of intimidation and aggression as a means of achieving power or position within a peer group. Others with similar outward behavioral symptoms have apparently obtained fuller personality development, including the capacity to form mutually rewarding relationships with others, and only exhibit such antisocial behaviors when "acting out" against authority. Still others possess very immature personality development with severe deficits in capacity for attachment, affect regulation, and behavioral control. This last description represents that majority of the incarcerated youth.

We have found the Psychodynamic Diagnostic Manual (PDM) (2006) to be very helpful in understanding the conduct disordered youth because it describes the fabric of the underlying character formation. Due to environmental factors and possibly constitutional factors, these youth have had significant interruptions in their social, educational, and psychological development along with longstanding functional difficulties. Using a descriptive continuum of personality development and organization, ranging from the healthy personality, to the neurotic, to the borderline, and finally to the psychotic, the authors of the manual state that the conduct disordered youth generally can be best understood as having developed, at best, a borderline personality organization (PDM, 2006). Because we do not wish to label youth who are still malleable to treatment with terms that have developed a pejorative connotation in practice, we urge the reader to understand the use of these terms as a description of the level of personality development rather than a description of adult clinical symptomatology as described in DSM-IV-TR (2000). Limited by a borderline level of personality development and organization, conduct-disordered youth generally have a limited ability to manage their internal life and to form stable attachments with others. Moreover, these youth have serious difficulty identifying their internal experiences, labeling their emotions, and regulating their emotional reactions. They also have difficulty identifying and understanding the feelings of others that likely contributes to their limited capacity to develop and maintain deep, lasting and intimate relationships. Their confidence and general self-regard are unstable at best. They characteristically have poor boundaries and lack a self-observing capacity. Further, as one might expect given the above, they have not yet developed a stable sense of morality or ideals from which to govern life choices.

Conduct-disordered youth employ a variety of defensive maneuvers to protect themselves from experiencing overwhelming affect and further psychological disorganization. Dissociation, projection, isolation of affect, avoidance, narcissism, and identification with the aggressor are psychological defenses commonly seen among conduct-disordered youth. It is the pattern of defensive behaviors that forms the "outward personality" (the presentation of self to others) and results in problems in adaptive functioning. Because the youth vary so much in their defensive patterns, it is expected that they will demonstrate personality patterns ranging from psychopathic, to anxious, to dissociative. Conduct-disordered youth with a psychopathic personality disorder and strong narcissistic character features believe that they are capable of doing anything. Their most common defense, perhaps as a result of identification with the aggressor as a means of survival, is to assume power and control over others. In contrast, those with anxious and dissociative personality disorders, who usually do not appear to have this inflated self-esteem, defend against a perceived hostile world through avoidance, even so severe, as is the case with dissociative types, that they "leave" reality. All of these conduct-disordered youths have one thing in common – a view that the world is hostile place where others can be potential victimizers. Substance abuse disorders are also customarily found in conduct-disordered youths, further encumbering their physical, psychological, and social development.

Psychotherapeutic considerations Professionals working with youth offenders with such severe personality disorders recognize that their impulse control problems and emotional regulation problems make traditional therapy difficult, if not ineffective. While most of the time these youth will employ defenses that avoid any exploration of affect, there will be episodes of extreme affective outburst accompanied by behavior that is difficult to manage. The more frequent and distorted from reality the outburst, the more severe the deficit in personality organization and development. The most severely damaged juveniles may resort to more primitive defenses of splitting, projective identification, dissociation, and regression. Lacking the ability to regulate their affect and their low tolerance for stress, these youth need a psychotherapeutic response that includes a stable structure and setting limits. A strong and stable structure helps them to manage their affect so they are not overwhelmed with it. Therapists can be helpful by coaching these youth on healthy coping strategies.

Not only does structure and limit-setting help youth offenders with borderline personality disorders to manage their affect, it is also necessary for the treatment of the psychopathic personality disordered youth who would devalue and distrust therapists who are too kind or allow boundaries and structure to be violated. These youth have often been attracted to gangs because of the consistency of structure and discipline. When there is a lack of consistent structure and discipline on the living unit or in the psychotherapeutic setting, these youth will assume the omnipotent power they seek yet desperately fear. Clinicians, as well as frontline staff, must provide an organizing and integrating capacity both in their individual encounters as well as group encounters. The need for safety and security serves a critical function in bringing about healthy changes in defense systems whether considering diagnoses of conduct, mood, anxiety, or PTSD. Without consistency in implementation of a behavior management program, the youth will not have the trust or respect necessary to risk making changes in their cognitive-affective view of themselves and others.

Treatment professionals often initially struggle with recognizing the therapeutic value of the facility structure as not only an essential component of an effective treatment program, but as "preconditional to the development of a therapeutic environment" (Gibbs et al., 1995). Structure in the form of behavioral expectations, schedules, and rules provide for the physical and psychological safety of the youth. Structure provides predictability, stability, and consistency, which environmental conditions were often lacking in the lives of our youth. Because youth offenders are also prone to behavioral and relational aggression, proactive measures to intervene in conflict before it escalates supports safety and provides an opportunity for the youth to learn important conflict resolution skills. When proactive measures fail, youth need reassurance from the adults that if any harmful behavior expresses itself, there will be immediate intervention. In some cases, separation and physical control may be necessary to reestablish equilibrium to the milieu.

Group-based interventions, whether in the milieu or in the group therapy setting, also provide the youth with a containing structure that gives them the opportunity to internalize the discipline and affective regulatory functions they lack in their everyday life. The peer culture webbed within the organizational structure of the living units also elicits the development of self-regulatory skills. Youth who have earned higher levels of status, which include certain desirable privileges, are role models and often take on peer leadership roles. These youth will utilize a variety of peer-based interventions to cultivate growth in their struggling peers. The process of the group operating within the structure and design of everyday life in the milieu provides a containing function that facilitates maturation and development of higher-level self-regulation and modulation of affect.

Countertransferential considerations The stories that youth offenders bring to the residential living situation are imbued with neglect, abandonment, violence, deprivation, boundary violations, and trauma. Since their arrival at the residential facility is usually not their first placement, their transferential targets are comprised of many different kinds of authority and caretaking figures. Their affective world often consists of disappointment, rage, aggression, shame, fear of abandonment, attachment, and rejection. Their internal world of object relations is projected onto all personnel in some fashion and may result in individual and collective replication of their early trauma. To further complicate the work, these youth often experience a developmentally based quest for identity formation. This quest necessarily leads to subtle and aggressive challenges to the prevailing authority around them as a way of asserting their own sense of personal authority and power (Stone, 2001). The behavioral manifestations of their developmental urges and the relational complexity of their internal object world interact with facility personnel in profound ways. Within each living unit, there is a group matrix that assumes a life of its own with each youth and staff member fully participating in the unfolding relational system.

The affective impact of the youth residents on all facility personnel, especially clinicians and direct care staff, is manifested in the interactions between staff and the residents. The staff will have countertransferential responses to the residents that can be dysfunctional and may even facilitate a replication of early trauma in the resident. The manifestations of residents' internal object world into dysfunctional behavior put the staff at risk for dysfunctional countertransferential responses. Facility staff is also at risk for the development of vicarious and secondary traumatic responses because of their constant exposure to the residents stories of trauma. This constant exposure may result in assuming protective or defensive ways of relating to the residents that are ineffective, dysfunctional, and counter-therapeutic (Stone, 2001).

This transference-countertransferential matrix challenges the staff to work very closely together and to cultivate a culture that is explorative and dialogical about the interplay of affect between the youth and facility personnel. Frequent and open conversations about the emotional impact of the work will help to hold and contain countertransference so that staff can stay on a therapeutic track and not contribute to the replication of residents' trauma experiences.

This section has attempted to give the reader a complete picture of the youth offender from several important perspectives. The youth offender presents with a complex array of concerns that defies the desire to put any one of them into simple categories. Each of the youth offenders has a personal story to be told in order for the MTT to arrive at a treatment path that offers hope for change. The demographic information and diagnostic viewpoints serve the purpose of giving the clinician starting points from which to begin the evolving process of making interventions individually and within the group. In the next section, we will talk in more detail about the structure and operation of the Multi-Disciplinary Treatment Team which can be central to compiling the starting points, rendering an attainable treatment plan, and designing behavioral interventions for youth offenders.

The Multi-Disciplinary Team: Structure and Process

Structural considerations

Multidisciplinary treatment models have been in operation for over half a century. The model originated in the medical field and was made popular in the mental health field with the introduction of the Child Guidance Center model in which a psychiatrist, psychologist, and social worker were teamed up to provide comprehensive services to troubled youth and their families. Fritz Redl (1966), who was a major proponent of the multidisciplinary treatment approach in residential treatment settings, critically evaluated the mental health field's application of the model referring to it as "implementational psychopathy" and accused the field of purposefully excluding the participation of both paraprofessionals and the children's primary caretakers. Redl further noted that even the best-intentioned initiatives to provide multidisciplinary treatment often still operated under the authority of medical staff and within the constraints of the medical model. As a result, these treatment teams were not genuinely multidisciplinary and often failed to consider the most valuable assessment and intervention opportunities embedded in the relationships among and between the children and their direct care staff.

In a truly multidisciplinary treatment model, all disciplines, professionals and paraprofessionals, actively participate in the collection, evaluation, synthesis and integration of information to form the most accurate comprehensive assessment possible. Such an assessment will, in turn, direct the creation of a collaborative and coordinated intervention plan. In keeping with the lesson learned from the parable of the blind men and the elephant, the MTT must authentically and equally value the unique perspectives of all participants in order to develop a single vision.

The development of a single vision from multiple perspectives requires an organizing and integrating function that is the most foundational and challenging function of the MTT. Much like the wise men in the fable, the various disciplines that observe different parts of the same phenomena are at risk of forever disagreeing about the true nature of the phenomena without the benefit of an integrating "all seeing" function. Persons in the various disciplines have differing backgrounds, training, and experience that allow them to accurately observe a particular aspect of a child and, like the wise men, are susceptible to concluding that their observation is the only perspective. The MTT provides the needed integrative function to bring about a transcendent view that is "greatly right" as failure to do so adversely impacts the effectiveness of treatment and risks re-traumatization of the children.

The task of the MTT is to oversee the on-going dynamic process of assessment and treatment planning. Together, members of the team develop and revise individual treatment plans as indicated, when new information is introduced and integrated into the clinical assessment. Members of the team usually include: counselor, teacher, nurse, probation officer, the unit supervisor, front line officers, psychiatrists recreation coordinator, and any other persons involved with the youth offender such as a caseworker for Child Protective Services, a community-based family therapist working with other members of the family, etc. Each of the MTT members needs to understand their functional roles and the expectations for the team meetings, but most importantly, they must all come together with a strong commitment to and trust in the wisdom of a multidisciplinary approach to treatment.

This model of the MTT will require full support from all other organizational parts of the facility. Changes at any level of an organization will affect changes in all other levels (Agazarian, 1992; Kibel, 1987); hence, even well-intentioned decisions or changes made in another area of the organization may unknowingly interfere with the MTT process. Uninformed of the need for a uniform approach, administrators may interfere by engaging in such activities such as:

1. Intervening directly with the youth, rather than working through the MTT to address concerns.
2. Making unilateral decisions without due consideration of the team's input.
3. Taking sides with one team member against another rather than encouraging mutual agreement and resolution by all members of the team, etc. (Gibbs et al., 1995).

Administrators who understand and support the containment and integrative functions of the MTT, and understand the way in which their decisions affect the MTT and the facility in general, will operate in a collaborative manner. They will maintain open and direct lines of communication with the MTT to consider what impact changes within the organization might have upon the stability of the MTT and the treatment milieu.

Function and process

Well-defined structure, including role definition, boundaries, and procedural guidelines, is critical to ensuring that the MTT effectively meets its objectives. While an overall climate of mutual respect, open and direct communication, acceptance of individual differences, and a firm belief in the strength and wisdom of the team as a whole is fostered, having clear structure is just as important to ensuring that the MTT functions collaboratively. Furthermore, in this model, the MTT needs to be empowered by the facility's administrative leadership to make decisions that address group needs, as well as the individual needs of each youth offender. In a correctional treatment facility, this is an important function as some behavioral interventions implemented by the MTT are directed at the entire living unit.

The mission of the facility, its core values, and guiding principles provide the outermost boundaries of the MTT's scope and function. The MTT understands that its scope does not extend to making substantive changes in "standard" programming, but that it has the authority and responsibility, to address the individual treatment needs of the youth by adapting "standard" programming as needed and to address issues within the milieu to ensure a stable functioning group setting for all, that is safe and fosters growth opportunities.

While treatment teams in traditional treatment settings such as hospitals or residential centers are typically "run" by professional staff, primarily medical staff, it has proven to be more productive and dynamic when the MTT is truly egalitarian, with no individual holding final and single decision-making power. An egalitarian approach requires full and active participation by all MTT members and requires that all decisions be made by consensus. In this case, consensus is defined to mean that all MTT members agree that the decisions made by the MTT are the best possible, albeit not perfect, solutions, while also knowing that each week presents a new opportunity to review and evaluate the decisions made. Additionally, and consistent with an egalitarian approach, is the notion that every member has the power and authority to "table" a decision. The press for consensus makes this an infrequent occurrence, but any member who simply cannot or will not agree with a proposed solution of the MTT can "table" a decision. Once a decision is "tabled," there is a decision-making structure for resolution at the next highest level of administration. If any member holds unilateral authority to change the decision of the MTT, that alone would undermine the value of the input provided by each of the disciplines and over time would lead to disillusionment, disinterest, and poor participation. Although the MTT is egalitarian, a Facilitator is necessary to lead the meetings. It is for this reason that we conceptualize the leader of the MTT as a Facilitator. The MTT Facilitator's role will be more fully explained in the next section.

Lastly, explicitly stating the functional roles and responsibilities of each participant assists each member of the MTT in recognizing their professional boundaries. Each MTT member is expected to report on the juvenile resident, based on that member's respective discipline, that is: nursing staff report on healthcare issues while teachers report on educational issues. Knowing one's own role and responsibilities prevents conflict that necessarily develops out of role confusion and resultant boundary violations. All the information shared by the disciplines is considered valuable to the task of the MTT to develop a comprehensive assessment of the youth's individual treatment needs.

Dynamic challenges to the team Having administrative and organizational support, understanding its charge, and having clear structural guidelines is not enough by itself to meet the day-to-day challenges presented by youth offenders. The MTT's cohesion and sense of trust in each other significantly determines its capacity to function as a container of the intense, unmodulated affect and psychological distortions often presented by youth offenders. The application of psychodynamic concepts to underlying individual psychopathology, group dynamics, and the functioning of the treatment team lends itself to creative opportunities for intervention. Together, MTT members can weather the storm better than any individual and provide not only a stabilizing and integrative function for the individual youth but also for the MTT and for the living unit as a whole in an effort to circumvent the possibility of participation in the reenactment of early traumatizing experiences.

Most commonplace in a correctional treatment facility is the projection by youth offenders of painful feelings of disappointment, rage, frustration and despair resulting from the traumatic early caregiver relationships onto the adults in authority in the facility. While the youth may, at times, have fully experienced and directly expressed these painful feelings toward caregivers, they are more likely to split off these feelings and project them onto other authority figures, especially those authority figures who are tasked with setting limits and possibly frustrating immediate needs as a result. Because of their predominant need to maintain attachments to caregivers, youth offenders have learned that projecting these painful feelings onto other authority figures allows them to preserve their attachment to their caregivers. Youth offenders often blame others rather than risk experiencing any painful introspective feelings of self-doubt, shame, or helplessness.

Staff from all disciplines need to be careful not to get pulled into the "splitting" defenses of the youth by accepting a youth's perceptions of those who manage behavior as "bad." Some staff might be tempted to be drawn into these splits because being the "good object" feels much better than being the "bad object." However, by being drawn into the split, the staff member reinforces the splitting defenses and misses an opportunity for healthy progress through integrative interventions designed to repair the split. This inherent "pull" to participate in splitting when working with traumatized youth can be managed by maintaining allegiance to the MTT model. Within the team process, these unconscious dynamics are identified as they occur in MTT members. The egalitarian approach, requiring full participation by all disciplines and consensus for all decisions, encourages the development of a more integrated vision and works to minimize the destructive processes "pulling" MTT members into the unconscious projections of the youth. When the youth experience the treatment team as cohesive, they experience a healthy containment of their efforts to use self-protective but maladaptive defenses.

Relational problems are typical among troubled youth sent to these facilities. Many youth offenders have endured frustrating, even traumatizing, experiences with early caregivers, resulting in the internalization of bad objects and deficits in the internalization of good objects. They bring with them the "compulsive" need to seek attachment to bad objects, which may have been the only objects they have had, in the "relentless hope" of reworking these internalized bad objects through the experience with loving caregivers (Stark, 1999). Rutan, Alonso, and Groves (1988) describe how young patients have a capacity "to create situations in which their prophesies about the world are fulfilled. How do they accomplish this task? Often they use a powerful defense know as projective identification" (Rutan et al., 1988: p. 467). Through this defense, the youth projects or splits off unwanted aspects of the self onto a worthy adult who identifies with these aspects and behaves accordingly. The youth and the adult unconsciously collude to fulfill the prophecies.

Working through projective identification, first described by Bion (as cited in Stark, 1999) in 1967 as the single most important and therapeutic intervention, is a critically important task for the MTT to effectively implement. Professional staff is very vulnerable to the failure of recognizing their unconscious participation in the relational process of the defense. Clinicians tend to recognize it in correctional officers quite easily, but clinicians have difficulty in seeing how they are participating in the defensive dynamic. Perhaps their narcissistic need to "know all and cure all" obscures their ability to see their own participation.

Abundant literature is available about the process of successful resolution of projective identification in a client-therapist relationship (Stark, 1999). As noted by Ogden (1981), projective identification serves as the only defense that bridges the intrapsychic and interpersonal worlds because of how the other becomes an active, yet unaware, participant. The literature discusses the significance of how the clinician manages the interpersonal relationship with the client to help resolve conflicts within the intrapsychic world, but only on a two-dimensional basis. Kibel (1987) expands on this notion to describe the projective identification process in three-dimensional terms when he says:

> ... the hospital therapist is at once the object of these projections and, at the same time, caught in rivalries and struggles with the staff that are induced by several elements, including these very projections. (Kibel, 1987: p. 23).

In other words, more than one MTT member can identify with split off parts of the child's personality and then reenact them, often resulting in conflict and splitting within the team.

The optimal resolution of this process can be achieved when the members of the MTT come together to:

1. Support and value the unique experiences each have had with the youth.
2. Process the information together to understand what clues their differing experiences provide them about the internal world of the youth.
3. Make collaborative intervention plans to assist the youth to work through and eventually learn to accept the previously unacceptable aspects of themselves.

> The net result is the patient's development of capacity (to tolerate previously unmanageable aspects of herself), where before she had the need (to deny their existence by disowning them). (Stark, 1999: p. 267).

The MTT's task of designing and implementing an effective treatment plan must include the way in which the resident's defenses infiltrate and affect the MTT members. The MTT's conversations will inevitably include strongly held positions about the resident's behavior that, at times, will be expressed in conflictual ways. The more the MTT is on the watch for how the resident's defenses appear in the MTT's conversation, the more likely will they be able to not only recognize the relational dynamics among MTT members, but also, through understanding of the purpose of the defenses, design finely-tuned behavioral interventions.

The Role of the Multidisciplinary Treatment Team Facilitator

The MTT is essentially a task-based group. The primary focus is the development, review, and modification of the youth resident's individual treatment plan. The MTT also has an eye on the overall functioning of the unit as the youth's shared living space along with the trickle down effect of facility-wide administrative activity. Since the MTT has an egalitarian approach, the MTT leader is defined as a Facilitator. In such a role, the MTT Facilitator has control over the structure and process of the meetings but has no direct or singular authority or responsibility for the decisions made by the MTT. Decisions are to be made by the MTT as a whole, and the MTT possesses the exclusive authority and the responsibility for their treatment decisions. The MTT Facilitator has three basic functions that need to be fulfilled in order for the MTT to effectively manage their complex group dynamics as described in the previous section. The three functions are maintaining, negotiating and containing.

Maintaining function

The MTT Facilitator's task of maintaining requires convening the meetings and upholding the collaborative team culture by cultivating open and direct communication, tolerating individual team member differences, effectively utilizing conflict resolution skills, and guiding the MTT in reaching a consensus on team decisions (Klein and Brown, 1987). The MTT Facilitator will need "to be active, serving as a catalyst who promotes and guides discussion." (Kibel, 1987: p 19) It should be clear to the other members from the MTT Facilitator's style of communication that divergent perspectives that are germane to better understand the youth resident are welcomed. A culture that tolerates member differences will create team trust and cohesion so that divergent ideas can evolve into convergent ideas and result in highly functional and effective treatment decisions. Fundamentally, it is important that the MTT Facilitator continually reinforces and models values that emphasize the youth offenders' capacity for growth, healthy coping, and mastery over their environment and themselves.

Effective MTT Facilitators should possess executive ego skills that assist them in mediating between the completion of the tasks before the team and the cast of characters that comprise the team (Klein and Brown, 1987). The Facilitator might be thought of as a social engineer (Yalom, 1985) who defines and regulates transactions across boundaries. The transactions are more manageable when the structure and operational format of the meetings are conducted in "a clear, logical, and predictable manner" (Klein and Brown, 1987: p. 229). The transactions within and between MTT members are partly informed by their role and function on the team. The MTT Facilitator needs to orient the members on the structure, tasks, time frame, communication process, and goals. Norms and group expectations must be established about gathering and sharing relevant and accurate information within a nonjudgmental atmosphere (Klein and Brown, 1987). Importantly, the MTT Facilitator needs to balance the process of dialogue by putting closure on discussion when necessary and promoting consensual decisions. For example, if a difference of opinion cannot be resolved within five to ten minutes after both sides have been given a full opportunity to articulate their position and the MTT has been given the opportunity to integrate the information into a cohesive picture, then the decision is to be automatically "tabled." The MTT Facilitator is also responsible for starting and ending the meeting on time. Finally, in regard to task and structure, the Facilitator would do well to heed Kernberg's (1978) recommendation to regularly identify the group task as "meaningful rather than trivial and feasible rather than overwhelming" (Kernberg, 1978: p. 4).

Negotiating function

Negotiating refers to the MTT Facilitator's task of negotiating between sub-systems that exist both within the MTT and outside of it. First, structural sub-systems, such as the medical services department, the school, and the probation department, each bring their own inherent value systems and institutional concerns to the meeting. In addition, sub-systems are also created by particular perspectives and affectively informed experiences that transcend structural sub-systems. The MTT Facilitator needs to be able to negotiate between these sub-systems outside of the MTT meeting and, most importantly, within and during the meeting.

The negotiations outside of the meeting refer to conversations that the MTT Facilitator might conduct with facility personnel so as to gather information about incidents in the facility or changes in policy or procedure. This might be thought of as the MTT Facilitator doing some homework in advance of the MTT meeting. It is no small task to have these conversations, as the MTT Facilitator will be digesting not only factual information, but also affectively-imbued opinions from people who may not attend the MTT meeting but still expect their strong opinions to be conveyed or even represented by the MTT Facilitator. Fostering the permeability of the boundaries of the MTT team to consider information from other sources is critical to making informed decisions. At the same time, the MTT Facilitator needs to be aware of the projections and introjects that come from individuals and sub-systems outside of the MTT. As discussed in the previous section, these projections and introjects need to be identified and managed within the MTT. The MTT Facilitator is responsible for fostering openness and collaboration between the MTT and the other sub-systems. The MTT Facilitator is also responsible for not allowing the projections and introjects coming from outside the MTT to manage the MTT. The MTT needs to be educated about projection, projective identification, introjects, and splitting (Ganzarain, 1992). Only then can the MTT identify and manage the inevitable projections that will infiltrate it.

The MTT Facilitator is systems conscious, meaning that he or she has an astute awareness of the multiplicity of variables within the overall system and "their reciprocal influences within the totality." (Ganzarain, 1992: p.454) The organizational sub-systems of all the disciplines in the systems are described by Kibel as "hierarchically and dynamically interrelated" (Kibel, 1987: p. 6). An abiding awareness of the influence of the system-as-a-whole and how administrative policies influence residents and the function of the MTT is very valuable. It is important that the MTT Facilitator does not minimize the competing priorities of the administration and all the treatment partners. The MTT Facilitator must hold the team to the task of staying open to new viewpoints and input so that there is movement away from the "vicious cycle" of despair and helplessness to a "virtuous cycle" of hope and growth (Ganzarain, 1992: p. 455).

Negotiating how sub-systems operate within the MTT and facilitating the resolution of differences between sub-systems are especially challenging. Agazarian (1992) has developed a method of working with sub-systems that assists the group leader in negotiating among them. In her model, an emphasis is placed on giving voice to the sub-systems as they evolve in the group process. The voice of each sub-system is allowed open expression so that the possibility of convergent views between sub-systems will develop through full articulation of each perspective that will then lead to consensual decisions. Decisions that are made from this process are more likely to be effective, as they have integrated the full body of knowledge available to the team. The MTT Facilitator accomplishes full articulation of the perspectives of each of the sub-systems by keeping the communication process within and between sub-systems "free of ambiguity, contradiction, and redundancy" (Agazarian, 1992: p. 180). Such communication is reflective of defenses that relate to Bion's Basic Assumptions. When the team is in "fight" mode and constrained by a win/lose configuration, the MTT Facilitator might begin to point out the similarities of each view. In "flight" mode, the MTT Facilitator might emphasize the differences between sub-systems to circumvent the retreat into ambiguities and vagueness. The "restraining forces" in groups, comprised of ambiguity, contradictions, and redundancies, inhibit the discriminating function that identifies differences as well as similarities and thereby prevents "integration of new information in new ways" (Agazarian, 1992: p. 201). By reducing the defenses and negotiating greater permeability between sub-systems, the MTT Facilitator promotes the integration of all relevant information and moves the MTT toward resolutions on treatment plan modifications. This team process becomes a mirror for the internal process a resident needs to have in order to resolve internal conflicts through an openness to the resident's own divergent and conflicted self-concept.

Containing function

The function of containment refers to the ability of the MTT Facilitator to tolerate the intense affect that can permeate the MTT and conduct a dialogue that lends itself to a better understanding of the attitudes and behaviors in question (Moss, 2008). There are two aspects to the role of container. One is to contain the affect, distorted cognitions, projections and transferences that arrive at the MTT Facilitator's doorstep as a result of this role. The other is to contain the myriad of defensive positions that MTT members, including the Facilitator, bring to the meeting. These are a combination of the MTT member's own unmetabolized anxieties about the resident and the politics of the institution along with the anxieties that they carry for others.

The anxieties and associated defenses of the MTT members are best understood as solutions to conflicts. Although these solutions may be unhealthy and dysfunctional, they serve functional purposes that need to be analyzed and understood so that healthier solutions can be found. Analyzing and understanding the MTT members' anxieties and defenses require the MTT Facilitator to use the executive ego skills previously mentioned in order to facilitate the MTT's ability to untangle the dysfunctional knots created by these defenses. A well-formed observing ego helps the MTT Facilitator to track the group process, knowing that there is no immunity to participating in the swirl of affect and defenses that can fill the MTT meeting room. Due to the primitive affective matrix of the residents, the MTT Facilitator can become rejective, uncompassionate, and hostile because of how his or her impulses and superego contents are triggered (Kernberg, 1978).

The observing ego, coupled with strong analytical skills, will help the MTT Facilitator move the team from an emotionally fettered position on the tasks at hand to one that points to rational and effective treatment team decisions. The team leader does this first by modeling for the team the ability to tolerate the dichotomous and conflicting experiences of the team: "good and bad, love and envy, anger and compassion" (Moss, 2008: p. 189). When splitting occurs in the MTT, the MTT Facilitator helps to contain the conflict by recognizing and pointing out the split to the MTT. Initially, this may include educating the team about the nature of splitting and the other primary defenses such as projection and projective identification. As the affect within the MTT is metabolized through tolerance, acceptance, and lack of judgment, the MTT is then ready to participate in what Bion described as "the very active process, which involves feeling, thinking, organizing, and acting" (in Moss, 2008: p. 190). The effective MTT Facilitator is paying close attention to the level of affect in the MTT meeting room and the need to stay in an empathic mode. Once the affective temperature is sufficiently lowered, then the Facilitator is able to promote an interpretative process aimed at understanding the MTT's dynamics and how to stay on task (Pines and Hutchinson, 1993). It is important to note that the structure and operational format of the MTT meeting also serves a containing function.

MTT Facilitators also need to be able to contain and manage the transferences and projections that will be superimposed on them as a result of their role as MTT Facilitators. In many ways, the MTT can be thought of as having an impossible task: that of making a difference with severely damaged and disturbed youth. Because the MTT carries the idealized function of designing treatment interventions that will promote change and growth, the MTT Facilitator becomes a target for devaluation, denigration, and judgment if the MTT fails to achieve its idealized goals (Klein and Brown, 1987). This transference and projection of disappointment, shame, and a sense of failure comes from outside the MTT as well as within it. Of course, some MTT Facilitators may initially be idealized and perceived as carrying all of the success of the team and the resident (Kernberg, 1984). This perception will not last as envy, greed, and resentment over perceived power, control, and authority take its place. The competing narcissistic drives of those on the MTT and outside of it require containment by the MTT Facilitator. When the MTT Facilitator is able to analyze and understand the motivating forces by staying objective and rational, the MTT is able to understand the competing and conflictual needs of the institution, the residents, and themselves. The MTT is then able to focus their attention on the demands of devising treatment plan interventions that have an optimal chance of making a difference.

The maintaining, negotiating, and containing functions all assist the MTT Facilitator in providing the necessary leadership for the MTT to achieve its purpose. As the reader can see, it is no small task to lead a team charged with the task of designing interventions that will lead to change and growth for a youth offender. There are a myriad of influences that impinge on the structure and the process of the MTT. The MTT Facilitator's role is to assist the MTT in managing, negotiating, and containing these influences so that the MTT's assigned tasks are effectively accomplished. Just as in group psychotherapy, the MTT Facilitator needs to trust the MTT's inherent ability to accomplish its work.

Conclusion

The criminal justice system will continue to be challenged with meeting the varying and complex treatment needs of youth offenders. As this system continues to operate residential correctional treatment facilities, the Multidisciplinary Treatment Team model will have significant relevance and centrality for the delivery of effective services to youth in these settings. The evolving body of psychodynamic and systems-based group concepts that seek to account for the plethora of psychological forces within these settings will continue to enhance the MTT's ability to be "all-seeing."

References

Agazarian, Y. M. (1992). Contemporary theories of group psychotherapy: A systems approach to the group-as-a-whole. *International Journal of Group Psychotherapy*, 42(2), 177–203.

American Psychiatric Association. (2000). *Diagnostic and statistical manual of mental disorders* (4th ed., Text Rev.). Arlington, Virginia: American Psychiatric Publishing, Inc.

Cocozza, J., & Skowyra, K. (2000). Youth with mental health disorders: Issues and emerging responses. *Juvenile Justice*, VII(1), 3–13.

Friedman, R. M., Katz-Leavy, J. W., Manderscheid, R. W., et al. (1996). Prevalence of serious emotional disturbance in children and adolescents. In R. W. Mandershcied & M. A. Sonnenschien (Eds.), *Mental health, United States, 1996*. Rockville, Maryland: US Department of Health and Human Services.

Ganzarain, R. (1992). General systems and object-relations theories: Their usefulness in group psychotherapy. *International Journal of Group Psychotherapy*, 441–456.

Gibbs, J. C., Potter, G. B., & Goldstein, A. P. (1995). *The equip program: Teaching youth to think and act responsibly through a peer-helping approach*. Champaign, Illinois: Research Press.

Kernberg, O. F. (1978). Leadership and organizational functioning: organizational regression. *International Journal of Group Psychotherapy*, 28(2) 3–25.

Kernberg, O. F. (1984). The couch at sea: Psychoanalytic studies of group and organizational leadership. *International Journal of Group Psychotherapy*, 34(1), 5–23.

Kibel, H. D. (1987). Contributions of the group psychotherapist to education on the psychiatric unit: Teaching through group dynamics. *International Journal of Group Psychotherapy*, 37(1): 3–29.

Klein, R. H., & Brown, S. L. (1987). Large-group processes and the patient-staff community meeting. *International Journal of Group Psychotherapy*, 37(2), 219–237.

Moss, E., (2008) The holding/containment function in supervision groups for group psychotherapists. *International Journal of Group Psychotherapy*, 58(2), 185–201.

Office of Juvenile Justice and Delinquency Prevention, Vol. VII, No. 1. Youth with Mental Health Disorders: Issues and Emerging Responses, April 2000.

Ogden, T. H. (1981). Projective identification in psychiatric hospital treatment. *Bulletin of the Menninger Clinic*, 45, 317–333.

Pines, M., & Hutchinson, S. (1993). Group analysis. In A. Alonso & H. Swiller (Eds.), *Group therapy in clinical practice* (pp. 29–47).Washington, DC: American Psychiatric Press, Inc.

PDM Task Force. (2006). *Psychodynamic diagnostic manual*. Silver Springs, Maryland: Alliance of Psychoanalytic Organizations.

Redl, F. (1966). *When we deal with children*. New York, New York: Free Press.

Rutan, J. S., Alonso, A., & Groves, J. E. (1988). Understanding defenses in group psychotherapy. *International Journal of Group Psychotherapy*, 38(4), 459–472.

Sickmund, M., Sladky, T. J., Kang, W., et al. (2008). *Easy access to the census of juveniles in residential placement*. Available: http://ojjdp.ncjrs.gov/ojstatbb/ezacjrp/

Saxe, J. G. (1878). The blind men and the elephant. In W. J. Linton (Ed.), *Poetry of America: Selections from one hundred American poets from 1776 to 1876* (pp. 150–152). London: William Clowes & Sons.

Stark, M. (1999). *Modes of therapeutic action.* Lanham, Maryland: The Rowman Littlefield Publishing Group, Inc.

Stone, D. T. (2001). Countertransference issues in adolescent residential settings. *Journal of Child and Adolescent Group Therapy, 11*(4), 147–157.

Teplin, L. A., Abram, K. M., McClelland, G. M., et al. (2006). Psychiatric disorders of youth in detention. *OJJDP Juvenile Justice Bulletin.*

Wachtel, E. F. (1994). *Treating troubled children and their families.* New York, New York: The Guilford Press.

Yalom, I. D. (1985) *The theory and practice of group psychotherapy* (3rd ed.). New York, New York: Basic Books, Inc, Third Edition.

Section Four
Diversity

Introduction

Culture counts. Norms, belief systems, and roles all contribute to mental health, impairment and recovery. Who is ill and who is well, who is deemed a healer, and the assumptions surrounding his curative powers contribute to the problems and possibilities of treating people who may be culturally different from the leader. Political concerns over the availability of accessible mental health treatment and the meaning of freedom also play a factor.

Without knowledge of the local assumptions regarding the definition of dysfunction and its etiology, and the nature of regional expectations about what could restore individuals and families to "normalcy," the group leader will face many obstacles to establishing and conducting an acceptable treatment group.

This section will prepare the prospective group therapist to gather information about the population with which she is working, decide whether a particular composition will work, and attend to cultural values and views of illness and cure, existent among the members. The two chapters that follow also alert the group leader to the impact of the risk that her own racial and ethnic identities as well as religious beliefs may become barriers to understanding and connection.

Siddharth Shah and Razia Kosi describe the way they identify and work through differences found in a group that flow from the surrounding culture. In "Diversity in Groups: Culture, Ethnicity and Race," they explain how to implement a positive approach to addressing prejudice and oppression. A more empathic interaction among members is then possible. They draw on extensive international experience, including working in regions struck by community trauma.

Alexis Abernethy, in "Approaches to Spirituality in Group," asks a number of questions about assessing the degree to which patients can tolerate differences in their respective belief systems. She also considers ways to address issues that group members

---

The Wiley-Blackwell Handbook of Group Psychotherapy, First Edition. Edited by Jeffrey L. Kleinberg.
© 2012 John Wiley & Sons, Ltd. Published 2012 by John Wiley & Sons, Ltd.

are facing in their spiritual lives, a component of their cultural identity, that influence key decisions.

Diversity is a much-neglected area in group work, but needs to be considered as one screens members for group and deals the "whole person." This section also spotlights the link between what happens in group and the tensions within the greater society. Friction among groups in the community often gets played out in small groups, and unless addressed by the leader, can sabotage the treatment. Throughout these papers, the therapist is urged to identify his own prejudicial assumptions.

33
Diversity in Groups: Culture, Ethnicity and Race
Siddharth Ashvin Shah and Razia Kosi

Introduction

Groups in which leaders orchestrate a positive exploration of diversity may experience several desirable therapeutic outcomes. Among those outcomes are the healing of painful discriminatory experiences, a deepening of interpersonal understanding (Abernethy, 2002) and the modeling of courageous enquiry. Given that psychotherapy groups recapitulate the groups from which members come, the larger social system in which they are embedded necessarily comes into play. Intergroup dynamics might be positively processed if the leader is informed by the theory, research and technical considerations that surround diversity in clinical practice. This chapter's discussion of actively resolving culture, ethnicity and race [CER] issues is termed Positive Diversity Processing, and it will be outlined systematically after the literature review.

A typical occurrence in mainstream psychotherapy practice is problematic explorations (or non-explorations) of CER diversity. The inattention to, avoidance of, and discounting of diversity issues has been described as "directly interfering with the therapist's ability to be open and neutral" (Abernethy, 1998: p. 2). Minority clients and therapists are consciously and unconsciously left "holding the bag" of justifying diversity in ways that marginalize them similar to our larger social system (Tummala-Narra, 2004). Finally, problematic dealings with diversity are thought to contribute to why clients of color underutilize counseling services and terminate treatment after the first session fifty percent more often than mainstream clients (Sue and Sue, 1999).

It must be said at the outset that dealing with diversity involves several complex narratives and creative tensions. In this chapter we will address "diversity" as the potential for conflict *and resolution* over cultural, ethnic and/or racial issues (Table 33.1).

Table 33.1 Diversity issues giving rise to Conflict over Difference.

Culture	Shared beliefs, practices, traditions and values that are socially transferred.
Ethnicity	An identification with a group that shares heritage, language, culture, country of origin or ancestral homeland.
Race	A construct upholding power and privilege for individuals in dominant groups; this construct has no defensible, consistent biological criteria.

While some of the arguments and guidelines of this chapter might be relevant in addressing other parameters of difference, we suggest that the reader seek out more readings to hone her awareness and competency *vis-à-vis* these parameters. Green and Stiers (2002) have drawn from the American Psychological Association the following parameters of difference that we do not explicitly cover: gender, sexual orientation, physical/mental disability, socio-economic status, age, national origin, indigenous heritage, religion.

Although the category distinctions among culture, ethnicity or race taken separately are significant for both theoretical and practical use, we will proceed in this chapter to address these categories together. We are not dispensing with the very real distinctions; however, in order to say something useful in the scope of this chapter, we are distilling CER to the essential issue of working with *difference*. It is worthy of note, however, that exploring race tends to heighten a mood of narcissistic vulnerability (Tummala-Narra, 2004). This is likely due to race's linkages to power and institutional dominance.

Any practical engagement with diversity must be anchored in context (e.g. history and location) because the ramifications of difference vary according to the time and place in which one practises group. The social meanings of difference are indeed varied and yet it is possible for a leader to encourage her group to positively process issues of diversity. To serve this end, this chapter presents four Principles for Positive Diversity Processing (PPDP): counter-transference management, safe space, uncovering oppressive patterns and leveraging differences. While these principles are not intended to be exhaustive, we believe that PPDP is a primer for healthy processing from a CER-difference standpoint.

Review of the Literature

A number of excellent publications exist on the impact of CER-difference on group dynamics. Green and Stiers (2002) point out that early multicultural group therapy literature (traced to the 1970s) focused on the targets of discrimination (disadvantaged groups). More recent trends in the literature (traced to the late 1990s) have brought attention to how those who are privileged knowingly (or unknowingly) benefit from discrimination and larger systems of oppression (e.g. colonialism, class, sexism, homophobia, poverty, racism).

In 1995, Davis, Galinsky and Schopler addressed multiracial group leadership with the **RAP** framework (Davis et al., 1995: p. 158):

- Recognize the critical importance of the racial dynamics of the group.
- Anticipate the sources of racial tension and help members deal with these tensions.
- Problem-solve if issues become problems.

In RAP, the authors emphasize that a leader's self-awareness of internal CER history/dynamics is as crucial to monitor as is member history and the group's unfolding dynamics.

In 2001, Matsukawa offered practical insights and case examples in a chapter entitled "Group Therapy with Multiethnic Members." Matsukawa offered the following four modifications of technique (Matsukawa, 2001: p. 259):

1. Encourage the explanation and exploration of ethnically derived values in order to help the members understand the interpersonal behavior that is the result of these values.
2. Help the members observe and understand nonverbal and symbolic forms of communication. Norms of self-expression will vary.
3. Explore the dynamics underlying the cultural transferences arising from group members, and examine cultural countertransferences occurring within the therapist(s).
4. Help the members examine their ethnic or racial prejudices in a safe environment that can contain the strong affects that may arise.

Finally, Matsukawa (2001) maintains that multiethnic groups may have special benefits over homogenous groups such as creating "a social microcosm in which members may safely try out new ways of relating, less restricted by customary ethnic and cultural boundaries and social circles." The opportunity to engage a multi-CER group offers both the group leaders and participants a chance to explore differences and develop new ways of interacting with differences. As will be discussed below, a group leader should be aware of his or her own responses to this new "social microcosm" and at appropriate times articulate the role of these responses in the group.

The American Psychological Association has published versions of Dr Pamela Hays' book on cultural complexities that includes the acronym "ADDRESSING." This acronym directs clinicians to recall important sources of privilege and disadvantage in the following way: **A**ge, **D**evelopmental and acquired **D**isabilities, **R**eligion, **E**thnicity, **S**ocioeconomic status, **S**exual orientation, **I**ndigenous heritage, **N**ational origin, and **G**ender (Hays, 2007). A deeper study of Hays' scholarship will reveal that attending properly to these parameters will bring focus to areas of difference that are arbitrarily omitted in group practice. Notably, the ADDRESSING model asserts that a leader who is a member of a disadvantaged group may have special empathy or knowledge of disadvantage but "this specific knowledge does not necessarily generalize to an understanding of the issues faced by all disadvantaged groups" (Green and Stiers, 2002: p. 235). That is, a group leader who is Asian-American does not automatically understand what blacks in America experience.

Green and Stiers (2002) further reference a common mistake made by leaders: the idea that difference in itself is what oppresses or harms individuals. It is the discriminatory and exclusionary practices that oppress an individual (Green and Stiers, 2002;

Robinson, 1999). Furthermore, individuals in a group who experience disadvantage in the larger social context are likely to perceive psychic impositions in any mixed group, and these impositions may be experienced as a silencing unless the group discourse can acknowledge that CER are at play.

Principles for Positive Diversity Processing (PPDP)

The following principles are intended to be a primer for healthy processing from a CER-difference standpoint. The principles distill best practices that might be adapted for a broad spectrum of group work.

Principles for Positive Diversity Processing (PPDP)

A. **Counter-transference management**
   1. Nervous avoider.
   2. Polite inquirer.
   3. Difference bridger.

B. **Safe space**
   1. Leader self-awareness of his/her own experiences.
   2. Participatory determination of ground rules.
   3. Regulating stuck energy.
   4. Managing interpersonal conflict.

C. **Uncovering oppressive patterns**

D. **Leveraging differences**
   1. Pushback to expose the leader as source of issues.
   2. Differences as assets/opportunities.

A. Counter-transference Management

Group leadership tends to flow from the designated leader(s) or therapist(s) and therefore we must begin with this position (Matsukawa, 2001). For the sake of discussion – not reification – we will consider three countertransference management patterns: nervous avoider, polite inquirer and difference bridger.

Countertransference in a nervous avoider may be composed of a leader's overwhelming anxiety, over-intellectualized evasions or perpetual delays in addressing diversity. Avoidance may take the form of ambivalence around interpretations of "politically correct" words to use for difference. Other avoidance stances are:

a. colorblindness in which "everyone is the same," and
b. CER are irrelevant to issues of clinical significance (Davis et al., 1995).

With these and other rationalizations, the nervous avoider may contribute to poor group functioning and covert processes of projection, scapegoating, and/or displacement.

The polite inquirer has managed countertransference partially and is therefore able to take some risks. He will actively ask group members involved in problematic diversity dynamics about their experience from a CER point of view ("what's it like for you (to be different)?"). The polite inquirer hopes that merely bringing up the issue will promote a healthy environment and psychological insight. Where the polite inquirer lags in his approach is fully bringing to awareness his own assumptions about difference and the value(s) he may attach to this difference. He identifies the difference, but he may not be fully open to valuing difference. When the difference is not valued, it still creates a situation where diversity is viewed as outside the norm and increases feelings of alienation for group participants. Even though the subject is being discussed, some may feel silenced and unsafe.

The difference bridger has managed countertransference most fully. She might be anxious about CER, but she models a way of working with it that acknowledges the anxiety of group members and ultimately relieves some of her own and the group's anxiety. Instead of over-intellectualizing the subject, she might display affect and an excited sense of hope in working with CER. At the healthiest level of countertransference management, the difference bridger is able to dive into problematic diversity dynamics as they are freshly experienced. She encourages respectful dialogue and questioning as a road to learning and strengthening; and she validates all perspectives to deepen trust and communication in the group.

B. Safe Space

For groups to be therapeutic for all members, safe space is necessary. Group leaders have to discern what a group will consider "safe space" and how CER differences will influence the space. The group leader's CER (whether different or the same) will evoke a reaction from the group. The opportunity to have a safe, trusting and positive relationship with the group leader can help influence relationships both within and outside the group. Across cultures, trust may have different connotations from safety. In the authors' view, groups in North America tend to proceed in the following sequence: an initial feeling of safety accrues from the "space" (formal rules established by people), then trust develops interpersonally (as a result of implicit rules being followed), finally a deeper interpersonal safety emerges (as a result of implicit rules being relied upon). Another way of putting this is that external safe space (ground rules) can facilitate the experience of internal safe space (deeper relatedness) (K. Nishimura, personal communication, July 15, 2011).

To promote safe space *vis-à-vis* CER difference the following factors are crucial for leaders:

1. **Leader self-awareness of his/her own experiences.** A leader may consider, for example, what has been the emotional impact of being a member of the dominant group culture – or being a member of a marginalized group culture? This can include the larger context of society, family, friendships, work and other group contexts. As leaders it is crucial to openly discuss the impact of difference with any co-leader prior to and during the life of groups (Davis et al., 1995). In this way, responses during and after the group can be studied so that problematic countertransferences can be minimized and other relational dynamics can be put productively into play during future group meetings. Co-leaders who articulate their experience of CER differences

to each other or to group members may model positive processing or provide pressure release. Sharing this experience becomes imperative if CER enactments in the group become pronounced.

2. **Participatory determination of ground rules.** Since confidentiality statements and "rules" for the group may seem similar for most group spaces, they are typically prefabricated and presented to the group for assent in order to move more quickly into the content of the sessions. However, offering a process for the group to create their own means for safe space may enhance trust and appropriate risk-taking in the group. Having each of the participants verbalize their desires for safety and concerns with confidentiality will engage each group member to foster a sense of responsibility and accountability to one another to preserve the safe space. Individuals who have not been well served by the dominant culture may be coming in with historical distrust and the leaders of the group need to build processes in which the trust is built upon in each session. One method, particularly suited for agency settings or cognitive-behavioral groups, is to deliberately spend time in the first session involving the participants in a discussion about trust and safety criteria. The statements of confidentiality and expectations of behavior, such as openness to differing experiences and refraining from judging any individual's choices, are then documented on a large sheet of chart paper. Each participant then signs the document created by the group as a symbolic gesture of their commitment to acknowledging the different needs of the women in the space on the issues of trust and safety. Depending on the norms that are desired for the setting, the leader can post this document at each session, amplifying the commitment of each participant to create a safe space.

3. **Regulating stuck energy.** Members in the group will have varying willingness or ability to let go of past CER hurt or trauma. A member may bring in supercharged stories and affect, and there will be a consequent change in the group's space. The charge (and feelings of a changed space) is colloquially termed "energy." Members in a group may feel less safe if they perceive group energy to be stuck. Leaders have to manage:

(a) the individual needs of the member bringing energy changes *and*
(b) the energy perceived by others in order to maintain the safe space.

For example, if a member continuously redirects CER discussions back to her views or validating experiences, overpowering the other members' voices, the group leader should be active. The leader can take a number of group interventions: asking others in the group their perspectives about the situation, verbalizing the observation that a particular member's voice is not being heard, pointing out the body language of detachment, or asking the member who is dominating to be aware of her "airtime." Ignoring stuck energy can erode safe space and result in members distrusting the group.

4. **Managing interpersonal conflict.** Conflict will arise in groups because of any range of CER factors: differences in opinions and perspectives regarding gender, ethnicity, cultural background, familial upbringing, religious beliefs as well as other differences that may surface with group members. The leader has to be prepared for conflict and maintain a safe space. This may include temporarily suppressive interventions, such as interrupting harmful comments (e.g. derogatory or mean-spirited comments to individuals in the group or stereotyping of groups). Stopping the derogatory comments can be followed by examining the group's responses about

how some perspectives are hurtful but nevertheless exist in society. Members can then be asked how to manage the interpersonal stress that resulted in the group as a result of the derogatory comments.

C. Uncovering oppressive patterns

Oppression for a group member can be located in two places: patterns within the group, and patterns that a member experiences outside the group. Frequently, a parallel process (similar patterns within and outside the group) can be discerned, interpreted and worked through. However, in cases of oppression, it is not recommended that a leader wait to see whether group patterns are re-enactments of outside patterns. In other words, it would be a mistake for a leader to delay intervention on a pattern discerned within the group that does not have a clear correlation for that member outside the group.

Maintaining a safe space is a prerequisite for a leader's pointing out oppressive patterns in the group. Attempts to uncover oppression in an overly risky environment will be avoided, rejected or veiled. Ground rules should be clear at any juncture when oppressive behavior is identified; if there is any ambiguity or doubt about those ground rules, a ritual of re-affirming those ground rules can ensure that each member shares freely and productively.

Davis et al., exhort the leader to "be aware of various forms of institutional discrimination and their impact on different populations groups"(Davis et al., 1995: p. 161). Individuals from oppressed CER groups may manifest this impact as additional layers of psychological and physiological stress within the therapy group. Group leaders can play a role in stress reduction by orchestrating a dynamic in which such individuals are able to ventilate negative experiences, improve self-efficacy, and bolster the ability to think constructively. This orchestration should provide support for coping with the intra-psychic and social effects of CER-difference.

D. Leveraging differences

Within "Recognize" in the RAP framework, leaders are exhorted to "know and respect the history, norms, and culture of the populations represented in the group" (Davis et al., 1995: p. 161). This exhortation is open to wide interpretation. What constitutes knowing? To what extent? While a group leader may seek out primary and secondary references to learn about populations – and this is usually fruitful – it is the view of these authors that maintaining positive principles of processing difference can provide benefits that do not accrue from data collection. Regulating the experience of difference is pivotal to the comfort and growth of the group.

For many leaders, diversity among members is construed as an extra, unwelcome challenge to deal with. That is, differences are automatically viewed as problems to be solved. Two drawbacks to this formulation include the following:

1. Members may experience the leader to be the source of CER issues; and
2. Differences are assets that can be put to use on behalf of the group's needs.

One method of leveraging difference that has been under-represented in the literature is that of actively inviting pushback. Pushback is phenomenon of a group expressing its resistance and/or providing redirection to a leader (Shah, 2011). A member or subgroup pushing back brings to light the possibility that the leader is the source of CER issues or problems.

When pushback comes, it always has a procedural complaint process (something is not good), and it may or may not have discernible complaint content ("this specifically is what is not good"). Actually noticing that pushback is procedurally occurring can be demanding for the leader, especially if there is not discernible content. Without a shared cultural lens by which to apprehend the complaint process, pushback can go unnoticed ("under the radar"). It may be then necessary for the leader to actively invite pushback.

Inviting pushback is part of a highly participatory, elicitive pedagogy that invites honest and active participation and asks that no one hold back (Wessells and Monteiro, 2004). Leaders inviting pushback onto themselves regarding CER can provide a corrective experience for those who have felt silenced and bring more CER issues into dialogue.

In the absence of a leader's actively inviting pushback, existing power asymmetries may snuff out resistance or redirection from those who are feeling marginalized from a CER standpoint. Inviting pushback can be thought of as eagerly asking for feedback or criticism (Shah, 2011). When it comes to delicate matters of diversity, feedback or criticism will be withheld until members perceive that the leader can handle the aggression of resistance (or the correcting nature of redirection).

Being "corrected," as happens when redirection is being provided, has the capacity to stimulate shame in a leader. If the complainer has group support, then anger will be mobilized by the group towards a leader. A leader's narcissism will determine how much shame and/or anger can be tolerated. If a leader cannot handle the shame or anger of the circumstance, he/she will withdraw, become more directive, become defensive, become combative or unconsciously discourage pushback. Protecting oneself from that shame or anger will take precedence over a group's needs. The leader who is able to tolerate these negative states for the group's benefit thus is able to send the message "I want your honest reactions to my way of dealing with these differences. If you push back, I can handle it." When a group realizes that the leader is OK with pushback, and that it will not be rejected, it amounts to a believable invitation to push back (Billow, 2010; Ormont, 1994; Shah, 2011). There will be difficult moments when a leader is put to the test, and a good leader will be able to maintain engagement with challenging members rather than hiding behind his/her leader role – or be defensive.

Even if one demonstrates a readiness to handle aggression and shame, asking for pushback directly may not meet with success. Many cultures discourage such direct communication, especially when it amounts to negative feedback. One's social location – gender, ethnicity, position in hierarchy, religious orientation, social class, and national origin – can impact the proclivity to pushback. While power asymmetries are unavoidable, social location can be negotiated through elicitive methods by which historically marginalized groups feel they have a voice. Proactively mentioning social location and systems of oppression can open the door to thinking about how to dismantle damaging power asymmetries. For a leader employing PPDP, it is important to work effectively with different sub-groups, building bridges between constituencies whenever possible (Debiak, 2007).

The possibility that differences are assets that can be put to use on behalf of the group's needs is also under-represented in the literature. Diversity and its CER differences can in fact be a source of new thinking, novel problem-solving and reintegration of disavowed psychic and social dynamics. The following statement from Green and Stiers seems to be consistent with the idea that diversity is an extra challenge:

> As group psychotherapists, we are placed in the precarious position of being arbiter of a potential array of socially constructed realities that are brought to life over the course of treatment. (Green and Stiers, 2002: p. 241).

Of course diversity presents special challenges; and yet the use of the word "precarious" emphasizes possible peril and de-emphasizes the idea that diversity offers rich opportunities as well.

Teaching Case 1

Women's Wellness Group for South Asian Women led by two South Asian female co-leaders

This author (RFK) is the executive director of Counselors Helping (South) Asians, Inc. (CHAI), a community-based organization in the Baltimore-Washington DC metro areas. One role of the author is to serve as the co-leader for a Women's Wellness Group that was established to respond to unmet needs for women of South Asian descent to find a safe space and dialogue. Both leaders for this group were cognizant of the stigma, based upon their own experiences as South Asian women living in the US, in the community in addressing mental health and the pressure to maintain the image of the "Model Minority." Understanding this community's perceptions and concerns, the author intentionally organized a group to meet weekly for the purpose of wellness (rather than psychotherapy), thereby minimizing stigma.

Several components of CER were considered for this group: the cultural needs of the women, shared ethnic identity, experiences of living in the US with a historical legacy of racism and current post 9/11 climate all influenced the thought processes of the author in creating a group to best meet the interests of underserved women. The author was purposeful in creating topics for the weekly sessions that included opportunities to discuss racism, stereotyping, microaggressions (Sue, et al., 2007), gender expectations, cultural conflict and taboo topics in the community. The advertised topics provided transparency to potential participants that this group was a space to uncover oppressive patterns outside of the group.

Wellness group models for ethnic minority women have proven to be effective (Rayle, Brucato and Ortega, 2006). However, this author felt it additionally important to co-create a space that was fluid and flexible to the needs of the women in the group while including wellness guidance. The leaders developed a hybrid using the Wheel of Wellness to incorporate the characteristics for healthy living into the seven Dimensions of Wellness – social, family, physical, spiritual, financial, career, and mental (Witmer, Sweeney and Myers, 1998).

The leaders made deliberate decisions on how to meet the needs of the candidates who were expressing interest. Given that all of the candidates were college-educated (minimum of bachelors degree, with several holding graduate degrees), had been in the US for a range of ten to thirty years or had been born in the United States, the leaders narrowed the dimensions of wellness that would be more relevant to the women. The leaders were critically aware that a group for college-educated, English-speaking women living in the Washington DC area who were free to attend a women's group on a Sunday afternoon is itself consistent with patterns of systemic oppression. Issues that can arise when working with ethnic minority groups, such as limited English proficiency, desire for intra-community communication or social isolation were not as prominent with this targeted group of participants. The issues that did arise for this group were: shared group identity as South Asian women, stressors in their lives and understandings of cultural beliefs/expectations.

During the comprehensive intakes, candidates identified the following barriers to their comfort in joining a mainstream [European-American] organization: cultural differences, language barriers, and religious practices. In various ways, the women expressed desires for a group that offered *universality, cohesion* and *guidance* (Yalom, 1995). What resulted was a group space that felt free of judgment, open to trust and thrived on the strengths of the women.

Participants discussed the negative effects of discrimination for being "different" in the larger society. Their feelings varied from "not fitting in" to narratives of blatant stereotyping and racism. The leaders highlighted the universality in the experiences of the women's shared South Asian heritage. Each woman individually had built networks of support or individual coping mechanisms to handle the day-to-day microaggressions. The power in having the women come to a group and openly share their experiences in order to collectively learn from each other became the foundation for the women to continue relationships beyond the group. The experiences of an South Asian woman in the US, are varied and yet similar with the struggle to balance expectations from both the South Asian community and negotiating the norms of dominant society. The opportunity for participants to freely express their challenges and triumphs in a collective space was a valued experience for both the participants and the group leaders.

It is important to note that even within a shared space of South Asian women, the leaders were cognizant of their own CER-based and non-CER countertransference and sought to surface their own assumptions and actions in the group. Debriefing post sessions would include voicing countertransference reactions about punctuality, women who were not as verbal or who took on the role of the victim and women who found a greater need to set themselves as unique from the group thereby challenging the universality factor. The punctuality issues were avoided by the leaders, partly because of their awareness that meeting start times are fluid and their own experiences within the South Asian community. Furthermore, avoidance of addressing this issue might have stemmed from the leaders' own inner conflict with Western norms for group and cultural norms.

Teaching Case 2

Post 9/11 Group work with Muslim teachers and school staff

In 2002, this author (SAS) was invited to provide technical assistance to Project Liberty, a post 9/11 program of the Federal Emergency Management Agency (FEMA) and New York Department of Health and Mental Hygiene. As part of this work, the author was invited to lead a community intervention at a school with primarily Muslim students and staff in Queens, New York. The objective of this one-time community intervention was to facilitate teachers and administrators at the school in a discussion of anti-Muslim bias incidents and traumatic impact on Muslims in the New York City metro area.

The beginnings of safe space for this community intervention came through a conversation with the principal of the school. The conversation started with the author saying "Assalaam Alaikum," to which the principal replied "Wa Alaikum Salaam. Are you Muslim?" Some negative countertransference emerged around this question because the author worried the "in-group/out-group" discourse to be possibly undermining to his mission of outreach and community cooperation. The author said, "No, I am not Muslim, but I have the highest regard for your faith and culture. I hope that will be helpful enough to your staff."

When the community intervention began with 35–40 staff members, the author introduced himself at length in order to reveal his motivations, and how he came to be interested in talking to them. The lengthy introduction (4–5 minutes) was intended to increase safety in the group by reducing what might be unknown or mysterious about the leader. At some point he expressed the following: "Given who I am, I am quite aware that my experience will not be similar to yours. And I have been a little worried that you will not accept me. My background gives me protection when it comes to anti-Muslim bias. Still, it is my hope that I can assist this group to discuss important experiences." This was an attempt to show up as a difference bridger, a level of countertransference management that acknowledged this author's anxiety and simultaneously expressed hope of working things out.

The author included one other element in the introduction: "Given that I occupy a different place in society, I rely on you as a group to push back and correct me when I have an inaccurate or problematic idea about what you are going through. It is my job to learn from what you teach me and not have bad feelings about your telling me I am wrong. My purpose is to provide an opportunity for all of you to discuss the negative consequences of being Muslim in a post-9/11 context. You may be accustomed to censoring yourself because there are subjects that are socio-culturally damaging to speak about. For example, Muslims in this country may be held to a different standard in their support of the Palestinian people. A Muslim risks being accused of being anti-Semitic or anti-American – and this puts him and his community at more risk for anti-Muslim bias." This statement had a dual purpose of freeing people to discuss oppressive patterns explicitly and inviting pushback (leveraging differences).

The above methods appeared to have been effective in facilitating a discussion of anti-Muslim bias. Participants expressed surprise and gratitude that someone representing greater NYC thought they should have the opportunity to speak about their special form of post-9/11 suffering. They catalogued how neighborhood kids and students from other schools were targeting the students at their school. Teachers expressed how helpless they felt in protecting vulnerable students. Other teachers expressed anger. There was a rift between Muslims born in the USA (in this case African-American individuals) and immigrant Muslims. Muslims born in the USA expressed more outrage and calls to action. Immigrant Muslims expressed that they could not afford to trust the results of action. They feared bad reactions from authorities and fellow New Yorkers. One immigrant turned to the author and said, "You see, we have our own differences here."

Teaching Case 3

Early Stage General Psychotherapy Group composed of all white members, one Jewish co-leader and one co-leader of color

This author (SAS) co-leads a new group in which he is the only person of color. While the group was formed with both co-leaders, one leader (not the author) is Jewish-American and has been seeing every member of the group in individual therapy. Therefore, the author is less known to the members of the group and is naturally the "outsider." In the second month of the group, one member (who has had long term relationships with black men) was asked by the white co-leader, "Can you describe why you are uncomfortable about Siddharth?" The member replied, while physically squirming, "He is just so foreign to me."

Both the author and his co-therapist registered the double sense of "foreign" in that he is the outsider and that he is a person of color. After the group concluded that day, during the de-briefing that was routine practice between the co-leaders, this author expressed intellectual curiosity about his "foreign" quality. The white co-leader acknowledged this and in her individual session with the member brought up the possibility that "foreign" referred to his being non-white or of Indian ethnicity. The white co-leader the following week shared with this author that the member denied with embarrassment that "foreign" referred to anything but his being the least known person in the room.

With his countertransference, this author finds himself nervously avoiding the subject because he does not want to make a big deal out of race when the member is likely to be defensive. His co-therapist is comfortable to explore this subject, and she would be supportive of his concerns were he to bring it up with the group. For two months, this author maintains many reasons (both rationalizations and intellectualizations) for not bringing up the subject. He worries that it may not be obvious how such a confrontation serves the member's (or group's) therapeutic needs. He worries that it would be dismissed in a way that he could not pursue the subject. And he worries that he might be negatively judged for being the one to bring up race in the group context.

In the sixth month, the Jewish-American co-therapist sensed that one day's themes might signal the group's readiness to talk about differences. She points to the group's attempts to cling to sameness after encounters of difference. She poses the questions: "Can we look at this? What differences do we have in group?" This author thought "It is now or never" and that he might be more accepted for exploring the use of the word "foreign" and the squirming member. He articulated his experience of being singled out as foreign and his feelings of awkwardness in bringing up the subject to the group. The co-therapist elaborated and sought to involve group members; however, the group equivocated. After a cursory denial and baffled silence, the group found a way to change the overt subject and proceeded to reinforce sameness among themselves.

A discussion of differences seemed premature for this early group. The attempt was made to bridge differences in what was an increasingly safe space. Perhaps it was not a safe enough space to uncover oppressive patterns or more could have been done to leverage differences. An alternative approach may include one of the therapists questioning his or her own handling of difference. An open exploration of a therapist's handling CER may invite pushback and model the courage that is helpful in hearing pushback.

Summary

As the world "flattens" and diverse groups are increasingly sharing the same space, it cannot be assumed that systemic oppression is disappearing. Without active intervention in leading groups, diverse settings may perpetuate patterns of oppression that arise from the values assigned to culture, ethnicity and race. This chapter suggests that four Principles for Positive Diversity Processing can be a guide for healthy dynamics and resolving oppressive patterns: countertransference management, safe space, uncovering oppressive patterns and leveraging differences.

The authors are pleased to know that scholarship – theoretical, descriptive and outcomes – is increasingly being devoted to the cause of broader, more accurate, empathy. Much of the literature focuses on a vast number of problems that can arise from difference; however, while there is potential for conflict, there is also potential for resolving patterns and stimulating healing on several levels. Furthermore, while CER discrimination seems to have analogues to the pain of other oppressions (such as homophobia, sexism, class hierarchy, ageism and able-bodied privilege), the authors want to acknowledge that each oppression has both its own historicity of perpetration and particularity of anti-oppression mobilization. The authors thus come full circle in acknowledging that culture, ethnicity and race each have historicity and particularity. All those who utilize Principles for Positive Diversity Processing will do well to discern how therapy groups give rise to their own historical moments and anti-oppression mobilizations.

References and Bibliography

Abernethy, A. D. (1998). Working with racial themes in group psychotherapy. *Group, 22*, 1–13.

Abernethy, A. D. (2002). The power of metaphors for exploring cultural differences in groups. *Group, 26*, 219–231.

Billow, R. M. (2010). Modes of therapeutic engagement Part I: Diplomacy and integrity. *International Journal of Group Psychotherapy, 60*, 1–28.

Davis, L. E., Galinsky, M. J., & Schopler, J. H. (1995). RAP: A framework for leadership of multiracial groups. *Social Work, 40*, 155–165.

Debiak, D. (2007). Attending to diversity in group psychotherapy: An ethical imperative. *International Journal of Group Psychotherapy, 57*, 1–12.

Green, Z., & Stiers, M. J. (2002). Multiculturalism and group therapy in the United States: A social constructionist perspective. *Group, 26*, 233–246.

Hays, P. A. (2007). *Addressing cultural complexities in practice: Assessment, diagnosis, and therapy* (2nd ed.). Washington DC: American Psychological Association.

Marsella, A. J., Johnson, J. L., Watson, P., et al. (2008). Essential concepts and foundations. In: A. Marsella, J. L. Johnson, P. Watson & J. Gryczynski (Eds.), *Ethnocultural perspectives on disaster and trauma* (pp. 3–13). New York, New York: Springer.

Matsukawa, L. A. (2001). Group therapy with multiethnic members. In W. Tseng & J. Streltzer (Eds.), *Culture and psychotherapy* (pp. 234–261). Washington, DC: American Psychiatric Press.

Ormont, L. R. (1994). Developing emotional insulation. *International Journal of Group Psychotherapy, 44*, 361–375.

Rayle, J., Brucato, T., & Ortega, J. (2006). The "comadre" group approach: A wellness-based group model for monolingual Mexican women. *The Journal for Specialists in Group Work, 31*, 5–24.

Robinson, T. L. (1999). The intersections of dominant discourses across race, gender, and other identities. *Journal of Counseling and Development, 17*, 73–79.

Shah, S. A. (2011). Ethical Standards for Transnational Mental Health and Psychosocial Support (MHPSS): Do No Harm, Preventing Cross-Cultural Errors and Inviting Pushback. *Clinical Social Work Journal.* doi:10.1007/s10615-011-0348-z

Sue, D. W., & Sue, D. (1999). *Counseling the culturally different* (3rd ed.). New York: Wiley.

Sue, D. W., Bucceri, J., Lin, A. I., et al. (2007). Racial microaggressions and the Asian American experience. *Cultural Diversity and Ethnic Minority Psychology, 13*, 72–81.

Tummala-Narra, P. (2004). Dynamics of race and culture in the supervisory encounter. *Psychoanalytic Psychology, 21*, 300–311.

Wessells, M. G., & Monteiro, C. (2004). Healing the wounds following protracted conflict in Angola: A community-based approach to assisting war-affected children. In U. P. Gielen, J. Fish & J. G. Draguns (Eds.), *Handbook of culture, therapy, and healing* (pp. 321–341). Mahwah, New Jersey: Erlbaum.

Witmer, J. M., Sweeney, T.J., & Myers, J. E. (2000). The wheel of wellness counseling for wellness: A holistic model for treatment planning. *Journal of Counseling and Development, 78*(3), 251–266.

Yalom, I., (1995) *Theory practice of group psychotherapy*, New York, New York: Basics Books.

34
A Spiritually Informed Approach to Group Psychotherapy

Alexis D. Abernethy

Introduction

My approach to addressing spirituality in group therapy is a spiritually informed interpersonal orientation to group psychotherapy. In describing this approach, I will begin by placing it in the context of my interpersonal orientation. As an interpersonally-oriented group therapist I have been heavily influenced by Yalom (Yalom and Leszcz, 2005). Most of my training in individual therapy was psychodynamically oriented and I had imagined that I might use this orientation in group therapy as well. My training during internship at Howard University Hospital exposed me to four critical group training opportunities. First, I was enrolled in a group therapy seminar where I was introduced to Yalom's interpersonal approach. Second, I observed my group therapy instructor and supervisor lead an inpatient and outpatient therapy group. Third, I was involved in a process group where we examined our interactions in the here-and-now as a means of learning about group process and deepening our self-understanding. Finally, I co-led an interpersonally oriented group of adults under the supervision of my group therapy instructor. This multidimensional exposure to an interpersonal approach to group therapy offered an immersion experience that facilitated my learning and skill development.

Critical features of the interpersonal approach that resonated with me included the following: viewing the therapy group as a social microcosm; understanding that the interpersonal patterns members experience in their lives will be present in the group process; and creating a rich therapeutic context for a corrective emotional experience while relating to others. The leader not only considers the individual dynamics and histories of individual members, but weaves interpersonal threads that will offer therapeutic opportunities for growth and change. A primary technique in recognizing these interpersonal threads is attending to the here-and-now rather than a primary focus on the there-and-then. As members share, the leader is reflecting on not only the content, but also the process of the communication. For example, what is communicated by the member's tone, at whom they are looking, or who are they avoiding in the group as they speak, and/or other non-verbal behaviors. The focus may be intrapersonal or interpersonal. If I comment on an intrapersonal aspect, then my optimal goal is to highlight a dimension that is not only useful for the member, but beneficial to the group; that is, a dimension that the group might be able to comment on or give feedback on in the future. While leaders may be more or less active in interpersonally-oriented groups, I was impressed with a key dimension of leadership: to facilitate members' ability to provide feedback to one another and to become more attuned to the here-and-now. In general, as groups develop, members move from an initial phase of a more tentative position of deciphering how the group works toward a more mature phase of familiarity and comfort with the group process. In interpersonally-oriented groups, the process of socialization intentionally enhances members' ability to help one another, to be not only self-observant, but also observant of others. This process increases members' ability to help one another especially in the mature phase where they play an active role in propelling the group, providing feedback to other members, and taking risks. An interpersonal approach maximizes the power and work of the group as a catalyst for change.

Another pivotal group training experience was my participation in a modified Tavistock group. Although I tend to be less active than many as a group leader, I still appreciate the importance of the leader shaping the norms and playing an active role in this process. My participation in a Tavistock group where there was little to no commentary or direction from the leader, deepened my appreciation for the process that occurs among members and transferentially toward the leader even in the absence of overt leader commentary. It helped me understand how dynamics are unfolding and always present. Prior to this experience, I was more focused on creating and establishing a group culture as if no culture was present. I now understand this as a collaborative activity where I still have a leadership role, but part of my task as a leader is to sense the emerging culture in the group and to seek to develop the adaptive elements of it. Although I still note transferential and countertransferential dimensions, attend to defensive maneuvers, and assess ego functions in screening, my primary attention in group is to create a safe interpersonal context where members will be able to display their interpersonal strengths and pathology.

Orientation to Spiritually Informed Group Therapy

My training in psychodynamic individual therapy and interpersonally oriented group therapy was not informed by a spiritual perspective. I have had ongoing interests in spiritually integrated therapy and engaged in reading Christian approaches to therapy, but I was not trained in this approach in courses or supervision.

This void was in some ways similar to my experience in addressing cultural issues. I had a little more didactic training and supervision in addressing cultural issues in individual work, but little to no exposure in addressing cultural issues in group therapy. As I became more attuned to addressing cultural issues in individual psychotherapy, I began to incorporate this lens in my group work. Even today, I continue to be amazed that I must remain vigilant to cultural dimensions to avoid defaulting to my training socialization. The field of mental health has suffered from this cultural blindness and general avoidance of spirituality. One perspective on spirituality is to consider it a cultural dimension. Spirituality shares common ground with culture although it is distinct from it. Approaches to incorporating cultural issues in therapy, provide an invaluable resource for addressing spiritual issues in therapy.

Although similar to my doctoral training, my formal internship training did not provide instruction in integrating a spiritual perspective. My primary supervisors attended to the cultural perspectives of their patients and encouraged my focus on this domain in my patients' lives. Their influence deepened my appreciation of the cultural context of individual's lives in general, if not a specific focus on spirituality, in particular. In my group work, my attention to cultural issues in general and spirituality, in particular, emerged from my observation of group dynamics and group composition challenges. As I followed the process of the group and some of the transferential themes and areas of interpersonal conflict, cultural and spiritual issues presented themselves. I have described the cultural dimensions related to racial identity in another article (Abernethy, 1998). Here, I will focus on the spiritual dimension. The vignettes at the end of this chapter are composites, but will illustrate this process.

Kenneth Pargament (2007) offers insight on addressing the sacred in psychotherapy and describes his approach as spiritually integrated psychotherapy. Some might argue whether all group therapy should be spiritually integrated, but I would argue that all group therapy should be spiritually informed. Pargament's delineation of the orientation of spiritually integrated therapy for the patient, therapist, and process of change supports the notion that a spiritual lens should be adopted in all work given the pervasiveness of spirituality. First, he argues as have others (Abernethy, 2004) that patients bring a larger cultural and spiritual context to therapy and spiritual concerns may be a salient dimension of their problem. For group members, this means that not only do members bring their spiritual context, but their perspective on their own and others' problems and how they relate to others may be informed by a spiritual lens. Second, as in individual therapy, the leader brings his/her own spiritual background to therapy and Pargament argues that the therapist needs to be spiritually literate and competent including spiritual knowledge, self-awareness, tolerance, openness, and authenticity. These characteristics would be important for the group therapist, but may be complicated by the interaction of members from diverse, contrasting, or feuding spiritual backgrounds. The therapist may need to be prepared to manage potential conflicts, misunderstandings, and stereotypes that may emerge or are implicit. Third, Pargament's argument for the role of spirituality in the process of change is consistent with Yalom's (Yalom and Leszcz, 2005) therapeutic factors. Originally, Yalom introduced his factors as healing factors. The instillation of hope remains an important factor and existential factors provide one way of categorizing spiritual factors in change.

The prevalence of religious belief provides an important context for spiritually informed practice. A recent US Gallup Poll (2006) found that 82% believe in God, 13% believe in a universal spirit or a higher power, and 5% do not believe in either. In addition, 49% indicate that they are religious; 40% describe themselves as spiritual but not religious and 7% indicate both. In terms of identification with Christianity, 74% view themselves as part of the Christian tradition, 6% in a non-Christian tradition, and 18% in no religious tradition. In terms of diversity within Christianity, the

Pew Research Council (2002) collected data on people who identified themselves as Christian and reported that 52% were Protestant, 24% were Catholic, and 2% were Mormon. The American Religious Identity Survey (ARIS) conducted in 2001 found that 77% of Americans are Christians, 13% non-religious, and 1% Jewish, and less than 0.5% Islam, Buddhist, Agnostic, Atheist or Hindu.

In efforts to address this religious diversity, spirituality has been defined in numerous ways. It has most commonly been contrasted with religion. In refining the definitions of religion and spirituality, a panel of leading researchers and scholars noted that two concepts were central to both: a sacred core and a search process (Larson, Swyers, and McCullough, 1998). They defined religion and spirituality as the "subjective feelings, thoughts, and behaviors that arise from a search for the sacred" (Larson et al., 1998: p. 22). Both are distinct from other experiences in their core focus on the sacred: "a socially influenced perception of either some divine being, or some sense of ultimate reality or truth" (Larson et al., 1998: p. 20). Religion and spirituality also involve a search process. Religion involves an identifiable reference group that is engaged in the search, whereas this is not necessarily the case for spirituality. Alternative views of spirituality include descriptions of it as primarily relational, a transcendent relationship with that which is sacred in life (Pargament, 1997; Seidlitz et al., 2002), or with something divine beyond the self (Emmons, 1999). Anthropologist Melford Spiro (Spiro, Kilborne, and Langness, 1987) defined religion "as an institution consisting of culturally patterned interaction with culturally postulated superhuman beings" (Spiro et al., 1987: p. 197). This definition is particularly enlightening for groups as it suggests that religion informs not only what people believe, but also how they interact. Spirituality would not be defined as an institution, but these other dimensions of this definition may be more or less relevant in spirituality – specifically culturally patterned interaction with superhuman beings. Clearly in groups, members may be identified with a specific religion, be atheist, be uninterested in spiritual issues, and/or be spiritual. For the purposes of this chapter, recognizing the limitations of using only one word, the term spiritual will be used to describe interest in sacred matters within and outside of a particular religious tradition.

Presenting Problems Addressed

Increased research and clinical interest in the role of spirituality in clinical practice and health have provided a more conducive context for considering spiritual factors. Early research in the area of psychology of religion by the pioneers, Stanley Hall (Hall, 1904) and William James (James, 1985), provided a foundation. More recent empirical research supports an association between church attendance and reduced morbidity and longer survival rates (Chida, Steptoe, and Powell, 2009; Powell, Shahabi, and Thoresen, 2003). In addition, in an American Psychological Association survey, 60% of psychologists noted that their patients often described their experiences in religious language and one-sixth presented concerns that directly involved religion or spirituality (Shafranske and Maloney, 1990). Perspectives on a range of issues that are commonly a focus of therapy are influenced by religion and spirituality: marriage, divorce, mourning, child-rearing, abortion, alcohol and drug usage, suicide, and sexuality. It is in the context of discussing issues related to marital roles, divorce, suicide, death, and sexuality, that issues related to spirituality have emerged most often in my groups.

Despite the prevalence of spiritual beliefs among people in the US, a framework that might allow for a spiritually informed if not spiritually integrated approach to therapy, and increasing receptivity to addressing spirituality by mental health professionals, opposition still exists. Common reasons include the following:

a. Concerns about imposing personal values and beliefs;
b. Negative attitudes toward religion;
c. Lack of training and the absence of a theoretical model for addressing religion;
d. Training that socializes therapists to avoid or minimize the importance of spirituality for patients;
e. An orientation that the spiritual domain is outside their scope of practice and more appropriate for clergy (Aten and Leach, 2009a).

These concerns are legitimate and pose a challenge not only for some therapists, but also for group members. One dilemma for group members is that even if their religion or spiritual perspective is important to them, will other group members assume that sharing their beliefs is an attempt to proselytize? Another concern is that discussing religion may evoke negative reactions from other members. Many patients have also had their spiritual perspectives ignored or even discounted by therapists. Patients may also struggle with what spiritual dimensions might be appropriate to address in a psychotherapeutic context. Johansen (2010) underscores this challenge well and notes that religion is often avoided as the focus becomes whether or not someone believes in a particular religious faith or adheres to certain tenets of that faith rather than focusing on having a respect for religious values and traditions. If raising spiritual concerns becomes a debate about whose perspective is right, this thwarts growth, limits interaction, and creates conflict. On the other hand, if members can develop a respect for religious and spiritual values and traditions that may be diametrically opposed to their own, then this reflects an achievement of a goal that is more difficult to attain even in the world external to group.

Pargament (2007) has highlighted seven psychological problems that based on clinical observations or research may be related to spiritual problems: depression, anxiety, addiction, eating disorders, marital problems, violence, and serious mental illness. For example, depression and eating disorders have been associated with anger toward God (Exline, Yali, and Sanderson, 2000) and fear of being abandoned by God (Richards, Hardman, and Berrett, 2007), respectively. Additionally in studies of hospital patients, widows, physically abused spouses, and combat veterans, 50–85% of study participants noted that their faith helped them cope with their situation (Pargament, 1997).

Consistent with increased attention to spiritual concerns, the Diagnostic and Statistical Manual-Fourth Edition (American Psychological Association [*DSM-IV*], 1994) added a new V code (V62.89) for religious or spiritual problems. In the more recent DSM-IV-TR, V codes have been renamed Other Conditions That May Be a Focus of Treatment (American Psychiatric Association (*DSM-IV-TR*), 2005). Spiritual concerns are in the category of identity problems and include the following domains: religious or spiritual problem: doubt, conversion, and problems with faith.

Given the diverse problems that might intersect with spirituality and religion and warrant a treatment focus on spiritual issues, the challenge is less whether these concerns might be relevant in group therapy (although some may still have this question), but rather how does a therapist assess their relevance and how does this inform therapeutic interventions?

Assessing the Spiritual Dimensions

Significant advances have been made in the assessment and measurement of religious and spiritual concerns. Measures have been developed that assess important domains including church attendance, subjective spirituality (e.g., spiritual transcendence), religious coping, and faith maturity (Hill and Hood, 1999; Seidlitz et al., 2002). Efforts have been made to identify those domains that are most clinically significant (Richards and Bergin, 2005). More recent efforts have focused on approaches to interviewing that include global questions followed by more in-depth questions (Pargament et al., 2009). Global questions typically assess the salience of spirituality and religion in general for the patient as well as their salience to the problem and the solution. If the patient indicates that these dimensions play a role, then the therapist has a range of follow-up questions for further inquiry: the location of the patient in their spiritual journey; the content of their spirituality including what the patient holds sacred; and the degree of support or conflict that they experience in their spiritual context (Pargament and Krumrei, 2009). These questions could emerge in the context of treatment, but ideally they will be part of an initial inquiry during group screening.

So how does this lens inform my approach to group therapy screening? First, if I am interviewing a patient who is new to the clinic, I would conduct an initial intake. Some of the above areas would be covered if I was adopting a spiritually informed approach; however, I will highlight specific ways that the screening interview would be tailored to get a sense of the person's spiritual background. As we noted in our article where we coined the terms, "religiocultural transference and countertransference" (Abernethy and Lancia, 1998), therapists need to consider their own and their patient's responses to the real and imagined religious background of the patient and therapist, respectively. In group therapy, this is even more complicated as the therapist needs to consider the patient, therapist(s), but also the composition of the group. Does this patient have the capacity to work in a group of religiously diverse members? Key factors that I weigh include the following: the patient's spiritual identity, their religious tolerance, my assessment of how their spiritual convictions might manifest interpersonally in the group, and the degree of fit with other members.

Before assessing these areas, I preface my comments by noting that some therapy groups are more homogeneous in terms of age, gender, and problem focus. Here is an excerpt of what I have typically said in recruiting members for a spiritually informed interpersonally oriented group. "My groups tend to be more heterogeneous and may include members from a wide age range of 21–75, mixed gender, diverse ethnic backgrounds, differing sexual orientations, and different spiritual backgrounds who may be dealing with different kinds of problems. One of the things that people have in common is difficulties in their relationships. One of the ways the group works is to look at how people interact in the group and use this as a way of understanding some of the issues that might come up in people's lives outside of the group. Sometimes people will feel connected to others and sometimes less connected. Both of these experiences are important to understand more about and sometimes more can be learned from our disconnection. Sometimes similarities, but more often differences can create disconnection that might feel difficult to handle. Based on some of the areas I mentioned before – gender, age, sexual orientation, religious background, or ethnicity – would any of these areas be particularly challenging for you if a member was different from you?"

As I listen to prospective members describe what might be more challenging for them, I am attending to what they are saying as well as how they are interacting interpersonally as they share. Typically, prospective members will note one or two of the cultural domains that are more salient for them and indicate their own identification. Then they often explain what their experiences have been with others that have been particularly challenging. They normally volunteer a narrative, but if not I ask for an example. As they are sharing their story, I gain a greater appreciation for their range of responses, their flexibility, and their sensitivity. At times I use their story as a template for assessing their openness, tolerance, and desire for growth, and if I need to gain more information beyond their narrative.

If prospective members mentioned their spirituality, I would build on this and inquire more. Obtaining a sense of the prospective members' spiritual identity on a global level is important for two reasons: content and process. Minimally, I would ask if they view themselves as a spiritual or religious person. If so, then I would ask about their affiliation. Secondly, I would inquire about whether spiritual or religious concerns are related to the issues that they are bringing to group. Their responses will provide some insight as to potential ways to tailor some of my interventions and comments in terms of language. I would also attend to the strength of convictions and emotions that might underlie their description of their spiritual background. Clearly, deeply held spiritual and religious beliefs can be accompanied by tolerance of other faith perspectives, but I would inquire about this specifically for clarification purposes. So the broader statement that addressed cultural differences more generally would be tailored to address spiritual differences specifically. "Given the strength of your identification as a Muslim, how would it be for you if the group included members from different faith backgrounds or those who did not have a particular spiritual belief?"

The responses to the aforementioned questions provide the therapist with insight regarding the salience of spirituality for the patient and the interpersonal implications of this for the group. The final consideration is the implication for group composition. A member being less tolerant of religiously different others is not a contraindication for selection, but the inclusion of two members who are less interpersonally skilled and also highly religiously intolerant from religious groups that have and are experiencing significant tensions, may not be the wisest composition. If spiritual concerns are particularly salient in the presenting issues of these two members, there could be a rich opportunity as these members might find important common ground or it could be destructive. What is most helpful is to be able to anticipate some of these issues and to explore this in screening. I have found that making a decision to include these members who might typically engage in conflict can work quite effectively if the members have some openness to engaging with others differently and also recognize that their current interpersonal style is no longer effective. A critical dimension of group preparation then would be to anticipate this expansion of their interpersonal repertoire in general, but in this domain specifically as a potential treatment focus. What has been the most unhelpful is not inquiring about these areas, feeling unprepared to address these tensions, not being aware of these polarizing differences, and not having a frame for working through these differences. The vignettes will demonstrate the challenges that arise from this and the potential opportunities.

Setting of Treatment

Spiritual approaches to group therapy can be readily implemented in a wide variety of settings including religious centers, private practice, hospitals, schools, and community clinics. Therapists have greater freedom in implementing spiritual interventions in religious settings. Support groups are a common offering in churches and synagogues. Treatment groups are frequently offered in church clinics and spiritually-oriented treatment centers. Group members attend these groups with the expectation that spiritual concerns would be addressed. In these settings, it would be reasonable to expect a clear articulation of the setting's approach to spiritually integrated group therapy. This setting would be identified in religious terms and it would be expected that the spiritual interventions would be consistent with the central tenets of this religion. The opportunities in this setting include shared fundamental beliefs and a common desire to be in an explicitly religious treatment setting. A few of the challenges include assumptions of homogeneity and agreement about what beliefs are fundamental. Even within narrower ranges of religious groups such as denominations, sects, and orthodoxy, there are still varying beliefs. Depending on the religious setting, it may be more or less important to achieve agreement on these differences. An important consensus for a group would be to be open to religiously informed interventions and assessment as an integral part of the work. This level of integration would vary from group to group, from group therapist to group therapist. While this is true for all groups, group members might have higher expectations for certain spiritual interventions to be incorporated and perhaps in similar ways that they are implemented in their religious settings, e.g., prayer. The wise group therapist might anticipate these expectations and the assumptions of homogeneity and provide the group with an opportunity to explore the opportunities and potential challenges that a group in a religious setting might offer. Expectations for how the group leader might conduct spiritual interventions may not only come from members, but also the religious organization. Advance work to anticipate and address organizational expectations and concerns, in addition to explaining the unique features of a treatment group, would be important preparation for a leader conducting these groups.

Depending on the size of the religious community, these groups may include members who know one another. This poses a challenge, but not an insurmountable one. This challenge is greater for insight-oriented groups rather than psychoeducational groups. The limits of confidentiality need to be addressed in light of this complexity. If the therapist is also from this community, multiple relationships will need to be explored to assess to what extent this may present a challenge and/or a unique opportunity. For some group members, the group leader sharing their faith may be an important prerequisite for their membership. Despite the challenges of working in religious settings, this provides a rich opportunity for religiously committed patients to explore their issues in a setting that is consistent with their values. Some patients exclusively choose these settings for therapy for religious and cultural reasons.

Private practice is another setting for spiritually informed practice. Therapists may establish their private practice with varying degrees of sensitivity to spiritual concerns. Some view their practice as spiritually integrated as a religious setting, while others engage in a spiritually informed practice. Informed consent forms have been developed that specifically address therapists' ability to incorporate spiritual interventions. This can range from a private practice model where the therapist notes her own orientation in terms of spiritual interventions, to consent for specific spiritual interventions, to a more general consent for addressing spirituality. The following is one example of a spiritually integrated approach.

> I specialize in helping individuals, couples, and families cope with the impact of illness, accidents, or other medical issues on their lives. My therapy work is characterized by holism and focuses on the ways people make meaning of their life circumstances. Holism means that I assess health and wellness in mental, emotional, social, physical, and spiritual facets of experience . . . It is my belief that many individuals approach life with moral beliefs or spiritual practices that inform their decisions and perspectives of life. Few people examine how these beliefs and practices are related to emotional issues or life circumstances. Such transcendent beliefs can provide tremendous support and meaning for the issues clients face or may even be associated with unpleasant emotions or exchanges. I typically invite my clients to discuss their religious beliefs and faith practices as a way to think through the challenges they face and to acquaint me with their worldview. Such discussions are for the purpose of enriching our understanding of the issues at hand and are not for the purpose of proselytizing or debating the correctness of our ideas. I am comfortable including religious practices in therapy, such as prayer, meditation, or discussion about guiding religious documents, if these things are valuable to you. (Leach et al., 2009: p. 81)

Patients are also told that they may elect to include or exclude any of their feelings, thoughts, and interventions. This more fully integrated model reflects a spiritual orientation in therapy that includes the use of explicit spiritual interventions. For the group therapist, this type of approach and informed consent would be consistent with practitioners whose expertise is in spiritually integrated practice. One would expect that this therapist would list this as a specialty area and have received training specific to this competency area. While a general process-oriented or cognitive-behavioral group might be led with this frame, this orientation is particularly suited to groups that might have a spiritual focus such as forgiveness, meditation, spiritually integrated eating disordered groups. Members would then expect to hear spiritual language in this group, be exposed to spiritual interventions, and have therapeutic goals that may be spiritually informed.

Some therapists in community agencies or hospitals might not offer this kind of extensive disclosure as this kind of professional self-disclosure might not be deemed appropriate or consistent with agency guidelines. What might be more common is that the therapist in an agency might seek informed consent for using a specific spiritual or religious intervention. This therapist may not identify her as a specialist, but would have likely received specialized training in the technique that she is offering, for example, using meditation in cognitive-behavioral group designed to address anxiety.

> Our therapists are trained to provide mental health counseling services. Many are also capable of integrating specific spiritual or religious practices with typical counseling practice. Your therapist may ask if you would like to integrate specific spiritual or religious practices into your treatment. These include, but are not limited to, praying with or for you, teaching and guiding you in meditation, assigning readings from scripture or sacred writings, encouraging you to practice specific religious or spiritual rituals, and helping you to access the resources of your spiritual or religious community. In all cases, the therapist will strive to provide you with interventions that are congruent with your spiritual or religious perspective and that fit within your faith tradition. You are free to decline these interventions at any time and request that your therapist refrain from including the spiritual or religious in therapy, if it makes you feel uncomfortable. (Leach et al., 2009: p. 81)

This consent would need to be modified for a group unless it was a religiously homogeneous group. Even in a religiously homogenous group, there would be variation in terms of receptivity and preferences, so tailoring would need to occur where the therapist assessed what practices might be more applicable. The therapist could remain in one faith tradition in a homogeneous group. In a heterogeneous group, the therapist would need to have assessed during intake the varying faith backgrounds of the patients and clarify whether all members have writings that they consider sacred, spiritual rituals, and a religious community. If so, then this more universal language could be used in incorporating a spiritual perspective for Muslims and Christians, and at times it would be helpful to mention the Koran as well as the Bible by name. If a member did not have religiously sacred writings, but some other source of meaning and purpose, then this would also need to be mentioned as other sacred sources were noted. One of the challenges associated with spiritual interventions is that some spiritual practices, such as meditation, while arising from Hinduism, may be practiced apart from a religious context. While some would argue that this separation is artificial, it would be important for therapists to be clear whether they are incorporating a more religious practice or a non-religious psychological technique that evolved from a traditionally religious practice.

A more general agency level approach to including spiritual assessment and inquiry if not specific interventions is the following consent. Given current standards in terms of culturally competent care as well as ethical guidelines for Psychologists (American Psychological Association, 2002), mental health treatment should include a consideration of the spiritual and religious dimensions of patients' experience as it is pertinent to their problem and care.

> It is our belief that spirituality and/or religion are important elements of many people's lives. We believe that religion and/or spirituality can have a significant effect on the types of problems for which many people seek therapy. These effects might be positive (e.g., religious beliefs helping someone to cope with their concerns) or negative (e.g., disconnection from a religious community that makes other problems more severe). As a result, we seek to include a client's spiritual or religious commitments in the therapy process whenever appropriate. You can expect some questions about your spiritual/religious beliefs and practices in the initial assessment phase of your therapy. If spirituality and/or religion are important elements in your life or appear to have a role in your presenting concerns, with your consent, your therapist will integrate these issues into your treatment. However, if at any time you are not comfortable discussing spiritual or religious issues with your therapist, you may decline to answer or otherwise share your discomfort with your therapist. Your therapist will also be able to help you by providing a referral, in addition to our services, to appropriate spiritual leaders or clergy within your faith tradition. (Leach et al., 2009: p. 80)

This frame for addressing spiritual issues would be consistent with a spiritually informed practice and a useful preface to the more specific statement noted earlier that I typically offer in screening. In practice, I have found it more helpful to place this specific focus in the context of a broader general orientation to addressing cultural issues. In the past, I would not have noted religious issues specifically or asked global questions about a prospective member's spiritual background. Now, I integrate this into my exploration of interpersonal flexibility in a way that does not overly attend to these issues, but allows room for them to surface as relevant. This is consistent with my interpersonal orientation. Several approaches to obtaining consent and introducing spirituality are provided in this section. It is hoped that therapists' approach will be guided by their theoretical orientation, group training, group goals, and group composition.

Overall Treatment Strategy

Spiritually-informed group therapy may be a group alone or augmented by individual therapy or other spiritual therapies and practices. Spiritual techniques, such as prayer and meditation, may be incorporated into relaxation training in cognitive-behaviorally oriented groups, forgiveness groups may be offered that are explicitly religious, and therapists may supplement some of the work within group that is spiritually focused with recommendations for members to follow up with religious leaders as appropriate. This approach is most effective when the therapist is actively collaborating with these leaders.

Clinical Tactics

The more structured spiritual therapies, such as forgiveness groups (Worthington, Mazzeo, Canter, Sperry, and Shafranske, 2005), provide a psychoeducational approach that details specific intervention techniques. There are spiritual interventions and techniques (Aten and Leach, 2009b) that could be incorporated in group therapy: prayer, forgiveness, sacred writings, meditation, spiritual assessment, spiritual history, clarification of spiritual values, accessing spiritual resources, spiritual journaling, spiritual life review, spiritual metaphors, and spiritual genograms.

Another approach to addressing the role of spirituality is to attend to psychospiritual themes in the therapeutic process (Richards and Bergin, 2005). In light of patient's hesitancy to use explicitly spiritual language in therapy, often spiritually neutral language is used. A common example of this is to refer to moral values when some people may mean religious values. Existential themes may emerge in group as a member shares about the death of a spouse. The leader has a choice to explore the communication using the language that the patient initially uses. This approach is generally a good first step. Following this, a leader might inquire and note that sometimes when people deal with death and loss this brings up a spiritual or religious dimension for them that is an important part of the experience. Even if this does not emerge for this member, it may be relevant as other members are listening. They may be concerned about incorporating their spiritual perspective or lack of perspective out of a fear of offending someone. They may mute their responses or even withdraw from other members not due to a lack of empathy, but in response to these other concerns.

Jacques (1998) made a significant contribution to our understanding of how to incorporate spiritual perspectives in group. She incorporates Rizzuto's work (1979) on God representations and applies this to group work. Technically, she conceptualizes the group as a spiritual community and explores religious content and themes similar to exploring dreams. She draws connections between God representations and family of origin issues and facilitates growth as new perspectives emerge.

Porter (2004) describes his Buddhist approach to group therapy. He argues that his approach incorporates Buddhist principles and that this can be applied to diverse existing approaches. The group structure might be modified by the addition of meditation, perhaps at the beginning. The posture of the leader might be modified as the leader is more in tune by focusing on being present, facilitating communion, and engaging in other Buddhist practices that might enhance the leader's consciousness in the group. The group members' participation in meditation may also facilitate their ability to be present with one another.

Spiritually informed group therapy for patients suffering from eating disorders may take many forms. One approach (Richards, Hardman, and Berrett, 2007) is to identify key aspects of these patient's lives that might be influenced by a spiritual perspective. Patients are provided with informed consent, including the right to decline participation, and interventions are then designed to challenge patients to reorient their perspective. One exercise, Kneeling at the Shrine of the Eating Disorder, has members explore the extent to which they are worshipping their bulimia or anorexia and have lost important aspects of themselves including God. Another task, Body Image Exercise, allows one person who particularly loathes his body to share with the group the negative experiences related to his body and its connection with the past. The group responds with compassion and at times members have connected with a more positive and divine sense of being created in God's image. Another exercise, Let Us See What Is Most Important to You, has members bring what is most valuable to them from their lives and they share this with group members. Members place what they find valuable in the center and share with the group their story and the symbolism. Then members turn their back on these items and share their feelings of loss as they contemplate not having these valued items. Frequently the objects symbolize spiritual themes such as love, God, peace, justice, and truth.

Evidence Base

In comparison to other interventions, few studies have been conducted on the efficacy of spiritual interventions and even fewer on spiritually integrated group therapy. The most recent review of religious and spiritual (R/S) therapies (Hook et al., 2010) suggests that certain R/S therapies are effective, but most of these approaches reflect an accommodation, that is adaptation, of an existing therapy. What remains unclear is what dimensions of the therapy were most effective. Criteria developed by Chambless and Hollon (1998) were used to determine efficacy. A treatment is considered efficacious if it meets one of these two criteria:

a. outperforms a no-treatment placebo, control group, or alternative treatment or
b. is equivalent to a treatment that is already established as efficacious in a study with moderate power to detect differences (Chambless and Hollon, 1998).

In addition, two independent research labs must obtain results that support its efficacy. Specificity means that the treatment is more effective than an alternative treatment. Clinical effectiveness refers to a treatment's ability to produce changes that are clinically meaningful. Significance means that the treatment has been demonstrated to work in clinical practice. In general, some R/S therapies were found to be effective in treating psychological problems of R/S clients and in a few cases (Christian accommodative cognitive therapy for depression and 12-step facilitation for alcoholism – views alcoholism as a spiritual and medical disease) (Project Match Research Group, 1997), these R/S therapies were more effective than alternative treatments.

In terms of group treatments, Christian accommodative and spiritual group treatments for unforgiveness, as well as Christian accommodative CBT group treatment for marital discord, were found to be possibly efficacious. Either only one lab or one study findings supported its efficacy. Spiritual Group Treatment for Eating Disorders (Richards, Hardman, and Berrett, 2007) offered in the context of an inpatient unit was found to be possibly efficacious and there was some support for its specificity.

Another meta-analysis of religious and spiritual therapies (Smith, Bartz, and Richards, 2007) offered empirical support for selected therapies. Of the 31 studies reviewed, 22 were group therapy. The common spiritual techniques across these studies included teaching spiritual concepts, religious meditation, religious imagery, client prayer, and reading sacred texts. The overall effect size for these studies was 0.56 and it was 0.58 for group as compared to individual therapy (0.42). Although the criteria for effectiveness were less stringent than the aforementioned review, this work lends some empirical support for the effectiveness of group therapy for eating disorders, stress, depression, and anxiety.

Cautionary Notes

The therapist's degree of openness significantly affects the extent to which spiritual issues will be addressed in group therapy. Zinnbauer and Pargament (2000) offer four different approaches to incorporating spiritual issues in therapy: rejectionism, exclusivism, constructivism, and pluralism. Rejectionists do not believe in God, tend not to respect their patient's religion, and do not discuss spiritual issues. Exclusivists take an opposing view to the rejectionists and have deeply held religious beliefs. The only religious perspective that they value is their own, so they either typically only see patients from their religious background or seek to convert those who do not share their religion. Constructivists do not have a personal belief in God and take no particular religious position, but they focus on the extent to which their patient's religious worldviews promote adaptive or maladaptive functioning. Pluralists have a personal belief in God, but they are open to patients who may take different spiritual paths and are able to explore these paths. Many therapists may experience some aspects from several of these orientations. Perhaps, what is most important is to examine one's orientation and to be open to consultation regarding one's assumptions and biases (Zinnbauer and Pargament, 2000).

In group therapy, the therapist's openness to addressing religion is complicated by varying positions that members might have regarding religion. These four categories may be applied to group members as well. The most challenging group composition would be a group of exclusionists, members who hold their religion deeply and would seek to be in a religiously homogeneous group or to proselytize members. Some exclusionists would self-select out as they might only choose a homogeneous group, but for members who might view their group experience as an opportunity to "witness", this could lead to early dropouts, scapegoating, and other destructive processes. A single exclusionist might be challenging, but multiple exclusionists could degrade into a religious battle. This might not only be problematic if members were from different religions. The diversity within religions and even within denominations and sects can also create significant tension related to differing beliefs and perspectives on issues such as sexual orientation and divorce.

The complexity and potential challenge associated with addressing issues that may be religiously connected is significant. Therapist and patient preparation are key factors in providing a group culture where these issues may be addressed as relevant. Key therapist factors include the following:

- the therapists' awareness of their own orientation, (i.e., degrees of rejectionist, exclusivist, constructivist, and pluralist) and their group members;
- their countertransferential response to the interreligious and intrareligious transferential reactions of group members toward one another and the therapist;
- therapists' ability to use spiritual language, recognize spiritual themes, and address process issues that may be linked to spiritual concerns; and
- receptivity and openness to psychological and spiritual consultation when necessary (Abernethy, 2004).

A common process issue that may emerge during screening or in the context of an ongoing group is patient inquiry regarding the religious affiliation of the therapist. Some therapists who adopt a spiritually integrated approach to therapy and who work in a religious setting may disclose their religious background as part of the expertise that they bring to spiritually integrated practice. For those in other settings where greater religious diversity is anticipated and in a spiritually informed practice, this disclosure may have a different meaning. Therapist self-disclosure will be informed by leader style and orientation as well as the process that is emerging in the group. One of the challenges of leader disclosure about their spiritual affiliation is similar to what was noted earlier about the homogeneity of religious settings. Members may make assumptions about what it means to be a Buddhist, a Christian, or an Orthodox Jew. How much detail should be given about this? Should a leader self-disclose about this aspect of his/her identity if no other personal information is shared? What does the question mean? For the spiritually informed and integrated group therapist, it would be important to process the meaning of this question, so that the leader can respond in a way that addresses the underlying concern. At times, I have noted this complexity by noting that if you knew whether I was a Christian or not, what about that would make what's going on more and less difficult or more of less comforting? Sometimes this arises in the midst of a moral issue or an imminent conflict in the group where sides might be taken.

In addition to reflection on one's spiritual background, given the powerful emotional pull of religious issues for some people, therapists should also be prepared to work with religious conflict that may occur between religiously different members. Patients from religious backgrounds that have experienced historical conflict may view other members from an opposing group as representative of a historical enemy and be less able to relate in the context of the group due to these powerful past experiences. While this may present a significant obstacle, the group also may provide an opportunity to address some of the interpersonal dimensions of this generalization that may cause difficulties in other relationships. Managing this conflict introduces several therapeutic challenges. Therapists must be comfortable with this tension, demonstrate an ability to contain this tension in the group, resist the temptation to take sides, and attempt to clarify the potential intersection of clinical and social identity issues in members' presentation as well as the group process (Green and Stiers, 2002).

Supervision and consultation are an invaluable contexts for addressing spiritual issues that emerge in groups and religiocultural countertransference. Many groups, particularly for therapists-in-training, are co-led. Co-therapists need to address many areas in their preparatory process for leadership (Roller and Nelson, 1991). Important areas for discussion include their religious values and how it might influence their role as leaders including the degree to which their orientation will be spiritually informed. Similar to group preparation, supervisors and consultants need to consider whether their supervision will be spiritually informed. Current approaches to supervision encourage a developmental approach. Stoltenberg and Delworth (1987) have identified eight domains in the Integrative Developmental Model:

a. intervention skills competence,
b. assessment,
c. interpersonal assessment,
d. client conceptualization,
e. individual and cultural differences,
f. theoretical orientation,
g. treatment goals and plans, and
h. professional ethics.

Aten and Hernandez (2004) applied this model to addressing spirituality in supervision. The supervisor should introduce their supervisees to spiritual interventions and approaches to assessment. Supervisors should help supervisees to be attuned to countertransferential issues and to address transferential issues that emerge in the therapeutic process. Supervisors should help their supervisees reflect on how their supervisee's theoretical orientation views religion in general and how pathological and healthy dimensions of religiousness are defined. Supervisors should include a consideration of spiritual issues in case conceptualization. Treatment goals and plans should be developed that are consistent with the patient's religious values. Supervisors need to model and assist supervisees in recognizing that state-of-the-art care includes a consideration of spiritual issues as relevant to an understanding of the problem, process, and treatment planning for the patient. The application of this model provides concrete examples of ways to frame the supervision of solo group leaders or co-leaders to include an appropriate focus on spiritual issues. Group leaders face an added challenge in tailoring interventions and treatment plans as the differing religious values of members needs to be weighed and processed as spiritual interventions are tailored to an individual member.

In order to illustrate some of the issues that have been discussed in this chapter, several critical exchanges in an ongoing interpersonally oriented group will be used. All depictions are a composite that illustrate key interactions. This is a group that was led by a psychology supervisor (Therapist A) and her trainee (Therapist B). At this point this therapist discussed typical areas of similarity and dissimilarity with her trainee leader, but there was not a specific discussion of spiritual issues. Cultural issues were discussed, but not spiritual issues. As spiritual issues emerged in group, then spiritual issues became a discussion for the therapists in their relationship. This vignette begins two years after the start of an ongoing group. The vignettes will reflect a progression for the supervisor therapist from a time when she did not attend to spiritual issues in the group despite her strongly held beliefs in God and ongoing readings in the area of spirituality and therapy to her increasing attention to these issues and their interface in the therapeutic process.

Clinical Illustration

This group was an interpersonally-oriented group of mixed gender for moderately functioning adults who were experiencing wide-ranging problems including depression, marital distress, work-related stress, and interpersonal difficulties. The group was ethnically diverse and included members from different religious backgrounds and sexual orientations.

The group had been meeting for two years, had formed a cohesive unit, and was in the mature phase. The group had eight members, six women and two men. Barbara is an African American divorced woman with Baptist roots in her mid 50s. Jennifer is a Mormon and married mother of three young children. Angela is a single woman of European descent in her 30's. Robert is a single man in his mid 40s with Catholic roots. Given the supervisor therapist's inattention to spiritual issues, with the exception of Jennifer, the spiritual backgrounds of these members were not assessed or explored during group screening.

Members were providing feedback to other members and challenging their growth. An older 60+ member, Mrs Tanya Jordan, shared that her chronically ill husband had died suddenly during the past week. This member came to group that following week for support in her mourning process. The following vignette occurred several weeks after her husband's death. Robert had joined the group in the past year and was very supportive of Mrs Jordan.

TANYA	I know my husband and I didn't get along and I often told you all about how he made me angry, but it is really hard to see how my life will go on without him. It just seems that taking care of him or being angry with him was the focus of my life.
THERPIST B	You are feeling loss and you feel at a loss right now.
TANYA	Yeah. . . .
THERAPIST B	I wonder whether other members can connect with this mixture of feelings of loss and anger.
JENNIFER	Yeah, I know how it is to feel angry at your husband for the things that he does and still love him for his other qualities. Sometimes being a wife takes over your whole life and you get lost in being a wife and mother . . .
THERAPIST A	Tanya, the group is connecting with your feelings of anger and sadness. You are grieving the loss of your husband including your anger, but also what it meant to have him as a part of your life. I wonder whether this group can be a place where you can continue to bring the pain that you felt in your relationship, but also the cherished memories from that relationship.

ANGELA	I feel for you, Tanya. You all were together for so many years. I admire you for being able to hang in there with your husband through the ups and downs, but I cannot even imagine how you can get used to him not being around. It's for better and worse. Well, this is even worse.
THERAPIST A	Angela, you appreciate and admire Tanya's strength and perseverance. This is helpful for Tanya to hear, but I wonder whether it might also help if you can connect her pain with something in your own life.
ANGELA	Nothing comes up for me right now.
ROBERT	Tanya, you were a devoted wife for so long and I know your husband appreciated it, even if he didn't let you know that. Just know that even if you don't feel it now, there is life after this. When I lost my mother, I thought I couldn't go on. I couldn't even imagine it. We were so close, but life does go on. My life began to mean something different. It had a new meaning.

The group continues on to support Tanya during this difficult time and the therapists make some final comments in support of her mourning, but also in an effort to instil hope.

THERAPIST B	It is so important that you have felt the group's support during this difficult time. I wonder whether the group might not only support you as you mourn the loss of your husband, but also as you consider what life will be like in the future.
TANYA	I don't know what you mean. It is hard to even imagine a future.
THERAPIST A	Yes, that may be the place where you are right now, unable to imagine the future, but maybe the group can help as you move from your current place of loss to imagining a new future. I was struck with Robert's comment about meaning. Sometimes with difficult transitions in life, it is an opportunity to find new meaning in life.

A member introduces a spiritual theme that has more universal implications. A reasonable question might be what is gained by viewing meaning from a spiritual frame or at least exploring the potential spiritual dimensions of it. An approach that was not spiritually informed might simply explore perspectives on meaning, the members' association to meaning and work with what emerges. A spiritually informed approach might do this, but also note the potential spiritual and religious connections and associations in particular. For a member who is feeling lost and unclear, one way to reconnect is to find those values that she may be deeply connected to or rooted in even if this is outside of her awareness. The key is to be open to exploring it, but not prejudging its salience. The notion of meaning does not necessarily have spiritual connections for all, but some people will consider this from a spiritual perspective. The leader flags this realizing that Tanya and the group are not really ready to explore this yet, but in the future it will be important to return to this. Members continued to share some of their mixed emotions in response to loss of familial and close relationships. A few months later, the group returns to this idea of finding new meaning.

TANYA	I really want to thank everyone for your words of support last week. It is still not easy. I take it day by day, but I don't know what I would do without the support of this group.
ROBERT	We are happy to be able to be here for you.
TANYA	That means so much. I am still a bit lost about what my life should be about now. I always connected my purpose in life to being a wife and mother. Now who am I?
THERAPIST A	Tanya, you are asking a deep question. Some people look to their religious, spiritual, family, or philosophical values for help with this. Are there any values that would help you in answering this?
TANYA	I am not a religious person. It is not that I don't believe in God, but the religious spiritual stuff is not so important to me. I do not want to offend some of you because I already know that for some of you your religion is very important to you.
JENNIFER	Yeah. I guess you are talking about me. As a Mormon, my religion is very important to me and it helps me in how I live my life. I see my role as a mother and wife as divine responsibilities and duties. I am deeply committed to fulfilling my responsibilities, but part of why I am here in this group is because sometimes I am just so overwhelmed. I am not complaining, but it just becomes too much, sometimes.
THERAPIST A	Jennifer, you have talked about feeling overwhelmed before and how difficult this is for you, but I am also hearing now that part of your sense of responsibility comes from your Mormon beliefs about how you should be as a wife and a mother.
JENNIFER	Exactly, for us family is a central part of what it means to be a Mormon. I am supposed to relate to my husband and support him. You see we believe that what I do for my family has eternal value. In fact, the most important thing that I do in my life is what I do for my family.
BARBARA	I mean I value family and it is part of my cultural values and even my religion, but the way you just said that . . . that puts a lot of pressure on. Whew!! Eternal! That's a long time. Whew! . . . and you have those three little children. No wonder you're so tired all the time.

Members continue to discuss the weight of this responsibility, the burdens, and the stress.

THERAPIST B	People have been talking about the weight of responsibility in being a wife and mother and for some this is connected to a divine purpose. I wonder whether there is any room here in the group to explore what it means to get in touch with your purpose outside of this role of being a wife and a mother. Tanya, this is part of the next step of your journey, Jennifer, being in touch with what this might feel like and what this means, could be important for you as you manage your family life. We may not only be able to draw on people's experiences outside this group, but also what happens right here in the group as a way of understanding more fully who we are and what we truly feel.

THERAPIST A	Angela, I remember when we were talking about meaning before and you didn't have much to say.
ANGELA	I still don't. I mean this is part of what I am struggling with. I know it's kind of old-fashioned, but I thought being married would define me. I have not got married and don't see that happening any time soon, so I am stuck with trying to figure out my life by myself.
THERAPIST A	So even though you and Tanya have arrived there from different positions, I wonder whether hearing more about your feelings of being lost could be helpful to Tanya.
ANGELA	Well, it doesn't feel good. It's confusing, it's frustrating, and sometimes embarrassing!!
TANYA	I can identify with that!

The group continues to explore some of these feelings and the interactions continue primarily among the women in the group. There appears to be significant energy as the women in the group focus in on continuing to share their experiences and the men seem to be marginalized, if not excluded. Therapist A comments on this process exploring the associated feelings.

ROBERT	Yeah, I am open to that.
THERAPIST A	Although there has been a focus on the roles of mothers and wives and it might seem natural to engage in this exploration with other women, we may also be learning something important about how you might relate to men. It felt at some points as if the men in this group were not even here. There can be many reasons for this, but just as these men here are seeking to be supportive, I wonder whether you might overlook some other men in your life who might lend support?

Clinical Illustration

A few members have just completed their course in group and engaged in a termination process and two new members, male and female, have joined. With the new members the group currently has six members, three male and three female. There were multiple factors that contributed to the dynamics that ensued in response to the addition of the new members. A major factor was that one of the members who had ended with the group was an older revered woman (Tanya Jordan) who had been a long-standing member of the group. Her departure was experienced as a deep loss for many and as a significant transition for the group. The leaders were aware of this to some extent, but one of the male members, Robert, carried the weight of this in a particular way. He had felt protective of this member and that extended to the group as a whole. The vignette will highlight the exchange between Robert and the new member, John. This exchange occurred during the second session after the new members joined.

JOHN	I am looking forward to being in this group because it will provide me an opportunity to address some of the issues that I need to focus on related to relationships.

> ROBERT   What do you need to work on?
> JOHN   Well, as a gay man, I want to be able to address some of the things that are emerging in my relationships.
> ROBERT   Now, why do you have to come out and say that. As a gay man! I am Catholic and I believe that being gay is a sin.
> JOHN   How can you say that to me! Don't you know how judgmental that is!!
> ROBERT   Well, I believe what I believe!
>
> This exchange develops very quickly and catches the leaders off guard. The leaders were aware that John was gay, but there were two additional surprises: the strength and boldness of Robert's response and his assertion that he was Catholic. It was also noteworthy that these two members had focused on the most potentially polarizing aspects of their identities and highlighted this in such an early phase of group. In retrospect, this might have been a helpful process comment to make. A spiritually informed approach would have included an exploration of some of these issues during group screening, specifically Robert's Catholicism and his attitudes toward people who are gay and lesbian.

If I had done then, what I do now, I would have anticipated Robert's potentially strong response to John and would have been more prepared to manage this intensity. More importantly, part of the work of the group would have been not only continued work on the ending, but also preparation for newer areas of difference and values. While it was clear that their interaction displayed competitive strivings including Robert's increased sense of protectiveness about the group and had less to do with religious affiliation and sexual orientation, it was also evident that any intervention would need to incorporate this content even if the goal was to address deeper underlying issues. Countertransferentially, the power of these conflicting positions seemed insurmountable. The affect in the room was palpable and it felt as if not only were these two men passionately presenting their own opinions and experiences, but that this also reflected some of the tensions in our larger culture. As I reflected on my own personal views and reactions, I found myself feeling trapped, but as I wondered what this meant for the group and why now, I began to gain a helpful perspective. Given my concern for the new member and the sense of connection with Robert, I decided to try to challenge Robert and assess the degree of flexibility that he might have in his position.

In contrast to the first example where spiritual issues were an integral part of the issues that the group was addressing and the exploration of these issues facilitated the work of the group, this example demonstrates the emergence of spiritual issues in a defensive way that fuels conflict. Spirituality is used as a means of erecting barriers between members. Clearly, this is a too uncommon occurrence in the larger world, but this conflict in such an early stage for this new group was very difficult to manage. The members were able to hear and respect one another and begin to establish some sense of tentative connection, but the end result was that John left the group prematurely. Fascinatingly, another male member, Tim, who was debating about coming out to the group shared some of his journey and found that despite the volatility of John and Robert's interaction, he felt sufficient support from John and the group to be more disclosing. Tim's interpersonal style was less abrasive and dominating and Robert found it more difficult to reject him outright since he had already established a connection with him. Productive work continued including addressing how religious issues surfaced in the group and how religion can be used as a powerful force for building community, but also be used destructively.

> ### Clinical Illustration
>
> The final brief example is a process-oriented interpersonally focused group for Christians. The group was composed of eight graduate students of mixed gender and included Christians from Presbyterian, Methodist, Baptist, and non-denominational backgrounds. The focus of the group was on providing support for graduate students. Members have expressed a wide range of feelings from feeling isolated and lonely to feeling thankful and grateful. As students reflected on the end of the group and their graduate student experience, there was also a way that this was giving birth to a new dimension in their lives. The stress and strain of graduate school at times obscured their sense of purpose, their vitality, and even their recognition that they had felt led by God to pursue this life course. The Christian therapist leader considered how to end the group and instead of following the lead of a member-led prayer, she decided to use a spiritual intervention, prayer, to end the group. On the one hand, this might seem like a superficial approach to bringing closure, but on the other hand, given that this is a valued practice for members of the group and allows the leader to include the multiple voices of the members, and to invoke a divine resource that can be viewed as a source of hope, the leader decides to pray. Other leader choice points included processing the prayer in advance or providing specific preparation for the leader's prayer, but the leader decided to do this in the flow of the group. She assured members that there was sufficient time for saying goodbye, addressing regrets, and other termination issues and then in the last couple of minutes prepared to pray.
>
> THERAPIST   We could end this group many ways today. What is coming up for me is to end in prayer. I tend to like to do open-eyed prayers so I will be looking at you as I pray, but feel free to adopt whatever position that is comfortable for you. Lord, I thank you for the time that we have had together. Time to cry, time to be angry, time to be thankful, time to be grateful. I appreciate the risks that people have taken here and the ways that they have been vulnerable. I am thankful that you can handle our anger and our frustration at you. Thankful that you understand the pain and loneliness. I am thankful for the ways that people have reached out to one another here. Even as this seems to be an end and even as it is an end to this group, I pray that it might also represent a beginning of a commitment to connecting in spite of the stress and strain of life, that we might remember this as a time when we made the time to connect in the midst of pain and that that might transfer to our lives beyond this group. In Jesus' Name. Amen.

This is a way of ending that would only be appropriate in a religiously homogeneous group where members were comfortable enough with an explicit intervention (Tan, 2001) that incorporated a spiritual practice.

These three vignettes provide three different examples of how spirituality may emerge in group processes: an integral part, as a divisive force, and as unifying symbolic ending. These examples highlight the thematic, interpersonal, and symbolic uses of spiritual issues as well. These examples also reflect an ongoing journey for this author of being increasingly open and gaining more skills in addressing spiritual issues in group. I hope that as group therapists we will continue to be more open to considering varied approaches to incorporating spiritual issues in group.

References and Bibliography

Abernethy, A. D. (1998). Working with racial themes in group psychotherapy. *Group*, 22(1), 1–13.

Abernethy, A. D. (2004). Special edition on spirituality in group therapy (Guest Editor). *Group*, 28(4), 13–29.

Abernethy, A., & Lancia, J. (1998). Religion and the psychotherapeutic relationship. Transferential and countertransferential dimensions. *The Journal of Psychotherapy Practice and Research*, 7(4), 281–289.

American Psychiatric Association. (1994). *Diagnostic and statistical manual of mental disorders: DSM-IV* (4th ed.). Washington, DC: American Psychiatric Association.

American Psychiatric Association. (2000). *Diagnostic and Statistical Manual of Mental Disorder: DSM-IV-TR* (4th ed.). Washington, DC: American Psychiatric Association. doi: 10.1176/appi.books.9780890423349.

American Psychological Association (2002). Ethical principles of psychologists and code of conduct. *American Psychologist*, 57, 1060–1073. doi: 10.1037/0003-066X.57.12.1060.

Aten, J. D., & Hernandez, B. C. (2004). Addressing religion in clinical supervision: A model. *Psychotherapy: Theory, Research, Practice, Training*, 41(2), 152–160. doi: 10.1037/0033-3204.41.2.152.

Aten, J. D., & Leach, M. M. (2009a). A primer on spirituality and mental health. In J. D. Aten & M. M. Leach (Eds.), *Spirituality and the therapeutic process: A comprehensive resource from intake to termination* (pp. 9–24). Washington, DC: American Psychological Association. doi:10.1037/11853-001.

Aten, J. D., & Leach, M. M. (2009b) *Spirituality and the therapeutic process: A comprehensive resource from intake to termination*. Washington DC: American Psychological Association.

Chambless, D. L., & Hollon, S. D. (1998). Defining empirically supported therapies. *Journal of Consulting and Clinical Psychology*, 66(1), 7–18. doi:10.1037/0022-006X.66.1.7.

Chida, Y. Steptoe, A., & Powell, L. H. (2009). Religiosity/spirituality and mortality: A systematic quantitative review. *Psychotherapy and Psychosomatics*, 78(2), 81–90. doi: 10.1159/000190791.

Emmons, R. A. (1999). Religion in the psychology of personality: An introduction. *Journal of Personality*, 67, 873–888. doi:10.1111/1467-6494.00076.

Exline, J. J., Yali, A. M., & Sanderson, W. C. (2000). Guilt, discord, and alienation: the role of religious strain in depression and suicidality. *Journal of Clinical Psychology*, 56(12), 1481–1496. doi:10.1002/1097-4679(200012)56:12<1481::AID-1>3.0.CO;2-A.

Green, Z., & Stiers, M. (2002). Multiculturalism and group therapy in the United States: A social constructionist perspective. *Group, 26*(3), 233–246. doi:10.1023/A:1021013227789.

Hall, G. S. (1904). *Adolescence: Its psychology and its relations to physiology, anthropology, sociology, sex, crime, religion and education* (Vol I). New York, NY: D. Appleton & Company.

Hill, P. C., & Hood, R. W. (1999). *Measures of religiosity*. Birmingham, Alabama: Religious Education Press.

Hook, J. N., Worthington, E. L., Jr., Davis, D. E., et al. (2010). Empirically supported religious and spiritual therapies. *Journal of Clinical Psychology, 66*(1), 46–72. doi:10.1002/jclp.20626.

Jacques, J. R. (1998). Working with spiritual and religious themes in group therapy. *International Journal of Group Psychotherapy, 48*(1), 69–83.

James, W. (1985). *The varieties of religious experience*. Cambridge, Massachusetts: Harvard University Press.

Johansen, T. (2010). *Religion and spirituality in psychotherapy: An individual psychology perspective*. New York, New York: Springer Publishing Co.

Larson, D. B., Swyers, J. P., & McCullough, M. E. (1998). *Scientific research on spirituality and health: A report based on the scientific progress in spirituality conferences*. Rockville, Maryland: National Institute for Healthcare Research.

Leach, M. M., Aten, J. D., Wade, N. G., et al. (2009). Noting the importance of spirituality during the clinical intake. In J. D. Aten & M. M. Leach (Eds.), *Spirituality and the therapeutic process: A comprehensive resource from intake to termination* (pp. 75–92). Washington, DC: American Psychological Association. doi:10.1037/11853-004.

Pargament, K. I. (1997). *The psychology of religion and coping*. New York, New York: Guilford.

Pargament, K. I. (2007). *Spiritually integrated psychotherapy: Understanding and addressing the sacred*. New York, New York: Guilford Press.

Pargament, K. I., Krumrei, E. J., Aten, J. D., et al. (2009). Clinical assessment of clients' spirituality. In J. D. Aten & M. M. Leach (Eds.), *Spirituality and the therapeutic process: A comprehensive resource from intake to termination* (pp. 93–120). Washington, DC: American Psychological Association. doi:10.1037/11853-005.

Porter, K. (2004). Who we really are: Buddhist approaches to psychotherapy and group Psychotherapy. *International Journal of Group Psychotherapy, 28*(4), 53–69.

Powell, L. H., Shahabi, L., & Thoresen, C. E. (2003). Religion and spirituality: Linkages to physical health. *American Psychologist, 58*(1), 36–52. doi:10.1037/0003-066X.58.1.36.

Project MATCH Research Group. (1997). Matching alcoholism treatments to client heterogeneity: Project MATCH posttreatment drinking outcomes. *Journal of Studies on Alcohol, 58*(1), 7–29.

Richards, P. S., & Bergin, A. E. (2005). A theistic view of psychotherapy. In P. S. Richards & A. E. Bergin (Eds.), *A spiritual strategy for counseling and psychotherapy* (2nd ed., pp. 153–185). Washington, DC: American Psychological Association. doi:10.1037/11214-006.

Richards, P. S., Hardman, R. K., & Berrett, M. E. (2007). A spirituality group for patients with eating disorders. In P. S. Richards, R. K. Hardman, & M. E. Berrett (Eds.), *Spiritual approaches: In the treatment of women with eating disorders* (pp. 155–185). Washington, DC: American Psychological Association. doi:10.1037/11489-008.

Rizzuto, A. M. (1979). *The birth of the living God: A psychoanalytic study*. Chicago: University of Chicago Press.

Roller, B., & Nelson, V. (1991). *The art of co-therapy: How therapists work together*. New York, New York: The Guilford Press.

Seidlitz, L., Abernethy, A., Duberstein, P., et al. (2002). Development of the spiritual transcendence index. *Journal for the Scientific Study of Religion, 41*(3), 439–453. doi:10.1111/1468-5906.00129.

Shafranske, E. P. & Malony, H. N. (1990). Clinical psychologists' religious and spiritual orientations and their practice of psychotherapy. *Psychotherapy, 27*, 72–78.

Smith, T. B., Bartz, J., & Richards, P. S. (2007). Outcomes of religious and spiritual adaptations to psychotherapy: A meta-analytic review. *Psychotherapy Research, 17*(6), 643–655. doi:10.1080/10503300701250347.

Spiro, M. E., Kilborne, B., & Langness, L. L. (1987). *Culture and human nature: Theoretical papers of Melford E. Spiro.* Piscataway, New Jersey: Transaction Publishers.

Stoltenberg, C. D., & Delworth, U. (1987). *Supervising counselors and therapists.* San Francisco: Jossey-Bass.

Tan, S.-Y. (2001). Integration and beyond: Principled, professional and personal. *Journal of Psychology and Christianity, 20*(1), 18–28.

The Gallup Organization. (2006). *The spiritual state of the union: The role of spiritual commitment in the United States.* Retreived from http://www.spiritualenterprise.org/archive/opinion/Final_Gallup_Report.pdf.

The Pew Research Center. (2002). *Americans struggle with religion's role at home and abroad.* Retrieved from http://people-press.org/reports/pdf/150.pdf.

Worthington, E. L., Jr., Mazzeo, S. E., Canter, D. E., et al. (2005). Forgiveness-promoting approach: Helping clients REACH forgiveness through using a longer model that teaches reconciliation. In L. Sperry & E. P. Shafranske (Eds.), *Spiritually oriented psychotherapy* (pp. 235–257). Washington DC: American Psychological Association. doi:10.1037/10886-010.

Yalom, I., & Leszcz, M. (2005). *The theory and practice of group psychotherapy* (5th ed.). New York, New York: Basic Books.

Zinnbauer, B., & Pargament, K. (2000). Working with the sacred: Four approaches to religious and spiritual issues in counseling. *Journal of Counseling and Development, 78*(2), 162–171.

Section Five
Through a Personal Lens

Introduction

This section is quite different from what is usually found in a book such as this. Among the authors I invited to write chapters, are three very experienced and thoughtful clinicians who chose to weave their personal stories into their professional presentations. I believe that they have given the reader a special opportunity to see the development of the group therapy field in tandem with the formation of one's professional identity and take away some lessons for her own personal growth. When viewed together, the three authors, living in different parts of the US, have provided insight into the forces that influenced the development of the group modality as well as their respective theoretical viewpoints. The three are characterized by a concern for what works, why it works and how they can use these findings to enhance treatment and training in ways compatible with their own personalities. Drs. Buchele, Stone and Aronson are no doubt superb clinicians, supervisors and teachers. This section will make it possible for you to get to know them, and to let them "speak" to your own evolving stance as a group therapist.

Walter Stone in "Group Psychotherapy as My Career Path" describes his personal journey through medical and psychiatric training and subsequent professional positions. Each phase provided him the opportunity to interact with many of the leaders in the mental health professions. It is interesting to read his insights into how group became prominent in treating the psychologically-impaired. You will also appreciate how he came to adapt Self-Psychology to the group setting. The innovations he introduced in institutional settings and his research and writing about group treatment have been groundbreaking.

Similarly, Marvin Aronson focuses on the factors that contributed to his development as a group clinician and reviews his experience in becoming an educator of generations of group therapists. In "My Development as a Group Therapist," he discusses the role of formal training in group. The ways in which senior therapists impart their knowledge to the less-experienced highlight the importance of institute-based training. Designing curriculum, selecting faculty, structuring supervision and giving trainees access to clinic groups were found to contribute significantly to leader development.

Bonnie Buchele, in "Group Psychotherapy with High Functioning Adults Or People Like Me!" discusses how she developed her own approach to patients, groups and organizations. Her increasing awareness of who she is and what influenced her personal development, her experiences in a variety of clinical settings, including work with incest survivors, and her tracking theoretical and neurobiological advancements, have led her to encourage group leaders to learn throughout the life span.

Realizing that effective group therapists have incorporated the wisdom of predecessors, clinical experience, and growing insights into their own growth process can be reassuring. Group leadership is a skill that develops over time. The openness of each of the authors to new theoretical positions equipped them to address the needs of emerging populations. Using the group modality for treatment and training reflect creativity and courage.

35

Group Psychotherapy as my Career Path

Walter N. Stone

> ... a memoir focuses on some specific periods of one's life, although ultimately it may well cover a good part of it.
>
> (Kurzweil, 2001: p. 7)

In the middle of the last century, a split existed between biological and dynamic-orientation of many psychiatric residency training programs. Among the leaders in teaching dynamic-analytic psychotherapy was Maurice Levine, a training analyst associated with the Chicago Analytic Society, who was the department director at the University of Cincinnati. Cincinnati had a unique organization of its faculty resulting from Levine's belief that teachers needed to actively practice in order to effectively teach. Thus, almost all faculty appointments were for 25 hours a week and the remainder of one's time could be spent seeing private patients. Several faculty members were conducting groups as part of their practice and served as a model for trainees. In addition, Roy Whitman who had co-authored the initial papers describing the group focal conflict, had been recruited from Chicago as a "full-time" faculty member.

Within the portion of psychiatric practice that focused on dynamic treatment, psychoanalysis had a preeminent-idealzed position. Levine created an atmosphere in the training in which "ordinary" psychotherapy could be seen as having an important status. In the brochure describing the departmental ideology, Levine had written that residents upon completing the program would be able to conduct a "self-respecting" psychotherapy, by which he implied that one did not have to receive psychoanalytic training to feel that he could conduct dynamic treatment. Group psychotherapy was included under that umbrella.

Interest in group treatment had been initially stimulated by W. Donald Ross, a psychoanalyst, who had joined the faculty from Canada in the early 1950s. Don encouraged faculty members to both teach and lead their own therapy groups. He regularly lead a group of diabetic patients who were hospitalized on a special ward for patients with psychosomatic problems at the Cincinnati General Hospital. A boost in interest in group treatments was created by Michael Balint (1968), a prominent London analyst, who had championed group process workshops for general practitioners in London. Balint had been a visiting teacher for a year in the late 1950s. He had conducted an experiential group for the faculty and served as a mentor during his visit.

One of the important elements in the department teaching was Levine's stance that the department needed regular outside stimulation, not only from psychiatry but from other intellectual disciplines. Each February, Margaret Mead visited the department for two weeks, creating renewed intellectual excitement. Lawyers, philosophers, historians, and economists from the University regularly presented at general departmental meetings linking their work to the more general human condition. In addition Heinz Lehman, annually visited the department from Canada to discuss the Canadian healthcare system and to describe the therapeutic milieu in Canadian hospitals, which included a great deal of group treatment. Most memorable was a pair of movies made of patients on the ward before and a year after implementing pharmacoptherapy and milieu treatment. The first showed patients sitting listlessly around the unit, many on the floor. The second illustrated a very interactive informal period where patients who were actively engaging with one another and with staff.

Reinforcing interest in group treatment as an area of specialization were several faculty members who had become actively involved with the AGPA and in the regional affiliate organization, the Tri-State Group Psychotherapy Society (TSGPS). Don Ross had led one of the first AGPA Institute groups. Others had presented at annual conferences. Don and Stanley Block had served as president of TSGPS. As I will describe in detail below, groups were a major portion of inpatient work and all residents led out-patient groups, beginning with a six month period as silent recorder observer. A sense of excitement about group treatment existed within the department. The "legitimacy" of group therapy was enhanced by practicing psychoanalysts who were also conducting and teaching group therapy. However, no formal training program existed. Training was embedded in the experiences of leading groups. I began my three year residency in 1961 in this dynamic, energetic milieu.

The Training Program

Group treatment was prominent in both in-patient and out-patient settings. In Cincinnati half of the three years was spent working in various hospital placements: the city hospital, the Veterans Administration, a private hospital and a state hospital. Lengthy hospitalizations were the norm. In centers such as Cincinnati, patients might remain in the teaching hospitals (VA and Cincinnati General Hospital) for six months. The idealized models for treatment were centers such as Chestnut Lodge and Menninger Foundation where patients were treated with intensive long-term psychotherapy to "cure" their illness. A brilliant and evocative description of intensive psychoanalytic-psychotherapeutic treatment of a schizophrenic person was described by Joanne Greenberg in her best-selling book, *I Never Promised You a Rose Garden*. The book served as an idealized treatment model.

I began my training with a six-month rotation at the VA hospital which was associated with the department and staffed by department psychiatrists. Two residents were assigned to a moderate size ward of 10–12 patients A generous size nursing staff included several registered nurses and two nursing assistants, who for the most part were men to help manage the all male wards. We had several types of groups. The primary one was the ward group check-in each morning. All patients, residents and staff were expected to be present. Patients were asked to comment on what had happened to them during the previous 24 hours. There was not much patient interaction expected, but I began to see how patients told their story and how they interacted with one another and the staff. The experience enabled me to be reasonably comfortable sitting with patients in a large group, and learning some of the fundamentals of group work that included patient showing respect for one another, and trying to describe their feelings. I became familiar with psychotic ramblings, patients anxieties about leaving the hospital and returning to the community, and I began to grasp the idea of metaphorical communication. Once a week, the staff and residents met with the ward supervisor to discuss ward functioning, and address any issues arising in the groups or among the staff and residents. This was a central aspect of seeing the treatment as an experience in living for both patients and staff; however, I do not recall any particular theory informing our work. Our task was primarily to help patients talk to one another in a respectful manner.

Opportunities also arose for residents to conduct a more traditional type of group therapy for selected patients, who seemed more capable of gaining insight. These were patients primarily categorized with personality disorder, often with major depressive affect. Some patients diagnosed with schizophrenia were treated in this group. Many of these patients lived in the Cincinnati area, and we were able to continue the group following their discharge from the inpatient unit. When I rotated to the outpatient department, I would return to the VA to lead the weekly treatment, which I continued during the remainder of my training and during my first year on the faculty. As I will describe below, after I began serving as an observer/recorder of an outpatient group, I worked from a theoretical base of the group focal conflict.

During this period, one of my most poignant experiences was listening to a young man, diagnosed with schizophrenia, talk about his failed hopes. He had been a star baseball player in high school and had dreams of playing professional baseball. His mental illness had derailed his hopes, and he seemed quite lost. I believe that working in the hospital setting with groups helped me focus on working with this population when I transitioned to teaching in the department outpatient setting of Central Clinic.

Group therapy in Central Clinic was organized in accordance with the model of the day: weekly, ninety minute sessions for individuals with neurotic and personality disorders. The groups were co-led by two advanced residents, and junior residents served as silent recorder, whose task was to take notes and present the material for the bi-weekly supervision!

I was asked to be a recorder at the beginning of my second resident year. Supervision was on Monday, and I spent part of Sunday evening immersed for more than an hour reviewing my process notes. The expectation was that I could formulate the process in terms of the group focal conflict (Whitman and Stock, 1957; Whitaker and Lieberman, 1964) which was the prevailing theoretical model. At the end of the six month mandatory recording experience, no groups were available to lead. I chose to continue recording for an additional six months, because the group was assigned a new supervisor who provided a different perspective. In my final year of training, I co-led an outpatient group in the clinic. Despite the limitations of the theory, the emphasis on group-as-a-whole processes and the rigor of the experience of recording were instrumental to my sense of growing mastery of this treatment modality.

The clinic also cared for a large population of patients requiring treatment following discharge from the hospital. Because these patients often regressed with change of resident rotations, a special clinic was formed where patients could come, wait with others and see whatever doctor was available. They might see a different resident at each visit, and not form an attachment to a particular individual. Transferences would be to the institution, not to the individual (MacLeod and Middleman, 1962). The patients were also invited to come to the clinic an hour before their scheduled appointment for coffee and snacks. They met with a clinic volunteer who was hostess. The volunteer's observations of patient interactions in these preliminary gatherings suggested that group processes were taking place. I found the actual contact with patients frustrating because I did not get to know them. I might not see the same person for several months. The model may have been good for patients, but I did not feel good about my work. As I will discuss below, my rethinking and revamping this clinic became the stimulus to develop a new model of group treatment for this deserving population.

Motivated by my academic ambitions, I began searching for opportunities to enhance my career by publishing. Two particular experiences during residency led to publications on group psychotherapy.

The first experience arose almost by accident. In the context of the 1960s psychotherapeutic culture dynamic psychotherapy for homosexuality was changing, but the general rule was to exclude gay/lesbian patients from mixed groups (at the time homosexuality was an official diagnosis). My co-therapist and I usually interviewed prospective members together. On one occasion, our schedules precluded this. He interviewed and really liked a woman candidate, and he minimized her lesbian orientation. I found her fully committed to a lesbian lifestyle. I liked her, felt she would likely fit in the group. My co-therapist had committed to her and I would not exclude her from the group because of the prevailing theory. She joined the group, and despite our concerns that members would leave they did not; the group went very well. I reviewed the literature, and submitted an abstract emphasizing countertransferential aspects of working "counterculture" for presentation at the annual AGPA conference in 1965 held in Philadelphia. The case report was subsequently published in the International Journal of Group Psychotherapy (Stone, Schengber and Seifried, 1966).

The second example emerged from my work as a silent recorder. My silence seemed to evoke paranoia both in the co-therapists and patients. I was often quite uncomfortable with all of the projections streaming my way. Excellent supervision helped me understand such processes, and their impact not only on myself but the therapists and the "treatment team." When I subsequently became a supervisor I was able to gain an additional perspective of the entire process. With these experiences,

I wrote a paper on the dynamics of the recorder observer (Stone, 1975). About one year after becoming training coordinator for group therapy, I discarded the training model, and subsequently therapists wrote their own process notes.

Beginning an Academic Career

Academics

Upon completing the residency in June 1964, I made a decision to remain at the VA Hospital as an instructor in the Department of Psychiatry. The VA, as I suggested earlier, was an integral part of the residency training. My responsibilities were ward chief and admitting officer. This was a 25-hour-a-week position, and in keeping with the department philosophy, I was provided an office in the outpatient wing of a private hospital to conduct my practice.

At the VA, I worked to try to further enhance my understanding of in-patient groups and find a focus for my career. Without many of the current: The *Health Insurance Portability and Accountability Act (HIPAA)* recquirements, I began videotaping in-patient groups. Some of these sessions were startling. In one meeting when the therapist was departing the hospital, a patient suggested that the group have a picnic. The meal would be the roasted doctor who they would then eat – a wonderful illustration of primitive incorporation of the departing object. I was invited to present in-patient group therapy at a national VA conference at Menninger clinic. This tape became "the star of the show."

Groups were on my mind. I suggested that I might provide a "support" group for six first- and second-year residents assigned to the VA and facing the difficulties inherent in working with the sickest patients. My model came from learning more about how staff could be supported in their work, and by a visit by Michael Balint, who spoke how GPs in London engaging in a group gradually became more in tune with their patients' emotional states and were more effective practitioners. The departmental chief approved the notion and we were able to go ahead. We kept the schedule at "low-intensity," meeting for fifty minutes biweekly. The power of group processes soon took hold and the residents looked forward to the meetings where they had a place to air their anxieties and gripes. Staff commented that the residents seemed more engaged in their work. I was very pleased with the direction things were going. When I became head of the group therapy program, I was able to establish "process groups" as part of the more extensive group therapy training.

I served as a Ward Chief for several years until the faculty member leading the day-hospital departed for another city. I was asked to replace him. This opportunity exposed me to another, somewhat less-ill, patient population. However, the experience was short lived as the VA system discontinued the service.

In 1970, as the day treatment center was discontinued, several faculty members departed, either to focus on psychoanalytic training at the newly formed Cincinnati center or for other faculty appointments outside the city. I was appointed coordinator of group therapy training for the department.

I was concerned that I could not influence or develop a group program while based at the VA, seemingly a "remote" one block down the hill from Central Clinic was where the residents did their outpatient work. I needed to be there to have hands-on contact. During my tenure at the VA, I was promoted from instructor to assistant professor.

Private practice

Patient referrals for psychotherapy were frequent, and I rather quickly accumulated more than 12 hours a week of individual treatment. Learning to interest patients in group treatment took a little more time. I approached the task by obtaining a history that included the patient's reasons for seeking treatment and a reasonably in-depth history of their illness; I then asked if they were interested in dyadic or group treatment. Often the suggestion of groups would startle them, and since I offered no particular reason for my suggestion, they usually said, "no." I then learned from my patients, and I recast my proposal to carefully formulate reasons and provide simple examples of how and why groups might be helpful. This direct approach was more successful and enabled me to recruit for a private group, but the process was slower than I had hoped for. I incorporated the experience into my writing about groups, as I found many beginning group therapists had little idea about how to help patients enter groups.

I had good fortune when Bill Powles, one of my more senior colleagues at the VA, asked if I would join him and co-lead his private group. I was startled and honored. I was able to refer a few of my patients to fill our co-led group to eight members. We were sufficiently successful recruiting members that within a short time we started a second group. These experiences proved invaluable, and we continued together until he left the city for another academic position. There are few opportunities to learn first-hand how others actually practice. We also had an opportunity to discuss theory, and although Bill had been one of my supervisors, he was not wedded to the group focal conflict. He began to show me the need to use more of my own emotions in responding, rather than the strict recommendations of focal conflict theory.

An additional opportunity to study groups arose in the context of the cultural revolution of the 60s and 70s when the T-group movement was flourishing. A religious organization had been sponsoring a series of intensive week-long T-group conferences and became concerned about psychological casualties. A colleague and I were consulted by the church leaders. We discussed the problem and proposed a tri-partite training model: personal history, psychological testing and a brief morning T-group experience. Our proposal was accepted, and it included the stipulation that we could decide the suitability of candidates to take on the rigors of the training. About 20% of the candidates were screened out by the psychological evaluation, their personal decision or by administrative decision. Although controversial, the administrative decisions were based on concerns regarding their psychological "safety" (Stone and Tieger, 1971). This was one of the early papers challenging the notion that T-groups were not harmful to participants. Within a short period, the more definitive evaluation was published by Lieberman, Yalom and Miles (1973).

Organizations and theory

Cincinnati was one of the main hubs of the active Tri-State Group Psychotherapy Society – Ohio, Kentucky and Indiana. The TSGPS held two weekend meetings each year focused on experiential learning and a meeting in which a nationally prominent lecturer would be the featured speaker. I was exposed to a wide variety of approaches, including transactional analysis and gestalt therapy. Seeing vastly differing approaches was a stimulus to sharpen my own theoretical knowledge.

I joined the AGPA, the gathering place for therapists from around the world. There, I became familiar with the intrapsychic theories of Slavson, Wolf and Schwarz, Durkin and Glatzer; group-as-a-whole theories of Bion, Ezriel, Foulkes, and Horwitz; the Interpersonal approach of Yalom and general system theories of Durkin and Aagazarian. My presentations at these meetings gained me some recognition, and beginning in the late 1970s, led to many invitations to speak at regional group therapy conferences across the country.

I did not ignore my local and state general psychiatric organizations. Soon I was invited to assume positions of responsibility, including program chair. I used these roles to invite group therapists to present their work at the meetings. This not only increased my exposure to prominent persons in the field, but stimulated interest in group treatment among my colleagues. Several then started their own groups, and later became group therapy supervisors.

Central Clinic

Structuring group training

With my new responsibilities as coordinator of group therapy and the support of Bob Stewart, the clinic director, I was able to implement a formal group therapy course with both experiential and didactic components. The first model was to have a brief series of readings on group dynamics, group development and understanding group function from the perspectives of a group-as-a-whole, interpersonal and intrapsychic stance. The experiential portion of the training went through several iterations: at first we used a one-day model (usually a Saturday) with a series of one-hour experiential sessions. We reserved time at the end of the day to review and integrate the participants' experiences with prior theory.

The model was unsatisfactory, primarily because the one-day model day did not allow for on-going reflection and learning of group processes. We then introduced a series of 12 weekly sessions in which the dynamics of the meeting could be conceptualized at the level of the individual and of group dynamics and developmental. These elements were explored in a discussion period immediately following the end of the group. Subsequently, we modified this model by videotaping the session and immediately reviewing the tapes to illustrate dynamic processes. The participants felt that this was a very effective model for learning. The tapes were erased after the review session, assuring confidentiality.

Participation in the groups was considered confidential and information about an individual learned in the group was not used for evaluation of the residents' academic performance. Group leaders were chosen from outside the core University faculty to further distance the training from the administration.

Conductors of these groups recognized the difficulties residents had in managing the complexity of people who worked together exposing less than optimal aspects of themselves. A part of the problem was solved, when we expanded the teaching to include clinic-based, advanced social work and psychology trainees. Competitive strivings became a much more prominent dynamic, and we were able to illustrate to the participants, the importance of not only intrapsychic phenomenon, but also the impact of social/cultural elements on the unfolding processes (Hall et al., 1981).

New clinical services

Caring for persons with chronic mental illness When I arrived at Central Clinic in 1970, a considerable portion of the patient population were described as "aftercare." As I noted above, I felt that the patient care was not optimal because of the model of institutional transference.

I altered the model by creating small teams of three doctors who were assigned a cohort of patients. The small teams would get to know each of the patients and be more effective in their treatment.

I felt a therapy group would be an optimal treatment for many of these patients. The patients had shown an ability to interact in the waiting room setting with a volunteer, and I thought that they could gain even more in a formal therapeutic setting.

I thought that group had several major advantages over the existing treatment model. Foremost, group would help patients develop opportunities for improved social relationships, which I believe not only would enhance their quality of life but would also diminish their need for re-hospitalization. Transferences would be to the group as well as the doctor, and changes in therapist would be less traumatic (Bachrach, 1992; Breier and Strauss, 1984; Hogarty, 1993). The presence of peers would offset some of their experiences of loss. Most groups were to be held during daytime hours, because few patients worked and they felt safer traveling in daylight. The group was held in a large room. Coffee was provided, as had been when the patients were in the waiting room. Patients could relieve tension by getting and drinking coffee, without having to leave the room, as they seemed to do as tensions arose during a session. The groups were to meet weekly.

I discovered that I had been rather naïve applying a traditional model of weekly group treatment for this population as we soon learned that patients with chronic mental illness had great difficulty regularly coming to group. The reasons were not only psychological, but included insufficient finances for transportation, intermittent, unexpected or regular obligations for family. Searching the literature, we discovered that others had noted the same problem, (de Bosset, 1982, 1988; Keith, and Mathews, 1984) and with this background, we began working on a new model, which we labeled, "The Flexibly Boundaried Group" (McIntosh, Stone and Grace, 1991; Stone, 1991, 1992a).

The fundamental change was that in preparing patients for group, they were asked to come for four consecutive successive weeks. Thereafter, in the group, they would decide how frequently they would like to attend, with a range of weekly to monthly. The model demonstrated that discussion of attendance, and by unspoken extension, other personal matters could take place within the group. Our experience and literature review (de Bosset, 1982) indicated that the group would develop a core group of 3–5 members who would consistently attend and a peripheral subgroup who came less frequently. Over time, the peripheral members would be integrated into a cohesive group. Groups were based on the premise of providing long-term, if not life-long care. Social work, psychology and psychiatric residents all served as co-leaders.

One of the unexpected aspects of the experience was that many of these patients brought small children or infants to the clinic. We learned that this was not a resistance, but actually represented the patients' motivation to come to therapy, since they had no alternative for caring for the child. We had no alternative but to include them in the group session. Much to our surprise, the children's presence yielded valuable clinical information; we watched both the caretaker and other members interact and play with the kids. They were warm and respectful, which seemed to serve as a stimulus for more peer interaction. We learned that children much over 2–3 years old would not sit still and solved that by having them meet with a volunteer who provided a play-hour (Stone, 1983).

Whenever possible, we arranged for group patients to receive their medications at the conclusion of the group session. In groups led by a resident, 15 minutes following the session were set aside to review and prescribe medications. This arrangement had several advantages. All group members could remain during the discussion and patients could comment on one another's propensity to adhere to or disregard the prescribed dosages. Members had considerable outside contact with one another and they could also make observations about various stresses or peculiar behaviors, suggesting impending difficulty. The added eyes and ears would often prevent or diminish the intensity of the impending psychic decompensation as patients told about one another's clinical state. For groups that were not led by a resident, another physician was assigned to care for the patients' medication needs, arriving at the group during this 15 minute period. The patients and therapists could fill in important clinical information. At times, therapists would have to arrange a separate consultation because of the complexity of the patient's problems.

To learn more about the processes, we formed several groups in which patients agreed to be video-taped, for teaching purposes. Patients seemed pleased to "do something in return" for their therapy, and recruiting members for these groups generally went smoothly.

As I gained experience, I decided to write a book about the model and the patients' experiences. The patients seemed truly appreciative of the format change, and were actually proud of being in a book that described their treatment. They willingly agreed to sign special permits that appropriately protected their identity and disguised clinical illustrations of their treatment (Stone 1996).

The model had increased salience with deinstitutionalization and emptying of state hospitals beginning in the 1980s. Treatment for persons with chronic mental illness moved to community mental health centers. In addition to their therapeutic aims groups provided social/peer contact that had been available in the hospital. I think this model was one of the major contributions of my career.

An important by-product of the model is the collaborative working across disciplines, with each bringing the particular discipline's perspective to bear on the entire treatment. As I worked with these therapists I developed a "slogan" for therapist behavior: Therapists are like the Physician's Desk Reference – the PDR: Predictable, Dependable and Reliable. I understood the PDR as alerting therapists to the inevitable breaks in their behavior as having an impact on the therapy. With the new structure, patients actually seemed to be more open about their lives and I found that we were more deeply and meaningfully engaged. I gained a deeper appreciation of their lives, and the internal and external barriers to their recovery. I began to care about them in ways that I had not anticipated when I had started.

Waiting list groups

Another innovation I implemented was a waiting list group. The Clinic regularly struggled with more requests for treatment than could be provided. Patients could be placed on a waiting list, often with an indeterminate wait for treatment. The problem was exacerbated following deinstitutionalization. Publicly supported clinics were required by law to provide prompt treatment or referral elsewhere. A group for patients who had to wait would provide immediate service and assure the clinic of a continuing flow of patients and additional income from the service.

The plan was to have a semi-structured weekly group meeting of 75 minute duration. Patients would be referred from the intake department, where a description of the group would be given to those interested. If they chose to join a group they were given a written handout describing the benefits of talking and listening to others. Those in acute crises were not appropriate for the group.

The groups were open-ended and new patients could be added. I co-led the group with a resident. We rarely had more than eight members for the co-led groups. We tried to limit the number of sessions a patient might attend to six. This limit might last an extended period because not all patients attended weekly as we suggested. We began each group by asking new patients to describe their problem for seeking treatment, and we asked returning members the status of their problem since their previous visit. The therapists actively tried to find commonalities in the patients' descriptions to facilitate their engagement with one another, and in the treatment. This process usually took 15–20 minutes and was followed by open discussion. At the end of each session, the therapists asked patients to consider personal goals for the next week.

Among things we learned, was that we should exclude patients who would only say they wanted to come to the group to receive medications. We could not responsibly assess and evaluate medication needs in the limited time available. For patients who were taking medications, the clinic director provided a psychiatrist who could meet with the patients after the group to discuss their medications. This was considered a separate service, and the clinic had assumed responsibility for the care of the patient.

Another lesson was the importance of marketing. Our initial label for the group was "The Preliminary Process Group." When we changed to "Immediate Treatment Group" we were more successful in recruiting patients from the intake service. We also learned that the group was most valuable during the late winter and spring when student therapists' caseloads were full, and therapy time was unavailable until new students arrived in the summer.

We believe that the groups provided an important treatment beginning. Patients were seen immediately, and hidden crises could be exposed. Patients also had the experience of psychotherapy, and they became more amenable to accepting "talking therapy," when they might have preferred merely brief contact and medication refill. Moreover, they became a conduit to the regular clinic groups as a result of their positive experiences. As was our custom, we publicized our work at various group meetings, and through publication of our findings. (Stone and Klein, 1999; Klein et al., 2001; Stone, Klein et al., 2006). I have informally surveyed a number of colleagues working in the public sector, and I was disappointed to learn that other clinics have not adopted the model.

Personal growth and support

Through my involvement in the various professional organizations, including international associations, I met therapists with many different perspectives. One of my more enriching experiences was a three-month sabbatical leave spent in the UK. My intention was to learn about group analysis, the dominant theoretical base for group therapy in most of Europe. I was able to gain appreciation for the theoretical and clinical applications of group analysis, in particular, the notion of an open system in which the therapist is to help members widen and deepen communication, ranging from the more conscious to increasingly subjective and unconscious fantasy. I observed how the group provides patients opportunities to discover similarities and differences through each member seeing him/herself in others. I was able to attend seminars and an international conference, where I could present some of my own work. Through these experiences, I had many personal encounters with theoreticians from around the globe. They helped me gain newer understanding of the work of Wilfred Bion, Melanie Klein, and Malcolm Pines, as they had influenced group analytic practice and training. In many instances, the collegial relationships overlapped into my social life. I renewed my friendship with Sigmund Karterud in Norway, and I became good friends with Earl Hopper. Both have read drafts of my papers and made helpful suggestions. I had a feeling often of being most welcome around the globe.

Reflection

Looking back at the first 10 to 15 years of my academic career, I can identify several strands, which were not always so clear to me at the time. A number of my publications were not focused on groups. They laid the groundwork for some later group-related studies. One example was collaborating on annual reviews of psychopharmacology. This led to surveying therapists' attitudes about including patients receiving medications in their groups (an early bias regarding the "purity" of psychotherapy) and the impact of psychosocial elements in conducting research or influencing treatment decisions (*see*, publications of Hofling, Winslow and Stone, 1996–1971). I knew that these were helpful for academic promotion, but they had an unanticipated result – I became known as someone who was knowledgeable about pharmacoptherapy, which was particularly helpful in my work with the chronically mentally ill.

My publications on groups began with clinical case reports or innovations in treatment models (the flexibly bound group, the intake group). Some of the observations in the literature did not fit with my clinical experiences. This led to several projects. The dropout literature came primarily from public sector and student-led groups. Scott Rutan and I reviewed our private long-term groups to see if we could discover factors that led to patients discontinuing treatment or, conversely, those factors that may have contributed to their becoming engaged and were committed to their group

(Stone and Rutan, 1984). We were both pleased with our findings and sought to expand our collaboration. We considered writing a paper together analyzing group sessions from our differing clinical perspectives. In the midst of these discussions, we broadened our horizon and decided to write a textbook on dynamic group psychotherapy. That led to our continuing collaboration for the next thirty plus years as we produced the first edition of Psychodynamic Group Psychotherapy, a rather thin volume, in 1980. Since then, three more editions have been published in what has become a standard textbook (Rutan, Stone and Shay 2007). The task of writing such a book consolidated my thinking about the field. Our goal in writing the book was to consider the particular advantages and disadvantages of each of the major theoretical models. In the third edition, we added a chapter that looked at the process of a group session from our differing theoretical perspectives. Thus, I gained broader perspective about theory and its applications.

I would add Scott to the list of people who have influenced me, as he not only was knowledgeable about group therapy, but also available as a consultant when I would hit snags in my organizational work. We alternated in preceding one another first as head of the AGPA institute, and later as AGPA president. I also pursued my interest in psychopharmacology exploring attitudes and practice of treating group patients with pharmacotherapy (Stone, Rodenhauser and Markert, 1991), and the associated question of inclusion of seriously mentally ill patients in "usual" private practice groups (Rodenhauser and Stone, 1993). These latter projects were further examples of expanding my collaboration with persons outside of Cincinnati.

Focusing and Consolidating

Introduction

The first 15 years of my practice was a period of considerable cultural turmoil. The civil rights movement and 1964 act seemed to spark the changes, which included women's rights, concern for the mentally ill leading to accelerated deinstitutionalization and the community mental health movement. Concomitantly, the cost of medical care was skyrocketing and managed care was the administrative "solution" to control costs. Although not specifically targeted, dynamic psychotherapy and psychoanalysis, with their subjective criteria for termination, became a particular target for cost control. Categories of illness were reviewed and revised, with more or less specific criteria for a diagnosable illness. If a person was not ill, the insurance would not pay. The handmaiden of changes in diagnostic nomenclature and rise of managed care was evidenced-based treatment. Time-limited interventions and behavioral therapies expanded treatment options which further threatened open-ended long-term treatments. Managed care altered patterns of payments that in turn impacted on who could afford treatment.

Expansion of government entitlement programs, Medicare and Medicaid, enabled many previously underserved people to access treatment. Paradoxically, managed care increased administrative overhead resulting in many clinics needing to increase patient fees, which affected the working poor. They could no longer easily afford long-term treatment. Many of my colleagues hoped that these changes would be an impetus for more referrals to group therapy, which had lower cost per session. However, this change was not as successful as hoped, because dynamic group treatments often extended for years. Even with the smaller fee per session, many patients chose to enter a time-limited dyadic treatment with predictable personal expense.

Rumblings of change were also taking place in psychoanalytic theory and practice. The hegemony of Freudian theory ended. In Ego Psychology the external world was considered of little importance in helping patients solve their problems. Treatment was facilitated by correct interpretation, and the personal therapist was of lesser importance. Kohut's seminal work on the psychology of the self shifted the focus to account for the impact of a person's real-life experiences in the development of their psychopathology. In treatment settings, the therapist through empathic understanding and responding contributed as a person (or selfobject) to the treatment. He was much more than a blank screen on which projections were placed. Kohut created a coherent two-person psychology. In the same timeframe, intersubjective and relational theoreticians added to the theoretical ferment, often evoking heated disagreements among theoreticians. The result was a period of concerted effort to examine actual practice and theory (Michels, 1999).

Self-Psychology

During the period of the late 1950s onward, Heinz Kohut was evolving his Psychology of the Self at the Chicago Psychoanalytic Institute. As part of the department culture, faculty matriculated to Chicago for analytic training. They began to expose departmental members to Kohut's "radical" ideas. Paul Ornstein conducted a series of seminars to familiarize faculty with both basic theory and clinical application of self-psychology. Paul would illustrate specific interventions from his own practice and discuss the change in technique compared with his previous ego-psychologically based interventions. In addition, Kohut began regularly visiting the department as a Visiting Professor. Thus, I was exposed to his ideas in his own words.

I experienced the impact of the theory when I entered a four-time a week psychoanalytic treatment with Anna Ornstein, who had matriculated for her training in Chicago, and was part of Kohut's initial inner circle. I began to understand my treatment with Anna Ornstein more clearly as I learned more theory from the seminars taught by Paul. The analytic experience with Anna was only part of her impact on my life and my work. Following a lengthy interval after completing my analysis, I began to consult with both Anna and Paul regarding my thinking and application of self-psychology to groups. They would make "little" (Paul's expression) suggestions, which would illuminate aspects of my work that I had not understood. Even though they were not group therapists, they could make very helpful observations about the therapeutic process as it unfolded in the group material. At times, they would watch the group videotapes and comment on what they had observed. On occasion, when Kohut would visit the department, Paul and Anna would have a reception at their home, and I would have an opportunity to have an informal chat with him. My recollection is that he was empathic with my efforts to apply self-psychology to groups, but indicated that he knew little about group work.

Contributions to theory Central to the understanding of self-psychology was the shift from a conflict-based theory of human development to one of growth through the availability of significant others, who were to understand and respond to the persons needs. This was a two-person psychology. From a consistent empathic stance the therapist was to respond as if he was an extension of the patient, that is under complete control of the patient. Kohut labeled this process as a self-object need. Kohut defined three primary self-object needs: merger with an idealized self-object; mirroring and twinship. An essential element in the treatment was for the therapist to be alert to failures in providing the patient's self-object needs. Responses to such failures were described as fragmentation of the self. Symptoms, usually marked by anger, withdrawal, or psychosomatic responses in the therapy setting or in the person's external life were understood as efforts to regain inner equilibrium.

Therapeutic progress took place when the therapist helped the patient understand the sequence of injury and response. The patient would internalize the therapist's response, labeled transmuting internalization, and gradually achieve a greater sense of inner stability. He could assume for himself some of the soothing response required from others. Later the therapist could add an "explanation," that is linking the in-treatment process to experiences in the patient's life outside or in childhood. This would consolidate the learning.

Kohut (1984) also understood that narcissism, which was implicit in the need for self-object response, continues throughout one's life. Autonomy was not a therapeutic goal. We are all vulnerable to narcissistic injury and varying states of self-disruption, which are neither as intense nor as prolonged as in persons with narcissistic personality disorders.

Another important element in the development of self-psychology was the focus on what the person was experiencing, that is the work was labeled "experience near." This was contrasted to more traditional theory which was "experience distant." Therapeutic "cure" followed from the base of patients having felt understood. Technically, clinicians learned to reflect their understanding of what had transpired in the process and engage the patient in discussion if the understanding was off base. In the treatment process inevitably patients would feel misunderstood. Through the processes of understanding and explaining, interpretation of historical contributions to the person's difficulties, the person would gradually assume the abilities to self-sooth or seek appropriate responsive others. In addition, others would be experienced as individuals with their own needs, and not primarily to provide self-object experiences. Patients would learn also to use non-human ways of soothing themselves such as listening to music, exercising, or playing with pets.

Self-Psychology in group therapy Self-psychology contributed to my understanding of my patients and some of their seeming problematic behaviors. The first was a way of thinking about patients labeled narcissistic or borderline. Their "pathology" could be reconceptualized as a disorder of the self, and their behavior could be understood as their efforts to stabilize a disrupted self. Anger, withdrawal, or psychosomatic reactions were thought of as likely responses to a narcissistic injury. Verbalizing my understanding of the process of the person's injury and their response as efforts to restore their inner balance on most occasions soothed the person. They would often follow such a response by deepening the process.

I came to understand the importance of responding in a fashion that was conversationally ordinary. I would be responsive to questions and when I gained the impression that the patient felt responded to, I would then explore the motivation for the question. Of course not all questions could be or should be answered, but I experienced increased freedom in how I responded.

I gained new understanding of patients' ordinary ways of orienting themselves when they entered a group by linking to one another, by asking where were you born, or what kind of work do you do as trying to find how they might be alike. These behaviors represented a search for a soothing twinship transference. Other "ordinary" experiences were understood in a new way. For instance, I understood my discomfort with being excessively idealized – my grandiosity was overstimulated. This helped me contain my emotions. I saw similar processes in the members when they had accomplished something new. Patients would excessively congratulate them and they would then minimize their accomplishment or find other ways of repairing a sense of fragmentation. For the patients, the possible meaning was that if they could idealize the group, their participation in it would add to their self-esteem.

I tried to get a handle on making empathic interventions to the entire group. I learned that any whole group intervention would likely be injurious to one or more members, even if I thought that I was "right on." Verbalizing my understanding of a patient's experience usually served to restore the patient's equilibrium. Such interventions likely strengthened the relationship with the entire group as they observed my efforts to understand (Stone and Whitman, 1980).

A frequent experience in groups is patients wanting to or actually terminating after only a few sessions. I understood this as a patient's experience of feeling deeply understood and their symptoms disappearing. Of course, for some, this represented resistance to engaging in the process. Others felt that having regained their balance, they could proceed on their own. Of course, these possibilities had to be explored.

I began intervening in my therapy groups from an empathic stance, responding to the therapeutic conversation with "understanding" comments. Self-psychological theory divided "interpretations" into two parts: understanding and explaining. The understanding portion reflected the therapist's understanding of the process, without linking the comments to deeper, unconscious processes. This latter element was labeled "explaining." Many tense moments seemed to disappear, and patients began working at deeper, more self-exposed levels. Indeed, one member commented to me after I had made what he experienced as a particularly in-tune intervention, "What meeting did you just go to?" In the spirit of the theory, I answered directly that I had been exposed to some new theory. My response represented an illustration of the more "friendly" stance of self-psychology.

As I gained experience, I wanted to write about my work and the applications of self-psychology to group treatment. I decided to ask Roy Whitman, who not only knew group theory but had received his analytic training in Chicago with Kohut, to collaborate on the project. The result was the initial publication in 1977 of the application of self-psychology to group dynamics and therapy (Stone and Whitman, 1977).

Understanding and applying self-psychology to groups then became the central focus of my writing and my career. I had a vision of exploring this paradigm shift as much as I could. I thought Anna Ornstein's formulation of the "curative fantasy" was applicable to group work. The curative fantasy, which contains both conscious and unconscious elements, is an organized wish for what the patient hopes to gain in therapy (Stone, 1985: p. 4). For example, one man, who used highly organized compulsive defenses slowly exposed his wish that therapy would help him think more clearly rather than understand his emotions. This was a curative fantasy that was not altered after three years of tumultuous group treatment; it seemed incompatible with group therapy. A common fantasy patients entering groups have is that they will be able to prove their worth to others and strengthen their sense of self, without having to become dependent on the therapist (parent). Another paper explored manifestations of self-object transferences, including merger, twinship and mirroring transferences (Stone 1989). Transference needs for mirroring often arise in therapy, not only for members' accomplishments in the external world, but for subtle empathic, insightful responses to others or sudden personal insight. Failure to acknowledge the achievement may be experienced as hurtful.

Basic issues in treatment were re-examined. A self-psychological perspective on envy illustrated how group members sensing others had attributes or resources that they lacked, experienced narcissistic injury, and their anger was an effort to destroy the offending object (Stone, 1992b). The self-psychological viewpoint also let me to explore other phenomena: the transference neurosis (Stone, 1997), the role of the therapist's affect in detection of empathic failure (Stone, 2001), and the group-as-a-whole (Stone, 2005), also, a termination when therapists leave practice (Stone, 2005). I also wrote with a number of colleagues, patients with borderline personality disorders (Stone and Gustafson, 1982). In this paper, we suggested a developmental approach that would enable a member to develop his "own individuality and sense of inner continuity, which in turn [would] help him acknowledge others as separate persons and decrease his need for self-defeating or self destructive solutions or problems" (Stone and Gustafson, 1982: pp. 30–31). Collaborating with Sigmund Karterud from Norway, we elaborated Kohut's concepts of the group-self (Karterud and Stone, 2003) in which members internalize the ideals and goals of the group. This concept helps explain some members and the therapist's inner experience of depletion when a valued member would terminate; the group-self felt depleted. We later wrote about self-dreams, in which the dreams represented various aspects of self-cohesion (Stone and Karterud, 2006). Understanding aspects of group development was the topic of the most recent paper (Stone and Spielberg, 2009).

A great deal of my focus on self-psychology impacted my other activities, including activities in AGPA, the International Association of Group Psychotherapy and opportunities to present my work to various organizations and contribute chapters to major psychiatric textbooks (Stone, 2002, 2008).

More on Organizations

As I became more comfortable presenting my work both at local and national group therapy meetings, I became interested in taking on leadership positions. These positions provided innumerable opportunities to reflect upon group dynamics in organizations. Certainly understanding group dynamics and applying those understandings to change dysfunctional organizations are not simple. Nevertheless, it provides a theoretical model. On many occasions, I was able to internally keep my balance when I tried to understand, from an empathic stance, an emotionally laden outburst or a previously active participant's withdrawal. I had learned that understanding does not always mean that an intervention is indicated or even correct. However, I felt more contained within myself with such understandings, and I could more comfortably await developments. I also understood the need for a leader to provide structure and responsiveness, different than that of a therapy group.

In the Tri-State Group Psychotherapy Society (TSGPS), I served as program chair, and as president. At the national level, I joined several AGPA committees, including the Institute committee. At the time I became co-chair I, believe my understanding that any change would be experienced as disruptive (a narcissistic injury) and might be met with anger, helped me make administrative changes in the selection of leaders for the Institute. We managed to loosen the hold of the "old-guard" and make space for newcomers. We limited the number of consecutive years of leadership and added an instructor designate group, for training purposes and offered a commitment to subsequently lead groups. These changes enabled therapists from around the country to lead Institute groups.

In 1978, I was elected to AGPA Board of Directors. For the next 14 years, I was involved with the administration and executive committee of AGPA, as secretary and president, and thereafter as chairman of the Group Psychotherapy Foundation. I began to gain broad understanding of the complexities of organizational life. I also made life-long friendships, forged in the heat of many administrative battles.

When I became president of AGPA in 1990, I believed that the organization needed to expand its membership in order to thrive. Money had finally been raised to purchase the new headquarters. Yet the organization seemed to be in a somewhat financially precarious position. At the time, the membership was about 3200. I felt we needed 4000 members to be financially more stable. Increasing membership by 800 was a greater task than merely recruiting new members. Most organizations lose about 12% of their members annually.

In response to my presentation, the BOD engaged in a heated, enthusiastic discussion. Marsha Block AGPA, CEO took hold of the idea and reorganized the staff to meet the new organizational priorities both by reducing membership loss and vigorously recruiting new members. These efforts were successful and by 1994 we had exceeded our goal, and membership exceeded 4000.

Strengthening the affiliate societies as key components of the overall organization became a second goal of my administration. To that end, we increased liaison to the affiliates and a number of new local societies were formed. I personally visited and actively helped start societies in St. Louis and Colorado. I was pleased with my presidency, my collaboration with Marsha, and what I learned from her about organizational administration, which differed from what I had learned at the University.

Academic leadership

As I gained experience in the psychiatry department, I was asked to take a number of leadership roles. I was requested to consult on the very hot political issue of the early 1970s, that of the hospital performing abortions. I had been providing psychiatric consultation and when appropriate, recommended abortion for Cincinnati General Hospital patients. The city of Cincinnati was politically very conservative, and anti-abortion protesters vigorously picketed obstetricians who performed abortions. Administrators feared that if the hospital became known for performing abortions that funding from the city would be cut. I was counseled not to approve abortions. I consulted with the hospital attorneys and in collaboration with a senior member of the gynecological service, we agreed that a small number of abortions could be performed monthly. We referred additional patients to Planned Parenthood. Not surprisingly, I was soon asked to be the psychiatric consultant to Planned Parenthood, where I was further educated on the interface between clinical services and politics. I learned the importance of public relations and kept information regarding abortions low key.

Politics also influenced several of my other departmental and medical center responsibilities. As a member of the medical school admissions committee, I learned that considerable subjectivity was involved in the decision-making process. On a number of occasions, I received phone calls from local politicians, university administrators or medical center faculty whose child or a child of a close friend was applying for admission. The admissions committee established a small committee headed by a vice-dean to meet with interviewers who were facing such pressure. The process was very supportive to the interviewers.

I was chair of the residency selection committee for the department. The committee met at intervals to review and rank applicants. In parallel fashion to the medical school admissions, we faced the same political pressures of relatives or children of university faculty or colleagues in the community who wanted to train in Cincinnati. I believe that our developing a working committee helped support everyone involved in the decision-making.

In 1980, Roy Whitman was appointed Department Director. He asked me to serve as vice-director and I agreed. Many of my relationships within the department shifted, not always positively. I was seen as a conduit to the director and often felt overtly and covertly pressured into using my position to influence Roy in his decision-making, primarily regarding salary. Other requests were directed at gaining assignments with more ready access to private patients or to recommendations regarding promotion or merit raises. At times, particularly when the re-appointments or promotions were being addressed, the tensions increased exponentially. One individual took me to the University grievance committee because I had not supported his promotion.

Initially I did not understand the boundary between Roy and myself. Only gradually did I understand that department directors relate to other directors or to the dean. Sorting out boundaries, authority and accountability was not easy because there was nothing written; these aspects of the work were learned experientially.

My experiences with these various responsibilities added another layer of understanding to the value of group processes. Certainly, these positions all carried real-life decision-making processes. They carried important emotional salience, in respect to organizational finances and career paths. How to organize support for decision makers varies and sometimes is limited by the nature of hierarchical systems.

The Future

My sense is that there is continuing ferment in the field of group therapy. Theory of group treatment continues to expand, applying intersubjectivity and relational theories to group work. The sometimes heated discussions regarding these applications is healthy, for they bring to the fore strengths and shortcomings of each theory. Of course, self-psychology has not stood still, and even after more than 30 since its introduction, the theory is being fine-tuned.

I see the need to think about how we can apply our knowledge of groups to the very short hospital stays. I believe that some model is needed that has very limited goals compatible with hospital stays of 5–7 days. Such a model would need to have limited goals. I see such goals as introducing patients to the value of speaking with others and sharing problems in a safe environment. This experience would serve as an introduction to therapy and may stimulate patients to seek similar treatment following discharge.

References and Bibliography

Bachrach, L. L. (1992). Psychosocial rehabilitation and psychiatry in the care of long-term patients. *American Journal of Psychiatry, 141*, 1455–1463.

Balint, M. (1968). The Basic Fault, London, Tavistock.

Breier A., & Strauss, J. S. (1984). The role of social relationships in the recovery from psychotic disorders. *American Journal of Psychiatry, 141*, 949–955.

de Bosset, F. A. (1982). Core group: A psychotherapeutic model in an outpatient clinic. *Canadian Journal of Psychiatry, 27*, 123–126.

de Bosset, F. A. (1988). Comparison of homogeneous and heterogeneous group psychotherapy models for chronic psychiatric outpatients. *Psychiatric Journal of University of Ottawa, 13*, 212–214.

Greenberg, J. (1964). *I never promised you a rose garden.* New York: Penguin Books.

Hall, J. M., Stone, W. N., & Kunkel, R. L. (1981). The development and exploration of group experiential training models. *Group, 5*(3), 3–12.

Hofling, C. K., Winslow, W. W., & Stone, W. N. (1966). New Drugs. In E. A. Spiegel (Ed.), *Progress in neurology and psychiatry* (pp. 586–607). New York: Grune & Stratton.

Hofling, C. K., Winslow, W. W., & Stone, W. N. (1969). Drug Therapy. In E. A. Spiegel (Ed.), *Progress in neurology and psychiatry* (pp. 478–497). New York: Grune & Stratton.

Hogarty, G. E. (1993). Prevention of relates in chronic schizophrenic patients. *Journal of Clinical Psychiatry, 54*, 18–23.

Karterud, S., & Stone, W. N. (2003). The group self: A neglected aspect of group psychotherapy. *Group Analysis, 36*, 7–22.

Keith, S. J., & Mathews, S. M. (1984). Schizophrenia: A review of psychosocial treatment strategies. In J. B. W. Williams & R. I. Spitzer (Eds.), *Psychotherapy research: Where are we and where should we go?* (pp. 70–86). New York: Guilford.

Klein, E. B., Stone, W. N., Reynolds, D. J., & Hartman, J. S. (2001). A systems analysis of a failure to test the effectiveness of the waiting-list group. *International Journal of Group Psychotherapy, 51*, 417–423.

Kohut, H. J. (1984). *How does analysis cure?* Chicago: University of Chicago Press.

Kurzweil, E. (2001). Introduction, autobiography, biography and memoir conference. *Partisan Review, 68*(1), 5–10.

Lieberman, M. A., Yalom, I. D., & Miles M. D. (1973). *Encounter groups.* First Facts: New York, Basic Books.

MacLeod, J. A., & Middleman, F. (1962). Wednesday afternoon clinic: A supportive care program: A preliminary evaluation of modifications of the prevalent pattern of treatment arrangements in a psychiatric clinic. *Archives of General Psychiatry, 6*, 56–65.

McIntosh, D., Stone, W. N., & Grace, M. (1991). The flexible boundaried group: Format Techiniques and Patient's Perceptions. *International Journal of Group Psychotherapy*, *41*, 449–464.

Michels, R. (1999). Pyschoanalysts' theories. In P. Fonagy, A. M. Cooper & R. S. Wallerstein (Eds.), *Psychoanalysis on the move: The work of Joseph Sandler* (pp. 187–200). London: Routledge.

Rodenhauser, P. & Stone, W. N. (1993). Combining psychopharmacotherapy and group psychotherapy: problems and advantages. *International Journal of Group Psychotherapy*, *43*, 11–28.

Rutan, J. S., Stone, W. N., & Shay, J. J. (2007). *Psychodynamic group psychotherapy* (4th ed.). New York: Guilford.

Stone, W. N. (1975). Dynamics of the recorder observer in group psychotherapy. *Comprehensive Psychiatry*, *16*, 49–54.

Stone, W. N. (1983). Some dynamics of children's participation in aftercare groups. *International Journal of Group Psychotherapy*, *33*, 333–348.

Stone, W. N. (1985). The curative fantasy in group psychotherapy. *Group*, *9*, 3–14.

Stone, W. N. (1989). Transferences in groups: Theory and research. In D. A. Halperin (Ed.), *Group psychodynamics* (pp. 44–61). Chicago: Year Book Medical Publishers.

Stone, W. N. (1991). Treatment of the chronic mentally ill: An opportunity for the group therapist. *International Journal of Group Psychotherapy*, *41*: 11–22.

Stone, W. N. (1992a). Group psychotherapy for chronic mentally ill patients. In A. Alonso, & H. Swiller (Eds.), *Group therapy in clinical practice* (pp. 71–91). Washington: American Psychiatric Press.

Stone, W. N. (1992b). *A Self Psychological Perspective on Envy in Group Psychotherapy*. Group Analysis, *25*, 413–428.

Stone, W. N. (1996). *Group Psychotherapy for Chronically Mentally Ill Persons*. Guilford Press, New York.

Stone, W. N. (1997). *A Self Psychological Perspective on Transference Neurosis in Group Psychotherapy: The Concept and the Reality*. International Journal of Group Psychotherapy, *47*, 211–225.

Stone, W. N. & Klein E. B.(1999). *The Waiting List Group*. International Journal of Group Psychotherapy, *49*, 417–428.

Stone, W. N. (2001). The role of the therapist's affect in the detection of empathic failures, misunderstandings and injury. *Group*, *25*, 3–14.

Stone, W. N. (2002). Psychodynamic group psychotherapy. In M. Henson & W. Sledge (Eds.), *The encyclopedia of psychotherapy* (pp 439–449). New York: Academic Press.

Stone, W. N. (2005a). Saying goodbye: Exploring attachments as a therapist leaves a group of chronically ill persons. *International Journal of Group Psychotherapy*, *55*, 281–303.

Stone, W. N. (2005b). The group-as-a-whole: A self psychological perspective. *Group*, *29*, 239–255.

Stone, W. N. (2008). Group psychotherapy. In A. Tasman, J. Kay, J. A. Lieberman, M. B. First & M. Maj (Eds.), *Psychiatry* (3rd ed., pp. 1904–1919). John Wiley & Sons.

Stone, W. N., & Karterud, S. (2006). Dreams as portraits of self and group interaction. *International Journal of Group Psychotherapy*, *56*, 47–61.

Stone, W. N., & Spielberg, G. (2009). A self psychological perspective of group development. *Group*, *33*, 27–44.

Stone, W. N., & Tieger, M. E. (1971). Screening for T-groups: The myth of healthy candidates. *American Journal of Psychiatry*, *127*, 1485–1490. Reprinted in M. Rosenbaum, & M. M. Berger, (Eds.), *Group psychotherapy and group function*. New York: Basic Books.

Stone, W. N., & Gustafson, J. P. (1982). Technique in group psychotherapy of narcissistic and borderline patients. *International Journal of Group Psychotherapy*, *32*, 29–48.

Stone, W. N., & Rutan, J. S. (1984). Duration of treatment in group psychotherapy: A private practice experience. *International Journal of Group Psychotherapy*, *34*, 101–117.

Stone, W. N., & Whitman, R. M. (1977). Contributions of the psychology of the self to group process and group therapy. *International Journal of Group Psychotherapy*, *27*, 343–359.

Stone, W. N., & Whitman, R. M. (1980). Observations on Empathy in Group Psychotherapy. In L. Wolberg (Ed.), *Group and family therapy: 1980* (pp. 102–120). New York: Brunner/Mazel.

Stone, W. N., Hofling, C. K., & Winslow, W. W. (1968). Drug Therapy. In E. A. Spiegel (Ed.), *Progress in neurology and psychiatry* (pp. 563–581), New York: Grune & Stratton.

Stone, W. N., Klein, E. B., Hicks, M. W., et al. (2006). Assessing the immediate treatment group: The systems impact of an explicitly communicated contract. *Group*, *30*, 25–35.

Stone, W. N., Rodenhauser, P., & Markert, R. J. (1991). Combining group psychotherapy and pharmacotherapy: A survey. *International Journal of Group Psychotherapy*, *41*, 449–464.

Stone, W. N., Schengber, J., & Seifried, F. S. (1966). Treatment of a homosexual woman in a mixed group. *International Journal of Group Psychotherapy*, *17*, 425–433.

Whitaker, D. S., & Lieberman, M. A. (1964). *Psychotherapy through the group process.* New York: Atherton Press.

Whitman, R. M., & Stock, D. (1957). The group focal conflict. *Psychiatry*, *21*, 269–276.

Winslow, W. W., Stone, W. N., & Hofling, C. K. (1967). Drug therapy. In E. A. Spiegel, (Ed.), *Progress in neurology and psychiatry* (pp. 509–528). New York: Grune & Stratton.

Winslow, W. W., Stone, W. N., & Hofling, C. K. (1970). Drug therapy. In E. A. Spiegel (Ed.), *Progress in neurology and psychiatry* (pp. 141–166). New York: Grune & Stratton.

36
My Development as a Group Therapist
Marvin L. Aronson

I was brought up in Borough Park, a heavily Jewish enclave in Brooklyn (now mostly Chassidic). During the summer months, we resided in a small town named Belmar on the Jersey Shore. The atmospheres of these locales were totally different. The two settings could have been a thousand miles away from each other. What they shared in common was that they were both extremely provincial in orientation.

My family was unusually friendly and accepting, so much so, that my friends would often "hang around" our home because they liked the permissive atmosphere. Eccentricity was easily tolerated. In some ways, my family's interaction was similar to that portrayed in the stage play "You Can't Take It with You!"

As a child, I especially looked up to my paternal grandfather and mother's step-father. Both were self-made businessmen who had emigrated to the United States from Europe as young men. Initially, my grandfather, who was very flamboyant and self-confident impressed me a great deal but as I grew older, I realized that he was fundamentally quite narcissistic and manipulative. My step-grandfather, on the other hand, seemed an increasingly admirable person to me as I grew up. In addition to being well-versed in Talmudic studies, he was a brilliant businessman who became quite wealthy during the Great Depression. He played an important role in financing the development of the State of Israel. Through him I met, as a teenager, and was able to interact with such Israeli luminaries as Chaim Weitzman, Moshe Sharett and Chaim Bialik. It was quite exciting to be exposed to such extraordinary individuals during this formative period.

Although they were not observant, my parents sent me to a religious Yeshiva until I was 14 years old. They did so in the belief that I would receive a better education there than in the local public school.

We spent four hours a day studying the Torah and Talmud in Hebrew-speaking classes and a similar amount of time studying the regular English curriculum that was being taught in the public schools.

As I look back, I am astonished to realize that the subject matter we studied in the Hebrew classes was at the same level of difficulty as courses taught in American law schools.

I believe a beneficial effect of this regimen was that we developed a sense of confidence in dealing with difficult intellectual matters. We also developed a level of patience in struggling with intellectual problems until we felt we had mastered them, at least partially. (I distinctly remember spending days on end discussing relatively short passages in the Talmud.) A side-effect of this type of concentrated study was that I developed an aversion to interminable "hair-splitting" arguments about minute differences of opinion between authority figures.

I grew increasingly restive with the Yeshiva as I approached adolescence because the classes were not co-ed. I was very pleased to enter the neighborhood public high school and enjoyed for the first time socializing with girls. I did very well in most of my courses (except for mathematics). By my senior year, I had become editor of the school newspaper and for a while was seriously interested in becoming a journalist.

In retrospect, I believe that becoming editor of the newspaper was probably the first indication that I possessed some leadership capabilities. In my senior year, I had my first encounter with political controversy. An editorial I had written about relations between the student body and the neighboring business community aroused the ire of the school administration and I was told in no uncertain terms to restrain my opinions in the matter. Also, around the same time, I inadvertently overheard angry interchanges between the school's administrators and certain faculty members. I remember feeling quite shocked and disillusioned at witnessing such strife because I had rarely experienced it in my family.

Entering Columbia College was a revelation. For the first time in my school experience, I found myself in classes in which many of the students seemed conversant with matters I had never even heard of. The student body consisted of exceptionally bright, motivated individuals. Some of the leading figures of the "Beat Generation" were matriculated at Columbia during this period. A high proportion of the students, it turned out later, ended up as college deans, university provosts, deans of medical schools, university presidents, etc.

Initially, I was completely unclear about my choice of a major. I entertained thoughts at various times of becoming a journalist, physician, lawyer, and factory production manager. One day I woke up from a nap with the conviction that I wanted to become a psychologist. This seems strange as I look back because I had only the vaguest idea of what psychologists did. Most of them, as far as I could tell, taught at universities: psychology practitioners, on the other hand, seemed mainly engaged in giving and interpreting tests. Clinical Psychology as we know it now barely existed. I cannot remember that any of my classmates chose Clinical Psychology as a career. The only Psychology professor I remember was Fred Keller. In a course on the history of Psychology, Keller expressed the belief that "all of psychology could be subsumed under behaviorism and all of behaviorism could be subsumed under the work of B.F. Skinner."

One of the distinctive features of the curriculum at Columbia were small classes in Humanities and Contemporary Civilization. The Humanities course focused on great books of Western Civilization from Homer to the present. Contemporary

Civilization dealt with Classical writings in history, economics and political philosophy.

What was memorable about these courses was that the classes were small, met four times a week and were conducted not by graduate assistants but by some of the most prominent university professors, some of whom were actually world-renowned. It was quite exhilarating to interact in this setting with outstanding teachers and fellow students. As I look back, it was something like the feeling of excitement one can obtain in a well-functioning therapy group.

Upon graduating from Columbia College in 1946, I enrolled in the masters program of the Psychology Department which was housed in the Faculty of Pure Sciences. In earlier years, Columbia had achieved a considerable reputation in experimental psychology. A leading proponent of experimental psychology was the venerable Robert S. Woodworth. Some of the outstanding facility members when I was in the Department were Otto Klineberg and Gardner Murphy. Murphy taught Personality Theory; Klineberg specialized in Social Psychology.

There was practically no reference to Clinical Psychology in this program. Clinical courses were, however, being offered at this time at Columbia's Teachers' College. There was a distinctly snobbish attitude in the Psychology Department toward Clinical Psychology. It had a much lower status than "scientific psychology." The prevailing expectation was that graduates of the PhD program would enter into academia: teaching, conducting research and publishing books and articles on aspects of Experimental Psychology and Learning Theory.

I did not feel particularly drawn to learning theory but eventually I realized that it did influence my thinking about psychotherapeutic processes, especially during the working through phases. It highlighted the need for rewards and positive reinforcement of the therapist's interventions. It also helped me to understand the patient's need for guidance on how best to utilize the properties of therapeutic groups in order to obtain maximum benefits.

I remember conducting a laboratory study on the relationship between one's level of expectation and level of achievement. I found that subjects who attempted to respond to multiple aspects of a brief discriminable stimulus were able to see less of anything as compared to those who focused on fewer aspects of the stimulus. The implications of this laboratory study proved useful to me later on in working therapeutically with perfectionistic patients.

After receiving my master's degree in 1947, I enrolled in the Clinical Psychology Doctoral Program at the University of Michigan in Ann Arbor, Michigan. The Department was in the process of expanding its Clinical Psychology component. During this period, Clinical Psychology was undergoing a great expansion nationwide. Psychologists who had obtained clinical expertise during World War II were increasingly entering academia. There was concomitantly a burgeoning of clinical services for returning servicemen under the auspices of the Veterans Administration.

Most psychologists were still involved in the administration and interpretation of projective techniques such as the Rorschach and T.A.T. Gradually they ventured into the field of psychotherapy. The few courses dealing with psychotherapy focused on Freudian and Rogerian psychotherapy as applied, usually, to college students.

I do not recall learning about group therapy in any of my courses at Michigan. There were active well-regarded programs in Lewinian Group Dynamics and Social

Psychology at Michigan at the time, but, unfortunately, contacts between these disciplines and Clinical Psychology were minimal.

My first experience with group therapy took place during my internship at the Fort Custer VA hospital in Battle Creek, Michigan. The Medical Director announced that he had recently received a request from Central Office that psychology interns should conduct therapy groups at the hospital. The first group that I ever led consisted of post-lobotomy patients! All I can remember of these sessions was an atmosphere of general chaos. Patients would faint during the sessions and would have to be wheeled out by their ward attendants.

It became clear that group therapy was regarded as a vaguely-defined modality that required minimal staffing and little planning. The prevailing attitude was that almost any novice could conduct therapy groups and that some group interaction was preferable to social isolation on the ward. Sixty years later, I find that these attitudes still prevail in many institutions and are reinforced by the fact that group therapy is cheaper to administer than is individual therapy. I could not envisage, at the time, that the group modality could be effectively employed for the evocation and working through of deep-seated personality problems.

My PhD dissertation consisted of "A Study of the Freudian Theory of Paranoia by Means of a Variety of Projective Techniques." The study revealed that paranoid patients did, in fact, possess more indications of latent homosexuality than control groups of non-paranoid psychotics and normals. Parts of the dissertation were published in an anthology and also in several journal articles.

My first job after receiving my PhD was at an outpatient VA clinic in New York. I left there after two years because I could not abide the bureaucratic atmosphere which pervaded the job situation, especially when I contrasted it with my previous exposure to highly competent and motivated colleagues at Columbia and Michigan. This proved to be my only full-time job!

In 1952, I enrolled as a full-time Fellow in the first full-time class of the Psychoanalytic Training Program of the Postgraduate Center for Mental Health in New York City. The Center had recently been founded by Lewis R. Wolberg, a prominent psychiatrist, and by his wife, Arlene. The faculty consists largely of psychiatrists, psychologists and psychiatric social workers who had broken away from more traditional psychoanalytic institutes. One of its salient characteristics was that it was completely multidisciplinary, a true rarity at that time. (Even in this setting one of my medical supervisors voiced the opinion that psychologists who conducted psychotherapy without medical supervision were violating medical practice laws of New York State.)

Most of the faculty were full-time private practitioners. Very few relied on the Postgraduate Center for their incomes. This fact contributed, in my opinion, to their intellectual independence. What drew them to the Center were primarily affiliative needs to interact professionally with respected colleagues. Although the faculty consisted of brilliant mavericks, the overall attitude was that three or four times a week of individual psychoanalysis was the ideal form of psychotherapy. Many of the faculty and students were of the opinion that group therapy was an ancillary form of therapy that could possibly be of some help to patients in need of socialization, but was not "really psychoanalytic."

My personal analyst was Dr Emil Gutheil, originally from Vienna, and a disciple of Wilhelm Stekel. (He reminded me in appearance of my paternal grandfather.) Dr Gutheil was very active in a number of psychiatric and other medical organizations. He also served as Editor of the American Journal of Psychotherapy. He strongly emphasized the importance of dreams and had written an excellent book on that topic. This served me in good stead as a group therapist in later years. Unfortunately, some group therapists, in their eagerness to promote interpersonal action in their groups, ignore the therapeutic significance of dreams.

Of special importance to me during my analytic training was Theodora M Abel. Tao, as she was called, practised well into her 90s. At one time, she had been an assistant to Titchener, a pioneering experimental psychologist at Cornell. Later, she did important work in Cultural Anthropology (she was a cousin of Margaret Mead). After a lengthy career as a psychoanalyst, she moved into the field of Family Therapy and contributed significantly to the training of family therapists in New Mexico.

As I look back on my analytic training, I find that I learned a great deal that I could apply to my private practice. This was supplemented by my training in the Center's Children's Clinic where I was exposed to some of the important contributions of Family Therapy. This material was most important to me in understanding the significance of multiple transferences in group therapy and how groups could evoke the overall atmosphere of the patient's family of origin.

A real limitation in my training in analytic therapy was that there was virtually no attention paid to the specific effects of therapeutic interventions on the patient's psychic equilibrium from moment to moment. It was common, at this stage of the field, to rely on strong opinions voiced by charismatic teachers and supervisors with minimal focus on clinical results. This state of affairs was true not only at the Postgraduate Center but permeated the field. I, myself, remember contributing a chapter on group therapy to a volume edited by Richie Heirink, entitled *250 Forms of Psychotherapy*.

Although group therapy was looked down upon by some of the faculty and analytic candidates, it became increasingly evident to me that many of the most interesting and dynamic teachers were utilizing combinations of individual and group therapy in their private practices. Most saw their patients individually in the initial phases of therapy and then introduced them into group therapy. They referred to this approved process as Combined Therapy. When one therapist saw patients individually and referred them to another therapist for group therapy they referred to this process as Conjoint Therapy.

Shortly after receiving my certificate in analytic psychotherapy, I enrolled in the first class of the Postgraduates Center's one-day-a-week Specialty Training Program in Analytic Group Therapy offered by the Center's Group Therapy Department. By this time (1957), its faculty boasted a roster of some of the most prominent group therapists in the United States. Some had already achieved international reputations as a result of their publications and presentations at professional meetings of the American Group Psychotherapy Association (AGPA) or the Eastern Group Psychotherapy Society (EGPS).

There was a definite feeling of excitement in the Department. Group therapy was enjoying increased status not only at the Postgraduate Center but in the field generally. Since regional associations of group therapists were not yet highly developed, it was not unusual for practitioners who lived far from New York to fly in one day a week to participate in the program. In some ways, the prevailing atmosphere of excitement and anticipation was reminiscent of my earlier experiences as a student at Columbia College.

The Department from its inception, was led by Asya L. Kadis. Although she had an atypical academic background, she was able to gain the respect of her eminent colleagues by dint of her enormous energy and her brilliant, intuitive mind. She served as Director from 1957 until her death in 1970. She appointed me Associate Director shortly after my graduation. During this period, I helped Asya run the Department with a particular focus on curriculum development. Jerome Leff was appointed Assistant Director with responsibility for coordinating departmental retreats and special workshops.

Some of the faculty members who introduced me to group therapy, and who influenced my understanding of it, include: Ruth Cohn, Helen Durkin, Samuel Flowerman, Edrita Fried, Henrietta Glatzer, Harold Leopold, Max Markowitz, Bernard Riess, Helene Papanek, Clifford Sager, Emanuel Schwartz, Arlene Wolberg, and Alexander Wolf.

The next two generations of the Specialty Training Program produced the following individuals each of whom influenced my thinking about the theory and practice of group therapy: Joan Adams, Frederick Arensberg, Fernando Astiguetta, Janet Bauman, Albert Brok, Judith Caligor, Karen D'Amore, Nancy Edwards, Jeff Kleinberg, Nina Fieldsteel, Elaine Gould, Arthur Gray, Priscilla Kauff, Henry Kellerman, Jerome Kosseff, Zanuel Liff, Michael Lindenman, Martin Livingston, Joseph Lynch, Herbert Rabin, Judith Rabinowitz, Peter Schlachet, Emanuel Shapiro, Robert Thorne, Janice Warner, Marcia Wood, and Rachel Wyman.

In addition to the regular program, candidates were exposed in Colloquium meetings and Special Workshops to such outstanding group therapies as S. H. Foulkes, Fritz Perls, Saul Scheidlinger, S. R. Slavson, Hyman Spotnitz, and Saul Tuttman.

There was, from the outset, a strong emphasis on publications in the Group Therapy Department: Caligor, Fieldsteel and Brok; Durkin; Kellerman; and, Wolf and Schwartz wrote basic textbooks on various aspects of group therapy. Liff edited a volume of invited articles in a Festschrifft dedicated to Alexander Wolf. Seminal articles on dynamic group therapy by Glatzer and Durkin appeared over the years in the International Journal of Group Therapy. Durkin was instrumental in introducing psychodynamic group therapists to Systems Theories.

The International Journal of Group Therapy was edited for a number of years by Zanvel Liff. The journal Group has been edited by Nina Fieldsteel, Jeff Kleinberg, Martin Livingston, Peter Schlachet and myself. Henrietta Glatzer became the first female president of AGPA. Jeff Kleinberg holds that title at the present time.

Albert Brok and Zanuel Liff became presidents of the Division of Psychoanalysis of the American Psychological Association. I founded and served as president of the section on Psychoanalysis and Groups, housed in the Division of Psychoanalysis.

As a student in the Department, I personally experienced the benefits, both emotional and intellectual, of belonging to a highly valued benevolent group. I was increasingly impressed with the potentialities of group therapy not only by my mentors but by close contact with my peers whom I greatly respected. We saw ourselves as part of the outstanding group therapy program in the United States, possibly in the world. All of this was tremendously ego-enhancing. In a sense, the feelings engendered in me were reminiscent of those I had experienced earlier at Columbia College.

During my 10 years as a student, I participated both in a group experience course and in personal group therapy in a group led by Alexander Wolf. What stays in my mind about the group experience led by Samuel Flowerman, was that he developed a brain tumor; took a leave of absence; returned to conduct the group for a few months; and died shortly thereafter. As a memorial, the group members decided to write a joint paper about our personal experiences. Over a period of several months, we brought in a number of leaders and consultants but quickly disposed of them all. It was only after many meetings that we came to the realization that we were blocked as a group by unconscious negative feelings towards Flowerman and various other authority figures in the Department. Once we became aware of our repressed hostility, we quickly finished the paper and published it. This was the first group therapy paper that I participated in.

My personal group therapy experience proved to be a real eye-opener. My previous individual analysis, several years earlier, was relatively placid and uneventful with its focus on dream material. To my amazement, the group's interaction brought out material which had not been touched on in my individual analysis. This experience brought home the realization that dynamic group therapy was an extraordinarily powerful vehicle for eliciting and working through core unconscious material. During this temporary period of emotional turmoil, I met individually with Alexander Wolf to try to integrate the meaning of the conflictual material which emerged in the group. Within a relatively short period of time, the storm departed and I learned a lot about myself in the process. All of this confirmed my belief that group therapy without earlier or concomitant individual [Combined Therapy] can lead to untoward eruption of repressed conflictual material.

Asya Kadis died in 1971 while she and I were leading a group in her office. (S.R. Foulkes, the renowned British group therapist, also died while leading a group.) Upon Asya's death, I took over the directorship of the Department. As I stated in an interview almost 20 years later, "My goal was to maintain the integrity of the Department. I was concerned that some of our senior faculty members (a number of whom were 20 or more years older than I) would go elsewhere, that they would feel Asya's departure signaled the permanent end of an era. To my great satisfaction, all of them remained actively involved in the Department."

One of the most memorable events during the early years of my directorship was a trip that about 12 members of the faculty took to visit group therapy colleagues in London. During the week that we went there, we met personally with S. H. Foulkes and some of his co-workers in the Trust for Group Analysis, including Malcolm Pines. We visited the famous Tavistock Clinic and participated personally in a demonstration group led by Henry Ezriel. We also met later with David Malan whose research cast some doubt on Ezriel's approach. Unfortunately, we did not have an opportunity to meet with Wilfred Bion who was an enormously popular figure in British psychoanalysis at the time. We had an interesting exchange with Joshua Bierer, a leader in the field of Social Psychiatry. Finally, we had informal exchanges with psychiatrists who were routinely working with large groups of individuals at St. George's Hospital. I could not relate very much to their work at the time, but later realized that some of their concepts were helpful to me in running the Group Department.

At around the same time that I assumed the directorship of the Group Therapy Department I was called upon to lead a group of fearful flyers. This group was originally organized by a phobic flyer who was convinced that he could only fly if he had a personal relationship with the other flyers. The group met for 15 sessions and then we all flew to a Caribbean Island together. The group proved extremely successful. Approximately 90% of the members were able to achieve their goal of flying in a group. A book which I wrote about the experience attracted a good deal of attention, as did several subsequent articles. I appeared on "The Johnny Carson Show" to talk about our experiences. (Fear of flying is a real problem for media celebrities because they are frequently required to fly as part of their work.)

Some of the dynamics underlying the effectiveness of flying groups are:

1. Group cohesiveness (which can accentuate resistance in psychodynamic groups) may serve as a motivation to overcome frightening situations;
2. Fearful flyers are not required to renounce gratifications, as in dieting groups;
3. The leader is often able to quickly help fearful flyers develop an array of non self-destructible maneuvers to minimize their anxieties; and
4. The leader's attention to minute changes in the physical and social environments during flight can often facilitate anxiety reduction.

Using short-term group methods to deal with a variety of anxiety reactions was an interesting change of pace from my usual efforts of trying to resolve intra-psychic conflicts in long-term psychodynamic groups. Since my initial work, with phobic flyers, I have led many anxiety alleviation groups in my private practice. These experiences have increased my sensitivity to the central role of anxiety in all human behavior. It has also led to the development of a number of therapeutic interventions that are essentially non-interpretive yet potentially quite effective.

Other short-term groups I have led consisted of psychiatric residents of Beth Israel Hospital in New York City and, many years ago, psychiatric members of the Wolverine Group Therapy based in Michigan. I have also taught group therapy to graduate students at Baruch College, the New School for Social Research and The Graduate Program in Psychology at New York University. It has been very interesting to field questions about the basic assumptions of group therapy from bright students who were not committed to being group therapists precisely because they had not been influenced by various mythological assumptions about the modality.

In 1974, Lewis Wolberg and I decided to edit an annual series of invited articles. From 1974 the series was entitled "Group Therapy – An Overview." It was published by Stratton Intercontinental. From 1980 through 1983, the series was renamed "Group and Family Therapy – An Overview." Wolberg and I felt it would be advantageous for practitioners to become aware of the considerable overlap between certain aspects of the two fields (cf. Couples Groups).

Each volume was dedicated to a professional who we felt had made important contributions to either group or family therapy or both. It might be interesting to enumerate these honorees at this time: Nathan Ackerman, Emanuel Schwartz, Jacob

Moreno, Donald Jackson, S.H. Foulkes, Paul Schilder, M. Peter Laquer, Wilfred Bion, Eric Berne, and Samuel Slavson. Bion, Foulkes, Moreno, Schilder, Schwartz, and Slavson were honored principally for their work in group therapy. The other four were selected for their contributions to family therapy.

As I achieved greater proficiency in my clinical practice of Combined Therapy, I became increasingly dissatisfied with the state of group therapy theories. Bion and Ezriel, two of the leading theoreticians, had, as far as I could tell, very little experience leading therapy groups of adults in private practice settings. Foulkes' writings seemed somewhat more pertinent but they tended, in my opinion, to overemphasize group dynamics. Wolf and Schwartz provided a salutary emphasis on individuals' dynamics in the group but they had relatively little to say about employing individual and group analysis in tandem.

In the course of organizing and administering the training program at Postgraduate Center, I tried to develop more effective ways of teaching group therapy and especially Combined Therapy to our students. The traditional regimen in psychoanalytic institutes had typically consisted of a combination of personal psychoanalysis, course work and clinical supervision, individually and in a group. This model often worked well in teaching the complicated skills required of a psychodynamic therapist. The drawbacks, however, are that it can inhibit the supervisee's independent creativity and foster excessive rigidity in the hierarchical structure of the institutes. Traditional supervision should in my opinion be accompanied by opportunities to observe senior group therapists working with live groups. Observational opportunities are pervasive in the training of physicians and attorneys. They also exist in the training of family therapists. Psychoanalytic group therapists, because of their awareness of the influences of unconscious countertransferential reactions, sometimes are skittish about having their interventions scrutinized by peers.

From the outset, I encouraged candidates of the Group Department to observe senior group therapists at work. At first, various faculty members would lead groups behind a one-way mirror. This presented a problem because some group patients found it difficult to attend the group at a designated daytime hour. In later years, improvements in technology allowed students to observe and discuss previously taped sessions. Often the actual group leader was available to discuss the observed session. On other occasions, a second senior instructor would discuss the session.

An interesting outcome of these sessions was that senior therapists, *regardless of their theoretical orientations*, would intervene essentially in the same way. It seems that at a given moment in an on-going group there is a definite limit to the number of effective interventions that can be made by competent therapists.

An important training innovation of the Group Department is an annual 3-Day Workshop dealing with some aspect of psychodynamic group therapy. These workshops which have been offered each spring for the past 53 years are attended by candidates and by strongly motivated therapists from all parts of the United States and abroad. Registrants participate in small groups, usually led by two leaders that meet five times over the weekend. In addition, they are offered the opportunity to observe another group led by a senior therapist. As a result of participation in these annual workshops candidates and other professionals are given the opportunity to deal with any personal issues that might be impinging on their work and to personally observe how a variety of skilled therapists handle emergent clinical phenomena. Isaac

"Zeke" Youcha has been exceptionally skilled at leading observation groups and has repeatedly demonstrated his skills over a period of many years.

Each Autumn, candidates, faculty and invited colleagues attend an annual Weekend Retreat. These two-day retreats are held in various towns on Long Island, New York. They have been effectively organized by Jerome Leff for more than 45 consecutive years. In addition to providing ample opportunities to interact with colleagues and with senior faculty members, these retreats have been highly instrumental in fostering and maintaining an atmosphere of friendliness and collegiality within the Department.

As indicated above, I feel that the basic ingredients in group therapy training and practice are personal group therapy; individual and group supervision; familiarity with theoretical formulations of group therapy and group dynamics; and, direct observation of experienced group therapists at work. To these experiences, I would add a special focus on the "nitty gritty" of treatment planning. Most of this planning takes place in the therapist's mind. It cannot be ascertained by simply observing the leaders interventions during group sessions.

I have attempted to highlight this aspect of group therapy in various courses and have written a number of articles outlining my ideas regarding it. The first step in Combined Therapy is obviously to form a working alliance with the patient. Fortunately, ample literature on this aspect of treatment is available in textbooks on psychodynamic therapy. I have found that group therapists often underestimate the emotional demands which are placed on patients when they move from individual therapy into a group. Even experienced group therapists can become overwhelmed by intense multiple transferences, identifications and projective identifications upon entry into a group. Therapeutic progress can be greatly facilitated if the leader orients the patient as to how to obtain maximal benefit from the group that he/she is about to enter. This orientation is based upon the therapist's formulation of the patient's core psychodynamics as revealed in the prior individual sessions. Mostly this preparation takes place during regular sessions. Some therapists supplement their preparations with relevant written material.

In training group therapists, I urge them to search for the repetitive actions which patients employ to contain their anxieties. (I have referred to these repetitive actions in various journal articles, as Core Behavioral Sequences – CBS's.) First, I ask them to ascertain the patient's characteristic interpersonal maneuvers. Then, we try to determine the specific external stimuli which precipitated particular interpersonal maneuvers. Whenever anxiety or turbulent emotionality, indications of anxiety, are manifested, we try to determine the underlying fantasies or impulses which have been evoked. Then we determine the defense mechanisms which have been automatically activated by the patient.

The anxieties which I focus on in psychodynamic therapy are usually based on fantasies of what would transpire if the patient drew closer to another individual. In working with phobic patients, I try to determine the fearful fantasies aroused by particular inanimate objects (e.g., planes, bridges, elevators, small spaces, etc.). Interpretations of the underlying fantasies are repeatedly pointed out by the therapist and eventually amplified by the other group markers. Finally, both therapist and group members recommend more effective ways of coping with the patient's anxieties and achieve greater interpersonal gratifications.

It is most important that the therapists look into his own countertransferences to the patients to make sure that he is not placing the patient into a group to avoid feelings of frustration about the course of the individual treatment. Also, some therapists who are overenthusiastic about the group modality are prone to place their patients into groups much too soon. A good rule of thumb is not to refer a patient to a group unless he/she has made substantial progress in prior individual therapy and is highly motivated to learn more about his or her personality dynamics. Needless to say, the therapist, prior to placing a patient into a group, should make sure that the group is minimally resistant and is operating at its optimal level of efficiency.

In recognition of my leading the Postgraduate Group Therapy Program, the National Registry of Certified Group Therapists in 2006, presented me with an "Award for Outstanding Contributions in Education and Training in the Field of Group Therapy."

Since retiring from the directorship of the Group Department, I have continued my full-time practice in Manhattan and in Mount Vernon, New York (about 15 miles away). During this period, I have become especially interested in the effects of aging on the Combined Therapy process. I have found that the aging therapist, assuming he or she is functioning at a high level, can provide certain ingredients that the younger therapist often cannot.

The aging therapist can provide inspiration and hope to the middle-aged patient who has experienced serious declines in the functioning of his or her older parents and fears that aging inevitably leads downhill. Many patients who were raised by absent or dysfunctional parents had the good fortune to be rescued by grandparents or other older individuals in their environment. The reactivation of this pattern via interaction with an older therapist can be very ego-enhancing. Finally, for lack of a better term, a competent older therapist can provide "wisdom" as a result of having experienced a wider range of experiences than the younger therapist.

The aging factor can also exercise a powerful influence on the therapists' countertransferential feelings. Some therapists feel comfortable with a patient who is a generation younger but are uneasy in working with patients who are two generations younger. The therapist may feel quite at ease with patients of his or her age, but by the same token, identify too much with these patients' insecurities. Increasingly, I find myself dealing in my clinical work with tensions that have developed between older patients and their adult children. There is very little written about these problems in either the popular or professional literature. Hopefully, as therapists gain more clinical experience with these issues, guidelines will become more available.

Another set of problems that have engaged my interest lately have to do with mandatory retirement (I have given a number of workshops on this topic). Individuals who have had a powerful impact on others most of their adult lives often find it extremely depressing that the people with whom they currently interact do not provide the respectful mirroring to which they had become accustomed and which had previously enhanced their functioning. A positive sharing of experience in a homogenous group, not necessarily accompanied by therapeutic interpretations, can be extremely salutary for these individuals.

I continue to find the private practice of Combined Therapy to be most satisfying. I believe that I am doing better therapeutic work than earlier. I see no reason to cease working as a therapist as long as my health holds up. I am extremely grateful that I have, from the outset of my career, earned my livelihood as a private practitioner and that no employer is in a position to decide when I should stop doing what interests me. Since I can control the amount of time I work and can select the kind of caseload that engages me, I do not feel held back from engaging in a wide variety of gratifying activities in my personal life.

None of this would have been possible without a long and most gratifying relationship with my wife, Helen. We have been married a very long time (around the same time as the State of Israel was established) and see ourselves as soul mates. We are fortunate to get along very well with our children and grandchildren and often visit or go on joint vacations with them. Our son David lives in Southern California and practices as a psychologist. His children are Claire and Neil. Our daughter is an official of the Development Staff of Brandeis University. Her sons Benjamin and Joshua live with her in Lexington, Massachusetts. I am increasingly impressed with the cliché that was often repeated by my grandparents: "The most important thing is your health!"

When I compare our current understanding of group therapy processes to the state of knowledge sixty years ago, I am quite impressed with the progress we have made. Numerous textbooks, anthologies and excellent articles in such publications as the International Journal of Group Therapy and GROUP – The Journal of the Eastern Group Psychotherapy Society, have added numerous insights to our field. Yet, as a private practitioner, I am often appalled by the ignorance about group therapy that still prevails among many patients and some individual therapists. One factor accounting for this state of affairs has been a long-standing resistance on the part of the individual psychoanalytic community. Psychodynamic group therapy did not appear on the scene until World War II or shortly thereafter. By that time, individual psychoanalysis had become firmly entrenched in medical schools and university settings. Many chairpersons of the major psychiatry departments were graduates of psychoanalytic institutes.

In the early days of the group therapy movement, most presidents of the American Group Psychotherapy Association were psychiatrists. Interpretations in psychodynamic groups mainly focused on projections onto the leader or the group-as-a-whole. It seemed obvious to therapists at the time that the most effective interventions consisted of intense interaction between the individual patient and a highly trained, highly credentialed practitioner. The fact that some prominent group leaders during the encounter movement were personally flamboyant and possessed dubious academic credentials did not help matters. Group therapy was generally considered helpful for patients in need of socialization but was thought to be too "diluted" or undisciplined to be taken seriously by most influential practitioners of the day.

Therapists who worked exclusively in one-to-one therapy had difficulty in accepting the idea that group therapy formats could not only elicit a wider range of transferences and identifications, but if employed by a sophisticated therapist, provide unique advantages in working through patients' core conflicts. The first therapists to understand this were those individuals who had obtained substantial expertise as individual therapists prior to their leadership of therapy groups. The Postgraduate Center's Group Therapy Department was truly a pioneer in that it offered a "Specialty Training Program in Psychodynamic Group Therapy" open only to therapists who had already developed competences as dynamically-oriented psychotherapists.

Most patients who I screen for therapy these days, have only a dim awareness of the potentialities of group therapy to help them deal with their core issues. Those individuals who spontaneously request group treatment tend to regard themselves as repositories of a cluster of symptoms and they often state that they have been diagnosed as possessing one or more of the most common DSM IV diagnoses. They may ask for "support groups" for generalized anxiety, phobias, depression, OCD, gambling, eating disorders, bereavement or the like. It is only after considerable individual therapeutic work that they begin to understand that their symptoms reflect disequilibrium in the coping mechanisms they characteristically employ to deal with untoward impulses and fantasies and in their efforts to achieve gratification in interactions with significant others.

Training of psychodynamic group therapists should, I believe, follow the model established by the Postgraduate Center Specialty Training Program in Psychodynamic Group Therapy. It will probably be necessary to make future programs less time-demanding since it looks as if most candidates in the future will need to hold full-time jobs during their training. The main change I would recommend is that such programs pay more attention to the treatment planning aspects of psychodynamic group therapy. Greater emphasis should be placed on how to select the best group constellation in which to elicit and work through those of the patient's central dynamics that have emerged in prior individual sessions.

Irrespective of the type of groups they lead, all future group therapists could, I believe, benefit from exposure to personal group therapy conducted by experienced leaders; knowledge of basic psychodynamic thinking; familiarity with small group thinking (especially leadership research); as well as competence in the application of time-tested cognitive behavioral techniques.

References and Bibliography

Aronson, M. L. (1954). Review of fundamental concepts in clinical psychology by G. Wilson Shaffer & Richard S. Lazarus. *American Journal of Psychotherapy*.

Aronson, M. L. (1964). Technical problems in combined therapy. *International Journal of Group Psychotherapy*, 14, 425–432.

Aronson, M. L. (1964). Acting out in individual and group psychotherapy. *J Hillside Hosp*, 1, 43–49.

Aronson, M. L. (1965). Organization of programs of conjoint psychotherapy in mental hygiene clinics. *Psychiatry Quart 39 (Supple)*, 299–310.

Aronson, M. L. (1967). Resistance in individual and group psychotherapy. *Am J Psychotherapy*, 21, 86–94.

Aronson, M. L. (1958). Discussion of paper by Blatner on patient selection in group therapy. *Voices*, 4, 93–95.

Aronson, M. L. (1971). *How to overcome your fear of flying*. New York: Hawthorn Books.

Aronson, M. L. (1972). Intensifying the group process: Techniques to raise intensity. *Psychiatry Ann*, 2(39), 56.

Aronson, M. L. (1972). Intensifying the group process: Certain theoretical considerations. *International Mental Health Research Newsletter, Postgraduate Center for Mental Health*, 14(1).

Aronson, M. L. (1973). A group process for overcoming the fear of flying. In L.R. Wolberg & E.K. Schwartz, (Eds.), *An overview*. New York: Intercontinental book Corporation.

Aronson, M. L. (1975). The leader's role in focusing. In L. Liff, (Ed.) *The leader in the group* (pp. 151–160). New York: Jason Aronson.

Aronson, M. L. (1978). Developments in psychotherapy during the past 25 years: An overview. *Colloquium: Journal of the Postgraduate Center for Mental Health, 1*(1), 7–8.

Aronson, M. L. (1979). Short-term approaches for overcoming the fear of flying. *Colloquium: Journal of the Postgraduate Center for Mental Health, 2*(6), 58–60.

Aronson, M. L. (1988). Discussion of "One Clinician's Thoughts about Paradoxical Invariants in Individual and Family Therapy" by C. Kahn, *Psychoanalysis and Psychotherapy, 6*(1), 77–78.

Aronson, M. L. (1989). Discussion of "Working with the Fragile Patient in the Initial Phases of Group Therapy" by J. L. Kleinberg. *Psychoanalysis and Psychotherapy, 7*, 59–62.

Aronson, M. L. (1990). A group therapist's perspectives on the use of supervisory groups in the training of psychotherapists. *Psychoanalysis and Psychotherapy, 8*, 88–94.

Aronson, M. L. (1990). Integrating Moreno's psychodrama and psychoanalytic group therapy. *Journal of Group Psychotherapy and Pyschodrama*, 199–203.

Krasner, J., Feldman, B., Liff, Z., Mermelstein, I., Aronson, M.L., & Guttman, O. (1970). Observing the observers. *International Journal of Group Psychotherapy, 14*, 214–217.

37

Group Psychotherapy with High-Functioning Adults Or, People Like Me!*

Bonnie J. Buchele

We spend a considerable amount of time being at odds with ourselves and with others – in conflict of one kind or another. Sometimes internal conflict leads to creativity but when it is painful and destructive or tears at our relationships, we struggle, and the quality of our lives is lessened. We also spend much of our lifetime in groups of one kind or another; they have the capacity to foster creativity and cause injury. My early life included some traumatic group experiences related to my family, the healing from which was facilitated by membership in many music performance groups (Buchele, 2008). Having internalized many of my good and bad experiences in group settings likely accounted, at least in part, for my attraction to learning about group psychotherapy at the beginning of my career at The Menninger Clinic.

In the following chapter, I will describe the theoretical orientation with which I worked in the early years and illustrate it with a brief clinical example taken from a book co-authored by me and my teacher and mentor, Ramon Ganzarain (Ganzarain and Buchele, 1989). The evolution of my theoretical perspective during the intervening years until today has been deeply influenced by my becoming a psychoanalyst. In other words, I was a practising group psychotherapist long before I was a psychoanalyst, combining two professions and professional groups that often do not relate well to one another while doing it in the reverse order, that is, group training followed by psychoanalytic training rather than the other way round, the order usually followed by those few individuals who do embrace training for both types of psychological treatment. I will explicate the evolution of my theoretical perspective in conducting psychotherapy groups for high-functioning adults and leading organizational or task groups, ending with how I would today understand the same clinical example originally discussed in 1989.

---

* This is a playful reference to my early days in mental health wherein I discovered that all of us, clinicians and patients, were more alike than different.

The Wiley-Blackwell Handbook of Group Psychotherapy, First Edition. Edited by Jeffrey L. Kleinberg.
© 2012 John Wiley & Sons, Ltd. Published 2012 by John Wiley & Sons, Ltd.

Interested in group psychotherapy in response to experiences as a music therapist at the Menninger Clinic in the 1960s and 1970s, I studied group psychotherapy under Ramon Ganzarain. We joined forces to treat and study incest survivors. At that time very little was known about this population. I was motivated from my personal perspective as a feminist (Lerner, 1976) and Ramon desired to pick up where Freud left off when he turned away from the seduction theory (Freud, 1931). Ramon was primarily an object relations theorist and clinician (Ganzarain, 1989) with an interest in general systems and group-as-a-whole theories (Ganzarain, 1977). We found object relations theory to be helpful in understanding how trauma in people's lives affects their internal worlds and then, their relationships with others. Little did we know that several decades later, neuroscientific findings would indicate that object relationships are stored in implicit memory, but more about this later.

Object Relations Theory: The Early Building Blocks

We are born seeking relationships with others which we then take in, making those experiences ours internally (Klein, 1946). This basic concept is dramatically evident when a child has been abused emotionally, physically or sexually by a trusted adult over time. The child can experience the abuse in a multiplicity of ways, but the totality of those experiences, each of which includes a self-experience, an experience of another/an object and an affect (Kernberg, 1966) is internalized. The close relationship between family member and child is intricate and ambivalent, then, containing many object relationships. In the incestuous family, these relationships can include the raging adult and the terrified child as well as the needy parent and the omnipotent child. A less obvious one is the wounded parent favoring the preferred child, each member of the dyad providing glowing narcissistic supplies for the other (Ganzarain and Buchele, 1989). Our patients, the incest survivors, were experienced as difficult patients, but were often misdiagnosed as borderline or accurately diagnosed as borderline with little or no emphasis on childhood trauma (Gabbard, 2000) because patients and clinicians alike overlooked or omitted the trauma in their histories. Our work with them, both in homogeneous groups and general groups, included quickly shifting, kaleidoscopic transferences, intense countertransferences, considerable acting out and, characteristically, scattered, unintegrated senses of self. Internal object worlds were played out on the stage of the group, at times chaotic and deskilling for the therapists. When understood theoretically and that understanding shared with the patients over time, however, the patients got better.

The work was exciting because we began to discover that what a number of theorists in other contexts had said before us had utility in facilitating these patients' improvement. Bion (1961) had postulated that the emotional life of an individual in a group was comparable to the experience of an infant with psychotic-like anxieties when interacting with the breast. Therefore, consistent with the primitive nature of this regressive experience in group psychotherapy, part-object transferences abounded and primitive defense mechanisms such as projective identification and splitting were expectable, a discovery that had been described by Ezriel (1952). As the clinical example below demonstrates, we found this to be the case. Ezriel opined that each group member projects his/her own unconscious fantasy-objects into other group members and is the recipient of these same projective identificatory defensive processes from others, patients and therapists alike. Horwitz further delineated these processes in his 1983 paper (Horwitz, 1983) where he discusses role suction, a concept first proposed by Redl (1963), as well as spokesperson and scapegoating. A description of a session during this period of my work follows:

> Karen's impulse to control the group had been gaining momentum for months. She would come late, leave early, and glower in silence, or have outbursts of anger at both therapists. Occasionally, she gave evidence of her perception that the therapists were ignoring her, rather than vice versa. . . . Examining her exchanges with Anna revealed that Karen was accusing Anna of abusing her with silent indifference, exactly as her father had. Karen's identification with the aggressor then became evident. In a private discussion precipitated by our frustration with this patient's controlling behavior, we diagnosed these unconscious defense mechanisms (and object relations). Realizing that any intervention made by the male therapist would be rejected out of hand, we agreed that the female therapist would confront Karen with her intimidating behavior and the group with their fearful response. We hoped that this would start the working through process.
>
> In the next session, Karen continued her angry, controlling behavior. As we attempted to interact with her, she furiously arose to leave the room. The female therapist then told Karen that she was intimidating everyone with her behavior. Karen halted, her hand on the doorknob. The word intimidation had brought an expression of astonishment to her face. Just as Karen hesitated at the door, before leaving silently, there was a remarkable release of tension in the room. As she left, everyone commented, for the first time . . . how intimidated they had been by her. Group members agreed with the therapist's confrontation and elaborated on it with a noncritical and understanding attitude. The matter-of-fact tone of the therapist's confrontation was serving them as a model.
>
> The following sessions were not characterized by an atmosphere of intimidation. Initially Karen participated silently. She said she would now be able to remain through entire sessions, adding, "I shall eventually be able to talk with you but right now do not talk to me, because I may not yet be able to take it." Although her words were addressed to both therapists, nonverbal indications made clear that she was talking primarily to the male therapist. The other members accepted and supported Karen without fearing her; no longer were they under her control (Ganzarain and Buchele, 1989).

Self-Psychology: Cohesion from the Scatter

We also found that the work of Heinz Kohut helped us to understand the psychopathology resulting from severe trauma. He describes how healthy self-esteem develops and is maintained when people close to us validate our sense of worth, that is: serve as good self objects (Kohut, 1968). Horwitz (1984) extended this concept into the arena of the group, postulating that belonging to a group can have significant positive impact on self-image through partnering, for example, having and actualizing the wish for experience of a mature, reciprocal relationship, and mirroring, such as, receiving and transmitting perceptions of the self. Sometimes hidden parts of the individual are disclosed in this way within the group environment facilitating the development of the sense of cohesiveness and higher self-esteem. In the group, being valued, needed and seen as desirable by others as well as being capable of contributing to others' welfare, give the self-esteem a boost. Without the mirroring back to us that affirms our sense of worth the psychological and bodily sense of self suffers. As we understood the extent to which our patients were struggling with the underdevelopment and damage to their sense of self, occurring as part of the childhood abuse, we sought to promote awareness of their numerous self states, and a better integration of them by facilitating the mirroring and partnering as well as offering self-objects within the group.

Where Does the Acting Out Come From?

The addition of attachment theory and neuroscience

In working with traumatized people, a primary clinical challenge contributing to its difficult nature was their inability to contain affect which could lead to acting out. Understanding of affect containment and acting out as well as how to work with these phenomena clinically took a leap forward with the findings of neuroscience in the study of the development of the brain and its relationship to attachment and human development in general, as reported by Cozolino (2002) and Schore (2003). We knew that when incest had occurred, most frequently it was but one manifestation of a disturbed family system. Usually the perpetrator was a male, but the relationship between mother and child was also troubled and we wrestled with how to understand it fairly – without blaming the mother in a misogynist-oriented way. Neuroscientific studies have revealed that the development of the right brain is extremely important and has shed significant light on the subject.

The capacity to regulate affect and the stress response are both located in the right brain; they are greatly impacted by the attachment relationship between caregiver and infant, and are experience dependent (Schore, 2003). During the first three years of life, the development of the right hemisphere is dependent on the emotional attunement of the primary caregiver to the infant. When mother can be attuned to the infant's distress and respond with appropriate soothing, the child internalizes an expectation that the disruption in emotional homeostasis will be righted – a healthy rhythm develops, distress leads to an expectation and experience of relief, and gradually this is internalized as a mature capacity to contain and regulate affect. When development goes well, the autonomic nervous system containing both sympathetic and parasympathetic arousal are coupled appropriately and are mutually responsive to one another, the child feels securely attached to the mother, and the capacity to contain affect and self-regulate is internalized.

We had observed for a long time that the mother of the incest patient was often unavailable emotionally for various reasons to comfort the abused child, but had not known that, related to the family disturbance, literally the development of the right brain of our patients may have been negatively impacted by an insecure or disorganized attachment which in turn resulted in affect dysregulation. The possibility opened up that, at least for some, the difficulty to contain and regulate affect that contributed to the acting out had a basis in the development of the brain and the capacity to securely attach. In addition, the stress response is located in the right brain and a hallmark of having experienced trauma is a severe dysregulation of both sympathetic and parasympathetic arousal. Thus, understanding broadened to include the fact that right brain development in persons traumatized in childhood was often negatively impacted as a result of caretaker misattunement leading to an insecure attachment and ongoing trauma activating the stress response located in the right brain as well. No wonder containing affect and self-regulation were problematic!

For the first time, an answer to the vexing question of why the same traumatic experience for two people might result in post-traumatic stress disorder for one and not for the other began to emerge: the best insurance against post-traumatic stress disorder is a secure attachment with a primary caregiver in childhood (Schore, 2003). When childhood abuse occurs it is usually within the context of lack of a consistent sense of security with caregivers. The research has also indicated that the right hemisphere is central to self-recognition and a coherent, consistent, cohesive sense of self, thus adding research support to early experiences in our groups that the sense of self in our patients was vulnerable to a scattered experience and lack of integration prior to trauma. The findings also yielded hope, however, and helped explain why our patients often improved even though the work was hard. Because of the brain's neuroplasticity, therapy that includes the experience of a secure attachment can impact the ability to contain affect and achieve improved self-regulation, thereby decreasing acting out and attaining a more fully integrated sense of self. When the therapist is able to be emotionally attuned, the attachment becomes more secure, the trauma is converted from implicit to explicit memory via the use of words, changes occur in the brain and the patient grows healthier.

The neuroscientific findings regarding the development of the right brain were compelling and immensely illuminating in their application to the traumatized population. This knowledge affirmed my clinical experience and led me to a fuller appreciation of the role of attachment in the development of psychopathology in general. Thus, I began to extend the use of attachment theory and right brain development as well as object relations and self-psychology to work with groups of high-functioning adults, without histories of traumatization. Now let me describe several clinical examples of treatment of individuals in a general group for highly functioning adults.

Clinical Illustrations

In an ongoing general group, use of self-psychology and attachment theory integrated with object relations theory has been quite helpful in understanding several individuals and their relationships with group members as well as outside the group.

Walter

Walter is an intelligent man in his fifties. He is highly trained in contemporary technology and is quite successful but he does not feel successful; his self-esteem is low and sense of shame great. He is involved in a longstanding chronically dissatisfying marriage. Although he has been in psychotherapy, either individual or group, for many years, he feels despondent about his life and says that therapy has not been particularly helpful. On the other hand, he says that group psychotherapy is much better for him than individual. For a brief period he participated in a combination of individual therapy and group psychotherapy, but withdrew from individual sessions, saying he could not justify such a large expenditure. However, he continues to regularly attend group, offers meaningful insights to others and intermittently works on himself in sessions. Walter does not feel understood when the therapist or group members comment on his positive qualities, trying to give him hope. Very easily the transference object relationship evoked in response to helpers is that of an arbitrary, righteous authority figure condemning him for an inadequacy – a condemnation that is shaming and one against which he must fight. Puzzled by how to help this stubbornly sad man, I began to realize that his attachment style is an avoidant one. Feeling attached puts him at risk for being quickly catapulted into a state of despair when the slightest misattunement occurs. I see him as having an attachment style in which the imbalance is comprised of a parasympathetic dominance resulting in an avoidant style evidenced by a low level of emotional expression, infrequent eye contact and a propensity to withdraw. In the group the attachment is less threatening; for one thing, no matter what his self-state, almost always someone understands and can be more attuned to him in the nuanced way he so needs. His alliance with the group improved once I told him that, as I understood him, the problem was not that he could not love others, but that when he did, he immediately experienced an insecurity that they would stay with him and be attuned to him so he would avoid them and other attachments. He and group members have found this helpful in their relationships with one another. Group members have been less insistent that he be optimistic since they understand how much risk feeling hopeful entails for him.

Stephanie

Stephanie is in her late fifties, a retired employee at the management level in an industry with significant sex bias. She, too, is quite smart, but extremely depressed. Her despondency can become so consuming that she stays in her home for days, failing to get dressed and playing computer games. Given her prior work history and capacity to function at a high level, she finds these episodes of immobilization mystifying and shameful. In group sessions, her eyes are taken off the therapist for only short periods, a behavior acknowledged by the leader and group members alike. This surveillance of the leader is not emanating from devaluation of other group members. Rather, she can have a negative maternal transference to me as the unwanted, inadequate daughter of a rejecting mother exacerbated by my referring her to a colleague for individual psychotherapy when she requested that I be both her individual therapist and her group therapist. The daughter of a mother who could become depressed herself and who felt threatened if her daughter acted in any way that reflected badly on her but also fostered the mutual experience of a stifling psychological cocoon, Stephanie is attached to me with wariness that is part of an insecure attachment style that bespeaks a dominance of dramatic shifts in sympathetic and parasympathetic arousal: in group sessions, when sympathetic arousal is high, she must keep her eyes on me at all times! Her vigilance of me seems necessary for two reasons:

1. she feels she must be watchful to ascertain that I am attending to her, and
2. she also needs to be on the alert for indications that I might shame her.

Despite her sympathetic arousal in my presence, once we are apart or I am not attuned, her insecure attachment is dominated by a parasympathetic arousal; she perceives me as not responding or at risk of being shamed by me. She withdraws, talking about herself in soft tones, at a slow pace and with lowered eyes. She treasures group members' input and her interaction with others is valued by them. Her abilities to function well in tasks with men, to be a good mother facilitating a secure attachment with her son and have a more secure attachment to the group may be due to a more secure attachment with her step-father at an early age. Security with him seems to have enabled her to experience a sense of earned autonomy on which she is able to rely in parenting her child and in some other areas.

Ona

Ona is an educator in her early sixties. Despite a history of anxiety and even panic attacks beginning in childhood, as well as disparate, unintegrated self experiences that contribute to her alternating states of lack of confidence and rebellion, her level of professional development is notable and she has maintained a successful marriage while raising healthy children. She grew up in a family where she was assigned the role of the "fragile" one and felt that she was different from her parents, especially her mother, and siblings – that she was "on the outside." I believe that this is her way of describing having been insecurely attached to her mother. The family had little vocabulary for emotions, but rather believed that feelings were signs of weakness to be risen above. Ona lived in a constant state of fear that if she did not do exactly as her mother wanted her to, something dreadful would happen to her. Yet, she felt lightheaded on many occasions, a symptom of her protest. The only way she could refuse what her parents insisted she act on was to become dizzy, requiring that she stop doing whatever she was doing. She now knows that she was anxious a fair amount of the time and needed to lodge a protest, but felt unsafe to do so openly; her dizzy episodes expressed this conflict. Ona also has significant gaps in her childhood memories and recently has begun to wonder why this would be so, asking herself if some traumatic happenings could have occurred that she needs not to remember.

Ona does everything fast. In the group she presents her dilemmas talking at breathtaking speed often giving no opportunity for anyone to interact with her. She is hypervigilant, being especially aware of nonverbal communication and looking for ways in which others might disagree with or disapprove of her. She has large amounts of energy, but also is often struggling with anxiety offering enormous amounts of detail when recounting her dilemmas. Initially when other members tried to clarify what it was that she wanted from them, she felt criticized by their inquiry. And if the therapist participated in this attempt at clarification, her eyes would widen much like a frightened deer, caught in headlights. At those moments her transference seemed to consist of expecting I would disapprove, withdraw from or even "disown" her if she in any way was noncompliant, an object relationship much like an outrageously demanding, arbitrary ruler and a terrified, compliant, non-complaining subject. Admiring her for her dedication to working hard in life and in her treatment and genuinely fond of this engaging woman, the group persisted despite her voiced interpretation of their queries as criticisms. Finally she responded that it was important for her to give the details so others would know that her feelings were justified and she would not have to be ashamed. She was shocked when all responded by telling her that her feelings needed no justification; it was sufficient that they belonged to her. As she lessened her "justifications," their response has been to be able to be attuned to her and she to them. It would appear that Ona was mismatched with her caretakers, who successfully managed life struggles and the attendant feelings with denial. She needed understanding to master the anxiety, something to which they could not be attuned. Ona, like Stephanie, has been able to establish and maintain a secure attachment later in life, in her case with her husband, who is almost always available to talk things through with her until resolution can be achieved. Thus, with this security she too has obtained an earned autonomy which has enabled her to parent effectively and maintain a healthy marriage. As she achieves a more secure attachment to the group, she is exploring aspects of her relationships that were outside her awareness despite years of therapy. It is indeed possible that some traumatic events occurred while she was very young and that the insecure attachment played a role in their not being spoken; thus, they may be unformulated and unthought until now.

Lowell

Lowell is in his late thirties and has been depressed for a decade. His withdrawal was severe following a divorce and the death of both his parents in the same year. He has no social life and little contact with his siblings, although he speaks with fondness of other living family members. His career is in business, but he is isolated except for the small group of co-workers from whom he keeps distance. Lowell's capacity to blame himself is noteworthy. He grew up in a large family, the child of substance abusers. He struggles mightily with his anger and feelings of self-loathing. He is ashamed of his hermit-like existence and blames himself for his limited career advancement. A positive result of a brief period of individual therapy before joining the group was his willingness to attribute some of his difficulties negotiating life to being depressed.

After joining the group he began his participation slowly, initially giving astute but kindly spoken feedback to other members as they worked on their difficulties. As group members began to grow fond of him, he shared more about his internal world. His mood started to improve and there were signs of his depression lessening. Then the group shifted into a period of time when Lowell shared little, participating nonverbally, but only commenting on the dilemmas of others and seldom even doing that. Finally at the beginning of a session when the other male members were absent so that the group consisted of Lowell and the women, one of them asked how he was doing. Heaving a large sigh, Lowell began by saying he had been fearful of discussing something that had been bothering him for weeks. With deliberation Lowell then recounted a story of how he had, years before, been pulled aside by a supervisor and told that someone had complained that he had been engaging in sexual harassment. Lowell was horrified because he could not imagine how any of his behavior could be construed as sexual harassment, nor who would say such a thing; in fact, he had been enjoying his co-workers and he had believed that they all liked him. The supervisor stated that the person or the exact complaint could not be divulged, but that Lowell should be exemplary in his behavior going forward. Since that time, Lowell had intentionally withdrawn even more and isolated himself in fear and anger, trusting no one while becoming more and more depressed. He went on to wonder aloud what he could have done and worrying that his judgment was impaired in some way. He had even worried that maybe he was "psychopathic," hurting people and possessing a poorly functioning conscience. Rather quickly one of the women in the group who had worked for many years in law enforcement, succinctly commented, "I am qualified to identify a psychopath. I can smell one a mile away and there's absolutely no way that you qualify!" Her comment was made with a tone of endearment, laced with humor. Lowell looked at her in amazement, realizing that what

> she was saying about her own experience was correct and then the relief was apparent in his face. The others laughed but then empathized with the unfair position he had been put in, especially the fact that his withdrawal had been necessary in a practical sense as well as a psychological one. The mirroring provided by all the group members, but especially the commenting member, initiated a period of growth for Lowell wherein he shared more freely about himself in sessions and began to attend a few social events in the rest of his life.

The Evolution of My Personal Group Theory

In the previous sections, I have addressed primarily the development of my theoretical formulations about how individuals make characterological changes. Now I will talk about the evolution of my understanding of group life, including the role of therapy groups in helping people change and the application of group psychotherapy principles to administrative or task groups. First, let us look at the psychotherapy group and its therapeutic action. As I said, I formally became a psychoanalyst rather late in my career, quite a while after I began practicing group psychotherapy. I obtained my training and started practicing psychoanalysis just at the time that a relational perspective within psychoanalytic thinking was on its ascendancy. My experience was that much of what I had been a part of and observed in groups – the importance of a relational context in understanding oneself and others – was finally being discussed and elaborated in psychoanalytic circles; I have loved that confluence of my two worlds. I believe the intrapsychic world of the individual can only be understood in relational terms; we are all responding internally to another person or persons. Relational concepts such as enactments, dissociation and the multiplicity of self states/experiences make sense in the world of my clinical experience with traumatized persons, the general adult population, groups and psychoanalysis. Relational theory resonates with the basic idea of systems theory – every part of a system is affected by every other part of a system so that it only makes sense that the psychotherapy group as a system includes the therapist who is embedded in the entire context with everyone else – and I really have felt a resonance between group psychotherapy and relational psychoanalysis within the clinical work.

Much of my thinking is validated by the recent neuroscientific findings that specifically relate to the functioning of the psychotherapy group. Badenoch and Cox (2010) suggest that the psychotherapy group is especially suited to be a source of regulation. Our relationships are governed by templates of implicit memory that can be changed because of the neuroplasticity of the brain. Maximization of this potential is achieved when the environment includes moderate emotional arousal, attuned interpersonal relationships, facilitation and support for exploring the experiential awareness of memories, and interpersonal experiences that disconfirm earlier relational, implicit models. The psychotherapy group that is functioning well possesses these conditions so that with the leadership of a therapist who is calm and containing, the implicit memory templates undergo change because the pattern of secure attachments within the group enables rewiring of the limbic system; emergence of memories including their emotionality allows transfer from implicit to explicit memory. Siegel (2010) adds to this conceptualization of the group as possessing a capacity to facilitate change by suggesting, that improved integration of the inner world is the goal of psychotherapy, that neuronal stimulation and growth are central to achieving increased integration, and that the conditions of compassion and empathy within the psychotherapy group can foster such change as individual members work themselves and observe others working. Flores (2010) agrees, saying that ideal conditions facilitating healthy change within the psychotherapy group include an optimal balance between security and arousal, protest and disagreement without violence or abandonment – conditions that constitute a secure group attachment which, then, facilitates improvement in self regulation.

The recent discovery of mirror neurons holds promise for the lending of support to the ideal nature of the group to facilitate characterological change. Mirror neurons are brain cells that fire in response to the actions of another, similarly to when one rehearses or performs the actions oneself. They fire in response to observing someone's goal-directed activity. Groups including psychotherapy groups seem replete with opportunities for activating the firing of mirror neurons. Schermer (2010) discusses the implications of this discovery for group psychotherapy. Most importantly, the evidence suggests that human beings are "hard-wired" to be relational, just as object relations theorists, group psychotherapists and relational psychoanalysts have been saying. Group-as-a-whole phenomena such as Bion's basic assumptions (Rioch, 1970) may then have a biological substrate based on individuals' nonreflective responses to similarities in others. Also, there are implications for the group therapist's role when one considers mirror neurons. In light of these functions, the leader would do well to be aware of ways he or she is part of the group, that is, within it rather than above it, because the leader is part of the process as Grossmark (2007a) suggests. Due to the nature of the processing done by the mirror neurons, they are more likely to fire in response to "I" statements from the therapist. Schermer (2010) suggests that group therapists may facilitate helpful mirror neuron functioning by employing interventions such as "wearing the attribution," being willing to explore with patients what it means to them if he or she is having the experience that the patient attributes to them (Lichtenberg, 2008). Not only can the patient explore the subjective experience of being with the therapist in this way, but as part of this process, the group therapist may become more aware of ways he or she is embedded in the group process. Healthy mirroring and identification may be best facilitated when an "I" intervention precedes one about the group; the latter reflects a more objective stance, since it requires awareness of the overall functioning of the group which does require some detachment. Good group psychotherapy leadership requires skillfully moving back and forth between these types of interventions. According to Flores (2010) this evidence reminds us that for the group leader paying attention to the manner in which he or she and group members express themselves is as important as what they say, both in terms of revealing information about implicit memory as well as potential activation of mirror neurons in others.

Grossmark (2007a) nicely articulates many of these concepts in different terms. In his view, from relational and dynamic systems perspectives there are multiple self states available in the group and the therapist is embedded in the inevitable group enactments that are constantly evolving within the group. An important change from prior theory here is that there is no assumption that the group therapist can stay outside the enactment, but that, in fact, he or she is inevitably involved. These enactments involve repetitive, unmentalized states that are self experiences coming from earlier in life which have not been understandable and never put into words. A major task of the treatment process is getting the enactments into words so that the "unmentalized" becomes "thinkable." By accessing different self states that are available *vis-a-vis* the meaningful relationships with other members and the therapist in the group, the enactments evolve and can be moved through. The "unmentalized" becomes "thinkable," it is put into words, new states of mutual regulation are established and a more secure type of attachment is attainable, thus facilitating change.

Another way of understanding the therapeutic action of the group is that a kind of thirdness is found through the multiplicity of group members themselves within the group. An enactment which involves a rigidity of the system is countered with a transitional space related to the presence of thirdness. The enactment is moved through and meaning emerges (Grossmark, 2007b). A subtle but important distinction in theory here is that the enactment evolves and is not lying underneath to be interpreted as would have previously been the understanding. Therefore, because the enactments occur in the natural course of events, timing is central to foster the evolving and developing of meaning. When the therapist can be attuned to the evolution and not intervene prematurely, the treatment is deepened and enriched. The "thirdness" involves creating a group space where the meaning of enactments can be explored.

In summary, then, my theoretical orientation has evolved in the following way: I began with a foundation in object relations theory blended with a background in group-as-a-whole theory and general systems theory. The context with which I began doing clinical work was with traumatized individuals in groups. I found self psychology, attachment theory and neuroscientific findings supporting and broadening these theoretical perspectives as well as the ongoing effects of traumatization, useful in my attempts to help people make characterological changes related to their trauma experiences. As my context broadened to include working with persons attempting to make characterological changes not always related to trauma, this blended theoretical view has been extremely helpful. Most recently, the relational and dynamic systems approach articulated by Grossmark (2007a) has contributed to my developing an even clearer understanding of how people might be able to make the changes that they desire and to help them do so in groups. As I see it, today relational psychoanalytic theory and the dynamic systems approach have at their core some variation of a primary concept: when two or more people interact, mutual effects on one another are inevitable and elaborating those effects, for example, opening up space for a "third" point of view, is a powerful tool in accomplishing psychological change. The neuroscientific research supports this idea because, as Denninger (2010) says, simply participating in group psychotherapy sessions changes the brain.

The Group in Action: Is it Safe to Rely on You?

This clinical example is from an ongoing group which has been meeting once per week for a number of years. There are seven members of this group with two original members, others joining at intervals. Attending the session below are three men and two women. The remaining two members are absent, one having told us the week before that he would be vacationing.

The session begins with Walter, Catherine, Lester and Sam present. As we enter my office from the waiting room, Ona comes rushing in. I have just listened to a voicemail message from her saying that she is coming, but has gotten lost on her way and might be late. I note that she has been attending group at this same location for several years so having trouble finding her way here might be worthy of exploration.

Once we are seated Sam looks directly across the room at Walter and says, "How are you doing?" Thoughtfully Walter answers, "Not well. I am coasting at work. We just completed a complicated project and now we are waiting to see if it takes off. I'm not in any trouble there. I'm just so-so. I think I might be pretty depressed for me. I just feel kinda normal for me, but down deep in there somewhere I think I'm pretty depressed. Susan is gone; she went to visit her family over the weekend. My eating is out of control. I almost didn't go to work yesterday not because I was sick but because I couldn't get my pants on. I don't think I'm suicidal or anything, but I could see me eating myself to death. A couple of times I got pretty close to making myself throw up. I'm just going through the motions. I mean what's the point. I don't see any end in sight."

I look around the room and somewhat to my surprise everyone is alert and listening intently. I, on the other hand, am experiencing a sense of hopelessness and helplessness that I have had before listening to Walter. He has been in treatment for a long time. Originally he came seeking help with bulimia, which he has been able to conquer. However, he continues to binge eat and is overweight. His marriage is unfulfilling, but he finds himself unable to make any changes in that relationship, a paralysis which extends to his not following my recommendation to add couples' counseling to his treatment regimen; he feels discouraged, hopeless and helpless. Group members are fond of him, but are aware that he does not receive help easily.

Lester asks, "When did Susan leave? How bad is the eating?" Walter looks at Lester and replies, "Susan is not with me when she's here. We just co-exist in the house." I realize that Walter has not answered Lester's question, in fact avoiding it, but is communicating his deeply felt sense of existential despair that includes no hope of things ever being better. I wonder if his avoidance will go unnoted and we will continue to lament the emptiness of Walter's life. Much to my surprise, Lester persists, "I know, but in the past when she is gone the eating is worse. How bad is it?" I feel relief. We have sidestepped getting stuck for the moment. Lester's object relationship of being the stubborn, silent kid struggling against the intrusive parent has been enacted and moved through.

Again, looking directly at Lester, Walter answers this time, "You're right. I think my pride just won't let me overeat in front of her so when she is gone I really let go. There's just no point to all of this." Remembering that Walter loves reading literature that examines the existential dilemmas of life and wanting to let him know that I hear the piercing pain of his distress, I say, "Do you mean it's an existential crisis: there isn't any meaning in anything?" Looking directly at me, he simply replies, "Yes." Ona inquires, "When was the last time you did anything with meaning?" Walter is silent and thoughtful for a short while, but then answers, "When I was mountain climbing. I mean I was close to this bunch of guys. My best friend was a machinist. He and I could climb anywhere. I didn't see them often, but there were many times when I would trust that friend with my life – in fact I would do that anytime. And also there were the times around the campfire. It's the best feeling in the world to be up there so many feet toward the sky soaring above everything." With considerable interest Ona queries, "What happened that you gave it up?" Walter responds, "In order to do it now, for starters I would have to lose 100 pounds. But when I married Susan, it would take whole weekends away from us. She didn't mind. She would actually tell me to go when I wanted to and she bought me equipment from time to time. She knew how important it was to me. But it just didn't seem right to take so much time away from us." Ona continues, "Have you ever thought of going back to it?"

At this point I repress an urge to intervene and protect him because it is so obvious that he is physically unable to return to the sport at this time and I worry he will feel shamed. I am also painfully aware that Ona can become concrete which can have the effect on the group of shutting off exploration by problem solving. In the past Walter has been annoyed with her when she does this, especially if it is done in a spirit of optimism. I also remember he can experience her as the intrusive parent. I remain quiet and, therefore, am surprised! Walter answers directly, saying "I couldn't do it right now." I notice the "right now" – he hasn't given up! "I'd have to lose at least 100 pounds first. I think, though, more than anything else there were just no more places to climb around here." I say, "So it got to be like walking the same old pathway."

Walter answers me in the affirmative and goes on, disclosing new information, "Susan and I have been seeing a couples' counselor but it just looks more and more like we should split up. We just aren't on the same page." Lester asks, once again persisting, "How would that help?" "Well, we aren't getting anywhere this way. We just aren't connected. We just can't seem to get unstuck." Catherine then volunteers, "I think you two splitting up is a very bad idea. Your eating would just get out of control and then you will just transfer the problem somewhere else." I decide to comment, "See what you think about this; I would be interested in your opinion. It seems to me that the problem is not splitting up. The problem is that when you begin to get attached and connected, very quickly you need to avoid the person – in this case, Susan, for fear she won't get you."

Walter coughs violently and I wonder if he is going to let me continue or override me as he has many times in the past, thereby avoiding deeper connection with me as well. But this time, he lets me speak and even says, "Go ahead, I want to hear what you have to say." I continue, "So many times in your life, starting with when you were very little, people were not attuned to you – they did not get you and it was so painful you just turned away. You try to avoid the connection. The misattunement for whatever reason between you and them had to be coped with and so very early, even at 2 or 3 years, you learned to try to avoid needing them because so often you had the painful experience of your parents not responding with understanding and even shaming you. It is almost wired into your brain, but the good news is that it can be changed." Catherine exclaims, "I think that is what happens with my foster daughter, Anne!" I nod in agreement.

I am pleased that I seem to have opened up a new space for Walter to think about himself because he muses, "From the time when I was little I didn't want to ask them (parents) for anything – I just wanted to do everything for myself. I was angry at them." "Yes," I say, "and that leads me to the rest of my thoughts. You would rather not have any needs, especially any connected to people. When you feel needy, you need food and eat; at least that is under your control." In a surprised tone Walter says, "I think you are right. It makes sense to me."

I then look around the room. Everyone is looking interested but silent so I say, "How is this for the rest of you?" Lester says, "I know that feeling of wanting to be close to someone, like a woman in my life I mean. And then feeling – oops! I don't want her too close because when she gets close I need to push her away. I also know how relieving it can feel to use food, like sometimes when I'm uneasy and can't tell what is wrong, I buy a bag of chips on the way home and by the time I get home, they are all gone." Catherine again joins the conversation, "My father never had any idea of what I needed." "And your mother was not very available because she was taking care of the other kids," I say. Catherine responds with a resounding "NO! She was taking care of HIM, my father!" Turning directly toward me she asks, "You say it can be changed, but how can we do that?"

I think how I should answer and then decide that reinforcing the glimmer of hope here might be helpful, so I say, "By taking the risk of having relationships. The trick is to push just a little beyond what feels safe and then understanding what is going on inside. The change really starts to take hold by having new relationships that can take many painful tries, but eventually are less disappointing." I think to myself that maybe the attachment to her father was as important as to her mother, given the gender bias toward males in her family and her subsequent identification with a male-oriented profession in choosing a career. "How is it for the rest of you? What do you think? Does avoiding as a way of coping with the hurt and being misunderstood ever serve as a way of protecting yourselves?" There is a short silence, so I address Ona directly, "I wonder if maybe that had something to do with your getting lost on your way here today." Initially in her quickly paced style Ona answers, "My sense of direction is terrible and I wasn't trying to miss." Realizing that she is feeling misunderstood and experiencing my question as an accusation that she purposefully tried not to attend the session against which she is defending herself, I clarify. "My thought was that you may have been preoccupied as you were driving because the last session in here was painful for you." Continuing to stay in her rather rigid stance when offered an opportunity to reflect that feels dangerous, she answers, "I have a terrible time knowing where I am going direction-wise." Irritated that she insists on closing the space, but sensing her behavior is related to her fear that I am trying to shame her as well as feeling that there might be some chance that she could partner with me in keeping the psychological space open to relate in a freer way, I, trying yet again, say, "True, but you have never gotten lost before and I thought avoidance might be pulling at you to help manage the fear of coming here."Ona looks thoughtful and responds, "True. Group therapy is the hardest thing I have ever done. My friends ask me how I can talk about myself in front of a bunch of people and I tell them that it is really hard. You have to trust. Parts of yourself you don't even know about come out – parts that are hidden." Suddenly Walter adds, "I don't trust anyone." Ona asks him, "Not even Bonnie?" Pensively Walter states, "I think maybe a little, only in the back of my mind, I can tell you this: I really have the feeling that if group doesn't work, that's it. I know nothing else will work. I need to speak more in here. Sometimes I let myself get by with just coasting." I then ask, "Are you also saying that sometimes we collude with you and let you get by with not talking?" He says, "Yes. Sometimes I need to be asked like Sam did today, but sometimes I have pushed you all away when you try."

There is a silence. As I look around I see everyone's eyes are downcast. After a few moments I remark, "I wonder what our silence is about." Catherine slowly says, "I am tired and at the end of my rope. Anne's so-called friends broke into my home and stole some of my things. Then she loaned them her car and they stole it." The group empathizes with her plight, expressing outrage for her, softly and respectfully offering suggestions. They ask if she has found a new place to live. She says, "I have found a new place and I will have to move without telling my daughter where I am living. She will wind up on the streets but I can't do anything else. I am so full of a crazy mix of feelings." At first I am puzzled by why this might be coming up at the end of the session and then I remember that anytime Catherine is aware of a feeling and speaks to it (she began group remarkably cut off from her feelings), we have taken a step forward in her growth and that she is proud when she is able to do so. Ona, apparently mindful of the approaching end of the session, offers support by asking, "Are you able to talk to family or friends about this?" Catherine responds, "Oh, yes, but it doesn't help much. I'm glad I have the group." I then announce, "Unfortunately, we have to stop here. See all of you next week."

Analysis: Opening Space

A primary accomplishment in the group described above is the opening up of a new space wherein members can experience parts of themselves and others that are relatively unknown or even hidden. As the session begins and Walter starts to talk I am filled with a sense of hopelessness and helplessness remembering how many years he has been in treatment and is still living with a pervasive lack of fulfillment. My experience actually may have begun before that with Ona's message that she was lost; internally I may have received her statement as an unconscious communication that she did not want to be in the group and then felt rejected and incompetent. At that beginning moment I wonder if I really am capable of helping these people or am I doomed to fail. I also am acutely aware of Walter's avoidant attachment style and wonder if he will need to withdraw as others try to help him. I expect them to be overwhelmed and discouraged too, but as I look around the room, they are not. Indeed, they are interested in his plight. Lester, who can be quiet, inquires about Walter's eating and his relationship. When Walter answers Lester's question in an avoidant way, Lester is not deterred, but persists. He is not afraid of Walter's avoidant style. Maybe I am holding the despair and that less secure sense of attachment for the group and they are able to move through an avoidant enactment. And, then, Walter does not get caught up in the stubborn child/intrusive adult object relationship with the attendant enactment, but seems able to identify with Lester's curious self, looking at him repeatedly directly in the eye and elaborating on his unhappiness.

Feeling relief that we have not gotten stuck in the enactment of a problem with no solution, I intervene, hoping to deepen the work. I know that Walter loves to read novels that examine the existential dilemmas of life, especially finding meaning and I know that a part of him, when feeling safe, can respond to my being attuned to him so I comment on his existential despair. Again, with direct eye contact, he lets us know he is not ashamed, but feeling understood. Much to my surprise, Ona, who also can be insecure, queries him about what gives him a sense of meaning in his life. I have temporarily forgotten that she has an insatiable appetite for reading, especially about the more vexing aspects of the human condition. I deliberate whether I should say something, knowing that she can become concrete and attempt to problem solve which intermittently infuriates him and can herald periods of stuckness in the group. I worry that his feelings of shame about his weight will kick in – I don't want to lose the moment! But I am very pleasantly surprised. He not only is not irritated, but identifies with her hopeful self and uses it to bolster his own fragile sense of hope. A transitional space, a thirdness, is getting bigger within the group and they are seeing things somewhat differently than usual. Being joined by her and accessing her self experience of hopefulness, he seems to feel more secure and explores his inner world more freely and we learn of new, hopeful developments. He would like to return to climbing someday – that hope is alive – and he and his wife have begun seeing a couples' therapist, a new disclosure, something the group and I have gently encouraged for months, but heretofore unknown to us. I intervene with my understanding of his avoidant attachment style, capitalizing on the opportunity and a growing willingness to think differently provided by the group. I decide to elaborate more about how he uses food to satisfy needs for others and this makes sense to him. The space is made larger when Catherine comments that her daughter relates to her in this same avoidant way. I sense nonverbally as Walter casts his eyes downward, that he has done enough for the moment.

I invite others to join. Lester, Catherine and Ona, all identify with Walter's avoidance. Lester discloses his identification with Walter's avoidant self when he says he knows how it feels to be too close to a woman, but we learn about a previously hidden part of himself as well: he can binge eat in an effort to soothe himself. They are feeling safe in the group-as-a-whole as evidenced by Catherine's free and easy disagreement with me when I inaccurately described her relationship with her parents as a child. I decide to answer Catherine's direct question about how relationships can be improved because I want to respond affirmatively to her interest, I want to affirm her and because I want to sustain the shaky sense of optimism that is now existing in the room. I also am aware that I am enacting the caretaking scenario that she so often experienced in childhood of being taken care of by her mother with answers that were suitable for the men in her family but were seldom "right" for her. I am encouraged that she is lodging a protest – telling me to get it right – in a way that was not allowed growing up.

Noting the enactment, I decide to try to broaden the space, so I invite others' thoughts about the use of avoidance. In the brief silence I remember another enactment that we have not addressed: Ona's getting lost. Ona at first retreats from my wondering if she needed to avoid the group this week because the prior week was painful for her. I want to encourage an open statement of protest and make it safe enough for her to be in touch with that protesting part of herself so I pursue my inquiry. She helps further the opening of the space by articulating that group therapy is the hardest thing she ever has done because "you discover hidden parts of yourself," the mirroring and partnering transferences (Horwitz, 1984) helping her in this way. Her statement about finding hidden parts of herself leads to talking about trust in the group with a qualified and fragile acknowledgement by Walter that he may trust me "a little" and that being prodded by other members is helpful. He takes ownership of his need to avoid closeness. Finally, the safety of an open space where relatively unknown self experiences can be examined in relation to others is confirmed by Catherine's disclosure that she is having a "crazy mix of feelings" about a situation in her life. During much of her early treatment she was unable to identify any feeling, but most frequently felt numb. That she can not only be aware that she is having feelings, but is able to make herself vulnerable by acknowledging that there is, not one, but "a crazy mix," is risky for her and truly indicative of growth. And, at this point, the group can contain her hopelessness and despair, empathizing with her excruciatingly painful dilemma with her daughter.

I have used a mixture of theoretical views to understand this group session. I am aware of the object relations of the individuals, especially that there is a wealth of self experiences of worthlessness and despair often felt in relationships. I note attachment styles, keeping in mind how the neuroscientific findings support these ways of trying to stay connected and try to explicate their experiences for them in that way. I am mindful of the enactments, especially associated with despair, that have emerged and are worked through by the group and how I am embedded in them with my sometimes containing the sense of helplessness so that it is in the room, but not overwhelmingly so for the group-as-a-whole. The multiplicity of self experiences, especially the hopeful parts of themselves that can be dissociated or hidden from themselves and each other, is noteworthy. Finally, members seem to be working toward integrating their many self experiences as they see themselves mirrored by and partnered with others. I feel privileged to be allowed to participate in these intimate interactions with them.

The Challenges and Rigors of Leadership

During the period of life when I was enrolled in my first seminars in group psychotherapy, I discovered I liked being in leadership positions. It happened fortuitously.

Exiting a troubled time, the upper-level management of the Menninger Clinic sent many staff members to Tavistock Group Relations Conferences (Horwitz, 2006; Menninger, 2006). The experience I had had in music groups growing up, that everyone has a unique role and everyone counts (a principle which can be understood as a variation on general systems theory) was affirmed in this totally different setting. What I learned is that as participants, all of us have impact; the only choice, really, is what one wants the personal impact to be, not whether or not one can have one. An awareness was illuminated: opting out is not an option, but only another way of exercising one's power, usually illusory and outside one's awareness. Taking my newfound knowledge back to the Clinic, I became a more active participant in treatment team meetings, believing I had a responsibility to exercise my power as a follower and feeling valued as my feedback was utilized. In the same time frame I reluctantly agreed to become President of the local Young Women's Christian Association (YWCA), the Chief Executive Officer (CEO) of which was a female politician who intuitively understood group functioning at an unconscious level, was clear about the task at hand so that she was a whiz at administration and was at ease using her power constructively. Thus began parallel and eventually intersecting lines of development for me in my identity as a group therapist and my identity as a leader. The combination has been an invaluable one for me. Exercising my interest as well as what I was learning in my clinical work led me to subsequently assume leadership positions at the Menninger Clinic beginning in the Activity Therapy Department and later as Director of the Group Psychotherapy Department. Later I became Treasurer and then President of the American Group Psychotherapy Association, Director of the Greater Kansas City Psychoanalytic Institute, and a member of the Board of Directors of the International Association for Group Psychotherapy and Group Processes. It seems to me that it is a natural step in the evolution of one's identity as a group therapist to become aware of and reflect on one's thoughts and feelings about being a leader as well as being a follower. The group dynamics are alive and well in administrative groups just as they are in psychotherapy groups. Leadership plays a crucial role in both settings, but the tasks are very different.

Unconscious processes in groups can be the curse and the blessing of group life. When they enhance the accomplishment of the task, phenomenal things can take place. The best of leaders know this – about themselves regarding their being leaders and/or followers – and about groups generally. As I have thought about this, it seems to me that effective leadership and its attendant functions are the same much of the time but the setting changes. Kotter (2001) states that organizations need two kinds of leadership functions: management and leadership. The management function concerns attending to the conditions that lead to maintenance of the complex organizational functioning. It seems to me that what Kotter defines as management is what we group therapists would conceptualize as creating and maintaining the frame (Langs, 1975; McWilliams, 2004). For instance, one central element to the management function is establishment of a clear definition of the task whether it is to provide group psychotherapy for people who want to change, to study the functioning of a group as it is in a Tavistock group, to govern an institution or to plan a class reunion. It is the role of the leader to help the group stay on task as well. Similar aspects of the management function would be establishing boundaries and maintaining conditions of safety and security. Kotter's other leadership function, leadership itself, is about having vision and the facilitation of change. Good leadership requires that the leader alternate between management and leadership functions.

Group psychotherapy training is extremely helpful in fostering an awareness of unconscious group forces, so that the leader can then harness them for accomplishment of the task. For instance, if the task is education, then facilitating that by skillfully managing what Bion (Rioch, 1970) describes as the dependency basic assumption, that is, when the group behaves as if its purpose is to get together and be nurtured by the leader, is indicated. I have found that in educational settings, the leader can behave in nurturing ways that mobilize the basic assumption of dependency and enhance the task of learning; it is likely that this works because the basic assumption of dependency which is unconscious is being constructively attended to. Creating a safe, predictable environment by adhering to time boundaries, providing comfortable physical space, having a welcoming atmosphere and presence, openly and firmly addressing attendance expectations and events as well as continuously defining and redefining the task so that role expectations are clear and without surprises, are some of the leadership responsibilities that create a safe, secure container wherein the basic assumption of dependency is harnessed to fuel the task of learning. Hopefully, members' yearnings for nurturance are appropriately met so that they trust and accept the leader's authority and their own responsibility which is learning. It is not unusual for me to provide food!

When a creative solution is required to a gnarly problem, fostering a contained regression so that disagreement and difference can emerge within the group and be channeled for creative purposes can work. In my administrative roles, when the group I am leading arrives at a critical juncture such as having a crisis, moving into a more mature level of development and/or functioning, or developing one or more schisms between subgroups, the leader is ultimately responsible for finding a resolution to the problem, but no solution will be operationalized unless every member of the organization takes part in a process wherein feelings about the decision are expressed and worked through. Another way of conceptualizing this is that the leader maintains conditions wherein the basic assumption of fight/flight is mobilized to enhance creativity. Also, here one of Foulkes's ideas (Foulkes, 1948) – that the group is greater than the sum of its parts – applies because often the solution arrived at by a group experiencing turmoil and ferment (if it is provided with a safe process/container and with the leader serving primarily as a conductor, another of Foulkes's concepts), is more creative than previous ideas voiced by any individual, including the leader. All members of the particular community then share in assuming responsibility for implementing the decision. Usually when such a process is facilitated, the crisis or dispute is resolved with little or no loss of members and responsibility is distributed equitably and appropriately throughout the group. Sometimes even as the resolution is achieved, a few individuals continue their dissent. For the leader this becomes a problem which leads me to a third example of how understanding of unconscious group dynamics can aid in effective leadership in administrative situations.

Scapegoating is a phenomenon to be avoided or worked through in a task group, but diagnosing it in an organizational setting can be difficult. As defined by Horwitz (1983), scapegoating is the use of projective identification by a group in which members unconsciously project into one person – usually the most vulnerable – some undesirable aspect of themselves and then proceed to attempt to extrude the scapegoat from the group, thereby unconsciously attempting to rid themselves of the undesirable attribute. The problem, of course, is that since what the scapegoat is carrying, in truth is jointly owned by the scapegoat and the group peers, members are unable to rid themselves of their contribution with the departure of the scapegoat. Thus, often in short order, the conflict or problem resurfaces in some other way.

The leader's role when this situation exists is crucial, difficult and lonely. First, the leader must try to ascertain if the dissenter is speaking for others besides himself or herself. It is wise to be very cautious about allowing any member to be extruded in this way because usually the speaker is not alone and creating a scapegoat is a two-way process between the individual and the group in an attempt to manage painful internal conflict on the stage of the group. If the scapegoated person is kicked out, in addition to the damage done to that individual, the process is destructive to the group because the problem is NOT solved: it only resurfaces! If a group process has occurred which includes everyone, even the dissenting voices, and the leader hears the dissenters as voicing their point of view as part of a group dynamic and not as a personal, isolated opinion, then the dissenting feelings can often be worked through and scapegoating is unlikely.

After a decision is made, it is the leader's role to facilitate each person's exercising responsibility and power in implementing the decision. Sometimes there will be minor dissensions about the decision and then it is helpful for the leader to reinforce the decision of the group so that the integrity of the organization is maintained. Usually the dissenting individual responds and the productive, cooperative functioning of the individual within the group resumes. However, on rare occasions these members are not speaking for the unconscious aspects of others, but simply cannot participate constructively in the life of the group. Two signals that this might be the case are when the same member repeatedly refuses to act in accordance with the group's decision or, in a related vein, when the leader spends such an inordinate amount of time attending to the dissenter that other major administrative tasks are neglected. Determining whether the behavior of a member is basically too destructive to the welfare of the group or whether the individual is being scapegoated can be a challenge for the most talented of leaders. In all of these situations, awareness of unconscious group processes on the part of the leader plays a large role in the leader's choice of how to proceed.

Leaders can do a better job if they have been followers themselves and know experientially what is required to exercise one's responsibility as a group member. The leader then can focus on creating and maintaining optimal working conditions for the group. Clearly defining and redefining the task is such a function. Another is observing and supporting the established lines of authority. Everyone can better find a place to contribute and feel securely worthwhile doing it, if who is responsible for what is stated and reinforced. Clarifying the lines of authority prepares the way for delegation. And delegation of authority provides structure for how each member can best exercise personal responsibility and participate in the task of the work group. I began learning this in the Tavistock Group Relations Conferences I attended and as I applied it to the work situation to which I returned. The leader has the responsibility for keeping the lines of authority clearly in view, reinforcing them, and delegating, but also has the responsibility to exercise the authority attendant to the leadership position and be able to appropriately assert that power in making decisions when necessary. People who are not at ease with their own aggression and power do not make good leaders, just as people who do not observe the lines of authority but act arbitrarily or micro-manage do not make good leaders either. The leader's capacity to be decisive in a fair way creates a sense of security within the group so that it can function well.

Enabling a group of people to work together is crucial. Just as in the case of the psychotherapy group, in task groups this is done by facilitating the building of bonds among members and being mindful of the functioning of the total system: what everyone does affects everyone else. It is also essential that the group has and feels ownership of the task. Leaders must artfully dance between advocating their points of view and stepping back into a neutral position where the primary concern is keeping watch that the necessary conditions for the work group to function are in place.

Another function of the leader is to stay standing while being hated. In the psychotherapy group, this takes the form of surviving the negative transference while in leading a board of directors this may mean containing the unhappiness and criticisms that come from disappointed members or those in the minority who would do things differently. Performing this difficult function may be a central reason why Goleman (1998) believes that emotional intelligence is absolutely a requirement for good leadership functioning; emotional intelligence consists of self-awareness, self-regulation, motivation, empathy and social skills. Tolerance of the hatred, when necessary, is better accomplished when the leader possesses that combination of qualities that together constitute what Goleman describes as emotional intelligence.

Finally, valuing generativity is important. Generativity supports the accomplishment of the group task because it provides for continuity and allows the leader to feel pride in the work of others. In this way the leader can value the contributions of all members and delegates but can also derive a sense of gratification from seeing others grow and having had a part in that growth. This sense of gratification can help the leader manage the narcissistic injury and perceived threats from members, both inevitably happening in the healthy group. However, leadership, although it can be rewarding, can be lonely. No one knows this better than the group psychotherapist who is destined to have moments of envy that the group members have one another while the leader is alone in the leadership role, responsibility and function.

Perhaps the good leader possesses the characteristics and training I have discussed, but there remains some mystery about why some people with these attributes make great leaders and others do not. It has been suggested that the greatest of leaders, the ones who are able to lead organizations from goodness to greatness, also have a combination of two additional personality traits that one would not necessarily expect: humility and fierce resolve. In task groups, especially, these personality traits may be very helpful.

Re-analysis of Early Clinical Vignette

So, decades later, I would likely intervene in the basically the same manner that my co-therapist and I did, but I now would have a deeper understanding of why I would do so. Let me explain. An enactment was evolving in which Karen and the group were enacting the experience of the powerful, terrorizing parent and the terrified, helpless child, an experience rife in all of their histories. While Karen was focusing on Anna as abusing her with silent indifference, in fact the entire group was silent. Everyone, including the co-therapists, was feeling at the mercy of Karen's angry, controlling behavior and rage. Multiple self states were present; Karen, identified with her aggressor in her self state, was terrorizing the members. Members and therapists had gone into a self state of paralysis, unmentalized, unformulated and dissociated. The helpless, dissociated self state was accessible to the group members given their history of childhood abuse which carried with it insecure and/or disorganized attachments with caretakers in childhood. For most of them it is likely that right brain development was negatively affected, resulting in difficulties containing and regulating affect. A dissociated self state was accessed to regulate the high arousal of the sympathetic nervous system when being terrorized and one component of the dissociated self state was an exaggerated parasympathetic counter-response. Therapists were caught up in the enactment as well, feeling helpless to intervene in any constructive way in response to Karen's rageful and/or glowering attacks. An additional important element in this enactment was the therapist's experiencing and playing the role of the caretaker, misattuned to the needs of the suffering child/children and caught up in the helplessness, much as these patients' nonabusing parent may have felt. Karen was in danger of being scapegoated as everyone attempted to disavow and project into her their own capacity to use power abusively, carrying with it the potential for doing damage to others.

The co-therapy pair was able to experience and contain their feelings of incompetence, rage and helplessness by using one another for comfort and gaining understanding, thus avoiding premature intervention and finding words to describe the experience. Together they formed a kind of thirdness, creating transitional space and countering the rigidity in the system. Tolerating this self state until the female therapist, perceived by the group as less terrifying and a safer source of nurturance, could speak the "unthinkable" and say Karen was intimidating the group, the female therapist's statement gave meaning to their experience, allowing the group to move through the enactment. Gradually the group was able to self regulate, re-stabilize, and re-establish itself as a safe and secure container; with that process the treatment deepened and was enriched. It is likely that their experience moved from implicit to explicit memory and object relationships changed.

Conclusion

More than other forms of psychological treatment and human discourse and because of the complexity, learning is incomplete in any group; there are always things unknown. It is exciting to learn that the functioning of mirror neurons may be one reason why nonverbal communication in groups is so powerful. That what we have conceptualized as object relationships exist as implicit memory in the function of the right brain and that the brain's neuroplasticity means that our idea that object relations can be changed throughout the lifespan bolsters our belief in the effectiveness of our work. Equally impressive is the disconfirmation of some theoretical beliefs. For instance, when we are nonresponsive intentionally, we miss out on maximizing the possibilities of change and may even do damage. I was originally trained to be nonresponsive and stay "outside" the group. AND, early on, I tried to behave that way! This is embarrassing, but even so I must struggle against the voices of beloved early teachers to incorporate what I have more recently learned that contradicts that position. But my point here is that the good group psychotherapist is an evolving entity which is exciting and sobering. We must attend to learning as long as we practice – difficult work in its own right, but exciting in ways never even dreamt about when we began.

References and Bibliography

Badenoch, B., & Cox, P. (2010). Integrating interpersonal neurobiology with group psychotherapy. *International Journal for Group Psychotherapy*, 60(4), 462–481.

Bion, W. R. (1961). *Experiences in groups*. London: Tavistock.

Buchele, B. (2008). The music of churches, gangs, and other groups. *Group*, 32(2), 97–104.

Cozolino, L. (2002). *The Neuroscience of psychotherapy: Building and rebuilding the developing social brain*. New York: Norton.

Denninger, J. (2010). Group and the social brain: Speeding toward a neurobiological understanding of group psychotherapy. *International Journal of Group Psychotherapy*, 60(4), 595–604.

Ezriel, H. (1952). Notes on psychoanalytic group therapy: II Interpretation and research. *Psychiatry*, 15, 119–126.

Flores, P. (2010). Group psychotherapy and neuro-plasticity: An attachment theory perspective. *International Journal of Group Psychotherapy*, 60(4), 546–571.

Foulkes, S. H. (1948). *Introduction to group analytic psychotherapy*. London: William Heinemann Medical Books Limited.

Freud, S. (1961). (Original work published 1931). Female sexuality. In J. Strachey (Ed. and Trans.), *The standard edition of the complete psychological works of Sigmund Freud* (Vol, 21, pp. 225–243). London: Hogarth Press.

Gabbard, G. (2000). *Psychodynamic psychiatry in clinical practice* (3rd ed.). Washington, DC: American Psychiatric Press, Inc.

Ganzarain, R. (1977). General systems and object-relations theories: Their usefulness in group psychotherapy. *International Journal of Group Psychotherapy*, 27, 441–456.

Ganzarain, R. (1989). *Object relations group psychotherapy*. Madison: International Universities Press.

Ganzarain, R., & Buchele, B. J. (1989). *Fugitives of incest: A perspective from psychoanalysis and groups*. Madison: International Universities Press.

Goleman, D. (2004). What makes a leader? *Harvard Business Review*, January, 82–91.

Grossmark, R. (2007). The edge of chaos: enactment, disruption, and emergence in group psychotherapy. *Psychoanalytic Dialogues*, 17(4), 479–499.

Grossmark, R. (2007). The rhythm of the group. *Psychoanalytic Dialogues*, 17(4), 529–537.

Horwitz, L. (1983). Projective identification in dyads and groups. *International Journal of Group Psychotherapy*, 33(3), 259–279.

Horwitz, L. (1984). The self in groups. *International Journal of Group Psychotherapy*, 34(4), 519–540.

Horwitz, L. (2006). Forty years of group psychotherapy at the Menninger Clinic. *International Journal of Group Psychotherapy*, 56, 221–243.

Kernberg, O. F. (1966). Structural derivatives of object relationships. *International Journal of Psychoanalysis, 47*, 236–253.

Klein, M. (1946). Notes on some schizoid mechanisms. In M. Klein (Ed.), *Developments in Psychoanalysis*. London: Hogarth.

Kohut, H. (1977). *Restoration of the self*. New York: International Universities Press.

Kotter, J. (2001). What leaders really do. *Harvard Business Review, December*, 85–96.

Langs, R. (1975). The therapeutic relationship and deviations in technique. *International Journal of Psychoanalytic Psychotherapy, 4*, 106–141.

Lerner, H. (1976). Parental mislabeling of female genitals as a determinant of penis envy and learning inhibitions in women. *Journal of the American Psychoanalytic Association, 24S*, 269–283.

Lichtenberg, J. (2008). The (and this) analyst's intentions. *Psychoanalytic Review, 95*, 711–727.

McWilliams, N. (2004). *Psychoanalytic psychotherapy: A practitioner's guide*. New York: The Guilford Press.

Menninger, R. (2006). On Horwitz (226) "Forty years of group psychotherapy at the Menninger Clinic." *International Journal of Group Psychotherapy, 56*, 363–370.

Redl, F. (1963). Psychoanalysis and group therapy: A developmental point of view. *American Journal of Psychoanalysis, 15*, 135–142.

Rioch, M. (1970). The work of Wilfred Bion on groups. *Psychiatry, 33*, 56–66.

Schermer, V. (2010). Mirror neurons: Their implications for group psychotherapy. *International Journal of Group Psychotherapy, 60*(4), 486–513.

Schore, A. (2003). *Affect dysregulation and disorders of the self*. New York: Norton.

Siegel, D. (2010). Reflections on mind, brain, and relationships in group psychotherapy. *International Journal of Group Psychotherapy, 60*(4), 483–485.

Author Index

Abernethy, A 665–6, 681–705
  (1998) 667, 683
  (2002) 667
  (2004) 683, 695
Abernethy, A and Lancia, J (1998) 686
Abramowitz, I and Coursey, R (1989) 277
Adams, KA (2006) 325
Adams, KA et al (2006) 576
Afifi, W and Faulkner, S (2000) 392
Agazarian, YM
  (1992) 655, 660, 661
  (1994) 114, 129, 480
  (1997) 114–17, 119, 121, 141, 147, 180
  (1999) 129
  (2002) 130
  (2003) 129, 134, 147
  (2006) 130
  (2010) 119
Agazarian, YM and Carter, F (1993) 462
Agazarian, YM and Gantt, S
  (2000) 115, 118, 122, 130
  (2003) 129, 134, 147
Agazarian, YM and Peters, R (1981) 436
Aichhor, A (1936) 589–90
Ainsworth, M et al (1978) 322
Alden, L (1988) 370
Alexander, F (1949) 346
Alexander, F and French, T (1946) 49
Alonso, A and Swiller, H (1993) 279

Altman, D (2010) 102
American Academy of Child and Adolescent
    Psychiatry (2001) 609
American Psychiatric Association
  (1994) 59
  (2005) 685
American Psychological Association
  (1994) 685
  (2002) 691
Anderson, CM et al (1972) 233
Andronico, M et al (2004) 511
Anzieu, D
  (1984) 65
  (1989) 489
Argyris, C and Schon, D (1974) 233, 234
Armstrong, T (1999) 104
Arnstein, S (1969) 626
Aron, L (1996) 60, 177, 253, 262, 459
Aronson, M 707–8, 731–44
Aronson, S 587, 589–607
  (1995) 590, 591
  (1998) 589
Aronson, S and Kahn, C (2004) 620, 621
Aronson, S and Scheidlinger, S (2002) 601
Aten, JD and Hernandez, BC (2004) 696
Aten, JD and Leach, MM
  (2009a) 685
  (2009b) 692

The Wiley-Blackwell Handbook of Group Psychotherapy, First Edition. Edited by Jeffrey L. Kleinberg.
© 2012 John Wiley & Sons, Ltd. Published 2012 by John Wiley & Sons, Ltd.

Atwood, G and Stolorow, R
  (1984) 60, 64
  (1993) 60
Aveline, MO (1993) 148
Azima, F (1972) 600
Azima, H and Azima, F (1959) 140

Bachrach, L (1992) 716
Badenoch, B and Cox, P (2010) 754
Baer, JS et al (1992) 370
Bales, R (1950) 139
Balint, M
  (1957) 525, 531
  (1968) 710
Barbato, A and D'Avanzo, B (2008) 451
Barris, R et al (1983) 139
Battegay, R (1990) 148
Beck, A
  (1948) 92
  (1976) 92
Beck, R 273, 571–85
Beck, R and Buchele, B (2004) 572, 574, 577, 578
Becker, D (2006) 520
Beebe, B and Lachmann, F (2002) 177
Beebe, B and Stern, D (1977) 177
Behr, H and Hearst, L (2005) 403
Bellak, L (1980) 45
Benjamin, J (1988) 192
Benne, K and Sheats, P (1978) 139, 147, 149, 163
Bennis, W and Shepard, H (1956) 119, 123, 139
Ben-Noam, S 272, 409–30
Berg, M et al (2009) 470
Berger, M 197–216
Bergin, A and Garfield, S (1990) 503
Berman, A 187–96
Berman, A and Berger, M (2010) 233, 235
Bernard, H (1999) 235
Bernard, H and Spitz, H (2006) 308
Bernard, H et al (2008) 42, 43, 257, 259, 504, 507
Bernard, J and Goodyear, R (2004) 234
Bettelheim, B (1987) 589, 594
Billow, R 169–85
  (2003) 64, 170, 254, 259, 262, 263, 264
  (2010a) 170, 172, 173
  (2010b) 183, 253, 674
  (2010c) 183
Bion, WR
  (1959) 28, 66, 123, 154, 165, 251
  (1961) 170, 171, 234, 746
  (1962) 66, 170, 171, 178, 182, 195, 237, 481, 593
  (1963) 170
  (1965) 170
  (1967) 233, 246
  (1970) 170, 237
  (1993) 489, 492
Blechner, M (1996) 177
Blinderman, C and Cherny, N (2005) 467
Blocher, DH
  (1974) 342, 343
  (1996) 342, 343
Blos, P (1962) 609
Boesky, D (2000) 170
Bogo, M et al (2004) 233
Bolen, R (2002) 418
Bollas, C
  (1987) 231, 240, 323
  (2000) 403
Booty, JE (1990) 467
Bornschein, D (2009) 518
Boss, P (2006) 502
Bowen, M (1971) 432
Bowlby, J
  (1969/1982) 321
  (1973) 322
Boyle, M (1990) 548
Boyle, P (1994) 410
Brabender, V (2002) 278
Brabender, V and Fallon, A (2009) 506
Brabender et al (2004) 631
Braddock Bromley, N (2007) 410
Bransford, CR (2009) 232, 233
Brantbjerg, M (2009) 131
Breier, A and Strauss, J (1984) 716
Brems, C (1994) 598
Briere, J and Spinazzola, J (2009) 413
Brodsky, A (1973) 383
Brok, AJ 272, 335–44
  (1973) 344
  (1976) 339
  (1996) 336, 344
  (1997) 339, 343, 344
Bromberg, P (1998) 191

Brook, M
  (2001) 250, 252, 255, 257, 261, 263
  (2006) 300
Brown, N (2003) 144, 148, 163
Brown, R (1980) 370
Buber, M (1996) 625
Buchele, BJ 707, 708, 745–69
  (2000) 420
  (2008) 745
Buchele, BJ and Spitz, H (2004) 503, 504
Burke, JP (1983) 139
Burlingame, G, Fuhrman, A and Mosier, J (2003) 387, 502
Burlingame, G, MacKenzie, K and Strauss, B (2003) 503
Burlingame, G et al (2002) 43
Burman, E (2002) 398
Burns, D
  (1980) 93, 99, 100
  (1999) 106
Butler, A and Beck, J (2001) 93

Calhoun, L and Tedeschi, R (2006) 632
Caligor, J et al (1993) 336
Callahan, K et al (2004) 276
Cammarota, J and Fine, M (2008) 636
Cannon, T and Mednick, S (1993) 548
Caper, R (1997) 171
Carlock, C and Martin, P (1977) 383
Carson, R (1982) 36
Carter, E et al (1998) 110
Cartwright, D and Zander, A (1968) 139
Caspary, A (1993) 593
Castelein, S et al (2008) 470
Chambless, D and Hollon, S (1998) 693
Chasen, L (2005) 590
Chazan, R (2001) 624, 625, 629, 632, 633
Chemtob, C et al (2002) 637
Chida, Y et al (2009) 684
Choi-Kain, L and Gunderson, J (2008) 52
Chused, J
  (1991) 177
  (1992) 170
Classen, C et al (2001) 417, 420
Cividini-Stranić, E
  (1996a) 555
  (1996b) 555
  (1980) 563

Coché, J 272, 431–56
  (1983) 444, 451
  (2010) 431, 434, 439, 442, 443, 445–9, 451–3
Coché, J and Coché, E (1990) 438, 439, 446, 450
Coché, J et al (2006) 452, 453
Cocozza, J and Skowyra, K (2000) 649
Cohen, A and Smith, R (1976) 159
Cohen, B (2000) 70
Cohen, B and Schermer, V (2002) 68
Cohen, P 271–2, 299–320
  (1996) 304
Cohen, S and Wills, T (1985) 275
Cohn, B (2005) 283
Coleman, M et al (2009) 234, 235, 236
Collins (2001) 766
Comisióde Esclarecimiento Histórico (1999) 517, 518
Committee on Treatment of Posttraumatic Street Disorder (2007) 417
Conacher, G (1998) 176
Connolly, J and Johnson, A (1996) 391
Connolly, J et al
  (1999) 391
  (2000) 391
Cooke, B and Kothari, U (2001) 638
Cooper, L (1976) 440
Cooperman, A (2005) 410
Corey, G and Corey, M
  (1977) 155
  (1982) 155, 159
Cory, M and Corey, G (2002) 601, 604
Counselman, E (2005) 290
Courtois, CA (2010) 410, 411, 415, 419
Cozolino, L (2002) 748
Crosby, G with Altoman, D 89–112
Csikszentmihalyi, M
  (1975) 147
  (1990) 147

Dalal, F
  (198) 204, 211
  (2002) 530
Damasio, A
  (1999) 448
  (2003) 211
Davenport, Y et al (1977) 276
Davies, J (1994) 177

Davis, K and Meara, N (1982) 448
Davis, L et al (1995) 668, 670, 671, 673
Dawson, D and Reid, K (1997) 106–7
Dayan, D (2010) 494
de Bosset, F
 (1982) 716
 (1988) 716
De Maré, PB
 (1972) 461–2
 (1975) 462
 (1998) 490
Debiak, D (2007) 398, 405, 674
DeLucia-Waack, J
 (1997) 619
 (2006) 619
Denninger, J (2010) 756
DeRubeis, R and Crits-Christoph, P (1999) 451
DeSchill, S (1973) 19
Dickinson, G (1975) 391
Dies, K (1991) 614
Dimen, M (1995) 400
Doll, L et al (2004) 410
Donadio, R (2010) 410
Dore, J (1994) 381, 388
Drewes, A (2005) 628
DSM-IV-TR 650, 651, 685
Duncan, J and Arntson, L (2004) 628, 631, 636
Dunphy, D (1963) 390
Durkin, H
 (1964) 26
 (1981) 615
Durkin, H and Glatzer, H (1973) 28

Edwards, N (1977) 22
Ehrenberg, D (1995) 177
Eigen, M
 (1977) 299
 (1981) 194
Eilenberg, M and Wyman, S (1998) 603
Elias, N 531
 (1978) 404
 (1994) 525
Elrick, M (1977) 383
Emmons, R (1999) 684
Erickson, EH (1968) 609
Erikson, E (1959) 339–40, 589, 594

Ernsberger, C (1991) 300
Ettin, M
 (1992) 180
 (1995) 308
 (1999) 245
Everly, G and Flynn, B (2005) 509
Everly, G and Mitchell, J (1999) 509
Everly, G et al (2006) 509
Exline, J et al (2000) 685
Ezriel, H 251
 (1952) 746
 (1973) 251–2

Fairbairn, RWD (1952) 60
Fehr, S (2003) 257, 258, 264
Feindler, E et al (1986) 386
Feiring, C (1996) 391
Fernando, G et al (2010) 625
Festinger, L (1953) 117
Fidler, G and Fidler, J (1978) 139, 141
Fidler, J (1989) 71
Fieldsteel, N (1996) 31
Figley, CR
 (1985) 412
 (1995) 520, 576
 (1999) 576–7
Finkelhor, D
 (1994) 410
 (2008) 410
Fisher, J and Corcoran, K (2007) 100
Fleckenstein, L and Horne, A (2004) 620
Flores, P (2010) 325, 755
Flowers, J and Booraem, C (1990) 52
Foa, E et al (2007) 63
Fonagy, P
 (2000) 490
 (2001) 60, 64
Fonagy, P and Bateman, A (2006) 47, 52
Fonagy, P and Target, M (1998) 171
Fonagy, P et al (2002) 322, 323
Fonagy, P et al (2004) 34
Fonagy, P et al (2005) 60, 69
Fook, J (2002) 233, 234, 235, 238, 244, 246
Ford, JD et al (2009) 417
Foreman, SA (1996) 36
Fosshage, J (2003) 65
Foucault, M 401

Foulkes, SH
  (1948) 200, 764
  (1957) 200
  (1964) 70, 180, 181, 200–1, 231, 233–5, 252, 490, 522, 523, 525, 531, 555, 565
  (1973) 488
  (1975) 472, 491, 494
  (1977) 187, 188, 191, 192
  (1983) 522, 523, 531
  (1986) 525
  (1990) 200
Foulkes, SH and Anthony, EJ 555
  (1957) 14, 27, 180, 235
  (1965) 562
  (1990) 201
Foy, D et al (2000) 503, 510
Framo, I (1982) 432
Frank, K (2002) 447, 452
Frank, M (1976) 590, 597
Frankiel, R (1985) 600
Freeman, J (2005) 410
Freeman, J et al (1997) 628
Freire, P
  (1972) 625
  (1973/2002) 625
Freud, S
  (1900) 479, 484, 485–6
  (1912) 22, 179
  (1913) 17
  (1914) 29
  (1921) 175–6
  (1931) 746
  (1933) 485
Friedan, B (1963) 383
Friedman, R 272–3, 479–97
  (1997) 169
  (2002) 484, 485, 487, 488, 491
  (2004) 492
Friedman, R et al (1996) 650
Fromm, E (1947) 192
Fromm-Reichmann, F (1953) 548

Gabbard, G
  (1995) 54
  (2000) 746
Gabbard, G and Wilkinson, S (2000) 318
Gable, S et al (2003) 447
Gable, S et al (2004) 447
Gabriel, B (1939) 590
Galea, S (2002) 71
Galt, A (2010) 70
Gans, J (2005) 154
Gans, J and Alonson, A (1998) 52
Gans, J and Counselman, E (2010) 285, 553
Gantt, S 113–17
  (2010) 116–17, 121
Ganzarain, R
  (1977) 746
  (1989) 746
  (1992) 660
Ganzarian, R and Buchele, B (1989) 745, 746, 747
Gardner, R (1977) 306
Garfield, S and Bergin, A (1994) 503
Garfield, S et al (1965) 614
Garland, C (1980) 214
Garland, C et al (1965) 139
Garland, C et al (1973) 601
Gayle, R (2009) 66
Garrett, A et al (2007) 631
Gartner, R (1999) 410
Gemelli, R (1996) 609
Gemmill, G (1989) 118
George, C et al
  (1984) 322
  (1985) 322
  (1996) 322
Gerson, B (1994) 177
Gibbs, J et al (1995) 652, 655
Giesler, R and Swann, W (1999) 34, 39
Gilbert, D (2010) 14
Gill, H et al (1972) 440
Gill, M
  (1982) 599
  (1994) 172
Gilmore, M 272, 321–34
Ginot, E (2007) 447, 452
Gladding, S (1998) 619
Glaser, K (1976) 383
Glatzer, H (1969) 29
Gloaguen, V et al (1998) 93
Gold, S et al (1999) 410
Goldstein, K (1995) 525
Goleman, D
  (1997) 453
  (1998) 766

Goodman, M and Weiss, D (2000) 257
Goodwin, P et al (2001) 386
Gordis, E (1987) 346
Gorman, C and Dolan, B (1991) 410
Gottman, J (1994) 447
Graber, R and Miller, W (1988) 370
Green, Z and Stiers, M (2002) 668, 669–70, 675, 696
Greenbaum, H (1983) 445
Greenberg, J
  (1964) 710
  (1995) 177
Greenfield, S et al
  (2007) 388
  (2008) 388
Greenson, R
  (1960) 261
  (1967) 66, 176
Greer, G (1972) 383
Griefen, M et al (1985) 346, 347, 348, 351
Grinberg, L et al (1957) 530
Grossmark, R
  (2007a) 69, 253, 262, 327, 755, 756
  (2007b) 263, 756
Grotjahn, M (1977) 227

Haddock, R and Viskari, S (2006) 132
Hall, J et al (1981) 716
Hall, S (2004) 684
Halton, M (1999) 181
Hammer, E (2008) 577
Harpaz, N (1994) 148
Hart, L (1977) 345
Hart, R
  (1992) 625, 638
  (1997) 625–6, 629, 634, 636, 638
  (2008) 625, 626
Harwood, I
  (1998) 254
  (2006) 67
Havens, L and Ghaemi, S (2005) 467
Haynal, A and Pasini, M (1984) 553
Hays, P (2007) 669
Heather, N and Robertson, I
  (1983) 371
  (1997) 371
Heather, N et al (1987) 370
Hegarty, P and Buechel, C (2006) 402
Hellwig, K and Memmott, R (1974) 440

Hensley, L (2002) 386
Herman, J 578
  (1992a) 412, 413, 415, 420, 421, 428
  (1992b) 413
  (1997) 63, 499, 500, 501, 512, 572
  (2000) 409, 410
Herr, K and Anderson, G (2005) 627, 634
Hester, R and Delaney, H (1997) 370
Hickey, S and Mohan, G (2005) 638
Hill, C and Knox, S (2009) 33
Hill, P and Hood, R (1999) 686
Hoffman, I 256
  (1983) 61, 227, 599
Hofling, C et al (1996–71) 719
Hofstede, G (2001) 459
Hogarty, G (1993) 716
Holmes, L
  (2002) 384
  (2009) 261
Hook, J et al (2010) 693
Hopper, E
  (2001) 299
  (2003) 72, 181, 204, 325, 459–60, 464, 471
Horowitz, L (1983) 178
Horowitz, L and Vitkus, J (1986) 34
Horwitz, L
  (1983) 118, 747, 764
  (1984) 747, 762
Howard, A and Scott, R (1965) 119
Howe, M and Schwartzberg, S (1986) 139
Howells, J and Guirguis, W (1985) 548
Hummelen, J (1994) 552
Hutton, D (2001) 625, 632, 636

Iacoboni, M (2008) 188
IASC (2007) 637
Imber-Black, E (1989) 110
Institute of Medicine (1990) 371, 372

Jacobs, G (2007) 633–4, 636, 637, 638
Jacobs, T (1991) 177
Jacques, J (1998) 692
James, D (1994) 468
James, W (1985) 684
Jarrar, L (2003) 462, 469
Jensen, H et al (2010) 276
Johansen, T (2010) 685

John, M (2003) 638
Johnson, S and Greenberg, L (1994) 447
Jordan, J (2001) 462, 467
Joseph, S and Linley, P (2008) 632
Joyce, At e al (2007) 260

Kadushin, A (1992) 234
Kahn, G 595, 597
Kanas, N
  (1986) 276
  (1996) 548, 549, 553, 565–6
  (2005) 276
Karles, J and Wondrei, K (1994) 231
Karterud, S and Stone, W (2003) 724
Kashner, T (1995) 276
Kaslow, F (1981) 445
Kauff, P 13–32
  (1977) 30
  (1979) 14
  (1993) 16
  (1997) 28
  (2002) 31
  (2009) 23, 30
Kauff, P and Kleinberg, J
  (2008) 506
  (2009) 31
Kauffman, E et al (1995) 388
Kauffman, S (2002) 504
Keith, S and Mathews, S (1984) 716
Kernberg, O
  (1978) 659, 661
  (1984) 662
Kernjack, F (2006) 517
Keyser, J et al (2000) 590
Khamphakdy-Brown, S et al (2006) 470
Kibel, H (1987) 655, 658, 659, 660
Kielhofner, G (2009) 139
Kiesler, D (1996) 34, 36, 39, 53–4
Kindon, S et al (2007) 637
Kinoshita, I (2007) 636
Kipper, D and Ritchie, T (2003) 387
Kishline, A (1994) 371
King, L (1978) 139
Kissane, D et al (2003) 386
Kivlahan, D et al (1990) 371
Klain, E (1996) 555
Klein, A (1972) 159
Klein, E et al (2001) 719

Klein, M 209, 251
  (1946) 746
  (1976) 383
Klein, R (198) 506
Klein, R and Brown, SL (1987) 659, 662
Klein, R and Phillips, S (2008) 503, 504, 507, 509, 511
Klein, R and Schermer, V (2000) 503, 504
Klein, R and Thomas, N (2003) 504
Klein, R et al (2007) 504
Kleinberg, J 1–7
  (1999) 235
  (2007) 417
Klingman, A and Cohen, E (2004) 627, 629
Kluge, P (1974) 440
Kohlberg, L (1981) 609
Kohut, H 256
  (1959) 60
  (1968) 747
  (1971) 60, 254
  (1977) 60
  (1982) 211
  (1984) 722
  (1989) 209
Konner, M (2004) 447
Kornblum, R (2008) 625
Kotter, J (2001) 763–4
Kreeger, L (1975) 461
Kripke, D and Robinson, D (1985) 276
Kris, E (1952) 598
Krugman, S (1987) 412
Kunneman, P and Ritz, H (2010) 115
Kurland, R and Salmon, R (1998) 611
Kurtenbach, S (2003) 518
Kurtz, L (1997) 277, 282
Kurtz, N and Reiger, M (1975) 345
Kurzweil, E (2001) 709

Ladden, L et al (2007) 132
Lambert, M (2003) 503
Lambert, M and Ogles, B (2004) 34
Langs, R
  (1975) 374, 763
  (1976) 68
Laquercia, T (1983) 218
Larmer, B (2010) 624
Large, T (2005) 289, 290, 294
Lathrop, D (1984) 310

Larson, D et al (1998) 684
Leach, M et al (2009) 689, 690, 691
Leaper, C and Anderson, K (1997) 391, 392
Leavy, R (1983) 275
Leibenberg, B (2009) 223
Leichter, E (1962) 432
Lenihan, G (1985) 387
Lerner, H (1976) 746
Levenkron, S and Levenkron, A (2007) 415
Levenson, E (1972) 599
Levine, R (2001) 221
Levy-Warren, M (1996) 609
Lewin, K 251, 529, 531
  (1947) 530
  (1951) 119, 122, 432, 436
Lewinson, P (1967) 93
Leszcz, M
  (1992) 33
  (1997) 33
Leszcz, M and Malat, J 33–58
  (2007) 33
  (2010) 33
Li, H 634
Lichtenberg, J
  (1982) 198
  (1985) 198
  (1989) 198, 219
  (2001) 60
  (2008) 755
Lichtenberg, J et al (1992) 254
Lieberman, M et al
  (1973) 714
  (1979) 383
Liegner, E (1991) 317
Lifton, W (1961) 139
Lim, L (2008) 624
Linehan, M (1995) 63
Lionells, M et al (1995) 60
List, L (2008) 634
Little, M
  (1951) 177
  (1958) 309
Livingston, M (2002) 490
Lorenz, K (1952) 176
Loughry, M and Eyber, C (2003) 636
Lubin, H and Johnson, D (2008) 417, 420, 423, 511

Lindquist, G et al (2006) 417, 420
Lyon-Ruth, K (1999) 328

Mack, M
  (1994) 469, 470
  (2004) 519
MacKenzie, KR
  (1977) 91
  (1987) 258
  (1990) 97–8
  (1994) 506
  (1996) 506
  (1997) 506
MacKenzie, KR and Grabovac, A (2002) 39
MacKenzie, KR and Tschuschke, V (1993) 43, 258
MacLeod, J and Middleman, F (1962) 712
Madonna, J and Caswell, P (1991) 620
Maglajlic, R (2010) 636
Mahler, M 561
Mahler, M et al (1975) 60, 65
Main, M
  (1946) 461
  (1991) 322, 323
Main, M and Solomon, J (1990) 322
Main, M et al (1985) 322
Malat, J and Leszcz, M
  (2005) 39
  (2008) 33
Malekoff, A (2004) 610, 618
Malone, K and Hartung, C (2010) 626, 631
Mandell, J et al (1989) 590
Mann, D (2003) 399
Manyena, SB et al (2008) 636
Margolin, G et al (2010) 636
Margolis, B (1983) 302
Markus, H and Abernethy, A (2001) 148
Marlatt, G (1998) 371
Marlatt, G et al (1993) 371
Maroda, K (1991) 218
Marsella, A and Christopher, M (2004) 636
Martin, DJ et al
  (2000) 43
  (2004) 34
Maslow, A (1970) 139
Masten, A (2001) 634
Matsukawa, L (2001) 669, 670
McAfee, J (2002) 595

McAuliffe, K (2007) 609
McCann, I and Pearlman, L (1990) 427, 573
McCarthy, KS and Coché, J (2008) 451, 452
McCullough, J
  (2000) 34, 35, 53
  (2006) 34, 35, 53
McFarlane, A and Girolamo, G (1996) 501
McGarry, D (1955) 256
McIntosh, D et al (1991) 716
McLaughlin, J (1991) 170, 177
McWilliams, N (2004) 763
Meadow, P (1996) 308
Meeks, J and Bernet, W (2001) 609
Mehl-Madrona, L (2010) 102
Meltzer, D (1983) 482
Metzel, E (2009) 634
Meyer, T and Mark, M (1995) 275
Michels, R
  (1999) 721
  (2011) 84
Miehls, D and Moffat, K (2000) 239
Mikulincer, M and Shaver, P (2007) 322
Milders, C (1994) 552
Miller, S et al
  (1992) 371
  (1997) 96, 98
Miller, W and Rolnick, S (2001) 372
Miller, W et al (1992) 371
Mishna, F and Muskat, B (2004) 590
Mishna, F et al (2002) 596
Mitchell, S 256
  (1996) 404
  (1988) 60, 599
  (1994) 34
  (2000) 188, 211
Moeller, M (2002) 403
Molkentin, G (2002) 517
Monson, C et al (2004) 451
Moreno, J (2007) 118
Moro, L (1996) 555, 564
Morran, D et al (1998) 49
Mosey, A (1970) 141
Moss, E (2008) 661, 662
Motherwell, L 271, 275–98
Motherwell, L and Shay, J (2005) 278
Muller, R (2009) 333

Nitsun, M 272, 397–408
  (1996) 564
  (2006) 397, 398, 403, 405
Norberry, L (1986) 276
Norman, E (2000) 502
Northen, H and Kurland, R (2001) 611
Nuttman-Shwartz, O and Shay, S 231–48
  (1998) 232–3
  (2006) 245, 246

O'Connor, N and Ryan, J (1993) 401
Oei, T and Browne, A (2006) 276
Ogden, T
  (1981) 658
  (1994) 231
  (1997a) 195
  (1997b) 195
Ogden, T and Gabbard, G (2010) 13
O'Neill, R (2010) 134
O'Neill, R and Constantino, M
  (2009) 132
  (2010) 134
O'Neill, R et al (2010) 134
Orange, D et al (1997) 59
Ormont, Lou 217, 220, 300
  (1962) 256, 257
  (1970) 255, 261, 262
  (1974) 265
  (1984) 259, 261, 262
  (1987) 257
  (1988) 255, 256, 259, 300, 304, 318
  (1989) 265, 266
  (1990) 47, 144, 147, 255
  (1991) 253, 255
  (1992) 173, 227, 258, 263
  (1993) 300
  (1994) 265, 300, 305, 674
  (1996) 300
  (1997) 255, 262
  (1999) 218
  (1999a) 255, 263
  (1999b) 261
  (2001) 255, 301, 305
  (2002) 255
  (2003) 224
ørner, R and Schnyder, U (2003) 502, 509
Orzack, M et al (2006) 386
Öttler, A (2004) 519
Oyard, L et al (2000) 276

Padesky, C and Greenberger, D (1995) 93
Palmer, S et al (1992) 386
Palombo, S (1992) 480
Papp, P (1976) 439
Pargament, K
  (1997) 684, 685
  (2007) 683, 685
  (2009) 686
Pargament, K and Krumrei, E (2009) 686
Parloff, M (1968) 183
Parson, E (1985) 420
Pearlman, L (1999) 511
Pearlman, L and Coutois, C (2005) 419
Pearlman, L and Saakvitne, K (1995) 511
Pedder, J (1986) 232
Peek, L (2008) 636
Percy-Smith, B and Thomas, N (2010) 638
Perls, Fritz (1973) 100
Peterson, J (1968) 432
Pew Research Council (2002) 683–4
Phelan, J (1974) 601
Phillips, S (2004) 511
Phillips, Sand Klein, R 273, 499–515
Phillips, S et al (2010) 581
Piaget, J (1972) 609
Pines, M 208
  (1981) 204, 459
  (1998) 203, 204
  (2000) 204
  (2002) 487
Pines, M and Hutchinson, S (1993) 662
Piper, W et al 276
  (1979) 440
  (1981) 440
  (2005) 43
Plante, T et al (1988) 552
Pojman, A 588, 609–22
  (2009) 610, 612, 617, 620
Pomerleau, O et al (1978) 371
Porter, K (2004) 692
Powell, L et al (2003) 684
Powers, M et al (2008) 451
Preston, J (2006) 106, 107
Prewitt, JO and Dayal, A (2008) 628
Prewitt Diaz, OJ (2008) 628
Prilleltensky, I (2010) 636
Prior, V and Glaser, D (2006) 69
Prochaska, J et al (1994) 96
Project Match Research Group (1997) 693

Psychodynamic Diagnostic Manual (PDM) (2006) 651
Puget, J (2002) 490
Pure, D 272, 381–96

Rachman, A (1995) 611, 613, 615, 616, 618
Rachman, A and Ceccoli, V (1996) 616
Racker, H (1968) 26, 169, 179
Rando, T (1993) 501
Rangell, L (1981) 67
Raphael-Leff, J (2010) 401
Ratey, J (2008) 105
Rausch, S et al (2006) 464
Ray, P (2010) 636
Rayle, J et al (2006) 675
Recuperación de la Memoria Histórica (1998) 518
Redl, F
  (1944) 590
  (1951) 611
  (1963) 747
  (1966) 590, 591, 592, 603
  (2006) 654
Reed, H
  (1982) 233
  (1984) 139
Reich, A (1960) 261
Reid, B (1993) 234
Reik, T (1983) 169
Reis, B (2009) 188
Renik, O (1993) 169, 170
Restek-Petrović, B et al (2007) 553
Reynes, R and Allen, A (1987) 307
Rice, C
  (1996) 159
  (2004) 510
Richards, P and Bergin, A (2005) 686, 692
Richards, P et al (2007) 685, 693, 694
Richards, R et al (1990) 386, 387
Richarz, B (2008) 253
Rioch, M (1970) 755, 764
Rizzuto, A (1979) 692
Robinson, T (1999) 670
Rodenhauser, P and Stone, W (1993) 720
Rodriguez-Srednicki, O and Thwaite, J (2006) 415
Rogoff, B (2003) 467
Rohr, E 273, 517–45

Roller, B and Nelson, V (1991) 696
Romanelli, L et al (2009) 470
Ronan, K et al (2008) 636
Roopnarino and Johnson (1994) 628
Rosati, M (2006) 636
Rose, N (1994) 548
Rosenthal, L 229
  (1987) 227
  (2005) 251
Rothke, S (1986) 49
Rubino, G et al (2000) 333
Rutan, J (2005) 265, 291
Rutan, J and Stone, W
  (1984) 440
  (1993) 251, 255, 256–7, 258, 263
  (2001) 180
Rutan, J et al
  (1988) 657
  (2007) 118, 278, 280, 283, 347, 381, 462, 465, 720

Saakvitne, K and Pearlman, L (1995) 511, 577, 580
Safran, J and Segal, Z (1990) 34, 35, 37
Salloum, A et al (2010) 631
Salvendy, J (1993) 277
Samide, L and Stockton, R (2002) 628
Sanchez-Craig, M et al (1984) 371
Saragovi, C et al (1997) 467
Sandison, R (1994) 552
Saxe, JG (1878) 645–6
Scanlon, C (2000) 233
Schames, G (1986) 594, 597
Schames, G et al (1997) 598
Schechtman, Z (2007) 599, 604, 613
Schechtman, Z and Gluck, O (2005) 591
Schechtman, Z and Mor, M (2010) 589, 590
Scheidlinger, S 598
  (1960) 590, 597
  (1974) 592
  (1982) 590, 592, 602, 603
  (1985) 590
  (1997) 552, 565
  (2004) 637
Schein, L et al
  (2003) 509
  (2006) 504, 509

Schermer, V
  (1994) 553
  (2002) 71
  (2008) 71
  (2010) 60, 755
Schermer, V and Rice, C 10, 59–87
Schiffer, M (1969) 590
Schindler, R 529, 531
  (1957–1958) 531
Schlachet, P (1989) 552
Schlapobersky, J (1993) 489
Schon, D
  (1987) 231, 233, 234, 238, 246
  (1991) 233
Schore, AN
  (1994) 210, 228
  (2003a) 129, 748, 749
  (2003b) 129, 419
Schwartzberg, S and Barnes, M 10, 139–67
Schwartzberg, S et al (2008) 139, 140, 148, 149, 150, 159, 163–6
Searles, H (1979) 177
Seidlitz, L et al (2002) 684, 686
Seligman, S
  (2002) 447, 452
  (2009) 188
Shadish, W and Baldwin, S (2003) 451
Shaffer, J and Galinsky, M (1974) 251, 252
Shafranske, E and Maloney, H (1990) 684
Shaked, J (2003) 469
Shah, S 673, 674
Shah, S and Kosi, R 665, 667–80
Shalev, A and Ursano, R (2003) 499
Shambaugh, P (1996) 614
Shannon, C and Weaver, W (1964) 119, 122
Shay, J (2009) 292
Shea, M et al (2009) 420
Shedler, J (2010) 33
Shen, Y (2002) 637
Shepherd (2004) 308
Sheppard, T (2008) 598
Shields, W (2001) 464, 468, 471
Sickmund, M et al (2008) 648
Siegel, D
  (1999) 419, 609
  (2006) 453
  (2010) 102, 754–5
Sikkema, K et al (1995) 275–6

Silverman, W and La Greca, A (2002) 636
Simon, A and Agazarian, Y (2000) 122
Skolnick, M (1994) 548–9
Skutle, A and Berg, G (1987) 371
Slack, D (2005) 410
Slater, P (1966) 523
Slavson, S
 (1943) 590
 (1950) 250–1, 590, 594
 (1973) 562
Slife, B and Canyon, J (1991) 49
Slochower, J (1996) 592
Smead, R (1995) 601, 604
Smith, M (1985) 70
Smith, T et al (2007) 694
Snyder, D et al (2006) 451
Sobel, M and Sobel, L
 (1976) 371
 (1984) 371
 (1993) 371
Soo, E (1991) 598
Speck, R and Attneave, C (1973) 108
Spezzano, C (1996) 170
Spiegel, D (1986) 418
Spiro, M et al (1987) 684
Spitz, H (1979) 435
Spotnitz, H 255, 300, 312
 (1969) 302
 (1976) 218, 226, 264
Springmann, R (1975) 461
Stamm, B (1999) 511, 575–6
Stark, M (1999) 657, 658
Steinitz, L (2009) 636, 638
Stern, D
 (1971) 177
 (1985) 34, 60
 (1990) 210
 (1998) 194
Stern, D et al (1998) 488
Stoller, R
 (1979) 402, 403
 (1985) 402
Stolorow, R
 (1994) 260
 (1997) 170
 (2010) 60
Stolorow, R and Brandchaft, B (1987) 254

Stolorow, R et al
 (1987) 34, 63, 254
 (2002) 480
Stoltenberg, C and Delworth, U (1987) 696
Stone, DT (2001) 653
Stone, DT and Beck, R
 (2009) 576–7, 578–9
 (2010) 576, 581
Stone, DT and Thomas, A 589, 645–64
Stone, L (1954) 62
Stone, W 707, 709–29
 (1975) 713
 (1983) 717
 (1985) 724
 (1989) 724
 (1991) 716
 (1992) 716, 724
 (1996) 39, 717
 (1997) 724
 (2001) 724
 (2002) 724
 (2005) 724
 (2008) 724
 (2009a) 64, 254
 (2009b) 254
 (2009c) 262, 263
Stone, W and Gustafson, J
 (1992) 724
 (2009) 263, 267
Stone, W and Karterud, S (2006) 490, 724
Stone, W and Klein, E (1999) 719
Stone, W and Rutan, J (1984) 719–20
Stone, W and Spielberg, G (2009) 724
Stone, W and Tieger, M (1971) 714
Stone, W and Whitman, R
 (1977) 723
 (1980) 723
Stone, W et al
 (1966) 712
 (1991) 720
 (2006) 719
Strasser, S (1985) 66
Strupp, H and Binder, J (1984) 35
Sue, DW and Sue, D (1999) 667
Sue, DW et al (2007) 675

Sullivan, HS 169
  (1953) 34, 36, 42, 60, 435, 589
Sultanoff, C (2000) 307
Sutherland, JD (1985) 251
Sutton-Smith, B (1986) 589
Szasz, T (1961) 20

Tan (2001) 703
Taylor, K et al (2003) 275
Tebb, S (1995) 470
Teplin, L et al (2006) 650
Thomas, N and Percy-Smith, B (2009) 636
Thyssen, B (1992) 398
Toseland, R et al (1990) 277
Towel, C (1972) 232
Triandis, H and Suh, E (2002) 467
Tronick, E
  (1989) 177
  (2007) 120
Trotter, W (1953) 176
Tschuschke, V and Dies, R (1994) 258
Tschuschke, V and Greene, L (2002) 148
Tuckman, BW
  (1965) 139, 280
  (1977) 280
Tylim, I (2003) 403
Tylin, I (1999) 232
Tummala-Narra, P (2004) 667, 668

Uhernik, J and Husson, M (2009) 509
Ullman, M (1996) 491
Ulman, K and Beck, R (2010) 579, 580, 581
UNCRC (1989) 636, 637
Underwood, M et al (2004) 631
Unger, W et al (2006) 510
UNICEF
  (2006) 627
  (2007) 631, 634, 636, 638
United Nations Development Program (2005) 518
United States Department of Health and Human Services (2001) 509
Urlić, I 273, 547–69
  (1989) 548
  (1994) 548
  (1999) 553, 561, 566
Ursano, R et al (2007) 625, 631, 636

Valenstein, A (1981) 67
Van der Kolk, B
  (1987a) 412
  (1987b) 420
  (1996) 412, 413
Van der Kolk, B and McFarlane, A (1996) 500
Van der Kolk, B et al (1996) 502, 625
Van Emde Boas, C (1992) 35, 432
Van Wagoner, SL 11, 249–67
  (2000) 154
  (2008) 260
Vannicelli, M 272, 345–79
  (1982) 346, 347, 348, 353, 365
  (1988) 346, 347, 348
  (1992) 346, 347, 348, 351, 353, 355, 357, 358, 361, 373
  (2001a) 346, 347, 348, 368, 374
  (2001b) 347, 370, 373
  (2002) 347, 370
  (2006) 286
Vannicelli, M et al
  (1984) 346, 347, 348, 356
  (1989) 346, 347, 348
Viederman, M (1993) 37
Vogel, J and Vernberg, F (1993) 636
Volkan, V (1988) 460
Volkmar, F et al (1981) 276
Von Bertalanffy, L
  (1968) 432
  (1976) 119
Von Thun, FS (1998) 533
Von Wallenberg Pachaly, A (2000) 413
Vostanis, P and O'Sullivan, D (1992) 148

Wachtel, E (2008) 59
Waldegrave, C (2009) 469
Walker, L (1981) 381, 382, 383
Wallin, D (2007) 323, 324, 325, 328, 333
Walter, M et al (2008) 447
Waltz, J et al (1993) 161
Wampold, B (2001) 33, 34
Wang, M (2003) 624
Wardi, D (1989) 159
Wasserman, H and Daforth, H (1988) 282
Wattenberg, M et al (2006) 510
Weber, A and Haen, C (2005) 590
Weber, R and Gans, J (2003) 148, 154
Weegmann, M (2007) 398

Weinberg, H (2007) 459
Weinberg, H and Schneider, S
  (2002) 462
  (2003) 457, 462, 463, 468, 469, 470, 471, 474
  (2007) 461, 473
Weinberg, H and Weishut, D 272, 457–78
Weiner, M (1993) 289
Weiner, M et al (1987) 339, 343, 344
Weiss, J (1993) 35–6, 49
Welzel, C and Inglehart, R (2010) 470
Wessells, M (209) 625
Wessells, M and Monteiro, C (2004) 674
Wessendorf, K (2009) 624
West, A (2007) 636, 638
West, A et al (2007) 638
Westefeld, J and Winkelpleck, J (1983) 387
Westen, D (1999) 36
Whitaker, C and Keith, D 433
Whitaker, D and Lieberman, M (1964) 279
White, J and Freeman, A (2000) 100
White, RW
  (1959) 139
  (1971) 139
Whitten, S et al (2008) 434
Whitman, R and Stock, D (1957) 712
Wilfley, D et al
  (1993) 386
  (2000) 42
Wilke, G (2003) 461, 464
Winnicott, D 593
  (1949) 177
  (1960) 592
  (1965) 190, 209
  (1969) 484, 491
  (1971) 65, 203, 209, 210, 234, 589, 598, 628
Witmer, J et al (1998) 676
Wolberg, L (1948) 346
Wolf, A 250–1, 737, 737
  (1975) 227
Wolf, A and Schwartz, E (1962) 251, 563, 739

Wolf, ES (1988) 65
Wolfsdorf, A and Zlotnick, C (2001) 417
Worden, B (2000) 233
Worthington, E et al (2005) 692
Wright, F
  (1987) 391
  (2000) 253, 254, 263
  (2004) 253, 254, 262, 263, 331
Wulsin, L et al (1988) 276

Yalom, I 252, 335, 398
  (1970) 97, 221
  (1980) 463, 467, 581
  (1983) 33
  (1985) 256, 261, 435, 553, 555, 659
  (1995) 33, 154, 180, 278, 279, 676
  (1998) 625, 629, 631
  (2005) 233, 235, 563
Yalom, I and Leszcz, M
  (1985) 253
  (1995) 598
  (2005) 33, 42–3, 47, 49, 53–5, 66, 114, 143–4, 162, 252, 258, 261, 262–4, 266, 302, 347, 417, 462–7, 504, 590, 599, 601, 681, 683
Yalom, I and Lieberman, M (1971) 566
Yerushalmi, H (1999) 235
Young, J (1999) 61
Young, J et al (2003) 93

Zabalegui, A et al (2004) 275
Zeisel, E 10, 217–29
  (2009) 220, 223, 224, 262, 263
Zeng, E 588, 623–43
Zeng, E and Silverstein, L (forthcoming) 626, 627
Zinkin, L 214
  (1983) 204, 208
  (1992) 204, 208–9
Zinnbauer, B and Pargament, K (2000) 694

Subject Index

ABC of caregiver care 511–12, 580–1
Abel, Theodora M 735
abortion 725–6
absence and absenteeism 19–20, 31, 43–4, 259, 445–6
  functional group models 154, 156, 159, 162
  supervision in Guatemala 521–2, 524
  mirroring 201–2, 207–8
  substance abuse 357, 359
abstinence 347–50, 352–4, 361–2, 367, 369–72, 376
abuse of children *see* sexual abuse
acceptance and commitment framework 96
acting out 483–4, 618, 748–9
action for change 96
action-oriented activities 627, 629, 631, 632
action program method 343
activities 617
activity gains 339, 340, 343
activity group therapy (AGT) 590
activity level 179–82
acute stage of trauma 502, 509
adaptation 139
adaptive interpersonal spiral 52, 54
addiction 33
  see also substance abuse
ADDRESSING 669

adolescents 588, 590, 609–21, 646–63
Adorno, Theodor 525, 531
Adult Attachment Inventory 322
affect 28–9, 188, 306, 413, 671
  interpersonal model 34, 37, 52
  intersubjective–relational groups 60, 69
  youth offenders 652, 653, 661
agency 470–1, 472, 475
AIDS/HIV 276, 277, 293, 590, 591
Ainsworth Strange Situation Studies 322
alcohol 345–77, 388, 693
  moderation training 370–3
Alcoholics Anonymous 277, 345, 349–52, 358, 361–2, 365–6, 369, 374, 376
Alexander, Franz 97
altruism 463, 465–6, 590, 591
American Association for Marriage and Family Therapy 449, 450
American Family Therapy Association 450
American Group Psychotherapy Association (AGPA) 6, 7, 91, 308, 763
  care for caregivers 573, 574
  career in group psychotherapy 710, 712, 715, 720, 724–5
  children and mass trauma 639
  couples group psychotherapy 450, 452
  development as group therapist 735, 742
  relational group therapy 173

American Group Psychotherapy Association
  (AGPA) (*cont'd*)
  support and process-oriented groups 293,
    296
  systems-centered therapy 114, 120, 135
  theoretical purity 249, 250
  trauma and disaster 504, 507, 511
American Psychiatric Association 59, 685
American Psychoanalytic Association 169
American Psychological Association 668–9,
  684, 685, 736
American Religious Identity Survey (ARIS)
  684
anger 118, 193, 243, 259, 386, 674
  adolescents 619, 620
  cognitive behavioral therapy 99, 102–3,
    105
  intersubjective–relational groups 67–8,
    71, 73, 75, 84
  maturational needs 218–21, 223, 225–6,
    227
anorexia 415, 693
antabuse 346, 352, 356, 367, 370, 376
antagonistic mirror reaction 204–5, 209
anti-group tendencies 398, 407
antisocial personality 62
anxiety 212, 219, 272, 670, 671
  adolescents 610–14, 618, 619
  care for caregivers 572, 578
  career in group psychotherapy 711, 713
  children 592, 595, 597, 599
  cognitive–behavioral therapy 92–3, 95–7,
    99, 100, 104–5, 110
  couples groups 451
  development as group therapist 738, 740
  dreams 485, 486, 493
  functional group model 147–9, 154, 159
  group facilitator development 235, 237,
    243
  high functioning adults 746, 751, 752
  interpersonal model 34, 46, 47, 49
  intersubjective–relational groups 77–9
  large groups 458, 459, 464, 473
  primitive defences 321, 324, 325, 327–8
  psychoanalytic groups 14, 15, 17, 24, 26,
    29
  psychosis 549, 560, 565
  relation group therapy 171, 178, 179,
    182
  resonance 188–90, 192–5
  sexual abuse 413–16, 418, 420–1,
    423–7
  sexual diversity 398, 403, 405
  single gender or mixed groups 383, 388,
    393
  spiritually informed therapy 685, 690,
    694
  structured techniques 335, 336, 337,
    343–4
  substance abuse 361, 365, 370
  supervision in Guatemala 519, 521, 513,
    529–34, 543
  support and process-oriented groups 275,
    278, 287
  systems-centered therapy 123, 124–7,
    128, 131, 132
  trauma and disaster 505–8, 510
  youth offenders 651, 652, 661
anxious/ambivalent attachment 418
Appleton Treatment Program 345–6
Aristotle 14, 171
Arnold, Roseanne 410
Arzù, President 519
assault 647, 648
assessment of developmental experience
  339–40, 343
Association for Applied and Therapeutic
  Humor 307
attachment and attachment theory 613,
  748–9
  couples groups 434, 445, 447–8, 452,
    453
  high functioning adults 748–9, 750–2,
    755–6, 761–2, 767
  interpersonal model 34, 43, 47
  intersubjective–relational groups
    59–60, 62, 64, 67–9, 74–6, 81–2,
    84
  primitive defenses 321–2, 323–33
  relational group therapy 177, 178
  sexual abuse 411, 412, 414, 418–19,
    427
  youth offenders 651, 653, 657
attention deficit 62–3, 590
attention deficit/hyperactivity disorder
  (ADHD) 105, 108, 595, 619–20
Attneave, Carolyn 108
attraction and sexual feelings 224–7

attunement 159, 191, 748–9, 750, 752
  interpersonal model 34–6, 50
  intersubjective–relational groups 65–9, 84
  systems-centered therapy 119, 120
authenticity 67–8, 253, 261–2
  intersubjective–relational groups 65, 67–8, 80, 83–4
authority 121, 123–9, 471, 472
autistic spectrum disorders 62–3
automatic thoughts 92–3
avatars 401–2
avoidance 651, 670, 676
  care for caregivers 573, 578
  trauma and disaster 500, 511
avoidance cluster 413
avoidant attachment 418–19, 761–2

Babette's Feast (film) 526, 543
Balint, Michael 529, 531, 710, 713
Balint Group 528, 531
barometric event 121, 123, 128–9
basic assumptions 251, 661, 755, 764
  group facilitator development 232, 233, 237–8, 240
relational therapy 171–2, 179
Beck, Aaron 92
Beck Anxiety Inventory (BAI) 100
Beck Depression Inventory (BDI) 100
beginning groups 1, 287–9, 335–6
behavioral theory 92–94, 98
beliefs *see* values and beliefs
Benedict XVI, Pope 402
Benson, Herbert 93, 102
bereavement 276–7, 278, 288, 290, 293
Bernard of Chartres 256
Bialik, Chaim 731
Bierer, Joshua 737
Bion, Wilfred R 64, 170–1, 209, 251, 335, 601
  career path 715, 719
  development as therapist 737, 739
  high functioning adults 755, 764
  psychosis 555
  supervision in Guatemala 529, 531
  youth offenders 657, 661, 662
bipolar disorder 89, 95, 276, 549
bisexuality 399, 402, 403
Blake, William 180

blind men and the elephant 645–6, 647, 654
Block, Marsha 725
Block, Stanley 710
bonding 95
borderline personality 208, 217, 278, 724, 746
  difficult patients 299, 308–9
  intersubjective–relational groups 62, 69
  sexual abuse 415
  theoretic purity 265
  youth offenders 651, 652
Bott, Elizabeth 107
boundaries and rules 131, 302, 332, 604
  adolescents 612–13
  children and mass trauma 627
  diversity 670–71, 673
  sexual abuse 424
  sexual diversity 405, 408
  support and process-oriented groups 275, 282–3, 285, 291, 293
  systems-centered therapy 130, 131, 133–4
  trauma and disaster 507
Boy Scouts of America 410
brain basics 101, 102
breast cancer 386, 387
breathing and stress management 101, 102–3
bridging 255, 262, 263, 305
Brown, Don 114
building the group stage 236–8
bulimia 329, 415, 693, 757
bullying 50–1, 595
burn out 273, 520, 528, 574–5, 576
Burns, David 93, 99, 100
Burrow, Trigant 70

caffeine 104–5, 107
campril 376
cancer 386, 387
  support groups 275, 277, 284, 288–9
capacity to develop as a group leader 5, 6
caregiver–child interaction 60, 67, 68–9
caregivers 511, 571–82
caretaking 113–14
catharsis 96, 276, 463, 466, 505, 590–1, 614
Central Clinic 711, 713, 715–20

check-in 99, 100–1
Chestnut Lodge 710
Child Guidance Center model 654
Child in Need of Supervision (CNS) referrals 648
children 587–8, 589–605
  couples therapy 433–4
  evacuated 460–1
  mass trauma 623–39
  stages of group development 601–2
  see also sexual abuse
Children's Protection movement 410
China 589, 623–39
chosen glories and trauma 460–1
client's concerns 95
climate of group 592
clinical emergencies 436
clinical psychology 733
closure stage 140, 154–60
clown 592
co-created meanings 66, 67, 70, 73–4, 76, 78, 81–3
code 591
cognitive–behavorial therapy (CBT) 10, 59, 89–112, 743
  adolescents 617, 619, 620
  core skills 102–9, 110
  couples 432, 434, 445–6, 448, 450, 453
  intersubjective–relational groups 61
  overall treatment strategy 99–102
  process-oriented groups 278
  response plan 110–11
  sexual abuse 420
  spiritually informed approach 690, 692, 694
  substance abuse 348
  support groups 276
  systems-centered approach 131, 135
  theoretic purity 250, 267
  trauma and disaster 504, 511
cognitive–didactic therapy 420
cognitive–interpersonal schema 35, 37–41, 44–5, 48, 50
cognitive theory 92, 93, 94 98
cognitive worksheet 109
cohesion of group 42–4, 55, 258–60, 463–4, 676, 716–17
  adolescents 611, 612
  children 590–2, 598, 601, 602, 603–4

children and mass trauma 627, 629–30, 631–3
  cognitive-behavioral therapy 92, 100, 101
  couples therapy 436, 437, 444, 451
  sexual abuse 421
  substance abuse 363
  support and process-oriented therapy 282
  trauma and disaster 505, 507, 509
  youth offenders 656, 657
Columbia College 732–3, 736, 737
combined therapy 30, 327–8, 735, 737, 739–41
communication 2, 279, 285, 323, 391
  children 590, 599
  couples therapy 433, 447, 448, 453
  difficult patients 302, 305–6
  diversity 669, 671
  dreams 492–3
  four-ear model 533–4
  functional subgrouping 117–19
  group facilitator development 233, 235
  large groups 462, 469–70, 471
  mirror reactions 197–8, 200, 202–3, 206–7, 213
  paraverbal 35, 39, 45
  progressive emotional 219–20
  psychosis 548, 549, 554, 555
  resonance 187–8, 191, 194
  sexual abuse 416, 424
  sexual diversity 397, 399, 403
  spiritually informed approach 682, 692
  systems-centered therapy 122, 131
  theoretic purity 256–7, 262, 263
  therapeutic meta 38, 44, 50, 53–5
  youth offenders 655, 659
  see also non-verbal communication
community action 627
community-based therapy 631–2, 636–8, 639
community mapping 628
compassion fatigue 573, 576, 577
complex post-traumatic stress disorder 413–15, 420
composition of group 14–15
  adolescents 611, 618
  diversity 15–17
  gender 381–94
  spiritually informed approach 687–8
conceptualization 236, 237–8, 245

conduct disorders 619, 620, 650–2
confidentiality 18–19, 256, 672, 715
  adolescents 588, 612–13, 618
  caregivers 580
  children 595, 598, 604
  couples 448–9
  functional group model 161
  large groups 473
  maturational needs 220
  psychosis 552, 565
  resonance 194
  sexual abuse 424
  sexual diversity 408
  spiritually informed approach 688
  substance abuse 357, 359–60
  support and process-oriented groups 275, 282, 283
  trauma and disaster 507
conflict 115, 433, 652, 745
  diversity 667, 668, 671, 676
  dreams 488
  group facilitator development 244–5
  large groups 458, 464, 468, 469, 471, 475
  maturational needs 218–19, 221, 222–3, 224
  psychosis 553, 563
  spiritually informed approach 683, 686, 695
  supervision in Guatemala 523, 525–31, 537–9, 541–4
  support and process oriented groups 279–82, 285–6
congruent therapy 30
conjoint therapy 735
constriction 500, 573, 574
constructivism 694, 695
consultation skills 5
contact functioning 304
contagious social moods 199–200, 211, 213
containment 593, 601, 661–2, 748
  dreams 479–80, 481–2, 484, 490–5
contemplation 96
context 71–2, 76, 82, 84, 130, 134
contract 15, 17–20, 332, 351, 365
  children 595
  difficult patients 303
  formal aspects 19–20

maturational needs 220, 224
substance abuse 346, 349–51, 356–7, 359, 365, 368–70
support and process oriented groups 283, 289
theoretic purity 256, 257–8, 259, 261
control mastery model 35
coping strategies 322–3, 363, 508–10, 621, 652
  support and process oriented groups 271, 275, 277–8, 281, 283, 295
CORE Battery–Revised 100
core behavioral sequences (CBSs) 740
corrective emotional experience 44, 49–52, 97
co-therapy 64, 90, 440
co-transference 65, 68, 70, 73, 76–81, 83–4
Counselors Helping (South) Asians, Inc (CHAI) 675–6
countertransference 290–1, 373–6, 599–601, 615–16, 653, 670–1
  adolescents 614, 615–16
  caregivers 572, 573
  development of group therapist 739, 741
  difficult patients 301, 310, 312–15, 317, 318
  diversity 668–71, 676, 678–9
  functional group model 153, 159
  group facilitator development 233, 240–1
  high functioning adults 746
  interpersonal model 40, 54
  intersubjective–relational groups 60–1, 64, 68, 84
  large groups 473
  maturational needs 217, 228
  modern analytic approach 255
  psychoanalytic groups 25, 27
  psychosis 548, 549, 553, 562
  relational group therapy 169, 181
  resonance 195
  sexual abuse 427
  substance abuse 350, 373–6, 377
  spiritually informed approach 682, 686, 695–6, 701
  supervision in Guatemala 532
  support and process oriented groups 279, 290–1, 296

countertransference (cont'd)
  theoretic purity 250, 253, 255, 258, 261, 266
  trauma and disaster 499, 508, 511
  youth offenders 647, 649, 653
couples group psychotherapy 2, 272, 276, 431–53
  clinical illustrations 433–4, 436–7, 441–2, 444, 446, 448
  existential base 432–3, 435
creativity 66, 200, 708, 739, 745, 764
  caregivers 581
  children and mass trauma 623, 629, 633
  couples 433
  maturational needs 226
  psychosis 567
  trauma and disaster 502, 508
crisis 441
culture 7, 223–4, 226, 665–6, 667–79, 716
  adolescents 610–13, 619
  caregivers 580
  children 589, 598
  children and mass trauma 628, 632, 634, 637
  intersubjectivity–relational groups 71–2
  large groups 457, 458–9, 462, 463, 467, 469
  sexual abuse 410
  sexual diversity 402
  spiritually informed approach 682–4, 687, 689, 691, 695–6, 701
  supervision in Guatemala 521–2, 526, 529–30, 543, 544
  trauma and disaster 502, 503, 507
  youth offenders 647, 648–9, 653, 659
curative fantasy 723–4
cybernetic feedback 70
cyboxin 346, 377

dance therapy 625, 627
death of group member 31, 75–7
death of therapist 30–1
defenses 66, 485, 548, 740
  large groups 459–60
  modification 122, 123–30, 131–4
  supervision in Guatemala 519, 536
  trauma and disaster 505, 508
  youth offenders 652–5, 657–8, 661, 662
dependency 171

depression 99, 324, 336, 557, 620
  adolescents 611, 619, 620
  caregivers 573, 578
  cognitive–behavioural therapy 89, 91–7, 99–101, 104–7, 109–10
  couples 433
  difficult patients 313
  functional group model 159
  high functioning adults 750–1, 753–4
  interpersonal model 37, 45–6, 51
  maturational needs 227
  mirror reactions 207–8
  psychoanalysis 15–16
  resonance 188, 193
  spiritually informed approach 685, 693, 694, 697
  substance abuse 365, 366, 413
  support and process oriented groups 275–6, 278, 283, 294–5
  systems centered therapy 128, 131
  trauma and disaster 503, 505, 508, 510
depth psychology 66, 450
derailments 68–9, 84
Derrida, Jacques 401
development stage 140, 149–54, 155, 159
developmental approach 382, 390, 392–3, 394
  romantic relationships 390–2
diagnoses and treatment populations 61, 62–3
dialectical behavior therapy 63, 267, 278
dialogic mirror reaction 206
Dickinson, Emily 172
didactic–education function of supervision 232
diet and nutrition 101, 102, 104–5
difference bridger 670, 671
differentiation stage of group 614
difficult patients 271–2, 299–319
  case studies 308–17
  support and process oriented groups 291–3
disaster 499–512
  mediating factors 501–3
  role of leader 505–6
  technique 506–7
disclosure 411, 422, 491
  see also self-disclosure
discrete intervention 11, 249–67

discrimination and integration of differences 114–15, 117–18, 135
displacement 670
disruptive behavior disorder 650
dissociation 321, 324, 754
 sexual abuse 411, 413, 414, 415
 trauma and disaster 500, 503, 508
 youth offenders 652, 653
distance group experiences 6–7
distortion 23–6
diversity 15–17, 468, 665–6, 667–79
 adolescents 619
 large groups 468, 472, 475
 psychosis 553
divorce 439, 448, 450, 619, 684–5, 753
 children 598
 support groups 276–7, 282–3, 287–8, 291, 293–4
domestic violence 386, 387, 648
Donne, John 467
doubt of others 36
dreams 22, 240, 272–3, 479–95, 724
 children and mass trauma 627–8
 development as group therapist 735, 737
 difficult patients 307, 310–12
 interpretation 250, 251
 large groups 459
 psychosis 551–2, 557–8
driving forces 121, 122–3
dropouts 2, 95, 100, 258
 support and process oriented groups 283, 285, 293–4
drug abuse 345–77, 388
Duque, Vilma 525
Durkin, Helen and Jim 114
dynamic-analytic psychotherapy 64, 708, 712

early recovery groups 349
Early Stage General Psychotherapy Group 678–9
earthquakes 588, 623–39
Eastern Group Psychotherapy Society (EGPS) 735
eating disorders 386, 757–61
 sexual abuse 414–15, 423
 spiritually informed approach 685, 690, 693, 694
Echo myth 203–4

education and youth offenders 647, 649
effectance motivation 139
embeddedness 325
embodied 331–2, 333
embodiment 403–4, 408
emotional attachment 272
emotional contagion 603–4
emotional co-participation 178–9
emotional intelligence 52, 453, 766
emotional vitality 263–4
emotional reinforcement 271, 275, 277
empathic immersion 254, 260–1
empathy 10, 11, 67–8, 98, 328, 722–4, 755
 caregivers 572, 573, 578–9
 children 591
 difficult patients 315–16
 diversity 669, 679
 functional group model 161
 interpersonal model 35, 47, 50, 52, 54
 intersubjective–relational groups 60, 63–8, 73, 80, 83–4
 maturational needs 226
 mirror reactions 205, 209
 process oriented groups 279
 psychosis 561, 565
 relational group therapy 178
 resonance 188, 189, 190, 193, 194
 sexual abuse 416, 418, 419, 422, 427
 substance abuse 354, 355, 368
 supervision in Guatemala 543
 support groups 277, 280
 trauma and disaster 511
empowerment 28, 470, 472, 475
 sexual abuse 415, 416, 417, 425
enactments 170, 261, 330–1
 couples 447, 452
 high functioning adults 754, 756, 761–2, 766–7
 primitive defenses 324, 327, 330–1, 333
 support and process oriented groups 285
 theoretic purity 253, 259–60, 261, 262, 265
energy organizing 119, 122–3
engagement 132, 177, 263, 549, 718
 interpersonal model 35, 43, 47, 48, 51, 55
 intersubjective–relational groups 62, 64
 maturational needs 217, 223, 225

erotic imagination 397, 403, 404, 407, 408
espoused theory 231–2, 233, 245, 247
ethics 449, 588, 605
ethnicity 665–6, 667–79
exclusion 95, 189, 518, 669, 694–5
  spiritually informed approach 694, 695
  sexual abuse 422–3
  sexual diversity 402, 407
exercise 101, 105–6
existential factors 171, 590, 683, 761
  couples 432–3, 435
  large groups 463, 467
expanding emotional range 219–21
expectancy, hope and placebo factors 98
expectations of large groups 474–5
experience 66–7, 68–9, 71
experimenting in large groups 475
exploring 123, 128–9
expression 66–7, 68–9, 71
expressive arts therapies 590
extra-group contact 19, 47, 256, 257–8
  adolescents 617–18
  couples 445, 448
  substance abuse 358
  support groups 283–4, 289
extra-therapeutic factors 98
Ezriel, Henry 737, 739

facilitators *see* therapists
fantasies 459
fear 36, 573, 738
  trauma and disaster 500, 503, 511
Federal Emergency Management Agency (FEMA) 677–8
feedback 763
  adolescents 617, 619
  children 591, 599, 602
  couples 442, 444, 449
  diversity 674
  functional group model 140, 144–7, 152–4, 158–9, 161
  group facilitator development 234–5
  interpersonal model 33–4, 36, 38–44, 46–7, 49–51, 53, 55
  large groups 465
  relational group therapy 170, 178, 182
  sexual abuse 416, 418, 420, 422, 427
  sexual diversity 407

spiritually informed approach 682
supervision un Guatemala 527
support and process-oriented groups 280, 292–3
theoretical purity 252, 258
feeling as a group therapist 3
fees 19–20, 415, 424, 595, 720
  financial commitment 2, 6, 15, 449
Fidler, Jay 114
Field Theory 251
fight subphase 121, 123, 128, 171
flight subphase 121, 123, 124–7, 128, 131, 171
Flowerman, Samuel 736, 737
focal conflict theory 714
focusing 475
food and children's groups 597
forgiveness groups 689, 692
formation stage 140, 144–9, 150, 159
formative approach 489–91, 494
forming 280, 601
Foulkes, Sigmund H 203, 208, 210, 251, 260, 764
  development of therapist 736, 737, 739
  sexual diversity 400, 404
  supervision in Guatemala 522–5, 524–5, 529, 531–2
four-ear model 533–4
free association 14, 17, 250, 251
  group facilitator development 235, 237–8, 240, 243
Feud, Anna 60
Freud, Sigmund 209, 228, 256, 289, 721, 733
  difficult patients 299, 302, 310, 315
  intersubjective–relational groups 60
  relational group therapy 170, 171, 183
  sexual diversity 399–400
  supervision in Guatemala 522, 524–5, 528–31
functional group model 10, 139–66
  common questions 161–2
  leader role 162
  member roles 163–5
functional group protocol 140, 141–4
functional subgroup 10, 113, 114–19, 130, 133–5
  theory of living human systems 119–23

Gamblers Anonymous 277
Ganzarian, Ramon 745–6
gender 272, 381–94
  adolescents 611
  clinical illustrations 384, 385–6, 387
  dreams 495
  psychoanalysis 15, 16
  sexual diversity 400
  specific problems 386–7
  trauma and disaster 502
  youth offenders 647, 649, 650
general system theories 715, 746, 754, 756, 763
generativity 766
genuineness 98
geriatric depression 33
German Technical Cooperation (GTC) 519–21, 526
gestalt therapy 100, 131, 250, 321, 530, 715
goal-directing 119, 122–3
goal orientation 130
goals 1, 20, 95, 444, 505
going around the group 20
Golani, Dr Ilan 199
Goodwill Industries 89–90
grandparents 142, 741–2
group agreements 257, 423
  support and process-oriented groups 282–5, 286, 289, 294
group analysis 200, 252, 522–5, 533–5, 547–67, 719
  large groups 459, 462
  supervision in Guatemala 522–7, 530, 533–41
group-as-a-whole 251, 252, 262–3, 328, 715, 724
  children 592, 593
  couples 436
  difficult patients 300
  high functioning adults 746, 755, 756, 761–2
  large groups 459, 461, 473
group as witness 397, 405, 407, 408
group assessment 140, 141–2
group building and maintenance role 164
group centered action 140
  functional group model 139, 140, 143, 146–50, 152–5, 159–60

Group Cohesion Scale 100
group development 149–54, 275, 278–81
  stages 140, 144–60, 236–41, 280–1, 601–2, 614
group dynamics 139, 250, 251–2
group member development 265–6
group morality 404, 407, 408
group narratives 140
  closure stage 154–60
  development stage 149–54
  formation stage 144–9
group process 14, 15, 17, 20, 22, 23
Group Psychological First Aid 509
Group Psychotherapy Foundation 725
group task roles 163–4
group tensions 165–6
group work stage 238
Guatemala 273, 517–44
  clinical illustrations 521, 524, 529, 532
guided self change 371
guilt and responsibility for others 36
guilt of success 36
Gutheil, Dr Emil 735

hallucinations 549, 550, 558–9
Harvard Health Plan 91–2
Hayes, Steven 96
Heirink, Richie 735
helplessness 500, 504, 511
here-and-now 46–9, 326–7, 335
  adolescents 618, 619, 621
  couples 444, 446, 451
  difficult patients 305, 316, 318
  group facilitator development 231, 235, 237, 241, 245
  interpersonal model 44, 45, 46–9, 52, 55
  large groups 458
  psychosis 549, 554, 555, 565–6
  sexual abuse 416, 417, 421
  sexual diversity 406–7
  spiritually informed approach 681, 682
  support and process-oriented groups 278, 283, 289
  theoretical purity 249, 252, 253, 263
  trauma and disaster 505, 508, 510
hermeneutic spiral 66, 70

heterogeneous groups 387, 439, 669
  gender 381–94
  sexual abuse 419, 410, 421–2, 428
  spiritually informed approach 686–7, 690, 697
  substance abuse 348–50, 363–70, 372
hierarchy 119–20
  defense modification 123–30, 131, 132
Hitler, Adolf 530
holding 237, 592, 599
holism 689
homework 95, 100, 343, 506, 660
  adolescents 617, 620
homogeneous groups 420–1, 439–40, 509
  gender 381–94
  sexual abuse 418, 419, 420–1, 428
  specific problems 382, 386–7, 394
  spiritually informed approach 688, 690, 695, 703
  substance abuse 348, 349, 350, 360–3
homosexuality 397–408
  clinical illustration 406–7
hope 98, 581–2
  see also instillation of hope
Hopper, Earl 719
Horkheimer, Max 525, 531
horror 500
hostility 25, 69, 191, 304
  interpersonal model 37–8, 39, 50, 55
  psychoanalysis 21, 22, 24, 25
  relational therapy 171, 176, 182
human conflict 170–2
human resources group 342
humanistic psychotherapy 321
humor 307
Hurricane Katrina 500
hurricanes 6, 500, 574
hyperarousal 412, 500, 508, 511, 573

I statements 70, 73–4, 84, 755
ideas v reality 343
identification 610, 612
imitative behavior 463, 466, 590
immediacy 300, 315
impact messages 39–40, 41
imparting information 463, 464, 590
implicit/unconscious meanings 67, 83

incest 410–13, 418–19, 425–7, 572
  boys 410, 572
  high functioning adults 746, 748–9
inclusion 95, 422, 557, 720
  adolescents 610, 614, 617
incongruity 500
individual roles 164–5
individuation 432, 433
infant observation 34, 35
influence 482
informative approach 484–9, 491
informed consent 689–91, 693
infrastructure 591
initial contact and consultation 20–2, 442–3
initial relatedness stage 614
insecure–ambivalent attachment 322–3
insecure attachment 412, 419, 427
insecure–avoidant attachment 322
insecure–disorganised attachment 322, 323
insight 2–4, 9–10, 29, 250, 707–8, 711, 724
  cognitive behavioral therapy 101–2, 109
  couples 448
  diversity 669, 671
  dreams 485
  functional group model 140, 161
  group facilitator development 234, 235, 239, 241, 742
  high functioning adults 750
  interpersonal model 33, 35, 36, 49, 54
  intersubjective–relational groups 61, 63, 66–7, 72
  large groups 465
  psychosis 549, 552, 554
  relational group therapy 170, 172, 174, 178–9, 182
  sexual abuse 416, 418
  spiritually informed groups 683, 687, 688
  supervision in Guatemala 521, 523–4
  support and process-oriented groups 272–3, 276, 279, 281
  theoretical purity 250, 262
  trauma and disaster 506
instillation of hope 279, 590, 599, 631, 683
  larger groups 463, 464
insulation barrier 300, 318
integrative developmental model 696

intergenerational frame 434
intergroup romance 382, 390–2
internal working models (IWMs) 322
International Association of Group
  Psychotherapy 724
International Association for Group
  Psychotherapy and Group Processes
  135
International Journal of Group
  Psychotherapy 250–1
internet 6, 401
interpersonal approach 2, 10, 33–55, 715
  adolescents 609, 610, 612–15, 617, 620
  children 599–600, 602
  clinical illustrations 37–8, 40–1, 43–8,
    50–3
  cognitive behavioral therapy 92, 93–4
  couples 435, 437, 451
  diversity 667, 669, 673
  dreams 480, 482–3, 485, 487–8, 491–2,
    494–5
  group therapist development 740
  large groups 472, 475
  primitive defenses 321, 333
  process oriented groups 276, 278–9, 293
  psychosis 561
  sexual abuse 417, 419, 421, 422, 428
  spiritually informed approach 681–2,
    686–8, 691, 696–7, 702
  substance abuse 345
  theoretic purity 249, 252–3, 261, 263,
    266
  youth offenders 658
interpersonal circumplex 39
interpersonal effectiveness 217–18, 224,
  229
interpersonal feedback 33
interpersonal interaction 33
interpersonal learning 33, 44, 52–3, 463,
  465, 631
  children 590, 591
  process oriented groups 271, 275, 278,
    283, 293–4
interpersonal neurobiology 419
interpretation 262–3
intersubjective–relational groups 10, 59–85,
  459, 721, 726
  dreams 480, 482, 484, 492
  illustrative vignette 72–83

maturational needs 228
primitive defenses 321, 331, 333
principles 64–72
relational therapy 170, 172, 175, 181,
  183
theoretical purity 260, 261
interviewing children 629, 635
intimacy 300, 305, 318, 433
intimacy stage 121, 123, 129–30, 614, 615
introjections 554, 560
intrusion 500, 510, 511
intrapersonal approach 472
intrapsychic approach 9–10, 60, 249, 473,
  715–16
  children 602
  difficult patients 307
  diversity 673
  primitive defenses 333
  psychosis 561
  relational group therapy 170, 174
  sexual abuse 416, 418
  supervision in Guatemala 525, 530,
    531
  support and process oriented groups
    278–9, 283, 293, 294
  youth offenders 658
isolation 467, 503, 506–7, 512
  caregivers 571, 572, 579
isomorphy 120, 122, 435–6

joining 190, 218, 441
  difficult patients 303, 304, 313, 317
  functioning subgroups 113, 114, 119,
    120, 129
Jungian psychology 485, 490
Juvenile justice system 647–8

Kadis, Asya 736, 737
Kaiser Permanente 90–2
Karterud, Sigmund 719, 724
Keller, Fred 732
Kierkegaard, Soren 170
Klein, Melanie 60, 719
  Relation group therapy 170, 171
Kleinberg, Otto 733
knowledge of multiple theories 5
Kohut, Heinz 721–4
Krier Juvenile Correctional Treatment
  Center 646–9

ladder of children's participation 625–6, 638
language 469–70, 473
large groups 272, 457–76
  clinical illustration 460
  leaders 472–4
  therapeutic factors 462–71, 475
  therapeutic value 461–2
lateness 445–6
Law of Optimum Distance 611
learning disabilities 590, 649
learning from others factors 98
leaving a group 259–60, 283
Leff, Jerome 736, 740
Lehman 710
leveraging differences 668, 670, 673–5, 677, 679
Levine, Maurice 709, 710
Lewinian Group Dynamics 733
Lewinson, Peter 93
life choices 433
Life Enrichment Counseling Approach 336–7
limit-setting 616
lithium 276
long term stage of trauma 503, 510, 511
Lorenz, Konrad 200

MacKenzie, Roy 91
maintenance 96, 164, 659, 662
major affective disorder 650
maladaptive transaction cycle (MTC) 36–7, 41–2, 49
Malan, David 737
malignant mirroring 208–9
managed care 346
manic-depressive illness 276
Marcuse, Herbert 525, 531
Marlatt, G Alan 110
Marsh, Cody 221
maturational needs 10, 217–29, 260, 266
  clinical illustrations 218, 221–3, 224–6
  difficult patients 317, 318
  modern analytic approach 255–6
Mead, Margaret 710, 735
mediation 541–4
Medicare and Medicaid 720
men in groups 384–6
Menninger Clinic 710, 745–6, 763

Men's Movement 383, 393
mental health factor 649–54
mental health hospitals 89
mentalization 60, 69, 84, 171
  primitive defenses 323, 325, 327, 328
metacognition 323, 325, 327
metaphors 306, 711
mindfulness therapy 59, 93, 96–7
mirror neurons 60, 188, 211, 228, 755, 767
mirroring 10, 197–214, 233, 243, 722, 724
  clinical illustrations 201–2, 205–8, 212, 213–14
  difficult patients 303, 304
  dreams 488, 492
  high functioning adults 748, 754, 755, 762
  intersubjective–relational groups 67, 68, 70
  patterns 204–9
  psychosis 547, 557, 560
  resonance 188, 192
misconstrual 35, 36
misconstrual–misconstruction sequence 35, 38, 42
model and technique factors 98
modeling 617, 620
moderation management 371, 376
moderation training 370–3
  substance abuse 347–50, 365, 369–73, 376
modern analytic therapy 249–50, 255–6, 258, 260–2, 264–6
  difficult patients 300–1, 302, 308, 318–19
  primitive defenses 321
monopolizer 591, 592
mood and anxiety disorders 276
mood disorder track 95
mood disorders 2, 451
mother groups 592, 633
motivational systems theory 60
moving on stage 614
multidisciplinary treatment team (MTT) 645–63
  dynamic challenges 656–8
  role of facilitator 656, 658–62
  structure and process 654–8

multiple self states 324–5
multiple transference 23–4, 523–4, 533, 740
Murphy, Gardner 733
music therapy 746

naltrexone 346, 357, 366, 370, 376
narcissism 265–6, 291, 731, 746
  career in group psychotherapy 722, 724
  difficult patients 299–302, 310, 313, 315–16, 318
  diversity 668, 674
  functional group model 148
  intersubjective–relational groups 62, 65, 70
  maturational needs 217, 226
  mirror reactions 209
  relational group therapy 176
  resonance 191
  self psychology 254, 266
  sexual abuse 423
  youth offenders 651, 662
narcissistic defense 301, 302, 316
Narcissus myth 203–4
Narcotics Anonymous 351, 357, 361, 365, 374, 376
narrative stage 238–9, 240
National Institute for Mental Health 90
National Registry of Certified Group Psychotherapists 294
natural disasters 2, 6, 573
  earthquakes 588, 623–39
  hurricanes 6, 500, 574
needs hierarchy 139
negotiating function 660–1, 662
nervous avoiders 670
neurobiology 419, 453
neuroscience 748–9, 754–5, 756, 762, 767
neutrality 21, 23–4
new members 18–19, 26–7, 43, 286–7, 700
  cognitive behavioral therapy 95, 96, 100–2
non-disclosure 411
non-verbal communication 20–2, 24, 752, 760, 767
  couples 447, 448, 453
  interpersonal model 35, 39, 45

non-psychodynamic therapy 267
norming 280, 601
"not me" experiences 34
numbing 573, 578

obesity 15
object feelings 219–20
object oriented questions 302, 304–5, 313–14
object relations theory 59, 251–2, 486, 746–7, 749, 755, 762
objectivity 21, 23, 60
Oedipal complex 66, 179, 183, 400, 486
operative principles of supervision model 236
oppositional defiant disorder 650
oppression 668, 670, 673, 679
orientation 95
Ormont, Louis R 217, 220
Ornstein, Ana 721, 723
Ornstein, Paul 721
outcome measures 99–100
out-of-group contact *see* extra-group contact
outpatients and psychosis 549–50, 553, 554–5, 556–7, 564, 566–7
Overeaters Anonymous 277
oversight 232

Padesky, Christine 93
pairing 171, 530
panic disorders 15, 95, 102, 104–5, 109
pan-theoretical approach 250
paradoxical interventions 617
parallel processes 240
paranoia 734
paraverbal communication 35, 39, 45
parental loss 15, 74, 79, 590–1
Parents Anonymous 277
participants 505
participation 631–2, 634, 636–8
pelicans 198, 199–200
performing 280, 601
personal growth 271, 275, 280
personality disorders 2, 207, 278, 711
personality integration 217, 221, 223
pharmacotherapy 548–9, 550, 553–4, 566–7, 710, 717–20
phenomenological field 64
Phillips, McKenzie 410

photography 629, 634, 639
Pines, Malcolm 719, 737
Planned Parenthood 726
play 263–4, 628, 630, 632–3
pleasant activities 93, 96, 103, 103–4
pluralism 468–9, 472, 474, 475, 694, 695
polite inquirers 670, 671
positive diversity processing 667
positive psychology 447, 453
positive regard 92, 98
post-acute stage of trauma 502–3, 510
Postgraduate Center for Mental Health 734–43
   Group Therapy Department 735–42
post-traumatic stress disorder (PTSD) 62, 652, 749
   caregivers 571, 573, 577
   disaster 501, 503, 508, 510, 511
   evacuated children 461
   sexual abuse 412–13, 414, 415, 423
power and control stage 614
power struggle in large groups 467, 469–71, 472–5
Powles, Bill 714
practical knowledge 231
pre-affiliation stage 601–2, 614
pre-contemplation 96
predictable problems 445–6
prejudice 398, 400–2, 405, 407
pre-oedipal disorder 265, 300, 301–2, 304
preparation and pre-group interviews 17, 96, 256–8, 716
   adolescents 610, 613–14, 618
   couples 440–1
   sexual abuse 423
   substance abuse 357–8, 362, 365, 368
   trauma and disaster 507
Present Centered Supportive Group 510
pretraining 440
priests and sexual abuse 410
primitive defenses 272, 321–33
   case study 324, 326, 329, 331–2
Principles for Positive Diversity Processing (PPDP) 668, 670–5, 679
probation 647–8
problem-solving 108
process commentary 163

process-oriented approach 271, 275–98
   clinical illustrations 278, 287, 288, 292
   example 284–5
   sexual abuse 417
procrastination 93, 106, 108
programs organizer 362–3
program proselytizer 361–2, 366, 685
projections 593, 670, 712
   psychosis 548, 552, 554, 557, 560, 561
   youth offenders 651, 657–8, 661, 662
Projective Identification-in-the-Dream 485, 487
psychiatric assessment 443
psychoanalytic approach 9–10, 13–32, 250–1, 399, 533–5
   career path 709, 710, 713, 720, 721
   couples 446–7, 452
   dreams 479, 482, 485, 486
   group therapist development 734–7, 739, 742
   high functioning adults 745, 754, 756
   intersubjective–relational groups 59–60, 61, 62, 64
   large groups 459, 462
   sexual abuse 418
   sexuality 399, 400–1, 406
   supervision in Guatemala 522–5, 530, 533–5
   theoretical purity 249, 250–1, 252, 256, 262
   see also modern analytic therapy
Psychoanalytic Training Program 734
psychobiological mirrors 200, 210–12
psychodrama 471
psychodynamic approach 6, 276, 278, 294, 650–1, 720–1
   couples 432, 434, 447–8, 453
   difficult patients 300
   group therapist development 739, 740, 742, 743
   large groups 457–9, 464, 471, 474
   primitive defenses 321
   psychosis 547–67
   sexual abuse 417, 418, 420
   spiritually informed approach 681, 682
   structured techniques 340–1, 344
   substance abuse 272, 345–77
   theoretical purity 250, 262, 263, 265–7

trauma and disaster 504, 511
youth offenders 645–63
psycho-educational groups 463, 464, 579, 590
  adolescents 612, 619, 620
  spiritually informed approach 688, 692
  systems-centered therapy 131, 135
  trauma and disaster 505, 507, 509–11
Psychological First Aid (PFA) 509
psychological testing 443
psychological work factors 98
psychological mindedness 15
psychopharmacotherapy 548–9, 550, 553–4, 566–7
psychosis 16, 63, 273, 547–67, 572
  role of leader 561–6
  youth offenders 650, 651
psychosocial group therapy 631–2, 637–8
psychosomatic symptomology 301
purposeful action 140
  functional group model 139–40, 143, 146–8, 150–2, 154–60
pushback 673–4, 677

qualifications of therapist 61
qualitative descriptions of leisure 340, 343–4

race 665–6, 667–79
RAP framework 668–9, 673
rape 386, 387
  see also sexual abuse
"Rashomon" effect 28
readiness group 349
recapitulation of family 464–5
  children 590, 591, 598
  large groups 463, 464–5, 468
recorder/observer 711, 712–13
re-experiencing 413, 500–1, 508, 573–4
reflection 302, 436–7, 719–20
  group facilitator development 233–4, 236–41, 243–7
  stage 236, 239–41
reflective action model 234–5
reflective examination 233, 234, 236
regression 28–9, 522, 611, 652
  psychosis 549, 553–4, 557, 560–3, 566–7

rejectionism 694, 695
relapse 93–4, 96–7, 101, 109–11
relapse prevention groups 348
relational approach 10, 59–85, 169–83, 253, 447
  career in group psychotherapy 715, 721, 726
  children 589, 599
  couples 445, 446, 447, 452
  high functioning adults 754, 755, 756
  illustrative vignette 72–83
  large groups 462
  primitive defenses 321, 331, 333
  principles 64–72
  theoretic purity 250, 253–6, 259–65
  youth offenders 658
relationship building 90, 93–4, 99
relaxation 101, 102
religion 7, 714, 731–2
  diversity 665, 669, 677–8
  spiritually informed approach 681–703
REM sleep 106
repetitive behavior 21, 29–30
representation of society 467–9, 472
required skills of therapist 4, 5
research 132–5, 307–8
  substance abuse 370–1
resilience 634, 636, 637
resistance 26–8, 244, 251–2, 289–90, 364, 534
  difficult patients 300–2, 304
  maturational needs 217, 219–20, 224, 226–9
  modern analytic approach 255–6, 262
  psychoanalytic approach 9, 14, 15–16, 19–20, 22, 25–30, 533–5
  sexual abuse 420
  single or mixed gender groups 392
  substance abuse 350, 362, 364
  supervision in Guatemala 519, 521, 533–6
  support and process oriented groups 279, 289–90
  theoretic purity 251–2, 257–60, 263, 265
  trauma and disaster 505
resolving authority issues stage 614

resonance 10, 213, 187–95
  clinical illustration 188–91
  dreams 488, 492, 494, 495
  psychosis 560
  subjective experience 193
  therapeutic value 191–3
respect 98, 282, 612–13, 627
response plan 101, 110–11
restoring structure and routine 627, 632–3
restraining forces 122–3, 128
risk issues 609, 617
Rogers, Carl 98
role lock phase 121, 123, 128–9
role of leader 162, 326–8, 505–6, 512, 561–6
  MTT 656, 658–62
role of members in children's groups 591–2
role play 358–9
Rorschach 733
Ross, W Donald 709, 710
Russian dolls 524–5
Rutan, Scott 719–20

safety 101, 111, 194, 671–2
  adolescents 620
  children 593–4, 599, 602–4
  children and mass trauma 623, 627
  diversity 668–9, 670, 671–2, 673, 679
  mirror reactions 198, 210
  sexual abuse 415–16, 420–3, 428
  sexual diversity 398
  single or mixed gender groups 393
  substance abuse 348, 354
  supervision in Guatemala 532
  support and process oriented groups 281–3, 291–2
  trauma and disaster 501, 503, 505–7, 509, 512
  youth offenders 652
Salisbury, John 256
San Francisco Psychotherapy Research Group 35
scapegoating 68, 173, 521, 670, 747, 764–5
  adolescents 615
  children 591, 595–6, 602–3
  functional subgroups 117–18, 135

  support and process oriented groups 289, 293
schizophrenia 89, 217, 276, 710, 711
  caregivers 572
  difficult patients 300, 301
  psychodynamics 547–9, 565
screening and selection of group members 1, 4, 422, 594–5, 714
  adolescents 588
  children 590, 54–5, 604
  cognitive behavioral therapy 95–6, 100
  couples 438–9
  intersubjective–relational approach 63–4
  maturational needs 218
  primitive defenses 326
  psychosis 553
  relational therapy 180
  sexual abuse 422–3
  spiritually informed approach 686–7, 691, 695
  structured techniques 335
  support and process-oriented therapy 275, 279, 285–7
  trauma and disaster 506–7
secondary post-traumatic stress disorder (SPTSD) 511
secondary traumatic stress (STS) 573, 576–7
secondary traumatization 520, 573, 653
secure attachment 322, 325, 328, 333
  sexual abuse 412, 419, 427
security 19
selection of group members see screening and selection of group members
self-disclosure 70, 77, 261–2
  adolescents 616, 619
  children 599, 600
  couples 443–4
  functional group model 161
  intersubjective–relational groups 70–1, 73–4, 80, 83–4
  mirror reaction 213–14
  relational group therapy 173–5, 176–8
  resonance 188, 190, 192–4
  spiritually informed approach 690, 695
  substance abuse 350, 363, 374
self-doubt 36
self-empowerment 28
self-evaluation of enjoyment 338, 342–3

self-exploration 13–14, 18–20, 23, 27
self-feelings 219–20
self-generated list of leisure activities 337–8, 339–42
self-harming 329, 415, 423
self-initiated action 139, 140, 143, 146, 148, 150–5, 158–60
selfobjects 254, 721, 722, 724
self-psychology 254, 707, 721–4, 727, 747–8
  dreams 490
  high functioning adults 747–8, 749, 756
  intersubjective–relational approach 59–60, 64–5, 67
  theoretic purity 250, 254, 256, 260, 262–3, 266
self-reflective capacity 5
self-revelation factors 97
self-verification theory 34
sense of self 34–5
separation stage 614
session evaluations 140, 146–7, 152–3, 158–9
setting 1–2, 4, 6, 337, 436, 764
  adolescents 610, 611, 613
  cognitive behavioral therapy 90, 94–5, 106
  couples 436–8, 445–8
  functional group model 140, 154, 161–2
  gender 382–4, 386–9
  interpersonal model 33, 42
  intersubjective–relational groups 61, 63–4
  psychoanalysis 13, 17, 27, 29–31
  sexual abuse 417, 420, 423
  spiritually informed approach 688–91
  support and process oriented groups 276, 278, 283, 285
  systems centered therapy 131–2, 135
sexual abuse 15, 53, 329, 409–28, 572
  boys 410
  children's groups 590, 591, 593, 600–1
  clinical illustrations 409, 414, 416, 424–6
  cognitive behavioral therapy 90, 97
  high functioning adults 746, 748–9, 767
  process oriented groups 272, 276
  youth offenders 648
sexual activity 342, 611
sexual compulsivity 386, 387, 389–90

sexual diversity 397–408
  as experimental 401–2
  as natural 401
  as perversion 399, 400–1, 404
  clinical illustrations 406–7
sexual orientation 15, 272, 397–408, 432, 712
  adolescents 618, 619
  gender 382, 387
  spiritually informed approach 684–7, 694, 697, 700–2
Shakespeare, William 108–9
shame 65, 67, 154, 290, 613, 575, 674
  caregivers 57, 575
  maturational needs 219
  resonance 188, 190–2, 195, 202, 206, 212
  sexual abuse 414, 415, 416, 423
  sexual diversity 397, 404
  substance abuse 372, 374, 375
  trauma and disaster 503, 507, 512
Sharett, Moshe 731
shellshock 522
sibling rivalry 175–6, 179, 183, 251, 524
  difficult patients 305, 311–12
silence 20, 712, 760
  children 591, 592
  difficult patients 301, 304, 305, 315
  dreams 490
  group facilitator development 241–3, 244
  mirror reactions 201–3, 213
  relational group therapy 172, 174, 176, 182
  support and process oriented groups 280, 289
Sisyphus problem 123
skills training 348
Skinner, B F 732
Skola, Atura *The Family* (film) 209–10
Slavon, Samuel 250–1, 590, 715, 736, 739
sleep hygiene 101, 106–7
social dynamic groups 531
social microcosm 33, 38, 42, 44–6, 49, 52, 55
social networks 107–8, 110
social psychologists 733–4
social unconscious 458–61, 468, 470, 473

social skills 10, 91
　adolescents 609–10, 612
socializing techniques 463, 465, 468, 590, 591
Socialshteimung 200
sociopathy 62
somatization disorder 276
special medical needs 649
special needs 587
　see also learning disabilities
specificity 33
spiritually informed approach 681–703
　clinical illustrations 697–701, 702
spontaneity 20
spontaneous action 139, 140, 143, 146–8, 150, 152–5, 158–60
Spotnitz, Dr Hyman 217
stages of group development 140, 149–60, 236–41, 601–2, 614
　intimacy 121, 123, 129–30, 614–15
states of mind 219–20
Stekel, Wilhelm 735
Stewart, Bob 715
storming 280, 601
stress 2, 93, 105, 107
structure of therapy 596–8
subjectivity 254, 260, 323, 328
　mirror reactions 198, 201, 206, 214
　relational group therapy 170, 172, 182, 183
　resonance 192, 193
substance abuse 67, 110, 272, 345–77, 618–19, 753
　adolescents 609, 613, 618–19
　children 592, 602
　couples 451
　recovery1related defenses 361–3
　sexual abuse 414, 422
　single or mixed gender groups 388
　spiritually informed approach 685
　trauma and disaster 510
　youth offenders 647, 649, 650, 652
sugar 104, 105
suicidal ideation 69, 75, 291–2, 324, 331–2
　adolescents 618
　caregivers 581
　cognitive behavioral therapy 95, 99, 104
　difficult patients 299
　psychosis 549–50

sexual abuse 423
　spiritually informed approach 684–5
　substance abuse 366
summary stage 241, 245
supervision 62, 94, 294, 296, 333, 335, 527–9
　career in group psychotherapy 711–12, 715
　caregivers 580
　children 589, 627, 639
　clinical illustrations 241–3, 521, 524, 529, 532
　couples 450–1
　difficult patients 307–8
　group therapist development 232–47, 264, 739, 740
　Guatemala 517–44
　sexual abuse 423–4, 428
　spiritually informed approach 681, 683, 696–7
　substance abuse 272, 377
　team 537–9
support groups 27, 271, 275, 276–98, 713
　clinical illustrations 276, 282, 287, 290
　couples 434
　development of group therapist 743
　example 284, 291, 295
　psychosis 548
　sexual abuse 417–18
　trauma and disaster 502, 504, 509, 511
supportive factors 97
supportive function 232
symmetry 632–3
systems centered therapy (SCT) 10, 113–36
　methods 130–1
　research 132–5
　TLHS 119–23
Systems Centered Training and Research Institute 132, 135
system-correcting 119, 122–3
system development 121, 123–30, 131

talkers and non-talkers 173–6, 177, 178–9
tattoos 649
Tavistock groups 464, 472, 682, 737, 763, 765
team supervision 537–9
tension 272
termination of group 30–1

children 602
couples 442
difficult patients 317–18
sexual abuse 421
spiritually informed approach 700, 702–3
substance abuse 357
support and process oriented groups 280, 287–9, 294
terrorism 2, 6
see also World Trade Center attack
testing of limits stage 614, 616
T-group movement 714
theme oriented group discussion 340–1
theoretical constructs 34–42
theory of living human systems (TLHS) 114, 119–23
theoretic knowledge 231
theoretic purity 249–67
clinical illustration 257
theory in use 231–2, 233, 245, 247
therapeutic alliance 257, 285–6, 560–1
adolescents 613, 615
difficult patients 301
maturational needs 224
primitive defenses 333
psychosis 549, 560–1, 563
sexual abuse 415, 416, 427
therapeutic factors 97–9, 504–5
therapeutic meta-communication 38, 44, 50, 53–5
therapists 3, 66–70, 227–9, 231–47, 264–5
qualifications 61
transparency 53–4
vicarious trauma 273
therapy relationship factors 98
there-and-then 241, 245, 283, 681
Thomas, Dylan (154) 175
torture 273
training 94, 294, 296
career path 709–29
development as therapist 731–44
difficult patients 301, 305, 318
transactional analysis 715
transference 9, 22–6, 68, 599–601, 615–16
adolescents 614, 615–16
career in group psychotherapy 712, 716, 723–4
children 599–601
couples 439, 440

difficult patients 301, 302, 309, 318
diversity 669
dreams 485
functional group model 153, 165
group analysis 523–4
group therapist development 735, 740, 742
high functioning adults 746, 750–2, 762, 766
interpersonal model 35, 36, 37
intersubjective–relational groups 60–1, 66, 68, 71
maturational needs 221, 222–3
modern analytic approach 255, 264
multiple 23–4, 523–4, 533, 740
primitive defenses 325, 333
process oriented groups 279, 289
psychoanalysis 9, 19, 20, 22–6, 28
psychosis 548–9, 553–5, 560–3, 567
relational group therapy 169, 177, 179, 180, 181
sexual abuse 418, 421, 423, 427
spiritually informed approach 682, 683, 686, 695
supervision in Guatemala 522–4, 532–3
theoretic purity 251–2, 253, 255, 261–3, 264
trauma and disaster 505–6
youth offenders 661, 662
transmuting internalization 254
transparency 261–2
trauma 2, 6, 273, 421, 422, 499–512, 620–1
adolescents 609, 619, 620–1
care of leader 511–12
caregivers 571–2, 573–80
children 587, 588, 590, 623–39
defined 412
diversity 672
Guatemala 518, 520
guidelines 507–8
high functioning adults 746–9, 752, 754, 756
intersubjective–relational groups 59, 62, 63
large groups 460–1
mediating factors 501–3
primitive defenses 321
process oriented groups 276

trauma (cont'd)
  role of leader 505–6, 512
  sexual abuse 409–20, 421–8
  vicarious 273, 427, 428
  youth offenders 653, 654, 656–7
trauma-focus group therapy 510
treatment constructs 42–55
treatment planning 1, 2–7
triggers 96, 103, 110, 111
Tri-State Group Psychotherapy Society (TSGPS) 710, 714–15, 725
trust 18, 92, 101, 259, 762
  adolescents 615
  caregivers 572
  children and mass trauma 627
  diversity 671, 672
  functional group model 149, 163
  MTT 656
  psychosis 551, 552, 560
  sexual abuse 410, 411, 415
  supervision in Guatemala 519, 521–2, 535, 543
  support and process oriented groups 280
  trauma and disaster 506, 507, 508
Trust for Group Analysis 737
truth 170, 171–2, 179, 182–3
tsunami 636
tuning in stage 236
twinship 722, 723, 724

unconscious 533–4
uncovering oppressive patterns 668, 670, 673, 679
understanding 66–7, 68–9, 71
unisex or mixed gender groups 381–94
  clinical illustrations 384, 385–6
  specific problems 382, 386–7, 394
universality 235, 463, 466, 590, 591, 631
  diversity 676
unthought known 323–4, 328

values and beliefs 231, 685
  spiritually informed approach 685, 689, 692, 696, 698–9, 701
vampires 207
vectoring 130, 133
verbalization 21
vicarious trauma and traumatization 273, 427, 428, 635
  ABCs 580–1
  caregivers 573–4, 576, 577, 580–1
  disaster 499, 508, 511
  youth offenders 653

waiting list groups 718–19
waiting room 712, 716
war 517–22, 571, 572–3, 576, 733
weekly organizer 108
Weitzman, Chaim 731
what and how 236, 245
Whitman, Roy 709, 723, 726
Wilde, Oscar 28
Winfrey, Oprah 410
wise men of Helm 198, 199
Wolberg, Lewis 734, 738
Wolf, Alexander 736, 737
women in groups 383–4
women's groups 418–19, 420–1, 428
Women's Movement 383, 393, 410
Women's Wellness Group 675–6
Woodworth, Robert S 733
work stage 121, 123, 130, 236, 602
working on self stage 614
working through 29–30
World Trade Center 31, 71, 84, 677–8
  caregivers 574, 578
  trauma and disaster 501, 503, 504

Youcha, Isaac "Zeke" 239–40
Young, Jeff 93
Young Women's Christian Association (YWCA) 763
youth offenders 589, 645–63
  demographics 648–54